A Military History of Scotland

In memory of
Wallace Cunningham DFC
(1916–2011)

A Military History of Scotland

Edited by

Edward M. Spiers, Jeremy A. Crang and Matthew J. Strickland

EDINBURGH
University Press

© in this edition Edinburgh University Press, 2012, 2014
© in the individual contributions is retained by the authors

First published in hardback in 2012
This paperback edition 2014

Edinburgh University Press Ltd
The Tun – Holyrood Road
12 (2f) Jackson's Entry
Edinburgh EH8 8PJ
www.euppublishing.com

Typeset in Miller Text by
Servis Filmsetting Ltd, Stockport, Cheshire
and printed and bound in Great Britain by
Bell & Bain Ltd, Glasgow

A CIP record for this book is available from the British Library

ISBN 978 0 7486 3335 7 (hardback)
ISBN 978 0 7486 9449 5 (paperback)
ISBN 978 0 7486 3204 6 (webready PDF)
ISBN 978 0 7486 5401 7 (epub)

The right of the contributors to be identified as authors of this work has been asserted in accordance with the Copyright, Designs and Patents Act 1988 and the Copyright and Related Rights Regulations 2003 (SI No. 2498).

Published with the support of the Edinburgh University Scholarly Publishing Initiatives Fund.

Contents

List of Illustrations viii
Acknowledgements xv
Foreword by Hew Strachan xvii

Introduction 1
    Edward M. Spiers

I Early Warfare and the Emergence of a Scottish Kingdom

1   War in Prehistory and the Impact of Rome 41
     Fraser Hunter
2   Warfare in Northern Britain, c. 500–1093 65
     James E. Fraser
3   The Kings of Scots at War, c. 1093–1286 94
     Matthew J. Strickland
4   The Wars of Independence, 1296–1328 133
     Michael Prestwich
5   The Kingdom of Scotland at War, 1332–1488 158
     Alastair J. Macdonald
6   Scotland in the Age of the Military Revolution,
     1488–1560 182
     Gervase Phillips
7   Warfare in Gaelic Scotland in the Later Middle Ages 209
     Martin MacGregor

II Forging a Scottish–British Military Identity

8   The Wars of Mary and James VI and I, 1560–1625 235
     Matthew Glozier

9	'Mercenaries': the Scottish Soldier in Foreign Service, 1568–1860 *Allan Carswell*	248
10	The Wars of the Three Kingdoms, 1625–60 *Martyn Bennett*	276
11	The Restoration and the Glorious Revolution, 1660–1702 *K. A. J. McLay*	298
12	Marlborough's Wars and the Act of Union, 1702–14 *John C. R. Childs*	326
13	The Jacobite Wars, 1708–46 *Christopher Duffy*	348

III Scotland in Britain and the Empire

14	The Scottish Military Experience in North America, 1756–83 *Stephen Brumwell*	383
15	The French Revolutionary and Napoleonic Wars, 1793–1815 *Charles J. Esdaile*	407
16	Internal Policing and Public Order, c. 1797–1900 *Ewen A. Cameron*	436
17	Scots and the Wars of Empire, 1815–1914 *Edward M. Spiers*	458
18	Commonwealth Scottish Regiments *Wendy Ugolini*	485
19	The First World War *Trevor Royle*	506
20	Internal Policing and Public Order, c. 1900–94 *Ian S. Wood*	536
21	The Second World War *Jeremy A. Crang*	559
22	The Cold War and Beyond *Niall Barr*	600

IV The Cultural and Physical Dimensions

23	Scottish Military Dress *Allan Carswell*	627
24	Scottish Military Music *Gary J. West*	648

25	The Scottish Soldier in Literature *Robert P. Irvine*	669
26	The Scottish Soldier in Art *Peter Harrington*	688
27	Castles and Fortifications in Scotland *Chris Tabraham*	706
28	The Archaeology of Scottish Battlefields *Tony Pollard*	728
29	Scottish Military Monuments *Elaine W. McFarland*	748
30	Scottish Military Collections *Stuart Allan*	776

Epilogue: Reflections on the Scottish Military Experience *Alistair Irwin*	795
Select Bibliography	813
Notes on the Contributors	828
Illustration Credits	834
Index	840

Illustrations

Maps

1.1	Scotland before and during the Roman era	42
2.1	Scotland in the Early Middle Ages, c. 500–1093	66
3.1	Scotland and northern England in the twelfth and thirteenth centuries	95
4.1	The Wars of Independence, 1296–1328	134
5.1	Scotland and northern England, 1332–1488	159
6.1	Southern Scotland and northern England in the sixteenth and early seventeenth centuries	183
7.1	Warfare in the Highlands and the Isles	210
10.1	Scotland and the Wars of the Three Kingdoms	277
11.1	Scotland from the Restoration to Culloden	299
21.1	Scotland and the Second World War	560

Figures

I.1	Bronze statue of Robert the Bruce, Bannockburn	8
I.2	Colonel Sir Robert Douglas of the Royal Scots	14
I.3	The Black Watch at Fontenoy, 1745	17
I.4	Lieutenant-Colonel Winston Churchill, with officers of the 6th battalion, the Royal Scots Fusiliers, 1916	21
I.5	*The Ross-shire Buffs*	26
1.1	Bronze spearheads discovered at Murrayfield	47
1.2	Woden Law hill-fort, Roxburghshire	51
1.3	Rough Castle, Stirlingshire	57
1.4	Detail from a Roman distance marker from the Antonine Wall at Bridgeness	58
2.1	Dunadd fort	67

2.2	Clyde Rock, Dunbartonshire	70
2.3	Aberlemno churchyard cross-slab	76
2.4	The Sueno Stone	85
3.1	Mote of Urr	98
3.2	Duffus castle	99
3.3	Walrus ivory chess piece found on Lewis	113
3.4	Cast of the Great Seal of King Alexander II	119
4.1	Robert the Bruce slaying Sir Henry de Bohun at Bannockburn	135
4.2	William Wallace in a stained glass window at the National Wallace Monument	142
4.3	Stirling castle	144
4.4	The Scottish siege of Carlisle in 1315	147
5.1	Mons Meg	162
5.2	Scottish longsword, c. 1400–20	170
5.3	Gravestone of Sir Gilbert de Greenlaw	173
5.4	Threave castle	174
6.1	The battle of Flodden in a contemporary woodcut by Hans Burgkmair	192
6.2	Tantallon castle	194
6.3	James Hamilton, earl of Arran and duke of Châtelherault	195
6.4	The battle of Pinkie Cleugh	199
7.1	Carving of a birlinn	213
7.2	Castle Sween	214
7.3	Tomb effigy of Bricius, or Gille-Brigde, fourteenth-century chief of the MacKinnons	224
7.4	Late seventeenth-century Scottish two-handed sword	226
8.1	The confrontation at Carberry Hill in 1567	237
8.2	Edinburgh castle from the east	238
8.3	Bronze statue of a border reiver	241
8.4	Smailholm tower	242
9.1	Highland soldiers at Stettin, 1631	260
9.2	Contemporary engraving of the battle of Breitenfeld, 1631	261
9.3	Sir Alexander Leslie	262
9.4	Cap worn by a grenadier officer of the Royal Écossais, 1745	267
10.1	Small brass cannon, probably used by the covenanters' army	283
10.2	David Leslie, from a lithograph of 1823	284
10.3	Cromwell at Dunbar	293

10.4	George Monck, Cromwell's commander-in-chief in Scotland	294
11.1	Thomas Dalyell of Binns	305
11.2	John Graham of Claverhouse	309
11.3	George Douglas, earl of Dumbarton	313
11.4	The 2nd battalion, the Royal Scots, on the march, 1688	314
12.1	George Hamilton, earl of Orkney	328
12.2	The Cameronians at Blenheim, 1704	334
12.3	The Royal Scots Dragoons (the Scots Greys) at Ramillies, 1706	335
12.4	David Melville, earl of Leven	341
13.1	John Erskine, earl of Mar	351
13.2	Corporal Malcolm MacPherson, executed at the Tower of London	361
13.3	Prince Charles Edward Stuart	363
13.4	Lord George Murray	366
13.5	Detail of a basket-hilted broadsword etched with Jacobite mottos	369
13.6	William Augustus, duke of Cumberland	373
14.1	Miniature of Captain John Peebles of the 42nd Royal Highland Regiment (the Black Watch)	384
14.2	Lieutenant James Hamilton Buchanan, 21st Royal North British Fusiliers	390
14.3	John Campbell, earl of Loudoun	392
14.4	Broadsword said to have been carried by a Highland officer at Quebec in 1759	399
15.1	Jane, duchess of Gordon	411
15.2	*The Fight for the Standard*	420
15.3	The eagle from the standard of the French 45th regiment captured by Sergeant Ewart	420
15.4	Piper Kenneth Mackay of the 79th (Cameron) Highlanders at Waterloo	425
16.1	Militia riot memorial, Tranent	437
16.2	The Scots Greys in Ireland, c. 1848	441
16.3	Sir Archibald Alison, Sheriff of Lanarkshire	442
16.4	Reading the Riot Act to crofters at Aignish farm	451
17.1	*The Wreck of the Birkenhead*	464
17.2	Sir Colin Campbell, commander of the Highland Brigade	466
17.3	Men of the 72nd Highlanders (later the 1st battalion, the Seaforth Highlanders) on their return from the Crimea	467

17.4	Officers of the 1st battalion, the Royal Scots, in Zululand	471
17.5	*At Last, the Bivouac at Omdurman (Gordon's Spirit at Rest)*	474
17.6	Soldiers of the 2nd battalion, the Black Watch, on the march in South Africa	475
18.1	Officers of the New South Wales Scottish Rifles, Sydney, 1895	489
18.2	Men of the 13th Canadian Infantry Battalion (Royal Highlanders of Canada) consolidating a captured trench	494
18.3	'Nancy', the springbok mascot of the 4th South African Infantry Regiment (South African Scottish)	496
18.4	The Transvaal Scottish, Addis Ababa	499
19.1	HMS *Repulse* at Clydebank, 1916	507
19.2	Soldiers of the 2nd battalion, the Argyll and Sutherland Highlanders, at Bois-Grenier	514
19.3	Piper of the 7th battalion, the Seaforth Highlanders, leads men back after an attack	520
19.4	Company Sergeant Major John Douglas and NCOs of the 16th battalion, the Royal Scots, France and Flanders, c. 1918	525
19.5	Sir Douglas Haig, 1918	528
19.6	Gallipoli veterans outside Greyfriars Church, Edinburgh	530
20.1	Men of the 1st battalion, the Gordon Highlanders, on strike duty in Sheffield, 1911	538
20.2	Tanks and soldiers brought in to quell the unrest in Glasgow in 1919	543
20.3	A King's Own Scottish Borderer closes the gates of the Royal Barracks in Dublin, 1914	546
20.4	The King's Own Scottish Borderers man a barrier, Belfast, 1970	549
20.5	Soldiers of the 1st battalion, the Argyll and Sutherland Highlanders, at Holy Cross Primary School, Belfast, 2001	552
21.1	Singer sewing machine factory, Clydebank, in the 1930s	561
21.2	Commandos training at Achnacarry	564
21.3	The Heinkel He-111 shot down near Humbie	567
21.4	Douglas Wimberley in the North African desert	574
21.5	The 'Highway Decorators', Sfax, Tunisia, 1943	575
21.6	Pipers of the 51st Highland Division parade in Tripoli	576
21.7	Men of the 7th battalion, the Seaforth Highlanders, 15th (Scottish) Division, advance during Operation Epsom, Normandy	583

22.1	Demonstration against Polaris in Paisley	604
22.2	Soldiers of the 1st battalion, the Black Watch, after the battle of the Hook, Korea, 1952	612
22.3	Lieutenant-Colonel Colin 'Mad Mitch' Mitchell	615
22.4	Disbandment service of the 1st battalion, the Cameronians (Scottish Rifles), 1968	616
22.5	Celebrating the news of the Argentine surrender: Scots Guards, 14 June 1982	618
22.6	The colours of the 1st battalion, the Black Watch, paraded during the Hong Kong handover ceremony	619
23.1	Cap badge of the Royal Regiment of Scotland	630
23.2	Private of the 43rd Highland Regiment (the Black Watch), 1742	634
23.3	Officer of the 79th (Cameron) Highlanders, c. 1833–6	638
23.4	Pipes and drums of the 2nd battalion, the King's Own Scottish Borderers, 1914	641
23.5	Pipers of the 12th Indian Pioneers with Pipe Major Duff of the 2nd battalion, the Royal Scots, c. 1904	642
24.1	Reconstruction of a carnyx based on the head of the original instrument discovered at Deskford	649
24.2	Piper George Findlater winning the Victoria Cross at Dargai	656
24.3	Pipe Major Daniel Laidlaw VC, 1934	660
24.4	Commandos of the 1st Special Service Brigade landing at Sword Beach on D-Day	661
25.1	Scene from *Black Watch*	670
25.2	Hamish Henderson, in Sicily in 1943, interrogates a captured German paratroop commander	678
25.3	Alec Guinness in the role of Jock Sinclair in *Tunes of Glory*	684
26.1	*The Death of General Wolfe*	691
26.2	*Wellington at Waterloo*	694
26.3	*The Departure of the Highland Brigade*	697
26.4	*Kandahar: The 92nd Highlanders and 2nd Gurkhas Storming Gaudi Mullah Sahibdad*	699
26.5	*All That Was Left of Them*	701
27.1	Dirleton castle	711
27.2	Doune castle	714
27.3	Balvaird castle	715
27.4	Craignethan castle	720
27.5	Tolquhon castle	721
28.1	Culloden battlefield	733

28.2	The Jacobite memorial cairn at Culloden battlefield	734
28.3	Lead shot from Culloden battlefield	737
28.4	Surveying Prestonpans battlefield	740
28.5	The siege of Leith, from the contemporary Petworth map	742
29.1	The National Wallace Monument, Stirling	751
29.2	The Black Watch Monument at Aberfeldy	757
29.3	The Cameronians' Regimental Memorial at Douglas	758
29.4	Service of commemoration at the Scottish National War Memorial	761
29.5	The Commando Memorial, Spean Bridge	766
29.6	The Thistle Foundation's Robin Chapel, Edinburgh	767
30.1	The Armoury Hall at Inveraray castle	780
30.2	Gallery in the Naval and Military Exhibition, 1889	785
30.3	John Buchan MP at the opening of the Scottish National Naval and Military Museum	787
30.4	Regimental displays in the Scottish United Services Museum	788
30.5	Regimental silver at the museum of the Argyll and Sutherland Highlanders	790
30.6	Pipe banner in the Cameronians' regimental collection, Low Parks Museum	791
E.1	Soldier of the 1st battalion, the Black Watch, in Iraq, 2003	797
E.2	Satirical engraving of Highland soldiers in Paris, 1815	801
E.3	Recruiting poster for the Scottish regiments, 1919	808
E.4	Soldiers from the Black Watch, 3rd battalion, Royal Regiment of Scotland (3 SCOTS), receive their gallantry awards for service in Afghanistan	809

Colour plates between pages 170 and 171

1. Bronze shield found at Moss of Auchmaliddie at New Deer
2. Adoration of the Magi from the *Hours of Étienne Chevalier* by Jean Fouquet
3. *The Romance of Alexander*, produced in Flanders c. 1338–44
4. Cap worn by a Grenadier officer in a Scottish unit of the army of William III, c. 1692
5. *The Battle of Killiecrankie*
6. *An Incident in the Rebellion of 1745*

7   Fort George, Ardersier
8   *Scotland For Ever!*
9   Sergeant Major John Dickson portrayed as an old man wearing his medals
10   *The 74th Highlanders, 1846*
11   *Engagement on the Heights above Waterkloof, 1851*
12   *The Thin Red Line*
13   *Jessie's Dream: The Campbells are Coming, Lucknow, September 1857*
14   *Lucknow, November 16th 1857*
15   *The Storming of Tel-el-Kebir*

Colour plates between pages 522 and 523

16   *The First Wounded, London Hospital, August 1914*
17   *Return to the Front: Victoria Railway Station*
18   *A Highlander Passing a Grave*
19   *Pipe Practice, 1918*
20   Lance-Corporal Robertson, 11th City of Edinburgh Battalion, Home Guard
21   *The 51st Highland Division Plans El Alamein*
22   The Argyll and Sutherland Highlanders on patrol in Aden, 1967
23   A detachment from the 1st battalion, the Scots Guards, as part of the procession for the lying in state of the Queen Mother, 2002
24   Edinburgh Military Tattoo
25   Funeral of Lance-Corporal Barry Stephen at St John's Kirk, Perth, 2003
26   A soldier from the Black Watch, 3rd battalion, Royal Regiment of Scotland (3 SCOTS), on operations in Afghanistan

Acknowledgements

In editing this volume we have accumulated many debts. We are grateful first and foremost to our contributors and to Professor Hew Strachan for agreeing to write the foreword.

National Museums Scotland has been an important collaborator in this project and special thanks are due to Dr Stuart Allan (who, as Senior Curator of Military History, has been an indispensable ally), Dr David Caldwell, Dr Fraser Hunter, Helen Osmani and Margaret Wilson.

We are indebted to a host of other museums, galleries, libraries and archives and we wish to express our gratitude to the following: the Argyll and Sutherland Highlanders Museum (Major Bob Elliot, Rod Mackenzie and Joyce Steele), the Black Watch Museum (Emma Halford-Forbes and Tommy Smyth), the Gordon Highlanders Museum (Jesper Ericsson), the Highlanders Museum (Dr Alix Powers-Jones), the King's Own Scottish Borderers Museum (Ian Martin), the Royal Highland Fusiliers Museum (Colonel Bobby Steele), the Royal Scots Museum (Colonel Robert Watson), the Royal Scots Dragoon Guards Museum (Lieutenant-Colonel Roger Binks and Major Robin Maclean), Low Parks Museum (Aileen Anderson), the National Army Museum (Juliet McConnell and Emma Lefley), the Imperial War Museum (David Bell and Yvonne Oliver), the Royal Armouries Museum (Chris Streek), Glasgow Museums (Dr Ralph Moffat, Winnie Tyrrell and Jane Whannel), the New South Wales Scottish Regimental Association (Ian Meek), Historic Scotland (Sean Conlon and Chris Tabraham), the Royal Commission on the Ancient and Historical Monuments of Scotland (Neil Fraser and Graham Turnbull), the National Records of Scotland (Morag Fyfe), the National Library of Scotland (Louise McCarron and Keith Skakle), the National Archives (Hugh Alexander), the British Library

(Martin Minz and Sandra Powlette), the Bodleian Library (Tricia Buckingham and Samantha Townsend), West Sussex Record Office (Alison McCann), the Scottish National Portrait Gallery (Philip Hunt), the McManus Art Gallery and Museum (Anna Robertson), York Art Gallery (Jackie Logan), the National Gallery of Canada (Belma Buljubasic), the Bridgeman Art Library (Charlotte Heyman), the Anne S. K. Brown Military Collection at Brown University (Peter Harrington), Defence News Imagery (Neil Hall and Mark Owens), Getty Images (Lisa Hancock), the Kobal Collection (Cheryl Thomas), the Herald and Evening Times Picture Archive (Kevin Turner), Scotavia Images (Gary Brindle), Canongate (Kirsty Wilson), the Press Association (Lucie Gregory), the National Theatre of Scotland (Emma Schad and Andrew Neilson) and the Design and Artists Copyright Society (Emma Mee).

Academic colleagues have provided helpful advice. Particular thanks are owed to Professor Ian Beckett, Professor Dauvit Brown, Professor Tom Devine, Professor Harry Dickinson, Professor Stephen Driscoll, Dr Julian Goodare, Professor Steve Murdoch, Dr Stephen Reid, Geoffrey Stell and Dr Debra Strickland. Dave Appleyard of the University of Leeds kindly prepared the maps. We also wish to acknowledge the generosity of the Carnegie Trust for the Universities of Scotland for providing a grant towards the cost of the colour illustrations.

We are grateful to the staff (past and present) at Edinburgh University Press. Special tribute should be paid to Roda Morrison for instigating this volume and bringing the editorial team together. We are further indebted to Esmé Watson, John Watson, Rebecca Mackenzie, Eddie Clark and Anna Stevenson for their invaluable guidance.

Last, but not least, we are beholden to our respective spouses, Fiona Spiers, Fiona Douglas and Debra Strickland, for their unstinting support during the long gestation period of the book. Edward Spiers would also like to thank Robert and Amanda for tolerating the production of this book.*

Edward M. Spiers
Jeremy A. Crang
Matthew J. Strickland
Leeds, Edinburgh and Glasgow

---

* In this paperback edition we have taken the opportunity to correct errors of fact that have come to our attention and to update the select bibliography.

Foreword

Until 2011, the baggage hall at Edinburgh airport greeted tourists arriving in Scotland's capital with a notice that said, 'Welcome to Edinburgh, home of the Enlightenment.' For those going to play golf at St Andrews or to catch fish on the Spey, the burden of this message may have been obscure. For those with the education to know what was being referred to, the claim that Edinburgh was as responsible for Voltaire or Rousseau as it was for David Hume may have been hyperbolic; it may even have offended, especially if you hailed from Glasgow, the academic home of Adam Smith. But the point here is that, from the moment the visitor to Edinburgh and its surrounding region leaves the terminal building, the visual images that assault the eye are less likely to be academic or cultural than military. From the Spitfire, moved to the airport roundabout from its home outside the mess of RAF Turnhouse, to the first sight of Edinburgh castle, as it dominates the city's skyline, Scotland proclaims its martial heritage. It is one with which I was brought up, all too aware of the battlefields of Bannockburn, Pinkie, Dunbar and Prestonpans, and a frequent visitor to the military architecture of Craigmillar, Dirleton, Tantallon and Stirling. At its heart was not just Edinburgh's castle, with its national war memorial and its Tattoo, but the National War Museum of Scotland (then called, more prosaically and less grandiloquently, the Scottish United Services Museum), in whose library and amidst whose collections my serious education as a military historian began.

And yet the distinction between the Scottish Enlightenment and Scotland's military identity may not be as stark as this juxtaposition suggests, not least because this book gives the lie to the notion that learning and war are uneasy bedfellows. In the eighteenth century Scotland's political economists were conscious that its military reputation, its capacity to produce soldiers for the rest of Europe, if not necessarily to win wars on its own behalf, might be holding back its growth as a prosperous and hence civilised community. Today the products of that civilisation can devote their skills and knowledge to unpicking the legacy of Scotland's battles, and to separate out myths and legends (of which there are far too many) from truth and reality.

The creation of *A Military History of Scotland* has forged at least two communities that bear testimony to the power of scholarship to provide a common vocabulary, even on a subject so nationally determined as military history. In the first place historians of Scotland have collaborated with military historians to produce this outstanding and innovative account. In the second place both groups no longer demand that you need to be a Scot (or for that matter a former soldier) to be admitted to their brotherhoods, and as a result have collaborated with a much broader range of scholars than they would once have done. Nor does the strength of the book rest solely on the fruitfulness of these two interactions. It is also interdisciplinary, with chapters by an archaeologist and by a literary scholar, and comparative, as it sets Scotland's military experience in context. Put simply, the range and quality of this volume mean that it could not have been written fifty years ago.

We have come a long way from the fancies and even fictions perpetuated by our forebears, sustained by a romanticised view of the Highlands in particular. That myth-making now looks old fashioned, but it at least contained a truth that is today also unfashionable in western liberal democracies – the domination of war in shaping nationhood and in making or (in Scotland's case) breaking states. That ringing endorsement of Scotland's independence, the Declaration of Arbroath, was the product not of the Enlightenment but of war in 1320, however modern its assertion that Scots were fighting 'not for glory, nor riches, nor honours', but 'for freedom'.

Civil war was the defining military experience for Scotland, with Scot fighting Scot as nobles and chiefs competed for internal supremacy, territorial control and economic advantage, and Scot fighting Scot as external pressures interacted with these domestic disputes – from the Wars of Independence of the thirteenth and fourteenth centuries, through the British civil wars (or 'the Wars of the Three Kingdoms' as they are called here) in the seventeenth century, to the Jacobite risings of the eighteenth. In 1707 the union of the English and Scottish parliaments made Scottish nationalism compatible with British. Indeed Scottish soldiers, ambitious for the possibilities that conjunction with England and its empire opened out, were overwhelmingly in favour of the union, even if its corollary was the extinction of a separate Scottish army. It is an irony often forgotten by many nationalists today that the much-vaunted accomplishments of the Scottish regiments over the next three centuries were achieved in the service of the British government that gave them life. Moreover, a cursory survey of the military heroes celebrated in the statues of Scotland's great cities shows that many were not Scots, but Anglo-Irish – from the duke of Wellington, commemorated in both Glasgow and Edinburgh, to Lord Roberts of Kandahar, whose equestrian figure stands at the summit of Kelvingrove Park in Glasgow.

Scottish soldiers served under the command of both generals, in the Peninsula and at Waterloo, and in Afghanistan and South Africa. Those who campaigned across Europe and the empire stood in direct succession to the Scottish mercenaries who had fought with the armies of many north European states in the sixteenth and seventeenth centuries. For both groups soldiering was an honourable profession. It was also a way of escaping the limitations of life in a small and relatively impoverished country on the periphery of Europe. Scottish regiments raised by the Hanoverian crown in the mid-eighteenth century mutinied when confronted with orders to serve abroad, but many Scots also saw foreign service as a path to maturity – to becoming 'a man of parts'. As Scotland prospered in the nineteenth century Scottish recruiting declined in relation to the rest of Britain, but in 1914 Scots responded disproportionately to Kitchener's call to arms. As the (unfounded) fears that war would produce unemployment multiplied, the relationship between enlistment and emigration resonated once again.

Those Scots who served in the Scottish regiments are the tip of a much larger iceberg. We do not know how many Scots left early modern Scotland to join other armies, but one calculation – given in this book – is that about 50,000, or one in five Scots males of military age, served in the Thirty Years War. As military service became nationalised in the eighteenth century, fewer Scots became 'soldiers of fortune', but many joined formations that were not directly Scottish: the army of the East India Company or regiments such as the Royal Artillery that recruited across Britain. Many Scots went south to England in search of work, and so enlisted not in Aberdeen or Dundee but in London or Birmingham.

As a result the military service of many Scots is simply unacknowledged. This is particularly the case in relation to service at sea. The dominant image of the Scottish serviceman today, that of the highlander (so much so that all Scottish infantry, whether recruited from the Highlands or not, now have to wear the kilt), ought in many ways to be that of war at sea, not on land. The archipelago of the west coast shaped its patterns of raiding and conquest, and they reached across to northern Ireland. Those who manned the Scottish fishing fleets or who crewed the country's merchant ships were part of the wider maritime nation on which British naval supremacy was founded. Many of Nelson's subordinates (and Nelson, an Englishman, was another hero of the union in Scotland) were Scots. As Scottish industry flourished in the nineteenth century it did so in large part on the back of shipbuilding, particularly on the Clyde. By the beginning of the twentieth century, when Britain's putative enemy was no longer France but Germany, the naval bases of the south of England, Portsmouth and Plymouth, lost their primacy to those that abutted the North Sea more directly, Rosyth and Scapa Flow.

So we might be more logical if we spoke as readily of the Scottish sailor as of the Scottish soldier. But we do not. Our image is of a warrior hewn from the land, tough and unyielding because those are also the qualities of so much of Scotland, however beautiful. It is a terrain that has itself been so militarised that its hill-forts and castles seem integral to it, rather than man-made additions. That observation applies also to the twentieth century's legacy to the landscape, the country's war memorials. The most striking – the Scottish National War Memorial (also a fusion of Scottish nationalism and British identity) in Edinburgh castle and the Commando memorial at Spean Bridge – seem to spring from the rock on which they stand, and so to belong to their locations as of right.

It is a geography that has shaped how Scotland has fought. Its unproductiveness helps explain Scotland's military backwardness in the fifteenth and sixteenth centuries. Scotland lacked the fodder and grazing to produce heavy horses fit for cavalry charges, and the country was slow to adopt gunpowder, favouring the use of pikemen and archers longer than was the case in much of the rest of Europe. Those areas that were naturally fertile, particularly East Lothian and Berwickshire, were also effectively the Low Countries of Britain, the natural invasion routes not least because they were best able to sustain an army in the field. They were therefore the most susceptible to being fought over, and this was one factor in slowing agricultural development. But to the north and north-west, as well as in the Borders, uplands and mountains naturally favoured defence, and so sustained Scottish independence. The Victorian enthusiasm for the Scottish soldier may have been linked to set-piece battles like Waterloo in 1815 and the Alma in 1854, but the natural form of fighting within Scotland was to raid, to hit and run, and to avoid battle: guerrilla warfare *avant la lettre*.

Scotland is naturally and geologically divided into two by the Great Glen, the fault that runs from Inverness through Loch Ness to Fort William. The kings of Scotland struggled to establish their writ to the north and west of the so-called Highland line. Those to the south saw the highlanders as backward and conservative: their resistance to the sorts of doctrine propagated by the French Revolution made them particularly attractive recruits in the 1790s. Their forms of warfare also seemed particularly brutal and bloody. Current scholarship in military history is much preoccupied with the origins of 'total war', and its association with atrocity and even genocide. Highlanders have not been exempt from their attentions. Fighting before the 1745 Jacobite rebellion could be uncompromising, however inflated the claims made for the so-called 'Highland charge' as a tactical device may now seem to be. The duke of Cumberland's suppression of the Highlands after the battle of Culloden in 1746 can therefore be seen to be as characteristic of warfare as practised in the north-west of Scotland as it was symptomatic of a determination to exterminate rebels operating in Britain's rear during a European war. And since their subsequent incorporation in the British order of battle Highland regiments have had a reputation for a prickly pride, a readiness to take offence, which can prove them fierce and ruthless opponents not just of the enemy but of other units of the British army.

If these attributes are the downside of the Scottish soldier, they should not be allowed to stick solely to the highlander. The 'debatable land' of the Borders proved as hard to govern in the fifteenth and sixteenth centuries as the Highlands, and its folk memories are as strong. In my childhood I was regularly told to behave or 'Black Douglas' would get me. Those stories were perpetuated in literature by Walter Scott, himself a Border laird at Abbotsford, and venerated in the woefully neglected war poetry of John Buchan, a product of Peeblesshire on his mother's side. Buchan, another Scot who made fame and fortune through service to the union and empire without losing his sense of Scottish nationalism, wrote in 1915 'the ordinary Borderer in peacetime looks like anybody else, but these men seem suddenly to have remembered their ancestry'.

Ultimately the Scots in Buchan's fiction are hybrids: Glaswegians who come from Galashiels, like John Amos in *Mr Standfast,* or who serve in Highland regiments. Buchan himself was born in Fife and educated in Glasgow, however much he identified with the Borders. The same point can be made of a more recent and popular Scottish literary lion, George MacDonald Fraser. In *Quartered Safe Out Here,* now one of the classic memoirs of the Second World War, he recorded his wartime service as a private soldier in Burma with the Border Regiment, which recruited in Cumberland and Westmorland. But after the war he was commissioned in the Gordon Highlanders, and his service with them produced two books, *The General Danced at Dawn* and *McAuslan in the Rough*, which hilariously capture the essence and ethos of a Highland regiment, above all through the prism of a hapless, militarily incompetent and presumed Glaswegian, the eponymous McAuslan.

Over the last fifty years Scotland's military identity has been vested in the Scottish regiments; indeed much Scottish nationalism has also ridden on their backs. Every restructuring of defence has fractured into regimental soul-searching as amalgamations and disbandments have forced hard and uncomfortable choices. Gregory Burke's play for the National Theatre of Scotland, *Black Watch*, that company's inaugural production in 2006, made the point, not just in its script but also in its timing. It was a wake for a regiment faced with extinction. Formally neither the Black Watch nor the Gordon Highlanders exist any more; they – like all the other Scottish infantry regiments of the line – are subsumed in the Royal Regiment of Scotland. There is a message here, albeit one tinged with sadness at the departure of the titles disseminated and made famous by two world wars.

The Scottish United Services Museum of my youth was organised in regimental sections, by seniority, beginning with the Scots Guards. The most senior of the infantry of the line regiments, the Royal Scots or First of Foot, came next. In 1881, like the other Lowland regiments, the Royal Scots had aped its more junior Highland colleagues by adopting some aspects of 'Highlandism', tartan trews and, for officers, claymores. As a result, for the casual and uncommitted visitor, and even for the scholar, the regimental divisions within the museum seemed repetitive and obscured a deeper truth: a common Scottish identity. The new displays implicitly recognise that nationalism is more important than localism, with their thematic, more revealing and instructive organisation. The title of the new Royal Regiment of Scotland makes a similar point. Like its predecessors, it forges Scots not only of those who enlist from the different cities and counties of Scotland, as well as those Scots who reside outwith Scotland, but also of those whose origins lie in other parts of the United Kingdom and even further afield. *A Military History of Scotland* is in this respect a metaphor for the same idea: that of multiple, sometimes incoherent and often competing identities, but of identities that are still capable of formation into a single and concrete whole.

Hew Strachan
Chichele Professor of the History of War
University of Oxford

Introduction

EDWARD M. SPIERS

In taking his leave of 51st Highland Division in August 1943, after a year of fighting overseas, from El Alamein to the Sferro hills of Sicily, Major-General Douglas Wimberley 'spent a long time' in his caravan composing his farewell 'Order of the Day to all Ranks'. In this order, he declared:

> By your deeds, it is not too much to claim that you have added to the pages of military history, pages which may well bear comparison with the stories of our youth, telling us of our kinsmen who fought at Bannockburn, Culloden, Waterloo, the Alma and at Loos. Further, in achieving this, you have earned, as is indeed your due, the grateful acknowledgements of your Country . . . All this can be summed up in one verse recently written of the Division in the Scots' Press.
>
> > Ye canna mak' a sojer wi' braid an' trappin's braw
> > Nor gie him fightin' spirit when his back's ag'in the wa'
> > It's the breedin' in the callan's that winna let them whine
> > The bluid o' generations frae lang, lang syne.[1]

These sentiments capture the self-belief of the Scot as a fighting man, a reputation developed over centuries, and often in fraught relations with English neighbours. This reputation, etched into the popular consciousness, underpins a sense of national identity forged in battle since before the Wars of Independence when Scotland, as Tom Devine reminds us, 'was born fighting'.[2] Accordingly, this volume has sought to provide a military history[3] of Scotland from the earliest times through the Wars of Independence, and thence the struggles of the Stewart kings to establish their royal authority, despite a military record described as 'abysmal' in the context of the sixteenth and early seventeenth centuries.[4] It encompasses the engagement of Scots in the wars of Europe, and thereafter as part of the British army in the imperial wars and through the massive challenges of two world wars to the present day.

It seemed timely to undertake this work after the surge of writing on Scottish history, including military history, in the late twentieth century,[5] and an opportunity to update a claim in *The Oxford Companion to Scottish History* (2001) that 'little has been written on the Scottish army before the 17th century'.[6] In the past decade major studies have appeared on ancient warfare in Scotland, Celtic fortifications, the Canmore and Balliol dynasties, several medieval Scottish kings, Wallace and Bruce, as well as scholarly works on Bannockburn, the Border wars, the Irish–Scottish wars and Highland clanship.[7] By assigning seven chapters to the earlier periods of Scottish history, we believe that the fruits of this scholarship can find a proper outlet in this volume. Comparable sections follow on the crafting of a Scottish–British military identity (through involvement in the religious, ideological and civil wars that consumed the military in the British Isles and on the continent in the seventeenth and early eighteenth centuries); on Scotland's role in the wars of empire, in providing military aid to the civil power, and in wars of national survival, the end of empire and beyond; and finally, on the manifold legacies of Scotland's military identity, explored culturally in literature, music and art, physically in fortifications, monuments and military collections, and materially in the evidence unearthed by battlefield archaeology.

Although this work has a clear chronological sequence, it is designed as neither a grand work of historical narrative nor a series of discrete and self-sustaining essays. Within the broad parameters set by the editors, contributors have been free to develop themes in their essays that relate to the evolving account of Scotland's military history, one from which attitudes towards the conduct of war gradually emerge, namely degrees of resilience, loyalty, bellicosity and a collective fortitude displayed on active service over the centuries. Such martial qualities may not be unique to the Scottish soldier but they became inextricably linked to his reputation for military prowess. If this reputation underpins a distinctive sense of military identity, both internally in the Scots' high level of self-esteem and externally in the perception of the fighting 'Jock', care must be taken in expounding upon any Scottish military tradition stretching over the centuries. Like the layered, and at times divergent, strands of the Irish military tradition,[8] Scotland has never had any single, uniform military tradition. If such traditions derive, at least partially, from modes of fighting over periods of time, then the patterns of fighting during the Wars of Independence, involving spearmen deployed in schiltroms (hedgehog-like formations to keep cavalry at bay), raids into the northern counties of England, the slighting of castles and a scorched-earth policy, bore scant resemblance to subsequent service in continental armies, in covenanters' armies, still less to the Highland charge.

Moreover, as Hew Strachan has rightly observed, the military reputation of Scotland could ebb as well as flow:[9] once at peace with the old enemy, Restoration Scotland recoiled from the costs of supporting a large standing army, and even the militia of Charles II, a partial reflection of the old traditions of universal military obligation, atrophied under his successors. For nearly a century Scotland lacked any militia,[10] leaving home defence to a British regular army, many of whose units were often serving abroad under the direction of a London-based executive. If some Lowland elites advocated the restoration of a Scots militia to promote 'self-respect and civic virtue' in non-Jacobite Scotland, soldiering appeared to have a limited appeal in the Lowlands and the Lowland regiments barely a discernible image. Whether, as Steve Murdoch suggests, this reflected an absorption with more profitable economic opportunities, or a satisfaction that the settlement of 1707 had secured the Kirk, or the competitive effects of naval recruiting, a real contrast is evident in the Highlands where military service had a much more positive appeal, albeit on a distinctively contractual basis.[11] Admittedly attitudes would change during the French Revolutionary and Napoleonic Wars, with the surge of military recruitment and volunteering throughout Scotland. The redoubtable achievements of Scottish regiments in these wars (and the imagery associated with the Highland units) would be celebrated in paintings, prints, and all manner of imperial iconography throughout the nineteenth century.

During this century the Highlandisation of Scottish military traditions gathered pace. At a time when Highland regiments were recruiting more heavily from the central belt, and so becoming more broadly 'Scottish' in composition, 'the signs and symbols of the Highland military tradition were increasingly adopted by Lowland Scots'.[12] Lowland fascination with the Highlands coincided with the heyday of Romantic writing in the first quarter of the nineteenth century. Sir Walter Scott's first novel, *Waverley* (1814), focused on the 'lost cause' of Jacobitism, and his invention of Highland traditions, complete with clan leadership and martial connotations, reached its apogee in August 1822 when, assisted by Major-General David

Stewart of Garth, he organised the celebrations for the first visit of a Hanoverian monarch to Edinburgh.[13] This mythologising of the Highlands provided an escapist outlet for those who recoiled from the rapid industrialisation and urbanisation of Lowland Scotland, implying that the essence of the nation was located in a mythical rural past, where the purported qualities of the highlander – stoicism, loyalty and martial prowess – were forged amid a rugged, unspoiled landscape.[14] Scotland's military, increasingly adorned with Highland accoutrements but still embodied fully within the British army, would find plenty of scope for demonstrating its fighting attributes, powers of endurance and *esprit de corps* over the next two hundred years. While the record was by no means uniform, involving moments of tragedy and pathos as well as occasions for triumph and acclaim, Scottish units, whether defending the heights of Balaclava or supporting the assault on Fallujah, would find ways of distinguishing themselves on active service.

So there are significant periods of continuity in Scotland's military tradition, but any review of the phenomenon has to take account of the discontinuities of the Scottish military experience, including internecine warfare within Scotland itself, and the varieties of tradition involved (including the periodic recurrence of a principled anti-war tradition).[15] Yet the notion of a broad military tradition, rooted in the experiences of war at home and abroad, seems relevant to any attempt to understand how the military history of Scotland evolved. This martial culture contributed to the establishment of a Scottish kingdom by gradually extending acceptance of the king's writ within Scotland, and by securing its territory. It came to express a distinctive sense of Scottish identity, albeit intertwined latterly within an encompassing British identity.[16]

Early warfare and the emergence of a Scottish kingdom

Fraser Hunter and James Fraser remind us that a fighting tradition has an ancient pedigree in what is now Scotland. There are signs of fighting from the Neolithic Age onwards, including weapons, hill-forts and skeletons of warriors, but nothing to suggest that the inhabitants of Caledonia were prepared for the shock of the three Roman invasions that drove as far north as the River Spey and occupied much of central and southern Scotland for several decades. As the first of three well-organised and equipped military machines that would leave a heavy imprint upon Scotland,[17] the Romans established precedents for future invaders. In advancing beyond the Solway and Tweed and usually up the east coast, where invading columns and fortified positions could be resupplied from the sea,[18] they exploited routes that others would follow. Similarly, the Romans demonstrated that overwhelming military superiority, if deployed properly, could prevail in encounter battles. Yet their pattern of limited conquest and occupation – 'in total, less than thirty ill-documented years'[19] – reflected the remoteness of the country, the difficulty of the topography, the severity of the winters in certain years and the vulnerability of supply lines as irreconcilable local inhabitants engaged in guerrilla warfare.

Violence, or the threat of ferocious retributive violence, remained a recurrent feature of early medieval northern Britain, with resources exchanged as a result of war or as the price of tribute to stave off the ravaging, plunder, mutilation and enslavement that characterised contemporary fighting. Military reputations became increasingly important, with battles and sieges written up in chronicle narratives and warriors commemorated in monumental sculpture. Wars also became the province of a military aristocracy involving kings, nobles and their retinues of clients and dependents, extending at times into 'common armies' of men, mustered in acts of duty to their immediate lord. Though the Scots were renowned as a people that fought primarily on foot, with small shields and long thrusting spears,[20] Matthew Strickland highlights the important catalyst for developing the king's forces begun by David I's extensive grants of land to Norman, English and Flemish followers in exchange for military service as heavily armed knights and serjeants (the latter serving with less expensive equipment and mounts, and sometimes as archers). Over some two centuries before the Edwardian invasion, there were only eight years of Anglo-Scottish warfare and, on each occasion, the king of Scots sought to exploit discord in England by invading the northern counties. Scottish failures, whether at the battle of the Standard (22 August 1138) or in various sieges, which exposed their lack of sophisticated siege weaponry, ensured that they could not retain any of their captured territory but their raids ravaged the lands and terrified northern communities. Discounting the accounts of their practices by English chroniclers as simply 'hostile propaganda' or as evidence that the Scots, in massacring or enslaving non-combatants, were merely waging war 'by different rules to the Anglo-Normans',[21] seems a relatively mild characterisation of the testimony adduced by Strickland. While Scottish troops would abandon the enslaving of captives by the thirteenth century, their reputation as wild and ruthless fighters was already a matter of common repute south of the border.

Scottish military capacities were then tested as never before by the way in which Edward I pressed his claims of overlordship over all other rulers in the British Isles, richly earning the sobriquet 'hammer of the Scots'. In chronicling the course of Edward's triumphant advance in 1296, and the ensuing Wars of Independence, Michael Prestwich assesses the attributes of the Scottish armies that won two remarkable victories against the odds. He also alludes to the importance of a Scottish leadership that displayed determination and imagination, factors that clearly had a bearing upon the development of Scotland's military tradition. William Wallace was one of the earliest leaders (alongside Andrew Murray, who died of wounds inflicted at Stirling Bridge) to raise the revolt on behalf of the deposed king, John Balliol. By killing the English sheriff of Lanark, he triggered a revolt in Lanarkshire, and with Murray plotted the ambush by which they exploited the blunder of sending English knights across the narrow bridge at Stirling. In the ensuing battle of Stirling Bridge (11 September 1297) the English were routed and their commander, John de Warenne, earl of Surrey, fled to bring news of the humiliation. In following up this triumph Wallace, now supported by more of the Scottish nobility, was able to clear most of Scotland of its English mastery[22] and launch a devastating five-week raid into England. As Fiona Watson remarks, 'Those living immediately south of the border doubtless came to the conclusion during those months that William Wallace could give Edward I a lesson or two in oppression.'[23] In March 1298 Wallace, a scion of minor gentry, reached his zenith as a political/military leader when he was knighted and appointed sole Guardian of Scotland.

Wallace's martial reputation then suffered a crippling blow (at least among contemporaries if not in legend) by his readiness to confront another invading army under Edward's personal command at Falkirk (22 July 1298). Deploying his infantry on high ground in schiltroms (intended to face onrushing cavalry), interspersed with archers and supported by cavalry in the rear, he found that this formation – after the Scots cavalry fled – invited annihilation by the combined assaults of English archers and heavy cavalry. Wallace abdicated the guardianship thereafter in favour of a collective leadership under the representatives of the leading families of Bruce and Comyn, later joined by Bishop William Lamberton. Little is known about Wallace's subsequent role in the continuing resistance but, after four years on the continent, he returned in 1303 to continue harrying English forces in the company of other noble commanders. Once the last embers of the revolt were suppressed in 1304, Wallace was captured by Sir John Menteith and earned lasting martyrdom by virtue of his trial and horrendous execution. For all his subsequent fame and iconic status, derived in part from Blind Harry's poem of the 1470s, fellow Scots did not erect any shrines or memorials to Wallace: as Alexander Grant observes, 'there was no contemporary cult of William Wallace'.[24]

Leadership passed to Robert Bruce after the slaying of John Comyn and the seizure of the Scottish crown in March 1306. Encountering opposition from the nobles and soldiers who had fought for Balliol, the kinsmen of Comyn and the English king in whose eyes he was a mere rebel, having broken an oath of allegiance made in 1302, Bruce had to display exceptional powers of leadership. In managing to survive the initial onslaught of his Scottish adversaries and then assume the offensive, he proved the master of unconventional warfare. He was able to recognise the weaknesses of his enemies, 'knowing when and how to fight them and how to employ his own limited forces to best effect'.[25] His castle-destruction policy, as analysed by Prestwich, can be seen as a strategy to undermine the political power of his enemies in the north of Scotland and to deny Edward II the forward bases from which he could project power south of the Forth, including from the three royal castles of Edinburgh, Roxburgh and Stirling.[26] This strategy seemed linked with Bruce's raiding deep into northern England from 1311 onwards, by which he raised resources from plunder and tribute to finance his siege warfare in Scotland.[27]

Bannockburn, in this context, was a battle Bruce did not wish to fight. Heavily outnumbered, he initially formed his schiltroms in a wooded park to resist the precipitate cavalry charges on 23 June 1314. Then, on learning that during the night the English army had manoeuvred itself into a dangerous and highly unfavourable position on the boggy Carse, intersected by the Bannock Burn and other water courses, Bruce seized the initiative. He moved his schiltroms forward the following morning to exploit this blunder and deny the enemy the time and space in which to deploy their larger numbers of horse and foot. After a hard-fought battle the Scots triumphed over the English, demoralised, poorly led and with a high command riven by internal discord. Although like many medieval battles Bannockburn would not prove decisive in itself, it would nonetheless pass into folklore as 'a victory of spirit over might'.[28] Bruce was now recognised within Scotland as king by military conquest, with all his internal opponents either forced to submit or sent into exile. In victory he behaved like a king; he treated the bodies of fallen nobility respectfully and returned them to England. He also returned the privy seal and shield of Edward II found on the field of battle, and exchanged

Figure I.1 Bronze statue of Robert the Bruce, Bannockburn. The statue, which was sculpted by Charles d'Orville Pilkington Jackson, was unveiled by Her Majesty the Queen in 1964 to mark the 650th anniversary of the battle.

the earl of Hereford, brother-in-law of the English king, for his wife and daughter, so establishing the prospect of a dynastic line.

Denied English recognition, however, Bruce had to persevere with his castle-destruction policy in Scotland (with the exception of Berwick, which was retained after its capture in 1318, possibly as a base from which to project power south of the border).[29] Meanwhile he dominated northern England by repeated raids but the opening of a second front in Ireland proved less productive when his brother, Edward, was killed at Faughart in 1318. Only willing to engage the enemy when the odds were in his favour, notably at Old Byland (14 October 1322), where he nearly captured the English king, Bruce generally avoided battle, having preferred scorched-earth tactics as in the previous summer when the English invaded. Ultimately his policies of calculated and ruthless aggression spared Scotland from further conquest, and achieved his objective of securing recognition as king of Scots by England at the Treaty of Edinburgh-Northampton (1328). If that treaty was a product primarily of internal strife in England following the overthrow of Edward II, Bruce had positioned himself to exploit such turmoil and secure a desired outcome. He had managed, as David Cornell argues, to avoid being seduced by Bannockburn 'into believing that a battle-seeking strategy could win the war against England'.[30]

The initial failure of Bruce's successors to learn the lessons of his success is analysed in depth by Alastair Macdonald. After a series of costly defeats, the Scots reverted to scorched-earth tactics whenever invaded after the 1330s, and mounted numerous raids into the northern counties in the hope of profiting from English distractions during the Hundred Years War, and of upholding commitments under the Auld Alliance. Dating at least as far back as William the Lion's alliance with Louis VII, and subsequently given formal expression in the Treaty of Paris (23 October 1295), the Auld Alliance was by no means always a mutually supportive arrangement; Balfour-Melville even argued that the alliance 'was always more cordial . . . when the two nations remained apart'.[31] Nevertheless, the alliance seemed particularly apposite at a time when the two countries faced huge challenges from the massive strength of the English war machine under kings like Edward III (r. 1327–77) and Henry V (r. 1413–22). It also provided opportunities for Scots to serve overseas, especially after the near annihilation of the French nobility at Agincourt (25 October 1415) and the virtual disintegration of the French government four years later. The dauphin of France begged Scotland for direct military assistance, and the Scots sent an expeditionary force to serve in France from 1419 to 1424. Foreign service, as the Scottish commanders experienced, involved the prospect of huge rewards and risks. After the victory at Baugé (21 March 1421), John Stewart, earl of Buchan, became constable of France, Sir John Stewart of Darnley was granted the lordship of Concressault and later Aubigny, and Archibald Douglas, earl of Wigtown, became count of Longueville. When Wigtown returned home his father, Archibald Douglas, fourth earl of Douglas, joined the expedition, becoming duke of Touraine. Within four months Douglas died fighting alongside Buchan and his second son, James, at the battle of Verneuil (17 August 1424).[32] Darnley, who lost an eye at the defeat of Cravant (1423) before being captured and exchanged, continued in service until he was killed alongside his brother, William, at the battle of the Herrings (12 February 1429), where a Franco-Scottish attack upon a supply convoy, carrying barrels of herrings amongst other supplies for the English forces besieging Orléans (1428–9), was routed. Despite the heavy losses of Scottish soldiers, particularly at Verneuil, a Scottish presence remained in the royal armies of France for the rest of the century and beyond, most notably La Garde Écossaise.[33]

Military pressures on Scotland and France were eased greatly by the ending of the Hundred Years War in 1453, the ensuing Wars of the Roses and the reign of the cautious and parsimonious English king, Henry VII (r. 1485–1509). The recrudescence of Anglo-French warfare under his son, Henry VIII, reactivated the Auld Alliance and plunged Scotland into further conflicts. Resilience, argues Gervase Phillips, was the most impressive aspect of the Scottish response as evidenced by the vast numbers ready to respond to musters and to fight in the host for Scottish kings. In the last major Anglo-Scottish war, Scots defended Edinburgh castle despite the sack of the city (1544), and won minor engagements at Haddon Rig (1542) and Ancrum Moor (1545). For invading English armies, such Scottish resilience compounded the difficulties of overcoming Scotland's topographical challenges, the precariousness of lengthening supply lines, the effects of scorched-earth tactics in Lothian and the Borders, the diversions of domestic instability and wars with France, and the mounting costs involved (including the expensive strengthening of the fortifications of Berwick).[34] Yet the inept conduct of five Scottish invasions of England, in 1522, 1523, 1542, 1545 and 1547, coupled with the salutary defeats of numerically superior Scottish forces at Flodden (9 September 1513), Solway Moss (24 November 1542) and in the last battle between Scotland and England as independent countries, Pinkie Cleugh (10 September 1547), indicated how little

Scotland had progressed as a military power. The Scottish rout at Pinkie reflected not only poor leadership, lack of horse and inferior artillery but also 'a lack of training' and professionalism in the use of the pike. Serving alongside the well-supplied French professional forces that came to Scotland's aid 'must have brought it home to many Scots that their host was not a credible fighting force except for purely local struggles'.[35]

Such struggles had plagued the Stewarts. Like many other medieval kingdoms, powerful magnates and regional lords had ignored, challenged and periodically rebelled against the crown. They had assassinated James I in 1437 and profited from the numerous royal minorities that blighted the Stewart dynasty to extend their territories and their political influence. As the Stewarts lacked any standing army and relied on nobles to contribute fighting forces, they had to exploit the many fractious rivalries between the nobility whenever they wished to enhance their internal authority. In this respect, as Martin MacGregor explains, Gaelic Scotland provided peculiar challenges. Quite apart from its physical remoteness and island fastnesses, the Isles, like Ireland, possessed a geostrategic significance as a potential second front in Anglo-Scottish rivalry. Moreover, the Lord of the Isles, who could recruit vast numbers of Islesmen, was the only magnate able to defeat the forces of the crown in pitched battles. Sometimes he made common cause with other regional magnates against the crown, as John MacDonald, the earl of Ross and fourth Lord of the Isles, would do with James, the ninth earl of Douglas in 1454. Accordingly, James II had to buy off Ross before he mounted his final assault on the Douglas estates in the Borders. The ravaging of the Douglas lands, with the storming of Abercorn castle and the routing of the clan at the battle of Arkinholm (1 May 1455), not only drove Douglas into exile but also led to the forfeiture of his estates and represented 'the assertion of the Scottish crown's authority on the principal military frontier of the realm'.[36] When the Lord of the Isles negotiated with Edward IV of England for a tripartite division of Scotland with the exiled Douglas under the delightfully named Treaty of Westminster-Ardtornish (1462), James III later used the treaty to justify the forfeiture of the earldom of Ross in 1475.

Even worse followed during the reign of Mary Queen of Scots when, as Matthew Glozier shows, she survived a Catholic rising and a rebellion by her own Protestant half-brother, Lord James Stewart, the earl of Moray, before the Marian civil war (1567–73) erupted. Once again James VI had to consolidate royal authority after his minority, and he led six expeditions (1587–94) to quell signs of disaffection by Catholic nobles, a separate challenge from the Protestant, Francis Stewart, fifth earl of Bothwell, and a rebellion by the Catholic earls of Huntly and Angus. James, though, was never able to press his claims for the crown of England by force of arms, prompting Keith Brown's observation that 'Scotland might have been an armed society, but it was not suitably armed for war ... The King of Scots had no army and no likelihood of ever having one unless parliament and, in particular, the nobility thought it necessary.'[37] The Union of the Crowns in 1603 transformed this state of affairs, enabling James VI and I to suppress the Border reivers ruthlessly and later to exert effective pressure in the Isles.

Forging a Scottish–British military identity

Despite the establishment of an executive in London, thousands of Scots, as Alan Carswell explains, still sought martial adventure and employment overseas, serving as mercenaries in Europe with many of them supporting the Dutch Revolt against Catholic Spain (1568–1648). During a period of relative peace in mainland Britain (1604–25), Scottish officers and other ranks derived much of their military training and experience from service on the continent. James VI and I also sanctioned small expeditionary forces to support his continental diplomacy. The Scottish privy council funded a separate Scottish intervention on behalf of the Protestant cause, led by King Christian IV of Denmark-Norway, while the marquess of Hamilton raised another 'British' force of 6,000 soldiers to fight for the Swedish king Gustav II Adolf.[38] As many as 25,000 Scots, including 2,000 officers, may have served in the Swedish army over the period 1629–48, and some veterans, such as Alexander Leslie, later first earl of Leven, returned to serve in the covenanters' armies, bringing the benefits of sound military training as well as tactical and administrative innovation.

This would prove hugely valuable in the opening exchanges of the religious and ideological wars that would engulf the Three Kingdoms. Martyn Bennett reviews both Scotland's role in these wars, and the early successes of the covenanters against royalist armies, but the climax found Scotland facing another major invasion from the New Model Army, led by Oliver Cromwell. It was preceded by an extensive and well-documented propaganda war steeped in religious ideology. Presbyterian Scots depicted the invading army as not so much an English army as an 'army of sectaries', that is, a sectarian army which tolerated heretical opinions and 'stood against and were a response to the expansionist policies of the established Church of Scotland'.[39] Following the challenge from the attempted imposition of the Book of Common Prayer by King Charles I in 1637, the Scots had sought to protect the Kirk by using the National Covenant (1638), and then the Solemn League and Covenant (1643), as justifications for the despatch of covenanters' armies into England to establish Presbyterianism and religious uniformity across both kingdoms. When this failed to materialise, and Charles I was executed (30 January 1649), the Scottish parliament proclaimed Charles II king of Great Britain and Ireland and required him to sign the covenant. Cromwell not only denounced the 'tyranny' of the Kirk's demands but also damned the Scots as malignant for imposing a king who had consorted with Catholics in Ireland and on the continent. English Independents, who predominated in the New Model Army, now regarded 'the defeat of the Scots' as 'vital to the establishment of a free state'.[40]

The pre-war propaganda had interesting effects. When Scotland's committee of estates ordered every male between the ages of sixteen and sixty to take all their provisions and gather in Edinburgh for the defence of the nation, the invading army found the Borders denuded of men and desolate.[41] Cromwell's taunts of religious malignancy, however, had prompted a purging of several thousand royalists and several hundred of their officers from the Scottish army. The latter still outmanoeuvred Cromwell's army for over a month before choosing to engage his force, now much weakened and numerically smaller, at Dunbar (3 September 1650) where the Scots held the high ground. Having redeployed his forces the previous night, Cromwell launched a surprise flank attack and, within an hour, 3,000 Scots lay dead and 10,000 surrendered at the cost of twenty English fatalities: Cromwell's cavalry, having pursued the fleeing Scots, sang Psalm 117 in triumph. Once suitably reinforced, the New Model Army exploited Scottish divisions and war-weariness; it secured the surrender of all Scotland's castles, sacked the last major stronghold, Dundee (1 September 1651), and drove Charles II into exile after the rout at Worcester (3 September 1651). Unlike previous occupations, Cromwell established military forts all across Scotland, including major citadels in Inverness and Inverlochy, and the Commonwealth ended Scotland's political independence. It enforced Protestant religious toleration under an English military government but treated Scotland with far less repression and punishment than Ireland.[42]

However readily Scotland embraced the restoration of the monarchy in 1660, and the recovery of its independent statehood, the Interregnum had confirmed that its military capacity had fallen far below that of England. Despite their successes in the Bishops' Wars, the covenanters' armies had foundered before the professional

Figure I.2 Colonel Sir Robert Douglas of the Royal Scots retrieves the regiment's colour at Steenkirke, 1692. Painted by Richard Simkin, c. 1900.

training, tactics and ordnance of the New Model Army, supported by the Cromwellian navy, 'one of the most powerful in Europe'.[43] Henceforth Scotland's political and military fortunes seemed inextricably bound with the development of a United Kingdom. If the Scottish standing army, as described by Keith McLay, was only a modest body, sufficient to deal with armed uprisings of covenanters, some of the regiments raised in this era would have a long association with Scotland. As the restored monarchy placed a premium upon loyalty to the crown, the new units included a third regiment of foot guards, formed in 1661, that became known as the Scots Guards, and Le Régiment de Douglas, brought back after nearly three decades of French service since its formation in 1633. As the oldest regiment on the English establishment, it saw service at home, in Europe and, under its ennobled colonel, the earl of Dumbarton, in Tangier from 1680 to 1684. For this first tour of duty by a British regiment outside Europe, fighting the Moors and staving off the ravages of disease and dissipation, it received a battle honour, 'Tangier 1680', and the title 'The Royal Regiment of Foot'. It became the senior line infantry regiment, the 1st of Foot (later the Royal Scots).[44] In fostering regimental spirit, such honours complemented the gradual equipping of these regiments with more modern weapons – flintlock muskets, bayonets and grenades for the grenadier companies – and with standard red-coated uniforms. Yet well-armed government soldiers, if maldeployed, could still be overwhelmed, as John Graham, Viscount Dundee, demonstrated at Killiecrankie (27 July 1689). Exploiting the favourable ground, he was able to 'combine the superior mobility of the Highlanders, their fierce appearance and reputation, and the shock power of the Highland charge'.[45]

Military allegiances rent by the dynastic struggle of 1688, and the accession of William of Orange, had triggered both a mutiny within the Royal Scots, objecting to their despatch to the Netherlands, and the abortive Jacobite rebellion of 1689. The Royal Scots, once purged of their leading mutineers, served with distinction in the Netherlands, fighting in the main battles of Steenkirke (1692), Landen (1693) and the siege of Namur (1695). Like several other Scottish regiments – the 21st (later Royal Scots Fusiliers), the 26th (later the Cameronians) and the Scots Greys – they also served under Marlborough in the War of the Spanish Succession (1701–14). Scots, as John Childs explains, comprised a significant proportion of Marlborough's officers and men and were to the fore in all the great victories of Blenheim, Ramillies, Oudenarde and Malplaquet. It is doubtful if many equalled the determination of Henry Gordon who, as a second lieutenant in the Scots Fusiliers, lost 'a legg & half of his thigh' at Blenheim before serving in another 'five campaigns' in the earl of Stair's Regiment of Dragoons until being 'shott through the other legg att the battle of Mons'.[46] Effectively the Scots, as Childs claims, had been serving in a *de facto* British army since 1689 and this experience of active service in Europe, coupled with the Whiggish views of many Scottish officers, ensured their overwhelming support for the union of 1707.[47] The ending of the small Scottish establishment was hardly a blow as martial accolades had been won through service in the armies of continental Europe over the past two centuries. Despite the continuing appeal of the Scots Brigade in the Dutch service,[48] the military service of Scots would now be predominantly in the British army.

Christopher Duffy, however, reminds us that the union received an immediate challenge in the Jacobite rising of 1708 before another three risings followed in 1715, 1719 and 1745. Of these rebellions, 1715 attracted by far the largest number of Scots but they were treated very lightly in its wake and much more lightly than the English Jacobites. The aftermath of the 'Forty-Five was very different, prompting the claims of Alan MacInnes that it reflected 'genocidal clearance verging on ethnic cleansing'. He admits that the numbers of victims are not known, and that the repression 'markedly slackened off' after the Young Pretender escaped to the continent in September 1746, but that the whole point of the policy was to 'inflict such a crushing defeat on the Jacobite clans that they would remember it for generations'.[49] Tony Pollard rightly contends that any characterisation of these events has to be placed in context, and that by comparison with the atrocities in the wake of several European wars of the mid-eighteenth century neither the scale nor the nature of the repression appears unique.[50] Underpinning the 'Forty-Five reprisals was a mixture of fear at the progress made by the Jacobites on this occasion, a dehumanising of the enemy, a desire for revenge after the mutilation of fallen government soldiers at the battles of Prestonpans and Falkirk, and a determination to ensure that another rebellion never erupted.[51] If prime responsibility for the repression subsequently inflicted on Highland communities rests with Cumberland and his military entourage, particularly William Anne Keppel, the second earl of Albemarle, who was gazetted commander-in-chief of Scotland on 23 August 1746, 'Lowland Scots', as Bruce Lenman avers, 'enforced Cumberland's orders with a degree of harshness which exceeded even that of the royal duke himself'.[52] Some Gaels, like Captain George Munro of Culcairn in Easter Ross and Captain Alexander Grant of Knockando in Strathspey, joined in the repression but several Whig commanders of Highland troops, including Major-General John Campbell of Mamore (the future fourth duke of Argyll) and especially John Campbell, fourth earl of Loudoun, were much more lenient in their exaction of reprisals.[53] Parliament sustained the process of pacification by the passage of the Disarming Acts of 1746 and 1747, disarming the Highlands, prohibiting the wearing of Highland dress and abolishing the traditional legal powers of many chieftains and Highland noblemen. Approval was also given to the construction of the new Fort George, which was built between 1748 and 1769 on the estuary of the Moray Firth, guarding the sea approach to Inverness.

Scotland in Britain and the empire

Highland redemption, as Stephen Brumwell indicates, gathered momentum in the vast numbers raised by aristocratic Highland families, Jacobite as well as Whig, to fight in North America, and in their valiant contributions at various battles, including Ticonderoga (8 July 1758), and on the Plains of Abraham (13 September 1759). This fighting capacity developed a potential first exemplified by the 43rd Foot (later renumbered as the 42nd Foot or the Black Watch) in the 1740s. When first ordered overseas (breaking the terms of enlist-

Figure I.3 The Black Watch at Fontenoy, 1745. Painted by William Skeoch Cumming, 1896.

ment for home defence), the regiment had mutinied, but its subsequent heroism at the battle of Fontenoy (11 May 1745) confirmed the fighting worth of highlanders in the Hanoverian cause.[54] The government's need for soldiers to fight its many wars in Europe and India, as well as in North America, led to the employment of Lowland regiments, too. The 'Year of Victories' during the Seven Years War included the memorable victory at Minden (1 August 1759), where the 25th Foot (later the King's Own Scottish Borderers) participated in the stunning victory over the French army.[55]

Similarly, Scottish soldiers found themselves engaged in fighting on several fronts during the French Revolutionary and Napoleonic Wars. Charles Esdaile reviews the widespread assumptions about the fighting reputation of soldiers from the Highlands in the European campaigns leading up to and including Waterloo itself. These soldiers, as Andrew Mackillop has argued, were coming from a militarised society, albeit one in which their 'warlike endeavour was now state-sponsored as opposed to the private, clan-based military activity' before the battle of Culloden.[56] They found an outlet for their bellicosity in the wars of the 1790s, wherein the successes of the French were only broken by the triumph of the British expeditionary army in Egypt (1801). Led by a Scottish commander, Sir Ralph Abercromby, this army included three Highland regiments, the 42nd, 78th and

92nd, as well as the Royal Scots and the 90th (Perthshire, later 2nd battalion, Cameronians). Despite Abercromby's death from a wound incurred at the battle of Alexandria (21 March 1801), the six-month campaign demonstrated immense improvements in the steadiness and discipline of the British regiments. The Highland Society in London struck a special medal for the Black Watch, and vast crowds turned out to cheer the regiment on its return to Edinburgh in 1802.[57] The Lowland regiments also contributed significantly to the subsequent victory over Napoleon: the Royal Scots, far from struggling to find recruits (the ostensible reason why six regiments lost the kilt), sustained four battalions during these wars, all of whom saw overseas service. The third battalion incurred 363 casualties out of its strength of 624 men at Quatre Bras and Waterloo.[58]

Scots also made their mark in India. During the period 1754–84 Scots formed half of the fourteen royal regiments, that is, 4,000 to 5,000 men, and from 1789 to 1800, Scots supplied 224 out of the 538 cadets entering the Bengal army, or about 41 per cent of the intake.[59] Whether serving in the East India Company (EIC), where commissions were free, or in the royal regiments, Indian service held the prospect of being able to better oneself with the allure of prize money or loot (as after the storming of Seringapatam on 4 May 1799),[60] and of undertaking duties that were much less onerous than those at home since 'all the fatiguing work is performed by the natives'.[61] Campaigning was often arduous, with disease and sunstroke likely to exact a heavy toll, but reputations could be enhanced as the 74th (later 2nd battalion, Highland Light Infantry), the 78th (later 2nd battalion, Seaforth Highlanders) and the 94th (Scots Brigade) found serving under Sir Arthur Wellesley, later the duke of Wellington, in the Mahratta War (1803–5). The 74th and 78th were to the fore in the battle of Assaye (23 September 1803) and the 94th in the storming of Gawilghur (15 December 1803). Of the 78th's assault at Assaye, Jac Weller observes that

> The Mahratta regular infantrymen were good soldiers, the best sepoys in India after those in the EIC units. But they had seen their guns taken with astonishing ease by white giants whose kilts and feathered bonnets made them seem more gods than men . . . [they] broke leaving only a few die-hards to perish on Scottish bayonets.[62]

Remarkably, fifty years later this same regiment under the command of another English general, Henry Havelock, again distinguished itself in the first relief of Lucknow (25 September 1857). The event would be impressed upon Scottish popular consciousness through songs and ballads about the 'dream' of Jessie Brown, who was purportedly a corporal's wife in the invested residency. Her experiences were captured in a drama in four acts, a painting by Frederick Goodall and several ballads including 'Jessie's dream at Lucknow', where she hears the pipes playing 'The Campbells are Coming' before the soldiers hear it, and gives thanks to 'Brave Havelock and his Highlanders/The bravest of the brave.'[63]

The British authorities, nonetheless, expected the Highland regiments to perform more prosaic duties, including aid to the civil power as addressed by Ewen Cameron and, later, by Ian Wood. While much of this service was in Ireland, from the response to the rebellion of the United Irishmen (1798) onwards,[64] Scots were also employed in assisting the English and Welsh magistrates, particularly during the industrial disturbances, Chartist agitation and the Rebecca riots of the early nineteenth century. In these highly stressful duties occasional lapses occurred,[65] but generally military discipline proved effective: 'The ranks of a standing army,' argued Quartermaster James Anton (42nd Highlanders), 'though composed of the sons of the working people, become by usage estranged from the political creeds and local grievances that excite cities, towns, and provinces to resist the civil magistrate . . . Trained to support the executive authority,' he continued, 'the soldiers' prejudices regarding civil rights, are more likely to flow in an opposite direction, than in unison with the current of the people's inclination.'[66]

More pleasing for the Scots, especially the highlanders, was the extent of royal patronage bestowed upon them by Queen Victoria, whose love of the Highlands and lengthy visits to Balmoral became a feature of her reign (1837–1901). Describing the 42nd as 'very handsome in their kilts', she took a close interest in her Highland guards of honour, regularly presented regimental colours at Balmoral and conferred a royal title upon the 79th, whereupon it became known as the '79th Queen's Own Cameron Highlanders'.[67] On 24 September 1845 the queen also presented colours to the Atholl Highlanders, thereby giving this private Highland regiment the right to carry arms, a unique honour. During the South African War (1899–1902) many Atholl Highlanders would serve in the Scottish Horse, a body raised at the suggestion of the Caledonian Society of South Africa by the marquess of Tullibardine, the eldest son of the seventh duke of Atholl.[68] This war was made famous not only by the sacrifices of the Highland Brigade at Magersfontein (11 December 1899), and the role of the Gordon Highlanders in the defence of Ladysmith, but also by the spectacle of thousands of Scottish citizen soldiers volunteering to serve their country at a time of national emergency.[69] Their service in Volunteer units, Imperial Yeomanry and new military bodies like the Lovat Scouts and the Scottish Horse complemented the response from the empire, where Australians, Canadians and New Zealanders joined loyal South Africans in fighting the Boers. As Wendy Ugolini observes, the Scottish diaspora rallied to fight in this war, a precursor to even more extensive service in the Great War.

Both the two world wars and the ensuing Cold War brought war or the threat of war to Scotland. Trevor Royle, Jeremy Crang and Niall Barr describe how Scotland contributed to these massive challenges in the provision of bases, training areas, industrial support and home defence as well as through the service of Scots in the armed forces, whether as volunteers or conscripts. Just as the challenges were unprecedented, so Scotland like the rest of the United Kingdom responded in an extraordinary manner, with the Royal Scots raising thirty-five battalions, and the Argyll and Sutherland Highlanders and the Cameronians each raising twenty-seven battalions in the Great War.[70] Scottish units also served in the highly professional, and rightly acclaimed, British Expeditionary Force that fought in France and Flanders (1914) from Mons to the first battle of Ypres. The high standards of pre-war training and the prompt return to the colours of the reserves served those battalions well,[71] but casualties mounted rapidly, prompting the vast expansion of New Army and Territorial units that Royle describes. In the process the local, territorial and national connections suffered dilution, with the 51st Highland Division accepting a Lancashire brigade as early as April 1915 and, the following month, the under-strength 11th battalion, Black Watch, sent recruiting parties off to Edinburgh, Glasgow and Manchester. When the 16th Highland Light Infantry (HLI) was based in Nieuport in 1917, it received a draft from the Nottingham, Derby and Yorkshire depots.[72] English officers were required, too, with Winston Churchill readily accepting command of the 6th battalion, Royal Scots Fusiliers. As he informed his wife:

> Now that I shall be commanding a Scottish battalion, I shd like you to send me a copy in one volume of Burns. I will soothe & cheer their spirits by quotations from it. I shall have to be careful not to drop into a mimicry of their accent! You know I am a vy gt admirer of that race. A wife, a constituency, & now a regiment attest the sincerity of my choice![73]

Churchill would prove a vigorous commanding officer, earning an accolade from his predecessor, Colonel A. E. Holland, that he had transformed 'his battalion from a moderate one into a d____ good one'.⁷⁴

If such units remained distinctively Scottish in ethos and cultural mores, morale was sustained in a structure of support that pervaded the British army as a whole. Using the example of the 2nd Cameronians at the battle of Neuve Chapelle (10–13 March 1915), Lieutenant-Colonel John Baynes argued persuasively that morale rested upon layers of support. The foundation lay in administrative support, namely good food, adequate rest, mail, proper medical care and welfare services, moving through smartness, discipline and attention to sanitary detail, and thence to cheerfulness and high spirits within the ranks, buttressed by pipe bands in camps, parades, on the line of march, in battle and at funerals, and culminating in a sense of 'bloody-mindedness' (a resolve to persevere irrespective of the conditions) and a nobility of spirit (that is, love of a cause, country, loyalty, *esprit de corps* and unselfishness) in action.⁷⁵

How far religion contributed to the wartime morale of Scottish soldiers remains a matter of dispute, not least the claims of several senior commanders, including Field Marshal Sir Douglas Haig, that army chaplains provided 'incalculable' support for the war effort.⁷⁶ Chaplains, usually supplied by the Church of Scotland, normally supported the Scottish war service units; sons of the manse sometimes served among the officers of Scottish battalions; and Scots serving in Territorial and New Army units apparently had a higher level of declared religious affiliation than their English counterparts (with

Figure I.4 Lieutenant-Colonel Winston Churchill (seated centre), with officers of the 6th battalion, the Royal Scots Fusiliers, near Ploegsteert, Belgium, 1916. Archibald Sinclair, who was Churchill's second-in-command and later served as his secretary of state for air during the Second World War, sits to the immediate right of Churchill.

the highest level of affiliation found among the Territorials of the 51st Highland Division). Even among the hardened regulars examined by Baynes, religion boosted morale in some cases but without permeating throughout the rank and file.[77] Despite evidence of spiritual loss or erosion during wartime, and examples of virulent criticism of wartime chaplains, belief in the rectitude of Britain's cause appeared widespread both at the outset of the war and during the dismal autumn of 1917: indeed, Scots served in the only major army that entered the war in 1914 but never experienced any widespread failure of morale in 1917 or 1918.[78]

Scots nonetheless adapted to the changing nature of war in the twentieth century. As the chemical war erupted in 1915, Major (later Major-General) Charles H. Foulkes became the principal gas adviser of the British army. A keen sportsman, who had formerly played football for Heart of Midlothian and captained the Scottish hockey team, he rose to command the Special Brigade (the chemical forces) and to serve as director of Gas Services in 1917, championing the use of gas in the interwar years and writing a major history of the Special Brigade.[79] Foulkes was too a keen photographer, who had devised and organised the photographic reconnaissance section of the army in the Anglo-Boer War, a precursor of the Army Film and Photographic Unit. Scots also contributed to the formation of British counter-espionage and espionage services (later MI5 and MI6 or the Secret Intelligence Service), when a Scottish secretary of state for war, Richard B. Haldane, requested his director of military operations, Sir John Spencer Ewart, a fellow Scot, to set up a British Secret Service Bureau in 1909. During the First World War intelligence work attracted several distinguished Scots, including John Buchan, Compton Mackenzie, Sir Alfred Ewing, who ran the Admiralty's cryptology unit (and was later vice-chancellor and principal of Edinburgh University), and Major-General Sir Stewart Menzies, a scion of a Scottish whisky family, who entered intelligence after being gassed on the Western Front in 1915. By 1939 he was director of the Secret Intelligence Service, and remained in that role throughout the Second World War and into the early years of the Cold War until his retirement in 1951.[80]

Of those engaged in unconventional forms of warfare during the Second World War, the Special Operations Executive (SOE), intent upon conducting espionage, subversion and propaganda behind enemy lines, trained many of its agents at Arisaig and at other properties in the Highlands. At their fullest extent of development in 1943, the Group A schools along the Road to the Isles and Loch Morar trained up to seventy-five students simultaneously, and overall these schools accepted 2,479 students out of the 6,810 trained by the SOE.[81] Among Scots who served in enemy-occupied countries, Sir Fitzroy Maclean earned renown as head of a military mission to Tito in Yugoslavia (1943–5). A Conservative MP and former Cameron Highlander, Maclean had joined the 1st Special Air Service regiment, a new unit founded by another Scot, David Stirling, in January 1942. The SAS raided installations deep into enemy-held territory, and Maclean, after being severely injured in one of these expeditions, described 'David Stirling's driving as the most dangerous thing in World War Two.'[82] In more conventional but still novel forms of warfare Sir Robert Watson-Watt, the pioneer of radar, had grown up in Brechin and had first developed an interest in radio waves while at University College, Dundee, then part of the University of St Andrews.[83]

Complementing the role of Scotsmen in innovative warfare was the enlistment of women in 1917 to undertake non-combatant duties in France. Hitherto Scots women had found extensive employment in nursing and the munitions industries during the Great War, and some had served in the FANY (First Aid Nursing Yeomanry), founded in 1907, to run field hospitals, drive ambulances and set up soup kitchens and troop canteens. In 1916, women responded to the burgeoning manpower crisis that was afflicting the army when Dr Mary 'Mona' Chalmers Watson, a distinguished Scottish doctor and sister of the director of recruiting at the War Office, Brigadier-General Sir Auckland Geddes, advocated the raising of a corps of women volunteers to undertake ancillary duties in support of the military. Asked to head the new Women's Army Auxiliary Corps (WAAC), which was formally instituted on 7 July 1917, Chalmers Watson set about the immense task of raising a corps of 40,850 women, of whom 17,000 served overseas but never more than 8,777 at any time.[84] While Chalmers Watson regarded this response as 'an advance of the women's movement and . . . a national advance',[85] it set a precedent that would be followed in the Second World War. By March 1943, when nearly 184,000 women were serving in the Auxiliary Territorial Service, Scotland supplied 22,296 women, or about 12 per cent of the force.[86]

The cultural and physical dimensions

Notwithstanding the novel military contributions of Scots in the twentieth century, Scottish military traditions remain rooted, as Alan Carswell observes, in military costume, its imagery and association with the wars of empire. Much of this imagery found reflection in the political decisions of 1881 to clothe all Scottish infantry soldiers in forms of Highland costume. When consulted on the matter, the Royal Scots Fusiliers 'raised strong objections, and the Scots Guards categorically refused',[87] but other Lowland regiments welcomed the changes. Doubtless they were aware of the publicity attracted by the kilted battalions, the appeal of the kilt among Lowland volunteers, where 'highland companies' were conspicuous by their attire, and the recruiting attractions of the kilt outside the Highland recruiting districts. A. F. Corbett, a Birmingham lad who joined the Seaforth Highlanders in 1891, recalled that it was 'our gorgeous Highland uniform . . . which I really think was the attraction to boys of our age at the time'.[88] Yet the battlefield serviceability of the kilt soon aroused controversy by its visibility on the veld during the South African War (1899–1902). After the heavy casualties sustained by the Gordon Highlanders at the battle of Elandslaagte (21 October 1899), drab aprons were issued to kilted units. Despite the debates over the wartime practicality of the kilt that persisted through the Great War and during the opening years of the Second World War,[89] the costume, so associated with Scottish identity, remained as important in planning for the formation of the Royal Regiment of Scotland in 2006 as it had been in the reforms of 1881.

The bagpipes, if not the only form of Scottish military music, as Gary West indicates, remained the other iconic symbol identified inextricably with the Scottish soldier, whether Highland or Lowland. Although piping fulfilled a diverse array of military functions, it was piping in action that captured the popular imagination. Often the central figure, or at least highly prominent, in battle paintings, the spectacle of a piper, bereft of personal protection, playing a musical instrument when under fire to encourage fellow soldiers embodied the virtues of courage and comradeship that lent itself to legends, myths and, in several cases, celebratory status.[90] Even as the kilt was phased out as a form of battledress, the pipes remained a conspicuous icon of Scottish identity, spanning generations and sustaining the military tradition.

For over a century that tradition, as Peter Harrington observes, had had powerful projection from the imagination and vision of battle painters. Whether these artists, like Robert Gibb, had a distinct Scottish agenda or, like Lady Butler, were attracted to kilted soldiers because 'these splendid troops were so essentially pictorial',[91] their representations of the highlander in exotic locations, in offensives at Kandahar, Tel-el-Kebir and Dargai, or in poignant scenes lamenting fallen comrades or taking leave of anxious wives and children, proffered powerful images of the Scottish soldier. In these works, accuracy other than in matters of costume and armament (for which military advice was often sought) was less important than the evocative characterisations. In *The Thin Red Line* (1881) Gibb employs artistic licence to depict Russian troopers falling before Scottish bayonets but captures magnificently the look of resolute defiance on the faces of the 93rd Sutherland Highlanders left isolated at Balaclava. In *All That Was Left of Them* (1899), Richard Caton Woodville portrays a stark evening after the defeat at Magersfontein, with highlanders, bereft of their drab khaki aprons, bringing in the dead and wounded but still looking defiantly at the enemy. If much of this imagery, and with it an element of Scottishness, fades during the First World War, part of the reason lay with the bans on the 'specials' from entering the war zones, strict censorship and the poor materials of the soldier-artists: a plethora of desolate landscapes, ruins and trench scenes ensued.[92]

Other forms of media, notably the imperial films of the interwar years, sustained the traditional imagery, with films like *The Black Watch* (1929), *Wee Willie Winkie* (1937), *The Drum* (1938) and *Gunga Din* (1939) exploiting the deeply rooted imagery of the Scottish soldier in the wars of empire to foster 'drama, dreams and myths'.[93] There was martial imagery of a more permanent kind in Scotland's military monuments, as examined by Elaine McFarland. Within the long tradition of erecting memorials from Pictish stones through to the present day, a surge of commemoration occurred during the Victorian era. Not all of these memorials were to Scots; when statues of Wellington were unveiled before vast crowds in Glasgow (1844) and Edinburgh (1852), they were commemorating a highly controversial political statesman, who had never had any Scottish connections. Yet these events were a display both of political support for 'an icon of Britishness' and of Scottish military pride in serving under a general who had led them to victory in India, the Peninsular War and at Waterloo.[94] Subsequently Scottish military service was commemorated throughout the Victorian era, with the South African War producing a profusion of memorials, including many to the citizen soldiers who volunteered to serve in South Africa.[95] While styles of memorial evolved during the twentieth century and encompassed more functional memorials and community remembrance after the Second World War, a traditional cairn like the one unveiled near Contalmaison's church on 7 November 2004 could still highlight Scotland's military traditions. The service commemorated the sacrifices of the 16th battalion, Royal Scots, or McCrae's battalion, which included several footballers from Heart of Midlothian at the battle of

Figure I.5 *The Ross-shire Buffs*: cover illustration for James Grant's 1878 novel of the 78th Highlanders (later the 2nd battalion, the Seaforth Highlanders) in Persia, 1857.

the Somme, and was led by the Reverend Dr Fiona Douglas, whose grandfather, Company Sergeant Major John Douglas, had served in the 16th.[96]

While memorials commemorated the leadership, heroism and achievements of Scottish military history, literary and historical commentary has tended to interpret and reinterpret the significance of this martial legacy. In modern literature, as Robert Irvine maintains, such reinterpretation includes critiques of the traditional paradigm, which reflect upon the fate of the ex-soldier, the burdens of regimental traditions and the salience of political causes in Scotland. Such works are a reaction in part to the stereotyping of the Scottish soldier in the nineteenth century, when writers in the Romantic Movement such as James Grant (1822–87) popularised the exploits of Scottish soldiers and regiments in numerous works, including *The Ross-shire Buffs* (1878), an approach reflected in theatrical melodramas, patriotic songs and the juvenile literature of the late Victorian era.[97] They are also a reaction to a greater awareness of the costs and controversies of modern wars, but insofar as contemporary writing has sought dramatic effect by its 'anti-Tattoo' critique, or by downplaying the heroic-warrior ideal, it has only reflected the enduring potency of the traditional imagery of the Scottish soldier.

Underpinning this imagery are the material reminders all across Scotland of its martial heritage. Castles and fortifications remain highly conspicuous, imprinting a military identity upon the Scottish landscape. As Christopher Tabraham explains, they reflect the readiness of owners to repair and restore impressive facades and romantic features, whether crenellated battlements, towers, gatehouses or dungeons. They demonstrate, too, the versatility of these fastnesses – some preserved as splendid stately homes like Blair castle, others used as military barracks (Fort George) or listed as historic monuments, preserving their military connections through regimental and other military museums. If Scotland's battlefields are less well preserved, with relatively few heritage sites, battlefield archaeology, as Tony Pollard maintains, has made significant finds at various sites, especially at Culloden where it has enhanced our understanding of the scale of the battle, the dispositions of the rival forces and the influence of terrain – all embodied in a revised interpretation at the new visitor centre opened by the National Trust for Scotland in 2008. Complementing these castles and battle sites are the rich collections of weaponry, costume, regimental silver and associated artefacts retained in the aristocratic seats, the great museums of Edinburgh and Glasgow, and the regimental collections. As Stuart Allan relates, the Scottish National Naval and Military Museum, now the National War Museum, held particular significance by virtue of its location in Edinburgh castle alongside the Scottish National War Memorial. Yet the Scottish regimental collections are not static reflections of a bygone past: as the Gordon Highlanders Museum in Aberdeen has demonstrated, museums can foster local connections and exploit the Heritage Lottery Funding to upgrade their facilities, and explore new ways to display, contextualise and promote their material.

A Scottish military tradition

A Scottish military tradition remains a viable and enduring concept. Over the centuries it has evolved and developed, leaving in its wake an enviable, if by no means uniform, record of military service, coupled with a potent mix of imagery, legend, myth and collective memory. Its roots lie in some of the seminal events of Scotland's history such as the Wars of Independence and the ever-controversial Jacobite risings or rebellions (where even the terminology remains contentious) – events that still arouse heated debate and voluminous publication, so ensuring that the military tradition retains a prominence in the national consciousness. Less controversial perhaps has been the evolution of that martial tradition within a British context, with service in famous regiments including ceremonial duties in royal guards and escorts, and opportunities for active service across a vast empire.[98] 'Common experiences,' as Allan Massie remarked, 'had made Scots and English alike British',[99] and this was particularly true of a military that secured (and later withdrew from) an empire, fought in two world wars and contributed through the British Army of the Rhine to the allied forces that contested the Cold War.

The Scottish military tradition, as Alistair Irwin affirms, is a living one based on high levels of self-esteem, staunch regimental affiliation and a sense of regimental family – a family that encompasses 'mothers, fathers, wives and children of members of the regiments as amongst the soldiers themselves'.[100] As several contributors acknowledge, it is an inclusive tradition that has enabled regiments to absorb recruits from outside of their designated recruiting areas, and from outside Scotland itself. When focused upon specific regiments, the tradition can excite fierce passions and loyalties among both serving and retired members of these units, and the eruption of such passions whenever the identity of these regiments is threatened. This is not a uniquely Scottish phenomenon, even if the intensity of these feelings may seem particularly high north of the border. Despite their distinctive names, attire, musical instruments and, in some cases, royal affiliations, the Scottish regiments were formed on the same structure and discipline as other British regiments, with an ethos forged in the Victorian era. The regiment, as John Keegan observed, 'with its complex and highly individual accretion of traditions, local affinities, annual rituals, inter-company rivalries, fierce autonomy and distinctive name . . . was an extension, indeed the creation of the Victorian public school system'.[101]

Even in the Victorian era, however, the tradition extended beyond specific regiments, and survived amalgamations, the loss of cherished regimental numbers in 1881 and the controversies that attended those events.[102] Scotland's military tradition found reflection, too, in wider loyalties to brigades and divisions, first in the Napoleonic Wars, later in the Highland Brigades of the mid- to late nineteenth century and then in the divisions formed from the Territorial and New Armies of the Great War, with the 9th, 15th, 51st and 52nd Divisions serving again in the Second World War. Just as regimental numbers and titles could be sources of pride and inspiration, so could the divisional signs and symbols, and some of Scotland's redoubtable commanders led brigades and divisions, namely Sir Colin Campbell, Andrew Wauchope and Douglas Wimberley. So Scottish military traditions could manifest themselves in different forms but within the small, professional army retained in peacetime, the regiment remained a prime source of identity and reputation. Perhaps the last word should therefore go to Brigadier Sir Bernard Fergusson in reflecting upon his decision not to follow in the footsteps of his father and grandfather, both of whom served in the Grenadier Guards:

> I would have hated soldiering in London and its environs, and I am glad to have spent so much of my life with Jocks. Somebody once said that The Black Watch was more like a religion than a regiment: I always thought of myself as being in The Black Watch rather than in the Army.[103]

Notes

I should like to acknowledge the constructive comments and criticism of my fellow editors, Jeremy Crang and Matthew Strickland, in the preparation of this Introduction. While I take full responsibility for any errors that occur, their support has been invaluable.

1. National Library of Scotland [hereafter NLS], Acc 6119, 'Scottish Soldier: An Autobiography by Douglas Wimberley', vol. 2, 'World War II' (1974), p. 200; see also J. B. Salmond, *The History of the 51st Highland Division 1939–45* (Edinburgh and London: Blackwood, 1953), pp. 130–1.
2. T. M. Devine, foreword, in S. Allan and A. Carswell (eds), *The Thin Red Line: War, Empire and Visions of Scotland* (Edinburgh: National Museums of Scotland, 2004), p. 8.
3. The editors would like to emphasise that this work does not purport to be 'the' military history of Scotland, only 'a' volume that seeks to bring together insights from contemporary scholarship and interpretations from contributors with a knowledge of the primary sources and relevant materials. It is also a work that focuses primarily upon the army as an institution until the age of 'interstate industrial war' in the twentieth century, when war, or the threat of war (as in the Cold War), had a broader impact upon Scotland as a whole. For his thesis on the interstate industrial warfare and its application to Cold War deterrence, see R. Smith, *The Utility of Military Force: The Art of War in the Modern World* (London: Penguin, 2006), pp. 3, 78–90, 105–47, 152.
4. H. Strachan, 'Scotland's military identity', *Scottish Historical Review*, vol. 85 (2006), p. 317.

5. 'More Scottish history,' as Michael Lynch observed in c. 1990, 'has been written since 1960 than in any generation before it', *Scotland: A New History* (London: Century Ltd, 1991), p. xv. Among the principal works on Scottish military history written in this period were J. Michael Hill, *Celtic Warfare, 1595–1763* (Edinburgh: John Donald, 1986); S. Wood, *The Scottish Soldier* (Manchester: Archive Publications Ltd, 1987); D. M. Henderson, *Highland Soldier: A Social Study of the Highland Regiments, 1820–1920* (Edinburgh: John Donald, 1989); E. M. Furgol, *A Regimental History of the Covenanting Armies, 1639–1651* (Edinburgh: John Donald, 1990); N. MacDougall (ed.), *Scotland and War AD 79–1918* (Edinburgh: John Donald, 1991); C. M. M. Macdonald and E. McFarland (eds), *Scotland and the Great War* (East Linton: Tuckwell Press, 1999); G. Phillips, *The Anglo-Scots Wars 1513–1550* (Woodbridge: Boydell and Brewer, 1999); S. Murdoch and A. Mackillop (eds), *Fighting for Identity: Scottish Military Experience c. 1550–1900* (Leiden: Brill, 2002); and a multitude of works on the Jacobites (see Chapter 13 in this volume).

6. M. Lynch (ed.), *The Oxford Companion to Scottish History* (Oxford: Oxford University Press, 2001), p. 688.

7. Most of these works are mentioned in the references to the first seven chapters but see also A. G. Beam, *The Balliol Dynasty, 1210–1364* (Edinburgh: John Donald, 2008); F. J. Watson, *Under The Hammer: Edward 1 and Scotland 1286–1307* (East Linton: Tuckwell Press, 1998); and C. McNamee, *Robert Bruce: Our Most Valiant Prince, King and Lord* (Edinburgh: Birlinn, 2006).

8. T. Bartlett and K. Jeffery, 'An Irish military tradition?', in T. Bartlett and K. Jeffery (eds), *A Military History of Ireland* (Cambridge: Cambridge University Press, 1996), pp. 1–25.

9. Strachan, 'Scotland's military identity', pp. 319–20.

10. B. P. Lenman, 'Militia, fencible men and home defence, 1660–1797', in Macdougall (ed.), *Scotland and War*, pp. 170–92; J. Robertson, *The Scottish Enlightenment and the Militia Issue* (Edinburgh: John Donald, 1985).

11. Lenman, 'Militia, fencible men and home defence', pp. 188–9; S. Murdoch and A. Mackillop, 'Introduction' and A. Mackillop, 'For king, country and regiment?: Motive and identity within Highland soldiering', in Murdoch and Mackillop (eds), *Fighting for Identity*, pp. xxiii–xliii and 203. For an earlier reflection on the problem of discerning a Lowland military image, see Sir H. Maxwell, Bt (ed. for the Association of Lowland Scots), *The Lowland Scots Regiments: Their Origin, Character and Services Previous to the Great War of 1914* (Glasgow: James Maclehose, 1918), pp. 24–7.

12. H. Streets, 'Identity in the Highland regiments in the nineteenth century: Soldier, region, nation', in Murdoch and Mackillop (eds), *Fighting for Identity*, pp. 214, 224.
13. H. Trevor-Roper, 'The invention of tradition: The Highland tradition of Scotland', in E. Hobsbawn and T. Ranger (eds), *The Invention of Tradition* (Cambridge: Cambridge University Press, 1983), pp. 15–41; C. Withers, 'The historical creation of the Scottish Highlands', in I. L. Donnachie and C. A. Whatley (eds), *The Manufacture of Scottish History* (Edinburgh: Polygon, 1992), pp. 143–56.
14. L. Leneman, 'A new role for a lost cause: Lowland romanticisation of the Jacobite Highlander', in L. Leneman (ed.), *Perspectives in Scottish Social History: Essays in Honour of Rosalind Mitchison* (Aberdeen: Aberdeen University Press, 1988), pp. 107–24.
15. W. H. Marwick, 'Conscientious objection in Scotland in the First World War', *Scottish Journal of Science*, vol. 1, part 3 (1972), pp. 157–64; W. Kenefick, 'War resisters and anti-conscription in Scotland: An ILP perspective', in Macdonald and McFarland (eds), *Scotland and the Great War*, pp. 59–80; 'Norman MacCaig', in I. MacDougall (ed.), *Voices From War and some Labour Struggles: Personal Recollections of War in our Century by Scottish Men and Women* (Edinburgh: Mercat Press, 1995), pp. 282–90.
16. For an essay that grapples with the many complexities involved in multiple national identities; see Murdoch and Mackillop, 'Introduction', in Murdoch and Mackillop (eds), *Fighting for Identity*, pp. xxxiii–xliii.
17. The other forces encountered by the Scots were the army of Edward I and the New Model Army of Oliver Cromwell.
18. Even with advance preparations seaborne support could prove tardy and unreliable, as Edward I experienced in his advance northwards in 1298, and the reports of famine sweeping through the English army may have contributed to Wallace's decision to seek battle at Falkirk. Watson, *Under the Hammer*, pp. 66–7.
19. G. Maxwell, 'The Roman experience: Parallel lines or predestination?', in Macdougall (ed.), *Scotland and War*, p. 5.
20. Lynch (ed.), *Oxford Companion to Scottish History*, p. 635.
21. Ibid. p. 636.
22. For example, Henry de Haliburton took possession of Berwick (but not Berwick castle); see C. J. McNamee, 'William Wallace's invasion of northern England in 1297', *Northern History*, vol. 26 (1990), p. 43. Roxburgh castle, however, held out against a Scottish siege; see F. Watson, 'Sir William Wallace: What we do – and don't – know', in E. J. Cowan (ed.), *The Wallace Book* (Edinburgh: John Donald, 2007), p. 32.

23. Watson, *Under the Hammer*, p. 51.
24. A. Grant, 'Bravehearts and coronets: Images of William Wallace and the Scottish nobility', in Cowan (ed.), *Wallace Book*, p. 105; see also F. Riddy, 'Unmapping the territory: Blind Hary's *Wallace*', in Cowan (ed.), *Wallace Book*, pp. 107–16.
25. M. Brown, *Bannockburn: The Scottish War and the British Isles, 1307–1323* (Edinburgh: Edinburgh University Press, 2008), p. 133.
26. D. Cornell, 'A kingdom cleared of castles: The role of the castle in the campaigns of Robert Bruce', *Scottish Historical Review*, vol. 87 (2008), pp. 233–57.
27. A. A. M. Duncan, 'The War of the Scots, 1306–23', *Transactions of the Royal Historical Society*, sixth series, vol. 2 (1992), p. 147.
28. D. Cornell, *Bannockburn: The Triumph of Robert the Bruce* (New Haven, CT and London: Yale University Press, 2009), p. 235; Brown, *Bannockburn*, p. 125.
29. Cornell, 'A kingdom cleared of castles', p. 253.
30. Cornell, *Bannockburn*, p. 249.
31. E. W. M. Balfour-Melville, *James I, King of Scots* (London: Methuen, 1936), p. 116; G. Donaldson, *The Auld Alliance: The Franco-Scottish Connection* (Edinburgh: The Saltire Society and L'Institut Français d'Écosse, 1985), p. 9; N. Macdougall, *An Antidote to the English: The Auld Alliance, 1295–1560* (East Linton: Tuckwell Press, 2001), pp. 70, 72, 74, 77; and generally on the Auld Alliance, J. Laidlaw (ed.), *The Auld Alliance: France and Scotland over 700 years* (Edinburgh: Edinburgh University Press, 1999).
32. B. Chevalier, 'Les Alliés écossais au service du roi de France au XVe siècle', in Laidlaw (ed.), *Auld Alliance*, pp. 47–57; Macdougall, *An Antidote to the English*, pp. 65–6, 69–71, 73, 77; on the Franco-Scottish military connection; see S. Wood, *The Auld Alliance: Scotland and France: The Military Connection* (Edinburgh: Mainstream Publishing, 1989).
33. M. K. Jones, 'The battle of Verneuil (17 August 1424): Towards a history of courage', *War in History*, vol. 9 (2002), pp. 375–411.
34. Lynch (ed.), *Oxford Companion to Scottish History*, pp. 636–8.
35. D. H. Caldwell, 'The battle of Pinkie', in Macdougall (ed.), *Scotland and War*, pp. 88–9.
36. M. Brown, *The Black Douglases: War and Lordship in Late Medieval Scotland 1300–1455* (East Linton: Tuckwell Press, 1998), p. 312; N. Macdougall, 'Achilles' heel: The earldom of Ross, the Lordship of the Isles, and the Stewart Kings, 1449–1507', in E. J. Cowan and R. Andrew McDonald (eds), *Alba: Celtic Scotland in the Medieval Era* (East Linton: Tuckwell Press, 2000), pp. 248–75.
37. K. M. Brown, 'From Scottish lords to British officers: State build-

ing, elite integration and the army in the seventeenth century', in Macdougall (ed.), *Scotland and War*, p. 135; see also S. Murdoch, 'James VI and the formation of a Scottish–British military identity', in Murdoch and Mackillop (eds), *Fighting for Identity*, pp. 3–31.

38. S. Murdoch, 'James VI and the formation of a Scottish–British military identity', pp. 12–15, 22–3.
39. For an excellent account of the religious propaganda battle, see R. Scott Spurlock, *Cromwell and Scotland: Conquest and Religion, 1650–1660* (Edinburgh: John Donald, 2007), p. 6.
40. A. I. Macinnes, *The British Revolution, 1629–1660* (Basingstoke: Palgrave, 2005), p. 194; see also Scott Spurlock, *Cromwell and Scotland*, pp. 13–28.
41. This compounded the logistical problems that Cromwell encountered in the provisioning and supply of his invading army. Despite support from 140 ships, his army languished initially in the Lothians, losing about one-quarter to one-third of its number from disease and desertion; see I. Gentles, *The New Model Army in England, Ireland and Scotland, 1645–1653* (Oxford: Blackwell, 1992), pp. 388–92; and J. D. Grainger, *Cromwell Against the Scots: The Last Anglo-Scottish War, 1650–1652* (East Linton: Tuckwell Press, 1997), pp. 37–40.
42. On Cromwell's battlefield triumphs, see Gentles, *The New Model Army*, pp. 392–411. A few castles and some Highland lords held out briefly after Dundee; see Grainger, *Cromwell Against the Scots*, ch. 10, but General George Monck established Cromwellian garrisons throughout Scotland; see Scott Spurlock, *Cromwell and Scotland*, pp. xv and 38.
43. Allan and Carswell (eds), *The Thin Red Line*, pp. 52–3.
44. R. H. Paterson, *Pontius Pilate's Bodyguard: A History of The First or The Royal Regiment of Foot, The Royal Scots (The Royal Regiment)*, 3 vols (Edinburgh: RHQ Royal Scots, 2000–7), vol. 1, pp. 23–31, 36–7, 110.
45. J. Michael Hill, 'Killiecrankie and the evolution of Highland warfare', *War in History*, vol. 1 (1994), p. 131.
46. The National Archives [hereafter TNA], WO 33/88 (3), p. 49 'Petition of Cornet Henry Gordon to Her Majesty, asking for a yearly gratuity on account of his wounds.' I am grateful to Stewart Stansfield for drawing my attention to this reference.
47. For a similar view, see B. P. Lenman, *The Jacobite Clans of the Great Glen 1650–1784* (Aberdeen: Scottish Cultural Press, 1995), p. 180.
48. S. Conway, 'The Scots Brigade in the eighteenth century', *Northern Scotland*, vol. 1 (2010), pp. 30–41.
49. A. I. Macinnes, 'The aftermath of the '45', in R. C. Woosnam-Savage (ed.), *1745: Charles Edward Stuart and the Jacobites* (Edinburgh:

HMSO, 1995), pp. 103 and 106–9; and A. I. Macinnes, *Clanship, Commerce and the House of Stuart, 1603–1788* (East Linton: Tuckwell Press, 1996), pp. 211–17; of some 3,400 rebels taken prisoner, 120 were executed (including 40 deserters, mainly prisoners of war coerced into service after Prestonpans), 750 died in the appalling prison conditions (over 80 officially recorded as fatalities and probably most of the 684 unaccounted for) and 1,287 were released. Most of the remainder were transported; see W. Speck, *The Butcher: The Duke of Cumberland and the Suppression of the '45* (Oxford: Basil Blackwell, 1981), pp. 181–2.

50. T. Pollard, 'Introduction: The battle of Culloden – more than a difference of opinion', in T. Pollard (ed.), *Culloden: The History and Archaeology of the Last Clan Battle* (Barnsley: Pen and Sword, 2009), p. 11; for an account of similar atrocities across contemporary Europe, see J. Black, *Culloden and the '45* (Stroud: Sutton, 1990), pp. 187–8 and on contemporary perceptions of the reprisals, Speck, *The Butcher*, p. 182.

51. C. Duffy, 'The '45 campaign'; S. Reid, 'The British army at Culloden', in Pollard (ed.), *Culloden*, p. 23 and pp. 83–5; Speck, *The Butcher*, p. 147. After Culloden, Jacobites continued to plot as late as 1759, with Dr Archibald Cameron the last Jacobite to be hanged for high treason in 1753, Daniel Szechi, 'The significance of Culloden', in Pollard (ed.), *Culloden*, p. 233; see also Lenman, *Jacobite Clans*, p. 185.

52. B. Lenman, *The Jacobite Risings in Britain 1689–1746* (Dalkeith: Scottish Cultural Press, reprinted 2004), p. 263.

53. Macinnes, *Clanship, Commerce and the House of Stuart*, pp. 212–13.

54. Lenman, *The Jacobite Clans*, p. 181; on Highland mutinies, see J. Prebble, *Mutiny: The Highland Regiments in Revolt, 1743–1804* (London: Penguin, 1977).

55. The 25th was the only regiment to fight at Killiecrankie, Sheriffmuir and Culloden; see R. Woollcombe, *All The Blue Bonnets: The History of the King's Own Scottish Borderers* (London: Arms and Armour Press, 1980), p. 23.

56. A. Mackillop, *'More Fruitful than the Soil': Army, Empire and the Scottish Highlands, 1715–1815* (East Linton: Tuckwell Press, 2000), p. 234. On the reputation of the highlander, see Leneman, 'A new role for a lost cause: Lowland romanticism of the Jacobite highlander', in Leneman (ed.), *Perspectives in Scottish Social History*, pp. 115–16.

57. D. Stewart, *Sketches of the Character, Manners and Present State of the Highlanders of Scotland; with Details of The Military Service of The Highland Regiments*, 2 vols (Edinburgh: n.p., 1822), vol. 1, p. 497; see also P. Mackesy, *British Victory in Egypt, 1801: The End*

of Napoleon's Conquest (London and New York: Routledge, 1995), pp. 236, 240–1.
58. Paterson, *Pontius Pilate's Bodyguard*, vol. 1, pp. 146, 148–9.
59. G. J. Bryant, 'Scots in India in the eighteenth century', *Scottish Historical Review*, vol. 64 (1985), pp. 23–4; V. Kiernan, 'Scottish soldiers and the conquest of India', in G. G. Simpson (ed.), *The Scottish Soldier Abroad 1247-1967* (Edinburgh: John Donald, 1992), p. 106.
60. The 73rd, 74th and 75th regiments were among those that shared the prize money of some £1,100,000 (apart from private plunder), Lt.Col. L. B. Oatts, *Proud Heritage: The Story of the Highland Light Infantry*, 4 vols (London: Thomas Nelson, 1952–63), vol. 2, p. 69; see also T. M. Devine, *Scotland's Empire 1600-1815* (London: Allen Lane, 2003), ch. 11; T. Quinney, *Sketches of a Soldier's Life in India* (Glasgow: privately published, 1853), p. 144 and D. Campbell (ed.), *Records of Clan Campbell in the Military Service of the Honourable East India Company 1600-1858* (London: Longman, 1925).
61. J. Pindar, *Autobiography of a Private Soldier* (Cupar: 'Fife News', 1877), p. 24.
62. J. Weller, *Wellington in India* (London: Greenhill Books, 1993), p. 182.
63. 'Jessie's Dream at Lucknow'. Available at http://digital.nls.uk/broadsides/broadside.cfm/id/15105, accessed on 21 November 2010.
64. T. M. Devine, *The Scottish Nation 1700-2000* (London: Allen Lane, 1999), pp. 210–11.
65. As at Preston in August 1842 when a small detachment of 72nd Highlanders fired on the mob, killing one man and wounding several others (of whom one later died), TNA, HO 45/268, Col. Arbuthnot to Sir James Graham, 13 August 1842; 'The Late Riots', *Preston Chronicle and Lancashire Advertiser*, 27 August 1842, p. 3.
66. J. Anton, *Retrospect of a Military Life, During the Most Eventful Periods of the Last War* (Edinburgh: W. H. Lizars, 1841), pp. 260–1.
67. D. Duff (ed.), *Queen Victoria's Highland Journals* (Exeter: Webb and Bower, 1980), journal entries for 6 September 1842 and 16 August 1872, pp. 25 and 161 respectively; 'The Seaforth Highlanders', *Highland News*, 7 October 1899, p. 2.
68. J. L. M. Stewart, *The Story of the Atholl Highlanders* (Blair Castle: The Atholl Highlanders, 2000), pp. 8–9, 15.
69. Scottish Volunteers, including the London and Liverpool Scottish, may have numbered at least 5,000, or about 10 per cent of the enrolled force, Major-General J. M. Grierson, *Records of the Scottish Volunteer Force 1859-1908* (Edinburgh: Blackwood, 1909), p. 95; see also E. W. McFarland, '"Empire-enlarging genius": Scottish Imperial Yeomanry

volunteers in the Boer War', *War in History*, vol. 13 (2006), pp. 299–328.
70. However impressive in Scottish terms, the Northumberland Fusiliers raised fifty-one battalions, the King's (Liverpool) Regiment forty-nine battalions and the Royal Fusiliers forty-seven battalions during the Great War, Brigadier E. A. James, *British Regiments 1914–1918* (London: Samson Books, 1978), pp. 42–3, 70–1, 107–8 and Appendix 1 Table B. This source also claims that the HLI raised thirty-three battalions – seven more than the regimental history acknowledges, Oatts, *Proud Heritage*, vol. 3, pp. vi and 404.
71. For a review of the pre-war BEF, including a case study of the 1st battalion, the Black Watch; see E. M. Spiers, 'The regular army in 1914', in I. F. W. Beckett and K. Simpson (eds), *A Nation in Arms: A Social Study of the British Army in the First World War* (Manchester: Manchester University Press, 1985), pp. 37–61.
72. Major-General A. G. Wauchope, *A History of The Black Watch [Royal Highlanders] in the Great War 1914–1918*, 3 vols (London: The Medici Society, 1926), vol. 3, p. 272; Major F. W. Bewsher, *The History of the 51st (Highland) Division 1914–1918* (Edinburgh: Blackwood, 1921), p. 8; T. Chalmers (ed.), *A Saga of Scotland: History of the 16th Battalion The Highland Light Infantry (City of Glasgow Regiment)* (Glasgow: John McCallum, 1930), p. 45.
73. W. S. Churchill to C. Churchill, 3 January 1916, quoted in M. Gilbert, *Winston S. Churchill, Vol. III, 1914–1916* (London: Heinemann, 1971), p. 629.
74. Col. A. E. Holland to C. Churchill, 18 February 1916, in M. Gilbert, *Winston S. Churchill*, vol. III Companion Part 2 (London: Heinemann, 1972), p. 1,431.
75. J. Baynes, *Morale: A Study of Men and Courage: The Second Scottish Rifles at the Battle of Neuve Chapelle 1915* (London: Leo Cooper, 1967).
76. M. Snape, *God and the British Soldier: Religion and the British Army in the First and Second World Wars* (London and New York: Routledge, 2005), p. 114; see Lt.-Col. W. D. Croft, *Three Years with the 9th (Scottish) Division* (London: John Murray, 1919), pp. 24, 291.
77. Snape, *God and the British Soldier*, pp. 115–16, 159–60; Allan and Carswell, *The Thin Red Line*, pp. 111–12; Baynes, *Morale*, pp. 202–5, 217.
78. Snape, *God and the British Soldier*, p. 115; on Scottish criticisms of wartime chaplains; see those quoted in E. M. Spiers, 'The Scottish soldier at war', in H. Cecil and P. H. Liddle (eds), *Facing Armageddon: The First World War Experienced* (London: Leo Cooper, 1996), p. 325.
79. D. Richter, *Chemical Soldiers: British Gas Soldiers in World War I*

(London: Leo Cooper, 1994), pp. 18–20; see also Brigadier-General C. H. Foulkes, *Gas! The Story of the Special Brigade* (Edinburgh: Blackwood, 1934).
80. A. Cave Brown, *The Secret Servant: The Life of Sir Stewart Menzies, Churchill's Spymaster* (London: Michael Joseph, 1988).
81. S. Allan, *Commando Country* (Edinburgh: National Museums of Scotland, 2007), pp. 157, 170–1.
82. 'Sir Fitzroy Maclean', *The Independent*, 19 June 1996, p. 14; see also F. Maclean, *Eastern Approaches* (London: Jonathan Cape, 1949).
83. P. Addison and J. A. Crang (eds), *The Burning Blue: A New History of the Battle of Britain* (London: Pimlico, 2000), p. 248.
84. D. Shaw, 'The forgotten army of women: The overseas service of Queen Mary's army auxiliary corps with the British forces, 1917–1921', in Cecil and Liddle (eds), *Facing Armageddon*, pp. 365–79; see also R. Terry, *Women in Khaki: The Story of the British Woman Soldier* (London: Columbus Books, 1998), pp. 48–74.
85. R. Terry, 'Watson, Alexandra Mary Chalmers', *Oxford Dictionary of National Biography* (Oxford: Oxford University Press, 2004), vol. 57, pp. 598–9.
86. TNA, WO 73/156, 'Nationalities – Auxiliary Territorial Service as at 1st February, 1943' in the 'General Return of the Strength of the British Army on 31 March 1943'.
87. J. Buchan, *The History of The Royal Scots Fusiliers (1678–1918)* (London: Thomas Nelson, 1925), p. 228.
88. A. F. Corbett, *Service Through Six Reigns, 1891 to 1953* (Birmingham: privately published, 1953), pp. 6, 8 and on the Volunteers, see Grierson, *Records of the Scottish Volunteer Force*, pp. 4–5, 234–5.
89. E. M. Spiers, 'The Scottish soldier in the Boer War', in J. Gooch (ed.), *The Boer War: Direction, Experience and Image* (London: Frank Cass, 2000), p. 162; Spiers, 'The Scottish soldier at war', in Cecil and Liddle (eds), *Facing Armageddon*, pp. 317–18; see also Chapter 21 in this volume.
90. Over fifty years after his piping on the beaches at Normandy, Bill Millan still received an obituary in an American newspaper, 'Bill Millan, Scottish bagpiper at D-Day', *International Herald Tribune*, 20 August 2010, p. 3.
91. E. Butler, *An Autobiography* (London: Constable, 1922), p. 99; see also P. Harrington, 'The man who painted THE THIN RED LINE', *Scots Magazine*, vol. 130 (1989), pp. 587–95.
92. P. Gough, 'The experience of British artists in the Great War', in Cecil and Liddle (eds), *Facing Armageddon*, pp. 841–53.
93. J. Richards, *Films and British National Identity: From Dickens to*

Dad's Army (Manchester: Manchester University Press, 1997), pp. 41, 210.
94. J. E. Cookson, 'The Edinburgh and Glasgow Duke of Wellington statues: Early nineteenth-century Unionist Nationalism as a Tory project', *Scottish Historical Review*, vol. 83 (2004), pp. 23–40.
95. E. W. McFarland, 'Commemoration of the South African War in Scotland, 1900–10', *Scottish Historical Review*, vol. 89 (2010), pp. 194–223.
96. 'McCrae's battalion of footballers honoured in France', *The Scotsman*, 8 November 2004, p. 9.
97. E. M. Spiers, *The Scottish Soldier and Empire, 1852–1902* (Edinburgh: Edinburgh University Press, 2006), pp. 13–14, 115–17, 210–11.
98. For his review of the Scottish martial tradition within an imperial context, and how it contributed to the popularity of the profession of arms up to the Great War and beyond; see T. M. Devine, *To the Ends of the Earth: Scotland's Global Diaspora 1750–2010* (London: Allen Lane, 2011), pp. 209–27.
99. A. Massie, *The Thistle and the Rose: Six Centuries of Love and Hate between the Scots and English* (London: John Murray, 2005), p. 285.
100. D. M. Henderson, *The Scottish Regiments* (Glasgow: HarperCollins, 1996), p. vii.
101. J. Keegan, *The Face of Battle* (London: Jonathan Cape, 1976), p. 274.
102. H. Strachan, *The Politics of the British Army* (Oxford: Oxford University Press, 1997), p. 205.
103. B. Fergusson, *The Trumpet in the Hall 1930–1958* (London: Collins, 1970), p. 278.

Part I
Early Warfare and the Emergence of a Scottish Kingdom

1
War in Prehistory and the Impact of Rome

FRASER HUNTER

While the recorded military history of Scotland starts with the northward march of the Roman legions, warfare and violence were nothing new. During the long millennia of Scottish prehistory, warfare was at times endemic and destructive, at times a major influence on society, at times a source of status and prestige as well as misery and death. While this prehistory of warfare is poorly known, archaeological evidence allows increasing insights. The main focus of this chapter is on later prehistory, from the late Bronze Age to the impact of Rome (c.1000 BC–AD 400), but it is prefaced with a broad overview of trends in warfare from the first post-glacial colonisation of the area some 10,000 years ago. This cannot be comprehensive: it is intended as a sketch of possibilities and problems.

Perceptions and prejudices

All historical studies are influenced by their contemporary context, but views of early warfare have been affected more than most. Sixteenth-century expeditions to the New World influenced depictions of naked, heavily armed Picts and Ancient Britons,[1] while Britain's own experience of imperial conflict led nineteenth- and early-twentieth-century writers to see conflict as inherent in the savage or barbarian societies of early Scotland.[2] As the complexities and time-depth of prehistory were realised new interpretations developed, yet violence and warfare continued to be a major feature of these narratives. Change, it was believed, was externally driven, brought by invaders and enforced at dagger or sword point: the first farming, the advent of metal, the 'Beaker people' and wave upon wave of 'Celtic invaders'. Monuments were interpreted with a military bent – the brochs and duns of northern and western Scotland became part

Map 1.1 Scotland before and during the Roman era.

of a 'castle complex', souterrains (underground cellars) were refuges and hill-forts, the chiefly strongholds of invading Celtic warriors.[3]

In the decades after the Second World War things began to change. Whereas for an older generation of scholars the experience of war had largely reinforced their view of its key role in prehistory, younger generations of scholars saw things rather differently. Invasions and conflicts were no longer the root source of change; economic and social motives were increasingly considered. Warfare slid down the intellectual agenda as attention focused on trade and exchange, landscape organisation and craft production. Rather than defensive strongholds, hill-forts were seen as expressions of community identity or status; rather than death-dealing weapons, swords and shields had ritualistic and prestige roles. As so often with intellectual trends, the pendulum swung too far. In the last decade or two, discussions of warfare have re-emerged – a trend itself hard to divorce from an unstable and threatening post-Cold War world. This chapter attempts to apply some of these emerging perspectives to the Scottish material.

Archaeology and anthropology of early warfare – setting the scene

Anthropology has been subject to similar debates and provides valuable parallels. Keeley's influential *War before Civilization* (1996) reacted against interpretations of 'primitive' societies as essentially peaceful.[4] His cross-cultural study noted the rarity of peaceful societies and the prevalence of warfare and violence in many different social and environmental settings. While lacking the military organisation and technology of medieval and post-medieval nations, early warfare could have major impacts on the smaller-scale groups involved. He notes that formal battles were often low impact, with hostilities ceasing after a few casualties; raiding and ambushes were the normal, more debilitating, mode of warfare.[5] His polemical approach has been criticised and he rather over-reports the incidence of war,[6] but his basic contention that evidence for prehistoric warfare requires explanation is entirely justified.

Warfare can have many roots. Motives and causes deduced from anthropology and history are equally relevant to prehistory, such as severe economic pressures from population growth, natural disasters or climatic change; conflict over desirable resources (such as food, marriage partners, status goods); and the spiralling of interpersonal violence and feuds in societies lacking centralised power to contain them. Technological innovations (notably in weaponry, but also in food technology and transport) could create tensions or put some groups at a marked disadvantage. To this must be added the prestige role of warfare: conflict offered a chance to gain, enhance or display prowess and status. It also had a crucial role in defining relations between people or groups, the threat of violence or war underpinning power relations. However, while violence and insecurity may have been facts of life for much of prehistory, groups were not permanently at war – there was variation in frequency, scale, nature and causes. To understand warfare we must understand its context, for it is a social construct. Warfare is used here to indicate violent actions or threats structured and sanctioned by a wider group and directed at another group, as opposed to the more individualistic nature of violence. Archaeologically, the symptoms can be hard to differentiate. We can investigate broad trends, but there are limitations for the evidence is partial and ambiguous. The three main sets of evidence are wounds on skeletons, weapons and equipment, and defended sites.[7]

The most direct evidence comes from weapon injuries on the skeleton. Unfortunately we are cursed by Scottish soils, which often inhibit bone preservation, and by a persistent reluctance in later prehistory to bury people, while much weapon trauma leaves little or no skeletal trace. Evidence may also be interpreted in different ways. The earliest clear sign of interpersonal violence comes from the early Neolithic tomb of Tulloch of Assery B in Caithness – a vertebra with an arrow tip of chert (a silica-rich stone which flakes like flint) still embedded in it.[8] But is this evidence of warfare, murder, a judicial or ritual killing, or even a hunting accident? A violent death does not necessarily represent warfare.

Our second category, weapons and equipment, again has its problems.[9] Many items would have been organic – leather armour, wooden shields – and would have survived only exceptionally. Moreover, in earlier prehistory there is no sign of specialised weapons for war. The weapons of the hunt – spear, arrow and club – served also for hunting humans. Only from the Bronze Age can specialist weapons be identified. But even here their use is often problematic. For instance, the thin, highly decorated bronze shields of the later Bronze Age, which rarely show any damage, are likely to have had ceremonial or ritual roles. Such ritualistic or prestige weapons certainly imply more practical counterparts and indicate the place of warfare in these societies. Yet weapons alone cannot show the frequency or context of their use.

Finally, defended settlements have interpretative problems. First, defence is not the only motive for enclosure. It can imply the marking of status or difference, enclosing livestock, providing central places for social gatherings and so on. There may thus have been social or practical reasons for communities to construct and maintain an enclosure and so a prevalence of enclosures cannot necessarily be equated with unstable times. The corollary is also problematic. Unenclosed settlements do not necessarily imply peaceful societies but may reflect low-intensity conflict or fighting restricted to particular social groups.[10] Despite these caveats, what does the archaeological record suggest?

Violence and warfare in early prehistoric Scotland (c. 8000–1000 BC)

It is tempting to proceed on the basis that insecurity, violence and warfare would be familiar to most generations in Scottish prehistory. For earliest prehistory, however, we must question this broad statement. While warfare is attested elsewhere in Mesolithic Europe, the Scottish evidence is ambivalent. Hunting weaponry is abundant – flint tips of arrows and spears are among the most common finds of the period – but gives no firm grounds to identify warfare. Anthropologically, while hunter-gatherer societies are rarely peaceful, warfare is often less prevalent in small-scale, loosely organised groups with a low population density.[11]

It is from the Neolithic period (c. 4200–2500 BC) that the first possible evidence of violent death in battle in Scotland emerges, with the discovery of the arrow-pierced backbone, mentioned above, in a Neolithic burial in Caithness. In other parts of Britain arrows were used systematically in warfare – enclosure sites in south-western Britain have dense clusters of arrowheads around the gateways from assaults, along with the skeletons of fallen victims.[12] This cannot be applied uncritically to Scotland, where such enclosures are unknown and settlement sites are not located with defensibility in mind, but it suggests the likely role of arrows in warfare in the region. Other likely weapons would be the wooden spear and club, stone-headed axe and mace. The evidence of their use from the skeletal remains of Neolithic Scotland is rare, although re-examination of burial assemblages elsewhere in Britain shows frequent wounds consistent with axes and clubs. Only in the earlier Bronze Age (c. 2500–1500 BC) do the first specialised weapons of war appear in the Scottish repertoire. Bronze daggers are more likely to have been used for warfare than hunting, while experimental work shows that the halberd (a dagger-like blade mounted transversely on a shaft), long considered a ceremonial weapon, would have possessed deadly effectiveness in battle.[13] It also provides our first example of a recurring phenomenon – participation in wider European trends. The Europe of prehistory was interconnected. People did not live isolated, sheltered lives, but were affected by and influenced wider events. Developments in technology, changes in subsistence, changing climates – all touched the lives of people in the landmass of what is now Scotland. This is not to return to an archaeology of dependency, where all influences were external, but to position Scotland in a broader context – a prehistoric Europe of the regions, where influences came and went, where connections rose and fell, and where the peoples of Scotland were sometimes peripheral, and at other times integral, players. This is particularly the case with weaponry. The halberd was a prestige weapon across Europe, from the bogs of Ireland to the rock carvings of Scandinavia and Italy.

Even with our knowledge of these first specialised battlefield weapons, it is hard to draw firm conclusions about the role of warfare in early Bronze Age Scottish society. The abundant burials provide few hints of violence – a male, 35 to 40 years old, from Cnip (Lewis) with serious (non-fatal) blunt weapon injuries being a rare exception.[14] Rich Beaker burials with flint-tipped arrows and bronze daggers (c. 2500–2000 BC), or later cremations with stone 'battle-axes' (axeheads often made from highly decorative stone, with a cylindrical perforation for the shaft, which were in use c. 2000–1600 BC), carry implications of the place of warfare in society, but were also symbols of power and position. Other specialist weapons, notably rapiers (slender bronze stabbing swords), had been developed by 1500 BC, though the narrowness and fragility of some suggests a prestige or ceremonial role. Only towards the end of the Bronze Age, from c. 1000 BC, does warfare become a more clearly recognisable feature of the Scottish archaeological record.

Later prehistoric warfare

In the archaeology of later prehistory (c. 1000 BC–AD 400), there are moments when warfare is barely visible and others when it forms a major part of the archaeological record. The period falls naturally into three parts. The first is the late Bronze Age and earliest Iron Age, c. 1000–700 BC, which saw a plethora of bronze weaponry and the first widespread construction of defensive enclosures. The second is the earlier Iron Age, c. 700–200 BC, the main era of hill-forts but largely lacking distinctive weaponry. Finally, from c. 200 BC onwards, iron weaponry in particular is increasingly in evidence. The

Figure 1.1 Bronze spearheads discovered at Murrayfield, Edinburgh. They form a hoard buried between c. 950 and 750 BC.

prominence of high-status bronze or iron weaponry is suggestive of periods when being identified as a warrior was socially desirable and exclusive. This contrasts with periods when such prestige weaponry was less evident, perhaps correlating with anthropological models of 'primitive warfare' as a non-specialist group activity to which most able-bodied males would contribute, either willingly or under peer pressure.

Before discussing the three periods outlined above in more depth, it is worth making some general points. It is often assumed that the active participants in warfare were male. Anthropologically this is the norm but is by no means an absolute.[15] It is notoriously hard to attribute gender roles from archaeological evidence, and seeing war as a purely male activity risks imposing modern stereotypes. For most of our period we have no clear evidence. Scandinavian late Bronze Age rock carvings depict visibly male warriors, as does available burial and iconographic evidence from the British Iron Age.[16] Yet Roman histories reveal female war leaders, notably Boudicca (d. AD 60/61) in southern Britain, while Gaulish coins also show female warriors. In truth, however, information is too sparse to draw firm conclusions in Scotland.

Three further points merit attention. The first is the absence of missile weapons in Scotland apart from hand-thrown spears and stones. Arrowheads are essentially unknown after the demise of flint examples by c. 1000 BC. The Romans used archery but their opponents did not, in either warfare or the hunt. The other obvious missile weapon, the sling, is well attested in southern England in the middle and later Iron Age, but not in Scotland – the massive caches of stones found in southern hill-forts are unknown in the north. It is hard to believe that the peoples of Scotland were unaware of the idea of missiles. This suggests a cultural taboo on 'impersonal' weapons designed to kill at a distance.

A second issue is the use of horses. They were introduced into Scotland in the late third millennium BC, but the available stock comprised small ponies. Such diminutive beasts would hardly make impressive mounts, and clear archaeological evidence for cavalry is lacking until the Early Historic period, although they feature in the southern English late Iron Age, and a Roman writing tablet from Vindolanda (Northumberland) makes reference to local cavalry.[17] On current evidence, however, horses seem to have been commonly used as draught animals for chariots.

The final area of concern is methodological – why and how does weaponry survive for archaeologists to find? Swords and spears, for example, were valued items which were not simply thrown away but were purposefully buried in graves or hoards, the latter often in bogs or lochs, and are best interpreted as votive offerings.[18] Yet these habits varied considerably. In some areas and periods it was considered appropriate to deposit weaponry in this way; in others it was not. And this need not correlate with warlike times and places. Thus in the late Bronze Age across Britain and Ireland weapons were placed in bogs and rivers, but during the Iron Age the habit was much more restricted and the archaeological record is thus thinner in this respect. This does not mean that Iron Age people did not use swords – it simply reflects biases in the evidence.

The warrior identity: late Bronze Age Scotland

The period c. 1000–700 BC saw the first major phase of defensive enclosures in Scotland, while weaponry became a dominant product of the bronze-worker – swords, spears, javelins and, more rarely, shields. An elite warrior's equipment may have included bronze helmets and body armour – both are attested on the continent, and their absence in Britain probably reflects different hoarding practices.[19] Although much of this bronzework was locally made, there were clearly some imports and knowledge of developments and fashions elsewhere. The nature of these contacts is opaque but some individuals no doubt travelled widely. Indeed, travel and adventuring may have been a rite of passage for young males, and one in which warfare may have played a role.[20] Travel beyond the normal boundaries also had a potency in pre-modern societies as a way for the traveller to acquire status and honour with the acquisition of exotic goods and the telling of colourful tales.[21]

Many fine bronze weapons ended their lives in hoards, often in wet locations and sometimes with a clear sense of occasion. From Duddingston Loch, Edinburgh, have come swords and spears which were broken up, bent and burnt. Discoveries elsewhere also show deliberate breakage – perhaps the killing of the weapon at the end of its life, to mark the owner's death or symbolise the end of some conflict. While single finds may be connected to an individual's life history, hoards often contain weaponry in abundance. One discovered in Grosvenor Crescent, Edinburgh, contained seven swords; another from Ballimore, Argyll, produced two swords and seven spears. Some show a clear pattern to their deposition – swords thrust upright into peat on the island of Shuna, Argyll, or shields placed in a circle at Beith, Ayrshire. There are also patterns to their locations – around special or sacred areas (such as the hills of Holyrood Park, Edinburgh); on remote mountain routeways like the Cairngorms; and in peatbogs or at the edge of cultivated land where the wildlands began.[22] Some may have been linked to the definition or contesting of boundaries between groups – perhaps even to ritualised warfare, with rivals competing in ever-grander ceremonies.[23]

The weapons themselves give evidence of active use. Sword edges show combat damage,[24] while repair and re-sharpening indicate that some lived long lives; perhaps, as in later heroic tales, weapons had lives of their own, acquiring names and stories. We cannot know how the damage occurred. Was it inflicted in the heat of massed battles, or the single combat of heroes and champions, or a ritualised exchange of blows before consigning the weapons to a watery fate? The details may be opaque, but the quantity and craftsmanship of this weaponry suggests a more visibly warlike society, where the display of weaponry (and the threat of violence) was prevalent. Swords were not rare – over 130 survive from Scotland. However, the way they were treated, repaired and buried indicates they were valued weapons, not available to everyone. We can perhaps talk for the first time of warriors – people who acquired and maintained prestige by the bearing of arms and who were in some sense specialists.

Enclosed sites, on hilltops, knolls and promontories, become more frequent at this time. They vary tremendously in scale and form:

some with timber palisades, others with ramparts and ditches. Their interpretation has been contentious – how far were they defensive, and how far statements of social differentiation? Since weaponry indicates a society that practised warfare, the defences must surely have had a practical military role, but the two ends of this debate are not mutually exclusive: ramparts and ditches can both defend and define a society.[25] Many enclosures were domestic in scale, for single houses or small clusters of an extended family or community. But this was also the age of the massive hill-forts: some of the largest in southern Scotland, at Traprain Law (East Lothian), Eildon Hill (Scottish Borders) and Burnswark (Dumfries and Galloway) originate from this time. Their massive scale (with over 1.5km of rampart surrounding Traprain at its peak) was very much a mark of status, their construction drawing on the labour of the surrounding land, and their role possibly included that of a communal focus at times of ceremony as well as a residence for the powerful.

A land of hill-forts: the earlier Iron Age (c. 700–200 BC)

In the earlier Iron Age, weaponry disappears from the archaeological record. This is not simply due to iron's poor survival in Scottish soils as elsewhere in Britain the sword vanishes as a weapon to be replaced by the less specialist spear, javelin and club. It is also because the warrior himself becomes less visible, perhaps suggesting that warfare, while still an unpleasant communal task, was not such an arena of marked social competition. This fits broader perspectives on earlier Iron Age societies, which seem rather inward-looking in comparison to those of the later Bronze Age – little in the way of exotic contacts or prestigious possessions, but a focus on the everyday and domestic.

The key military monument of these times is the aforementioned hill-fort – a diversity of enclosures, varying in scale, fortification method and topographic location. For much of the first millennium BC they were a common, at times dominant, part of the landscape. Yet, as in the late Bronze Age, their diversity must conceal a range of functions. A role as refuges in times of need has been argued, but excavation has shown that most were inhabited. A few do appear empty of occupation, such as the Caterthuns in Angus, but here the large number of entrances suggests defence was not a priority; rather, they indicate the likely role of such sites as foci for the surrounding communities to gather on high days and holy days.[26]

The twin roles of defence and social display are seen in a number of recurring features. At some hill-forts ramparts are still visible today

Figure 1.2 Woden Law hill-fort, Roxburghshire. The fort's multiple ramparts developed in a number of phases during the first millennium BC.

which suggests continuing efforts to maintain and refurbish the defences. At others, ditches were dug and promptly allowed to silt up, hinting that it was the act of display that was uppermost. This display element is seen particularly at entrances, which were often built to impress the approaching visitor. Indeed, some have little substance beyond the entrance. A would-be attacker could simply go round the back of the site and enter over a low bank or fence.[27] This cautions against approaching these sites with a solely military purpose in mind.

Among the most dramatic examples of these hill-forts are the vitrified forts, their timber-framed stone walls partly melted and fused by great heat. Their origin has long been contentious – early commentators even viewed them as extinct volcanoes – but they were widespread and long-lived across Scotland.[28] The vitrification of these walls was unlikely to have been a deliberate defensive measure to make the wall impregnable as the results would have been unpredictable, with some ramparts being heavily vitrified, others only partially. It is equally unlikely as a besieging strategy: experiments revealed great difficulties in lighting a wall and this would be made all the harder with the hostile attentions of the besieged. Vitrification was most likely a deliberate act at the end of the site's life, rendering it unusable in a very dramatic manner, with the glow of the fires visible for miles. This could be linked to a site's capture by hostile forces or an act of closure when an old site was abandoned.

Scotland was not, however, covered solely in hill-forts. They are markedly rarer in the north-east, where unenclosed settlements were the norm, and even more so on the Atlantic edges of the country, where small stone-walled enclosures and stone-built roundhouses (duns and brochs) predominated. But we should not mistake unenclosed settlements, or isolated sturdy houses, for evidence of peaceful societies as spears and sword fittings from some indicate warlike tendencies, while brochs were often set on defensible locations with accompanying enclosures. In truth, we cannot yet characterise the prevalence or role of warfare in these areas. The variety in settlement types indicates differing societies and warfare would play different roles in different areas.

Warriors once more: the later Iron Age c. 200 BC–AD 100

Towards the end of the first millennium BC changes become apparent. The construction of hill-forts declines. While the sites often remained in use, the defences became denuded, with settlement spreading over them. In contrast, weaponry becomes once again more visible. In England, swords reappear from the fourth century BC; in Scotland, on current evidence, around the second century BC.[29] During this period we see increasing evidence of iron swords with decorative bronze scabbards or fittings. This correlates with a growth of decorative material in other fields – personal ornaments, horse harnesses and feasting gear, often adorned with Celtic art. These trends become particularly strong from the first century AD, though their roots are visible earlier. They indicate an increasing differentiation between individuals in terms of status, age, gender, community and so forth through material culture. Within these increasingly status-conscious societies, warfare becomes once more an arena for social display and competition: the warrior was back.

This is well illustrated by a group of burials in east central Scotland. Formal burial was always rare in the Iron Age, restricted to particularly significant or unusual people. Yet occasionally grave goods give a picture of the dead person's identity – how their family or community chose to represent them in the grave. Some were clearly buried as warriors. The six known examples are ranged round the Forth, from Fife to East Lothian,[30] and were isolated burials, perhaps reflecting a certain ambiguity over the role of the warrior: defender of the community, but also man of violence. A recent find from Alloa provides a vivid picture of one such warrior. The man lay extended on his back in a drystone cist (stone-lined burial chamber). He was clothed in his finery, a pin by his throat preserving traces of a fur-trimmed cloak, with a glass bead pendant and rings on his toes. Round his waist a leather sword belt was fastened by bronze rings. The sword was drawn and laid across his chest; subtle bronze fittings drew the eye's attention to the hilt. A spear accompanied him, its head wedged between the stones as it was too long for the grave. If he had a shield, it was entirely wooden, as no trace survived.

The sword was the symbol *par excellence* of the warrior. In burials, iconography and hoards, these weapons were given a special status.[31] Some were decorated, the motifs probably having a magical, apotropaic or ritual significance. Fittings on some scabbards show they were worn strapped to the back and drawn over the shoulder, an unusual habit attested from Yorkshire to the Forth.[32] Evidence from elsewhere suggests the well-equipped warrior could also have worn body armour, notably mail, and perhaps a helmet, but these were rare, or at least too valued to be buried for archaeologists to find. Marked differentiation in weaponry and equipment points to major social differences between individuals. The warrior with sword and perhaps armour and helmet would have stood out in a raiding party. Most others may have simply gripped a spear and huddled nervously behind a shield.

While there is no evidence of cavalry, according to Roman sources the chariot was used in warfare at this time in Scotland,[33] although battle was only one role among many for these high-status vehicles. The same is true of the magnificent carnyx, the boar-headed trumpet which would rally warriors and terrify the opposition – the surviving Scottish example, from Deskford (Banffshire), would have been equally at home marking rituals and ceremonies. Indeed, it emphasises the elements of drama and show which must have accompanied formal battles.[34]

What was the nature of warfare at this date? It seems to have had an increasingly important social role for gaining and marking prestige, but we know nothing of its frequency, scale and impact. There is occasional evidence of violent death, such as the remains of a male aged between twenty-five and thirty-five from Mine Howe (Orkney) with spear and sword wounds.[35] There are also signs of an interest in gathering human heads, perhaps as trophies, but this widely attested cross-cultural phenomenon cannot necessarily be linked to warfare; there are parallels both for the taking of enemy skulls and the curation of venerated ancestors.[36] What is lacking is evidence of an extensively militarised society. If we turn to the continent, a range of mass weaponry deposits suggests well-organised raiding bands of tens or hundreds of individuals travelling considerable distances for inter-regional conflicts, while from the third century BC onwards it was much more common than in Britain for adult males to be buried with weapons.[37] This seems more than just differences in burial and hoarding habits: it suggests societies geared to endemic large-scale warfare, as evidence of conflicts with the Mediterranean world indicates.[38] There is little sign of this in Scotland.

This raises the key issue of the social structures of warfare – in particular the development of the war band, with retinues of warriors cutting across kin-based structures through loyalty to a leader, becoming highly volatile agents in sustaining and increasing a cycle of violence. Kin-based feuds can, of course, persist for generations and lead to bloody violence, while war bands could be raised for a specific purpose, the participants returning to their families afterwards. But such bands could develop into a retinue of specialist warriors, with little link to everyday agricultural production and sustained in large measure by plunder. Success then breeds a larger war band, which in turn needs more warfare to sustain the group. Identifying such war bands is far from easy but we shall return to this question once we consider the gathering storm on the horizon – the coming of the Romans.

Conquering Caledonia: Roman interventions in Scotland

In the late 70s AD, the rules of warfare changed irrevocably as the Roman army marched northwards. In southern England, with its much longer history of pre-conquest contact, members of the local elite served in the Roman army, returning home with Roman military equipment and knowledge.[39] There is no such evidence from Scotland, where pre-conquest contact was very limited. The arrival of the Roman forces would have been a major shock. It is worth emphasising how different, how alien the Roman battle train would have been. There was its sheer size – the invasion army in the first century was some 20,000 men and would have stretched over several kilometres on the march. There was its equipment – in contrast to Iron Age societies, where only certain warriors had swords and even fewer had body armour and helmets, every Roman soldier was fully equipped with armour, helmet, sword, shield and spears, and drilled for combat as a truly professional army. Then there were other military wonders – cavalry forces, mobile artillery and a supply chain to keep them on campaign for months with no concerns over tending cattle or harvesting crops. Apart from this, the sheer visual impact of a first encounter with the Roman army – the scale, the weaponry, the clank of armour, the crunch of nailed shoes – must have been quite overwhelming.[40]

Roman incursions into Scotland have left a disproportionate amount of evidence for the short time they were in the region. From the campaigns we can derive information from the string of temporary camps, erected on the march and serving as overnight stops, bases for the supply chain and centres for longer-term campaigning in particular areas. From the various occupations we have the forts and fortlets covering much of Lowland Scotland and linked by a network of roads, the sinews of the Roman war machine which dissected the country and allowed troops to move rapidly to trouble spots. The wealth of excavated material left behind by the army gives a vivid picture of life on the frontier.[41]

Historical sources record three major campaigns – in the late first, mid-second and early third centuries. The first, from c. AD 78 to 84 under the governor Agricola, brought much of the Lowlands under Roman sway and culminated in a major battle against the local tribes, who uniquely came together en masse against this alien force under a war leader called Calgacos ('swordsman'). This battle, Mons Graupius, has been a major source of contention. Revisionist histories have downplayed its significance and even argued it never took place, but this extreme view is implausible. Our one source, the biography of Agricola by his son-in-law, Tacitus, is undoubtedly biased and exaggerated, but it is inconceivable that the battle was simply invented; there were enough veterans among the book's readership to gainsay any such distortion.[42] Its location has, however, been heavily debated, with possible sites from Fife to Sutherland.[43] We are, in truth, little closer to establishing this; in the absence of a victory monument, or firm traces such as weaponry deposits, speculation is entertaining but largely futile. In many ways the location is unimportant – what mattered was that the Romans seemingly had succeeded in conquering the south and north-east of Scotland. The consolidation of the new territories was well under way, with further campaigns into the Highlands being contemplated, when the order came to withdraw. As so often with Roman Scotland, this was due to circumstances far away; more important frontiers needed troops, and Scotland was given up, with a staged withdrawal from AD 87 onwards to the Tyne–Solway line.

This line was fossilised in stone under the Emperor Hadrian, apparently in response to considerable frontier unrest. Prolonged construction started in AD 122. The design of Hadrian's Wall created a military zone with the linear barrier of the wall facing north and garrisons along its length; a matching earthwork to the south, the Vallum, suggests, however, that threats came from within as well as beyond the wall. Such frontiers were not solely a fortification in the medieval sense: they were a line where movement could be controlled (and taxed). And Rome's interests did not stop at the wall. A series of outpost forts provided patrols and surveillance, with any hostile incursions met in the field, not fought from the battlements.[44]

Following Hadrian's death, his successor, Antoninus Pius, rapidly ordered the legions northwards, probably due both to unrest in Lowland Scotland and his desire for a quick military victory to secure his position. The Lowlands were reconquered and regarrisoned in AD 139–42, and a new wall of turf, timber, earth and clay built from the Forth to the Clyde to control movement; once again outpost forts show that the Romans had interests in fertile areas north of the wall.[45]

The Antonine Wall was short-lived: parts were barely finished by the time it was abandoned in the 160s AD, probably shortly after Pius's death, because of a combination of stretched resources and local hostility. The frontier story for the remainder of the second century is one of intermittent and increasing hostility, apparently driven by tribes in the Forth valley and the north-east, the Caledonians and Maeatae. Eventually the emperor himself, Septimius Severus, led two major campaigns in 209 and 210 into these trouble spots, seemingly intent on taking them within the empire. Campaigning was hard – the locals practised guerrilla warfare rather than the unsuccessful massed battles of an earlier generation – but with Severus's death in York in AD 211 the attempt was abandoned and peace secured by treaties and bribes.[46]

Such an outline history inevitably misses details: the small-scale raids, patrolling, punitive expeditions and day-to-day realities of frontier life. Yet it was not solely a story of war. Roman finds from Iron Age sites show that some elements of local society were keen to acquire Roman goods as status items.[47] The wealth of Roman material from Traprain Law, for example, and the virtual absence of Roman garrisons from East Lothian, suggests this was a pro-Roman area. In contrast, it seems Dumfriesshire was particularly

Figure 1.3 Rough Castle, Stirlingshire, one of the smallest but best-preserved Roman forts on the Antonine Wall. On the left of the picture the wall runs from top to bottom, its deep ditch crossed by a causeway leading into the fort and its annexe.

troublesome, as a heavy garrison network of small fortlets in the Antonine period provided intensive supervision; the siege works around the hill-fort at Burnswark, long considered as practice works, are increasingly suggestive of an active, if short-lived, siege.[48] Overall, these northern lands clearly represented an active Roman frontier, as snatches of 'informal' history hint at: a tombstone from Vindolanda to a centurion who 'died in the . . . war'; an altar from Carlisle recording 'the slaughter of a band of barbarians'. Indeed, tombstones for cavalry soldiers, and triumphal sculptures from the Antonine Wall with Roman cavalrymen killing local barbarians, speak of a daily reality of conflict and violence in these parts.[49]

What of the Roman army itself? The campaigning force consisted of both legionaries (heavy infantry composed of citizen soldiers) and auxiliaries (both infantry and cavalry, recruited from the provinces). After the campaigns, the legions did much of the building work, but the bulk of garrison duty was left to the auxiliaries. These were drawn from conquered groups across the empire, a strategy to harness troublesome young men for the Roman good and send them far from their homeland. A similar strategy may well have been employed after the Scottish conquests, but any such units are anonymous – we know of cohorts of Britons, but none of Caledonians, Votadini or Novantae. Yet as time went on and the empire became less expansionist much recruitment into the auxiliaries would have been locally based, with sons of soldiers following fathers into the army.

Figure 1.4 Detail from a Roman distance marker, erected c. AD 142, from the Antonine Wall found at Bridgeness, West Lothian. A Roman cavalryman rides down the enemy who are depicted as naked barbarians.

The impact of Rome

Whether as conqueror or aggressive neighbour, Rome was a pervasive influence on Scotland for over 300 years. What was the impact on her native peoples? An effect on local societies is inevitable, not least in warfare. Empires often lead inadvertently to the creation of a 'tribal zone', an extensive area beyond the formal frontier that witnesses drastic changes.[50] These changes are varied but frequently include the formation of new, larger-scale social units and enhanced volatility. Conflict may have arisen, for instance, over access to Roman goods or in the acquisition of slaves, furs and animals to trade in return. There is no suggestion that the peoples of Scotland were peaceful before the Romans arrived – quite the reverse. However, it seems likely that the proximity of Rome indeed caused considerable social change and led to greater violence, reflected dimly in the persistent Roman records of problems on the northern frontier. This is very hard to track archaeologically, but one indication of this is the emergence of the group known as the Picts.

The Picts were one of the 'problem peoples' of the later Roman period – and have proved no less problematic to archaeologists and historians – but they can be seen as a major new political group created by Roman policies.[51] From the late third century AD they appear in the sources as a persistent thorn in the side of the Romans, sufficiently irritating for the Emperor, Constantius Chlorus, to lead a field army against them in AD 305. The extent of their seaborne raids into Roman-controlled territory is indicated by the erection of a series of signal stations down the Yorkshire coast to warn of their approach. They raided and plundered deep into the province; a knife handle from Norfolk inscribed with Pictish ogham gives a hint of their reach.[52]

How did this happen? The emergence of the Picts is often seen as the product of a coalition of pre-existing tribes, but this over-simplifies a complex problem. An alternative reading sees their emergence as due to persistent Roman interference in the north-east of Scotland as they tried to build alliances and create internal tensions.[53] In the short term, this seems to have created social upheaval, leading to the relative peace of the third century; but in the longer term it may have contributed to the forging of new, better organised and more implacably hostile groups.

Yet how could the Picts, apparently a small-scale grouping with little evidence of major power centres, pose such a threat to the Roman state? How could they conduct campaigns at such a distance from their homeland? This takes us back to the question of war bands, with leader and retinue bound together by plunder rather than blood. The war band, able to operate for longer periods of time and thus at greater range, would facilitate such long-range raids, with success breeding larger and ever more dangerous groups. If we wish to explain the emergence of such groups, so significant in the Early Historic period, this may be the place to look – the inadvertent creation of the very Roman state that they threatened. In a situation where existing social bonds and groupings had been disturbed or destroyed by Rome's activities, new bonds and new connections could have been made much more easily.

Although archaeological evidence is frequently ambiguous, there are persistent signs that warfare played a significant part in Scottish prehistory from at least the Neolithic. This is no evolutionary story as patterns shifted between small-scale endemic warfare (doubtless varied in character) and rarer periods when warfare seemed to assume considerable social importance. What we see here is an opportunity for some players in society to create or reinforce their position, as reflected in specialist, ornate weaponry, or in the construction of such features as hill-forts, which combine a defensive role with motives of display and demarcation. Warfare was never a purely military exercise.

The impact of Rome has invariably been examined from the viewpoint of the Romans, with studies of their camps, forts, campaigns and army organisation. Yet the indigenous peoples, at the sharp end of Roman swords, lost, gained and changed. The loss was physical – of land and people. The gain was in material wealth – through access to Roman objects and economic transactions with the occupiers. The change, in the long term, was the creation of new social groupings, notably the Picts, emerging from the disastrous effects of Roman interference to pose a severe military threat to the empire. With them we may dimly glimpse the appearance of a new unit, the war band or military retinue, bound by loyalty to its leader rather than by community. This marked the rise of a new dynamic in the land that would come to dominate the history of warfare in the succeeding centuries.

Notes

I am grateful to a First Millennia Studies Group seminar in 2004 which stimulated much debate on this topic, and to David Clarke and James Fraser for valuable discussions.

1. S. Piggott, *Ancient Britons and the Antiquarian Imagination* (London: Thames and Hudson, 1989), pp. 73–5; K. Sloan, *A New World. England's First View of America* (London: British Museum, 2007), pp. 153–63.
2. For example, J. MacKinnon, *Culture in Early Scotland* (London: Williams and Norgate, 1892).
3. For example, V. G. Childe, *The Prehistory of Scotland* (London: Kegan Paul, 1935), pp. 190–235; T. G. E. Powell, 'The coming of the Celts', in S. Piggott (ed.), *The Prehistoric Peoples of Scotland* (London: Routledge and Kegan Paul, 1962), pp. 105–24, especially pp. 120–4.
4. L. H. Keeley, *War before Civilization* (New York and Oxford: Oxford University Press, 1996).
5. Keeley, *War before Civilization*, pp. 59–69.
6. R. B. Ferguson, review of Keeley, *War before Civilization*, in *American*

Anthropologist, new series, vol. 99, no. 2 (1997), pp. 424–5; J. Chapman, 'The origins of warfare in the prehistory of Central and Eastern Europe', in J. Carmen and A. Harding (eds), *Ancient Warfare: Archaeological Perspectives* (Stroud: Sutton, 1999), pp. 101–41, especially pp. 101–2.

7. Battlefields are mostly invisible in the absence of readily recoverable ordnance such as shot or iron arrows (although see P. S. Wells, *The Battle that Stopped Rome* (London: Norton, 2003) for an exception), while with other evidence of destruction, such as burnt houses, the cause is generally unclear.
8. J. X. W. P. Corcoran, 'The excavation of three chambered cairns at Loch Calder, Caithness', *Proceedings of the Society of Antiquaries of Scotland*, vol. 98 (1964–6), pp. 1–75, especially p. 44.
9. Usefully discussed by Chapman, 'The origins of warfare', pp. 107–8.
10. For instance, Iron Age Denmark, where open settlements dominate, produces clear evidence of warfare; K. Randsborg, 'Into the Iron Age: A discourse on war and society', in Carmen and Harding (eds), *Ancient Warfare*, pp.191–202, especially p. 198.
11. S. Vencl, 'Stone Age warfare', in Carmen and Harding (eds), *Ancient Warfare*, pp. 57–72, especially pp. 58–60; I. J. N. Thorpe, 'The ancient origins of warfare and violence', in M. Parker Pearson and I. J. N. Thorpe (eds), *Warfare, Violence and Slavery in Prehistory* (Oxford: British Archaeological Reports, 2005), pp. 1–18, especially pp. 10–12; R. C. Kelly, *Warless Societies and the Origin of War* (Ann Arbor, MI: University of Michigan Press, 2000).
12. R. J. Mercer, 'The origins of warfare in the British Isles', in Carmen and Harding (eds), *Ancient Warfare*, pp. 143–56.
13. R. O'Flaherty, 'A weapon of choice – experiments with a replica Irish Early Bronze Age halberd', *Antiquity*, vol. 81 (2007), pp. 423–34.
14. I. Macleod and B. Hill, *Heads and Tales: Reconstructing Faces* (Edinburgh: National Museums of Scotland, 2001), pp. 16–19.
15. Keeley, *War before Civilization*, p. 35; Thorpe, 'The ancient origins of warfare', p. 5.
16. J. Coles, *Images of the Past: A Guide to the Rock Carvings and other Ancient Monuments of Northern Bohuslän* (Uddevalla: Hällristningsmuseet Vitlycke, 1990), especially pp. 23–4, fig. 11; F. Hunter, 'The image of the warrior in the British Iron Age – coin iconography in context', in C. Haselgrove and D. Wigg-Wolf (eds), *Iron Age Coinage and Ritual Practices* (Studien zu Fundmünzen der Antike 20; Mainz: Von Zabern, 2005), pp. 43–68.
17. A. K. Bowman and J. D. Thomas, *The Vindolanda Writing Tablets (Tabulae Vindolandenses II)* (London: British Museum, 1994), no. 164; P. R. Sealey, *A Late Iron Age Warrior Burial from Kelvedon, Essex* (East

Anglian Archaeology 118; Colchester: Colchester Museums, 2007), p. 40; Hunter, 'Image of the warrior', pp. 61–2.
18. R. Bradley, *The Passage of Arms: An Archaeological Analysis of Prehistoric Hoards and Votive Deposits* (Cambridge: Cambridge University Press, 1990), especially ch. 3.
19. R. Osgood and S. Monks, *Bronze Age Warfare* (Stroud: Sutton, 2000), pp. 23–32.
20. K. Kristiansen and T. B. Larsson, *The Rise of Bronze Age Society: Travels, Transmissions and Transformations* (Cambridge: Cambridge University Press, 2005).
21. M. W. Helms, *Ulysses' Sail: An Ethnographic Odyssey of Power, Knowledge and Geographical Distance* (Princeton, NJ: Princeton University Press, 1988).
22. J. M. Coles, 'Scottish Late Bronze Age metalwork: Typology, distributions and chronology', *Proceedings of the Society of Antiquaries of Scotland*, vol. 93 (1959–60), pp. 16–134, especially pp. 102–7, 118–19; T. G. Cowie, *Magic Metal: Early Metalworkers in the North-East* (Aberdeen: Anthropological Museum, 1988); I. A. G. Shepherd, 'The use of bronzes in "frontier locations": some new Late Bronze Age objects from Upper Deeside, Aberdeenshire', in W. H. Metz, B. L. van Beek and H. Steegstra (eds), *Patina: Essays Presented to Jay Jordan Butler on the Occasion of his 80th Birthday* (Groningen: privately published, 2001), pp. 493–501.
23. Bradley, *The Passage of Arms*, pp. 138–42.
24. S. D. Bridgford, 'Mightier than the pen? (An edgewise look at Irish Bronze Age swords)', in J. Carmen (ed.), *Material Harm: Archaeological Studies of War and Violence* (Glasgow: Cruithne Press, 1997), pp. 95–115, especially pp. 106–7.
25. I. Ralston, *Celtic Fortifications* (Stroud: Tempus, 2006); I. Armit, 'Hillforts at war: From Maiden Castle to Taniwaha', *Proceedings of the Prehistoric Society*, vol. 73 (2007), pp. 25–37.
26. A. Dunwell and R. Strachan, *Excavations at Brown Caterthun and White Caterthun Hillforts, Angus, 1995–1997* (Perth: Tayside and Fife Archaeology Committee, 2007), pp. 91–3.
27. Ralston, *Celtic Fortifications*, pp. 38–40, 75–6.
28. Ibid. pp. 143–63.
29. I. M. Stead, *British Iron Age Swords and Scabbards* (London: British Museum, 2006).
30. Hunter, 'Image of the warrior', pp. 50–6; for subsequent finds see *British Archaeology*, vol. 87 (2006), p. 9; S. Mills, 'Alloa: A Bronze Age woman and an Iron Age warrior', *Current Archaeology*, vol. 191 (2004), pp. 486–9.
31. Hunter, 'Image of the warrior', pp. 45–6, 55–8, 61.

32. Stead, *Iron Age Swords*, pp. 61–3, 68.
33. Tacitus, *Agricola*, 35.3; *Cornelii Tacitii De Vita Agricolae*, ed. R. H. Ogilvie and Sir Ian Richmond (Oxford: Clarendon Press, 1967), p. 115. A good recent translation is by A. R. Birley, *Agricola and Germany* (Oxford: Oxford University Press, 1999).
34. F. Hunter, 'The carnyx in Iron Age Europe', *Antiquaries Journal*, vol. 81 (2001), pp. 77–108.
35. N. Card and J. Downes, 'Murder at Mine Howe?', *Scottish Archaeological News*, vol. 51 (2006), pp. 1–2.
36. I. Armit and V. Ginn, 'Beyond the grave: Human remains from domestic contexts in Iron Age Atlantic Scotland', *Proceedings of the Prehistoric Society*, vol. 73 (2007), pp. 113–34, especially pp. 127–30; I. Armit, 'Inside Kurtz's compound: Headhunting and the human body in Prehistoric Europe', in M. Bonogofsky (ed.), *Skull Collection, Modification and Decoration* (Oxford: British Archaeoleological Reports, 2006), pp. 1–14.
37. K. Randsborg, *Hjortspring: Warfare and Sacrifice in Early Europe* (Aarhus: Aarhus University Press, 1995); J.-L. Brunaux, *Guerre et religion en Gaule* (Paris: Errance, 2004), pp. 90–124; J. Collis, *The European Iron Age* (London: Batsford, 1984), pp. 127, 130–3.
38. B. Cunliffe, *The Ancient Celts* (Oxford: Oxford University Press, 1997), pp. 68–90.
39. J. Creighton, *Coins and Power in Late Iron Age Britain* (Cambridge: Cambridge University Press, 2000), especially ch. 4.
40. The Roman army has a huge literature; for introductions see G. Webster, *The Roman Imperial Army*, third edition (London: A. & C. Black, 1985); M. C. Bishop and J. C. N. Coulston, *Roman Military Equipment from the Punic Wars to the Fall of Rome*, second edition (Oxford: Oxbow, 2006).
41. For introductions, see D. Breeze, *Roman Scotland: Frontier Country*, second edition (London: B. T. Batsford for Historic Scotland, 2006); G. S. Maxwell, *The Romans in Scotland* (Edinburgh: James Thin, 1989); G. Maxwell, *A Gathering of Eagles: Scenes from Roman Scotland* (Edinburgh: Canongate for Historic Scotland, 1998).
42. J. E. Fraser, *The Roman Conquest of Scotland: The Battle of Mons Graupius AD 84* (Stroud: Tempus, 2005), pp. 15–16.
43. G. Maxwell, *A Battle Lost: Romans and Caledonians at Mons Graupius* (Edinburgh: Edinburgh University Press, 1990); Fraser, *Roman Conquest*, pp. 67–78.
44. From an extensive literature, see D. J. Breeze, *J. Collingwood Bruce's Handbook to the Roman Wall*, fourteenth edition (Newcastle: Society of Antiquaries of Newcastle-upon-Tyne, 2006); D. J. Breeze and B. Dobson, *Hadrian's Wall*, fourth edition (London: Penguin, 2000).
45. For the Antonine Wall, see D. J. Breeze, *The Antonine Wall* (Edinburgh:

John Donald, 2006); W. Hanson and G. Maxwell, *Rome's North-West Frontier: The Antonine Wall* (Edinburgh: Edinburgh University Press, 1983).
46. A. R. Birley, *Septimius Severus: The African Emperor* (London: Routledge, 1999), pp. 170–87.
47. F. Hunter, 'Roman and native in Scotland: New approaches', *Journal of Roman Archaeology*, vol. 14 (2001), pp. 289–309.
48. D. B. Campbell, 'The Roman siege of Burnswark', *Britannia*, vol. 34 (2003), pp. 19–33.
49. A. R. Birley, 'A new tombstone from Vindolanda', *Britannia*, vol. 29 (1998), pp. 299–306; R. G. Collingwood and R. P. Wright, *The Roman Inscriptions of Britain, I* (Oxford: Oxford University Press, 1965), no. 946; L. J. F. Keppie and B. Arnold, *Corpus of Sculpture of the Roman World, Great Britain I:4, Scotland* (Oxford: British Academy, 1984); S. Bull, *Triumphant Rider: The Lancaster Roman Cavalry Tombstone* (Lancaster: Lancashire Museums, 2007); F. Hunter and L. Keppie, 'Tombstone of a Roman cavalry trooper discovered', *History Scotland*, vol. 8 (2008), pp. 7–8.
50. R. B. Ferguson and N. L. Whitehead, *War in the Tribal Zone: Expanding States and Indigenous Warfare*, second edition (Santa Fe, NM: School of American Research Press, 1999).
51. F. Hunter, *Beyond the Edge of the Empire: Caledonians, Picts and Romans* (Rosemarkie: Groam House, 2007). For general treatments, see J. E. Fraser, *From Caledonia to Pictland: Scotland to 795* (Edinburgh: Edinburgh University Press, 2009); S. Foster, *Picts, Gaels and Scots*, second edition (London: B. T. Batsford for Historic Scotland, 2004).
52. R. R. Clarke, 'An ogham inscribed knife-handle from south-west Norfolk', *Antiquaries Journal*, vol. 32 (1952), pp. 71–4.
53. J. Mann, 'The Northern Frontier after AD 369', *Glasgow Archaeological Journal*, vol. 3 (1974), pp. 34–42; P. Heather, 'State formation in Europe in the first millennium AD', in B. E. Crawford (ed.), *Scotland in Dark Age Europe* (St Andrews: Committee for Dark Age Studies, University of St Andrews, 1994), pp. 47–70; Hunter, *Beyond the Edge*, pp. 4–9, 23–7, 32–6, 50–4.

2
Warfare in Northern Britain, c. 500–1093

JAMES E. FRASER

Violence was endemic in the early medieval Latin West, and evidence relating to it abounds in the texts pertaining to northern Britain from the sixth to the eleventh century.[1] Such conflict provides the 'background noise' in the decorative programmes of many of the carved stone monuments that testify to the social and cultural achievement of the peoples of Scotland in this otherwise elusive period.[2] The twin engines that powered this violence were social norms obliging men to rally round their kin in times of trouble, and for such kindreds to resolve their differences through mutual hostility. The right of 'normal freemen' – that is freemen with full legal status – to take revenge for injuries to their person, property or good name was not usually questioned, while to allow injured kin to go unavenged was a disgraceful dereliction of familial duty.[3] Military service was an integral part of life for many over these six centuries; for others, it was fear of, and victimisation by, fighting men that loomed large. The underlying social forces involved were doubtless ancient by the sixth century, and they remained influential in Scotland well beyond the eleventh century.

For most of this period northern Britain was home to four main ethno-linguistic groups, the longest of pedigree being the North Britons, whose British tongue, ancestor of modern Welsh, appears to have been spoken throughout the country in the Roman Iron Age. By AD 700 those regarding themselves as Britons were essentially confined to districts south of the Clyde, but also of the Forth, where they had been under considerable pressure for the better part of two centuries from the expanding political power of the Anglo-Saxon peoples dwelling north of the River Humber. The seventh century had seen most of the North Britons of southern Scotland brought into the realm of the mightiest of these Northumbrian English groups

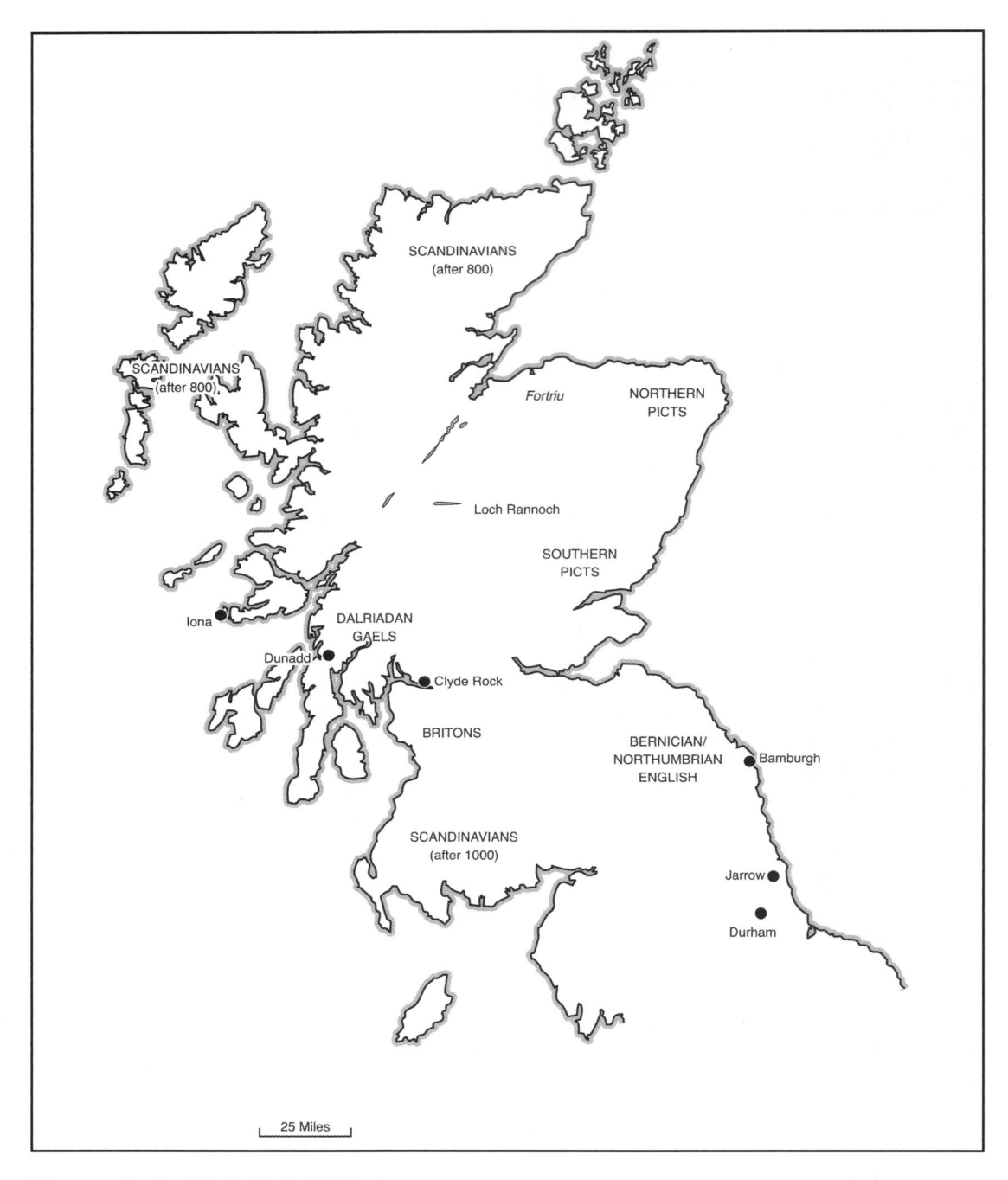

Map 2.1 Scotland in the Early Middle Ages, c. 500–1093.

Figure 2.1 Dunadd fort, Argyll, one of the chief centres of the early Scottish kingdom of Dalriada.

– the Bernicians – whose main royal centres included Bamburgh, Dunbar and sites in the Tweed basin, and probably Edinburgh. By the middle of the eighth century, the Bernicians had subdued south-west Scotland, and the kingdom of Clyde Rock (or Dumbarton) had become the last of the major North British kingdoms. Further north, the British-speaking population of the country had assumed a different name. In Latin they spoke of themselves as *Picti*, a name that the Romans had coined for the 'painted' natives of Scotland in the second half of the Roman Iron Age. The period between c. 650 and c. 750 saw these 'Picts' achieve a degree of political coherence under the dominion of the kings of Fortriu in and around Moray, who out-competed the Bernician English for primacy in the fertile and strategic country between the Grampians and the Forth.

To the west of Pictland, Atlantic Scotland was home to the fourth of the country's main ethno-linguistic groups, who spoke the Gaelic language and named themselves *Scoti* in Latin, traits they shared with the neighbouring Gaels of Ireland. The seventh century saw a major kingdom develop in Argyll – Dál Riata or Dalriada – but this realm appears to have been smashed by the Picts in a succession of campaigns in the 730s. There followed one of the most important but obscure periods of Scotland's history, during which the Picts became ethnic Gaels, setting aside the name *Picti* in favour of *Scoti*. At the same time Scandinavian incomers were carving out settlements on the western seaboard, including the Northern Isles and the south-west. Scandinavian armies caused widespread disruption in northern Britain, especially among the Northumbrian English. The impact of the Scandinavians on the military history of western Europe has been much studied, but unfortunately evidence is extremely sparse in a specifically Scottish context. Instead, surviving texts relating to warfare and society in these centuries come mainly from eighth-century commentators, though it would be unwise to apply an eighth-century template to our whole period, save as something to be tested with earlier and later evidence.

Around 700, Adomnán, abbot of Iona, described in his *Life of Columba* how a would-be monk at his monastery who had killed a man was 'held in chains as the one condemned', presumably by his victim's kin. One of his wealthy relatives, however, arranged for his acquittal, probably by offering acceptable compensatory payment, and thus redeemed his kinsman from execution.[4] Similar values are evident in the story related by Bede of Wearmouth-Jarrow, writing c. 730 in his *Historia Ecclesiastica*, of how when a Bernician king lost his brother in battle against the king of Mercia in 679, the result was 'cause for fiercer fighting and prolonged hostilities'. A settlement was nevertheless brokered by Archbishop Theodore of Canterbury, with 'no further lives of men being demanded for the death', because of the 'obligatory compensation-payment paid to the avenging king'.[5] The realm of the Bernician English spanned the present-day Anglo-Scottish border when these words were penned, and it seems very likely that neighbouring Pictish, British and Gaelic societies across Scotland were regulated by similar notions of bloodfeud or 'customary vengeance' which were ubiquitous across the early medieval west. Anthropological analogy also suggests that military activity, whether on a small or larger scale, in the non-state societies of early medieval northern Britain was understood at the time and legitimised by the participants principally as the avenging of wrongs.[6] In these eighth-century stories, the kin of both killer and victim take the law into their own hands but do so lawfully; violent reprisal is threatened, and the payment of compensation by one side to the other defuses the situation. Peace prevails through the power of retributive military activity as a deterrent, not so much to would-be offenders as to would-be pursuers of indiscriminate vengeance.[7]

Societal norms did not keep men from settling personal grudges violently, whether in 'private' disputes between kindreds or in international ones between kings. Far from being condemned, revenge was 'a duty one owed to the community, for the maintenance of law and order'.[8] Individual acts of homicide seem to have been common and jurisprudence largely unconcerned with its eradication. Victims and their kin were entitled to blood, and, as has been observed from continental evidence, 'might be excused almost anything' before blood cooled, upon which disputes were expected to succumb to 'the natural pulls inherent in feud-society towards settlement'.[9] It was the power of these pulls that law was chiefly concerned to invigorate, and these two stories from Adomnán and Bede suggest that in northern Britain (as elsewhere) it was effective in preventing simmering antagonisms from boiling over and destabilising whole regions or networks of interconnected kindreds.

Yet if fear of terrible retributive violence was a major incentive to seek a settlement,[10] compensation might equally be 'no long-term substitute for equalling the score violently'.[11] Bede spoke optimistically of a peace treaty between the Pictish and Northumbrian kingdoms facing one another across the Forth in the early 730s, but strife had boiled over by 740.[12] Treaties between nations, as between kindreds, were temporary suspensions of hostilities as long as effort, nerve, attention and faith held, or until some flashpoint ignited old grudges.[13] Over the early medieval centuries a sizeable number of battles and sieges are recorded in northern Britain, principally in Irish chronicles, though with depressingly little detail. Nevertheless, while we are hampered by the paucity and character of the available sources, it may be that such major engagements were exceptions, newsworthy for this very reason, and that more often pitched battles were consciously avoided. For while social pressures on men to initiate hostilities were considerable, it seems that so too were expectations that confrontation should generally result in settlement with a minimum of bloodshed.

Sieges and dispute settlement

To Scottish armies of the central Middle Ages, castles were high-profile military targets, not least because their defensibility could be suspect in the face of dedicated assault by sizeable forces. Such major assaults, however, were rare, and castle defences were arguably geared primarily towards intimidating raiders on more common small-scale plundering campaigns.[14] The hill-forts and other defended sites of early medieval northern Britain may perhaps be understood in similar terms, as providing effective protection to even small numbers of occupants from the relatively ephemeral but common threat posed by marauders. In his *Life of St Wilfrid*, Stephen of Ripon describes how during a siege of Bamburgh in 704, 'the minds of the [besieging] enemies were changed; very hastily they all plighted their

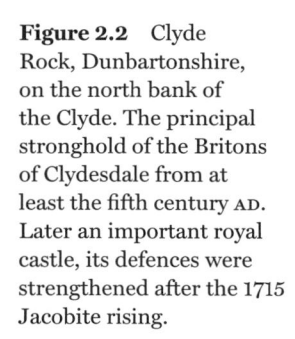

Figure 2.2 Clyde Rock, Dunbartonshire, on the north bank of the Clyde. The principal stronghold of the Britons of Clydesdale from at least the fifth century AD. Later an important royal castle, its defences were strengthened after the 1715 Jacobite rising.

friendship to us with an oath, by opening the gates we were freed from constraint, [and] our enemies were put to flight'.[15] Though admittedly literary, this account makes no mention of direct combat, but rather seems to reflect the kind of hostile posturing, coupled with the avoidance of direct fighting and inclination to settle, noted above. Such apparently bloodless stand-offs may not have been unusual in sieges (*obsessiones*) during this period. Evidence from Adomnán and Bede suggests that ramming or setting fire to the gates of fortified places was a common way of attacking them, yet we have no explicit accounts of strongholds being taken by storm.[16] The local account of the disastrous Scottish siege of Durham in 1006, where the Scots were heavily defeated by a relief force, provides no indication of attempts of a direct assault on the defences, though in a further siege of Durham in 1039, the Scots are said to have 'laboured greatly to reduce (*expugnare*) it, but vainly'.[17]

The apparent rarity of siege warfare across much of the Latin West in the early Middle Ages, including most of Britain and Ireland,[18] makes the prominence of sieges in the record from northern Britain quite distinctive. Rather than relentless assaults, sieges might be concluded by the forging of some kind of formal understanding by protagonists who faced one another across the ramparts, or across the water between a besieged island and the mainland.[19] Perhaps the most striking example is the investment of Clyde Rock, the predecessor stronghold to Dumbarton castle, by combined Pictish and Northumbrian forces in 756, where the inhabitants 'accepted terms', apparently without bloodshed.[20] Storming a stronghold was a high-risk tactic of the first order: the odds were securely in the defenders' favour until the fortifications were breached, and even then attackers risked being surrounded within and massacred.[21] Another less risky tactic seems to have been preferred, termed *combustio* in the Irish chronicles and exemplified in the following description by Bede:

> A hostile Mercian army led by Penda, cruelly devastating Northumbrian districts far and wide, reached the royal stronghold (*urbs*) called [Bamburgh]. As he could not capture it either by arms or by siege (*obsidio*), he attempted to set it in flames; and he broke up settlements which he found near the stronghold, and brought to it an accumulation of many beams, timbers, wattle hurdles, and roofing thatch. He built them up to an immense height around that side of the fortress that faced the land, and then a favourable wind arose, and he set it on fire, attempting to burn up the stronghold.[22]

Here there is no negotiation, forging of terms or peaceful disengagement as in the encounters described above: instead Penda attempts to destroy Bamburgh and its occupants by firing it. According to the *Chronicle of the Kings of Alba*, one of the crowning achievements of the military career of Cinaed son of Alpín was his burning of the English stronghold of Dunbar in the middle of the ninth century.[23] A generation later a Scandinavian force sacked and destroyed Clyde Rock after a four-month siege.[24]

A related scenario provides the backdrop to a story told in the *Life of Columba*, in which a much humbler dwelling (*domus*) is surrounded, and lay devotees of the saint 'escaped unhurt from the hands of their enemies, among flames, swords and spears', unlike others who perished there.[25] *Obsessio* and *combustio* were clearly not the exclusive preserve of kings and great strongholds, but featured in the struggles of men and kindreds further down the social scale: evidence suggests that similar arson attacks killed several notables in Scotland during this period.[26] The decisive role of fire in such encounters explains the appeal of the crannog on its artificial island, which would also have been very difficult to surround.[27] A breakout similar to that engineered by the devotees of St Columba perhaps lies behind an Irish chronicle's statement that in 734 Donngal son of Selbach, king of Lorn, 'fled into Ireland' after Dún Leithfinn, a stronghold in Argyll whose location is unknown, was 'destroyed after the wounding of Donngal'.[28]

Plundering and the pull towards settlement

Bede's portrayal of invaders marauding across Northumbria reminds us that early medieval war could be total war. Adomnán noted how the 'neighbouring folk' of an Ionan monastery in northern Ireland fled 'for refuge to the church with their women and children because of an attack by enemies'.[29] Contemporaries needed no reminding about the wisdom of such flight; elsewhere in the *Life of Columba*, similar raiders brutally ravage a district on Loch Rannoch, much to the distress of a native whom Columba comforts with the news that his wife and sons had 'escaped by fleeing to a mountain', leaving their cattle and chattels to the marauders (*uastatores*).[30] Real or imaginary, such scenes of devastation, flight and loss abound in this and other texts. Their offhand, matter-of-fact handling by authors implies that the threat of *uastatio* can never have strayed far from the minds of ordinary people across Scotland in this period.

Uastatio, the plundering raid, was everywhere the central reality of early medieval campaigning.[31] Even with thin evidence, the conformity of northern Britain is clear, and marauding remained 'the most immediate and fundamental expression of enemy hostilities' well into the central Middle Ages.[32] It could take place on a small scale, as in our Loch Rannoch example above, or on a large one, as in the devastations wreaked by Penda, or indeed by Scandinavian forces in the ninth and tenth centuries, who could ravage for months.[33] Anthropology conditions us to envisage lives lived against a backdrop of frequent plundering and attacks on settlements, which could be cumulatively devastating to kindreds or kingdoms.[34] The precious vignettes provided by Adomnán suggest that flight was commonly the response to news of enemy campaigning. No doubt households had escape plans, taught carefully to children by anxious adults. It did not always avail them. Why else did Adomnán, by Herculean effort, secure royal and ecclesiastical undertakings across Ireland and northern Britain to uphold his *Lex innocentium* in 697? The text of this 'Law of Innocents' is frank: women, children, penitents and clerics, *innocentes* all (literally 'harmless'), were in dire need of greater protection from butchery, mutilation, enslavement and degradation, and their plight was far from uncommon in the early medieval west.[35] Even where they managed to avoid such grisly fates, the inhabitants of plundered countrysides faced hardship and want, if not utter ruin. The farming people of early medieval Scotland, as elsewhere, must have been prepared, socially and psychologically, to cope, showing a resilience that is difficult to fathom today. Historians must, of course, remain vigilant for exaggeration of the woeful vices of a sinful world on the part of the monks who serve as their sources, but Adomnán's violent depictions of society share much in common with other contemporary writing.

Insofar as they were designed with military functions in mind, the hill-forts and related strongholds of early medieval Scotland can be seen, like the castles of later centuries, as being geared towards convincing marauders to move on to softer targets, thereby providing indirect evidence of *uastatio*. When other commentators of Adomnán's generation reported that Northumbrian English raiders were marauding, literally 'depopulating' (*depopulans*), in Pictland in 685,[36] and that Pictish forces annihilated (*deletae sunt*) Orkney in 681,[37] we have little cause to doubt them. Not lightly, after all, can folk have fled their homes in the manner imagined by Adomnán, sometimes perhaps seeking refuge at local strongholds. The consequences of *deletio* and *depopulatio* were surely as dire as they sound, and so incentivised the acceptance of arbitration. Such methods of plunder were a feature of Hebridean warfare long before the first Vikings appeared in Atlantic Scotland, and Adomnán tells of one group of sixth-century sea raiders in Argyll sacking churches as well as settlements.[38] Other observers at Iona recorded marauding and slaying by Argyll men ranging as far afield as Ulster, Donegal and Orkney in the pre-Viking period.[39] The massacre of sixty-eight people during the third recorded Viking assault on Iona in 806 was outrageous because the victims were denizens of the great monastery, but it need not be doubted that slaughter on this scale featured in many plundering campaigns in this period.[40]

Devastation (*vastatio*) was a deceptively complex feature of early medieval society. The exchange of resources lay at the heart of political relationships, with dominion and subjection formally signalled by the giving and accepting of gifts, or, in more fraught situations, the demanding and payment of tribute and hostages.[41] Plundering was the implicit threat that overshadowed expectations of tribute, and *uastatio* could affirm, restore or overturn unequal bonds between men without the higher levels of risk involved in sieges and pitched battles. Here again brutality may have incentivised settlement. Disturbing the lives of ordinary folk could be a political act, dishonouring those whose duty it was to protect them. Robbing farms of their principal sources of essential labour – cattle, servants and slaves – must commonly have created knock-on political and economic effects.[42] Whether resources changed hands as a result of plundering, or as the price of tribute or compensation paid to stave off the threat of ravaging, military activity (or the threat of it) was clearly a central factor in the exchange relationships of early medieval northern Britain, all too often encompassed by scholars today under the more inoffensive umbrella of 'trade'.

We know little about even the generalities of campaign life on military expeditions. There may have been little in the way of organised logistics, but a chance detail in a story related by Bede reveals that camp-followers of a sort – local farmers willing or coerced to provide victuals – featured in some campaigns.[43] Forces on the move may have subsisted in the main on plunder rather than baggage borne by pack animals, creating natural windows of greatest opportunity within the annual cycle of planting, transhumance and harvesting. Yet it is difficult to believe that the vital matter of provisioning was left entirely to the chance of plundering; and the availability of pack animals would have been useful for the removal of booty. According to the *Life of Columba*, the Bernician king Oswald described himself as 'encamped (*castrametatus*) in readiness for battle' before an engagement in 634, 'sleeping on his pillow in his tent'.[44] These meagre details, like those relating to Penda's efforts in pulling down settlements in order to fire the walls of Bamburgh, beg the question of whether or not warriors undertook the manual labour of making and breaking nightly camps, setting up tents, loading pack animals or stacking timber against the walls of strongholds. If they did not, Bede's evidence of camp-followers from the locality hints at potential sources of the necessary labour involved in such campaign activities, but it is difficult to say much more about this important subject.

The face of battle

Ravaging, however common, may have been considerably less effective in bringing disputes to decision than riskier and potentially costlier sieges like the one described by Bede or by the ninth-century *History of the Britons* at the unidentified *urbs Iudeu* on the Firth of Forth in 655. Negotiations took place on that occasion, and the Bernician defenders turned over treasures, with the proviso that the Mercian attacker (Penda again) 'would cease to plunder (*uastare*) the districts of his realm', but residual hostilities soon led to a subsequent clash on the battlefield.[45] Such pitched battles were more decisive than sieges, but with higher risks that made them a last resort.[46] Battle was big news in early medieval Scotland, and prominent enough in the collective memory to be used in narrative writing to provide chronological signposts; Adomnán, for instance, observed that St Columba left Ireland for Britain 'in the second year after the battle of Cúil Dreimne' c. 561.[47] We have no detailed descriptions of major engagements in this period, and more generally there has been increasing scepticism about the value of such 'battle-pieces' in chronicle narratives.[48] Pitched battles must, of course, have varied widely, but the sources permit the sketching of some general features. A king or warlord gets wind of trouble and quickly prepares an expedition to challenge his foes. Having located the enemy and settled on battle, he and his council form a plan. Overnight manoeuvres followed by dawn assaults, flanking manoeuvres, ambushes and feigned flights can be glimpsed in the record. In each case, the tactical objective seems to be an element of surprise, though potentates tend to be praised in the sources for their personal valour and prowess rather than for tactical brilliance. Such emphasis, however, is a better reflection of narrative conventions than the actual strategic or tactical abilities of these warlords and their men. One must remain wary of the old paradigm among military historians regarding 'the art of war' as moribund in the Middle Ages because the genius of commanders could not flourish among warriors infatuated by cultivating their personal honour and renown.[49]

As regards battlefields themselves, riversides were common, and fortified places like hill-forts and old Roman installations seem often to have stood nearby. Kings or war leaders may commonly have congregated at such sites to consider enemy action and to decide whether to withdraw, to stay put and endure siege or to deploy nearby in preparation for battle in the open. A single sea battle (*bellum maritimum*) is on record in our period, fought in 719 between rival kindreds of Dál Riata, but there is too little evidence to enable further discussion of naval encounters.[50] Forces entered battle with the objective of turning the enemy to flight, and either killing enemy leaders or delivering them as captives into the hands of their own commanders. There are hints that banners were carried, and depictions of trumpets and horns on monumental sculpture suggest these may have been used for signalling men in battle.[51] Shield-walls, mentioned particularly in panegyric poetry, were apparently the usual infantry formation, encouraging poets to mobilise the image of the shattered shield to symbolise death and defeat.[52] Images of shield-bearing spearmen in file on the Dupplin Cross and the Pictish slab from Birsay may perhaps represent shield-walls, but the comparable image on the Aberlemno churchyard cross-slab must represent a stylised deployment in an array of three ranks.[53] The use of archery in battle

Figure 2.3 The Aberlemno churchyard cross-slab, Angus, possibly dating from the late seventh or early eighth century AD, depicts a battle scene that may portray the defeat of the Northumbrian English by the Picts at Nechtanesmere (Dún Nechtain) in AD 685.

is implied by images of archers on a panel of the Sueno Stone and by finds of arrowheads, for example at Dunadd, while other sculptural images suggest the deployment of cavalry alongside infantry.[54] The clash of arms does not last long. Having succeeded in driving its foes from the field, the victorious army pursues and massacres enemy fugitives. Afterwards, men take no great care for wounded and slain foes, perhaps mutilating or beheading them, and pass any prisoners over to their commanders for judgement.[55]

The call to arms: prestige, patriotism or practicality?

The character of war glimpsed above reflected the ways in which the services of fighting men were secured. The best evidence for recruitment in our period is provided by the much considered *Míniugud senchasa fher nAlban* ('Explanation of the Genealogy of the Men of Alba'), a tenth-century tract as we have it, which contains seventh- or eighth-century breakdowns of various Argyll districts and kindreds into numbers of houses (*tige*) pertaining to each, mainly in twenty- or thirty-house groupings.[56] The total size of each kindred's hosting force (*fecht áirmi*) is expressed here without any obvious use of a calculation based on these housings or groupings, but the size of its seafaring host (*fecht immorra for imram*) is expressly calculated as two seven-bench vessels per every twenty-house grouping.[57] Problems and inconsistencies bedevil these data.[58] Nevertheless, the tract is important because it establishes that military obligations linked to landed status were in place, in Argyll at least, by about 700. Broadly similar household-based military obligations are attested across the west.[59] Unfortunately, this text says nothing about who fulfilled the obligations to form the land and sea forces it describes, and thus who fought the wars of early medieval Atlantic Scotland.

The earliest Anglo-Saxon evidence of household-based military obligations is roughly contemporary with *Míniugud senchasa fher nAlban*. Conventional notions that these obligations were shared by all normal freemen in respect of their landed status have been challenged. Richard Abels has observed, for example, that there is 'remarkably little evidence' of mass levies of free farmers – the Old English *fyrd*, paralleled by the Gaelic *slóg* and the British *llu* – in the wars of Anglo-Saxon England. The evidence from northern Britain until the middle decades of the tenth century encourages similar circumspection.[60] Like the rest of western Europe, the country was dominated by a military aristocracy whose wars seem largely to have been the province of specialist fighting men, who adhered to them as retainers and received maintenance from them. The *Life of Columba* relates tales about a Pictish exile joining such a retinue (*comitatus*) on Islay and how 'the leader of the retinue (*cohors*) of Geona', a good pagan elder, was brought before St Columba in Skye by 'two youths (*iuuenes*)' for baptism before his death and burial by his companions (*socii*).[61] The household (*familia*) of one Pictish king secured victory over another king in 729.[62] The term *familia*, like its Gaelic equivalent *muinter*, could be applied to entire households and to monastic communities, as well as more narrowly to armed retinues. The defeat of an Argyll king and his *muinter* in 640 is an example of the latter.[63] A Northumbrian king slain in battle in Pictland in 685 is said in one Northumbrian source to have fallen with the *regalia*, the royal household, and in another with the best unit (*optimus exercitus*) in his strike force (*agmen*), which by implication contained other lesser units.[64] Another Northumbrian leader (*praefectus*) who fought Picts and defeated them in 711 is elsewhere called 'the leader second [in rank] to the king' (*secundus a rege princeps*) in 704, when he stood by his king in the face of a succession challenge. His social position was thus that enjoyed in British contexts by the commander (*penteulu*) of a king's retinue (*teulu*), and this man's record of military activity and loyalty certainly encourages the conclusion that he was serving the same function in eighth-century Northumbria.[65]

The armed retinue came to symbolise lordliness across the west including, it seems, northern Britain, limited though our information is. The Merovingian royal retinue was, in Wallace-Hadrill's estimation, 'rather more of an army than a bodyguard', and when the king went to war it formed 'the nucleus of his field force'.[66] There were practical and tactical considerations as well as strong social and ideological reasons for warlords to place such reliance upon retainers in war. The armies described above seem to have required operational flexibility – now surrounding fortifications, now ravaging the countryside, now withdrawing, now destroying settlements, now engaging in pitched battle. It may have been uncertain at the outset of a campaign whether or not siege or battle was going to feature. With plundering and burning dominating warfare, military effectiveness must often have depended on striking without warning to minimise the risk of flight or the organisation of armed resistance. Ideally, units ought to have been small enough to elude detection by prospective victims, and sufficiently mobile to strike quickly, hit-and-run style, and to stay one step ahead of pursuit.[67] There can have been few items of military technology more precious than the horse or, in Atlantic Scotland and other maritime environments, the warship, and few skills more valuable than equestrian and nautical ones. Scenes of men demonstrating these skills are accordingly common on the surviving sculpture of the age.

Ensuring that they had such well-trained fighters at their disposal must have been a central concern of potentates. The retinue was as close to being a standing, professional fighting force as early medieval society produced. Within it, training, experience and familiarity bred discipline, *esprit de corps* and a capacity to contemplate, plan and execute complex battlefield manoeuvres.[68] At the battle of the

Two Rivers in c. 671, a Pictish force remained concealed from its Northumbrian enemies until battle was joined, but its attempted ambush apparently failed to secure victory.[69] At the battle of Dún Nechtain, or Nechtanesmere, in 685, another Pictish force enjoyed distinctly greater success over a Northumbrian army by executing a feigned flight.[70] The culture of loyalty associated with the retinue must have enhanced its appeal to lords still further. Across the west, normal freemen tended to be sensitive about their rights and divided in their loyalties, and their attitude to summonses to arms could be fickle and unpredictable. Retainers, being permanently beholden to their lord, were consistently more reliable. Whether or not, or in what circumstances, the obligations of 'common armies' in Scotland extended to campaigns outwith their homeland is unclear even in the central Middle Ages, but crucially these forces were entitled to disband after a fixed period of time. After discharging his tour of duty – a maximum period of forty days is attested in thirteenth-century Scotland[71] – the normal freeman expected to head home to attend to his family, farm and fields. Retainers had no such rights, so that retinues had the advantage of staying power and long-distance operations over common armies.

The development from the early twelfth century of 'free' or knight service in Scotland, 'owed by a particular individual for a particular estate', is regarded as having been superimposed upon the older 'common army' service that normal freemen had been obliged to provide since early times.[72] Military obligations of the latter type, discharged by furnishing a set number of men per unit of land assessment, are implicit in *Míniugud senchasa fher nAlban*. Yet the aristocratic practice of conferring lands upon 'military settlers' may not have been new in the twelfth century. Lordly grants of land in return for military (and other) service are anticipated in early Irish law, and Abels has argued that royal grants of this kind were being made among the Northumbrian English and other Anglo-Saxons as early as the seventh century.[73] Similarly, a panegyric addressed to the sixth-century British king Urbgen envisions that he granted 'splendid lands in abundance'.[74] Military services associated with clientship in early Irish law included pursuing outlaws, patrolling strategic areas, escorting the lord and supporting him in customary vengeance.[75] Rather than summoning normal freemen to discharge compulsory military obligations in the Anglo-Saxon *fyrd*, the Gaelic *slóg* and the British *llu*, lords and kings are now thought to have more often simply mustered their own clients and dependants. Instead of trusting to patriotic sentiment or dutifulness of common levies, they relied almost exclusively on the recruiting power of lord-client relationships in mobilising forces for war beyond those of their retinues.[76]

Bonds between lords and clients, rather than national duty, may therefore have been the means through which normal freemen were recruited into 'common armies' in northern Britain in this period. In contrast to the evidence of military households, there is little in the thin record to suggest that such armies enjoyed a very significant role in the wars of early medieval nobles and kings.[77] Before Máel Coluim son of Cinaed marched on Durham in 1006, according to *De obsessione Dunelmi* ('Concerning the Siege of Durham'), he 'collected the army of the whole of Scotland'.[78] Earlier examples of such grand forces, however, are largely absent anywhere in Britain prior to the middle decades of the tenth century, when King Æthelstan of Wessex 'ravaged a great part' of Scotland with land and sea forces in 934, and Máel Coluim son of Domnall 'pillaged the English to the River Tees' a decade or so later, seizing men and cattle in what seems to have been a very famous raid.[79] In the previous generation 'the men of Alba' (*fir Alban*) under Máel Coluim's uncle Constantín son of Áed, who faced Æthelstan at the great battle of Brunanburh in 937, had defeated an army of four Scandinavian retinues in battle beside the River Tyne in 918, weathering a successful Scandinavian ambush in such a way that 'neither king nor mormaer [a regional prince with responsibilities to muster and lead the common army of their district] was lost' among the Scottish dead.[80]

The scale of these campaigns and phrases such as 'the men of Alba' thus suggests that the role of normal freemen in the wars of their betters became increasingly significant by the tenth century.[81] We have seen that they and their kin are likely to have been engaged frequently in customary vengeance, and no doubt they got caught up from time to time in pursuing brigands and dealing violently with other threats to their property, including victimisation by raiders when their home districts happened to become the theatres of larger-scale wars. Few will have been innocent of the brutal ways of war practised in this period; yet the clashes between warlords that pepper our earlier sources are likely to have been fought largely without their close involvement, recruitment or deployment, by the retainers of kings and lordly men. And not just men: Bede speaks of one king's retainer who had formerly served in the retinue of a queen, though there is no record that women personally led their retinues in the field in northern Britain.[82]

All the same, normal freemen must have fought in a share of the military encounters on record in early medieval Scotland, even before the tenth century. For example, the terse record of the battle of Cnoc Coirpri in north Argyll in 736 describes an encounter between the Dál Riata of Argyll and the Foirtrind, the Picts of Fortriu, probably denoting the presence of 'common armies' raised in both realms.[83] Such forces were seemingly formed from levies of normal freemen, whose obligation and right to be mustered were probably expressed and understood primarily in terms of duty to their immediate lords rather than to king or nation. Hostings were important public affirmations of the rights of freemen as against those of more servile classes. They also provided kings, lords and mormaers with occasions for affirming their rank, while they may well have been opportunities to disseminate political doctrine and calls for action.

Levies were doubtless obliged to turn up suitably armed and provisioned for the full tour of duty. Though archaeological corroboration is thin, precious depictions such as those found on slabs at Aberlemno, Glamis and Birsay suggest that they commonly carried a long spear, a targe-type shield and perhaps a handful of javelins, and wore a knee- or ankle-length jack-type tunic. Household retinues appear similarly equipped, with perhaps qualitative differences, but with the addition of a thigh-length sword and, crucially, a horse. These warriors were quite capable of fighting from the saddle, including throwing javelins mid-gallop, when circumstances called for it.[84] By the standards of these retainers, levies of freemen must always have seemed amateurish, and both strategically and tactically limiting. The time and effort required to muster them must have been prohibitive in most strategic circumstances, and such issues as absenteeism, desertion and short-termism, not to mention the logistical and command challenges of maintaining them in good order, good health and good spirits on the march, must often have further discouraged their deployment.

The unleashing of large numbers of comparatively undisciplined men to ravage into enemy territory may have been a particularly effective way of bringing about a pitched battle, or else humiliating enemies who refused to fight one. When battle was joined, however, levies of freemen were probably limited to simple and straightforward manoeuvres, though not necessarily ineffective ones. Compared with household retinues, they were less predictable, more prone to ill-discipline and panic, and more apt to take flight – the single greatest risk in warfare of this period. Certainly the jealous guarding of rights, freedoms and obligations that is likely to have been a feature of free status is at odds with the ethos of extremes of loyalty and attention to duty idealised in the panegyric court poetry of the age.[85] Normal freemen and armed retainers formed different relationships with their respective lords, and ideas about duty may have sharply differentiated elites from non-elites.

All across the west, retainers were mainly young men. They tended to be of high birth: Bede noted exiled Northumbrian princes fleeing from their homeland 'with young nobles'. Serving in a lord's retinue was a form of apprenticeship for such noble youths who had not yet inherited lands from still-living fathers, but retinues could also include men of foreign or humbler birth.[86] Fighting on the frontlines in a war-torn society, retainers enjoyed considerable prestige, even if landless, and may have formed lifelong bonds with their lord and with one another. Competition for places was doubtless keen. At fourteen, the future St Wilfrid was outfitted by his father, mounted and (presumably) armed, and sent to serve in the Northumbrian royal household, with which his father was already connected.[87] Nonetheless, he was instead placed in the service of one of the king's elderly retainers. Irish evidence highlights a more sinister alternative for some noble youths excluded from royal or aristocratic retinues: they might fall in with an unattached gang of such youths, the *fían*, which had a black reputation in Ireland for criminal behaviour.[88]

Adomnán's *Life of Columba* tells of twelve retainers who adhered to a Northumbrian prince even in exile, and accepted baptism with him.[89] Settlement archaeology in northern Britain and parallel Insular evidence suggests a rough estimate of between thirty and fifty men for typical armed retinues, a figure that the tenth- and eleventh-century kings of Alba and some of their Pictish antecedents might have been able to double.[90] The military assessment of Argyll outlined in *Míniugud senchasa fher nAlban*, though problematic, produces armies several hundred strong for each Dalriadan kingdom. Yet ravaging was probably most effective where it was perpetrated by relatively small and mobile bands, and the evidence consistently indicates that the practical, logistical and strategic effectiveness of military leadership, particularly in the earlier centuries of our period, depended on limiting the size of armies to fewer – and perhaps often considerably fewer – than about 500 men. That fact helps us to understand the treatment of one apparently close-run pitched battle in the *Life of Columba*, in which the victors suffer 303 casualties. Towards the end of our period, however, the kings of Alba may have been capable of assembling several such armies together under the auspices of their mormaers, and thus of leading more than 1,000 men into battle.[91]

The bloodiness of their primary role did not necessarily mean that retainers were simple or brutish men. St Wilfrid is said by his hagiographer to have overseen the tutelage of young nobles, not all of whom were destined for ecclesiastical careers.[92] Away from the battlefield, Adomnán and Bede provide examples of retainers assuming roles as 'service aristocrats', as Halsall has termed such men, bearing their lord's messages or dispensing largesse on his behalf.[93] At the end of their martial careers, slowed down by age or injury, or simply having come into their inheritance, retainers could be given gifts, including lands.[94] Wilfrid's father seems to have been such a man, who envisioned a similar career path for his son. His parting gifts in hand, having accrued prestige in service to his lord, as well as personal affiliations and even a certain amount of diplomatic and political experience, the retainer was set for what remained of his life. Such were the rewards of the armed service he had provided at great risk of life and limb, fighting alongside countless less fortunate other men whose bones mouldered beneath the grass.

War and society: final thoughts

Our period ends with the long reign of Máel Coluim son of Donnchad (r. 1057/8–93), also known as Malcolm III Canmore (Ceann Mór, or 'Big Head'), whose military exploits included pitched battles, sieges and numerous episodes of marauding.[95] However much the shape of society had changed since c. 700, along with military obligations and the size and constitution of armies, in many key respects war at the end of the eleventh century still resembled the conflicts familiar to Adomnán and Bede. Quite apart from the damage it continued to inflict upon early medieval Scotland, both in terms of property and psychology, the endemic warfare of the age also shaped, and itself was moulded by, the social structure and the economics of prestige, which encouraged elites to acquire and disseminate resources in part through plundering. It is important, however, not to confuse the social and economic effects of early medieval warfare with the motives behind it. Customary vengeance was the main spur to violence in this period, and there is little sign in the sources of other practical motives for hostilities, such as testing a new king's mettle, that have been adduced by some scholars.[96] Whatever may have been the political and economic gains for potentates who took to the warpath, these do not in themselves appear to have been accepted justifications for fighting. Retainers, in their own minds, almost certainly did not fight primarily for such rewards, even if they felt it keenly if their lord withheld them. They risked their necks for loyalty and duty, steeped in an ethos of mutual commitment between lords and their retinues. Subsisting on his hospitality, and basking in his prestige, retainers undertook to fight for their lord, and even to die to protect him from harm or dishonour.[97]

If in a cynical age we require reassurance that such men could really have been willing to die as an act of loyalty, we need look no further than the stark realities that confronted Imma, a king's retainer wounded, according to Bede, fighting on the losing side in a battle between the Northumbrians and the Mercians in which his lord was killed. Having been taken captive, an enemy magnate (*comes*) identifies him and declares Imma worthy of death 'because all my brothers and kin were killed in that fight'.[98] The ransoming of prisoners of war is attested in various sources – this tale itself ends with Imma being sold into slavery but subsequently offered a chance to ransom himself – but these are secondary developments, arising after he has first managed to avoid summary execution.[99] The implication is that the killing of captives was normal, a conclusion reinforced by what seems to be images of systematic beheadings carved alongside scenes of combat on the Sueno Stone at Forres. Willingness to fight to the death thus seems easier to understand where surrender and capture were known to incur enslavement or ignominious death.[100] Alongside their physical and military training, new recruits to a lord's retinue must have been taught to despise mercy, flight and surrender.

In keeping with such brutal military norms, few retainers who ended up in enemy hands may ever have seen home again. This grim reality was reflected in the stark social expectations of retainers to fight to the bitter end, but surely also in the comparative rarity of battle and, apparently, the surprisingly low levels of violence associated with sieges in our extant sources. Flight, of course, was an alternative to surrender, but experienced retainers also appreciated that victorious armies butchered opponents who fled from them. The most effective means of ensuring one's survival in an age of endemic warfare at all levels of society was to cultivate a healthy reluctance to allow the norms of customary vengeance to lead to unfettered fighting and bloodshed, when they were just as capable of leading to honourable, if uneasy, peace. We are all too familiar in our own times with fraught political relationships around the world in which the protagonists profess sincere desires for peace and yet are haunted by old grudges; concerned in their posturing to demonstrate their willingness and capacity to redress new grudges through violent means, they find themselves locked in

Figure 2.4 The Sueno Stone, Morayshire, dating from the tenth century AD, celebrates a great victory, perhaps that of the men of Moray over the Scots king, Dubh, at Kinloss in 966. Rows of decapitated bodies, their hands bound, attest to the fate of the vanquished.

depressing cycles of war- and truce-making. Society and politics in early medieval Scotland were shaped from top to bottom by similar norms which envisaged order as a function of establishing an optimum balance between encouraging and discouraging extreme acts of violence. The idea was already ancient in the sixth century, and the comparatively recent criminalisation of customary vengeance and all its trappings in 1598 surely represents a watershed in the social history of Scotland at least on a par with that associated with industrialisation and urbanisation.

Notes

1. Studies of particular relevance include J. M. Wallace-Hadrill, 'The bloodfeud of the Franks', *Bulletin of the John Rylands Library*, vol. 41 (1959), reprinted in J. M. Wallace-Hadrill, *The Long-Haired Kings* (London: Methuen, 1962; reprinted Toronto: University of Toronto Press, 1982), pp. 121–47; R. P. Abels, *Lordship and Military Obligation in Anglo-Saxon England* (London: British Museum, 1988); N. T. Patterson, *Cattle-Lords and Clansmen: The Social Structure of Early Ireland*, second edition (Notre Dame and London: University of Notre Dame Press, 1994); T. M. Charles-Edwards, 'Irish warfare before 1100', in T. Bartlett and K. Jeffery (eds), *A Military History of Ireland* (Cambridge: Cambridge University Press, 1996), pp. 26–51; G. Halsall, 'Violence and society in the early medieval west: An introductory survey', in G. Halsall (ed.), *Violence and Society in the Early Medieval West* (Woodbridge: Boydell and Brewer, 1998), pp. 1–45; R. A. Fletcher, *Bloodfeud: Murder and Revenge in Anglo-Saxon England* (London and New York: Penguin, 2003); S. Davies, *Welsh Military Institutions, 633–1283* (Cardiff: University of Wales Press, 2004).
2. The key recent Scottish studies are L. Alcock, *Kings and Warriors, Craftsmen and Priests in Northern Britain AD 550–850* (Edinburgh: Society of Antiquaries of Scotland, 2003), especially pp. 119–202; N. Aitchison, *The Picts and the Scots at War* (Stroud: Sutton, 2003). 'Background noise' is the phrase of A. D. Lee, *War in Late Antiquity: A Social History* (Oxford: Blackwell, 2007), p. 3.
3. On the links between the obligations in an Irish context, see Patterson, *Cattle-Lords and Clansmen*, pp. 183–7, 259–71. On 'normal freemen', see T. M. Charles-Edwards, 'Kinship, status and the origins of the hide', *Past and Present*, vol. 56 (1972), pp. 3–33.
4. A. O. Anderson and M. O. Anderson (eds), *Adomnán's Life of Columba*, second edition (Oxford: Clarendon Press, 1991) (hereafter, Adomnán, *Vita sancti Columbae*), bk ii, ch. 39. For discussion see R. Sharpe (trans.), *Adomnán of Iona: Life of St Columba* (London: Penguin, 1995), pp. 338–9.
5. Bede, *Historia ecclesiastica gentis Anglorum*, ed. and trans. B. Colgrave and R. A. B. Mynors as *Bede's Ecclesiastical History of the English People*, second edition (Oxford: Clarendon Press, 1991), bk iv, ch. 21. For discussion see D. Whitelock, *The Beginnings of English Society* (London: Penguin, 1952), pp. 38–45; Patterson, *Cattle-Lords and Clansmen*, pp. 53–4, 261–3.
6. See in particular L. H. Keeley, *War before Civilization* (New York and Oxford: Oxford University Press, 1996), pp. 115–17; and for the early

medieval period, G. Halsall, *Warfare and Society in the Barbarian West, 450–900* (London and New York: Routledge, 2003), p. 16.

7. For Irish and English parallels see, for example, Patterson, *Cattle-Lords and Clansmen*, pp. 349–50; D. A. E. Pelteret, *Slavery in Early Mediaeval England* (Woodbridge: Boydell and Brewer, 1995), p. 29. For continental parallels, see Wallace-Hadrill, *Long-Haired Kings*, pp. 121–47; Halsall, *Violence and Society*, pp. 2–26.
8. D. Whitelock, 'Anglo-Saxon poetry and the historian', *Transactions of the Royal Historical Society*, fourth series, vol. 31 (1949), p. 84.
9. Wallace-Hadrill, *Long-Haired Kings*, pp. 124–5.
10. Whitelock, 'Anglo-Saxon poetry and the historian', p. 84.
11. Halsall, *Violence and Society*, pp. 21–2; see also P. Wormald, '*Lex Scripta* and *Verbum Regis*: Legislation and Germanic kingship, from Euric to Cnut', in P. H. Sawyer and I. N. Wood (eds), *Early Medieval Kingship* (Leeds: University of Leeds, 1977), pp. 111–12. For consideration in a northern British context, see Alcock, *Kings and Warriors*, pp. 122–3.
12. Bede, *Historia ecclesiastica*, bk v, ch. 23.
13. For discussion in an Anglo-Saxon context, see Abels, *Lordship and Military Obligation*, p. 12.
14. M. Strickland, 'Securing the North: Invasion and the strategy of defence in twelfth-century Anglo-Scottish warfare', in M. Strickland (ed.), *Anglo-Norman Warfare: Studies in Late Anglo-Saxon and Anglo-Norman Military Organization and Warfare* (Woodbridge: Boydell and Brewer, 1992), pp. 213–16.
15. B. Colgrave (ed.), *The Life of Bishop Wilfrid by Eddius Stephanus* (Cambridge: Cambridge University Press, 1927), ch. 60.
16. I. Ralston, *Celtic Fortifications* (Stroud: Tempus, 2006), pp. 108–9.
17. *De obsessione Dunelmi*, in T. Arnold (ed.), *Symeonis Monachi Opera Omnia*, 2 vols (Rolls Series, London: Longman, 1882), vol. 1, pp. 215–20, for the 1006 siege; see also S. Mac Airt and G. Mac Niocaill (eds), *The Annals of Ulster (to A.D. 1131)* [hereafter *AU*] (Dublin: Dublin Institute for Advanced Studies, 1983), s.a. 1006. For the 1039 siege, see D. Rollason (ed.), *Libellus de exordio atque procursu istius, hoc est Dunhelmensis, ecclesie: Tract on the Origins and Progress of this the Church of Durham* (Oxford: Clarendon Press, 2000), bk iii, ch. 9.
18. Halsall, *Warfare and Society*, pp. 215–16, 218–19; and on the Insular dimension, Davies, *Welsh Military Institutions*, pp. 207–8.
19. *Historia Brittonum*, ch. 63; E. Faral (ed.), *La Légende Arthurienne: études et documents*, vol. 3 (Paris: H. Champion, 1929), pp. 4–62, records the siege of Lindisfarne by Urbgen. The encounter at *Iudeu* may be another example of an island siege; see A. Woolf, 'Caedualla *Rex*

Brettonum and the passing of the old north', *Northern History*, vol. 41 (2004), p. 10.
20. Symeon of Durham, *Historia regum*, in *Symeonis Monachi Opera Omnia*, vol. 2, s.a. 756, pp. 30–68.
21. M. D. Reeve (ed.), *Vegetius: Epitoma Rei Militaris* (Oxford: Clarendon Press, 2004), bk iv, ch. 12, §§ 1–4; bk iv, ch. 25, §§ 1–3.
22. Bede, *Historia ecclesiastica*, bk iii, ch. 6.
23. *Chronicle of the Kings of Alba*, § 4; M. O. Anderson, *Kings and Kingship in Early Scotland* (Edinburgh and London: Scottish Academic Press, 1973), pp. 149–53.
24. *AU* 870.6.
25. Adomnán, *Vita sancti Columbae*, bk i, ch. 1.
26. For example, *AU* 643.4; W. Stokes (ed.), *The Annals of Tigernach* [hereafter *AT*] (Felinfach: Llanerch, 1993), vol. 1, 644.5; *AU* 1032.2 and W. M. Hennessy (ed.), *Chronicum Scotorum: A Chronicle of Irish Affairs from the Earliest Times to A.D. 1135* [hereafter *CS*] (London: Longman et al., 1866), 971.1, but cf. *AU* 971.
27. Aitchison, *Picts and Scots at War*, p. 100; Alcock, *Kings and Warriors*, p. 200.
28. *AU* 734.7.
29. Adomnán, *Vita sancti Columbae*, bk i, ch. 20.
30. Adomnán, *Vita sancti Columbae*, bk i., ch. 46. On the identification of *stagnum Crog reth* as Loch Rannoch, see W. J. Watson, *The History of the Celtic Place-Names of Scotland* (Edinburgh and London: Blackwood, 1926), p. 78.
31. On *uastatio* in early medieval Ireland and Britain, see respectively Charles-Edwards, 'Irish warfare', p. 32; and Davies, *Welsh Military Institutions*, pp. 37–8, 89–111, 219–23.
32. Strickland, 'Securing the north', p. 217.
33. For example, *Chronicle of the Kings of Alba*, § 5; *AU* 866.1 (and see also *Chronicle of the Kings of Alba*, § 11); S. Irvine (ed.), *The Anglo-Saxon Chronicle: A Collaborative Edition* [hereafter *ASC*], vol. 7 (Cambridge: Brewer, 2004), 'E', s.a. 875; *Chronicle of the Kings of Alba*, § 20; *AU* 904.4 (see also *Chronicle of the Kings of Alba*, § 24).
34. Keeley, *War before Civilization*, p. 48, provides the anthropological corrective to underestimations of casualty rates.
35. Adomnán, *Cáin Adomnáin*, §§ 34–6, 40, 44, 46, 50; M. Ní Dhonnchadha, 'The law of Adomnán: A translation', in T. O'Loughlin (ed.), *Adomnán at Birr, AD 697: Essays in Commemoration of the Law of the Innocents* (Dublin: Four Courts Press, 2001), pp. 53–68. See also Aitchison, *Picts and Scots at War*, pp. 136–40; Alcock, *Kings and Warriors*, pp. 123–4, 202.

36. *Vita sancti Cuthberti anon.*, bk iv, ch. 8; B. Colgrave (ed.), *Two Lives of Saint Cuthbert* (Cambridge: Cambridge University Press, 1940), p. 122.
37. *AU* 682.4.
38. Adomnán, *Vita sancti Columbae*, bk ii, ch. 22 and bk ii, ch. 24.
39. *AU* 580.2 (also 581.3), 672.2, 691.3; Adomnán, *Vita sancti Columbae*, bk iii, ch. 5b.
40. *AU* 806.8; *CS* 806.3. There were also Irish maritime plundering campaigns in Atlantic Scotland during the Viking Age, for example *CS* 941.5.
41. F. Kelly, *A Guide to Early Irish Law* (Dublin: Dublin Institute for Advanced Studies, 1988), p. 5.
42. On cattle raiding in northern Britain see, for example, 'Taliesin', *Arwyre gwyr Katraeth*, line 2; I. Williams (ed.), *The Poems of Taliesin* (Dublin: Dublin Institute for Advanced Studies, 1968), II (translated in T. O. Clancy (ed.), *The Triumph Tree: Scotland's Earliest Poetry AD 550–1350* (Edinburgh: Canongate, 1998), pp. 79–80); 'Taliesin', *Ar vn blyned*, lines 8–9; Williams (ed.), *Poems of Taliesin*, V (trans. Clancy, *Triumph Tree*, pp. 83–4). On slaving, see Aitchison, *Picts and Scots at War*, pp. 140–2; Davies, *Welsh Military Institutions*, pp. 45, 223–4.
43. Bede, *Historia ecclesiastica*, bk iv, ch. 22. See also A. D. Carr, '*Teulu* and *Penteulu*', in T. M. Charles-Edwards et al. (eds), *The Welsh King and His Court* (Cardiff: University of Wales Press, 2000), pp. 73–4; Davies, *Welsh Military Institutions*, p. 53, for some logistical discussions.
44. Adomnán, *Vita sancti Columbae*, bk i, ch. 1.
45. Bede, *Historia ecclesiastica*, bk iii, ch. 24; *Historia Brittonum*, §§ 64–5.
46. Davies, *Welsh Military Institutions*, pp. 111–12; see also Vegetius, *Epitoma*, bk iii, ch. 9, lines 2–3; bk iii, ch. 9, line 20; bk iii, ch. 11, lines 1–2; and bk iii, ch. 26, line 4.
47. Adomnán, *Vita sancti Columbae*, *praefatio*, Ii, and ibid. bk ii, ch. 46.
48. The classic discussion is J. Keegan, *The Face of Battle* (London: Penguin, 1976), pp. 35–45.
49. For a brief discussion of this paradigm, see J. F. Verbruggen, *The Art of Warfare in Western Europe during the Middle Ages from the Eighth Century to 1340*, second edition (Woodbridge: Boydell, 1977), pp. 2–5. On comparable Welsh evidence, see Carr, '*Teulu*', p. 76.
50. *AU* 719.7; *AT* 719.5. Aitchison, *Picts and Scots at War*, pp. 111–29, makes the most of the scraps of evidence available.
51. *Battle of Brunanburh*, in J. M. Bately (ed.), *The Anglo-Saxon Chronicle: A Collaborative Edition*, vol. 3, 'A' (Cambridge: Brewer, 1986), s.a. 937, line 49 (for a recent translation see A. Woolf, *From Pictland to Alba*,

789-1070 (Edinburgh: Edinburgh University Press, 2007), pp. 172–3). This may imply that the Scottish forces bore banners (*cumboles*) at that engagement. On the use of horns for signalling, see Aitchison, *Picts and Scots at War*, p. 78.

52. Examples of shield-walls linked with forces from northern Britain include, among others, 'Taliesin', *E bore duw Sadwrn kat uawr a uu*, line 15; Williams (ed.), *Poems of Taliesin*, VI (trans. Clancy, *Triumph Tree*, p. 85); 'Aneirin', *Y Gododdin*, 'A-text', line 122; I. Williams (ed.), *Canu Aneirin* (Cardiff: Gwasg Prifysgol Cymru, 1938) (trans. Clancy, *Triumph Tree*, pp. 47–67); *Brunanburh*, line 6. For discussion see Aitchison, *Picts and Scots at War*, pp. 84–6; Davies, *Welsh Military Institutions*, pp. 180–3.

53. J. E. Fraser, *The Battle of Dunnichen 685* (Stroud: Tempus, 2002), pp. 69–70; Aitchison, *Picts and Scots at War*, pp. 86–8.

54. A. Lane and E. Campbell, *Dunadd: An Early Dalriadic Capital* (Oxford: Oxbow, 2000), pp. 160–2; Aitchison, *Picts and Scots at War*, pp. 62–4, 78–82; Alcock, *Kings and Warriors*, pp. 149–50. Davies, *Welsh Military Institutions*, pp. 151–4, discusses the comparable lack of textual and sculptural evidence of archery in a British context.

55. Stephen, *Vita sancti Wilfrithi*, ch. 19; B. Colgrave (ed.), *The Life of Bishop Wilfrid by Eddius Stephanus* (Cambridge: Cambridge University Press, 1927); Adomnán, *Vita sancti Columbae*, bk i, ch. 1 and bk i, ch. 9; *Vita sancti Cuthberti anon.*, bk iv, ch. 8; Bede, *Historia ecclesiastica*, bk iii, ch. 18.

56. *Míniugud senchasa fher nAlban*, chs 32–4, 42, 45, 47, 50–2; D. N. Dumville, 'Ireland and North Britain in the earlier Middle Ages: Contexts for *Míniugud Senchasa Fher nAlban*', in C. Ó Baoill and N. R. McGuire (eds), *Rannsachadh na Gàidhlig 2000* (Aberdeen: Clo Gaidhealach, 2002), pp. 201–3.

57. *Míniugud senchasa fher nAlban*, chs 35–7, 43–4, 50–2.

58. Dumville, 'Ireland and North Britain', pp. 207–10, does 'not believe a single word which has been written in interpretation' of the data. The most recent attempt to wrestle with it (and to 'correct' the figures) is Aitchison, *Picts and Scots at War*, pp. 15–20.

59. On general trends involving changes over time in these obligations, see Halsall, *Warfare and Society*, pp. 93, 105. The essential comparative study of Insular evidence is Charles-Edwards, 'Kinship'; and see also J. Campbell, *The Anglo-Saxons* (London: Penguin, 1982), p. 58; G. Barrow, 'The army of Alexander III's Scotland', in N. H. Reid (ed.), *Scotland in the Reign of Alexander III 1249–1286* (Edinburgh: John Donald, 1990), p. 133.

60. Abels, *Lordship and Military Obligation*, pp. 13–15; Aitchison, *Picts*

and Scots at War, pp. 14–32, is not so circumspect. On *slógad* in Irish law, see Kelly, *Guide to Early Irish Law*, p. 4. The use of *slógad* in *Míniugud senchasa fher nAlban*, § 35, implies that the text deals here with the obligations of normal freemen.

61. Adomnán, *Vita sancti Columbae*, bk i, ch. 33 and bk ii, ch. 23. Aitchison, *Picts and Scots at War*, pp. 33–4, does not address D. Dumville, '"Primarius cohortis" in Adomnán's Life of Columba', *Scottish Gaelic Studies*, vol. 13, no. 1 (1978), pp. 130–1; see also Carr, '*Teulu*', pp. 77–9; Davies, *Welsh Military Institutions*, pp. 32–7.
62. *AU* 729.2. See Adomnán, *Vita sancti Columbae*, bk i, ch. 1 and bk ii, ch. 32, for *familia* plainly used to denote a household; see also Carr, '*Teulu*', p. 80 and Davies, *Welsh Military Institutions*, pp. 18–20, for its use to denote *teulu*, and for the distinction sometimes made between the bodyguard (*teulu*) and the wider household (*gosgordd*), which included non-military retainers.
63. *AT* 638.1. The usual British terms are *teulu* (bodyguard) and *gosgordd* (household).
64. *Vita sancti Cuthberti anon.*, bk iii, ch. 6; Stephen, *Vita sancti Wilfrithi*, ch. 44.
65. *AU* 711.3; *AT* 711.3; *ASC*, 'E', s.a. 710; Bede, *Historia ecclesiastica*, bk v, ch. 24, s.a. 711; Stephen, *Vita sancti Wilfrithi*, ch. 60. On the *penteulu*, see Carr, '*Teulu*', pp. 77–8.
66. Wallace-Hadrill, *Long-Haired Kings*, pp. 32, 165.
67. See, for example, Vegetius, *Epitoma*, bk iv, ch. 31, line 6.
68. See, for example, Davies, *Welsh Military Institutions*, p. 39. Aitchison, *Picts and Scots at War*, p. 88, argued that images on Pictish sculpture suggest highly organised, disciplined and trained forces. Alcock, *Kings and Warriors*, pp. 173–5, is unnecessarily sceptical.
69. Stephen, *Vita sancti Wilfrithi*, ch. 19.
70. Bede, *Historia ecclesiastica*, bk iv, ch. 26; Fraser, *Battle of Dunnichen*, pp. 56–7.
71. Barrow, 'Army of Alexander III's Scotland', p. 135; similarly Davies, *Welsh Military Institutions*, p. 81, who concludes that the number was borrowed from the Anglo-Normans.
72. Barrow, 'Army of Alexander III's Scotland', pp. 133–4.
73. Kelly, *Guide to Early Irish Law*, pp. 29–31; Abels, *Lordship and Military Obligation*, pp. 24–5.
74. 'Taliesin', *Eg gorffowys*, line 4; Williams (ed.), *Poems of Taliesin*, IV (trans. Clancy, *Triumph Tree*, pp. 82–3); and see also Davies, *Welsh Military Institutions*, pp. 48–9.
75. Kelly, *Guide to Early Irish Law*, p. 31; Patterson, *Cattle-Lords and Clansmen*, p. 168.

76. Abels, *Lordship and Military Obligation*, pp. 19–22; Patterson, *Cattle-Lords and Clansmen*, pp. 49–50, 225–6; Davies, *Welsh Military Institutions*, pp. 63–6. Kelly, *Guide to Early Irish Law*, pp. 4, 19, 31, also supposes that men formed up into units consisting of the clients of particular lords.
77. See, for example, Aitchison, *Picts and Scots at War*, pp. 14, 31, 149. Patterson, *Cattle-Lords and Clansmen*, pp. 168–9, 225–6, argued much the same for Ireland.
78. *De obsessione Dunelmi*, ch. 1 (1006).
79. *ASC*, 'E', s.a. 934; *Chronicle of the Kings of Alba*, § 35 (Máel Coluim's raid). Æthelstan's forces reached the Mounth, with his ships pressing further north as far as Caithness, Symeon, *Historia regum*, in *Symeonis Monachi Opera Omnia*, vol. 2, s.a. 934.
80. *AU* 918.4.
81. Davies, *Welsh Military Institutions*, pp. 50–2, 66–70, provides a British perspective on a similar trend.
82. Bede, *Historia ecclesiastica*, bk iv, ch. 22.
83. *AU* 736.2, and for other probable examples *Chronicle of the Kings of Alba*, § 39; *CS* 953.3 (and the less detailed *AU* 954.2).
84. For thoroughgoing discussion of arms, see Aitchison, *Picts and Scots at War*, pp. 44–70.
85. See, for example, 'Taliesin', *Eg gorffowys*, lines 6–7; *Ardwyre Reget*, line 46; Williams (ed.), *Poems of Taliesin*, VII (trans. Clancy, *Triumph Tree*, pp. 85–6); *Uryen Yrechwyd*, line 14; Williams (ed.), *Poems of Taliesin*, III (trans. Clancy, *Triumph Tree*, pp. 80–1).
86. Bede, *Historia ecclesiastica*, bk iii, ch. 1. See also Carr, 'Teulu', p. 63; Davies, *Welsh Military Institutions*, pp. 26–32.
87. Stephen, *Vita sancti Wilfrithi*, ch. 2.
88. K. R. McCone, 'Werewolves, Cyclopes, *Díberga*, and *Fíanna*: Juvenile delinquency in early Ireland', *Cambridge Medieval Celtic Studies*, vol. 12 (1986), pp. 1–22; K. R. McCone, *Pagan Past and Christian Present in Early Irish Literature* (Maynooth: An Sagart, 1990), pp. 203–7; see also Patterson, *Cattle-Lords and Clansmen*, pp. 97–8, 122–5, 215–16, 345–6. For British parallels, see Davies, *Welsh Military Institutions*, pp. 47–8.
89. Adomnán, *Vita sancti Columbae*, bk i, ch. 1; and for the duty of retainers to follow their lord into exile, see Abels, *Lordship and Military Obligation*, pp. 16–17; Davies, *Welsh Military Institutions*, pp. 39–40.
90. Davies, *Welsh Military Institutions*, pp. 22–6.
91. Adomnán, *Vita sancti Columbae*, bk i, ch. 8. Davies, *Welsh Military Institutions*, pp. 53–62, provides a complementary discussion of British evidence.

92. Stephen, *Vita sancti Wilfrithi*, chs 2, 21.
93. Halsall, *Warfare and Society*, p. 21. See, for example, Adomnán, *Vita sancti Columbae*, bk ii, ch. 33, where retainers bear royal messages, and Bede, *Historia ecclesiastica*, bk iii, ch. 6, who speaks of a retainer 'whose duty it was to relieve the needy'.
94. See, for example, 'Taliesin', *Eg gorffowys*, lines 4–5, 19–20.
95. Battles: Symeon, *Historia regum*, s.a. 1070; *ASC*, 'E', s.a. 1093. Sieges: Aelred, *De sanctis ecclesiae Hagulstadensis*, bk i, ch. 2; M. L. Hutton (ed.) and J. P. Freeland (trans.), *Aelred of Rievaulx: The Lives of the Northern Saints* (Cistercian Father Series 71, Kalamazoo: Cistercian Publications, 2006), pp. 69–74; Symeon, *Historia regum*, ch. 39. Marauding: Aelred, *De sanctis ecclesiae Hagulstadensis*, bk i, ch. 2; Symeon, *Historia regum*, ch. 143 (s.a. 1061); William of Malmesbury, *Gesta regum*, iii. 249 (c. 1070); Symeon, *Historia regum*, chs 155–6; *ASC*, 'E', s.a. 1079, 1091, 1093.
96. Aitchison, *Picts and Scots at War*, pp. 2, 35, 42–3, 130, 136, is a recent example; see also Alcock, *Kings and Warriors*, pp. 121, 123.
97. See, for example, T. M. Charles-Edwards, 'The authenticity of the *Gododdin*: An historian's view', in R. Bromwich and R. B. Jones (eds), *Astudiaethau ar yr Hengerdd/Studies in Old Welsh Poetry* (Cardiff: University of Wales Press, 1978), pp. 44–71; Carr, 'Teulu', pp. 74–5; Davies, *Welsh Military Institutions*, pp. 38–40.
98. Bede, *Historia ecclesiastica*, bk iv, ch. 22.
99. *AU* 725.3, 726.1, 733.1, 731.3; Adomnán, *Vita sancti Columbae*, bk i, ch. 11. See also Aitchison, *Picts and Scots at War*, pp. 141–2.
100. For beheadings, see for example *De obsessione Dunelmi*, ch. 1; *Libellus de exordio atque procursu*, bk iii, ch. 9; and *AU* 986.2. Keeley, *War before Civilization*, pp. 83–5, shows that quarter tended to be neither given nor expected in anthropological contexts because prisoners not summarily killed were often publicly humiliated and tortured to death.

3

The Kings of Scots at War, c. 1093–1286

MATTHEW J. STRICKLAND

On 13 November 1093, King Malcolm III 'Canmore' was ambushed and killed by Norman forces close to the River Alne as he led an army into Northumberland.[1] The monastic chronicler Simeon of Durham regarded his death as the just judgement of God, for during his reign (1058–93) Malcolm had invaded northern England no fewer than five times, 'harried it with savage devastation, and carried off the wretched inhabitants as captives, to reduce them to slavery'.[2] His campaigns, exploiting the complex and troubled politics of Northumbria, reflected the expansionist ambitions of the kings of Scots. Yet what is most striking is that Malcolm was able to take the offensive at all. For, between 1066 and 1075, the Norman invaders under William the Conqueror had crushed resistance in Anglo-Saxon England, secured their conquest by widespread castle-building and had begun to make deep inroads into Wales, divided by a multiplicity of warring princelings. Such successes have been seen as part of a wider pattern of conquest during the eleventh century, whereby aggressive and land-hungry warrior aristocracies from the heartlands of France and Germany used a highly effective combination of heavy cavalry, castles, crossbows and siege equipment to effect sweeping territorial gains in the more peripheral lands of Europe, whether in southern Italy, Sicily, the eastern frontiers of Germany or Britain.[3]

It is doubtful whether Malcolm III could have long withstood a sustained campaign of invasion by the Normans deploying this superior military technology. Yet, alone of the polities within the British Isles, the kingdom of the Scots was not to experience such an onslaught.[4] When Franco-Norman settlers came, it was at the invitation of Scotland's twelfth-century kings, who were swift to harness the military potential of heavy cavalry and castles to bolster

THE KINGS OF SCOTS AT WAR, C. 1093–1286   95

Map 3.1   Scotland and northern England in the twelfth and thirteenth centuries.

and expand their own authority. For the death of Malcolm heralded the beginnings of a period of profound political, cultural and military change. Between 1093 and 1135, the close relations between the four sons of Malcolm III who in turn succeeded to the kingdom of Scots (Duncan II, Edgar, Alexander I and David I), and the Anglo-Norman kings, to whom the former looked for military support and patronage, ensured a period of sustained détente.[5] The new Anglo-Norman chivalric dimension of Scottish kingship was symbolised by the seal of Duncan II (r. 1094), modelled on that of the Conqueror and of William Rufus, depicting him as a mounted knight, in hauberk (mail shirt) and helmet, carrying a lance with a long, two-tailed pennant, or gonfanon.[6] Moreover, David I (r. 1124–53) had actually been brought up at the Anglo-Norman court and was enriched by his brother-in-law, King Henry I of England (r. 1100–35) with lands in Normandy and a great English earldom centred on Huntingdon, Northampton and Cambridge.[7] He may have fought for Henry in Normandy, and his subsequent military reforms within Scotland and tactical thinking were strongly influenced by contemporary Anglo-Norman practice.[8]

Knights, fiefs and castles

The knights employed by Duncan II, Edgar (r. 1097–1107) and Alexander I (r. 1107–24) were predominantly stipendiaries, forming the core of the king's military household (*familia regis*) and, from at least the reign of Alexander, were commanded by the constable, the king's chief military officer.[9] From c. 1113, however, when his elder brother Alexander ceded him a large appanage in Lothian and Cumbria north of the Solway, David began to make extensive grants to his Norman, English and Flemish followers in return for military service as heavily equipped knights and serjeants. With only a nascent monetary economy, and many renders to the king still paid in kind, distribution of lands offered an effective means of securing the permanent availability of a heavily equipped force of cavalry. As king, David continued this process of land settlement, and under his grandson, Malcolm IV (r. 1153–65), further military tenures were established in the Clyde valley, the coastal regions of Galloway and in Fife. During the reign of Malcolm's brother, William the Lion (r. 1165–1214), they spread further north, into Angus, Gowrie and Mearns.[10]

These settlers, coming to form a new military aristocracy, did not receive their lands as freeholders but as military tenants, subject to a range of obligations, chief of which was the provision of knight service and castle guard at the king's fortresses. The basic unit of tenure was the knight's fief (also fee or feu, from the Latin *feodum*), an estate that might vary considerably in size, but whose revenues were expected to allow its holder to serve the king as a fully equipped knight.[11] Lords granted great estates (known as 'honours') were expected to furnish a quota of knights, commensurate with their holdings. Robert de Brus, for example, held Annandale for the service of ten knights, though the size of this lordship and its military obligation appears to have been exceptional, reflecting its strategic importance on the frontier with Galloway.[12] The native aristocracy was not invariably displaced by the process of settlement, but those who retained power came under increasing pressure to accept these new forms of tenure. By 1136 at the latest one of the greatest indigenous nobles, Duncan of Fife, had received his earldom from David I as a fief, an arrangement that strengthened the crown's position and defined more sharply the extent of military service owed.[13]

Estates were also granted out to serjeants, serving with less expensive equipment and mounts. Some were archers, horsed for speed of movement but dismounting to shoot their longbows. Highly effective troops for operating in broken country unsuitable for heavy cavalry, they were also more cost effective, with a serjeant's fief being valued roughly at a quarter of that of a knight. Though charters granting such serjeantries are only extant from the reign of Malcolm IV onward,[14] mounted archers are likely to have been introduced by David I, who had witnessed their important role in the military households of the Anglo-Norman kings.[15]

Castles, which had been first introduced into Britain by the Normans, formed an integral element of the new settlements, rapidly transforming the strategic as well as the physical landscape of the kingdom.[16] Combining the needs of defence against an often hostile local population with the high status accommodation appropriate to a lordly dwelling, they also served as centres for the administration of lordships. Motte and bailey castles, such as the great Mote of Urr in Galloway, constructed between c. 1130 and c. 1160, were a common but by no means universal form.[17] Though many were initially built of earth and timber, these might be of considerable sophistication and strength and, with a smaller ground area than communal fortifications such as hill-forts or burghs, they could be garrisoned by a comparatively small number of men. From such protected bases, mounted forces could impose their authority on the locality, enforcing taxation and labour services and seizing supplies in time of war.

Figure 3.1 The Mote of Urr, Kirkcudbrightshire, constructed between c. 1130 and c. 1160 on the troubled marches of Galloway. The earthworks were originally topped by strong timber palisades, with a wooden keep on the motte.

Equally, they could act as jumping-off points for further conquest. Thus, for example, the defeat of Angus, mormaer of Moray, by David I's forces in 1130 was followed by the annexation of the province, redistribution of lands and the construction of castles, such as the fine motte and bailey built by Freskin the Fleming at Duffus.

Nevertheless, despite these military developments, and concomitant royal efforts to expand burghs, mints and trade, the economy remained predominantly rural and its growth restricted. Scottish kings accordingly remained heavily dependent, as in earlier centuries, on the common army of unpaid and poorly equipped levies for the bulk of their troops. For warfare against England, this reliance was to impose significant strategic and tactical limitations. By contrast, the troops of the common army were better suited to fighting less heavily armed opponents in broken terrain, circumstances that characterised much of the warfare against internal dynastic opponents or enemies on the kingdom's northern and western frontiers.

Figure 3.2 Duffus castle, Morayshire, built c. 1150 by Freskin the Fleming following King David I's annexation of Moray. The stone keep and bailey wall, constructed c. 1350, replaced the timber defences of the original motte-and-bailey castle.

The scope of war

Between the eleventh and thirteenth centuries, the kings of Scots were confronted by a number of potential enemies, each with differing traditions and capabilities of waging war. Of all these, the most formidable was the kingdom of England. Yet with the important exception of William Rufus's annexation of Carlisle and southern Cumbria in 1092, no Anglo-Norman or Angevin king of England before Edward I (r. 1272–1307) ever attempted the whole or even partial conquest of Scotland, nor did they permit predatory marcher lords to undertake private conquests across the border as was the case on the Welsh frontier.[18] For the strategic priorities of the kings of England now lay primarily across the Channel, in the defence or expansion of their continental domains. From the kings of Scots they demanded acknowledgement of their hegemony within Britain but also sought a *modus vivendi* to ensure peace on their northern border. The Scots could not, of course, always be expected to share such a strategic view. A longstanding *casus belli* was the control of Cumbria and Northumberland, an issue that was to bedevil Anglo-Scottish relations from David I's reoccupation of Carlisle in the winter of 1135–6 until Alexander II (r. 1214–49) finally renounced his claims to the northern counties by the Treaty of York in 1237.[19]

Yet between the deaths of Malcolm III in 1093 and Alexander III in 1286, there was open war only in 1136–8, 1173–4 and 1215–17, and on each occasion it was the king of Scots who initiated hostilities and invaded the northern counties. Beyond these major campaigns, there were occasional alarums, as in 1209 when King John led an army to Norham on the Tweed, forcing the elderly William the Lion into an abject capitulation, and in 1244 when Alexander II mustered his army to resist a threatened invasion by Henry III. But the overall pattern, with only some eight years of outright war in nearly two centuries, emphasises just how radical a shift occurred with Edward I's invasion of Scotland in 1296.[20] Ironically, most of what we know of the operations and military forces of the Scots from the late eleventh to the mid-thirteenth century comes from the more extensive narratives of English writers concerning the Scottish incursions during these few years of intensive conflict.

War with England

David I ruthlessly exploited the mounting challenges to King Stephen's authority to launch sustained invasions of northern England between 1136 and 1138, aiming thereby to secure Cumbria and obtain the earldom of Northumberland for his son, Earl Henry.[21] In 1138, at the head of probably the most powerful army yet mustered by a king of Scots, David pushed over the Tees into Yorkshire where on 22 August, just north of Northallerton, he was met by a strong Anglo-Norman force. The English, rallied by Archbishop Thurstan of York to fight a holy war against the invading Scots, massed under 'the Standard', a collection of religious banners hoisted from a ship's mast which gave the battle its name.[22] David's intention had been to place his knights in the front ranks, supported by archers, in emulation of the battle-winning tactics his brother-in-law, King Henry I, had employed in Normandy.[23] The men of Galloway, however, angrily claimed the right to lead the attack, and David was forced to concede to their demands in order to contain a dangerous dispute within his own army. Yet, as the king had feared, the onrush of these lightly armed troops foundered against the densely formed ranks of the dismounted English knights, supported by spearmen and archers, whose arrows took a terrible toll. The Galwegians and other units, including the men of Lothian, finally broke in flight. A gallant charge by Earl Henry failed to stem the now general rout, but by scattering the horses of the dismounted Anglo-Norman knights kept to their rear, his division saved the Scots from an effective pursuit and the possible capture of David himself. Instead, the king retreated in good order with his household knights to Carlisle, although many of the Scots were killed on the field or as they struggled back to the border.

Despite the humiliating and potentially disastrous defeat of the Scots at the battle of the Standard, King Stephen's position was so weakened by civil war that he had little choice but to acknowledge David's *de facto* annexation of the northern counties. The 'Scoto-Northumbrian realm' thus formed represented the high-water mark of the power of the kings of Scots.[24] The resulting increase in revenues not only strengthened David's military might within Scotland but also allowed costly building works in stone, notably at Carlisle, where David probably completed the great keep.[25] However, the premature death in 1152 of Earl Henry, lauded by English chroniclers as a paragon of chivalry, meant that David I was succeeded by his grandson, the young Malcolm IV. Faced by the overwhelming might of Henry II (r. 1154–89), Malcolm had no choice but to yield Cumbria and Northumberland back to the English crown in 1157. Attempts to recover these lands by force underlay the two major but unsuccessful invasions of William the Lion in 1173 and 1174, when he sided with Henry II's rebellious elder son, Henry 'the Young King', who headed a powerful coalition against his father, including Louis VII of France, Count Philip of Flanders and many dissident nobles within the Plantagenet domains. For the Scots, however, the war ended in catastrophe when in 1174 William the Lion was captured by an English force whilst besieging Alnwick castle, and was only released after conceding the unequivocal feudal submission of his kingdom to Henry II by the Treaty of Falaise. Subsequently, Alexander II sought to exploit growing noble opposition within England to King John, Henry II's youngest son, to again invade the northern counties between 1215 and 1217. His efforts proved equally fruitless.[26]

Much of the explanation for the Scots' lack of success lay in the increasing importance of castles in Anglo-Scottish warfare.[27] Under Malcolm III, plundering and devastation of the land, involving widespread killing of the local inhabitants, had been the Scots' primary mechanism of waging war: in none of his five campaigns of invasion is he recorded as laying a siege or building his own fortifications. Although the kings of Scots undoubtedly regarded such reigns of terror, inspired by the ferocious conduct of their Galwegian and Scots troops (the latter a general term for those dwelling north of the Forth in 'Scotia'), as an instrument of policy,[28] the northern counties of England could not be effectively occupied and held without obtaining control of their key castles. Ravaging remained an essential mechanism of war, inflicting economic damage and allowing the invaders to live off the land, but it was increasingly a means to the end of taking strongholds. The Anglo-Norman poet Jordan Fantosme recounts that in 1173 Count Philip of Flanders gave William the Lion's messengers the following advice:

> Let him destroy your enemies and lay waste their land: let it all be consumed in fire and flames! Let him not leave them, outside their castles, in wood or meadow, so much as will furnish them a meal on the morrow. Then let him assemble his men and lay siege to their castles. They will not get succour or help within thirteen leagues around them. This is the way to begin a fight, to my way of thinking: first lay waste the land, then destroy one's enemies.[29]

Yet siege warfare was long to prove the Achilles' heel of Scottish armies. David had occupied Carlisle and Newcastle in early 1136 more by guile than force. In subsequent campaigns, by contrast, the stronghold of Wark on the Tweed repeatedly resisted siege artillery and direct assault, and yielded in 1138 only after months of blockade had reduced its garrison to starvation. In 1173–4, William the Lion took a number of lesser castles, including Appleby (probably betrayed to him) and Brough, but despite the use of Flemish auxiliaries as assault troops, every attempt to capture major fortresses, such as at Carlisle, Wark and Prudhoe, met with defeat. In truth, he faced a far harder task than his grandfather David I, for Henry II had heavily refortified England's northern border and upgraded its major strongholds. Advances in fortress design could only be countered by more sophisticated siege engines, which in turn demanded a corps of specialist engineers, and the kings of Scots struggled to compete with the far wealthier Angevins in such a costly arms race.[30] The considerable damage wrought by Alexander's engines during his successful siege of Carlisle in 1215 suggests that efforts had been made to improve the royal siege train,[31] but Norham defied his attack the following year and he was also forced to withdraw from Mitford without success.[32]

Lengthy sieges were not only expensive but also strategically disadvantageous as they slowed an invader's progress and made his forces a static target for a defending field army. Given their inferiority to Anglo-Norman armies in terms of heavily armoured troops, there was little option for the Scots but to avoid pitched battle and retreat as swiftly as possible when threatened by the arrival of English relief forces. David had aggressively sought battle in 1138 but his heavy defeat at the Standard impressed upon his successors the wisdom of the time-honoured strategy of raid and rapid retreat. If English forces pursued them into Scotland, the Scots would avoid battle and withdraw to inaccessible areas of forest, hill or marsh. Such defensive, or 'Vegetian', warfare was, however, by no means passive.[33] Scottish commanders could severely hamper an invader's operations by keeping its armies within range, harassing enemy foraging parties and setting ambushes. In 1138, for example, David attempted, though without success, to lure King Stephen's army into a trap at Roxburgh, while in 1216 Alexander's aggressive defence of Lothian culminated in harrying John's retreating army as far as Swaledale in Yorkshire.[34]

In reality, the kingdom of Scots itself suffered but little at the hands of its southern neighbour in these periods of hostility. The fact that kings of Scots only committed themselves to war when England was troubled by civil war or rebellion meant that English counter operations against Scotland were restricted to retaliatory raids of short duration and limited geographical scope. In 1054, 1072 and 1091 kings of England had launched great combined land and naval expeditions against the Scots, yet by contrast punitive English raids between 1136 and 1217 rarely if ever penetrated beyond the Forth and were often curtailed to meet pressing strategic threats elsewhere. In 1173, the English justiciar, Richard de Lucy, cut short his ravaging in Lothian to hurry south to confront the landing in East Anglia of the rebel of Leicester with an army of Flemish mercenaries.[35] Similarly, in January 1216 rebellion and the fear of French invasion ensured that King John's brutal punitive raid into Lothian lasted less than a fortnight, though it left Haddington, Dunbar and Berwick in ashes. These English incursions, however, were not invasions but only fast-moving raids, unencumbered by ponderous siege trains: no attempts were made to besiege Edinburgh, Stirling or other major Scottish strongholds.[36] When in 1175 the key fortresses of Lothian fell into English hands, it was without a blow, surrendered by William the Lion to Henry II as sureties for his adherence to the Treaty of Falaise.[37] They were to remain garrisoned by English troops for well over a decade before being returned to the king of Scots by negotiation.

War north of the Tweed and Solway

The ill-fated Scottish invasions of England between 1136 and 1217 demanded an all-out military effort. But the great majority of campaigning undertaken by the kings of Scots in this period took place north of the Tweed and Solway, for the kingdom of the Scots by no means encompassed the geographical area of modern Scotland. 'Scotia' referred only to the kingdom's ancient heartlands, which lay between the Forth and the Spey.[38] Control of Lothian, confirmed by Malcolm II's major victory over the Northumbrians at Carham on the Tweed in 1018, had not been challenged by the kings of England. Nevertheless, as late as the reign of David I the men of Lothian could still be referred to as 'English', at a time when the equipment and fighting methods of its thanes and drengs (a type of substantial freeman owing a variety of services including military ones) may still have reflected the influence of Anglo-Scandinavian Northumbria.[39]

To the south-west, English occupation of Cumbria south of the Solway in 1096 had truncated the former kingdom of Strathclyde, leaving the virtually autonomous lordship of Galloway under the uneasy hegemony of the Scots kings. The Galwegians were to furnish important contingents to the armies of the kings of Scots, notably in the invasions of northern England in 1136–8 and 1173–4, yet they fiercely resisted attempts by the Canmore dynasty to impose more direct rule. Moreover, Galloway's proximity to Ireland and the Western Isles, where mercenary fleets could easily be raised, meant that it continued to pose a serious threat as a potential base for dynastic rivals.[40] In 1160, Malcolm IV led no fewer than three campaigns into Galloway, establishing settlers and castles there. The extent to which these could be regarded as instruments of a repressive occupation was graphically revealed when, following the capture of William the Lion by the English in 1174, the lords of Galloway expelled all royal officials, killed English and French settlers, and destroyed the castles established by the king of Scots.[41] Despite subsequent attempts to re-establish royal overlordship, the lords of Galloway remained powerful figures. It was said of Alan of Galloway (d. 1234) that he 'was the greatest warrior at that time. He had a great army and many ships. He plundered about the Hebrides for a long time.'[42] Furthermore, their independent ambitions might draw the kings of Scots into wider conflict. Alan's attempts to conquer Man for his bastard son Thomas in 1230 provoked a major Norwegian incursion, including an attack on Bute and the storming of Rothesay castle, only repelled by the timely intervention of Alexander II. In 1235, the latter suppressed a serious rebellion in Galloway and the harsh rule he established thereafter had the stamp of a military occupation.[43]

The twelfth century also witnessed increasing attempts by kings of Scots to subdue and absorb Moray and Ross. Between c. 1130 and c. 1150 Wimund, a renegade bishop of the Isles who claimed to be the son of Angus, mormaer of Moray, led sporadic raids against royalist forces.[44] Subsequently, the capture of William the Lion ushered in an extended period of uprisings, primarily west of the Great Glen.[45] These were led by the family of MacWilliam, who took their name from William fitz Duncan, David I's cousin and loyal commander, and laid claim to the kingship through a dynastic connection to his father Duncan II. They, in turn, were supported by the Macheths, a family who pressed their right to the earldom of Ross by frequent rebellion. William's response was a major campaign in 1179, accompanied by the construction of castles at Redcastle on the Black Isle, and at Dunskeath, Ross-shire.[46] Nevertheless, a fresh insurrection led by Donald Ban MacWilliam, a son of William fitz Duncan, appears to have gained control of much of Ross and Moray and rebels under Aed, son of Donald Macheth, even attacked Coupar Angus in 1186.

The king's ability to wage war in campaigns against such dynastic rivals was hampered by fears of disloyalty and treachery. In 1187, suspecting betrayal, William chose to remain at Inverness while his army advanced against MacWilliam, for some of his nobles were believed to favour the enemy. Eventually, it was decided to send out a picked force of 'warlike youths' (*juevenes bellicosos*), drawn from the military households of Roland of Galloway and other magnates, to confront the rebels and they soon proved their dependability by defeating them in battle on 31 July at 'Mam Garvia' (unidentified, but probably near Inverness). MacWilliam, and perhaps as many as 500 of his men, were killed and his head sent as a trophy to William.[47] Nevertheless, in 1211 the king was again forced to lead a major expedition to drive out Donald's son, Guthred MacWilliam, whose uprising was said to be 'with the assent of several of the nobles of Scotland'.[48] Mercenaries were an effective, if costly, weapon against suspect or rebellious nobles and the following year King John sent William the Lion a force of the notorious Brabançons, whose loyalty was as assured as their ruthlessness.[49]

Campaigns by the Scots kings and their enemies in regions such as Moray, Ross and Galloway appear to have consisted primarily of the burning of dwellings, destruction of crops, seizure of livestock and all too indiscriminate slaying. In 1212, Guthred was said to have 'depopulated a great part of the land, and put to death many of both sexes and all ages', while the previous year William the Lion had 'left behind him the lifeless corpses of many men, when he pursued the son of MacWilliam, Guthred, and destroyed those responsible for subverting him'.[50] Such acts differed little from the brutal conduct displayed towards the inhabitants of the northern English counties by the Scots and Galwegians during the invasions of 1138 and 1173–4. Furthermore, as in Wales and Ireland, the killing or mutilation of political opponents, even if kinsmen, was still commonplace,[51] and the fact that the kings of Scots regarded dynastic rivals, such as the MacWilliams and Macheths, as rebels served to exacerbate still further the savagery displayed towards them. In 1230, after forces loyal to Alexander II defeated one MacWilliam pretender, his infant daughter had her brains dashed out against the market cross at Forfar after a royal proclamation by the public crier.[52] The rebels themselves could expect little mercy. In 1212, betrayed and captured, Guthred was beheaded at Kincardine in the presence of young Prince Alexander and his corpse hanged by the feet.[53]

Little is known about the size or composition of the forces commanded by the dynastic rivals to the kings of Scots, but they were probably not large and may have depended heavily on allies or mercenaries raised in Ireland or the Western Isles. In marked contrast to their strategy when facing Anglo-Norman forces, the kings or their deputies appear to have pursued an aggressive battle-seeking approach, as at Mam Garvia, to exploit their superiority in numbers and better-armed troops. Conversely, their enemies employed exactly those defensive tactics used by kings of Scots themselves to counter incursions into southern Scotland by English armies. Wimund, for example, made repeated raids during the 1130s and 1140s against the lands of the king of Scots, but, as William of Newburgh noted

> when the king's army was dispatched against him, he retired to more distant forests or took refuge on the sea, and thus frustrated that entire war-machine (*apparatus bellicus*); once the army had retired, he would burst out again from his hidden lairs to molest the regions.[54]

In 1235, the Galwegians carried out a scorched-earth policy, burning their own and neighbouring dwellings so that Alexander II's army 'might not find lodging or food'.[55]

War in the west

Much of the north and west remained under Norse influence, reinforced in 1098 when King Magnus of Norway led a great fleet 'west beyond the sea', taking control of the Orkneys, Man and the Western Isles. The Norse earls of Orkney and the Gaelic lords of the Isles remained largely independent and powerful players in the politics of the western seaboard.[56] This was a theatre of war where the longship and the birlinn – the west Highland galley – reigned supreme. The operations of galley fleets were increasingly linked to a number of sea-girt castles of distinctive form such as Castle Sween, Tioram and Mingary.[57] Decisive battles might occur at sea, such as in 1156 when the power of Godred Crovan, Norse ruler of Man and the Hebrides, was broken by Somerled, who annexed his territories to rule as 'king of the Hebrides and *regulus* (kinglet) of Argyll and Kintyre'.[58] Gaelic-Norse rulers such as Somerled (whose Scandinavian name means 'summer warrior') could serve the kings of Scots as allies, but might equally pose a threat, reflected by the establishment of royal castles along the Clyde estuary. In 1164, Somerled landed near Renfrew with a great fleet from Argyll, the Hebrides and Dublin, but was defeated and killed by local forces.[59]

The naval dimension of royal campaigns in the north and west becomes increasingly visible from the later twelfth century.[60] The fleets of the lords of Galloway played a key role, not only in supporting the king's land forces but also in launching seaborne offensives. In 1212, for example, Thomas, earl of Atholl, the younger brother of Alan of Galloway, allied with the sons of Ragnall, Somerled's son, to raid Ulster with a force of seventy-six ships, attacking bases used by the MacWilliams, while in 1221 he won a major naval battle off the Irish coast against a Hebridean fleet. The lords of Galloway also appear to have acted as brokers, assembling stipendiary galleymen from the Isles, Ireland and Man, and supplying ships to the kings of England as well as to those of the Scots.[61]

Under Alexander II royal authority was increasingly asserted in the west. A naval expedition to Argyll in 1221 established control over Cowal, Knapdale and possibly Kintyre, consolidated by the construction of major stone castles, such as at Rothesay, Dunstaffnage and Tarbet, which commanded the isthmus at the head of Loch Fyne.[62] Alexander III (r. 1249–86) exerted a further sustained challenge to Norwegian hegemony on the western seaboard and in 1262 a Scottish fleet under the earl of Ross attacked the Isles. This provoked a major retaliatory expedition by King Hakon IV in 1263, which took Rothesay and, using ships dragged across the isthmus at Tarbet to Loch Lomond, even raided into the Lennox. Yet, dogged by a number of setbacks and adverse weather, the Norwegians achieved little and when part of the fleet was blown ashore at Largs it was sharply engaged by a local Scottish force comprising both infantry levies and cavalry.[63] Though the battle of Largs was to gain an exaggerated significance in national mythology (it has featured, for example, alongside the battles of Stirling Bridge (1297) and Bannockburn (1314) in William Hole's spirited murals (1897–1900) at the National Portrait Gallery in Edinburgh), it was in reality only a skirmish, itself indecisive enough for both sides to claim victory.[64] Nevertheless, the expedition's failure, and Alexander's purchase of control of the Isles under the Treaty of Perth in 1266, highlighted the waning Norwegian influence in the region.

Forces

From the reign of David I, the ability of the kings of Scots to raise both a general infantry levy by common army service and an elite mounted arm by knight service considerably increased their forces' military potential and strategic flexibility, for the cavalry could be called out separately, as well as in conjunction with the common army.[65] The total number of enfeoffed knights and serjeants available to the twelfth-century Scots monarchs was, however, never large. Unlike in Anglo-Norman England, the lands of abbeys and bishoprics, even those newly founded from the twelfth century, were never burdened with an obligation to provide quotas of knights.[66] Nevertheless, in open ground against poorly equipped or ill-disciplined infantry, even a comparatively small number of such heavily armed and well-trained knights could have an impact quite disproportionate to their numbers.[67] While horsemen in the armies of earlier kings of Scots had fought as skirmishers with javelin, sword or axe, Anglo-Norman knights fought in highly disciplined units, charging in close order and delivering a powerful attack with couched lances. It was the availability of such knights that probably helped David I defeat the challenge to his succession by Alexander I's son, Malcolm, in two 'sufficiently fierce battles' in 1124, just as it was the king's knights led by the constable, Edward son of Siward, who 'overwhelmed, captured and routed' a rebel army of Angus of Moray at Stracathro in 1130.[68]

Such tactics required much training. While the cavalry raised from military tenants holding by knight service were a significant asset, it was the knights of the king's military household who provided monarchs with a small corps of professional troops at the heart of their forces. They served variously as bodyguards, as crack frontline troops and as units to stiffen armies predominantly composed of ill-disciplined and poorly trained levies. At the Standard in 1138, Earl

Henry commanded such a division of knights comprising 'the English and Normans who lived in his father's household'.[69] During his siege of Alnwick castle in 1174, William the Lion sent the bulk of his army to devastate the surrounding region, keeping with him only his immediate military household (*privata familia sua*). It was these knights who put up a spirited, if hopeless, resistance against the surprise attack by an English force under Ranulf de Glanville.[70]

Effective forces, however, depended on adequate finance. Our understanding of this crucial dimension of warfare is hampered by the absence of surviving royal accounts before the reign of Alexander III, but the Anglo-Norman chronicler Orderic Vitalis had already noted that David I had defeated Malcolm's forces in 1124, 'being wiser, more powerful and wealthier'.[71] Furthermore, his ability to field some 200 knights (*loricati milites*) at the Standard was directly linked to his acquisition, through the occupation of southern Cumbria from 1135, of the silver mines at Alston.[72] Aside from booty, war could be made to pay by selling peace. During the war of 1173–4, the barons of Northumberland purchased a temporary truce from William the Lion for 300 marks of silver.[73] In 1215–16, by contrast, a powerful group of rebel barons from northern England, several of whom were linked to Alexander II by kinship or marriage, pledged a substantial monetary contribution to his war expenses against King John.[74] Indeed, exiles or dissident English lords and their knights helped swell the ranks of Scottish armies, notably in 1138 and 1173–4. Nevertheless, the number of heavy cavalry available to kings of Scots by the thirteenth century probably rarely exceeded the low hundreds. Matthew Paris was guilty of considerable exaggeration when he stated that Alexander's army in 1244, mustered against a threatened Henry III of England, contained 'a thousand armed knights'.[75]

The common army

The basic form of military service owed to the king by all free men remained the common army service (*communis exercitus*), also known as Scottish service (*servitium Scoticanum*). Whereas knight service was tenurial (that is, owed in respect of the holding of a specific fief), this more ancient obligation was territorial, by which each local unit of land assessment was assigned a quota of men it had to provide at the royal summons.[76] These forces were led on campaign by the earls, the king's regional governors. In 1173, William the Lion's army included contingents led by Colban, earl of Buchan, and Gillebridge, earl of Angus.[77] Gospatric II, earl of Dunbar, was probably the 'leader of the men of Lothian' at the Standard in 1138 and when he was struck by an English arrow his contingent broke in flight.[78] The men of Galloway formed a distinct element in the king's armies and by this time were claiming as customary the privilege to lead the first attack 'to arouse the rest of the army by their courage'.[79] During the incursion into the northern counties in 1138, William fitz Duncan led a force deep into Yorkshire and Lancashire, winning a notable victory over local Anglo-Norman forces at Clithero by the fierce charge of the Galwegians.[80]

How these regional contingents were themselves organised is unknown, though doubtless local noblemen and their retinues provided a degree of cohesion. Richard of Hexham noted that in 1138 David I entrusted the siege of Wark to 'two of his thanes, that is barons', while one raiding party that attempted to pillage Hexham was led by 'a man powerful and rich in the land of his birth'.[81] Trumpets, used to signal basic manoeuvres, are mentioned in both 1138 and 1174,[82] while it is probable that banners were used to identify and rally various detachments. David himself adopted a banner 'blazoned in the likeness of a dragon and easily recognized', such as had been carried by the later Anglo-Saxon kings of England, thereby perhaps consciously evoking his direct descent from the kings of Wessex through his mother's line.[83]

The fact that in 1215 Alexander was compelled to raise his siege of Norham after forty days and retire across the border suggests that, as in later centuries, this was the maximum length of unpaid service the king could demand.[84] In periods of exceptional military activity, kings might raise a host on more than one occasion in the year. In 1138, David launched no fewer than three separate invasions of Northumbria; Malcolm IV invaded Galloway three times in 1160; William the Lion invaded northern England twice in 1174; and Alexander II raised the common army in February 1216 and then in May, July and September 1217. It is possible that some form of rotation was in operation in such cases, while the extent of summonses varied according to strategic circumstances. To meet a threat of invasion, every able-bodied man was expected to serve,[85] but a charter of David stipulated that Edmund, son of Forn of Pinkie, could decline to join the king's army 'unless that army be so universal that the men of Inveresk cannot stay at home, in which case he must send one man'.[86] The army that David led at the Standard is likely to have been an example of the so-called 'universal army' since it is said to have been composed of contingents drawn from Galloway, Cumbria and Teviotdale, Lothian, Lorn and of the Isles, Moray and 'Scotia', north of the Forth.[87] Failure to perform common army service might be punished by heavy fines. In 1221, an edict issued by Alexander II set penalties by rank at six cows and one bull for a thane (*thanus*), fifteen sheep or six shillings for a lesser lord (*ogtigern*), and one cow and one sheep for a peasant (*rusticus*).[88] That such fines were levied not in cash but in kind highlights the predominantly rural, and in many areas pastoral, nature of the economy.

It is unclear how far afield the levies were obliged to serve, but as well as the limits imposed by a fixed term of service, it would have been an impossible feat of discipline and logistics to take large numbers of such troops further into England than Yorkshire.[89] In July 1216 Alexander II raised an army only from the southern areas of his realm, taking payment in lieu of service from the Scots dwelling north of the Forth. After taking Carlisle, and an unsuccessful attack on Barnard Castle, he dismissed the bulk of the southern levies and marched south with the more elite units of knights and serjeants as far as Dover to meet Prince Louis of France.[90] Although part of his route must have led through the territories of his rebel English allies, Alexander's bold strike successfully evaded John's attempts to catch him and has rightly been hailed as a 'a stunning feat of arms'.[91]

Some troops might serve further afield, not as levies but as picked auxiliaries. Anglo-Norman and Angevin kings regularly employed native troops from one frontier region to help subdue another, utilising their skills in warfare in difficult terrain in which knights and other heavily armed troops could not operate effectively. In 1212, King John of England required of Alan of Galloway that 'as you love us you send to us a thousand of your Galwegians, the best and most vigorous', to join his army mustering to attack north Wales.[92] It may well be that similar Galwegian units numbered among the 1,000 or so troops brought by Alexander I to assist Henry I's campaign in 1114 against Gwynedd and Powys,[93] and also among the forces contributed by Malcolm IV to Henry II's expedition against the Welsh in 1165 which penetrated as far as the Berwyn mountains.[94] The employment of such troops necessitated unit commanders capable of enforcing strict discipline to prevent disputes and violent outbreaks that were all too common within hybrid armies whose contingents were separated by custom and language.[95]

Arms and equipment

Observers were consistently struck by the lack of equipment, and even of clothing, of the bulk of Scottish troops. A canon from the region of Cambrai noted of a party of Scots, probably en route to join the Second Crusade in 1147, that whereas knights and townsfolk wore underwear, 'the rest make do with a general covering, which is closed over at the front and the back, but which underneath is open at the sides', so that their lack of drawers was readily apparent.[96] Hence the derogatory reference that David I's former steward, Abbot Ailred of Rievaulx, places in the mouth of the Anglo-Norman commander, Walter Espec, before the Standard in 1138: 'Who then would not laugh, rather than fear, when to fight against such men [as the Normans] runs the worthless Scot with half-bare buttocks?'[97]

Mail shirts or helmets of iron were owned only by the wealthy few. For most, body armour – if worn at all – was of hardened leather. Shields, perhaps similar to later Highland targes, were of wood and leather, although Ailred also mentions shields of calfskin.[98] One of the earliest known depictions of Scottish infantry, on an English royal charter illustrating the siege of Carlisle in 1315, shows them wearing large hooded cloaks, seemingly as their only defence, though one has a rudimentary helmet. To Anglo-Norman observers, it was lack of armour as much as clothing that made these troops 'naked people',[99] and such a deficiency left them extremely vulnerable, especially to archery, as the fighting at the Standard so starkly demonstrated. By contrast, as knightly equipment became heavier during the late twelfth and thirteenth centuries, so the invulnerability of fully armed knights to poorly armed infantry became all the greater. In 1247, Roger de Quincy, earl of Winchester and the constable of Scotland, found himself besieged in a castle in Galloway by a large force of local men rebelling against his harsh rule. 'Armed to the teeth and mounted on a valuable horse', Roger burst out of its gates with a small following and 'cut a way for himself through the midst of his enemies . . . they fell to either side of him; and so he cleft and scattered the whole army, and narrowly escaped from danger and death'.[100]

For levies of the common army, offensive arms included axes, javelins and long spears, while some, particularly from areas such as the Forest of Selkirk, were archers.[101] *Hakon's Saga* recounts how at the battle of Largs in 1263 the Scottish infantry 'had mostly bows and Irish axes'.[102] The latter were two-handed weapons of Scandinavian origin, much favoured among the Irish and the Hiberno-Norse. A twelfth-century axehead found at Lumphanan, Aberdeenshire, already displays the distinctive lengthening of the upper part of the blade that would characterise later Scottish axes, while some surviving examples are finely decorated with silver.[103] Capable of severing limbs, or even killing horses, such axes were long to remain a primary

Figure 3.3 A walrus ivory chess piece of a warder or foot soldier, originally made in Scandinavia in the late twelfth century, found on Lewis.

weapon of the galloglass warriors of the western seaboard.[104] Some of the more affluent warriors of the Isles and the north-west may well have had other equipment reflecting strong Norse influence, with helmets and shields perhaps similar to those depicted on the famous Lewis chessmen, probably of Scandinavian manufacture and dating to the second half of the twelfth century.[105]

The English chronicler Ralph of Diss described the Galwegian troops in William the Lion's army in 1173 as 'athletic, naked, remarkable for their baldness, equipped at their left side with knives formidable to armoured men, skilled at throwing spears even from a distance and holding their long spears aloft like a standard when advancing to battle'.[106] Ailred of Rievaulx was similarly struck by the great length of the Scots' spears.[107] Using only a small amount of iron, a scarce and expensive commodity in Scotland,[108] the long spear was a natural weapon for impoverished infantry.[109] Such spears may have had a long ancestry: the late seventh- or early eighth-century Aberlemno stone, which probably represents the Picts' victory over the Northumbrian king Egcfrith at Nechtanesmere in 685, clearly shows a Pictish infantryman holding a long spear in two hands, with a shield hanging over his shoulder from a baldric, confronting a heavily equipped horseman. At the battle of Falkirk in 1298, William Wallace's innovation, if such it was, lay not in developing a new weapon, but rather in drilling his spearmen to stand fast in effective formations against Edward I's cavalry.

Cohesion, morale and discipline

The sources allow only the rarest glimpses of how troops were motivated in combat. At the Standard, the men of Galloway were said to have given three great yells 'after their custom' before commencing their wild onrush, doubtless to strike fear into the enemy and arouse their own courage.[110] The Scots' war cry was 'Albani, Albani!' – referring either to the kingdom of Alba or possibly to *Albannaig* – 'the men of Scotland'.[111] Religious preparations before battle, such as prayer, confession and absolution by priests, were also undoubtedly important. Alexander III's infantry, assembled in 1244 to counter a threatened invasion by Henry III of England, were said to be 'all of one mind, and . . . having made confession, and been encouraged by the consoling words of their preachers that they were about to fight in a just cause on behalf of their country, had very little fear of death'.[112] Indeed, defence of the *patria* or homeland was always held to be the most just of wars, and the proclamation of such defensive campaigns as a holy war against the invader would become a marked feature of the Scottish response to Edward I's campaigns of invasion from 1296.

Relics and religious banners might be carried with the army to invoke divine aid and protection. In 1211, when William the Lion was campaigning against the MacWilliam rebellion, he confirmed to Arbroath abbey custody of the *Brecbennoch* and granted 'to God, St Columba and the Bracbennach' lands of Forglen (Banffshire), on condition that the monks perform service in the army with it, doubtless through their local tenants.[113] Serious doubt has now been cast on the traditional identification of this *Brecbennoch* with the small house-shaped casket known as the Monymusk reliquary. It may rather have been a sacred war banner, perhaps incorporating relics of fabric associated with St Columba, akin to the standard of St Cuthbert kept at Durham cathedral priory.[114] If so, its use may be analogous with that of the sacred Oriflamme banner, ritually brought out by the kings of France from the royal abbey of St Denis for major campaigns.

The acquisition of booty was a pervading aspect of warfare. In enemy territory, or even on home soil, the moveable wealth of churches and monasteries in particular offered an all too tempting target for troops hungry for plunder. Kings, however, might grant charters of protection to religious houses. David I did so to Hexham priory in 1138 and sent guards from his own men to defend it.[115] Sometimes it proved impossible to enforce royal commands to respect churches. In 1216 Holme Cultram abbey was plundered despite Alexander II's express prohibition, while in 1235 his troops also sacked Glenluce and other abbeys in Galloway during his absence.[116] The acquisition and proper division of more licit plunder was a crucial aspect of campaigning, especially as the great majority of troops were unpaid.[117] A mid-fifteenth-century Scottish ordinance that stated that no man should leave the host, on pain of death for treason, until the spoil 'be thriddyt and partyt' (thirded and divided), probably reflected a much older custom.[118] The king himself was entitled to a share, most likely a third.[119]

Well into the twelfth century Scots and Galwegian troops enslaved captives taken in war and such hapless folk were divided up along with other booty. Finding such slaving repugnant, but evidently unable to prohibit the practice, David I and his Anglo-Norman vassals set at liberty those who fell to their share by lot during the campaigns in northern England between 1136 and 1138, sending them to safety at Carlisle.[120] Nevertheless, the internal quarrels to which such a process of division might give rise is suggested by an incident in 1138 when, as David's army lay encamped at Durham, 'a serious sedition arose because of a certain woman', and the Galwegians 'threatened to destroy the king and his followers'.[121]

This ugly confrontation highlighted the fact that while most medieval commanders were plagued with problems of discipline, desertion and effective coordination of disparate units, the hybrid nature of Scottish armies confronted twelfth-century kings with peculiar difficulties of command and control. Bitter tensions between native elements and an 'alien' elite patronised by the king are evident as early as 1094, when Duncan II only achieved reconciliation with his rebellious nobles 'on the condition that he should no more introduce into Scotland either English or Normans, or allow them to give him military service'.[122] Long simmering resentment of the influence enjoyed by David I's Anglo-French vassals came dramatically to the fore at the Standard, when the Galwegians vociferously opposed the king's attempt to place his knights in the front ranks of the Scottish army, claiming this as their established right. Malise, earl of Strathearn, and Alan de Percy, one of David's Anglo-Norman followers, thereupon traded insults and with the quarrel threatening to erupt into open violence David reluctantly conceded to the Galwegians' demands, with catastrophic results.[123] Even as his defeated army was fleeing in headlong rout, fights broke out between its rival factions. This so incensed the king that he later imposed heavy fines on those he held responsible and extracted oaths and hostages 'that they would never again desert him in battle'.[124]

Atrocity and chivalry

In addition to the fundamental elements of ravaging – the destruction of crops, the killing or seizure of livestock and the burning of dwellings, mills and barns – widespread atrocities were imputed to the Scots during their invasions of northern England. The accounts by Anglo-Norman chroniclers, often vague and formulaic, were powerfully informed by the developing perception of the Scots, together with other Celtic peoples, as barbarians on the fringes of a civilised Christendom, set apart by their uncouth language and dress, outmoded ecclesiastical practices, deviant sexual habits and ferocious conduct in war.[125] Such a view depicted the Scots as formidable fighters, but also as wild savages, 'barbarous and filthy, neither overcome by excess of cold nor enfeebled by severe hunger, putting their trust in swiftness of foot and light equipment; in their own country they care nothing for the awful moment of the bitterness of death, among foreigners they surpass all in cruelty'.[126] Even the anonymous Lowland Scottish author of the *Gesta Annalia*, writing in or before 1285, could note how in 1173 William the Lion had invaded England 'with the highland Scots, whom they call brutes (*brutos*) and the Galwegians, who knew not how to spare either place nor person, but raged after the manner of beasts'.[127] Such men seemed capable of any outrage. The Galwegians, it was said, slew babies and drank their blood mixed with water.[128] As late as 1745, during the Jacobites' march to Derby, a bemused Cameron of Lochiel found himself having to assure a terrified woman, upon whom he had been billeted, that he would not eat her children.[129]

Beyond such lurid fantasies, however, lay a stark reality: the warfare waged by Scots and Galwegian troops in the eleventh and twelfth centuries was characterised by widespread slaving and the indiscriminate killing of non-combatants. Indeed, those who were too old, ill, pregnant or otherwise unable to keep up with the raiders, were despatched out of hand as mere encumbrances to the march.[130] The enslavement of prisoners-of-war had once been ubiquitous in early medieval Europe, while the ruthless killing of the local populace still remained a common feature of war in Wales and Ireland. Yet such conduct was becoming increasingly unacceptable, particularly to the Church, who condemned the enslavement of fellow Christians and legislated for the protection of the unarmed (*inermes*) – women, children and the clergy.[131] Thus it was that when the papal legate Alberic, cardinal bishop of Ostia, met with David I at Carlisle in 1138 as part of his efforts to bring peace, he obtained pledges from the Galwegians and the Scots 'that they should bring back to Carlisle . . . all captive girls and women whom they might have and restore them to liberty there'. In addition, he made them swear not to violate churches, and to spare women, children, the sick and the old, and 'thenceforth slay no-one at all unless he opposed them'.[132]

The practice of enslaving captives by Scottish troops had ceased by the thirteenth century.[133] A legacy of ruthlessness continued, nevertheless, to mark the Scots' conduct in war. An Irish annalist noted of the Bruce invasion of Ireland between 1315 and 1318 that while other armies merely ravaged and burned the Scots also killed.[134] During the Flodden campaign of 1513, a Gaelic praise poem could exhort Archibald, earl of Argyll, to be merciless:

> Let us make harsh and mighty warfare against the English . . . The roots from which they grow, destroy them, their increase is too great, and leave no Englishman alive after you nor Englishwoman there to tell the tale. Burn their bad coarse women, burn their uncouth offspring, and burn their sooty houses, and rid us of the reproach of them. Let their ashes float down-stream after burning their remains, show no mercy to a living Englishman, O chief, deadly slayer of the wounded.[135]

But such sentiments had no place in the developing chivalric ethos of the aristocracy, which enjoined clemency towards a defeated opponent and sought to regulate the practice of war – at least towards other members of the knightly elite – by conventions of ransom, truces and negotiated surrenders. In 1138, David I acknowledged the bravery of the English garrison of Wark by permitting them to go free without exacting ransom and, as they had eaten their own horses during the prolonged siege, he gave them new mounts.[136] In turn, the English knights who surprised William the Lion at the siege of Alnwick in 1174 took care not to kill or seriously wound their Scottish counterparts, but to capture them for ransom, while their brave defence of their king was praised by Jordan Fantosme.[137] The contrast with the earlier ambush of Malcolm III near the River Alne in 1093, when neither quarter nor ransom had been afforded to the Scots, could not be more revealing.

In terms of its martial culture, the nobility of twelfth- and thirteenth-century Scotland was now both a cross-border and a cross-channel aristocracy. In 1159, Malcolm IV, who had enthusiastically answered Henry II's summons to join his great expedition to besiege Toulouse, was knighted by the king himself outside the walls of Périgueux. Malcolm then in turn dubbed his younger brother William and thirty of his young noble companions as knights.[138] William the Lion and his nobles showed themselves equally enthusiastic participants of the tournament circuit of north-eastern France and it is likely that the tournament had emerged within Scotland itself well before the first chance references to it from the mid-thirteenth century.[139] These sporting combats, fast becoming an integral feature of noble society, trained knights to fight in close order as a team, honed weapon skills, offered profit through ransoms and provided a cosmopolitan social forum.[140] As a spectacle and an arena to display prowess, it was the tournament, rather than battle, that stimulated the development of heraldry from the mid-twelfth century. It is probable that the royal arms of the lion rampant were adopted by King William, but the device first appears unequivocally on the seal of Alexander II, who also adopted the fine 'double tressure' border of fleurs de lys.[141] More tangibly, the great castles of Bothwell, Direlton and Kildrummy proudly proclaimed the influence of their French model of Coucy-le-Château in the design of their *donjons* (keeps or great towers).[142]

The influence of this Anglo-French chivalric culture extended well beyond the Lowlands. Roland, lord of Galloway, who was both justiciar and royal constable, chose the Norman-French version of his name in preference to the Gaelic Lachlan.[143] He may also have commissioned the Anglo-French romance that transformed his grandfather, the Gaelic lord Fergus of Galloway, into the eponymous hero of an Arthurian tale that based Arthur and the Round Table at Carlisle and the castle of Fergus's lady Galiene at Liddell, and made

Figure 3.4 Cast of the Great Seal of King Alexander II (r. 1214–49). His shield bears the earliest known representation of the royal arms of Scotland.

Dunnottar the seat of a murderous hag armed with a giant scythe.[144] Roland's effigy in Dundrennan abbey depicts him with hauberk, mail coif, surcoat and shield, as does that of Walter Stewart, earl of Menteith, in Inchmaholm priory.[145] Both the equipment and the image of knighthood they convey are indistinguishable from noble effigies south of the border. To the west, the fusion of Anglo-French and Hebridean symbols of chivalric lordship is neatly encapsulated by the seal of Somerled's son, Ragnall, which was said to depict on one face 'a ship filled with men at arms; on the reverse side, the figure of an armed man on horseback with a drawn sword in his hand'.[146] The image of the mounted warrior even caught the imagination of the Norse *Hakon's Saga*, which approvingly recounts the gallant exploits of a young Scottish knight, Fergus, at the battle of Largs in 1263 who, splendidly accoutered, charged ahead of his comrades and 'rode through the ranks of the Norwegians and back to his men' before being killed.[147]

Yet the repulse of the Norwegians at Largs had been achieved as much by Scots foot soldiers as by the knights.[148] The combined force of local infantry, levied by common army service, and of cavalry, raised by knight service, symbolised the effective fusion of the old and the new in Scottish armies. The unsuccessful attempts by the Scots kings to restore the 'Scoto-Northumbrian realm' by their invasions of the northern counties had highlighted the limitations of Scots armies when confronting an English opponent far superior in resources, heavily armed troops and sophisticated fortifications. But further north, Scottish royal armies had served their purpose with much greater success, enabling kings gradually to extend their authority over the whole mainland and into the Western Isles. The battle of Largs represented the last serious military engagement of Alexander III's reign. Indeed, it was indicative of the peaceful state of the kingdom that the bitterest fighting subsequently experienced by Scots was once more to be in England, when in 1264 a number of leading Scottish nobles were captured and many of their infantry killed, fighting for King Henry III against the rebel forces of Simon de Montfort.[149] The peace would, however, have a price. When war came again to Scotland with Edward I's invasion of 1296, the strategic wisdom of avoiding pitched battle, and of defeating incursions by Vegetian tactics, had all but been forgotten – with catastrophic consequences for the Scots.

Notes

I would like to thank Dauvit Broun, David Caldwell, Stephen Marritt, Ralph Moffat and Alice Taylor for valuable discussions which have helped to shape this chapter. It has also greatly benefited from Jeremy Crang's judicious and constructive editing.

1. *The Anglo-Saxon Chronicle* [hereafter *ASC*], in D. C. Douglas and G. W. Greenaway (eds), *English Historical Documents, 1042–1189*, second edition (London: Routledge, 1981), 'E', 1093; Simeon of Durham, *Historia Regum*, in T. Arnold (ed.), *Symeonis Monachi Opera Omnia*, 2 vols (London: Rolls Series, 1882, 1885), vol. 2, pp. 221–2.
2. Ibid. p. 222.
3. R. Bartlett, *The Making of Europe: Colonization, Conquest and Cultural Change, 950–1350* (London: Penguin, 1993), pp. 24–59, 60–84.
4. For wider context and comparisons, see R. R. Davies, *Domination and Conquest: The Experience of Ireland, Scotland and Wales, 1100–1300* (Cambridge: Cambridge University Press, 1990); and R. R. Davies, *The First English Empire: Power and Identities in the British Isles 1093–1343* (Oxford: Oxford University Press, 2000).

5. R. L. G. Ritchie, *The Normans in Scotland* (Edinburgh: Edinburgh University Press, 1954), remains a valuable overview.
6. Duncan's seal is reproduced in A. M. Duncan, 'Duncan II', *Oxford Dictionary of National Biography* [hereafter *ODNB*] (Oxford: Oxford University Press, 2004) vol. 17, pp. 219-20. R. Oram, *The Canmores: The Kings and Queens of the Scots, 1040-1290* (Stroud: Tempus, 2002) also reproduces the seals of Malcolm's sons and subsequent kings. For the wider context of the adoption of such imagery, see D. Crouch, *The Image of Aristocracy in Britain, 1000-1300* (London: Routledge, 1992).
7. R. Oram, *David I. The King who Made Scotland* (Stroud: Tempus, 2004), pp. 49-73.
8. For the wider context of David's policies, see G. W. S. Barrow, 'David I of Scotland: The balance of old and new', in G. W. S. Barrow, *Scotland and her Neighbours in the Middle Ages* (London: Hambledon, 1992), pp. 67-90.
9. M. Chibnall (ed.), *The Ecclesiastical History of Orderic Vitalis*, 6 vols (Oxford: Oxford University Press, 1969-1980), vol. 4, pp. 274-5; G. W. S. Barrow (ed.), *Regesta Regum Scottorum, I: The Acts of Malcolm IV, King of Scots 1153-1165* (Edinburgh: Edinburgh University Press, 1960), pp. 31, 34-5.
10. This process of settlement is analysed in detail by G. W. S. Barrow, *The Kingdom of the Scots*, second edition (Edinburgh: Edinburgh University Press, 2003), ch. 12, 'The beginnings of military feudalism' and ch. 13, 'Scotland's Norman families'; and G. W. S. Barrow, *The Anglo-Norman Era in Scottish History* (Oxford: Oxford University Press, 1980).
11. For a rare indication of the monetary value of a knight's fief, see G. W. S. Barrow (ed.), *The Charters of David I: The Written Acts of David I King of Scots, 1124-53, and of his son Henry, Earl of Northumberland, 1139-52* (Woodbridge: Boydell and Brewer, 1999), no. 94; and Barrow, 'The beginnings of military feudalism', p. 262.
12. Barrow (ed.), *Charters of David*, no. 16; G. W. S. Barrow (ed.), *Regesta Regum Scottorum, II: The Acts of William I, King of Scots 1165-1214* (Edinburgh: Edinburgh University Press, 1971), no. 80. Of the major acts of landed settlement made by David to leading barons, only this charter of enfeoffment for Annandale and the castle of Annan survives.
13. Barrow, 'The beginnings of military feudalism', pp. 253, 269-70; G. W. S. Barrow, 'The earls of Fife in the 12th century', *Proceedings of the Society of Antiquaries of Scotland*, vol. 87 (1952-3), pp. 51-62.
14. For example, Barrow (ed.), *Regesta Regum Scottorum, I*, pp. 55-6, 152, 284; and Barrow (ed.), *Regesta Regum Scottorum, II*, pp. 55-7, 389.

15. Aelred of Rievaulx, *Relatio de Standardo*, in R. Howlett (ed.), *Chronicles of the Reigns of Stephen, Henry II, and Richard I*, 4 vols (London: Rolls Series, 1884–9), vol. 3, p. 189; J. Bradbury, 'Battles in England and Normandy, 1066–1154', *Anglo-Norman Studies* [hereafter *ANS*], vol. 6 (1983), pp. 1–12, and reprinted in M. Strickland (ed.), *Anglo-Norman Warfare* (Woodbridge: Boydell and Brewer, 1992), pp. 189–90; M. Strickland (ed.), *The Medieval Archer* (Woodbridge: Boydell and Brewer, 1985), pp. 39–57; M. Strickland and R. Hardy, *The Great Warbow: From Hastings to the Mary Rose* (Stroud: Sutton, 2005), pp. 69–83.
16. G. G. Simpson and B. Webster, 'Charter evidence and the distribution of mottes in Scotland', in K. J. Stringer (ed.), *Essays on the Nobility of Medieval Scotland* (Edinburgh: John Donald, 1985), pp. 1–24; F. Watson, 'The expression of power in a medieval kingdom: Thirteenth-century Scottish castles', in S. Foster, A. Macinnes and R. MacInnes (eds), *Scottish Power Centres from the Early Middle Ages to the Twentieth Century* (Glasgow: Cruithne Press, 1998), pp. 59–78. For an important discussion of the extent of continuity in form and function of lordly dwellings, see R. D. Oram, 'Royal and lordly residence in Scotland c. 1050 to c. 1250', *The Antiquaries Journal*, vol. 88 (2008), pp. 165–89.
17. C. J. Tabraham, 'Norman settlement in Galloway: Recent fieldwork in the Stewartry', in D. J. Breeze (ed.), *Studies in Scottish Antiquity Presented to Stewart Cruden* (Edinburgh: Edinburgh University Press, 1984), pp. 114–16. For early castles in Scotland, see Chapter 27 in this volume.
18. For the nature of the border, see W. M. Aird, 'Northern England or Southern Scotland? The Anglo-Scottish border in the eleventh and twelfth centuries and the problem of perspective', in J. C. Appleby and P. Dalton (eds), *Government, Religion and Society in Northern England, 1000–1700* (Stroud: Sutton, 1997), pp. 27–39.
19. For valuable overviews of Anglo-Scottish relations, see A. A. M. Duncan, *Scotland: The Making of the Kingdom* (Edinburgh: Oliver and Boyd, 1975), pp. 216–56; and J. Green, 'Anglo-Scottish relations, 1066–1174', in M. Jones and M. Vale (eds), *England and Her Neighbours, 1066–1453* (London: Hambledon, 1989), pp. 53–72.
20. R. Bartlett, *England under the Norman and Angevin Kings, 1075–1225* (Oxford: Clarendon Press, 2000), pp. 78–81.
21. G. W. S. Barrow, 'The Scots and the North of England', in E. King (ed.), *The Anarchy of Stephen's Reign* (Oxford: Clarendon Press, 1994), pp. 231–53, and reprinted in Barrow, *Kingdom of the Scots*, pp. 130–50.
22. Richard of Hexham, *De Gestis Regis Stephani et de Bello Standardii*, in

Howlett (ed.), *Chronicles*, vol. 3, pp. 162-3. The sources for David I's campaigns and the battle of the Standard are usefully collected in A. O. Anderson (ed.), *Scottish Annals from English Chroniclers, AD 500 to 1286* (London: David Nutt, 1908, reprinted Stamford: Paul Watkins, 1991), pp. 176-213. For the context of the battle, see K. J. Stringer, *The Reign of King Stephen* (London: Routledge, 1993), pp. 28-33 and Oram, *David I*, pp. 135-40. For a valuable, if not always convincing, revisionist analysis of the battle, see R. Toolis, '"Naked and unarmoured": A reassessment of the role of the Galwegians at the battle of the Standard', *Transactions of the Dumfriesshire and Galloway Natural History and Antiquarian Society*, third series, vol. 78 (2004), pp. 79-92.

23. Aelred of Rievaulx, *Relatio*, p. 189. For the tactics of Henry's victories, see Bradbury, 'Battles in England and Normandy', pp. 1-12, reprinted in Strickland (ed.), *Anglo-Norman Warfare*, pp. 182-93.

24. K. J. Stringer, 'State-building in twelfth-century Britain: David I, King of Scots, and Northern England', in J. C. Appleby and P. Dalton (eds), *Government, Religion and Society in Northern England, 1000-1700* (Stroud: Sutton, 1997), pp. 40-62; K. J. Stringer, 'King David I (1124-1153): The Scottish occupation of Northern England', *Medieval History*, vol. 4 (1994), pp. 51-60; G. W. S. Barrow, 'King David I, Earl Henry and Cumbria', *Transactions of the Cumberland and Westmorland Antiquarian and Archaeological Society*, new series, vol. 99 (1999), pp. 117-27; G. W. S. Barrow, 'The Scots and the North of England', pp. 130-47.

25. R. A. Brown, H. M. Colvin and A. J. Taylor (eds), *A History of the King's Works, vol. II, The Middle Ages* (London: HMSO, 1963), pp. 595-6; M. R. McCarthy, H. Summerson and R. G. Annis (eds), *Carlisle Castle: A Survey and Documentary History* (London: Historic Buildings and Monuments Commission, 1990), pp. 121-2.

26. For an excellent discussion of Alexander II's campaigns, see K. J. Stringer, 'Kingship, conflict and state-making in the reign of Alexander II: The war of 1215-17 and its context', in R. Oram (ed.), *The Reign of Alexander II, 1214-1249* (Leiden: Brill, 2005), pp. 99-156, especially pp. 120-30.

27. For a fuller discussion, see M. J. Strickland, 'Securing the North: Invasion and the strategy of defence in twelfth-century Anglo-Scottish warfare', *Anglo-Norman Studies*, vol. 12 (1989), pp. 177-98, reprinted in Strickland (ed.), *Anglo-Norman Warfare*, pp. 208-29.

28. M. J. Strickland, *War and Chivalry: The Conduct and Perception of War, 1066-1217* (Cambridge: Cambridge University Press, 1996), pp. 323-9; and I. A. MacInnes, '"Shock and awe": The use of terror as a psychological weapon during the Bruce-Balliol civil war, 1332-1338', in

A. King and M. Penman (eds), *England and Scotland in the Fourteenth Century: New Perspectives* (Woodbridge: Boydell and Brewer, 2007), pp. 40–59.

29. R. C. Johnston (ed.), *Jordan Fantosme's Chronicle* (Oxford: Clarendon Press, 1981), lines 443–50.
30. Johnston (ed.), *Fantosme*, lines 443–50, 1242–59. For the wider context, see A. Stevenson, 'The Flemish dimension of the Auld Alliance', in G. Simpson (ed.), *Scotland and the Low Countries, 1124–1994* (East Linton: Tuckwell Press, 1996), pp. 28–42.
31. Subsequent repairs reveal that the keep had been damaged and one of the towers breached, while his sappers had mined part of the bailey walls, Brown, Colvin and Taylor (eds), *History of the King's Works*, p. 596.
32. Stringer, 'Kingship, conflict and state-making', pp. 120–5.
33. So called after the late Roman military theorist Vegetius, whose *De Re Militari* advocated the avoidance of battle where possible and the defeat of the enemy through denying him supplies. For recent discussions, see C. J. Rogers, 'The Vegetian science of warfare in the Middle Ages', *Journal of Medieval Military History*, vol. 1 (2002), pp. 1–20; S. Morillo, 'Battle seeking: The contexts and limits of Vegetian strategy', *Journal of Medieval Military History*, vol. 1 (2002), pp. 21–42, and the rejoinder by J. Gillingham, 'Up with orthodoxy! In defense of Vegetian warfare', *Journal of Medieval Military History*, vol. 2 (2003), pp. 149–58.
34. Richard of Hexham, *De Gestis Regis Stephani*, p. 155; *John of Fordun's Chronicle*, ed. W. F. Skene, 2 vols (Edinburgh: Edmonston and Douglas, 1871–2), vol. 1, p. 284; Walter Bower, *Scotichronicon*, ed. D. E. R. Watt et al., 9 vols (Aberdeen: Aberdeen University Press, 1987–8), vol. 5, pp. 82–5; Stringer, 'Kingship, conflict and state-making', p. 123.
35. A. O. Anderson and M. O. Anderson (eds), *The Chronicle of Melrose Abbey* (London: Percy Lund Humphries & Co. Ltd, 1936), pp. 62–3.
36. In 1216, John was only able to burn Roxburgh because it had been abandoned by Alexander II, Anderson and Anderson (eds), *Chronicle of Melrose*, p. 62.
37. W. Stubbs (ed.), *Gesta Regis Henrici Secundi Benedicti Abbatis*, 2 vols (London: Rolls Series, 1867), vol. 1, pp. 97–8; D. W. Hunter Marshall, 'Two English occupations of Scotland', *Scottish Historical Review* [hereafter *SHR*], vol. 25 (1927), pp. 20–3; Barrow (ed.), *Regesta Regum Scottorum, II*, p. 8, and n. 31. Edinburgh was restored to William in 1186, but Berwick and Roxburgh not until 1189.
38. Barrow (ed.), *Regesta Regum Scottorum, I*, pp. 39–40.
39. Ibid. p. 45.

40. S. Duffy, 'Irishmen and Islemen in the kingdoms of Dublin and Man, 1052-1171', *Ériu*, vol. 43 (1992), pp. 93-133; R. A. MacDonald, 'Rebels without a cause? The relations of Fergus of Galloway and Somerled of Argyll with the Scottish kings, 1153-1164', in E. J. Cowan and R. A. McDonald (eds), *Alba: Celtic Scotland in the Medieval Era* (East Linton: Tuckwell Press, 2000), pp. 166-86.
41. Stubbs (ed.), *Gesta Henrici*, vol. 1, pp. 67-8, 126.
42. A. O. Anderson, *Early Sources of Scottish History, A.D. 500-1296*, 2 vols (Edinburgh: Oliver and Boyd, 1922; Stamford: Paul Watkins, 1990), vol. 2, p. 464; K. J. Stringer, 'Periphery and core in thirteenth-century Scotland: Alan, son of Roland, lord of Galloway and constable of Scotland', in A. Grant and K. J. Stringer (eds), *Medieval Scotland: Crown, Lordship and Community. Essays Presented to G. W. S. Barrow* (Edinburgh: Edinburgh University Press, 1993), pp. 82-113.
43. Duncan, *Scotland: The Making of the Kingdom*, pp. 530-2. The insurrection had resulted from the king's enforced partition of the lordship between Alan of Galloway's three daughters and heiresses, each married to a major Anglo-Scottish magnate.
44. William of Newburgh, *Historia rerum Anglicarum*, in Howlett (ed.), *Chronicles*, vol. 1, pp. 73-6; A. O. Anderson, 'Wimund, bishop and pretender', *SHR*, vol. 7 (1909-10), pp. 29-36.
45. Barrow (ed.), *Regesta Regum Scottorum, II*, p. 8.
46. Ibid. p. 292.
47. Stubbs (ed.), *Gesta Regis Henrici*, vol. 2, p. 8; Barrow (ed.), *Regesta Regum Scottorum, II*, p. 12.
48. *Fordun*, ed. Skene, vol. 1, pp. 278-9; Anderson, *Early Sources*, vol. 2, pp. 389-90.
49. *Annals of St Edmunds*, in T. Arnold (ed.), *Memorials of St Edmunds Abbey*, 3 vols (London: Rolls Series, 1890-6), vol. 2, p. 20.
50. Ibid. p. 20; Anderson and Anderson (eds), *Chronicle of Melrose*, p. 56.
51. See J. Gillingham, 'Killing and mutilating political enemies in the British Isles from the late twelfth to the early fourteenth centuries: A comparative study', in B. Smith (ed.), *Britain and Ireland 900-1300: Insular Responses to Medieval European Change* (Cambridge: Cambridge University Press, 1999), pp. 114-34.
52. J. Stevenson (ed.), *Chronicon de Lanercost* (Edinburgh: Maitland Club, 1839), pp. 40-1.
53. *Fordun*, ed. Skene, vol. 1, pp. 278-9. When in 1235 the men of Glasgow defeated an Irish force supporting Thomas, the illegitimate son of Alan of Galloway, they beheaded all those they caught, while two of their leaders were taken to Edinburgh where they were pulled apart by horses, Anderson and Anderson (eds), *Chronicle of Melrose*, pp. 84-5.

54. William of Newburgh, *Historia rerum Anglicarum*, p. 74; William of Newburgh, *The History of English Affairs*, trans. P. G. Walsh and M. J. Kennedy, 2 vols (Warminster: Aris and Phillips, 1988–2007), vol. 1, p. 105.

55. Stubbs (ed.), *Gesta Regis Henrici*, vol. 1, p. 348: H. R. Luard (ed.), *Matthæi Parisiensis, monachi Santi Albani, Chronica Majora* [hereafter *Matthew Paris*], 7 vols (London: Rolls Series, 1872–83), vol. 3, pp. 364–6; Anderson and Anderson (eds), *Chronicle of Melrose*, p. 84. Alexander was only saved from disaster by the timely intervention of Farquhar MacTaggart, earl of Ross, whose forces routed the Galwegians with great slaughter.

56. R. A. McDonald, *The Kingdom of the Isles: Scotland's Western Seaboard, c. 1100– c. 1336* (East Linton: Tuckwell Press, 1997); D. W. H. Sellar, 'Hebridean sea kings: The successors of Somerled, 1164–1316', in Cowan and Macdonald, *Alba*, pp. 187–218.

57. D. Rixson, *The West Highland Galley* (Edinburgh: Birlinn, 1998); Cruden, *The Scottish Castle*, pp. 18–49; *Argyll Castles in the Care of Historic Scotland* (extracts from Royal Commission on Ancient and Historical Monuments Scotland [hereafter RCAHMS] inventories of Argyll, vols 1, 2 and 7 (RCAHMS and Historic Scotland, 1997).

58. McDonald, *The Kingdom of the Isles*, pp. 39–67; W. D. H. Sellar, 'Somerled (d. 1164), king of the Hebrides', *ODNB*, vol. 51, pp. 562–4.

59. Anderson, *Early Sources*, vol. 1, pp. 254–8; Barrow (ed.), *Regesta Regum Scottorum, I*, p. 20.

60. A fleet, for example, was assembled in 1196 for William the Lion's major expedition to Caithness against Harald Maddason, earl of Orkney, *Chronica Magistri Rogeri de Houvedene*, ed. W. Stubbs, 2 vols (London: Rolls Series, 1868–71), vol. 4, p. 10; Barrow (ed.), *Regesta Regum Scottorum, II*, pp. 15–16.

61. R. Oram, 'Thomas, earl of Atholl (d. 1231)', *ODNB*, vol. 54, pp. 272–3. Thomas commanded a fleet hired by King John for his aborted expedition in 1204–5 to regain Normandy, and again for his more successful campaign in Poitou in 1206.

62. Duncan, *Scotland: The Making of the Kingdom*, p. 528; J. G. Dunbar and A. A. M. Duncan, 'Tarbert castle', *SHR*, vol. 50 (1971), pp. 1–17.

63. Anderson, *Early Sources*, vol. 2, pp. 607–42. For a detailed analysis of the campaign, see E. J. Cowan, 'Norwegian sunset – Scottish dawn: Hakon IV and Alexander III', in N. Reid (ed.), *Scotland in the Reign of Alexander III, 1249–1286* (Edinburgh: John Donald, 1990), pp. 103–31.

64. Duncan, *Scotland: The Making of the Kingdom*, pp. 578–9.

65. Barrow, *The Anglo-Norman Era*, pp. 164–5.

66. G. W. S. Barrow, *Kingship and Unity: Scotland, 1000–1306* (Edinburgh: Edinburgh University Press, 1989), pp. 45–6.
67. This is clearly revealed by the more detailed evidence of the Anglo-Norman invasion of Ireland from 1169. See *Giraldus Cambrensis, Expugnatio Hibernica: The Conquest of Ireland*, ed. A. B. Scott and F. X. Martin (Dublin: Royal Irish Academy, 1978), pp. 36–7, 76–83, 90–1, and R. Rogers, 'Aspects of the military history of the Anglo-Norman invasion of Ireland, 1169–1225', *Irish Sword*, vol. 16 (1986), pp. 135–46.
68. Chibnall (ed.), *Orderic Vitalis*, vol. 4, pp. 276–7; *ASC*, 'D', 1130; Barrow (ed.), *Regesta Regum Scottorum, I*, p. 34.
69. Henry of Huntingdon, *Historia Anglorum*, ed. D. Greenway (Oxford: Clarendon Press, 1996), pp. 716–19.
70. Stubbs (ed.), *Gesta Regis Henrici*, vol. 1, p. 6; Johnston (ed.), *Fantosme*, lines 1, 746– 1,892.
71. Chibnall (ed.), *Orderic Vitalis*, vol. 4, pp. 276–7.
72. *The Chronicle of John of Worcester*, ed. R. R. Darlington and P. McGurk, 3 vols (Oxford: Oxford University Press, 1995, 1998), vol. 3, pp. 254–5: I. Blanchard, 'Lothian and beyond: The economy of the "English Empire" of David I', in R. H. Britnell and J. Hatcher (eds), *Progress and Problems in Medieval England* (Cambridge: Cambridge University Press, 1996), pp. 23–45.
73. Stubbs (ed.), *Gesta Regis Henrici*, vol. 1, p. 64.
74. *Acts of the Parliaments of Scotland* [hereafter *APS*], ed. T. Thomson and C. Innes, 12 vols (Edinburgh: n.p., 1814–75), vol. 1, p. 108; Duncan, *Scotland: The Making of the Kingdom*, p. 521.
75. Luard (ed.), *Matthew Paris*, vol. 4, p. 380.
76. Barrow, *The Anglo-Norman Era*, pp. 161–8; Barrow, 'The army of Alexander III', in Reid (ed.), *Scotland in the Reign of Alexander III*, pp. 133–4.
77. Johnston (ed.), *Fantosme*, lines 471–4 and 1,342–3, where he states that in 1174 'the earls of Scotland lead the detestable people whom pity never made refrain from devilries'.
78. Huntingdon, *Historia Anglorum*, pp. 716–17.
79. Aelred of Rievaulx, *Relatio*, pp. 189–90.
80. Richard of Hexham, *De Gestis Regis Stephani*, pp. 155–6; John of Hexham, *Historia*, in Arnold (ed.), *Symeonis Monachi Opera Omnia*, vol. 2, pp. 289, 291; Aelred of Rievaulx, *Relatio*, p. 190; Anderson, *Early Sources*, p. 198.
81. Richard of Hexham, *De Gestis Regis Stephani*, p. 158; John of Hexham, *Historia*, p. 289.
82. Aelred of Rievaulx, *Relatio*, p. 195; Johnston (ed.), *Fantosme*, lines 469 and 1,347–8.

83. Aelred of Rievaulx, *Relatio*, p. 197.
84. Anderson and Anderson (eds), *Chronicle of Melrose*, p. 61; *APS*, vol. 1, p. 339, cl. 33, and vol. 2, p. 45, cl. 3; G. Dickinson, 'Some notes on the Scottish army in the first half of the XVI century', *SHR*, vol. 28 (1949), p. 144 and n.10.
85. Barrow, *Anglo-Norman Era*, p. 168; Barrow (ed.), *Regesta Regum Scottorum, II*, p. 57 and nos 197, 513.
86. C. Innes (ed.), *Registrum de Dunfermelyn* (Edinburgh: Bannatyne Club, 1842), p. 191, no. 301; Barrow (ed.), *Regesta Regum Scottorum, II*, p. 57.
87. Richard of Hexham, *De Gestis Regis Stephani*, p. 152; Aelred of Rievaulx, *Relatio*, pp. 190–1.
88. *APS*, vol. 1, p. 398, cl. 2.
89. See Barrow, 'The army of Alexander III's Scotland', pp. 135–6. The force brought by David I to the aid of his niece, the Empress Matilda, at the siege of Winchester in 1141 can only have comprised his household knights and some of his military tenants, *Gesta Stephani*, ed. K. R. Potter and R. H. C. Davis (Oxford: Clarendon Press, 1976), pp. 128–9, 134–5.
90. Anderson and Anderson (eds), *Chronicle of Melrose*, p. 63; Duncan, *Scotland: The Making of the Kingdom*, p. 523.
91. Stringer, 'Kingship, conflict and state-making', pp. 121, 127–9. We should note here the implication that Alexander had access to first-rate intelligence of John's movements. The expense of the expedition into England, however, forced the king to raise an aid, paid in hides, some of which may have been seized from Scottish burgesses, C. Innes (ed.), *Liber S. Thome de Aberbrothoc* [hereafter *Arbroath Liber*], 2 vols (Edinburgh: Bannatyne Club, 1848–56), vol. 1, no. 110; Duncan, *Scotland: The Making of the Kingdom*, p. 523.
92. *Rotuli litterarum clausarum in Turri Londinensi asservati*, ed. T. D. Hardy, 2 vols (London: Eyre and Spottiswoode, 1833–44), vol. 1, p. 131; Anderson, *Early Sources*, vol. 2, p. 392.
93. *Brut Y Tywysogion or The Chronicle of the Princes. Peniarth MS. 20 Version*, trans. T. Jones (Cardiff: University of Wales Press, 1952), pp. 37–8; J. E. Lloyd, *A History of Wales*, 2 vols (London: Longmans, 1911), vol. 2, p. 463.
94. J. W. ab Ithel (ed.), *Annales Cambriae* (London: Rolls Series, 1860), p. 50, s.a. 1166; *Brut y Tywysogion*, s.a. 1163.
95. Hence King John's order to Alan of Galloway concerning the Galwegians sent to him in 1212: 'Place over them such an officer as shall keep peace with our army, and shall know how to oppress our enemies' (*Rotuli litterarum clausarum*, ed. Hardy, vol. 1, p. 131).

96. A. Macquarrie, *Scotland and the Crusades, 1095–1560* (Edinburgh: John Donald, 1985), p. 19.
97. Aelred of Rievaulx, *Relatio*, p. 186; W. M. Aird, '"Sweet civility and barbarous rudeness": A view from the frontier: Abbot Ailred of Rievaulx and the Scots', in S. G. Ellis and L. Klúsaková (eds), *Imagining Frontiers, Contesting Identities* (Pisa: Edizioni Plus, 2007), pp. 49–73.
98. Aelred of Rievaulx, *Relatio*, p. 186.
99. Huntingdon, *Historia Anglorum*, pp. 714–15; Johnston (ed.), *Fantosme*, line 475, 'nue gent', and line 569 'od armee gent et nue'.
100. Luard (ed.), *Matthew Paris*, vol. 4, p. 653; Anderson, *Scottish Annals*, p. 359. Earl Roger, who had married one of the daughters of Alan of Galloway, is depicted in just such equipment, both mounted and on foot, on his fine seal (c. 1234), *Catalogue of Seals in the Public Record Office. Personal Seals, Volume II*, ed. R. H. Ellis (London: HMSO, 1981), p. 87, no. P1916, and plate 25.
101. Barrow, 'The army of Alexander III's Scotland', pp. 134–5.
102. Anderson, *Early Sources*, vol. 2, p. 630.
103. D. C. Nicolle, *Arms and Armour of the Crusading Era, 1050–1350*, 2 vols (New York: Kraus, 1988), vol. 1, p. 388, and vol. 2, p. 840, nos 1,021–2.
104. D. H. Caldwell, 'Some notes on Scottish axes and long shafted weapons', in D. H. Caldwell (ed.), *Scottish Weapons and Fortifications, 1100–1800* (Edinburgh: John Donald, 1981), pp. 253–314; A. Mahr, 'The Galloglach axe', *Journal of the Galway Archaeological and Historical Society*, vol. 18 (1938–9), pp. 66–8.
105. D. H. Caldwell, M. A. Hall and C. M. Wilkinson, 'The Lewis hoard of gaming pieces: A re-examination of their context, meanings, discovery and manufacture', *Medieval Archaeology*, vol. 53 (2009), pp. 155–203; D. H. Caldwell, M. A. Hall and C. M. Wilkinson, *The Lewis Chessmen Unmasked* (Edinburgh: National Museums of Scotland, 2010), pp. 37–8.
106. *Radulphi de Diceto Decani Londoniensis Opera Historica*, ed. W. Stubbs, 2 vols (London: Rolls Series, 1876), vol. 1, p. 376; Barrow, 'The army of Alexander III's Scotland', p. 144, n. 23.
107. Aelred of Rievaulx, *Relatio*, p. 186.
108. As the *Chronicon de Lanercost*, p. 233, remarked: 'iron is scarce in Scotland'.
109. Hence Gerald of Wales noted in the 1190s that they were also the traditional weapon of the men of Gwynedd, and that when thrown at short range they could penetrate a mail hauberk, J. S. Brewer, J. F. Dimock and G. F. Warner (eds), *Giraldus Cambrensis Opera*, 8 vols (London: Rolls Series, 1861–91), vol. 6, p. 123.

110. Aelred of Rievaulx, *Relatio*, p. 196.
111. Huntingdon, *Historia Anglorum*, pp. 716–17; Anderson, *Scottish Annals*, p. 202, n. 5.
112. Luard (ed.), *Matthew Paris*, vol. 4, p. 380.
113. Barrow (ed.), *Regesta Regum Scottorum, II*, pp. 57, 453–4 (no. 499); Innes (ed.), *Arbroath Liber*, vol. 1, no. 5.
114. D. H. Caldwell, 'The Monymusk reliquary: The *Breccbennach* of St Columba?', *Proceedings of the Society of Antiquaries of Scotland*, vol. 131 (2001), pp. 267–82.
115. Barrow (ed.), *Charters of David*, no. 66; Richard of Hexham, *De Gestis Regis Stephani*, p. 153; John of Hexham, *Historia*, pp. 289–90.
116. Anderson and Anderson (eds), *Chronicle of Melrose*, pp. 63, 84.
117. D. Hay, 'Booty in Border warfare', *Transactions of the Dumfriesshire and Galloway Natural History Society*, vol. 31 (1954), p. 146.
118. *APS*, vol. 2, pp. 44–5. By the fifteenth century, there was apparently a link between shares of spoil and the extent of a soldier's equipment, *APS*, vol. 2, p. 716b; Hay, 'Booty in Border warfare', pp. 160–1.
119. Hay, 'Booty in Border warfare', p. 148.
120. Richard of Hexham, *De Gestis Regis Stephani*, pp. 156–7.
121. Ibid. pp. 155–6.
122. *John of Worcester*, ed. Darlington and McGurk, vol. 3, p. 68.
123. Aelred of Rievaulx, *Relatio*, pp. 189–90.
124. Richard of Hexham, *De Gestis Regis Stephani*, pp. 165–6.
125. J. Gillingham, 'The beginnings of English imperialism', *Journal of Historical Sociology*, vol. 5 (1992), pp. 392–409, and J. Gillingham, 'Conquering the Barbarians', *The Haskins Society Journal*, vol. 4 (1992), pp. 67–84, with both papers reprinted in J. Gillingham, *The English in the Twelfth Century* (Woodbridge: Boydell and Brewer, 2000), pp. 3–18, 41–58.
126. *Gesta Stephani*, ed. Potter and Davis, pp. 54–5.
127. *Fordun*, ed. Skene, vol. 1, p. 262, and vol. 2, pp. 257–8; D. Broun, 'Attitudes of *Gall* to *Gaedhel* in Scotland before John Fordun', in D. Broun and M. MacGregor (eds), *Mìorun Mòr nan Gall, 'The Great Ill-Will of the Lowlander'? Lowland Perceptions of the Highlands, Medieval and Modern* (Glasgow: Centre for Scottish and Celtic Studies, University of Glasgow, 2009), pp. 74–7.
128. Aelred of Rievaulx, *Relatio*, p. 187; Richard of Hexham, *De Gestis Regis Stephani*, p. 152; Luard (ed.), *Matthew Paris*, vol. 3, p. 365.
129. The Chevalier de Johnstone, *Memoirs of the Rebellion in 1745*, cited in H. McCorry (ed.), *The Thistle at War: An Anthology of the Scottish Experience of War in the Services and at Home* (Edinburgh: National Museums of Scotland, 1997), p. 9. As the woman told Lochiel, 'every-

body said that the Highlanders ate children and made them their common food', ibid. p. 9.
130. Richard of Hexham, *De Gestis Regis Stephani*, pp. 151–2.
131. For the wider context of these changes, see M. J. Strickland, 'Rules of war or war without rules? Some reflections on conduct and the treatment of non-combatants in medieval transcultural wars', in *Transcultural Wars from the Middle Ages to the Twenty-First Century*, ed. H. H. Kortüm (Hamburger Institut für Sozialforschung and the University of Regensburg, 2005), pp. 107–40.
132. Richard of Hexham, *De Gestis Regis Stephani*, pp. 170–1; Anderson, *Scottish Annals from English Chroniclers*, pp. 211–12.
133. Nevertheless, Alexander II was careful not to deploy Galwegian troops during his incursions into northern England in 1215–17, doubtless fearing that their excesses would alienate his allies there, Stringer, 'Kingship, conflict and state-making', pp. 125–6.
134. J. Lydon, 'The Scottish soldier in medieval Ireland: The Bruce invasion and the Galloglass', in G. G. Simpson (ed.), *The Scottish Soldier Abroad, 1247–1967* (Edinburgh: John Donald, 1992), p. 4.
135. *A Celtic Miscellany*, ed. K. H. Jackson (Harmondsworth: Penguin, 1971), pp. 239–410.
136. Richard of Hexham, *De Gestis Regis Stephani*, pp. 171–2.
137. Johnston (ed.), *Fantosme*, lines 1780, 1848–85.
138. *Continuatio Beccensis*, in Howlett (ed.), *Chronicles*, vol. 4, p. 323; A. C. Lawrie, *Annals of the Reigns of Malcolm IV and William, Kings of Scotland, AD 1153–1214* (Glasgow: James Maclehose & Sons, 1910), pp. 43–4. For the great significance of dubbing to knighthood within chivalric culture, see M. Keen, *Chivalry* (New Haven, CT and London: Yale University Press, 1984), pp. 64–82.
139. C. Edington, 'The tournament in Scotland', in M. J. Strickland (ed.), *Armies, Chivalry and Warfare in Medieval Britain and France. Proceedings of the 1995 Harlaxton Symposium* (Stamford: Paul Watkins, 1998), pp. 46–62.
140. Keen, *Chivalry*, pp. 83–101; D. Crouch, *Tournament* (London: Hambledon, 2005).
141. J. Malden, 'Alexander II and the double tressure', in Oram (ed.), *The Reign of Alexander III*, pp. 214–15. In heraldic terminology, the royal arms of Scotland thus became *Or, a lion rampant Gules armed and langued Azure within a double tressure flory counter-flory Gules*.
142. Cruden, *The Scottish Castle*, pp. 18, 40, 64–83; C. Tabraham, *Scottish Castles and Fortifications* (Edinburgh: HMSO, 1986), pp. 35–9. For Coucy, built between 1225 and 1242 by Enguerrand III, whose daughter Marie had married King Alexander II in 1239, see J. Mesqui,

Châteaux forts et fortifications en France (Paris: Flammarion, 1997), pp. 135–8.
143. Stringer, 'Periphery and core', pp. 82–113.
144. Guillaume le Clerc, *Fergus of Galloway, Knight of King Arthur*, trans. D. D. R. Owen (London: Dent, 1991). On the romance of Fergus, see D. D. R. Owen, *William the Lion: Kingship and Culture, 1143–1214* (East Linton: Tuckwell Press, 1997), pp. 114–53.
145. Nicolle, *Arms and Armour*, vol. 1, p. 389, and vol. 2, p. 841, no. 1029 (Roland), and no. 1027 (Mentieth).
146. R. A. McDonald, 'Images of Hebridean lordship in the late twelfth and early thirteenth centuries: The seal of Raonall Mac Sorley', *SHR*, vol. 74 (1995), pp. 129–30.
147. Anderson, *Early Sources*, vol. 2, p. 632.
148. Anderson and Anderson (eds), *Chronicle of Melrose*, p. 123.
149. H. R. Luard (ed.), *Flores Historiarum*, 3 vols (London: Rolls Series, 1890), vol. 2, pp. 488, 496. When the following year Henry's son, Edward, took bloody revenge at the battle of Evesham among those who were ruthlessly slain with De Montfort was his standard bearer, the Scottish knight Guy de Balliol, Anderson and Anderson (eds), *Chronicle of Melrose*, p. 131.

4
The Wars of Independence, 1296–1328

MICHAEL PRESTWICH

The first stage of the Wars of Independence was one of astonishing success for the Scots. The English war machine, developed during Edward I's conquest of Wales between 1277 and 1295, stuttered and was defeated several times in battle. It failed in face of opponents with far fewer resources in terms of men, material, experience and organisation. Yet much about the nature of the Scottish armies remains obscure; little is known about how they were recruited and deployed. Of their courage and resilience there is no doubt, while their leadership displayed determination and imagination.

The war began in 1296. It was the product of the excessive demands made by Edward I on his client king of Scots, John Balliol, and of the alliance formed between the Scots and the French. Edward's campaign appeared decisive. The Scots were defeated at Dunbar and Edward led his army on a triumphant progress as far as Banff and Elgin. John Balliol, totally discredited, was deprived of his kingship at Montrose. In the following year, however, the Scots, headed by Andrew Murray and William Wallace, achieved a major success at Stirling Bridge, where the victor of Dunbar, Earl Warenne, was roundly defeated. Edward avenged this at Falkirk in 1298, and with campaigns in 1300, 1301 and 1303–4 steadily ground down the Scots. The final act of this phase of the war was the English siege of Stirling castle.

Robert I's seizure of the Scottish throne in 1306 re-ignited the conflict, which soon took on a very different character. After an initial defeat at Methven, Robert tasted success at the battle of Loudoun Hill in 1307, with a victory over another English force three days later. The following years saw remarkable achievements, as one English-held castle after another fell to the Scots. From 1311 the Scots were in a position to take the war to the English, launching devastating raids

Map 4.1 The Wars of Independence, 1296–1328.

Figure 4.1 Robert the Bruce slaying the English knight Sir Henry de Bohun at Bannockburn, 1314. Painted by John Duncan, c. 1914.

into the north of England. At midsummer, 1314, Robert's army won a justly celebrated victory at Bannockburn over Edward II, one of the great medieval triumphs of dismounted and predominantly infantry forces against heavy cavalry. In 1315 a new front was opened when Robert's brother, Edward, launched an invasion of Ireland. Here, successes were limited and in 1318 Edward Bruce was killed at the battle of Faughart.

Meanwhile, the raids into the north of England continued and in 1319 the English failed to recapture Berwick, which they had lost the previous year. A large-scale English invasion of Scotland in 1322 achieved nothing and after he had retreated across the border Edward II was almost captured by a Scottish army at Old Byland in Yorkshire. A truce was finally agreed in 1323, but it was broken on the accession of Edward III to the English throne in 1327. The Scots invaded again, and an English army failed to engage them in battle in Weardale. Finally, by the Treaty of Edinburgh–Northampton in 1328 Bruce gained recognition as king of an independent Scotland. Despite the failure in Ireland, the achievements of the Scots were remarkable. Against all the apparent odds, they had maintained the independence of Scotland and humiliated the English.

The evidence for the Scottish armies of this period is limited. Charters and royal legislation provide some clues about military structures, but there are none of the elaborate pay accounts and horse valuation lists that exist to provide a detailed picture of English forces. Nor are there good contemporary chronicle accounts written in Scotland. The most important narrative source is John Barbour's life of Robert Bruce, written in about 1375, in which the events are viewed through a somewhat distorted lens. Barbour was anxious to depict the achievements of his heroes – Robert I and his celebrated commander, Sir James Douglas (the Black Douglas) – in a chivalrous light. His work was dependent on a number of sources, whose quality varied. Inevitably, he concentrated on the achievements of the great men and revealed little about the ordinary people who made up the bulk of Scottish armies. He enjoyed describing the din of battle, as weapons struck armour, spears were thrust and broken, and blood and brains were spattered. Detailed description of the composition of armies, unsurprisingly, was not a part of his story.[1] English chroniclers provide some information, and an excellent account of the 1327 Scottish invasion of northern England was provided by Jean le Bel, a Hainaulter accompanying the English army.[2]

The cavalry

The cavalry was the elite of a medieval army. The role of traditional cavalry, knights with lance and sword, in Scottish armies of this period has received little emphasis, for it was by fighting on foot that the Scots achieved their successes in battle. At the outset of the war, the Scottish nobility had little military experience. The battle of Dunbar in 1296 was a crushing defeat inflicted by the English under Earl Warenne, a veteran of Edward I's Welsh wars (yet a man who had not himself seen battle since 1265), and it seems that an ill-disciplined cavalry charge, when the Scots wrongly thought the English were in retreat, led to the defeat. Many high-ranking Scots were taken to imprisonment in England. According to the English chronicler Walter of Guisborough, three earls, four barons and thirty-one knights were captured.[3] Following this, it is not surprising that the Scots made little use of cavalry at the battles of Stirling Bridge and Falkirk. At the latter engagement the Scottish horsemen were placed to the rear and fled without striking a blow.[4] This, however, was not the end of cavalry warfare.

An English account of a Scottish ambush near Cupar in Fife describes a pure cavalry action which ended with the English commander, Thomas Gray, capturing 180 horses.[5] There are also many accounts of mounted engagements in Barbour's life of Bruce. It is difficult, however, to tell to what extent the author was transferring the realities of late fourteenth-century warfare back to Robert I's reign, or how far he deliberately exaggerated the role of mounted men in order to enhance the chivalric credibility of his account. In describing Edward Bruce's actions in Galloway in 1308, Barbour depicted him with a force of fifty cavalry, well armed and mounted. He charged an English force, broke through, turned and charged again. Meanwhile, the infantry had been removed to safety.[6] At Bannockburn in 1314, cavalry under Sir Robert Keith, the marischal of Scotland, played an important part in the later stages of the battle, when they were used to rout the English archers.[7] In another battle in Ireland in 1317, Edward Bruce's cavalry were harassed by archers, but the core of the engagement was between the mounted men on both sides. 'Horses came charging there, head to head, so that many fell to the ground.'[8] On a further occasion, Barbour describes the bishop of Dunkeld, William Sinclair, fighting on horseback with a following of some sixty men, routing an English force that had invaded by sea.[9]

The cavalry clearly remained a significant element in Scottish armies, but this was not composed of the heavily armoured knights on great warhorses of France or England. There is no evidence to suggest that the Scots possessed large chargers (*destriers*). These were expensive to buy and costly to keep. Instead, the Scots relied on smaller mounts. At Bannockburn, Robert Keith's men were 'well horsed on light steeds'.[10] In 1327, according to Jean le Bel, the Scots were mounted on what he described as rounceys and hackneys.[11] This was not a disadvantage; indeed, in 1327 the English were encouraged to bring light horses on campaign with them, rather than their great chargers.[12]

Feudal service

There was a traditional feudal obligation to provide cavalry service, which is referred to in a number of charters issued by Robert I. In many cases, grants simply stated that customary service was due, without defining what that service was.[13] The largest quotas were ten knights for Annandale and eight for Moray. These were, however, exceptional regalities (the highest feudal dignity, with extensive rights of jurisdiction); it has been calculated that the average quota for a barony was 0.82 knights.[14] Such a level of service was hardly sufficient to enable Robert I to recruit the cavalry forces he needed, and, as was the case in England, strict feudal obligation represented a somewhat outmoded survival from the past, far more significant in legal and financial terms than in military reality.

It has been argued that by the late thirteenth century strict feudal service had been merged, or was merging, with a much wider obligation owed by the able-bodied population, while at the same time service of archers and others was becoming increasingly feudalised.[15] The evidence here is limited. A formula book contains what is almost certainly a summons issued by the Guardians of Scotland on Alexander III's death in 1286. This mentions 'free service', and 'Scottish service', adding with a note of some desperation 'any other service'. All who owed service of whatever type were required to be ready at twenty-four hours' notice, and to bring foodstuffs with them for a period of forty days.[16] 'Free service' is probably to be equated with knight service, and 'Scottish service' to a more general duty, but how far such a summons as this effectively merged the two is not clear. What was the case was that the old-fashioned knight service was increasingly irrelevant, and that in times of emergency a general appeal of arms was what was needed. There is no evidence to show that, as in England, lords brought much larger contingents with them than their formal quotas, but this seems highly probable. Barbour describes the way in which some of the major lords came to fight at Bannockburn with substantial retinues.[17]

The common soldier

Descriptions of the Scottish common soldiers, who played such a major part in the Scottish triumphs of this period, are few. The author of the *Life of Edward II* described them at Bannockburn. Every infantryman was in light armour and had an axe to his side; spears were wielded as they advanced in tight formation.[18] Barbour also refers to axes and spears as the main infantry weapons; in his description of Bannockburn he also mentions the role of Scottish archers.[19] Legislation in 1318 set out the requirements for the military equipment that everyone who had goods worth ten pounds should possess for the defence of the realm. This was a haketon (or padded tunic), a bascinet (or light helmet) and gauntlets. Lance and sword were also required. Should anyone not possess haketon and bascinet, some other form of body armour and an iron cap would suffice. Anyone possessing goods to the value of one cow should have a spear, or a bow with a quiver containing two dozen arrows.[20] Such regulations were similar to the English assize of arms, and cannot have been enforceable; rather, they help to provide some indication of how Robert I would have liked to see his soldiers equipped. In practice, the bulk of the common soldiers would have had no armour and only rudimentary weapons.

The legislation made no reference to the fact that ordinary soldiers might be mounted. One of the features of the armies of this period was the use of hobelars, men lightly armed with sword and lance, who rode nimble, inexpensive mounts. Such men were initially recruited in Ireland, but were soon to be found in the north of England.[21] It has been suggested that the Scots copied this, and made use of hobelars themselves.[22] Although many of those who raided England were mounted on small horses, however, the word hobelar was not applied to Scottish troops. When it came to set-piece battle, as at Myton in 1319 or Byland in 1322, the Scots would dismount and fight in familiar manner, whereas the true hobelar fought on horseback.

Very little is known about how the common soldiers were recruited. There was a general obligation to serve in what was termed 'the army of Scotland', which clearly worked well in times of national emergency. In 1306 Robert Bruce charged those who had done fealty to him to be ready to go on campaign, taking sufficient victuals for nine days, at twenty-four hours' notice.[23] This may well have represented traditional practice. Recruitment could be very effective. Documents from Coldingham priory show that a large number of tenants, perhaps as many as sixty, fought for the Scots at Falkirk in 1298.[24] Lands at nearby Ayton, held by Walter of Upsetlington and worth 13s. 4d., were noted as being forfeited 'because he was killed at Falkirk'.[25] Armies were recruited from the townspeople as well as from the countryside. In a parliament held at Inchture in 1312 it was laid down that the burghs could only negotiate over military service with the Chamberlain of Scotland or his deputies.[26] An undated summons, from the fourteenth century, asked for 120 men from a town, whose name is not given, to serve for sixty days.[27]

The regulations of 1318 made no mention of archers, but there were some in Scottish armies. At Falkirk in 1298 archers stood between the solid ranks of the schiltroms. One group was recruited from Selkirk Forest.[28] At Bannockburn, according to Barbour, the Scottish archers, although far outnumbered by their English equivalents, did much damage to the English cavalry.[29] In 1317, at Lintalee, if Barbour's account of the engagement is to be believed, an important part was played by the Scottish archers, demoralising the English before the hand-to-hand fighting began.[30] It is striking that in a number of grants of land from this period the service of archers was stipulated. This made excellent sense: Robert I was anxious to improve his armies and this was an arm that needed reinforcement. The largest number of archers required was ten, from the barony of Manor in Peeblesshire, which in the thirteenth century had been held for one knight.³¹ Other charters specified much smaller numbers. In 1325 William de St Clair received the barony of Cessford for the service of four archers.³² Richard Yung, barber, received Thornton in Angus for the service of one archer.³³ David Graham also owed service of a single archer by a grant of 1326, and William Olifant three archers for Auchtertyre in Angus.³⁴ One charter specified half the service of an archer.³⁵ The scale of these grants was not such as to suggest the introduction of a form of military service that transformed Scottish armies; they are, however, a reflection of the realities of early fourteenth-century warfare. The evidence suggests that feudal service, at least in the form of archers, was still a reality in Scotland, and that it had not been commuted into a form of taxation.³⁶

There is nothing in the surviving sources to indicate that any of those who served in Scottish armies were paid. This, however, is not the sort of information that chronicles would provide and unfortunately there are no surviving accounts. It is very probable that men were persuaded to serve voluntarily at their own expense, in some cases to assist in a time of national emergency, in others in the expectation of gaining booty from raids into England. Nevertheless, pay should not be ruled out. Exchequer records show that the earl of Menteith had maintained a force of 120 men in Ayr castle in 1263 and that other payments were made to troops at that time.³⁷ The fact that similar records do not survive for the period of John Balliol, the Guardians and Robert I does not mean that no payments were made to Scottish troops.

Logistics

The size of Scottish armies can only be guessed at for this period. Barbour's statement that Bruce had 80,000 men in 1322 has to be disbelieved, and his figure of 30,000 men at Bannockburn, while more credible, is unlikely to have had any real foundation.³⁸ It is possible to calculate the numbers in English armies from pay records, and to show, for example, that Edward I had about 25,700 men at Falkirk in 1298.³⁹ This was almost certainly the largest single army of this period, and was very substantially greater than any the Scots could put into the field. It is obviously dangerous to extrapolate from the numbers of English troops, but they provide an order of magnitude. The most plausible guess puts the size of the Scottish army at Bannockburn at between 7,000 and 10,000, of whom between 5,000 and 6,000 were actually engaged in the fighting.⁴⁰ This is, however, no more than a guess. Most Scottish forces will have been much smaller than this.

Food supply was always an issue for armies, but there is little indication of the measures taken by the Scots in this period to provide much-needed victuals. In the legislation of 1318 lords were required to attend with sufficient carriage and supplies to meet their needs. If they came from too far away to be able to bring food with them, they were to have sufficient money with them to buy what they needed.[41] This was highly optimistic. The crown could use a power of compulsory purchase of food supplies to assist in the task of supplying armies. Exemption from prise, as this power was termed, was clearly worth possessing and was granted in many charters. In 1326 the king agreed to end the practice, save for the traditional requirements of his own household.[42] Such a concession was easier to make in time of truce than during a period of open warfare.

Command

Medieval armies did not have complex command structures and relied heavily on the single individual in charge. It was highly unusual for a man to emerge from obscurity to become a major military leader; William Wallace was exceptional. Indeed, it was extraordinary for a man whose expertise was not that of a mounted knight, but that of a bowman, to emerge, as he did, as commander of an army.[43] His rise reflects Wallace's personal charisma, and also perhaps an element of social revolution in the rising he led. Yet Wallace had no successors. After him, leadership reverted to noble hands, to members of a new nobility created by Robert I.

Robert's brother, Edward, was, unsurprisingly, given important commands. He took charge of a partially successful campaign in Galloway in 1308, and conducted the siege of Stirling, which led to the battle of Bannockburn. At that engagement he commanded one of the divisions of the army.[44] His major role, however, came with the invasion of Ireland in 1315. Edward emerges from the pages of Barbour's *Bruce* as a chivalrous hero, worthy of comparison with Judas Maccabeus. His marital misadventures, though, which saw him discard Isabella of Atholl in favour of Isabella Ross, did him little credit.[45] Edward was the least successful of the Scottish commanders of this period, although he was unfortunate in the problems he faced in Ireland which were as much political as military. He had an impetuous side to his character, which contrasted with his brother Robert I's wiser disposition.

Figure 4.2 William Wallace portrayed in a stained glass window designed by James Ballantyne & Son, 1886, at the National Wallace Monument, Stirling.

Thomas Randolph was the son of Robert I's half-sister and in 1312 was created earl of Moray. He led the Scots in the capture of Edinburgh castle that year. Subsequently he commanded one of the divisions at Bannockburn and he led troops both in Ireland and in raids into England. After Edward Bruce's death at Faughart in 1318, Moray became the most important Scottish commander after the king himself. It was his force that won the battle of Myton in 1319 and he played a leading part in the defeat of Edward II's army at Byland in 1322. Moray's virtues were described by Barbour, but in such conventional terms that the real abilities of the man remain hidden. He was said to have been of moderate height, with a broad, pleasant face. He was always courteous, and loved loyalty, exalting honour and generosity.[46] His role in the wars was central, but it is somewhat obscured by the emphasis that Barbour places on another of Robert I's commanders, James Douglas.

Pale and black-haired, Douglas had, according to Barbour, a record of fifty-seven victories to thirteen losses. Barbour makes much of him; after Robert I himself, he is the hero of his book. Douglas was a man to lead by example, but that example might be one of brutality. The 'Douglas Larder' of 1308 famously demonstrated this: he beheaded his prisoners and mixed their blood with the foodstuffs in the cellar of Douglas castle so that 'meal and malt and blood and wine all ran together in a mush that was disgusting to see'.[47] His capture of Roxburgh castle in 1314 was a particularly notable feat and he was knighted on the eve of Bannockburn, where he served under Edward Bruce. As the war continued, Douglas took an increasingly important military role, though on the 1319 raid which culminated in victory at Myton he was subordinate to Moray.[48] At Byland in 1322, when the Scots came close to capturing Edward II, Douglas and Moray advanced side by side in a narrow pass.[49] In 1327 Douglas led the Scots army that raided the north of England, along with Moray, Earl Donald of Mar, James Stewart and his brother Archibald Douglas.[50] Here he showed that he was capable of acting with caution; according to Barbour, it was he who was responsible for leading the Scottish army away from the English host in 1327, so avoiding the risk of battle.[51]

In avoiding battle, James Douglas was following an established strategy. The Scots had learned some hard lessons in the early years of the war. In 1296 their ill-disciplined army had proved no match for an English force under Earl Warenne at Dunbar. Success at Stirling Bridge in 1297 was followed by Wallace's disastrous defeat at Falkirk in the following year. Battle was clearly a risky strategy, and after

Figure 4.3 Stirling castle: the strategic key to central Scotland.

1298 Scottish commanders avoided engaging large invading English armies. Robert I was prepared to meet an English force under Aymer de Valence at Loudoun Hill in 1307, but this was little more than a skirmish, for Valence's was not a full-scale invading army. The exception to the rule was Bannockburn. This was the result of a deal struck by Edward Bruce, probably in May 1314: if besieged Stirling castle were not relieved by the English before midsummer, it would be surrendered to the Scots. This set up a challenge to the English. The Scots must have thought it unlikely that an English army could be recruited in time to attempt this, but they were mistaken and Robert I was faced with no option other than to fight.[52] The triumph at Bannockburn did not persuade Robert that he should aim to confront the English in battle again. In 1319, rather than challenge the English force besieging Berwick, the Scots launched a diversionary raid into England. In 1322 they withdrew in face of a large invading force, emptying the land in a highly effective strategy, so that the English ran desperately short of supplies. Edward Bruce, however, was not persuaded that battle was best avoided; his Irish campaign stood in contrast to his brother's strategy, and battle took place at Connor in 1315, at Ardscull early in 1316 and, disastrously, at Faughart in 1318.

Battle

The battles that were fought by the Scots were characterised by the success of their infantry forces against the heavy cavalry of the English. The all-conquering mounted knight had met his match. There is no simple explanation for this. In the great Scottish successes they had the advantage of favourable terrain. At Stirling Bridge they were able to surprise Warenne's army before it had completed the crossing of the bridge and rushed down from a height onto the hapless and unprepared English. Yet the victory can be attributed at least as much to English stupidity as to Scots bravery and skill.[53] At Loudoun Hill, Robert I also chose his ground carefully. A road ran over a wide field, with boggy ground to either side. The Scots cut deep ditches at right angles to the road, to block the English cavalry's advance and to funnel them towards a gap where they met the Scottish spearmen.[54] At Bannockburn the Scots were similarly able to dictate where the fighting took place. The terrain was unsuitable for cavalry and, to make matters worse for the English, parts of the battlefield were carefully prepared with pits to trip the horses as they charged.[55]

Battlefield tactics were dominated by the use of the schiltrom. According to the chronicler Walter of Guisborough, at Falkirk in 1298 William Wallace organised his troops in these tight circular formations. The men were held in place by ropes and each schiltrom, with firmly held lances projecting all round, presented a fierce obstacle to the English.[56] 'I have brought you to the ring, now hop if you can' were Wallace's words, no doubt more inspiring on the day than they appear now in print.[57] At Falkirk the schiltroms were motionless, awaiting the English attack; at Bannockburn, however, Bruce showed that these dense infantry formations could be manoeuvred tactically on the field of battle. There is nothing to suggest that the use of the schiltrom was a traditional Scottish tactic; rather, it was a highly intelligent response to the problem of how to deal effectively with the English armies and their weight of cavalry. Nor is it clear that the schiltrom necessarily took the circular shape adopted, without eventual success, at Falkirk. It is more likely that the term was used for any tightly packed infantry force, and that this might take different forms. On the first day of Bannockburn Moray ordered his men to form a schiltrom so as to deal with Clifford's cavalry force: 'Don't be afraid of their menace, but set your spears before you, and form yourselves up back to back, with all the spears pointed outwards.'[58]

There is regrettably little information about the battle tactics used by the Scots in Ireland. According to Barbour, at Ardscull the Scots all fought on foot. The Anglo-Irish were mounted, but Scottish spearmen proved more than equal to the task of dealing with their charge.[59] Accounts of Edward Bruce's defeat at Faughart are, however, too imprecise and, in some cases, fanciful for any proper analysis. Barbour, for example, includes the extraordinary story of how Edward's minstrel, Gib Harpour, wore his master's armour, and so was mistaken for him. It was therefore Gib's head, not Edward's, that was sent in triumph to Edward II, salted and in a box.[60]

Much of the warfare of this period was characterised by small-scale skirmishes and ambushes, many of which have left little historical record. The author of the *Life of Edward II* describes the way in which Robert I's men were concealed in caves and woodland and suddenly emerged to slaughter a party of English and Welsh foragers.[61] It was in an ambush in 1303 at Roslin that the cofferer of Edward I's wardrobe, Ralph Manton, was killed. Sir John de Segrave, the king's lieutenant in Scotland, was fortunate to escape.[62] In 1317 James Douglas ambushed an English force at Lintalee, near Jedburgh.[63] In another engagement, Robert Neville, 'the peacock of the north', was killed.[64] In 1322 Douglas again ambushed an English force of hobelars near Melrose, when they were out foraging. As a result of this action, no one dared to leave the main army in search of food.[65] In this guerrilla warfare the Scots had the advantage of knowing the terrain, and, as success followed on success, of superior morale.

Castles

The English hold on Scotland under Edward I depended very considerably on the castles that they held. Most notable were those of Edinburgh and Stirling; Lochmaben and Caerlaverock in the southwest; and Berwick, Jedburgh and Roxburgh on the border in the east. North of the Forth the English garrisoned few castles, relying instead on Scottish allies. For the Scots, the capture of English-held castles was essential. They lacked the capacity for traditional siege warfare, however, and had few siege engines to deploy.[66] The Scots were able to force the surrender of some powerful castles by means of lengthy blockade and starvation, such as at Stirling in 1299 and Carrickfergus in Ireland in 1316.[67] But when it came to besieging Carlisle in 1315 the great movable siege tower they constructed became bogged down and could not be shifted up to the walls. The stone-throwing trebuchet they erected, illustrated in a Carlisle charter, was similarly ineffective.[68] Some castles proved impregnable. Norham resisted all efforts of the Scots despite lengthy sieges. Even when the outer bailey fell

Figure 4.4 The Scottish siege of Carlisle in 1315, as depicted in a later drawing of the decorated opening initial of Edward II's charter to the city rewarding its successful defence. The Scots, whose lack of armour is clearly shown, attempt to undermine the walls with picks and prepare to fire a trebuchet or counter-weight siege engine.

through treachery, the inner bailey and the keep remained in English hands.[69]

Despite their limitations in siege technology, in the years leading up to Bannockburn the Scots under Robert I and James Douglas nevertheless achieved astounding successes in taking English-held castles, using equipment no more sophisticated than rope ladders. When the English saw examples of these, left after an unsuccessful attempt on Berwick in 1312, they were astonished by the ingenious way they were constructed.[70] In 1307 Robert took Inverlochy, and razed Inverness, Nairn and Urquhart. Other castles in the north offered little resistance. The English-held castles in southern Scotland were more formidable, but still fell like skittles. Barbour had remarkable stories to tell, and while there must be some literary exaggeration in his account, it is clear that time and again the English failed to deal with surprise attacks. The Scots first took Douglas castle by disguising themselves as traders with pack-horses; on a second occasion they attacked the garrison when it had come out to attend church on Palm Sunday.[71] Forfar fell to a simple assault with ladders.[72] At Linlithgow a local man, William Bunnock, led his cart through the castle gate. Soldiers were concealed under the load and, as the cart entered the castle, the traces were cut. The men jumped out and after a brief fight the castle fell into their hands.[73] At Roxburgh Douglas and his men advanced at dead of night to the castle walls, carrying rope ladders and going on all fours so that the watchmen thought that they were cattle.[74] Edinburgh fell to a small group who climbed up the great rock on which the castle stands. The route was identified by William Francis, who had been a member of the garrison in his youth and had used it to get in and out in search of an amorous liaison in the town. Moray was the third man to reach the top.[75] The Scots had little option other than to utilise these methods of surprise attack; but what they did amounted to a revolution in castle warfare. As success after success was achieved, the English must have been increasingly demoralised and reluctant to offer sterner resistance.

Once the castles were taken from the English, there was the question of what to do with them. The Scots did not have the men or the resources to maintain effective garrisons and so the strategy was to slight them. Robert Bruce used the tactic early: after Falkirk, Edward I marched to Ayr, only to find the castle empty and burned.[76] After Linthithgow was taken, the king 'had it knocked to the ground'. At Roxburgh, Edward Bruce came 'with a large company, and made them work so hard that tower and wall were knocked to the ground in a short time'.[77] An English chronicler explained that 'all that beautiful castle the Scots pulled down to the ground, like the other castles that they had succeeded in capturing, lest the English should ever again rule the land by holding the castles'.[78] These were extreme measures: the demilitarisation of castles meant that one possible defence against English invasion was removed. The calculation was clear, however. The danger that the castles represented when they were in English hands was greater than any advantage that they might give to the Scots.[79]

Raids

Raiding northern England was central to Scottish strategy from the outset of the war. The chronicler Jean le Bel, a Hainaulter who accompanied the English army on the campaign in Weardale of 1327, provides a celebrated description of a Scottish raiding force. The soldiers were all mounted, the knights and squires on substantial rounceys and the remainder on small hackneys. There was no baggage train, for where possible they relied on eating captured cattle, the meat being boiled in the animals' hides. When this upset their stomachs, they made oatcakes on heated griddles, using supplies of oatmeal brought with them in saddle-bags. Speed was vital for such a force; it moved rapidly through the north of England, burning and ravaging as it went.[80]

Scottish raids began at the outset of the war in 1296. At this stage many of the troops were on foot. The first incursion saw seven earls leading an army to Carlisle. This was followed up by a more devastating attack on Northumberland. English propaganda emphasised the horrors of the raids, reporting such events as the alleged burning alive of two hundred children by blocking the doors of their school and setting it alight.[81] Wallace's incursion in the autumn of 1297 brought fire and sword to a swathe of territory extending from Cockermouth to the east coast. He offered protection to Hexham priory, but he could not control his followers who were set on robbing a wealthy church.[82]

In the latter years of Edward I's reign the Scots were in no position to invade England, faced as they were by major English attacks, but from 1311 raiding began again in earnest. In that year there were two incursions; in one of them, Robert Bruce 'burned all the land of the lord of Gilsland and the vill of Haltwhistle and a great part of Tynedale, and after eight days he returned to Scotland, taking with him a great booty of animals'.[83] In 1312 a further raid saw Corbridge and Hexham burned, and much of the city of Durham sacked on market day. There, as elsewhere, the castle proved no protection. The best solution for the English was to buy truces, but this merely encouraged further raids when a truce ended. The pattern of raids and truces continued, though the invasion of Ireland in 1315 by Edward Bruce distracted the Scots from the north of England to some extent.

In 1318 and 1319 raids came further south into Yorkshire and Lancashire. Though the Scottish strategy was not intended to goad the English into battle, in 1319 they defeated a motley force at Myton, close to York. The raiders, mounted on light horses, moved too quickly to be caught by English forces and were able to ride where they chose at will. It was highly unusual for five Scots to be captured in 1316 or 1317, as they were, by Roger Mauduit as they plundered Tynedale.[84] Castles were no obstacles. In 1322 Edward II rebuked the constables of the powerful northern castles of Warkworth, Dunstanburgh and Bamburgh for their inactivity, but there was, in reality, little that they could do. In 1327 Edward III's troops pursued the Scots army under Moray and Douglas, the route marked by burning villages. Hopes that they had cornered the Scots were, however, in vain; rather than risk battle, Moray, Mar and Douglas's men made a rapid exit by night from their encampment overlooking the Wear.[85]

There is no doubt that the impact of these raids on England was serious, but it is not possible in any overall assessment to distinguish between the effects of Scottish actions and those of the famine of 1315–16. Nor can the profit that the Scots made from a combination of booty and tribute be calculated; to assume that the £20,000 promised by the Scots in 1328, in return for peace and a marriage settlement, represented the sum that they had exacted from the north makes no sense.[86] The proceeds of truces alone probably came to over £20,000. But the money raised was vital to the Scots. It meant that the war against the English was effectively self-financing. Bruce did not need to tax his people.

Chivalry

Despite Barbour's attempts to cast a chivalric light on the careers of Robert I and James Douglas, this war was not characterised by courtesy and the pursuit of individual feats of arms. There was much about it that was certainly not chivalric. English tales about William Wallace depicted him as what in modern times would be termed a war criminal. That he forced naked English men and women to sing for him in a mixed choir was one of the milder charges against him. The body of Edward I's official, Hugh Cressingham, for example, was skinned after the battle of Stirling Bridge so as to provide the Scots with convenient mementoes. After the engagement at Lintalee, James Douglas is said to have beheaded an English clerk, Elias, and shoved his face up his backside.[87] Nor, of course, were the Scots alone in being guilty of atrocities. Edward I treated his opponents with savagery after Robert I's seizure of the Scottish throne, even imprisoning Robert's sister, Mary, and the countess of Buchan in cages. For him, the Scots were rebels, not to be treated as equals.

Nevertheless, as the war proceeded it made increasing sense for both sides to adopt the normal conventions of the time. For the Scots, the war was one between two equal nations, in which case the accepted laws of war should apply. For the English, it was foolish to mistreat the Scots in case the latter reciprocated in kind. Accordingly, most prisoners taken at Bannockburn were ransomed. Ralph Neville, for example, was charged a ransom of 2,000 marks. Meanwhile, the earl of Hereford was exchanged for Bruce's womenfolk and the bishop of Glasgow, while five Scottish knights were freed in exchange for John de Segrave.[88] The distinguished English knight Marmaduke Thweng, and Ralph de Monthermer, who had formerly been the king's lieutenant in Scotland, were simply released.[89] Similarly, Robert I freed the French noble Henry de Sully, who was captured at Byland in 1322, without demanding any ransom.[90]

Discipline

Discipline was hard to maintain in a medieval army, and there is nothing to suggest that the Scots had found the answer to this problem. Wallace, as we have seen, was unable to deal as effectively as he wished with looters at Hexham priory.[91] The legislation of 1318 contains indications of some of the disciplinary problems that might occur. Those on their way to a muster might commit homicide, rape or theft on their route and it was made clear that they should not be exempt from punishment. They might also seize food as they travelled – the solution being that they should provide properly for themselves, either by bringing food with them or by paying for what they took.[92] Yet when the Scots took Berwick in 1318, it proved impossible to restrain the troops from running amok through the town, desperate to acquire booty.[93]

Naval warfare

The war had a significant naval dimension. Although Robert I owned a 'great ship', there was, in contrast to England, no Scottish royal fleet in this period.[94] The crown did have the right to summon naval service, though this was confined to the west coast. During Robert's reign, more ancient obligations of ship service and their means of assessment were increasingly replaced by the definition of lords' estates as fiefs, held of the crown for a stipulated number of galleys.[95] A charter records that in 1315 Colin Campbell, son of Neil Campbell of Lochawe, held by barony for the service of a ship with forty oars. Similarly, Duncan Campbell held by barony for a ship of twenty-six oars,[96] and no doubt there were many others who owed similar ship service. In addition, it would of course have been possible to commandeer ships for naval duties, though the scale on which this took place is not known. Numbers of ships were, however, not large. The figure of 300 vessels taking Edward Bruce to Ireland is hardly to be credited; more plausible is that of the four ships that came to his rescue when he needed to cross the River Bann.[97]

It was in the west that naval activity was most important. The ships used here were usually described as galleys; these were almost certainly oared vessels of Viking type, also known as birlinns.[98] There was a need to prevent the English from receiving assistance from Ireland, and to control those chieftains in the Isles who saw an alliance with Edward I and his son as being in their best interest. In addition, the Scots needed effective naval support in order for them to take the war to Ireland. It seems certain that the ships of Angus Og MacDonald were vital to Robert I in the difficult days of the winter of 1306–7, when he fled from the Scottish mainland. A fleet was also available to take his brothers, Thomas and Alexander, on their ill-fated expedition to Galloway in February 1307. In 1313 the Scots again showed their capabilities at sea by successfully invading the Isle of Man, though by 1315 John of Argyll, who supported the English, had retaken it. Yet mastery of the sea largely remained with the Scots. In the same year Robert I was able to establish his lordship in the Western Isles, surprising the local lords by dragging his ships overland at Tarbert,[99] and when Edward Bruce launched his invasion of Ireland his sea crossing was unopposed.[100] An important Scottish sea captain, Thomas Dun, also took the war to Wales, with a raid on the harbour at Holyhead in Anglesey.[101] Dun's capture, by the Anglo-Irish John of Athy in 1317, was, however, one demonstration that the Scots did not have the complete control of the western seas that they sought.[102]

In the east, the evidence suggests that it was the allies of the Scots, particularly the Flemings, who were able to do most to impede the route used by English vessels bringing victuals north to armies and castle garrisons.[103] There were many English complaints in the years leading up to Bannockburn about the hostile activities of Flemish and German sailors. Nevertheless, when Berwick was under siege by the Scots in 1315 and 1316, Scottish ships were able to prevent the English from supplying the town by sea. Moreover, once the town was in the hands of the Scots, and it came under siege from the English, the latter's ships did not present a serious threat. The contrast between the days of Edward I, when English ships had been able to bring supplies north with little apparent difficulty, and those of his son became very clear in 1322, when the English supply effort failed disastrously. Edward II's army was to have been supplied by a fleet bringing much-needed foodstuffs from Newcastle to Leith, but the operation failed. This, however, was the consequence of wind and weather, with some assistance from Flemish pirates, rather than of any Scottish naval action.[104]

Overall, this was less a period of the transformation of Scottish armies than of their creation. When the Wars of Independence began, there was little tradition or experience of how to fight major campaigns in a sustained defensive or offensive war and the events of 1296 suggested that the Scots could not possibly resist the weight of experienced English armies. The adoption of techniques of guerrilla warfare, with surprise attacks and ambushes, offered one way forward. In battle, a tactical revolution came with the development of the schiltrom, which gave spearmen an advantage over heavily armed cavalry. The mobility of Scottish armies was transformed with the development of mounted raiding forces that terrorised the north of England. Yet the Scots were also fortunate for much of this period in facing English opponents who, under Edward II, lacked effective leadership. In contrast, first Wallace, and then Robert I and his lieutenants Moray and Douglas, provided the inspiration that underlay their remarkable achievements.

Notes

1. John Barbour, *The Bruce*, ed. and trans. A. A. M. Duncan (Edinburgh: Canongate, 1997). For an important discussion of Scottish armies, see A. A. M. Duncan, 'The War of the Scots, 1306–23', *Transactions of the Royal Historical Society*, sixth series, vol. 2 (1992), pp. 125–51.
2. *Chronique de Jean le Bel*, ed. J. Viard and E. Déprez (Paris: Société de l'histoire de France, 1904), pp. 44–77; translated in extract in C. J. Rogers, *The Wars of Edward III. Sources and Interpretations* (Woodbridge: Boydell and Brewer, 1999), pp. 4–19.
3. *The Chronicle of Walter of Guisborough*, ed. H. Rothwell (London: Royal Historical Society, 1957), Camden third series, vol. 89, pp. 278–9. Bartholomew Cotton, *Historia Anglicana*, ed. H. R. Luard (London: Rolls Series, 1859), p. 312, gives similar figures.
4. *Guisborough*, ed. Rothwell, p. 328.
5. Sir Thomas Gray, *Scalacronica 1272–1363*, ed. A. King, Surtees Society, 209 (Woodbridge: Boydell and Brewer, 2005), p. 69.
6. Barbour, *The Bruce*, pp. 348–52.
7. Ibid. pp. 482–3.
8. Ibid. pp. 588–9.
9. Ibid. pp. 608–13.
10. Ibid. pp. 482–3.
11. *Chronique de Jean le Bel*, ed. Viard and Déprez, p. 51.
12. *Rotuli Scotiae*, ed. D. Macpherson et al., 2 vols (London: n.p., 1814–19), vol. 1, p. 208.
13. As, for example, *Regesta Regum Scottorum*, V, ed. A. A. M. Duncan (Edinburgh: Edinburgh University Press, 1988), p. 566.

14. *Regesta*, ed. Duncan, p. 50.
15. G. W. S. Barrow, 'The army of Alexander III's Scotland', in N. H. Reid (ed.), *Scotland in the Reign of Alexander III 1249–1286* (Edinburgh: John Donald, 1990), pp. 134–5.
16. *Formulary E. Scottish Letters and Brieves 1286–1424*, ed. A. A. M. Duncan (Glasgow: University of Glasgow, Scottish History Department, 1976), no. 88.
17. Barbour, *The Bruce*, pp. 416–17.
18. *Vita Edwardi Secundi*, ed. W. R. Childs (Oxford: Oxford University Press, 2005), p. 90.
19. Barbour, *The Bruce*, pp. 474–5, 484–5.
20. *Regesta*, ed. Duncan, p. 414.
21. C. McNamee, *The Wars of the Bruces* (East Linton: Tuckwell Press, 1997), pp. 23–4, 155–6.
22. G. W. S. Barrow, *Robert Bruce and the Community of the Realm of Scotland*, fourth edition (Edinburgh: Edinburgh University Press, 2005), p. 308.
23. *Anglo-Scottish Relations*, ed. E. L. G. Stones (London: Nelson, 1965), p. 131.
24. G. W. S. Barrow, 'Lothian in the first War of Independence', *Scottish Historical Review*, vol. 55 (1976), pp. 155–70.
25. *The Priory of Coldingham*, ed. J. Raine, Surtees Society, 12 (London: J. B. Nichols & Son, 1841), pp. xci, c. Even within the Coldingham estates, levels of involvement in the war varied. There were, for example, no forfeitures at Eyemouth.
26. *Regesta*, ed. Duncan, p. 303.
27. *Formulary E*, ed. Duncan, no. 59.
28. *Guisborough*, ed. Rothwell, pp. 327–8.
29. Barbour, *The Bruce*, pp. 484–5.
30. Ibid. pp. 600–3.
31. *Regesta*, ed. Duncan, p. 294; Barrow, *Robert Bruce*, p. 373.
32. *Regesta*, ed. Duncan, p. 537.
33. Ibid. p. 540.
34. Ibid. pp. 552–3, 554.
35. Ibid. p. 581.
36. Ibid. p. 615. As in England, service was, at least technically, for forty days; a charter of 1329 required a foot soldier with sword and lance, and sufficient supplies to maintain himself for that duration.
37. Barrow, 'The army of Alexander III's Scotland', p. 142.
38. Barbour, *The Bruce*, pp. 684–5.
39. M. C. Prestwich, *War, Politics and Finance under Edward I* (London: Faber, 1972), p. 94.

40. Barrow, *Robert Bruce*, p. 273.
41. *Regesta*, ed. Duncan, p. 407.
42. Ibid. p. 583.
43. For Wallace as an archer, see A. A. M. Duncan, 'William, son of Alan Wallace: The documents', in E. J. Cowan (ed.), *The Wallace Book* (Edinburgh: John Donald, 2007), pp. 49–56.
44. Barrow, *Robert Bruce*, pp. 234–5, 255, 275.
45. Barbour, *The Bruce*, pp. 504–5, 536–7.
46. Ibid. pp. 374–5.
47. Ibid. pp. 64, 210–11, 312–13.
48. Ibid. p. 644.
49. Ibid. pp. 686–7.
50. Barrow, *Robert Bruce*, pp. 328–9.
51. Barbour, *The Bruce*, pp. 730–5.
52. I follow Duncan's analysis in Barbour, *The Bruce*, p. 402, rather than accepting Barbour's statement that the deal was made in the summer of 1313.
53. M. C. Prestwich, 'The battle of Stirling Bridge: An English perspective', in Cowan (ed.), *The Wallace Book*, pp. 66–71.
54. Barbour, *The Bruce*, pp. 298–307.
55. There have been many studies of the battle of Bannockburn; among the most recent are M. Brown, *Bannockburn: The Scottish War and the British Isles, 1307–1323* (Edinburgh: Edinburgh University Press, 2008), and D. Cornell, *Bannockburn: The Triumph of Robert the Bruce* (New Haven, CT and London: Yale University Press, 2009).
56. *Guisborough*, ed. Rothwell, p. 327.
57. *Willelmi Rishanger, Chronica et Annales*, ed. H. T. Riley (London: Rolls Series, 1865), p. 187.
58. Barbour, *The Bruce*, p. 434.
59. Ibid. pp. 534–5. I have accepted Duncan's interpretation that this is indeed an account of the battle of Ardscull, and not of some other engagement.
60. Barbour, *The Bruce*, pp. 670–1, 674–5. On the battle see G. O. Sayles, 'The battle of Faughart', in *The Irish at War*, ed. G. A. Hayes-McCoy (Cork: Mercier Press, 1964), pp. 23–34; D. Mac Íomhair, 'The battle of Fauchart', *Irish Sword*, vol. 8 (1967–8), pp. 192–209.
61. *Vita Edwardi Secundi*, ed. Childs, pp. 22–5.
62. *Guisborough*, ed. Rothwell, pp. 351–2.
63. V. H. Galbraith, 'Extracts from the *Historia Aurea* and a French *Brut*', *English Historical Review*, vol. 43 (1928), p. 208; Barbour, *The Bruce*, pp. 600–3.
64. Gray, *Scalacronica*, pp. 78–9.

65. Ibid. pp. 88–9.
66. Before his accession Robert Bruce only had one substantial trebuchet and had considerable difficulty in trying to transport its great beam to the siege of Stirling in 1304, *Calendar of Documents Relating to Scotland*, ed. J. Bain, 5 vols (Edinburgh: HM General Register House, 1881–8), vol. 2, no. 1,510.
67. McNamee, *Wars of the Bruces*, p. 180.
68. *Chronicon de Lanercost*, ed. J. Stevenson (Edinburgh: Maitland Club, 1839), p. 230; M. C. Prestwich, *The Three Edwards* (London: Weidenfeld and Nicolson, 1980), illustrations.
69. Gray, *Scalacronica*, pp. 84–5.
70. *Lanercost*, ed. Stevenson, p. 220.
71. Barbour, *The Bruce*, pp. 204–11, 312–15.
72. Ibid. pp. 334–5.
73. Ibid. pp. 368–73. Duncan notes a suspicious resemblance between this tale and the story of the fall of Edinburgh in 1341, when one William Bullock played a significant role.
74. Barbour, *The Bruce*, p. 380.
75. Ibid. pp. 388–9.
76. *Guisborough*, ed. Rothwell, p. 328.
77. Barbour, *The Bruce*, pp. 372–3, 386–7.
78. *Lanercost*, ed. Stevenson, p. 223.
79. D. Cornell, 'A kingdom cleared of castles: The role of the castle in the campaigns of Robert Bruce', *Scottish Historical Review*, vol. 87 (2008), pp. 233–57.
80. *Chronique de Jean le Bel*, ed. Viard and Déprez, pp. 51–2.
81. *Guisborough*, ed. Rothwell, pp. 272–3, 276–7; *Anglo-Scottish Relations*, ed. Stones, p. 107.
82. *Guisborough*, ed. Rothwell, pp. 305–6.
83. *Lanercost*, ed. Stevenson, p. 194.
84. *Calendar of Documents Relating to Scotland*, ed. Bain, vol. 3, no. 539.
85. This campaign is fully analysed by R. Nicholson, *Edward III and the Scots* (London: Oxford University Press, 1965), pp. 26–36.
86. *Anglo-Scottish Relations*, ed. Stones, p. 168; Barrow, *Robert Bruce*, p. 338. In 1322 Bruce had been prepared to pay 40,000 merks, or £27,000: *Regesta*, ed. Duncan, p. 480.
87. William Rishanger, *Chronica et Annales*, ed. H. T. Riley (London: Rolls Series, 1865), pp. 180, 226; *Guisborough*, ed. Rothwell, p. 296; Galbraith, 'Extracts from the *Historia Aurea*', p. 208.
88. Barbour, *The Bruce*, p. 516; *Calendar of Documents Relating to Scotland*, ed. Bain, vol. 3, nos 402, 527; Barrow, *Robert Bruce*, pp. 302, 318; A. King, '"According to the custom used in French and Scottish wars":

Prisoners and casualties on the Scottish marches in the fourteenth century', *Journal of Medieval History*, vol. 28 (2002), p. 272.
89. Barbour, *The Bruce*, pp. 506–7; Thomas Walsingham, *Historia Anglicana, 1272–1422*, ed. H. T. Riley (London: Rolls Series), p. 141.
90. Barbour, *The Bruce*, p. 694 and note to line 543.
91. *Guisborough*, ed. Rothwell, pp. 305–6.
92. *Regesta*, ed. Duncan, p. 407.
93. Barbour, *The Bruce*, p. 146.
94. For the naval history of this period, see W. Stanford Reid, 'Sea-power in the Anglo-Scottish War, 1296–1328', *Mariner's Mirror*, vol. 46 (1960), pp. 7–23, and the wide-ranging discussion by S. Duffy, 'The Bruce brothers and the Irish sea world', *Cambridge Medieval Celtic Studies*, vol. 21 (1991), pp. 55–86.
95. Barrow, *Robert Bruce*, p. 375.
96. *Regesta*, ed. Duncan, pp. 333, 617. Ship service is discussed by Barrow, *Robert Bruce*, pp. 375–6.
97. McNamee, *Wars of the Bruces*, p. 170; Barbour, *The Bruce*, pp. 540–1.
98. The term 'berlinn' is discussed by W. Sayers, 'Fourteenth-century English balingers: Whence the name?', *Mariners' Mirror*, vol. 93 (2007), pp. 7–10.
99. Barbour, *The Bruce*, pp. 564–5. This story of dragging the ships, assisted by a favourable wind, may be one of Barbour's exaggerated tales.
100. Barbour, *The Bruce*, pp. 520–1.
101. McNamee, *Wars of the Bruces*, p. 176.
102. Duffy, 'The Bruce brothers and the Irish sea world', p. 63.
103. The war in the North Sea is discussed fully by McNamee, *Wars of the Bruces*, pp. 207–19.
104. M. C. Prestwich, 'Military logistics: The case of 1322', in M. Strickland (ed.), *Armies, Chivalry and Warfare in Medieval Britain and France* (Stamford: Paul Watkins Press, 1998), pp. 283–4.

5

The Kingdom of Scotland at War, 1332–1488

ALASTAIR J. MACDONALD

Defending the realm

Robert I's military successes led to his great achievement of 1328: English recognition of Scottish independence under a Bruce dynasty. Renewed war, however, came soon after his death. The young and capable English king Edward III adopted a new technique in seeking to subdue Scotland: an innovative combination of direct English rule in the southern counties of the kingdom and support for the quiescent regime of a restored Balliol dynasty in the north. Edward Balliol, son of the deposed King John, invaded Scotland in 1332 and gained a major victory over the Scots at Dupplin Moor by deploying a formidable tactical combination of dismounted men-at-arms supported by longbowmen in a strong defensive position. He could not secure a lasting conquest but did enough to encourage the direct intervention of Edward III who, by adopting similar tactics, inflicted another great defeat on the Scots at Halidon Hill in 1333. If Robert I, as tradition maintains, had passed on deathbed advice not to face major English forces in battle, the counsel was completely ignored by the Scottish leadership to disastrous effect.[1] These events amounted to a sudden and dramatic military reversal. The war machine of Robert I had established an impressive ascendancy in North Britain. Yet a few years later at Dupplin the Bruce Scots found themselves charging in a disorganised mass against a greatly outnumbered enemy, clambering over each other and dying in a great heap of bodies.[2] Notwithstanding this reverse, the Scots again advanced to defeat at Halidon against a much stronger English force the following year.

One can suggest reasons for the battlefield failures of 1332–3, such as overconfidence born of years of military success, dissensions among

The Kingdom of Scotland at War, 1332–1488

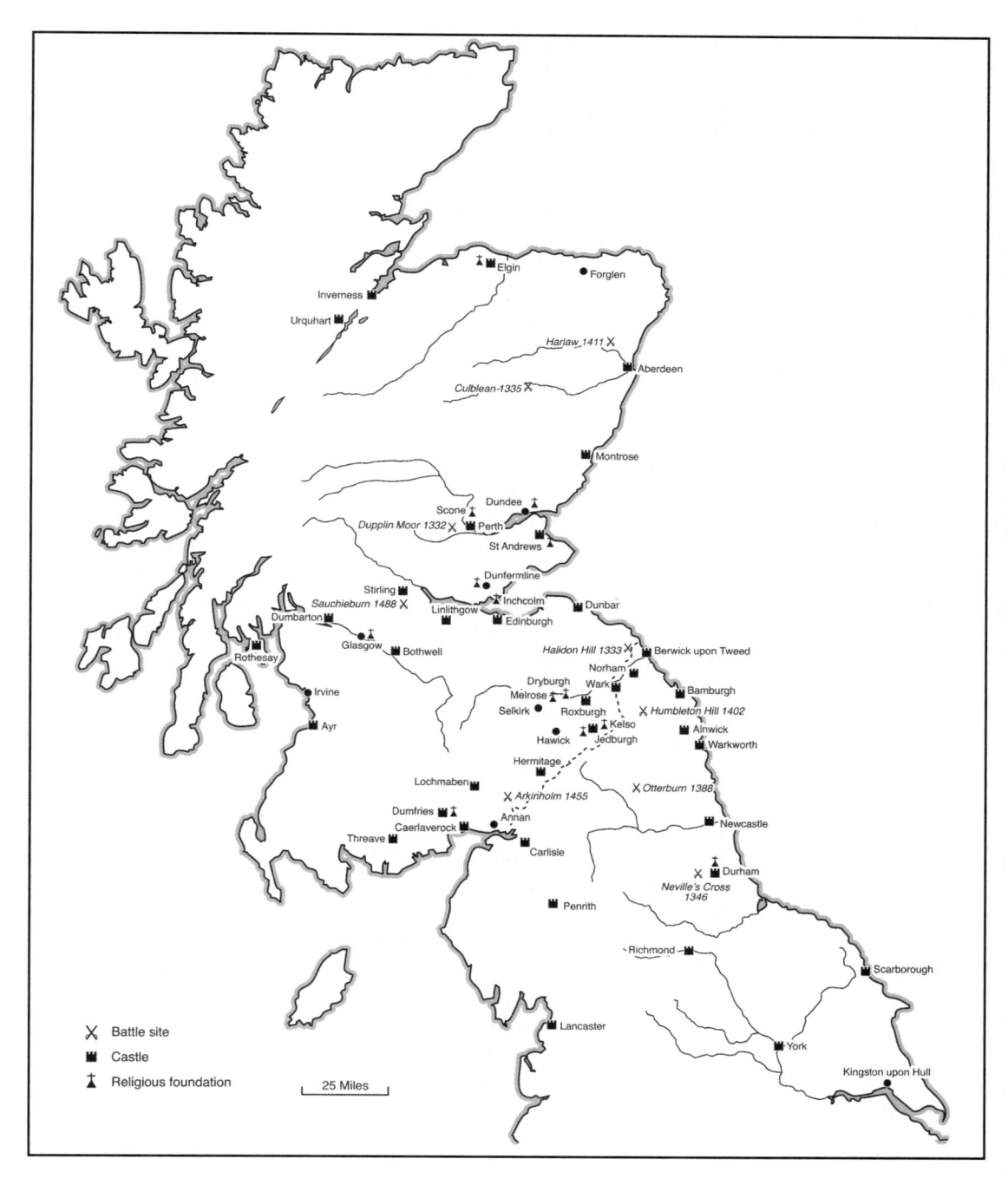

Map 5.1 Scotland and northern England, 1332–1488.

the commanders and the recent deaths of many capable leaders of the war effort under Robert I. But while this rapid descent from highly effective to fatally incompetent cannot be ignored and raises serious issues for assessing Scottish military effectiveness, the Scots still demonstrated remarkable resilience in resisting conquest: the Bruce regime did survive the challenges of the 1330s, even if the young Scots king, David II, had to be sent to France for his own safety in 1334. The formidable resources of the English crown were thrown into the task of subduing the Scots until 1337, when a war with France commenced that would increasingly absorb Edward III's attention and his finances. By 1338 an English attempt to take the castle of Dunbar, famously defended in robust fashion by the countess of March, 'Black Agnes', was allowed to peter out in failure.[3] An ill-judged winter campaign in southern Scotland in 1341 seems to have disheartened Edward III in relation to the whole Scottish venture.[4] The English king, now fully committed to more promising continental conquests, would campaign in Scotland only once more.

If the outbreak of Anglo-French hostilities was a major factor in the maintenance of Scottish independence a number of other military issues were vital in the kingdom's durability after 1332. A new generation of capable military leaders appeared on the scene, often lesser nobles like Sir Alexander Ramsay. These men developed skills in the small-scale activity of raiding and guerrilla actions. Such figures were vital in coercing local communities to accept Bruce authority. They also sought to establish their own regional positions. Members of the Douglas family in particular were adept at imposing their authority and enhancing their landed position through localised, small-scale warfare.[5] The Scots had also learned – finally – not to face major English invading armies in battle. In the campaigns he mounted between 1333 and 1356, Edward III was never again offered battle by the Scots. Similarly, Richard II, invading in 1385, and Henry IV in 1400, were not confronted on the battlefield. Indeed, the Scots would not give battle to a major English invasion force again until 1547, with predictably disastrous results. Instead, the Scottish response to major English invasions was a policy of scorched earth, carried out on numerous occasions to great effect, and the harassment of outlying elements of English armies.

Outside assistance also helped the Scots to hold out in the 1330s. Aid from France in the form of money and supplies bolstered Scottish resistance, while the French crown exerted diplomatic pressure on Edward III. Help for the Scots was on a scale significant enough to be one of the direct causes, perhaps even the most important, of the

Anglo-French conflict in 1337, the start of what came to be termed the Hundred Years War.[6] Another key to explaining Scottish survival in the 1330s, and beyond, was that the English crown lost the will to continue the struggle. Edward III eventually turned to diplomacy, rather than warfare, in attempting to assert some form of dominance in Scotland – an aspiration never to be abandoned by the English crown. But after the mid-fourteenth century hopes for Scottish conquests were generally distant and rarely the focus of governmental planning and resources.

One of the keys to controlling Scotland militarily was being able to hold on to fortified places from which the surrounding countryside could be policed. English possession of such sites was an important arena of Anglo-Scottish competition. Ruses and stratagems were frequently the means by which the Scots were able to regain strongpoints from English control: Roxburgh castle, for instance, was taken by surprise on Easter Day, 1342.[7] Treason might also be effective, and when Lochmaben fell to the Scots in 1384 the English keeper of the castle was carted off to face charges in London.[8] Conventional sieges could bring success too, as at Perth in 1339 and Stirling in 1342, but alternative means were usually more effective and the Scots often appeared ill-equipped for siege operations. A notable failure was the attempt to take both Roxburgh and Berwick in 1417, an escapade of sufficient ignominy to earn the popular appellation 'The Foul Raid'.[9] The Scots made few attempts to besiege strongpoints in England and were rarely successful when they did. One such reverse occurred at the gates of Carlisle in 1385. We might suspect that a lack of expertise and resources in conventional siege warfare more readily explains this mishap than the timely supernatural intervention of Carlisle's patron saint, the Virgin Mary.[10]

An important issue in siege warfare was the developing importance of gunpowder weaponry. The Scots were very slow to embrace this technology, not having the use of these weapons until the personal reign of James I (1424–37).[11] Gunpowder weapons had by this time been prominent in the military activities of England, France and other powers for many decades. In a sense, this hesitance is puzzling: the Scots had ample opportunity to witness the potency of these new weapons in English operations, most strikingly in 1405 when Henry IV regained Berwick castle by blasting down the walls.[12] Embracing the new technology was certainly expensive, however, and personal royal interest was probably important in its eventual appearance in Scotland. In the event, James I's gunpowder weaponry could not take Roxburgh in 1436 nor prevent a shambolic retreat, leaving his

Figure 5.1 The great bombard, known as Mons Meg, weighing some six tons and with a 20-inch (510mm) calibre, fired stone balls of approximately 400lbs. Now in Edinburgh castle, it was cast in 1449 at Mons and presented to James II by Philip the Good, duke of Burgundy, in 1457.

ordnance in English hands.[13] James II was even more enthusiastic and it was during his reign (1437–60) that the great bombard, Mons Meg, arrived in Scotland, a happy offshoot of new diplomatic affinities with Philip the Good, duke of Burgundy. The artillery amassed by James, together with gunners hired from the continent, had some success in taking domestic strongpoints for the king. It was also employed to good effect at the siege of Roxburgh in 1460, although James himself was killed in one of the less fortunate moments for the Stewart dynasty when an artillery piece exploded near the king.[14]

The use of strongpoints as bases of English control explains the Scottish policy of dismantling major fortifications to prevent them falling into their hands. Such steps were taken in the 1330s and after the capture of Lochmaben (1384), Jedburgh (1409) and Roxburgh (1460). The great Scottish royal castles of Dumbarton, Stirling and Edinburgh were, however, maintained as bulwarks of the crown's power and their defences were developed, an example being the construction of a great new tower at Edinburgh in the late fourteenth century.[15] Only the most determined of enemy operations would have been able to capture these places and, from 1342, when Stirling was recaptured, they all remained in Scottish hands. The greatest prize of border conflict, Berwick, remained, however, a special case. The town fortifications and the castle had been maintained after their capture by Robert I in 1318.[16] One consequence of this decision was the Scottish defeat at Halidon Hill when trying to relieve the besieged town in 1333.[17] Brief interruptions aside, Berwick remained the focal point of the English administration in Scotland until the Lancastrians delivered it in 1461 to the regency administration during James III's minority. James was determined to hold on to the town and was set on offering battle to invading English forces in 1482 when a major noble revolt – no doubt fortuitously – ended his plans. Berwick was taken by the English for good.[18]

The Scottish offensives

Contest for control made Scotland a major arena of conflict, but raiding into England was also a prominent aspect of Scottish military activity during the period. In fact, the Scots were overwhelmingly the aggressors in war with England after the 1330s. Major English forays into Scotland after this were responses to Scottish attacks until the 1480s when Edward IV's regime embarked once more on campaigns aimed at northern expansion.[19] In the late fourteenth and mid-fifteenth centuries, in particular, Scottish incursions caused widespread damage and dislocation in the English north and it remained a staple of Scottish foreign policy to mount attacks on the now well-established enemy when circumstances allowed. Offensives were carefully timed to harmonise with heavy English entanglements in foreign war or domestic crises. There were ample opportunities to exploit such conditions.

We have no compelling description, such as Jean Le Bel's earlier account of Scottish raiding forces, for the post-1332 period. It was still the intention, clearly, that the Scots should be fast-moving and elusive. They were expected to carry their own victuals or buy what was needed while they were on native soil.[20] Once over the border they were to live off the land, obviating the need for slow-moving baggage trains. We can sometimes see the confusion caused in England by what do appear to be rapidly moving Scottish forces, for instance during the Otterburn campaign of 1388.[21] It is unlikely, however, that all Scots were mounted in anything other than relatively small raiding parties. Great battlefield defeats – especially if they took place deep in England, such as that at Neville's Cross in 1346 – must have led to a significant loss of horseflesh. There were clearly governmental concerns about lack of horses in Scotland from at least 1372 when legislation forbidding their export was passed.[22]

Scottish forces undertaking the dangerous business of invading the well-guarded north of England needed to be cohesive and disciplined.

Unfortunately, command and control structures are difficult subjects to explore from contemporary source materials. Undoubtedly it was hoped that orders would be followed, as shown by ordinances laid down in 1385 and 1448.[23] But quite what mechanisms were in place to ensure responsiveness to commands is unclear. War banners, the rallying points of medieval armies, formed one sinew of command. The Scots certainly utilised these, but we know less about their role in helping to coordinate army activities than their relationship to issues of military motivation. The Scottish leadership was clearly aware of the potential benefits of battle standards in this latter respect. This explains why lairds of Forglen in Aberdeenshire were expected to provide the service of bearing the *Breccbennach*, probably a sacred war banner, in Scottish armies.[24] The royal standard also had motivational power. Its symbolic authority had at times considerable impact on domestic enemies of the Scottish crown. Indeed, in 1429 two Highland clans defected to join royal forces once the banner had been unfurled.[25] Other national and religious symbols could enhance military cohesion. One of the holiest of such artefacts was the Black Rood of St Margaret. Seized by Edward I in his conquest of Scotland in 1296, the relic may have been borne against the Scots alongside the frequently victorious banner of St Cuthbert at the battle of Neville's Cross.[26]

In terms of leadership, as elsewhere in Christendom, social class was paramount in a hierarchical structure of command. An adult reigning monarch was at the apex of the system and could provide prominent military leadership as did David II (early in his personal rule) and James II. Even without the personal involvement of the monarchy, however, the great Scottish magnates could be very active militarily, notably in the reigns of Robert II (1371–90) and Robert III (1390–1406). This is partly because the military system in Scotland was relatively decentralised, with the higher nobility exercising broad powers of leadership over the regional affinities they brought to the field. Wardens of the Marches, for example, had important command responsibilities, alongside judicial and disciplinary authority, and their regional position as great nobles gave them the means to exercise these wide powers. So, in the 1380s, military successes were attributable to the personal leadership of such figures as George Dunbar, tenth earl of March, James, second earl of Douglas, and Sir Archibald Douglas, lord of Galloway, rather than the approving, but less active, royal establishment.[27] Below the level of the magnates, the lesser nobility also had roles of leadership in particular localities. Again this is suggestive of devolved and regionalised structures of military command, and can be seen at a lower level still in legislation mentioning 'vinteners', officers drawn from the worthy men of border parishes with responsibilities for military leadership.[28]

In this period the Scots did produce some highly capable military leaders. Perhaps the greatest of these was George Dunbar, ninth earl of March. Prominent in the Scottish war effort in the 1370s and 1380s, he regained extensive disputed border lands and had much the better of raiding exchanges and a number of small engagements. His leadership was also vital in the Scottish success at Otterburn in 1388 when a force raiding Northumberland was brought to battle by Sir Henry Percy, known as 'Hotspur'. Dunbar led the Scots to victory after James, second earl of Douglas, was killed on the field.[29] After defecting to the English in 1400 Dunbar continued to enjoy success in battle, but now in the service of his new royal master, Henry IV. Dunbar appears to have played a considerable role in the defeats of both the Scots at Humbleton (or Homildon) Hill in Northumberland in 1402 and the Percys, who were in rebellion against the English king, at Shrewsbury in 1403.[30]

Dunbar's military success was exceptional, due to a combination of natural aptitude and the experience gained from years of campaigning. This happy combination of circumstances was not often replicated. In the dangerous business of pursuing a military strategy heavily dependent on launching cross-border raids there were many potential pitfalls. Overconfidence, for instance, might lead swiftly to disaster. In the campaign that led to Neville's Cross in 1346 it seems likely that the Scots expected success because, encouraged in this belief by their French allies, they thought England would be empty of fighting men, who instead would all be on campaign in France.[31] For David II and his fellow commanders this was a disastrous misapprehension. Inexperience could also be deadly and the battlefield was a challenging place to learn on the job. Archibald, fourth earl of Douglas, represented a new, belligerent, but inexperienced, Scottish military leadership at the turn of the fifteenth century. His clumsy and inept invasion culminated in total defeat for the Scottish army at Humbleton Hill.[32] This was a turning point. Scottish incursions into northern England did not stop, but there was now a tendency for them to be of smaller scale and less deep in penetration. Moreover, this reinforced the Scots' reluctance to risk battle with sizeable English armies. In 1417, for example, the Scots hastily withdrew from their sieges of Roxburgh and Berwick on the approach of an army under the dukes of Bedford and Exeter, while in 1436 James I did not linger to confront the English forces coming to the relief of Roxburgh once again.

Soldiers and their impact, home and abroad

It is clear that the Scots were able to put significant forces in the field. In theory there was a general obligation on able-bodied males aged between sixteen and sixty to serve in Scottish armed forces. In practice, this can hardly have been the case, particularly for the humblest social classes who would have had little or no military equipment. Firm statistics are lacking, but estimates of up to 10,000-strong armies for the most prominent campaigns are usually accepted. On these occasions forces from north of the Forth supplemented the southern contingents which more regularly operated in Anglo-Scottish warfare. For the ill-fated Halidon Hill campaign in 1333, for example, soldiers were drawn from the Highlands and the Western Isles.[33] The manpower from the west, however, was dependent on good relations between the crown and magnates of the region, especially the MacDonald Lords of the Isles, and this was an increasingly rare circumstance. Indeed, contests for local dominance in Scotland continued to be carried out by small forces based on the retinues of nobles and their closest followers. Telling interventions in the wider Anglo-Scottish conflict could, however, be made by such contingents. A pivotal moment in the struggle of the 1330s was the defeat and death of Edward Balliol's lieutenant north of the Forth, David of Strathbogie, earl of Atholl, at the battle of Culblean in 1335. The Bruce force responsible was centred around noble leaders from north and south, the southern contingent numbering only some 800 combatants.[34]

A crucial issue for the armed forces was payment. It is usually said that Scottish armies were unpaid and this is true to the extent that no regular system of wage payment for crown military service developed.[35] However, at times the crown did pay troops. David II did so in 1363, and James I in 1429.[36] Moreover, in the face of imminent English invasion in 1482 plans were made to pay a 500-strong garrison at Berwick, while a further 600 paid troops were to hold lesser border strongholds.[37] The crown also paid for military service by offering annuities to the most belligerent members of the nobility in the late fourteenth century,[38] and offered further encouragement by waiving its right to inheritance payments from the successors of nobles killed in national war. Another significant source of payment was the French crown. Enormous sums, for example, were offered to encourage the Scots to attack England in 1355 and 1385.[39] Yet these fiscal arrangements did not allow for the regular payment of troops. This meant that forces could be put in the field cheaply, but this could do nothing other than adversely affect their combat effectiveness when matched against professionals.

Nonetheless, warfare offered the possibility of other financial rewards. Booty was one incentive for Scots to engage in raids into England. Military regulations produced in 1430 and 1448 make this very clear. They also make manifest tensions between effective military activity and the quest for material gain. Severe punishments were to be enacted, for example, against those who left the host in pursuit of plunder without permission. Individuals had the right to seek enrichment, but there had to be careful constraints on this if Scottish armies were not to become merely acquisitive rabbles.[40] Even at a relatively humble social level, it seems that Scots felt that war could line their pockets; the ordinary people were said to be enraged by the agreement of a truce in 1389 that denied them the prospect of rich pickings in England.[41] Perhaps, though, material gain was more likely to be achieved through joining foreign armies. Sir John Swinton returned to Scotland a wealthier man in the 1380s, having benefited from English service,[42] and others were able to prosper in the pay of the French crown in the fifteenth century. Military activity could also bring rewards that were not straightforwardly material. Obtaining the favour of great magnates or the crown for prowess in war was one means of social advancement. David II, for instance, highly favoured a group of his subjects who shared his crusading and chivalric enthusiasms.[43]

If war could bring rewards it could of course bring enormous suffering too. We have far better evidence for the impact of Scottish raids in England than for the effects of war north of the border. Throughout this period the complaints of northern English communities can be traced and estate records give indications of serious economic decline.[44] Yet we must treat evidence relating to Scottish attacks carefully. Atrocity stories about a barbaric enemy cannot always be taken at face value. No doubt the Scots were vicious enough in their depredations on English soil, but it is doubtful that they had the leisure time while on lightning raids, as one chronicler alleges, to pause for games of football with the decapitated heads of their victims.[45] Even grim financial records are open to varied interpretation. In a time of plague and falling land values it is hard to know to what extent long-term economic depression was caused by Scottish raiding. Nonetheless, it is clear that at times the Scots could bring great misery to vast areas of the English north. One indication, among many, of the impact on the region comes in the form of the mid-fourteenth-century register of the bishop of Carlisle. It is written on very poor quality parchment, a circumstance that may be explained by a lack of sheepskin, the Scots having destroyed the bishop's flocks.[46]

We can hardly imagine that the Scots suffered much less, especially in the 1330s when the ferocious Anglo-Scottish war was fought mostly north of the border and took place alongside a brutal conflict for allegiance and control at the local level that had much of the character of civil war. Scottish chroniclers provide hints of widespread misery, as in the contention that war caused famine and severe depopulation in Lothian.[47] The burning of Aberdeen by Edward III in 1336 provides a glimpse of the impact of war on one community. Impressive coin hordes were hidden in the burgh prior to its destruction,[48] but the fact that these remained undisturbed until modern times suggests that many of the town's inhabitants did not survive the attack. An urban community like this, far removed from the southern epicentre of conflict could, and did, go on to recover and prosper. Not so for a contested border burgh like Roxburgh. During the fifteenth century it ceased to exist as an urban centre. Nevertheless, after the 1330s, the worst was over for Scottish communities. English raiding in the border region would continue, and occasional larger-scale forays were intended to be punitive, such as the tellingly named 'Burnt Candlemas' of 1356.[49] But for most Scots, most of the time, war ceased to be a regular threat to lives and livelihoods.

In theory, of course, many non-combatant groupings should have been protected from the worst effects of war in the Anglo-Scottish sphere, as elsewhere in Christendom. One example of such protection is in the ordinances for war of the Scots and their French allies in 1385 which stipulated punishments for harm done to women, children and churches.[50] Yet enforcing such theoretical protection may not have been easy, especially given a style of warfare that rested heavily on terrorising enemy non-combatants.[51] On some occasions it was hardly possible to spare theoretically protected property, as in 1333 when English siege engines destroyed the Berwick *maison dieu* or hospice.[52] It was a different matter, however, deliberately to attack church buildings and it is telling that when this did occur it attracted the outraged attention of chroniclers, sometimes from both sides of the border. The normally patriotic English chronicler Walsingham expressed his sadness at the destruction of Melrose abbey by his countrymen in 1385.[53] Generally it was not in the interests of combatants to step outside the accepted conventions of war, which in any case provided plenty of scope for personal enrichment and causing damage to the enemy.

The reason for such damage, from the governmental perspective, was to pursue political objectives. For the Scottish crown, the goal appears to have been recognition of national independence. Sometimes, in propitious international circumstances, the aim may have been even more ambitious: the final destruction of the great enemy, the English state. A high point of this ambition came in 1385 when a major French expeditionary force arrived to invade northern England alongside the Scots in the expectation of a simultaneous full-scale invasion in the south.[54] This southern landing did not materialise and the allies' relationship in the north was marked by disagreement and rancour. Another moment of high ambition came in the 1450s. Defeated on the continent, England had entered a phase of debilitating civil conflict. In these circumstances James II was keen to wage energetic war against the old enemy, again with French assistance, until his early death in 1460.[55]

As well as close involvement with the Scottish war effort, France itself offered another arena in which the Scots could confront their English enemy and receive wages for the pleasure. Significant Scottish contingents saw French service from the mid-fourteenth century until a remarkable peak early in the fifteenth. A striking number of troops – reckoned to have totalled 15,000 – was despatched to France between 1419 and 1424, led by great Douglas and Stewart magnates.[56] The victory of a largely Scottish force at Baugé in 1421 interrupted a sequence of English military successes as Henry V attempted to conquer France.[57] Heavy defeats at Cravant in 1423 and Verneuil in 1424, however, wiped out most of the Scots serving the French crown. Verneuil, in particular, was a bloody and hard-fought encounter at which the Scots present, led by Archibald, fourth earl of Douglas, were killed almost to a man. With around 6,000 dead, this may have been the biggest Scottish battlefield loss of life during the period.[58] A Scottish presence in French royal armies would nonetheless persist for the rest of the century and beyond. Indeed, in 1418 a Garde Écossaise had been established by Charles VII as a personal bodyguard to the French monarchy, and Scots continued to serve in this company into the seventeenth century.[59]

One prominent aspect of Scottish service in France at this time was that many of the soldiers involved were archers. Their arrival in their thousands, it has been argued, was a factor in the shift of the French armies towards the inclusion of a greater proportion of missile troops.[60] This is puzzling to the extent that, although there had always been archers in Scottish armies, they do not appear to have been particularly numerous nor to have performed as effectively as English bowmen. Scottish monarchs were certainly very aware of how useful archery could be on the battlefield and James I's legislation of 1424 to develop these skills among his subjects was echoed by similar enactments later in the century.[61] But whether this did much to change the choice of weaponry of the common soldiers must be doubted; it certainly did not succeed in halting rival leisure activities that were felt to be less to the common benefit, such as football and golf.[62] It seems that the characteristic weapons of ordinary Scottish soldiers remained the spear, sword and axe. The latter was sufficiently identified with Scots for one version of the weapon to be specifically known as the 'Scotte axe' in early-fifteenth-century Northumberland.[63] Expertise in the use of weapons no doubt varied, but it was certainly a consistent governmental concern to ensure that wapinshawings – occasions for demonstrating material readiness, and practising in the use of arms – were held in both urban and rural communities.[64]

Ordinary Scottish soldiers no doubt remained lightly armoured, irrespective of governmental legislation detailing desired levels of protection and stipulating heavy fines for failure to comply. Noble warriors, however, would have been equipped much as other elites in north-western Europe. Indeed, much Scottish aristocratic armour and weaponry came from abroad. The Scots used London and Flanders as marketplaces to purchase such equipment. The government was also keen for merchants to purchase suitable military materials abroad and passed legislation to that effect.[65] Meanwhile, the Scots' French allies provided weapons and armour as a means of encouraging Scottish belligerence against England. Scottish aristocrats believed themselves to be encased in the latest and most effective armour in both 1346 and 1402, a factor tending to overconfidence that may have played a part in the military defeats of those years.[66] Funeral effigies give us some indication of how the knightly class was armed in this period with many fifteenth-century examples depicting nobles in full plate armour.[67]

Figure 5.2 Scottish longsword, c. 1400–20. The style of the hilt, whose wooden grip is missing, is distinctively Scottish, but an inlaid gold mark in the form of a running wolf suggests that the blade was imported, probably from Germany.

Plate 1 Bronze shield, probably used for ceremonial purposes, found at Moss of Auchmaliddie at New Deer in Aberdeenshire. It is likely to have been deposited in a watery area as a gift to the gods, some time between 950 and 750 BC.

Plate 2 Adoration of the Magi from the *Hours of Étienne Chevalier* by Jean Fouquet, c. 1445. Charles VII of France, depicted as one of the three Magi, is accompanied by his Garde Écossaise.

Plate 3 *The Romance of Alexander*, produced in Flanders c. 1338–44, depicts Alexander the Great (shown in the top left and bottom right registers) bearing a coat of arms notably similar to that of the kings of Scots. Although no firm evidence links the manuscript to David II, it illustrates the type of arms and equipment used by the king and his leading nobles during this period.

Plate 4 Cap worn by a Grenadier officer in a Scottish unit of the army of William III, c. 1692. Embroidered thistles flank the royal crown and cypher of William and Mary.

Plate 5 *The Battle of Killiecrankie* by Alan B. Herriot, 1993. The Jacobite clans charge downhill towards the government line, 1689.

Plate 6 *An Incident in the Rebellion of 1745*, traditionally attributed to David Morier, c. 1745–50. The Jacobites confront the bayonets of the government troops.

Plate 7 Fort George, Ardersier, near Inverness. Built to help pacify the Highlands after the Jacobite rising of 1745, the fort was completed in 1769.

Plate 8 *Scotland For Ever!* by Lady Elizabeth Butler, 1881. The charge of the Scots Greys at Waterloo, 1815.

Plate 9 Sergeant Major John Dickson portrayed as an old man wearing his medals. Artist unknown. As a corporal Dickson had taken part in the Scots Greys' charge at Waterloo. He retired from the army in 1834 and lived in Crail, Fife, until his death in 1880.

Plate 10 *The 74th Highlanders, 1846.* Contemporary painting by David Cunliffe. This picture celebrates the return of the 74th (later the 2nd battalion, the Highland Light Infantry) to Highland dress in 1846 after a gap of thirty-seven years.

Plate 11 *Engagement on the Heights above Waterkloof, 1851.* The 74th Highlanders are depicted by eyewitness artist, Thomas Baines, under attack in the Amatola mountains during the Eighth Frontier War in South Africa.

Plate 12 *The Thin Red Line* by Robert Gibb, 1881. The stand of the 93rd (Sutherland) Highlanders at Balaclava, 1854.

Plate 13 *Jessie's Dream: The Campbells are Coming, Lucknow, September 1857* by Frederick Goodall, 1858. Jessie Brown, purportedly the wife of a corporal besieged in Lucknow during the Indian Mutiny, hears the pipes of the approaching highlanders playing 'The Campbells are Coming'.

Plate 14 Orlando Norie's *Lucknow, November 16th 1857. The 93rd Highlanders Entering the Breach at the Storming of the Secundrabagh*.

Plate 15 *The Storming of Tel-el-Kebir* by Alphonse Marie de Neuville, 1883. Dawn assault by the 1st battalion, the Black Watch, on the Egyptian defences, 1882.

Martial culture on sea and land

As well as seeking to create well-equipped armies on land, the Scottish crown tried to compete with England at sea. The Scots were certainly able to capture enemy vessels and even on occasion mount attacks on English maritime communities such as the assault on Scarborough in 1378.[68] There is also evidence of the existence of royal ships, such as the barge built for James I at Leith.[69] It is probable, however, that a nascent Scottish royal navy cannot yet have been of scale enough to play a great role in war. Instead, the Scottish merchant fleet was called upon, bolstered by foreign vessels often supplied by the French crown. In 1402 when David Lindsay, earl of Crawford, preyed on English shipping in the Channel it was at the head of a mainly French fleet.[70]

But despite the best efforts of the Scots and their allies, the strong impression remains of an English naval ascendancy. It seems clear that the Scots suffered much more in maritime losses than they gained, partly because they needed to traverse the east coast of England to reach the main focus of foreign trade in the Low Countries. And even with foreign assistance, the Scots could not oppose major fleets such as those habitually used to support English land invasions. The whole length of the Scottish North Sea coast remained vulnerable to maritime assault. The Forth estuary was a particularly tempting target: in 1421 the monks of Inchcolm Abbey, the chronicler Walter Bower among them, were forced to abandon their island there in fear of English naval assault.[71]

English naval superiority in the western seas was not, however, such a clear-cut issue. The Irish Sea world was a zone where the Scottish crown felt it could exploit English weaknesses, evident in their contracting lordship in Ireland and sometimes uncertain hold on Wales. In 1388 Scottish naval landings were made in Ireland, where Carlingford was plundered, and in the Isle of Man.[72] The Scots clearly hoped to benefit from the Welsh rising of Owain Glyn Dwr and in 1401 a Scottish ship was captured after naval activity off the Welsh coast.[73] The English maritime presence was not nearly as strong in the west as the east, explaining the Scots' repeated use of the Irish Sea route to maintain links with their continental allies. The western port of Dumbarton, in particular, was vital in this regard, a place where supplies arrived, Scottish soldiers embarked for foreign service and where David II took ship for his refuge in France in 1334.[74] Meanwhile, the galley fleets controlled by the nobility of the western Highlands and Islands were a prominent presence on the western seas. These vessels maintained contact with Ireland and facilitated the service of thousands of Scottish mercenary galloglass troops in the wars there. James I saw possibilities for the exploitation of such fleets by the crown and legislated to encourage them.[75] In truth, however, western galley fleets largely lay beyond the effective control of Scottish monarchs.

In this connection the west was not just a zone of possible English naval weakness, but also a source of vulnerability for the Scottish crown. The most serious and consistent domestic military threat to royal government came from this region in the form of the Lords of the Isles. At Harlaw in 1411 a major invasion force from the west, led by Donald of the Isles, battled a royal army defending Aberdeenshire to a standstill in a famously bloody encounter.[76] The defending force at Harlaw was drawn from the communities of north-eastern Scotland, including the burgh of Aberdeen, and the army's performance in battle suggests a high level of military preparedness in the region.[77] In turn, the lordship could not be lastingly cowed by military force, a key moment coming when a government expedition to the Highlands was defeated in 1431.[78] In the areas north of the Forth, as well as in the regions bordering England, local society clearly retained pronounced militarised characteristics.

Not all military encounters between the crown and its subjects took place in a Highland context. Much recent historiography is in fact dominated by studies of what is depicted as a highly competitive and violent political society throughout Scotland at both local and national levels. There were, of course, aspects of a Bruce–Balliol civil war in Anglo-Scottish conflict, most prominently in the 1330s. But thereafter, in terms of direct military confrontations between the crown and its subjects, the scale of violence actually seems rather muted.[79] The major rebellion against David II in 1363 was put down with relative ease and no prominent casualties, while political upheavals in the reigns of Robert II, Robert III and James I were accompanied by remarkably little internal military activity. The destruction by James II of the mightiest of magnate families, the Black Douglases, did involve military campaigns. Yet the crown's triumph seems to have been smoothly achieved and the Douglas defeat at Arkinholm in 1455 was hardly of sufficient magnitude to be considered a full-scale battle.[80] It is telling of the king's military priorities that while besieging the Douglas stronghold of Threave in the same year he felt able to detach troops to attempt a surprise seizure of English-held Berwick.[81] When James III faced his rebellious subjects at Sauchieburn in 1488 the encounter was a confused series of skirmishes with few notable casualties other than the king himself.⁸² There may indeed have been a high level of competition in Scottish political life, but – problems of crown control in the Highlands aside – it rarely manifested itself in significant military clashes between crown and nobility.⁸³

One factor tending towards unity between king and subjects was a shared martial culture. Not all kings were warriors in person but a warlike ethos infused the self-perception and projected image of the royal establishment. Royal knighting ceremonies surely expressed a sense of chivalric expectation. David, duke of Rothesay, heir to Robert III, was knighted at a tournament organised for the purpose; the knighting of the future James II took place alongside noble children intended to be his companions in arms in struggles to come; and the infant James III was dubbed alongside one hundred others in 1460 as the campaign that had just claimed his father's life continued.⁸⁴ There is also abundant evidence that martial prowess was a vital part of aristocratic self-identity. In two late fourteenth-century wills of Sir James Douglas of Dalkeith, a magnate not particularly notable for his military activities, prominent items included romances of knightly adventure, as well as arms, armour and horses.⁸⁵ In the mid-fifteenth century Sir Gilbert Hay made vernacular translations of popular chivalric treatises in order to satisfy aristocratic demand for these documents.⁸⁶

The context for Scottish martial culture, for aristocrats and royalty alike, was in the international world of chivalric endeavour. In the fourteenth century the formative military experiences of the young

Figure 5.3 Gravestone of Sir Gilbert de Greenlaw, killed at the battle of Harlaw in 1411, in Kinkell churchyard, Aberdeenshire.

Figure 5.4 Threave castle, Kirkcudbrightshire. In front of the great tower, built c. 1370 by Archibald 'the Grim', third earl of Douglas, is the purpose-built artillery fortification, erected c. 1450, which helped resist a siege by King James II for some three months in 1455. It was the king's money, rather than his bombards, that finally induced the garrison to yield up the castle.

David II occurred in France, while one of his greatest subjects, William, future earl of Douglas, was knighted on campaign by the French king.[87] The military activities of the Scots at home and abroad were presented to an international audience by continental writers such as the late fourteenth-century Netherlandish chronicler Jean Froissart. Scottish arms are also well represented in the folios of the *Armorial de Gelre* from the same region.[88] Furthermore, there was royal endorsement of continental chivalric connections, represented by James II presiding when Burgundian jousters, led by the renowned Jacques Lalaing, competed with prominent Scots in tournament combat in 1449.[89] That the Scottish crown did not develop its own order of knighthood in this period should not thus be taken to suggest a lack of chivalric aspirations.[90] But it might indicate a certain slowness to embrace military change, a conservatism that may have had much to do with lack of finance as well as the lengthy periods when there was no adult monarch in command to push through new initiatives. In any event, the Scottish crown had a secure military role in Christendom: the chastisers of the English, and recognised as such by popes and kings.

This role may help to explain the limited involvement of Scots on crusade.[91] Small numbers can be traced regularly enough in crusading activity, but opportunities to face the hated enemy closer to home were more attractive to many. It is no surprise that when the unity of crusade was split by national discord, the Scots and their English rivals were the culprits: the Scottish chivalric paragon, Sir William Douglas of Nithsdale, was killed in Königsberg in 1391 during a clash with an English crusading party.[92]

Socially humbler Scots, who formed the bulk of armies, also embraced a military ethos. Indeed, war played a part in the elevation of some burgess families to knightly rank, as in the case of the Forresters of Corstorphine whose funeral monuments express their new sense of belonging to the chivalric elite.[93] At a lower social level the martial values of common soldiers are hard to identify individually. That they were accepted as being part of a military community, however, seems obvious from literary works. In Harry's *The Wallace*, for instance, written in the 1470s, ordinary Scots like John the Carpenter play a significant role in battle alongside their social betters.[94] In long wars against a national enemy class distinctions were to some extent blurred.

If a communal sense of military purpose existed it may explain a certain disregard for social niceties in the Scottish conception of chivalry. The chronicler Bower depicts Sir William Dalzell engaging in a contest of arms with an English opponent in London around 1390. But he is also shown engaging in repartee that took an irreverent view of chivalric convention. Accused of breaching an agreement to fight on equal terms, Dalzell suggests that for true equality his English opponent should lose an eye to mirror the injury he had suffered at Otterburn.[95] This says something about medieval humour, but also touches on the realm of courage. From kings to commoners, Scots displayed great bravery in war. David II was wounded in the head by arrows before being captured still fighting gamely at Neville's Cross. The fourth earl of Douglas fought on, despite the loss of an eye and a testicle, until his death in combat in 1424.[96] Courage was as celebrated a virtue as any in later medieval Scotland, and many had the scars to prove themselves in this regard.

Warfare played a significant role in the late medieval Scottish state and affected all the kingdom's inhabitants. Although military structures give the appearance of being somewhat rudimentary, they had the resilience to ensure Scottish independence in the 1330s and were a factor in discouraging English attempts at conquest thereafter. Taking war to a more powerful enemy – Scotland's strategic dilemma in the later Middle Ages – was fraught with danger, but the struggle with England had become a prominent aspect of Scottish martial identity and a vital component of foreign policy. Such aggressive policies led to some failures but there were notable periods of success as well. The military performance of the Scots was a big factor in a small state punching above its weight on the international stage.

Notes

1. R. Nicholson, *Edward III and the Scots: The Formative Years of a Military Career, 1327–1335* (London: Oxford University Press, 1965), p. 111.
2. C. J. Rogers, *War Cruel and Sharp: English Strategy under Edward III, 1327–1360* (Woodbridge: Boydell and Brewer, 2000), pp. 40–5.
3. Walter Bower, *Scotichronicon*, ed. D. E. R. Watt, 9 vols (Aberdeen: Aberdeen University Press, 1987–98), vol. 7, pp. 126–31.
4. Sir Thomas Gray, *Scalacronica, 1272–1363*, ed. A. King, Surtees Society, 209 (Woodbridge: Boydell and Brewer, 2005), p. 134.
5. M. Brown, *The Black Douglases: War and Lordship in Late Medieval Scotland, 1300–1455* (East Linton: Tuckwell Press, 1998).
6. J. Sumption, *The Hundred Years War: Trial by Battle* (London: Faber and Faber, 1990), pp. 123–84.
7. Gray, *Scalacronica*, p. 131.
8. A. J. Macdonald, *Border Bloodshed: Scotland and England at War, 1369–1403* (East Linton: Tuckwell Press, 2000), pp. 76–7.
9. R. Nicholson, *Scotland: The Later Middle Ages* (Edinburgh: Oliver and Boyd, 1974), p. 249.
10. *Knighton's Chronicle, 1337–1396*, ed. G. H. Martin (Oxford: Oxford University Press, 1995), pp. 336–7.
11. D. H. Caldwell, 'The Scots and guns', in A. King and M. Penman (eds), *England and Scotland in the Fourteenth Century: New Perspectives* (Woodbridge: Boydell and Brewer, 2007), pp. 60–72.
12. J. H. Wylie, *History of England under Henry IV*, 4 vols (London, 1884–98), vol. 2, pp. 272–3.
13. M. Brown, *James I* (East Linton: Tuckwell Press, 1994), pp. 163–4.
14. C. McGladdery, *James II* (Edinburgh: John Donald, 1990), pp. 111, 154–6.
15. S. Cruden, *The Scottish Castle* (Edinburgh: Nelson, 1981), p. 114.
16. On Bruce's policy towards fortifications, see D. Cornell, 'A kingdom

cleared of castles: The role of the castle in the campaigns of Robert Bruce', *Scottish Historical Review* [hereafter *SHR*], vol. 87 (2008), pp. 233–57.
17. Nicholson, *Edward III and the Scots*, pp. 111–38.
18. N. Macdougall, *James III: A Political Study* (Edinburgh: John Donald, 1982), pp. 58, 154–5, 168–9.
19. A. J. Pollard, *North-Eastern England during the Wars of the Roses: Lay Society, War and Politics, 1450–1500* (Oxford: Clarendon Press, 1990), pp. 235–44.
20. *The Records of the Parliaments of Scotland to 1707* [hereafter *RPS*], ed. K. M. Brown et al. (St Andrews, 2007), 1385/4/2, 1385/6/4. Available at www.rps.ac.uk/mss/1385/4/2 and www.rps.ac.uk/mss/1385/6/4, accessed on 29 August 2011.
21. R. B. Dobson, 'The Church of Durham and the Scottish Borders, 1378–88', in *War and Border Societies in the Middle Ages*, ed. A. Goodman and A. Tuck (London: Routledge, 1992), pp. 127–8.
22. *RPS*, 1372/3/3. Available at www.rps.ac.uk/mss/1372/3/3, accessed on 29 August 2011. Acts relating to horse exports were regular thereafter.
23. *RPS*, 1385/6/4. Available at www.rps.ac.uk/mss/1385/6/4, accessed on 29 August 2011; *Acts of the Parliaments of Scotland* [hereafter *APS*], ed. T. Thomson and C. Innes, 12 vols (Edinburgh: n.p., 1814–75), vol. 1, pp. 714–16.
24. D. H. Caldwell, 'The Monymusk reliquary: The *Breccbennach* of St Columba?', *Proceedings of the Society of Antiquaries of Scotland*, vol. 131 (2001), pp. 267–82.
25. Bower, *Scotichronicon*, vol. 8, pp. 262–3.
26. L. Rollason, 'Spoils of war? Durham cathedral and the Black Rood of Scotland', in D. Rollason and M. Prestwich (eds), *The Battle of Neville's Cross* (Stamford: Shaun Tyas, 1998), pp. 57–65.
27. Macdonald, *Border Bloodshed*, pp. 45–116.
28. *RPS*, 1430/34. Available at www.rps.ac.uk/mss/1430/34, accessed on 29 August 2011.
29. *The St Albans Chronicle: The Chronica Majora of Thomas Walsingham, I, 1376–1394*, ed. J. Taylor et al. (Oxford: Clarendon Press, 2003), pp. 856–7.
30. Bower, *Scotichronicon*, vol. 8, pp. 44–7; *The Chronica Maiora of Thomas Walsingham, 1376–1422*, trans. D. Preest (Woodbridge: Boydell and Brewer, 2005), pp. 327–8.
31. C. J. Rogers, 'The Scottish invasion of 1346', *Northern History*, vol. 34 (1998), pp. 51–69. See also the appendix to this article: C. R. Rogers and M. C. Buck, 'Three new accounts of the Neville's Cross campaign', pp. 70–82.

32. Bower, *Scotichronicon*, vol. 8, pp. 44–9; *Chronica Maiora of Thomas Walsingham*, trans. Preest, p. 323.
33. M. Penman, *David II, 1329–71* (East Linton: Tuckwell Press, 2004), p. 50.
34. Nicholson, *Edward III and the Scots*, p. 232.
35. D. Hay, 'Booty in Border warfare', *Transactions of the Dumfriesshire and Galloway Natural History and Antiquarian Society*, third series, vol. 31 (1952–3), p. 158.
36. *Johannis de Fordun, Chronica Gentis Scotorum*, ed. W. F. Skene, 2 vols (Edinburgh: Edmonston and Douglas, 1871–2), vol. 1, pp. 380–1; *RPS*, 1430/29. Available at www.rps.ac.uk/mss/1430/29, accessed on 29 August 2011.
37. *RPS*, 1482/3/44. Available at www.rps.ac.uk/mss/1482/3/44, accessed on 29 August 2011.
38. S. Boardman, *The Early Stewart Kings: Robert II and Robert III* (East Linton: Tuckwell Press, 1996), pp. 115–16.
39. J. Campbell, 'England, Scotland and the Hundred Years War in the fourteenth century', in J. R. Hale, J. R. L. Highfield and B. Smalley (eds), *Europe in the Later Middle Ages* (London: Faber and Faber, 1965), pp. 199–200, 209.
40. *RPS*, 1430/32-53. Available at www.rps.ac.uk/mss/1430/32-53, accessed on 29 August 2011; *APS*, vol. 1, pp. 714–16.
41. *St Albans Chronicle*, ed. Taylor et al., pp. 868–9.
42. G. C. Swinton, 'John of Swinton: A Border fighter of the Middle Ages', *SHR*, vol. 16 (1918–19), pp. 261–79.
43. M. A. Penman, 'Christian days and knights: The religious devotions and court of David II of Scotland', *Historical Research*, vol. 75 (2002), pp. 261–5.
44. R. Lomas, 'The impact of Border warfare: The Scots and South Tweedside, c. 1290–c. 1520', *SHR*, vol. 75 (1996), pp. 143–67.
45. *St Albans Chronicle*, ed. Taylor et al., pp. 306–7.
46. *The Register of John Kirkby, Bishop of Carlisle, 1332–1352*, ed. R. L. Storey, 2 vols (Woodbridge: Boydell and Brewer for the Canterbury and York Society, 1993–5), vol. 1, pp. xiii, 2, no. 500.
47. Bower, *Scotichronicon*, vol. 7, pp. 126–7.
48. N. Mayhew, 'Alexander III – a silver age? An essay in Scottish medieval economic history', in N. H. Reid (ed.), *Scotland in the Reign of Alexander III, 1249-1286* (Edinburgh: John Donald, 1990), p. 60.
49. Bower, *Scotichronicon*, vol. 7, pp. 290–1.
50. *RPS*, 1385/6/4. Available at www.rps.ac.uk/mss/1385/6/4, accessed on 29 August 2011.
51. I. A. MacInnes, '"Shock and awe": The use of terror as a psychologi-

cal weapon during the Bruce-Balliol civil war, 1332–1338', in King and Penman (eds), *England and Scotland in the Fourteenth Century*, pp. 40–59.
52. *Calendar of Documents Relating to Scotland*, ed. J. Bain, 4 vols, with a supplementary vol. 5, ed. G. G. Simpson and J. D. Galbraith (Edinburgh: HM General Register House, 1881–1986), vol. 3, no. 1,105.
53. Thomas Walsingham, *Chronicon Angliae*, ed. E. M. Thompson (London: Rolls Series, 1874), p. 364.
54. A. J. Macdonald, 'The apogee of the "Auld Alliance" and the limits of policy, 1369–1402', *Northern Scotland*, vol. 20 (2000), pp. 38–40.
55. McGladdery, *James II*, ch. 6.
56. B. G. H. Ditcham, 'The employment of foreign mercenary troops in the French royal armies, 1415–70' (unpublished PhD thesis, University of Edinburgh, 1979).
57. J. H. Wylie, *The Reign of Henry the Fifth*, 3 vols (Cambridge: Cambridge University Press, 1914–29), vol. 3, pp. 293–310; J. D. Milner, 'The battle of Baugé, March 1421: Impact and memory', *History*, vol. 91 (2006), pp. 484–507.
58. M. K. Jones, 'The battle of Verneuil (17 August 1424): Towards a history of courage', *War in History*, vol. 9 (2002), pp. 375–411.
59. See W. Forbes-Leith, *The Scots Men-at-Arms and Life Guards in France from their Formation until their Final Dissolution AD 1418–1830*, 2 vols (Edinburgh: Paterson, 1822).
60. P. Contamine, *War in the Middle Ages*, trans. M. Jones (Oxford: Blackwell, 1984), p. 129.
61. *RPS*, 1424/20, 1458/3/7, 1471/5/6. Available at www.rps.ac.uk/mss/1424/20, www.rps.ac.uk/mss/1458/3/7 and www.rps.ac.uk/mss/1471/5/6, accessed on 29 August 2011.
62. For the contention that James I did effect a temporary change in the balance of Scottish armies, see M. Strickland and R. Hardy, *The Great Warbow: From Hastings to the Mary Rose* (Stroud: Sutton, 2005), pp. 351–3.
63. R. B. Dobson, 'Politics and the Church in the fifteenth-century north', in A. J. Pollard (ed.), *The North of England in the Age of Richard III* (Stroud: Sutton, 1996), p. 9.
64. G. Dickinson, 'Some notes on the Scottish army in the first half of the sixteenth century', *SHR*, vol. 28 (1949), pp. 133–45.
65. *RPS*, 1426/5, 1471/5/6. Available at www.rps.ac.uk/mss/1426/5 and www.rps.ac.uk/mss/1471/5/6, accessed on 29 August 2011.
66. Geoffrey Baker, *Chronicon Galfridi le Baker de Swynebroke*, ed. E. M. Thomson (Oxford: Clarendon Press, 1889), pp. 87–8; *Chronica Maiora of Thomas Walsingham*, trans. Preest, p. 323.

67. K. Stevenson, *Chivalry and Knighthood in Scotland, 1424–1513* (Woodbridge: Boydell and Brewer, 2006), pp. 125–9.
68. *St Albans Chronicle*, ed. Taylor et al., pp. 222–3.
69. *The Exchequer Rolls of Scotland*, ed. J. Stuart and G. Burnett, 23 vols (Edinburgh: HM General Register House, 1878–1908), vol. 3, pp. 55, 651; vol. 4, pp. 578–9, 626, 666.
70. By this expedient it could be claimed that the current Anglo-French truce remained unbroken. See C. J. Ford, 'Piracy or policy: The crisis in the Channel, 1400–1403', *Transactions of the Royal Historical Society*, fifth series, vol. 29 (1979), pp. 63–77.
71. Bower, *Scotichronicon*, vol. 8, pp. 136–7.
72. Ibid. pp. 412–15.
73. R. R. Davies, *The Revolt of Owain Glyn Dwr* (Oxford: Oxford University Press, 1995), pp. 189–90.
74. Penman, *David II*, p. 52.
75. *RPS*, 1429/10/4, 1430/21. Available at www.rps.ac.uk/mss/1429/10/4 and www.rps.ac.uk/mss/1430/21, accessed on 29 August 2011. For recent work on galloglass troops see S. Duffy (ed.), *The World of the Galloglass: Kings, Warlords and Warriors in Ireland and Scotland, 1200–1500* (Dublin: Four Courts Press, 2007).
76. D. J. Sadler, 'The Reid Harlaw', *History Scotland*, vol. 2, no. 4 (July/August 2002), pp. 35–40.
77. Andrew Wyntoun, *The Original Chronicle of Andrew of Wyntoun*, ed. A. Amours, 6 vols (Edinburgh: Scottish Text Society, 1903–14), vol. 6, pp. 371–4. A similar reaction of rapid mobilisation and combativeness had greeted an earlier Highland incursion into Angus in 1392.
78. Brown, *James I*, pp. 137–9.
79. For an influential and divergent view, see M. H. Brown, 'Scotland tamed? Kings and magnates in late medieval Scotland: A review of recent work', *Innes Review*, vol. 45 (1994), pp. 120–46.
80. Nicholson, *Scotland*, p. 370, calls the encounter a 'fight'.
81. McGladdery, *James II*, p. 97.
82. Macdougall, *James III*, pp. 255–63.
83. A. Grant, 'Crown and nobility in late medieval Britain', in R. Mason (ed.), *Scotland and England, 1286–1815* (Edinburgh: John Donald, 1987), pp. 34–59 provides an important discussion of political violence.
84. Stevenson, *Chivalry*, pp. 18, 183.
85. *Registrum Honoris de Morton* (Edinburgh: Bannatyne Club, 1853), nos 193, 196.
86. *Gilbert of the Haye's Prose Manuscript (AD 1456)*, ed. J. H. Stevenson, 2 vols (Edinburgh: Scottish Text Society, 1901–14).
87. Penman, *David II*, pp. 71–2; Brown, *Black Douglases*, p. 211.

88. A. H. Dunbar, 'Facsimiles of the Scottish coats of arms emblazoned in the "Armorial de Gelre", with notes', *Proceedings of the Society of Antiquaries of Scotland*, vol. 25 (1890–91), pp. 9–19.
89. C. Edington, 'The tournament in medieval Scotland', in M. Strickland (ed.), *Armies, Chivalry and Warfare in Medieval Britain and France* (Stamford: Paul Watkins, 1998), pp. 55–6.
90. The idea that there was a fifteenth-century Scottish chivalric order has been shown to lack substance: K. Stevenson, 'The unicorn, St Andrew and the thistle: Was there an order of chivalry in late medieval Scotland?', *SHR*, vol. 83 (2004), pp. 3–22.
91. D. Ditchburn, *Scotland and Europe: The Medieval Kingdom and its Contacts with Christendom, c. 1215–1545, Volume 1: Religion, Culture and Commerce* (East Linton: Tuckwell Press, 2000), pp. 65–73.
92. Ditchburn, *Scotland and Europe*, p. 70.
93. Stevenson, *Chivalry and Knighthood*, pp. 15–16, 127–8.
94. Blind Harry, *The Wallace*, ed. A. McKim (Edinburgh: Canongate, 2003), pp. 178–9.
95. Bower, *Scotichronicon*, vol. 8, pp. 14–19.
96. M. Prestwich, 'The English at the battle of Neville's Cross', in Rollason and Prestwich (eds), *The Battle of Neville's Cross*, p. 12; Bower, *Scotichronicon*, vol. 8, pp. 58–9, 126–7.

6
Scotland in the Age of the Military Revolution, 1488–1560

GERVASE PHILLIPS

'O what a noble and triumphant courage was thys for a kynge to fyghte in a battayl as a meane souldier!' So declared the English chronicler Edward Hall in admiration of the reckless bravery of James IV the King of Scots, slain in the thickest press of the *mêlée* at Flodden field on 9 September 1513.[1] It was a tribute rooted in the old ideal of a warrior king who led but did not command and whose conspicuous courage was itself 'triumphant', even in defeat. Viewed thus, history might judge James as little more than a relic of an obsolete chivalry. Scotland's armies of this age, too, seemed archaic hosts – commoners mustered through ancient bonds of personal loyalty and social obligation. They dutifully followed their lairds and noblemen to war, and to three catastrophic defeats at the hands of the English: Flodden (1513), Solway Moss (1542) and Pinkie (1547). This grim succession of disasters left a powerful impression of an enfeebled capacity for warfare.

In continental Europe, soldiers were transforming the conduct of war: they had rediscovered Roman order; they were perfecting the battlefield use of gunpowder weapons; they built sophisticated artillery fortifications; and they took service with powerful centralised states with the financial resources to sustain professional military forces. This, it has been argued, was the age of Europe's 'military revolution', when the modern nation state was born out of the welter of organised violence.[2] Yet Scotland's apparently archaic way of war seems of little relevance to historians of tactical reform and technological innovation in the early modern period. Indeed, early-sixteenth-century Scottish armies have been viewed merely as the English crown's 'most backward of adversaries'.[3]

It may appear that any attempt to challenge this view would flounder after those triple defeats of Flodden, Solway Moss and Pinkie.

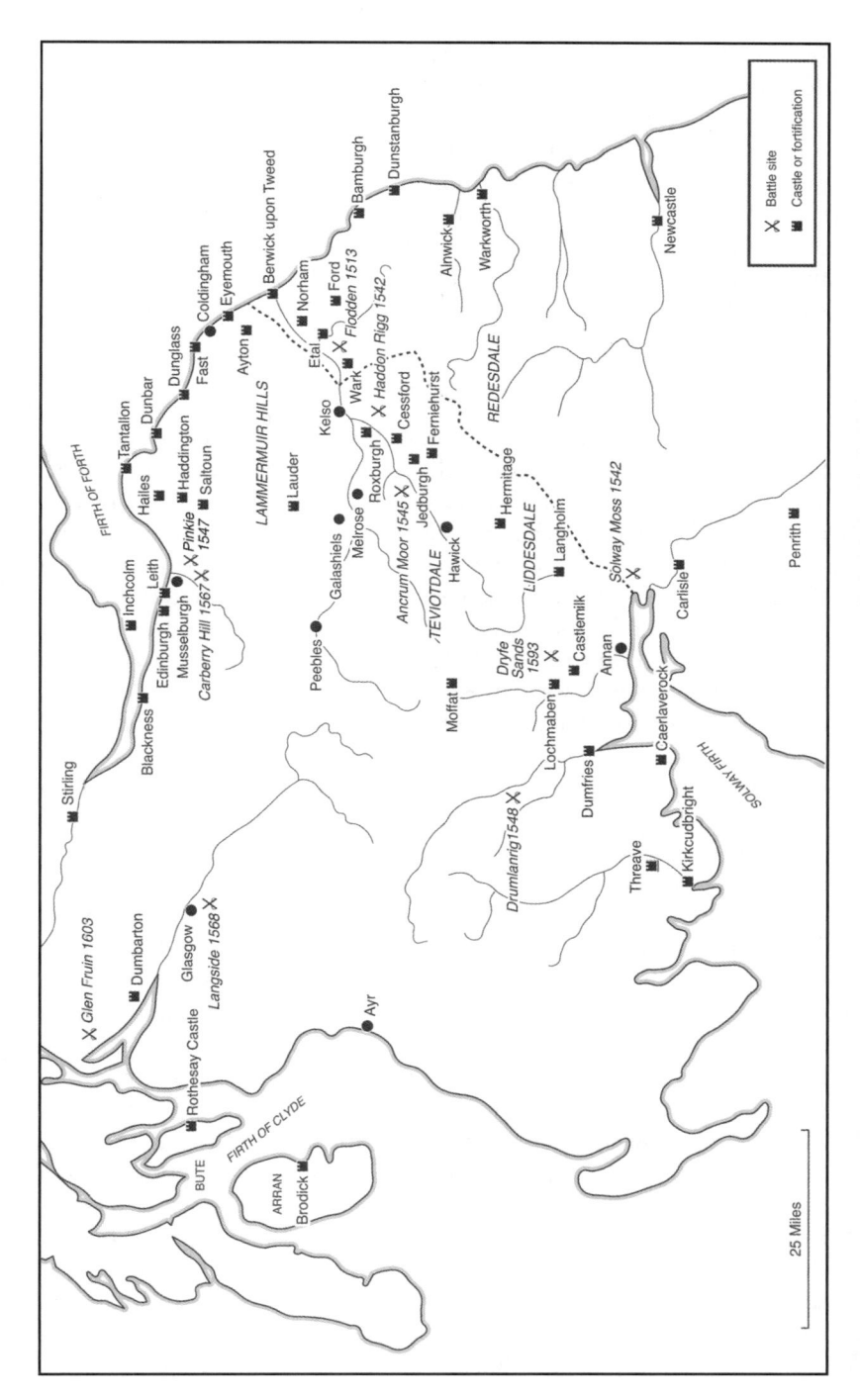

Map 6.1 Southern Scotland and northern England in the sixteenth and early seventeenth centuries.

But the memory of these fields has obscured an essential truth about Scotland's military capacity: Scottish soldiers endured, even in the aftermath of disaster, and Scotland escaped English hegemony. Furthermore, an appreciation of this capacity for sustained resistance necessitates a revision of a common understanding of the Anglo-Scots wars of the sixteenth century. They were not futile English campaigns that delayed the (otherwise inevitable) dynastic union between the two countries: they were a triumph of Scottish resilience that demonstrated the fundamental viability of an independent Scotland.[4]

Recruitment, troop types and equipment

Underpinning this resilience was a military system that allowed the Scottish crown to raise large, well-equipped armies at short notice. There were relatively few in Scotland who could be described as professional soldiers, although the tradition of highlanders serving as mercenaries in Ireland persisted. Others had gained experience in the service of France and whenever those 'weill besene and practissit in weirs' could be found they were put to good use in the field: at the battle of Haddon Rig in 1542, the Scottish vanguard was led by Sir Walter Lyndsay, a veteran Knight of St John.[5] For the most part, however, Scotland depended on men levied for specific campaigns.[6] Forces were raised by privy letters from the crown to lairds and magnates who, via the bonds of 'manrent', a formal contract between a man and his lord, could muster large bodies for service. Yet there was always the risk that these could become private armies. More reliance was, therefore, placed upon a national militia system.[7]

It should not be assumed that such a levy inevitably produced 'backward' armies. All men between the ages of sixteen and sixty were obliged to serve for a maximum of forty days per year at their own expense. They were to possess arms and armour appropriate to their station. Musters known as wapinshawings (weapon showings) were held two to four times each year to ensure that this obligation was met. For the wealthy, this meant donning 'white harness' (plate armour) for they took their place in the front rank of Scottish 'battles' (as large tactical units were called). Those who led the columns at Flodden, noted Hall, were 'all chosen men with speres on foote . . . the most assuredlyest harnessed that hath bene sene'.[8] As for the men they led to war, the Englishman William Patten, who served at Pinkie, noted in 1547 that the Scottish infantry 'cum to the felde well furnished all with jak [lightweight body armour of metal plates sewn into a leather garment] and skull [helmet], dagger, buckler [shield], and swoordes'.[9]

By the early sixteenth century the pike had become the preferred weapon for lowlanders but other arms, generally an axe or pole-arm, were considered acceptable.[10] The 'wild Scots' of the Highlands and Western Isles preferred bows for engaging at a distance, then a combination of axe, broadsword and targe (shield), or the *claidheamh-mor* – a fearsome double-handed sword – for 'handstrokes'. Some of these highlanders wore a protective linen garment 'sewed together in patchwork, well daubed with wax or pitch, and an overcoat of deerskin'.[11] Their chiefs wore the hauberk (mail shirt) and, with shields on one arm and 'Danish' axes cradled in the other, they would not have looked so very far removed from the Viking warriors who had once raided and settled western Scotland.

The lowlanders' adoption of the pike, and the aggressive use of the assault by pike column on the battlefield, were emulations of the most successful continental infantry of the day: the Swiss and the Germans. At Flodden, the Scots advanced 'in good order, after the Almaynes [German] manner'.[12] Even the tactical deployment of Highland contingents as skirmishers in front of the main formations had contemporary equivalents on the continent. In the early sixteenth century armies conventionally manoeuvred in three large 'battles', the forward (or vanguard), the main battle and rearward, but smaller bodies of troops might be thrown out as 'wings' to the flanks or as an advance guard ahead of the forward. At Céresoles in 1544, for example, the battle was opened by a fast-moving combat between several hundred Imperialist and French arquebusiers,[13] while Henry VIII recruited mercenary Irish kern (lightly armed troops) especially for this service.[14]

Scottish mounted troops were overwhelmingly light horse, mostly raised in the Borders. For raiding and 'scouring' (reconnaissance) these light cavalry, or Border Horse, were highly prized. The French, for example, eagerly employed them. Of the 1,600 light horse garrisoned in Péronne in 1558, 600 were Scottish, serving under their own captains.[15] The English had also developed an effective battle cavalry and bred appropriate chargers. The passing of the War Horses Act of 1542 obliged the wealthy to provide both horses and men to serve as 'demilancers' (lancers in three-quarter armour).[16] James V strove to meet this challenge and did much to encourage horse breeding. Yet making a significant impact on the quality of the national herd took years and it was only in the latter half of the century that progress was evident.

Although generally outweighed, the Scottish mounted arm was nonetheless able to make its presence felt on campaign. Indeed, the first half of the sixteenth century witnessed a striking rise in the importance of cavalry in warfare within Britain. This is perhaps most clearly illustrated by contrasting the composition of forces at Flodden in 1513 and Pinkie in 1547. At Flodden the Scottish army, perhaps 26,000 strong, had fought entirely on foot while the English, numbering around 22,500, fielded 1,500 cavalry, all of whom were Border horsemen. Yet by the battle of Pinkie, a Scottish army of again around 26,000 included some 1,500 light cavalry compared with the English army, numbering 18,000 in total, which included 2,000 light and 4,000 heavy horse.[17] During the three-year struggle that followed Pinkie, with the English seeking to maintain isolated garrisons across Lothian and the Borders, Scottish mounted forces threatened their survival, ambushing convoys and patrols. In these conditions their small, hardy horses were far less likely to succumb to exposure, lack of fodder and overwork than the larger mounts of the English demilancers.

For missile support, Scotland's armies fielded substantial numbers of bowmen. Both English bowyers and French crossbow manufacturers worked under royal patronage in Edinburgh in the 1530s, an indication of the value placed on their crafts.[18] It might be tempting to view this adherence to the bow as evidence of isolation from the mainstream of continental warfare, where the arquebus was increasingly dominating battlefields. Yet the pattern of adopting handheld firearms in Scotland largely mirrors the experience of other European powers during the same period. In this regard, the closest parallel was England. So long as both countries could muster an appreciable number of skilled bowmen, widespread adoption of firearms was unnecessary. Although lacking the armour penetration of a gunpowder weapon, the bow had its own advantages in combat, most significantly a higher rate of fire. Even Humphrey Barwick, an Elizabethan critic of archery, accepted that an archer could loose six arrows in forty seconds compared with the arquebusier's single shot.[19] Bowmen displayed their utility well into the sixteenth century. Thus, for example, John Erskine of Dun repelled an English amphibious assault on Montrose with archery in 1548.[20]

The rise of gunpowder weapons

If adherence to the bow was particularly pronounced within the British Isles it was not unique, and French armies of the day retained a considerable proportion of crossbowmen.[21] But the potential of handheld gunpowder weapons was now recognised by all, including the Scots. There was an established import trade for firearms and small numbers of hand-gunners had taken the field with Scottish armies throughout the latter half of the fifteenth century. Thereafter, there is plentiful evidence for the gradual proliferation of firearms: in 1522 a force under John Stewart, duke of Albany, levied to invade England, possessed a 'marvelous greate number of hand gonnes' and many *arquebus à croc* (large firearms mounted on wagons); in 1541 there were 413 arquebuses held in Edinburgh castle; at the battle of Haddon Rig in 1542, the vanguard was led by 500 bowmen and 500 'hagbuttis'; and by 1553 it was a legal requirement for Scottish Borderers to arm themselves with a 'hagbut'.[22]

The crucial decade in the widespread adoption of gunpowder firearms was, however, the 1540s. Having seized Boulogne in late 1544, Henry VIII's expeditionary forces in France had found themselves caught in a prolonged war of emplacement around the port. Both sides constructed impressive earthworks: angled bastions, gun emplacements and forts on the modern *trace italienne* model. To the English, it was a fast-paced education in modern military engineering and an incentive to increase the number of arquebusiers, who were more useful than bowmen in the defence of deep trenches, narrow parapets, confined casements and small gun loops.[23] Once the English, and latterly the French, began constructing similar fortifications in Scotland between 1547 and 1550, there was an urgent requirement, on all sides, for arquebusiers.[24] By the end of the decade, Scottish battlefields were dominated by the fire of gunpowder small arms. As Franco-Scottish forces fought to drive an English garrison from Haddington in 1549, Lord Methven reported to the Dowager Queen, Mary of Guise, 'daly and nychtlie is at all ouris carmoshe of hacbuttis'.[25]

The use of larger gunpowder weapons, both siege cannon and lighter 'field' pieces, is of even greater importance. It has been suggested that the increased use of artillery was of particular significance in the rise of the early modern state in Europe. As only kings and emperors were wealthy enough to manufacture and purchase artillery trains and keep them supplied in the field, it is argued, they established a monopoly on their use. The castle-shattering capacity of their cannon brought greater control over 'over-mighty subjects', the peripheral regions of their own kingdoms and weaker neighbours. Greater control brought greater tax revenues, which paid for more guns and more soldiers and saw, therefore, yet more power gravitating to the political centre.[26]

In Scotland's case, while it might be an overstatement to credit cannon with creating a modern state, they nevertheless appear to have played some part in the process of nation-building. Towards the end of his reign, James III (1460–88) furnished a number of coastal and border castles with defensive artillery, largely supplied from France. But there is little indication that he attempted to employ artillery to defend his crown from rebel forces, with his son James, duke of Rothesay, at their head at the battle of Sauchieburn on 11 June 1488. This was a scrappy affair, with royal forces disintegrating as they were pursued from the field and the king overtaken and killed near Bannockburn. It was, however, Rothesay, crowned as James IV, for whom cannon became a more integral instrument of policy. Faced with rebellion in 1489, he used the royal artillery to capture smaller castles, such as Duchal and Crookston, but Dumbarton defied the young king. In 1491, in a contest with the powerful Douglas family, James's artillery was back in the field, laying siege to their castle at Tantallon.[27] The king appreciated the need for more and better cannon. Although he imported both guns and gunners from France, in 1511 he appointed a Scottish master gunner, Robert Borthwick, to maintain a royal artillery train that soon boasted fine guns of Scottish manufacture.[28]

The history of James IV's artillery cannot be properly separated from that of his navy. For the king to project military force across the whole of his realm required both guns and ships. In this sense, Scotland's geography imposed its own logic on the nation's military development. Annual expenditure on the navy showed a dramatic rise over the course of James's reign: from about £140 per annum between 1488 and 1498 to £5,000 per annum between 1505 and 1507, and £8,710 10s per annum between 1511 and 1513. The most impressive product of this investment was the *Great Michael*. Launched in 1511, it had a keel of perhaps 240 feet in length and was armed with twenty-four cannons in broadside, three larger 'basilisks' and 300 smaller guns, ranging from light cannon, 'falcons and quarter falcons', to anti-personnel pieces. It carried 300 mariners and 120 gunners, with the capacity to transport up to 1,000 soldiers. Not only was it bigger than any potential rival, but its weight of ordnance indicates that it was designed to sink opposing ships or bombard land fortifications with stand-off gunfire, rather than simply serving as a troop platform (the *Great Michael*'s only action in Scottish service was, in fact, a shore bombardment of the English garrison of Carrickfergus in Ulster in 1513).[29]

Guns and ships gave James the capacity to undertake amphibious operations. Although on a smaller scale than the contemporary joint military-naval campaigns waged by the monarchs Ferdinand of Aragon and Isabella of Castile during the final stages of the *Reconquista* of Nasrid Spain, his expeditions to enforce royal authority in the Highlands and Isles between 1494 and 1499 were examples of 'cannon conquest'.[30] The large, semi-independent maritime empire ruled by John MacDonald, Lord of the Isles, did not survive James's expeditions. The lordship was forfeited to the crown and John died a court pensioner in 1503. Resistance under John's grandson, Donald Dubh MacDonald, was similarly defeated in 1506 by a force supplied by the king with guns, ships and money. The royal cannon, however, failed to overawe another rebel, Torquil MacLeod of Lewis, who, secure in his remote island fastness, remained active until his death in 1511.[31]

The creation of an impressive artillery train had important implications for Anglo-Scottish relations. Acting in support of the Yorkist pretender, Perkin Warbeck, James invaded England in September 1496. It was an audacious intervention into English affairs and a logistical triumph: cannon, munitions and a mass of associated equipment had been carried across the Tweed. The invasion itself, however, was little more than a grand foray, and James fell back when an English army under Thomas Howard, earl of Surrey, approached. Yet the lesson was clear: James could transport his artillery train overland from Edinburgh and across the border into England. This gave him considerable leverage over the English crown, and the following year he repeated the feat, besieging Norham castle.[32]

Although Norham resisted successfully, and the king again withdrew before the advance of an English army, the incursions of 1496 and 1497 bolstered James's authority in Scotland. His avoidance of a major battle demonstrated military prudence while his behaviour in combat was courageous to the point of recklessness. This was only proper, since, as the king explained to the Spanish ambassador Don Pedro de Ayala, he expected his subjects to serve him in just and unjust quarrels and hence he should be the first in harm's way.[33] It was a principle he would uphold until his death at Flodden in 1513 and was widely shared by contemporaries across Europe. Gaston de Foix, duke of Nemours, for example, threw his life away in a chivalric but pointless charge against the rearguard of a beaten Spanish army at Ravenna in 1512, while King Francis I of France was unhorsed and taken prisoner at Pavia in 1525. James's risk-taking on the battlefield was characteristic of the age.

Here again, the Scottish way of war fits well into the broader European context. Scotland was part of the late fifteenth-century 'resuscitation' of chivalry under the sponsorship of James IV. Chivalry could find peacetime expression in pageantry and tournament, with the king himself taking on the allegorical, but not inappropriate, role of 'the wild knight' in 1507. Yet the chivalric ethos also served a practical military function. James's habit of dubbing men while on campaign rewarded exemplary behaviour on the battlefield, fostered strong ties of personal loyalty and ensured that in combat his men would be led by proven captains. Knights drawn in this way from the lesser nobility and gentry assumed positions of military responsibility and, to a degree, performed the functions of a professional officer corps. John Ogilvy of Finglask, for example, was knighted during the Border wars of the 1490s and went on to serve as the constable of Inverness castle and sheriff of Inverness.[34]

James's initial campaigns also demonstrated that a well-developed chivalric sense did not preclude sound military judgements. When a retaliatory English raiding force pushed into Scotland and sacked Ayton in August 1497, the king would not be goaded into a battle, allowing instead Henry VII's lack of funds, and the English army's tenuous supply lines, to force his enemy to retreat. James, the tactical risk-taker, was also a cautious strategist whose pursuit of 'limited objectives' (as Niall Barr has described them) was vindicated by the campaigns of 1496–7.[35] Henry VII certainly had to take James seriously, for he had twice demonstrated the vulnerability of north-east England to Scottish attack. In the ensuing negotiations, James reaped considerable diplomatic dividends, including his marriage to Henry's daughter Margaret. War, as an instrument of policy, had served James well.[36]

The Flodden campaign, 1513

It is in this context that the decision to embark upon the ill-fated Flodden campaign of 1513 should be judged. With Henry VIII campaigning in France, James had the opportunity to attack England, demonstrate his commitment to Louis XII of France and win fresh personal laurels on the battlefield. James moved against Norham castle on 24 August with an army probably in excess of 30,000 men, although desertion (the bane of all pre-modern armies) reduced it to around 26,000 by the day of the encounter at Flodden.[37] Norham's fate, however, was sealed by cannon, not by numbers. James's siege train was much enhanced since 1497; it included the famous 'seven sisters', heavy guns, probably cast by Borthwick, which smashed down the castle's walls in five days.[38] Three smaller castles, Etal, Chillingham and Ford, rapidly succumbed to the threat of Scottish artillery.

On 6 September the earl of Surrey, at the head of 22,000 Englishmen, located the Scottish army well entrenched on Flodden Edge. One of its flanks was protected by marshy ground, the other by steep slopes, so that the only clear approach was across a field and straight at Borthwick's guns. Surrey's army, moreover, was tired after its forced march north, short of food and out of beer. With Scottish scourers soon reporting that the English army was on the move, it must have seemed to James that Surrey was making either for Scotland, to execute some retaliatory raid, or for Berwick to revictual. It was only mid-morning on 9 September when the truth dawned: Surrey had executed a flank march and would soon be taking up a position between the Scottish army and home. As the English moved to seize Branxton Edge in the Scottish rear, James had to act. Abandoning his position, he placed his trust in the assault by close-order pike. Surrey described five Scottish battles 'in grete plumps', each 'an arrowe shotte from the othre', advancing 'after the Almaynes manner withoute spekyng of eny worde'.[39] As the two armies closed, there was a brief exchange of artillery fire, but Borthwick's cannon, attempting to fire downhill, did little damage: 'our bullets . . . did thame na hurt, bot flewe ouer thair heidis'. Meanwhile, English cannon balls crashed into the oncoming columns 'to breke and constreyn the Scottisshe great army'.[40]

Charging from the Scots' left flank, Home and Huntly's forces swept away the hopelessly outnumbered English vanguard. The whole English right flank wavered momentarily before a timely charge by 1,500 Border Horse under Lord Dacre crashed into the Scots and brought their advance to a standstill. To the right of Home's column, Montrose and Crawford led their men against the English battle commanded by Surrey's son, Thomas Howard, the Lord Admiral. Beyond them, the king drove his column into Surrey's main battle. On Surrey's left, however, the English rearward took the offensive, scrambling up Branxton and coming quickly to 'hand-strokes' with Argyll's highlanders. The Scots found 'the Englishmen not fleeing, but manfullie standing at resistance, so that there was a right hard incounter', while a Northumbrian veteran recalled 'it is not to be doubted, but the Scotts faught manly, and were determined outthir to wynne or to dye'.[41] Slowly the English hacked their way into the now disordered pike columns. It was a 'right hard incountre' but, ultimately, as the Cheshire bard Leigh of Baggerley sang, 'we blanked

Figure 6.1 The battle of Flodden, 1513, depicted in a contemporary woodcut by Hans Burgkmair. The Scottish pikemen are routed by the English infantry (seen to the right) who wield bills, a weapon better suited to close combat than the cumbersome pike. King James IV lies slain in the foreground.

them with billes through all their bright armor'.⁴² The magnitude of Scotland's defeat was reflected in the toll of the dead: James was slain alongside most of his country's nobility and gentry and 5,000 of their compatriots. The English army lost some 1,500 men, but claimed a spectacular victory. Surrey sent James's bloodied surcoat to London and hauled his captured artillery to Etal.⁴³

James's death threw the kingdom onto the defensive, for Henry VIII resolved that Scotland should be punished for the invasion. Thomas Lord Dacre favoured launching a large number of fast-moving raids to strike at dispersed targets, but Henry insisted upon two grand forays converging on Jedburgh. These took time to organise, allowing the Warden General of the Scottish Marches, Alexander Home, to prepare his defences. Dacre's forces were harried at every turn, and Home even launched small forays of his own into England.⁴⁴ In 1522, John Stewart, duke of Albany and now 'Governor' (regent) to the infant James V, even mustered a Franco-Scottish army for a counter invasion of England, but his men refused to follow their arrogant and overbearing French officers across the border.⁴⁵

The campaigns of 1523

To meet the threat from England, the burgh council of Edinburgh constructed a wall around vulnerable parts of the city which, although unable to withstand a formal siege, could hold a large foray at bay. Older fortifications were upgraded to counter the use of cannon, and Albany had a massive masonry blockhouse added to Dunbar castle. Elsewhere, as at Cessford castle, the medieval 'barmkin' (outer) wall was strengthened with a 'rampire' (a sloping earthwork that could absorb cannon shot) to the front and an earthen 'countermure' to the rear. The results of this innovative military architecture proved startlingly effective.⁴⁶

In May 1523, the earl of Surrey (the Lord Admiral of Flodden) led a column against a series of Scottish strongpoints. Cessford, however, stopped the foray in its tracks, for Surrey's guns made little impression on the earth-strengthened walls. The castle's surrender was eventually negotiated but it was a hollow victory for Surrey: he had been stalled too long, using up his victuals and munitions, and could now only withdraw to England.⁴⁷ His renewed campaign in September profited the English little. Though Jedburgh was sacked and burned, its defenders had fought stubbornly, as did those of nearby Ferniehurst castle. Again the English soon withdrew from Scotland, bloodied and weary.⁴⁸ Albany's counter-offensive, however, was poorly supported and, after a failed campaign, he withdrew, disillusioned, to France,⁴⁹ leaving the new regent, Angus, to establish a truce with England in 1525.

In 1528 the young James V attempted to assert his personal rule. Major Douglas strongholds including Tantallon and Coldingham priory were besieged but successfully resisted. Force, however, remained an integral means of re-establishing royal authority. For example, the king issued 'letters of fire and sword' to James, earl of Moray, instructing him on how to deal with the unruly Clan Chattan: 'invaid thame to thair utter destructioun, be slauchtir, byrning, drowning, and uthir ways; and leif no cretur levand of that clan, except preistis, wemen and bainis'.⁵⁰

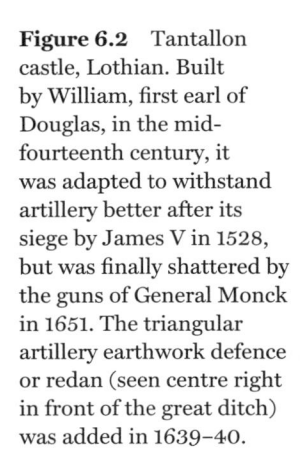

Figure 6.2 Tantallon castle, Lothian. Built by William, first earl of Douglas, in the mid-fourteenth century, it was adapted to withstand artillery better after its siege by James V in 1528, but was finally shattered by the guns of General Monck in 1651. The triangular artillery earthwork defence or redan (seen centre right in front of the great ditch) was added in 1639–40.

The battle of Solway Moss, 1542

James remained committed to close ties with France and hostile to the Reformation. His choice of a French bride, Mary of Guise, and the raising of David Beaton to cardinal, demonstrated his unwillingness to bend to the will of England's king. By 1541, Henry had accordingly resolved to brutalise Scotland into passivity while he waged war on France. On 24 August 1542, a 3,000-strong English foray under Robert Bowes, accompanied by the earl of Angus, entered Teviotdale. The Scots, however, were able to round up the numerous small forays sent out by Bowes, while his main base at Haddon Rig was overrun by George Gordon, earl of Huntly.[51] A second English expedition in October commanded by Thomas Howard, duke of Norfolk, was another failure, lasting just six days.[52]

Despite initial problems in mustering troops, James switched to the offensive. On 24 November, Robert Maxwell and Oliver Sinclair led an army some 18,000 strong across the border, hoping to catch the English off guard. But while it was dangerously strung out across the boggy ground of Solway Moss, 700 English Border Horse galloped out of the mist and struck into the dense mass of troops. The invading force simply collapsed. The number of slain on both sides was small but 1,200 Scots were made pris-

Figure 6.3 James Hamilton, earl of Arran and duke of Châtelherault, after a portrait attributed to Arnold Bronckorst, 1578. Governor Arran had to resist constant English military incursions.

oner, including many prominent lords. Generously treated while guests of the English crown, they would form the core of a pro-English party among the Scottish nobility. On 14 December, three weeks after he received the news from Solway Moss, James V died.[53]

He left his week-old baby daughter, Mary Queen of Scots, as his successor. Henry's Scottish captives dutifully requested that he take her under his protection with a view to her eventual betrothal to his son, Edward. Mary's regent, the Governor James Hamilton, earl of Arran, was judged to be favourably inclined to the Reformation, and the prospects for dynastic union seemed real. Yet the peaceful future promised by the union agreed at Greenwich on 1 July 1543 was illusory. Henry crassly offered Arran English troops to crush the opposition faction now coalescing around Beaton and Mary of Guise, and Scots resolved to defend their liberty. The new mood was signified by Arran himself, who heard Mass and received the Sacrament from Beaton. Henry therefore sought to win the bride for his son by force of arms. The 'Rough Wooing' had begun.

The 'Rough Wooing'

Henry instructed Edward Seymour, earl of Hertford, to 'put all to fire and sword' and 'burn Edinburgh town'.[54] Hertford's large fleet allowed an amphibious strike deep into Lothian in conjunction with a land campaign across the border. Henry also opened a new front in the Highlands: Donald Dubh MacDonald, John MacDonald's grandson, sought to reclaim the lordship of the Isles with English financial support. With another English ally, Matthew Stewart, earl of Lennox, he fomented conflict across the Highlands and by 1545 was engaging in seaborne raids against Bute, Arran and Argyll. English strategy was now to seize and hold strongpoints within Scotland in order to create an English Pale, peopled by those known as 'assured Scots', who took an oath of loyalty to the English crown.[55]

Any assessment of Governor Arran's defence of the realm during the fighting of 1544–5 must acknowledge the particular difficulties he faced. Judging where to concentrate forces to meet any threat was complicated by the vulnerability of both the land border and the coastline. Manpower and resources were diverted away from the defence of the Borders by the pressing need to pacify the Highlands, and protracted siege operations exposed one undeniable weakness of the Scottish militia-based armies – they were not obliged to remain in the field longer than forty days. Arran perforce adopted a largely Fabian strategy: battle avoidance; retreat before overwhelming numbers; and the husbanding of resources. It was a policy that may have seemed like weakness, but it allowed for the re-establishment of his authority over the Highlands and created the opportunity, in early 1545, for a striking victory for Scottish arms at Ancrum Moor.

The battle of Ancrum Moor, 1545

On 4 May 1544 Hertford's army disembarked near Leith and his vanguard of archers and arquebusiers quickly overran the earthwork defences Arran had prepared.[56] The city walls of Edinburgh held the English up for some time before Canongate was finally stormed. The garrison withdrew successfully to defend the castle, which defied bombardment, but the city itself, including the palace and Holyrood House, was pillaged and fired.[57] Hertford's men then harried and burned across Lothian, meeting little organised resistance, while the English navy carried destruction along the length of the eastern coast.

Yet Scotland weathered the storm. Arran made common cause with Mary of Guise and Beaton and together they forged a more unified opposition to Henry VIII's onslaughts. Militarily, the most important figure in a reinvigorated Scottish defence was the earl of Angus, formerly an ally of England. Angus's land, his kin and his tenants had been harried hard by English borderers under three ambitious knights, Sir Ralph Eure, Sir Brian Layton and Sir George Bowes. Henry rewarded their endeavours with title to the lands they had ravaged, and many of the estates thus granted to Eure and Layton belonged to Angus. When the latter heard the news he promised to write his *sasine*, the document proving ownership of land, on their skins 'with a sharp pen and bloody ink'.[58]

On 27 February 1545 Angus ambushed the two English knights as they rode through Teviotdale with 5,000 men. A feigned retreat by a small body of Scottish light horse across Ancrum Moor then tricked the raiders into a reckless pursuit. They were led straight into a solid phalanx of pikemen which Angus had positioned across a narrow section of Dere Street. The local population (including, according to folklore, the courageous 'Maid of Lilliard' fighting to avenge her murdered lover) joined in the slaughter. Some 1,000 were taken captive and 800 were slain, Layton and Eure among them.[59]

There was now much to be optimistic about from a military perspective. Five well-attended general musters held in Scotland over the course of 1545 demonstrated the nation's will and capacity to sustain the war. The earl of Huntly had hunted down the adherents of Donald of the Isles and soon Highland levies were once again available for service in the Lowlands.[60] Arran, maturing as a military commander, recaptured Threave, Lochmaben and Caerlaverock castles from English garrisons. Realising the limitations of reliance on a national militia, he established a semi-permanent band of 1,000 light cavalry to guard the Merse and Teviotdale, funded by a special tax.[61]

When necessary, Arran chose to avoid battle rather than risk defeat, trusting Scotland's defence to weaknesses in English logistics. Hertford brought another army of 16,000 men into Scotland in September 1545, but dwindling supplies forced him to withdraw and the raid's political impact was fleeting.[62] By the end of the year the governor's authority was strengthened and parliament had begun prosecuting those 'sitting under assurance of the King of Ingland'. When England and France signed the peace treaty of Camp on 6 June 1546, Scotland was included in its terms.[63]

Henry, however, continued to meddle in Scottish affairs, sending munitions to the 'Castilians', the Protestant conspirators who, on 29 May 1546, had seized St Andrews and put Cardinal Beaton to the sword. A garrison of English Borderers strongly fortified Langholm castle in the Scottish West March, converting its lowered tower into a gun platform and countermuring the stairs, windows and chimney with earth. In July 1547 Arran had to mobilise 20,000 men and a considerable siege train, 'the starkest host and the monest and with the best order that was sen Flodden', to take this ancient 'pile'.[64] It required the arrival of French auxiliaries in the same month under Leo Strozzi, a Knight of St John, to breach the walls of St Andrews castle.[65]

Somerset's invasion of 1547 and the battle of Pinkie Cleugh

Following Henry VIII's death on 28 January 1547, Edward Seymour, now duke of Somerset, became lord protector of England and regent to his nephew, the boy king Edward VI. Late that summer, he renewed the English offensive with two simultaneous invasions. The main 'Army Royal' of 18,000 men advanced from Berwick, supported by an armada of eighty ships, while in the west 2,000 foot and 500 horse (300 of whom were assured Scots) under Lord Wharton and the earl of Lennox took Annan and established garrisons in Castlemilk and Moffat.[66] Despite difficulties, Arran assembled an army of some 26,000 foot, 4,000 archers, 1,500 light horse and a train of at least twenty-five guns, plus some *arquebus à croc* at Fala Muir by 31 August.[67] Dependent upon tenuous supply lines, Somerset needed a quick victory. Arran, however, had deployed his army in earthwork fortifications defending the line of the River Esk, along the raised ground of Edmonston Edge between Musselburgh and Inveresk. His left flank rested on the coast, his right on the boggy ground of the Shire Moss. The most mobile elements were employed as wings: Argyll's highlanders on the shoreline and the Border Horse flung out to the right, on the western edge of Fawside Brae, a hill overlooking the English encampment at Prestonpans. The Scottish army's flanks could not be turned on land and a frontal assault on his position would have been reckless folly. Yet Arran could not counter Somerset's fleet and his powerful cavalry force, led by William, Lord Grey of Wilton.[68] When around 1,500 Scottish light horse 'bickered' at the English on Fawside Brae, trying to tempt them into a pursuit onto the pikes of 500 Scottish foot lying concealed behind them, Grey had 2,000 of his horsemen charge just as the Scots wheeled before them. Caught by surprise, Arran's mounted arm was badly mauled, losing around 800 men.[69]

Nevertheless, the following morning, 10 September, the Scottish position still appeared strong. Somerset offered to withdraw his army from Scotland and pay for the damage caused if only the Scots would consent to the marriage of Mary and Edward. Arran rejected the proposal. He was conscious of his numerical superiority and hoped that a fleet of sixty-two French ships would arrive in a timely fashion to deal with the English fleet under Lord Clinton.[70] Meanwhile, Somerset seemed in no hurry to seek battle that day. He commanded a considerable weight of ordnance, including Clinton's ships, now in the Firth of Forth, which could bombard the Scottish left. Moreover, if his forces could seize two prominent points, Carberry Hill, overlooking the Scottish right flank, and St Michael's Church of Inveresk on Pinkie Cleugh, overlooking their centre, they could establish batteries that could pummel the whole Scottish line. But what Somerset failed to anticipate, as his army meandered somewhat carelessly across the face of the enemy position, was that Arran might take the offensive.

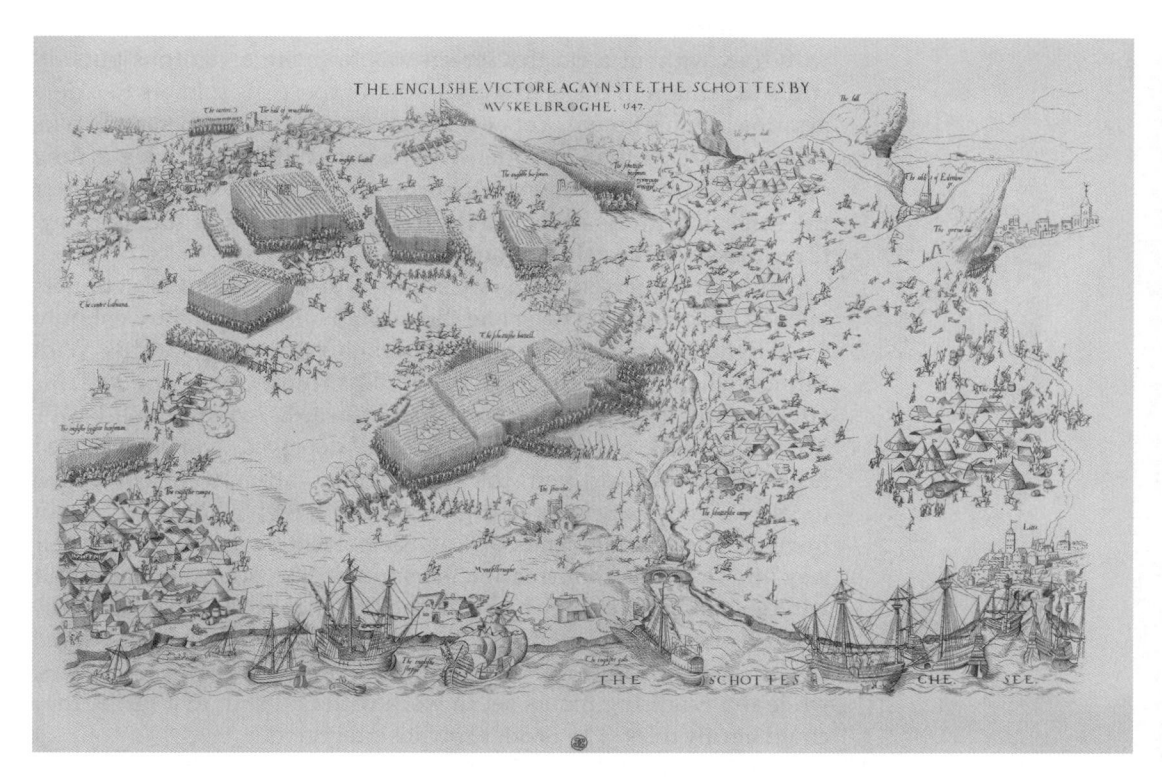

This audacious stroke was not born of consensus in the Scottish camp. Angus, commanding the Scottish vanguard, at first refused to attack and only obeyed a second order 'under pain of treason'. In retrospect, his hesitancy may seem wise, but Arran's options were limited. Given the superiority of the English mounted arm, to

Figure 6.4 The battle of Pinkie Cleugh, 1547, from a contemporary English engraving. In the centre, the three divisions of Scottish pikemen are heavily engaged and repel an English cavalry attack, but some of their rear ranks are already breaking in flight towards the river Esk.

withdraw without a cavalry screen was to invite a vigorous pursuit, while to remain in the field works would expose his soldiers to a devastating bombardment. Yet he had over 20,000 pikemen and the pike column was essentially an offensive weapon. With the invaders strung out before him, Arran saw an opportunity for a swift stroke to shatter the English army as it deployed. Just after 8 o'clock in the morning, three massive pike columns advanced on the English.[71]

Although Somerset's plans were now in disarray, Clinton's gunners opened fire on Argyll's wing and the earl of Huntly's rearward column. The Highland archers faltered and began to stream backwards. With cannonballs tearing through his ranks, Huntly also checked his advance and swung his column inland towards Arran's main battle. To halt the pike columns while his army deployed, Somerset hurled his heavy cavalry at them; the Scots, noted Patten, were 'compelled to sway a good way back and give ground largely', but they did not break.[72] The leading ranks of English horsemen tried to fight their way into the Scottish formation, hacking with swords and maces, but without success. Yet they had won the time needed for the rest of the English army to deploy. Both foot and mounted arquebusiers poured a withering fire into the now stationary mass of Scottish soldiers, while the English gunners set to work with hail shot at a target they could hardly miss. The Scots' army disintegrated.[73]

Arran rode for Edinburgh while Angus escaped the field by playing dead. Huntly, having held a ford across the Esk to cover the flight of his compatriots, surrendered with an English borderer's lance at his throat, one of 1,500 Scots made prisoner that day. Of the 6,000 or so killed, more died in the rout than in the fierce fighting. The English dead perhaps numbered 800. But catastrophic as it was, Pinkie did not mark an end to Scotland's capacity to resist. Much of the shattered army sheltered in Edinburgh and its castle. Somerset had won only the opportunity to plant his garrisons.

French allies and the transformation of warfare, 1547–60

The next three years saw a dramatic intensification of military activity in Scotland. Far from being peripheral to the mainstream of continental warfare, Scotland became a principal theatre of operations in a broader European struggle. In particular, the active intervention of the French, who not only filled Scotland's war chest but also despatched a substantial expeditionary force composed of professional soldiers, was a powerful catalyst in the transformation of insular warfare.

That process, however, was begun by the English invaders. Even before Pinkie, a modern *trace italienne* fort (with angled bastions designed to resist shot and provide flanking fields of fire for defending artillery) was under construction at Eyemouth, among the first of its kind in the British Isles. Garrisons were also established at Inchcolm in the Firth of Forth, Broughty Craig on Tayside, Home castle and at Roxburgh. Medieval 'piles' (peles or towers) were seized and strengthened with earthworks; the tower at Broughty was supported by a new fort on Balgillo Hill.[74] After Somerset returned to London, command in Scotland passed to Lord Grey. Under his direction forts were constructed at Lauder, Dunglass and, most significantly, at Haddington, which was large enough for a garrison of 2,500 men. The castles of Fast, Ferniehurst, Hailes and Saltoun now flew the cross of St George.

Scots responded by fighting at a local level. The Broughty garrison struggled to maintain control over the people of nearby Dundee, whose initial 'assurance' to the English crown swiftly lapsed. A tough Scottish captain named Jamie Dog rallied resistance, drove landing parties from Clinton's ships back into the sea and penned the garrison behind its walls. Similarly, James Stewart, prior of St Andrews, routed English raiders when they attempted to land at St Monans, taking 300 captives.[75] Prolonged local resistance, and the retaliation it provoked, revealed the English garrisons not as protectors of 'assured Scots' but as an army of occupation, rapacious and ruthless. English captains in the field often had to pay compensation to 'loyal' Scots for deprivations committed by their men.[76] As resistance stiffened, the principled advocates of union began to despair. The prominent Edinburgh Protestant James Henrisoun asked Somerset 'whether it was better to conquer hearts without charges, or burn and build forts at great charges, which will never conquer Scotland?'[77]

Sustained Scottish resistance revealed the inherent fragility of English strategy. The Borders and much of Lothian had been harried and fought over for years. Few could live off this land; its people and the planted garrisons faced starvation. Scottish garrisons, such as that at Dunbar, fought to sever Grey's poorly organised and slow supply convoys sent from Berwick.[78] French aid, first arriving in December 1547, tipped the balance against the English. By June 1548, 10,000 French troops were in Scotland, including some of the most famous European soldiers of their day. Francis Philip, the Rhinegrave count of Salm, and the Italian *condottiere* Pietro Strozzi directed siege operations against Haddington. André de Montalembert, Sieur d'Essé, brought German *Landsknechte*, Italian arquebusiers and pistol-armed French *chevauleger* cavalry into the field. Paul de la Barthe,

Sieur de Thermes, arrived with a further 1,200 reinforcements in June 1549 and drove the English from Inchkeith.[79]

Now on the strategic defensive, the English garrisons clung tenaciously to their earthwork walls. Haddington withstood two ferocious sieges. Broughty was besieged by land and bombarded by French galleys from the sea. Yet they could not win the battle to secure their supply lines. On 17 July 1548, a relief force attempting to batter its way into Haddington through the Franco-Scottish besiegers was bloodily repulsed and pursued for eight miles (the engagement became known as 'Tuesday's Chase'), losing some 700 men.[80] There was a striking victory in the west too. On 20 February 1548 Thomas Wharton led 3,000 men into an ambush at Drumlanrig planned by Angus. During the fighting, 400 of the assured Scots, Maxwells whose lands had been despoiled by English raiders, turned on their erstwhile allies. Wharton suffered some 500 casualties, but it was the desertion that had done the real damage. The assurance system in the south-west collapsed.[81]

Meanwhile, back in the east the smaller English garrisons were being picked off, one by one, and Franco-Scottish forces raided into England. D'Essé led a *chevauchée* to the gates of Newcastle and Chapelle de Biron struck at Ford castle.[82] The English cause was in tatters, not just militarily but also politically: Mary was now betrothed to the French dauphin. After Somerset's fall from power, his successor, John Dudley, earl of Warwick, prolonged the war in the vain hope of salvaging the proposal for the royal marriage. Yet Haddington was abandoned because of the critical supply problems in September 1549 and Broughty fell to a Franco-Scottish *camisado* (surprise assault) in February 1550. Most of the other garrisons were under severe pressure by the time a peace treaty with France stipulated that the English were to return Boulogne and abandon their remaining garrisons in Scotland.

Many Scots prospered from the alliance with France, especially Arran, elevated to the French dukedom of Châtelherault in 1549. Yet the relationship had been fractious; French soldiers were unpopular, especially in Edinburgh where they had rioted in the summer of 1548.[83] Much of the credit for keeping Scotland so firmly in France's orbit for so long belonged to Mary of Guise. By 1554, she had replaced Arran as regent, and when in 1557 the Valois-Habsburg War reignited, she committed Scotland to fight on France's behalf.[84] Although her attempts to wage war in the Marches were unsuccessful, Mary's engineers built impressive modern fortifications at Eyemouth and Leith. By 1559 the latter had become the first town in the British Isles to be wholly enclosed by a *trace italienne* system of fortification.[85]

These were expensive undertakings and the heavy burden of taxation Mary imposed alienated many Scots. Nevertheless, the mass of the people remained largely passive as the Lords of the Congregation drove the regent's forces back to Dunbar before they were stalled before the walls of Leith. With some 4,000 troops, and confident of resupply by sea, Mary could probably have held out indefinitely. An English fleet, however, despatched by the young Queen Elizabeth, cut the supply lines to France, and it was an English army that forced the capitulation of Leith, a process eased by the death of the indomitable Mary in Edinburgh castle on 11 June 1560.[86]

By the Treaty of Edinburgh, concluded on 6 July 1560, it was agreed that English and French troops should withdraw from Scotland. Just as they had already slighted the old English strongholds, the Scots moved swiftly to demolish the walls and bastions left by the French so that the last of the strangers' earthworks were cast down. After many dreadful years of conflict, during which the Scots had shown a remarkable capacity to resist and endure, their nation had finally emerged free from foreign domination.

Notes

1. Edward Hall, *The Triumphant Reigne of Kyng Henry the VIII*, ed. C. Wimbley, 2 vols (London: T. C. & E. C. Jack, 1904), vol. 1, p. 108.
2. See G. Parker, *The Military Revolution: Military Innovation and the Rise of the West, 1500-1800* (Cambridge: Cambridge University Press, 1988), and C. J. Rogers (ed.), *The Military Revolution Debate: Readings on the Transformation of Early Modern Europe* (Boulder, CO: Westview Press, 1995).
3. G. J. Millar, *Tudor Mercenaries and Auxiliaries* (Charlottesville, VA: University Press of Virginia, 1980), p. 3.
4. I owe this notion primarily to conversations with the late Dr Marcus Merriman.
5. A. McKerral, 'West Highland mercenaries in Ireland', *The Scottish Historical Review* [hereafter *SHR*], vol. 30 (1951), pp. 1-14; Robert Lindesay of Pitscottie, *The Historie and Cronicles of Scotland from the slaughter of King James the First to the ane thousande five hundrieth thrie scoir fyftein zeir*, ed. A. J. G. Mackay, 3 vols (Edinburgh: Blackwood, 1899-1911), vol. 1, pp. 396-7.
6. *Calendar of State Papers and Manuscripts relating to English Affairs existing in the Archives and Collections of Venice and in other libraries*

of northern Italy, 1202–1675, ed. R. Brown et al., 40 vols (London: Longmans, 1864–1947), vol. 1, 1509–19, p. 316.
7. *Calendar of State Papers Relating to Scotland preserved in Her Majesty's Public Record Office, London*, ed. J. Bain, 5 vols (Edinburgh: HM Register General House, 1881–8, 1986), vol. 1, 1547–63, pp. 34, 40; G. Dickinson, 'Some notes on the Scottish army in the first half of the sixteenth-century', *SHR*, vol. 28 (1949), pp. 133–45.
8. Hall, *Kyng Henry the VIII*, vol. 1, p. 109.
9. William Patten, 'The expedition into Scotland, 1547', in A. F. Pollard (ed.), *Tudor Tracts 1532–1588* (Westminster: Constable, 1903), p. 112.
10. D. Caldwell, 'Some notes on Scottish axes and long shafted weapons', in D. Caldwell (ed.), *Scottish Weapons and Fortifications 1100–1800* (Edinburgh: John Donald, 1981), pp. 253–314.
11. *John Major's History of Greater Britain*, ed. A. Constable (Edinburgh: Scottish Historical Society, 1892), pp. 49–50.
12. 'Articules of the bataille betwix the Kynge of Scottes and therle of Surrey in Brankstone felde the 9 day of September', in H. James (ed.), *Facsimiles of National Manuscripts from William the Conqueror to Queen Anne*, 4 vols (Southampton: Ordnance Survey, 1865–8), pt 2, p. 2.
13. Blaise de Monluc, *The Valois-Habsburg Wars and the French Wars of Religion*, ed. I. Roy (London: Longman, 1971), pp. 104–14.
14. D. G. White, 'Henry VIII's Irish kern in France and Scotland, 1544–1545', *Irish Sword*, vol. 3 (1958), pp. 213–25.
15. D. Potter, *War and Government in the French Province*s (Cambridge: Cambridge University Press, 1993), pp. 166, 183.
16. J. Goring, 'The military obligations of the English people 1511–1558' (unpublished PhD thesis, London University, 1955), pp. 39–41, 232–9.
17. Patten, 'The expedition into Scotland', pp. 77–8, 101; N. Barr, *Flodden* (Stroud: Tempus, 2003), p. 149.
18. G. Buchanan, *The History of Scotland*, 3 vols (Edinburgh: James Kay, 1821), vol. 3, p. 62; D. H. Caldwell, 'Royal patronage of arms and armour making in fifteenth and sixteenth-century Scotland', in Caldwell (ed.), *Scottish Weapons and Fortifications*, p. 83; K. Stevenson, *Chivalry and Knighthood in Scotland 1424–1513* (Woodbridge: Boydell and Brewer, 2006), pp. 175–6.
19. Humphrey Barwick, 'A Breefe Discourse, Concerning the force and effect of all manuall weapons of fire' [1594], in E. G. Heath (ed.), *Bow Versus Gun* (Wakefield: The Scholar Press, 1973), p. 12.
20. Buchanan, *The History of Scotland*, vol. 3, p. 62.
21. See, for example, Monluc, *The Valois-Habsburg Wars*, p. 41; and 'A diary of the siege and capture of Boulogne, 1544', ed. J. Leslie, *Journal of the Society for Army Historical Research*, vol. 1 (1922), p. 196.

22. *Letters and Papers, Foreign and Domestic, of the Reign of Henry VIII*, ed. J. S. Brewer, 22 vols (London: Longmans, 1864–1932), vol. 20, pt 1, p. 347; A. Maxwell-Irving, 'Early firearms and their influence on the military and domestic architecture of the Borders', *Proceedings of the Society of Antiquaries of Scotland*, vol. 103 (1970–1), p. 201; *Calendar of State Papers, Henry VIII*, 11 vols (London: n.p., 1830–52), vol. 1, pt 1, p. lxi; Patten, 'The expedition into Scotland', pp. 97, 111; Pitscottie, *The Historie and Cronicles of Scotland*, vol. 1, p. 397; *The Register of the Privy Council of Scotland*, ed. J. H. Burton, 14 vols (Edinburgh: HM General Register House, 1877–94), vol. 1, 1545–69, p. 80.
23. H. M. Colvin, 'The king's works in France', in H. M. Colvin (ed.), *The History of the King's Works*, 8 vols (London: HMSO, 1963–82), vol. 3 (1485–1660), pt 1, pp. 337–94.
24. M. Merriman and J. Summerson, 'The Scottish Border', in Colvin (ed.), *The History of the King's Works*, vol. 4 (1485–1660), pt 2, pp. 607–728.
25. *The Scottish Correspondence of Mary of Lorraine*, ed. A. Cameron, Scottish History Society, third series, vol. 10 (Edinburgh: T. and A. Constable, 1929), p. 249.
26. B. D. Porter, *War and the Rise of the State: The Military Foundations of Modern Politics* (New York: Free Press, 1994), p. 31; Rogers, 'The military revolutions of the Hundred Years War', in Rogers (ed.), *The Military Revolution Debate*, p. 75.
27. N. MacDougall, *James IV* (Edinburgh: John Donald, 2006), pp. 42–4.
28. Caldwell, 'Royal patronage of arms and armour making', pp. 73–93.
29. N. MacDougall, 'The greattest scheip that ewer saillit in Ingland or France: James IV's "Great Michael"', in Macdougall (ed.), *Scotland and War*, pp. 36–59.
30. W. F. Cook, Jr, 'The cannon conquest of Nasrid Spain and the end of the Reconquista', *Journal of Military History*, vol. 57 (1993), pp. 43–70.
31. D. Gregory, *The History of the Western Highlands and Isles of Scotland, AD 1493–AD 1625* (Glasgow: Thomas Morison, 1881), pp. 86–113; MacDougall, *James IV*, pp. 101, 180–91.
32. A. Goodman, *The Wars of the Roses* (London: Routledge, 1991), pp. 111–13; MacDougall, *James IV*, pp. 132–41.
33. MacDougall, *James IV*, p. 133.
34. Stevenson, *Chivalry and Knighthood*, pp. 185–9.
35. Barr, *Flodden*, p. 135.
36. MacDougall, *James IV*, p. 141.
37. For the strengths of the armies at Flodden see F. Elliot, *The Battle of Flodden and the Raids of 1513* (Edinburgh: Blackwood, 1911), pp. 196–204.
38. *Letters and Papers*, ed. Brewer, vol. 1, no. 4457.

39. 'Articles of the bataille betwixt the Kynge of Scottes and therle of Surrey', p. 2.
40. Leslie, *Historie of Scotlande*, p. 145; 'The trewe encountre or batayle lately don betwene Englande and Scotlande: In which batayle the Scotsshe kynge was slayne', ed. D. Lang, *Proceedings of the Society of Antiquaries of Scotland*, vol. 7 (1866–8), pp. 147–8.
41. Raphael Holinshed, *Historie of Scotland*, in *Holinshed's Chronicles of England, Scotland and Ireland*, 6 vols (London: J. Johnson, 1805), vol. 5, p. 481; 'Trewe encountre', ed. Lang, p. 150.
42. Leigh of Baggerley, 'Scotish feilde', in I. Baird (ed.), *Scotish Fielde and Flodden Feilde, Two Flodden Poems* (London: Garland, 1982), lines 329–30.
43. For casualty figures see Barr, *Flodden, 1513*, pp. 117–22.
44. Dacre's account of the 'Great Raid' can be found in H. Ellis (ed.), *Original Letters Illustrative of English History*, 3 vols (London: Triphook and Lepard, 1824), vol. 1, pp. 92–9.
45. *Calendar of State Papers, Henry VIII*, vol. 1, pt 1, p. lxi; Hall, *Kyng Henry the VIII*, vol. 1, pp. 271–3.
46. I. MacIvor, 'Artillery and major places of strength in the Lothians and the East Border, 1513–1542', in Caldwell (ed.), *Scottish Weapons and Fortifications*, pp. 94–118; D. H. Caldwell, 'A sixteenth-century group of gun towers in Scotland', *Fort*, vol. 12 (1984), pp. 15–24.
47. *Calendar of State Papers Relating to Scotland*, ed. Bain, vol. 1, p. 44; *Letters and Papers*, ed. Brewer, vol. 3, pt 2, no. 3039.
48. Hall, *Kyng Henry the VIII*, vol. 1, pp. 300–1.
49. Ibid. pp. 304–5.
50. G. Donaldson (ed.), *Scottish Historical Documents* (Edinburgh: Scottish Academic Press, 1970), pp. 103–4.
51. G. Macdonald Fraser, *The Steel Bonnets* (London: Collins Harvels, 1989), p. 248.
52. G. Bruce, 'The English expedition into Scotland in 1542', *Archaeologia Aeliana*, third series, vol. 3 (1907), pp. 191–212.
53. J. Bain (ed.), *The Hamilton Papers*, 2 vols (Edinburgh: HM General Register House, 1890–2), vol. 1, 1532–43, no. XVI.
54. Bain (ed.), *The Hamilton Papers*, vol. 2, p. 207.
55. M. Merriman, 'The assured Scots', *SHR*, vol. 47 (1968), pp. 10–34.
56. J. P. Balfour, 'Edinburgh in 1544 and Hertford's invasion', *SHR*, vol. 8 (1911), p. 121.
57. *Letters and Papers*, ed. Brewer, vol. 19, pt 1, p. 472; 'The late expedition into Scotland', in Pollard (ed.), *Tudor Tracts 1532-1588*, pp. 37–52.
58. Pitscottie, *The Historie and Cronicles of Scotland*, p. 35.
59. G. Ridpath, *The Border History of England and Scotland* (Berwick:

Philip Ridpath, 1848), p. 381; *Letters and Papers*, ed. Brewer, vol. 20, pt 2, p. 301.
60. Leslie, *Historie of Scotlande*, pp. 280–2.
61. G. Donaldson, *Scotland, James V – James VII* (Edinburgh: Oliver and Boyd, 1965), p. 72; Ridpath, *The Border History of England*, p. 382.
62. *Letters and Papers*, ed. Brewer, vol. 20, pt 2, pp. 347, 533.
63. M. Merriman, *The Rough Wooings: Mary Queen of Scots 1542–1551* (East Linton: Tuckwell Press, 2000), pp. 161–3.
64. *Calendar of State Papers Relating to Scotland*, ed. Bain, vol. 1, p. 21.
65. Holinshed, *The Description of Scotland*, p. 547; Leslie, *Historie of Scotlande*, p. 295.
66. *Calendar of State Papers Relating to Scotland*, ed. Bain, vol. 1, pp. 42, 44.
67. *Calendar of State Papers Relating to Scotland*, ed. Bain, vol. 1, p. 23; Patten, 'The expedition into Scotland', p. 108; Pitscottie, *The Historie and Cronicles of Scotland*, vol. 2, p. 96. For the battle, see D. H. Caldwell, 'The battle of Pinkie', in N. MacDougall (ed.), *Scotland and War AD 79–1918* (Edinburgh: John Donald, 1991), pp. 61–94.
68. *Calendar of State Papers Relating to Scotland*, ed. Bain, vol. 1, p. 266.
69. Sir Philip de Malpas (ed.), *A Commentary on the Services and Charges of Lord Grey of Wilton 1508–1562 by his son Arthur, Lord Grey of Wilton* (London: J. B. Nichols & Son, for the Camden Society, 1847), p. 12.
70. Patten, 'The expedition into Scotland, 1547', pp. 104–5.
71. Ibid. pp. 109–10.
72. Ibid. p. 110.
73. Ibid. pp. 116–17.
74. *Calendar of State Papers Relating to Scotland*, ed. Bain, vol. 1, pp. 160, 176, 183; British Library MS Cotton Caligula BVII, f. 339.
75. *Calendar of State Papers Relating to Scotland*, ed. Bain, vol. 1, p. 332; Thomas Churchyard, *A Generall Rehearsall of Warres* (London: 1579), p. 64.
76. See, for example, *Rutland Manuscripts* (London: Historical Manuscripts Commission, 1905), p. 355.
77. *Calendar of State Papers Relating to Scotland*, ed. Bain, vol. 1, p. 357.
78. *Holinshed's Chronicles of England, Scotland and Ireland*, vol. 3, pp. 906–7.
79. British Library MS Cotton Titus BV, f. 33; Holinshed, *Historie of Scotland*, pp. 564–5.
80. Bain (ed.), *The Hamilton Papers*, vol. 2, p. 452.
81. *Calendar of State Papers, Domestic, Elizabeth I, 1601–1603, with Addenda 1547–1565*, ed. M. A. E. Green (London: Longman, 1870), p. 393.

82. J. B. Brown, 'The French troops in the Borders in 1548', *Transactions of Hawick Archaeological Society* (1905), pp. 43–5.
83. H. Ellis (ed.), *Original Letters Illustrative of English History*, third series, vol. 3 (London: Richard Bentley, 1846), p. 292.
84. G. Ferrers, 'The winning of Calais by the French, January 1558', in Pollard (ed.), *Tudor Tracts*, p. 293.
85. S. Harris, 'The fortifications and siege of Leith: A further study of the map of the siege in 1560', *Proceedings of the Society of Antiquaries of Scotland*, vol. 121 (1991), pp. 359–68.
86. W. Fergusson, *Scotland's Relations with England: A Survey to 1707* (Edinburgh: John Donald, 1977), pp. 63–73.

7
Warfare in Gaelic Scotland in the Later Middle Ages

MARTIN MACGREGOR

Contemporary testimony of many hues marks out late medieval Gaelic Scotland as a society of remarkable military capacity. Command of this resource, or access to it, was disputed or desired by MacDonalds and Campbells, come the sixteenth century locked in a struggle for what the high literary tradition termed *ceannas nan Gàidheal*, or the headship of the Gaels; and by lords of Lowland Scotland and Gaelic Ireland, Stewarts and Tudors, and the crowned heads of Europe. Here we would seem to have plausible antecedents for the region's later eruptions onto the British and imperial stages. Yet with the partial exception of mercenary activity in Ireland,[1] the phenomenon remains lightly touched by scholarship.

One school of thought has posited a continuous and distinctive 'Celtic warfare' extending from classical antiquity to the modern era, and attributed the outcomes of Flodden in 1513 and Glenlivet in 1594, key battles of the covenanting and Jacobite epochs, and even the American Civil War, to Highland, Gaelic or 'Celtic' indiscipline and savagery.[2] Of like mind were the late medieval Scottish Lowland literati who deployed time-honoured paradigms of civility and barbarity to explain the relationship between Gaelic and non-Gaelic Scots, and portrayed the former as 'contemporary ancestors' of the 'ancient Scots' they found in their classical exemplars. Late medieval Gaels no less than ancient Scots were, according to John Mair, 'full of mutual dissensions, and war rather than peace is their normal condition'.[3] The idea that resorting to arms was a Gaelic reflex extended to the mode of warfare practised. John Mair compared the descent of Bruce's Gaelic contingent upon the English host at Bannockburn with the rush of wild boars, and the Highland 'caterans' who inspired such dread from the late fourteenth century onwards were described as a force of nature.[4] The pejorative flavour evident in some of these

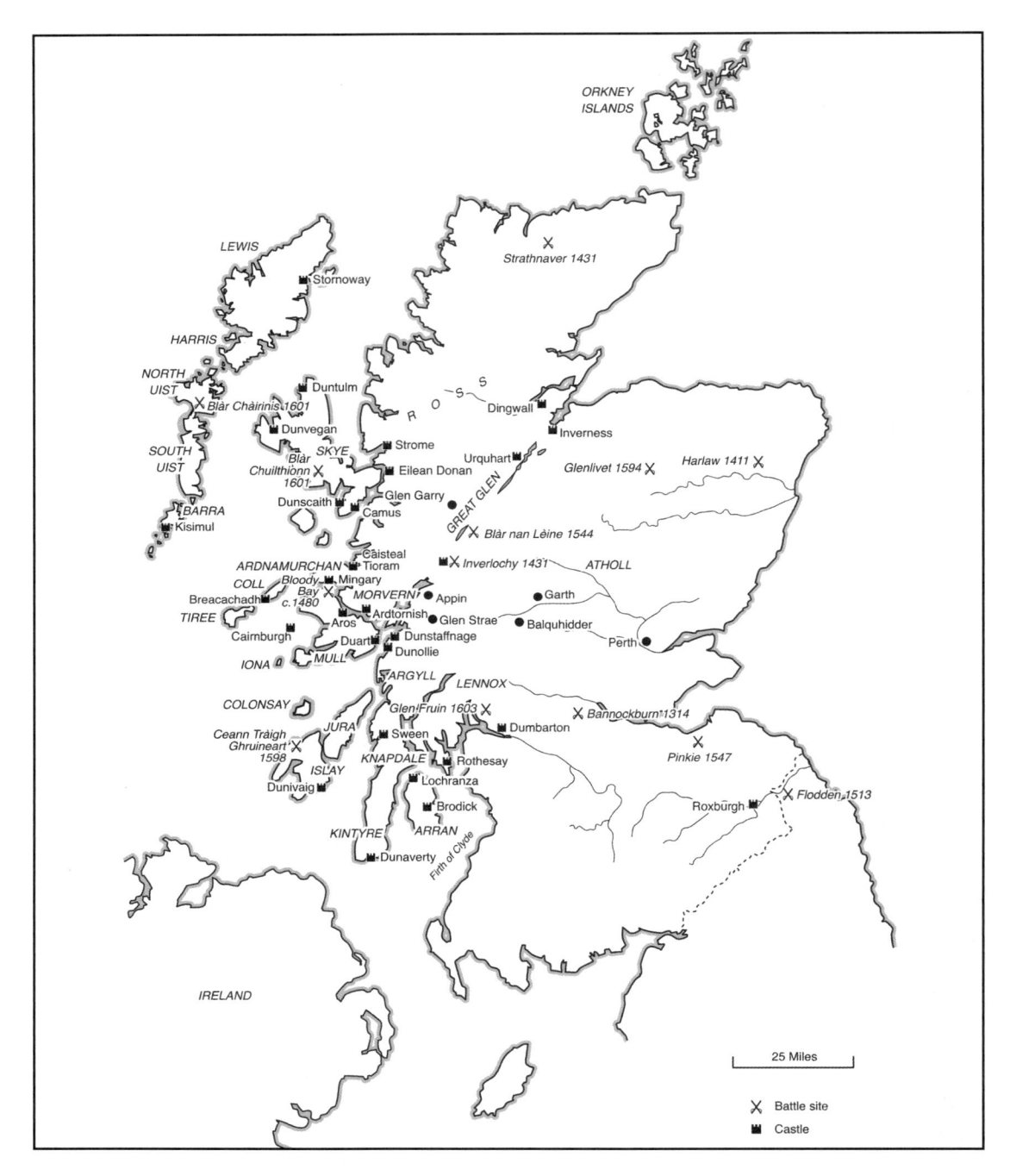

Map 7.1 Warfare in the Highlands and the Isles.

accounts of Gaelic primitivism may reflect a wider backlash against a perceived national obsession with an outmoded warrior ideal which, it has been argued, was a feature of Renaissance and Reformation discourse in Scotland.[5] Yet this would not be incompatible with a nostalgic yearning for the martial prowess of old Scotia identified now, and not for the last time, with Gaelic Scots. 'Highlandism' was not the monopoly of the age of empire. The sixteenth-century historians took a real interest in the material culture of Gaelic warfare,[6] while to Hector Boece at least, continuing fidelity to the military life had allowed Gaelic Scots to maintain a host of virtues now fading fast from the face of the Lowlands. Devotion to hunting was a means of waging war in peacetime, and thus of retaining a capacity for self-defence which the nation to its shame no longer possessed.[7]

This chapter shall explore why, by whom and how war was waged in Gaelic Scotland in the later Middle Ages. The evidence is diverse and plentiful, and its Gaelic component, mainly contemporary poetry and later prose tradition, as vital as it is neglected.[8] Gaelic Ireland is both an integral part of this story and an important comparator, and the work of Katharine Simms provides a basis for testing the hypothesis of a common Gaelic or 'Celtic' warfare.[9] We must begin with broader strategic considerations, foremost among them being the exercise of sovereignty within Britain and Ireland. It was an axiom of Anglo-Scottish enmity from the First War of Independence to the Reformation that each side competed to harness the Isles to open a second front: Scottish monarchs by fomenting trouble or pursuing dynastic ambitions in the English lordship of Ireland, English monarchs by seeking to recruit the men of the Isles as a 'fifth column'. As English strategy towards Ireland moved towards conquest in the later sixteenth century, so the seasonal movement of 'redshanks', or Scottish Gaelic mercenaries across the North Channel – a trend originating in the previous century – escalated in proportion. After 1603 James could now train the resources of his three kingdoms onto the Isles to cauterise the wound. But in truth there was probably no need, for the mercenary trade gave its last great flourish in 1595 before dying off as policing of the Irish Sea intensified and English conquest neared fulfilment. The internalisation of the mercenary dynamic was one likely cause of the escalation of warfare on the home front in the immediate aftermath of 1595, not only in frequency but also in intensity and brutality, and in apparent sympathy with the climate of 'total war' then prevailing in Ireland.[10] By 1615 and the Islay rising, when a government army led by the seventh earl of Argyll crushed the supporters of Sir Seumas MacDonald of Clan Donald South, the military capacity of the west Highlands and Islands seems to have fallen away dramatically. While the steadily rising profile of public law in resolving disputes was a likely contributory factor, the obvious explanation is the end of the Irish mercenary trade, suggesting that in part at least this military capacity was demand-led and artificially distended by the Irish market.

Another relevant aspect of sovereignty, and a difference between the experience of Gaels in Scotland and Ireland, was that the existence of a unitary late-medieval Scottish kingdom under one monarch and one common law meant that Gaelic no less than non-Gaelic Scots were expected to respond to national hostings and fight for their country. The reality of the Isles as Scotland's late-medieval 'Achilles' heel', and the stereotype of the Gael as rebel and traitor, indeed non-Scot, have for too long obscured the existence of a counter-narrative. There were significant Gaelic presences in James II's army in Ettrick forest in his second assault on the Douglases in 1455; in the royal army prior to the siege of Roxburgh in 1460; in James IV's northern English campaigns of the late 1490s; at Flodden in 1513 and at Pinkie in 1547.[11] Here are grounds for believing that Gaelic attachment to the Stewarts long predated the century between Tibbermuir in 1644 – the first of Montrose's victories over a covenanters' army – and Culloden in 1746.[12] By around 1600 thousands of Scottish Gaels were already fighting in the Stewart interest as mercenaries in the continental sphere.[13] Mercenary activity was no less characteristic of Lowland than Highland Scotland, the preferred theatre being Scandinavia or the continent rather than Ireland.[14] In civil wars as in national campaigns, lowlanders and highlanders fought under the same banner; twice in 1559 the Lords of the Congregation raised composite Lowland and Highland armies for the cause of religious Reformation. The kin basis common to both societies engendered a mindset capable of transcending difference in language and meant that private war, the bloodfeud and the system of private arbitration designed to regulate it, operated throughout the kingdom until the reign of James VI.[15]

At the same time, warfare allows obvious contrasts to be drawn between Highlands and Lowlands, both in its scale and significance within society, and in how it was waged, a key factor being the distinctive topography of the physical highland zone with which Gaelic Scots had increasingly come to be identified. Immediately apparent is the virtual invisibility of the horse, marking the region out not only from the Lowlands but also from Gaelic Ireland, where an elite mounted strike force, the lord in its number, was basic to combat.[16] In the west, the birlinn, or galley, underpinned the military power of

Figure 7.1 Carving of a birlinn, or west Highland galley, from the tomb of Alexander MacLeod of Dunvegan, dated 1528, in St Clement's church, Rodel, Harris.

the Isles in the era of contested sovereignties in the Irish Sea world, giving Hebridean warlords a reach extending from Ireland and Man to Orkney.[17] It was natural that the great internal battles determining lordship over the western seaboard should take place at sea, in 1156 off Islay and again at Bloody Bay in the Sound of Mull probably in the early 1480s. Emphatic confirmation of the passing of the naval power of the Isles came with the Islay rising, essentially a land-based campaign fought in a maritime environment with ships reduced to a transport rather than a strike role.[18]

The castle was another universal feature, markedly earlier than in Gaelic Ireland, and pivotal to lordship and warfare across the later Middle Ages. Landward, the strategic primacy of the Great Glen was staked out with fortresses from Inverlochy to Urquhart to Inverness and Dingwall, all scenes of repeated siege, sacking or battle. In the west castle and galley formed a perfect symbiosis, 'a network of stone and ships'.[19] There was no point in a naval strategy without a castle strategy, and consolidating or reducing castle-based authority

Figure 7.2 Castle Sween, Argyll, built c. 1200 on the east shore of Loch Sween. Such castles helped control the western seaboard in conjunction with fleets of galleys.

was impossible without naval power. Castle keepership and naval command went together, whether to collect rent or tribute in peace, or to muster and lead in war. The head of the MacLeans held major castles in the west for the Lord of the Isles, and was also his military right-hand man, acting as 'principal leader' of his army at Harlaw in 1411, and commander of his fleet at Bloody Bay.[20] The rationales for the great coastal castle and the galley died together. In the Islay rising it was inland sites on freshwater lochs in Colonsay and Islay that Sir Seumas MacDonald was concerned to fortify, while the simultaneous abandonment and demise of Dunivaig, proud symbol of the power of Clan Donald South for more than 200 years, was an epitaph for an era.

Meshing the matter of sovereignty with the role of galleys and castles permits identification of nodal points on the strategic and military map of the late medieval Highlands. Of first importance was the Firth of Clyde, where the lordships of Stewarts, MacDonalds and Campbells met and clashed. Dumbarton was the jewel in the crown of the remarkable concentration of fortresses in the region, impregnable until finally taken by stratagem in 1545 after successfully resisting Henry VIII's forces under the earl of Lennox.[21] Henry's 'Rough Wooing' lit up the zone's significance when questions of sovereignty loomed. While Dòmhnall Dubh was leading the forces of the Lordship of the Isles to Ireland, Irish and English troop fleets joined Lennox and Scottish levies, including Gaels, to attack targets across the region. As north met south on the Firth of Clyde, so east met west in Lochaber, scene of major battles at Inverlochy in 1431 and 1645, and Kinlochlochy, or Blàr nan Lèine – probably the largest inter-clan battle of the later Middle Ages – in 1544. On the ground, virtually permanent volatility was guaranteed by the competing territorial claims of the Camerons, MacDonalds of Keppoch, MacLeans and Macintoshes. At the level of lordship, Lochaber was both the launchpad for MacDonald expansionism eastwards and, travelling in the opposite direction down the Great Glen, a destination for the western ambitions of the Gordon earls of Huntly. This was the scenario underlying Blàr nan Lèine, when Huntly's incursion into Lochaber to assert regional authority saw one of his client kindreds, the Frasers, intercepted and decimated by the Clanranald on the homeward journey. As the Campbells supplanted the MacDonalds as regional lords in Lochaber during the sixteenth century, so they inherited the rivalry with Huntly which culminated in 1594 at Glenlivet.

Causation

The late medieval Lowland literati, such as John Leslie and George Buchanan, with one eye on their classical sources, claimed that Gaelic Scots made constant war for reasons of nature, nurture, environment, and social structure and ethos. Children were raised within a society obsessed equally by a culture of revenge in which the hurt suffered by one was taken up by all and feud 'was nevir put in the buke of oblivione', and by a cult of everlasting fame fuelled by the poets. Militarism was a benchmark of honour and high social status, while glory was not to be found in accumulating wealth or tilling the soil.[22] Modern historians have kept faith with the line that Gaels would revert to nature unless well governed by arguing that warfare flourished in a 'frontier' society where 'the land was hilly and the king remote'.[23] They have also added an economic case, that where good land and other natural resources were allegedly scarce they had to be fought over.[24] If so, this would render Gaelic Scotland directly analogous to late medieval Gaelic Ireland, which Katharine Simms has described as a society founded upon force, where lordship came to be virtually synonymous with the ability to billet one's soldiery upon a subject population.[25]

There is certainly evidence for the contention that this society possessed no 'book of oblivion'. Within a kin-based milieu where concepts of honour counted for so much, perceived personal insult could spark a feud which might escalate into bloody and prolonged local war. Nevertheless, a fresh appraisal of causation suggests right – to land, chiefship and lordship – as a predominant theme, and the rightful ruler as a predominant figure. The era abounds in instances of the exiled lord setting out to reclaim his own, his legitimacy confirmed by society's willingness to rise on his behalf, and prefiguring the Gaelic response to the Stuart cause. Economic motives were at their clearest in the deals struck by the Lords of the Isles with various English kings, but more consistently in the seasonal Irish mercenary trade of the fifteenth and sixteenth centuries. The fundamental form of warfare was the *creach*, or cattle raid, but it can be argued that what was at stake here was less the control of finite resources than both a ritual need to give honour and legitimacy to the aspirant warrior or ruler, and the assertion of lordship, with the resources taken representing not random spoil but the rent and tribute either denied or appropriated by another party.[26]

War was a means of asserting or challenging fitness to rule. Up to about 1600 contested successions to chiefships were a significant source of instability within the tiny ruling elite at the apex of clan society, and in the right circumstances could lead to civil war or worse. The MacLeods of Lewis in the late sixteenth century were a classic case of a kindred that imploded over a disputed succession, with devastating consequences. Equally profound was the relationship between war and land. The principle of *còir a' chlaidhimh*, or 'sword-right', was one means of winning land and lordship. The strength of the bond engendered between kindred and homeland was immense, and explains the need for warfare in attempts to break it, peaking with four great state-sanctioned expropriations in the reign of James VI and I: Clan Donald South from Islay and Kintyre; the MacGregors from Glen Strae; the MacLeods from Lewis and the MacIains from Ardnamurchan. In late medieval Gaelic Ireland it seems to have become increasingly unusual for freeholders within a lordship to be obliged to give military service as a condition of their tenure. The vacuum was filled by various types of mercenary, supported off the land, and some of whom might be rewarded with land; but it is instructive that once the MacQuillins established actual lordship over what came to be known as the

Route in north County Antrim, they ceased mercenary activity and became a conventional territorial kindred.[27] In Gaelic Scotland, by stark contrast, freeholders did give such service to their lord, and ultimately to the crown, and levies for service on both sea and land could be raised in proportion to land values, while the granting of land within a military contract was quite common.[28] In other words, land was a prerequisite for military service, which in turn was deemed to generate a right to land, a belief equally pertinent in the age of simultaneous clearance and imperial service on either side of 1800, notably in Sutherland, and in the age of the land raids in the wake of both world wars.

The explanation for what seems to be a crucial difference between Gaelic Ireland and Gaelic Scotland may lie in the influence of royal authority and common law. In demanding military service from all its subjects, Gaelic or otherwise, the crown could use land to make this explicit, to reward service given and to dictate the form of service sought. A distinctive case in point was the charter stipulating galley service, a central tool of the west Highland settlements of both Robert I and, following his annexation of the Lordship of the Isles, James IV. However, national institutions and frameworks did not automatically confer greater stability. There were many instances of local conflicts in the late medieval Highlands whose roots lay in Scots law, in the shape of conflicting legal title to land or pursuit of the rights of an heiress. It was in all probability the claim to the earldom of Ross he inherited through his wife that brought Dòmhnall Lord of the Isles to Harlaw with 10,000 men, a right his successors made good and fought to keep. Late medieval Stewart monarchs had to negotiate the practical limits to their power set by limited wealth and military resources. James IV's introduction of aggressive feu-ferme policies in Lochaber and Rannoch – a fiscal expedient designed to boost royal income in the short term through a one-off down payment and a fixed, increased annual rent – provided a vivid illustration of the violent reactions the crown could provoke if local society deemed its actions ill-considered, precipitate or excessive.[29] There were many junctures across the fifteenth and sixteenth centuries when the crown was in a minority or otherwise vulnerable and needed to make concessions to win support. In localities this could translate into vacuums of authority or abrupt policy shifts. The crown might employ agents with scores to settle or little regional legitimacy; it might deliberately foment local instability in order to serve its own strategic ends or need for self-preservation.

Personnel

Who participated in warfare in late medieval Gaelic Scotland? An emphasis upon small numbers and single combat allowed individuals to make the difference, and poetry raised to the level of a cult the persona of the warrior chief to whose military prowess the well-being of the kindred was tied. However, there is clear and interesting evidence that the war leader of the kindred was not necessarily the chief, but a surrogate. Dòmhnall Ballach, first cousin of Alasdair Lord of the Isles, was effective military commander of the Clan Donald for much of the fifteenth century, winning Inverlochy in 1431 and leading the great expedition on the Firth of Clyde around 1452. Alasdair, brother of the chief Ruairi Mòr, led the MacLeods of Harris in their defeat at Blàr Chuilthionn in 1601 and was captured there. Eoin Dubh, brother of the MacGregor chief Alasdair Ruadh, was likewise the brains behind the MacGregor battle strategy at Glen Fruin in 1603, where he died in single combat in the pursuit and was subsequently eulogised as an outstanding warrior. There are instances where such a figure performed the role of experienced military foil and acting warrior leader for a prospective claimant who had returned from imprisonment or exile to reclaim his inheritance. The outstanding example is Colla mac Ghilleasbuig, Sir Seumas MacDonald's right-hand man during the Islay rising.[30] Here we have prototypes of later famous pairings: Colla's son, Alasdair, as Montrose's brilliant general and likely architect of his victories in his *annus mirabilis* in 1644–5; and Lord George Murray and Charles Edward Stuart during the 'Forty-Five.

Beyond this we can invoke an Irish template with which to draw comparisons and contrasts. In Ireland, Simms posits a threefold division. The *teaghlach* or *luchd-taighe* seems to correspond to the small core of mounted noble warriors who formed the immediate retinue of the chief. It may have been drawn from his freeholders or leading clients, but perhaps with input from a knightly mercenary class, itinerant and landless. It formed the van and strike force in the onset, a protective shield in the pursuit. The *cethern* – landless infantry mercenaries of lower status – provided the essential muscle on the ground, rounding up cattle and torching dwellings. Those who could afford them employed *gall-óglaich* or galloglass, the permanently settled, elite infantry mercenaries of Scottish extraction (sometimes of Irish origin with Scottish officers); or the seasonal Scottish mercenaries who supplanted or complemented them from the fifteenth century onwards. A mercenary culture was therefore endemic. Rather than serving him militarily, his kin and freeholders provided their chief and lord either with mercenaries or with the economic wherewithal to engage or support them.[31]

Gaelic Scotland looks profoundly different, almost a mirror image. Its smallest military unit was *lèine-chneis* (also *lèine-chrios*), which seems to denote the chief's irreducible core retinue, a bodyguard or corps presumably accommodated within his household. Traditional accounts agree that it was twelve in number, which seems consistent with the limitations to chiefly retinues proposed in the blueprint for reform of the Isles, the Statutes of Iona, in 1609, and with the small-scale military needs that normally prevailed. The term *luchd-taighe* in Scotland may have been a synonym of *lèine-chneis*, according to Martin Martin's definition 'a competent number of young gentlemen called lucht-taeh or *guard de corps*, who always attended the chieftain at home and abroad'.[32] *Teaghlach* was certainly used, sometimes in contrast to terms of clearly broader application. It seems to refer to close kinsmen of the chief, as in *Is Maith an Cairt Ceannas nan Gàidheal* ('A good charter is the headship of the Gaels') where the poet systematically enumerates the levies due to the earl of Argyll, concluding with the Campbells themselves:

> A stalwart household (*teaghlach*) around Gill'Easbaig of his own blood, the better its might; their fame is fabled, I will not conceal it: each mettlesome man is of Duibhne's blood. His mustering amid his soldiers for MacCailein is the start of his force.[33]

If we regard the Irish *cethern* as precise equivalents of the *caterani* who feature in Scottish sources, notably in the service of Alexander Stewart, the 'Wolf of Badenoch', in the late fourteenth century, then there were landless mercenaries in late medieval Gaelic Scotland. Such a conclusion may be premature, however, for across the timeframe and region there is no sense of the mercenary culture as operative in Ireland. Instead, the sources insist that the basic building block of society, the territorial clan, was also the essential military unit. Thus Gaelic Scotland and Ireland complemented one another, with the Scots reserving their mercenary activity for the Irish theatre. Even then, in their Scottish context these warriors were not independent military castes, but members of territorial kindreds, such as the MacLeans, MacDonalds and Campbells, who served on that basis in the fifteenth and sixteenth centuries, with their chiefs presumably making the contracts and profits. Gaelic Scotland may well have contained kindreds that were militarised in the sense that this was a prime function they performed on behalf of a larger lineage: Clann Donnchaidh (the Robertsons of Atholl) for Robert Stewart (the future Robert II) and perhaps his son Alexander after him; the Macraes for the MacKenzies; and the MacGregors for the Campbells. But these were all landed clans, not floating entities on hire to the highest bidder. The fact that the Campbells employed territorial kindreds in their wars with the MacGregors, and on the basis of grants of land, suggests that employment of landless mercenary bands for a season was not an option.

Land and militarism thus again appear conjoined, and participation in war as pervading society rather than grafted onto it. How far down the social scale did participation run? Its correspondence to the landed upper echelons of society is consistent with Leslie's views noted earlier, while the military census of the Isles in 1593 draws a line at the tillers of the soil: 'in raising or furthbringing of thair men ony time of yeir to quhatsumevir cuntrie or weiris, na labourers of the ground are permittit to steir furth of the cuntrie quhatevir thair maister have ado, except only gentlemen quhilk labouris not'.[34] There are possible hints of penetration of intervening strata in references in the 1490s to Clan Donald's *daoine coitcheann*, or 'common men', as 'most steadfast', and to Lachlann Mòr MacLean's loss of 80 kinsmen and 200 common soldiers at Ceann Tràigh Ghruineart in 1598; nor can we forget the expectation that in times of national emergency all adult males should respond to their sovereign's summons. Finally, it seems clear that on the fringes of settled clan society there were what the parliamentary record came to term 'broken men': outright *banditti* and pirates, autonomous and landless, living through theft or extortion on land and sea.[35]

Typology, scale and recruitment

The nature and scale of warfare can again best be approached via comparison with late medieval Gaelic Ireland. There, the *creach*, or cattle raid, was likewise ubiquitous, as was the harrying raid designed to inflict material damage. Warfare was highly mobile and avoided head-on contact with the enemy if at all possible: the norm was raid and retreat, with the spoil being defended from the pursuit. Thus, 'running away was an important part of Irish warfare', while the numbers involved were often extremely modest.[36] In Gaelic Scotland, the national dimension made for greater variety of warfare and a fuller and longer escalator of violence. A conspicuous theme was how far up that escalator conflict worked its way. According to John Mair, writing of a battle in Strathnaver in 1431, in such fashion did these wild men fight that on both sides scarce one escaped with his life; for the conflict was, as it were, by an equal number of duels, and every man made an end of his antagonist, or contrariwise.[37]

A cult of single combat and fight to the death found judicial expression in the extraordinary duel fought before Robert III at Perth in 1396, involving thirty picked men representing rival kindreds.[38] In fact, the evidence as a whole suggests a very powerful predisposition against large-scale and head-on confrontation, and against over-committing too many human resources at the one time, or in the face of superior odds. This made sense if the clan were the normal fighting force, for to behave otherwise was to run the risk of destroying the clan itself, a fate that almost befell the Frasers in 1544, when only five out of nearly three hundred reportedly survived. Set-piece clan battles on the grand scale were rare, and even then the Clanranald only committed at Blàr nan Lèine once the Frasers split off from Huntly's invading coalition, while both Ceann Tràigh Ghruineart in 1598 and Glen Fruin in 1603 followed directly upon failed arbitrations. The classic pattern was 'tit for tat' warfare with each side attacking in turn, or simultaneously but in different locations, or in the absence of the other party or its leader. The choreographing of conflict according to the rhythm of an unwritten gentleman's agreement allowed for preservation of life, the salvaging of chiefly honour, pause and perhaps resolution. The regularity of hostage taking underlined the importance of negotiation, the presumption against indiscriminate slaughter and the value placed upon the human resource. A pointer towards the advent of a 'total war' mentality around 1600 was that maltreatment of hostages, and summary execution of prisoners rather than the taking of hostages, became more prevalent.[39]

Since the chief embodied the military worth of his kindred, one way of making war, or rather achieving the ends that might otherwise necessitate a war, was to neutralise him by assassination, execution, prolonged imprisonment or exile. Closely connected to this was domestic warfare within the ruling lineage, typically where the present chief had had children by more than one partner, as was common. These dynastic disputes, such as the fratricidal strife within Clann Uisdein about 1500, were pursued by stratagem, duplicity, ambush and targeted killing. They involved tiny numbers but had the potential to pull in both the wider clan in terms of factional support for rival candidates, and other kindreds connected to the candidates by ties such as marriage or fosterage. Dubhghall Stewart may have failed to follow his father as lord of Lorn, but traditional sources claim that he succeeded in defeating the MacDougalls and taking a portion of his patrimony in Appin with the help of his mother's people, the MacLarens of Balquhidder.[40] One moved by degrees to confederal conflict, seen at its fullest in the struggle for territorial and regional supremacy between Clan Donald South and the MacLeans which climaxed at Ceann Tràigh Ghruineart in 1598 and which sucked many of the clans of the west into its vortex. The opposing coalitions here took their broad outlines a century earlier, in the rift between the MacDonalds, backing Eoin Lord of the Isles, and their vassal kindreds, backing his son Aonghas Òg, resulting in the battle of Bloody Bay. The partial healing of this divide after 1598 paved the way for the Islay rising and the reasonably broad alliance that rallied behind Sir Seumas MacDonald. Also confederal on the grand scale were the various risings for Aonghas Òg's son, Dòmhnall Dubh, especially in 1545, and the clear theme here, as with the Islay rising, was the attempt to restore or recreate the MacDonald Lordship of the Isles and what it represented.

The lynchpins of military organisation, and a significant continuity with early medieval Scotland, were the intermediate tier of earls or major provincial lords. Their right and duty to gather and lead those within their lands and jurisdictions – either on their own behalf or on that of the crown – can be attested for Atholl, the Lennox, the Isles and Argyll, to give the most obvious examples, across the later Middle Ages. In 1478 Niall Stewart of Garth, head of a prominent Atholl kindred and a crown tenant-in-chief, bound himself to participate in royal hostings under the earl's banner.[41] In Argyll the mechanisms for raising men on the basis of territorial division and land assessment were long established and sophisticated. In 1596, however, Argyll and Lennox were asked to contribute from their earldoms only a very modest proportion of a royal muster against the Isles, the bulk of which consisted of mercenaries and forces to be raised by the burghs. This can be taken as representative of a shift away from the older mechanisms of national military recruitment to a rainbow coalition taking shape under James VI, and which became more pronounced once regal union gave the scope to add English and Irish elements. The Islay rising of 1615 saw a symbolic contrast of modes of recruitment: on the one hand the clans who flocked to the standard of Sir Seumas MacDonald as he made a dramatic quasi-inaugural progress through the west Highlands and Islands; and on the other the earl of Argyll – 'the special person of power and friendship in the Highlands' – at the head of a state army including levies from his earldom certainly, but also other Scottish militia, 400 mercenaries and Irish and English ships, troops and ordnance.

Ways and means of warfare

Finally, consideration must be given to the ways and means of combat: tactics, weaponry and dress. The sources suggest that certain universals applied across time and space, less because of conservatism, poverty or isolation than because Gaelic Scots had developed ways of waging war that suited their environment and society. The classic battle sequence, on land or sea, was the approach, discharge of the throwing weapon, charge, engagement at close quarters with the sword and pursuit (*tòir*) or rout (*ruaig*). The archetypal warrior was the foot soldier armed with both a throwing implement – spear, bow and arrow, or gun – and a sword. He was not defined by weapon or role, but multifunctional. Mobility, agility, speed and endurance were his essential attributes: he was no behemoth but a nimble, swift and sinewy athlete who could leap, evade and pursue over potentially long distances such as the estimated ten-mile rout at Glen Fruin in 1603.

On the basis of the disposition of the Scottish army at Pinkie, David Caldwell has speculated that the 'Highland charge', which played so conspicuous a part in the battles won by armies composed largely of Gaelic Scots in the early modern era, was not the invention of Alasdair mac Cholla, as David Stevenson had argued, but had earlier origins.[42] All the late medieval evidence points to the centrality of the charge. The approach to battle was dictated by the need to take the higher ground to give impetus to the charge, and to ensure security in the rear. Even on the flatlands of western Islay, the battle of Ceann Tràigh Ghruineart turned on both sides' attempts to gain a nearby eminence, while Argyll at Glenlivet and Alasdair MacLeod at Blàr Chuilthionn in 1601 both occupied the high ground on the mountain shoulder. Inseparable from the charge was the volley preceding it. At Blàr nan Lèine, for example, both sides discharged their arrows at a distance and once these were exhausted rushed to close combat. At sea, galleys were used as launchpads for missiles as they closed in on a target. As late as the eighteenth century a Jacobite poet could state that the ideal was to 'be at close quarters as was ever your custom'.[43] However, the volley was no hollow gesture preceding the main event; rather it served the dual purposes of discomfiting and thinning the ranks of the enemy to render the charge more effective. In an engagement between the galleys of MacKenzie and MacDonald of Glengarry in 1601, a salvo of musketry and arrows resulted in the capsizing of the Glengarry galley and the drowning of the chief himself.[44] At Blàr Chàirinis, the superior range achieved by MacDonald archers reduced MacLeod numbers to the point where the charge became realistic. At Glen Fruin, the MacGregors first retreated to the place where their bowmen were concealed, and, once concentrated arrow fire had taken a heavy toll, charged and turned the Colquhouns, instigating a long and bloody rout.[45]

The mode of warfare dictated the armour and weaponry used. The first impression is of profound conservatism, on two particular counts. Whereas the rest of Europe had turned to plate armour from about 1300, Gaelic Scotland continued to favour the *luireach*, or coat of mail. Plate does appear in west Highland monumental sculpture in the century following 1450, but in no decisive manner, and many sources confirm the dominance of mail in the later sixteenth century. The explanation must lie in the paramount need for speed, mobility, agility and flexibility. Indeed, the desire for lighter equipment may mean that the thickly quilted *cotún*, or tunic, so prominently depicted on a series of contemporary effigies from the west Highlands, was sometimes worn as the principal form of body armour, rather than in conjunction with the mail shirt as was more common elsewhere in Europe. Second, the gun only started to play a significant role in the later sixteenth century, notably later than elsewhere in Europe including Ireland. Its role in warfare is best approached through Gaelic terminology. *Làmhach*, originally a spearcast, had by the eighteenth century become applied to a volley of musketry or cannonfire.[46] *Urchair*, 'gunshot', originally meant a slingshot. It could be that continuity in language here is masking the fact that the coming of the gun meant a real and dramatic change in how war was waged. But when actual battle accounts are also brought to bear, the much more likely implication is that the gun was adapted to perform the role played within the prevailing scheme of engagement by other throwing weapons such as sling, spear or bow.

The sword was throughout the preferred weapon at the fulcrum of battle. An alternative existed in the *lamhagh* (also *tuagh*), or axe, the definitive piece of equipment of the Scottish galloglass serving in Ireland, but its role in domestic warfare seems to have been marginal by comparison. The single-handed sword was sup-

Figure 7.3 Tomb effigy of Bricius, or Gille-Brigde, fourteenth-century chief of the MacKinnons, from Iona abbey, Iona, showing the military dress and equipment typical of the west Highland elite of the period. He wears a bascinet (*feilm*, *clogas*, *ceannbheart*) with a mail tippet or aventail (*sgaball*), and a thickly quilted coat, known as a *cotún* or aketon.

planted by the double-hander around 1500[47] but came back into vogue around 1600, suggesting three distinct phases. In the older mould, the single-hander was linked to shield and spear, and the onset of the attack signalled by the launching of spears, two being the poets' favoured number. The shield was presumably slung on the warrior's back at this point, as is attested in Irish sources, and brought into play once the single-hander was drawn and battle engaged. It has been stated that the heater- or iron-shaped shields found in sculptural depictions were likely to be purely ornamental, but classical poetry supports their existence and use down to c. 1500, possibly implying that the circular *targaid*, or targe, was either a later development, or at first confined to a lower social level.[48] The introduction of the double-hander necessitated a reorganisation of warfare. The shield was now redundant, while the missile role previously performed by the spear seems to have been subsumed by the bow, which the sources invariably associate with the double-hander.[49] The year 1600 was clearly a time of transition. Particularly revealing is Lord Ochiltree's agenda for disarming the Isles in 1608, enjoining the inhabitants to abstain from the use of guns, bows and two-handed swords, confining themselves instead to targe and single-hander.[50] The single-hander could now be coupled with a new 'throwing' weapon in the form of the pistol. When Aonghas MacDonald faced up to his son, Sir Seumas, in Kintyre in 1598, he 'tuke his swerd in his hand with his targe, and had lykwys ane pistollet in his uther hand': a prototype of the Highland warrior of the covenanting and Jacobite eras.[51]

The bow dominated the sixteenth century as the Highland strike weapon *par excellence* and relinquished that status only very slowly in the seventeenth century. Such tenacity suggests deeper origins, as does the remarkably rich and secure material culture surrounding the bow and arrow in vernacular and proverbial verse, even if the vagaries of source survival mean that this evidence largely postdates 1500.[52] References in earlier classical poetry and depictions in sculpture are strikingly sparse, but when fleshed out by the documentary record there can be little doubt that expertise with the bow existed across the later Middle Ages. We find 'archiers escos sauvages' in the hire of the duke of Burgundy in 1411; James V directing 500 archers from the Isles to Ireland in 1532; and a company of 200 MacNaughton bowmen being recruited for war with France in 1627.[53] The adoption of the two-handed sword may indeed have enhanced the role of the bow, but it is perfectly possible that its social and military role was already significant, although perhaps not among the elite of the classical poetry with whom the throwing spear is invariably associated. By the late sixteenth century there are hints that its importance may have been recognised, at home as abroad, in terms of dedicated units. At Glen Fruin the Colquhouns were led into an ambush where havoc was wrought by two divisions of MacGregor bowmen, who nevertheless participated fully in the ensuing charge and pursuit.

Handguns and light artillery were coming into use in Gaelic Ireland around 1500, but they made slow progress in Gaelic Scotland, perhaps in the first instance as a prestige item at the individual chiefly level, and for hunting rather than war.[54] Few of the 3,000 men Dòmhnall Dubh took to Ireland in 1545 had guns. By the 1590s, however, accounts of the weaponry of the men of the Isles, and of Argyll's forces at Glenlivet, suggest that the gun was making real inroads and that, perhaps mimicking the pattern of development with the bow, specialist divisions employing firearms were being created. The outcome of Glenlivet was in part determined by a volley of artillery at the outset that was said to have discomfited Argyll's forces because they were unused to it. Yet the gun was not part of the kit of the MacLean and MacDonald warriors in Ireland in 1594 and seems to have played no role to speak of in the clutch of clan battles around 1600. It was a volley of arrows, combined with musketry, that caused MacDonald of Glengarry's galley to capsize in 1601. On the eve of the Wars of the Three Kingdoms the bow continued to hold its own, although perhaps not without active intervention. There is evidence c. 1600 of bowmanship having to be artificially sustained, and indeed resurrected, by the Fraser chiefs in the eastern Highlands.[55] The Highland elite, no less than central government, may have harboured concerns about the social and economic implications of widespread availability of firearms, as suggested by attempts to restrict their use in the Isles either to those in royal service, or to the chiefly class for hunting purposes, in early seventeenth-century enactments.[56]

Warfare in late medieval Gaelic Scotland was without doubt governed by continuities and universals. New fashions and technologies were tested, rejected or absorbed into paradigms, fidelity to which derived not from genetic programming but from sober appreciation of their durability. The perceptible contraction in militarism across the region in the aftermath of 1600, at its starkest in the west with the demise of the Irish mercenary trade, galley and coastal castle, demarcated a clear horizon, and the apparent hiatus between that point and Gaelic Scotland's thoroughgoing engagement in the Wars of the

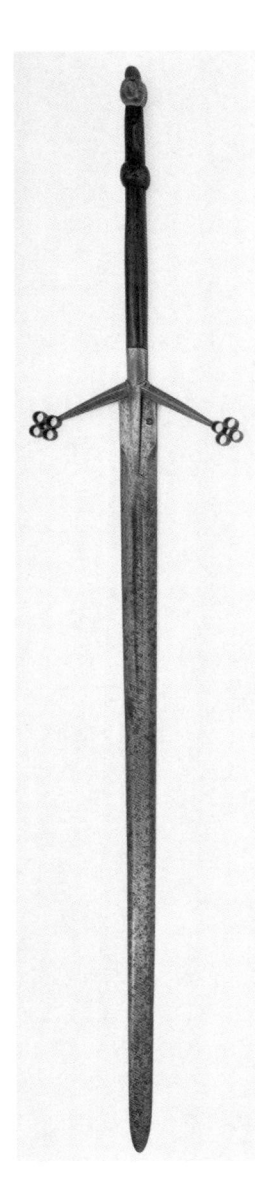

Figure 7.4 A late seventeenth-century example of a Scottish two-handed sword (*claidheamh dà làimh*), also referred to as a *claidheamh mòr* or 'great sword'.

Covenant needs research and explanation. If 'Celtic warfare' is held to mean a commonality of approach across Gaelic Ireland and Scotland, then it did not exist. Whether in the guise of galloglass or redshank, the attraction of Gaelic Scots to Irish chiefs may have lain as much in their distinctive approach to warfare as in their numbers and availability. In Gaelic Scotland the hallmark of warfare was integration: with the environment, with social and tenurial structures, and in the very person of the multipurpose Highland soldier. It was on foreign fields that specialisation set in, as Gaelic Scots adapted to military regimes organised by function and weapon.

Notes

1. See most recently S. Duffy (ed.), *The World of the Galloglass: Kings, Warlords and Warriors in Ireland and Scotland, 1200–1600* (Dublin: Four Courts Press, 2007).
2. D. Gregory, *The History of the Western Highlands and Isles of Scotland, from A.D. 1493 to A.D. 1625* (Edinburgh: John Donald, 2008), pp. 112, 258, 413; G. McWhiney, 'Continuity in Celtic warfare', *Continuity*, vol. 2 (1981), pp. 1–18; G. McWhiney and P. D. Jamieson, *Attack and Die: Civil War Tactics and the Southern Heritage* (Tuscaloosa, AL: University of Alabama Press, 1982); J. M. Hill, *Celtic Warfare 1595–1763* (Edinburgh: John Donald, 1986); J. M. Hill, 'The distinctiveness of Gaelic warfare, 1400–1750', *European History Quarterly*, vol. 22 (1992), pp. 323–45.
3. John Mair, *A History of Greater Britain, as well England as Scotland*, ed. and trans. A. Constable (Edinburgh: Scottish History Society, 1892), p. 49.
4. Ibid. p. 240; S. Boardman, *The Early Stewart Kings: Robert II and Robert III 1371–1406* (East Linton: Tuckwell Press, 1996), p. 83; A. Wiseman, 'Chasing the deer: The hunt in Scottish Gaelic history and tradition' (unpublished PhD thesis, University of Edinburgh, 2007), p. 109.
5. K. M. Brown, *Bloodfeud in Scotland 1573–1625: Violence, Justice and Politics in an Early Modern Society* (Edinburgh: John Donald, 1986), pp. 184–214; R. Mason, 'Chivalry and citizenship: Aspects of national identity in Renaissance Scotland', in R. Mason and N. Macdougall (eds), *People and Power in Scotland: Essays in Honour of T. C. Smout* (Edinburgh: John Donald, 1992), pp. 62–7.
6. E. G. Cody and W. Murison (eds), *The Historie of Scotland written first in Latin by the most reverend and worthy Jhone Leslie, Bishop of Rosse, and translated in Scottish by Father James Dalrymple*, 4 vols (Edinburgh:

Scottish Text Society, 1888), vol. 1, pp. 90–1; George Buchanan, *The History of Scotland*, trans. J. Aikman, 4 vols (Glasgow: Blackie, Fullarton & Co., 1827), vol. 1, p. 41.

7. *The History and Chronicles of Scotland: written in Latin by Hector Boece, canon of Aberdeen; and translated by John Bellenden*, 2 vols (Edinburgh: W. and C. Tait, 1821), vol. 1, pp. lix–lxii.
8. For contrasting approaches to the sources, see P. Harbison, 'Native arms and armour in medieval Gaelic literature, 1170–1600', *The Irish Sword*, vol. 12 (1975–6), pp. 173–99, 270–84; D. H. Caldwell, 'Having the right kit: West Highlanders fighting in Ireland', in Duffy (ed.), *The World of the Galloglass*, pp. 144–68.
9. K. Simms, *From Kings to Warlords* (Woodbridge: Boydell and Brewer, 1987), pp. 116–28; 'Warfare in the medieval Gaelic lordships', *The Irish Sword*, vol. 12 (1975), pp. 98–108; 'Images of warfare in bardic poetry', *Celtica*, vol. 21 (1990), pp. 608–19; 'Gaelic warfare in the Middle Ages', in T. Bartlett and K. Jeffery (eds), *A Military History of Ireland* (Cambridge: Cambridge University Press, 1996), pp. 99–115.
10. Simms, 'Images of warfare', p. 617.
11. S. Boardman, *The Campbells 1250–1513* (Edinburgh: John Donald, 2007), pp. 168, 332–3; Gregory, *History*, p. 45; Caldwell, 'Having the right kit', pp. 163, 167; see also J. Goodare, *State and Society in Early Modern Scotland* (Oxford: Oxford University Press, 1999), pp. 137–8.
12. Gregory, *History*, p. 333; D. Stevenson, *Highland Warrior: Alasdair MacColla and the Civil Wars* (Edinburgh: Saltire Society, 1994), p. 267.
13. S. Murdoch, 'More than just Mackays and mercenaries: Gaelic influences in Scandinavia, 1580–1707', *Transactions of the Gaelic Society of Inverness* [hereafter *TGSI*], vol. 60 (1997–8), pp. 161–86.
14. Ibid. pp. 161–86; J. E. A. Dawson (ed.), *Campbell Letters 1559–1583* (Edinburgh: Scottish History Society, 1997), p. 47.
15. Brown, *Bloodfeud*, pp. 6–7; J. Wormald, 'Bloodfeud, kindred and government in early modern Scotland', *Past and Present*, vol. 87 (1980), pp. 54–97.
16. See n. 9.
17. Boardman, *Campbells*, pp. 169–71, 175 and n. 37, 179; Gregory, *History*, p. 290.
18. Gregory, *History*, pp. 366–90.
19. Boardman, *Campbells*, p. 56.
20. Gregory, *History*, p. 69.
21. Ibid. pp. 164, 175.
22. Cody and Murison (eds), *Historie*, pp. 92–3, 96; Buchanan, *History*, pp. 65–7, 94–7.

23. T. C. Smout, *A History of the Scottish People 1560–1830* (London: Collins, 1969), p. 43; see also Simms, 'Warfare in the medieval Gaelic lordships', p. 98.
24. R. Dodgshon, *From Chiefs to Landlords: Social and Economic Change in the Western Highlands and Islands, c. 1493–1820* (Edinburgh: Edinburgh University Press, 1998), p. 87.
25. Simms, *From Kings to Warlords*, pp. 127–8; Simms, 'Gaelic warfare in the Middle Ages', p. 115.
26. D. MacLeod (ed.), *A Description of The Western Islands of Scotland circa 1695, by Martin Martin, Gent.* (Edinburgh: Birlinn, 1994), pp. 165–6; Dodgshon, *From Chiefs to Landlords*, p. 88; A. Cathcart, *Kinship and Clientage: Highland Clanship 1451–1609* (Leiden: Brill, 2006), pp. 136–40; Boardman, *Campbells*, pp. 152–4.
27. Simms, 'Gaelic warfare in the Middle Ages', pp. 108–10.
28. C. Innes (ed.), *The Black Book of Taymouth* (Edinburgh: Bannatyne Club, 1855), pp. 206–8, 408–9, 416–17; Boardman, *Campbells*, p. 129; Dawson, *Campbell Letters*, p. 45.
29. Boardman, *Campbells*, pp. 275–83, 311–19.
30. Gregory, *History*, pp. 366–90.
31. Simms, *From Kings to Warlords*, pp. 19, 126–8.
32. Martin, *Description of the Western Islands*, p. 167.
33. W. McLeod and M. Bateman (eds), *Duanaire na Sracaire: Song-Book of the Pillagers. Anthology of Scotland's Gaelic Verse to 1600* (Edinburgh: Birlinn, 2007), pp. 146–9.
34. W. F. Skene, *Celtic Scotland: A History of Ancient Alban*, 3 vols (Edinburgh: David Douglas, 1880), vol. 3, p. 439.
35. A. D. M. Forte, 'A preliminary account of an early sixteenth-century episode of Highland piracy', in C. Ó Baoill and N. R. McGuire (eds), *Caindel Alban: Fèill-sgrìobhainn do Dhòmhnaill E. Meek/Scottish Gaelic Studies*, vol. 24 (2008), pp. 207–14; A. I. Macinnes, 'Lochaber – the last bandit country', *TGSI*, vol. 54 (2004–6), pp. 1–21.
36. Simms, 'Warfare in the medieval Gaelic lordships', pp. 101, 105.
37. Mair, *History*, pp. 361–2.
38. G. MacKenzie, 'The rarest decision recorded in history: The battle of the clans in 1396', *TGSI*, vol. 59 (1994–6), pp. 420–87.
39. Gregory, *History*, pp. 234, 239.
40. S. Boardman, 'The tale of Leper John and the Campbell acquisition of Lorn', in E. J. Cowan and R. A. MacDonald (eds), *Alba: Celtic Scotland in the Middle Ages* (East Linton: Tuckwell Press, 2000), pp. 219–47.
41. C. P. Stewart (ed.), *Historic Memorials of the Stewarts of Forthergill* (Edinburgh: W. and A. K. Johnston, 1879), pp. 74–5.

42. Caldwell, 'Having the right kit', p. 167; Stevenson, *Highland Warrior*, pp. 82–4.
43. J. L. Campbell (ed.), *Highland Songs of the '45* (Edinburgh: Scottish Gaelic Texts Society, 1984), pp. 12–13.
44. Gregory, *History*, p. 299.
45. M. Newton, *Bho Chluaidh gu Calasraid: From the Clyde to Callander. Gaelic Songs, Poetry, Tales and Traditions of the Lennox and Menteith in Gaelic with English translations* (Stornoway: Acair, 1999), pp. 190–211; see also Wiseman, 'Chasing the deer', p. 307, for the employment of similar tactics at Bealach Mhalagan c. 1580.
46. R. Black, *An Lasair: Anthology of 18th Century Scottish Gaelic Verse* (Edinburgh: Birlinn, 2001), pp. 44, 196.
47. K. A. Steer and J. W. M. Bannerman, *Late Medieval Monumental Sculpture in the West Highlands* (Edinburgh: The Royal Commission on the Ancient and Historical Monuments of Scotland, 1977), pp. 5–6, 167–70; Gregory, *History*, pp. 161, 166, 171, 257; W. McLeod, *Divided Gaels: Gaelic Cultural Identities in Scotland and Ireland c. 1200–c. 1650* (Oxford: Oxford University Press, 2004), p. 47.
48. Steer and Bannerman, *Sculpture*, pp. 26, 172; Caldwell, 'Having the right kit', pp. 160–1.
49. For the survival of the spear into the sixteenth century, see The Iona Club (ed.), *Collectanea de Rebus Albanicis* (Edinburgh: Thomas G. Stevenson, 1847), p. 28, and Appendix, pp. 31–3, 36–7; Newton, *Bho Chluaidh gu Calasraidh*, pp. 168–9, line 42; National Library of Scotland [hereafter NLS], Wod. Qu. XX, f. 70r. My thanks to Dr Aonghas MacCoinnich for the last reference.
50. For other references to the targe dating to the 1590s, see NLS, Wod. Qu. XX, f. 70r; A. Matheson, 'Documents connected with the trial of Sir James MacDonald of Islay', *Transactions of the Gaelic Society of Glasgow*, vol. 5 (1956–7), p. 215; see also Wiseman, 'Chasing the deer', p. 246.
51. Matheson, 'Trial of Sir James MacDonald', p. 215.
52. Wiseman, 'Chasing the deer', pp. 121, 172.
53. A. Cathcart, 'James V King of Scotland – and Ireland?', in Duffy (ed.), *The World of the Galloglass*, pp. 128–9; Archives départementales de la Côte-d'Or, Dijon, B1570, f. 36v; J. R. N. Macphail (ed.), *Highland Papers*, 4 vols (Edinburgh: Scottish History Society, 1914), vol. 1, pp. 113–16. My thanks to Dr David Ditchburn for the Burgundian reference.
54. W. MacGill (ed.), *Old Ross-shire and Scotland as seen in the Tain and Balnagown Documents* (Inverness: Northern Counties Newspaper and Printing and Publishing Co., 1909), pp. 264–5 (no. 673). My thanks to

Dr Aonghas MacCoinnich for this reference. D. S. Thomson (ed.), *The Companion to Gaelic Scotland* (Edinburgh: Edinburgh University Press, 1983), p. 10.
55. Wiseman, 'Chasing the deer', p. 117.
56. M. MacGregor, 'The Statutes of Iona: Text and context', *Innes Review*, vol. 57 (2006), pp. 148–50.

Part II
Forging a Scottish–British Military Identity

8
The Wars of Mary and James VI and I, 1560–1625

MATTHEW GLOZIER

In the aftermath of the Treaty of Edinburgh in 1560 the withdrawal of the professional and well-equipped French regiments forced the crown back on what military resources it could muster. Chief among these remained the general levy of men raised, as for many centuries, by common army service, supplemented by the retinues of magnates, producing armies that would not have been so dissimilar from those raised by Robert the Bruce in the early fourteenth century.[1] Although royal castles such as Edinburgh, Stirling, Dumbarton and Blackness remained strategic strongholds across the land, the efforts of previous monarchs to modernise and expand the crown's artillery were not continued, and in 1558 attempts to establish a native gun foundry were abandoned.[2] Yet the times of trouble were far from over. To prevent the French from taking control of Scotland, Elizabeth I, the Protestant queen of England, had successfully supported the Lords of the Congregation against Mary of Guise and, in 1560, the Scots parliament had established the Protestant religion. Scotland's newly returned queen, Mary Stewart, Queen of Scots, however, was not only a Catholic but was also allied to France, and she herself had a claim to the throne of England. Renewed conflict seemed inevitable.

Mary, daughter of James V and Mary of Guise, had been sent to France as a child and in 1558 she married the dauphin Francis. The following year Henry II was accidentally killed by a lance splinter when jousting and Francis and Mary became king and queen of both France and Scotland. After Francis's death in 1560, Mary returned to Scotland in August 1561, only to become immediately embroiled in bitter religious disputes. Viewed with suspicion by many of her Protestant subjects, she was denounced from the pulpit by John Knox for her 'popery' and alleged extravagance and frivolity. Without the backing of French troops, Mary was forced to rely on the support of her Protestant half-brother, Lord James Stewart, the earl of Moray. Indeed, in 1562 he assisted her in putting down a rebellion in the north-east Lowlands by George Gordon, fourth earl of Huntly, one of Scotland's leading Catholic magnates. Meanwhile, Mary sought to repair relations with Elizabeth, but refused the English queen's attempts to neutralise her through a proposed marriage to Elizabeth's favourite, Robert Dudley, earl of Leicester.

Instead, in 1565 Mary married her cousin, Henry Stewart, Lord Darnley (who at the time of his marriage was posing as a Protestant, but a few months later was professing to be a Catholic). Infuriated by this match, Moray led a rebellion against the queen. Mary, however, had the support of a number of loyalist nobles. With a pistol in her belt, she accompanied an army in pursuit of her brother in the 'Chaseabout raid'. Moray was forced to flee to England. Mary's son, the future James VI, was born in 1566, but the following year Darnley was assassinated in Edinburgh. The queen's subsequent marriage to James Hepburn, the Protestant earl of Bothwell, who was widely believed to have been involved in the plot to murder Darnley, inflamed both Protestant and Catholic nobles. The stage was set for another military confrontation and it came on a summer day in East Lothian in 1567.

The Marian civil wars (1567–73)

On 15 June the rebel lords and their men confronted the forces of Mary and Bothwell at Carberry Hill near Musselburgh. The former carried a banner depicting the murdered Darnley and his son James kneeling beside him invoking God with the legend 'Judge and avenge my cause, O Lord'. The queen was able to assemble an army of 2,600 loyalists, but after a lengthy stand-off, and with temperatures soaring and dehydration setting in, many of her troops drifted away from the battlefield. Realising the game was up, she negotiated her husband's safe withdrawal before she herself rode into the rebel lines and captivity. The queen was taunted with cries of 'Burn the whore! Burn the murderer!'[3] She was subsequently imprisoned in Loch Leven castle and forced to abdicate on 24 July in favour of the infant James. Her personal rule was over.

Mary, however, escaped in 1568 and headed west. A cross-section of mainly Protestant nobles rallied to her cause and within a few days she had raised an army of approximately 6,000 men under the command of Archibald Campbell, the fifth earl of Argyll. In the meantime, Moray, who had returned to Scotland and been appointed regent for the boy king James VI, once again gathered forces to oppose her. Mary's forces headed for the stronghold of Dumbarton

Figure 8.1 The confrontation at Carberry Hill, near Musselburgh, in 1567 between Mary's forces (positioned on the hill to the right) and the lords opposed to her, as depicted in a contemporary drawing.

castle but while marching there her soldiers encountered those of Moray, who had drawn up his army at Langside, near Glasgow. As the royalist army tried to force its way through the village on 13 May it was met with pikes and hagbut fire and, with Argyll said to have suffered a fainting fit, it broke away in disarray. The battle of Langside lasted just forty-five minutes, with some 300 men killed.[4] Mary fled to England where Elizabeth I was to keep her captive for the next nineteen years before her eventual execution in 1587.

Her flight left Scotland in turmoil. In 1570, Moray was assassinated and bitter factional fighting broke out between the 'king's men' and the 'queen's men'. Gradually, however, James's supporters gained the upper hand and by 1571 Edinburgh castle, the last major stronghold held by her adherents, was placed under a lengthy siege: the 'lang siege'. Sir William Kirkcaldy of Grange, the castle's keeper, along with his allies, defended the castle against a succession of regents backing the claims of James, but their resistance cost the lives of further Marianists. Eventually, the Regent Morton was forced to request help from the English in order to capture the castle. In May 1573, English cannons and 1,000 troops took just ten days to compel the rebels to surrender the stronghold. The survivors numbered 164 men, 34 women and 10 boys.[5]

The length of the siege highlighted the dearth of effective military capacity north of the border. Yet some innovation did occur at Edinburgh castle as a result of the bombardment by Elizabeth's guns. The cannon had destroyed two medieval towers within the castle

Figure 8.2 Edinburgh castle from the east. The castle entrance is dominated by the Half-Moon Battery constructed after the 'lang siege' of 1571–3, during which the castle suffered extensive damage.

complex, David's Tower and the Constable's Tower at the castle's gates. As a result of the damage, the outer defences of the castle were slowly rebuilt. Most notably, David's Tower was replaced by the Half-Moon Battery flanking the castle entrance. This was begun in 1573 on the orders of the Regent Morton and completed in 1588.[6] It resembled the round defensive structures for cannon experimented with by Henry VIII for England's coastal defences and remained the most modern element of the castle's fortifications for generations.

The common army and wapinshawings

James VI, who assumed power in the mid-1580s, relied, as had his predecessors, on the common army, the traditional armed levy. Service was owed to the crown by all men between the ages of sixteen and sixty, and was unpaid. In theory, the maximum period of service was forty days in one year, but in practice armies rarely stayed in the field for so long. In 1575 instructions were issued to improve the efficiency of the wapinshawings, or official musters of fighting men, within specific districts of the kingdom. These were supposed to be held regularly as a means of assessing the eligibility to serve and of ensuring that men possessed the equipment relative to their status and wealth required of them by statute. Such musters, however, remained infrequent in Scotland and did not do much to improve military proficiency.[7]

As there was only a small state armoury, the crown relied on the weapons of lairds and nobles. There were not many muskets in private hands, so the vast majority of weapons possessed by Scots levies were pikes, swords, axes and spears, with a few handguns among the wealthier men. The poor equipment is illustrated by a muster of 900 men in Moray in 1596, the surviving records of which have been analysed by Julian Goodare.[8] This muster, which may have been typical of Scottish forces of the period, comprised 5 per cent horsemen, 18 per cent well-armed footmen, 35 per cent lightly or non-armed infantry and 42 per cent non-combatants (presumably support personnel). There were only nine firearms.[9] Scots armies also continued to reflect structures of local lordship that were typically clannish. Lairds would arrive at wapinshawings on horseback, with their 'heill kynne, freindis, and servandis'. John Grant of Freuchie brought 500 men to the muster of Moray in 1596, all of whom were his dependants and servants.[10]

In the Lowlands, the last military challenge to the Scottish crown was mounted by the so-called Catholic earls, a group of north-eastern magnates. With their surrender in 1594, and subsequent exile, James, who had personally led his army in the campaigns against them,[11] had less to fear from Scottish nobles and their private forces. There were, however, other dangers. England and Spain had been fighting an undeclared war since 1585 and Scotland, although never an active participant in the conflict, was officially allied to England from 1586. The Spanish Armada of 1588, and its successors in 1596 and 1597, were recognised as threats to Scotland as well as to England. Moreover, in the late 1590s James feared that when Queen Elizabeth died this might lead to a war of the English succession in which Scotland might have to fight – a fear that continued until he received secret assurances from Sir Robert Cecil in 1601. There was thus the need for an effective force to deal with such challenges. Sheriffs were instructed to appoint parish captains to drill the 'common army' to ensure its fitness for war. Weaponry, however, remained of poor quality, and the king believed that his men had to be better armed if they were to form a credible fighting body. The answer was to acquire newer and better arms. In 1599 Sir Michael Balfour of Burleigh was granted a monopoly on the importation of weapons. In the Netherlands he was said to have purchased 6,000 corslets, 10,000 pikes and 4,000 muskets and calivers, but had the greatest difficulty in selling them on to James's reluctant subjects.[12]

The situation was yet more bleak in regard to maritime power. The earlier efforts by Scots kings to create a naval force had not been sustained after the death of James V, despite largely uncontrolled piracy. In 1614, however, a forty-ton warship – possibly named the *Golden Fleece* (later the *Charles*) – was bought from John Mason, its English owner, and was charged with collecting assize herring duties from Dutch fishermen in Scottish waters. In 1621, in poor condition and needing expensive repairs, it was ordered south of the border and the short-lived Scottish navy came to an end.[13]

Border reiving and feuds

The Border region in southern Scotland, along with the northern English counties of Cumberland and Northumberland, had been severely destabilised by the protracted Anglo-Scottish wars. Feuds between local families had become endemic, marked by the reiving (theft) of cattle, kidnapping, arson, extortion and murder.[14] Attempts to assert royal authority had been made, including the appointment, from the fourteenth century, of Wardens of the Marches: officials, usually local magnates, who worked on behalf of the Scottish crown, often in cooperation with their English counterparts on the other side of the border.[15] Such was the scale of the banditry, however, that the authority of the Wardens often counted for little.[16]

Many surnames became infamous as Border reivers. They are immortalised in the balladry collected by Sir Walter Scott, himself descended from one of the most notorious reivers: Sir Walter ('auld Wat') Scott of Harden (d. 1629).[17] Such men lived intermittently beyond the law, yet they also formed part of the social fabric of the region and, as landed lairds, a number obtained rank and title. One such figure was Sir Robert Ker of Cessford, head of one of the great branches of the Ker kindred in the borderland. During the 1590s he took part in many violent feuds with local families, including the murder of one of his kinsmen, William Ker of Ancrum. In 1600, however, he was created Lord Roxburghe (and in 1616 earl of Roxburghe, Lord Ker of Cessford and Caverton).[18]

One of the most prominent Border conflicts of the period was the Maxwell-Johnstone feud. It began as a private disagreement between two reiver families who were rivals over the wardenship of the West

Figure 8.3 Bronze statue of a border reiver, Galashiels, by Thomas J. Clapperton, 1925.

Marches, and escalated into a bloody regional struggle that left Dumfriesshire in a more or less permanent state of war. In 1593 this smouldering dispute burst into flames at the battle of Dryfe Sands near Lockerbie. The Johnstones, who were positioned atop a slope beside the River Annan, charged down into the Maxwells and cut them to pieces. John, Lord Maxwell, and 700 of his kinsmen, were killed, many the victims of downward sword strokes by horsemen that became known as 'Lockerbie licks'.[19] It was reported of Lord Maxwell that the Johnstones 'did cut af baith his hands, and careit the same with thayme on speir points, as a memorial of his perfidie, and for ostentatioun of ther awin glore'.[20]

With the Union of the Crowns in 1603, the Borders were no longer a remote frontier region, becoming instead 'the Middle Shires' of James's realm of Great Britain. The king was thus determined to bring order once and for all to these troublesome lands. Lord Home was appointed lieutenant of the three Scottish Marches, with the earl of Cumberland holding a similar position on the English side of the border, and the reiver families were ruthlessly suppressed. In 1603 alone, thirty-two members of the Johnstones,

Figure 8.4 Smailholm tower, Roxburghshire, dating from the fifteenth century. It was one of a series of fortified tower houses built in the Scottish borders to protect against raiders.

Elliots, Armstrongs and Batys were hanged, one hundred and forty were outlawed and fifteen were banished. 'Jeddart justice' became a local term for the summary punishments meted out: hang first and try later.[21] In 1605 cross-border military cooperation become more formalised when the king instituted an Anglo-Scottish Border commission to safeguard the security of the 'middle shyes of this yland'.[22]

In the Highlands, these sorts of internecine struggle were more difficult to control. A quarrel between Clan MacGregor and Clan Colquhoun in the south-west Highlands, sparked reportedly by the summary execution of two MacGregor men for slaying a sheep on the Colquhoun lands after they had been denied hospitality, is an example of such local conflicts. At the battle of Glen Fruin near Loch Lomond in 1603 the MacGregors, who had assembled an army of 400 men, defeated a numerically superior force of the Colquhouns and slew some 200 of them.[23] James, however, sought to extend his influence over the western seaboard by a mixture of military pressure and the granting of hostile areas to pro-Stewart clans.[24]

Meanwhile, pressure was brought to bear on the Scottish nobility to submit disputes to royal justice. In 1598 an 'Act Anent Removing and

Extinguishing of Deidlie Feuds' became law. The act specified that current feuding parties were to appear before the king and the privy council. Arbitrators would be appointed to settle the greviances, but if agreement could not be reached the king, or the privy councillors or judges appointed by him, would rule on the dispute. Such judgement would have the status of an act of the privy council, and there was no right of appeal. As for feuds in the future, the party to whom an offence was done was not to seek private vengeance; any killings that occurred in the course of such vengeance would now be treated as murder by the criminal courts.[25]

As a result of coercion and persuasion – along with increased political stability, the desire of Scottish nobles to share in the spoils of regal union by currying favour with the king and the impact of the Calvinist church, which was strongly opposed to the ideology that underpinned these violent episodes – the number of feuds declined in Scotland. By 1625 they were under control. The state now had a virtual monopoly over the use of armed force. 'The successful attack on private violence and the confinement of feuding to the less governable parts of the highlands,' notes Keith Brown, 'was one of the major achievements of Jacobean government.'[26]

The royal guard

During the period a small permanent royal guard was established in Scotland to protect the person of the monarch. Mary created such a body of men early in her personal reign. Her guard comprised nineteen archers, and, in contrast to foreign monarchs who sometimes stocked similar guards with expatriates from other kingdoms to ensure loyalty and trustworthiness, the queen's archers were all Scots. This first guard disappeared from Scotland with Mary, but from 1580 James possessed a royal guard, which was seen as 'part of the equipment of monarchical rule'. In 1582 his guard consisted of thirty horsemen under the command of the duke of Lennox. The unit, however, fell into abeyance after the Ruthven Raid to abduct the young James. A fresh start was made in 1584, with another guard raised by an order for forty gentlemen 'hable, honest, and weill horssit and having sum reasounable levingis of thair awin'. In 1590 a new guard was recruited, consisting of 100 horsemen and 100 infantry, but it was disbanded the following year. From 1595 to 1603 there was little or no regularly constituted guard.[27]

After the Union of the Crowns the king no longer needed personal protection from a permanent royal guard in Scotland. In 1603 a new guard of forty horsemen was nevertheless instituted to perform police functions on behalf of the privy council. In 1611 this force was disbanded but eight of its soldiers were temporarily redeployed to arrest tax defaulters. Meanwhile a Border guard had been formed and when its operations were extended to cover all the Lowlands its number was raised from twenty-five to forty men. From 1615 these guards arrested habitual outlaws, especially debtors. In 1621 it too was stood down on the grounds that the country had become sufficiently compliant for it not to be needed.[28]

Looking abroad

Scots served in significant numbers as foreign mercenaries during the period. Between 1560 and 1590 approximately 25,000 fought in Ulster. They were known as 'redshanks' to the English, reputedly because of the colour of their exposed legs.[29] Sorley Boy MacDonnell became the chief conveyor of these itinerant Scots to Ulster and he used them to extend his areas of control there. Indeed, the MacDonnells came to be regarded as a key obstacle to stability in the region, and in 1575 the earl of Essex instigated a massacre of the clan's non-combatants, including women and children, on Rathlin Island whilst Sorley Boy's forces were concentrated near Ballycastle on the mainland. Over 500 were slaughtered.[30]

As Allan Carswell explains in Chapter 9, the Dutch Revolt of 1568 provided further employment for Scottish mercenaries willing to assist the northern Protestant provinces of the Netherlands in their struggle against Catholic Spain. This event witnessed a great wave of Scottish military emigration to the European continent and between 1573 and 1579 licences were granted for at least 3,100 Scots to be recruited for service in Flanders and the Low Countries,[31] perhaps in part reflecting English agent Sir Henry Killigrew's 1572 observation that 'the number of able men for service [was] very great'.[32] Britain was at peace from 1604 to 1625, prompting more Scots to pursue a career in arms abroad. In 1620 a regiment of 1,500 men was raised in Scotland to fight on the continent for Frederick V, Elector Palatine and (briefly) King of Bohemia, during the early stages of the Thirty Years War.[33] Geoffrey and Angela Parker's analysis of the recruiting grounds of Europe's armies between 1550 and 1650 indicates that Scottish soldiers came from a broad swathe of Scotland, encompassing both Lowland and Highland regions.[34] Foreign service provided opportunities for Scottish commanders too. Not only did it promise financial rewards, but it also called for a new level of military professionalism. This saw the practice of the 'art of war' become a source of profit and honour for gentlemen across Europe and a tenable career for the Scottish landed elite.[35] Some of the Scots mercenaries returned home and put their new military skills to use in the service of the crown. A veteran of the Netherlands wars, Andrew Stewart, Lord Ochiltree, led an expedition against the Western Isles in 1608 before taking part in James's plantation of Ulster in 1611.[36] Others sought to pass on their military experience in more literary form. Sir Thomas Kellie of Eastbarns, who served in the army of Christian IV of Denmark-Norway, published a military manual, entitled *Pallas Armata, or Militarie instructions for the learned: and all generous spirits, who affect the profession of armes* (1627). 'A well affected Subject,' he noted, 'ought to enable himself to doe service to his Countrie, by the studies, both of Mars & Minerva.'[37] But few of those who ventured abroad – especially the poorer sort – returned to Scotland, instead either dying in service or integrating into local populations.[38]

By the end of James's reign, Scotland was devoid of domestically based military expertise and the necessary gear of war. Yet, as Keith Brown reminds us, it was to the Scottish nobles that the crown still had to turn for military resources to help officer and recruit the new state-authorised armies, whether to crush internal risings, such as those on Orkney in 1614 and Islay the following year, or to assist in confronting external enemies, such as the duke of Buckingham's expedition to stir up a rebellion against the French at La Rochelle in 1627.[39] These local elites were also expected to display the same martial qualities as their forebears. In the 1620s the young earl of Sutherland was instructed to 'lead fourth your countreymen your selfe in persone; so shall they obey the willingly, and fight with better courage'.[40]

Notes

1. J. Goodare, *State and Society in Early Modern Scotland* (Oxford: Oxford University Press, 1999), p. 133.
2. D. H. Caldwell, 'The royal Scottish gun-foundry in the sixteenth century', in A. O'Connor and D. V. Clarke (eds), *From the Stone Age to the 'Forty-Five: Studies Presented to R. B. K. Stevenson* (Edinburgh: John Donald, 1983), p. 430.
3. J. Guy, *'My Heart is My Own': The Life of Mary Queen of Scots* (London: Harper Perennial, 2004), pp. 343–9; A. Fraser, *Mary Queen of Scots* (London: Weidenfeld and Nicolson, 1969; Phoenix, 2009), pp. 409–12.

4. Fraser, *Mary Queen of Scots*, pp. 452–3; Guy, '*My Heart is My Own*', pp. 368–9; A. M. Scott, *The Battle of Langside 1568* (Glasgow: Hugh Hopkins, 1885), passim.
5. H. Potter, *Edinburgh under Siege, 1571-1573* (Stroud: Tempus, 2003), pp. 119–41.
6. I. MacIvor, *Edinburgh Castle* (London: B. T. Batsford for Historic Scotland, 1993), pp. 67–71.
7. Goodare, *State and Society*, pp. 151–2.
8. Ibid. pp. 137–9.
9. Ibid. p. 138.
10. Ibid.
11. S. Murdoch, 'James VI and the formation of a Scottish–British military identity', in S. Murdoch and A. Mackillop (eds), *Fighting for Identity: Scottish Military Experience c. 1550–1900* (Leiden: Brill, 2002), p. 6.
12. Goodare, *State and Society*, pp. 153–7.
13. Ibid. pp. 165–6; *The Register of the Privy Council of Scotland*, ed. D. Masson, 14 vols (Edinburgh: HM General Register House, 1877–94), vol. 11 (1616–19), pp. 593–4, 602–3.
14. G. MacDonald Fraser, *The Steel Bonnets: The Story of the Anglo-Scottish Border Reivers* (London: Barrie and Jenkins 1971; HarperCollins, 1995), passim.
15. See T. I. Rae, *The Administration of the Scottish Frontier 1513–1603* (Edinburgh: Edinburgh University Press, 1966).
16. Fraser, *The Steel Bonnets*, p. 137.
17. Ibid. pp. 103–4.
18. Ibid. pp. 321–2; A. R. MacDonald, 'Ker, Robert, first earl of Roxburghe (1569/70–1650)', *Oxford Dictionary of National Biography* [hereafter *ODNB*], Oxford University Press, 2004. Available at www.oxforddnb.com/view/article/15456, accessed on 29 December 2010.
19. Fraser, *The Steel Bonnets*, pp. 174–80; K. M. Brown, *Bloodfeud in Scotland 1573–1625: Violence, Justice and Politics in Early Modern Society* (Edinburgh: John Donald, 1986), pp. 74–5.
20. Quoted in J. R. M. Sizer, 'Maxwell, John, earl of Morton (1553–1593)', *ODNB*, online edn. Available at www.oxforddnb.com/view/article/18404, accessed on 30 December 2010.
21. Fraser, *The Steel Bonnets*, pp. 363–9.
22. Murdoch, 'James VI and the formation of a Scottish–British military identity', pp. 11–12.
23. W. Scott, *Manners, Customs and History of the Highlanders of Scotland: Historical Account of the Clan MacGregor* (Glasgow: Thomas D. Morison, 1893; New York: Barnes and Noble, 2004), pp. 80–2.

24. Murdoch, 'James VI and the formation of a Scottish–British military identity', p. 10.
25. Goodare, *State and Society*, pp. 75–6; Brown, *Bloodfeud*, pp. 241–3.
26. Brown, *Bloodfeud*, p. 259. See also A. Groundwater, *The Scottish Middle March, 1573-1625: Power, Kinship, Allegiance* (Woodbridge: Boydell and Brewer, 2010), p. 204.
27. Goodare, *State and Society*, pp. 145–9.
28. Ibid. pp. 149–50.
29. M. Glozier, *Scottish Soldiers in France in the Reign of the Sun King: Nursery for Men of Honour* (Leiden: Brill, 2004), p. 21; C. Falls, *Elizabeth's Irish Wars* (London: Constable, 1996), pp. 79–80.
30. H. McDonnell, 'MacDonnell, Sorley Boy (b. in or before 1508, d. 1590)', *ODNB*, online edn. Available at www.oxforddnb.com/view/article/17465, accessed on 29 December 2010; J. M. Hill, *Fire and Sword: Sorley Boy MacDonnell and the Rise of Clan Ian Mor, 1538-1590* (London: The Athlone Press, 1993), pp. 163–6; G. A. Hayes-McCoy, *Scots Mercenary Forces in Ireland (1565-1603)* (Dublin and London: Burns Oates and Washbourne, 1937), p. 120.
31. I. R. Bartlett, 'Scottish mercenaries in Europe, 1570–1640: A study in attitudes and policies', *Scottish Tradition*, vol. 13 (1984–5), p. 18.
32. Quoted in M. Lynch, *Scotland: A New History* (London: Century, 1991), p. 252.
33. Murdoch, 'James VI and the formation of a Scottish–British military identity', p. 19.
34. G. and A. Parker, *European Soldiers, 1550-1650* (Cambridge: Cambridge University Press, 1977), p. 23.
35. K. M. Brown, *Noble Society in Scotland: Wealth, Family and Culture from Reformation to Revolution* (Edinburgh: Edinburgh University Press, 2000), pp. 2–3.
36. Goodare, *State and Society*, pp. 160–1; M. Sheane, *Ulster Blood: The Story of the Plantation of Ulster* (Ilfracombe: Arthur H. Stockwell, 2005), pp. 44–57.
37. T. Kellie, *Pallas Armata* (Edinburgh: heirs of Andrew Hart, 1627), p. 1; S. Murdoch, 'Introduction', in S. Murdoch (ed.), *Scotland and the Thirty Years' War 1618-1648* (Leiden: Brill, 2001), pp. 3–4.
38. Goodare, *State and Society*, p. 167.
39. Brown, *Noble Society in Scotland*, p. 2.
40. Quoted in Brown, *Noble Society in Scotland*, p. 3.

9

'Mercenaries': the Scottish Soldier in Foreign Service, 1568–1860

ALLAN CARSWELL

Nowadays, the term 'mercenary' provokes an almost universally negative response. The word dredges up a litany of the worst and most unwholesome aspects of war and military service – greed, violence, brutality and amorality – reinforcing the long-held belief that mercenaries are an unacceptable element of armed conflict; that fighting (and therefore killing) for money is morally inferior to fighting for a belief; and that professional soldiers are tolerable only if they serve the nation in which they happen to have been born.[1] Yet in Scotland the word can provoke a different reaction. The Scottish soldiers who for centuries travelled far and wide to fight other people's wars are regarded by many Scots with a surprising, and slightly brazen, sense of pride. Why should this be?

One answer could be that many of these 'mercenaries' were not motivated exclusively by financial gain and so do not really deserve the label, with all its unsavoury modern connotations. Quite so, but just as many did fight for the money alone and neither they nor their contemporaries would have seen anything especially shameful in that. A more persuasive argument is that the Scottish 'mercenary' is seen as a variation on an enduring (and popular) military tradition which holds that soldiering is an honourable occupation, and that as long as it is done honestly and well, politics can be left largely to others. The oft-quoted lines of James Turner, a Scottish mercenary of the Thirty Years War, though written late in life and more in mitigation than justification, express the notion in stark terms: 'I had swallowed without chewing, in Germanie, a very dangerous maxime, which militarie men there too much follow: which was, that so we serve our masters honnestlie, it is no matter what master we serve.'[2]

While some have taken this as evidence with which to condemn Turner and his like as unprincipled outcasts, others regard them as honest professionals and treat their individual successes – foreign honours, high rank, reputation and trust – as a source of national pride. It helps that the Scottish mercenary can also be seen as a manifestation of another well-polished facet of the national self-image: the individual Scot taking his chances in the wider world. The resilience of the overlapping attributes inherent in these twin archetypes of the soldier and the 'lad o'pairts' – courage, aggression, hardiness, loyalty, ambition, enterprise and self-reliance – as hallmarks of national character reveals how important interpretations of Scotland's past still are in forming a sense of identity. But are we correct to see these 'mercenaries' simply as either heroes or villains?

The bulwark of the republic

Although the tradition of Scots serving abroad precedes 1568 by at least two centuries, it was the outbreak of the Dutch Revolt that shaped the nature of subsequent Scottish foreign service. The overriding factor in the war that broke out in Flanders between the United Provinces (from 1588, the Dutch Republic) and Spain was religion – the Dutch being Protestant and the Spanish, together with their supporters in the rest of the Netherlands, Catholic. As well as foreshadowing the divide that was to lead to the outbreak of conflict throughout much of the rest of Europe for the next eighty years, the Dutch experience influenced how states would employ foreign soldiers, or allow their subjects to go abroad in such a capacity. The religious divide (and the cultural, political and dynastic distinctions bound up within it) transcended purely national concerns, creating a class of military manpower that was neither thoroughly 'mercenary' in its character, nor the manifestation of a full-blown interstate alliance. Scotland, avowedly Protestant since 1560 and with a military tradition to rival any in Europe, yet often lacking the royal will, political unity and financial means to intervene at a national level, became a prime exporter of this type of soldier.

As war spread throughout Europe, the massive demand for troops, and the Scots' willingness to meet it, allowed the Stuart kings (or their regents) to manipulate the supply of this military manpower as a tool of their foreign, domestic and dynastic policies. The sheer numbers of Scottish soldiers who flowed overseas, either as a direct consequence of this policy or from less regulated forms of recruitment, were unprecedented. What had been an irregular flow before 1568 grew into a steady stream; after 1618, and the outbreak of the Thirty Years War, it became a torrent. The Scottish soldier abroad therefore became a proxy both for Scottish popular support for the international Protestant cause and the ambitions of the house of Stuart. As such he came to be seen as a principal agent for national endeavour.[3]

Yet he carried a double-edged sword. The creation of bodies of trained military manpower that existed beyond the direct control of the Scottish and, after 1603, the British throne helped sow the seeds of destruction for the Stuart dynasty. The consequences of these troops' domestic interventions between 1568 and 1745 were far-reaching, both in shaping the new British state and defining Scotland's place within it. In addition, a legacy of the divisions and conflicts born of this process, in the shape of communities of political exiles, would ensure a continuing reservoir of Scottish military manpower for foreign employment up until at least the 1780s.

Political or dynastic considerations had, of course, always been a factor in Scottish service abroad – La Garde Écossaise in France being the best-known example. Nor by any means were all Scots who fought abroad after 1568 motivated purely by religious scruple, or placed there by some grand design of their sovereign – individual motivations for military service were as varied as they had ever been. These larger trends, however, were important, not least in their influence on Scotland's developing military tradition and its link with national identity.

The modern concept of a national 'standing' army was still in its infancy in 1568, and most forces were a temporary mix of dwindling feudal levies, conscripted militias and hired help. Yet the relentless warring of European states meant that armies were growing ever larger as well as having to maintain themselves for longer periods of service. The economic, administrative and social consequences for wealthier states of removing large parts of the productive population had always been severe, so the expedient of buying in manpower from elsewhere had much appeal. In the view of one French commander, the employment of a single foreign soldier was worth three men – one more for France, one less for the enemy and one Frenchman left to pay taxes.[4]

Yet life as a professional soldier was harsh. Even pay, the principal inducement for the vast majority, was usually hopelessly in arrears, a situation compounded by employers routinely hiring more troops than they could afford in the hope that the victories achieved would bring in the means of payment, either through loot, prize money or the acquisition of new territory. When neither the victories nor the pay chest materialised, soldiers were forced to take what commodities they could, by whatever means, or starve, making war an even more brutal experience. When even this failed, armies degenerated into mutinous rabbles, or defected wholesale to whoever was better able to pay them. Modern notions of military discipline, patriotism, legal restraint and respect for non-combatants were almost unheard of; compliance to a vague code of individual gallantry and personal honour was about all that could be hoped for. These professionals, or mercenaries, consequently tended to come from regions where options for a secure future were limited and where conflict was endemic. Remote or peripheral 'border' regions of Europe like Scotland, Ireland, the Balkans and the Swiss Alps were well established as sources for military manpower and areas where men could always be found by military 'entrepreneurs' – individuals with the capital, political influence and experience necessary to organise and transport military forces to anywhere they were required for anyone willing to pay. Recruits were largely pushed out by local circumstance – famine, economic hardship and over-population being the usual ones for those destined for the ranks – rather than being pulled in by the promise of vast wealth or adventure. Those responsible for recruiting on behalf of the main contractor were usually men from the lower rungs of the local nobility who could exploit traditional family or clan structures to bring in sufficient recruits to confirm them in their future officer rank. For such men, military service was seen as a continuation of a noble warrior culture, a view shared by some of those they recruited.

The tactics and organisation of armies were also to develop in particular ways during the late sixteenth century. The impetus for many of these changes came from the protracted war in the Netherlands. The Dutch provinces in revolt against their Spanish overlords had the advantage, initially at least, of significant collective wealth, but the disadvantage of little central organisation – ideal preconditions for the employment of foreign mercenaries. William of Orange, the first leader of the Revolt, began in 1568 by hiring a force of mainly German mercenaries. Yet as the war deepened, and their money ran low, it became clear to the Dutch leaders that they had to think creatively about how best to utilise their limited resources – what men they had, or could afford to employ. Pre-eminent amongst these leaders was Prince Maurice of Nassau. From 1585 he developed new strategies and tactics favouring the kind of defensive war the Dutch had to fight. Many of these innovations, however, required a new focus on individual training and discipline, supported by greatly improved standards of military administration, especially for pay and supply. For example, the new method of continuous volley firing in extended ranks adopted by the Dutch forces in the 1590s required soldiers to perform complex drill movements. They also had to develop the individual discipline and mental toughness to stand steady in relatively exposed formations – qualities less required in the densely packed squares (or *tercios*) favoured by the Spanish. Such tactics also required better systems of command, so smaller units with a higher ratio of officers became the norm. All of these factors favoured the growth of the thoroughly trained and disciplined soldier, while simultaneously creating greater career opportunities for those with the class credentials to recruit and command him.[5]

Yet the rigours of the Dutch model worked against the established practices of mercenary troops and the short-term needs of many of their employers. There was little incentive for mercenary commanders to husband their resources by spending long periods learning complicated new drill movements. Instead, they could rely on sheer weight of numbers to bludgeon their way to victory, often making good their losses by recruiting amongst the defeated enemy. Besides, those who employed mercenaries paid them to fight, not train. Nor did the need for strict central control, efficient logistics and personal discipline sit comfortably with a mercenary culture of transient, freebooting individuals, ambitious entrepreneurs and unscrupulous employers. There was therefore still plenty of demand for the old type of crude, ready-made mercenary armies.[6]

Scottish troops of conventional mercenary type had figured in William of Orange's initial efforts to recruit foreign troops for the Dutch Revolt. In June 1572, with Scotland's 'Marian' civil war petering out, and in the midst of a period of 'hunger, dearth and scarcitie', the privy council ordered the removal of all 'hable men and suldartis' from Edinburgh so that they 'be not drawn to any desperate necessity'. If they were unable to support themselves elsewhere in Scotland, the proclamation gave permission for the unemployed soldiers 'to pas to the Warres in Flanders or other foreign countries' – Sweden's war with Muscovy being the other favoured destination.[7] A year later, however, rising sympathy in Scotland for the plight of the Protestant Dutch forced a change in the nature of Scottish military involvement. In contrast to the official expediency of the previous year, this popular support encouraged a more positive stance by the Scottish state. During the summer of 1573 the privy council granted licences to three Scottish captains each to raise a company of 300 'wageit men of weare' for Flanders. Many more were to follow in the next six years.[8]

It was stated explicitly by the privy council that the troops were being recruited to serve 'in the defence of Goddis trew religioun agains the persecutiouris thairof', and that they were forbidden to 'serve with Papistis agains Protestantis'. There were other more pragmatic conditions – no men already in royal service were to be recruited without additional permission, any stocks of arms taken abroad were to be replenished and no captain was to muster his men within sixteen miles of Stirling castle, home of the infant King James VI. In attempting to control the flow of manpower abroad, the King's regent and the privy council struck a balance between supporting their 'friendis and conferdirattis' in Flanders and preserving domestic security. How far they succeeded is debatable, as much unlicensed recruitment clearly went on, and not just for the service of the Dutch. By the 1580s, when for reasons of their own the king and his privy council needed to severely restrict foreign recruitment, it was found necessary to make it a capital crime to levy and transport troops without proper authority.[9]

Initially, the Scots fared badly as the Dutch Revolt faltered in the face of both superior Spanish forces and inadequate organisation. Arrears in pay and Spanish intrigue undermined the loyalty of a few. During the 1580s, before the advent of Prince Maurice's reforms, several towns with Scottish garrisons simply 'sold out' to the attacking Spanish forces. Those Scots who chose to defect to the Spanish side would have found many compatriots already serving there, some of whom were committed Roman Catholics but others who were simply fighting for the money.[10]

Yet the determination of the Dutch revived, and the Scots' contribution to their cause was consolidated initially as part of an Anglo-Scottish brigade (often referred to as the 'Anglo-Dutch Brigade'), then as a distinct Scots brigade of three regiments – a formation which, remarkably, was to continue in existence until 1782. Although the Scots were a small part of the Dutch army overall, they were never more than around 7 per cent of the total; they and their English comrades made a much larger contribution to the Dutch field armies, as opposed to the static garrison forces. For most of the extended period of the Dutch war (from 1568 until 1648 – the so-called 'Eighty Years War'), around half the infantry of these field forces were Anglo-Scottish.[11] The Scots, in particular, gained a formidable reputation among both Dutch commanders and foreign observers. Frederick William, the younger brother of Prince Maurice of Nassau, described the Scots as 'the bulwark of the Republic' after they suffered heavy losses holding off the main Spanish attack at the battle of Nieuwpoort in 1600. An Englishman wrote in 1622 after the siege of Bergen-op-Zoom that 'the Scottish are like Beanes and Peas among chaffe. These are sure men, hardy and resolute, and their example holds up the Dutch.'[12] If ever there were epithets that express the Scottish military tradition of the last four hundred years or more, these are they. The experience of Dutch service, especially after the introduction of Prince Maurice's reforms of the 1590s, was to be a formative influence on a generation of Scottish soldiers. Instead of being seen as basically cheap and available manpower, Scottish soldiers, especially their officers, were now regarded as seasoned professionals whose skills were soon to be much in demand.

The northern world

Scottish economic and cultural contact with Scandinavia and the Baltic had flowed back and forth for centuries, creating strong bonds and precious vested interests. The struggle between the established power of Denmark-Norway against the aspirations of Sweden, Russia and Poland from the sixteenth century onwards was therefore of great concern to Scotland, emphasised further by the marriage of King James VI to Anne of Denmark in 1589. Whilst royal support lay with Denmark-Norway, the rising influence of Sweden attracted increasing attention in Scotland. As a Protestant state with a small population, but one in need of military power to assert itself, Sweden developed as an important employer of Scottish soldiers from the 1550s onwards. As elsewhere in Europe this was facilitated through a group of military entrepreneurs. However, rather than access to capital being their first qualification as recruiters, it was the family networks of these Scots that were key to putting together regiments for Swedish service. As experience from the Netherlands filtered through, the Scots gradually developed a reputation for dependability. This was later contrasted with soldiers from other parts of Europe, including from elsewhere in the British Isles. Irish troops, for example, lacked the cultural and religious affinity the Swedes came to recognise in the Scots and were thought too prone to desertion. This closeness was greatly helped by the willingness of senior Scottish officers like Sir James Spens to align themselves with Sweden's interests and work at the level of court diplomacy for what they saw as the mutual benefit of both countries.

For Scottish officers generally, this burgeoning relationship meant an opportunity for long-term service under a favourable employer. It also held out the possibility of reward for distinguished service in the form of military promotion, social advancement and the award of land – all commodities in short supply elsewhere, particularly in

Scotland. The opportunity of gaining such preferment, especially through as honourable a means as the profession of arms, was therefore highly attractive.[13] Even the 'rank and file' could benefit from the Swedish custom of offering promotion to officer rank for an exceptional soldier. This was also a time when Scots were beginning to leave their homes in increasing numbers in search of better lives elsewhere. Places as diverse as Poland and Ulster experienced substantial Scottish immigration during the late sixteenth and early seventeenth centuries. Some of this movement was the result of official Stuart policy, such as the schemes for the Ulster Plantation and the abortive Lowland settlement of the island of Lewis in which, interestingly, Sir James Spens also played a leading role.[14] Military opportunities in Sweden can therefore be seen as part of a wider picture of the economic migration of Scots, encouraged and harnessed by nascent British policies towards colonisation, internal subjugation and commercial entrepreneurship.

For the Scottish crown, attempting to control access to this military resource could be a valuable diplomatic lever. From the 1560s permission for the Swedes (or the Danes) to levy troops in Scotland, in a similar manner to the Dutch, was used as a way of exerting pressure on Denmark-Norway to resolve its disputes with Sweden, thereby promoting stability and helping protect both Scotland's economic interests and the occasionally conflicting dynastic concerns of the Stuart crown.[15] The accession to the Swedish throne of the young and aggressive King Gustav II Adolf in 1611 heralded a shift, both in the balance of power in Scandinavia and in Scottish–Swedish relations. The military element of this relationship, building on firm foundations, was about to become even more important.

The 'Winter Queen'

The revolt of the Protestants of Bohemia against the Catholic Habsburg Holy Roman Emperor in 1618, and their invitation to Elector Frederick V of the Palatinate to become their king, set off a chain reaction along the religious and dynastic fault lines of Europe which led to thirty years of devastating war. For Scotland, events in Bohemia had a particular significance through Frederick's wife, Elizabeth Stuart, daughter of King James VI and I. The plight of the 'Winter Queen', both through her family, her nationality and her religion stirred the hearts of many leading Scots. The salvation of 'the Delight of the World, the Jewel of Europe' therefore became a matter of national honour – this was Scotland's fight as much as anyone else's.[16]

Typically, however, the first Scottish military involvement came indirectly, via the Netherlands. In early 1620, the Dutch Republic despatched around 1,200 of their Scots troops to help their Protestant allies in Bohemia. The following year the Republic's dormant war against Habsburg Spain reignited. Meanwhile, a concerted recruiting effort was about to begin in Britain when Sir Andrew Gray, a Scottish officer of Elizabeth Stuart's household, was sent by Elector Frederick to London to raise military support from his father-in-law. Although King James was anxious to avoid openly provoking the Habsburg dynasty, which held both the thrones of Spain and the Holy Roman Empire, permitting foreign recruitment of his subjects, ostensibly to protect the Elector and his family rather than fight for Bohemia, was one way he could materially support his family's fortunes. Over the next two years around 8,000 recruits left Britain for Bohemia; it is believed around 5,000 of them were Scots.[17]

In its complexity, the character of this contingent reveals much about Scotland's reaction to the war. For a start, Gray and several of his officers, most notably Sir John Hepburn, were Roman Catholics. As an experienced professional soldier, who had previously served in Protestant Sweden, Gray clearly did not see his personal faith as a determining factor as to who he served. Nor, at this stage, did Hepburn as he sought to embark on what was to become one of the most successful careers of any Scottish professional soldier of the period. For men like these, in this particular campaign, loyalties to the house of Stuart and career opportunity were more important factors than religion.

As for the composition of the ranks, the privy council in Scotland, in as much as it had the power, was again keen to use foreign enlistment for its own domestic ends. Beggars and 'masterless vagabonds' were encouraged to join up on pain of a whipping or being burnt on the cheek for a first refusal, and hanging for a second.[18] Convicted criminals were offered the chance of enlistment as an alternative to execution. The council also saw an opportunity to neutralise certain sectors of Scottish society that retained a capacity for serious violence. The termination of 'Border warfare' after 1603 had left a turbulent class of men used to a life of lawlessness and conflict whose adherence to their old ways was seen as a threat by both the Scottish and the English authorities. In 1605, for example, 150 men of the Graham clan were sentenced to be sent to the wars in Flanders in the hope that most of them would not come back.[19] In May 1620 the council ordered that all incorrigible outlaws and masterless men already identified from the Border counties as being a threat to the peace were to come to

Edinburgh, on pain of death, and sign up with Sir Andrew Gray. Such moves were in line with wider efforts to ensure that the use of violence was now to be a monopoly of the king. Parliament's acceptance in 1598 of the principle that justice was the prerogative of the state, not a matter for private vengeance, demonstrated how Scottish society was developing.[20]

It is not known what proportion of the 5,000 Scots recruits for Bohemia resulted from these official efforts, but it certainly was not all. As for the rest, they came from the familiar sources that were to sustain Scottish recruiting for the next twenty years and more: the extended kin of regimental commanders (often younger sons looking to improve their prospects as junior officers and recruiters themselves, or as soldiers), fugitives of one kind or another, the adventurous, the desperate and the poor. Among the class of fugitives were some who had got on the wrong side of the Kirk – men whose moral behaviour had been found wanting by local presbytery courts.[21] The adventurers included plenty who saw the defence of a Protestant queen of Stuart lineage as a natural cause for a Scot and the act of taking up arms as the first step in an honourable profession. At least one account of Scottish units bound for Bohemia comments on the 'quality' of many of the Scottish recruits compared to their English comrades.[22] For such men, social mobility was also a strong incentive for military service. The prospect of future officer status, with its automatic privileges and social cachet, was so appealing that many aspiring young Scots carried with them 'birthbrieves' – documents setting out their family lineage – as a means of establishing their suitability for higher rank. Both in 1620 and later, however, illegal enforcement was also frequently used to fill the ranks, achieved by straightforward abduction, or by false arrest and imprisonment, followed by 'authorised' release into the hands of an unscrupulous recruiter.[23]

Despite British support, the war went badly in Bohemia and the torch of the Protestant cause passed to King Christian IV of Denmark-Norway in coalition with his brother-in-law King James (and after 1625 with his nephew, Charles) and the United Provinces. Scottish troops constituted a major element in the alliance, with the privy council authorising the recruitment of 13,400 men for service under Danish command in Germany between 1626 and 1628.[24] Given that Scottish taxation was actually subsidising these levies, and that the Danes themselves regarded the Scots (and English) as *hjælptropper*, or 'help' troops, of an allied nation, rather than as *lejotrupper*, or 'rented' troops, as they did the Germans who served alongside the Scots, the label 'mercenary' is misleading.[25] In contrast to earlier, more entrepreneurial levies, the role of powerful aristocratic and political figures like the earl of Nithsdale and Lord Spynie in raising these troops demonstrates both the level of state leadership to the project and the manner in which the Scottish nobility were now willing to combine their traditional influence with the developing mechanisms of centrally funded and directed national military service.[26]

Another significant aspect of the Danish levy was the appearance of a distinctly Highland element. This was the regiment recruited by Sir Donald Mackay, later Lord Reay, head of his clan and a major figure in the north of Scotland. In contrast to other units, Mackay's regiment was brought up to strength – 3,600 men – remarkably quickly. A Gaelic phrase that long outlived Mackay and his regiment translates as 'he that is down on his luck shall get a dollar from Mackay'.[27] The regiment was immortalised in what is reckoned to be the first published regimental history of a British military unit – *Monro, His Expedition with the Worthy Scots Regiment called Mac-Keyes Regiment*. The work of Colonel Robert Monro, the book was first published in 1637 and gives a rare insight into the experience, motivation and self-esteem of Scottish soldiers of the time.[28]

In comparison to the rest of Scotland, the Highlands had developed a particular tradition of 'mercenary' service. This was largely linked to Ireland where from the early thirteenth century warriors from the western Highlands and Islands had found regular employment. These *gall-óglaich* ('foreign soldier' or 'foreign young warrior'), or galloglass as they became known, were an established part of Celtic warfare and many settled in Ireland forming elite military dynasties. In the sixteenth century they were joined by other Highland soldiers, colloquially known as 'redshanks', brought over to Ulster by local magnates to fight in the myriad conflicts both for and against the invading English, or their own local rivals. In the 1590s, according to an English intelligence report, there were more than 6,600 of these 'redshanks' or *buannachan* ('household men', that is members of a retinue) available in the Western Isles alone.[29] The Scottish crown's inability to control their seasonal movement to Ireland (along with the activities of the Border clans) was the cause of frequent complaint by the English during the protracted period of rapprochement that preceded James VI's eventual accession to the English throne in 1603. Consequently, military efforts were undertaken to extend Scottish state control to parts of the west Highlands in the 1590s using manpower and experience gleaned from Scottish service in the Dutch wars.[30] One rather cyclical consequence of such campaigns, and of other royally commissioned 'fire and sword' operations against particularly unruly clans, was the creation of pockets of destitute military manpower ripe for continental recruitment.[31]

The lion of the north

Although raised for the campaign in Bohemia, Mackay's regiment was transferred to Danish service in 1626. Three years later, with the defeat of the Danes, it entered the service of Sweden. With French financial backing, and limited British military support, the Swedish army had become the last hope for the anti-Imperialist cause and its arrival in Germany in 1630 had a dramatic effect on the war. In King Gustav II Adolf, the allies found an aggressive and inspiring military leader whose tactical and organisational innovations had already transformed his forces. Although based around an established system of conscription, the Swedish army was heavily augmented by foreign troops, amongst whom the Scots were prominent. During the 1620s this balance between national and foreign recruits had been shifting as Gustav Adolf expanded the army, both to fight the Poles in Livonia and in the expectation of greater involvement in the war in Germany. From around 15 per cent in 1621, the proportion of foreign troops had grown to 50 per cent by 1630. It is estimated that around 14,000 of these were Scots – approximately 20 per cent of the total army and 40 per cent of the foreign contingent.[32] The proportion of foreign troops grew as the Swedes advanced deep into Germany, rising to 72 per cent by 1631.[33] Between 1629 and the end of the war in 1648, it is estimated that around 25,000 to 30,000 Scots served in the Swedish army, about 2,000 of whom were officers.[34]

The remarkable success of the Swedish forces, especially in the period leading up to the death of King Gustav II Adolf at the battle of Lützen in 1632, was partly the consequence of tactical innovation combined with sound training. By refining the methods of the Dutch and applying them more offensively, the Swedes significantly influenced the course of European warfare. Key to this success was a hard core of seasoned, highly trained and loyal troops. Forming just under a quarter of the Swedish field army in Germany, Scottish units constituted a major part of this core. Similarly, the influence of hundreds of experienced Scottish officers throughout the army (again, providing just under a quarter of the total number of officers), especially in positions of senior command, was crucial to Swedish success.[35]

Seen as more adaptable and reliable than other foreign troops, and with the religious and cultural affinity already highlighted, the Scots were frequently placed in key tactical roles. When the men of

Figure 9.1 Highland soldiers at Stettin, 1631, in the service of King Gustav II Adolf of Sweden, from a contemporary German engraving.

MacKay's regiment transferred to Swedish service in 1629, a vital clause in their new contract stipulated that they must be willing and able to undertake the digging and construction tasks necessary for modern Dutch-style field and siege works.[36] The decisive role the Scots played in Swedish victories, such as Breitenfeld in 1631, greatly enhanced their national reputation. In the words of Robert Monro, Gustav Adolf owed much to his Scottish soldiers, achieving his victories 'with the helpe of the nation which was never conquered by any forraine enemy, the invincible Scots'.[37]

For the Scots, King Gustav II Adolf's willingness to preserve them in largely national units – the famous Green Brigade being the best known – while simultaneously inculcating a sense of religious or moral purpose for the entire army, encouraged a sense of loyalty to the Swedish cause. When coupled to Gustav Adolf's personal appeal as a charismatic and heroic leader, this loyalty could come close to devotion. In addition, by embracing the cause of the 'Winter Queen', Swedish service became all the more honourable for many Scots. The distinctive coherence and scale of the Scottish contribution to the anti-Imperialist cause therefore strengthened the link between notions of national identity and military service.

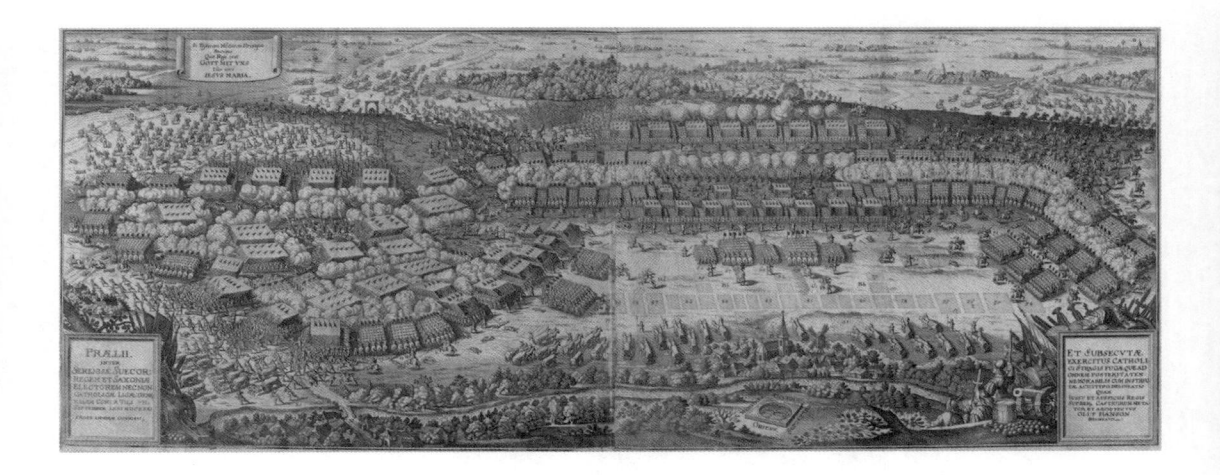

Figure 9.2 A contemporary engraving of the battle of Breitenfeld, 1631, Gustav Adolf's victory over the Catholic forces led by Tilly.

There were, however, negative factors. For the Swedes, a reliance on highly trained troops meant that replacing losses invariably led to a dilution of quality. This was particularly true of the Scots, who found themselves to be victims of their own success, being repeatedly deployed as assault troops and suffering heavy losses accordingly. After the Swedish defeat at Nördlingen in 1634, Scottish casualties were such that the role of these national units in the Swedish army sharply diminished, even if the importance of Scottish officers remained high. Relations between these officers and the Swedes could also be complicated. Despite loyal and distinguished service, Colonel Sir John Hepburn left the Swedish army for the French following a dispute with Gustav Adolf, apparently after the latter made a disparaging remark about King Charles. Some sources also cite Hepburn's Catholicism as a source of friction with the king, as well as Scottish resentment at occasionally being slighted in favour of Swedish troops. Such tensions notwithstanding, the Scots' part in the campaigns in Germany both enhanced their military reputation and secured their place as trusted allies of the Swedes. It was an alliance that was about to be tested.

Veterans

In 1637 King Charles attempted to impose a new prayer book on his Protestant Scottish subjects. Religious trouble had long been brewing and the Scots' response crystallised in the National Covenant in defence of their Presbyterian faith. This was soon followed by the need for a more temporal defence against their king. With the

Figure 9.3 Sir Alexander Leslie, from an engraving of 1642. A veteran of the Swedish army, he was to play a prominent role in the British civil wars.

domestic military apparatus moribund through years of neglect, the *de facto* covenanter government, as Martyn Bennett notes in Chapter 10, quickly looked abroad for a means of salvation. The presence in Scotland of Sir Alexander Leslie, a senior officer in the Swedish service (and a veteran of the Dutch and Bohemian wars), immediately opened a channel of negotiation for the recall of veteran Scottish soldiers from the war in Europe.

After some debate, the Swedish response was positive both in accepting that the Scots had a duty (indeed, a right) to return home to defend their nation, and in acknowledging a sense of obligation to individual Scots for their loyal service. Political self-interest also figured in that the Swedes were well aware that King Charles had recently been courting alliances with both their old rival Denmark-Norway and even with Habsburg Spain. With Swedish assistance, including naval escorts (partly officered by other Scots) and shipments of arms (arranged through Scottish merchants in Sweden and the Netherlands), an estimated 300 Scottish officers prepared to return home; the vast majority were to side with the Covenant, a minority with the king.[38]

Their return, however, meant far more than physical manpower and matériel: they also brought experience and understanding of new tactical and administrative doctrines which were to have far-reaching effects. One such consequence was the adoption in Scotland of a Swedish model of conscription, dividing the country into military districts with a hierarchy of representative committees reporting to a national committee for war. With the active participation of the Kirk and its organisation the results of this system were remarkable. By 1640 the Scots had put up to 25,000 men in the field (a mobilisation on a par with the best the Swedes could achieve themselves), plus around another 15,000 called out by clans in the west Highlands and the north-east. Although it was expedient that the nobility should play the leading role in this army, the covenanter leadership stipulated that the lieutenant-colonel and major of each regiment, and the ensign and two sergeants of each company, were to be veteran professional soldiers.[39] They also insisted that overall command of the army should go to Alexander Leslie. With such stiffening, the Scots army quickly became a formidable prospect, so much so that it quite over-awed the royal forces sent against it in 1639, and again in 1640, in the so-called Bishops' Wars.[40]

The political consequences that stemmed, in part, from this royal humiliation were profound – over ten years of civil war throughout Britain and Ireland, the execution of one king, and the exile and eventual restoration of another. For Scotland, the ability to mobilise such a formidable pool of veteran military manpower not only allowed it to defend a national interest, but also provided the means to project that interest elsewhere, for better or for worse, for the next ten years. There may not have been any climactic Bannockburn-like clash of arms in 1639–40, but seldom was the link between Scotland's military tradition and a sense of national purpose more clearly defined.

The veterans' return did not mean the end of Scottish recruitment, either for the Swedish service or for the war in Europe in general;

indeed, many of the vacancies created in Sweden were soon filled by new officers from Scotland. The absorption of much of the country's military manpower in the domestic campaigns of the next ten years, however, weakened Scotland's international position and so its influence in the European Protestant cause. Catholic Bourbon France had also reasserted itself as a major employer of Scottish soldiers, especially following the country's full entry into the war against the Habsburgs in 1635. As the war evolved from one of religion into an overt dynastic struggle, French service became an attractive option for many Catholic Scots.

The strategic shift in favour of France was actively encouraged by King Charles. Between 1633 and 1642, the Scottish privy council issued licences for the recruitment of 10,200 men for French service.[41] In the run-up to the first Bishops' War in 1639, Charles even attempted to use additional recruitment for France as a means of reducing the military threat developing under covenanter leadership.[42] By using Scottish troops as collateral for his foreign policies, Charles was simply following the lead of his father. However, just as there had previously been tensions between the often 'unregulated' Scottish recruitment for Sweden and royal (and English) support for Denmark – rival forces narrowly avoided coming to blows in 1612 – so there were contradictions for the Scots in now openly supporting Catholic France. There had also been instances since 1625 when Charles's policies as king of England had gone against Scottish interests, even if it had meant the hiring of Scottish troops for English service. In 1627, for instance, when his policy opposed Louis XIII, Charles had hired 2,000 Scots as part of an English force sent to support Protestant Huguenots at La Rochelle against the French king, much to the disruption of Scottish trade with France.[43] In 1641 Charles, with the backing of the English parliament, had hired a whole army of Scots for service in Ulster which included much of the European trained manpower recalled in 1638.

A mix of factors, including Catholicism, had also led an unknown number of Scots into Imperial/Habsburg service in the same way it had previously encouraged Scottish enlistment in the Spanish forces in Flanders. Although outnumbered by Irish troops, these Scots gained some notoriety, especially after the involvement in 1634 of two officers, Colonel John Gordon and Major Walter Leslie (both of whom happened to be Protestants, with Leslie a veteran of the Dutch army), in the Imperial conspiracy to assassinate Count Albrecht von Wallenstein, the notorious Bohemian mercenary commander. The majority of these Scots were officers recruited on a 'freelance' basis, many of whom had drifted eastwards in search of employment.

The ever-present threat from the Ottoman Empire and Poland-Lithuania's wars with Sweden and Russia provided plenty of opportunity. Scots recruited amongst immigrant communities in Poland could also find themselves serving under Imperial command.[44]

It is impossible to say exactly how many Scots fought during the Thirty Years War. The records of the privy council confirm that licences were issued for the enlistment of 47,110 men between 1625 and 1642.[45] Whether all these quotas were filled is unknown. Nor does the figure take account of the unlicensed recruiting that certainly went on, or the recruitment amongst Scots already abroad. A figure of around 50,000 is now, however, reckoned to be likely.[46] Given a population of roughly a million over the period, this works out to around one in five of the male population of military age – a staggering proportion. The impact on Scottish society must have been severe, especially on marriage and birth rates, made all the more stark by the fact that most of these young men never returned home, the majority dying either of disease or on the battlefields of Germany. For those few 'old beaten blades of soldiers' who survived their long years of service, retirement amongst expatriate Scottish communities would probably have been a better option than attempting to return home. A proposal in 1634 by Colonel Robert Monro to establish a charitable hospital for returning veterans in Edinburgh came to nothing.[47] Naturally, the fate of surviving officers was different, with many achieving their goal of wealth and social advancement in their adopted homes. Around eighty Scottish officers in Swedish service were ennobled during the course of the seventeenth century.[48]

The conclusion of the Thirty Years War in 1648 did not mean the end of Scottish service abroad even though the nature of European armies was changing. In the aftermath of the war, nation states became more clearly defined, with fixed borders requiring static defences and more full-time garrison troops. Instead of relying on unaccountable and self-serving military entrepreneurs, states now wanted disciplined permanent 'standing' armies which could be relied upon to fight when needed and to remain loyal. Although a recovery in population numbers and a willingness amongst local elites to embrace fresh career opportunities could provide the bulk of the manpower for these new forces, there was still a market for foreign troops. The difference was that the deals were now done at state level, something the governors of Scotland were well used to.

Throughout the rest of the seventeenth century, official approval (given by a mix of authorities for a mix of motives) allowed both Sweden and the Netherlands to continue recruiting in Scotland for both officers and men, albeit on a reduced scale. France also maintained several Scottish regiments. Following the Restoration of the Stuart monarchy in 1660, these units were kept on, partly as a kind of offshore investment – a way of sustaining a loyal military force away from the direct control of the English parliament, ready for periodical recall as and when needed. They were also a valuable source of income to the British crown as the French paid a subsidy for their continued use. The principal regiment was that commanded by the earl of Dumbarton, originally raised by Sir John Hepburn in 1633.[49] It saw heavy fighting in French service, particularly during the 1670s, and its replenishment ran to thousands of Scottish recruits.

Exiles

The end of the Thirty Years War also roughly coincided in Scotland with the start of a hundred years of constitutional and religious turmoil, which cast out political exiles of every colour – royalists, Catholics, Presbyterians and Jacobites. This created an alternative source of Scottish soldiers who took service as a means of survival, usually for states at odds with the prevailing regime in Britain. The fact that many of these exiles joined established Scottish military enclaves across Europe, most of which had, at some point, enjoyed official support, highlights the mercurial nature of foreign employment at the time. Once again, it also reveals the risks of establishing extra-territorial military bodies outside the control of the home government: forces whose loyalties, already weakened by distance and the vicissitudes of international politics, could be manipulated by whatever faction happened to be in opposition and might have need of their services. The central role played by the Anglo-Scots Brigade in William of Orange's successful invasion of Britain in 1688 is a clear example of this danger, even if the consequences of its actions in securing the Protestant cause in Scotland were wholly compatible with the Brigade's origins. It is also ironic that Scottish troops under foreign command should have been so crucial in both undermining the last Stuart king and thereby releasing the next wave of military exiles, given that dynasty's former enthusiasm for trading manpower for influence.

Although it was expected that France would become the natural sponsor of Jacobite military service, the defeat of King James's forces in Ireland and Scotland by 1691 undermined French confidence in the cause. The establishment of James and his exile court at St Germain-en-Laye, and the influx of Irish troops into French service (the so-called 'Wild Geese'), may have raised Jacobite hopes of addi-

Figure 9.4 Cap worn by a grenadier officer of the Royal Écossais, 1745.

tional French financial support, but attempts to create Scottish units came to very little. A few hundred men were gathered, mainly deserters from Scottish regiments now serving with the Williamite British army in Flanders. Unsurprisingly, the largest number came from Dumbarton's regiment, whose previous long service in France and lingering loyalty to the house of Stuart had clearly (for the moment) undermined its reliability.[50]

In 1743 a distinct Scottish Jacobite regiment was successfully created in the French army – Le Régiment Royal Écossais – which along with elements from the Franco-Irish Brigade saw service in the 1745 rising. Two further regiments were created in 1747, but they were principally a belated means of providing an income as French officers for the exiled leaders of the 'Forty-Five. With the possible exception of the Royal Écossais, the proportion of Scots in the ranks of these units never exceeded around 30 per cent, and all were disbanded by 1762.[51]

With France reluctant to hire large numbers of Jacobite exiles, alternative sources of military employment were sought. Russia was one such destination, where the most recent Scottish military presence had been established in the 1630s through contacts with Sweden.

Its leader, Alexander Leslie of Auchintoul, was the first officer in the Russian service to bear the rank of general. As a state keen to modernise its armed forces, Russia began to attract further experienced Scottish officers, many of whom were senior political exiles like the royalists Thomas Dalyell and William Drummond. Both returned to Scotland after the Restoration and played an active role in the suppression of the religious 'Troubles'. Dalyell, in particular, was vilified in covenanter propaganda as 'Bluidy Tam' and the 'Muscovy Beast', for using all manner of barbarous tactics – such as thumb-screws – allegedly picked up during his service in Russia against the Turks and the Tartars.[52] Younger exiles, like Patrick Gordon of Auchleuchries, needed employment as much as a refuge and stayed on in Russia (sometimes under duress, as Gordon's diaries attest) to achieve senior positions in the tsar's forces.[53]

There was, however, an important difference between the service of these Scots and their predecessors. The one resource Russia was never short of was manpower, so what was needed most was a corps of experienced officers to mould this raw material into an effective military organisation. As other European armies also expanded through the conscription of their own subjects, a similar need arose. That this coincided with an exodus of political exiles from Scotland, many of whom had the necessary skills and social background, was fortuitous. Many of these exiled Scottish officers achieved high rank in Russia and elsewhere. James Keith (1696–1758), for example, served in the Spanish and Russian armies before being killed in action as a field marshal in the Prussian service.

The employment of exiles could also have a political dimension. While Scottish Jacobites were welcomed by Tsar Peter the Great and his successors, particularly after 1715, principally for their military (and naval) skills, growing Anglo-Russian rivalry gave their employment additional meaning. The use of politically neutral foreign officers in Russia, especially in senior positions, was also seen as a necessary safeguard to the domestic stability of the state. As ever before, personal ambition was another factor in attracting recruits to the east. Swingeing financial cuts in the British army and Royal Navy in 1717, for example, forced many half-pay officers onto the international market. Their continuing ability to convert close-knit webs of kinship into professional military service meant a high proportion of these unemployed officers were Scots.[54]

If the international market for Scottish officers continued well into the eighteenth century, recruitment of Scots for the ranks of foreign forces was falling away. An expanding British army needed all the manpower it could get and Scotland was seen as a rich seam, especially by those Scots keen to capitalise on the professional military opportunities accelerated by the 1707 Act of Union. Yet continuing Jacobite conspiracies, especially involving the Highlands, threatened this fragile new British unity. Attempts at foreign (mainly French and Prussian) recruitment in the Highlands, especially when linked to disaffected exiles, therefore had to be sharply dealt with – a priority both for the government in London and for its adherents in Scotland. A key duty of the Highland Independent Companies from 1725 (until their regimentation as the Black Watch in 1739) was the prevention of such recruiting and its corrosive effect on southern perceptions of Scotland's political reliability.[55]

Some traditional patterns of overseas recruitment continued. Economic hardship, for example, caused by an exceptionally harsh winter in 1739–40, led to heavy recruitment in the Highlands for the Scots Brigade in the Netherlands. Dutch service was also seen by the British government as one means of demilitarising the Highlands after 1745, with the Dutch being seen as reliable allies against the French.[56] It is doubtful if this later policy was ever implemented, for the raising of new Highland regiments for the British army was soon absorbing most of the available manpower. Certainly, by the late eighteenth century the Scots Brigade in the Netherlands had ceased to recruit Scots into the ranks. It did, however, still attract young Scots as officers, often as an informal pre-qualification to a commission in the British army.[57] Yet even this was to come to an end. In 1776 the British government requested that the Brigade be recalled for service in the unfolding American War of Independence. The Dutch refused, stating that 'Janissaries rather than troops of a free state should be used to subdue colonists'.[58] The allusion to the regiments of Christian-born soldiers in the pay of the Ottoman Empire pre-empted Britain's widespread employment of Hessian mercenaries in America while also expressing the contrasting Dutch view of the Scots in their own service. Four years later Dutch sympathy with the American colonists led to open war with Britain, and in 1782 the officers of the Brigade were given an ultimatum to either renounce their nationality and swear allegiance to the Dutch Republic or forfeit their commissions. Only about a third of the 153 officers chose to resign and return home, but after 200 years' service the Brigade finally lost its distinctive Scottish identity. Appropriately, in light of the direction in which the Scottish military tradition was now heading, a rump of the returning officers reformed the Brigade in 1793 for British service in India.[59]

The assimilation of Scotland into the British imperial state (a process perhaps nowhere more successful than in the armed forces) meant an end to the nation's role as a pool for significant foreign recruitment. Yet the demand for such troops never fully disappeared, and Scots continued to serve other masters than the British crown. From the early nineteenth century, emerging nations, from South America to Italy, appealed to foreign 'volunteers' to join their wars of liberation. Quasi-colonial and commercial organisations such as the British East India Company were also happy to recruit military manpower outside the framework of the nation state. As before, motivating factors for foreign service traversed the scale between ideological commitment and material gain.

Liberators

In the aftermath of the Napoleonic Wars, a harsh economic climate and a revival of radical politics encouraged recruitment throughout Britain and Ireland for service in the newly founded republics of South America against the Spanish empire. Over 5,000 men were raised, about a third of whom were probably ex-soldiers and half-pay officers.[60] Although heavily outnumbered by the Irish, the Scots were still well represented, partly as a consequence of a continuing enthusiasm for emigration and by their military reputation, enhanced through the twenty years of war with France. Under pressure from the Spanish government, Britain passed the Foreign Enlistment Act in 1819 which, while not eliminating such recruitment, certainly curtailed it. A few years later civil wars between constitutionalist and absolutist factions, first in Portugal (the Miguelite War, 1828–34), then in Spain (the First Carlist War, 1833–40), prompted further British recruiting. With public opinion and the Liberal government favouring the constitutionalists, especially in Spain, there were calls for direct British military intervention. Politically, this was deemed too provocative so a compromise was reached whereby the Spanish government was permitted to recruit a force of 10,000 men in the United Kingdom – in reality the vast majority were to come from Ireland. This British Auxiliary Legion included three nominally Scottish regiments (2,104 men and 69 officers) recruited largely from Glasgow and Edinburgh.[61] Many of these recruits were former handloom weavers, a group whose radical views, as much as their straitened circumstances, may have influenced their decision to fight for the liberal cause in Spain – a precedent in some small way for Scottish involvement in the Spanish Civil War of the 1930s. Such an outlook, however, did not help once the Legion reached Spain, where poor organisation, disputes about terms of service and rampant disease destroyed much of its capacity to fight as well as its reputation.

Political sympathy was certainly to take 260 Scottish volunteers from Glasgow to Italy in 1860 as part of the British Legion of 600–800 men raised to assist Giuseppe Garibaldi's campaign in Sicily. The fact that the Legion was created in response to successful Papal appeals for Irish volunteers (some of whom were found in Glasgow) to defend Rome from Garibaldi's anti-clerical republicans only strengthened support in Scotland, where the cause of Italian reunification had attracted considerable support since the 1840s. In an echo of the Netherlands in the 1570s, many Protestant Scots, particularly those of a radical or reforming outlook, saw the struggles for liberation in Italy and elsewhere as part of an older battle against autocratic and reactionary forces, manifested in the shape of 'Popery' and the power of the Catholic Church.[62] Yet one of the many differences between 1570 and 1860 was that Scotland's military manpower was now committed elsewhere and the country's ability to act nationally tempered by union and empire.

A store of men

This chapter began by posing a question – whether it was right to see the experience of Scottish soldiers in foreign service as a single phenomenon and to judge them accordingly. It is to be hoped that the foregoing account shows that a single label of 'mercenary', implying a single motivation, is misplaced, as are any general verdicts, either good or bad, on the moral probity of those thousands of Scots involved. If their story is too complex to justify either pride or revulsion, what then might it tell us?

First, it indicates that Scotland's people have long adapted to their circumstances by seeking better prospects elsewhere. Foreign military service should therefore be looked at as a form of emigration, made possible by the close-knit nature of Scottish society and the survival of a warrior ethos among the fringes of a teeming nobility. The prospect of honourable employment and the chance of social advancement, linked to religious, national and dynastic sympathies, provided a powerful stimulus for many Scots to take up arms abroad. Hunger, poverty, obligation and exile were often just as strong motives. For many, the outcome was an early death, far from home; for a few it was the rank, income and future they desired. For the rest, it probably was not much more than a life of hardship, danger and violence, redeemed perhaps by the budding reputation of the Scottish soldier.

Second, it testifies that foreign service was long used as a method of projecting, defending and developing a variety of national interests in circumstances when diplomatic or conventional military means were either beyond the wherewithal of a Scottish state, or when the interest was not wholly shared by those in power. The soldier therefore became a form of capital to be traded in return for influence or profit, otherwise unattainable either by Scotland's monarch or by many of its elite. As the reputation of these soldiers grew, so did foreign demand, thus increasing their value as capital and perpetuating the networks of supply. The prevalence and prestige of these soldiers abroad, both individually and as national units, also established a synergy between a developing Scottish identity, especially as defined by its choice of religion, and military service.

When Scotland's fragile structures of state were eventually subsumed within a Protestant Great Britain, it was natural that military service abroad should continue as a means both of attaining influence and profit and remaining a focus for national identity. The culture of military service, largely created by the opportunities and demands of foreign employment, was thus sufficiently durable and flexible to meet the growing needs of Britain and the empire. In so doing it helped secure a place of honour for Scotland and a global role for its soldiers. The 'sure men, hardy and resolute' were set to continue for a while yet as Scotland's face to the world.

Notes

1. S. Percy, *Mercenaries: The History of a Norm in International Relations* (Oxford: Oxford University Press, 2007), pp. 49–67.
2. Sir James Turner, *Memoirs of his Own Life and Times, 1632–1670*, ed. T. Thomson (London: Bannatyne Club, 1829), p. 16.
3. The author acknowledges here the wealth of recent published work on this topic, especially that by Steve Murdoch and Alexia Grosjean.
4. H. Strachan, *European Armies and the Conduct of War* (London: George Allen and Unwin, 1983), p. 9.
5. G. Parker, *The Military Revolution: Military Innovation and the Rise of the West, 1500–1800* (Cambridge: Cambridge University Press 1988), pp. 18–24.
6. J. Childs, *Warfare in the Seventeenth Century* (London: Cassell & Co., 2001), pp. 34–8.
7. H. Dunthorne, 'Scots in the Wars of the Low Countries 1572–1648',

in G. G. Simpson (ed.), *Scotland and the Low Countries, 1124–1994* (East Linton: Tuckwell Press, 1996), p. 109; J. Ferguson (ed.), *Papers Illustrating the History of the Scots Brigade in the Service of the United Netherlands, 1572–1782*, 3 vols (Edinburgh: Scottish History Society, 1899–1901), vol. 1, p. 5.

8. Licences were issued for the levying of at least 3,100 men between 1573 and 1579; I. R. Bartlett, 'Scottish mercenaries in Europe, 1570–1640: A study in attitude and policies', *Scottish Tradition*, vol. 13 (1984–5), p. 18.
9. Bartlett, 'Scottish mercenaries', pp. 17–18; Dunthorne, 'Scots in the Wars of the Low Countries', p. 110; *The Register of the Privy Council of Scotland*, ed. J. H. Burton, 14 vols (Edinburgh: HM General Register House, 1877–94), vol. 2 (1627–8), pp. 237, 256–7.
10. Dunthorne, 'Scots in the Wars of the Low Countries', p. 107.
11. R. B. Manning, *Apprenticeship in Arms: The Origins of the British Army, 1585–1702* (Oxford: Oxford University Press, 2006), p. 53.
12. Dunthorne, 'Scots in the Wars of the Low Countries', pp. 114–15.
13. K. M. Brown, 'From Scottish lords to British officers: State building, elite integration and the army in the seventeenth century', in N. Macdougall (ed.), *Scotland and War AD 79–1918* (Edinburgh: John Donald, 1991), pp. 142–3.
14. Scotland, Scandanavia and Northern European Biographical Database. Available at www.st-andrews.ac.uk/history/ssne/index.php, accessed on 25 July 2011.
15. A. Grosjean, *An Unofficial Alliance: Scotland and Sweden 1569–1654* (Leiden: Brill, 2003), p. 15.
16. S. Murdoch, 'The House of Stuart and the Scottish professional soldier, 1618–1640: A conflict of nationality and identities', in B. Taithe and T. Thornton (eds), *War: Identities in Conflict, 1300–2000* (Stroud: Sutton, 1998), pp. 45–6.
17. Ibid. pp. 43–4.
18. J. Miller, *Swords for Hire: The Scottish Mercenary* (Edinburgh: Birlinn, 2007), p. 103.
19. Parker, *The Military Revolution*, p. 49.
20. Brown, 'From Scottish lords to British officers', p. 134.
21. Manning, *Apprenticeship in Arms*, p. 50.
22. Murdoch, 'The House of Stuart', p. 45.
23. M. Glozier, 'Scots in the French and Dutch armies', in S. Murdoch (ed.), *Scotland and the Thirty Years War, 1618–1648* (Leiden: Brill, 2001), p. 122.
24. Bartlett, 'Scottish mercenaries', p. 21.
25. S. Murdoch, 'Introduction', in Murdoch (ed.), *Scotland and the Thirty Years War*, p. 15.

26. J. Goodare, *The Government of Scotland 1560–1625* (Oxford: Oxford University Press, 2004), pp. 310–11.
27. Murdoch, 'Introduction', p. 14, n. 53.
28. W. S. Brockington (ed.), *Monro, His Expedition with the Worthy Scots Regiment called Mac-Keyes Regiment* (Westport, CT: Praeger, 1999); and W. S. Brockington, 'Robert Monro: Professional soldier, military historian and Scotsman', in Murdoch (ed.), *Scotland and the Thirty Years War*, pp. 215–41.
29. A. I. Macinnes, *Clanship, Commerce and the House of Stuart, 1603–1788* (East Linton: Tuckwell Press, 1996), p. 57.
30. M. Lynch, 'James VI and the Highland problem', in J. Goodare and M. Lynch (eds), *The Reign of James VI* (East Linton: Tuckwell Press, 2000), p. 220.
31. Manning, *Apprenticeship in Arms*, p. 81.
32. Grosjean, *An Unofficial Alliance*, pp. 57–62.
33. A. Grosjean, 'Scotland: Sweden's closest ally?', in Murdoch (ed.), *Scotland and the Thirty Years War*, p. 143.
34. Ibid. pp. 150–1.
35. Grosjean, *An Unofficial Alliance*, pp. 105–8.
36. T. A. Fischer, *The Scots in Germany: Being a Contribution Towards the History of the Scot Abroad* (Edinburgh: Otto Schulze & Co., 1902), p. 280; F. G. Bengtsson, 'Robert Monro', in J. Berg and B. Lagercrantz (eds), *Scots in Sweden* (Stockholm: Nordiska Museet, 1962), pp. 79–100.
37. Brockington, 'Robert Monro', p. 237.
38. Grosjean, *An Unofficial Alliance*, pp. 165–90.
39. This was probably more of an aspiration than an accomplished fact. On this basis, if a maximum of 300 officers returned from Swedish service, this would only have provided enough officers to staff nine regiments, but in 1639 the covenanters' army had at least sixteen non-'Highland' infantry regiments.
40. E. M. Furgol, *A Regimental History of the Covenanting Armies, 1639–1651* (Edinburgh: John Donald, 1990), pp. 1–14; and E. M. Furgol, 'Scotland turned Sweden: The Scottish Covenanters and the Military Revolution 1638–1651', in J. Morrill (ed.), *The Scottish National Covenant in its British Context* (Edinburgh: Edinburgh University Press, 1990), pp. 134–54.
41. Bartlett, 'Scottish mercenaries', p. 21.
42. Glozier, 'Scots in the French and Dutch armies', p. 121.
43. Brown, 'From Scottish lords to British officers', p. 159, n. 13.
44. D. Worthington, 'Alternative diplomacy? Scottish exiles at the courts of the Habsburgs and their allies, 1618–1648', in Murdoch (ed.), *Scotland and the Thirty Years War*, p. 63.

45. Bartlett, 'Scottish mercenaries', p. 21.
46. Murdoch, 'Introduction', pp. 14, 20.
47. Bartlett, 'Scottish mercenaries', p. 22.
48. Manning, *Apprenticeship in Arms*, p. 70.
49. The regiment's ultimate recall to Britain in 1679 led to its eventual transformation into the 1st Regiment of Foot or the Royal Scots, the senior line infantry regiment of the British army. It continued as a distinct unit until its incorporation into the Royal Regiment of Scotland in 2006.
50. M. Glozier, *Scottish Soldiers in France in the Reign of the Sun King: Nursery for Men of Honour* (Leiden: Brill, 2004), pp. 231–49.
51. H. C. McCorry, 'Rats, lice and Scotsmen', *Journal of the Society for Army Historical Research*, vol. 74 (1996), pp. 1–38.
52. One source actually credits this innovation to Dalyell's comrade, William Drummond (later Viscount Strathallan), who seems to have had a disposition equal to Dalyell's reputation. Prior to their time in Russia, both had served under Robert Munro in the Scots army in Ulster. See J. Grant, *The Scottish Soldier of Fortune* (London: George Routledge, 1889), p. 3.
53. P. Dukes, 'Problems concerning the departure of Scottish soldiers', in T. C. Smout (ed.), *Scotland and Europe, 1200–1850* (Edinburgh: John Donald, 1986), pp.143–56.
54. R. Wills, *The Jacobites and Russia, 1715–1750* (East Linton: Tuckwell Press, 2002), pp. 21–37.
55. A. Mackillop, *More Fruitful than the Soil: Army, Empire and the Scottish Highlands, 1715–1815* (East Linton: Tuckwell Press, 2000), pp. 20–2.
56. Mackillop, *More Fruitful than the Soil*, pp. 22, 57.
57. S. Conway, 'The Scots Brigade in the eighteenth century', *Northern Scotland*, vol. 1 (2010), pp. 30–41.
58. A. Mockler, *Mercenaries* (London: MacDonald & Co., 1970), p. 114.
59. Ferguson, *Papers Illustrating the History of the Scots Brigade*, vol. 2, pp. 396–402.
60. M. Brown, *Adventuring through Spanish Colonies: Simon Bolivar, Foreign Mercenaries and the Birth of New Nations* (Liverpool: Liverpool University Press, 2006), pp. 22–7.
61. E. M. Brett, *The British Auxiliary Legion in the First Carlist War, 1835–1838* (Dublin: Four Courts Press, 2005), pp. 40–4.
62. H. Fraser, *Scottish Popular Politics* (Edinburgh: Polygon, 2000), pp. 72–4, 80.

10
The Wars of the Three Kingdoms, 1625-60

MARTYN BENNETT

In the mid-seventeenth century Scotland played a key role in the political destiny of the British Isles. During this period five wars enveloped the three kingdoms (or four nations) of the geographic archipelago. On no fewer than four occasions Scottish armies invaded England. Scotland also sent an expeditionary force into Ulster that remained there for almost a decade. Most of the major engagements across Britain and Ireland involving Scottish troops were fought using tactics practised on the continent (the so-called Celtic charge was generally the product of opportunism on the field or a response to deficiencies in armament or training). One feature that remained distinctive was the nature of the cavalry or horse wing of the army. Scottish horses were generally smaller than those of their adversaries and therefore Scottish cavalry was 'light' when compared with 'heavy' English harquebusiers. The relative shortage of horses in Scotland also meant that the ratio of horse to foot in the Scottish armies was closer than in English armies to what was considered the military ideal on the continent.

After his accession to the throne in 1625 Charles I pursued policies that were increasingly unpopular to many of the governing elite. In 1637 rebellion in Scotland followed the introduction of his revised liturgy.[1] The king refused to acknowledge his Scottish subjects' genuine concerns about creeping episcopalianism and he geared up for war whilst maintaining a facade of negotiation through the marquess of Hamilton. The Scots realised that they had to respond accordingly. The largest pool of trained and experienced Scotsmen was serving in Europe in the armies fighting in the continental wars of religion. To recover this lost asset the king's Scottish opponents, known as the covenanters following their promulgation of a National Covenant binding the Scottish people to God's cause, began recalling

The Wars of the Three Kingdoms, 1625–60

Map 10.1 Scotland and the Wars of the Three Kingdoms.

veterans from the continent in late 1638. Of these, the most prominent was Sir Alexander Leslie, who was given command of the covenanters' army. Leslie suggested that the Scots follow the Swedish recruitment model of assigning conscription targets to districts, broken down into shire targets. It was a system that would subsequently be adopted across the British Isles.[2]

The first and second British wars in southern Scotland and northern England

The Scottish army raised for this first 'Bishops' War' was larger than anything mustered in Scotland for decades. The most experienced domestic cadre, once the new earl of Argyll (formerly Lord Lorne) joined the cause, would probably have been the Campbells and their allies, with recent Highland campaigns under their belt. Yet their training was outdated and, moreover, these men spoke Gaelic – the erse that the lowlanders could not or would not hear and a language inaccessible to Edinburgh.[3] Veterans from Europe, however, brought much-needed expertise, while from the Netherlands came the weapons required to replace the ageing stock available in Scotland.

The covenanters had established a *de facto* government led by a series of representative committees, or tables, that in turn furnished members of an executive committee known as the fifth table. This principal table assessed the numbers of soldiers required from each shire and by the spring of 1639 produced seventeen regiments of foot, thirteen 'regiments' of horse and a series of 'retinues' (generally groups of mixed arms formed of family and client clans).[4] The foot regiments reflected contemporary European models, incorporating some 1,200 men, but the horse 'regiments' were smaller formations, almost troop size, perhaps numbering sixty. Alongside the notables placed in command because of their social standing, veterans were incorporated into these regiments. Each colonel would have veterans as lieutenant-colonels and majors, and in each company there would be an experienced ensign and two veteran sergeants, thereby providing training and leadership for the inexperienced recruits. Army leadership nevertheless remained firmly in the hands of the upper strata of covenanter society: the colonels and other leaders numbered thirty-one aristocrats and one heir to an aristocratic title. Ten regiments were raised by baronets and knights, and a further twelve by various tutors, lairds and masters. Just one regiment each was raised by a burgh and a sheriff. In contrast to the signing of the covenant, which publicly embraced the breadth of Scottish society, the military wing of this rebellion was given the veneer of aristocratic 'respectability'.

The regiments and retinues served chiefly in three areas: in the west to deal with possible threats from Ireland and the MacDonalds of the Isles; in the east around Aberdeen where the major fighting took place; and in the southern Lowlands where the king was expected to target his main forces. The fighting in the east was centred upon the royalist marquess of Huntly's attempt to hold Aberdeen in readiness for the arrival of the king's forces by sea led by Hamilton. When this landing did not materialise, the covenanter general, the earl of Montrose, credited with creating the 'uniform' of blue sash and ribbon which marked the covenanters' armies, spent the early summer of 1639 alternatively occupying Aberdeen and seizing several opponents' castles. On 19 June he defeated Lord Aboyne, son of Huntly, at the battle of the Bridge of Dee and occupied the town for the third and final time. Meanwhile, Leslie did not have much of a war in the southern Lowlands either, for when his advance troops spotted an English scouting force in the area of Kelso on 4 June 1639, neither side was greatly tested; the English forces fled quickly across the border, effectively halting the fighting. Negotiations ended the conflict, but most realised that this was only a temporary pause and that Charles was playing for time.

No sooner had the first Bishops' War been brought to an end by the Pacification of Berwick than both sides sought to prepare for the next round. In November the executive established war committees in each county, comprising four lairds from each presbytery in the shire. The convenor of each committee was in direct contact with Edinburgh, with two committee members staying in the capital at all times (there were fewer representatives from the committees in the far north). The committees levied troops and raised money in consultation with local ministers.[5] The surviving papers of the Kirkcudbright committee give us a good idea of how the financial aspects of the system operated. The committee had eight towns in its charge. Within these, thirty-one men and one woman were identified as the wealthiest inhabitants who could provide funds, while twenty-one others were thought to be able to make loans and donate silverware. 'Anti-covenanters' were singled out, including two noble women who had their lands commandeered for the cause. Objectors and the obstructive were imprisoned and obliged to petition the Scottish estates (parliament) for relief or reconsideration.[6]

Preparations for war continued apace.[7] In 1640 the king gathered his forces again, despite having failed to get parliamentary backing in England and Wales. The Scottish estates were suspended by him until June, by which time he hoped to have defeated the covenanters. In response, the estates set up a committee of estates to continue their business and declared the king's action illegal. Government north of the border was thus reorganised in a revolutionary manner and a financial levy for the war effort of one-tenth of land value or commercial income was ordered. Wapinshawings were also held in the burghs. In April men of military age were mustered in Edinburgh while 500 men were gathered in nearby Leith, funded by loans raised in the city. Royalist supporters' castles were besieged and the king's loyal garrison in Edinburgh castle was cut off.

The army of the covenant had been largely disbanded at the end of the previous war. It was now reassembled. Argyll held rendezvous in June and created three regiments from his followers. In total, forty foot regiments, nine horse regiments and six retinues were raised. The European veterans were again prominent but the commanders were still drawn from the social elite. They included thirty-one aristocrats, nine baronets and knights, ten lairds and a further knight who, in his capacity as sheriff of Teviotdale, commanded one of the two regiments raised and named after a region. Additionally, there was one burgh regiment of foot from Edinburgh.[8]

The second Bishops' War was to be fought to a Scottish agenda: an invasion of England. In the previous war, the Scots had been reticent to cross the border, but this time they had sufficient evidence of the king's aggressive intent to overcome their qualms. On 20 August 17,775 men of the covenanters' army under Leslie, accompanied by government representatives, entered the north of England. They bypassed the Berwick garrison and headed towards Newcastle, where Charles had concentrated his forces.[9] This town's coal resources were an important source of fuel for London, and holding it, and the Tyne, was an important component of the king's strategy.

The English and Welsh forces drew back from the north bank of the Tyne, choosing instead to hold the bridge at Newburn against an expected attack. The problem for the king's army was that it had too few men to defend the bridgehead and hold Newcastle simultaneously. Fighting began on the afternoon of 28 August after the armies had eyed each other warily all morning. Whilst Leslie had the advantage of having double the king's forces, the English had fortified their bank of the Tyne. The Scots, however, had larger numbers of artillery, outnumbering the English guns by a ratio of five to one, if not ten to one. English musketeers were unable to target the Scottish gunners yet the Scots were able to pick off the English gunners because their defence works proved to be too low. Moreover, by mid-afternoon the tide had gone out, lowering the river level: it was now fordable. Scottish horse pushed across the river, allowing Leslie to move the rest of his army over. A final rally by the English foot failed to stem the Scots, and the battle ended with the attackers firmly planted on the south bank of the Tyne. The king's strategy collapsed.[10] Newcastle surrendered at the end of August and the Scottish covenanters' army occupied northern England.

This military occupation formed a barrier to any future incursions from Charles into Scotland. Furthermore, the presence of Scottish forces occupying the northern English counties provided the king's political opponents with real muscle to back their dominance at Westminster. Edinburgh made ratification of any peace treaty dependent on parliamentary approval on both sides of the border and Charles was forced to pay £850 a day to cover the costs of occupation on top of the funds required by the English and Welsh army still in the field. The king was now confronted by the total collapse of his government in England and Wales in the face of unified parliamentary opposition in the three kingdoms.

The covenanters' army was based chiefly between the River Tweed and north Yorkshire. Much of it was in quartered in Northumberland, but an advance guard, including the earl of Home's regiment, was stationed in south County Durham, maintaining the pressure on the English forces across the county border. The funds to pay the Scots were, in part, directly collected by their army within Newcastle, Northumberland and County Durham.[11] The occupiers enacted a version of their homeland taxation, with landlords registering their estate values and incomes and then over four weeks handing over one quarter of their value as a loan to be repaid or offset once the weekly tax ordered by Westminster began to come into the treasury. In the meantime, Scottish troops began to cross to the west of England to get the food which could be neither supplied readily enough from home nor bought in the depressed English markets in the east. The situation had hardly improved before August 1641 when the army returned home to disband.[12]

The third British War: war in Ireland

After only a brief respite, Scotland was once again embroiled in war. In October 1641 Charles came to Edinburgh to ratify the peace treaty negotiated at Ripon, but also to try and provoke a counter revolution among a group of covenanters, centred on Montrose, who were suspicious of Argyll, now the most powerful noble in Scotland. Charles's plot, known as 'the incident', was discovered and imploded just as Ulster erupted in rebellion. On the night of 22 October prominent castles in the north-east of the Irish province were seized, while over the next days and weeks the rest of Ireland experienced a rebellion, first of the native Irish and then of Anglo-Irish Catholics. The potential for a further damaging rupture between Scotland and the king, with a Catholic rebellion only some twenty miles off the Scottish coast, forced a very public, but ultimately fragile, show of unity. Both the Scottish estates and Westminster decided to send armed forces to Ulster: the Scots were to be led by Leslie, newly ennobled as the earl of Leven by his defeated king, with Sir Robert Monro, another veteran of foreign service, as his second.

In April 1642 2,500 Scottish soldiers led by Monro arrived in Ulster. This army had been raised in a different manner from those fielded in the two most recent wars as the government did not appoint veterans to second the nobles who dominated the high-level commissions. This caused resentment amongst those professionals dragged from their long-term careers in Europe and now suddenly rendered unemployed by the swift military defeat of Charles and subsequent disbandment of the covenanters' army. The Scottish army on this occasion consisted of ten foot regiments, three of which were in existence already, and it was shipped across the Irish Sea from Ayr.[13]

The initial impact of the Scottish troops was dramatic. The rebels were pushed onto the defensive in Ulster and the Scots stormed Newry in May. But there was to be no complete victory. Funding for the war, amounting to £400,000 to be raised in England and Wales, faltered when the developing political crisis there resulted in the money being used instead to raise troops for king and parliament. Nevertheless, Lord Leven arrived in August with a further 7,000 men and by the following year it was clear to the rebels that if the Scots' control of Ulster was to be eased then pressure needed to be placed on the latter's home soil. The seeds of Alasdair MacColla's attack on Scotland in 1644 were sown.[14] In the meantime, the rebels reorganised and the Scots were unable to extend their control far into the centre of Ulster from their bases in Armagh and Antrim. The war became a repetitive pattern of incursion and repulsion, with no side able to inflict a decisive defeat on the other.

Figure 10.1 A small brass cannon, probably used by the covenanters' army. The inscription on the barrel records that it was made by James Monteith in Edinburgh, 1642.

The fourth British war: war in Scotland and in England

Hostilities broke out in England and Wales in the summer of 1642 when Charles felt confident enough to challenge the Westminster parliament's growing political hegemony. The Scots' immediate reaction was to try and mediate, wary of a king who, if victorious in the south, might become vengeful towards his adversaries north of the border. The king's attitude towards his Scottish subjects confirmed their suspicions. Convinced of victory in the spring of 1643, he played cat and mouse with the covenanters, whom he despised. On one occasion, he rudely dismissed them from his presence, but then asked his queen, Henrietta Maria, to flatter them as they returned home via her base in York.

Events across the Irish Sea also influenced Scottish attitudes. Not only was it discovered that the Catholic marquess of Antrim had been plotting an invasion of Scotland with the queen, but it was also the case that the earl of Ormonde, the king's army commander in Ireland, was obliged by his master to seek a cessation of hostilities because Charles wanted the return of the trained English and Welsh troops sent there during 1641–2. In Scotland, this was seen as a dangerous move. If these regiments were withdrawn from Ulster, this could leave the Irish Catholic confederation in control of Ireland and thus expose

Figure 10.2 David Leslie, from a lithograph of 1823. He commanded the Scottish horse in the anti-royalist army at Marston Moor in 1644.

Scotland to a Catholic power as a near neighbour. In the autumn of 1643 a truce was duly agreed and the king's troops began to be shipped home. Against this backdrop, the Scots and the Westminster parliaments entered into an alliance against the king known as the Solemn League and Covenant. As part of this arrangement the Scots promised to send forces to help the English parliamentarians. The mechanism of war again swung into action and money was raised to create a new army.[15]

On 19 January 1644, 21,000 Scottish soldiers (18,000 foot, 3,000 horse and 500–600 dragoons) crossed the English border under Leven. The new army was composed of twenty-one regiments of foot, nine regiments of horse and one regiment of dragoons.[16] There were fewer members of the nobility in charge this time, but they remained well represented in the elite branch of the army – the horse – where nobles commanded a majority of the regiments. The lieutenant-colonels who had experience of fighting on the continent were also present once again. This army was, however, different in that the horse had been reorganised in 1643–4, with troop-size 'regiments' of cavalry now combined into full regiments. This reform was probably linked to the arrival of another veteran of European wars, the cavalry commander David Leslie, son of Lord Lindores, who also introduced the regiment of dragoons into the army.[17] As in 1640, representatives of the government followed the army, but this time they were in contact with the joint executive based in Westminster and conjoined with parliamentarians under the title of the 'Committee of Both Kingdoms'. The principal figures on the committee were Argyll and Sir William Armyne, with authority that stretched from issuing billeting orders to summoning the town of Newcastle to surrender.

This second invasion of England, greeted with optimism on both sides of the border, initially seemed reminiscent of the events of 1640. Once again the main royalist forces waited in the Tyne valley. But this time the opposition, under the marquess of Newcastle, were experienced troops who had been in arms since 1642. Furthermore, the town of Newcastle had been refortified and was prepared to withstand a siege. When the royalist field forces withdrew before his advance, Leven was forced to leave six regiments to watch Newcastle and its garrison in his rear, dividing his forces in the face of the enemy. He struck southwards, capturing a fort at South Shields, but the marquess pushed him back to Sunderland.

The Scottish general's failure to make significant progress after crossing the Tyne raised questions about his military capabilities. This, however, was unfair for in the end the campaign in the north was successful.[18] Simply by his presence in the region Leven had caused the royalists to drain their southern command, enabling English parliamentarians to defeat them in south Yorkshire. This caused the marquess to withdraw to York. Leven then advanced quickly and arrived outside the city on 22 April, where he was joined by an English army under Lord Ferdinando Fairfax. The immediate business was to prise the marquess out of York, which had been reinforced by modern defences. Surrounding the city, however, required more resources than Leven and his allies could muster and it was only on 1 June, with the arrival of the earl of Manchester's eastern association army, that the city was finally hemmed in.[19]

The siege of York ended dramatically on 1 July when Charles's young nephew, Prince Rupert, advanced with an army on the city from the west of England, forcing Leven and his allies to withdraw rapidly south-westwards. The following day Leven, Fairfax and Manchester led their troops towards Tadcaster. In response, the royalists moved out of York and began to follow them. Skirmishes developed between the villages of Long Marston to the east and Tockwith to the west. Eventually the rival armies drew up facing each other.

As the long summer's day settled into evening the battle of Marston Moor began.[20]

The battle of Marston Moor, 1644

Leven's soldiers were spread across the allied army. The lighter-mounted horse regiments were unsuited to meet the heavily armoured royalist horse head on in the first attack, so the regiments of Kirkcudbright and Balcarres were grouped under Leslie in the third line of the left flank behind the eastern association horse under Oliver Cromwell. Cromwell commanded about 3,000 cavalry in the first two lines, Leslie about 1,000 in the third or reserve, with Fraser's regiment of dragoons on the extreme left with the eastern association dragoons.[21] To Leslie's right were the Scottish foot regiments formed up as part of each of the three lines of the allied centre: Lieutenant-General William Baillie led the four Scottish regiments in the frontline (Crawford-Lindsay's, Lauderdale's, Hamilton's and Rae's); the second line comprised Scots regiments alone (Loudoun's, Buccleuch's, Cassilis's, Douglas of Kelhead's, Dunfermline's, Coupar's, Livingston's and Hay of Yester's) commanded by Major-General Sir James Lumsden; and in the third line was Erskine's. On the far right of the field, further Scots horse regiments were in the third line (Leven's, including Balgonie's lancers, Dalhousie's and Eglinton's). This spread of the Scottish regiments ensured that the full gamut of the battle's vicissitudes was visited upon them.

The Scottish and parliamentarian forces advanced on the royalists. Cromwell's regiments charged into Lord Byron's horse, catching it somewhat at a disadvantage on broken ground. The latter's regiments began to break and head towards York, but Cromwell was rushed from the field with what seemed a serious wound. Leslie's forces pressed home the attack. Peter Young has suggested that it was Leslie who 'tipped the scales against Rupert'.[22] Peter Newman and Paul Roberts, by contrast, are less certain of Leslie's impact on the battle and, more recently, Malcolm Wanklyn is even less convinced of his influence – a view held by contemporary commentators on the Scottish role at Marston Moor.[23] Whatever significance historians of the battle have ascribed to its actions, the Scottish horse wheeled inwards onto the royalist foot, which had been holding the Scots and parliamentarian foot back, and turned the tables on them. With some of Cromwell's regiments working round to the rear of the royalist centre, and Leslie's men putting pressure on the centre itself, the enemy were now under intense strain.

On the opposite flank the allies had been defeated by the royalist commander, Lord Goring, in a mirror image of Leslie and Cromwell's success on the left. This setback was said to have caused Leven and his some of his fellow commanders to flee the field thinking all was lost. Goring's victory, however, could not be sustained once the royalist centre began to crumble behind him. Retreating towards the ground from whence he had started, he was cornered by the troops from Leslie and Cromwell's flank and defeated. This struggle marked the end of the main fighting and the defeated royalists attempted to retreat towards York.

After Marston Moor, the Scottish forces remained concentrated in the north of England, where royalist control collapsed almost immediately, Prince Rupert having retreated westwards and the marquess of Newcastle gone into exile. Rather than playing a role further south, the Scots instead devoted a great deal of resources to capturing Newcastle, which was eventually in their hands by October. Although there were those who began to question Scotland's role in the joint war effort, Leven's hold on the north remained of great strategic value, allowing the principal English and Welsh forces to concentrate exclusively on the south Midlands and the south-west of England in 1645; it was these forces that failed to win the war in the autumn of that year, not Leven's strategy. Furthermore, as Peter Newman has pointed out, the potential for northern royalists to stage a revanche was ever present. If sufficient external support had arrived the region might have been wrested from the king's enemies. It was largely Leven's strategy of pinning down the isolated royalists and closing the borders that prevented any such resurgence. Scottish forces played an equally important role in holding the Irish confederate forces in check within eastern Ulster, thereby strengthening the otherwise tenuous hold that English forces had in Ireland, and eventually allowed for the launch of a war of reconquest in 1649.

Meanwhile, royalists' attempts to weaken the Scottish influence on events by using Ireland to draw their forces away from England merged with the realisation in Ireland that to limit the effectiveness of Monro's troops in Ulster an attack on the Scots' homeland was necessary. With the backing of the confederate, the marquess of Antrim's kinsman, Alasdair MacColla, was given command of a small invasion force which left Ireland at the end of June 1644 to begin a campaign in the Western Isles and the renegade covenanter, Montrose, went north to join him.[24] The latter's ambitions, however, went beyond MacColla's desire to grab back his clan's ancestral

MacDonald lands lost to the Campbells, and even beyond the idea of diverting Scottish forces from England. Instead, Montrose sought a war in the Lowlands that would bring down the covenanter government. Initially, MacColla was confronted by his Campbell rivals, led by Argyll, but when Stirling was menaced Edinburgh began to raise fencible units to combat the threat. A government army under Lord Lothian was beaten by Montrose and MacColla at Tippermuir near Perth on 1 September. But growing opposition to the incursion forced the royalists northwards and, after defeating Lord Burleigh at Justice Mills in Aberdeen on the 13th, Montrose forced his way into the town where the Irish troops caused havoc.

Such actions made it difficult for Montrose to raise a thoroughly royalist war in Scotland. Potential allies, such as the Gordons, disliked the Irish complexion of Montrose's army and, moreover, their clan head, the marquess of Huntly, had been vanquished in the first Bishops' War by Montrose. As MacColla moved westwards to attack garrisons in the Highlands, Montrose remained in the east where Argyll followed him. Fighting continued as winter set in. By early 1645 Montrose had moved north but appeared to be bottled up in the Great Glen. In a surprise move, however, he and MacColla attacked Argyll's forces at Inverlochy on 2 February in a battle that became part of Highland folklore. The lowlanders on the latter's flanks fled the field after the initial musket fire, and the battle turned into a contest between the Campbells and the MacDonalds and their respective allies. It was Gael against Gael: a fight that the royalists won.[25] The military effect of Montrose's victory was dazzling. The forces assembled by the Sinclairs to the north changed sides and joined the royalist cause, while the Gordons softened their stance, sending Montrose a much-needed contingent of horse. Dundee was captured in April, forcing Edinburgh to raise a new army, under a Marston Moor veteran, William Baillie, and the former royalist Sir John Hurry to deal with the invaders. The royalists, however, abandoned Dundee and attacked the home army when it was divided. Montrose defeated Hurry at Auldearn on 9 May then Baillie at the Bridge of Alford on 2 July.

Montrose's spectacular victories were somewhat offset by Charles's defeat at Naseby in the English Midlands on 14 June; they would remain a sideshow unless the king's fortunes south of the border could be significantly improved, or a really decisive victory won in Scotland. It looked briefly as if the latter was in reach. Montrose headed for Glasgow and en route defeated Baillie again at Kilsyth on 15 August. The collapse of the regime seemed certain and Montrose, in the king's name, summoned the estates to Glasgow for a meeting in mid-September. Yet ironically, one of the original strategic goals of the incursion was now achieved: David Leslie was despatched home from England with part of the army of the Solemn League and Covenant. At Philiphaugh on 17 September Montrose's Scottish adventure came to an end. Leslie caught the scattered royalist army and inflicted a heavy defeat from which it never recovered. Guerrilla warfare continued in the Highlands for some months but this was now no more than a minor distraction to the government in Edinburgh. Montrose fled into exile.

Leven and the end of the 'English civil war'

Leven was criticised for his inaction after the battle of Marston Moor, but with the growing potency of the royalist campaigns within Scotland he had taken the sensible precaution of attempting to seal Scotland off from England. He was right to do so for the royalists tried, and failed, to send reinforcements to Scotland after Philiphaugh, using one of the routes he barred so effectively. With Leslie on his way back to England, and the Borders controlled, Leven now led the Scottish army into the English Midlands in November 1645 to join the siege of Newark. Leven's intervention was crucial: this major royalist garrison could now be effectively ringed and isolated for the first time. The harsh winter prevented much activity, but with the labour of local villagers circumvallation was completed.[26] On 5 May 1646 Charles arrived at nearby Southwell in disguise and announced that he intended to surrender to Leven. The king was seeking to divide the Scots from their Westminster allies by associating with the Scottish commander, but Leven refused to fall in with the plan and announced Charles's arrival to the commander of the English northern army and to parliament.

Back in Ulster, Montrose's campaign had caused Monro to shift some of his troops back to Scotland. In 1646 those remaining in Ireland suffered a military reverse. Armed with cash and supplies from the pope, the Irish confederate general of Ulster, Owen Roe O'Neill, defeated the Scots at Benburb on 5 June. The confederate hailed the battle as a major triumph, and it was celebrated in Rome. Although the Scots lost 2,000–3,000 men, and their ability to hold east Ulster was seriously compromised, the victory was not exploited. In the end it left little changed: Monro hung on and in 1648 he was again in a position to despatch troops to the mainland, but this time for a different cause.

The engagement

Charles's plan to divide the Scots from Westminster was not a complete failure; it just took a little time to come to fruition. After the surrender of Newark, Leven headed to Newcastle in triumph with the king in his baggage train. The negotiations to end the war were a tripartite affair, with the king attempting to play off his allied adversaries and prevent a deal from being struck. At the start of 1647 the Scots accepted back pay for their army in return for sending the king southwards. Leven led the army home and it began to disband.

At the end of the year, whilst imprisoned at Carisbrooke castle on the Isle of Wight, Charles signed a treaty known as the 'engagement' with a faction of the Scottish covenanters. This promised that he would support the establishment of Presbyterianism in England for a period of three years in return for a military alliance with the Scots. As Charles himself refused to take the covenant personally, the Scottish Kirk was not persuaded of his sincerity and many of the army commanders who would be expected to come to the aid of the king, including Leven, refused to subscribe to the engagement. However, when it became clear that the English were not going to restore Charles to power (instead parliament made it illegal to discuss peace with him) a Scottish royalist army was raised under the duke of Hamilton to fulfil the treaty. The relative calm in Ulster allowed for 3,000 troops to be shipped over, led by Monro himself.[27]

The third Scottish invasion of England in eight years was launched on 8 July 1648. Hamilton's army of 18,000 troops took the western route into England, unlike Leven's previous invasions, partly because it was believed that there would be significant support from English royalists there. Indeed, Marmaduke Langdale and a force of royalists at Carlisle joined up early on. Hamilton, however, moved so slowly once he had arrived in England that, whilst Lord Thomas Fairfax was tied down at the siege of Colchester, Cromwell was able to conclude successfully the siege of Pembroke before marching northwards to deal with the invasion. At Wetherby he met up with the other parliamentary forces, led by John Lambert, that had been shadowing the Scots from east of the Pennines.

Although he could have crossed into Yorkshire through the passes at Ribblesdale and Craven, Hamilton decided to continue along the western route into the Midlands; as Monro's forces had still not arrived, he must have been convinced that the disadvantage of their absence would be offset in battle by the fact that, as Langdale insisted, the enclosed fields of Lancashire were excellent for infantry engagements but not for Cromwell's horse. The latter's regiments had now crossed the Pennines to the north of Hamilton's army and followed at a day's distance. This was a risk-laden move since 3,000 experienced veterans under Monro were to his rear and Cromwell had marched so swiftly that he had left his artillery behind to follow him as it could.

Hamilton continued to press southwards towards Cheshire. By 17 August the engager army had reached Preston Moor but Monro was still thirty miles north of it, with Cromwell in between. Moreover, Hamilton's horse was strung out on the route southwards, some as far as twenty miles away from Preston. Langdale was guarding the northern approaches to the town and Cromwell decided to attack by simply barging down the road towards his centre with three regiments of horse in column.[28] There was confusion as some engager regiments continued to head south across the Ribble bridge while others attempted to turn back towards the fighting. In the end the line collapsed and fell back on Preston. The Scots' only objective now was to keep the bridge open long enough to extract Langdale's men. Most of Hamilton's horse were too far away to reach the field, and by the time the majority began to head north, the battle was over and a two-day retreat to Wigan began.

The engager army was larger than Cromwell's force and, if able to reunite, would still be a formidable adversary. He was thus determined to prevent it from doing so. Constant skirmishing and a more serious fight at Winwick decided the matter. Although the relatively unscathed Scottish horse made off into the English Midlands, Hamilton's foot regiments surrendered at Warrington on 20 August. Cromwell subsequently turned north and crossed the border into Scotland. The engager government there soon collapsed, leaving Argyll and the kirk party to form an administration that sought immediate revenge on their political opponents. Cromwell remained in southern Scotland whilst Argyll and his party established themselves in power and then returned to England.

Revolution

Over the next few months Argyll and his supporters watched with increasing alarm as their native-born king was arraigned and tried at Westminster by a 'kangaroo court', set up by a parliament shorn of its Presbyterian MPs and acting alone without the House of Lords. All attempts at intercession from Edinburgh were ignored and on 11 February 1649 the news that Charles had been executed at Westminster arrived in the Scottish capital. With little delay the Scots proclaimed his son Charles, prince of Wales, as king of Great Britain. It was tantamount to a declaration of war and the English republic responded by abolishing the monarchy altogether. Fortunately for Scotland, long exhausted by war, the republic followed the military priorities set by Cromwell and attacked Ireland instead.

By 1650, the war in Ireland had become a lost cause for the new Charles and he focused his attention on Scotland. He authorised Montrose to test the waters for a royalist revival and exert pressure on the covenanters with a military expedition into the Highlands. He also began talking to Argyll's representatives. Charles himself then arrived in Scotland only to find out that he had been lured into a theological trap: not only was he obliged to sign the covenant, and undergo religious and personal 're-education', but he also had to renounce both the church of his birth and his parents' 'errors'. Furthermore, he had to disown Montrose, who had been duly captured and executed. It was all for very little gain: Argyll kept Charles as an uninstalled figurehead.[29]

When the republic turned its attention northwards, Scotland created a new army and its commander-in-chief, David Leslie, prepared to lure the English into a war of attrition in the Lowlands.[30] When the English commander, Fairfax, stepped down, unwilling to go to war with the Scots with whom he, or perhaps more realistically his wife, shared a common religious outlook, Cromwell took command and in July invaded Scotland. It was tough going for him. Leslie had denuded the approach to Edinburgh of men, matériel and food. He kept the Scottish army back and tempted Cromwell on but then dodged away again, leaving Cromwell dependent upon long and fragile supply lines. It was a fine tactical response and as the enemy succumbed to disease and dearth it looked as if it was a success.

While Leslie kept back the enemy, the kirk purged the Scottish army of those it regarded to be of dubious faith. This denuded it of experienced soldiers and left it tactically vulnerable. Nonetheless, it had the upper hand in the campaign and by early September Cromwell was in retreat. The Scots pursued him to his supply base at Dunbar and cut off his retreat to England. But then Leslie threw it all away. Moving from the security of his unassailable position on Doon Hill overlooking the town, he fell prey to the inexperience of his officers, who reacted slowly when Cromwell rolled up the Scottish regiments from east to west on 3 September.[31] As a result of the battle of Dunbar, the eastern Lowlands came under English control with Edinburgh taken at Christmas.

Figure 10.3 Cromwell at Dunbar, 1650. Painted by Andrew Carrick Gow, 1886.

Following this defeat there was some hope that the extreme covenanter faction – the remonstrants – could negotiate an end to the war by persuading Cromwell that they had common (anti-royalist) cause, but he destroyed their hastily created army at Hamilton on 1 December, thus securing the west. Instead, the more moderate covenanters under Argyll crowned Charles at Scone on 1 January 1651 and allowed him command of their army. Under the new king, the army grew quickly and effectively and, partly because of Cromwell's illness in the spring, was able to keep the English out of the fertile lands of Fife. Charles, however, wanted to use Leslie's army as a tool to crack England. It is possible that Cromwell realised this too.

In the summer Charles spotted a gap in the republic's positions and dashed through it into England. Following Hamilton's route, he reached Worcester by late August, but the advance then stalled. The invasion was not popular. Most now saw the Scots as invading foreigners, rather than allies, who disturbed their long-desired peace. Moreover, while Charles's army had declined in size to about 12,000 during the march south, so Cromwell's had grown to 28,000. The latter had in the meantime left General George Monck to deal with the remaining forces in Scotland, a task which

Figure 10.4 George Monck, Cromwell's commander-in-chief in Scotland, after a portrait by Samuel Cooper, c. 1660.

he completed over the ensuing year.³² On 3 September, exactly one year after the battle of Dunbar, Cromwell attacked Worcester with overwhelming force. Despite a brave show by the Scottish troops, the battle and siege combined lasted less than a day.³³ Charles fled the scene, leaving the dead and dying Scots in the streets and fields of Worcester. The defeat condemned his captured comrades to transportation and a life as indentured servants: the future redshanks of the Caribbean.

Cromwell described the battle of Worcester as a 'crowning mercy' and so it was for the republic. For Scotland it was the end of an era. Although there was a royalist uprising in the Highlands under the earl of Glencairn during 1653–4, this was crushed by Monck – a new 'hammer of the Scots' – who combined vigorous military action with diplomatic efforts amongst the clans to isolate the royalists. The failure of the rising underlined the fact that Scotland was now firmly under an army of occupation, no matter how much the country was incorporated politically into the republic.

For over a decade Scotland had played a significant role in driving revolutionary politics and had been almost constantly at war. Yet scratch the surface and it was still predominantly a monarchist nation that trusted the crown – even if the monarch was captive, politically emasculated or forcibly re-educated – to preserve its godly covenant from earthly jealousies. In 1660 an army once more marched from Edinburgh into England and, wittingly or not, facilitated a restoration of the monarchy. But it was the English army of occupation returning to its home nation rather than a Scottish army with Charles at its head.

Notes

1. See M. Bennett, *The Civil Wars in Britain and Ireland* (Oxford: Blackwell, 1997), ch. 2, for a full discussion of this.
2. For a comprehensive biographical record of emigrant Scottish soldiers in the period, see the database at the University of St Andrews (available at www.st-andrews.ac.uk/history/ssne/about.php, accessed on 16 September 2011) and the associated work by Steve Murdoch on connections between Scotland and northern Europe, for example S. Murdoch, *Britain, Denmark-Norway and the House of Stuart, 1603-1660: A Diplomatic and Military Analysis* (East Linton, Tuckwell Press, 2000).
3. E. Furgol, *A Regimental History of the Covenanting Armies* (Edinburgh: John Donald, 1990), p. 2.
4. Ibid. pp. 16–39.
5. Bennett, *The Civil Wars*, pp. 64–6.
6. J. Nicholson (ed.), *Minute Book kept by the War Committee of the Covenanters in the Stewartry of Kirkcudbright* (Kirkcudbright: J. Nicholson, 1855), pp. 6, 9–11, 24, 25, 26, 30–6.
7. For an excellent account of the mobilising of forces and matériel for the two Bishops' Wars see M. C. Fissell, *The Bishops' Wars: Charles I's Campaigns against Scotland, 1638-1640* (Cambridge: Cambridge University Press, 1994).
8. Furgol, *A Regimental History*, pp. 40–79.
9. C. S. Terry (ed.), *Papers Relating to the Army of the Solemn League and Covenant*, 2 vols (Edinburgh: T. and A. Constable for the Scottish History Society, 1917), vol. 1, p. lxxiii.
10. Fissel, *The Bishops' Wars*, pp. 54–8.
11. Northumberland Archives, Swinburne papers, ZSW 7/32, 33.
12. M. Bennett, *The Civil Wars Experienced* (London: Routledge, 2000), p. 21.
13. Furgol, *A Regimental History*, pp. 5, 80–108.
14. P. Lenihan, 'Confederate military strategy 1643-7', in M. O'Siochru (ed.),

Kingdoms in Crisis: Ireland in the 1640s (Dublin: Four Courts Press, 2001), pp. 163–5.
15. National Records of Scotland, Edinburgh, PA8/2, 'Charge of Loan and Tax of the Whole Kingdom for the Supply of the Army in Ireland, conform to Act of Convention of Estates, 15 August 1643'; D. Stevenson, 'Financing of the cause of the covenanters, 1638–1651', *Scottish Historical Review*, vol. 52, no. 152 (1972), pp. 100–1.
16. Furgol, *A Regimental History*, pp. 109–94.
17. Ibid. p. 8.
18. The best discussion of this campaign is to be found in P. R. Newman, *The Battle of Marston Moor* (Chichester: John Bird, 1981), ch. 1.
19. The most detailed account of this siege is P. Wenham, *The Great and Close Siege of York* (Kineton: Roundwood Press, 1970).
20. The foremost study of the battle is P. R. Newman and P. R. Roberts, *Marston Moor, 1644* (Pickering: Blackthorn Press, 2003), although Newman's earlier work, *The Battle of Marston Moor*, is still very valuable. P. Young, *Marston Moor, 1644: The Campaign and Battle* (Kineton: Roundwood Press, 1970), provides details of the regiments involved.
21. Newman and Roberts, *Marston Moor, 1644*, p. 72.
22. Young, *Marston Moor*, p. 108.
23. Newman and Roberts, *Marston Moor, 1644*, p. 81; M. Wanklyn, *Decisive Battles of the English Civil War* (Barnsley: Pen and Sword, 2006), p. 128.
24. The best account of this campaign remains D. Stevenson, *Highland Warrior: Alasdair MacColla and the Civil Wars* (Edinburgh: Saltire Society, 1994), chs 5–9. See also C. V. Wedgwood, *Montrose* (London: Collins, 1952; Stroud: Alan Sutton, 1995), pp. 61–125; S. Reid, *The Campaigns of Montrose* (Edinburgh: Mercat Press, 1990) and P. Lenihan, 'Confederate military strategy, 1643–7', pp. 158–75.
25. Stevenson, *Highland Warrior*, pp. 155–8.
26. S. B. Jennings, *'These Uncertaine Times': Newark and the Civilian Experience of the Civil Wars, 1640–1660* (Nottingham: Nottingham County Council, 2009), ch. 2.
27. For a discussion of the engagement, and the subsequent process of mobilising support in Scotland, see Bennett, *The Civil Wars*, pp. 284–90.
28. For good accounts of this battle, see S. Bull and M. Seed, *Bloody Preston: The Battle of Preston, 1648* (Lancaster: Carnegie Publishing, 1998), and Wanklyn, *Decisive Battles*, pp. 191–9.
29. For accounts of Montrose's venture in 1650, see Wedgwood, *Montrose*, pp. 135–42, and Reid, *The Campaigns of Montrose*, p. 177.

30. A very useful study of this campaign is J. Grainger, *Cromwell Against the Scots* (East Linton: Tuckwell Press, 1997).
31. Grainger, *Cromwell*, pp. 47–50.
32. M. Bennett, *Oliver Cromwell* (Abingdon: Routledge, 2006), pp. 191–4.
33. Grainger, *Cromwell*, pp. 139–44.

11
The Restoration and the Glorious Revolution, 1660–1702

K. A. J. McLay

Scotland's military contribution to the Restoration of 1660 was precipitate rather than substantive and hardly reflective of a national martial tradition. On 2 January 1660 the Cromwellian commander in Scotland, General George Monck, at the head of his own foot regiment, marched the forces in Scotland from Coldstream to arrive about a month later in London. The capital had been in turmoil since May 1659 when Oliver Cromwell's son and successor, Richard, was ousted from the role of lord protector by an increasingly radical republican army. Richard's dismissal hastened the implosion of the Protectorate as the army first restored the Rump of the Long Parliament, which had instigated the war against Charles I in 1642, and then briefly imposed its own rule before deferring again to the Rump by the end of the year. Throughout the British Isles the mood was running against the Rump and the army in favour of a full and freely elected parliament which, it was widely anticipated, would invite the return of the monarch. Once in London, Monck and his troops from Scotland restored order and put themselves at the head of this constitutional sentiment, obliging the Rump first to reinstate those members purged by Colonel Pride in 1648 and more recently by the army, and then to dissolve itself; the subsequent Convention Parliament which met in April restored Charles II from his exile in the United Provinces.[1]

Neither Monck's army nor his own regiment was by origin Scottish. The troops were initially drawn from Cromwell's English New Model Army and, notwithstanding the popular confusion prompted by the styling of Monck's regiment the Coldstream Guards upon his death in 1670, the Coldstreamers' heritage derived from the north-east of England.[2] To an extent, however, following the country's conquest by Cromwell and the 1654 ordinance effecting union under one

Map 11.1 Scotland from the Restoration to Culloden.

commonwealth, the military's nationality in Scotland in the late 1650s was largely immaterial.[3] This lack of a national martial distinction seemed to be confirmed by the general rejoicing – both civilian and military – throughout the three kingdoms at the return of the king in whom military identity was then vouchsafed through four separate armies – the force commanded by Monck, the Cromwellian establishment in Ireland, the brigade based in Dunkirk and Mardyke, and Charles's own troops in exile.[4]

In London, the diarist John Evelyn caught the prevailing mood of the Restoration when he 'stood in the strand, & beheld it, & blessed God'[5] while his fellow chronicler in Edinburgh, the Glaswegian lawyer John Nicoll, remarked that 'Our bellis and bonefyres did proclame his Majesteis guidnes, and the pepillis joyes'.[6] The modest garrison force that Monck had left behind in Scotland proved as effusive. At the official proclamation of the king at Edinburgh's Mercat Cross on 14 May, three volleys rang out from the castle while one of the garrison issued a panegyric that hoped that 'Long may His Princely Scepter bear Command,/Over our Kingdoms both by Sea and Land'.[7] Charles's command, though, was not going to be exercised through a large standing army in any of his kingdoms. Distrust and dislike of such a force within the British Isles had a long lineage bolstered by recent experience. Not only was there an appreciation of the theoretical arguments set out against a permanent standing army in Machiavelli's Renaissance text on the art of war, and an enduring belief that the militia might provide security to an island nation, but also the explicit militarism and recent dominance of Cromwell's New Model Army, including in particular the two-year rule (1655–7) of the major-generals, was thought to have trampled upon both personal and parliamentary liberties.[8] According to Lois Schwoerer, by 1660 opinion on a standing army was shaped by the notion that a free parliament, rather than the executive, should control the country's military, and that with locally raised militia forces counteracting the army, the state's military clout over an individual should be restrained.[9] This thinking was not wholly embraced within the Restoration military settlement – the monarch retained executive military control over both the established army and the militia and, provided he possessed the funds, could raise as many troops as he pleased while serving military officers were not debarred from being legislators. The New Model Army was still disbanded and the subsequent army establishments for the three kingdoms – England/Wales, Ireland and Scotland – were substantially limited.

The Scottish establishment fared the worse. John, earl of Middleton, the veteran army officer and a leader of the royalist revolt in Scotland between 1653 and 1654, whom Charles first appointed as both commander-in-chief in Scotland and lord high commissioner to the Scottish parliament, tried his best to ameliorate the force reduction.[10] Ultimately, his political skills and endurance were no match for the Secretary of State, John Maitland, earl (later duke) of Lauderdale, described with typical acuity by Bishop Gilbert Burnet as 'the coldest friend and the violentest enemy'.[11] By 1663 Lauderdale had engineered Middleton's downfall and removal from his offices, and the remaining English troops north of the border (two regiments of foot and a troop of horse) were withdrawn and the fortresses of Ayr, Inverness, Leith and Perth abandoned.[12] The formal Scottish establishment stood at a troop of Horse Guards commanded by Sir James Livingston, first earl of Newburgh (which was transferred to the English establishment in 1707), a regiment of Foot Guards (subsequently the Scots Guards) comprising only five, rather than the traditional eight, companies, commanded by George Livingston, third earl of Linlithgow, and sundry independent companies of foot and horse that contributed to the garrisons of the three strategic castles of Dumbarton, Edinburgh and Stirling.[13] This small establishment was socially exclusive with the officer corps dominated by Scottish noblemen and their sons, thereby emphasising that its function might extend as a royal bodyguard in the unlikely event (given his poor impression formed in the 1650s) that Charles II travelled to his northern kingdom.[14] In turn, this conclusion confirmed that in Restoration Scotland military tasks beyond royal protection might require the raising of additional regiments or the deployment of a militia force.

Bruce Lenman has demonstrated that there was limited contemporary Scots understanding of the term militia. In early modern Scotland, the phrase 'fencible men' was used instead but it embodied the same type of military force – the king's male subjects discharging their civic duty by being temporarily under arms through an obligation to serve and defend the interests of the realm – which was considered distinct from, and less threatening than, a permanent standing army.[15] In late September 1663 the Scottish parliament passed an act enabling the king to raise, according to proportions, an armed and provisioned (for forty days) militia force of 20,000 foot and 2,000 horse.[16] By empowering Charles to deploy these troops throughout his three kingdoms 'for suppressing any forraigne invasion, intestine trouble or insurrection',[17] the legislation envisaged this force as not exclusively Scottish in military purpose. Initially, the king did not take up the Edinburgh parliament's offer – Westminster had previously passed a Militia Act affording him authority to raise and command militia troops throughout his kingdoms[18] – but, as Lenman notes, the outbreak of the second Anglo-Dutch War and the simmering religious unrest in Scotland from the early 1660s altered circumstances.[19] Thus, by 1668 not only was a Scottish militia force established but the prevailing theme in the military history of Restoration Scotland emerged, namely the use of a military force, both permanent and temporary, as an instrument of civil power.

The Restoration religious settlement in Scotland was, and remained, contentious. Notwithstanding Gordon Donaldson's view that the arrangement was a compromise, offering peace between the different strains of Protestantism, the historical record supports the conclusion of Keith Brown that it represented a 'fundamental blunder'.[20] Despite the majority of Scots, and certainly those in the Lowlands, being Presbyterian, the legislation passed by the covenanting parliaments of the 1640s, which had established and maintained Presbyterianism as the national religion and church, was repealed by the Rescissory Act.[21] Charles – unsympathetic to Scottish Puritanism while seeking religious consistency throughout his kingdoms and greater control over the Church – took advantage of the powers afforded by the 1661 Act Concerning Religion and Church Government to condemn Presbyterianism as unsuited to 'our monarchiall estate' and to direct the restoration of the prelacy.[22] By the summer of 1662 the Edinburgh parliament had done the king's bidding, and not only was episcopacy reinstated but lay patronage as well, with the latter strengthened by the sanction that those post-1649 minsters who failed to obtain a patron and episcopal support were to be removed from their charge.[23] These measures were followed by acts that demanded compliance to the episcopacy and the renunciation of the Presbyterians' religious and political lodestars, the National Covenant and the Solemn League and Covenant.[24] Estimates vary, but at least a third of the clergymen in Scotland left the Church as a consequence and, contrary to the government's hopes, only one minister from amongst the front-rank moderate Resolutioner Presbyterians – James Sharp of Crail, Fife – accepted a see (St Andrews).[25]

Opposition to the religious settlement in Scotland was widespread, with the king, according to Samuel Pepys, 'doubtful'[26] of the whole country in 1663; but demonstrable discontent was concentrated geographically. In the south-west below Glasgow, where the loss of incumbency had been greater than elsewhere, many of the deprived ministers attracted popular support as they took their ministry to their homes and fields.[27] As Edinburgh had anticipated these developments, the act requiring compliance to the bishops also banned house meetings or field conventicles – open-air prayer meetings which often attracted large numbers.[28] While the attitudes of the king's ministers in Scotland towards religious non-conformity ranged across the spectrum, from Middleton's uncompromising zeal for suppression to Lauderdale's political moderation, the legislation required enforcement, and that task fell to the small Scottish standing army and militia forces.

Initially the approach was targeted at specific towns, parishes and presbyteries where reports indicated conventicler activity or the legislation being obviously flouted. In 1663 disputes flared in Kirkcudbright between parishioners and the conformist ministers while at least one non-conformist preacher, Alexander Robertson, had taken to leading worship in the vacant church of Anworth. In September Lieutenant-Colonel Sir James Turner was despatched to the town with sixty of the Foot Guards to join one hundred of the same under Captain Rattray, which had arrived earlier. Turner remained active in the town and surrounding area for nearly a year, suppressing the illegal meetings, levying fines upon those not attending church and trying to restore the bonds betweens the ministers and their flocks.[29] Despite his modest success, the outbreak of the second Anglo-Dutch war in May 1665, combined with the publication of the Reverend John Brown's pamphlet lamenting the sufferings of the Presbyterians since 1660 and asserting the legitimacy of acts of resistance, increased the ministry's fear of a pro-Dutch revolt in the south-west.[30] John Leslie, seventh earl of Rothes, who was just over a year into his three-year term as captain-general of the Scottish forces, led two troops of Horse Guards and some infantry into the south-western shires in November 1665 as the first phase of what he referred to as 'disarming the west'.[31] This was followed by the dispersal of smaller parties of soldiers throughout the region, but particularly in Galloway, and it was Turner to whom Rothes turned, appointing Sir James as the commander of all these forces in the west, charged to quieten the region as a whole.[32]

Gilbert Burnet described Turner as a 'naturally fierce'[33] soldier and one who was punctilious in following orders. His inherent severity, combined with the blind eye he turned to the excesses of his troops, only increased the militancy of the Presbyterian opposition. Worshippers turned up at conventicles armed, and not solely for defensive purposes. Thus, when in Dalry on 13 November 1666 a band of Presbyterians (labelled covenanters because of their commitment to the National Covenant and Solemn League and Covenant) sprung one of their own from the grasp of a small party of soldiers, shooting and injuring a trooper in the process, and then followed that action two days later by capturing Turner himself in Dumfries in an attempt to prevent reprisals, it was the prelude to a more widespread rising in the south-west.[34] As they began their march upon Edinburgh, there was surprise and then uncertainty, both in London and Edinburgh, about the scale of the rebellion. Pepys for one did not set much weight upon the story when told of it on 20 November, and the *London Gazette* did not carry the report until two days later, while the Scottish privy council nervously, and erroneously, informed Rothes on 27 November that the rebels had arrived just east of the Pentland Hills, rendering Edinburgh 'surrounded'.[35] The ministry, however, had prepared to meet such a rebellion by augmenting the small Scottish standing army. In July two recently returned veterans of Tsar Alexander I's service, William Drummond and Thomas Dalyell of Binns, had been commissioned to raise a cavalry regiment of six troops and an infantry battalion of ten companies, while the Foot Guards were increased by the reassignment of three companies from the (primarily Scottish) regiment of Lord George Douglas (subsequently the earl of Dumbarton) which was listed on the English establishment.[36]

In the late autumn of 1666, Dalyell assumed the field command of Scottish forces despatched to deal with the rebellion. Since leaving Dumfries in the second week of November the rebels, led by 'Colonel' James Wallace, a veteran of the covenanters' armies during the 1640s and 1650s, progressed north-west through Kirkcudbrightshire to Ayr and then north-east through Lanarkshire. En route they increased their number from around 300 to over 1,000,[37] though the majority of these recruits were 'ill-armed peasants'.[38] If it had not been for the wildly inaccurate reports that the rebels numbered 3,000 plus, Dalyell should have been fairly confident setting out from Glasgow on 23 November with over 2,000 foot comprised of his and Linlithgow's battalions, along with a contingent of Guards and some 600 horse organised into six troops.[39] As it was, Dalyell's advance party of horse, which came upon the rear of Wallace's men half a mile from Lanark, declined battle – rightly, according to Turner, given the poor state of the terrain – allowing the rebels to march onwards through Bathgate towards Edinburgh, albeit shadowed from the following day by Dalyell's force.[40] On three occasions during the march Wallace was offered an immunity deal but only on the third opportunity did he indicate any interest. By then the privy council in Edinburgh, reassured by Dalyell's efforts and by the mobilisation, as ordered, of all

Figure 11.1 Thomas Dalyell of Binns. Portrait by L. Schuneman, c. 1670. Dalyell's suppression of the covenanters earned him the nicknames 'Bluidy Tam' and the 'Muscovy Beast'.

fencible men in the Lothians, Fife, Perth, Renfrew, Ayr and Lanark, had hardened in opinion and would only offer a chance to petition for mercy following a surrender of arms.[41] Wallace considered the offer a 'Trick and Amusement'[42] as he marched into 'a Net betwixt Two Armies'.[43] Thus, with Dalyell in his rear, and the militia along with the remaining government forces in Edinburgh, Wallace decided to retreat towards Linton and Biggar in the hope that Teviot might be safely reached where a decision could be taken to regroup or disperse.[44]

The rebels were by this stage in a fairly sorry state. Significantly reduced in number – Wodrow labelled them 'weary, faint, half-drowned, half-starved'[45] – Wallace bivouacked at Rullion Green on 28 November to allow stragglers to come up. Dalyell, having tracked the rebels since Lanark, and with news reaching him that they had turned back though the Pentlands, sought to cut them off. At noon Wallace began to deploy his men in an 'admirably chosen'[46] defensive position on the high ground, which caused Dalyell's advance party of horse to hesitate before attacking down into, and then uphill from, Glencorse valley. Only when the main body arrived later in the afternoon did Dalyell launch a series of assaults by horse and flanking infantry against Wallace's left which, at the third attempt, plunged the latter's force into sufficient disorder to allow the former to unleash decisive attacks against its centre and right. As darkness enveloped the Pentlands, the rebels fled, save for the fifty fatalities and the eighty men taken prisoner. This first set-piece engagement for the Royal Scottish army had resulted in a victory, but hardly a compelling one.[47]

The Restoration Scottish military forces also suppressed localised crime and social unrest in the Highlands during the 1660s and 1670s.[48] In the summer of 1667 John Murray, second earl (later first marquess) of Atholl, a veteran of Rullion Green, was appointed commander of the Highland Watch with a commission to raise an independent company to secure the passes into the Lowlands. In addition, he was to be helped by the establishment of five garrisons north of the Tay which would pool and distribute information about potential threats.[49] This military policing in the Highlands was enhanced two years later when the Highland Watch, then commanded by Sir James Campbell of Lawers, was bolstered by the some 225 regulars, principally drawn (to a total of 200) from Linlithgow's battalion, with both Atholl's and Rothes's troops of Horse Guards contributing fifteen and ten troopers respectively. The total strength of this independent company was placed, and annually renewed from 1669, at 150 men compared with 100 for the companies of the standing army.[50] There is thus merit in Macinnes's argument that the Highlands proved a 'training ground for military suppression',[51] and when religious discontent flared up again in the south-west in the 1670s and 1680s, newly raised troops from the Highlands were deployed.

Following the defeat of the Pentland Rising, and the subsequent suppression of lingering dissent, the duke of Lauderdale feared that such repression was not only expensive but also counterproductive.[52] In 1669, and again in 1672, Indulgences were issued enabling the privy council to appoint peaceable outed ministers to vacant parishes on full pay, provided they accept the benefice from the bishop. Meanwhile, in 1668 the regulars were withdrawn as the principal policing presence within the provinces and replaced by a militia along the lines of the force first offered by the Scottish parliament in 1663 (some 22,000 men).[53] Largely free from the traditional hostility shown towards the regulars, it was hoped that a militia drawn from the localities would have greater success stifling dissent and ensuring adherence to the Restoration religious settlement. An Act of Supremacy affirming Charles's government of the Church in Scotland was passed in 1669 while both the parliament and the privy council enacted other measures, such as the decree demanding landowners to report the organisers of conventicles on their land and a sliding scale of punishments targeted at those both directly and indirectly involved in these meetings.[54] By the mid-1670s, Lauderdale's policy was looking increasingly threadbare: conventicler activity had only intensified, with more churches remaining vacant and the indulged ministers subject to attack while the Episcopalians feared the weakening of the Church–state axis.[55] Between 1674 and 1677 a resolution was sought in stricter legislation, principally through the issuing of a bond that made the Scottish landowners responsible for their tenants' adherence to the law in all its forms.[56] To a number of estate holders, this seemed unreasonable and unenforceable and, following the example of William Douglas, third duke of Hamilton, many refused the bond. News of this opposition enraged the king, who determined again upon a military solution to circumvent the landowners and enforce the law.[57]

Although periodically supported by the standing forces commanded by Major-General George Munro, including his new regiment of foot and two additional companies for the Foot Guards and three troops of horse, the response and success of the local Lowland militias established in 1668 proved patchy in the face of mounting unrest. The king lacked confidence in their ability to pursue his new vigorous military strategy and at the beginning of 1678 he ordered the creation of a Highland Host. This force of some 8,000 militiamen, which mustered in Stirling on 24 January, was only two-thirds highlander, with the remaining 2,000 Lowland regulars or local militia. Yet its symbolic potential was enough to convince a number of landowners, particularly in Fife, to submit to the bond and enforce the legislation. Others, however, mainly to the south and west of Glasgow, held out.[58] For nearly two months the Host was visited upon towns in Lanarkshire, Ayrshire, Dunbartonshire and Renfrewshire to much opposition and little effect. Tales – admittedly embellished by Presbyterian propagandists – of its atrocities soon emerged but it was pulled out primarily because it had proved ineffective and counterproductive; a reversion to a regular military force undertaking policing duties was anticipated.[59]

The Scottish army was increased threefold. In May 1678 two new companies of dragoons were levied, along with a similar number of foot companies designated for service in the Highlands. In the autumn a further company of dragoons and three new troops of horse, the latter commanded by James Ogilvy, second earl of Airlie, James Home, fifth earl of Home, and John Graham of Claverhouse were raised in addition to a new infantry battalion (subsequently the Royal Scots Fusiliers) under the charge of Charles Erskine, twenty-first earl of Mar.[60] Apparently because of his opposition to the Host, Sir George Munro had been replaced as field commander by the earl of Linlithgow in 1677 and, with his enlarged command, the latter rode through the south-west in an attempt to bring order. Such was the discontent caused by the billeting of the Host, however, that one progress by Linlithgow was never going to be sufficient. As an older soldier in his last command, he was subsequently replaced by Claverhouse who, in turn, sought to pacify the region where a second rising by the disaffected Presbyterians was widely expected.[61]

Based at Dumfries with his sixty-strong troop of horse, and the services of John Inglis's dragoon company on call, Claverhouse had to cover an area of some 200 square miles in which the outlawed field conventicles were attracting thousands of worshippers and, more significantly, armed bands for their defence. As a courtier – he was close to James, duke of York – as well as a soldier, he recognised that his task was as much political as military; the conventicles had to be suppressed but in so doing his men had to maintain their discipline, avoid excess and work with the local parishes to smooth relationships in the manner that Sir James Turner had tried in 1663.[62] Presbyterian historians and propagandists have generally damned Claverhouse's conduct in the west and south-west during the late 1670s and early 1680s, giving rise to the sobriquet 'Bluidy Clavers'.[63] Modern biographers have been kinder, arguing that, by the standards of the time, he showed restraint and demanded that his soldiers adhere to the regulations on conduct first promulgated a decade earlier and reissued in 1678.[64]

As in 1666, when a wider rising grew from a single event, in early May 1679 the snowball effect was initiated by the assassination, just outside St Andrews, of the Archbishop James Sharp. The Presbyterian assassins fled on horseback to the west, provocatively attending mass conventicles and drawing up a manifesto of grievances, which was posted in Rutherglen on the king's birthday, 29 May. Although Claverhouse and the Glasgow garrison commander, Lord Ross, agreed that the threat posed by the rebels was no greater than before, the former rode out to investigate and on the following Sunday, 1 June, his troop and Inglis's dragoons (nearly 150 men in total) encountered some 250 armed covenanters arranged defensively on boggy moorland near a farm named Drumclog. Admittedly, the latter's armament was poor – only about half held muskets with the remainder brandishing pikes, halberds and, reputedly, pitchforks –

Figure 11.2 John Graham of Claverhouse. Contemporary miniature by David Paton. In contrast to the 'Bluidy Clavers' sobriquet, Claverhouse's leadership qualities and youthful good looks led his supporters to eulogise him as 'Bonnie Dundee'.

but their commander, William Cleland, knew how to make best use of the terrain and maintain the discipline of his men. After resisting Claverhouse's opening probe to the edge of the bog by his dragoons, Cleland ordered a general charge through the marsh and in the ensuing hand-to-hand fighting the superior numbers and determination of the covenanters told, despatching Claverhouse's troops in full-scale retreat. If not a rout for the covenanters, the battle of Drumclog was a notable success which, combined with the albeit unsuccessful attack subsequently mounted on Glasgow, resonated loudly in Westminster.[65]

As the English dissenter Roger Morrice noted, such was the concern within the English privy council that it met on three occasions from the Saturday of the following week and on its agenda was the growing rebellion in Scotland.[66] Claverhouse's defeat at Drumclog was only one symptom of the covenanters' momentum; another was the timidity of Linlithgow's response. Despite possessing the troops to succour Glasgow, following the rebuff of the covenanters' attack after Drumclog Linlithgow ordered Lord Ross to evacuate his men and join him at Stirling. Linlithgow's conduct was further questioned when the Scottish privy council summoned the militia and sought to concentrate a force in Edinburgh prior to moving against the covenanters, only for delay to be occasioned by the poor repair of the army's logistics and supply.[67] Guided by his council, Charles decided that remedial military action in Scotland was required to suppress the revolt and he appointed James Scott, duke of Monmouth, his son with mistress Lucy Walter, temporary captain-general of the Scottish standing army and militia. Monmouth, with military experience at home and abroad, was then serving as captain-general of the English forces, albeit without (for reasons of court politics) a formal commission.[68]

Monmouth relieved Linlithgow of command at Blackburn, East Lothian, on 19 June. It had been anticipated that he would bring with him from England three troops of Horse Grenadiers, the earl of Feversham's Regiment of Dragoons, Lord Gerard's Horse and Colonel Strother's troop of dragoons, but the resources to raise these regiments could not be found and they remained as ghost entries on the English establishment. Monmouth did have some English forces, however: contemporary accounts mention upwards of five dragoon troops and it is known that the English majors, Oglethorpe and Maine, and Captain Corenewall, were present with their troopers. Although he also had a couple of militia regiments apiece from East Lothian and Fife, along with an Angus regiment and the marquess of Atholl's Perthshire regiment, his command was smaller than he would have hoped.[69] The sources are contradictory but it would seem that the government force was in excess of 3,000 men, which was a good deal fewer than the reported 6,000 troops the covenanters had brought together.

Now led by Robert Hamilton, the covenanters had entered Glasgow following the garrison's departure but made camp between Bothwell and Hamilton on the west bank of the River Clyde near Bothwell Bridge. In contrast to events at Drumclog, disunity and ill-discipline reportedly beset the covenanters and they were unable to agree a course of action. Thus, in a poorly prepared state, Hamilton and his men were forced onto the defensive by Monmouth, who approached Bothwell Bridge with his vanguard of dragoons and a troop of horse in the early hours of 22 June. Monmouth afforded half an hour for an offer of terms to be rejected before bringing his four cannon to bear over the bridge. Commendably, from behind their barricades, the covenanters repelled his initial probe across the river and maintained possession of the bridge for over two hours. Eventually, however, the government's artillery wreaked damage and Monmouth crossed the bridge with his main force before the left of the covenanters' line panicked and broke in retreat, followed by the centre and right. Monmouth's pursuit was vigorous, yielding over 1,000 prisoners and leaving around 800 dead.[70] Scottish forces, augmented by two new companies for Mar's regiment and a regiment of dragoons (subsequently the Royal Scots Greys) commanded by Thomas Dalyell (who returned as commander of the Scots forces in the autumn of 1679),[71] subsequently maintained a reportedly brutal policing presence in the south-west during the early 1680s. The Presbyterian rebellion in 1679, and the potential for further revolts, was thus crushed but it had required an Englishman to achieve it.

If the reign of Charles II had been notable for the deployment of military force against internal Scottish opponents, then it proved business as usual at the outset of his brother's rule. The national quiescence that accompanied the accession of the Roman Catholic James VII and II surprised many, including Secretary Middleton.[72] The calm did not, however, last. James's early reassurances that he would 'preserve this government both in church and state as it is now by law established'[73] provided some comfort, but it failed to forestall plotting abroad, particularly in the United Provinces. There, in exile, was the duke of Monmouth, a Protestant with popular appeal and martial links, whom some of the Exclusionist Whigs had adopted as an alternative monarch during their campaign in the late 1670s to exclude James, duke of York, from the throne. Such supporters discredited Monmouth in the eyes of James, who removed him from his military offices, and the former's subsequent incrimination in the 1683 Rye House plot to assassinate both his father and uncle forced him to flee into exile.[74]

Ironically, given his role at Bothwell, joining him in the Low Countries were many Scottish Presbyterians, who had fallen foul of the High Anglican and Tory reaction of early 1680s, and also of the Scottish Test Act of 1681, which demanded oaths of loyalty to Protestantism but also (more problematically) to absolute royal supremacy over the Church.[75] The portents of the latter provision under a Roman Catholic monarch were contradictory and unacceptable to many, and prominent among their number was Archibald Campbell, ninth earl of Argyll and son of the covenanting eighth earl, whom Charles II had had executed because of his close involvement with Cromwell. A capital charge hung over Argyll at the Restoration but he managed to get this repealed and made peace with the Stuart monarchy, being appointed a privy councillor in 1664. Argyll, however, initially refused to take the 1681 Test and when, under pressure, he submitted, he bound his oath in caveat leading to the charge that it was false and thus ultimately to his conviction on the charge of treason. Once again a capital sentence was sent down but the government lacked the appetite to create a martyr and a rather lax guard at Edinburgh castle enabled Argyll to escape to England at the end of 1681, where, like Monmouth, he was implicated in the Rye House assassination plot and so forced to seek sanctuary in the United Provinces.[76]

The exile community around Monmouth and Argyll considered that James's throne was ripe for a Protestant challenge and, although both men did not meet in person, a plan was developed to undertake synchronised landings and risings in Scotland and south-west England.[77] Burnet subsequently recorded that 'Argyll might have given much trouble'[78] but his landing and rebellion were desultory affairs, posing little threat. Having gathered around 300 men, yet carrying arms for 20,000, Argyll sailed from Amsterdam on 2 May 1685 and made slow progress up the east coast and round the head of Scotland, before landing on the Kintyre peninsula on 20 May. By the time he sailed out from Campbeltown with his standard unfurled – its legend read 'For God and Religion against Poperie, Tyrrany, Arbitrary Government, and Erastianism'[79] – he had augmented his force to over 1,000, though this was less than he had anticipated and proved insufficient. The government's decision to recall the three Scottish regiments then in the service of the Anglo-Dutch Brigade in Holland as a supplement to the standing forces, commissioning in the process their commander, Colonel Hugh Mackay, as major-general, while also ordering out the militia, proved an over-reaction.[80] Argyll, beset by indecision and friction within his council of war as to whether he should concentrate on raising more men from the Campbell Highlands or march into the Lowlands, moved to Bute, setting up a base at Eilean Dearg at the top end of Loch Riddon. From here, he despatched a raid on Inveraray and on 10 June marched out south-east, heading for the Clyde valley and Glasgow. The rebels were tracked and beaten twice en route. A day after the start of the march, the marquess of Atholl, commanding 300 militia, came upon and defeated 400 foot and eighty horse in Argyll's van. A week later, the earl of Dumbarton's party of horse and dragoons dispersed the rebels into smaller groups, thereby signalling the end of the rising. On the following day, 18 June, Argyll was picked up by a weaver at Inchinnan and taken first to Glasgow before being transferred to Edinburgh castle to await his inevitable execution.[81]

It had not proved possible to synchronise the risings of Argyll and Monmouth – undoubtedly to Argyll's disadvantage – but the duke retained some momentum following his accomplice's beheading

Figure 11.3 George Douglas, earl of Dumbarton. Portrait attributed to Henri Gascars, c. 1680. Dumbarton helped to put down Argyll's rebellion in 1685 and later followed James VII and II into exile.

on 30 June. Monmouth's venture had in any event attracted more support since his landing at Lyme Regis on 11 June while the leadership proved more adept and less divided. It gave the king a genuine scare when the duke and his men initially brushed aside the woeful English militia companies sent against them.[82] As a consequence, and supported by parliament, James moved quickly to increase the English establishment. Not only were some nine new infantry battalions and the same number of new troops of horse raised in 1685, but also the three Scottish regiments of the Anglo-Dutch Brigade were diverted from landing at Leith to land at Gravesend. Meanwhile, within Scotland the military forces, except for the standing army, were stood down.[83] The increase in the English establishment proved decisive at the battle of Sedgemoor on 6 July when Monmouth's night attack was comprehensively repulsed. Captured within a couple of

Figure 11.4 The 2nd battalion, the Royal Scots, on the march, 1688, by Bernard Granville Baker, 1939.

days of fleeing the battlefield, the duke was executed on Tower Hill on 15 July. His rebellion had endured longer than Argyll's, but not by much. For the rest of James's short reign, the lack of other internal challenges and an aggressive foreign policy meant that the size of the Scottish military home establishment remained at around 2,200 men, only rising to near 3,000 in the spring of 1688.[84]

During the 1680s the army in Scotland was not immune from James's policies promoting the interests of his Roman Catholic co-religionists through two Declarations of Indulgence (in 1687 and 1688). These Declarations afforded Catholics, and Protestant Dissenters, freedom to worship and ultimately access to civil and military office.[85] Indeed, bolstered by the 1686 Godden versus Hales test case, which upheld the king's right to assert the reputed ancient power of dispensation, and thus relieve an individual from the obligations of parliamentary statute, the king commissioned Roman Catholics across all his army establishments.[86] In Scotland, these commissions were issued against the advice of the new commander, William Drummond (Viscount Strathallan from 1686), who had succeeded the Catholic earl of Dumbarton in October 1685 following the latter's return to London and senior command at James's side. In March 1686 a second battalion of Dumbarton's First Regiment of Foot arrived in Leith. Originally raised as a Scottish regiment in the service of Louis XIII, the First of Foot had been restored to the English establishment in 1662 and styled first the Royal Regiment and subsequently the Royal Scots. Save for service in England between 1678 and 1680, it had mainly been stationed abroad and the arrival of the second battalion in Scotland was the first posting north of the border for a regiment that James reputedly viewed as a 'flagship' for 'military Catholicism and professionalism'.[87] Furthermore, the senior office of governor and constable of Edinburgh castle went to the Catholic George Gordon, first duke of Gordon, while Captains Charles Carney and William Oliphant – men labelled 'papists' by Sir John Lauder[88] – raised two new companies for the Foot Guards. Two years later, in March 1688, one of three new regiments paid for by the French king, Louis XIV, was mustered in Musselburgh and commanded by the Catholic Colonel John Wauchope, who later served as major-general of the Jacobite army in Ireland opposing the Williamite conquest during the early 1690s.[89] In practical terms, such commissions did not represent a re-Catholicisation of the Scots force, but along with those issued in England, they contributed to the perception that this was James's intent. Thus, when the birth of the Prince of Wales in June 1688 raised the prospect of an enduring Catholic monarchy, the stadtholder of the United Provinces and James's son-in-law, Prince William of Orange, was invited by seven members of the English political elite, reputedly supported by 'nineteen parts of twenty of the people', to come over and reverse his father-in-law's policies.[90]

Upon news reaching James in the early autumn of 1688 that William was gathering forces, he turned to his armies throughout his kingdoms. The soldiers of the English establishment were already encamped and exercising on Hounslow Heath and, as reinforcements, James ordered all the Scottish forces to cross the border into England. Recognising that this left Scotland without defence, orders were issued to raise militia forces under the overall command of Sir George Munro, which yielded ten companies in Glasgow and four in Fife where a troop of horse was also mustered. In the event, the militia forces proved inadequate and failed to quell the outbreak of anti-Catholic rioting in the winter of 1688.[91]

Meanwhile the Scottish standing forces, led by Lieutenant-General James Douglas, reached York by mid-October and then London at the end of the month, before marching as part of James's army to Salisbury plain where a battle was anticipated against the prince of Orange, who had landed at Torbay on 5 November with some 14,000 troops. James, however, fled Salisbury plain on 21 November. Not only had he been suffering from an intermittent, though heavy, nose bleed for three days but also, and more significantly, some senior military commanders, including the army's second-in-command, John Churchill, had defected with many of their men to the prince's camp. Among the Scottish forces, the defection of just over a company of Douglas's own regiment, led by Corporal Kempe, was a minor event but notable nonetheless.[92]

James's return to London signalled that the prince of Orange was now dominating the course of the Revolution of 1688. By Christmas, with William's Dutch troops surrounding London, the king had fled to France, not only dropping the Great Seal in the River Thames en route but also irresponsibly ordering the earl of Feversham to disband the army. Predictably this led to disorder and confusion. Within regiments scores were settled, usually against the Roman Catholics, while the populace vented their anti-standing army ire against many of the now rather forlorn former regulars. Fortunately, Feversham's writ extended only to those men over whom he had immediate command (about 4,000) and a number of wiser heads prevailed at regimental level, so preventing precipitous disbandment. One of these was the new acting commander of the Scots forces, Lord George Livingstone, who had taken over from Douglas when he laid down his commission upon James's departure for France. Livingstone asked William if he might march the Scots army back home in one unit, to which the prince, in the interests of security and cohesion, was only too happy to agree.[93]

The absence of a significant military engagement during the Revolution of 1688 in England and Wales gave rise to the label 'Bloodless Revolution'. Modern historiography, however, favours a multi-kingdom interpretation of this event and thus highlights the military conflicts in Scotland, and later in Ireland, that belie such a peaceful leitmotif.[94] In March 1689 Claverhouse, who had been created Viscount Dundee by James in 1688, left a meeting of the Estates in Edinburgh and a month later raised the Jacobite standard of rebellion on Dundee Law. Previously, the chief of Clan Cameron, Sir Ewen Cameron of Lochiel, had set about organising a confederation of clans in support of James, and Dundee now travelled north to seek its support, along with any other men he could recruit. The government, meanwhile, had mobilised a force of over 3,000 men, commanded by Major-General Hugh Mackay, to suppress the rebellion. The backbone of Mackay's detachment was the three Scottish regiments of the Anglo-Dutch Brigade, which had originally been recalled to help defeat the Monmouth and Argyll uprisings three years earlier and had then come across with William in 1688. In addition, there were two home-grown Scottish regiments: the foot battalions of Alexander Gordon, fifth viscount Kenmure, and David Melville, third earl of Leven.[95]

During his travels north and then back to the Lowlands, Dundee had managed to raise only some 2,000 men, so he was significantly outnumbered when he engaged Mackay at the pass of Killiecrankie, near Blair Atholl, on 27 July 1689. The subsequent Jacobite victory was credited to Dundee's position on the ridge above the pass and the ferocity of the Jacobite clans' charge, which ripped through and destroyed the centre of Mackay's line. The Jacobites, however, lost not only their inspiration and unifier, Dundee, who was fatally wounded, but also nearly one-third of their force. At Dunkeld a month later the Jacobite force, now commanded by Alexander Cannon, was defeated by Lieutenant-Colonel William Cleland at the head of a newly raised regiment of Cameronians (covenanters, many of whom subscribed to the teachings of Richard Cameron, 'The Lion of the Covenant', who had been formed as a regiment by James Douglas, earl of Angus). A year later all vestiges of the Jacobite revolt arising out of the Revolution of 1688 were extinguished when the Inverness garrison commander, Sir Thomas Livingstone, defeated a force of James's supporters, led by Thomas Buchan, at Cromdale on the banks of the River Spey.[96]

The battles of Killiecrankie, Dunkeld and Cromdale were not the only occasions when Scottish regiments were deployed against their own in order to secure William's crown in Scotland. While success against Dundee and his Jacobite adherents might have ensured William's writ as king within southern Scotland, the same could not be said for the north. In August 1691 those Jacobite clans that had participated in the 1689 rebellion, as well as those that were otherwise unreconciled to the new regime, were offered a pardon provided the clan chief swore the oath of allegiance by the deadline of 1 January 1692. Many submitted in time but others did not, including Alastair

MacIain, chief of the MacDonalds of Glencoe, a small sept of the Clan MacDonald. Having initially wrongly presented himself at Fort William, MacIain was delayed three days by the weather and, upon reaching Inveraray, another three days were to pass before the sheriff of Argyll, Sir Colin Campbell, returned from holiday to administer the oath. The unyielding lord advocate, the Master of Stair, Sir John Dalrymple, who was also one of William's two secretaries of state covering Scotland, decided that an example should be made of the MacDonalds of Glencoe. His resolution gave rise to the massacre, whereby two companies from the regiment recently raised by the tenth earl (later first duke) of Argyll, led by Captain Robert Campbell, put the clan to the sword during the night of 12 February 1692 having previously accepted the highlanders' hospitality. Thirty-eight out of one hundred and forty clan members were killed in this notorious incident, which created a political storm for William and hardly bound the Highlands closer to his monarchy.[97]

Notwithstanding his uneasy relationship with his northern kingdom, and the mutiny among Jacobite and other discontented elements of the Royal Scots at Ipswich in March 1689 just prior to their embarkation for the United Provinces (an event that led to the passage of the first Mutiny Act),[98] the king was determined to draw upon Scottish military resources for the war against Louis XIV's France. This conflict (the Nine Years War, 1688–97), which broke out in the autumn of 1688, involved a Grand Alliance of states principally seeking to check the threat posed by France to the nascent balance of power within the European state system.[99] From the Revolution of 1688 through to the conclusion of the Nine Years War in 1697, William commissioned some twenty new Scottish regiments. The majority were temporary expedients and did not survive the general disbandment at end of the war. Indeed, only the regiments of the earls of Leven and Angus endured to the modern period (the King's Own Scottish Borderers and the Cameronians respectively). Nevertheless, these Scottish regiments participated in some of the principal battles of the Nine Years War, thereby gaining extensive service experience in the line of battle.[100]

The military history of Scotland between the Restoration and the Glorious Revolution is one of increasing competence in the profession of arms and the consolidation of a national martial character, albeit not manifest in a separate national force. In the years immediately following Charles's Restoration, the small Scottish establishment, assisted by militia forces, enforced the civil law and later suppressed Argyll's rebellion. Although the Scottish troops and their various commanders rarely demonstrated decisive skill-at-arms in these tasks, they typically prevailed even if this only became apparent in the longer term. In the same way that the arrival of William III transformed British constitutional, political and financial history, so his accession proved a watershed for Scottish military forces. Lowland troops helped secure the Scottish crown by defeating the Jacobites between 1689 and 1690, and the number of Scottish regiments – both foot and horse – was substantially increased for the wars against France during which their professionalism further improved. The organisation of these forces as part of a British army contingent within the Grand Alliance's force ranged against Louis XIV in the Nine Years War inevitably led to a dilution in the identity of a separate Scottish establishment. However, and perhaps ironically, a distinctive Scottish identity in martial characteristics and traditions was maintained and even emphasised within this larger military enterprise as regiments from north of the border served with distinction under the duke of Marlborough in the forthcoming war of the Spanish Succession.

Notes

1. T. Harris, *Restoration: Charles II and his Kingdoms* (London: Penguin, 2006), pp. 15, 43–4.
2. B. Denton, *Regimental History of the New Model Army: Lloyd's Regiment, Monck's Regiment, The Coldstream Guards* (London: Partisan Press, 1994), pp. 25, 35.
3. P. Gaunt, 'The battle of Dunbar and Cromwell's Scottish campaign', *Cromwelliana* (2001), pp. 2–9; *The Constitutional Documents of the Puritan Revolution, 1625–1660*, ed. S. R. Gardiner (Oxford: Clarendon Press, 1906), pp. 418–22.
4. H. Strachan, 'Scotland's military identity', *Scottish Historical Review*, vol. 85 (2006), p. 319; J. Childs, 'The Restoration army', in D. G. Chandler and I. Beckett (eds), *The Oxford History of the British Army* (Oxford: Oxford University Press, 1996), p. 46.
5. *The Diary of John Evelyn*, ed. E. S. de Beer (London: Oxford University Press, 1959), p. 406.
6. J. Nicoll, *A Diary of Public Transactions and other Occurrences, Chiefly in Scotland, From January 1650 to June 1667*, ed. D. Laing (Edinburgh: Bannatyne Club, 1836), p. 284.
7. Ibid. pp. 283–4; *A Congratulation for His Sacred Majesty, Charles, the third Monarch of Great Britain, His Happy Arrival at Whitehall. By a Loyal Member of His Majesties Army* (Edinburgh: n.p., 1660).
8. R. B. Manning, *An Apprenticeship in Arms: The Origins of the British*

Army 1585–1702 (Oxford: Oxford University Press, 2007), pp. 265–6; P. Bondanella and M. Musa (eds), *The Portable Machiavelli* (Harmondsworth: Penguin, 1979), pp. 480–517; A. Grey, *Debates of the House of Commons, From the Year 1667 to the Year 1694*, 10 vols (London: T. Becket and P. A. De Hondt, 1769), vol. 1, p. 218.

9. L. G. Schwoerer, *'No Standing Armies!' The Antiarmy Ideology in Seventeenth-Century England* (Baltimore, MD: The Johns Hopkins University Press, 1974), p. 71; H. Strachan, *The Politics of the British Army* (Oxford: Oxford University Press, 1997), p. 47.
10. B. Lenman, 'Militia, fencible men, and home defence, 1660–1797', in N. MacDougall (ed.), *Scotland and War AD 79–1918* (Edinburgh: John Donald, 1991), p. 173.
11. M. J. Routh (ed.), *Bishop Burnet's History of His Own Time*, 6 vols (Oxford: Clarendon Press, 1823), vol. 1, p. 174.
12. A. Robertson, *The Life of Sir Robert Moray* (London: Longmans, Green & Co., 1922), pp. 122–3; C. Dalton, *The Scots Army 1661–1688* (London: Eyre and Spottiswoode, 1909), part I, pp. 2–3.
13. Dalton, *The Scots Army*, part I, pp. 3–4; part II, pp. 3–4, 13, 31; Manning, *An Apprenticeship in Arms*, pp. 284–5.
14. Manning, *An Apprenticeship in Arms*, p. 284.
15. Lenman, 'Militia, fencible men, and home defence', p. 175.
16. T. Thomson and C. Innes (eds), *Acts of the Parliaments of Scotland* [hereafter *APS*] (Edinburgh, 1820), vol. 7, pp. 480–1.
17. Ibid. p. 481.
18. C. M. Clode, *The Military Forces of the Crown*, 2 vols (London: John Murray, 1869), vol. 1, p. 33.
19. Lenman, 'Militia, fencible men and home defence', p. 176.
20. G. Donaldson, *Scotland: James V–James VII* (Edinburgh: Oliver and Boyd, 1978), pp. 358–84; K. M. Brown, *Kingdom or Province? Scotland and the Regal Union, 1603–1715* (London: Macmillan, 1992), p. 150.
21. Harris, *Restoration*, p. 108; *APS*, vol. 7, pp. 86–7.
22. *APS*, vol. 7, pp. 87–8; C. Jackson, *Restoration Scotland, 1660–1690* (Woodbridge: Boydell and Brewer, 2003), p. 110; *The Register of the Privy Council of Scotland* [hereafter *RPCS*], ed. P. Hume Brown, 10 vols (Edinburgh: HM General Register House, 1908–70), third series, vol. 1, p. 28.
23. *APS*, vol. 7, pp. 370–4, 376.
24. Ibid. pp. 379, 405–6.
25. I. Cowan, *The Scottish Covenanters, 1660–1688* (London: Gollancz, 1976), pp. 52–3; J. Buckroyd, *Church and State in Scotland 1660–1681* (Edinburgh: John Donald, 1980), pp. 41–5.

26. R. Latham and W. Matthew (eds), *The Diary of Samuel Pepys*, 11 vols (London: HarperCollins, 1995), vol. 4, p. 168.
27. Cowan, *The Scottish Covenanters*, pp. 53–4.
28. *APS*, vol. 7, p. 379.
29. J. Turner, *Memoirs of His Own Life and Times*, ed. T. Thomson (Edinburgh: Bannatyne Club, 1829), pp. 140–1.
30. J. Brown, *An Apologeticall Relation of the Sufferings of the Faithfull Ministers & Professours of the Church of Scotland since August 1660* (Edinburgh: n.p., 1665); Harris, *Restoration*, p. 118.
31. O. Airy (ed.), *The Lauderdale Papers*, 3 vols (London: Camden, 1884), vol. 1, p. 222.
32. Airy (ed.), *The Lauderdale Papers*, vol. 1, p. 235; Turner, *Memoirs*, pp. 142–6; R. Mitchison, *A History of Scotland* (London: Methuen, 1970), p. 252.
33. Routh (ed.), *Bishop Burnet's History*, vol. 1, p. 364.
34. Turner, *Memoirs*, pp. 146–61.
35. Latham and Matthew (eds), *The Diary of Samuel Pepys*, vol. 7, p. 377, n. 4; Airy (ed.), *The Lauderdale Papers*, vol. 1, p. 246.
36. Dalton, *The Scots Army*, part I, p. 13.
37. R. Wodrow, *The History of the Sufferings of the Church of Scotland*, 2 vols (Edinburgh: J. Watson, 1721), vol. 1, p. 246.
38. Mitchison, *A History*, p. 253.
39. Wodrow, *The History of the Sufferings*, vol. 1, p. 242; R. Law, *Memorialls, Or, The Memorable Things That Fell Out Within This Island of Britain from 1638–1684*, ed. C. K. Sharpe (Edinburgh: Constable, 1819), p. 16. It is incautious to rely exclusively on Wodrow for Dalyell's troop numbers for he refers to the total establishment Dalyell could have called upon but most certainly did not, and Wodrow, as the Presbyterians' historian, had an interest in exaggerating the government forces.
40. Airy, *The Lauderdale Papers*, vol. 1, p. 249; Turner, *Memoirs*, p. 172; J. Kirkton, *The Secret and True History of the Church of Scotland, from the Restoration to the Year 1678*, ed. C. K. Sharpe (Edinburgh: John Ballantyne, 1817), p. 240.
41. Kirkton, *The Secret and True History*, pp. 238–42; Wodrow, *The History of the Sufferings*, vol. 1, pp. 246–9.
42. Wodrow, *The History of the Sufferings*, vol. 1, p. 249.
43. Ibid. p. 247.
44. Kirkton, *The Secret and True History*, p. 242; Thomas M'Crie (ed.), *Memoirs of Mr William Veitch and George Brysson* (Edinburgh: Blackwood, 1825), pp. 415–16.
45. Wodrow, *The History of the Sufferings*, vol. 1, p. 247.

46. C. S. Terry, *The Pentland Rising & Rullion Green* (Glasgow: James Maclehose, 1905), p. 66.
47. This account of the battle of Rullion Green is based on the following sources: Kirkton, *The Secret and True History*, pp. 240–4; Airy, *The Lauderdale Papers*, vol. 1, pp. 249–51; M'Crie, *Memoirs of Mr William Veitch*, pp. 416–19, 429–32; Wodrow, *The History of the Sufferings*, vol. 1, pp. 250–2.
48. A. I. Macinnes, 'Repression and conciliation: The Highland dimension 1660–1688', *Scottish Historical Review*, vol. 65 (1986), pp. 171–3.
49. Hume Brown, *RPCS*, third series, vol. 2, pp. 324–9; Macinnes, 'Repression and conciliation', pp. 178–9.
50. Hume Brown, *RPCS*, third series, vol. 3, p. 356; Macinnes, 'Repression and conciliation', p. 183.
51. Macinnes, 'Repression and conciliation', p. 185.
52. Harris, *Restoration*, p. 120.
53. Hume Brown, *RPCS*, third series, vol. 3, pp. 38–40, 586–9; *APS*, vol. 7, pp. 554–5.
54. *APS*, vol. 7, pp. 554, 556–7; Hume Brown, *RPCS*, third series, vol. 3, pp. 61–2; *APS*, vol. 8, pp. 8–12.
55. Harris, *Restoration*, pp. 122–3.
56. Hume Brown, *RPCS*, third series, vol. 4, pp. 197–201; Ibid. vol. 5, pp. 206–9.
57. Historical Manuscripts Commission, *Supplement Report on the Manuscripts of the Duke of Hamilton*, ed. J. H. McMaster (London: HMSO, 1935), pp. 95–9; Harris, *Restoration*, p. 124.
58. Mitchison, *A History*, pp. 263–4; W. Mackay, 'The Highland Host (1678)', *Transactions of the Gaelic Society of Inverness*, vol. 32 (1924–5), pp. 67–81.
59. Mitchison, *A History*, pp. 263–4; Harris, *Restoration*, p. 124.
60. Dalton, *The Scots Army*, part I, p. 44.
61. Ibid. p. 41; M. Linklater and C. Hesketh, *Bonnie Dundee* (Edinburgh: Canongate, 1992), pp. 33–5.
62. Linklater and Hesketh, *Bonnie Dundee*, p. 33; M. Barrington, *Grahame of Claverhouse, Viscount Dundee, 1648–1689* (London: Martin Secker, 1911), pp. 45–82.
63. Linklater and Hesketh, *Bonnie Dundee*, p. 127.
64. See the biographies by Linklater and Hesketh, and Barrington, for a critical but balanced assessment; *Laws & Articles of War, For the Government of His Majesties Force within the Kingdom of Scotland* (Edinburgh: Evan Taylor, 1667); *Articles and Rules for the Better Government of His Majesties Forces in Scotland* (Edinburgh: Andrew Anderson, 1678).

65. This account of the battle of Drumclog is based on the following sources: W. Aiton, *A History of the Rencounter at Drumclog, and the Battle of Bothwell Bridge* (Hamilton: W. M. Borthwick & Co., 1821), pp. 53–60; T. Brownlee, *A Narrative of the Battles of Drumclog and Bothwell Bridge* (Edinburgh: William Duncan, 1823), pp. 13–22; Linklater and Hesketh, *Bonnie Dundee*, pp. 40–8.
66. J. Spurr (ed.), *The Entring Book of Roger Morrice, II: The Reign of Charles II, 1677–1685* (Woodbridge: Boydell and Brewer, 2007), p. 160.
67. Airy, *The Lauderdale Papers*, vol. 3, pp. 169–70.
68. Ibid. pp. 258–60; Dalton, *The Scots Army*, part I, pp. 52–4.
69. Dalton, *The Scots Army*, part I, pp. 50–1, 55–6.
70. This account of the battle of Bothwell Bridge is based on the following sources: Aiton, *A History of the Rencounter*, pp. 66–76; Brownlee, *A Narrative of the Battles*, pp. 23–32; *A Fresh Relation from the King's Army in Scotland* (London: n.p., 1679); *The Great Victory Obtained by His Majesties Army Under the Command of His Grace the Duke of Monmouth, Against the Rebels in the West of Scotland* (Edinburgh: n.p., 1679); Barrington, *Grahame of Claverhouse*, pp. 61–7; Linklater and Hesketh, *Bonnie Dundee*, pp. 51–5.
71. Dalton, *The Scots Army*, part I, p. 61.
72. Bodleian Library, Oxford, MS Eng. Hist. c. 51, Middleton to Carlisle, 2 Feb. 1685.
73. Sir J. Dalrymple, *Memoirs of Great Britain and Ireland* (London: W. Strahan and T. Cadell, 1771), vol. 2, part II, pp. 103–4.
74. T. Harris, *Revolution: The Great Crisis of the British Monarchy, 1685–1720* (London: Allen Lane, 2006), pp. 74–5.
75. *APS*, vol. 8, pp. 143–5; J. Willcock, *A Scots Earl in Covenanting Times* (Edinburgh: Andrew Elliot, 1907), pp. 252–3.
76. D. Stevenson, 'Archibald Campbell, ninth earl of Argyll (1629–1685)', *Oxford Dictionary of National Biography* (Oxford: Oxford University Press, 2004), vol. 9, pp. 716–21; Harris, *Revolution*, pp. 73–4.
77. *A Letter Giving ane short and true Accoumpt of the Earl of Argyls Invasion in the Year 1685* (1686), pp. 6–8; Stevenson, 'Archibald Campbell', pp. 721–2.
78. Routh, *Bishop Burnet's History*, vol. 3, p. 27.
79. Sir J. Lauder of Fountainhall, *Historical Observes of Memorable Occurrents in Church and State from October 1680 to April 1686*, ed. A. Urquhart and D. Laing (Edinburgh: Bannatyne Club, 1840), p. 177.
80. Dalton, *The Scots Army*, part I, p. 68.
81. Lauder, *Historical Observes*, pp. 164–85, 193; *An Account of the Proceedings of His Majesties Army In Scotland* (Dublin: n.p., 1685), pp. 3–8; *A Letter Giving ane short and true Accoumpt*, pp. 16–26.

82. D. Chandler, *Sedgemoor 1685* (Staplehurst: Spellmount, 1995), pp. 19–41; P. Earle, *Monmouth's Rebels* (London: Weidenfeld and Nicolson, 1977), pp. 82–106.
83. J. Childs, *The Army, James II and the Glorious Revolution* (Manchester: Manchester University Press, 1980), pp. x–xii; Dalton, *The Scots Army*, part I, p. 68; Hume Brown, *RPCS*, vol. 11, p. 90.
84. Childs, *The Army*, pp. 2, 4.
85. E. Cardwell, *Documentary Annals of the Reformed Church of England*, 2 vols (Oxford: Oxford University Press, 1839), vol. 2, pp. 308–15.
86. W. Cobbett, *Cobbett's Complete Collection of State Trials*, 33 vols (London: Hansard, 1809–26), vol. 11, pp. 1195–9.
87. Dalton, *The Scots Army*, part II, p. 152, note designated as *; R. H. Paterson, *Pontius Pilate's Bodyguard: A History of The First or The Royal Regiment of Foot, The Royal Scots (The Royal Regiment)*, 3 vols (Edinburgh: RHQ Royal Scots, 2000–7), vol. 1, pp. 1–40; J. Childs, *The British Army of William III, 1689–1702* (Manchester: Manchester University Press, 1987), p. 22.
88. Sir J. Lauder, *Historical Notices of Scottish Affairs*, ed. D. Laing (Edinburgh: Constable, 1848), p. 693.
89. R. Bell (ed.), *Siege of the Castle of Edinburgh* (Edinburgh: Bannatyne Club, 1828), p. 5; Dalton, *The Scots Army*, part I, p. 75, part II, pp. 147–8; J. Ferguson (ed.), *Papers Illustrating the History of the Scots Brigade in the Service of the United Netherlands, 1572–1782* (Edinburgh: Scottish History Society, 1899), vol. 1, p. 478.
90. Dalrymple, *Memoirs*, vol. 1, pp. 228–31.
91. Harris, *Revolution*, p. 370; Hume Brown, *RPCS*, third series, vol. 7, p. 328.
92. F. Holmes, *The Sickly Stuarts* (Stroud: Sutton, 2005), pp. 159–63; Childs, *The Army*, pp. 184–90; Dalton, *The Scots Army*, part 1, p. 83.
93. Childs, *The Army*, pp. 168–202.
94. L. Glassey, 'In search of the mot juste: Characterizations of the revolution of 1688–1689', in T. Harris and S. Taylor (eds), *The Final Crisis of the Stuart Monarchy: The Revolutions of 1688–91 in their British, Atlantic and European Contexts* (Woodbridge: The Boydell Press, 2013), pp. 1–32.
95. Harris, *Revolution*, pp. 410–11; Mitchison, *A History*, pp. 280–3.
96. H. Mackay of Scourie, *Memoirs of the War carried on in Scotland and Ireland, 1689–1691* (Edinburgh: Bannatyne Club, 1833), pp. 49–60; Barrington, *Grahame of Claverhouse*, pp. 333–79; *A True and Real Account of the Defeat of General Buchan, and Brigadeer Cannon, Their High-Land Army, at the Battel of Crombdell* (Edinburgh: n.p., 1690).

97. Mitchison, *A History*, pp. 285–8; also see J. Prebble, *Glencoe* (Harmondsworth: Penguin, 1966) and P. Hopkins, *Glencoe and the End of the Highland War* (Edinburgh: John Donald, 1998).
98. C. D. Ellestad, 'The mutinies of 1689', *Journal of the Society for Army Historical Research*, vol. 53 (1975), pp. 4–21; R. E. Scouller, 'The Mutiny Acts', *Journal of the Society for Army Historical Research*, vol. 50 (1972), pp. 42–5; Paterson, *Pontius Pilate's Bodyguard*, pp. 40–2; Childs, *The British Army*, pp. 22–4.
99. J. Lynn, *The Wars of Louis XIV, 1667–1714* (London: Longman, 1999), pp. 191–99; M. Sheehan, 'The development of British theory and practice of the balance of power before 1714', *History*, vol. 73 (1988), p. 30.
100. See Childs, *The British Army*, and his operational history, *The Nine Years' War and the British Army* (Manchester: Manchester University Press, 1991).

12
Marlborough's Wars and the Act of Union, 1702–14

JOHN C. R. CHILDS

Since the Restoration in 1660 the separate armies in England, Ireland and Scotland had enjoyed close association. A *de facto* British army, characterised by frequent interchange of national units and extensive collaboration, was created during 1689. By 1702 the transfer of Scottish regiments to and from the English establishment had become a well-lubricated procedure administered by the secretaries of state, the respective national treasury assuming financial responsibility whenever a unit crossed the border.[1]

In 1702, near the beginning of the War of the Spanish Succession (1701–14), the Scots army numbered 2,934 men at an annual charge of £65,740 14s (Scots). The cavalry comprised one troop of Life Guards, commanded by John Campbell, second duke of Argyll, and a single troop of Horse Grenadiers led by William, Lord Forbes. There were two marching regiments of infantry – the Scottish Foot Guards under George Ramsay and Brigadier James Maitland's battalion – plus independent foot companies in the Highlands, commanded by Captains Alexander Campbell and William Grant, and in garrison at Blackness Fort and the castles of Dumbarton, Stirling and Edinburgh. This permanent establishment was increased in March 1708 by the addition of a second troop of Horse Grenadier Guards, commanded by William Montgomery. The administrative staff was commensurately small. Major-General (Lieutenant-General from 15 February 1703) George Ramsay was commander-in-chief, succeeded on 2 March 1706 by Lieutenant-General David Melville, third earl of Leven, a client of Marlborough. On the fall of his patron in 1712 Leven was replaced by Argyll, although the duties were executed by two deputies, Major-Generals Thomas Whetham (d. 1741), who had previously commanded the expedition to Canada in 1709, and Joseph Wightman, lieutenant-general from 1710 (d. 1722).[2] Captain

George Somerville (lieutenant-colonel from 29 January 1703) served as adjutant-general whilst Muster Master-General, renamed Commissary-General of the Musters in 1713, Thomas Bruce, supervised the distribution of pay and the maintenance of the army's numerical strength. The quartermaster-general was Captain Charles Stratton, who also commanded a company in the Scottish Foot Guards. The secretary at war, a civilian, was little more than the commander-in-chief's personal clerk. John Aitkin, a follower of Leven and Marlborough, occupied this office until his replacement by James Cockburn, whose patron was Argyll, on 12 July 1712.[3]

In peacetime this tiny force was sufficient to prevent trouble in the Highlands from spreading south, to watch over the covenanters in Dumfries and Galloway, and to police the Lowlands. In wartime it gained the additional role of providing troops for service overseas. Following the formation of the Second Grand Alliance against France in 1701, preparations were made to mobilise Scottish manpower through the creation of 'hostilities-only' units. A nine-company infantry regiment was recruited by John Erskine, sixth or twenty-second earl of Mar, in the spring of 1702, Alexander Grant of Grant succeeding as colonel on 4 March 1706. In the same year, William Gordon, Lord Strathnaver, usually known as the Master of Strathnaver, son of John Gordon, fifteenth earl of Sutherland, raised an infantry battalion of nine companies, increased to twelve in 1710. Two dragoon regiments, each comprising six troops, were founded during 1703 by William Kerr, second marquess of Lothian, and John Carmichael, first earl of Hyndford.[4] George Macartney levied a twelve-company regiment of foot in January 1704. These five units were disbanded in 1713. Lord Mark Kerr's foot battalion of thirteen companies was formed in January 1706 specifically for service in Spain and was filled mainly with drafts from the battalions of Maitland, Grant and Strathnaver. It was demobilised in Gibraltar during 1712. Thus was the Scots establishment augmented to 5,315 by 1708, the peak year for the expansion of the British forces.[5]

The hunt for replacements was a major annual undertaking. On 11 May 1704 1,600 levies and drafts were ready to sail for the Low Countries from Leith. Drafting out of regiments remaining in Scotland was standard procedure: Strathnaver's, Maitland's and Mar's were 'almost broke' by drafting in April 1704 and had to recover their numbers through vigorous recruiting. This, however, was easier ordered than achieved because the English Press Acts,[6] which permitted partial, selective conscription, did not apply north of the border and the lake of 'volunteers' was already beginning to run dry, obliging

Figure 12.1 George Hamilton, earl of Orkney. Portrait by Sir Godfrey Kneller, 1710. Orkney was one of Marlborough's most able commanders during the War of the Spanish Succession.

Scottish colonels on both establishments to accept recruits from England. The Act of Union corrected this anomaly, enabling Scotland to resume its primary military function of providing soldiers for campaigns overseas.[7]

The official establishment was but one Scottish military contribution. From time to time during the War of the Spanish Succession, Scotland provided two regiments of dragoons and six battalions of infantry on the English establishment, plus six battalions in the Scots Brigade in the Dutch service. In addition, there were many Scots officers and men serving in nominally English regiments. At Blenheim in 1704 Englishmen led seven regiments, Scotsmen five and Irishmen four. Of the four lieutenant-generals attached to the British corps, one was Scottish – George Hamilton, earl of Orkney. One of the three major-generals was a Scot, Charles Ross, and three out of the eight brigadiers: James Ferguson, Archibald Rowe and Lord John Hay. Two of the seven brigade majors were Scottish, Captains Alexander Irwin and Patrick Gordon. On the eve of union, Scotland provided 10 per cent of regimental colonels in the English army and a disproportionate number of the rank and file. The expansion of the British army after 1707, plus the heavy casualties suffered at Oudenarde (11 July 1708) and Malplaquet (11 September 1709), augmented opportunities for Scotsmen. Between 1714 and 1763 Scots comprised approximately 25 per cent of British subalterns and 20 per cent of regimental colonels.

During the Nine Years War (1688–97), Andrew Fletcher of Saltoun opined that a population of about one million had provided between 7,000 and 8,000 Scots in the English fleet and a further 2,000 or 3,000 in the Dutch navy, whilst the English army contained twenty Scottish battalions and six squadrons of cavalry, a total of over 30,000 men: one in every five men in William III's British forces was either Scottish or Scots-Irish. In return for this considerable human investment, observed Fletcher, Scotland had been left in poverty and its commercial ventures allowed to founder. In 1706 Daniel Defoe reiterated Fletcher's argument – 'Scotland is an inexhaustible treasure of men' – but enlarged its scope by reminding his readers that large numbers of Scots were also serving in the armies of Sweden, the Netherlands, Russia, the Holy Roman Empire, Poland and France. By the time of the Great Northern War (1700–21), several Scottish families were well established in Sweden. Many Swedish Scots took part in the battle of Poltava in 1709 and there were fifty Scottish names amongst those who spent the ensuing thirteen years as prisoners of the Russians. Malcolm Hamilton (1635–99), a nephew of Malcolm Hamilton, archbishop of Cashel, and son of Captain John Hamilton, went to Sweden in 1654 and rose to become a baron, major-general and governor of northern Sweden. His brother Hugo (1655–1724) was a lieutenant-general under Charles XII. Had all these men been available to fight on the domestic establishments, said Defoe, Britain's power would have been substantially enhanced. Union was thus partly motivated by the need to secure permanently these martial resources for employment overseas in England's subsequent wars.[8]

The army of the Dutch Republic contained the largest permanent concentration of Scots on foreign service. After the Glorious Revolution, the remnants of the three English regiments in the Anglo-Dutch Brigade were added to the English establishment, but the three Scottish regiments returned to the Netherlands as the Scots Brigade. At the end of the Nine Years War in 1697, in an effort to save troops from parliamentary assault, William transferred three Scottish regiments – the Cameronians (led by Colonel James Ferguson, d. 1705), Lord Strathnaver's and Colonel George Hamilton's – to the Netherlands to bring the scarlet-coated Scots Brigade up to a strength of six battalions. These corps rejoined the English establishment in 1698 and 1699 but in 1701, with war imminent, Strathnaver's and Hamilton's were posted back to the United Provinces together with the battalion of David Colyear, first earl of Portmore (1657–1730). This restored the Scots Brigade to six regiments, an establishment that it retained until 1717 when the three youngest regiments were disbanded.[9]

In 1702 the three 'old' regiments were led by George Lauder, Robert Murray and Walter Colyear, distinguished officers who achieved high rank and recognition within the Dutch hierarchy and retained their colonelcies until 1716, 1719 and 1747 respectively. Colyear, Lord Portmore's brother, became a major-general in 1704, whilst Lauder and Murray were promoted to lieutenant-general in 1709. Of the three 'new' regiments, George Hamilton, promoted to brigadier in 1704, retained his colonelcy throughout the war but the command of the other two changed frequently. When Lord Portmore transferred to the colonelcy of the Queen's (Second) Foot in 1703 his replacement was John Dalrymple, who held the colonelcy until he took over the Cameronians in 1706. William Borthwick's short tenure ended with his death at Ramillies in 1706 whilst his successor, John Hepburn, was mortally wounded at Malplaquet. Brigadier James Douglas then assumed command. Lord Strathnaver transferred out of the Scots Brigade in 1702 to raise a new battalion in Scotland and was succeeded by John Campbell, Lord Lorne (second duke of Argyll from 1703), who held the colonelcy until 1708 when he was followed by John Murray, marquess of Tullibardine, the eldest son of the first duke of Atholl. Tullibardine was killed at Malplaquet in 1709 and his place taken temporarily by John Campbell until 1710, and then permanently by Sir James Wood.

The reorganised Scots Brigade saw extensive active service. Colonels Dalrymple and Lord Lorne distinguished themselves at the siege of Venlo (11–24 September 1702), participating in John, Lord Cutts's unorthodox assault on Fort St Michael. At Ramillies in 1706 Major-General Murray was posted on the left of the second line and enjoyed the distinction of personally saving Marlborough from capture. Argyll, commanding a brigade composed of Scots battalions and one of Dutch Guards, led the charge that evicted the French infantry from Ramillies village and was lightly wounded by three spent bullets. Colonel William Borthwick was killed at the head of his regiment and Major Edward Halkett of Colyear's also fell. The Scots Brigade probably took part in the rapid exploitation that followed the victory: Lauder's was certainly present at the siege of

Menin, which capitulated on 21 August. Four Scots and six Danish battalions garrisoned the key post of Courtrai over the winter of 1706–7.

Major-General Murray was involved in the unsuccessful attempt to recapture Ghent in June 1708 and Colyear's and Tullibardine's fought at Oudenarde on 11 July, young Tullibardine leading the attack on the left at the head of 500 detached grenadiers. Although Murray, Colyear, Lauder and Hamilton were present as general officers at the battle of Malplaquet in 1709, only the battalions of Tullibardine and Hepburn were on the field, forming part of the first line under George Hamilton. The prince of Orange personally led forward the nine first-line battalions through the Wood of Lanières to attack the French entrenchments covering Villars's right flank. Orange ploughed on through heavy, enfilading musketry and cannon fire that swept away entire ranks. His horse shot from under him, he continued on foot until reaching the entrenchment where, on a wave of his hat, the Dutch and Scots charged through with the bayonet and expelled the French 'with such a butchering that the oldest general alive never saw the like'. Before they could deploy, they were driven out by a French counter attack. Hamilton was carried from the field, wounded. One veteran, John Scot, recalled that

> These triple entrenchments and blocks of trees,
>   Co[a]st our Hollands armie right deare.
> Our regiments was beat and sadly defeate,
>   They retired and rallied againe.[10]

Orange mounted a fresh horse, which was soon shot, gathered the nearest troops, seized a standard and marched back to the entrenchment where he planted the colours in the ground and shouted, 'Follow me, my friends, here is your post.' The Scottish and Dutch infantry pressed forward again but failed to consolidate on their objective; Tullibardine was shot through the thigh, an injury that proved mortal, and his lieutenant-colonel, Charles Swinton, died along with his brother, Captain James Swinton, and Captains David Graham and James Brown. In Colonel Hepburn's battalion, the colonel was mortally wounded and Captain René de Tascher killed. The dead, wrote Lord Orkney,

> lye as thick as ever you saw a flock of sheep; and where our poor nephew Tullybardine was, it was prodigious. I really think I never saw the like: particularly where the Dutch Guards attacked, it is a miracle. I hope in God it

will be the last battle I ever see. A very few of such would make both parties end the war very soon.

Although five battalions took part in the prince of Orange's attack on St Venant in 1710, the Scots Brigade was mostly engaged in garrison duties for the remainder of the war.[11]

Because the three 'old' or 'standing' regiments of the Scots Brigade were on continuous loan to the Dutch army for two centuries, the officers became introspective and cliquish. Sons followed fathers into the same regiments: Stedmans, Halketts, Cunninghams, Stuarts, Douglases, Mackays, Lillingstones and Lamys turned the brigade into a series of family businesses. Many officers married local women, becoming more Dutch than Scottish. Although they were at liberty to resign their commissions at any time and return to Scotland very few did, largely because they lacked the patronage and means to purchase places on the British establishment. Money was always in short supply and what little the officers possessed often had to be used to pay their men, whose wages were frequently in arrears.[12] Turnover amongst the rank and file was much higher, especially in wartime. At the end of every campaigning season officers returned to Scotland to recruit – during the winter of 1703–4, 500 levies were shipped to the Netherlands, suggesting that the brigade suffered an annual wartime 'wastage rate' of between 15 and 20 per cent – but, towards the end of the War of the Spanish Succession, there was a sharp reduction in available native manpower and the brigade began to seek recruits amongst other European nationalities, beginning the process that saw the common soldiery gradually lose its specifically Scottish identity. In 1709 the Scots Brigade was substantially under strength, its recruiting parties having found the homeland 'already greatly depopulated', a situation exacerbated by the intensive recruiting drive that had taken place in all Scotland's parishes during the winter of 1708–9 to fill up British regiments. On 23 May 1712, whilst in garrison at Menin following the winter recruiting season, Wood's battalion mustered 468 private soldiers and NCOs, 192 below the establishment strength of 660. By 1715 it contained only 342 effective men, a shortfall of 318.[13]

The situation of wives and families of Scots Brigade soldiers who died or deserted was unenviable. The illiterate Mary King petitioned the States General on 20 February 1708 following the death of her husband, Daniel Maclean, a soldier in Lauder's battalion, eighteen months previously at Ramillies. 'Burdened with two young children in a foreign country and overtaken by poverty', she sought from their High Mightinesses a passport to allow her to travel to Düsseldorf, within the jurisdiction of Brandenburg, where she had 'a brother living'. Unsuccessful, she petitioned again on 31 July. Duncan Buchanan, formerly a soldier in Lieutenant-Colonel Walter Bowie's company in Hamilton's battalion, deserted and, fearing for his life if apprehended, enlisted in the Dutch navy. Buchanan then sought to rejoin his company under the umbrella of a general amnesty issued by the States General but he was too slow and the time limit expired. On behalf of her disorganised husband, Agnes Vermeer-Buchanan petitioned for his retrospective inclusion within the official pardon.[14]

Scottish regiments on the English establishment and units from the regular Scots army also saw much active service in the Low Countries.[15] Lord John Hay's 'Grey Dragoons' performed effectively at the Schellenberg in 1704. Shortly after 1900 hours Hay's men dismounted and joined Marlborough's infantry in the second, unsuccessful, attack upon the heavily fortified hill. Louis of Baden then discovered and exploited a weak point in the defences between the Schellenberg and Donauwörth, and Hay's dragoons quickly remounted and joined the pursuit.[16] They lost seven troopers killed and seventeen wounded. A detachment of 130 men from the Cameronians was also present, suffering nineteen killed and sixty wounded. Both battalions of the Royal Scots (First of Foot) went to Flanders in 1701 as part of Marlborough's initial expeditionary corps of 10,000 men. The first battalion, commanded by Lieutenant-Colonel John White, lost thirty-nine killed and one hundred and six wounded in the frontal assaults on the Schellenberg.

No British regiment in Marlborough's army served at more sieges than the Royal Scots, but they also fought in all four great battles. At Blenheim (13 August 1704) the first battalion (Lieutenant-Colonel John White) fielded thirty-seven officers, fifty-nine NCOs and 542 private soldiers whilst the second, under Major Andrew Hamilton, comprised thirty-eight officers, fifty-eight NCOs and 487 private soldiers. To attack Blenheim village on the banks of the Danube, Lord Cutts commanded four brigades of infantry and two lines of horse, the latter including Hay's 'Grey Dragoons' (twenty-five officers, ten sergeants, seventeen corporals and 288 troopers). In the first line of foot, comprising five battalions commanded by Brigadier Archibald Rowe, were the Royal Scots Fusiliers, another formation that took part in all Marlborough's major actions. Brigadier James Ferguson's brigade formed the second line and contained his own regiment, the Cameronians. Rowe took his brigade to within 150 metres of Blenheim where they lay down behind a fold in the ground, enduring

Figure 12.2 The Cameronians at Blenheim, 1704, by Richard Simkin, c. 1900.

a cannonade from a six-gun battery. At 12.30, Rowe dismounted and led them forward in silence – he had instructed that there was to be no firing until he struck the palisades with his sword – towards the strongpoints, barricades and loop-holed walls. When they were thirty metres distant, the French defenders opened fire, but Rowe's battalions closed up, dressed ranks and pressed on until their leader brought down his blade on the nearest stockade. Rowe fell mortally wounded and, having suffered 33 per cent casualties, the brigade staggered back. Cutts advanced three more times, on each occasion sustained by a fresh brigade from the column, but could make no impression on the village. However, by drawing the bulk of the Franco-Bavarian infantry into the village Cutts's tactical contribution was decisive. After Marlborough had penetrated the Franco-Bavarian centre and unleashed his cavalry, 'Lord John Hay's dragoons and others got in upon the Regiment du Roy, which they beat intirely'.[17]

In 1705 the 'Grey Dragoons' made two charges during the operation to pierce the Lines of Brabant and captured Lieutenant-General Yves, marquis d'Alègre. At Ramillies (23 May 1706), they supported Lord Orkney's attack on the right wing and participated in the pursuit. Soon after the battle, Lord Hay died of fever at Courtrai and

Figure 12.3 The Royal Scots Dragoons (the Scots Greys) at Ramillies, 1706, by Christopher Clark, c. 1920.

John Dalrymple, Viscount Stair (second earl of Stair from 1707), was awarded the colonelcy but the effective leadership fell to Lieutenant-Colonel James Campbell. The regiment was present at Oudenarde (11 July 1708) but took no part in the main action although Stair was chosen by Marlborough to convey the official despatches of victory to Queen Anne.[18] At Malplaquet (11 September 1709) the dragoons formed part of General d'Auvergne's cavalry force that eventually broke through the French centre following preparatory action by Orkney's infantry: 'Jemmy Campbell, at the head of the grey dragoons, behaved like an angel, broke through both lines.'[19] William Kerr's Dragoons did not arrive in Flanders until 1711, too late to take part in any action, and served in garrison at Brussels and Ghent.

The Cameronians had sailed to Flanders in 1702. Many of these covenanters from Dumfries and Galloway heartily disliked assisting their persecutors' cause. The excruciatingly pious Major John Blackader recorded on 23 May 1708: 'A sad Sabbath both by fatigue and ill company. Marching all day in the middle of an English army. I need say no more to give notion of what a hell on earth it is', although the pouring rain and abominable roads no doubt exacerbated his sourness. At Ramillies, Marlborough posted the Cameronians on the right wing away from the main battle; indeed, 'we did not think the action at first so considerable, but the effects of it are very remarkable and surprising . . . all we lost was by cannonading'. Similarly, at Oudenarde, they 'were obliged to stand in cold blood, exposed to the enemy's shot, by which we had several killed and wounded, for there was heavy firing for about two hours'. A detachment from the regiment, under the command of Colonel George Preston, fought alongside a battalion of the Royal Scots at Wynendael in 1708 but suffered no casualties apart from an officer who lost a finger. At Malplaquet, they were not involved in the main action but suffered severely from 'cannonading', including the loss of Colonel James Cranston, killed by a cannonball as he sat on horseback at the head of the regiment. Despite their somewhat peripheral service in the big battles, the Cameronians nevertheless made important contributions at the sieges of Dendermonde, Ath, Lille and Douai.[20] Meanwhile, in October 1708 the Master of Strathnaver's and Alexander Grant's battalions were transferred from Scotland to Flanders. Both regiments were largely employed in garrison duties but Grant's fought at the siege of Mons in 1709 and Strathnaver's may also have been present. Grant's battalion was drafted in 1711 to complete the battalions detailed for Major-General John Hill's Quebec Expedition and it was never subsequently recruited back to health. Strathnaver's, commanded by Colonel John Pocock from 1710, served at the siege of Bouchain in 1711.

Two Scottish regiments on the English establishment served in Spain and Portugal. George Macartney's campaigned for two years in Flanders before joining the expedition to Cadiz commanded by Richard Savage, fourth Earl Rivers, during October 1706. At the battle of Almanza in 1707 the battalion was obliged to surrender and Macartney was taken prisoner.[21] Lord Mark Kerr's was also broken at Almanza and both regiments had to return their cadres to Scotland to recruit but could only make good their numbers by accepting some English levies. Macartney's then proceeded to Flanders, where it undertook garrison duties until disbandment whilst Kerr's returned to Spain in 1710. It was present at the siege of Pratz del Rey in October 1711. The first battalion of the Scots Guards sailed to Spain in 1709 but was decimated at the battle of Brihuega in 1710. Some Scottish general officers commanded in Spain. Lord Portmore accompanied the duke of Schomberg's expedition to Portugal in 1704 and continued in Iberia, rising to become commander-in-chief in 1710 with the rank of full general. Appointment as governor of Gibraltar followed in 1713. Portmore was succeeded as commander-in-chief by the duke of Argyll who, assisted by Brigadier John Stewart of the Scots Guards, supervised the evacuation of the remaining forces in Spain to Minorca during the summer of 1712.[22]

Although the majority of the soldiers who left diaries and memoirs of Marlborough's wars were English and Irish, one Scottish soldier, Donald McBane, published an autobiography. It is, however, difficult to evaluate: racy memoir, picaresque novel or a mixture of truth and fiction after the manner of *Simplicissimus the German* and Defoe's *Memoirs of Captain George Carleton* and *Major Alexander Ramkins*? McBane, who frequently rose to the rank of sergeant but suffered equally frequent demotion, was not over-attentive to his military duties. Instead, he organised protection rackets, gambling schools and tented brothels in the camp whilst his 'wife' sold wine and beer. He also indulged in extortion and 'partizaning'.[23] Most of these activities appear to have been condoned, or at least connived at, by his officers. One of the highlights of McBane's rather fanciful memoirs occurred at Malplaquet when, apparently, he went into action with his baby shoved into a knapsack. Whatever the accuracy of his book, it does illuminate the generally easy relations between officers and men and the ways in which soldiers eked out a living when army pay was insufficient to keep a man from death by starvation. Aping their officers, soldiers duelled with swords over arcane details of honour and more mundane differences. Indeed, officers appear to have encouraged the settlement of quarrels with the sword rather than incur the attentions of the provost marshal and more formal disciplinary procedures.[24]

In wartime, the Scottish army was charged with defending the country against invasion. When, in 1705, the Chevalier de Saint-Pol Hécourt sailed from Dunkirk with six ships it was feared that he intended to land French soldiers in Scotland in order to foment rebellion. In fact, his target was an English merchant convoy which he successfully attacked at the cost of his own life, but the emergency revealed Scotland's military vulnerability: there were insufficient troops; the garrison companies in Edinburgh, Stirling and Dumbarton castles did not answer to the field command but only obeyed their own governors; and Maitland's battalion at Fort William and the three independent companies in the Highlands were too far removed from the central Lowlands and Borders to be of any use. On 5 February 1706 the master of the Scottish Ordnance Office and governor of Edinburgh castle, Lord Leven, made public the parlous state of the Scottish magazine. The anorexic condition of the Scots army was known to the Jacobites and encouraged the invasion attempt of 1708. The duke of Hamilton estimated that 30,000 Scots, besides highlanders, could have been raised for the Franco-Jacobite cause in the event of war with England. In addition, the invasion fleet of Claude, comte de Forbin, carried 6,000 French soldiers plus arms to equip 13,000 men.[25] Against these actual and potential numbers, the 2,000 available soldiers of the Scots army standing on Leith Sands would have appeared somewhat inadequate.

There was no defence against invasion and such a serious affront to British security could only be contained by retrieving troops from Flanders. Under Major-General William Cadogan and Brigadier Joseph Sabine, ten battalions – two of which were Scottish – departed from Ostend on 17 March 1708 in a convoy commanded by Rear Admiral John Baker. Despite persistent gales, the expedition battled into the mouth of the Tyne on 21 March and anchored under Tynemouth castle to await orders. The men had 'only the bare deck to lye upon, w[hi]ch hardship caused abundance of our men to bid adieu to the world'. Baker sailed for the Firth of Forth on 1 April and came into Leith Roads on the following afternoon but Admiral Sir George Byng had already chased Forbin's ships north towards Inverness whence they returned to France without landing a single soldier. Cadogan's battalions were sent back to Ostend on 17 April.

Yet a major battle would not have caused more casualties. John Marshall Deane records that

> While we lay on board we had a continual destruction in the foretop, the pox above board, the plague between decks, hell in the forecastle and the Devil at the helm . . . And so sharp weather that for one while I shall not care for any more voyages to the Northward.[26]

A plan to raise a mass Scottish militia was an immediate victim of 1708: Whitehall had no mind to arm potentially rebellious Scots.[27]

Maintenance of internal law and order was the second duty of the Scots army. In the Highlands, Maitland's battalion and the three independent infantry companies adopted a non-interventionist strategy, simply watching and relying upon the clans to police themselves with the assistance of bribes to the chiefs from Edinburgh. In the Lowlands, however, 2,000 men were expected to take a more active role in keeping the peace. The Scottish parliament did not confirm the Act of Settlement of 1701 and, during the final illness of William III in the following year, the earl of Nottingham observed that Scotland represented a chink in the national armour through which might slip James VIII and III, the 'Old Pretender'. The Scottish privy council recognised that this gap was wider than it might have been because Rowe's and Ferguson's battalions were embarked at Leith ready for Flanders and no steps had been taken to replace them. At its meeting on 11 March 1702, unaware that William had died on 8 March, the council delayed the departure of Rowe's and Ferguson's and put the whole Scots army on alert. These reinforcements were welcome, but Anne's succession was achieved without disorder or rebellion and the regiments were released to continue their journey to the Low Countries.

Because there had been a *de facto* British army since 1689 both English and Scottish military elites were, to some extent, more committed to the concept of a British state than the generality of the nobility and landed gentry. Although patronage and inducement played a part in determining pro-union attitudes, the Scottish officer-politicians were also influenced by wider issues concerning British security. They also appreciated that, when peace returned, their martial careers were more likely to prosper in a British army than within a narrowly Scottish establishment. One of the principal purposes of the 'garrison' armies maintained by many small European states, a category that included the royal standing armies in all three kingdoms after the Restoration, was to institute reservoirs of patronage from which the monarch might reward loyalty and services rendered. Government 'placemen', army officers prominent amongst them, in the Scottish parliament were expected to support the union and crown policies and most obliged, although additional douceurs were sometimes proffered. When Alexander Grant of Grant was made colonel of Lord Mar's regiment on 4 March 1706, he was presented with a number of blank commissions and took the opportunity to appoint his own relatives and associates: at least seven 'Grants' appeared in the regimental lists in 1706 and 1707. Such official nepotism guaranteed the future loyalty of both colonel and regiment. Lord Orkney was promoted to major-general in 1706, in recognition both of distinguished service in Flanders and of his canvassing on behalf of union. Lord Dalrymple's promotion to brigadier was probably in acknowledgement of the hard work of his father, the first earl of Stair, for the unionist cause, but Dalrymple quickly realised that the situation was ripe for exploitation and let it be known that the cost of his own vote was promotion to major-general. Promptly, he was made colonel of the Royal Scots Greys on 24 August 1706 followed by elevations to major-general in 1709, lieutenant-general in 1710 and full general in 1712. The duke of Argyll pointed out to Sidney, first earl of Godolphin, the Lord Treasurer in London, in August 1705 that certain placemen had recently voted against the government, amongst them Captain James Sandilands, seventh Baron Torphichen (Mar's Foot), and Lieutenant-Colonel William Cunningham, twelfth earl of Glencairn, governor of Dumbarton castle. Torphichen responded positively to a word of warning and voted for both the first article of union on 4 November 1706 and ratification of the treaty on 16 January 1707. Glencairn was more resistant and his eventual conformity cost £100. In December 1706 the earl of Mar complained about the voting record of Lieutenant-Colonel William Maxwell (Maitland's), who was subsequently made to realise the error of his ways. Six Scottish peers had previously served in either the Scottish or the English armies whilst twenty-seven were active commissioned officers, twenty-one of whom supported the union. Only two opposition lords were associated with the military. Of nineteen other army officers sitting in January 1707, all but one voted in favour of the union.[28]

The threat of intimidation was also important in swaying the Scottish political nation towards accepting union. The campaign of military pressure began in earnest on 17 July 1703, when Godolphin hinted to James Ogilvy, first earl of Seafield, then lord chancellor and a future treaty commissioner, that the alternative to union was war between Scotland and England, a warning repeated on 9 September 1705.[29]

Figure 12.4 David Melville, earl of Leven. Portrait by Sir John Baptiste de Medina, 1691. Leven was commander-in-chief in Scotland in 1707 and an enthusiastic promoter of the union of the parliaments.

Godolphin was intent on securing a Scottish commander-in-chief who possessed martial ability and sound political credentials and could be relied upon to support English concerns. The Scottish privy council expressed similar views and looked to the army leadership to suppress anti-union violence. General Ramsay, the commander-in-chief in Scotland, died on the afternoon of Sunday 2 September 1705 following a heavy drinking bout with William Douglas, earl of March, second son of the duke of Queensberry and captain of Edinburgh castle. Marlborough's initial thought was to put forward the best available soldier, Major-General Robert Murray (d. 1719) of the Scots Brigade but, on being informed that the earl of Leven had applied to Godolphin for the vacancy on the grounds that he was the senior major-general on the Scottish establishment, Marlborough began to appreciate the value of a more political appointment. Such a sensitive position, he mused, required a man who would 'entirely depend upon' Queen Anne. That ruled out Argyll, who had also expressed interest, because 'his temper is very warm and I should think he is too young to have that command'. On 25 October Marlborough recommended to Anne the appointment of Lord Leven, a sound, reliable Whig and avowed Hanoverian.[30]

Godolphin was in receipt of intelligence suggesting violent Scottish reactions to union. He informed Marlborough on 1 November 1706 that 'the mob is uneasy at the Union in Scotland and has been very unruly . . . they begin to find that it cannot be resisted but by tumult and open force'. Daniel Defoe, a principal informant, stated on 16 November that 15,000 Cameronians were busy training 'with arms and drums' and posed a potential danger to Glasgow. Godolphin, however, was sceptical and thought such menaces inchoate: provided that the business was hurried through the Scottish parliament troublemakers would be denied the necessary time to organise. Queensberry in Edinburgh could not afford such an Olympian view and requested that troops be advanced to the border. During November and December 1706 three Irish cavalry regiments, one of dragoons and an infantry battalion, a total of 2,000 men, marched into Ulster. In an emergency these troops would have embarked for Scotland – transports were ordered to stand by at Carrickfergus – but their principal task was to discourage sympathetic, anti-union demonstrations amongst the Scots-Irish. Despite the English army being heavily over-committed in Flanders and Spain and suffering a manpower crisis, troops were scraped together and deployed into the north of England towards the Scottish border. Colonel George Carpenter's regiment of dragoons moved to Leeds with a view to advancing on Edinburgh along the Great North Road, and the earl of Essex's dragoons took station in Lancaster ready to ride across Shap Fell towards Glasgow. Colonel John Livesay's infantry battalion, recently returned from the West Indies and thus considerably under strength, was posted to York. Stationed at Hull was the foot battalion of James Barry, fourth earl of Barrymore, which was ordered to push forward detachments to Richmond, Ripon, Bedale, Masham and Middleham in North Yorkshire. The Royal Horse Guards were stretched along the border from Alnwick to Cockermouth whilst the earl of Orrery's and Thomas Erle's battalions were also detailed into the north. In total, there were about 800 cavalry and 2,500 infantry under the operational command of Lieutenant-Colonel William Dobbins, the lieutenant-governor of Berwick-upon-Tweed, who was authorised to issue arms and ammunition from the Berwick magazine, should occasion arise. English troops wintering at Ghent were placed on alert too. The executive decision on whether to summon this assistance rested with Queensberry. Had he so decided then Dobbins would have supervised the march to the border whence the Edinburgh government would have assumed direct command. Naturally, these arrangements were secret and remained so: discovery by anti-unionists and Jacobites might have jeopardised the passage of the act. At the very least, there would have been demonstrations of a size and significance to dwarf the protests made in 1704 when the first earl of Stair's scheme to maintain the Scots army via a grant from the English Treasury had been uncovered.

These precautions proved unnecessary. Since the Restoration, riot control in Glasgow and Edinburgh had been performed by the militia and the town guards, the Scots army acting as a reserve of last resort. Scottish infantry was called in by Queensberry to contain and disperse threatening crowds in Edinburgh on 22 and 23 October 1706, and dragoons stood ready to intervene during the disturbances in Glasgow in late November and early December, but the town guard managed unaided to restore order. During the sitting of the union parliament Lord Leven concentrated the majority of the army close to Edinburgh and took the unprecedented step of marching the Scottish Life and Foot Guards along the High Street to Parliament Close and actually billeted some troops within the city precincts, an action without precedent during a parliamentary session. More serious trouble, which had been widely expected and predicted, never occurred. Atholl's 6,000 highlanders did not march on Edinburgh nor did the covenanters in Dumfries and Galloway cause trouble, partly because of the clandestine manoeuvrings of a network of government agents, spies and bribe-masters managed by Brevet Major James Cunningham (Royal Scots). Following union, and the attempted Jacobite landing the following year, Scotland's questionable loyalty caused the central Lowlands to be relatively heavily garrisoned.[31]

The earl of Mar blamed the peaceful outcome of union on the season of the year and bad weather. He may have been right but the fact that so many Scottish officers and soldiers were already serving in the English army, and thus effectively pre-committed to union, was also important. In addition, the majority of Scots on both the English and Scottish establishments were Whig and pro-union. For most, therefore, the union made little practical difference because the loyalty of the Scottish regiments to the Whitehall government was not in question and required scant realignment. When Lord Cadogan selected the ten battalions to go to Scotland in 1708, two were Scottish – the Royal Scots and the North British Fusiliers – there being no doubt about their allegiance to the new order. The pro-union stance of the Scots army and the absence of violence in both 1706–7 and 1708 enhanced the proud Scottish military tradition, which had been principally acquired not via the home establishment, but through distinguished service in the armies of continental Europe during the previous two centuries. Indeed, the transfer of Scottish military identity onto the broader British polity was to enhance and burnish that tradition through the unique Scottish contribution to Britain's wars of empire during the eighteenth century.[32]

From 1 May 1707 the Scots army was replaced by Her Majesty's Forces in Scotland, a regional command of the British army financed from London. There was a proposal in 1708 to revive a distinct Scottish establishment but it was impractical because there was no longer a Scottish Treasury from which to meet the costs. Also, Godolphin was anxious to remove all traces of Scotland as a discrete political and military entity so the words 'Scots' or 'Scottish' were erased from regimental titles. The Scots Life Guards went to London as the 4th Troop of Life Guards whilst the Scots Grenadier Guards, now the 2nd Troop of Horse Grenadier Guards, also travelled south.[33] Maitland's was reclassified in 1709 as a marine battalion but this was only an accounting device and the unit remained in garrison at Fort William. The Scots Dragoons were renamed the Royal North British Dragoons whilst the Scots Fusiliers re-emerged as the North British Fusiliers. Technically, the Test Acts of 1673 and 1678 now applied to Scottish regiments, and this would have affected the Cameronians, but a blind eye was turned. In 1708 the Scottish regiments were formally listed on the English establishment and their strengths commensurately increased. Something called a 'Scottish Establishment' – a handful of staff officers charged with administering the independent companies in the Highlands, the garrison companies at Fort William and in the castles at Edinburgh, Stirling and Dumbarton, and the Company of Gunners at Edinburgh – continued to exist for a few years after the union but was discontinued from the accession of George I in 1714.[34]

Notes

1. J. Childs, *The Army of Charles II* (London: Routledge and Kegan Paul, 1976), pp. 64, 199–203; J. Childs, *The Army, James II and the Glorious Revolution* (Manchester: Manchester University Press, 1980), pp. 4, 180, 182; J. Childs, *The British Army of William III, 1689-1702* (Manchester: Manchester University Press, 1987), pp. 4–33; K. M. Brown, 'From Scottish lords to British officers: State building, elite integration and the army in the seventeenth century', in N. MacDougall (ed.), *Scotland and War, AD 79-1918* (Edinburgh: John Donald, 1991), pp. 148–9. It should be noted that S. H. F. Johnston, 'The Scots army in the reign of Anne', *Transactions of the Royal Historical Society*, fifth series, vol. 3 (1953), pp. 1–21, pioneered the study of this topic.

2. C. Dalton, *George the First's Army, 1714-1727*, 2 vols (London: Eyre and Spottiswoode, 1910), vol. 1, pp. 48-54, 164-5.
3. *Calendar of State Papers Domestic, 1702-1703* [hereafter *CSPD*], ed. R. P. Mahaffy (London: HMSO, 1916), pp. 68-70; C. Dalton, *English Army Lists and Commission Registers, 1660-1714*, 6 vols (London: Eyre and Spottiswoode, 1892-1904, reprinted London: Francis Edwards, 1960), vol. 5, pp. 207-28; vol. 6, pp. 205-20.
4. Lord Hyndford was succeeded in the colonelcy by his son, James, Lord Carmichael, on 2 March 1706.
5. R. E. Scouller, *The Armies of Queen Anne* (Oxford: Oxford University Press, 1966), pp. 347-9.
6. A series of annual English Recruiting Acts, popularly known as 'Pressing Acts', began in 1704 (2 & 3 Anne c. 18). They provided the context for George Farquhar's play, *The Recruiting Officer*, first performed in 1706 at the Drury Lane Theatre, London.
7. Johnston, 'The Scots army', pp. 10-12; Scouller, *The Armies of Queen Anne*, p. 125.
8. A. Åberg, 'Scottish soldiers in the Swedish armies in the sixteenth and seventeenth centuries', in G. G. Simpson (ed.), *Scotland and Scandinavia, 800-1800* (Edinburgh: John Donald, 1990), pp. 90, 98; J. Berg and B. Lagercrantz, *Scots in Sweden* (Edinburgh: Royal Scottish Museum, 1962), pp. 49-50; A. Fletcher, *The Political Works of Andrew Fletcher Esq.* (London: n.p., 1737), pp. 89-91; D. Defoe, *An Essay at Removing National Prejudices against a Union with Scotland* (London: n.p., 1706), part I, pp. 27-8; B. P. Lenman, 'Militia, fencible men, and home defence, 1660-1797', in MacDougall (ed.), *Scotland and War*, pp. 185-6; Brown, 'From Scottish lords', p. 149; C. A. Whatley with D. J. Patrick, *The Scots and the Union* (Edinburgh: Edinburgh University Press, 2006), p. 113.
9. J. Childs, 'The Scottish Brigade in the service of the Dutch Republic, 1689-1782', *Documentatieblad Werkgroep Achttiende Eeuw*, vol. 16 (1984), pp. 59-61. The Scots Brigade was finally dissolved in 1782.
10. John Scot, Soldier, 'The Remembrance, or The Progress of a Regiment commanded by my Lord Portmore in the year 1701 and 1702, &c.', in *Papers Illustrating the History of the Scots Brigade in the Service of the United Netherlands, 1572-1782*, ed. J. Ferguson, 3 vols (Edinburgh: Scottish History Society, 1899-1901), vol. 3, p. 487.
11. H. H. E. Craster, 'Letters of the first Lord Orkney during Marlborough's campaigns', *English Historical Review*, vol. 19 (1904), pp. 319-20.
12. See the petition of Major-General George Lauder to the States General, 31 January 1708, in *Papers*, ed. Ferguson, vol. 2, pp. 80-3.
13. *Papers*, ed. Ferguson, vol. 2, pp. 3-105, 128-9; Childs, 'The Scottish

Brigade', pp. 66–70. See also *The Journal of John Gabriel Stedman*, ed. S. Thompson (London: Mitre Press, 1962).
14. *Papers*, ed. Ferguson, vol. 2, pp. 83, 87, 91.
15. Th. A. Fischer, *The Scots in Germany: Being a Contribution towards the History of the Scot Abroad* (Edinburgh: John Donald, 1982), pp. 118–19.
16. R. Holmes, *Marlborough: England's Fragile Genius* (London: Harper Press, 2008), pp. 273–4.
17. Craster, 'Letters of the first Lord Orkney', p. 315.
18. F. Taylor, *The Wars of Marlborough, 1702–1709*, 2 vols (Oxford: Basil Blackwell, 1921), vol. 2, p. 147.
19. Craster, 'Letters of the first Lord Orkney', p. 319.
20. *The Life and Diary of Lieut. Col. J. Blackader*, ed. A. Crichton (Edinburgh: H. S. Baynes, 1824), pp. 277, 314, 320, 330.
21. *Historical Manuscripts Commission* [hereafter *HMC*], *House of Lords MSS*, new series, vol. 7, 'Forces for Portugal', pp. 447–9; A. D. Francis, *The First Peninsular War, 1702–1713* (London: Ernest Benn, 1975), pp. 245, 316–19, 359; J. A. C. Hugill, *No Peace without Spain* (Oxford: Kensal Press, 1991), pp. 253, 342.
22. Johnston, 'The Scots army', p. 9.
23. 'Partizaning': groups of soldiers, often led by NCOs, were allowed to conduct small raids behind enemy lines to capture prisoners who were then held to ransom and their horses and field equipment sold. The proceeds, apart from an agreed percentage paid to the officer(s) who had granted permission, were divided amongst the participants. Less often, *ad hoc* bodies of adventurers and volunteers were assembled, commanded by 'officers' equipped with temporary commissions. 'Partizans' here resembled naval privateers issued with 'letters of marque'. A 'partizan' might also refer to a scout or guide, usually not a member of regular forces, who claimed a particular knowledge of a locality or region. See, P. Drake, *The Memoirs of Captain Peter Drake, Containing an Account of Many Strange and Surprising Events &c.*, 2 vols (Dublin: S. Powell, 1755), vol. 1, pp. 68–70; G. Satterfield, *Princes, Posts and Partisans: The Army of Louis XIV and Partisan Warfare in the Netherlands, 1673–1678* (Leiden: Brill, 2003), pp. 102–14.
24. D. McBane, *The Expert Sword-Man's Companion: or the True Art of Self-Defence. With an Account of the Authors Life and his Transactions during the Wars with France. To which is Annexed the Art of the Gunnerie* (Glasgow: n.p., 1728). See also I. A. Morrison, 'Survival skills: An enterprising Highlander in the Low Countries with Marlborough', in G. G. Simpson (ed.), *The Scottish Soldier Abroad, 1247–1967* (Edinburgh: John Donald, 1992), pp. 81–96; S. Anglo, *The Martial Arts of Renaissance Europe* (New Haven, CT and London: Yale University Press, 2000).

25. *The Correspondence of Colonel Nathaniel Hooke*, ed. W. D. Macray, 2 vols (Edinburgh: Roxburghe Club, 1870-1), vol. 1, pp. 393-8.
26. J. M. Deane, *A Journal of Marlborough's Campaigns during the War of the Spanish Succession, 1704-1711*, ed. D. G. Chandler (London: Society for Army Historical Research, 1984), special publication no. 12, pp. 53-5; J. S. Gibson, *Playing the Scottish Card: The Franco-Jacobite Invasion of 1708* (Edinburgh: Edinburgh University Press, 1988), pp. 106-31; *The Marlborough-Godolphin Correspondence*, ed. H. L. Snyder, 3 vols (Oxford: Oxford University Press, 1975), vol. 1, pp. 500, 504; vol. 2, p. 739.
27. J. Robertson, *The Scottish Enlightenment and the Militia Issue* (Edinburgh: John Donald, 1985), pp. 50-3.
28. P. W. J. Riley, *The Union of England and Scotland* (Manchester: Manchester University Press, 1978), pp. 327, 335; Dalton, *English Army Lists*, vol. 5, p. 223, vol. 6, pp. 214-15; Brown, 'From Scottish lords', pp. 151-2.
29. HMC, *14th Report, Appendix Part III*, p. 198; George Baillie of Jerviswood, *Correspondence, 1702-1708* (Edinburgh: Bannatyne Club, 1842), pp. 122-3.
30. *Marlborough-Godolphin Correspondence*, ed. Snyder, vol. 1, pp. 500, 504, vol. 2, p. 739; Johnston, 'The Scots army', pp. 15-17.
31. HMC, *Mar and Kellie MSS*, pp. 353, 356; *Marlborough-Godolphin Correspondence*, ed. Snyder, vol. 2, p. 727; Riley, *The Union*, pp. 284-5; Dalton, *English Army Lists*, vol. 5, p. 166; K. Bowie, *Scottish Public Opinion and the Anglo-Scottish Union, 1699-1707* (Woodbridge: Boydell and Brewer, 2007), pp. 62-3, 142-3, 150-2; Scouller, *The Armies of Queen Anne*, pp. 165-6; *CSPD*, pp. 279-80; HMC, *Portland MSS*, vol. 4, pp. 341, 352.
32. Johnston, 'The Scots army', pp. 15-21; D. Horsbroch, '"Tae see oursels as ithers see us": Scottish military identity from the Covenant to Victoria, 1637-1837', in S. Murdoch and A. MacKillop (eds), *Fighting for Identity: Scottish Military Experience, c. 1550-1900* (Leiden: Brill, 2002), pp. 105-9, 114-19. See also *Military Governors and Imperial Frontiers, c. 1600-1800*, ed. A. Mackillop and S. Murdoch (Leiden: Brill, 2003).
33. B. White-Spunner, *Horse Guards* (London: Macmillan, 2006), p. 164.
34. Dalton, *George the First's Army*, vol. 1, pp. 235-7, vol. 2, p. 347.

13

The Jacobite Wars, 1708–46

CHRISTOPHER DUFFY

The Jacobites are elusive, and not just in the sense of the people that the duke of Cumberland's redcoats sought to hunt down in the Highlands after the battle of Culloden in 1746. As a movement that endured for generations, and assumed many varied forms, Jacobitism is something that must be redefined constantly in terms of time and place.[1]

The term 'Jacobite' derives from 'Jacobus', the latinised form of 'James', and was first applied to the supporters of King James VII of Scotland and II of England, who fled from England in 1688 in the face of opposing Protestant magnates and an invading Dutch army headed by Prince William of Orange. This 'Glorious Revolution' was virtually bloodless in the English perspective, but it precipitated a long and costly British civil war that terminated on the mainland of Scotland when the last remaining Jacobite force of any size was surprised and beaten on the Haughs of Cromdale on 1 May 1690. The final Jacobite refuge, the Bass Rock in the Firth of Forth, surrendered on 18 April 1694.

Over the following decades the help for the Jacobite cause from abroad (effectively from France and Spain, with expressions of support from Sweden and Prussia) was fitful, and no single group of Jacobites, and not even 'Bonnie Prince Charlie' himself, embraced what might be termed the whole of the Jacobite agenda. Catholics remained a minority in the movement, which took in a number of Scottish Presbyterians and found the bedrock of its support in various Scottish and English forms of Protestant Episcopalians. Many Jacobites, like many adherents of the established government, were guided simply by considerations of personal or local advantage.

When all of this is borne in mind, it is fair to ask why Jacobitism has come to be associated so closely with Scotland. One reason is that public perceptions even now are coloured by romantic notions, dating from the 1820s, which link Jacobitism exclusively with the Scottish Highlands. The misunderstanding is natural, for the Jacobite forces of the 'Forty-Five, lowlanders as well as highlanders, were termed the 'Highland army', and the tartan was adopted as a unifying symbol for the Jacobite cause throughout the British Isles. Only in Scotland, moreover, did it remain possible for Jacobitism to generate significant armed force. The region was geographically remote from the government's seat of power in southern England, yet accessible (with luck and a fair wind) to seaborne assistance to the Jacobites from abroad. Scotland also retained forms of land tenure, and clan and feudal obedience, which allowed local Jacobite elites to summon up powerful followings in a way that was beyond their counterparts in England.

Scotland, lastly, encapsulated more forms of Jacobitism than did any other part of Britain, and Scottish Jacobitism gained coherence by greater or lesser degrees of resentment against the parliamentary union of the two kingdoms, which came into force on 1 May 1707. Many Scots began to conceive of the dispossessed Scottish dynasty of Stuart as embodying their hopes of regaining independence. One of the concessions to Scottish particularism, the recognition of Presbyterianism as the Church of Scotland by Law Established, actually hardened the opposition of the Episcopalian gentry and communities of the eastern coastlands.

The expedition of 1708

The exiled James II died in 1701, and the Jacobite legitimists now looked for leadership to his son James Francis Edward, as King James VIII of Scotland and III of England, later known to his enemies as 'The Old Pretender'. The Stuart court had found refuge in France, which was locked in the War of the Spanish Succession against a coalition led by Britain and Habsburg Austria. Between 1705 and 1707 the French sustained a number of defeats in the theatres of war in continental Europe, and in his frustration Louis XIV looked to the Jacobites to help him to make trouble for the British at home. His agent in Scotland, Colonel Nathaniel Hooke, assured him that 30,000 Scots would spring to arms once James Francis Edward came ashore with a French expeditionary force.[2]

The springboard of the invasion was Dunkirk, where the comte de Gacé assembled 5,000 French troops, to be conveyed by transports and warships under the command of Admiral Forbin, an impatient individual who had little confidence in the enterprise. After an acrimonious delay the expedition set sail on 6 March 1708. A favourable turn of wind enabled Forbin to evade the British blockading squadron and he reached the coast of Fife on the 12th of that month. A small party landed at Pittenweem, but no proper contact could be established with sympathisers on shore, and Forbin took alarm when British warships hove into view. He upped anchor and sailed north up the coast, ignoring the pleas of James Francis Edward to be put ashore by the castle of Slains to meet the earl of Erroll, his principal supporter. By the end of the month the expedition was back in France without a blow having been struck in Scotland.

Described in these terms, the enterprise of 1708 has every appearance of being a fiasco. It was not so regarded by the British authorities, for the infant union had undergone an almost immediate challenge and the French had managed to convey a respectable invasion force to the east coast of undefended Scotland. From July of that year Captain Theodore Dury began a major programme of military construction that embraced new barracks and officers' accommodation at Edinburgh castle, a substantial new barrack block at Fort William in Lochaber and an elaborate front of fortification in the modern bastion style at the entrance to Stirling castle.

The 'Fifteen

Out of the four Jacobite episodes under review, the rising of 1715–16 was the only one that was totally devoid of foreign help, and yet it commanded by far the widest base of support in Britain. All the celebrated clans of the 'Forty-Five were to take part, as well as some who held back on that occasion, together with the lairds and magnates of the lands between the firths of Moray and Tay, and the fishing and trading towns of the coast. There was common cause, if little or no concert, with the like-minded Viscount Kenmure and his companions in south-west Scotland, the feudal nobility of Northumberland, the Catholics of Lancashire, the conservative gentry of south-west England and the riotously inclined proletarian Jacobites of Newcastle and the English West Midlands.[3]

In England, at least, Jacobite militancy was for a time muted by the knowledge that the reigning queen, Anne (r. 1702–14), was a daughter of James II. A Tory ministry came into office in 1710 and hopes arose among some of its party that in spite of the Act of Settlement (1701), which lodged the succession in the heirs of the electress of Hanover, something might still be worked out in favour of James Francis Edward. Yet divisions and hesitations among the

Figure 13.1 John Erskine, earl of Mar, after a contemporary portrait by Sir Godfrey Kneller. Mar led the Jacobite rising of 1715.

Tories enabled the Whigs (committed supporters of the legacy of the Glorious Revolution) to place Elector George of Hanover on the throne after Queen Anne died in 1714. The new King George I proved to be even more foreign than had been expected, and the Tories were shocked to find that they were being excluded from office almost altogether. In their dismay a number of them turned to active Jacobitism.

The discontents north of the border found an unlikely channel in John Erskine, earl of Mar. He had been one of the promoters of the union and had been appointed to the secretaryship for Scotland in 1713. He now sought to make his mark with the new regime, but King George made it brutally clear that he had no use for his services. Mar returned to his native Deeside, where he brought together gatherings of Jacobite supporters. At Braemar on 6 September 1715 he signified the start of the rising in Scotland by proclaiming James Francis Edward as the rightful king of Scotland, England and Ireland. The task of maintaining the Protestant succession lay in the hands of Lieutenant-General John Campbell, second duke of Argyll, who took up the post of commander-in-chief in Scotland on 14 September.

The already slender 'wasp's waist' of Scotland, between the firths of

Clyde and Forth, was narrowed further by high grounds and marshes, and the effect was to confine the land passage between the north and south of Scotland to a narrow corridor by Stirling, some of it lying literally under the guns of the castle. Seeking to break the deadlock, the earl of Mar detached William Mackintosh of Borlum in a strategic outflanking move across the Firth of Forth. 'Old Borlum' joined the Jacobites of the Borders and Northumberland at Kelso and, under pressure from the English leader Thomas Forster, he committed the joint force to an invasion of England. The march progressed almost unopposed as far as Preston, where the forces of the government converged with unexpected speed. On 13 November the Jacobites beat off a first attack on their barricades at Preston, but the odds were turning against them and their morale gave way. Although some defenders succeeded in slipping away, Forster surrendered the remaining 1,485 officers and men unconditionally on 14 November, which exposed them to the vengeance of the government as captured rebels.

Meanwhile Argyll and Mar were in confrontation between Perth and Stirling. Mar's Jacobites grew to some 9,000 troops by contingents from the great estates of the earls of Seaforth and Huntly, and by Major-General Gordon of Auchintoul who arrived with clansmen from the west. On 11 November 1715 Mar finally advanced on Stirling. Argyll moved to meet him with some 3,700 troops, which was all he could bring together. On the 13th the two forces met in a ragged encounter battle on the high ground of Sheriffmuir to the north-east of Dunblane. The combat in itself was indecisive, for the Jacobites forced back Argyll's left wing, but fled before his right. The losses of the two sides cannot be established with any certainty, but the outcome was clearly to the advantage of Argyll, for the Jacobites simply fell back to their quarters in Strathearn and made no further attempt to force their way through the narrows at Stirling.

Argyll was now joined by the troops that were set free by the victory at Preston, and by the hired Dutch and Swiss troops who were brought from the continent by the energetic and uncompromising Lieutenant-General William Cadogan. On their side the Jacobites were weakened by the departure of the earls of Seaforth and Huntly to defend their lands against the earl of Sutherland. It was true that Prince James Francis Edward landed at Peterhead on 22 December and reached Perth on 9 January 1716, but he brought nothing beyond his person, for the French regent Orléans was adamant that he would not put his peace with Britain at any risk.

In the New Year Argyll launched reconnaissances in force from Stirling and towards the end of January the Jacobites set fire to the towns and villages of Strathearn, seeking to deny shelter to Argyll if he took the risk of opening the campaign in the depths of winter. Argyll was undeterred. He got his men on the move on 27 January and the resolve of the Jacobites at once collapsed. They evacuated Perth on the 31st and scuttled back through the eastern coastlands. They reached Dundee on 1 February and two days later arrived at Montrose, from where the prince and the earl of Mar took ship for France on the 4th.

The abandoned army, now numbering fewer than 4,000 men, continued its retreat. Argyll was ready to accept the surrender of individual Jacobites and release them on parole, in defiance of the instructions from London, and it seemed to Cadogan that the duke always contrived to be one or two marches behind the rebels. The unconvincing pursuit came to an end at Aberdeen on 8 February. The remaining Jacobite forces continued on their way to Ruthven in Badenoch, from where they dispersed on the 15th. The Jacobite army as such had ceased to exist. Argyll was succeeded in command by Cadogan, who in the spring launched a final offensive into the western Highlands. All resistance came to an end in May, except on the part of the defiant MacKenzies.

Leadership and forces

The 'Fifteen was, in the words of Daniel Szechi, 'a much dowdier bird' than the 'Forty-Five, with its romantic connotations, but still 'full of drama and potential'.[4] All told the number of Scots who bore arms in the Jacobite cause reached 20,000, which was 'certainly the largest number ever mobilised in any of their risings in Scotland'.[5] Added to these were the English who rose, or were ready to rise, in the Jacobite cause.

The question arises as to why the 'Fifteen turned out to be much less of a threat to the regime in London than the more narrowly based 'Forty-Five. There is a first clue in the characteristic way in which the Jacobites of the 'Fifteen formed, which was by an amoeba-like drifting together of elements rather than by purposeful concentration. The decision-making of the Jacobites was typically slow. The root cause of the failings may thus be traced to the nature of the rising itself, which sprang from numerous and diverse local initiatives. It was unfortunate for the Jacobites that the earl of Mar was essentially a plotter and opportunist and that Thomas Forster's main qualification as leader of the Northumberland Jacobites was that he was a Protestant, and therefore deemed to be more acceptable among the

English communities than was James Radcliffe, the Catholic earl of Derwentwater.

There was undeniable strength in the lower echelons of command. 'Old Borlum' was tough, intelligent and enterprising, and he helped to make up for some of Forster's deficiencies during their joint invasion of north-west England. Mar's own circle of officers took in Lieutenant-Colonel William Clephane (who had been a major in the British service), the former Dutch major-generals George Hamilton and Alexander Gordon of Auchintoul, and two young brothers, George Keith, the tenth hereditary Earl Marischal of Scotland, and James Keith. In their later careers the latter two both entered the Prussian service and Frederick the Great valued them highly both as professionals and as men. James was killed as a Prussian field marshal at Hochkirch in 1758, and a painting of his funeral cortege hangs in the university in Old Aberdeen.

What was lacking was a leader who combined demonstrable talent with hereditary authority. 'The Old Pretender' came on the scene only in December 1715, and even then his coming did not amount to much. His illegitimate half-brother, James Fitz-James, duke of Berwick-upon-Tweed, was of a different order entirely, being a marshal of France and one of the leading soldiers of his generation. He was appointed captain-general of the Jacobite forces on 13 October 1715. He sought leave to travel to Scotland, but was forbidden by the duke of Orléans, the French regent, who was determined to observe the peace with Britain. Berwick felt bound to obey, for he was a serving French officer, but James Francis Edward never forgave him.

Among the regular government forces, Scots elements comprised about 1,000 troops, along with shifting populations of militia, bands of zealots and other local volunteers, bodies of horse raised by the Whig gentry, and roughly 3,000 highlanders from the Campbells, Grants, Frasers and northern clans. It has been claimed that about 9,000 Scots took an active part on the side of the government, which was much less than the 20,000 combatants of the Scottish Jacobites, but together they amounted to about 12 per cent of the adult male population of Scotland. 'If we throw in women and children who saw their husbands, fathers, brothers and sons taken off to fight (sometimes never to return), or witnessed the passage and/or casual depredations of the marching armies,' writes Daniel Szechi, 'the lives touched in Scotland by the rising may have been in the region of 50 per cent of the population.'[6]

Regarded as a whole, the leadership of the government's forces in the 'Fifteen shows up well. Major-General George Wade[7] acted energetically to crush the centre of the plotting of the south-west English Jacobites in Bath. Another Protestant Anglo-Irishman, Cadogan, brought to the 'Fifteen his experience as chief of staff to John Churchill, the duke of Marlborough. As we have seen, Cadogan was chosen to convey the reinforcement of 6,000 Dutch and Swiss from the continent and, like Cumberland in 1746, he had little regard for Scottish sensibilities when it was a question of bringing the rising to an end.

Cadogan arrived with his Dutchmen and Switzers after the balance had already been turned in favour of the government by his old rival Argyll, who was ruthlessly self-aggrandising, to the degree that he had demanded and gained from London an English peerage and promotion to major-general as his price for promoting the union. He advanced to lieutenant-general in 1709, led the British contingent in Catalonia in 1711 and 1712, and as commander-in-chief in Scotland, bore the prime responsibility of confronting the great rising of 1715. He was on bad terms with Cadogan, and his grandiose style alienated him from his own second-in-command, Major-General Joseph Wightman, which adds to posterity's generally unfavourable view of his character and military abilities. Argyll nevertheless displayed sound strategic instincts, together with a redeeming awareness of a wider Scottish society independent of the allegiances of the moment. To him, the Jacobites were wayward neighbours with whom he had to learn to live over the long term.

Consequences

The captured English Jacobites, and the Scots taken with them, were treated severely, as was justified by the letter of the law. 'Old Borlum' escaped from Newgate Prison, but Kenmure and Derwentwater were among the forty who were executed, and the confiscation of the latter's great estates was a blow from which Jacobitism in Northumberland never fully recovered. About 640 of the lesser prisoners extended their lives only by consigning themselves to labour in North America as indentured servants.

In contrast, the Jacobites in Scotland escaped very lightly indeed. Most of the leaders had got away in good time from the west coast. The single execution was that of a soldier who had been implicated in a plot to seize Edinburgh castle, and the prisoners, who numbered fewer than eighty, were finally released without having come to trial. Large-scale confiscations of rebel land were certainly decreed, but were mostly frustrated by legal expedients and the goodwill of Whig neighbours, who were brought up on Scottish traditions of mutual help, reinforced by the knowledge that fortune might one day turn in favour of the Jacobites.

It is a moot point whether the leniency did or did not favour the survival of militant Jacobitism in Scotland. There were many committed Jacobites who felt obliged for their freedom and property to their Whig kin, friends and neighbours, and for that reason held back from 'coming out' in the 'Forty-Five.[8] Conversely the Highland clan society remained intact, together with its military potential, and irredeemably Jacobite magistrates were still entrenched in the local administration.[9] The duke of Cumberland was convinced that the evil of Jacobite rebellion had not been properly addressed and in 1746 he was to enforce a solution of a permanent kind.

The expedition of 1719

The 'Fifteen, for all its shortcomings, had been something of a general British rising. After it had failed, James Francis Edward had to look once more to foreign support, which proved to be a disillusioning process. His court in exile was hounded from one refuge to another, under pressure from the British government, while hopes of Swedish intervention rested on nothing more than contacts with individual officials.[10]

Quite unexpectedly, James Butler, duke of Ormonde, found himself in the position of being able to mastermind a projected invasion of Britain. He had been a late convert to the cause. During Anne's last years he had been captain-general of the British army, no less, but after George I came to the throne Ormonde became one of those Tories who were treated as virtual public enemies. The opportunity for Ormonde and the exiled Jacobite leaders came with one of those sudden revivals of energy and ambition that overtook Spain in the eighteenth century. The driving force in Spanish politics was Queen Elisabeth Farnese, whose dynastic aims brought Spain into conflict with Britain and Austria. Frustrated in the Mediterranean by the British fleet, she found in Ormonde and the Jacobites her instruments of revenge.

Ormonde devised a two-pronged strategy, whereby the main blow would be struck by an expeditionary force of 5,000 Spanish troops who would sail from Cadiz, pick up James Francis Edward and reinforcements at Corunna, and sail on to England, there to land and thrust 15,000 muskets into the hands of Jacobite militants. Purely as a diversion, Keith, the Earl Marischal, was to make for western

Scotland with two frigates bearing some 300 Spanish infantry and a further 2,000 muskets.

Ormonde's expedition took to sea early in March 1719 but ran into stormy weather and scattered. Only the remnants got into Corunna. There was no possibility of putting the force together again and so Ormonde (like Marshal Berwick in the 'Fifteen), was destined to remain one of those Jacobite commanders who might-have-been. On 8 March the young George Keith had sailed from Passages (the port of San Sebastian) with his two frigates and the 307 white-coated infantry of the regiment of Don Pedro de Castro. Arriving safely in Stornoway harbour in Lewis, the force was joined on the 24th by a vessel that had set out surreptitiously from Le Havre, bearing a number of Scottish notables. The newcomers included men of weight in their localities, notably Campbell of Glendaruel, John Cameron as acting chief of Clan Cameron, the earl of Seaforth (chief of the unsubdued MacKenzies) and the marquis of Tullibardine, who was the dispossessed Jacobite heir of the duke of Atholl.

The newcomers brought with them a fatal dissension. Contrary winds, together with disputes about authority and strategy, delayed the landing on the Scottish mainland, on the shores of Loch Alsh, until 13 April. Further arguments gave time for a powerful little squadron of the Royal Navy to cut off all communication by sea and capture the castle of Eilean Donan, together with its Spanish garrison and its large store of ammunition.

The expedition now depended entirely on whatever forces could be collected from the western clans. Contingents were brought in by Lord George Murray,[11] John Cameron of Lochiel, Rob Roy and, most significantly, by Seaforth, who returned on 7 June with some 500 of his followers from the lands of the MacKenzies, which brought the total force to about 250 Spaniards and rather more than 1,000 Scots. That was to be the limit, for news of the failure of Ormonde's invasion had spread through Scotland, which deterred further recruiting in the Highlands and ruled out altogether any support from the Lowland Jacobites.

The British authorities, put on their guard by warnings from the French government, were better primed to counter the threat than in 1708 or 1715, or indeed than they were to be in 1745. Military affairs in Scotland were under the direction of Major-General Joseph Wightman, who was one of the best horses in the British stable. He had had to take second place to Argyll in the 'Fifteen, but he had done very well at Sheriffmuir and now in 1719 acted energetically to deal with the Spanish and the Jacobites who had shown their noses in the far west. The total numbers available to Wightman in June are difficult to establish, but his returns for July show three small regiments of dragoons and six regiments of foot, making a total of 3,120 of all ranks, exclusive of Dutch auxiliaries.

Wightman reinforced the garrison of Inverness in good time and for the present expedition assembled some 120 dragoons, 850 foot, 130 highlanders from the northern Whig clans of Monro and MacKay, the Dutch regiment of Huffel and four companies of that of Amerongen. He took with him four light 'coehorn' mortars, a type of piece ideally suited for operations in the Highlands.

The dragoons, the redcoats, the Dutch, the highlanders and the mortars were all brought into play by Wightman in the hot little action of 10 June 1719, when he evicted the Jacobites and Spanish from their position at the narrows of Glenshiel. Twenty-one of Wightman's men were killed and 121 wounded, and the Jacobite losses were probably of the same order. The Jacobite leaders nevertheless recognised that they could no longer hold their men together and they accordingly told the highlanders to disperse, while the Spanish remained to surrender the following day. In Scotland there was no pursuit or repression such as was to follow on Culloden in 1746. The Jacobite leaders escaped, and Wightman was content to burn houses in Seaforth's country.

Scots, forts and roads: instruments of government control between 1716 and 1745

Commissioners had been appointed to manage the forfeiture of the estates of the 'traitors' after the 'Fifteen. The confiscations certainly helped to break the back of Jacobitism in the north-east of England, but in Scotland their work was frustrated by local solidarity, the wit of lawyers and obstruction on the part of the superior civil court, the Court of Session. That could not have been reasonably foreseen by the government in London. Entirely predictable, however, was the debacle that attended the Disarming Act of 1716, which required the highlanders to surrender their weapons. The hardline Jacobites and the thieves handed in a few rusty arms as a token, while the clans of the Whig chiefs complied loyally and were to find themselves at a severe disadvantage when they were overtaken by the new rising in the late summer of 1745.[12]

The basic problems had not been addressed, as was pointed out by the charismatic but totally unscrupulous Simon Fraser of Lovat, the chief of the Frasers. In 1724 it suited him to draw up a memorandum 'concerning the State of the Highlands', in which he drew attention to the deplorable habits of the highlanders, who were sustained in their ignorance and their violent ways by their chiefs. It would be fitting, argued Lovat, to police the Highlands by reviving the Independent Companies (of which more later), and to load good men like himself with offices and distinctions.

King George I commissioned one of his most reliable and tough-minded generals to look into the matter. As an heir of the Cromwellian land settlement in Ireland, Lieutenant-General George Wade was in the habit of exercising authority over an alien and resentful native population. Another formative experience was the British expedition to the rugged island of Minorca in 1708, which brought home to him the importance of good communications.

Wade travelled to Scotland and found that Lovat's analysis was true in substance. He recommended an updating of the system of fortifications, the establishment of a local judiciary and (with some reservations) the revival of the Highland Independent Companies in the style recommended by Lovat. He was aware that William III had made a first experiment in companies of this kind, but that they had been disbanded in 1717 on grounds of corruption.

The new Independent Companies were raised by virtue of a warrant of May 1725. They were set to work searching for arms and Catholic priests, suppressing 'blackmail' (protection money to buy off cattle thieves) and quelling disorder among the clans. As superior officers, Lovat and other notables indulged the patronage that was now at their disposal, while clan gentlemen and tacksmen gained opportunity for employment and local advantage. Service even in the ranks was considered an honour, and many of the private soldiers were genuine 'gentleman rankers'. Estimates of the combined strength of the six companies vary from 324 to 555, not least because company commanders were given to keeping 'ghost' soldiers on their books and pocketing their pay, and Lovat's corruption became so outrageous that he had to be relieved of the command of his company. The companies were already becoming known as 'the Black Watch' (*Am Freicheadan Dubh*), which has been ascribed to the supposedly dark hues of their tartan.

The distinctly qualified success of the Independent Companies did not deter the respected lord advocate of Scotland, Duncan Forbes of Culloden, from proposing in 1738 that the government should recruit up to five full regiments of highlanders for service in the British army. The plan in its original form was altogether too ambitious, but in 1739, when war was looming with Spain, Walpole's government decided to augment the number of companies to ten and to incorporate them as a regiment. The body was entrusted through a warrant of 25 October to John earl of Crawford and Lindsay, and became known as 'Crawford's Highland Regiment', the first of a complicated series of designations. With the coming of new colonels it was transformed into 'Sempill's' on 14 January 1741, then to 'Murray's' on 25 April 1745, the name by which it was known at the time of the great rising. In order of seniority it was ranked originally as the 43rd of Foot, and with the formal numbering of regiments it settled down in 1751 as the '42nd Highland Regiment of Foot'.

The government was now looking to the Highlands as a source of manpower to serve British interests wherever they might be engaged, and the Black Watch, under its various titles, was the first Scottish regiment of its kind, which makes it a landmark in Scottish military history. The highlanders had joined on condition of serving only in Scotland, but in the early spring of 1743 they were ordered to London on the pretext that they were to be reviewed by King George II. This was already a betrayal of the culture of trust that existed between the clansmen and their traditional superiors, for the intention was to ship them to service in Flanders. The rumour spread that the destination was the fever-ridden West Indies, and in a celebrated mutiny more than 100 men broke away and tried to escape to Scotland. They were overhauled and brought back for trial.

On 18 July 1743 three of the mutineers were shot in the Tower of London as an example (Private Farquharson Shaw from Lochaber and the Corporals Samuel and Malcolm MacPherson from Badenoch). All the others were transported to hard labour in the Mediterranean garrisons, Georgia or the West Indies, and many of these unfortunates also hailed from traditional Jacobite areas. Afterwards the loyalties of the Black Watch were never again put to such a direct test. As an integral part of the army the regiment fought well at Fontenoy in May 1745 and was shipped back with the rest in the crisis of the 'Forty-Five, but deployed exclusively for the defence of south-east England. By that time a second Highland regiment, Loudoun's 64th, had just come into being. It was more avowedly Whiggish than the Black Watch, being drawn heavily from 'well-affected' clans, but its story must be held over until a little later, as it was linked so directly with that of the great rising.

The notion of nailing down the Highlands by fortified bases formed an integral part of Wade's proposals in 1725. He had found that the Cromwellian citadels of the 1650s were all decayed and out of commission, as well as being mostly in the wrong places. A desultory

Figure 13.2 Corporal Malcolm MacPherson, executed at the Tower of London, 18 July 1743.

programme of barrack building had extended from 1717 to 1724, and established defensible posts at Glenelg at the short crossing to the Isle of Skye, at remote Inversnaid in MacGregor country near Loch Lomond, at Kilcumein (Kiliwhimen) near the head of Loch Ness and at Ruthven in Badenoch in upper Strathspey.

Wade was unimpressed and he fastened on the need to secure the axis of the Great Glen. The one well-sited and strong work available to him was the bastioned Fort William in the 'disaffected' country of Lochaber. Towards the middle of the glen the four-bastioned Fort Augustus was built close to Kilcumein barracks but on the actual shore of Loch Ness. Inverness at the north-east end of the Great Glen was overlooked by Fort George (not to be confused with the later Fort George on Ardersier Point). The hill site was cramped and unstable, but rather than begin afresh Wade had the old tower house encased in a tight circuit of bastioned works. Away from the Highlands the useful castle of Dumbarton on the Firth of Clyde was furnished with a neat bastion (King George's Battery), and at the same time a zig-zag wall with distinctive pepper-pot sentry boxes was cast around the western crags of Edinburgh castle.

'Marshal Wade' is remembered above all for his road building, even though it did not feature in his original reports, and he did not become a field marshal until 1743, three years after he laid down his command in Scotland, and longer still after the work under his personal supervision was complete. By ambitious blasting and bridging Wade established a road along the length of the Great Glen, from Fort William to Inverness. Another important route (corresponding with the A9) ran from Dunkeld over the dreary Drumochter Pass to Ruthven, and thence over the Slochd Pass to Inverness. A side route out to the west followed an ancient track by way of the Sma' Glen, while a branch from the 'A9' climbed the Corrieyairack Pass by a zig-zag road (one of Wade's proudest achievements) and descended to the Great Glen near Fort Augustus.

Taken together, Wade's various activities were comprehensive and ingenious, but they did not confront the fundamental issues of law and order, which demanded a powerful living military presence in the Highlands.

The 'Forty-Five

The most celebrated of all the Jacobite risings was launched when the cause appeared to be at a low ebb.[13] Hostilities had broken out between France and Hanoverian Britain in 1743, but a scheme for a French invasion of south-east England was abandoned early in 1744 and James Francis Edward could no longer be counted as an active campaigner for a Jacobite restoration. The torch had been taken up by his elder son and heir, Prince Charles Edward Stuart (b. 1720),[14] who was aware that the Jacobite supporters in Britain would be willing to 'come out' only if they could be assured of overt French intervention. His dilemma was that such an invasion would be unlikely as long as he could not present King Louis XV and his ministers with demonstrable success in a new rising.[15]

In his dilemma Prince Charles turned not to the contacts he had long cultivated among the Jacobites of Scotland, England and Wales, but to the prosperous Irish Catholic merchant community in France. The prince and the Irishmen fitted out a little expedition with the 'deniable' connivance of some of the French authorities and on 4 July their two ships met off the coast of Brittany and sailed together for Scotland. The enterprise already amounted to very much less than an invasion and on 9 July it lost all its fighting capacity when it encountered the sixty-four-gun HMS *Lion* to the west of the Lizard. The *Elisabeth*, the larger of the two vessels, was so badly mauled that she had to put back to France with her cargo of weapons and 700 regular troops of the Irish Brigade in the French service. The privateer *Doutelle* sailed on alone and on 25 July Charles reached the western Scottish mainland at Arisaig with his seven companions, none of them of particular credit in the Highlands.

Deploying all his powers of persuasion, together with assurances (unfounded though they mostly were) of support from France and the English Jacobites, the prince was able to win over figures of such stature as Donald Cameron Younger of Lochiel, who was the leading chief of Lochaber,[16] and the respected eastern laird John Gordon of Glenbucket. Charles was aided by the remoteness of the region of Arisaig, and over the longer term by the fact that the rising of 1745 was growing by increments from this one tiny source, unlike the much more widespread 'Fifteen which never gained cohesion.

From Arisaig Charles took a roundabout route to the rallying point of his promised supporters in Glenfinnan. The glen was disturbingly quiet when he arrived on 19 August, but over the following hours the successive arrivals of the MacDonalds, the Camerons and their septs, and the Keppoch MacDonells gave the prince at least 1,100 men and the beginning of an insurrection. Gathering strength all the time Charles marched inland, circumvented Fort William and made for Wade's new route over the Corrieyairack Pass.

The government's forces in Scotland at this time amounted to the garrisons of the strong points and 4,000 troops of generally poor quality, the whole standing under the command of Lieutenant-General Sir John Cope.[17] Upon the first reliable reports of what was brewing in the west, Cope gathered 1,500 men and a convoy of arms and marched from Stirling into the Highlands. He hoped to repeat what Wightman had done in 1719, namely to augment his force from

Figure 13.3 Prince Charles Edward Stuart. Portrait by Louis-Gabriel Blanchet, 1739. The prince arrived from France to lead the Jacobite rising of 1745 and on 19 August the royal standard was raised at the head of Loch Shiel at Glenfinnan. It was blessed by the Catholic bishop of Morar to cries of 'King James the Eight ... prosperity to Scotland and no Union'.

the 'well-affected' highlanders on the way and crush the rebels before they could emerge from the remoter west.

For all parties a constant feature of the 'Forty-Five was the reluctance of potential supporters, made wise by generations of revolutions, to venture their lives until they had some sense of the way the wind was blowing, and on this occasion Cope was let down badly by the Whig magnates of the Highlands. The race for the top of the Corrieyairack Pass came down to a number of hours, and on 27 August Cope shrank from the prospect of having to force the seventeen zig-zags on the near side with the forces at his disposal. Then, to general astonishment, he marched at top speed northeast for Inverness. He told his subsequent court martial that his considered motive was to secure Inverness as a place to rally the northern Whig clans, and he was given the benefit of the doubt. It was a different story at the time, for he feared that the Jacobites were in close pursuit and could cut him off at Slochd Pass short of Inverness, and in his near panic he gave the enemy an open route to the Lowlands.

With a clear sense of strategic purpose, Charles left Cope to one side and took up Wade's road over the Drumochter Pass and down through Atholl and into the fringes of the Lowlands. From 4 to 11 September the prince and the Jacobite leaders were at Perth, gathering reinforcements, and shaping them into the semblance of an army. On 13 September the Highland army passed the upper Forth by the Fords of Frew, and Ben Lomond, the last peak of the Highlands, was soon lost to view. Glasgow was in high alarm, for Charles could easily have turned in that direction, but on this momentous day he took up the road to Edinburgh and the column passed within distant cannon shot of Stirling castle, which was being held for the government. The only mobile forces available to the enemy, two bad regiments of dragoons recruited in Ireland, gave ground without a fight. Edinburgh was a politically divided town, unlike the almost solidly Whiggish Glasgow, and preparations to defend its feeble Flodden Wall dissolved in chaos. The prince entered without opposition on 17 September.

Cope was meanwhile acting with some energy to punish the supposed Highland *banditti* for their impudence. He marched his sorely tried force from Inverness to Aberdeen and took ship there for the Firth of Forth. Owing to contrary winds and tides he was just too late to anticipate Charles at Edinburgh, but during the course of 17 and 18 September he was able to disembark at Dunbar, which was reliably anti-Jacobite.

Early on the morning of 21 September, another of the defining days of the 'Forty-Five, the two forces fought at Prestonpans in a strength of about 2,400 each.[18] Cope responded skilfully to the first manoeuvres of the enemy, but the Jacobites found an unguarded pathway across a bog and were able to fall on the left flank of the redcoats. The ordeal of being charged by highlanders with cold steel was too much for Cope's shaky troops. They broke within a matter of minutes and fled in the direction of Berwick-upon-Tweed. The Jacobite victory at Prestonpans was significant in two respects. It established among the forces of both prince and government a sense of the psychological and tactical superiority of the highlanders, and it convinced Louis XV and his advisers that the Jacobite cause was once more worth supporting. A treaty of alliance was signed by the representatives of the king and Charles at Fontainebleau and the French not only revived the project of landing in England, but also began to despatch contingents of arms and troops direct to the eastern Scottish ports.[19]

The Scots Jacobites were all devoted to a greater or lesser degree to the dissolution of the union. Their commitment to the prince, however, did not necessarily extend to full-blooded support for an invasion of England, by which alone Charles could realise his ambition of restoring the Stuarts to both British thrones. The 'Fifteen had failed partly on account of its lack of focus, and the prince now had to address himself to what was to prove one of his most dangerous challenges, which was to hold the movement together.

After a finely balanced debate the Highland army, reinforced and intensively drilled, left its camps to the east of Edinburgh for the great undertaking in England. There was heavy desertion on the march through the Borders (as had been the case in like circumstances in 1715), but the force emerged into England on 9 November still about 5,500 strong. Lieutenant-General George Murray, who had growing doubts about the enterprise, was nevertheless largely responsible for the skilful manoeuvres that carried the army deep into England. By entering by the north-west, the Jacobites evaded the former army of Cope, now commanded by Field Marshal Wade, who was stranded by snow to the east of the Pennines.[20] The Highland army received the surrender of the border town and castle of Carlisle on 15 November and crossed the Ribble at Preston (dispelling the sinister associations of the place), and the Scots were welcomed into Manchester on the 28th.

A final push into the north Midlands carried the Jacobites to Derby on 4 December, after they had dodged the forces that the

Figure 13.4 Lord George Murray. Contemporary miniature by Sir Robert Strange. Murray was one of Prince Charles's key commanders during the 'Forty-Five.

duke of Cumberland had brought back in haste from the war in Flanders.[21] The junior officers and clansmen of the Highland army were buoyed up by their progress, and, when all circumstances are taken into account, the rate of recruiting among Jacobite sympathisers in Lancashire held up well compared with that in Scotland. The support in England, however, had fallen short of what Charles had promised to the clan leaders and there was no news of the intended French invasion of the south (which in fact was being postponed, and was finally abandoned). The prince was keen to press on to London, but Lord George Murray and the chiefs were all too receptive to a story planted by a spy, to the effect that an additional enemy army was hovering in the Midlands, and after a typically stormy debate at Jacobite headquarters the Highland army turned back north on 6 December.

No consensus is likely to be reached about the rights and wrongs of this, probably the most contentious of all the resolutions of the 'Forty-Five. It certainly closed off an important course of action that had been open to the Jacobites, but it did not lead inevitably to the fatal day of Culloden on 16 April 1746. Many options still remained open to Charles and his generals, and some of them might well have saved the Highland army from its ultimate destruction.

The Jacobites retreated along the path they had taken through the north-west of England, keeping just ahead of a flying column under the command of the duke of Cumberland, and on 18 December Lord George Murray fought a successful rearguard action at Clifton, a couple of marches short of the Scottish border. He had enabled the Highland army to continue its march in safety and he had upheld its reputation in combat.

The Jacobites forded the River Esk at Longtown and entered Scotland on 20 December. Behind him the prince had left a garrison of some 400 men in Carlisle as a strategic bridgehead into England. The place came under siege by the duke of Cumberland and on 30 December surrendered 'at discretion', a phrase signifying that the garrison was abandoned to the exiguous mercy of the government. On the face of it, Charles had been guilty of an irresponsible blunder. A second Jacobite army, however, had meanwhile been a-building in Scotland through intensive recruiting in the areas under Jacobite control, as well as through the arrival of substantial help that had been shipped from France in the shape of artillery and technicians, together with 800 regular troops from the Irish and Scottish regiments in the French service. The prince had called on the force to join him, but the self-willed Lord John Drummond had seized effective command from Viscount Strathallan and refused to budge.

Charles continued his retreat into the Lowlands and, after a brief pause to enjoy the forced hospitality of Glasgow, he made for Stirling. Drummond consented to make a short march to meet him and on 4 January 1746 the two forces came together outside Stirling in a strength of some 9,500 men. With heavy artillery and a solid element of regular troops at his disposal, the prince laid siege to Stirling castle. His decision was not wrong in principle, but the tactical execution was badly flawed for he renounced the opportunity to attack from the more accessible town side (out of consideration for the townsfolk) and his engineer, the Franco-Scot Mirabelle de Gordon, established his siege battery on the mound-like Gowan Hill, ridiculously close under the eastern ramparts and totally exposed to plunging fire.

Charles had abandoned Edinburgh when he first marched for England, and the town had come under a creeping occupation by the enemy, first by troops who were moved up from Berwick, and then by the reinforced army of Wade, which was now standing under the command of Lieutenant-General Hawley. This new leader underestimated both the numbers and the temper of the Highland army and marched to relieve Stirling. The two forces clashed on the high ground to the south-west of Falkirk on 17 January 1746. The battle scarcely registers in the public consciousness today and the detail was not particularly creditable to either side, yet it was bigger in terms of numbers than Culloden and ended with Hawley's army abandoning its artillery on the muddy slopes and in full flight on Edinburgh.

The prince had won his greatest victory. He commanded the largest and best-balanced army that ever stood under his orders and its tactical supremacy had been vindicated once again. It seems incredible that forces were now set in motion that set the Jacobites on the path to Culloden. Charles was falling prey to an ill health symptomatic of the weariness that was affecting the high command in general and extended to the staff work, which showed the first signs of falling away from its former high standards. Increasing numbers of highlanders were forsaking the ranks, not so much through outright desertion as by availing themselves of that prolonged absence without leave that was part of the seasonal ebb and flow of Highland campaigning. In this respect, the prince understood his highlanders better than their own clan chiefs and Lord George Murray, who feared that the army would disintegrate altogether unless it fell back to Inverness and the clan officers had the opportunity to recruit strength in their homelands over the rest of the winter.

After an impassioned debate on 29 January the Jacobites abandoned their siege of Stirling and retreated across the Fords of Frew. The operation was muddled and Murray put the blame on Colonel John O'Sullivan, the chief of staff, who was a member of Charles's innermost circle.[22] A second and decisive council came together on 2 February at Crieff, the gateway to the Highlands, and forced through a detailed plan of retreat all the way to Inverness, the Highland Division marching by way of Atholl and Badenoch, and the Lowland Division through the eastern coastlands. The resolution brought with it a number of evil consequences, just as Charles predicted. It abandoned the faithful eastern Episcopalian coasts and hinterland, with their recruiting and taxation base, and the ports by which alone reinforcements could still have arrived from France. Over the long term also it brought about a dispersal of effort, as Jacobite leaders attended to local objectives, with no guarantee that they could bring their forces together again at the outset of the next campaigning season.

Hawley's defeated army had just come under the direction of Cumberland, who breathed fresh heart into the troops and advanced from Edinburgh to Stirling. He was, however, in no state to mount

Figure 13.5 Detail of a basket-hilted broadsword etched with Jacobite mottos.

an active pursuit of the Jacobites. The prince and his highlanders conducted a measured retreat by the inland road. Murray regretted within a matter of days that the Jacobites had not after all mounted a stand at Crieff, but he marched his lowlanders with unaccountable haste and abandoned the eastern ports one after another. A French convoy carrying 700 regular troops arrived off Aberdeen on 27 February but had to bear again after learning that the Jacobites had already left and that the enemy were about to arrive.

The two divisions converged on Inverness where Major-General John Campbell, the fourth earl of Loudoun, had inherited Cope's original task of raising the northern clans for the government. He escaped from the town in the nick of time, but on 20 February an expedition under the command of the duke of Perth broke his final line of defence behind the line of the Dornoch Firth and River Shinn. The Whiggish highlanders disintegrated and Loudoun sought refuge on the Isle of Skye.

All parties were extremely busy in the weeks before spring returned. Cumberland was at Aberdeen, gathering provisions, revising his tactics and putting his troops in a state to take to the field. Charles and his headquarters remained at Inverness, but the concentration had been broken up in the interests of recruiting in the lands of the western clans and reducing the enemy strongpoints along the Great Glen. With the help of French experts, the Jacobites captured the isolated Fort George at Inverness on 21 February and then Fort Augustus on 5 March. The siege corps marched on against Fort William at the far end of the Great Glen, but the place resisted everything that could be thrown against it and the Jacobites abandoned their costly operation on 3 April.

In a particularly unfortunate episode a French warship, *Le Prince Charles* (the ex-Royal Navy sloop HMS *Hazard*), was chased by a British flotilla and on 25 February ran herself aground in the Kyle of Tongue in the far north of Scotland. She was carrying a consignment of gold coins that was vital for the pay of the Jacobite army. The company got the treasure ashore, but the whole was captured by the Whiggish MacKays under the command of Lord Reay. The logistic base of the Highland army was undermined, for the troops depended heavily on their pay for their survival, and a rescue column under the earl of Cromartie diverted still further forces from those available to the prince, and was itself captured.

Time was running out for the Jacobites. Cumberland was determined to open the campaign as soon as the melt waters of the lower Spey subsided. He set out from Aberdeen on 8 April 1746, and his meticulous planning helped him to ford the river on 12 April with scarcely any loss. On the far side he continued his systematic march in the direction of Inverness, where Charles was still trying to gather in his scattered forces. They had still not all come together by the time the duke reached Nairn, within one march of Inverness. The Jacobite troops were exhausted by an abortive attempt to surprise Cumberland in his camp on the night of 15–16 April, and on the next day the prince's army made its do-or-die stand at Culloden on Drumossie Moor.[23] The merits of the choice of ground (like that of the decision to retreat from Derby) will always be a matter of dispute, but wherever the Jacobites had chosen to fight the outcome would probably have been the same, given the redcoats' advantages in numbers, artillery, training, morale and physical condition.

The Highland core of the defeated army was still full of spirit when it came together at Ruthven in Badenoch on 17 April 1746, but Charles's resolution had at last broken and he was unwilling to approve the guerrilla-type resistance that could still have maintained his cause. He sent word to his supporters to disperse and see to their own safety.

Leadership and forces

If we need proof of the credibility of the Jacobite threat to the Hanoverian dynasty in Britain, we will find it in the government's plans to defend London in December 1745, its recall of virtually all the British forces from the war in Flanders and the massive fortifications of the new Fort George that sprang up on the Moray Firth after the 'Forty-Five.

The character of the challenge had been influenced by the prince's insistence that he was waging a just war, not an insurrection, on behalf of his father King James VIII and III. He set up complete civil administrations in the regions that were under his control for any length of time and he structured his army on regular lines. Charles also sought to exercise authority in the sense of command. He was physically fit and active (which impressed the highlanders), he had the instincts if not the formal training of a soldier and strategist, and on contentious issues he was right more often than he was wrong. He nevertheless lacked a record of conventional command, and was under cripplingly heavy obligations to the clan chiefs and the Lowland grandees. A combination of circumstances therefore favoured the rise of the restless Lord George Murray, the most controversial figure of the 'Forty-Five.

A former subaltern of the Royal Scots, Murray had very little experience of active service, which did not prevent him from carrying off the part of the veteran with total conviction. His inspirations and his fits of energy helped the Highland army to penetrate as far into England as it did in 1745, but did not save him from being overcome by sudden doubts or prolonged glooms. Murray had an extraordinarily vindictive nature, which sowed divisions in the high command and gave rise to unfounded suspicions that he was a traitor to the cause.

The highest numbers the Jacobites brought together in any one place were the 9,500 or so assembled by the prince and Lord John Drummond outside Stirling early in January 1746. Some 15,000 troops in all were raised on behalf of Charles in the 'Forty-Five, of whom less than half were clansmen. Most of the rest came from the Highland fringes and the eastern coastlands. Volunteers made a striking and significant contribution to the whole, though most of the Scots rank and file of all kinds were recruited through some kind of obligation or compulsion, whether from the conditions attached to land tenure, or the conscript levies such as those enforced by Lord Lewis Gordon in the north-east.

The infantry, both Lowland and Highland, remained the core of the

Jacobite army and were supplemented in the later stages by contingents of Irish and Scottish regulars from the French service. Among the cavalry, the most versatile troops were undoubtedly the hussars, being employed extensively in reconnaissances, diversionary movements and raids. The small units of medium and heavy horse were never brought together as a single striking force on the battlefield and their contribution was essentially ornamental. It is tempting to apply the same comment to the artillery, but the gunners had performed well on occasion and their poor showing at Culloden was probably due to the absence of their commander, Colonel James Grant, who had been wounded at the siege of Fort William.

The prowess of the Jacobites in combat derived from a combination of conventional and traditional Highland modes of fighting. The literal cutting edge of the Highland army was its first line of battle, composed of clan gentlemen (armed with broadsword, pistols and targe) and their followers. The less flighty lowlanders made up the second line. At Falkirk a decisive part was played by the small but formidable third line, or reserve, comprising the regular Irish and Scottish troops from France.

Although the leadership of the Jacobites was divided, it was demonstrably stronger than anything available to the forces of the government in Scotland until surprisingly late in the history of the 'Forty-Five. Cope was left behind by the pace of events at the outset of the rising. The aged, demented and deluded Hawley combined professional ignorance with a contempt of the Scots and near sadistic savagery, and he went down in his turn to defeat at Falkirk.

Truly valuable services were nevertheless performed by Loudoun, who was one of the more personally sympathetic figures of the period of the 'Forty-Five. In October 1745 he sailed to Inverness to assist Duncan Forbes of Culloden, who had remained to build up the government's forces in the north of Scotland after Cope set sail from Aberdeen to the Firth of Forth. Loudoun raised four companies for his new regiment of foot (Loudoun's 64th Highland Regiment), while Forbes recruited a number of independent companies from the MacLeods and other Whig clans. Although eventually hounded from his last refuge behind the line of the Dornoch Firth and the River Shinn, he had performed the crucial task of denying the Jacobites access to the human and material resources of the far north-east.

William Augustus, the duke of Cumberland, arrived to take effective command of Hawley's defeated army at the end of January 1746. The favourite son of George II, the duke combined the prestige of high birth with personal courage and a clear and ruthless vision of what was needed to settle Scottish affairs over both the short and long terms. He sought to meet the Jacobite threat at every level and proceeded from the principle that he must deny the enemy all authority as lawful combatants. In matters of personal leadership his undoubted model was Charles himself. He ameliorated Hawley's murderous disciplinary regime and further endeared himself to his troops by ensuring that they were well lodged and fed.

In the mid-1740s the British army mustered rather more than 60,000 officers and men, of which Cope had a nominal 3,850 originally under his orders in Scotland. With the Highland army's retreat to Scotland, the main concentration of the government's forces was shifted north of the border. Hawley had about 8,100 troops under his command at Falkirk and essentially the same force made up Cumberland's army for the final campaign and its culmination at Culloden, where the duke mustered about 7,000 troops. These numbers do not take in the forces that the earl of Loudoun and Forbes recruited in northern Scotland, or the contingents of the hired Dutch and Hessian troops who saw little or no action.

Figure 13.6 William Augustus, duke of Cumberland. Contemporary portrait by David Morier. Cumberland commanded the government forces at Culloden and his ruthless treatment of the Jacobites in the wake of the battle earned him the nickname the 'Butcher'.

Among the units engaged on the government's side in the 'Forty-Five, a number were known to be specifically Scots: the First of Foot (St Clair's, or the Royal Scots) on the unusually high strength of two battalions, the second battalion of which fought at Culloden; the 13th of Foot (Pulteney's), which fought at Falkirk and Culloden; and another two units at Culloden, the 21st of Foot (Campbell's, or the Scots Fusiliers) and the 25th of Foot (Sempill's). The sole regiment of Scottish horse, the 2nd Royal North British Dragoons (Scots Greys), was stranded in Flanders by storms.

All the regiments listed above represented long-established elements of the British army. The Black Watch, guarding the Kent coast, had, however, been incorporated as a regiment only in 1739, while ill-luck dogged Loudoun's 64th Highland Regiment, which was raised just before the rising after the costly British defeat at Fontenoy in May. The new regiment suffered heavily under Cope's command at the outset of the 'Forty-Five and was not reconstituted as a unit, though three of its Campbell companies fought at Falkirk and another did important service under Colin Campbell of Ballimore at Culloden.

Further units were raised through local Whiggish initiatives during the course of the 'Forty-Five. The loyalties of Edinburgh were divided, and the local Whigs were on their mettle to provide a number of volunteers for the established government. One of the companies was present at the battle of Falkirk and the regiment was kept on the strength even after Cumberland gave permission to disband in March 1746.

The Whigs of Glasgow raised a regiment of 600 volunteers in just nine days in 1745. This regiment, together with the neighbouring Paisley volunteers, marched out with Hawley's army and by its own account 'made no bad appearance in the action near Falkirk whereby they had one officer and eighteen private men killed, about as many wounded and upwards of three officers and twenty private men taken prisoner'.[24] The volunteers staged a riotous return to Glasgow, but their service was at an end.

The far more substantial Argyll Militia was an expression of the role of the main branch of the Clan Campbell in defence of the Protestant interest in Scotland. By 3 January 1746 the number of Campbell levies reached 1,989 and at the battle of Falkirk two weeks later Lieutenant-Colonel John Campbell commanded a joint force of twelve companies of his militia, three of the 64th Highlanders and one 'additional' (temporary recruit) company of the Black Watch. Many of the militiamen were now deployed in outposts and a number of those in Atholl were captured in the course of the great Jacobite raid on the night of 16–17 March. Another exposed detachment was overwhelmed at Keith four nights later.

On 16 April 1746 Captain Campbell of Ballimore (at the cost of his life) redeemed the tainted reputation of the militia when he led three of the companies, and one of his own 64th, into the Culchunaig enclosure at Culloden and opened a destructive fire into the right flank of the Jacobite infantry. A number of companies were disbanded after the battle, but from May twenty surviving units were employed in the western Highlands and Islands in reducing the rebels.

It was one thing for the government to establish a general superiority of force, but quite another to bring that force to bear to eliminate its dangerous and persistent enemy. The groundwork for Cumberland's final campaign lay in preparation during the final weeks of the winter about Aberdeen. He was careful to build supplies capable of sustaining the army when it took to the field with the return of spring, and he planned a route that would enable a flotilla of store ships to keep pace with him offshore. The men were kept in good condition and Cumberland's purposeful drilling (especially with the bayonet) bred confidence in themselves and their chief. The British artillery had failed at Prestonpans and Falkirk, but now the professional gunners of the Royal Artillery gave the army the chance of thinning out the charging highlanders even before they closed to within musket range.

In the two earlier battles the redcoats had been embroiled in action before they had a chance to get their bearings. Now, under the guidance of the tactical expert Major-General Humphrey Bland, the army would move forward with great caution, after due reconnaissances and taking care to secure the natural obstacles on the way. If the enemy were thought to be near, the army would break into multiple columns (each just three files wide, on the Jacobite model), capable of being deployed at speed into line whether to front or flank.

At Culloden, the most important decision of Cumberland was initially to do nothing, apart from standing in his lines and allowing his cannon and coehorn mortars to pound away at the enemy. In the Jacobite experience the redcoats were acting out of character, and the ordeal of the cannonade finally goaded the Highland army into launching its attack across open ground. Now the deadly work of Cumberland's artillery and bayonets was supplemented by an outflanking movement of cavalry out to the right, and another of cavalry and Campbell highlanders out to the left. The effect was to tease out the lines of the outnumbered Jacobites and, just as importantly, force them to divert the Irish infantry to support the threatened northern wing, and to send the Royal Écossais towards the enclosures in the south. The precious reserve of the Highland army was therefore broken up and Charles was deprived of all further means of influencing the course of events.

Did, finally, more Scots fight against the prince than for him at Culloden, as has often been asserted? The answer is almost certainly 'no'. While the numbers can never be established with precision, by putting together the complements of the 1st, 13th, 21st and 25th of Foot, and the companies of the Argyll Militia and the 64th, we arrive at a probable total of fewer than 2,100 men. When every allowance is made for discrepancies, the sum will always fall short of the approximately 4,670 Scots who fought for Charles on that fateful day.

Notes

1. On Jacobitism, and the Jacobite wars in general, see J. Allardyce (ed.), *Historical Papers Relating to the Jacobite Period 1699-1750*, 2 vols (Aberdeen: New Spalding Club, 1894-6); E. Cruickshanks and J. Black (eds), *The Jacobite Challenge* (Edinburgh: John Donald, 1988); T. M. Devine (ed.), *Conflict and Stability in Scottish Society 1700-1800* (Edinburgh: John Donald, 1988) and *The Scottish Nation* (London: Allan Lane, 1999); T. M. Devine and J. R. Young (eds), *Eighteenth Century Scotland: New Perspectives* (East Linton: Tuckwell Press, 1999); B. P. Lenman, *The Jacobite Risings in Britain 1689-1746* (Dalkeith: Scottish Cultural Press, 1995), *The Jacobite Clans of the Great Glen* (London: Methuen, 1984) and *The Jacobite Cause* (Edinburgh: Richard Drew for the National Trust for Scotland, 1986); A. Mackillop, *'More Fruitful than the Soil': Army, Empire and the Scottish Highlands, 1715-1815* (East Linton: Tuckwell Press, 2000); M. McKerracher, *The Jacobite Dictionary* (Glasgow: Neil Wilson, 2007); F. J. McLynn, *The Jacobites* (London: Routledge, 1985); C. Petrie, *The Jacobite Movement* (London: Eyre and Spottiswoode, 1932) and *The Jacobite Movement: The Last Phase, 1716-1807* (London: Eyre and Spottiswoode, 1950); M. G. Pittock, *Jacobitism* (Basingstoke: Macmillan, 1998); J. Robbins, *The Jacobite Wars: Scotland and the Military Campaigns of 1715 and 1745* (Edinburgh: Edinburgh University Press, 2002); and D. Szechi, *The Jacobites, Britain and Europe 1688-1788* (Manchester: Manchester University Press, 1994).
2. For the expedition of 1708, see J. S. Gibson, *Playing the Jacobite Card: The Franco-Jacobite Invasion of 1708* (Edinburgh: Edinburgh University Press, 1998).
3. The rising of 1715 has been treated comprehensively in J. Baynes, *The Jacobite Rising of 1715* (London: Cassell, 1970), with a predominantly military emphasis, and is also excellently covered in D. Szechi, *1715: The Great Jacobite Rebellion* (New Haven, CT and London: Yale University Press, 2006).
4. Szechi, *The Great Jacobite Rebellion*, p. 2.
5. Ibid. p. 127.
6. Ibid.
7. On Wade, see S. Brumwell, 'Wade, George (1673-1748)' in H. G. C. Harrison and B. Harrison (eds), *Oxford Dictionary of National Biography* (Oxford: Oxford University Press, 2004), vol. 56, pp. 658-61.

8. M. Sankey, *Jacobite Prisoners of the 1715 Rebellion: Preventing and Punishing Insurrection in Early Hanoverian Britain* (Aldershot: Ashgate, 2005), p. 20; Szechi, *The Great Jacobite Rebellion*, especially pp. 238–50, 257–9.
9. E. K. Carmichael, 'Jacobitism in the Scottish commission of the peace, 1707–1760', *Scottish Historical Review* [hereafter *SHR*], vol. 58 (1979), pp. 58–69.
10. For the expedition of 1719, see W. K. Dickson (ed.), *The Jacobite Attempt of 1719: Letters of James Butler, Second Duke of Ormonde, relating to Cardinal Alberoni's Project for the Invasion of Great Britain on Behalf of the Stuarts, and to the Landing of a Spanish Expedition in Scotland* (Edinburgh: Scottish History Society, 1895); T. Constable (ed.), *A Fragment of a Memoir of Field-Marshal James Keith, Written by Himself 1714–1734* (Aberdeen: Spalding Club, 1843); and C. S. Terry, 'The battle of Glenshiel', *SHR*, vol. 2 (1905), pp. 412–23.
11. For Lord George Murray, see K. Tomasson, *The Jacobite General* (Edinburgh and London: William Blackwood, 1958), though the name of the subject is missing from the title, and M. G. Pittock, 'Murray, Lord George', *ODNB*, vol. 39, pp. 897–900.
12. For the government's forces, forts and road-building in Scotland between the two great risings, see P. A. Simpson, *The Independent Companies 1603–1760* (Edinburgh: John Donald, 1996); C. Tabraham and D. Grove, *Fortress Scotland and the Jacobites* (London: B. T. Batsford for Historic Scotland, 1995); and W. Taylor, *The Military Roads in Scotland* (Newton Abbot: David and Charles, 1976).
13. On the 'Forty-Five in general, see G. Bailey, *Falkirk or Paradise! The Battle of Falkirk Muir, 17 January 1746* (Edinburgh: John Donald, 1996); J. Black, *Culloden and the '45* (London: Grange, 1997); C. Duffy, *The '45* (London: Phoenix, 2007); M. Lynch (ed.), *Jacobitism and the '45* (London: Historical Association Committee for Scotland and the Historical Association, 1995); R. Mackenzie et al., *The Swords and the Sorrows: An Exhibition to Commemorate the Jacobite Rising of 1745 and the Battle of Culloden 1746* (Edinburgh: National Trust for Scotland, 1996); G. Plank, *Rebellion and Savagery: The Jacobite Rising of 1745 and the British Empire* (Philadelphia, PA: University of Philadelphia Press, 2006), a bold attempt to link the suppression of the rising with British colonial methods in general; and L. Scott-Moncrieff (ed.), *The '45: To Gather an Image Whole* (Edinburgh: Mercat Press, 1988).
14. The standard biography of Prince Charles is likely to remain that by F. McLynn, *Charles Edward Stuart: A Tragedy in Many Acts* (London and New York: Routledge, 1988); see also M. G. Pittock, 'Prince Charles Edward Stuart', *ODNB*, vol. 11, pp. 145–50.

15. The many printed sources and standard reference books include the following: R. F. Bell (ed.), *Memorials of John Murray of Broughton, Sometime Secretary to Prince Charles Edward Stuart, 1740–1747* (Edinburgh: Scottish History Society, 1898), a memoir of a notorious turncoat; W. B. Blaikie, *Itinerary of Prince Charles Edward Stuart From His Landing in Scotland, July 1745, to His Departure in September 1746* (Edinburgh: Scottish History Society, 1897) and *Origins of the 'Forty-Five and other Papers Relating to that Rising* (Edinburgh: Scottish History Society, 1916), which includes John Daniel's 'Progress'; R. Chambers, *History of the Rebellion in Scotland in 1745, 1746*, 2 vols (Edinburgh: Constable, 1827), based in part on interviews with eyewitnesses; E. Charteris (ed.), *A Short Account of the Affairs in Scotland in the Years 1744, 1745, 1746 by David, Lord Elcho* (Edinburgh: David Douglas, 1907; facsimile reprint, James Thin, 1973); H. R. Duff (ed.), *Culloden Papers, Comprising an Extensive and Interesting Correspondence From the Year 1625 to 1748* (London: T. Cadell and W. Davies, 1815), which incorporates a first selection of the papers of Duncan Forbes of Culloden; D. Warrand (ed.), *More Culloden Papers*, 5 vols (Inverness: Robert Carruthers, 1923–30), which includes those relating to the 'Forty-Five in vol. 4; R. Forbes (ed.), *The Lyon in Mourning, or, a Collection of Speeches Letters Journals etc Relative to the Affairs of Prince Charles Edward Stuart*, 3 vols (Edinburgh: Scottish History Society, 1895–6), a most important collection of original materials assembled by the non-Juring Episcopal bishop of Ross and Caithness; J. Home, *The History of the Rebellion in Scotland in 1745* (Edinburgh: Peter Brown, 1822), by a versatile writer who had been captured as a Whig militiaman in 1746 and who made extensive use of the memories of other participants in the preparation of his history; A. Livingstone of Bachuil, C. W. H. Aikman and B. S. Hart (eds), *No Quarter Given: The Muster Roll of Prince Charles Edward Stuart's Army, 1745–46* (Glasgow: Neil Wilson, 2001); J. Maxwell of Kirkconnell, *Narrative of Charles Prince of Wales' Expedition to Scotland in the Year 1745* (Edinburgh: Maitland Club, 1841), the most judicious of the Jacobite memoirs; B. Rawson (ed.), *The Chevalier de Johnstone: A Memoir of the 'Forty-Five* (London: Folio Society, 1958); B. G. Seton and J. G. Arnot, *Prisoners of the '45* (Edinburgh: Scottish History Society, 1928–9); and C. S. Terry (ed.), *The Albemarle Papers, Being the Correspondence of William Anne, Second Earl of Albemarle, Commander-in-Chief in Scotland 1746–47* (Aberdeen: New Spalding Club, 1902).
16. Donald Cameron of Lochiel has been given a fine scholarly treatment in J. S. Gibson, *Lochiel of the '45: The Jacobite Chief and the Prince* (Edinburgh: Edinburgh University Press, 1998).

17. For Sir John Cope, see R. Cadell, *Sir John Cope and the Rebellion of 1745* (Edinburgh: William Blackwood, 1898).
18. On the military history of the 'Forty-Five, see S. Reid, *1745: A Military History of the Last Jacobite Rising* (Staplehurst: Spellmount, 1996); and K. Tomasson and F. D. J. Buist, *Battles of the '45* (London: Batsford, 1962).
19. On French links with the 'Forty-Five, see F. J. McLynn, *France and the Jacobite Rising of 1745* (Edinburgh: Edinburgh University Press, 1981).
20. J. Oates, 'Field Marshal Wade and the Forty-Five', *Journal of the Society for Army Historical Research*, vol. 84 (2006), pp. 95–108.
21. There is ample treatment of the duke of Cumberland in J. Oates, *Sweet William or the Butcher?* (Barnsley: Pen and Sword, 1998); W. A. Speck, *The Butcher: The Duke of Cumberland and the Suppression of the '45* (Oxford: Blackwell, 1981) and 'William Augustus, Prince, duke of Cumberland', *ODNB*, vol. 59, pp. 105–13; and R. Whitworth, *William Augustus: Duke of Cumberland: A Life* (Oxford: Oxford University Press, 1992).
22. For John O'Sullivan, see his autobiography: A. Tayler and H. Tayler (eds), *1745 and After* (London: Thomas Nelson, 1938). O'Sullivan's name does not appear in the title, which probably accounts for the neglect of this important testimony.
23. On Culloden, see T. Pollard (ed.), *Culloden: The History and Archaeology of the Last Clan Battle* (Barnsley: Pen and Sword, 2009); J. Prebble, *Culloden* (London: Secker and Warburg, 1961); S. Reid, *Like Hungry Wolves: Culloden Moor, 16 April 1746* (London: Windrow and Greene, 1994); and Chapter 28 in this volume.
24. National Library of Scotland, Fletcher of Saltoun papers, MS 17527 (157), 'Memorial stating the facts relative to the conduct of the town of Glasgow during the present rebellion; with the proper vouchers', 1746.

Part III
Scotland in Britain and the Empire

14
The Scottish Military Experience In North America, 1756–83

STEPHEN BRUMWELL

Saturday, 30 November 1776 found Lieutenant John Peebles of the 42nd Regiment in cheerful mood. After a hesitant beginning, Great Britain's war effort against its rebellious North American colonies was gathering a seemingly unstoppable momentum. A fortnight before, on 16 November, Peebles and his Scottish grenadiers had watched from their reserve position on the banks of the Harlem River as a force of redcoats and Hessian mercenaries launched a successful assault on Fort Washington, a key patriot strongpoint on the Hudson River above New York. So, when Peebles 'sat down to celebrate the day which is always kept with festivity & mirth by the wandering sons of St Andrew', there were more than the usual causes for joviality. As Peebles noted in his diary, he and his brother officers enjoyed 'a good dinner, pour'd a libation to the saint, and did justice to his memory, with a hearty glass'.[1]

During a further five years of North American service, John Peebles never failed to mark the anniversary of his country's patron saint. On campaign or in cantonments, St Andrew's Day was duly observed, not only by Peebles, but also by thousands more of his countrymen who were fighting to keep North America British. Taken alone, the rare detail and insight of Peebles' diary would entitle him to open this chapter. But Peebles has other telling qualifications. First, his military career encapsulates the timeframe considered here: he not only fought through the American Revolutionary War, but he had also previously served with Britain's 'American Army' during the Seven Years War. As will be seen, for Scots such experience of both conflicts was by no means exceptional. Second, although commissioned in perhaps the most famous of all Scottish military formations – the 'Black Watch', or 'Royal Highland Regiment' – Peebles was a lowlander, born in Ayrshire. He provides a useful reminder that while

Figure 14.1 Miniature of Captain John Peebles of the 42nd Royal Highland Regiment (the Black Watch), c. 1778.

then, as later, popular perceptions of the Scottish soldier within the British army would be dominated by the kilted and bonneted highlander, Scotland's contribution was more wide-ranging, harnessing the manpower of the country as a whole.

By serving the British state, John Peebles typified the vast majority of his countrymen who fought in North America between 1756 and 1783. Yet it is nonetheless necessary to acknowledge those Scottish soldiers who were atypical, and who fought against the British army during those same years, either as members of the military establishment of New France, or in the service of Congress. The Edinburgh-born James Johnstone – the self-styled 'Chevalier de Johnstone' – exemplifies the first category. During the 'Forty-Five, he was aide-de-camp to the Jacobite army's field commander, Lord George Murray, and occasionally to Prince Charles Edward Stuart himself. After Culloden, where he charged with the clans, Johnstone fled to France and then embarked upon a career with the French army in North America. Initially in garrison at Louisbourg on Cape Breton, he was elsewhere, on Prince Edward Island, when the fortress and its defenders were captured by the British in July 1758. At

Quebec, Johnstone resumed his old role, serving as aide-de-camp to the second-in-command of the French troops, François-Gaston, duc de Lévis, and ultimately to their commander, Louis-Joseph, marquis de Montcalm. He was present when Montcalm was defeated and mortally wounded on Quebec's Plains of Abraham on 13 September 1759; on that occasion, as he recalled, 'my usual destiny precipitated me fruitlessly into a tremendous fire, to extricate me afterwards when on the point of sharing his fate'.[2]

A different trajectory was followed by Hugh Mercer, a former Jacobite who subsequently served both alongside and against the British army in America. Born in Aberdeenshire in 1725, Mercer was a regimental surgeon with the Jacobite army at Culloden. By 1747 he had reached America, where he prospered, and in early 1758 was major to the third battalion of Pennsylvania's provincial regiment. Promoted to colonel-commandant, he led his unit during that year's gruelling, but ultimately successful, expedition against Fort Duquesne under Brigadier-General John Forbes. After the American colonies rebelled, in June 1776 Mercer's proven military credentials earned him promotion to brigadier-general in the Continental army. Widely recognised as a brave and capable officer, he died of wounds sustained after he was unhorsed and bayoneted by redcoats in the confused early phase of George Washington's defeat of a British brigade at Princeton on 3 January 1777.[3]

Also present at Princeton was another Scot who had served with the British during the French and Indian War, only to switch allegiance to Congress in the ensuing conflict. Born at Thurso, Caithness, in 1736, Arthur St Clair was commissioned ensign in the 60th Foot, or Royal American Regiment, in 1757. He participated in the conquest of Canada but resigned his lieutenancy in 1762 following marriage to a wealthy Bostonian. Like Mercer, St Clair became a brigadier-general in the Continental army, playing an important role in the council of war that convinced Washington to strike at the isolated garrison of Princeton. By February 1777 St Clair had risen to major-general, although his subsequent career was controversial. He faced a court of inquiry for abandoning Ticonderoga without a fight in the face of General John Burgoyne's 1777 invasion from Canada. St Clair was exonerated, but worse followed in the Republican era: in November 1791 his expedition against the 'Western Confederacy' of Ohio tribes ended at 'St Clair's Defeat' – the costliest ever sustained by the US army at Indian hands.[4]

While underlining the diversity of Scottish military experience in North America during the second half of the eighteenth century, men like Johnstone, Mercer and St Clair were exceptions to a more general rule: just as most Scots living in the American colonies in 1775 proved loyal to George III, so, during the 1750s and after, even those who had once sported the white cockade of the Stuarts were more likely to be found fighting for the crown than against it. Commencing just a decade after Culloden, the large-scale deployment of British regular troops in North America was crucial for the rehabilitation of Scotland's former Jacobites. It also created opportunities for highlanders in general who, regardless of their political sympathies, had suffered indiscriminately under the British government's measures to ensure that the Highlands never again hosted rebellion. Besides brutal punitive expeditions to stamp out the last embers of Jacobitism, these had included legislation calculated to eradicate the 'martial culture' of the highlanders. The Disarming Act of August 1746 outlawed the broadswords and dirks that many highlanders considered to be part of their daily dress; significantly, it also banned the wearing of tartan clothing except by soldiers of the British army.[5]

In 1756, when the escalation of the Seven Years War into a global conflict left Great Britain desperate for soldiers, the Highlands offered a rich potential reservoir. Even erstwhile rebels were now able to salvage something from the wreckage of the 'Forty-Five, exploiting the British army's manpower crisis to rebuild bridges with the Hanoverian regime, and to profit from its needs. This process operated on different levels: clan leaders or major landowners capable of mobilising their tenants en masse in the state's interest gained command of entire regiments, while, from 1747, individuals who had fought as officers under Prince Charles Edward Stuart could take advantage of an amnesty to swear allegiance to King George II and restart their careers within the British army.[6]

Not surprisingly, the recruitment drive that gathered momentum in the Highlands from late 1756 was initially viewed with alarm by some within the government. Writing in the summer of 1757 to the British army's captain-general, William Augustus, duke of Cumberland, the secretary at war, William Wildman, Lord Barrington, emphasised that nine additional companies being recruited to bolster the Black Watch and the two new Highland battalions of Archibald Montgomery and Simon Fraser 'should go to America as fast as the Companies were raised, and none of them remain in the Highlands'. As an extra safeguard, the raising of these companies, like Fraser's and Montgomery's battalions, would be entrusted to the unquestionably loyal Archibald Campbell, third duke of Argyll, who would also 'recommend', or nominate, the officers.[7]

Despite lingering Whig fears, this systematic recruitment in the

Highlands did not yield units composed overwhelmingly of hardened former rebels. Indeed, surviving evidence suggests that most rank-and-file highlanders were too young to have fought during the 'Forty-Five. For example, of ten men recruited for Major James Clephane's company of Fraser's battalion in early 1757, the oldest was only twenty-four, and the youngest seventeen.[8]

Far from being veteran fighters, these recruits were military novices. In early 1758, as he assessed the troops that he would lead against Fort Duquesne, Brigadier-General Forbes was forced to make the admission, galling for a regular officer, that the three additional companies of Montgomery's battalion were currently 'of less use for service than the same number of militia, as none of them has ever as yet burned powder, or is any ways used to arms'. Much the same was true of recruits destined to form the second battalion of the Black Watch, who faced their baptism of fire at Fort Louis, Guadeloupe, in February 1759. Lieutenant John Grant recalled that his men were only given their arms on the day of the landing itself. He added, 'I had charge of a platoon of 25 men and I showed them the way to load, describing the manner of pushing down the cartridge.' Yet when Grant inspected the muskets, he discovered that fifteen men had rammed down the ball before the powder needed to propel it.[9]

The highlanders' officers, however, were a very different proposition from the rank and file: their numerous veterans included men who had recently fought for Bonnie Prince Charlie. While here, too, it is important to avoid exaggeration, the presence of active former Jacobites, or men from families with strong connections to the exiled Stuarts, is striking. For example, James Murray, who was appointed captain of one of the Black Watch's three additional companies in 1757, was the second son of the man who had come closer than anyone to toppling George II from his throne in 1745: Lord George Murray. James Murray soon proved his own loyalty in the most unequivocal way, suffering wounds at Ticonderoga in July 1758, and again in command of the 2nd/42nd's grenadier company at Martinique in January 1762. He subsequently rose to lieutenant-general in the British army – the same rank that his father had held under the Young Pretender.[10]

For John MacDonell, son of the die-hard Jacobite Donald MacDonell of Lochgarry, hard service with Fraser's Highlanders – during which he was wounded in both the September 1759 and April 1760 battles before Quebec – outweighed his family background. As Major James Abercrombie of Fraser's wrote in 1761, MacDonell, the regiment's senior captain, was 'a very worthy good Officer, (although his father was mistaken in the 45)'. Like Murray, MacDonell continued to rise within the British army, serving as major to the first battalion of the 71st Foot raised in 1775 at the onset of the American Revolutionary War, and gazetted lieutenant-colonel commandant of another Highland unit, the 76th Foot, in December 1777.[11]

That neither Murray nor MacDonell was proscribed by the sins of their fathers is remarkable enough. Even more so is the British army's ready acceptance of men who had actually fought for the Jacobites. Donald MacDonald was among several such officers granted commissions in Fraser's Highlanders. MacDonald's military career began with the Irish and Scottish regulars in French service. In 1742 he was a cadet in Rooth's regiment of the Irish Brigade, and two years later he gained command of a company in the newly raised Royal Écossais. In November 1745 he accompanied his regiment to Scotland – where his close relatives had been among the first to draw their broadswords for the Young Pretender – as part of Louis XV's belated effort to bolster the rebellion. Wounded during the siege of Stirling castle in 1746, MacDonald was imprisoned after the Jacobites' surrender, but, as a French officer, swiftly released. Renouncing his old allegiance, he became a captain in Fraser's regiment in January 1757. He was wounded at Louisbourg in July 1758, yet it was in the following year, at Quebec, that he really made his mark, playing a crucial role in paving the way for Major-General James Wolfe's famous victory. Early on the morning of 13 September, after Wolfe's troops had slipped down the St Lawrence River, MacDonald was among the first of the advanced-guard to land and scramble up the cliffs above Quebec. When he and his men gained the heights they were challenged by a sentry whom the Scot coolly duped 'from his knowledge of the French service'. On 28 April 1760 MacDonald led a company of volunteers screening the British army's left flank. This was a hazardous post: he was ambushed by 'Savage Indians and Canadians' lurking among rocks and bushes, and butchered along with most of his company. Described as 'a good Soldier, a Brave officer, and a Bold, Enterprizing man', his fate was attributed to his 'being truly animated with Zeal for His Majesty's Service, as well as to procure a laurel for his own Brow'.[12]

MacDonald's career was cut bloodily short, but other former Jacobites rose higher within the British army. Allan Maclean of Torloisk, Mull, had joined the Young Pretender's army in 1745 at the age of twenty, fighting at Culloden as a lieutenant in his clan's battalion. He fled to the Netherlands and, like so many of his countrymen, enlisted in the Dutch Scots Brigade. In 1747 he was captured when the French stormed Bergen-op-Zoom, a bloody episode in which the Brigade was distinguished by its stubborn resistance. Maclean returned to Britain in 1750 following the royal amnesty and in January 1756 was commissioned lieutenant in the Royal American Regiment. Serving in the 4th/60th, he was wounded at Ticonderoga in July 1758 and accompanied the force that captured Niagara in 1759. In 1775, when the gathering imperial crisis threatened to escalate into full-scale war, Maclean proposed the formation of a loyalist regiment from disbanded Highland soldiers living in North America. On 12 June he was empowered to 'raise a corps of two battalions . . . to be called the Royal Highland Emigrants'. He became lieutenant-colonel commandant of the regiment – which was taken onto the regular establishment as the 84th Foot in 1779 – exercising personal command of its 1st battalion. In 1776 he was appointed adjutant-general and in 1777 promoted to brigadier-general, responsible for defending the vital Richelieu River route into Canada.[13]

Maclean's metamorphosis from hunted rebel to trusted defender of the British empire illustrates a pattern common to other erstwhile Jacobites: their integration was eased by sterling service, leading to increased responsibility and, ultimately, acceptance. The British army's swift absorption of ex-rebels, without apparent animosity on either side, was expedited by the shared code of Europe's international officer corps. To James Wolfe, for example, the Jacobites he had faced at Falkirk and Culloden were rebels, plain and simple. Indeed, his frank musings on the suitability of highlanders as expendable manpower for distant Nova Scotia in 1751 – 'hardy, intrepid . . . and no great mischief if they fall' – have often been quoted as evidence of his ruthlessness. Yet less attention has been focused upon Wolfe's own eagerness to command one of the two new Highland battalions raised in 1756–7, and his unstinting praise for the officers and men of Fraser's Highlanders whom he encountered on active service in 1758. In April 1759, after part of the regiment arrived in New York bound for Quebec, one New England newspaper noted that Fraser's Highlanders were participating 'at the particular Request of Major General WOLFE, who experienced their Bravery at the Siege of Louisbourg'. For Wolfe, as for other professional soldiers, what mattered were an officer's abilities and zeal, not his past.[14]

While significant in its own right, the role of ex-Jacobites merely hints at the true scale and breadth of Scotland's contribution to Britain's war effort in North America between 1756 and 1783. Surviving data is patchy, but it leaves no doubt that this was out of all proportion to Scotland's population, which, throughout the period

Figure 14.2 Lieutenant James Hamilton Buchanan, 21st Royal North British Fusiliers (later the Royal Scots Fusiliers), c. 1780.

in question, accounted for roughly 12% per cent of the British Isles' total.

An unusually large sample, based upon returns for units serving in North America in 1757, reveals that Scots provided no less than 27.5 per cent of the rank and file. The proportion of Scottish officers was even higher, at 31.5 per cent. As these returns are incomplete, and fail to include a large and exclusively Scottish formation, Fraser's Highlanders, and another nine companies en route from Scotland to reinforce that battalion and the other two Highland regiments in America (the 42nd and Montgomery's Highlanders), the true percentage of Scots would undoubtedly have been even higher.[15]

Although precise figures are lacking, the same basic pattern emerges for the American Revolutionary War. Inspection returns for forty-eight infantry battalions in Great Britain and Ireland between 1774 and 1777 show that Scots accounted for 24 per cent of the rank and file, and 27 per cent of the officers. The percentage of Scots serving across the Atlantic would certainly have been greater, however, not least because of the recruitment of new regiments within Scotland as the conflict dragged on. The 71st Foot, raised in 1775 by the same Simon Fraser who had headed the old Fraser's Highlanders (78th Foot), was a large two-battalion regiment, which briefly reached a brigade-strength peak of three battalions in 1777. After that autumn's disaster at Saratoga, followed by France's entry into the war, other Highland units – John Campbell's 74th Foot and Lord MacDonald's 76th – were raised specifically for American service. Along with another two non-Highland Scottish formations, the 80th, or 'Edinburgh Regiment', and the duke of Hamilton's 82nd Foot, these battalions reached North America during 1779.[16]

Scotland's disproportionate contribution of manpower during both American wars is only partially explained by the deployment of battalions recruited inside its boundaries. Just as highlanders and lowlanders alike had traditionally soldiered abroad, particularly within the armies of Sweden, France, Russia and the Dutch Republic, so, from its very birth, they had formed an important component of the more readily accessible British army. This phenomenon was not restricted to units such as the 1st Foot ('Royal Scots'), 21st Foot ('Royal North British Fusiliers'), 25th Foot ('King's Own Scottish Borderers') or the 26th Foot ('Cameronians'), which had links with Scotland. British regiments of the Georgian age were itinerant, drumming up recruits wherever they could find them, so significant clusters of Scots developed within ostensibly 'English' battalions. Their numbers could rise dramatically as the vagaries of recruiting and drafting transformed 'English' regiments into predominantly Scottish ones. For example, in the summer of 1757, Scots formed a clear majority (56 per cent) of the NCOs and men in Perry's 55th Foot, a unit with no obvious Scottish ties. This reflected the regiment's presence in Scotland during the enforcement of the 1756 Press Act, by which it received the pressed men of seven Lowland and Highland shires. In addition, the town of Perth had offered 'a Guinea & a half' to every man who enlisted in the Black Watch, or Perry's. In America, the daughter of one of its officers subsequently observed that the 55th 'might be considered as a Scotch regiment'.[17]

The presence of Scots, both Highland and Lowland, in the unlikeliest of British army regiments is highlighted by two Revolutionary War veterans of the 23rd Foot – the 'Royal Welch Fusiliers' – who came before the Board of Chelsea's Royal Hospital to be examined for their pensions in May 1787. Besides their customary qualification of 'being old and worn out in the Service', Neil McKoy (sic) and William Sample bore the scars of combat. Private McKoy, aged forty-four, and a weaver from Inverness, had served for fourteen years in the 47th Foot, being 'wounded in the left Knee at the action of Bunker's Hill' in June 1775, followed by another eight years and four months in the

Figure 14.3 John Campbell, earl of Loudoun. Portrait by Allan Ramsay, 1747. Loudoun had raised a regiment of pro-government highlanders during the Jacobite rising of 1745.

23rd. Private Sample, aged forty-nine, of West Kirk, Edinburgh, who had been a tailor before enlisting, had already served for twenty-three years and ten months in the 26th Foot before spending seven years and eight months in the 23rd. During that time he was wounded in the left cheek at the battle of Guilford Courthouse, in March 1781.[18]

Scots were even more prevalent among the redcoat officer corps in America. For example, they seized the opportunity offered by the formation of the Royal American Regiment in 1756 to become the single largest ethnic group within a unit originally intended to draw its personnel from continental Europe and the American colonies. The regiment expanded into a sprawling four-battalion formation, and according to the 1757 returns, of the 150 officers listed, more than a third (fifty-six) were Scots. In fact, in all of its battalions, Scottish officers outnumbered the 'foreigners and Americans'. This once again reflected the willingness of Scots to soldier wherever they could find employment, but also revealed the influence of the Royal Americans' first colonel-commandant, John Campbell, earl of Loudoun, commander-in-chief in North America from mid-1756 to early 1758.[19]

As Loudoun's papers reveal, he took a close interest in his countrymen's careers. The officer-candidates he approved included the future Continental army general, Arthur St Clair; as Loudoun noted, he had 'Caryed Armes' and was 'Recomended [sic] by Sutherland of Gower and the McKays'. James Dalyell was another Scot whose credentials caught Loudoun's eye. Dalyell's military apprenticeship with the Dutch Scots Brigade, including an expedition to Surinam, helped win him a lieutenancy in the Royal Americans in 1756. He then consolidated his reputation as a tough and daring officer: his readiness to accompany the celebrated New England ranger, Robert Rogers, on hazardous scouts earned him a captaincy in the newly formed Gage's Light Infantry. Dalyell subsequently transferred, with the same rank, to the more prestigious Royal Scots, securing the plum appointment of aide-de-camp to the commander-in-chief in North America, Major-General Jeffery Amherst. In 1763 he took time off from his staff duties to lead reinforcements to the garrison of Detroit, which was blockaded by Indians under the Ottawa war leader Pontiac. Like Donald MacDonald of Fraser's, Dalyell was both ambitious and aggressive. He shared his fate, being killed leading a sortie on 31 July.[20]

Not surprisingly, the over-representation of Scots within Britain's army in North America led to ill-feeling and grumbling among other nationalities. In early 1758, for example, Lord Loudoun informed the duke of Argyll that Brigadier-General Daniel Webb had been heard to complain that, when it came to promotion, the American army was 'a Scotes Expedition and no favour ... was to be expected for English or Irish Men'. In the circumstances, Webb had grounds for his gripes: not only was Loudoun a Scot, but so were his second-in-command and successor, Brigadier-General James Abercromby, his adjutant-general, Colonel John Forbes, and his aide-de-camp, Captain James Abercrombie. Soon after, when Forbes was promoted to brigadier-general in America, with command of the Fort Duquesne expedition, he too relied heavily upon yet another Scot, describing Major James Grant of Montgomery's Highlanders as his 'only plight anchor'.[21]

Grant found himself the target for similar anti-Scottish sentiment in 1776, when, as a brigadier-general, he was suspected of wielding undue influence over the commander-in-chief, William Howe. From Boston, Hugh, Earl Percy wrote that Grant's hold upon Howe would convince radicals in London that 'the Scotch influenced the Cabinets here as well as at home'.[22]

Resentment at the proliferation of Scots within Britain's military establishment was balanced by widespread recognition of their contribution to the war effort. James Grant is a case in point. Although best known for his rash pledge to the House of Commons in January 1775 to march from one end of America to the other with just 5,000 grenadiers, there was clearly more to the portly laird of Ballindalloch than mere bluff and bluster. Indeed, when he uttered his notorious boast Grant was poised to embark upon his third world war and was already, by any standard, an exceptionally experienced officer. In 1745, as a captain in the Royal Scots, he had survived the bloody battle of Fontenoy. Captured by the French and Indians in September 1758 after his attempt to surprise Fort Duquesne backfired, he clearly learned from his mistakes: exchanged, and promoted to lieutenant-colonel, he played an important role in two expeditions sent against the Cherokee Indians in 1760–1; in command of the second, he waged an effective campaign over punishing terrain.

In August 1776 Grant was prominent in the rout of Washington's inexperienced troops at Brooklyn Heights. Choosing words that have since proved irresistible to American popular historians, he wrote, 'If a good bleeding can bring those Bible-faced Yankees to their senses, the fever of independency should soon abate.' Soon after blamed for underestimating his enemy, and allowing the devastating attacks on Trenton and Princeton over the coming Christmas and New Year, Grant redeemed himself at the head of reinforcements sent to the Caribbean in 1778, capturing St Lucia and skilfully rebuffing a determined French assault on the island.[23]

The circumstances under which John Peebles entered the Black Watch also hinged upon hard service and merit rather than blatant nepotism. In 1758 he was surgeon's mate to the Second Virginia Regiment, a provincial unit in John Forbes' army. He was subsequently appointed to the same position in Montgomery's Highlanders (77th Foot) and accompanied the task force sent to retake St John's, Newfoundland, from the French in 1762. In the following summer, when 'Pontiac's War' erupted on the western frontier, Peebles obtained permission to serve with Montgomery's as a volunteer. That August he distinguished himself at the battle of Bushy Run, an extremely hard-fought two-day action against the Ohio Indians, in which the 42nd and Montgomery's Highlanders won the plaudits of their commander, the Swiss mercenary Colonel Henri Bouquet of the Royal Americans, who described them as 'the bravest men I ever saw'. The only volunteer present, Peebles, was 'dangerously wounded'. His conduct at Bushy Run and on 'former Occasions, particularly at Newfoundland' convinced Jeffery Amherst that he deserved an ensign's commission in the 42nd, with none of the customary fees to pay.[24]

The ongoing importance of the Scottish contribution, in terms both of units and of the individuals who composed them, is epitomised by the two regiments raised by Simon Fraser, the Master of Lovat, between 1756 and 1775. The original Fraser's Highlanders was especially important during the 1759 Quebec campaign. Not only was it by far the largest battalion in Wolfe's army, but its officers had a decisive impact upon the campaign's outcome. The exploits of Donald MacDonald have already been noted; equally valuable were those of another quick-thinking officer, the colonel's namesake, Captain Simon Fraser. In the early hours of 13 September, as the British boats were descending the St Lawrence, it was Fraser who calmly silenced an inquisitive French sentry, so preserving the secrecy of the entire operation. He was yet another graduate of that influential finishing school for Scottish officers – the Dutch Scots Brigade – and went on to have a lengthy and distinguished career across three major wars. He was a brigadier-general when sniped by a rebel rifleman at Saratoga in 1777.[25]

The second unit raised by Fraser, the 71st Foot, played a no less significant role during the American Revolutionary War, participating in almost every major engagement. For example, at the close of 1778, Lieutenant-Colonel Archibald Campbell of the 71st was sent with about 3,000 men, including two battalions of his own regiment, to retake Georgia. Occupying Savannah in late December, during the following weeks his force spread out through Georgia, ousting the rebels and restoring British prestige. With understandable pride, Campbell announced, 'I have taken a Stripe and Star from the Rebel flag of America.'[26]

Nothing illustrates the true extent of the 71st's service better than a remarkable document left by two of the ordinary soldiers who underwrote Campbell's boast. The story of Malcolm McKenzie and his comrade, Neill Thomson, survives in a letter they prepared in 1790 to support their belated applications for Chelsea pensions. After stating that both had served as private soldiers in the 71st 'faithfully & honestly for eight years', as their discharge papers proved, they proceeded to detail a lengthy roll call of battle honours. Mingling a strong measure of *esprit de corps* with a dash of exasperation, their testament provides a useful reminder that, for many British soldiers, the 'American rebellion' was an experience dominated by victory, not defeat.

Before even setting foot on American soil, McKenzie and Thomson had 'been in an Engagement upon the Coast of Boston' after their transport ships were intercepted by privateers. Once ashore, the pair embarked upon a series of rambling campaigns between summer 1776 and autumn 1781 that took them from one end of the American colonies to the other:

> [they] stood an Engagement or Balle with the rest of his Majesty's army on Long Island, another at York Island, one at Brandy wyne Creek, being also at the taking of Woolmington, Philadelphia, Savannahtown, at the Balle of Briers Creek, the siege of Savannah, that of Charlestown, the Balle of Cambden, balle of Gilpharl Court House, at the Balle of James town point and numberless petty skirmishes too tedious to mention. At last being taken prisoner with Lord Cornwallis at Lille York, Virginia all which is well known to most of the officers in said Regiment . . . it is expected Government will be pleased to consider the numberless dangers they have encountered and grant them a pension as a Recompense for their faithfull services equal to that bestowed upon some of the surviving soldiers of said Regt.[27]

While this chapter has sought to emphasise the national scope of Scotland's contribution to the British army in the Americas, the testimony of McKenzie and Thompson highlights the undeniable importance of the Highland battalions. Indeed, if Scotland's contribution to the British army in America was out of all proportion to its overall population, then that of the Gaelic-speaking Highlands – less than a third of the total – was even more so.

The highlander's enduring image as the quintessential Scottish soldier, a status resented by less picturesque units, at least rests upon solid and venerable foundations: although it has been argued that the Highland regiments only gained a high profile in consequence of well-publicised exploits during the French Revolutionary and Napoleonic Wars, their glamorisation was already under way by the closing years of the Seven Years War. In 1758, for example, the performance of Fraser's Highlanders at Louisbourg and of the Black Watch at Ticonderoga both prompted extensive coverage in British and North American newspapers, and such interest only intensified during the *annus mirabilis* of 1759.[28]

Looking back nostalgically from a post-Waterloo perspective, one Black Watch veteran, Colonel David Stewart of Garth, maintained that the highlanders who served in the Americas during the 1750s and 1760s were a vanishing breed: not only tougher, but also characterised by a stronger sense of honour and cultural integrity than the men who followed them.[29] The myopic Stewart of Garth undoubtedly viewed his subjects through rose-tinted spectacles, yet his wistful and romanticised *Sketches of the Highlanders* have had a lasting impact: for all their distortions and inaccuracies, they contain some basic truths that can be substantiated from contemporary evidence. For example, the highlanders who served under Amherst and Wolfe were clearly believed to be better behaved than the bulk of the redcoats. In the spring of 1758, while Brigadier-General Charles Lawrence had felt obliged to quarter his own battalion of the 60th inside Boston's isolated fort, the men of Fraser's were to be billeted in the town itself. Justifying this decision, Lawrence wrote that 'the Highlanders are thrifty, consequently sober & therefore less likely to get into squabbles'. His scheme proved 'highly agreeable' to Boston's Select Men, who had already heard glowing reports 'of the Behaviour & regularity of those Highlanders that passed the Winter [in] Connecticut'.[30]

But as deserter descriptions suggest, it would be naïve to assume that all highlanders were paragons of virtue. Anyone unlucky enough to encounter Archibald Montgomery, of Montgomery's Highlanders, who absconded at New York in the early summer of 1760, was unlikely to make such an assumption: aged forty-five, Montgomery had 'large grey eyes' and 'remarkably large' eyebrows, which, like his beard and hair, blazed 'red'. His complexion was likewise 'ruddy' – heightened by his tendency to both drink and take snuff 'to excess'.[31]

In his *Sketches*, Stewart of Garth noted that the highlanders who fought in the Americas during the Seven Years War were distinctive in several respects: language, ethnic coherence, clothing and weaponry all set them apart from the rest of the troops. The presence of Gaelic speakers is again reflected in deserter descriptions. Neil MacDonald, another man who quit Montgomery's battalion in the summer of 1760, was a highlander, who spoke 'little or no English'; while 'John M'Invin', who was born in the 'Shire of Argyle, and Parish of Morvin' and deserted from the 1st/42nd at Staten Island on 31 July 1761, spoke 'very bad English'. Nearly three decades later, in the wake of the Revolutionary War, surprisingly little had changed. Writing on behalf of four veterans of the 76th Foot seeking Chelsea pensions, their former commanding officer, Francis Needham, explained, 'These poor ignorant Highlanders not speaking a word of English are not able to state their own case when called upon.'[32]

But by no means all those who served in the Highland battalions between 1756 and 1783 were Gaelic-speaking highlanders. John Peebles was not the only lowlander to serve with Montgomery's. Robert Kirkwood, like Peebles, was born in Ayrshire. He too fought at Bushy Run, leaving a unique private soldier's account of the battle in his published memoirs. During the American Revolutionary War, what Stewart of Garth regarded as the contamination of Highland battalions by non-highlanders continued. For example, the men of the 71st included Corporal Robert Anderson of St Ninians, Stirling. A former maltster who had been 'miserably Frostbit' and crushed by a cart during a forced march across Long Island in December 1779, Anderson served for three years in the 71st, followed by a further four in the 80th.[33]

While not a highlander, Anderson was at least Scottish. The enlistment of non-Scots into Highland regiments was another matter. In August 1779 John Peebles registered disquiet at the 'Strange mismanagement of the Recruits at home, drafting them with great impropriety, & prejudice to the service, & the Regts. they belong to'. Highland recruits had been sent to other regiments, and vice versa – a policy 'hurtfull to the Recruiting business, & productive of mutiny & desertion'. He had good cause for concern: back in Britain there had been a rash of mutinies among Highland recruits who viewed drafting to non-Highland units as a breach of faith. It was with evident relief that Peebles soon after reported how most of the 'English & Irish recruits sent out for the 42d. [were] exchanged for Scotsmen from the 26th'.[34]

Alongside their group identity, and in Stewart of Garth's opinion, a major factor behind the formidable reputation of the first Highland regiments was their characteristic dress and armament. Both undoubtedly excited great curiosity, particularly within the American colonies. In the spring of 1759, for example, Rhode Island's *Newport Mercury* carried an advertisement inviting subscriptions for a series of prints 'consisting of six Representations of Warriors, who are in the Service of their Majesties the King of Great-Britain, and the King of Prussia, designed after the Life'. Alongside such exotic fighting men as Prussian hussars and uhlans, the British army's sole representative was 'A Scottish Highland Soldier (formerly called the Highland Watch) now the Royal Scots . . . whereof there are many now in North America'. Despite this confusion over regimental titles, the highlander's selection was surely significant, reflecting not only the prominence of such troops within Britain's 'American Army', but also a broader fascination with their novel appearance.[35]

In 1759 the highlanders looked very different from the rest of the regulars: they wore the belted plaid, short red coat, blue bonnet and diced hose. It was an eye-catching ensemble, but not best suited to back-breaking bateaux work on Lake Champlain, or footslogging in the strength-sapping heat of the Carolinas. Just as the ethnic composition of the highlanders gradually changed between 1756 and 1783, so did their appearance, with the tartan panoply of 'traditional' Highland

Figure 14.4 Broadsword said to have been carried by a Highland officer at Quebec in 1759.

dress increasingly replaced on campaign by more practical kit. This transformation began as early as the spring of 1759, when Black Watch company commanders were 'desired to order breeches and leggings for the men to be made with all dispatch possible'. That April the regiment was reviewed, both in full dress, with the men 'well kilted', and in their new fatigue clothing. By the end of the next war it had discarded kilts and plaids altogether on active service. When the regiment was inspected at Halifax, Nova Scotia, in 1784 it could not appear in full uniform as the commanding officer had disposed of its plaids during the 'late War, to purchase a more commodious dress . . . for the American service', consisting of white trousers and short black gaiters.[36]

Like their clothing, the weapons of the first highlanders to arrive in America set them apart. In theory at least, they carried a light carbine with short bayonet, a single all-metal 'side pistol' and a basket-hilted broadsword. Here too, the realities of American campaigning led to change, and, from the start, not all highlanders were equipped as tradition dictated. Via his agent Henry Drummond, in early 1759 Lord John Murray, the colonel of the Black Watch, made repeated attempts to have his regiment issued with 'a new stand of Lighter arms, with short Bayonets such as Coll Montgomery & Fraser's Battalions have', instead of their conventional, heavier 'firelocks'; and of the twenty companies in his two battalions, Murray added, only the seven raised most recently had been issued with pistols.[37]

The highlanders' traditional weapon *par excellence* was the yard-long broadsword. Wielded against the redcoats at Prestonpans, Falkirk and Culloden, its subsequent employment by highlanders fighting for King George in the Americas was highlighted in published letters. For example, in July 1760 an officer of the 2nd/42nd at Oswego told how ten 'French Indians' had come into camp to make peace. These warriors had been with Lévis's army before Quebec that April and, noticing the Black Watch's Highland dress, asked whether they too had fought there, 'as they said they saw such [Fraser's Highlanders] at the Battle, and that they killed many Frenchmen with their long knives (meaning their Broadswords)'. Yet despite such feats, by the end of the Seven Years War the men of the Black Watch had begun to regard their swords as encumbrances, preferring to rely upon their bayonets.[38]

The abandonment of the highlanders' characteristic weaponry reflected their tactical integration within the British army. From the outset, Highland units were viewed as conventional infantry rather than semi-tribal irregulars. They were trained in standard drill, with an emphasis on musketry, both aimed individual fire and collective volleys. Although the broadsword was ultimately discarded, the 'Highland charge' – essentially a sharp burst of short-range fire power backed by a vigorous application of cold steel – was itself absorbed within the British army's own increasingly aggressive tactical doctrine. During the early 1750s a more disciplined version of much the same battlefield elements was already being promoted by regular officers like Wolfe and in 1759 proved its worth at Niagara and Quebec. This trend continued during the American Revolutionary War, when the redcoats increasingly sought to intimidate their enemies – and minimise time spent within the 'killing zone' of the latter's muskets and rifles – by brisk advances with the bayonet.[39]

Just as the Highland battalions were integrated into the British army between 1756 and 1783, so their military services, and those of other Scottish soldiers, helped to achieve a more general – albeit more grudging – acceptance of their countrymen as bona fide 'Britons'. It was a slow process, set back by periodic outbreaks of 'Scottophobia' among Englishmen, such as that prompted in 1762 by the influence of George III's favoured first minister, John Stuart, Lord Bute. The American Revolutionary War, with its second major mobilisation of

Scottish manpower, gave fresh momentum to this rapprochement. Only in its wake, it has been argued, were prevailing English perceptions of Scots as plotting Jacobites or shock troops of despotism replaced by more positive images.[40]

Intriguingly, military service in America between 1756 and 1783 also helped to bond Scottish society itself, healing old wounds among Highland clans with traditions of feuding. Writing to his father from Fort Edward Camp in the summer of 1759, Major Alexander Campbell of Montgomery's Highlanders observed that his brother officer, Sir Allan Maclean, was 'doing very well and is very much esteemed'. Campbell added, 'If I survive the Campaign I shall be more full on the subject – when the Knight getts a little Drunk he swears that he scarce knows the difference in his affections betwixt a Bredalbane [sic] Campbell and a McLean.'[41]

Despite his arduous American service, John Peebles lived to be an old man, dying in 1823 aged eighty-four. The year before, Stewart of Garth had published his *Sketches*. They noted that 'Captain Peebles, wounded at Bushy Run, and residing in Irvine, and Major John Grant, late of the Invalids', were the last surviving officers to have served in the Black Watch during the Seven Years War. Peebles and Grant – who as a young lieutenant had led his raw recruits ashore at Guadeloupe in 1759 – lived long enough to see the events in which they had participated grow tinged with legend. Yet the experience of Scottish soldiers – both highlanders like Grant, and lowlanders like Peebles – was real enough. Their conspicuous, and costly, role in Britain's imperial wars in North America between 1756 and 1783 marks a key phase in the formation of Scotland's own 'military identity'.[42]

Notes

1. I. D. Gruber (ed.), *John Peebles' American War: The Diary of a Scottish Grenadier, 1776-82* (Stroud: Sutton Publishing, for the Army Records Society, 1997), p. 65. Peebles was promoted to captain of the 42nd's grenadier company in 1777.
2. T. A. Crowley, 'Johnstone, James', in F. G. Halfpenny (ed.), *Dictionary of Canadian Biography*, 13 vols (Toronto: Toronto University Press, 1966–94), vol. 4, pp. 400–1; *Memoirs of the Rebellion in 1745 and 1746. By the Chevalier De Johnstone*, second edition (London: Longman, Hurst, Rees, Orme and Brown, 1821), p. 447.
3. E. E. Curtis, 'Mercer, Hugh', in D. Malone (ed.), *Dictionary of American Biography*, 20 vols (New York: Charles Scribner's Sons, 1928), vol. 6, pp. 541–2.

4. G. Evans Dowd, 'St Clair, Arthur', in J. A. Garraty and M. C. Carnes (eds), *American National Biography*, 24 vols (New York: Oxford University Press, 1999), vol. 20, pp. 583–5; D. Hackett Fischer, *Washington's Crossing* (New York: Oxford University Press, 2004), pp. 314–15.
5. W. A. Speck, *The Butcher: The Duke of Cumberland and the Suppression of the '45* (Oxford: Basil Blackwell, 1981), pp. 171–7.
6. B. Lenman, *The Jacobite Clans of the Great Glen, 1650–1784* (London: Methuen, 1984), pp. 178–9; A. Mackillop, *'More Fruitful than the Soil': Army, Empire and the Scottish Highlands 1715–1815* (East Linton: Tuckwell Press, 1999).
7. Barrington to Cumberland, 8 July 1757, in S. Pargellis (ed.), *Military Affairs in North America, 1748–65: Selected Documents from the Cumberland Papers in Windsor Castle* (New York: D. Appleton-Century, 1936), pp. 381–2.
8. National Records of Scotland, Edinburgh [hereafter NRS], GD (Gifts and Deposits) 125/22/16/17.
9. NRS, 4/86/1 (microfilm), note on preparations for the 1758 expedition, in Forbes' hand; NRS, 4/77 (microfilm), journal of Lieutenant John Grant, 2nd/42nd, 1758–62, pp. 33–4. As Grant testified, although untrained, these men 'pressed on with the courage of old and tried soldiers'. In contrast to those raised in 1756–7, the highlanders who fought during the American War of Independence were often seasoned veterans of the previous conflict. For example, John McCallum, a labourer from Fortingall, Perth, and aged sixty when he applied for a pension in 1790, had served in the 74th Foot for six-and-a-half years, during which time he 'was shot through the thigh at Penobscot' in Maine. McCallum had already spent 'seven years in the 78th Regiment, the war before last and received a ball under the knee where it still remains'. See The National Archives, Kew [hereafter TNA], War Office Papers [hereafter WO], 121/8, Board of 1 February 1790.
10. Huntington Library [hereafter HL], Loudoun papers, 5484, Duncan Richardson to the earl of Loudoun, New York, 28 January 1758; see also casualty returns in TNA, WO 1/1, f. 203 (Ticonderoga), and TNA, WO 17/1489, f. 13 (Martinique).
11. HL, Loudoun papers, 6316, Abercrombie to Loudoun, Quebec, 27 August 1761. MacDonell never took command of the 76th, being captured by an American privateer while on passage to Scotland.
12. A. G. Doughty (ed.), *An Historical Journal of the Campaigns in North America for the Years 1757, 1758, 1759, and 1760, by Captain John Knox*, 3 vols (Toronto: Champlain Society, 1914–16), vol. 2, p. 96 (author's note); 'Memoirs of the Quarter-Master Sergeant', in A. G. Doughty and

G. W. Parmelee (eds), *The Siege of Quebec and the Battle of the Plains of Abraham*, 6 vols (Quebec: Dussault and Proulx, 1901), vol. 5, p. 127.

13. *The Loyal Americans: The Military Role of the Loyalist Provincial Corps and Their Settlement in British North America, 1775-1784* (Ottawa: National Museums of Canada, 1983), pp. 18-19; TNA, WO 1/1, f. 203.

14. S. Brumwell, *Paths of Glory: The Life and Death of General James Wolfe* (London: Hambledon Continuum, 2006), p. 123; *Newport Mercury*, 24 April 1759.

15. S. Brumwell, *Redcoats: The British Soldier and War in the Americas, 1755-1763* (New York: Cambridge University Press, 2002) pp. 318-19.

16. Inspection returns in TNA, WO 27, 30, 32, 34-6, cited in Gruber (ed.), *John Peebles' American War*, p. 10 (introduction). Stephen Conway believes that Scotland's contribution in 1775-83 was 'even more impressive... than in previous 18th century wars'. See his *The British Isles and the War of American Independence* (Oxford: Oxford University Press, 2000), p. 188.

17. On Scots abroad and in the British army, see H. Strachan, 'Scotland's military identity', *Scottish Historical Review* [hereafter *SHR*], vol. 85 (2006), pp. 319-20. For the 55th Foot, see Brumwell, *Redcoats*, p. 318, table 5; TNA, WO 4/51, p. 325, Barrington to Perry, 29 March 1756; HL, Loudoun papers, 999, Humphrey Bland to Loudoun, Edinburgh, 1 April 1756; *Memoirs of an American Lady... By Mrs Anne Grant* (London: n.p., 1808; reprinted New York: Dodd, Mead & Co., 1901), part I, p. 64.

18. TNA, WO 121/1 (Board of 12 May, 1787).

19. Brumwell, *Redcoats*, p. 319, table 6; A. V. Campbell, 'Atlantic microcosm: The Royal American Regiment, 1755-1772', in N. L. Rhoden (ed.), *English Atlantics Revisited: Essays Honouring Professor Ian K. Steele* (Montreal: McGill-Queen's University Press, 2007), p. 285. Scottish officers in America during the Seven Years War outnumbered those in the British army as a whole, in which 'something like one-fourth of all the regimental officers... were Scottish'. See J. Hayes, 'Scottish officers in the British army 1714-63', *SHR*, vol. 37 (1958), p. 25.

20. For St Clair see 'List of Commissions Granted By His Excellency The Rt Honbl The Earl of Loudoun', in Pargellis (ed.), *Military Affairs*, p. 365; and for Dalyell, HL, Loudoun papers, 6739: 'List of Lieutenants & Ensigns proposed for the Royal Americans March 17th: 1756'; also *Army List 1757*, p. 95; *1758*, p. 134; *1762*, p. 54.

21. HL, Loudoun papers, 5599, Loudoun to Argyll, 14 February 1758; Forbes to General James Abercromby, Raystown Camp, 16 October 1758, in A. P. James (ed.), *Writings of General John Forbes, Relating to His Service in North America* (Menasha, WI: Collegiate Press, 1938), p. 234.

22. Cited in S. Conway, *The War of American Independence 1775–1783* (London: Edward Arnold, 1995), p. 200.
23. Grant to Edward Harvey, 2 September 1776, cited in D. McCullough, *1776: America and Britain at War* (New York: Simon and Schuster, 2005), p. 179; see also P. D. Nelson, *General James Grant: Scottish Soldier and Royal Governor of East Florida* (Gainesville, FL: University Press of Florida, 1993).
24. NRS, GD 21/488, Captain James Dalyell to Major Lobel, New York, 14 June 1763; British Library [hereafter BL], Add MSS [Additional Manuscripts], 21, 649, f. 316, Bouquet to Lieutenant James MacDonald, 28 August 1763; TNA, WO 34/40, f. 322, Bouquet to Amherst, Camp at Edge Hill, 5 August 1763; BL, Add MSS, 21, 634, f. 359, Bouquet to Amherst, Fort Pitt, 11 August 1763; and TNA, WO 34/41, f. 122, Amherst to Bouquet, New York, 25 August 1763.
25. For Fraser see 'Journal of the particular transactions', in Doughty and Parmelee (eds), *The Siege of Quebec*, vol. 5, p. 187. According to Brigadier-General George Townshend, Fraser had acquired his fluency in French while in 'the Dutch service'. See 'Townshend's Rough Notes', in *The Northcliffe Collection* (Ottawa: King's Printer, 1926), p. 424. For the Dutch Scots Brigade, see S. Conway, 'Scots, Britons and Europeans: Scottish military service, c. 1739–1783', *Historical Research*, vol. 82, no. 215 (February 2009), pp. 114–30.
26. BL, Add MSS 34, 416, f. 246, Campbell to William Eden, 19 January 1779.
27. TNA, WO 121/8 (Board of 8 June 1790). McKenzie was a thirty-five-year-old labourer from Ardchatton, Fort William; Thompson's details are not given. Both men must have served in the 2nd/71st: the first battalion was captured at Cowpens, South Carolina, on 17 January 1781.
28. J. E. Cookson, 'The Napoleonic Wars, military Scotland, and Tory Highlandism in the early nineteenth century', *SHR*, vol. 78 (1999), p. 63. P. J. Marshall considers that the highlanders 'began their long career as popular British military heroes' in 1758. See his *The Making and Unmaking of Empires: Britain, India and America, c. 1750-1783* (Oxford: Oxford University Press, 2005), p. 99. Contemporary coverage of the Black Watch at Ticonderoga was especially fervent in the *Scots Magazine*. See N. Westbrook (ed.), '"Like roaring lions breaking from their chains": The Highland Regiment at Ticonderoga', *Bulletin of the Fort Ticonderoga Museum*, vol. 16 (1998), pp. 16–19, 44–5, 54–8.
29. Col. D. Stewart, *Sketches of the Character, Manners and Present State of the Highlanders of Scotland, with Details of the Military Service of the Highland Regiments*, 2 vols (Edinburgh: n.p. 1822), vol. 1, p. 292. For thoughtful critiques of Stewart of Garth and his *Sketches*, see J.

Prebble, *Mutiny: Highland Regiments in Revolt, 1743-96* (London: Penguin paperback edition, 1975), p. 27, and also the introduction to I. Macpherson McCulloch, *Sons of the Mountains: The Highland Regiments in North America, 1756-67, Vol. 1, A History of the Regiments* (Fleischmanns, NY: Purple Mountain Press, 2006).

30. HL, Abercromby Papers, 99, Lawrence to James Abercromby, Boston, Massachusetts, 2 April 1758.
31. 'Description of deserters from the Hon. Col. Montgomery's regiment', *New-York Gazette*, 9 June 1760.
32. Ibid. 9 June 1760 and 3 August 1761; TNA, WO 121/8 (Board of 3 May 1790).
33. I. McCulloch and T. Todish (eds), *Through so Many Dangers: The Memoirs and Adventures of Robert Kirk, Late of the Royal Highland Regiment* (Fleischmanns, NY: Purple Mountain Press, 2004; originally published Limerick: J. Ferrar, 1775), pp. 90-5. Originally in Montgomery's 77th, the author was drafted into the 42nd in October 1763. As the 42nd's muster rolls prove, his real name was Kirkwood (see TNA, WO 12/5478, f. 96). For Anderson see TNA, WO 121/1 (Board of 12 February 1787).
34. Gruber (ed.), *John Peebles' American War*, pp. 289, 291. For highlander mutinies in Britain, see Prebble, *Mutiny*, especially pp. 91-259.
35. *Newport Mercury*, 24 April 1759.
36. Col. R. F. H. Wallace (ed.), 'Regimental routine and army administration in North America in 1759: Extracts from company order books of the 42nd Royal Highland Regiment', *Journal of the Society for Army Historical Research*, vol. 30 (1952), p. 10; P. Sumner, 'Army inspection returns, 1753-1804', *Journal of the Society for Army Historical Research*, vol. 5 (1926), pp. 26-7.
37. TNA, WO 1/978, pp. 249-50, Drummond to Barrington, Whitehall, 14 February 1759; also TNA, WO 1/979 (not paged or foliated), Murray to Barrington, London, 12 April 1759.
38. 'Extract of a letter from Oswego, dated July 16, 1760' in *New-York Mercury*, 11 August 1760; inspection return cited in J. Houlding, *Fit for Service: The Training of the British Army, 1715-1795* (Oxford: Oxford University Press, 1981), p. 151 (note).
39. See orders for April 1759 in Wallace, 'Regimental routine', p. 11; Brumwell, *Paths of Glory*, pp. 112-13, 283; M. H. Spring, *With Zeal and With Bayonets Only: The British Army on Campaign in North America, 1775-1783* (Norman, OK: University of Oklahoma Press, 2008). Given the chronology, the possibility of a link between the British army's experience of the 'Highland charge' during 1745-6 and its own adoption of 'volley and bayonet' tactics in the 1750s deserves further investigation.

40. S. Conway, 'War and national identity in the mid-eighteenth century British Isles', *English Historical Review*, vol. 116 (2001), pp. 874–5; L. Colley, *Britons: Forging the Nation, 1707–1837* (Newhaven, CT: Yale University Press, 1992), p. 117; see also Conway, *The British Isles and the War of American Independence*, pp. 180–2.
41. NRS, GD/87/1/85, Campbell to John Campbell of Barcaldine, Fort Edward Camp, 19 June 1759.
42. Stewart of Garth, *Sketches of the Highlanders*, vol. 1, p. 588 (note).

15
The French Revolutionary and Napoleonic Wars, 1793–1815

CHARLES J. ESDAILE

If there is one image of the British soldier in the Revolutionary and Napoleonic Wars that is predominant over all others, it is that of the Scottish highlander. Kilted and feather-bonneted, this is a figure that is not only instantly recognisable, but also stands out from the ranks of the rest of the armed forces of King George III as one that is as dashing as it is exotic. Amongst contemporaries and later historians alike, meanwhile, there is a strong perception that the men of the Black Watch and the rest were at the very least first-class soldiers. In a book entitled *Sword of Scotland: Jocks at War*, it is only natural, perhaps, that we should find words such as the following:

> By the close of the eighteenth century, Scotland was making a significant contribution to the British army . . . But it was Scotland's part in the wars against Napoleon that will be best remembered because of the many outstanding actions fought by her cavalry and infantry regiments . . . Scottish troops served in every theatre of war and fought in every battle . . . There were seventy-two regimental engagements which were rewarded by the grant of a battle honour to be borne on the colours . . . From the time the Black Watch was raised until the end of the Napoleonic war [sic], the Highlands provided no [fewer] than fifty battalions of regular infantry . . . All these were volunteers and the quality was superb.[1]

But it is not just among such panegyrists that Britain's Scottish troops have won admiration. Let us here quote the French general Foy, for example: 'There are no regiments in the service of the King of England which are more steady in battle than the Scotch.'[2] And then we have the word of an English officer who fought in the Peninsula, John Patterson:

> Were I at liberty to choose a party upon whose steadiness in camp and quarters, and upon whose fidelity to orders, I might depend, and who, from love of country, take pride in the most implicit obedience to their officers even while suffering all the miseries of hard service, cold and famine, commend me to the Scotch. Their esprit de corps and faithful attachment to their chiefs and clans, is proverbial . . . prompting them to follow their leaders even 'to the cannon's mouth' while the pibroch is ringing in their ears. Talk to a highlander of his heaths and mountains, and remind him of his honour, [and] his blood gets up and he will burn with ardour to signalize himself for the honour of his people.[3]

We have, then, a glowing record, even the makings of a myth. What this chapter sets out to do is to examine this record for excellence, whilst at the same time discussing such issues as the organisation and composition of Britain's Scottish troops, not to mention the very important role played by images of the Revolutionary and Napoleonic Wars in the subsequent history of Scotland.

In attempting such a chapter, one issue that needs to be addressed is what we mean when we discuss 'Scottish troops'. In so far as this is concerned, it is obviously easiest to concentrate on the various overtly Scottish units – both Highland and others – that will be enumerated below. The picture is a complicated one, however. In the first place, Scots did not just serve in Scottish units. On the contrary, many hundreds, indeed possibly thousands, of Scots enlisted in non-Scottish units, the fact being that recruiting parties roamed the nation without paying much heed to the districts with which their units were theoretically associated. In May 1812, for example, the 68th Foot – the Durham Light Infantry – contained no fewer than 109 Scots out of a total of 608 men under arms, while in the period 1795–1810 21 per cent of the rank and file of the Royal Artillery were Scottish.[4] According to the best prosopographical source that we have on recruitment to the British army in the Revolutionary and Napoleonic Wars – a survey of fourteen regiments of foot, four regiments of cavalry and three sources relating to the artillery that incorporates details of 7,250 recruits who joined the army between 1793 and 1815 – out of the 1,145 Scots it lists, only 755 joined the four Scottish units that were examined by its compiler, Edward Coss (these were the 3rd Regiment of Foot Guards, together with the 1st First (Royal Scots), 42nd and 79th Regiments of Foot). But at the same time many Englishmen and Irishmen enlisted in Scottish regiments. According to the same survey, the four Scottish units it covers got no fewer than 543 men from England and 578 from Ireland. The inclusion of both the Scots Guards and the Royal Scots – both of them regiments that had little specifically Scottish about them other than the name – may help to account for this: the two Highland regiments gained 440 of the Scottish recruits as opposed to only thirty of the Englishmen and thirty-five of the Irishmen, whereas the Royal Scots, which was one of the regiments with the largest number of recruits in the survey, drew 79 per cent of the recruits in its ranks from non-Scottish sources (in a separate survey, based on a rather small sample of 206 recruits listed in the so-called 'description book' kept by the Scots Guards, T. H. McGuffie has shown that only thirty-two of these men came from Scotland).[5] Meanwhile so bad did the situation become in another such regiment – the 21st Foot, or Royal North British Fusiliers – that by 1811 it was known as an Irish regiment and so little associated with Scotland that it was felt safe to send it to suppress a revolt that was supposedly about to break out in Sutherland in protest at the growing tide of evictions.[6]

The presence of a solid Scottish contingent in non-Scottish regiments is therefore clear enough, as is that of a rather smaller English and Irish one in Scottish regiments, but for the sake of simplicity this problem will be overlooked.[7] Who, then, are we discussing? In terms of organisation, the Scottish units of the regular army that served in the Revolutionary and Napoleonic Wars can be grouped into two main categories. First, we have the troops who were already on the strength prior to the outbreak of hostilities in March 1793. These were as follows: the 3rd Regiment of Foot Guards (the Scots Guards); the 2nd Regiment of Dragoons (the Royal North British Dragoons); the 1st Regiment of Foot (the Regiment of Royal Scots); the 21st Regiment of Foot (the Royal North British Fusiliers); the 26th Regiment of Foot (the Cameronian Regiment); the 42nd Regiment of Foot (the Royal Highland Regiment, or, more colloquially, the Black Watch); the 70th Regiment of Foot (the Glasgow Lowland Regiment); the 71st Regiment of Foot; the 72nd Regiment of Foot; the 73rd Regiment of Foot; the 74th Regiment of Foot; and the 75th Regiment of Foot (these last five units did not have names at this time, but were all Highland regiments).

With the war becoming ever more serious, however, it soon grew necessary to raise more troops and for this task Scotland was an obvious target. In part, the rationale for this was strategic: only fifty years having passed since the rebellion of 1745, it was common sense to drain the Highlands, in particular, of manpower. Yet other ideas were at play. The secretary of state for war, Henry Dundas, was convinced that Scotland was an ideal recruiting ground for new regiments and that the highlander was potentially a splendid soldier (it has been said of Dundas, indeed, that he was an early example of a Lowland gentleman who romanticised the Highlands and saw in their image a way of strengthening Scottish distinctiveness within the union). His views on recruitment were, at best, only partly right, but these were not the only issues that moved him. What almost certainly mattered more to Dundas was a keen appreciation of the aspirations of his fellow grandees and the lower gentry that flocked around them. As had already been proven during the American War of Independence, the Scottish gentry were quite capable of raising fresh regiments for the crown and they also had a strong interest in doing so.

For men such as Sir James Grant of Strathspey, raising new units of infantry and cavalry allowed them at one and the same time to curry favour with the authorities in London, play the part of the traditional clan chief and dispense considerable quantities of patronage in the form of commissions. Indeed, the importance of their regiments to the lairds was underlined by a famous incident that occurred in respect of the 79th Foot – then the Cameronian Volunteers – in 1795. Ordered to bring his regiment, which had lost 200 casualties in the campaign in Flanders, up to its full strength of 1,000 men, the colonel, Alan Cameron of Erracht, had difficulty doing so and was in consequence told that his troops were to be drafted to other regiments. Much angered – aside from anything else, he had not received a penny from the government to aid with the costs of recruiting and had therefore borne the whole weight on his own shoulders – Cameron rushed to London from the regiment's station on the Isle of Wight to protest. In London, however, he was confronted by the duke of York, who, as commander-in-chief, was ultimately in charge of all such matters: either accept his men being drafted to other regiments or see the entire regiment sent to the West Indies. Cameron's response was forthright – 'You may tell the King your father from me that he may send us to hell if he likes ... but he dauna draft us' – and he and his men were shipped off to Martinique. This minor victory was dearly bought. Within two years over 500 officers and men were dead of yellow fever, the regiment being so badly hit that its remnants were broken up and Cameron left to recruit it from scratch back in Scotland (it appears to be at this point that his command was given the better-known designation of the Cameron Highlanders).[8]

Yet it was not just a question of power and influence on the local stage. Underpinning the formation of the new regiments was a useful political message in that, for all that it had long since begun to break

Figure 15.1 Jane (popularly known as Jean), duchess of Gordon, helped to raise the 92nd (Gordon) Highlanders. She is said to have offered a kiss as an incentive to anyone joining her husband's regiment. Painted by William Skeoch Cumming, 1897.

down, the relationship between the humble clansman and his chief seemed to represent an ideal that the turbulent nature of the times made more than worth restating. Indeed, Scottish lairds had no more reason to like the French Revolution than English lords, and more than one of them hated it with immense passion. A wealthy country gentleman from Perthshire, Sir Thomas Graham, famously formed the 90th Foot – and thereby immediately obtained the rank of colonel for himself – after his wife's coffin had been desecrated in France. Concerned for his wife's health, Graham had taken her to the south of France in 1792. Unfortunately, the lady died, but, on trying to get her body back to Scotland, Graham fell foul of the revolutionary authorities. Accused of espionage, he was arrested, while his wife's casket was broken open and searched for incriminating papers.[9]

Soon after the outbreak of war Dundas was thus canvassing plans for the organisation of many new Scottish regiments and within a few years the army had received many units of just this type. To repeat the previous exercise, these comprised the following: the 78th Regiment of Foot; the 79th Regiment of Foot (the Cameron Highlanders); the 90th Regiment of Foot (the Perthshire Volunteers); the 91st Regiment of Foot (the Argyllshire Highlanders); the 92nd Regiment of Foot (the Gordon Highlanders); the 93rd Regiment of Foot; and the 94th Regiment of Foot (the Scotch Brigade). Again, neither the 78th nor the 93rd received names in the first instance (the latter later became the Sutherland Highlanders), but both were composed of highlanders. In all, then, by 1800 Scotland's nominal share of the British army consisted of one regiment of dragoons, one regiment of guard infantry, six regiments of line infantry and eleven regiments of highlanders.[10]

Before we look at the performance of Scottish troops in the Napoleonic Wars, it is worth taking a closer look at the issue of recruitment in Scotland. The first point to make here is that anyone who imagines throngs of sturdy highlanders eagerly springing forth to fight for king, clan and country is sadly deluded. In fact, such evidence as we have suggests a very different picture. Judging from the limited information that is available, recruitment to the regular army was not particularly buoyant in Scotland. Despite strenuous efforts that often had a specifically Scottish flavour – determined to bring his 92nd Foot up to strength, for example, the duke of Gordon would turn out in the streets in person with his wife and family and a team of pipers and let any man who enlisted dance with his daughters[11] – many units do not appear to have been able to obtain sufficient recruits from recruiting districts north of the border. In 1799, for example, the rebuilt Cameron Highlanders could only muster 268 Scots out of 702 enlisted men, the result being that in 1809 the 72nd, 73rd, 74th, 75th, 91st and 94th Regiments of Foot – all of them originally highlanders – were stripped of their kilts and bonnets on the grounds that Highland dress was a positive obstacle to recruitment, this suggesting, of course, that they had perforce to look for recruits in England and Ireland.[12] Indeed, many of the residents of the Highland counties who were procured for service were in effect pressed by estate managers acting on the instructions of the lairds. This process was certainly used in connection with the 93rd Foot.[13]

Meanwhile, the number of men that Scotland was providing to the army overall seems to have been in decline for some time. During the American War of Independence 24 per cent of the common soldiers and non-commissioned officers in the British army were Scottish, along with 27 per cent of the officers, but, according to Coss, the same description could be applied to only 1,145 – some 15.7 per cent – of the 7,250 recruits he sampled for the period 1790–1815.[14] In respect of the officer corps, the figure remained much higher, for a military career was an obvious choice for sons of the gentry and middle classes alike – it is the opinion of the leading expert, John Cookson, that Scotland retained the 25 per cent share of the officer corps that it had enjoyed ever since the Act of Union, and that despite the fact that the officer corps grew fivefold between 1793 and 1814[15] – but even when the economic situation was very difficult, there was a reticence among the humbler ranks of society to join up. According to Coss's figures, the peak year for recruiting across Britain as a whole was 1806, which was a time of high bread prices and great misery, and yet in that year the 1,097 recruits he traced included just eighty-six Scots (7.8 per cent of the total).[16]

To pick up on a point implied earlier, tying these figures to individual regiments makes for surprising reading. In 1794–5, the 90th Foot had twice as many men from Manchester and Birmingham as it did from Perthshire, with which it was associated, while the 94th Foot was only 54 per cent Scottish.[17] Indeed, the commander of the 79th Foot faced so many recruiting problems that he even tried to obtain the services of a substantial batch of Prussian deserters.[18] Permission to do this was not granted, but, even so, the issue appears to have been taken on board by the authorities. When legislation was subsequently introduced allowing militiamen to volunteer for service in the regular army, serious efforts were made to ensure that Scottish recruits gained in this manner were only allowed to join Scottish regiments, and, together with other measures designed to exclude recruiting parties from English and Irish regiments from Scotland, this transformed the situation. By 1813, 70 per cent of Scots serving in the infantry were doing so in just ten regiments – the 26th, 42nd, 71st, 72nd, 78th, 79th, 91st, 92nd, 93rd and 94th, of which none was below 60 per cent Scottish and five were above 80 per cent.[19]

As to why there should have been such difficulty in raising men for the army, the principal reasons were related to factors that were common to other parts of Britain and, more especially, England and Wales. First and foremost, service as a common soldier in the army enjoyed an evil reputation and offered few rewards, while there were many alternatives. Men from coastal communities with experience of seafaring, for example, could always find higher bounties in the Royal Navy and with them the chance of prize money (it is worth noting here that 7 per cent of the men who fought at Trafalgar were of Scottish origin).[20] For the rest, there was always service in the militia or the various Volunteer units that were established to help resist the

French should they invade. None of these categories of troops ever needed to worry about being sent overseas, while they also came with added attractions.

With respect to the militia, which had been revived in Scotland and extended to all its counties in 1797 in response to the demands of the war against France, recruitment was theoretically conducted by means of conscription (in the first instance for three years), but the purchase of substitutes – a role that had plenty of takers given the substantial payments on offer to anyone willing to step forward in this fashion – was permitted, while service in its ranks carried with it the promise of an allowance for the recruit's family.[21] As for the units enlisted for home defence by means of direct voluntary enlistment, these came in three forms. First, and most important, there were the fencibles, which were full-time units of infantry and cavalry trained and equipped in the same way as the regular army that, like the militia, could be required to serve anywhere in Britain, but whose men received a substantial bounty for signing on. Second, there was the yeomanry, a voluntary part-time cavalry force officered mainly from the propertied classes. Recruits normally had to pay the costs of their own uniforms and equipment, so enjoying a guarantee of social exclusivity, but could be asked to volunteer to serve outside their home counties and received generous allowances for doing so. And, third, there were the Volunteers, these being men who served on a part-time basis in their counties of origin only, received a small allowance that was limited to the days on which they actually served and came in units of a variety of different shapes and sizes, not to mention some of the gaudiest uniforms seen in Britain during the whole period (which incidentally in Scotland included large amounts of tartan – something that only a few years before would have been all but unthinkable). As the militia was greatly expanded during the course of the wars and the various auxiliary units were raised in large numbers – in the Revolutionary Wars alone there were 14 regiments of fencible cavalry, 44 regiments of fencible infantry and 228 units of yeomanry or Volunteers – the result was that the regular army could not but be starved of recruits.[22]

We come here to another point. Just as the Highlands were expected to provide seven of the twenty-three new infantry regiments raised for the British army in the course of the Revolutionary and Napoleonic Wars, so they were expected to provide twenty-three of Scotland's forty-four regiments of fencibles. According to John Prebble, the reason for this was simple. In brief, the Highlands may have been politically suspect in one respect, but in another they were deemed to be absolutely reliable in that, politically, they were dominated by the principle of loyalty to the clan chief and therefore, by extension, far removed from the social and political agitation that was increasingly a feature of the Lowlands. To quote the words of an anonymous memorandum written in 1797, they were 'strangers to the levelling and dangerous principles of the present age'.[23] The reasons for this were never articulated very well – they lay, of course, in the area's geographical remoteness and economic backwardness – but the thinking was nonetheless acute enough in its general principles, and all the more so as the highlanders could with some reason be expected to bear a grudge against the lowlanders who had so consistently stood against them in the wars of the previous century, but had now, at least potentially, been transformed into militant revolutionaries. If so many of the fencibles, in particular, were originally envisaged as Highland units, it was because it was felt that this would boost their value in terms of policing. In short, it was not so much that a martial tradition existed amongst the clans, but rather that one was invented.[24]

All too evidently, then, the idea that Scottish recruitment was in some way boosted by longstanding instincts and habits of behaviour does not seem to be very plausible. Many thousands of Scots certainly served in the armed forces, and it is quite clear that they did so in numbers that far outweighed their share of the population. In 1811 Scotland was home to approximately 10 per cent of Britons and yet, according to Coss, it supplied 15 per cent of the regular army's recruits. Meanwhile, according to Cookson, in 1797 36.4 per cent of the Volunteers were raised in Scotland. Although this figure had slipped to 16.7 per cent by 1804, it still represented an impressive proportion.[25] However, setting aside the obvious fact that most men who enlisted did so in capacities that would keep them out of harm's way, there are two points that have to be made in qualification of this phenomenon. In the first place, genuine highlanders were surprisingly few in number. Of this there is much evidence. In 1794 the 895 men who made up the first battalion raised for the 92nd Foot, then numbered the 100th Foot, contained only 354 representatives of the Highlands.[26] Even the Black Watch – a unit of great prestige and one that would gain a colonel of great charm and popularity in the person of the marquess of Huntly – only drew 51 per cent of its men from the Highlands in 1798.[27] As for the fencibles and Volunteers, even units associated with areas such as the Western Isles seem never to have managed to recruit more than 70 per cent of their strength from the local population.[28] This is not to say that the Highlands did not make an extraordinary effort in terms of recruitment – one estimate is that they put 74,000 men into uniform out of a population of some 300,000[29] – but in the end such was the determination of the Highland aristocracy to share in the variety of benefits conferred upon them by the formation of new regiments of one sort or another that the duke of Argyll and the rest were simply asked to support far more units than they could possibly manage. By the late 1790s, just 3 per cent of the population of Great Britain were being expected to sustain the needs of eleven regiments of infantry, twenty-three regiments of fencibles and at least ten regiments of militia, together with a considerable number of auxiliary units of one sort or another (according to figures supplied by Spiers, about half of Scotland's Volunteers came from north of a line stretching from Dumbarton to Fife).[30]

The second point to make is that the vast majority of those men who did enlist did so because they were in desperate economic straits. In the late eighteenth century Scotland was undergoing a period of intense social and economic change. The population was increasing rapidly; the Highlands were in the grip of the mass evictions known as the Clearances; the main towns and cities – all of which, of course, were situated in the Lowlands – were under great pressure; and many farming districts were being affected by a variety of improvements and other changes in agricultural practices that had the effect of forcing many small tenant farmers off their holdings and converting them into wage labourers. Absorbing these developments was by no means easy. The industrial revolution was 'taking off' in Glasgow, but in the course of the Revolutionary and Napoleonic Wars there were repeated slumps that cut back opportunities for the poor, while the problem of destitution was exacerbated by serious harvest failures, not to mention the fact that wages throughout tended to lag behind prices. In general, the period is one in which the lower classes experienced, at the very best, a stagnation in living standards. With plenty of money on offer and conditions of service in the many non-regular units relatively easy, and in the face of a Poor Law that could not do more than keep paupers alive at the barest level of subsistence, there was therefore every incentive for men to 'go for a soldier'.[31]

But in the end it is evident that military service was not an option that was embraced with open arms. Even recruitment of the fencibles met with problems, those Highland chiefs who wished to raise them frequently engaging in compulsion. To quote Robert Clyde:

> The great majority of senior officers in the regiments during this period were Highland gentry and used their power as landlords to procure the necessary recruits; essentially, tenants and others residing on a certain

estate gave up their sons for military service in exchange for promises that they would not be evicted.[32]

In Glengarry the appearance of a recruiting party bent on obtaining men for such a regiment even provoked wholesale flight on one occasion.[33] Meanwhile, when the militia system was extended to Scotland in 1797 the response was an outbreak of serious rioting. Starting at Eccles in Berwickshire on 17 August crowds set upon the magistrates and other local worthies who had been charged with drawing up the lists of those eligible for conscription and destroyed their papers while in some instances also planting 'liberty trees'. According to some accounts, indeed, the disturbances were fomented by sympathisers with the French Revolution who had set up a secret society modelled on those of England and Ireland known as the United Scotsmen. For the most part the riots passed off without serious harm to anyone, but in the coal-mining district of Tranent, east of Edinburgh, things were very different. In an angry meeting at the village of Prestonpans on 28 August a large crowd, in which women were very prominent, denounced the new measures and sacked the house of the local schoolmaster before dispersing to their homes. Much alarmed at the radicalism of the crowd, the local pit-owners called in the troops and the next day a small column of soldiers turned up to restore order. There followed an angry confrontation and very soon firing broke out. Twelve members of the local community were killed and many more wounded, while the soldiers then added insult to injury by going on a drunken rampage. Nor was this the end of the trouble. Inspired by the news of the riot at Tranent, a number of revolutionary agitators – all of them members of the United Scotsmen – organised what has been described as a full-scale insurrection in the valley of the River Tay. Thus, a large crowd descended on Menzies castle, which they occupied as their base, and sent deputations off in all directions to compel the local gentry to declare against the militia. Plans were afoot, it seems, to seize arms and launch a guerrilla war, but prompt action by the nearest troops soon had the would-be rebels fleeing for their home villages, though it seems that a few men who had got hold of firearms sought to harass the soldiers as they retired to their home base.[34]

Strathspey was a particular source of trouble, for already in 1794 and 1795 the (partly) locally raised Strathspey Fencibles had twice mutinied in the face of unfounded rumours that they were to be compelled to serve outside Scotland, the second and more serious instance having ended in the execution of two of the ringleaders.[35] Mutiny and riot, meanwhile, were but one response to the imposition of military service in forms of which the populace disapproved. In so far as the militia was concerned, for those who could afford it, there was a much simpler way out, and that was to purchase a substitute. Evidence for the extent to which this took place is limited, but such data as can be found is certainly revealing. Thus, in 1804 the Bute Militia did not have a single 'principal' – a soldier who had fallen victim to the ballot – every one of its men being someone who was serving in the place of someone else. In contrast, out of 601 men sent to the militia from Edinburgh in 1799 only 179 fell into this latter category.[36]

Taking the argument still further, the social provenance of the rank and file certainly suggests that recruitment was concentrated amongst groups that were likely to be particularly exposed to the vicissitudes of economic change and harvest failure. If we examine the figures presented by Coss, we discover that of the 1,111 Scottish soldiers whose occupation is recorded, 412 were labourers (a category that almost certainly includes many tenant farmers who had been driven from their lands), 402 textile workers and 297 workers in other trades.[37] Meanwhile, moving on to the sample of the 'description book' of the Scots Guards previously referred to, we find that, out of the 206 entries, 106 were labourers, 33 weavers, spinners, framework knitters or stockingers, and the remainder almost all skilled workers or artisans, the residue – four shopkeepers, an optician and a musician – all presumably being men who had either failed in business, become social misfits or otherwise fallen on hard times.[38]

In short, while there may have been some men who craved adventure and others who, to paraphrase Wellington, enlisted for drink or were seeking to evade the consequences of some roll in the hay, most men joined up out of necessity. Yet simply because military service was chiefly the recourse of the desperate does not necessarily mean that Scottish soldiers could not fight hard once they finally got into action. Let us now, then, move on to a discussion of the record of the Scottish regiments in battle. As was observed at the beginning of this chapter, this has generally been held to be excellent. Indeed, if heed is paid to some of the more popular representations of Britain's struggle against Napoleon, the highlanders, especially, could almost be deemed to have won the war single-handed. As witness of this one need only look at the illustrations contained in books about the battle of Waterloo. In almost all of these, highlanders (the only non-Highland unit featured with any regularity is the Scots Greys) appear in far more pictures than is warranted by their participation in the battle, at which they were represented by just five infantry battalions out of the twenty-nine British units of this type involved in the campaign. For example, in H. Lachouque's *Waterloo* (1972), out of thirty-nine depictions of British soldiers, sixteen feature Highlanders (to this latter figure could be added six others relating to the famous charge of the 2nd Dragoons or Scots Greys). In Lord Chalfont's *Waterloo: Battle of the Three Armies* (1979), there are fourteen such pictures, of which five show highlanders. And in Ian Fletcher's *A Desperate Business: Wellington, the British Army and the Waterloo Campaign* (2001), the same totals come to twenty-one out of sixty-three. What is even more striking is that highlanders often appear in contexts in which the artist had no particular need to feature them. Thus, alongside the pictures of French cuirassiers charging Highland squares, or Highland regiments marching out of Brussels on the evening of 15 June, highlanders are strewn at the feet of Wellington's horse having their wounds dressed, escorting French prisoners back to Brussels and even witnessing the meeting between Wellington and Blücher at La Belle Alliance. In short, the highlander is ubiquitous – almost a universal symbol for the entire British army.[39]

That this should have been the case is by no means surprising. With their ostrich feathers, kilts and sporrans, highlanders were inherently exotic figures and, as such, attracted much attention wherever they went. 'Many young Scots found their dress not an encumbrance when they courted the young ladies of Belgium,' writes John Sutherland. 'Even then there seemed to be unusual interest in what a Scot might wear under his kilt.'[40] But for reasons that were as much as anything historical they were lionised from the earliest days of British success. For the best part of a century England had lived in fear of Scotland and, more especially, the Highlands, and the fact that men in kilts were now fighting bravely for the crown meant that many dark terrors had now evaporated. In the period since 1745, meanwhile, the image of the highlander had been steadily changing from that of an outright barbarian to that of a noble savage, and it seemed to be a matter of celebration that the inherent qualities that had hitherto largely been at the service of an enemy cause should now be reinforcing the armies of Great Britain.[41] No sooner had highlanders begun to participate in British victories – the first example came at the battle of Alexandria in 1801 – than they were celebrated as heroes, and all the more so as it was doubtless perceived that this would stimulate further recruitment.

As the wars continued, so various deeds of Highland courage presented themselves as timely exemplars, a case in point being that of Piper George Clark of the 71st. Wounded in the legs at the battle of

Figure 15.2 Richard Ansdell's *The Fight for the Standard*, c. 1848, showing Sergeant Charles Ewart of the Scots Greys capturing the standard of the French 45th infantry regiment at Waterloo.

Figure 15.3 The eagle from the standard of the French 45th regiment captured by Sergeant Ewart.

Vimeiro on 21 August 1808, he continued to play the men into action as they advanced to defeat the French.[42] It was the Waterloo campaign, however, that really cemented the claim of the Scottish troops to the gratitude of the nation (whether British or Scottish). In their one and only action of the entire Napoleonic Wars, the Scots Greys launched a heroic charge at a key moment in the battle that saw Sergeant Ewart cut his way though crowds of desperate Frenchmen to capture the eagle of the 45th Line.[43] Meanwhile, regiments such as the 42nd, the 79th and the 92nd alternately withstood hour after hour of bombardment and repeated cavalry charges. After the battle many admiring stories circulated about the Scots. According to Cavalié Mercer, captain in the Royal Horse Artillery:

> The road was covered with [Allied] soldiers, many of them . . . apparently untouched. The numbers thus leaving the field appeared extraordinary . . . My countrymen will rejoice to learn that amongst this dastardly crew, not one Briton appeared . . . One redcoat we did meet – not a fugitive, though, for he was severely wounded. This man was a private of the 92nd (Gordon Highlanders), a short, rough hardy-looking fellow with . . . a complexion that spoke of many a bivouac. He came limping along, evidently with difficulty and suffering. I stopped him to ask news of the battle, telling him what I had heard from . . . others. 'Na, na, Sir, it's aw a damned lee; they war fechtin' yat an I left'em, but it's a bludy business, and thar's na saying fat may be the end on't. Oor ragiment was nigh clean swapt off, and oor colonel kilt jist as I cam awa.' Upon enquiring about his . . . wound, we found that a musket ball had lodged in his knee . . . Accordingly, [we] seated him on the parapet of a little bridge . . . extracted the ball in a few minutes, and, binding up the wound, sent him hobbling along towards Nivelle, not having extracted a single exclamation from the poor man, who gratefully thanked [us] as he resumed his way.[44]

As further witness to the esteem in which the Highland regiments, in particular, were held in 1815 let me quote here David Stewart, an officer who had reached high rank in the Black Watch:

> Some time after the surrender of Paris, the regiment passed over to England, and from thence marched to Scotland . . . It was understood that they were to march into Edinburgh Castle on the 18th of March. A crowd of idle spectators is not so easily collected in Edinburgh as in London, but on this occasion it seemed as if two-thirds of the houses and the workshops in the city had been emptied of their inhabitants. Several hours before the regiment arrived, the road to Musselburgh was covered with carriages,

horsemen and pedestrians. At Portobello the crowd was great, and, on entering the Canongate, it was a solid moving mass, pressed together as if in a frame. The pipers and the band could not play for want of room, and were obliged to put up their instruments. Many of the crowd, on raising their hands to take off their hats to wave them in the air, could not without difficulty get them replaced by their sides . . . Of the soldiers little was seen except their bonnets and feathers.[45]

Finally, we have the words of the poet and journalist Robert Southey, who, on visiting the battlefield in October 1815, wrote, 'The Scotchmen – "those men without breeches" – have the credit of the day at Waterloo.'[46] Thus far, thus good, but did the Highland regiments really deserve the extraordinary reputation they earned during this period and which they have enjoyed ever since? At the time, there was more than a little grumbling among the rest of the army. Of this, we find a very good expression in the memoirs of John Leach, an officer in the 95th Rifles who served both in the Peninsular War and at Waterloo:

In the encampment near Saint Denis I one day overheard the following curious dialogue between some soldiers of our division. An Irishman who was washing his linen under a hedge close to my tent observed to some of his comrades similarly employed, 'I'm tould the newspapers is come from England, and, by Jasus, thim Highlanders have got al the cridit for the battle.' To this, a Highlander, who was on the opposite side of the hedge and had heard the remark, replied, 'And sa they ocht', meaning, I presume, 'so they ought'. The Irishman, however, appeared by no means disposed to cede that point, and very naturally proceeded, 'Sure, didn't we do our duty as any of thim Highland regiments, and lose as many men?' I much doubt, however, whether honest Pat's logic carried with it that conviction . . . which it most indisputably ought to have done . . . No man will deny that the Highlanders displayed invincible courage, and that they nobly upheld the honour of their country and of their respective regiments . . . The myriads of letters, however, with which the newspapers were constantly inundated for some months after the battle from Highlanders to their friends in the north actually had the effect of convincing nine tenths of the people in England, and 999 out of every 1,000 people in Scotland, that the Scottish regiments were the only people who pulled a trigger . . . throughout the whole of that protracted struggle, and that they, unaided, defeated the reiterated attacks of the imperial legions . . . Various panoramic exhibitions have also strongly tended to convince the good people of England that John Bull and Pat were little better than spectators . . . In a panorama at Edinburgh some months after the battle, the Highlanders and Scotch [sic] were depicted as giants, and placed in the foremost ranks, cutting, slashing, charging, bayoneting and sending headlong to the devil everything in the shape of a Frenchman, whilst the other poor dear harmless little regiments . . . were represented as mere pygmies in size and stature and placed in the background.[47]

Leach certainly has a case in so far as the representation of Waterloo, in particular, is concerned, yet many instances can still be found of Scottish gallantry. To take just one instance, let us discuss the action at the Puerto de Maya on 24 July 1813. In brief, what had happened was that a large French army had been thrown into an offensive in an attempt to relieve the besieged fortresses of Pamplona and San Sebastián. Pushing across the Pyrenees they encountered a thin line of Anglo-Portuguese defenders. They put up a good fight everywhere, but particular glory was earned by a half-battalion of the 92nd Foot which found itself blocking a narrow ridge in the very teeth of the French advance. One of the Gordons concerned was Lieutenant James Hope:

The right wing of the 92nd Regiment had now for some time to sustain the brunt of the combat. Their numbers did not exceed 370 men, whilst that of their enemies could not be fewer than 3,000 veterans. Colonel Cameron, on seeing the enemy, withdrew his little band about thirty paces in order to draw them forward, that he might have an opportunity of charging them. They greedily swallowed the bait – they advanced – but, as soon as the 92nd halted, the enemy did the same. The French now opened a terrible fire of musketry on the Highlanders, which they returned with admirable effect. For a quarter of an hour the French officers used every means in their power to induce their men to charge us, but their utmost efforts were unavailing. Not one of them could they prevail on to advance in front of their line of slain, which in a few minutes not only covered the field, but in many places lay piled in heaps. The Highlanders continued to resist the attacks of their numerous and enraged opponents till their numbers were reduced to 120 and all their officers wounded and borne from the field, except two young lieutenants. The senior of these [that is, Hope himself], seeing no support at hand and finding that the ammunition of those with him was nearly exhausted, conceived that a retreat was the most advisable measure he could adopt. With this handful of men, he retired from the bloody field, on which he left thirty-three that had been killed or mortally wounded during the action.[48]

To an extent, then, the image can be sustained, but if we look at the statistical evidence it does appear that any idea of the highlander as the ideal soldier and, indeed, the most capable soldier in the British army is open to challenge. Of course, neither courage nor discipline nor military efficiency can ever really be measured by recourse to figures, but these can certainly serve as useful indicators. Let us begin with the issue of casualties. In a recent survey that has been undertaken of the casualties suffered by thirty-four British battalions in the major actions of the Peninsular War, the seven Scottish battalions featured are shown to have suffered 4,015 rank-and-file casualties out of the total of 15,320. However, if the battalions are split up by classification (such as the Light Division, English line, Irish line, Guards, Highlanders) it quickly becomes apparent that the Scots did not suffer the heaviest loss rate. Whilst the price they paid was certainly very heavy at 574 men per battalion, the group heaviest hit was the Irish. Also represented by seven battalions, these units lost 4,319 casualties, or 617 men per battalion.[49] If the same exercise is repeated for Waterloo, the five Highland battalions that fought there lost 734 rank-and-file casualties out of a total for the British infantry of 4,255. In other words, whilst the average loss per battalion was 164, for the Highland units it was 147 (in view of the wild reception given to the Black Watch when they arrived in Edinburgh, it is worth noting that it suffered just five dead and thirty-nine wounded; equally, no Highland unit lost more than 225 casualties, whereas the 3rd Foot Guards – a very non-Scottish unit despite its appellation of the Scots Guards – lost 327, and the 27th Foot, 463).[50] In so far as these figures suggest anything it is that the Scottish performance on the battlefield was praiseworthy, but not particularly outstanding. Yet it was a Scot who produced what was arguably the greatest single act of individual heroism that the British army witnessed on the Waterloo battlefield. With his battalion assailed by wave after wave of French cavalry, and suffering grievously from the attention of the French artillery, Piper Kenneth Mackay of the Cameron Highlanders stepped out of the safety of the square into which it had been formed and paced round its outer faces playing a stirring Scottish air.[51]

As for the performance of the Scottish forces off the field, here too there is evidence that the Scots had nothing to be ashamed of, particularly during the two worst experiences to befall the British army during the Peninsular War, namely the retreat of Sir John Moore to Corunna in the winter of 1808–9, and the retreat from Burgos and Madrid to Ciudad Rodrigo in the autumn of 1812. In both these campaigns demoralisation, exhaustion, want of food and miserable

Figure 15.4 Piper Kenneth Mackay of the 79th (Cameron) Highlanders at Waterloo. Painted by William Lockhart Bogle, 1893.

weather combined seriously to erode the strength of the troops, many of whom fell by the roadside and were later in many instances swept up as prisoners. The loss rate was not uniform, however. In general, regiments in which the bonds of duty and *esprit de corps* were strong held together well, the heaviest losses being concentrated in units where these factors were weaker. Applying ourselves to the casualty figures of the British infantry, we find that Corunna campaign cost Moore 6,464 casualties, or a loss rate of 185 men per battalion, whereas his five Highland battalions – the 42nd, 71st, 79th, 91st and 92nd – lost 795 men or a loss rate of 159 per battalion.[52] Expressed in percentage terms, the figures are even clearer. Whereas the infantry as a whole lost 25.37 per cent of its strength, the figure for the highlanders was only 17.89 per cent. Although the Scots were only lightly engaged on the battlefield, the highlanders appear to have sustained their reputation for discipline and relative sobriety during the retreat.

Regrettably, a similar analysis of the losses suffered in the retreat to Ciudad Rodrigo is not possible because of the fact that the totals only ever seem to have been reported by division and not by regiment.

According to Oman, total losses due to straggling came to 4,752 men, of whom 2,073 came from British infantry regiments. In the course of these events the Scots suffered just as much as everyone else. Trudging along with the 94th Foot was a miserable and bedraggled Private Joseph Donaldson:

> I never saw the troops in such bad humour. Retreating before the enemy at any time was a grievous business, but in such weather it was doubly so. The rain, now pouring down in torrents, drenched us to the skin, and the road, composed of a clay soil, stuck to our shoes so fast, that they were torn off our feet. The ... cold wind blew in heavy gusts, and the roads became gradually worse ... Few words were spoken ... A savage sort of desperation had taken possession of our minds, and those who had lived on the most friendly terms in happier times now quarrelled with each other, using the most frightful imprecations on the slightest offence. All former feeling of friendship was stifled and a misanthropic spirit took possession of every bosom. The streams which fell from the hills were swelled into rivers, which we had to wade, and vast numbers fell out ... having been ... reduced to the most abject misery.[53]

Yet in this instance, too, the highlanders may just possibly have shown themselves to better advantage than their peers in that the First, Second and Third Divisions, each of which had two battalions that were strongly Scottish (that is, five Highland plus the largely Lowland 94th), averaged losses of 8.1 per cent, whereas the rest of the infantry averaged losses of 10.1 per cent. Whilst the cheerful hardiness that is very much a part of the mythology of the Scottish soldier in the Napoleonic Wars was certainly under great strain, it does not seem to have collapsed altogether.

To conclude, what we have seen in this chapter is yet another example of the vulnerability of historical myths. Both at the time and since, the soldiers that Scotland sent to fight in the Napoleonic Wars, and especially the highlanders, have been remembered as 'bonnie lads' and 'braw fighters' – men who cheerfully marched forth under the leadership of their traditional clan chiefs and won unending glory on battlefield after battlefield. This version of events, however, is partial at best. Presented with an excellent political opportunity by a government in London that was anxious to neutralise the last vestiges of the threat of a Jacobite rising, the clan chiefs were certainly very active in the mobilisation of Scotland's manpower, helping to form many new regiments and either directly or indirectly providing many of their officers. Under their leadership and, in addition, that of many Lowland magnates, Scotland made what was in all probability the greatest military effort in its history. The idea that the Scots rushed willingly into battle is, however, a myth. On the contrary, recruitment met with much resistance and was concentrated in parts of the armed forces that enjoyed guarantees that they would never have to fight beyond the confines of the United Kingdom, and, very often, indeed, Scotland. Once in the army, the highlanders and their fellow Scots fought well enough, and sometimes very bravely, but, while they were clearly steady troops, whether they really merited their heroic reputation is a moot point. Nor did the highlanders for the most part even wear the kilt. Several regiments were, as we have seen, stripped of them for recruitment purposes, while the rigours of campaigning in the Peninsula soon forced even those units who retained them to adopt the grey trousers worn by the rest of the infantry. It is probable that Highland garb was only ever on display en masse at Waterloo, most of Wellington's British troops arriving there straight from the depots of Great Britain.[54] Scotland, then, did not win the wars, but it did win the peace, for, with the nation mesmerised by visions of loyal kilted clansmen, England at last both accepted it as an integral part of the union and recognised its separate cultural identity. Military occupation was ended too. From the 1790s onwards, home defence was entirely in the hands of local auxiliaries, while after 1800 only Scottish regiments of the regular army were based north of the border. Furthermore, after Waterloo 'highlandism' may be said to have conquered Scotland, thereby helping to heal the political divisions that had bedevilled the country for so long. With the Highlands themselves already partially cleared, not least by the extraction of so much of their surplus manpower, it was truly the end of an era.[55]

Let us, however, end this chapter not with abstract discussions of the social and political consequences for Scotland of the Napoleonic Wars, but rather with the figure of the individual Scottish soldier. If the following anecdote is anything to go by, the many men who failed to return from the wars were not forgotten. Amongst the many traditional folk songs that have come down to us from the Napoleonic period is 'The Ballad of Jamie Foyers'. This recounts in considerable detail the fate of a young man from Campsie who, having first enlisted in the Perthshire Militia, elects to transfer into the Black Watch. Exactly when this happened we do not know, but it was undoubtedly in the period from February 1809 to March 1812, during the whole of which time the first battalion of the Black Watch – the unit that Foyers must have joined – was in England, and very likely towards the end of this period. This, however, is irrelevant: as the song tells us, in 1812 Foyers's battalion was sent to Spain to join Wellington's army and in mid-September duly found itself confronting the fortress the French had constructed overlooking the city of Burgos. Here, the careers of Foyers and many of his comrades were cut tragically short. On the night of 19 September – as the song recounts, the very first night of the siege – the 1st/42nd was ordered to take part in an assault on an outlying earthern redoubt called the Hornwork of San Miguel. While some of the highlanders advanced on the work from the front with orders to keep down the fire of the defenders, two parties were ordered to attack it from the flank as the spearhead of larger columns of Portuguese troops. It was a formidable task: the glacis of the fort was entirely devoid of cover, while the walls that the two ladder parties had to assault were at least thirty feet high. The result was a bloodbath. Out on the exposed glacis, the firing party was cut down in droves by French canister and musketry, while in the ditches the assault troops discovered that their ladders were too short. Undaunted, the highlanders tried to scale the wall by improvising extra steps with their bayonets, but the enemy fire was too strong for them and the attack would have failed had not an enterprising officer named Cocks led a small group of men round to the relatively unprotected rear face of the fort and got his men inside there. In all, 204 of the highlanders were killed or wounded, and among the former was Foyers, who the song tells us was hit by a cannonball while climbing a ladder. Mortally wounded, he dies in the arms of his comrades though not without first asking them (at some length) to bid farewell to his friends and family.[56]

This tale is worth telling because it transpires that Foyers was a real-life soldier, being listed as Sergeant James Foyer in the casualty return submitted by his battalion the day after the assault on the Hornwork. Quite why or how this one soldier came to be remembered in song is not known. The earliest written version of the ballad dates to the 1850s, but by that time the song had long since become a firm favourite in the north-east of Scotland. At least one dead highlander thus became revered in folk memory and it is scarcely fanciful to imagine that the popularity of the song that commemorated him was in part a reflection of a wider sense of pride and, indeed, loss: as the chorus poignantly reminds us, the bones of such men as Foyer were in many instances not even properly buried, but left to 'lie scattered on the rude soil of Spain'. They lie there still: in the course of recent explorations of the fortress of Burgos by a team headed by the author, human remains were found inside the fort where Foyer died.[57]

Notes

1. A. Leask, *Sword of Scotland: Jocks at War* (Barnsley: Pen and Sword, 1996), pp. 98–108 passim.
2. M. Foy, *History of the War in the Peninsula under Napoleon, to which is prefixed a View of the Political and Military State of the Four Belligerent Powers*, 2 vols (London: Treuttel and Würtz, Treuttel Jun. and Richter, 1827), vol. 1, p. 196.
3. J. Patterson, *The Adventures of Captain John Patterson with Notices of the Officers, etc., of the Fiftieth or Queen's Own, Regiment from 1807 to 1821* (London: T. and W. Boone, 1827), pp. 354–5.
4. P. Haythornthwaite, *The Armies of Wellington* (London: Arms and Armour Press, 1994), p. 75; R. Holmes, *Redcoat: The British Soldier in the Age of Horse and Musket* (London: HarperCollins, 2001), p. 55.
5. For the relevant details of this survey, see E. J. Coss, 'All for the King's shilling: An analysis of the campaign and combat experience of the British soldier in the Peninsular War, 1808–1814' (unpublished PhD thesis, Ohio State University, 2005), pp. 335–7. This has since been published as E. J. Coss, *All for the King's Shilling: The British Soldier under Wellington, 1808–1814* (Norman, OK: University of Oklahoma Press, 2010). For McGuffie's contribution to the debate, see T. H. McGuffie, 'Recruiting the ranks of the regular British army during the French Wars: Recruiting, recruits and methods of enlistment', *Journal of the Society for Army Historical Research*, vol. 34, no. 139 (September 1956), p. 125.
6. R. Clyde, *From Rebel to Hero: The Image of the Highlander, 1745–1830* (East Linton: Tuckwell Press, 1995), p. 172.
7. At the level of the rank and file, this probably makes no odds in that the Scottish soldiers fighting in English regiments were roughly cancelled out by the English ones fighting in Scottish regiments (here defined as units that primarily recruited in Scotland, imbued with Scottish cultural associations or traditionally possessed of associations with Scotland). But a word must here be said in honour of the large numbers of Scottish officers who held commissions either temporarily or permanently in non-Scottish regiments or served in other capacities. Typical of the men caught up in this traffic, which for a variety of reasons was largely one way, was the Glaswegian Sir John Moore, whose service as a regimental officer in the French Wars included periods with the 60th, 51st and 52nd Foot; less so was John Downie, a failed merchant and sometime South American revolutionary from Blairgorts, who enlisted as a commissary in 1808 and after many adventures ended up as a Spanish general, his story being recounted in C. J. Esdaile, 'Guerrillas, bandits, adventurers

and commissaries: The story of John Downie', in C. Woolgar (ed.), *Wellington Studies, IV* (Southampton: Hartley Institute, 2008), pp. 94–125.

8. For this story, see 'Record of the formation and services of the Seventy-Ninth Cameron Highlanders: A transcription of an original hand-written document'. Available at www.qohldrs.co.uk/html/cameron_hldrs-full_hist1.htm, accessed on 5 January 2009; cf. also S. Reid, *Wellington's Highland Warriors: From the Black-Watch Mutiny to the Battle of Waterloo, 1743–1815* (Barnsley: Frontline Books, 2010), pp. 55–75. In testimony to the strength of family connections in recruiting such regiments, according to the website of the museum of the Argyll and Sutherland Highlanders no fewer than fifteen of the Argyllshire regiment's first thirty-three officers were Campbells. See www.argylls.co.uk/history-of-the-regiment/the-91st-argyllshire-highlanders-1794-1881/ 1794-1881, accessed on 1 August 2011.
9. For details of the life of Sir Thomas Graham, see A. M. Delavoye, *Life of Sir Thomas Graham, Lord Lynedoch* (London: Richardson & Co., 1886).
10. The role of Henry Dundas is discussed in J. E. Cookson, *The British Armed Nation, 1793–1815* (Oxford: Clarendon Press, 1997), pp. 130–8. For a handy guide to the regiments of the British army at this time, see R. Partridge and M. Oliver, *Napoleonic Army Handbook (I): The British Army and her Allies* (London: Constable, 1999), pp. 35–48. After this point no new regiments were formed. As will be observed from the text, the designation of the British army regiments was rather complex, with regiments being given not just a number but also a name. To create still more problems, a few units used nicknames – the Royal North British Dragoons was always the Scots Greys and the Royal Highland Regiment the Black Watch, while the otherwise unnamed 78th became the Ross-shire Buffs – or became known by unofficial names (the 71st, for example, was always referred to as the 71st Highlanders before eventually being redesignated as the Highland Light Infantry).
11. Coss, 'All for the King's shilling', p. 116.
12. Haythornthwaite, *Armies of Wellington*, p. 76. The units concerned did not just adopt the standard infantry uniform, however: on the contrary the 71st affected trews and versions of the Highland bonnet.
13. Clyde, *From Rebel to Hero*, p. 171.
14. Holmes, *Redcoat*, p. 55; Coss, 'All for the King's shilling', p. 79.
15. Cookson, *The British Armed Nation*, p. 127.
16. Coss, 'All for the King's shilling', p. 77.
17. Cookson, *The British Armed Nation*, p. 137.
18. Ibid. p. 132.

19. Ibid. p. 146. These figures are scarcely representative of the war as a whole, but the dramatic increase in Scottish recruitment that they suggest has nonetheless enabled pro-Scottish commentators to take shelter in statistics that at first sight appear most favourable to them. For example, railing against the decision to strip the 91st Foot of its kilts, which it attributes to the hostile public reaction that the latter garb attracted in England, the website of its regimental museum claims that between 1800 and 1818 its first battalion raised 970 Scots, 171 English, 218 Irish and 22 foreigners, and that between 1809 and 1814 the same figures for its second battalion were 599, 168, 142 and 197. This, however, proves nothing, though it does seem to be the case that, when first mustered in 1794, the regiment was almost entirely made up of Scots, albeit in large part from Glasgow and Edinburgh rather than the Highlands. See www.argylls.co.uk/history-of-the-regiment/the-91st-argyllshire-highlanders-1794-1881/1794-1881, accessed on 1 August 2011.
20. P. Hore, 'Trafalgar: 200 years on – the sailors', *BBC History Magazine*, vol. 6, no. 10 (October 2005), p. 21.
21. The problem caused by the purchase of substitutes for the militia outbidding direct recruitment to the army was in part resolved by the practice of periodically authorising the enlistment of militiamen into the army, which thus received many men who came ready-trained. At the same time, particularly after Wellington began to win victory after victory in the Peninsula, the practice was very successful: once they had been drawn into the militia, men tended to lose their suspicions of life in the army, and even increasingly wanted to test themselves as 'real' soldiers.
22. For the Volunteer units, see Leask, *Sword of Scotland*, pp. 106–7. In his *Mutiny: Highland Regiments in Revolt, 1743–1804* (London: Secker and Warburg, 1975), John Prebble notes that the number of Fencible regiments was thirty-seven, rather than forty-four; it may, however, be that some units never came to fruition.
23. Quoted in P. Womack, *Improvement and Romance: Constructing the Myth of the Scottish Highlands* (London: Macmillan, 1989), pp. 49–50.
24. For all this, see Prebble, *Mutiny*, pp. 271–2.
25. Cookson, *British Armed Nation*, p. 128.
26. Ibid. p. 130. The regimental historian found a somewhat larger proportion of highlanders from his analysis of the Description Roll of 1794, but he confirmed that the regiment had to find recruits from outside of the Highlands. Lt.-Col. C. Greenhill Gardyne, *The Life of A Regiment: The History of the Gordon Highlanders from its Formation in 1794 to 1816* (London: The Medici Society, 1901), p. 14.
27. Holmes, *Redcoat*, p. 55.
28. Cookson, *British Armed Nation*, p. 129.

29. T. M. Devine, *Clanship to Crofters' War: The Social Transformation of the Scottish Highlands* (Manchester: Manchester University Press, 1994), p. 43. For an insight into what this effort meant in human terms in just one small corner of the kingdom, and, in particular, details of seventy-four men from the area around Thurso and Wick who volunteered for service abroad, see Anon., 'The military tradition in Caithness, Part 2: The territorial road to 1914'. Available at /www.internet-promotions.co.uk/archives/Caithness/tradition2.htm, accessed on 1 August 2011.
30. E. M. Spiers, 'Highland soldier: Imperial image and impact', *Northern Scotland*, vol. 1 (2010), p. 77. In one respect, however, the Highlands were spared. For reasons that are not quite clear, no yeomanry units appear to have been raised north of Perthshire and Forfar. At the same time, some lessening in the burden occurred from 1799 onwards thanks to the successive disbandment of all the fencible regiments (unlike the Volunteers, moreover, these were not resuscitated in 1803). For details on the fencible movement, in particular, see R. McGuigan, 'The forgotten army: Fencible regiments of the British army, 1793–1816'. Available at www.napoleon-series.org/military/organization/fencibles/c_fencibles.html, accessed on 26 October 2010.
31. For some suggestive material on the social and economic background, see T. M. Devine and R. Mitchison (eds), *People and Society in Scotland, vol. I: 1760–1830* (Edinburgh: John Donald Publishers, 1988), pp. 9–69, 188–203, 252–67 passim, and T. M. Devine, *The Great Highland Famine: Hunger, Emigration and the Scottish Highlands in the Nineteenth Century* (Edinburgh: John Donald Publishers, 1988), pp. 1–27.
32. Clyde, *From Rebel to Hero*, p. 165.
33. Ibid. p. 166.
34. For all this see K. J. Logue, 'The Tranent Militia riot of 1797', *Transactions of the East Lothian Antiquarian and Field Naturalists' Society*, vol. 14 (1974), pp. 34–61; D. Fraser, '1797 and Tranent: The United Scotsmen'. Available at http://kennysheerin.blogspot.com/2007/03/1797-and-tranent-by-donnie-fraser.html, accessed on 2 August 2011.
35. Prebble, *Mutiny*, pp. 263–391 passim.
36. Coss, 'All for the King's shilling', p. 107.
37. Ibid. pp. 118–19; Cookson, *British Armed Nation*, p. 107.
38. McGuffie, 'Recruiting the ranks of the British army', p. 125.
39. As a further point of interest here, it might be observed that when the plastic figure and kit manufacturer Airfix brought out its range of Napoleonic plastic war games figures in 1971 the very first set was composed of highlanders (inevitably, perhaps, there immediately followed a set of French cuirassiers).
40. J. Sutherland, *Men of Waterloo* (London: Frederick Muller, 1967), p. 66.

41. For the background to this development, see Womack, *Improvement and Romance*, pp. 27–80.
42. For the Clark incident, see, for example, G. Wood, *The Subaltern Officer: A Narrative* (London: Septimus Prowett, London, 1826), p. 56. Wounded in the groin, Clark is supposed to have shouted, 'De'il ha' my saul, if ye shall want music', and to have continued to play throughout the action. His heroism is commemorated in a well-known print that has appeared in numerous books on the British army in the Napoleonic Wars. Happily, Clark survived his wound and eventually returned home to Scotland where he was presented with a commemorative set of pipes by the Royal Highland Society. Of course, one point that is worth making here is that the Scots had the pipes and the others did not: such judgements are by their very nature most subjective, but it is hard to deny the stirring quality of the pipes even now.
43. The charge of the Scots Greys gave rise to one of the enduring images of the battle of Waterloo in that a number of artists picked up on a story to the effect that, as the Scots Greys charged forward, so the Gordon Highlanders seized hold of the stirrups of the horsemen and thereby hurtled themselves into the fight. As recent research has shown, however, this is little more than a myth. What appears to have occurred is that, as the Greys moved forward – at a sedate trot rather than the full gallop shown in most of the pictures – so they had to pass through a Gordon skirmish line. A few of the men thus deployed were ridden down and saved themselves from being trampled underfoot by grabbing at some of the riders as they rode by. What is incontestable is that the coincidence of Greys and Gordons at this moment of great crisis evoked much enthusiasm - the cheers that they exchanged of 'Scotland for ever' are no invention – and that the Gordons surged forward more or less spontaneously in the wake of the cavalry. See Reid, *Wellington's Highland Warriors*, pp. 196–202.
44. C. Mercer, *Journal of the Waterloo Campaign kept throughout the Campaign of 1815*, ed. J. Fortescue (London: Peter Davies, 1927), p. 138.
45. D. Stewart, *Sketches of the Character, Manners and Present State of the Highlanders of Scotland, with Details of the Military Service of the Highland Regiments* (Edinburgh: Archibald Constable & Co., 1822), vol. 1, p. 593.
46. R. W. Southey to J. Rickman, 2 October 1815, quoted in C. C. Southey, *The Life and Correspondence of the Late Robert Southey* (London: Longman, Browne, Green and Longman, 1850), vol. 4, p. 131.
47. J. Leach, *Rough Sketches of the Life of an Old Soldier during a Service in the West Indies at the Siege of Copenhagen in 1807, in the Peninsula and the South of France in the Campaigns from 1808 to 1814 with the Light Division in the Netherlands, [and] in the Netherlands in 1815, including*

the Battles of Quatre Bras and Waterloo, with a Slight Sketch of the Three Years passed by the Army of Occupation in France (London: Longman, Rees, Orme, Brown and Green, 1831), pp. 397–9.

48. J. Hope, *Letters from Portugal, Spain and France during the Memorable Campaigns of 1811, 1812 and 1813 and from Belgium and France in the Year 1815*, ed. S. Monick (Heathfield: Naval and Military Press, 2000), pp. 167–8. Lest this account be thought to be overdramatic, it is corroborated by B. Stuart (ed.), *Soldiers' Glory, being 'Rough Notes of an Old Soldier' by Major-General Sir George Bell* (London: G. Bell & Sons, 1956), p. 83.

49. I owe this information to my good friend, Mr Nicholas Dunne-Lynch, a freelance scholar who is currently working on the Irish war effort in the Revolutionary and Napoleonic period.

50. For a breakdown of the British casualties at Waterloo, see www.britishbattles.com/waterloo/waterloo-casualties.htm, accessed on 1 August 2011. In fairness to the Black Watch, it did suffer terribly at Quatre Bras on 16 June, where, amongst other misadventures, it was badly cut up by French cavalry in the act of forming square. In all, the butcher's bill came to 45 dead and 242 wounded.

51. For this incident, see Leask, *Sword of Scotland*, p. 105.

52. These figures should be regarded as approximate: in particular, few units kept separate records of soldiers lost in the retreat and soldiers lost in the battle that took place outside Corunna on 16 January 1809. See C. Oman, *A History of the Peninsular War*, 7 vols (Oxford: Clarendon Press, 1902–30), vol. 1, pp. 64–8.

53. J. Donaldson, *Recollections of the Eventful Life of a Soldier* (Edinburgh: Robert Martin, 1852), pp. 178–81.

54. For the issue of kilts in the Peninsula, see P. Haythornthwaite and M. Chappell, *Uniforms of the Peninsular War, 1807–1814* (Poole: Blandford Press, 1978), p. 103. Two actions that certainly saw entire battalions wear them were Vimeiro in 1808 and Burgos in 1812, the units concerned being the 71st and the 42nd.

55. For an excellent introduction to the aftermath of the Napoleonic Wars in Scotland, see Devine, *Clanship to Crofters' War*, pp. 84–99.

56. For a near contemporary account of the attack on the hornwork of San Miguel, see J. T. Jones, *Journals of the Sieges carried out by the Allies in Spain in the Years 1811 and 1812* (London: T. Egerton, 1814), pp. 190–1.

57. The lyrics of 'The Ballad of Jamie Foyers' may be found at www.mudcat.org/thread.cfm?threadid=3009, accessed on 20 September 2010, while a recorded version may be heard on Strawhead's *A Soldier's Life: Songs and Music from the Great French War, 1793–1815* (for full details, see www.strawhead.org.uk). The record of Foyer's death can be found in The

National Archives, Kew, War Office Papers, 12/5490, First Battalion, Forty-Second Regiment of Foot – Battalion Quarterly Pay Lists from 25 June 1812 to 24 December 1812. I am much obliged to Mr M. McDonagh for this information.

16
Internal Policing and Public Order, c. 1797–1900

EWEN A. CAMERON

In the early afternoon of 29 August 1797 Adam Blair, an East Lothian schoolboy, had an educational experience. He was pursued by soldiers through the fertile corn fields outside Tranent, twice wounded and left for dead. He was fortunate, certainly more so than John Adam, a collier from nearby Macmerry, who was shot dead in the same incident, and ten others who died that day. Blair would later go on to be a prominent Presbyterian clergyman and scholar of ecclesiastical history and, not surprisingly, remembered that day as having been characterised by 'bloody work'.[1] The context for these dramatic events, as Charles Esdaile has alluded to, was the passage of the Militia Act in July 1797, its extreme unpopularity in Scotland and the determination of the authorities to implement it, with military force if necessary.[2]

The controversy over the raising of a militia was a long-running one in eighteenth-century Scotland. In 1757, when an English militia had been raised, Scotland was excluded from the legislation. It was felt that with Jacobitism such a recent memory the risks of popular militarism were too high. Some elements of opinion felt that Scottish loyalty had been slighted and the equal partnership of the union undermined.[3] Nevertheless, by the late eighteenth century, and in view of the pressures created by the war with France, the situation was different. Despite awareness that the implementation of a Scottish Militia Act might be unpopular, the government required men for home defence and a militia seemed the obvious solution to their manpower problems. A militia, a compulsory force drafted from the young male population for home service for the duration of the war, was cheaper than the fencible regiments (also restricted to home service) and more flexible than the somewhat amateurish Volunteers. It was chosen by ballot but the well-to-do could pay for a

Figure 16.1 Militia riot memorial, Tranent, by David Annand, 1995.

substitute, something that was beyond the pockets of the colliers and farm servants of East Lothian who rioted against its terms in August 1797. The riots were widespread across Scotland, from Berwickshire to Aberdeenshire. Although troops were required to put down the disturbances, the events at Tranent, while sharing many characteristics with the other disturbances, were, in the words of their principal historian, 'unique' in the 'hostility' of the crowd and the 'ruthlessness' of the authorities.[4] Soldiers of the Royal Cinque Ports Light Dragoons and the Pembrokeshire Cavalry had been taunted and pelted with stones by a large crowd that had taken control of the main street in Tranent, where the local elite was meeting in a public house to draw up the list of those to be balloted for the militia. Among those present in the street and attempting to organise the troops was Lord Adam Gordon, the commander-in-chief of the army in Scotland, who had his sword knocked out of his hand by a stone and carried off by one of the protestors. Gordon believed that the crowd of colliers and salters who gathered at Tranent came with 'a positive determination of conquering or dying'.[5] In confused circumstances the troops opened fire on the crowd and there were several fatalities. There was then an attempt to disperse the crowd which was 'transformed . . . into bloody rout and a massacre'.[6] It was during this latter phase of the operation that Adam Blair and John Adam came into contact with the troops.

There is no question that the authorities were extremely panicky in Scotland in the late eighteenth century and that this created conditions where, with local mismanagement, events like the Tranent massacre could occur. The combination of the ongoing war with France, and the fear that the militia rioters were informed and inflamed by the movements for democratic reform, especially the Society of United Scotsmen, that were active in Scotland at this time, evoked concern. There were many other occasions during the 1790s when the army was called out to deal with disturbances. The most prominent of these was the despatch of soldiers of the 42nd Regiment from Fort George in 1792 to counteract an attempt to disrupt the sheep-farming economy of Sutherland and Easter Ross.[7] Closer to home were the riots on the King's Birthday in June of the same year. Soldiers from the 53rd Regiment (later 1st battalion, Shropshire Light Infantry) had to be ordered out from Edinburgh castle to protect such points as Parliament House and the houses of leading government officials, including that of the lord advocate, Robert Dundas, at George Square.[8] The government feared the effect of the increasingly alarming events in France, and although the impact on the crowd of radical ideas should not be underestimated, they assumed vast proportions in the official mind. The same fear of external influence would be evident in perceptions of Chartist activity in 1848 and even in the crofters' protests of the 1880s. In each case, however, it was possible that the presence of troops, although effective in the short term at quelling a crowd, was counterproductive. Military and judicial harshness ran the risk of producing martyrs which could keep alive a tradition of radical protest. This was especially the case with the executions of John Baird, Andrew Hardie and James Wilson, who had clashed with some 10th Hussars and the Kilsyth troops of the Stirlingshire Yeomanry at Bonnymuir, near Falkirk, in April 1820. This attempt at a general rising in Scotland was the culmination of four years of radical activity in the fraught economic conditions in the aftermath of the Napoleonic Wars.[9]

The events at Tranent were so shocking because it seemed that the civil power had lost control and the military had run amok. Indeed, at the trial of the rioters the question of who gave the initial order to fire could not be resolved and it has been suggested that this confusion was deliberately manufactured in order that responsibility could be avoided.[10] The issue behind the riot, the suspicion, perhaps sustained by deliberate misinformation, that the state was planning widespread compulsory military service – and that it could not be trusted about the matter of home service – added a popular theme to the civil-military tensions. One historian has gone so far as to argue that events such as the militia riots 'produced in Scotland an ambivalent attitude to the armed forces'.[11] This did not, however, seem to reduce the belief among leading elements of the civil power in Scotland that a body of soldiers could not only intimidate but also induce awe and respect among disorderly civilians.

The resources available to the civil power in Scotland were, until the late 1850s, extremely weak. It was only with an act of 1857 that a nationwide police force was created in Scotland and sheriffs outside the main cities given some resources to deal with disturbances.[12] Even then, however, the relative weakness of Scottish local government outside the burghs, and the fact that the landowners and their representatives were both the main agents of local government – as the Commissioners of Supply – and the principal sources of revenue to pay for services, meant that in many areas of Scotland the police forces were small, rudimentary and widely regarded as being the agents of the proprietorial class.[13] This is why advocates of the creation of a systematic police force argued that it should be funded from a compulsory assessment, rather than at the discretion of the Commissioners of Supply, and that there should be a reserve force of police kept at the disposal of central government, rather than the county or burgh authorities.[14] The need for greater centralisation of police would be a familiar refrain of those with experience of dealing with disorder in Scotland in this period.[15] This was a particular problem during the crofters' protests of the 1880s, when there was widespread disorder in remote areas where the police were thin on the ground and the logistics of using the army in support of a weak civil power were very difficult.[16] In addition the crofters' actions were unusual in their scale, more like some of the events of the 1790s than anything else in the post-1857 period. These protests were also characterised by a government in a state of near panic, being convinced that the crofters were replicating the politically charged protests of the Irish Land League. Unlike Tranent, however, there was no repeat of the civil power losing control of the troops called in to support their attempts to restore law and order.

The principal agent of the civil power in the matter of dealing with disorder in Scotland was the sheriff. As a meeting of sheriffs noted in 1909:

The Sheriff is the King's direct representative and executive officer. His primary and most important duty is the preservation of the King's peace in his Sheriffdom, and he is responsible for the means taken to fulfil that duty. The police force of the County is subject to his orders; and he has, in virtue of his office, the right to call upon the lieges and the King's forces to aid him in quieting disturbances.[17]

In the period from the 1740s to the 1880s, when the administration of Scotland was fairly weak, and the lines of communication between the lord advocate in Edinburgh and the sheriffs in the localities were fairly clear, shrieval 'sovereignty' was reasonably uncomplicated. After 1885 there was the additional complication of the presence of the Secretary for Scotland, but senior civil service opinion, drawing on legal material, re-emphasised the primacy of the sheriff.[18] This became problematic during the crofters' protests of the 1880s when there was a clash of personalities between Arthur Balfour, Secretary for Scotland, and the sheriff of Inverness, William Ivory. Ivory, as will be seen below, sought frequently to use military forces to deal with the troublesome crofters. In 1909 the relationship between the civil magistrate and the commanding officer of a military force called out to deal with disorder was reviewed after soldiers had been involved in quelling a riot in Belfast in 1908. As a result the King's Regulations were amended and it was suggested that the commanding officer could refuse to obey the order of a magistrate (although there was at least some history of soldiers believing that the civil power was too timid in cases of emergency). Whatever may have been the case in England, this did not seem either practical or legally correct in Scotland and the sheriffs resisted this perceived intrusion into their authority.[19]

The maintenance of order is the fundamental duty of central and local government. This much is clear and uncomplicated. Beyond this, however, the methods by which this duty was carried out are revealing of government attitudes towards the people, both orderly and disorderly. This chapter will explore the issues arising from some uses of the military to support the civil power in Scotland in the period from the late eighteenth to the early twentieth century. The problem of keeping order in Scotland reveals much about its place within the union and the empire during this period. While martial law was a strategy frequently adopted by colonial governors, at least up until the 1860s, it was unheard of in Britain. Ireland was a slightly different case. The rebellions of 1798 and 1916 were the episodes that induced states most closely approximating to martial law in the

Figure 16.2 The Scots Greys in Ireland, c. 1848. Contemporary painting by Michael Angelo Hayes.

United Kingdom. Furthermore, the ongoing agitation in Ireland throughout the nineteenth century necessitated frequent temporary coercive measures that gave the police exalted powers to deal with mass meetings and other forms of protest.[20] To assist the civil authorities, between 15,000 and 30,000 British troops were deployed across the Irish Sea at various times during the period. In the late 1860s, when the Fenian threat was at its height, the commander-in-chief in Ireland was Sir Hugh Rose (Baron Strathnairn), whose old regiment, the 92nd Highlanders, had been deployed to keep the peace and enforce the collection of tithes in Cork and Tipperary during the 1830s. He was particularly alive to the dangers presented by the Irish republicans and believed in the greater efficacy of troops in maintaining law and order compared to Ireland's rudimentary police force. Scottish regiments, including the 71st, 72nd, 73rd, 74th and 93rd Highlanders, were stationed in Ireland at this time and Rose prevented any serious insurrection.[21] Other Scottish troops, including the 1st battalion, Highland Light Infantry, were prominent during the agitation over the land question and home rule in the 1880s. Interestingly, in some of the unionist propaganda that portrayed the horrors that would ensue if home rule was granted the Scottish regiments were perceived as the last bastions against inevitable anarchy when home rule became 'Rome rule'.[22] The methods of dealing with internal agitation in Scotland, where the civil powers were more

Figure 16.3
Sir Archibald Alison, Sheriff of Lanarkshire. He vigorously upheld the authority of the state, especially against the early Scottish trade unions.

developed and refined, were more akin to those of England than Ireland. But the civil authorities still had frequent recourse to military support in their attempts to deal with disorder and we will examine in detail three such cases: industrial protests in Lanarkshire from the 1830s to the 1850s; food riots on the coast of the Moray Firth in 1847; and the crofters' protests of the 1880s. The final case came closest to pushing the government into a different legal dimension but the primacy of civil authority was retained.

Industrial protests

In his memoirs Sheriff Archibald Alison recalled the two great incidences of industrial disorder with which he had had to deal in his career as sheriff of Lanarkshire, the most populous and heavily industrialised county in Scotland. It was at the centre of the industrial revolution, which had transformed the west of Scotland in the space of a couple of generations and was subject to stresses and strains that often produced disorder. In May 1837 a strike of cotton spinners began in Glasgow and soon spread to the surrounding area and to other important trades. The spinners were exceptionally well organised and, combined with the coal miners in the semi-rural areas of Lanarkshire, posed, in the sherriff's mind, a serious threat to public order. Alison, a confirmed Tory who was of the opinion that most of the evils he faced in his day-to-day work had been unleashed by the French Revolution – a theme on which he published a multi-volume work – believed that there was no point in appealing to the Whig government for support as the ministry had been 'preserved in power by sedition, not unfrequently aided by treason'.[23] Yet he was handicapped by the lack of a reliable police force. At the end of June 1837 he attempted to use civil power to deal with demonstrations at a cotton mill at Oakbank. He swore in 100 special constables but only one turned up to face the crowd of striking cotton spinners. Alison recalled that he then 'went to the barracks and got a troop of horse, and the sight of the vanguard of red-coats at once dispersed the assemblage'. According to his account of events, a 'violent clamour' greeted his action.[24] Nevertheless, this did not hold him back and he dealt with the 'conspiracy' with extreme harshness, especially after the murder of a strike-breaker on the High Street in Glasgow in July 1837.

The defeat of the cotton spinners' strike had a profound effect on trade unionism in Scotland, which – with the exception of the miners – remained very weak for much of the century. It also influenced the nature of Chartism in Scotland which, it has been argued, remained bound to 'moral force' rather than 'physical force' tactics.[25] This is not to say, however, that Scottish Chartists did not adhere to the notion of the right to bear arms or present a challenge to the authorities which necessitated the use of the military. The most serious trouble occurred in 1848, especially the rioting in Glasgow in early March, when a mob had the run of the city before soldiers were called in and shots were fired. Perhaps learning something from these events, the authorities in Edinburgh, faced with the prospect of large Chartist meetings at Bruntsfield Links and Calton Hill, brought out the 33rd Regiment (later 1st battalion, duke of Wellington's Regiment) and stationed it at strategic points in the city in an attempt to prevent rather than react to violence.[26]

In 1856, faced with an equally challenging strike of colliers, Alison recalled in his memoirs that although there were two regiments of Lanarkshire Militia on hand to assist the civil powers the reason why this strike was occasioned by less violence than that of 1837 was the presence of 'strong bodies of police . . . located in the villages most immediately threatened'.[27] We are fortunate, however, in also having access to the sheriff's correspondence with the lord advocate and the military authorities at this time, and this evidence casts a slightly different light on proceedings. In these documents he emphasised the role of the military in his management of the crisis and lamented the weakness of the civil forces. Yet Alison also referred to the difficulties of using the army to deal with a strike which had no real centre of activity but which was spread around a variety of locations, especially in North Lanarkshire. He noted that as a result of the dispersal of the troops they had to act more like policemen, which reduced their efficiency as soldiers and meant that they could not be deployed as a surprise and in the overwhelming numbers required to overawe the large bodies of strikers.[28] Although the sheriff was in no doubt that a military force could only act in support of the civil power, he was equally emphatic that the civil power had to take advantage of its special qualities. He believed that the army should be deployed in numbers, never fewer than two cavalrymen or four foot soldiers, and preferably double that number. An element of surprise was also thought necessary in dealing with riots and a 'sudden advance either with fixed bayonets or swords drawn was the most efficacious means of proceeding'. He further concluded (and he could almost have had the tragic events at Tranent in 1797 in mind here) that

> in the event of the military being called out the magistrate doing so would do well to recall that the soldiers should be kept as much as possible out of view and never if it can possibly be helped to be kept standing to be pelted at by the mob. When brought out they should be made to act at once and with the utmost rigour consistent with humanity but if possible without discharging fire arms.[29]

Alison, and other sheriffs in areas of west and central Scotland affected by the 1856 miners' strike, tried to put these strategies into practice and, while the dispute was characterised by extreme distress and large gatherings of colliers, the violence was on a much smaller scale than had been evident during the cotton spinners' agitation. Although the principal force used was the local militia (and there did not seem to be particular worries about its loyalty in dealing with such a combustible situation in its own locality), the presence of dragoons, sent from Newcastle and quartered in the barracks in Hamilton, was also important in preventing further trouble.

After the cotton spinners' strike of 1837, and the miners' strike of 1856, a third series of industrial disputes in the late 1880s in the heartland of Scottish disorder in Lanarkshire provides another lens through which to examine the use of the military in dealing with these events. In February 1887 a young officer of the 4th Hussars reported in the following terms to his superior officer:

> I left Maryhill Barracks, Glasgow, at 3.30pm the 8th inst in aid of the Civil Power at Stonefield, Blantyre, with a detachment of 4th Hussars, consisting of 1 Officer and 42 rank and file. On my arrival at Stonefield, Blantyre, to meet the Civil Authorities, a few stones were thrown, two men were slightly cut, the Riot Act had been read, but on the arrival of the military the mob immediately dispersed; the streets were then quiet for the remainder of the night.[30]

This report indicated that the deterrent effect of a military force, especially cavalry, was as potent, if it was used properly, in the 1880s as it had been thirty years earlier. Yet what was impressive about the way in which the authorities dealt with riots and mass meetings during this strike was the cooperation between the civil and military forces. As well as the men of the 4th Hussars, who were on patrol, the Sheriff of Lanarkshire also secured reinforcements from the Glasgow and Edinburgh police forces. No shots were fired, no miners were injured and by late February 1888 the strike had petered out.[31]

The unit of cavalry that was so important in supporting the civil power in this instance came from Maryhill barracks in Glasgow, and the civil authorities felt keenly the removal of the cavalry detachment from Hamilton barracks in 1877. Protests were made at the time, but the War Office responded that

> Glasgow is moreover more central with reference to the great bulk of the manufacturing and mining population and the great centres of industry. Glasgow with its great population and wealth appears to be the chief place requiring protection in case of riot.[32]

The closure of the barracks at Hamilton was the first stage in the gradual removal of cavalry from Scotland. This was something that the civil authorities deeply regretted as they felt that the prospect of socialistic agitation was increasing all the time and that the cavalry had a greater deterrent effect on potential rioters and was a more 'humane' force (presumably because they could disperse crowds by the act of riding through them, rather than by firing shots, although this tactic had been a signal failure at Tranent in 1797) than infantry.[33]

Food riots

In contrast to Alison's rather blunt views on order and disorder in Scottish society was the more measured approach of Sheriff Cosmo Innes of Moray. This approach was vital as Innes had to deal with a very delicate situation in the north of Scotland in the early months of 1847. This arose from what have been called 'the last Scottish food riots'. These took place in ports along the coast of the Moray Firth from Banffshire to Caithness and occurred against a background of rising food prices and extreme food shortages in the Highlands, as a consequence of the widespread failure of the potato crop, and popular resentment against the activities of farmers and grain merchants seeking to profit from the inflation by exporting food. The riots that took place sought to regulate the price of food and prevent, by force if necessary, grain exports.[34] Although there were numerous incidences of disorder arising from this issue, the one that achieved the greatest prominence, and which might easily have become another Tranent, was a riot at Wick Harbour in late February 1847 at which shots were fired by men of the 76th Regiment (later 2nd battalion, Duke of Wellington's Regiment) who had been assailed by stones thrown by the crowd attempting to prevent the shipment of grain from the harbour.[35] Lurid press coverage of this event led to the lord advocate having to defend in parliament the actions of the sheriff and troops.[36] This was only one of a series of disturbances with which the civil authorities had to contend. The sheriffs involved, principally Innes, were, as we have seen elsewhere, hamstrung by the weakness and unreliability of the civilian forces at their disposal. Although the sheriffs could swear in special constables and deploy Chelsea Pensioners, neither were a match for the large and determined crowds with which they were faced (and the Pensioners were not so numerous as they had been after the war).[37] In a revealing comment, the crown agent in Edinburgh assured Innes that he was doing everything in his power to secure military support but he enjoined the sheriff to 'for heaven's sake work hard to increase your civil power. This is ever the pride of a Civil Officer.'[38]

There were two problems here in regard to the use of military force. The first was the relatively low numbers of troops in Scotland, estimated at around 1,800. Although Fort George, which had been constructed in order to cow rebellious northerners, was in the heart of the disturbed district, there were only some fifty troops there. Second, the frequency of protests and the diversity of their locations posed a logistical challenge in trying to ensure that the forces available could be deployed rapidly but were not divided into units which were too small.[39] The answer to these conundrums was discovered in the use of a small ship, the *Cuckoo*. Despite the fact that it was 'but a small ship originally fitted as a packet and is not fit for the transport of troops', it was used to ferry soldiers up and down the coast, landing them at the locations where they were most needed. This surprised the rioters and produced, in the opinion of Innes, a very positive result.[40]

As would later be the case during the crofters' protests of the 1880s, it was argued by some local officials, but in vain, that a permanent force in the north was required.[41] The objective, as in other cases, was to use the troops as a means of intimidating and overawing potential food rioters. This effect was not easily achieved, however, as social relations between the populace, on the one hand, and the farmers and merchants, on the other, were extremely tense and the blunt instrument of a body of troops could as easily inflame as pacify a crowd. The troops, and the authorities in general, also faced the problem that they could be perceived to be on the side of the farmers and merchants, as their mission was to create conditions whereby grain could be shipped. Such shipments were part of regular political economy, as opposed to the 'moral economy' aspired to by the crowd, and it was the job of the authorities to facilitate this as much as to keep law and order.[42] In the event, the disorder faded away as quickly as it had arisen, principally due to price movements, and this relieved the soldiers who had been sent to the north from the almost impossible task of dealing with people who were in fear of starvation.[43]

Crofters' protests

Much more unexpected for the civil authorities was the outbreak of agitation among the crofters of the north of Scotland. Although, as was pointed out to the home secretary in 1883, there was a long tradition of protest among the highlanders and the despatch of military forces to deal with them,[44] over the course of the nineteenth century a careful image of these people as peaceable and loyal had been constructed. Nevertheless, protests in Lewis and Wester Ross in the 1870s gathered pace in the early 1880s and much prominence was given by newspaper reports to disputes over access to grazing land at Braes and Glendale in Skye in 1882 and 1883. From this period down to the early months of 1888, when there was a series of violent incidents on the island of Lewis, the Highlands of Scotland seemed to be aflame. Meanwhile, Highland Land Law Reform Associations were formed to organise protests and to coordinate political activity. At the general elections of 1885 and 1886 the crofters used their newly won right to vote to elect a group of so-called 'Crofter MPs' who took the cause of the crofters to parliament. Gladstone's second administration had established a Royal Commission to examine the grievances of the crofters and his short-lived third administration passed the Crofters' Holdings (Scotland) Act 1886. This granted security of tenure to the crofting population but did little to address their principal grievance – shortage of grazing land – and violence continued.[45] Such was the disbelief of the authorities that the passive highlanders could sustain an agitation of this nature on their own that much of it was blamed on Irish 'agitators'. While there were links between Ireland and the Scottish Highlands in this period, the relationship was by no means one of inspiration by Irish example: there was much suspicion of the Irish on religious, racial and political grounds.[46] Nevertheless, in the minds of the government in London the highlanders seemed to be following the Irish and this pushed the grievance of the crofters up the official agenda and encouraged the government to use coercive, as well as conciliatory, tactics.

The initial outbreak of concerted agitation in the Highlands in 1882 was characterised by the problem that the authorities had faced in earlier disturbances: the balance between the use of police and military force. At Braes, near Portree in Skye, the Inverness-shire Commissioners of Supply faced the problem of trying, with an inadequate police force of only 135 men, to arrest crofters who had deforced (a legal term to describe the act of preventing an officer of the crown from carrying out his duty) the sheriff's officer serving interdicts on behalf of the landowner, Lord MacDonald, whose land had been invaded by the crofters. They were compelled to seek support from other local authorities in Scotland, some of whom were none too keen to expose their men to perceived risk, and the arrests were only made with the assistance of Glasgow policemen. The government was reluctant to despatch military forces to Skye. Not only did it fear, probably rightly given later events, that any force that was sent would get bogged down in a long drawn out civil operation, but it was also keen that the county authorities take full responsibility, including financial, for dealing with the disorder. The lord advocate, John Balfour, concluded:

> Recourse should not be had to military aid unless in cases of sudden riot or extraordinary emergency, to deal adequately with which police cannot be obtained; and soldiers should not be employed upon police duty which is likely to be of a continuing character.[47]

When renewed trouble erupted in late 1882 at Glendale in the north-west of the island, assistance was, however, sought from the Admiralty. A troopship and a body of marines were sent to support the civil power in making the arrests. This was the first in a series of events in which the diminutive sheriff William Ivory indulged his taste for leading military expeditions to Skye. Some of the operational details of these expeditions exemplify the difficulties of using military force to deal with civil disturbances.

Ivory led two expeditions to Skye, in 1884–5 and 1886, their significance for our purposes being the tactical innovations of 1886 based on lessons learned from the earlier expedition. The first expedition had been reluctantly launched by the government after widespread publicity had been given to the humiliating defeat of a party of police in the north of the island in late 1884. The military force assembled consisted of 350 marines on board HMS *Assistance* and two gunboats, the *Forester* and the *Banterer*. The troops were quartered on the local population on Skye and this was held to have reduced their effectiveness in quelling the trouble as there was a degree of fraternisation with the local population. This arrangement also meant that the force was scattered and their movements obvious to the crofters. John Balfour had sent fairly strict conditions on the use of the troops: they were not to be used to protect sheriff officers acting in civil cases between landlord and tenant. Ivory thus attempted to use them in an intimidatory fashion, marching them around the island to deter the local population. This, however, had very little effect on the crofters, who were now confident and determined. While the marines were on the island deforcements and other protests continued virtually unabated and the government, much to Ivory's frustration, withdrew the troops in May 1885.[48]

The 1886 expedition was conducted on different principles.[49] This expedition was sent to Skye to support the civil power in the issuing of writs for non-payment of rates. Ivory had claimed that the landlords were unable to pay their rates because they, in turn, had received no payments of rent and compounded rates from the crofters and that extreme difficulties in the discharge of local government were likely to ensue.[50] Arthur Balfour, the new Secretary for Scotland, was, however, determined to avoid a repetition of the mistakes of the first expedition. He believed that a force of 100 marines kept on a Royal Navy troopship, which could convey them readily to the points at which they were required, would constitute a much more effective force.[51] This was a similar tactic to the one used in 1847 in response to the food rioters. He also recognised the diplomatic importance of the troops not being perceived as the agents of the landlords, for whom he had no great regard, and reminded Ivory of the importance of being even-handed.[52] Although Balfour came to the view that he had been manipulated by the sheriff (whom he and his civil servants referred to as 'Poo-Ba') into the granting of military support to the civil power,[53] the troops did not on this occasion encounter large-scale resistance from the crofters who, contrary to the position in 1884–5, now had the benefits of the Act of 1886 and the promise of the arrival of the Commissioners appointed under that act to adjudicate on their rents. Over the next five years or so this Commission made a considerable contribution to taking the heat out of the agitation by dealing with some of its underlying causes, something which a military expedition could not do.[54] Nearly 400 writs were served, with Ivory deciding to land the marines only in the most troubled areas of the island, at Glendale, Valtos and Waternish.[55]

The expeditions to Skye were relatively straightforward in terms of access. There were railheads at Mallaig and Strome Ferry and most of the main areas of crofting settlement on the island were accessible by ship. The same could not be said for the north-west coast of Sutherland and the use of military force in an attempt to effect arrests demonstrated, in almost comical form, some of the limitations of using troops in this capacity. In May 1887 two of the duke of Sutherland's farms at Clashmore on the west coast of his estate were raided by crofters seeking access to more grazing land. In the usual pattern, the sheriff officer attempting to serve interdicts was deforced and the criminal law was invoked.[56] The county sheriff, John Cheyne, believed that arrests could not be carried out by the police alone (the entire force in the county amounted to only fourteen men) and there ensued a debate about whether soldiers (from Glasgow) or a gunboat and a squad of marines (from Plymouth) would be most appropriate. This involved the War Office and the Admiralty, neither of whom were very helpful in the matter. Given the fact that Clashmore was over fifty miles from the nearest railway station, it was decided that marines, who could be landed with an element of surprise, would be the best force, despite the fact that Cheyne felt that the crofters would be more likely to be intimidated by 'redcoats'. Nevertheless, the debate dragged on over the summer, with the ringleaders of the deforcement still at large, and a concerted attempt to make arrests was not made until December when forty marines, who had been sent to the island of Lewis to deal with a large land raid at the Park Deer Forest, were brought in HMS *Jackal* to Sutherland. Cheyne reported that he was not sanguine about the likelihood of making a successful

Figure 16.4 Reading the Riot Act to crofters at Aignish farm near Stornoway, Lewis, 1888.

arrest and this lack of confidence proved to be correct as only one of the accused was brought to book.⁵⁷

These events, and further trouble in Lewis in early 1888, prompted wider reflections about the use of the military to deal with disturbances in the north of Scotland. There was a growing consensus that, rather than dealing with incidents as they arose, and entering into fraught negotiations with the War Office or the Admiralty, it would be better if there was a permanent force cruising the north-west coast and the Hebrides, along the lines of what had been proposed in the north-east after the food riots of 1847. As well as the improved potential for dealing with lawlessness one important landowner and former Conservative MP, Donald Cameron of Lochiel, felt that such a force would have manifold benefits:

> The presence of soldiers would I believe be highly popular in the locality where they were stationed. This would especially be the case if the troops were selected from some Highland Regiment. The necessary expenditure both on the part of officers and men on money in the district must in some degree be felt by the small tradesmen and crofters and be to an appreciable extent a boon to the whole community. It would stimulate recruiting and this, while welcome to the military authorities, would of itself tend to

relieve that congestion of population which to a large extent contributes to the poverty of the country.[58]

A variant of this idea was expressed by the Conservative lord advocate, John Macdonald, in late 1885 when he argued that although the population of the island of Lewis 'was in a ferment against their local superiors', they belonged 'to a race which have a very high idea of the powers and position of the sovereign and of those who serve under her in the Navy and Army'. He thus recommended that naval officers should be used to investigate the grievance of the crofters and fishermen in the island. This idea did not, however, receive much favour from the Admiralty.[59]

In 1888 the Secretary for Scotland, Lord Lothian, received a proposal to station three or four gunboats, and a force of around 300 marines, on the north-west coast. This would, it was envisaged, be a flexible force which could respond rapidly to events as they arose and operate in a degree of secrecy and with an element of surprise, all of which would help to deter further lawlessness.[60] Although this proposal made eminent sense (assuming that the Admiralty would cooperate) it proved to be unnecessary as a combination of better seasons, improved prospects for temporary migration and the favourable decisions of the Crofters' Commission reduced the levels of agitation in the crofting districts.[61] Although there were further protests on the land question in the Edwardian period, and in the years immediately following the Great War, the advent of County Councils in 1889 meant that the police forces were better organised and resourced and military support for the civil power was not required to deal with these later phases of protest.

The evidence presented here suggests that, although the civil authorities placed a high value on the potential of military force to deal with disorder, it was a blunt instrument that was likely to have only short-term effects. Disorder of the type examined above was a symptom of deep-seated political, social or economic problems, and marines, infantry or cavalry could do little to deal with those. Sometimes the presence of the military could be useful in buying time and space for the implementation of political measures, as during the crofters' protests in the 1880s. When military action tipped over into the indiscriminate use of force, as at Tranent in 1797, huge damage was done. A turning point was the creation of more effective police forces in Scotland from 1857, after which the troops began to be used less frequently by the civil authorities. Although the crofters' actions stand out for the scale of their apparent challenge to the forces of law and authority in the second half of the nineteenth century, the further strengthening of local government in Scotland in the late 1880s provided more resources for the provision of police and by 1914 a corner seemed to have been turned in the use of the military to support the civil power in Scotland. Nevertheless, the police required a degree of public consent to operate effectively and when the authorities panicked in Glasgow in 1919 in the wake of 'Red Clydeside' soldiers stood ready to intervene.

Notes

1. K. J. Logue, *Popular Disturbances in Scotland, 1780–1815* (Edinburgh: John Donald, 1979), pp. 92–3.
2. J. R. Western, 'The formation of the Scottish militia in 1797', *Scottish Historical Review* [hereafter *SHR*], vol. 34 (1955), pp. 1–18. A twelfth died later.
3. J. Robertson, *The Scottish Enlightenment and the Militia Issue* (Edinburgh: John Donald, 1985).
4. K. J. Logue, 'The Tranent militia riot of 1797', *Transactions of the East Lothian Antiquarian and Field Naturalists' Society*, vol. 14 (1974), p. 37.
5. National Records of Scotland, Edinburgh [hereafter NRS], RH2/4/81 f. 18v, Lord Adam Gordon to Lord Advocate, 3 Aug. 1797.
6. Logue, *Popular Disturbances*, p. 89.
7. E. Richards, *A History of the Highland Clearances: Agrarian Transformation and the Evictions, 1746–1886* (London: Croom Helm, 1982), pp. 249–83.
8. B. Harris, 'Political protests in the year of liberty, 1792', in B. Harris (ed.), *Scotland in the Age of the French Revolution* (Edinburgh: John Donald, 2005), pp. 50–62.
9. W. H. Fraser, *Conflict and Class: Scottish Workers, 1700–1838* (Edinburgh: John Donald, 1988), pp. 111–12; G. Pentland, '"Betrayed by infamous spies": The commemoration of Scotland's "Radical War" of 1820', *Past and Present*, vol. 201 (November 2008), pp. 145–9.
10. Logue, 'The Tranent militia riot', p. 45.
11. W. Ferguson, *Scotland since 1689* (Edinburgh: Mercat Press, 1978), p. 263.
12. H. M. Dove, 'The role of the police and other law enforcement agencies in their application of the law relating to popular disturbances in central Scotland, 1850–1914' (unpublished M.Phil thesis, the Open University, 1994), pp. 13–14.
13. NRS, HH55/78, David Monro (Chief Inspector of Constabulary for Scotland) to Sandford, 15 Aug. 1886; ibid. John MacKay (Chief Constable

of Argyll) to Monro, 13 Sept. 1886; ibid. Alex McHardy (Chief Constable of Inverness-shire) to Monro, 7 Sept. 1886.
14. NRS, AD56/309/2, Alison to Lord Advocate, 7 May 1856.
15. NRS, HH55/78, David Monro (Chief Inspector of Constabulary for Scotland) to Sandford, 15 Aug. 1886; NRS, HH55/341, Fifeshire Constabulary, Private and Confidential Memorandum to the Standing Joint Committee of the County of Fife, 1 May 1912.
16. E. A. Cameron, *Land for the People? The British Government and the Scottish Highlands, c. 1880-1925* (East Linton: Tuckwell Press, 1996), p. 17.
17. NRS, HH55/264, Excerpt from Minute of Meeting of Sheriffs of Scotland, 16 Nov. 1909.
18. NRS, HH55/1, William C. Dunbar, Powers of the Secretary for Scotland in Cases of Riot & c. [in Counties], 7 Jan. 1891.
19. NRS, HH55/264, Excerpt from Minute of Meeting of Sheriffs of Scotland, 16 Nov. 1909; C. Townshend, *Making the Peace: Public Order and Public Security in Modern Britain* (Oxford: Oxford University Press, 1993), p. 45; E. M. Spiers, *The Army and Society, 1815-1914* (London: Longman, 1980), pp. 82-3.
20. C. Townshend, 'Martial law: Legal and administrative problems of civil emergency in Britain and the Empire, 1800-1940', *Historical Journal*, vol. 25 (1982), pp. 167-95.
21. C. Townshend, *Political Violence in Ireland: Government and Resistance since 1841* (Oxford: Oxford University Press, 1983), pp. 88-101, 140-7; V. Crossman, 'The army and law and order in the nineteenth century', in T. Bartlett and K. Jeffery (eds), *A Military History of Ireland* (Cambridge: Cambridge University Press, 1996), pp. 358, 360; B. Robson, 'Rose, Hugh Henry, Baron Strathnairn (1801-1885)', *Oxford Dictionary of National Biography* (Oxford: Oxford University Press 2004), online edn. Available at www.oxforddnb.com/view/article/24093, accessed on 7 August 2011.
22. J. Poster, *Home Rule in 1884: The Personal Experience of a Citizen of Dublin* (London: Trübner & Co., 1874), pp. 14-16; *The Great Irish Rebellion of 1886. Retold by a Landlord* (London: Harrison & Sons, 1886), p. 41.
23. A. Alison, *Some Account of My Life and Writings: An Autobiography by the Late Sir Archibald Alison*, 2 vols (London: Blackwood, 1883), vol. 1, pp. i, 374; M. Michie, *An Enlightenment Tory in Victorian Scotland: The Career of Sir Archibald Alison* (East Linton: Tuckwell Press, 1997), pp. 64-91; M. Milne, 'Archibald Alison: Conservative controversialist', *Albion*, vol. 27 (1995), pp. 419-43. It might be noted that Alison's son, Lieutenant-General Sir Archibald Alison, commanded the Highland

Brigade at the storming of Tel-el-Kebir in 1882. I am grateful to Dr Jeremy Crang for drawing this to my attention.
24. Alison, *Some Account*, vol. 1, p. 376.
25. Fraser, *Conflict and Class*, pp. 162, 170.
26. A. Wilson, *The Chartist Movement in Scotland* (Manchester: Manchester University Press, 1970), pp. 218–19, 231–7; T. Clarke, 'Early Chartism in Scotland: A moral force movement?', in T. M. Devine (ed.), *Conflict and Stability in Scottish Society, 1700–1850* (Edinburgh: John Donald 1990), pp. 106–21.
27. Alison, *Some Account*, vol. 2, p. 214.
28. NRS, AD56/309/2, Alison to Lord Advocate, 7 May 1856.
29. Ibid. Letter from Alison [possibly to Lord Advocate], 26 Apr. 1856; Memo of Chief Constable of Lanarkshire, 6 Feb. 1909, quoted in Townshend, *Making the Peace*, p. 50.
30. NRS, HH55/89, Lt. Starkey, 4th Hussars, to Adjutant General, 9 Feb. 1887.
31. Ibid. Robert Berry (Sheriff of Lanarkshire) to Home Secretary, 9 Feb. 1887; ibid. Berry to Home Secretary, 11 Feb. 1887; ibid. Telegram, Wallace McHardy (Chief Constable Lanarkshire) to Secretary for Scotland, 8 Feb. 1887.
32. Ibid. Lanarkshire Commissioners of Supply to Sandford, 4 Jun. 1887; NRS, HH55/91, J. Vivian, War Office, to Under Secretary of State, Home Office, 8 Jun. 1875.
33. NRS, HH55/91, Memorial of the Police Committee of the County of Lanark to the Secretary of State for War, 4 Mar. 1887; ibid. Ralph Vaughan (War Office) to Sandford, 29 Apr. 1887; ibid. Lanarkshire County Council to Under Secretary for Scotland, 17 Jan. 1893; ibid. Lanarkshire County Council to Under Secretary for Scotland, 22 Jan. 1907; Logue, 'Tranent militia riot', p. 45.
34. E. Richards, *The Last Scottish Food Riots*, Past and Present Supplement 6 (Oxford: Oxford University Press, 1982) is a full exploration of the background.
35. NRS, AD56/308/2/77, Captain Gordon, 76th Regiment, Commanding at Wick, to the Adjutant-General, 24 Feb. 1847.
36. *Parliamentary Debates*, third series, vol. 90 (4 Mar. 1847), cols 832–4.
37. NRS, AD56/308/3/2, Sheriff Currie (Banff) to Officer Commanding, HM Force, Barracks, Aberdeen, 26 Jan. 1847; NRS, AD56/308/3/6, Sheriff of Elginshire (Innes) to Crown Agent, 27 Jan. 1847; NRS, AD56/308/4, Innes to Lord Advocate, 27 Jan. 1847; NRS, AD56/308/4/35, Report by the Procurator Fiscal at Thurso of the state of the Thurso district of Caithness, 17 Feb. 1847; NRS, AD56/308/6/48, Lt.-Col. Goodman,

Commanding 27th Regiment at Invergordon, to Assistant Adjutant General, 3 Mar. 1847.
38. NRS, AD56/308/3/36, John Lindsay to Cosmo Innes, 30 Jan. 1847; NRS, AD56/308/3/44, 44, Lindsay to Lord Advocate, 29 Jan. 1847.
39. NRS, AD56/308/4/11, North Britain. Strength of the Troops at the Several Stations. Adj.-Gen. Office, 28 Jan. 1847; NRS, AD56/308/2/63, Crown Agent to Procurator Fiscal, Dingwall, 15 Feb. 1847.
40. NRS, AD56/308/4/2, Lindsay to Lord Advocate, 28 Jan. 1847; NRS, AD56/308/4/69, Innes to Lord Advocate, 30 Jan. 1847.
41. NRS, AD56/308/6/47, Sheriff Alex Currie, Banffshire, to Major Gardiner, 13 Feb. 1847.
42. NRS, AD56/308/2/30, John Jardine to Lord Advocate, 21 Feb. 1847.
43. NRS, AD58/69, Letter to Sheriff of Banffshire, 18 Jan. 1847.
44. Bodleian Library, Oxford, MS Harcourt Dep 114, ff. 101–2, Alexander Nicolson to Harcourt, 14 Mar. 1883.
45. J. Hunter, *The Making of the Crofting Community* (Edinburgh: John Donald, 1976), pp. 131–83; I. M. M. MacPhail, *The Crofters' War* (Stornoway: Acair Press, 1989).
46. A. G. Newby, *Ireland, Radicalism and the Scottish Highlands, c. 1870–1912* (Edinburgh: Edinburgh University Press, 2007); J. Hunter, 'The Gaelic connection: The Highlands, Ireland and nationalism, 1873–1922', *SHR*, vol. 54 (1975), pp. 178–204; E. A. Cameron, 'Communication or separation? Reactions to Irish land agitation and legislation in the Highlands of Scotland', *English Historical Review*, vol. 120 (2005), pp. 633–67; C. W. J. Withers, 'Rural protest in the Highlands of Scotland and Ireland, 1850–1930', in S. J. Connolly, R. A. Houston and R. J. Morris (eds), *Conflict, Identity and Economic Development, Ireland and Scotland 1600–1939* (Preston: Carnegie Publishing, 1995), pp. 172–88.
47. NRS, AD56/5, Copy of a letter from Lord Advocate [J. B. Balfour] to Sheriff of Inverness-shire [W. Ivory], 3 Nov. 1882.
48. I. M. M. MacPhail, 'The Skye military expedition of 1884–5', *Transactions of the Gaelic Society of Inverness*, vol. 48 (1972–4), pp. 62–94.
49. Ibid. 'Gunboats to the Hebrides', *Transactions of the Gaelic Society of Inverness*, vol. 53 (1982–4), pp. 542–52.
50. NRS, HH1/1, Arthur Balfour to Lord Advocate, 10 Aug. 1886.
51. NRS, HH1/711, Confidential Memorandum by Balfour, 15 Sep. 1886.
52. NRS, HH1/58, Balfour to Ivory, 6 Oct. 1886.
53. NRS, HH1/47, Ivory to Scottish Office, 5 Oct. 1886; NRS, HH1/458/6, Dunbar to Balfour, 6 Oct. 1886.
54. Cameron, *Land for the People?*, pp. 40–61.
55. NRS, HH1/461, Ivory to Balfour, 17 Oct. 1886.
56. See A. M. Tindley, 'The Sutherland Estate, c. 1860–1914: Aristocratic

decline, estate management and land reform' (unpublished PhD thesis, University of Edinburgh, 2006).
57. There is very extensive correspondence and other material relating to this incident at NRS, HH1/ 917, and in the papers of Lord Lothian, Balfour's successor as Secretary for Scotland, at NRS, GD40/16/4/24–48. Material relating to the Park Deer Forest raid can be found at NRS, AF67/35.
58. NRS, AF67/41, Donald Cameron of Lochiel to R.W. Cochran-Patrick, 4 Feb. 1888.
59. British Library, London, Cross MSS, BL Add MSS [Additional Manuscripts] 51276, ff. 148–9, J. H. A. Macdonald to Duke of Richmond and Gordon, 19 Sept. 1885; BL, 51275, ff. 110–11, George Hamilton (Admiralty) to R. A. Cross, 24 Sept. 1885.
60. NRS, GD40/16/12/63–8, Confidential Memorandum to the Secretary for Scotland on the Best Way of Employing an Armed Force in the Highlands and Islands.
61. E. A. Cameron, '"They will listen to no remonstrance": Land raids and land raiders in the Scottish Highlands, 1886 to 1914', *Scottish Economic and Social History*, vol. 17 (1997), pp. 43–64.

17
Scots and the Wars of Empire, 1815–1914

EDWARD M. SPIERS

The nineteenth century proved a crucial century for the reputation of Scotland as a nation that bred warriors and soldiers. Following the exalted achievements of Scottish soldiers in the Napoleonic Wars, and at Waterloo, meriting rapturous receptions in England and Scotland for returning regiments,[1] Scots found military service and further renown throughout the empire. Although Scots served in all the corps and regiments of the British army, including Private John W. Roy, who won a Distinguished Conduct Medal with the 1st battalion, 24th Foot at Rorke's Drift,[2] many served alongside Englishmen and Irishmen in the Scottish infantry regiments. Each of these regiments, as Stuart Allan and Allan Carswell affirm in *The Thin Red Line*, forged their own identity and traditions, and it was during the Victorian era that they lost their historic numbers, coming to use (or in some cases gain) evocative names: the Royal Scots, the Royal Scots Fusiliers, the King's Own Scottish Borderers, the Cameronians, the Black Watch, the Highland Light Infantry, the Seaforth Highlanders, the Queen's Own Cameron Highlanders, the Gordon Highlanders and the Argyll and Sutherland Highlanders. In addition there were the distinctively Scottish components of the cavalry and guards: the Royal Scots Greys and the Scots Guards.[3] Operating within an army whose numbers were slashed after Waterloo, falling to nearly 100,000 in the 1820s (with an active strength in excess of 200,000 only restored on a sustained basis in the 1890s),[4] Scottish infantry regiments undertook lengthy periods of service in India and the colonies, juxtaposed with service at home often involving protracted tours of duty in Ireland.

In spite of the accolades earned by Scottish soldiers, recruiting in Scotland proved increasingly difficult. Initially Scots were over-represented in the British army, supplying 13,800 non-commissioned officers (NCOs) and men or 13.6 per cent of the army in 1830, when

Scotland contained 10 per cent of the United Kingdom's population. By 1899, when the English and Welsh had quadrupled their numbers to nearly 165,000 soldiers, Scotland supplied only 17,280 men, or 8 per cent of the army below its 10 per cent of the UK's population. Even in the early nineteenth century, when Scottish recruiting was relatively buoyant, some Lowland regiments depended upon a preponderance of English and Irish recruits,[5] while Highland regiments, though overwhelmingly Scots in composition, struggled to find recruits from Highland counties as migration within Scotland compounded the effects of emigration from the Highlands. Even the 93rd (Sutherland) Highlanders, renowned for possessing a 'great majority' of Gaelic-speaking soldiers as late as 1857, found difficulty in sustaining the flow of recruits from the Highland counties.[6] National proportions could oscillate, as the 78th (later the 2nd battalion, Seaforth Highlanders) found when its proportion of Scottish soldiers slumped from 91 per cent in the years preceding 1844 to 47 per cent in 1846–53 following a catastrophic loss of 535 officers and men from cholera in India (as well as 202 wives and children). Desperate for drafts, the depot companies of the 78th had to seek men from across the UK, including 100 volunteers from the 2nd Queen's regiment.[7]

Nevertheless, recruiting improved in the mid-1850s and 1860s possibly on account of patriotism engendered, and accolades won, by Scottish regiments during the Crimean War and Indian Mutiny (but doubtless assisted by adverse economic conditions in parts of the country). By 1878, seven Highland regiments, the 42nd, 71st, 72nd, 78th, 79th, 92nd and 93rd, each claimed 60 per cent of their men as Scots, whereas three Lowland and two nominally Highland regiments – the 1st, 25th, 73rd, 75th and 99th – found less than 15 per cent of their men from Scotland.[8] Scottish units benefited from the localisation reforms of 1881 whereby they were linked in four-battalion regiments, each with a permanent depot and recruiting district in Scotland, leaving the Queen's Own Cameron Highlanders as the sole one-battalion regiment. Though helpful, these measures hardly transformed the recruiting base of Scottish regiments in general and of the Highland regiments in particular. As Lieutenant-Colonel A. Y. Leslie (Cameron Highlanders) remarked, 'Inverness-shire as a regimental district is miserable in its unproductiveness', and so when a 2nd battalion of the Camerons was approved in 1897, it was given all of Scotland as its recruiting district.[9] All Scottish regiments became increasingly dependent upon recruiting from the industrial belt of central Scotland, where the cities, like their English counterparts (still significant sources of supply for Scottish regiments), were characterised by swathes of overcrowding, poverty and unemployment. As Heather Streets observes, 'in the late nineteenth century, the men who enlisted in the Highland regiments were increasingly urban and from the lower working classes, in contrast to the rural, clan-based, Highland-born warriors of popular legend'.[10]

Scots enlisted from a myriad of personal motives. J. W. Moodie, a soldier-evangelist, recalled being 'entranced' by the sight of 'a stalwart Highlander, dressed in red coat and kilt, with feathers in his bonnet'; Private John Pindar (42nd, later 1st battalion, Black Watch) and Sergeant John Menzies (45th, Nottinghamshire Regiment) sought escape from the monotony or drudgery of their lives as a miner and ploughman respectively; Private William Duguid (93rd) enlisted like many others after finding himself drunk in the company of a recruiting sergeant; and the radical Alexander Somerville enlisted in the Scots Greys 'while moneyless' and in a 'black prism of despair'.[11] Dire circumstances drove many men to enlist throughout the nineteenth century, often in defiance of their family wishes[12] as military rates of pay, barrack-room life and protracted tours of overseas duty had scant appeal for respectable, working-class families. In the pre-Crimean army, regiments such as the 42nd recruited heavily from the unemployed handloom weavers in the west of Scotland, and when Scotland raised three regiments in 1835 to serve with the British Legion in the First Carlist War, a 'great number of those composing the Scotch regiments were', in Somerville's words, 'of an unfortunate class; that is, the handloom weavers of the west of Scotland; so it was the force of circumstance . . . that led many of them to go to Spain'.[13]

Until 1871, officers in the guards, cavalry and infantry regiments served within a purchase system in which they had to purchase their commissions and steps in rank up to the level of lieutenant-colonel. Socially exclusive in its own right, the effects of the system were buttressed by derisory rates of pay, expensive uniform costs, considerable regimental expenses, and a nomination system in which prospective officers required the nomination or approval of the colonel of their chosen regiment (or of the commander-in-chief if they wished to enter the guards). By these means Scottish regiments, like regiments throughout the British army, restricted access to the offspring of the landed classes, both aristocracy and gentry, or to the sons of old officers or those supported by influential patrons. They ensured, thereby, that military service remained a traditional and highly regarded career for landed families, carrying social status and respectability (or confirming it for the sons of magnates who, having made their money in industry, commerce and speculation, had moved on to the land).[14]

What Scottish regiments could not do was ensure that their officers' messes remained exclusively Scottish. Purchase facilitated promotion by encouraging a large proportion of subalterns and captains to serve for limited periods and then sell out, and it accommodated a system of exchanges that enabled English, Irish and Scottish officers to move between regiments (often allowing wealthier officers to avoid overseas service). In her analysis of Highland regiments during the period 1820–72, Diana Henderson found that only the kilted regiments were able to preserve a predominantly Scottish presence. Elsewhere English and Irish officers comprised over half of the officers in each of the five trews, or line regiments, reducing the Scottish presence in the 73rd (later 2nd battalion, Black Watch) and the 75th (later 1st battalion, Gordon Highlanders) to 15 and 16 per cent respectively.[15] Admittedly some officers born in England, Ireland or India came from Scottish stock, like John Alexander Ewart, who exchanged from the 35th Foot (Sussex Regiment) into the 93rd in 1846, later rising to become lieutenant-colonel of the 93rd and ultimately a general. Many Scottish officers were also the product of public schools and the Royal Military College Sandhurst, acquiring anglicised accents and so minimising differences to an outsider: as Henry Stanley said of the Black Watch when they disembarked on the Gold Coast in December 1873, 'They are mostly all young men of very good families, with cream-coloured complexions, light hair and whiskers, as if they had all been turned out of one mould – they appear to be so very much alike.'[16] Finally, although the purchase army suited wealthy and well-connected families, and enabled their sons to indulge in field sports and social entertainment,[17] it did not preclude entirely the entry of officers of modest means, like Colin Campbell (later Baron Clyde), the son of a Glaswegian carpenter. Yet even this doughty fighter, who rose by promotions in the field to the rank of captain during the Peninsular War, required funding from friends and family to purchase his majority and lieutenant-colonelcy in the post-war years.

The abolition of purchase did not alter radically the social composition of the officers in Scottish regiments. Family tradition remained a powerful factor, readily embraced by some, like Ian Hamilton, who exchanged as quickly as he could into the Gordon Highlanders, but more meekly by Archibald Wavell, who entered the Black Watch despite lacking any military ambitions:

> but it would have taken more independence of character than I possessed at the time to avoid it. Nearly all my relations were in the Army. I had been brought up amongst soldiers; and my father, while professing to give me

complete liberty of choice, was determined that I should be a soldier. I had no particular bent towards any other profession, and I took the line of least resistance.[18]

Like their English and Irish counterparts, Scottish officers reflected the increasing professionalisation of the late Victorian army; they passed entrance and promotion examinations, and several, including Douglas Haig and Spencer Ewart, passed the Staff College (despite a disdain of this institution in some Highland regiments).[19] Scotland still produced legendary, battle-hardened commanding officers, like Sir Archibald Alison (the eldest son of Sir Archibald Alison, the Tory sheriff of Lanarkshire), who served for over twenty years after losing an arm during the Indian Mutiny, and Andrew G. Wauchope, an intrepid Black Watch officer, who incurred severe wounds in several campaigns and, as a wealthy Conservative mine owner, opposed Gladstone in the Midlothian election of 1892, slashing his majority by over 80 per cent: they followed Colin Campbell as commanders of successive Highland Brigades. Distinguished service in the field also produced a rare promotion from the ranks, namely Hector Macdonald, whose achievement in rising from the ranks within the Gordon Highlanders to become a major-general, and then distinguishing himself in command of a Sudanese brigade at Omdurman (2 September 1898), earned him accolades on his return to Scotland and later command of the Highland Brigade in South Africa.[20]

Over the course of a century officers flourished in some contexts but struggled in others (not least when they had to cope with the influx of a large numbers of drafts).[21] If the messes were not always harmonious, as reflected in the survival of 'subalterns' courts', some Scottish regiments prospered under inspiring and innovative commanding officers. Often concerned about the effects of the demon drink and dissipation, these commanding officers introduced all manner of distractions. Lieutenant-Colonel Duncan MacGregor (93rd, 1827–33) introduced Bible reading classes and a regimental school, while Sir Charles Gordon, entering the 42nd as commanding officer in 1828, abolished the sergeants' annual Waterloo Ball and curtailed the hours of the 'wet' canteen. He introduced a regimental library (that would have 3,000 volumes by 1854) and persuaded the War Office to introduce a rota system for units quartered in the Mediterranean garrisons. Lieutenant-Colonel (later General Sir) George Bell, upon assuming command of the 1st Foot (later the Royal Scots) in 1843, introduced a Bible class, lectures on politics and world affairs, regimental sports and certificates of education, as well as starting a regimental library. During his twelve years in command, he neither permitted nor authorised a flogging.[22]

Although the effects of dissipation, and medical ailments, such as venereal disease, whether at home or overseas became less pronounced by the end of the century, service in tropical conditions sometimes in filthy and unsanitary quarters took its toll. Of all the overseas deployments, the West Indies with its trying climate, monotonous duties, consumption of rum and bouts of yellow fever was probably the worst. The 91st Argyllshire Regiment lost twenty officers and 616 NCOs and other ranks when quartered in Jamaica from 1822 to 1831; the 25th (later King's Own Scottish Borderers) lost two officers and 307 NCOs and men after serving in various West Indian islands from 1828 to 1835; and the 21st (later the Royal Scots Fusiliers) suffered from 'the usual record of boredom and ill-health' in 1860–4 before yellow fever swept through the ranks in Barbados.[23] Disease, as already stated, could exact a heavy toll in the Indian sub-continent but it also did so in the Mediterranean area: of the 367 Cameron Highlanders lost in Bulgaria and the Crimean War, only nine died as a result of enemy action.[24]

Even travelling to overseas stations could prove hazardous. The *Premier*, carrying the headquarters and several companies of the 1st Foot (later Royal Scots), foundered in the Gulf of the St Lawrence (4 November 1843); HMS *Transit*, with the left wing of the 90th Perthshire Light Infantry (later the 2nd battalion, Cameronians), was wrecked in the Banka Straits off northern Sumatra (10 July 1857); and the *City of Paris*, carrying the 2nd battalion, 21st to Zululand, almost foundered in Simon's Bay (21 March 1879). The worst disaster befell the *Birkenhead*, carrying 638 passengers and crew when it struck the rocks off the Cape of Good Hope on 26 February 1852. Of the twelve officers and 490 NCOs and men, Lieutenant-Colonel Alexander Seton of the 74th (later the 2nd battalion, Highland Light Infantry (HLI)) was the senior officer, and the 73rd, 74th and 91st regiments all had sizeable contingents on board. Officers and men maintained impeccable discipline as they enabled the women and children to escape. Only 193 persons survived the shark-infested waters, with the largest number of military fatalities, fifty-six, being incurred by the 73rd, but the heroism and discipline of the soldiery impressed royalty across Europe and captured the public imagination. In his painting *The Wreck of the Birkenhead* (c.1892), Thomas Hemy immortalised the scene of trews-clad soldiers calmly awaiting their fate on the deck of the ship.[25]

In the early nineteenth century Scottish units fought in relatively

Figure 17.1 *The Wreck of the Birkenhead* by Thomas Hemy, c. 1892.

few wars, as they were not heavily committed in India, other than the 2nd battalion, 1st Foot, which served through the Third Mahratta War (1817–18) and was the only British unit in the battle of Nagpur (1817). It later lost nine officers and 418 NCOs and men mainly from disease in the First Anglo-Burmese War, 1824–6.[26] Scots still had important duties to perform, not least in consolidating British rule in Canada, where their units received warm receptions in places like

Toronto, Quebec and Nova Scotia (and many Scots sought to remain in Canada, applying for transfers when their regiments were due to leave).[27] In Montreal, a town split between English- and French-speaking Canadians, with a substantial Irish Catholic minority, relations were much more sensitive, with election riots and small-scale insurrections along the American border in the 1830s and 1840s. The 71st (later the 1st battalion, HLI) arrived in Montreal in 1838, just after one rebellion but in time to suppress the second when it fought alongside an irregular militia, the Glengarry Highlanders. Although the 71st took part in the pillaging and burning of disaffected villages, the regiment, argues Elinor Senior, 'probably did more to heal rebellion wounds than any other . . .' Several officers spoke French and the regiment forged close links with British and French Montrealers, including 'young ladies [belonging] to the old French families'. The pipe band, which had arrived in Montreal playing 'Voulez-vous danser, Mademoiselle?' performed at social and sporting events over the next fourteen years. They appeared at house parties, balls and processions, even escorting French Canadians as they returned from Sunday morning mass to the quickstep 'Vive la Canadienne'.[28]

Scottish units undertook their share of duties in aid of the civil power in Britain and recurrently in Ireland; they also suppressed slave revolts in the West Indies.[29] In Cape Colony, they fought in the Sixth, Seventh and Eighth Frontier Wars. In 1834–5, the 72nd (later 1st battalion, Seaforth Highlanders) and the 75th participated in the combined-arms expedition to punish the Xhosa tribesmen for their raids upon settler communities. Assisted by Cape Mounted Rifles and Mfengu and Khockhoi levies, they exacted retribution by burning villages, capturing cattle and dispersing the enemy. Similar fighting occurred in 1846–7, when companies of the 73rd and 91st took part in convoy duty, the defence of Fort Peddie and the abortive assaults on the Xhosa stronghold in the Amatola Mountains. They often marched twenty to thirty miles a day in severe heat to locate tribesmen hiding in the *kloofs* (thickly wooded valleys).[30] When the Xhosa launched further raids in 1850, and gained defections from the Khockhoi (Hottentots), the 74th were part of the reinforcements sent to the Cape. Wearing serviceable kit (replacing plaids and bonnets by forage caps with leather peaks, dark canvas blouses and lighter pouches), they pursued the enemy through the bush, burning villages and crops, capturing cattle and driving the Xhosa from their villages and mountainous strongholds. Several of the actions in which the 74th were involved were depicted by Thomas Baines, an eyewitness artist, including one known as the *Engagement on the Heights above Waterkloof, 1851*. Although Captain

Figure 17.2 Sir Colin Campbell, commander of the Highland Brigade in the Crimean War and commander-in-chief in India during the Mutiny.

W. R. King applauded the Xhosa as guerrilla warriors, he was not alone in deploring their 'fetish-like cruelties' and the torture and murder of captured soldiers. Like Captain James Alexander, a Black Watch staff officer who fought in the Sixth Frontier War, he was dismayed by radical and missionary support for the tribesmen at home.[31]

The Crimean War (1854–6) proved a sterner test for Scottish units in a conflict that examined every facet of the army's organisation and received extensive coverage in the press at home. Within days of landing in the Crimea, the Highland Brigade (42nd, 79th and 93rd), serving under Sir Colin Campbell in the British frontline, stormed the Russian positions on the heights above the River Alma (20 September 1854). Soldiers faced 'incessant' firing and 'deafening noise' but followed Campbell, with the 42nd claiming to have reached the top first.[32] The Royal Scots Greys and the 93rd would later add to their laurels at Balaclava (25 October 1854). While the Greys were part of the Heavy Brigade that scattered a mass of Russian cavalry, six companies of the 93rd (550 men and 100 invalids) formed two lines under Campbell's command, to repel another body of Russian cavalry with three volleys from their Minié rifles. This resolute stand earned

Figure 17.3 Men of the 72nd Highlanders (later the 1st battalion, the Seaforth Highlanders) on their return from the Crimea, 1856.

paeans of praise partly, as Colour-Sergeant J. Joiner (93rd) recalled, because the other deployed forces, 'the cowardly Turks ran away', and partly from the misquoting of William Howard Russell's description of the 'thin red streak tipped with a line of steel' as the 'thin red line'.[33]

The heroism of the Greys and 93rd Highlanders somewhat obscured the services of other Scottish regiments, including the Scots Fusilier Guards defending their colours at the Alma, and these same Guards, the 1st battalion, Royal Scots and the 21st employing the bayonet in close-quarter fighting in the bloody battle of Inkerman (5 November 1854). As Lord Raglan's army endured the misery of serving through the first winter in the Crimea, with many units suffering in the trenches before Sevastopol, Scottish units appeared as reinforcements, including the 2nd battalion, Royal Scots, 71st, 72nd, 90th and 92nd. Like other soldiers, Scots eagerly read the press, posed for photographers and, in many cases, commended the writings of Russell. The latter's 'letters in the Times', wrote Captain Thomas Montgomery (42nd), 'are very good, they really leave very little to write about'.[34] That did not stop the Scots, who kept diaries or wrote home in prodigious numbers, whereupon the recipients passed this material on to the local press. As the latter was then preoccupied with the plight of the ordinary soldier, it readily published the correspondence.

Soldiers wrote of the harrowing sights after the battle of the Alma and the sufferings of the wounded or described their own wounds in gruesome detail.[35] They commented on the horrendous conditions of the first winter, working in the trenches or living in tents amidst tempests, rain and heavy snow, the recurrence of cholera and the mounting toll of sickness and death. 'Cholera and diarrhoea,' wrote Private D. McBean (93rd) just before his death, 'are killing more than the enemy, and from constant feeding on salt rations many are suffering from the scurvy'.[36] Yet Scots professed remarkable stoicism; some praised the much-criticised Lord Raglan and the French, if not the Turkish, allies, and many more lauded Campbell's leadership. They appreciated, too, the clothing and provisions sent from home, a testimony to the impact of the early reporting from the front. Sergeant W. Morrison, a Fifer serving in the Scots Guards, even asserted that in spite of living in a tent during the intense cold, 'I never was better off, or liked anything so well since I have been a soldier.'[37] In fact, those highlanders quartered near to the sea and ships at Balaclava enjoyed better rations and conditions than soldiers in the trenches before Sevastopol. Healthier than many English regiments, they also undertook the relatively 'tame expedition' to Kerch in the summer of 1855, so incurring resentment from those who had suffered more heavily in the trenches and received less coverage in the wartime press.[38] Little though could detract from the Scottish achievements, even if they were not involved in the final storming of Sevastopol, or from the pride aroused in Scotland. With scant sense of proportion, the *Glasgow Herald* wrote: 'The Scottish regiments of horse and foot not only bore the brunt of battle, but it was mainly due to their indomitable courage and unflinching bravery that the victories were won.'[39]

Even greater accolades followed the suppression of the Indian Mutiny (1857–9), where the bloody revolt of sepoys in Meerut (May 1857) provoked an orgy of looting, arson and murder of Europeans. In the ferocious response, Scots served in the European regiments of the East India Company,[40] or in the few Queen's regiments then stationed in India, including the 75th, one of the regiments that stormed and recaptured Delhi (14–20 September 1857), but most came in the wave of reinforcements. The 78th, following a decisive triumph in the Persian War, returned to serve under Brigadier-General (later Sir) Henry Havelock as his column battled into Cawnpore just after the infamous massacre of women and children. Bolstered by further reinforcements, including part of the 90th,[41] Havelock's column broke through the siege of the residency at Lucknow (25 September 1857), with the 78th playing the pipes as they did so. Although the 78th earned eight Victoria Crosses and the sobriquet 'Saviours of India',[42] relief of the residency had to await the arrival of Sir Colin Campbell's army (17 November 1857) after it had stormed Sikandarbagh (depicted in a notable watercolour by Orlando Norie) and the Shah Najaf mosque. At Sikandarbagh the 93rd, aided by Sikhs and Campbell's artillery, killed nearly 2,000 sepoys, determined to spare 'not a man of them'.[43]

Only able to evacuate the women, children, sick and wounded, Campbell had to assemble a much larger army with more artillery before he could rout the rebels at Cawnpore (6 December 1857) and capture Lucknow (21 March 1858). Criticised for his caution and favouritism towards the highlanders,[44] he moved on Bareilly, capital of Rohilkhand, defeating the army of Khan Bahadur Khan (5 May 1858) with a Highland Brigade (42nd, 79th and 93rd) in the frontline. While he pursued rebels in the Ganges valley, Sir Hugh Rose (later Baron Strathnairn) commanded a Central India Field Force (January–June 1858), including the 71st in its second brigade, which endured severe climatic conditions (and shortages of food, water and ammunition) in the course of destroying the organised rebel armies. Thereafter British forces, including the 72nd, 73rd, 74th, 92nd and 99th, spent another six months extinguishing the last embers of rebellion. As the Company's army was then disbanded after the 'white mutiny' (1859), several battalions embarked on lengthy tours of duty in India.[45]

Once again soldiers' letters had aroused considerable interest at home. Appalled by the sepoy atrocities, particularly at Cawnpore, where the sights, as a lance-corporal of the 78th recalled, 'made our blood boil with rage',[46] many soldiers took vows of vengeance. 'They will never get any mercy,' wrote a soldier of the 93rd, 'for we must be revenged for the barbarous way they used the women and children'.[47] In meting out reprisals and leaving corpses piled in heaps or hanging from gallows, Scots, like the other European soldiers, did so partly as retributive punishments and partly to terrify local communities. They had little respect for the 'cowardly rascals',[48] who increasingly fled 'like chaff before the wind',[49] as British guns, cavalry and infantry, often accompanied by loyal Indian forces, approached.

From the mid-century onwards Scottish military participation expanded beyond the regular army with a surge of enrolment into the auxiliary forces. Only two regiments of mounted yeomanry (Ayrshire and Lanarkshire) had survived in the early Victorian years but after invasion scares there was a revival of the voluntary militia in 1854 and then the Volunteers in 1859. Forming uniformed rifle clubs and joining the more prestigious artillery units proved hugely popular in the Highland counties, among the professions of Edinburgh, Glasgow and Aberdeen (where bankers, accountants and solicitors all formed companies), and in the industrial areas of Lanarkshire. When Queen Victoria reviewed the Scottish Volunteers in Holyrood Park on 7 August 1860, some 200,000 to 300,000 spectators covered the slopes of Arthur's Seat. Although the composition of the Volunteers changed over the subsequent decades, becoming increasingly urban and working class, Scottish enrolment remained buoyant. By 1871 Scotland had raised twice as many men per head of the male population as the rest of the UK, and by 1881 Scotland had over 47,000 Volunteers (about 5.5 per cent of the available population). Under the amalgamations of 1881, militia and Volunteer battalions were attached to the double-battalion infantry regiments in their respective regimental districts.[50]

Volunteering flourished during another invasion scare and the controversy over relieving Major-General Charles 'Chinese' Gordon in the Sudan (1884–5). It reflected a mixture of motives including patriotism, acceptance of martial values (wearing uniform, learning elementary military duties and obeying orders) and, in many cases, a desire for comradeship, respectability and the opportunity to undertake rifle-shooting and other leisure pursuits.[51] Some of these volunteer values, coupled with the Victorian cult of the Christian soldier,[52] found reflection in the formation of the Boys' Brigade by William Alexander Smith in Glasgow in 1883. A Volunteer and Sunday school teacher, Smith sought to propagate the manly Christian virtues of obedience, reverence, discipline and self-respect through Sunday school and Bible class attendance, the wearing of uniform and the inculcation of discipline and drill. By 1890 Scotland had 260 Boys' Brigade companies (122 in England) and by 1899 276 companies (470 in England).[53]

In the last forty years of the century, Scottish regiments encountered a diverse array of enemies in imperial service often in daunting climatic and topographical conditions. On the north-west frontier,

Figure 17.4 Officers of the 1st battalion, the Royal Scots, in Zululand, 1888.

brief but bloody fighting in the Ambeyla expedition (1863) involved both the 71st and the 93rd, two battalions otherwise mainly involved in home or garrison duty.[54] Active service also varied considerably; whereas the 1st battalion, Royal Scots, served in a bloodless expedition in Bechuanaland (1884) and incurred only one accidental fatality in Zululand (1888), the 2nd battalion fought in a major Anglo-French war with China (1860). In China the British forces served under the command of a redoubtable Scottish cavalry officer, Sir James Hope Grant, a veteran of several wars in India, who was also an accomplished cellist and had recently distinguished himself by commanding cavalry units with fanatical zeal during the Mutiny. Following his orders, the 2nd battalion, Royal Scots, participated in the three-week assault on the Taku Forts, which succeeded on 21 August, opening the way for three subsequent battles and an entry into Peking (Beijing) on 6 October. The emperor's Summer Palace, already looted, was then sacked in revenge for the death and mutilation of members of a British peace delegation.

Military action was just as diverse for other units. While the 1st battalion, 25th repelled Fenian border raids in Canada (1866), the 26th (later 1st battalion, Cameronians) won a battle honour on the lines of communication in the Anglo-Abyssinian War (1867–8) without a single casualty.[55] In the Asante War (1873–4), the 42nd battled through tropical rain forest and fought in a mobile square to rout a vast army and capture the Asante capital. The 90th, having engaged in bush warfare during the Ninth Frontier War (1877–8), had to adapt to fighting under Boer advice within a laager at Khambula (29 March 1879).[56] As some 2,086 British officers and men repulsed over 20,000 Zulu, this vindicated the confidence of a Crieff soldier: 'we are old warriors (for this is our second war) and are used to fighting darkies'.[57] Similar crushing victories occurred when the British fought in open squares, including the 91st at Gingindlovu (2 April 1879) and the 2nd battalion, 21st and the 90th at Ulundi (4 July 1879), leaving Scots in admiration of the bravery and skirmishing of the Zulu.[58]

The 2nd battalion, 21st (soon the Royal Scots Fusiliers) had to adapt more than most: after Zululand it moved through the heat and bush of the eastern Transvaal to breach Chief Sekhukhune's mountainous stronghold (1879) but later found its companies dispersed, and under siege, in isolated garrisons (Pretoria, Rustenburg and Potchefstroom) throughout the Anglo-Transvaal War (1880–1). Some of its officers were next in action fourteen years later, trying to suppress armed dacoits in the malarial rain forests on either bank of the Irrawaddy river (Third Anglo-Burmese War, 1885–9).[59] Fortunes could change as quickly as the nature of the fighting. Both the 72nd and 92nd (Gordon Highlanders) revelled in the hill fighting of the Second Afghan War (1878–80). Serving alongside Gurkhas, they defeated Afghan regulars at Charasiab (6 October 1879), defended cantonments near Kabul from mass attack, and participated in the much-vaunted march over 300 miles from Kabul to Kandahar before routing an Afghan army on the day after their arrival (1 September 1880). Lauded for these achievements, the 92nd (2nd battalion, Gordon Highlanders) travelled to Natal, where a detachment was overwhelmed by Boer farmers in the humiliating defeat on the summit of Majuba hill (27 February 1881). Meanwhile the 72nd moved onto Egypt, where it charged Egyptian guns along the southern bank of the Sweetwater canal at the battle of Tel-el-Kebir (13 September 1882); as one Seaforth wrote, 'about the shortest fight that ever I had, and as cheap a medal that ever any army got'.[60]

On the northern bank, where Sir Garnet Wolseley deployed the bulk of his forces, a Highland Brigade (1st battalions, Black Watch,

Camerons, Gordons and 2nd battalion, HLI) advanced at night and stormed the Egyptian fortifications. They attacked 'in the old Scotch style – by the bayonet'[61] and bore the brunt of the casualties. Crushing Arabi Pasha's revolt in Egypt, however, only ensured that the British forces in Egypt encountered a more formidable challenge from the Mahdist insurrection in the Sudan, then an Egyptian province. The 1st battalions, Black Watch and Gordon Highlanders engaged Mahdist tribesmen at El Teb and Tamai (29 February and 13 March 1884), with Tamai proving a particularly bloody battle after the Mahdists broke through a gap in one of the two squares to kill sixty-one Black Watch and wound another thirty-three before British firepower prevailed. Both units were then involved in the Gordon relief expedition (1884–5), with the Black Watch fighting alongside the South Staffordshire in assailing the Mahdist positions at Kirbekan (10 February 1885). As the relief force withdrew down the Nile after failing to relieve Gordon in Khartoum, the Cameron Highlanders took part in the rearguard victory at Ginnis (30 December 1885), the last battle fought by British forces wearing red.

Further accolades followed in the 1890s, involving several expeditions on the north-west frontier. In the Chitral relief expedition (1895), the 1st battalion, Gordon Highlanders and the 2nd battalion, King's Own Scottish Borderers took part in the storming of the Malakand Pass (3 April). Assisted by the 60th King's Royal Rifle Corps, and the cover of artillery and Maxim machine guns, they scaled heights varying from 1,000 to 1,500 feet to scatter an estimated force of 12,000 Pathans. The Gordons earned even more plaudits when they stormed Dargai Heights (20 October 1897) against a similar force of Afridis. Dubbed 'a second Gibraltar', the heights had defied the efforts of Gurkha and English soldiers and so the Gordons' triumph, inspired by their wounded piper, George Findlater, who won the Victoria Cross, became an imperial epic immortalised in poetry, paintings and imperialist iconography.[62] Finally, the 1st battalions of the Cameron and Seaforth Highlanders served as part of Sir Herbert Kitchener's Anglo-Egyptian army in reconquering the Sudan. The Camerons led the advance in line across open ground, firing volleys, against the Mahdist zareba at the battle of the Atbara (8 April 1898), where 'our fellows had revenge for Gordon', as Corporal Farquharson (Seaforths) recalled, shooting fleeing Mahdists like 'a rabbit drive at home'.[63] The firepower of both battalions contributed to the slaughter of Mahdists at the battle of Omdurman.

None of this experience prepared the Scots, or the rest of the British army, for their greatest imperial challenge, the South African War (1899–1902). Facing highly mobile Boers, armed with smokeless

Figure 17.5 *At Last, the Bivouac at Omdurman (Gordon's Spirit at Rest).* Print after Richard Caton Woodville, 1899.

magazine rifles and adept at the use of cover, British forces found crossing fire zones a costly experience. Despite victory at Elandslaagte (21 October 1899) officers of the 2nd Gordons, kilted and carrying claymores, incurred 70 per cent casualties, and at Modder River (28 November 1899), the 1st Argylls, though wearing aprons over their kilts, suffered 122 casualties out of 478 officers and men engaged.[64] Even worse followed at Magersfontein (11 December 1899), where Wauchope's Highland Brigade (2nd battalions, Black Watch and Seaforth and the 1st battalions, HLI and Argylls) was caught by 'terrific fire' from unseen Boer trenches at daybreak. With Wauchope killed and the brigade pinned to the ground for hours, the Scots, including the 1st Gordons, who came up in support, incurred most of the 948 killed, wounded and missing. The bulk of these casualties occurred when 'retire' was shouted in early afternoon and, as an HLI soldier recalled, 'we did – well, not retire, but a stampede: 4,000 men like a flock of sheep running for dear life'.[65]

Magersfontein was one of three defeats (with Stormberg and

Figure 17.6 Soldiers of the 2nd battalion, the Black Watch, on the march in South Africa, c. 1900.

Colenso) in the 'Black Week' of 10–15 December 1899. Although news of the disaster shocked Scotland, it prompted a surge of patriotic recruiting. Reservists and Volunteers responded to the call: in 1900 Scotland sent eleven Volunteer special service companies and four companies of Imperial Yeomanry to serve in South Africa (another wave of Volunteers followed in 1901, and a smaller one in 1902, ensuring that 5,000 Scots, including the London and Liverpool Scottish, served in the war, or about 10 per cent of the enrolled force).[66] Henceforth Scots took part in the major victory at Paardeberg (18–27 February 1900), in the combined arms operations that relieved Ladysmith (where the 2nd Gordons had survived the 118-day siege), and in the capture of the Boer capitals. As the Boers reacted by waging a protracted guerrilla campaign, Scots, like the rest of the British army, had to adapt. They undertook prodigious marches across the veld, fought in open-order formations and served in various roles as mounted infantry or in lines of communication, convoy protection and garrison duties.[67]

Faced with a highly mobile enemy operating across a vast country, the Highland Brigade was broken up and Scottish battalions dispersed in smaller units. Some served in the flying columns that chased the Boers across the veld, profiting from the reconnaissance skills of the three contingents of Lovat Scouts.[68] Scots also engaged in the burning of farms, the destruction of crops and livestock, and the rounding up of Boer families – distasteful work for many, but 'clearing off the people', as Sergeant William Hamilton (HLI) observed, 'has destroyed their principal means of intelligence'.[69] Whatever their own thoughts on the war, many Scottish soldiers deplored the expression of pro-Boer sentiments at home and favoured even more repressive policies if these would subdue the Boers.[70] Latterly Scottish units were split into even smaller bodies, manning some of the 8,000 blockhouses in Kitchener's elaborate, costly but ultimately successful attempt to bring about a Boer surrender (31 May 1902).

In short, Scots had performed impressively through the imperial wars of the nineteenth century. Despite their recruiting difficulties, five kilted regiments had emerged from the amalgamations of 1881, another Highland regiment, the HLI, wore trews and the Lowland regiments (save for the 99th which became an English regiment) were 'highlandised' by the imposition of doublets, trews and claymores. Distinctively Scottish in appearance and culture, they prospered under royal patronage, enjoyed a prominence within imperial iconography and earned huge popularity as reflected in the crowds that gathered whenever regiments left or returned to Scotland. This popular acclaim reached a crescendo during the South African War, where vast crowds cheered regulars and Volunteers off to war. Sergeant Will Greening (2nd Cameronians) recalled the difficulty of trying to march through the crowds to Finnieston Dock as 'people broke up our ranks, carried our rifles and kits' and plied the men with whisky, tobacco, cigars and money: 'I was kissed by several damsels of sorts, some sober and some otherwise. The cheering was deafening, and all Glasgow turned out to see us off, and the houses, windows and roofs were black with people.'[71] Such scenes were replicated following the relief of Ladysmith, Mafeking and the capture of Pretoria, and huge crowds gathered when Scottish soldiers returned, reportedly 'many thousands' at Musselburgh to greet six returning Volunteers.[72] By the end of the century the Scottish soldier not only embodied the country's national identity within the union but also discharged a valued mission, namely the defence of empire.

The South African War, nonetheless, had proved an unexpectedly protracted, costly and unpopular conflict. If Scottish soldiers were still welcomed home effusively, the somewhat muted celebrations at the end of the war reflected an awareness that the human and financial costs had escalated beyond anyone's expectation. Some 448,435 British and colonial soldiers had served in a war that cost £201 million, with 5,774 men killed in action, another 16,168 deaths from disease and 75,430 returned as sick or wounded. Scots had borne their share: after the first year's campaigning, Scottish units had incurred a greater proportion of the killed and wounded but had lost a lower proportion of men through capture or death from disease than any of the nationalities fighting in the imperial cause. The 2nd Black Watch, the principal victim at Magersfontein, had suffered the highest number of killed and wounded of any battalion in that year, and the 2nd Seaforths the highest number of killed.[73] After the war, Scottish soldiers found that they had additional garrison duties to perform in South Africa, with the 2nd battalion, Cameron Highlanders protecting Pietermaritzburg during the Zulu rebellion of 1906. On the north-west frontier, the 1st Seaforths served in the Zakka Khel and Mohmand expeditions of 1908 but Scottish soldiers never experienced another imperial triumph before 1914.

The South African legacy dominated the early years of the Edwardian era. Scots commemorated the achievements and sacrifices of their regiments in memorials erected all over Scotland and not only in traditional sites such as castle esplanades, churches and the High Kirk of St Giles but also in the centre of cities (on the North Bridge, Princes Street and the Mound in Edinburgh), towns, villages and in municipal parks (Dumbarton, Hawick and Glasgow), symbolising the deepening links between Scottish communities and their soldiery. They also did so in South Africa where the Scottish Horse (a volunteer formation from the war) and the Transvaal Scottish (formed after the war) paraded for the unveiling of the Scottish war memorial on the Kensington estate in Johannesburg.[74] Finally, Scots turned out in vast numbers after the deaths of imperial heroes (at the graveside of Sir Hector Macdonald despite the controversy over his suicide on 25 March 1903) and at the funeral of Sir Archibald Alison (9 February 1907).

Senior Scottish officers, too, were in the forefront of those who sought to learn the lessons of recent warfare. Sir Ian Hamilton despatched a major report from the Russo-Japanese War (1904–5) where he saw the effects of modern rifle and artillery fire and confirmed his view, formed in South Africa, that cavalry armed with sword and lance was obsolete on the modern battlefield. Conversely Douglas Haig, who had also seen extensive service in South Africa, championed the retention of the mounted arm albeit by a cavalry equipped with rifles as well as its traditional weapons. Both men rendered another Scot, Richard Burdon Haldane, considerable service when he launched wide-ranging reforms of the army as secretary of state for war (1905–12).[75] Although Haldane became aware of a possible continental commitment for the army as early as January 1906, and encouraged planning for this aim (with Spencer Ewart as director of military operations (1906–10) providing valuable support), he only reformed the army within the constraints of a politically acceptable budget, the voluntary system of enlistment and, as publicly stated, a potential imperial purpose.[76]

The reforms included the reorganisation of the home army units into the British Expeditionary Force, a body of six divisions and one cavalry division intended for rapid mobilisation in the event of war. Equipped with new rifles and artillery since South Africa, this would become a highly trained army, practised in the arts of fire and movement as embodied in the *Field Service Regulations* that Haig, when director of staff duties, had introduced. The 1st battalion, Black Watch, part of the 1st Division at Aldershot on the eve of the Great War, exemplified the remarkable standards attained in musketry, field craft and proficiency in night work and combined arms operations.[77] Scots also served in Haldane's second-line army, the Territorial Force raised for home defence, a much more organised and better-equipped force than the old Volunteers and yeomanry. Scots served in two divisions (Highland and Lowland) out of the fourteen Territorial divisions but recruiting across the UK never filled the peacetime establishment (about 312,000 men), falling to 236,389 men by 30 September 1913. Just as regular recruiting had struggled in Scotland, falling from 21,852 in 1904 to 17,282 or only 7.5 per cent of the army in 1913, so part-time service in the Territorials had limited appeal. As Lord Reith recalled, the Territorials in which he served encountered jeers and derision in parts of Glasgow.[78] Neither the endemic recruiting difficulties nor the promotion of compulsory service by the National Service League nor the surge of emigration to Canada daunted Haldane, who continued to tour Scotland (as he did England) beating the drum for Territorial recruits. He reminded audiences that Scots had rallied in the last 'great imperial emergency' and expressed confidence that they would do so again.[79]

Ultimately he was right, but in peacetime the imperial focus was both a strength and weakness for the reputation of Scottish soldiery. Reports and images of Scots, often in kilts and accompanied by bagpipes, serving in exotic locations undoubtedly stirred passions at home. The Scottish soldier, including the citizen soldiers who served in South Africa, embodied a sense of national identity, though firmly within a British context and charged with an explicit imperial mission. The Territorials, argued Haldane, were 'citizens of a great Empire'.[80] Yet the imperial role, when bereft of stunning triumphs, seemed far removed from much of ordinary, everyday life in Edwardian Scotland. Levels of pay and conditions of service remained unattractive and so the army remained a lowly career choice for the rank and file even if still a highly respected and increasingly professional institution. The paradox of Scottish attitudes towards military service was as evident in 1914 as it had been in the early nineteenth century.

Notes

I should like to acknowledge the British Academy for its award of a Small Research Grant to undertake the research for this chapter.

1. J. Anton, *Retrospect of A Military Life, during the Most Eventful Periods of the Last War* (Edinburgh: W. H. Lizars, 1841), pp. 247–53.
2. He served in the 1st Battalion, 24th Foot (the 2nd Warwickshire regiment), N. Holme, *The Noble 24th: Biographical Records of the 24th Regiment in the Zulu War and the South African Campaigns 1877–1879* (London: Savannah, 1999), pp. 315–16.
3. S. Allan and A. Carswell, *The Thin Red Line: War, Empire and Visions of Scotland* (Edinburgh: National Museums of Scotland, 2004), p. 19.
4. E. M. Spiers, *The Army and Society, 1815–1914* (London: Longman, 1980), p. 36; S. Wood, *The Scottish Soldier* (Manchester: Archive Publications, 1987), p. 52.
5. H. J. Hanham, 'Religion and nationality in the mid-Victorian army', in M. R. D. Foot (ed.), *War and Society* (London: Paul Elek, 1973), pp. 159–81, 318–20; J. C. Leask and H. M. McCance, *The Regimental Records of The Royal Scots* (Dublin: Alexander Thom, 1915), pp. 385, 414, 417.
6. Surgeon-General W. Munro, *Reminiscences of Military Service with the 93rd Sutherland Highlanders* (London: Hurst and Blackett, 1883), pp. 201–2; Brigadier-General A. E. Cavendish, *An Reisimeid Chataich The 93rd Sutherland Highlanders* (London: privately published, 1928), pp. 60, 87; D. Henderson, *Highland Soldier: A Social Study of the Highland Regiments, 1820–1920* (Edinburgh: John Donald, 1989), pp. 25, 38.
7. Lieutenant-Colonel A. Fairrie, *'Cuidich 'N Righ': A History of the Queen's Own Highlanders (Seaforth and Cameron)* (Inverness: Regimental HQ, Queen's Own Highlanders, 1983), p. 18.
8. Hanham, 'Religion and nationality', pp. 165–6; see also Lieutenant-Colonel L. B. Oatts, *Proud Heritage: The Story of the Highland Light Infantry*, 4 vols (London: Thomas Nelson, 1959), vol. 2, pp. 335–6 and A. Robb, *Reminiscences of a Veteran; Being the Experiences of a Private Soldier in the Crimea and during the Indian Mutiny* (Dundee: W. & D. C. Thomson, 1888), p. 2.
9. Lieutenant-Colonel A. Y. Leslie, q. 12256, appended to the *Report of the*

Committee on the Terms and Conditions of Service in the Army, C. 6582 (1892), vol. XIX, p. 416.

10. H. Streets, *Martial Races: The Military, Race and Masculinity in British Imperial Culture, 1857–1914* (Manchester: Manchester University Press, 2004), p. 177; Henderson, *Highland Soldier*, pp. 26–30.
11. J. W. Moody, *A Soldier's Life and Experience in the British Army* (Ardrossan: A. Guthrie, n.d.), p. 3; J. Pindar, *Autobiography of a Private Soldier* (Cupar: Fife News, 1877), p. 3; Sergeant J. Menzies, *Reminiscences of an Old Soldier* (Edinburgh: Crawford and McCabe, 1883), p. 4; Argyll and Sutherland Highlanders Museum [hereafter ASHM], N-B93 DUG, Duguid, diary, p. 3; A. Somerville, *The Autobiography of a Working Man* ed. J. Carswell (London: Turnstile Press, 1951), p. 114.
12. The Highlanders Museum [hereafter HM], 'The Autobiography of Donald Dickson Farmer, V.C.', p. 1.
13. A. Somerville, *History of the British Legion and War in Spain* (London: James Pattie, 1839), p. 6; E. and A. Linklater, *The Black Watch: The History of the Royal Highland Regiment* (London: Barrie and Jenkins, 1977), p. 95.
14. G. Harries-Jenkins, *The Army in Victorian Society* (London: Routledge and Kegan Paul, 1977), pp. 21–3; A. Bruce, *The Purchase System in the British Army 1660–1871* (London: Royal Historical Society, 1980), pp. 45, 73–4.
15. Henderson, *Highland Soldier*, p. 91; see also Bruce, *Purchase System*, pp. 69, 82–3.
16. H. M. Stanley, *Coomassie and Magdala* (London: Sampson Low, 1874), p. 103.
17. For remarkable shooting, fishing and hunting accounts of officers, see Black Watch Regimental Archive [hereafter BWRA] 0028, Colonel J. W. Wedderburn, diary, 1848–50, and HM, 83-77, Lieutenant W. Parke, diary, 1845–7.
18. J. Connell, *Wavell, Scholar and Soldier* (London: Collins, 1964), p. 34; I. B. M. Hamilton, *Happy Warrior: A Life of General Sir Ian Hamilton* (London: Cassell, 1966), pp. 11–12, 17.
19. Hamilton, *Happy Warrior*, p. 19; Henderson, *Highland Soldier*, p. 112.
20. T. Royle, *Fighting Mac: The Downfall of Major-General Sir Hector Macdonald* (Edinburgh: Mainstream Publishing, 1982), ch. 10.
21. After the 1st battalion, Seaforths received 500 drafts from the 2nd battalion en route to the Sudan, Lance-Sergeant Colin Grieve reflected that 'this Regiment is not what it used to be – that lot that joined us in Malta have played the mischief with it', National Army Museum (NAM), Acc No 1979-06-139, Grieve MSS, Grieve to Tommie, 16 February 1898.
22. Cavendish, *An Reisimeid Chataich*, p. 64; Linklater, *Black Watch*, pp.

89–90; B. Stuart (ed.), *Soldier's Glory being 'Rough Notes of an Old Soldier' by Major-General Sir George Bell* (London: G. Bell, 1956), pp. 176–7; on drinking habits, R. P. Dunn-Pattison, *The History of the 91st Argyllshire Highlanders* (Edinburgh: Blackwood, 1910), pp. 95, 108 and Robb, *Reminiscences*, p. 40.

23. Dunn-Pattison, *91st Highlanders*, pp. 95–6; Captain R. T. Higgins, *The Records of The King's Own Borderers* (London: Chapman and Hall, 1873), pp. 295–6; J. Buchan, *The History of The Royal Scots Fusiliers (1678–1918)* (London: Thomas Nelson & Sons, 1925), p. 223.
24. Fairrie, *'Cuidich 'N Righ'*, p. 33.
25. 'The Wreck of the "Birkenhead"', *Highland Light Infantry Chronicle*, vol. 1 (1894), pp. 260–3; see also C. Lowe, 'The 1st Royal Scots, of Lothian Regiment', *The Thistle*, new series, vol. 1 (1904), pp. 178–9; P. Wickins (ed.), 'The Indian Mutiny journal of Private Charles Wickins of the 90th Light Infantry', *Journal of the Society for Army Historical Research*, vol. 36 (1958), pp. 96–108; Buchan, *Royal Scots Fusiliers*, pp. 237–8; D. Bevan, *Drums of the Birkenhead* (Cape Town: Purnell, 1972).
26. 'The Royals in Burma in 1825', *The Thistle*, vol. 5 (December/January 1898–9), p. 335.
27. ASHM, N-B93 DOC, Dr. Mackenzie's diary, 24 May, 19 and 25 June and 24 September 1839; Stuart, *Rough Notes*, pp. 157–9; Linklater, *Black Watch*, p. 94.
28. E. Senior, 'An imperial garrison in its colonial setting: British regulars in Montreal 1832–54' (unpublished PhD thesis, McGill University, Montreal, 1976), pp. 230–1, 261, 277, 477–82.
29. For a sample of these activities, see Anton, *Retrospect*, pp. 257–61, 300–5; Buchan, *Royal Scots Fusiliers*, pp. 186–7; Dunn-Pattison, *91st Highlanders*, pp. 98–9.
30. Fairrie, *'Cuidich 'N Righ'*, p. 8; Lt.-Colonel C. Greenhill Gardyne, *The Life of a Regiment: The History of the Gordon Highlanders*, 3 vols (London: The Medici Society, 1903–29), vol. 2, pp. 208–10; Dunn-Pattison, *91st Highlanders*, pp. 109–11.
31. Capt. W. R. King, *Campaigning in Kaffirland* (London: Saunders and Otley, 1853), pp. 17, 27, 45, 90–2, 94, 96, 115, 135, 144–5, 158, 167, 209, 247, 272; Capt. J. E. Alexander, *Narrative of a Voyage of Observation among the Colonies of Western Africa, in the flag-ship Thalia: and of A Campaign in Kaffirland, on the staff of the Commander-in-Chief, in 1835*, 2 vols (London: Henry Colburn, 1837), vol. 2, p. 288.
32. BWRA 031-032, Sir P. A. Halkett, 'My Military Life'; 'Another Letter', *Inverness Courier*, 16 November 1854, p. 6; Lieutenant-Colonel A. Sterling, *The Highland Brigade in the Crimea* (Minneapolis, MN: Absinthe Press, 1995), pp. 44–6.

33. 'From a Colour-Serjeant [sic] of the 93rd Highlanders to his friends in Glasgow', *Glasgow Herald*, 19 February 1855, p. 10; ASHM, N-B93NAI, 'Military Career of Wm. Nairn'; E. M. Spiers, *The Scottish Soldier and Empire, 1854–1902* (Edinburgh: Edinburgh University Press, 2006), p. 5.
34. BWRA 0231, 'Letters from the Crimea of Captain Thomas Montgomery', p. 22; 'From an Officer of the 79th Highlanders', *Glasgow Herald*, 29 December 1854, p. 6; see also Wood, *Scottish Soldier*, p. 62.
35. BWRA 0214, 'Diary of David McAusland', p. 13 and 'Letters from the Crimea', *Glasgow Herald*, 27 October 1854, p. 5; see also letters in the *Glasgow Herald*, 8 and 29 December 1854, pp. 4, 6.
36. 'Soldiers' Letters from the Camp', *Inverness Courier*, 22 February 1855, p. 6; see also letters in the *Glasgow Herald*, 27 October 1854, p. 5 and *Inverness Courier*, 25 January 1855, p. 6.
37. 'From a Fifeshire Fusilier Serjeant [sic], to a Friend in Glasgow', *Glasgow Herald*, 19 March 1855, p. 5; see also letters in *Inverness Courier*, 19 April 1855, p. 6; *Glasgow Herald*, 25 December 1854, p. 5; 19 February 1855, p. 10; and 30 April 1855, p. 5.
38. 'Letter from a Corporal in the 42D to a Friend in Glasgow', *Glasgow Herald*, 18 June 1855, p. 5; see also Spiers, *Scottish Soldier and Empire*, pp. 5–6 and Oatts, *Proud Heritage*, vol. 1, pp. 186–7.
39. *Glasgow Herald*, 19 October 1855, p. 4.
40. D. Campbell (ed.), *Records of Clan Campbell in the Military Service of the Honourable East India Company 1600–1858* (London: Longmans, 1925); 'Letter from India', *Inverness Courier*, 5 November 1857, p. 5.
41. Low Parks Museum, CAM.H045, Lt.-Gen. J. C. Guise, diary, 16–26 September 1857.
42. Fairrie, *'Cuidich 'N Righ'*, pp. 20–3.
43. 'Letter from India', Supplement to the *Glasgow Herald*, 16 April 1858; Lieut.-Colonel W. Gordon-Alexander, *Recollections of a Highland Subaltern* (London: E. Arnold, 1898), pp. 85–105; C. Hibbert, *The Great Mutiny: India 1857* (London: Allen Lane, 1978), pp. 339–43.
44. Hibbert, *The Great Mutiny*, pp. 334, 338.
45. B. Robson (ed.), *Sir Hugh Rose and the Central India Campaign 1858* (Stroud: Sutton Publishing, for the Army Records Society, 2000); Oatts, *Proud Heritage*, vol. 1, pp. 190–201, vol. 2, pp. 329–37; Fairrie, *'Cuidich 'N Righ'*, pp. 10, 34.
46. *Inverness Courier*, 29 October 1857, p. 3.
47. 'Letter from a Soldier in the 93rd Regt.', *Glasgow Herald*, 12 April 1858, p. 5.
48. Ibid.
49. 'Letter from India', *Glasgow Herald*, 31 December 1858, p. 3; see also

letters in the *Glasgow Herald*, 25 November 1857, p. 4; 28 April 1858, p. 6; and 11 August 1858, p. 7.
50. J. M. Grierson, *Records of the Scottish Volunteer Force, 1859–1908* (Edinburgh: Blackwood, 1909), pp. 3–5, 13, 19, 37–8, 57, 68–70, 79; R. E. Wood, *Records of the Lanarkshire Yeomanry 1819–1910* (Edinburgh: privately published, 1910), p. 26; H. Cunningham, *The Volunteer Force: A Social and Political History, 1859–1908* (London: Croom Helm, 1975), pp. 18, 46–50.
51. Cunningham, *Volunteer Force*, pp. 27–30.
52. O. Anderson, 'The growth of Christian militarism in mid-Victorian Britain', *English Historical Review*, vol. 86 (1971), pp. 46–72.
53. J. O. Springhall, *Youth, Empire and Society: British Youth Movements, 1883–1940* (London: Croom Helm, 1977), pp. 17, 22–8.
54. M. Barthorp, *Afghan Wars and the North-West Frontier 1839–1947* (London: Cassell, 1982), ch. 6. The 93rd (2nd battalion, Argyll and Sutherland Highlanders) served in the Tochi expedition (1897–8).
55. S. H. F. Johnston, *The History of the Cameronians (Scottish Rifles) 26th and 90th*, 2 vols (Aldershot: Gale and Polden, 1957), vol. 1, p. 261.
56. Brigadier-General R. B. Fell, 'The Zulu War', *The Covenanter*, vol. 6, no. 2 (July 1926), p. 38.
57. 'The Zulu War', *Strathearn Herald*, 5 April 1879, p. 2.
58. ASHM, N-C91.1, Crauford MSS, Lt. W. R. H. Crauford to his father, 4 April 1879.
59. Buchan, *Royal Scots Fusiliers*, pp. 241–51.
60. 'Letter from another Crieff Soldier', *Strathearn Herald*, 21 October 1882, p. 2.
61. 'The Black Watch at Tel-el-Kebir', *Stirling Observer*, 12 October 1882, p. 2.
62. 'The Charge at Dargai', *North British Daily Mail*, 17 November 1897, p. 5; Spiers, *Scottish Soldier and Empire*, pp. 120–34.
63. 'At the Battle of Atbara', *Northern Scot and Moray & Nairn Express*, 21 May 1898, p. 3.
64. T. Pakenham, *The Boer War* (London: Weidenfeld and Nicolson, 1979), pp. 137, 197, 202; Greenhill Gardyne, *Life of a Regiment*, vol. 3, pp. 25–6; Dunn-Pattison, *History of the 91st Argyllshire Highlanders*, p. 270.
65. Major-General Sir F. B. Maurice and M. H. Grant, *History of the War in South Africa 1899–1902*, 4 vols (London: Hurst and Blackett, 1906), vol. 1, p. 329; 'Some Highland Comments', *Western Morning News*, 11 January 1900, p. 8.
66. Grierson, *Records of the Scottish Volunteer Force*, pp. 93, 95; T. F. Dewar, *With the Scottish Yeomanry* (Arbroath: T. Bungle, 1901), p. 7.
67. Of the many accounts of Scottish military service, see L. Gordon-Duff,

With the Gordon Highlanders to The Boer War & Beyond (Staplehurst: Spellmount, 1997); H. Wilson, *Blue Bonnets, Boers and Biscuits* (London: The Rotawise Printing Co., 1998); and P. Mileham (ed.), *Clearly My Duty: The Letters of Sir John Gilmour from the Boer War 1900–1901* (East Linton: Tuckwell Press, 1996).

68. M. L. Melville, *The Story of the Lovat Scouts 1900–1980* (Kinloss: Librario Publishing, 2004).
69. 'Letter from the Front', *Argyllshire Herald*, 6 April 1901, p. 3.
70. Spiers, *Scottish Soldier and Empire*, pp. 188, 192–4.
71. NAM, Acc, 1983-07-121, Greening diary, 24 October 1899.
72. 'Musselburgh's welcome', *The Scotsman*, 18 June 1901, p. 6.
73. 'Casualties in Scottish Regiments', *Aberdeen Journal*, 12 October 1900, p. 7; see also E. M. Spiers, 'The Scottish soldier in the Boer War', in J. Gooch (ed.), *The Boer War: Direction, Experience and Image* (London: Frank Cass, 2000), pp. 152–65, 273–7.
74. J. M. MacKenzie with N. R. Dalziel, *The Scots in South Africa: Ethnicity, Identity, Gender and Race, 1772–1914* (Manchester: Manchester University Press, 2007), pp. 255–6.
75. J. Lee, *A Soldier's Life: Sir Ian Hamilton, 1853–1947* (London: Macmillan, 2000), ch. 5 and pp. 98–107; G. J. De Groot, *Douglas Haig, 1861–1928* (London: Unwin Hyman, 1988), pp. 116–30.
76. E. M. Spiers, *Haldane: An Army Reformer* (Edinburgh: Edinburgh University Press, 1980), ch. 9.
77. E. M. Spiers, 'The regular army in 1914', in I. F. W. Beckett and K. Simpson (eds), *A Nation in Arms: A Social Study of the British Army in the First World War* (Manchester: Manchester University Press, 1985), pp. 37–61.
78. Lord Reith, *Wearing Spurs* (London: Hutchison, 1966), p. 25; *The Annual Return of the Territorial Force for the year 1913*, Cd. 7,254 (1914), LII, p. 125; *The General Annual Report on the British Army for the year ending 30th September 1913*, Cd. 7,252 (1914), LII, p. 92.
79. 'The New Army Act', *Dundee Advertiser*, 16 September 1907, p. 7; on recruiting difficulties, see 'Lord Haldane and the Territorials', *Edinburgh Evening News*, 9 January 1912, p. 2.
80. 'The Territorial Force', *Glasgow Herald*, 11 January 1912, p. 9.

18
Scottish Commonwealth Regiments

WENDY UGOLINI

In his poem 'Rabbie still be with us', the Canadian poet Milton Acorn (1923–86) commemorates:

> Canucks wha hae bled beside Mackenzie -
> last man to retreat from Montgomery's Tavern -
> haven't we got a Scottish situation?
> Much more in common than good whiskey . . .
> On a hundred foreign fields crosses and shattered corpses
> Commemorate our pointless victories.[1]

The war poetry of Acorn, who enlisted in a Canadian Highland regiment in 1941 to 'the skirl of pipes',[2] not only illuminates the long-standing contribution of the Commonwealth nations to Britain's war effort but also highlights the complex ways in which these countries have absorbed and utilised notions of Scottishness to represent their own military histories. Between the 1820s and the First World War over two million people emigrated from Scotland, settling primarily in North America, Australia, New Zealand and South Africa.[3] One of the most distinctive ways in which the influence of the Scottish diaspora in the dominions and overseas territories expressed itself was through the formation of military units which adhered to outwardly Scottish regimental forms.[4] In the 1880s particularly, 'a wave of manifestations of Scottish identity' ran through the colonial world, largely orchestrated by the new phenomenon of Caledonian societies.[5] Regiments with exotic names such as the Cape Breton Highlanders, the Transvaal Scottish and the New South Wales Scottish Rifles emerged across the empire. A significant number of these units became affiliated with the Scottish regiments of the British army and some formed strong links, the overseas regiment being considered almost as an extension of the home-based regiment.[6] Additionally, a number of Scottish military companies existed for a time in Malaya, Singapore, Southern Rhodesia, Calcutta, Bombay, Hong Kong, Rangoon and Shanghai, usually as a constituent company of a regiment of British expatriates.[7] This chapter provides an overview of the nineteenth-century emergence of 'a global politics of military Scottishness' and explores how the construction of Scottish military identity has evolved in the different Commonwealth countries.[8] In particular, it looks at the ways in which the volunteer regiments of the Scottish diaspora sought to draw upon, and align themselves with, the tradition of martial valour that the Highland regiments represented.

Nineteenth-century Scotland 'rejoiced' in its self-proclaimed status as a nation of 'empire builders'. Imperial success in the missionary, entrepreneurial and military fields was used to give expression to what were believed to be intrinsic Scottish national characteristics, enabling Scotland to assert its own distinctiveness as a nation.[9] Concurrently, the post-1746 pacification of the Highlands had stimulated the growth of 'Highlandism' whereby so-called Highland 'traditions', such as the kilt, tartan and Ossian verse, were, in the words of Tom Devine, 'absorbed freely by Lowland elites to form the symbolic basis of a new Scottish identity'.[10] Romanticised notions of the Highlands flourished, facilitated by the novels of Sir Walter Scott and the willingness of successive monarchs to embrace its traditions, symbolised in 1848 by Queen Victoria's acquisition of Balmoral. The notable successes of Highland regiments in Britain's overseas campaigns during this period meant that these regiments played a central role in imperial constructions of Scottishness. With their distinctive Scottish national dress making them exotic, colourful and 'painterly', the reproduction of their regimental achievements in sheet music, popular advertisements and the illustrated papers served to reinforce public perceptions regarding Scottish military valour and prowess.[11] As Heather Streets has noted, 'Tartanry had risen triumphant, and placed at its pinnacle the image of the kilted Highland soldier.'[12]

Up to the early 1840s, British North America, which became the Dominion of Canada in 1867, served as the most popular destination for Scottish emigrants, with distinctive Scottish communities being well established in the maritime provinces and Upper Canada by that time.[13] Meanwhile, between 1788 and 1900 approximately 230,000 Scots immigrants arrived in Australia and, by 1901, nearly 48,000 of the inhabitants of New Zealand had been born in Scotland.[14] By the close of the nineteenth century, however, southern Africa had overtaken Australia and New Zealand as the primary destination for Scots, with 'a particularly powerful influx' of immigrants arriving between 1893 and 1907.[15] In these overseas settlements there was an interactive relationship between the Scottish disapora and the homeland.[16] As Richard Finlay has pointed out, the activities of the Scottish immigrants – in the form of Burns societies, Highland games, and Caledonian and St Andrew's organisations – had the effect of reinforcing imperial notions of Scottish identity and locating it on a broad historical canvas available to all settlers.[17] Elizabeth Buettner confirms the pervasiveness of recently 'invented traditions' amongst Scottish diasporic communities in the heyday of British imperialism. Using India as a case study, she explores how prominent Scots promoted visible manifestations of Scottishness through the medium of public St Andrew's Day celebrations.[18] Significantly, these formal occasions incorporated both Scots and non-Scots, thus asserting an identity that was at once 'narrower and wider than is evident at first glance'.[19] The inclusive nature of 'Scottishness' is relevant to the history of the development of Scottish military units overseas.

Early formation

The first military units with a specifically Scottish dimension had their roots in Britain's colonial wars of the eighteenth century.[20] In June 1775, during the American War of Independence, General Thomas Gage, commander-in-chief of British forces in North America, issued orders to Lieutenant-Colonel Allan Maclean, son of Maclean of Torloisk, Mull, to raise a regiment consisting of two battalions, each of ten companies, to be clothed, armed and accoutred like the Black Watch and 'to be called the Royal Highland Emigrants'. The idea was that the Emigrants should find their recruits both among former soldiers who had served in Highland regiments in the campaigns of 1756–63, and subsequently settled in North America, and among the wider diasporic population. As inducements to enlist, each man was given one guinea levy-money on joining and promised a grant of land at the expiration of hostilities. The Emigrants played a notable part in the siege of Quebec in December 1775.[21]

It was, however, during the second half of the nineteenth century that the Scottish diaspora regiments became more firmly established. In anticipation of the proposed withdrawal of British troops from the partially or wholly self-governing colonies in 1870, the latter were encouraged to develop their own small standing armies supplemented by militia units. In Canada, the Militia Acts of 1855 and 1859 provided for the organisation of volunteer regiments and enthusiasm for the Scottish military tradition led to the formation of such units as the 48th Highlanders in Toronto in 1891 and the 91st Highlanders (later Argyll and Sutherland Highlanders) in Hamilton in 1903. The 5th battalion, Royal Light Infantry, first organised in 1862 in Montreal, was re-designated as the 5th battalion, Royal Scots of Canada, in 1884 and then the Royal Highlanders of Canada (Black Watch) in 1907.[22] In New Zealand, several 'distinctly Scottish' volunteer units were formed under the 1858 Militia Act, the first being the Caledonian Ranger Company of the Wanganui Rifle Volunteers in 1863. In 1885 the Dunedin Highland Rifles unit was raised, followed some time later by Highland Rifle groups in Wanganui (1900), Wellington (1900), Canterbury (1900) and Auckland (1900), as well as a mounted unit, the Scottish Horse Mounted Rifles of Waipu (1906).[23]

Australia also participated in the formation of volunteer militia units that were 'explicitly Scottish'.[24] In New South Wales, the first unit with Scottish associations was formed in 1868, primarily as a patriotic gesture by Scots emigrants following the attempted assassination of Prince Albert, duke of Edinburgh, on a visit to Sydney. Generally known as 'the Duke of Edinburgh's Highlanders', the unit disappeared after ten years when the volunteer land order system – by which volunteers were granted fifty acres of land on completion of five years' 'efficient' service – came to an end.[25] Events in the Sudan and the death of General Gordon at Khartoum in 1885, however, galvanised patriotic fervour amongst diasporic communities, while tensions between Britain and Russia, and the latter's territorial aggressiveness, aroused fears of an invasion of Australia. 'In such a climate of concern,' comments Martin J. Buckley, '. . . it was only to be expected that the Scotsmen in the community should consider the formation of a Scottish company or regiment.' At public meetings in Sydney in 1885 local Scottish notables Sir John Hay, president of the Highland Society, and Dr Normand MacLaurin outlined their plans for a Scottish regiment entitled the Sydney Scottish Volunteer Rifles (ultimately known as the New South Wales (NSW) Scottish Rifles) and enrolment sheets were placed in thirty-one locations around the city.[26] In a rather ambiguous statement, it was declared that members would 'be Scottish or of Scottish sympathies'.[27] At first the members mainly consisted of Scotsmen over the age of twenty born in Scotland but, in 1906, the vast majority of the members were eighteen or nineteen and, though of Scottish extraction, were Australian born.[28]

Scottish military formations in South Africa were also based

Figure 18.1 Officers of the New South Wales Scottish Rifles, Sydney, 1895.

initially on diasporic, first-generation Scots immigrants – a group which had achieved prosperity on the basis of imperial projects such as shipbuilding, railway manufacture, steel and heavy engineering and which identified closely with the empire.[29] Like their Australian counterparts, the local Scots behind the initiative to form Scottish units were 'mindful of the various colonial and imperial problems' of the late nineteenth century. In 1885 the Cape Town Highlanders were established.[30] Attracting a respectable 160 volunteers, the unit was said to have indulged in 'extravagant manifestations of Scottishness'. It imported a stag as a regimental mascot and offered classes in Gaelic.[31] As the local newspaper wryly noted, 'When toasts were exchanged in bars, the traditional Gaelic "Slainche Mhor" was given by people who had never been within 7,000 miles of Oban.'[32]

With the kilt as 'the sartorial badge of Highlandism and Scottishness', regiments formed overseas with Scottish associations were keen to adopt full Highland uniform.[33] The Cape Town Highlanders wore the tartan of the Gordon Highlanders with the sporran, spats and hose of the Sutherland Highlanders, so linking itself 'with the most fabled traditions of national valour'.[34] The Highland attire for the NSW Scottish Rifles was based on the accoutrements of the Black Watch. At a cost of eight pounds per private, it was an expensive investment but considered to be one of the reasons for the 'success' of the unit.[35] Indeed, when in 1912 the government in Australia reorganised its military forces, the proposal to 'kill the kilt' caused an outcry in Scottish circles. Protests, published in the *Newcastle Herald and Miners' Advocate*, were framed around the concept of the importance of this customary Highland dress. The Scottish community, it was asserted, 'consider that the desire to live up to the high traditions of those who have worn [the kilt] on the battlefields of history is the strongest incentive to the production of the best and bravest soldierly qualities in the wearers of today'.[36]

Affiliation was another way of plugging into the narrative of Scottish marital valour and many of the overseas units sought, and obtained, affiliation with Highland line regiments of the British army – the NSW Scottish Rifles, for example, becoming linked to the Black Watch and the Cape Town Highlanders to the Gordons. Canada's Cape Breton Highlanders – originally founded in 1871 as the 94th Victoria Regiment but converted to a Highland unit in 1879 – appears to be the exception with its affiliation in 1931 to an English line regiment: the Cheshire Regiment. This decision, however, based on the fact that the Cheshire Regiment had been posted to British North America in 1758 and participated in the capture of Louisbourg from the French, aroused internal 'criticism' on the grounds that it was not in accordance with tradition. The following year, the unit requested and received permission to adopt the uniform (regimental badges excepted) of the Argyll and Sutherland Highlanders (Princess Louise's), with the Black Watch tartan.[37] Thus the Cape Breton Highlanders, with their Gaelic motto '*Siol na Fear Fearail*' (the breed of manly men), were still able to assert the physical indicators of their Scottish heritage, despite affiliation with a regiment from south of the border.

The South African War (1899–1902)

The South African War provided one of the first opportunities for members of the Scottish volunteer units to engage in active service overseas. More than fifty members of the Royal Scots of Canada, including five officers, volunteered to serve in the 2nd battalion, Royal Canadian Regiment, which was formed for the campaign in

Africa. Two men were killed at the battle of Paardeberg in February 1900 and the Scottish unit was later granted the battle honour 'South Africa 1899–1900'.[38] The NSW Scottish Rifles also received a South African battle honour after eighty-five of its members served with various Australian contingents in the conflict.[39] Amongst the regiment's seven casualties was Lieutenant Keith Mackellar, brother of the poet Dorothea Mackellar and grandson of Scottish settlers, who was killed in action whilst serving with a British cavalry regiment, the 7th Dragoon Guards.[40] Meanwhile, members of the Cape Town Highlanders took part in several actions, including the relief of Kimberley.[41]

In South Africa new Scottish units were raised in the wake of the war. In 1902 the marquess of Tullibardine, who served as an army officer in the conflict and was later to become the eighth duke of Atholl, established the Transvaal Scottish (the regimental tartan becoming the 'Murray of Atholl' and the regimental march 'The Atholl Highlanders'). Many of those who joined were Scotsmen who had fought with British regiments in South Africa and had decided to settle in the country on the cessation of hostilities. Local Caledonian societies – organisations that, according to John Mackenzie, 'combined their devotion to the tartan image of Scotland with fierce loyalty to King and Empire' – played an integral role in recruitment for such units.[42] On 4 December 1902, in the Witwatersrand region of the Transvaal, a Caledonian society hosted a smoking concert at the Durban-Roodepoort gold mine hall in celebration of St Andrew's night. The Scottish standard was prominently displayed and 'all Scotsmen' urged to join the Transvaal Scottish.[43] By the end of 1903, no fewer than 10 per cent of the eligible male population of the Rand had volunteered. Whilst some of the appeal for recruits was exemption from poll tax and jury service, plus the ability to travel by rail at special rates when in uniform, the historian of the unit acknowledges that 'the lure of the kilt was a great help'.[44] Those in command attempted to adhere to a policy of 'strict ethnicism' and recruit those with at least one Scottish parent, but in reality the shortage of 'real' Scots meant that the Transvaal Scottish struggled to maintain its Scots character.[45]

The raising of the Scottish volunteer regiments in South Africa partly stemmed, it has been claimed, from concerns about 'what the Native problem might hold in store'.[46] Prominent members of the Scottish diaspora in South Africa were conscious of the fact that, with their 'intimidating reputation', these newly created Highland units could be utilised in response to internal disorder. Indeed, it can be argued that Scottish regiments were instrumental in maintaining the racial hierarchy within South Africa.[47] The first real fighting seen by the Cape Town Highlanders was during their involvement in the suppression of the Bechuanaland rebellion of 1897, whilst the Transvaal Scottish was first summoned into action in the Bambatha rebellion in Natal during 1906 and took part in the massacre at the Mome Gorge.[48] It was ironic that this latter unit was also involved in the suppression of white workers, many of whom were themselves Scottish. In 1913–14 the regiment helped to quell the Rand strikes and round up the leading labour activists, who included James Thompson Bain from Dundee.[49] In 1922 it took part controversially in the crushing of the Rand revolt.[50] As Hyslop has noted, this highlights 'a fascinating ideological division between colonial establishment Scots and left-wing Scots as to who were the real legatees of Scottish tradition'.[51]

The First World War

The formation of imperial service forces during the Great War had an important impact on Scottish diasporic units. The Canadian Department of Militia and Defence ignored existing militia units and enlisted men into a series of numbered Canadian Expeditionary Force (CEF) battalions. There was, however, some concession to the 'popularity of the new kilted units' with several of the battalions given Scottish designations. Of the three Scottish units grouped in the 3rd Canadian Infantry Brigade, the 13th battalion CEF carried the name 'the Royal Highlanders of Canada', the 15th battalion 'the 48th Highlanders of Canada' and the 16th battalion 'the Canadian Scottish'. Although their officers and men wore the kilt, none of these battalions was composed solely of Canadian Scots or, indeed, Scots living in Canada.[52] The 16th Canadian Scottish battalion, for example, included English, Irish, French, Americans, Italians, Dutch, Danes and Mexicans, as well as Scots.[53]

Likewise, the federal government of Australia organised an Australian Imperial Force (AIF). Existing members of militia units were required to volunteer for one of the new units of the AIF if they were to serve overseas. In this way, the ethnic identity of the Scottish units was again subsumed. However, of the three brigades of the First Division AIF, two were commanded by 'ex-Scottish' officers, the 1st brigade by Colonel Henry MacLaurin, son of one of the founders of the NSW Scottish Rifles, who was killed at Gallipoli.[54] Moreover, diasporic organisations continued to be key sources of recruitment. In remote areas such as Kalgoorlie sixty members of the local

Caledonian society joined up, whilst the South Australian Caledonian society contributed 110 of its members. It has been calculated that, in total, 226 MacDonalds, 195 Campbells, 191 Scotts, 181 Stewarts, 145 Johnstons, 137 Murrays, 129 MacKenzies, 117 Rosses, 113 Camerons and 100 Mackays were killed in the First AIF.[55]

Following the creation of the dominion of the union of South Africa in 1910, the military units of the four provinces had been reorganised in a single national army.[56] As Mackenzie notes, the sweeping up of the Scottish regiments into this new force meant that 'it was no longer possible to maintain the alleged ethnic purity of these regiments'.[57] Yet during the First World War the highly popular poetry of the Scots-born Charles Murray (a founding officer of the Transvaal Scottish) still encouraged volunteers to join up on the basis of 'a specifically Scottish patriotism' with verses intoning: 'Wha bears a blade for Scotland? She's needin' ye sairly noo, What will ye dae for Scotland for a' she has done for you?'[58] Following an offer from the South African prime minister, General Louis Botha, of a brigade of four battalions to the British government, a South African Scottish regiment was created, comprising members of the Transvaal Scottish and Cape Town Highlanders, as well as new recruits drawn in through the Caledonian societies. The latter had enthusiastically endorsed a campaign to ensure that one of the battalions was kilted, sending telegrams declaring that 'The heather is afire'.[59]

On the Western Front identification with a 'Highland ideal' could function to strengthen regimental morale amongst Scottish diasporic units.[60] The Royal Highlanders of Canada (Black Watch) distinguished themselves at the second battle of Ypres in April 1915 when, despite enduring heavy enemy shelling and one of the earliest chlorine gas attacks, they held the line for several days until relieved by British battalions.[61] Despite suffering grievous losses of twelve officers and 454 other ranks, the battalion was said to have 'gallantly upheld the finest fighting traditions of the Black Watch' and won 'immortal glory' for the Canadian branch.[62] Indeed, following the 13th battalion's brave stand at Ypres, its 'parent' Black Watch regiment in Scotland proudly added to its recruiting posters: 'With which is allied the 13th Canadian Battalion, RHC.' This highlighted the importance of reciprocity: not only did Scottish-named regiments share in the glory of their 'parent' regiment's martial record but they could also enhance that reputation through their own actions.

The psychological value of Highland accoutrements for Scottish-named regiments was also recognised. When Lieutenant-Colonel Cyrus Peck was appointed the new commander of the 16th

Figure 18.2 Men of the 13th Canadian Infantry Battalion (Royal Highlanders of Canada) consolidating a captured trench, 1916.

battalion, the Canadian Scottish, in 1917 he was 'adamant' that its Highland heritage would be maintained and insisted on five pipers, one each for the companies and a fifth personal piper, accompanying the troops into battle. He defended his policy in the following terms:

> When I first proposed to take pipers into action, I met with a great deal of criticism. I persisted, and as I have no Scottish blood in my veins, no one had reason to accuse me of acting from racial prejudices. I believe that the purpose of war is to win victories, and if one can do this better by encouraging certain sentiments and traditions, why shouldn't it be done?[63]

Furthermore, the heroism of soldiers serving in Scottish diasporic regiments was celebrated as part of an ancient martial tradition. Eight of the Canadian winners of the Victoria Cross between 1914 and 1918 were members of Canada's Highland battalions and George Stanley characterised these men as walking 'erect among the shades of those heroic Scots who, if not necessarily their progenitors, were the inspiration of the tradition which the Canadians, as members of Scottish units, had willingly embraced'.[64] Scottish-born VC winner Piper James Richardson, who was killed in October 1916, is often represented as embodying the essence of the Canadian-Scottish military tradition.[65] Richardson arrived in Canada with his parents in 1911–12, at the age of sixteen. In 1914 he volunteered for service in the Canadian Expeditionary Force and was taken on strength as a private and piper with the Canadian Scottish. As part of the Somme offensive of 1916, his battalion was involved in an attack on Regina Trench on Ancre Hill. According to the official history, the advancing company encountered a storm of fire and enemy wire that had not been cut by the artillery. With the company commander killed, casualties mounting, and morale and momentum almost gone, Richardson turned to the sergeant major and asked, 'Wull I gie them wund?', to which the latter replied, 'Aye mon, gie 'em wind.' Richardson was later killed during the battle but his posthumous VC citation reads 'The effect was instantaneous. Inspired by his splendid example the company rushed the wire with such fury and determination that the obstacle was overcome and the position captured.'[66]

The Scottish military tradition could be upheld too by Scottish diasporic units fighting with a Scottish formation. The South African Scottish – the 4th regiment of the 1st South African Infantry Brigade – was deployed on the Western Front as part of the 9th (Scottish) Division.[67] John Buchan, the historian of the South African forces in France, admitted that 'there were many in the Brigade who had still quick in their hearts an affection for the northern islands from which they had sprung; but there were many to whom Britain was only a faint memory, and many in whom her name woke no enthusiasm'.[68] Nevertheless, the South African Scottish (which wore the Murray Atholl tartan), along with the rest of the brigade, fought valiantly under the 9th Division. Its most famous engagement occurred during the battle of the Somme, on 15 July 1916, when the troops were ordered to capture the outer edge of Delville Wood. Encircled by a 'curtain of shells', they held their position for six days under 'violent and continuous' assault with the wounded filling the trenches.[69] The brigade was reduced in number from 121 officers and 3,032 men to a total of 750 in what Buchan terms 'an epoch of terror and glory scarcely equalled in the campaign'.[70] 'For some,' writes Hyslop, 'the Delville Wood battle story seemed like a basis for a South African equivalent of the Australian myth of Gallipoli.'[71]

Figure 18.3 'Nancy', the springbok mascot of the 4th South African Infantry Regiment (South African Scottish), Delville Wood, 1918.

Interwar

As a defining moment in the construction of nationhood amongst Commonwealth countries, it could be argued that the First World War also served to 'denationalise' the Scottish diaspora regiments, in terms of both uniform and personnel.[72] In addition to the ethnically diverse composition of the units, the practice of issuing khaki aprons to kilted regiments to camouflage the distinctive colours of the kilt, started during the Boer War, continued during the Great War. The potency of the Highland soldier image, however, endured across the diasporic militias. The NSW Scottish Rifles, for example, had by now evolved into the kiltless 30th infantry battalion, but Martin Buckley notes that there was still 'a yearning in the hearts of many of the Scots community to one day have a kilted regiment', culminating in 'persistent agitation' to achieve this by organisations such as the local Highland Society.[73] Whilst there were those within New South Wales who saw the re-formation of a kilted regiment as a 'decidedly retrograde step', and dismissed the wearing of Highland accoutrements as 'fancy dress innovations', on New Year's Day 1935 the president of the Highland Society, Captain J. R. Patrick, announced that such a Scottish regiment would be re-formed in Sydney.[74] The Black Watch tartan was to be worn and a new regimental badge adopted based on that Scottish regiment's Glengarry badge. Recruits had to be medically fit, of Scottish descent and prepared to pay two pounds to regimental funds before a uniform would be issued.[75] As the approximate cost to turn out a fully kilted regiment would be in the vicinity of £5,000, a subscription fund was opened by the Highland Society. This fundraising campaign 'to clothe and equip every man in Highland Military Kilt Uniform' was justified on the grounds that it would make for efficiency in the men, would act as an incentive for recruiting and would 'bring pride to every Scottish heart'.[76]

During the 1930s the kilted 30th battalion helped to sustain a sense of Scottish identity in New South Wales through public commemorative rituals and traditions, such as the annual church parade at the local Scots church where a wreath would be laid in remembrance of those members of the NSW Scottish Rifles who had died during the Boer War.[77] The regiment also paraded annually for the traditional Highland Gathering on New Year's Day where it 'roused to vociferous enthusiasm the Scottish blood of the twenty-thousand Australian Scots who had gathered'. By the outbreak of the Second World War, diasporic Scots had become so attached to the 30th battalion that they were said to have spoken of it in terms of 'our Scottish'.[78]

The Second World War

In contrast to the position during the previous conflict, on the outbreak of the Second World War the Canadian Defence Department mobilised a number of Scottish militia units for service overseas. The Essex Scottish, for example, was despatched to the UK and took part in the Dieppe raid in August 1942, returning from the blood-stained beaches of northern France with only two officers and forty-nine other ranks.[79] When the Canadians landed in France two years later the diaspora units again 'paid heavily for their victories'.[80] The Black Watch of Canada was in 'the thick of the bitter fighting'. Its regimental historian records how, after heavy action at Vaucelles, while crossing the Orne, and at Ifs, 'its bitterest day came in July 1944 at St André when it lost its young Commanding Officer, Lt.-Col. S. S. T. Cantlie, and was practically wiped out'.[81] The Cameron Highlanders of Canada also played a prominent role in north-west Europe. During the bitter Reichswald battle in February 1945 Lieutenant-Colonel Martin Lindsay, commanding the 1st Gordon Highlanders in the 51st Highland Division, recalled that his battalion pipers, and those of the nearby Canadian Camerons, played regimental tunes during the fighting in order to prevent the two allied units shooting at one another in the confusion of the advance through the forest.[82]

The South African government made use of its Scottish units too. Among them, three battalions of the Transvaal Scottish were sent overseas. The 3rd battalion was annihilated in the field at Sidi Rezegh in Libya in November 1941. The 2nd battalion fought at Sollum in Egypt in January 1941 but was captured at Tobruk later that year.[83] The 1st battalion, however, fared better. It first went into action at El Wak on the Kenya–Somaliland border in December 1940 and took part in the advance into Italian Somaliland and Ethiopia. Switching to the western desert, it participated in the Crusader campaign in 1941, sharing in the 1st South African Brigade's stand at Taieb el Essem. It subsequently helped to defend the Gazala and Alamein lines before participating in the great British and Commonwealth victory of El Alamein in October–November 1942.[84]

Although the ethnicity of the Scottish units was inevitably diluted during the war, with many becoming more 'Afrikaans in their character', during its military engagements the 1st Transvaal Scottish sought to assert its Scottishness. In East Africa, the battalion flew the Scottish standard from the main tower when it occupied the Wajir fort; it marched through Addis Ababa to the tune of 'The Atholl Highlanders'; and at Amba Alagi, the governor-general of Italian East Africa, the duke of Aosta, surrendered to the skirl of the Transvaal pipes.[85] The commanding officer of the 1st South African Infantry Brigade, Major-General Dan Pienaar, affectionately termed the battalion 'my Jocks'.[86]

In 1943 the Transvaal Scottish returned to South Africa. But this was not to be the end of the war for a number of its veterans. Individuals were permitted to carry on the fight if they wished and South Africans eagerly filled gaps among the officers of their affiliated Scottish regiment, the Black Watch, serving in the theatre. Bernard Fergusson, the historian of the Black Watch, noted that up until this time the alliance between the Transvaal Scottish and his regiment had 'existed mostly on paper, largely in the exchange of cards at Christmas and cables on St. Andrew's Day', but now 'the "paper alliance" gave place to one of flesh and blood'.[87]

Meanwhile, the Cape Town Highlanders had fought in the western desert and at El Alamein – losing a quarter of their men in this battle – and were subsequently transferred to Italy. During this campaign the regiment temporarily 'married up' with South Africa's First City Regiment – another Scottish unit, whose regimental march was

Figure 18.4 The Transvaal Scottish, Addis Ababa, 1941.

'Bonnie Dundee' – and this composite force fought from Monte Cassino through to the Alps. Its war culminated in the storming, at bayonet point, of the strategic heights of Monte Sole near Bologna in April 1945. This was said to have broken the back of the German resistance in Italy and served to avenge the SS massacre of hundreds of Italian civilians that had taken place a few months earlier in the area.[88]

At the start of the war the NSW Scottish regiment volunteered as a unit for the AIF but the Australian government was unwilling to send militia regiments overseas at this time in light of the invasion threat from Japan and the needs of home defence. As a result, individual members were distributed throughout the AIF, some 7,000 joining the force with over 250 being commissioned. Every combatant unit of the AIF included an ex-NSW Scottish soldier and of the first five military decorations won by the AIF during the conflict, four were awarded to former members of the regiment. After Japan entered the war in December 1941, the 30th served for a period on beach defence duties, but in January 1944 was despatched to New Guinea. As part of the 8th Australian Infantry Brigade, it took part in the capture of Madang and won a battle honour for its involvement in the liberation of the island from the Japanese.[89]

Scottish diaspora units continued to play a role in Commonwealth armies in the post-war era. The Black Watch of Canada, for example, served in the Korean war, was stationed in Germany with NATO forces and took part in the UN peacekeeping mission in Cyprus. In recent times it has sent troops to Afghanistan.[90] For the South African Scottish regiments, however, the Second World War came to symbolise the 'high water mark' of their prestige. With the inception of apartheid in 1948, the Transvaal Scottish and the Cape Town Highlanders – representing a traditionally apolitical and conformist Anglophone elite – took part in operations in Namibia and Angola and helped to suppress insurrections in the black townships. In the view of Hyslop, 'They took refuge in the ideology of serving the government of the day, and in the romance of the Scottish military tradition.'[91] It was perhaps a sign of the changing times that when South Africa's first all-race parliament was sworn in at Johannesburg in 1994 the guard of honour included a party from the Cape Town Highlanders.[92]

This chapter has outlined the ways in which, during the nineteenth century, a military Scots identity was reinvented and 'forged at the colonial periphery'.[93] The 'appropriation of outwardly Scottish accoutrements', such as bagpipes, kilts and tartans, was an important way in which diasporic units overseas could access and utilise the inspirational narrative of the highlander, a phenomenon increasingly independent of whether or not recruits were actually Scottish-born.[94] At the outset, the creation of Scottish-named units enabled the more elite members of the Scottish diaspora to cling to some form of ethnicity within an imperial context, as well as assert the importance of their own role within civic society in the land of settlement. By the twentieth century, however, those who joined were likely to utilise military service as an opportunity to assert their distinctive sense of Scottish ancestry and traditions. As Hyslop notes, 'Colonial life tended simultaneously to stimulate and to dissolve Scottish identity. The nostalgia of the immigrants and the version of it transmitted to their children tended to sharpen Scottish identification.' Yet at the same time, as Scottish-named regiments and pipe bands flourished, the Scots themselves were becoming part of a new social world, with new identities forming across boundaries of ethnicity, language and race.[95] Whilst Commonwealth regimental histories clearly valued and promoted the Scottish military tradition, that identity had to be placed within the context of the lands of settlement. It was indicative of this process that when a new Scottish regiment was raised in South Africa on the outbreak of the Second World War on the initiative of the Transvaal Caledonian societies – the Pretoria Highlanders, which went on to take part in the invasion of Madagascar in 1942 – its cap badge bore a shield with thistles and a protea intertwined: thus was the 'South Africanisation' of the Scottish regiment 'expressed in botanical form'.[96]

Notes

1. M. Acorn, *More Poems for People* (Toronto: New Canada Press, 1972) p. 12.
2. E. Waterston, *Rapt in Plaid: Canadian Literature and Scottish Tradition* (Toronto: University of Toronto Press, 2003), p. 37.
3. T. M. Devine, *The Scottish Nation 1700-2000* (London: Penguin, 2000), p. 468.
4. J. M. Mackenzie with N. R. Dalziel, *The Scots in South Africa: Ethnicity, Identity, Gender and Race, 1772-1914* (Manchester: Manchester University Press, 2007), p. 241.
5. J. Hyslop, 'Cape Town Highlanders, Transvaal Scottish: Military "Scottishness" and social power in nineteenth and twentieth century South Africa', *South African Historical Journal*, vol. 47, no. 1 (2002), p. 102.
6. P. Mileham, *The Scottish Regiments 1633-1996* (Staplehurst: Spellmount, 1988), p. 298. Mileham provides a comprehensive list of overseas regiments.
7. Ibid. p. 298.
8. Hyslop, 'Cape Town', p. 97.
9. R. Finlay, 'The rise and fall of popular imperialism in Scotland, 1850–1950', *Scottish Geographical Magazine*, vol. 113, no. 1 (1997), p. 13.
10. Devine, *Scottish Nation*, p. 233.
11. Mackenzie, *The Scots in South Africa*, p. 253; H. Streets, 'Identity in the Highland regiments in the nineteenth century: Soldier, region, nation', in S. Murdoch and A. Mackillop (eds), *Fighting for Identity: Scottish Military Experience c. 1550-1900* (Leiden: Brill, 2002), p. 219.
12. Streets, 'Identity in the Highland regiments', p. 219.
13. Devine, *Scottish Nation*, pp. 470-1.
14. M. D. Prentis, *The Scots in Australia: A Study of New South Wales, Victoria and Queensland, 1788-1900* (Sydney: Sydney University Press, 1983), p. 54; G. Donaldson, *The Scots Overseas* (London: Robert Hale, 1966), p. 179.

15. Hyslop, 'Cape Town', p. 103.
16. Mackenzie, *The Scots in South Africa*, p. 252. See also J. M. Mackenzie, 'Empire and national identities: The case of Scotland', *Transactions of the Royal Historical Society*, sixth series, vol. 8 (1998), p. 220.
17. Finlay, 'The rise and fall', p. 16.
18. E. Buettner, 'Haggis in the Raj: Private and public celebrations of Scottishness in late imperial India', *Scottish Historical Review*, vol. 81, no. 2 (2002), pp. 212–39.
19. Buettner, 'Haggis in the Raj', p. 228.
20. T. M. Devine, *Scotland's Empire* (London: Penguin, 2004), p. 131.
21. G. F. G. Stanley, 'The Scottish military tradition', in W. S. Reid (ed.), *The Scottish Tradition in Canada* (Toronto: McClelland and Stewart, 1976), pp. 146–7.
22. Stanley, 'Scottish military tradition', p. 150. See also P. P. Hutchison, *Canada's Black Watch: The First Hundred Years 1862–1962* (Montreal: The Black Watch of Canada, 1962), p. 44.
23. G. L. Pearce, *The Scots of New Zealand* (Auckland: Collins, 1976), pp. 174–5.
24. M. Prentis, *The Scots in Australia* (Sydney: University of New South Wales Press, 2008), p. 144.
25. M. J. Buckley, *Scarlet and Tartan: The Story of the Regiments and Regimental Bands of the NSW Scottish Rifles (Volunteers)* (Sydney: The Red Hackle Association, 1986), p. 3.
26. Buckley, *Scarlet and Tartan*, pp. 6–7.
27. Ibid. p. 6.
28. Buckley, *Scarlet and Tartan*, p. 172.
29. Hyslop, 'Cape Town', p. 99.
30. Mackenzie, *The Scots in South Africa*, p. 253.
31. Hyslop, 'Cape Town', p. 103.
32. T. Newark, *Highlander: The History of the Legendary Highland Soldier* (London: Constable, 2009), pp. 184–5.
33. C. Withers, 'The historical creation of the Scottish Highlands', in I. Donnachie and C. Whatley (eds), *The Manufacture of Scottish History* (Edinburgh: Polygon, 1992), p. 150.
34. Newark, *Highlander*, pp. 184–5; Hyslop, 'Cape Town', p. 103.
35. Campbell, *Twenty One Years*, cited in Buckley, *Scarlet and Tartan*, p. 174; Buckley, *Scarlet and Tartan*, p. 8.
36. Buckley, *Scarlet and Tartan*, p. 41. These pleas fell on stony ground and on 1 July 1912 the NSW Regiment of Scottish Rifles ceased to exist with most of the men transferring to the 25th Infantry Battalion.
37. A. Morrison and T. Slaney, *The Breed of Manly Men: The History of*

the *Cape Breton Highlanders* (Toronto: Canadian Institute of Strategic Studies, 1994), p. 64.
38. Hutchison, *Canada's Black Watch*, p. 37.
39. Buckley, *Scarlet and Tartan*, pp. 12, 290.
40. Ibid. p. 14.
41. See www.cthighlanders.co.za/cth/cthf1.htm, accessed 7 November 2010.
42. Mackenzie, *The Scots in South Africa*, p. 243; H. C. Juta, *The History of the Transvaal Scottish December 1902 to July 1932* (Johannesburg: Horters Ltd, 1933), p. 6.
43. Juta, *History*, p. 6.
44. Ibid. p. 7.
45. Hyslop, 'Cape Town', p. 104; Mackenzie, *The Scots in South Africa*, p. 256.
46. Juta, *History*, p. 3.
47. Mackenzie, *The Scots in South Africa*, p. 253; Hyslop, 'Cape Town', p. 98.
48. Newark, *Highlander*, p. 186; Hyslop, 'Cape Town', p. 105.
49. Mackenzie, *The Scots in South Africa*, p. 256.
50. Juta, *History*, p. 21.
51. Hyslop, 'Cape Town', p. 98.
52. Stanley, 'Scottish military tradition', p. 150.
53. Ibid. p. 151.
54. Buckley, *Scarlet and Tartan*, p. 44.
55. Prentis, *The Scots in Australia* (2008), p. 147.
56. Hyslop, 'Cape Town', p. 105.
57. Mackenzie, *The Scots in South Africa*, p. 257.
58. Hyslop, 'Cape Town', p. 106.
59. Juta, *History*, p. 121.
50. Streets, 'Identity in the Highland regiments', p. 236.
61. Hutchison, *Canada's Black Watch*, pp. 74–6.
62. Ibid. p. 76.
63. M. Zuehlke, *Brave Battalion: The Remarkable Saga of the 16th Battalion (Canadian Scottish) in the First World War* (Mississauga: Wiley, 2008), p. 148.
64. Stanley, 'Scottish military tradition', p. 151.
65. D. M. Henderson, *The Scottish Regiments*, second edition (Glasgow: HarperCollins, 1996), pp. 180–1.
66. Zuehlke, *Brave Battalion*, p. 139.
67. Hyslop, 'Cape Town', p. 105.
68. J. Buchan, *The History of the South African Forces in France* (London: Thomas Nelson & Sons, 1920), p. 261.

69. Ibid. pp. 58–66.
70. Ibid. pp. 73–4.
71. Hyslop, 'Cape Town', p. 106.
72. On the centrality of the First World War to constructions of national identity amongst Commonwealth countries, see A. Thomson, *Anzac Memories: Living with the Legend* (Oxford: Oxford University Press, 1994); F. H. Underhill, 'The Canadian forces in the war', in C. Lucas (ed.), *The Empire at War. Vol. II* (London: Humphrey Milford, 1923) and J. Bourne, P. Liddle and I. Whitehead (eds), *The Great World War 1914–45, Vol. 2* (London: HarperCollins, 2001). Stanley, 'Scottish military tradition', p. 154.
73. Buckley, *Scarlet and Tartan*, pp. 53–5.
74. Ibid. p. 55.
75. Ibid. p. 58.
76. Ibid. pp. 69–70.
77. Ibid. p. 76.
78. Buckley, *Scarlet and Tartan*, p. 74.
79. Stanley, 'Scottish military tradition', p. 152.
80. Ibid. p. 153.
81. P. P. Hutchison, 'The Black Watch of Canada during the Second World War', *The Red Hackle*, vol. 78 (1946), p. 24.
82. M. Lindsay, *So Few Got Through* (London: Arrow Books, 1968), pp. 170, 182.
83. C. Birkby, *The Saga of the Transvaal Scottish Regiment 1932–1950* (Cape Town: Hodder and Stoughton, 1950), pp. 5–6.
84. Ibid. p. 4.
85. Ibid. pp. 74, 260; see www.jocks.co.za/, accessed on 7 November 2010.
86. Birkby, *Saga*, p. 74.
87. B. Fergusson, *The Black Watch and the King's Enemies* (London: Collins, 1950), p. 211.
88. See www.cthighlanders.co.za/cth/cthf1.htm, accessed on 7 November 2010; www.rfdiv.mil.za/2010news.html, accessed on 7 August 2011.
89. Buckley, *Scarlet and Tartan*, p. 88.
90. See www.blackwatchcanada.com, accessed on 7 November 2010.
91. Hyslop, 'Cape Town', pp. 110–12.
92. See www.cthighlanders.co.za/cth/cthf1.htm.
93. Mackenzie, *The Scots in South Africa*, p. 260.
94. L. Leneman, 'A new role for a lost cause: Lowland romanticisation of the Jacobite Highlander', in L. Leneman (ed.), *Perspectives in Scottish Social History: Essays in Honour of Rosalind Mitchison* (Aberdeen: Aberdeen University Press, 1980), p. 120.

95. Hyslop, 'Cape Town', p. 98.
96. J. Lambert, '"Their finest hour?" English-speaking South Africans and World War II', *South African History Journal*, vol. 60, no. 1 (2008), p. 73; Mackenzie, *The Scots in South Africa*, p. 260.

19
The First World War

TREVOR ROYLE

The First World War touched Scotland in many different ways. Although the actual fighting was carried out far away from the Scottish homeland, the conflict was a fact of everyday life and there was no lack of evidence that hostilities were actually taking place. Following the declaration of war in August 1914 the rush to join the armed forces produced a steady flow of recruits as young men answered the call for volunteers 'to fight the Hun'. The warships of the Grand Fleet had already taken shelter in Scapa Flow in Orkney at the end of July following the annual summer manoeuvres and they were later joined in the Firth of Forth by the three battle cruiser squadrons of Vice-Admiral Sir David Beatty's Battle Cruiser Fleet. Other naval assets were based at Invergordon in the Cromarty Firth. At the same time the Highlands west and north of the Great Glen became a restricted area in order to safeguard the northern naval bases and coastal defences and were closed to anyone without the relevant permit. Naval patrol boats kept watch on the Caledonian Canal and to all intents and purposes the Highlands became an appendage of the navy and its force of auxiliaries.[1]

In the central belt the war brought new life to the heavy industries which were expanded and revitalised by the need to produce war matériel. The war had an immediate impact on the Clydeside shipyards where 90 per cent of Scotland's shipbuilding capacity was concentrated and where the bulk of Britain's biggest commercial and naval warships were built – in 1913 the Clyde shipyards had produced a record tonnage of ships, at 757,000 tons a third of the British total and superior to the tonnage of ships produced in German yards (646,000 tons).[2] A year later, those shipyards had full order books, with three battleships (the *Barham*, *Valiant* and *Ramillies*), three Arethusa class light cruisers and six destroyers under construction

Figure 19.1 HMS *Repulse* at Clydebank, 1916.

and the promise of more to come. Because of the exigencies of the naval war – the need for more surface warships, especially destroyers, and the growing loss of merchant ships – the Clydeside yards entered a profitable period with a total of 481 warships, aggregating almost 760,000 tons, being constructed between 1914 and 1918.[3]

In the steel-working industry in 1914, Scotland produced 1.2 million tons of the United Kingdom's total production of five million tons and the demand for munitions meant that the Scottish figure had doubled by 1918 with 24,000 men in full employment in the Clyde valley. By that same year 90 per cent of the country's armour plate was being produced in Glasgow. Coal underpinned everything and although the stocks of the west of Scotland fields were gradually being diminished, in 1913 they still accounted for 25.5 million tons, or roughly 10 per cent of the entire British output. In the east of Scotland production remained lower at seventeen million tons, a result of the loss of exports to Germany and the Baltic and a higher than average local recruitment of miners into the army.[4]

The creation of a state armaments industry under the Ministry of Munitions in May 1915 revolutionised weapons production and by the end of the war it had expended £2 billion and employed 65,000 civil servants. To ensure continuity and expansion of employment in the heavy industries the United Kingdom was divided into twelve areas, two of which were in Scotland under the control of a Director of Munitions. This job was given to Sir William Weir (later Lord Weir), a prominent Glasgow industrialist and millionaire who ran the family firm of marine engineers G. & J. Weir which supplied ancillary machinery for the engine rooms of the new generation of warships. Having been appointed managing director at the early age of twenty-five in 1902 he emerged as a confident, if conservative, leader who turned the company into a successful international business; he was, however, also a perfervid anti-trade unionist and a great believer in rationalising practices within the workplace.

Diversification became part of the remit of the Ministry of Munitions and under its direction the Clydebank heavy engineering firm of William Beardmore built a number of aircraft types at Dalmuir under licence. These included Sopwith Pup fighters, Wight seaplanes and giant four-engined Handley Page V/1500 bombers. The construction of a huge steel-framed airship hangar at Inchinnan allowed the construction of airships including the R34, which became the first machine to fly the Atlantic in both directions in July 1919. Beardmore also moved into the construction of artillery pieces, notably six-inch howitzers and eighteen-pounder field guns, while the shipbuilding firm of John Brown built a number of Mark IV tanks in 1917.[5] All this brought employment and wealth into Glasgow and the surrounding industrial area – a conurbation that embraced Clydeside, Lanarkshire, Renfrewshire, Dunbartonshire and North Ayrshire.

Scottish women found that they had a role to play in the war effort and one statistic sums up their contribution and the great changes that took place during the course of the war. The population census of 1911 showed that 185,442 men were employed in the heavy industries of Clydeside but apart from the 2,062 women employed in the Singer sewing machine factory at Clydebank there were only 3,758 women in full employment in the heavy sector, most of them in the chemical industry, itself a minor contributor to the region's economy. Five years later, by the middle of 1916, the number of women involved in heavy industries in the same area had climbed to 18,500 and by the end of the war 31,500 women were working in the munitions industry in Scotland.[6]

Unlike other parts of the United Kingdom, the Scottish mainland did not suffer any major German assault during the war: only twice did the enemy manage to strike a blow. On the night of 2–3 April 1916 two airships bombed Edinburgh. One of them, *L14*, made landfall at St Abbs Head and attempted to attack the naval facilities at Rosyth and the Forth Railway Bridge but only succeeded in bombing the centre of Edinburgh, hitting the Castle Rock and George Watson's College, and damaging property in Marchmont and the Grassmarket areas. A second airship, *L22*, arrived over Newcastle and attacked Edinburgh from the south, destroying several properties in Lauriston Place. The only recorded attack from the sea came on 15 May 1918 when the remote island of St Kilda was shelled by a German U-boat. Over seventy rounds were fired, damaging the church and two houses, one of them occupied by the island's nurse. No lives were lost because the German captain gave a general warning before opening fire – his target was an Admiralty radio station which formed part of the country's coastal defences.[7]

For most families, though, the war was about the fighting on the main battlefronts – France and Flanders, Gallipoli, Italy, Mesopotamia, Egypt, Palestine and Salonika – where thousands of Scottish soldiers saw active service. It was from these operational theatres that news came of breakthroughs, setbacks, triumph and disaster and, of course, the steady loss of casualties. In the army there were four operational infantry divisions with Scottish appellations, each numbering roughly 18,000 soldiers; two were New Army divisions, 9th (Scottish) and 15th (Scottish), and two were Territorial Force divisions, 51st (Highland) and 52nd (Lowland). All served on the Western Front while the 52nd (Lowland) Division also saw service in Gallipoli, Egypt and Palestine. Scots also served in Scottish regiments that were part of other infantry divisions and, of course, large numbers of Scots served in other military formations as well as in the Royal Navy and Royal Flying Corps. Although it is difficult to be precise about the numerical extent of Scottish involvement in the war's main theatres, Scots made major contributions in terms of personnel to the fighting in Gallipoli and to the following large-scale battles on the Western Front – Loos (1915), the Somme (1916) and Arras (1917).

The man responsible for the creation of the wartime armies was Field Marshal Horatio Herbert Kitchener, the hero of the reconquest of Sudan in 1898, and the later Boer War, and generally considered to be the greatest British soldier of the period. Shortly after the outbreak of war the prime minister, Herbert Asquith, had taken the bold move of appointing him secretary for war and Kitchener took up his post with characteristic energy. From the outset he predicted that the war would be long and bloody and he disagreed with the idea that the fighting in Europe would be curtailed because no nation could survive the strains that would be placed on their economies. He also believed that Britain's professional army was too small to offer anything but limited support to France – about 100,000 men in the initial deployment of the British Expeditionary Force (BEF) – and that huge new armies would have to be raised if the country was to make any impact on the direction of the war.

On 7 August 1914 Kitchener called for the first 100,000 volunteers aged between eighteen and thirty, the aim being to create an army of seventy divisions, approximately 1.2 million men, by 1917. Its arrival would come at a time when Germany's resources would be overstretched and Britain would then be in a position to crush the enemy and dictate the peace. Instead of expanding the part-time soldiers of the Territorial Force which had been raised for home defence in 1908, he built on the existing regimental structure of the British regular army. No new formations were raised but the existing infantry regiments expanded their numbers of battalions to meet the demand for men. These were known as 'special service battalions'. In that way, argued Kitchener, the volunteers could be assimilated quickly and no new machinery would have to be assembled to deal with them.[8]

By 12 September the first 100,000 men had been recruited; they signed on for three years or the duration of hostilities and formed the First New Army consisting of six divisions, 9th to 14th. By the end of the following month there were sufficient men to form twelve new divisions which formed the Second New Army (15th to 20th Division) and the Third New Army (21st to 26th Division). In Scotland, as in other parts of the country, the call to arms was shrill and insistent. 'I feel certain that Scotsmen have only to know that the country urgently needs their services to offer them with the same splendid patriotism as they have always shown in the past,' Kitchener told Sir Alexander Baird of Urie, Lord Lieutenant of Kincardineshire, in a letter that was given considerable prominence in the Scottish press. 'Tell them from me, please, that their services were never more needed than they are today and that I rely confidently on a splendid response to the national appeal.'[9]

His words did not fall on deaf ears. Within a day of the declaration of war the army's recruiting office in Edinburgh's Cockburn Street was doing brisk business under the judicious eye of Captain William Robertson, a Gordon Highlander who had won the Victoria Cross in the Boer War, and by the end of August the *Glasgow Herald* reported that 20,000 men had been processed through the recruiting office in the Gallowgate.[10] From other parts of Scotland came news of equally high figures of enlistment during August – 1,500 from Coatbridge, 900 from Clydebank, 940 from Dumbarton and 750 from Alloa.

A number of factors prompted those volunteers from all over Scotland to take the King's Shilling. Workers doing repetitive or menial jobs saw a chance to escape the drudgery of their existence. The Scots' inherent respect for militarism also encouraged many a young man who thought he would look a god in a kilt and a Glengarry bonnet. In those days, too, words such as duty, honour and patriotism were not idle concepts but the cornerstone of many young lives: within a year the Rev Duncan Cameron, Church of Scotland minister of Kilsyth, claimed that 90 per cent of the country's ministers had seen their offspring ('sons of the manse') volunteer for duty in the armed forces.[11] Unskilled workers or the unemployed looked forward to the prospect of a steady wage but, as *The Scotsman* reported, the recruits in Cockburn Street came from all walks of life: 'Men of all types and classes passed along, some in professions and trades – well groomed and spruce – and others with whom the world had dealt more hardly, but all curious to take their places in the ranks and shoulder a rifle.'[12] During this period soldiers of the Territorial Force were given dispensation to serve overseas and the vast majority of part-time soldiers accepted. Few seem to have given any thought to the dangers that lay ahead or even that warfare would bring casualties.

One of the most popular manifestations of the volunteering craze was the formation of 'pals' battalions – so called because they kept together volunteers from the same cities or towns, or from working, sporting or social clubs. All told, 215 'pals' or locally raised battalions had been formed across the UK by the summer of 1916 and although the title was never fully recognised in Scotland, the concept of men serving together did catch on, especially in the big cities. In Glasgow, at the beginning of September 1914, the corporation gave the go-ahead for the formation of a battalion to serve with the local regiment, the Highland Light Infantry (HLI), which would be drawn from the city's public transport service. Wearing their green uniforms and marching behind a pipe band, the motormen and conductors paraded through the city where they presented themselves for enlistment on 7 September. Under the direction of James Dalrymple, Glasgow's transport manager, the Coplawhill tramways depot became a giant recruiting hall and it took just sixteen hours to enlist the members of what would become the 15th (Tramways) Battalion, HLI.

Encouraged by that success, official approval was given to the Boys' Brigade to form a 16th (Boys Brigade) Battalion, a move that caused a great deal of public excitement in the city. 'Never will it be said that men who were connected with the Boys' Brigade throughout the length and breadth of the United Kingdom and Ireland funked in the hour of Britain's need,' noted a patriotic journalist in the *Glasgow Post*. A few days later, a third 'pals' battalion, numbered 17th, was formed at the instigation of the Glasgow Chamber of Commerce with recruits being enrolled in the Lesser Hall of the Merchants House.[13]

Edinburgh also followed suit; the first calls for a regiment of city volunteers appeared in *The Scotsman* on 12 August but it was not until 12 September that Lord Provost Robert Kirk Inches announced that a 'City of Edinburgh Battalion' would be formed. By then the local regiment, the Royal Scots, had formed three service battalions for the New Armies (11th, 12th and 13th) but Inches was keen to see a designated Edinburgh regiment which would be the equal of the three Glasgow battalions – then as now rivalry between the two cities needed no excuse to be encouraged. The result was the formation of two battalions that served with the Royal Scots as, respectively, 15th (1st City of Edinburgh, Service) and 16th (2nd City of Edinburgh, Service). As they both owed their existence to local commanding officers they were also known as Cranston's Battalion and McCrae's Battalion.

Both men were prominent members of the local business community. Sir Robert Cranston had served as provost and had interests in local drapery stores and temperance hotels and, like many of his class, enjoyed a long association with the old Volunteer movement. Sir George McCrae was equally well regarded, a self-made man who had set up in the drapery business on his own account. Hard work had made him a wealthy man and he was elected to parliament as a Liberal MP in 1899; like Cranston he had also served as a Volunteer. Both battalions were raised in the latter months of 1914 and both went on to serve on the Western Front, but McCrae's battalion was unique in that it contained a large number of footballers, most of whom played for the Heart of Midlothian football club. Shortly after the battalion was raised one of the new recruits penned a suitable verse for McCrae to read out when he appeared in uniform at a special performance of the annual Christmas pantomime in the King's Theatre: 'Do not ask where Hearts are playing and then look at me askance. If it's football that you're wanting, you must come with us to France.' By then McCrae had recruited over a thousand officers and men and his battalion assembled in George Street on 15 December with each volunteer being told to bring with him 'one pair good Boots, Topcoat, two pairs Socks, and shaving outfit'.[14]

Despite initial doubts, the volunteer principle worked: by the end of 1915 the British total was 2,466,719 men, more than would be achieved after the introduction of conscription and just under half the wartime total of 5.7 million men who served in the army during the war years. Of their number, 320,589, or 13 per cent of the total, were Scots. By the end of the war, the number of Scots in the armed forces amounted to 688,416, consisting of 71,707 in the Royal Navy, 584,098 in the army (Regular, Territorial and New) and 32,611 in the Royal Flying Corps and Royal Air Force.[15] It was not until 1916 that the supply of volunteers slowed down, resulting in the introduction of conscription under the Military Service Act of May 1916.

The first major test for the volunteer soldiers came in the early morning of 25 September 1915 when 70,000 British infantrymen steeled themselves to go into the attack across the flat landscape of Flanders. Their target was the German defensive line in the industrial complex formed by the coal-mining triangle of Loos-Lens-Liévin. Shortly after five o'clock in the morning thin wisps of chlorine gas drifted from the British lines towards the German trench system, the first time that chemical weapons had been used by the allies in the war. In some sectors it drifted listlessly towards the German lines on the soft south-westerly wind but to the north it blew back on the soldiers of the 2nd Division, causing the division to halt its attack along both banks of the La Bassée canal. Its role was to provide flanking cover for the 9th (Scottish) Division's attack on the formidable obstacle of the Hohenzollern Redoubt and Fosse 8 where the German observation posts were sited.

As the Scots pushed their way through the smoke and gas with four battalions in line, each battalion split into three waves, the lead units of 26th Brigade started suffering heavy casualties – 6th King's Own Scottish Borderers on the right lost twelve officers killed and seven wounded in the opening minute and 10th HLI on the left had its battalion HQ signalling staff wiped out by a shell blast. But some units achieved their objectives – shortly after eight o'clock 8th Gordon Highlanders had reached the German second line trenches and the German trenches on the faces of the redoubt had been taken by 7th Seaforth Highlanders and 5th Cameron Highlanders with 8th Black Watch in support.[16] Further to the south the attack of the 15th (Scottish) Division was more successful and by eight o'clock the town of Loos was in British hands although the next objective, Hill 70, was fiercely contested by the German defenders.

Loos has been called many things both by the soldiers who fought in it and by the historians who have picked over its bones, but most are agreed that the best description is that it was an unnecessary and an unwanted battle. In strategic terms the result was meaningless. The attacking divisions gained a salient two miles deep and in the early

Figure 19.2 Soldiers of the 2nd battalion, the Argyll and Sutherland Highlanders, at Bois-Grenier, 1915.

stages of the battle some Scottish battalions had the heady sensation of advancing steadily across no man's land – 'the scene resembled nothing so much as a cross-country race with a full field'[17] was the comment in one battalion war diary – but the end result did little to help the French offensive to the south in Artois and Champagne, the main reason for the battle. During the fighting the Germans showed that they had learned the lessons of allied attacks earlier in the year and had created second defensive lines on the reverse slopes to compensate for their lack of reserves and by occupying the higher ground they enjoyed an open field of fire for their artillery and machine guns. Both were used to good effect when the allied offensive opened and the high casualty figures tell their own story.

Although Loos was fought at the request of the French, the commander of the British First Army, General Sir Douglas Haig (scion of a Scots Border family and commander-in-chief of the BEF from December 1915), was optimistic and noted in his diary on 24 September that his men were on the eve of 'the world's greatest battle'.[18] He counted on surprise and placed great confidence in the use of chlorine gas: the plan was to unleash the gas after an artillery bombardment that would increase in intensity over several hours and then to attack with six infantry divisions in line along a broad front.[19]

Of those divisions two were New Army and composed entirely of volunteers (9th Scottish and 15th Scottish), one was Territorial Force

(47th) and three were from the old Regular Army (1st, 2nd and 7th), but the overwhelming representation came from Scottish battalions. In addition to the twenty-four battalions, which made up the two Scottish New Army divisions, a dozen other Scottish formations were serving in the three Regular Army divisions – 1st Black Watch, 1st Camerons and the London Scottish with the 1st Division; 2nd HLI, 1st/9th HLI, 1st Cameronians, 1st/5th Scottish Rifles and 2nd Argyll and Sutherland Highlanders with the 2nd Division; 2nd Royal Scots Fusiliers, 1st/4th Camerons, 2nd Gordon Highlanders and 1st/6th Gordon Highlanders with the 7th Division. Loos deserves to be called a Scottish battlefield: some 35,000 Scots took part in the attack; not since Culloden in 1746 had so many Scots been involved in such a serious military undertaking.[20]

In view of their fate it is tempting to write off the battle as a waste of the lives of men who were ill-prepared to face the shock of modern warfare. Certainly, in the aftermath of the war that was how Loos came to be viewed. 'There is not a name on the list of those who died for Scotland which is not familiar to us,' wrote the novelist Ian Hay, who served in 10th Argyll and Sutherland Highlanders. 'Big England's sorrow is national; little Scotland's is personal.'[21] But at the time the soldiers in the two Scottish New Army divisions had a good conceit of themselves and their ability to take on the enemy. As 6th Camerons waited in the frontline trenches on the eve of battle Private John Jackson exulted in the idea that the 15th (Scottish) Division was finally to be tried in battle after the long months of training and preparation. Having been issued with their rations and 250 rounds of ammunition apiece the men set about preparing themselves to put their training into practice. Ten years later Jackson was still able to recall in his memoirs the hours before his battalion went over the top:

> Instead of going to rest for a few hours in the usual manner, we gathered in groups talking over our chances in the morning. Then the absolute coolness of everyone was shown by the fact that we commenced singing. All the old favourites were sung one by one, bringing back memories of training days, and old scenes of sunny, southern England. Then friends wished each other 'Good Luck', friends who knew that the next day would find many of them in the casualty list.[22]

Soldiers in other Scottish battalions were also optimistic about the outcome. As 10th Gordons made its way to the frontline the men passed other kilted regiments of the 9th (Scottish) Division in the darkness and Private Jack Russell remembered the glee each encounter provoked amongst his fellow soldiers. 'One would shout to a kent face, "Whaur do ye come frae?" "Fife." "Fife! Gies your haun'. Whit part o' Fife?" "Kirkcaldy." "Kirkcaldy! Gies yer ither haun'. Gies baith hauns!"'[23] These were not sheep going to the slaughter but men who were confident in their abilities and training and who took comfort in the fact that they were going into battle in the company of friends.

The battle eventually ground to a halt in mid-October and the newspapers of the day were thick with the casualty lists and heroic descriptions of the fighting. Press reporting of the war was constrained by the Defence of the Realm Act of 1914 which created a system of strict censorship of war stories, but that did not stop news from the front being published in soldiers' letters, albeit with the names of places and military formations omitted. Loos was no exception. Readers of the *Inverness Courier*, for example, were spared the exact details of what actually happened, but in a published letter from Lieutenant-Colonel Donald Walter Cameron of Lochiel, written while he was on leave at his estate at Achnacarry, they were left in no doubt that the men of their local regiment, the Camerons, had just experienced a testing and no doubt bloody and terrifying battle.

'A lance-corporal, finding the [telephone] connection between the Brigadier and myself cut, climbed to the top of a slag heap to get into visual communication,' wrote Cameron of Lochiel who had played the leading role in founding the 5th Camerons in August 1914. 'Here he went on waving his flags amidst a perfect tornado of shell fire, until finally a shell burst right over him, and all that was found afterwards was a piece of his kilt and his notebook.'[24]

That refusal to be downhearted was typical of the soldiers' response to the fighting at Loos and as the military historian Sir John Keegan has pointed out in his study of the First World War feelings ran deeply amongst the Scots in the two New Army divisions who seemed 'to have shrugged off casualties and taken the setback only as a stimulus to renewed aggression'.[25] His assessment is backed up by much of the contemporary evidence. In the wake of the battle another officer in the 4th Camerons published a letter telling the people of Inverness-shire that the battle had provided his men with an important rite of passage and that they should be proud of what they had achieved:

> The men were in splendid spirits and feel that they have passed from what might be called the drudgery of war to the romance of war, where, instead of the monotonous trench life so long endured, they can now view war in a broader state and see something of that dash and glory which have appealed to the soldier nature from time immemorial.'[26]

The total casualty list was 20,598 dead and three times that number wounded and of that number roughly one-third served in Scottish regiments, the largest concentration of casualties in the eighteen to forty-one age group of any battle fought in the First World War. The Scottish losses were so appalling that scarcely any part of the country was unaffected. So high were they in Dundee that each year on the anniversary of the opening day of the battle the light still shines from the city's granite war memorial on The Law to remember the city's war dead at Loos. The majority were killed while serving in the six battalions of the Black Watch that took part in the battle; one of them, 9th Black Watch, was an assault battalion and lost 680 casualties (killed, wounded or missing) in the first hours of the fighting.

After the battle of Loos Scotland would never again provide half the number of infantrymen for a massed attack on the Western Front, but there were to be two other battles in which Scots played a leading role and suffered a disproportionate number of casualties. These were the Somme in 1916 in which three wholly Scottish divisions took part as well as Scottish battalions serving in other divisions (fifty-one battalions in total) and Arras in 1917 which saw the deployment of forty-four Scottish battalions on the first day plus seven Scottish-named Canadian battalions, making it the largest concentration of Scots ever to have fought together. The novelist and historian John Buchan estimated that the Scots' presence at Arras was seven times greater than the army that fought under Robert the Bruce at Bannockburn in 1314 and it was substantially larger than the total number which had fought at Loos.[27]

The next test for the volunteer forces was the battle of the Somme, which began on 1 July 1916 and continued over 140 days until the middle of November. It was to be remembered not for the expected breakthrough but as the killing ground of the British army – no other battlefield of the First World War created more casualties per square yard and the opening hours of the battle produced the bloodiest day for the infantry regiments that took part in the initial attack. From the eleven divisions which began the assault 57,470 men became casualties – 21,392 killed or missing, 35,493 wounded and 585 taken prisoner. As happened in the rest of the United Kingdom, whole areas were affected when the casualty lists began to appear and Scottish infantry regiments were no exception. In the Royal Scots both Cranston's and McCrae's battalions took part in the initial assault with 34th Division, which attacked the heavily fortified German position at La Boiselle and suffered accordingly. The 15th battalion lost 18 officers and 610 soldiers killed, wounded or missing, while the casualties in the 16th battalion were 12 officers and 573 soldiers.

Once again contemporary accounts show that despite the casualties enthusiasm for the fighting did not wane. Bucked up by the sound and fury of the bombardment on the first day, most of the men in the first wave were confident that nothing could have survived, and while naturally nervous and anxious they believed that they were about to participate in one of the glorious moments of the war. David Laidlaw, commanding 16th HLI, remembered that his men were 'singing and whistling as if they were going to a football match instead of one of the most serious encounters in the world's history'.[28] Senior commanders encouraged a feeling of optimism to build up morale, but it did not take long for the attacking soldiers to find that they were engaging well-defended positions and that the wire had not always been cut by the artillery fire. Accuracy was poor, far too many shells failed to explode and shrapnel proved useless in destroying the heavier barbed-wire defences. In the opening hours of the attack on the Leipzig Salient 16th HLI lost 20 officers and 534 men, most of them members of the Boys' Brigade from the Glasgow area and in the days that followed the casualty lists in the *Glasgow Herald* were thick with local names.

Little did those HLI volunteers know that they would fight over nearby ground on the last days of the battle to attack German positions north of Beaucourt and east of Beaumont Hamel. During the assault on 13 November the British failed to take two German defensive systems called Munich Trench and Frankfurt Trench. An attempt to put that right was launched on 18 November when 32nd Division attacked the objectives in what the *Official History* described as dreadful conditions: 'whirling sleet which afterwards turned to rain, the infantry groping their way forward as best they could through half-frozen mud that was soon to dissolve into chalky slime'.[29] Amongst the attacking battalions were 16th and 17th HLI, but the assault fizzled out with the division sustaining 1,387 casualties killed or wounded, most of them from the 16th HLI. Of the 21 officers and 650 other ranks who went into action, 13 officers and 390 other ranks did not make it to the final roll call three days later. But it was not the end of the suffering for the Boys' Brigade 'pals' from Glasgow. During the attack three platoons of D Company had fought their way into the Frankfurt Trench where they were marooned with a small party from 11th Border Regiment while the rest of the force withdrew. About a hundred men remained and finding themselves cut off with no hope of escape they set about barricading a section of the trench to repel the expected German counter attack.

It soon became painfully clear that the men of 16th HLI were in no position to offer protracted resistance – of their number only half were uninjured and they only had four Lewis guns with limited ammunition – but they possessed a stubborn will and fierce pride. They were also well led by their senior NCO, Company Sergeant Major George Lee, who had been a roads foreman with Glasgow Corporation in civilian life, and against the odds they managed to hold out until 25 November, a week after the original attack. Frantic attempts to save them were made by men of the 16th Lancashire Fusiliers, but the men from Glasgow were on their own.[30] To their credit the Germans sent a party under a white flag to try to encourage them to surrender but the offer was spurned, even though food had run out and the Scots had been without water for several days.

Eventually the Germans lost all patience and mounted a huge attack on the position only to find that the opposition had been reduced to fifteen able-bodied men and around thirty wounded who were 'isolated, exhausted with little ammunition left'. The rest, including Lee, were dead. Understandably the Germans were not amused and ordered the exhausted Scots to remove the dead and wounded from the trench. With tensions running high the survivors fully expected to be executed, especially when a sudden British barrage killed a German soldier, but they were treated with grim respect by the senior officer present. 'Is this what has held up the brigade for more than a week?' he asked as the unkempt Scots were brought before him.[31] The last stand of 16th HLI marked the end of the battle of the Somme. Winter had now arrived and offensive operations were no longer possible.

Arguments still rage about the winners and losers of a battle that came to symbolise the worst of the slaughter on the Western Front. The allies lost 600,000 casualties, two-thirds of them British, while the German losses cannot have been much less. In the cold statistical analysis of modern warfare the allies did better out of the battle than the Germans and most modern military historians are agreed that it was 'a win on points'. Although the expected breakthrough never occurred and the ground gained was a modest return for the expenditure of so many lives, pressure had been taken off the French and valuable lessons had been learned. After the war senior German commanders complained that the Somme was 'the muddy grave of the German field army' while their opposite numbers in the British army argued that their inexperienced divisions came of age during the battle, even though most of the lessons were bloodily learned.[32]

Figure 19.3 A piper of the 7th battalion, the Seaforth Highlanders, leads men of the 26th Brigade, 9th (Scottish) Division, back from the trenches after an attack on Longueval, 1916.

The battle of the Somme also forced the enemy to reappraise their options.[33] Rightly fearing the renewal of a bigger allied offensive in the same sector in the new year, the German high command decided to shorten the line between Arras and the Aisne by constructing new and heavily fortified defences which would be their new 'final' position behind the Somme battlefield. Known to the Germans as the *Siegfried Stellung* and to the allies as the Hindenburg Line, this formidable construction shortened the front by some thirty miles and created an obstacle which would not be taken until the end of the war. The withdrawal began on 16 March 1917 and as the Germans retired they laid waste to the countryside, leaving a devastated landscape in which the cautiously pursuing allies had to build new trench systems. To meet this new challenge, the allies planned a new spring assault on the shoulders of the Somme salient with the French attacking in the south at Chemin des Dames while the British and Canadians would mount a supporting offensive at Arras and Vimy Ridge.

The resulting battle of Arras began in the early morning of 9 April in a biting wind which sent snow flurries scudding across the countryside, but despite the wintry weather the portents were good. For the first time the assault battalions found that the artillery had done its job by destroying the wire and new types of gas shells had fallen in the rear areas, killing German transport horses and making the movement of guns impossible. Within a few hours the German line had been penetrated to a depth of two miles and in one of the most astonishing feats of the war the Canadian divisions swept on to take the previously impregnable German positions on the gaunt features of Vimy Ridge. The first day of the assault was a triumph for the British and the Canadians, who succeeded in taking their first objectives and then regrouped to attack the second and third lines of defence. According to the War Diary of 12th Royal Scots, the advance was 'effected just like a drill parade, correct dressing and distances between "waves" being maintained throughout' and, overall, the 9th (Scottish Division) likened their advance to 'a Salisbury Plan ceremonial manoeuvre'.[34]

The first phase of the battle encouraged hopes that this might be the long-awaited breakthrough and some units were surprised both by the ease of their attack and by the lack of German resistance. For example, all five Seaforth battalions achieved their first-day objectives and 1st Gordons, attacking towards Monchy-le-Preux with 3rd Division, were at the German front or Black Line within twenty minutes of leaving their trenches. At Rolincourt 1st/8th Argylls succeeded in capturing second (Blue) and third (Brown) lines, 7th/8th King's Own Scottish Borderers found themselves half a mile beyond their objective near Monchy, and in other sectors Scottish battalions enjoyed equal levels of success, some moving forward so quickly that they came under friendly fire from their own guns. It was at this point that things began to fall apart.

Despite the initial successes the British advance had been irregular and some units were held up by German defensive positions which had escaped the barrage and were still able to inflict heavy casualties on the attacking forces. A huge explosion triggered by the deliberate detonation of a German ammunition dump held up the attack of 1st/5th Seaforths, while 1st/4th Gordons lost so many men in the opening hour – 24 officers and 570 other ranks – that it ceased operating as a coherent unit. In the assault on the Blue Line near Bois de la Maison 15th Royal Scots was reduced to four officers with around a hundred men and according to the regimental historian 'once again raw courage was called for before the enemy could be silenced and officers and men immediately rose to the challenge'.[35] The British commander, General Sir Edmund Allenby, was anxious to continue the momentum and ordered forward units 'to press the enemy leaving any strongpoints to be dealt with by parties in the rear' but already the steam was running out of the assault. As night fell the weather deteriorated leaving the infantrymen in forward positions exposed, hungry and bitterly cold as they had been forbidden to wear or carry their greatcoats during the attack. Battalion war diaries spoke of men lying huddled together for warmth, their condition being made worse by the failure of supplies to get through to them because of congestion on the roads behind Arras.

Despite those problems Allenby ordered the attack to be resumed the following day with an assault on the final German line, the Green Line, at Monchy. He was optimistic of success but already the opposing German commander in the Arras-Vimy sector, General Ludwig von Falkenhausen, had started moving his reserves from their pre-battle positions fifteen miles behind his lines. Monchy fell on 12 April but time was fast running out for the ever more exhausted allied assault battalions. Increased German resistance and reinforcement meant higher casualties for the attackers: 11th Royal Scots lost 150 casualties and 12th Royal Scots 250 casualties in the course of an attempt to take the unlovely village of Rœux with its chemical works north of the Scarpe between Fampoux and Plouvain. On 15 April, almost a week after the first attack, Haig succumbed to reason and to the pleas of his divisional commanders and called a halt to the first phase of the battle to allow reinforcements to be brought up.

At the same time the French launched their attack on the German lines on the Aisne between Reims and Soissons with a huge creeping bombardment preceding the infantry attack, but this ended in disappointment. Not only was the barrage mismanaged but as a result of lapses in French security the Germans had reinforced the area and their machine-gunners were able to mow down the advancing French forces. Within five days it was clear that the offensive had failed, with the French army losing 134,000 casualties in return for minimal gains. Worse, the high attrition rate led to mutinies in many front-line formations as battle-weary soldiers refused to continue fighting. Under pressure from the French, Haig ordered Allenby to resume the offensive on 23 April but by then the Germans had not only reinforced their defensive positions but were able to counter attack. The result was that the roles were reversed and the British came under a heavy artillery bombardment.

This time there were to be no easy gains and the British attack faltered as the assault battalions came up against stronger German opposition, leaving the historian of the 9th (Scottish) Division to lament, 'Little can be said in defence of this battle, which the Division fought with great reluctance. The preparations and arrangements were hurried to a deplorable degree.'[36] For men who had been in con-

Plate 16 *The First Wounded, London Hospital, August 1914,* by Sir John Lavery, 1915.

Plate 17 *Return to the Front: Victoria Railway Station* by Richard Jack, 1916.

Plate 18 *A Highlander Passing a Grave* by Sir William Orpen, 1917.

Plate 19 William Bruce Ellis Ranken's *Pipe Practice, 1918*. Pipers of the Scots Guards in 'undress' uniform, which for pipers of this regiment was a kilt of Royal Stewart tartan and a white 'drill' jacket. As a foot guards regiment, only the pipers of the Scots Guards were kilted.

Plate 20 Lance-Corporal Robertson, 11th City of Edinburgh Battalion, Home Guard. Portrait by Eric Kennington, 1943.

Plate 21 *The 51st Highland Division Plans El Alamein* by Ian Eadie, 1949. The divisional commander, Major-General Douglas Wimberley (kneeling on the right), briefs his officers before the desert battle in 1942. The division codenamed its objectives after Scottish towns associated with its Highland regiments.

Plate 22 The Argyll and Sutherland Highlanders on patrol in Aden, 1967.

Plate 23 A detachment from the 1st battalion, the Scots Guards, marches onto Horse Guards from the Mall as part of the procession for the lying in state of Her Majesty, the Queen Mother, 2002.

Plate 24 The Edinburgh Military Tattoo.

Plate 25 Killed in action in Iraq: the funeral of Lance-Corporal Barry Stephen, 1st battalion, the Black Watch, at St John's Kirk, Perth, 2003.

Plate 26 A soldier from the Black Watch, 3rd battalion, Royal Regiment of Scotland (3 SCOTS), on operations in the Upper Sangin Valley, Afghanistan, 2009.

tinuous action in the first phase of the battle, this second assault along the Scarpe proved to be a battle too far and five days later Allenby was forced to scale down the offensive. Some of the fiercest fighting was at Rœux, which had been captured briefly by the 51st (Highland) Division, only for it to be retaken by the Germans. On 28 April a fresh assault on the village was made by 34th Division and in common with other operations at this stage of the battle it was hurried and improvised. The preceding artillery barrage failed to unsettle the German defenders who were in the process of rushing reinforcements into the village for an attack of their own. In the confusion forward elements of 16th Royal Scots found themselves cut off, having reached their objective ahead of the other attacking battalions, and as a result sustained heavy losses. The *Official History* referred to Rœux simply as 'a melancholy episode' while the historians of the 15th (Scottish) Division called it 'a black day for the British Army', but a Scottish private offered a soldier's perspective of the fighting when he commented later, 'To be in the Comical [chemical] works made a body windy whether it was shellin' or not.'[37]

By the time that the fighting ended at the beginning of May any hope of defeating the Germans at Arras had disappeared and the losses had multiplied. The British suffered around 159,000 casualties, a daily rate of 4,076 (higher than the Somme's 2,943), and the stuffing had been knocked out of many of the formations that had been involved in a month of hard fighting against a heavily reinforced enemy. Given that so many Scottish battalions were involved in the fighting, a high proportion of the casualties were Scots; one brigade in the 51st (Highland) Division lost 900 casualties in the final and bloodiest phase of the battle, the majority being killed or wounded by shrapnel.[38] Later in the year, at the Third Battle of Ypres, also known as Passchendaele, all three Scottish divisions were again involved in the fighting which aimed to deepen the British-held Ypres Salient. The battle lasted four months and accounted for a quarter of a million casualties, 70,000 of them killed or drowned in the lagoons of mud that covered the battlefield.[39]

The stalemate on the Western Front encouraged thoughts of opening a second front and the opportunity was provided by Turkey's entry into the war in December 1914. The target was Constantinople, capital of the Ottoman Empire, which could be attacked through the Dardanelles to allow a joint British and French fleet to enter the Black Sea following the destruction of the Turkish forts on the Gallipoli peninsula. At that point it would have been safe to land ground forces to complete the capture of the peninsula and to neutralise the

Turkish garrison. The plan was stymied, however, by the sinking of several allied capital ships and a consequent loss of nerve in the high command. Following the failure of the naval operations to destroy the Turkish forts, it was decided to land troops at Cape Helles on 25 April but the landings were opposed by the Turks, who offered stout resistance. By the end of the month the British had suffered around 9,000 casualties, one-third the size of the attacking force in return for little ground gained. Reinforcements were required and amongst them were the Scottish Territorial infantry battalions of 52nd (Lowland) Division which began landing on the peninsula in the first week of June.[40]

After spending some time in the trenches to acclimatise and become used to the enervating operational conditions on the peninsula, the division first saw battle on 28 June when it attacked the Turkish positions at Helles. The operation was a fiasco as the British artillery had failed to suppress the enemy's machine-gun positions and the attacking battalions paid a heavy price. For example, when 156th Brigade went into the attack, 1st/4th and 1st/7th Royal Scots fought their way through to the Turks' second line but 1st/8th Scottish Rifles ran into heavy fire and within five minutes had lost over 400 casualties killed or wounded.[41] Acting as brigade reserve, 1st/7th Scottish Rifles reinforced the assault but it fared no better, losing 14 officers and 258 soldiers. The Edinburgh battalions had also suffered heavily: 1st/4th Royal Scots lost 16 officers and 204 soldiers killed or missing while 1st/7th Royal Scots had been reduced to 6 officers and 169 soldiers, roughly the size of a company. As the casualty lists started appearing in the Edinburgh newspapers it was impossible to disguise the fact that whole areas of the city had been affected and that, as a local paper reflected, death had been unsparing of class or background:

> In its ranks are many former pupils of such schools as George Watson's College, not a few of whom joined after the outbreak of the war. There is something at once inspiring and pathetic in the fate of these young fellows. They had grown up together almost from infancy, sitting on the same bench at school, romping in the playground together, running shoulder to shoulder on the football field, and then after the parting that comes at the end of school life, finding themselves side by side once more on the field of battle, playing the biggest game that men have ever played.[42]

The sentiment comes close to delineating the ethos of the Scottish volunteer battalions, their tight solidarity and their optimism in the face of hardship and violent death.

Figure 19.4 Company Sergeant Major John Douglas (seated centre) and NCOs of the 16th battalion, the Royal Scots, France and Flanders, c. 1918. Twenty-three-year-old Douglas, who before the war had been a plumber at the Dalzell steel works in Motherwell, won the Distinguished Conduct Medal for 'conspicuous gallantry and devotion to duty' at the battle of the Lys in April 1918.

Despite the arrival of reinforcements – in all, the senior British commander General Sir Ian Hamilton was given five new divisions – the deadlock could not be broken and the men on the peninsula were becoming increasingly weakened. An ambitious amphibious landing at Suvla Bay failed in August because the Turks were able to rush reinforcements into the area to prevent the creation of a bridgehead. In October the inevitable happened: Hamilton was sacked and was replaced by General Sir Charles Monro, a veteran of the Western Front. Having taken stock of the situation he recommended evacuation, although this was not accepted until the beginning of November when Kitchener visited the battlefront and agreed that the difficulties were insuperable. In a brilliant operation, which was all the more inspired after the fiascos that preceded it, the British finally withdrew their forces at the end of 1915, remarkably without losing any casualties.[43]

In addition to Gallipoli Scottish regiments also saw action on the fronts in Salonika, Italy and Mesopotamia but the fulcrum of the fighting in 1918 remained the Western Front. The year opened with a major German offensive on 23 March, which was to be their last attempt to defeat the allies before the US Army brought much-needed reinforcements to the Western Front. (The US had entered the war in 1917.) The German strategy was brutally simple: its armies would drive a wedge between the two opposing armies, striking through the old Somme battlefield between Arras and La Fère before turning to destroy the British Third and Fifth Armies on the left of the allied line. It almost worked too. In their defensive positions in the Cambrai sector near Beaumetz the 51st (Highland) Division had their first inkling that something was afoot when scouting parties observed thousands of German infantrymen entering the frontline trenches carrying weapons but leaving behind their heavy packs, clearly preparing for an assault. In the first minutes C company of 1st/8th Argylls was wiped out and the battalion was forced to retire with 542 casualties while 1st/7th Argylls, in reserve at the time, had to fight for its very existence as did every battalion in the division, which lost three out of ten battalion commanders.

By the beginning of April the Germans had advanced twenty miles along a fifty-mile front, creating a huge bulge in the allied line, and had pushed themselves to within five miles of Amiens. If this key city and railhead had fallen it would have been a disaster for the allies. The French would have been forced back to defend Paris and the British would have been left with little option but to retreat to the Channel ports and the war would have hung in the balance. However, the Germans had already shot their bolt by failing to concentrate the main thrust of their assault and dispersing the effort to take their targets.

Following the failure of the attack the German commander General Erich von Ludendorff turned his attention to the French armies along the Aisne. Once again his assault forces achieved an initial success by breaching the opposition's defences and by 30 May they had reached the Marne, creating a salient twenty miles deep and thirty miles wide. Vigorous counter attacks by the French and US armies frustrated the German advance, and British forces were also involved when the newly formed XXII Corps was deployed in support of the French army in Champagne. Amongst its four divisions were 15th (Scottish) and 51st (Highland) and both of them took part in the second battle of the Marne, which finally halted the German advance in the middle of July. At the end of the action 1st/6th Black Watch was given the special honour of being awarded the Croix de Guerre for its support of French forces in the field during the battle of Tardenois in the Reims sector. This battle represented the last chance for the Germans to win the war for although they had captured large tracts of enemy ground all the salients had vulnerable flanks which were prone to counter attack. The Germans had also taken huge casualties and for the survivors it was dispiriting to see that so little had been gained for so much effort. The beginning of the end came on 8 August when Australian and Canadian forces attacked the German positions to the east of Amiens with a British and a French corps guarding the flank to the north and south. The attack achieved complete surprise and the allies were able to advance eight miles in one day, taking over 12,000 German prisoners in the process. With the war entering its final hundred days the advantage had swung inexorably towards the allies; applying relentless pressure the advance continued throughout October and into November as the Germans withdrew steadily back from their positions on the Western Front.

By that stage of the war, too, many of the army's pre-war battalions were regular in name only and the dilution caused problems for career officers who found that standards had slipped. When James Jack took over command of the 1st Cameronians in the summer of 1918 there were only two surviving pre-war officers and on meeting the brigade commander he received an unpleasant shock when he was told that the battalion was 'below form' and required 'smartening up'.[44] Differences between Regular, Territorial and Service battalion also became blurred during the latter stages of the war and some units disliked being reinforced by men from other regiments. In the summer of 1917 Lieutenant-Colonel the Hon. William Fraser, commanding 1st/6th Gordon Highlanders, complained in his diary about the arrival of a draft of sixty from the Argyll and Sutherland Highlanders: 'it does not make for esprit de Corps', he noted.[45] On the other hand, bucking the trend, the 9th (Scottish) Division found that its drafts of replacements measured up to what was required when they arrived to replace battlefield casualties in the summer of 1918: 'They were largely composed of lads who had been taken at the age of seventeen, and were splendid examples of the beneficial effects of good training, regular exercise and military discipline on young Scotsmen.'[46]

Figure 19.5 Sir Douglas Haig, photographed in 1918.

Any examination of the allied prosecution of the First World War has to consider the role played by Douglas Haig. Although he ended the war on a high note, in command of an army just under two million strong, it was his fate to be condemned as an inept battlefield commander and to be vilified for his apparent lack of sympathy for those who suffered as a result of his decisions. From being the highly respected commander-in-chief who had won the war, Haig was slowly transmogrified into an incompetent figurehead who had on his conscience the lives of thousands of men. Later historians have revised that assessment by arguing that Haig's tactics eventually wore down the Germans and that he and his colleagues were involved in a steep learning curve as they came to terms with the lessons of modern industrialised warfare.[47] As Haig himself expressed it in his Final Despatch, which was published on 21 March 1919:

> It is in the great battles of 1916 and 1917 that we have to seek for the secret of our victory in 1918 . . . the moral effects of those battles were enormous,

both in the German Army and in Germany. By their means our soldiers established over the German soldier a moral superiority which they held in an ever-increasing degree until the end of the war, even in the difficult days of March and April 1918.[48]

Like any other soldier who has been involved in the dirty business of warfare Haig knew that battles could only be won by careful planning and the determination and resolve of the men who fought them.

The precise numbers of Scottish war dead between 1914 and 1918 are difficult to compute but it is possible to reach some conclusions about the level of the losses. At the end of the war the official figure was put at 74,000 but this was decided by the unsound method of dividing the British total by ten to reflect the fact that Scots made up ten per cent of the United Kingdom's population. Later, when plans were being made to build a national war memorial for Scotland in the 1920s this was revised to 100,000, or 13 per cent of the British total.[49] Later still, the same memorial recorded the names of 148,218 Scots from around the world 'killed in the service of the Crown' and the figure is still being increased as new information becomes available.[50] It has also been suggested that the Scottish death rate was only exceeded by Serbia and Turkey: this is based on a statistic that the total Scottish casualties as a percentage of those mobilised was 26.4 per cent – whereas the percentage in Serbia and Turkey was, respectively, 37.1 per cent and 26.8 per cent.[51] With a total of 690,235 Scots having been mobilised, however, this would make the Scottish total 182,222, a figure that is unsustainable. As with all statistics from the conflict the figures have to be handled with caution. The original tally of 74,000 is far too low but the higher figure, which is double that amount, is also suspect as it contains the names of Scots-born soldiers who served in the forces of the dominions and there may also be some duplication. Part of the problem lies in the nature of the conflict. In the initial casualty lists men who were recorded as wounded later died as a result of their injuries, and the opposite was also true. There are other imponderables: men who died of wounds after the war or who had premature deaths as a result of their experiences are not counted and the names on the regimental rolls of honour also include soldiers who were not Scots-born but died wearing Scottish uniforms.

Although it is impossible to get absolute agreement on the exact number of Scottish war deaths, the available regimental and municipal figures suggest that the total is probably higher than the generally accepted 100,000. One regiment alone, the Royal Scots, suffered 11,213 killed in action, most of whom came from Edinburgh and

Figure 19.6 Gallipoli veterans outside Greyfriars Church, Edinburgh, 1971.

the east of Scotland. The Highland Light Infantry lost 10,000, the Gordon Highlanders 9,000 and the Black Watch 8,000. Of the 13,568 men who volunteered from Scotland's four universities, 2,026 were killed on active service. In Glasgow 18,000 young men, or one in fifty-seven of the city's population, did not come back from the war, while Dundee's death toll was 4,213 out of a population of 180,000.[52]

As with countless other soldiers from the warring nations, thousands of Scots returned home, picked up the pieces and got on with their lives as best they could. There was, of course, a darker side. Many of the four million survivors were disabled and of those incapacitated at least 13 per cent would have been Scots; others could not find work or became homeless; and there was an overwhelming need to tackle the problems that faced them on their return to civilian life. A number of associations and ex-servicemen's clubs already catered for the veterans but being independent of each other they lacked political and financial cohesion and the different factions were often at loggerheads over the best way forward. It was not until 1920 that the first steps were taken to forge some unity, and the guiding figure was Haig, who had retired from the army in January 1919 and had long insisted that the needs of former service personnel warranted urgent attention. As a result of his efforts the British Legion and the British Legion Scotland came into being in 1921, and by the end of the following year the Legion in Scotland was able to report that it had dealt with 7,645 cases in respect of pensions, medical claims and arrears of pay.[53] That year also saw the first 'poppy' appeal, made by the Earl Haig Fund, the charity for raising funds for ex-service personnel in Scotland. By then the first Armistice Day commemoration had also been held as the nation kept two minutes' silence on 11 November at eleven o'clock in the morning. Although the practice fell into disuse in the 1960s, it was revived in 2006 to remember the dead of the First World War and subsequent conflicts.

Notes

1. D. T. Jones, J. F. Duncan, H. M. Conacher and W. R. Scott, *Rural Scotland during the War* (Oxford: Oxford University Press, 1926), pp. 18–19. On the impact of the war upon Scotland's economy generally, see C. H. Lee, 'The Scottish economy and the First World War', in C. M. M. Macdonald and E. W. McFarland (eds), *Scotland and the Great War* (East Linton: Tuckwell Press, 1999), pp. 11–35.
2. C. Harvie, *No Gods and Precious Few Heroes: Scotland since 1914* (Edinburgh: Edinburgh University Press, 1993), pp. 3–5.
3. W. R. Scott and J. Cunnison, *The Industries of the Clyde Valley during the War* (Oxford: Oxford University Press, 1924), p. 19.
4. Cmd 7439, 7, HM Inspector of Mines for Scotland, 1913 Report, p. 29.
5. I. Johnston, *Beardmore Built: The Rise and Fall of a Clyde Shipyard* (Clydebank: Clydebank District Libraries and Museums, 1993), pp. 89–90; I. Johnston, *Ships for a Nation: John Brown & Company* (Clydebank: West Dunbartonshire Libraries and Museums, 2000), pp. 155-7.
6. Scott and Cunnison, *The Industries*, p. 98.
7. National Records of Scotland, Edinburgh, HH31/39, St Kilda: Damage to buildings due to a bombardment by German Submarines. Details of damage. Parliamentary questions. Correspondence etc, 15 May 1918.
8. For Kitchener's armies, see P. Simkins, *Kitchener's Army: The Raising of the New Armies, 1914–16* (Manchester: Manchester University Press, 1988); P. E. Dewey, 'Military recruiting and the British labour force

during the First World War', *The Historical Journal*, vol. 27 (1984), pp. 206–21.
9. *The Scotsman*, 12 August 1914, p. 6. On Scottish recruiting in general, see D. R. Young, 'Voluntary recruitment in Scotland, 1914–1916' (unpublished PhD thesis, University of Glasgow, 2001) and in the Highlands, E. A. Cameron and I. J. M. Robertson, 'Fighting and bleeding for the land: The Scottish Highlands and the Great War', in Macdonald and McFarland, *Scotland and the Great War*, pp. 81–102.
10. *Glasgow Herald*, 2 September 1914, p. 6.
11. D. Cameron, *Sons of the Manse: Muster Roll of Those Who answered Their King and Country's Call to Arms in the Great War* (Edinburgh and Glasgow: W. M. Hodge, 1915), editor's note, p. 7.
12. *The Scotsman*, 8 August 1914, p. 9.
13. *Glasgow Herald*, 8 September 1914, p. 6. See also T. Chalmers, *An Epic of Glasgow: History of the 15th Battalion The Highland Light Infantry (City of Glasgow Regiment)* (Glasgow: John McCallum, 1934), p. x; T. Chalmers (ed.), *A Saga of Scotland: History of the 16th Battalion The Highland Light Infantry (City of Glasgow Regiment)* (Glasgow: John McCallum, 1930), pp. 2–3; J. W. Arthur and I. S. Munro (eds), *The Seventeenth Highland Light Infantry (Glasgow Chamber of Commerce Battalion) Record of War Service 1914–1918* (Glasgow: D. J. Clark, 1920).
14. J. Alexander, *McCrae's Battalion: The Story of the 16th Royal Scots* (Edinburgh: Mainstream Publishing, 2003), pp. 54–90.
15. T. Royle, *The Flowers of the Forest: Scotland and the First World War* (Edinburgh: Birlinn, 2006), p. 35.
16. J. Stewart and J. Buchan, *The 15th (Scottish) Division 1914–1919* (Edinburgh and London: William Blackwood, 1926), p. 34. On the gas blowback at Loos, see D. Richter, *Chemical Soldiers: British Gas Warfare in World War I* (London: Leo Cooper, 1992), pp. 61–93.
17. J. Ewing, *History of the 9th (Scottish) Division 1914–1919* (London: John Murray, 1921), p. 60.
18. G. Sheffield and J. Bourne, *Douglas Haig: War Diaries and Letters 1914–1918* (London: Weidenfeld and Nicolson, 2005), p. 153.
19. On Haig's gas assumptions, see J. P. Harris, *Douglas Haig and the First World War* (Cambridge: Cambridge University Press, 2008), pp. 164–70.
20. E. Linklater and A. Linklater, *The Black Watch: The History of the Royal Highland Regiment* (London: Barrie and Jenkins, 1977), p. 144.
21. I. Hay, *The First Hundred Thousand* (Edinburgh and London: William Blackwood, 1916), p. 47. On the writings of 'Ian Hay', the pseudonym of John Beith Hay, see G. Urquhart, 'Confrontation and withdrawal:

Loos, readership and the first hundred thousand', in Macdonald and McFarland, *Scotland and the Great War*, pp. 125–44.
22. J. Jackson, *Private 12768: Memoir of a Tommy* (Stroud: Tempus, 2004), p. 51. For Scottish reflections in the trenches, see D. Young, *Forgotten Scottish Voices from the Great War* (Stroud: Tempus, 2005), pp. 72–103, and E. M. Spiers, 'The Scottish soldier at war', in H. Cecil and P. Liddle (eds), *Facing Armageddon: The First World War Experienced* (London: Leo Cooper, 1996), pp. 314–35.
23. J. Russell, *Diary of a Kitchener's Recruit: Being the experience of a Gordon Highlander during the first two years of the Great War, August, 1914, to September, 1916* (Aberdeen: privately published, 1916), p. 35.
24. Inverness Courier, *The Cameron Highlanders at the Battles at Loos, Hill 70, Fosse 8, & the Quarries* (Inverness: Inverness Courier, 1924), p. 14.
25. J. Keegan, *The First World War* (London: Hutchinson, 1998), p. 218.
26. Inverness Courier, *The Cameron Highlanders*, p. 22.
27. J. Buchan, *History of the War*, 24 vols (London and Edinburgh: Thomas Nelson, 1915–19), vol. 3, p. 417.
28. Chalmers, *A Saga of Scotland*, p. 32.
29. J. E. Edmonds (ed.), *History of the Great War, Based on Official Documents: Military Operations, France and Belgium*, 14 vols (London: HMSO, 1922–49), *1916*, vol. 1, pp. 492–3.
30. Chalmers, *A Saga of Scotland*, p. 57.
31. Ibid. p. 67.
32. Ewing, *History of the 9th (Scottish) Division*, p. 142.
33. A recent major reappraisal of the Somme is W. J. Philpott, *Bloody Victory: The Sacrifice on the Somme and the Making of the Twentieth Century: The Battle, the Myth, the Legacy* (London: Little, Brown, 2009).
34. The National Archives (TNA), WO 95/1773, War Diary 12th Royal Scots; Ewing, *History of the 9th (Scottish Division)*, p. 197.
35. R. H. Paterson, *Pontius Pilate's Bodyguard: A History of The First or The Royal Regiment of Foot, The Royal Scots (The Royal Regiment)*, 3 vols (Edinburgh: RHQ Royal Scots, 2000–7), vol. 1, p. 327.
36. Ewing, *History of the 9th (Scottish) Division*, p. 205.
37. Edmonds, *History of the Great War, 1917*, vol. 1, pp. 509–16; Stewart and Buchan, *The 15th (Scottish) Division*, p. 212; F. W. Bewsher, *The History of the 51st (Highland) Division 1914–1918* (Edinburgh and London: William Blackwood, 1921), p. 174.
38. For an assessment of the battle of Arras, see G. D. Sheffield, *Forgotten Victory: The First World, War Myths and Realities* (London: Headline, 2001), pp. 190–9.

39. On Passchendaele, see R. Prior and T. Wilson, *Passchendaele: The Untold Story* (New Haven, CT: Yale University Press, 1996) and P. H. Liddle (ed.), *Passchendaele in Perspective* (London: Pen and Sword, 1997).
40. For the experiences of two Lowland battalions, see G. Richardson, *For King and Country and the Scottish Borders: The Story of the 1/4th (Border) Battalion The King's Own Scottish Borderers on the Gallipoli Peninsula, 1915* (Hawick: Buccleuch Printers, 1987) and I. S. Wood, '"Be strong and of a good courage": The Royal Scots' Territorial battalions from 1908 to Gallipoli', in Macdonald and McFarland, *Scotland and the Great War*, pp. 103–24.
41. TNA, WO 95/4321, War Diary 4th Royal Scots; War Diary 7th Royal Scots.
42. *Evening Dispatch*, 8 July 1915, p. 5.
43. Recent major studies of Gallipoli include T. Travers, *Gallipoli 1915* (Stroud: Tempus, 2004) and R. Prior, *Gallipoli: The End of the Myth* (New Haven, CT and London: Yale University Press, 2009). For a sympathetic appraisal of Hamilton, see J. Lee, *A Soldier's Life: General Sir Ian Hamilton 1853–1947* (London: Macmillan, 2000), especially Chapter 9.
44. J. Terraine (ed.), *General Jack's Diary: War on the Western Front 1914–1918* (London: Cassell, 1964), pp. 245–6.
45. D. Fraser (ed.), *In Good Company: The First World War Diaries of The Hon. William Fraser, Gordon Highlanders* (Wilton: Michael Russell, 1990), p. 122.
46. Ewing, *History of the 9th (Scottish) Division*, p. 293.
47. On Haig, see J. Terraine, *Douglas Haig, the Educated Soldier* (London: Hutchinson, 1963); T. Travers, *The Killing Ground* (London: Unwin Hyman, 1987) and *How the War was Won* (London: Routledge, 1992); G. J. de Groot, *Douglas Haig 1861–1928* (London: Unwin Hyman, 1988); B. Bond and N. Cave (eds), *Haig: A Reappraisal 70 Years On* (London: Leo Cooper, 1999); W. Reid, *Architect of Victory: Douglas Haig* (Edinburgh: Birlinn, 2006); Harris, *Douglas Haig and the First World War*; and G. Sheffield, *The Chief: Douglas Haig and the British Army* (London: Aurum Press, 2011).
48. Sheffield and Bourne, *Haig Diaries*, p. 523.
49. R. Finlay, *Modern Scotland 1914–2000* (London: Profile Books, 2004), p. 36; Harvie, *No Gods*, p. 24.
50. Royle, *The Flowers of the Forest*, p. 285. On the Scottish National War Memorial, see A. Calder, 'The Scottish National War Memorial', in W. Kidd and B. Murdoch (eds), *Memory and Memorials: The Commemorative Century* (Aldershot: Ashgate, 2004), pp. 61–75 and

I. Hay, *Their Name Liveth: The Book of the Scottish National War Memorial* (East Kilbride: Edinburgh Trustees of the Scottish National War Memorial, 1985).
51. J. M. Winter, *The Great War and the British People* (London: Macmillan, 1985), p. 75.
52. Finlay, *Modern Scotland*, pp. 36–7.
53. J. A. Lister, *Sixty Years On: The History of the Royal British Legion Scotland* (Edinburgh: Royal British Legion Scotland, 1982), pp. 7–14.

20
Internal Policing and Public Order, c. 1900–94

IAN S. WOOD

Alexander Somerville, a young Scottish cavalry trooper in the Royal North British Dragoons, or Scots Greys as they became better known, was bound tightly to a ladder bolted at an angle to a barrack yard wall. Sentence on him was due to be carried out. At a court martial on 29 May 1832 it had been pronounced that he would 'receive two hundred lashes in the usual manner of the regiment.'[1] Somerville later wrote of how a farrier and a trumpeter took it in turns to swing the cat, or leather flail, across his back as the assembled regiment watched.

His account of his agony is graphic reading. As an attendant sergeant counted the fiftieth stroke, he recalled that 'I felt as if I had lived all the time of my real life in pain and torture, and that the time when existence had pleasure in it was a dream long, long gone by.'[2] By then he was coughing up mouthfuls of blood and had bitten his tongue almost in two because of his resolve not to cry out as the strokes fell. He had to endure a further fifty before his punishment was commuted on account of his youth. His ostensible offence had been to refuse to mount an obviously unmanageable horse which had been deliberately assigned to him in a training exercise.

Somerville had started his working life as a Berwickshire farm hand and was literate and politically aware. His real crime had been to write a letter from his barracks in Birmingham to a radical newspaper, the *Weekly Dispatch*, at a time of crisis in the passage through parliament of the Whig government's Reform Bill. With the duke of Wellington attempting to form a ministry which would block the bill, and Thomas Attwood's Political Union capable of mobilising mass support on the streets, Somerville had dared to query whether the civil authorities had unconditional claims on the army's obedience. He and his fellow troopers, he wrote, would obey lawful orders but would never 'raise an arm' against the cause of liberty.[3] Rather than have others punished, Somerville confessed to authorship of the letter which was represented by senior officers as a libel on the regiment. It was hardly that, but it still made him an obvious target for retribution. Though his case became a *cause célèbre* for the reform movement and associated well-wishers, it bought him a discharge from the army.[4]

Had the Greys in fact been ordered into action against the Birmingham reform crowds like the Manchester Yeomanry at Peterloo in 1819 it would have been simply a further instance of Scottish troops being called upon to give aid to the civil power against the threat of popular unrest. They had been doing this since the Hanoverian Riot Act of 1714, both regular and fencible units raised for home service in times of emergency being deployed by the authorities in Scotland, and on the English side of the border, when it became necessary to 'read' the act as a way of calling upon crowds to disperse.[5]

The act was still a statutory weapon for the state as the twentieth century opened with a wave of strikes. Scotland saw its share of this militancy as major employers went on the offensive to break such workplace organisation as there was. Alongside this, American-inspired management theory, based upon the aggressive gospel of 'Taylorism', was applied to the workforce, constituting what has been called a pincer movement against organised labour in Scotland.[6] Unions fought back, especially in the Glasgow area, preparing the ground for the heroic wartime and post-war legend of 'Red Clydeside' to grow in. There were also big strikes in England, and in Ireland, often involving Scottish troops in support of police. In 1912 the English syndicalist Tom Mann went to prison with others for circulating a leaflet, entitled *Don't Shoot*, which appealed to soldiers to refuse to take part in the coercion of strikers. Mann's prosecution came during the national miners' strike for a minimum wage which was strongly supported in the Scottish coalfields. From the Labour benches at Westminster Keir Hardie, a former Lanarkshire miner, rose to condemn Mann's conviction and to reiterate his appeal to soldiers not to act against strikers: 'Take the consequences of refusal to shoot them down, but do not murder your brother and your comrade who is fighting for your cause as well as his own.'[7]

The minimum wage was secured and, like others in Scotland prior to 1914, the strike passed without any major confrontation with the army. Events in Ireland, however, threw into very sharp focus the issue of military obedience when it began to appear that officers with unionist sympathies, and based at the Curragh camp in County

Figure 20.1 Men of the 1st battalion, the Gordon Highlanders, on strike duty in Sheffield, 1911.

Kildare, might be excused from any action involving the imposition of home rule on Loyalist Ulster.

One young officer in the Black Watch was Archibald Wavell, who would rise to the highest rank in the army. At the height of the Curragh crisis he wrote of his anxieties to his father: 'The idea of officers of the army going on strike, which I think is what it really amounts to over this business, is to my mind absolutely disastrous. What about the men? They can't resign whatever their opinions are.'[8] He was right, and soldiers certainly could not with impunity refuse orders for strike duty.

Some advocates of Ulster's cause, as well as its opponents, began to talk of civil war, as did others before 1914 who feared it could come on the back of militant strikes and suffragette law-breaking. For those with such fears conscription began to commend itself as an instrument of social order and also as a way to give the population military training. Since 1901 the National Service League had been making this case, much influenced by a European continent where conscription was the norm. There, it has been said, army service was a social initiation rite: 'the introduction to manhood and membership of the community'.[9]

In France republicans saw conscription as egalitarian while the clerical and royalist right shrank from it initially, haunted by the spectre of the 1871 Paris Commune and the risk, as Adolphe Thiers had put it, of 'rifles on the shoulders of Socialists'.[10] Acceptance of military service for all in a country of diverse regional cultures took time to be accepted but by 1914 it was widely viewed as a useful schooling in republican patriotism.[11] In Germany conscription was proof of the power of the unified state. Those who justified it, like Bismarck, also argued that the imperial state, through its social welfare policy, was benign to the new working class. But the danger that in a country with Europe's biggest socialist party not all conscripts might see it that way was recognised by the Kaiser's officer corps. In 1909 General von Eichorn sent out a document on political education to all units serving under him. This read in part that

> The young soldier's mind is like a piece of clay on which every sort of impression can be made. Many of course have already been infected by Social Democracy before they were called; but they are young, their sickness is superficial, and their service with the colours must work like a healing spring and wash the sickness out of their system.[12]

In Britain the conscriptionist case could only succeed through the brutal imperatives of war after 1914. Making the case for it, certainly in Scotland, ran against the grain of a still strong anti-militarism within the working class. Socialist leaders, such as Hardie and Ramsay MacDonald, gave a voice to this feeling, though perhaps less eloquently than the great Jean Jaurès did. He in fact favoured a citizens' militia for France, based on the Swiss model,[13] but in 1914 he accepted his country's need to fight a war of republican defence.

Popular anti-militarism in England and in Scotland was mainly directed at the regular army. Part-time soldiering in the rifle volunteer movement formed in 1859 in response to a French invasion scare was popular and had the approval of observers as different in outlook as Engels and Lord Tennyson. So too, in relative terms, was the Territorial Force, formed in 1908, though six years later Kitchener was sceptical of its military competence.[14] When Britain went to war in 1914 there were those among the rapidly constituted officer corps of Kitchener's New Army who saw the mobilisation of this new force as a bonding experience that could transcend the labour conflicts and class tensions of the previous decade. Liberal journalist A. G. Gardiner had written the year before in a book hostile to the National Service League that 'a drilled and disciplined proletariat is their hope against an insurgent democracy'.[15] A number of the New Army's 'raisers' might have had this thought even as they invoked at recruiting rallies the language of liberal internationalism, the sanctity of treaties and the rights of small nations.

Their appeals worked alongside many other motivations. Some of the raisers, like the Liberal Edinburgh businessman Sir George McCrae, always had faith in workers doing their national duty. This went back to his time in the Territorial Force before he became famous for recruiting the 16th New Army battalion of the Royal Scots. In November 1913 he had written to the War Office about territorial recruitment problems and how summer camps necessitated industrial workers taking time off work and losing pay while '[t]he middle class fellow gets his fortnight's holiday – at best his pay is not stopped. By attending camp he sacrifices only his leisure or convenience.'[16]

The triumph of New Army recruitment was to bring both artisan and 'middle class fellow' to the colours in huge numbers, nowhere more so than in Glasgow, despite its advanced Labour politics and trade union strength. The socialist city councillor, John Wheatley, never compromised over his opposition to the war but he recognised the potency of working-class patriotism and never mocked it, though he resented its exploitation.[17] Harry McShane, a militant engineering worker in the city, was so hostile to the conflict that he decided to join the army so that 'our propaganda should be directed at the military themselves'.[18] He was supported by his branch of the Marxist British Socialist Party, which the charismatic agitator John MacLean had joined, but it was an abortive venture. McShane deserted nine months later and was realistic about what he had attempted: 'It might have been possible to get further with socialist propaganda in the conscripted army of 1916; but among the volunteers of 1914 it was impossible to persuade any of them that the war was wrong.'[19]

The theme of Scottish working class volunteers' pro-war enthusiasm and how socialists, once enlisted, reordered their class loyalties looms large in one of the First World War's best-selling books, *The First Hundred Thousand*, which emerged from serial form into book length in good time for the Christmas 1915 market. Its author, Ian Hay, was a product of Fettes College and Cambridge, where he went back to teach prior to taking a commission in a New Army battalion of the Argyll and Sutherland Highlanders.[20] In his account of the formation and bonding of a Scottish New Army battalion, drawn heavily from his own experience at home and then on the Western Front, he created for his readers a vivid tapestry of characters. One of them was Private McSlattery, a class-conscious Clydebank shipyard worker of republican views:

> To such Royalty is simply the head and cornerstone of a legal system which officiously prevents a man from being drunk and disorderly and the British Empire an expensive luxury for which the working man pays while the idle rich draw the profits.[21]

In little time at all, McSlattery leads the cheers when the king and his family review the battalion and in due course the 'reformed revolutionary' distinguishes himself in battle.[22] At a later point in his narrative Hay has the battalion toiling by night to extend their trench system when someone mentions newspaper reports of strike action in the Welsh coalfields. Private Mucklewame's response is, for Hay, 'quite simple and eminently sound'. He merely remarks, 'All the decent lads are out here.'[23]

An even more popular writer than Hay was John Buchan, who shared his faith in the patriotism of the working-class recruits to the New Army as well as the conscripts of 1916. In *Mr Standfast*, not published until after the war, the plot requires Richard Hannay to be seconded from a command on the Western Front to intelligence and counter espionage work. He has to take on the identity of a South African opposed to the war and in this guise attends a rowdy anti-war meeting in Glasgow in 1917. At this the main speaker is a noted agitator who has already been deported from the city. To much applause the speaker vilifies both the government and war profiteers. The mood of the audience changes when he moves to the subject of the army and its effete officer caste of 'gentry pups' and cowardly generals, who wantonly sacrifice the other ranks in useless offensives. This enrages a Royal Scots Fusilier in the audience who calls the speaker a liar and threatens him. Violent chaos ensues and Hannay, to maintain his cover, has reluctantly to trade punches with 'a second Jock, a broad thickset fellow, of the adorable, bandy-legged stocky type that I had seen go through the railway triangle at Arras as if it was blotting paper'.[24]

Hay and Buchan both saw the success of working-class recruitment as a template for post-war society. In a sequel to his best-seller, Hay wrote of a new class unity being forged by the shared experience of war service. He has an older officer on leave telling a younger colleague how this will happen once the war finishes:

> What I mean is this. You can't call your employer a tyrant after he has shared his rations with you and never spared himself over your welfare and comfort through weary months of trench warfare, neither when you have experienced a working man's courage and cheerfulness and reliability on

the day of battle, can you turn round and call him a loafer and an agitator in time of peace, can you?[25]

Reality when peace came proved rather different, in Britain as a whole and certainly on the Clyde. Within weeks of the armistice Glasgow was in the grip of strike action. Engineering workers in the munitions industry feared for their future as wartime contracts ended and employers sought to reverse such gains as the war had brought for organised labour. Their union, the Amalgamated Society of Engineers (ASE), launched a national strike in January 1919 for a maximum working week. Essentially this was a defensive action and there was disagreement between the Glasgow district of the ASE and its national executive over what the sought-after maximum should be, though what followed has entered labour history as the engineers' forty-hour strike. Support nationally was uneven but in Glasgow it was solid, with heavy picketing to bring out electricity power workers and other strategic groups to back the forty-hour claim.

The strike failed to secure the forty-hour week but it reached its climax on Friday 31 January with a huge rally in Glasgow's George Square outside the council chambers after the lord provost had agreed to communicate on the strikers' behalf with the cabinet in London. A deputation, including the Communist Willie Gallacher, entered the chambers to talk to the lord provost but this was overshadowed by the build-up of a restless crowd in the square whose caps and red flags have become an iconic image in Scottish working-class history. Police action following the reading of the Riot Act was heavy-handed, with truncheons freely used, and this provoked the crowd. For a time the police lost control and one account has called what happened a police riot.[26]

In the aftermath of the 'battle of George Square' troops drawn from various English and Scottish regiments were deployed on the streets of Glasgow to prevent further unrest. Tanks were stationed at the Saltmarket and machine guns set up at key points across the city. Writing in 1936, Gallacher argued that the protesters should have marched to Maryhill barracks on 'bloody Friday': 'If we had gone there we could easily have persuaded the soldiers to come out and Glasgow would have been in our hands.'[27] But what Gallacher and his comrades would have done after that is unclear, and on the day his actions were not those of a revolutionary since he was among the speakers who urged the strikers and their supporters to leave George Square.

Meanwhile, Harry McShane was in the thick of the action and, on

Figure 20.2 Tanks and soldiers brought in to quell the unrest in Glasgow in 1919 proceed along Trongate.

hearing that soldiers were being brought into the city, he went with other militants to Buchanan Street station in the hope of talking to them arriving from points north of Glasgow: 'I remember those young soldiers very well,' he wrote nearly half a century later:

> They were recruits with no experience and they were very aggressive; they had no knowledge of the labour movement or anything else and were quite prepared to use their weapons – one of them pointed to his rifle and said: 'This is better than bottles' [which had been used against the police earlier on]. The others and I tried to talk to them on the road down to George Square, and the officers kept trying to get between us. But there was no need: those young ones would have shot us down.[28]

Like Gallacher, he thought that the Maryhill barracks men might have acted differently 'because they were old soldiers who had been at the front and couldn't be relied upon to act against us'.[29] Many of the garrison were, however, members of the Highland Light Infantry (HLI), a regiment with a ferocious reputation, so these later thoughts are only conjecture.

The Scottish Secretary in Lloyd George's cabinet, Thomas McKinnon Wood, described the events in Glasgow as a 'Bolshevist uprising'.[30] It was never that and state power will always survive such situations for as long as police and troops carry out their orders. McShane was a realist and stressed that the forty-hour strike and the mass action it generated was best seen 'not as a revolution but as a beginning. Other things would follow.'[31] They did, with unions in the docks, railways and coalfields banding together in a new Triple Alliance and engineering workers striking again in 1922. The coalition government's Emergency Powers legislation of 1920 claimed that the main role for troops would be to replace key workers on strike rather than coercing them,[32] but in April 1921 a Fife newspaper compared Cowdenbeath to an armed camp as the Argylls moved in to back up the police.[33]

The civil power was alert for strike action and the military was well briefed too. This is clear from an account of the role of the 1st Argylls: 'Elaborate preparations to deal with such trouble had long been made by the military authorities and vast masses of orders of the most complicated and secret description were taken over from our Third Battalion.'[34] This account then slipped into flippancy as it described the unit's deployment to guard locations in Edinburgh: 'one captain became so fond of a certain gasworks that he was with great difficulty restrained from moving his family there from the Caledonian Hotel'.[35] The Highland Light Infantry were deployed to the coalfields of Bonnyrigg in Midlothian. Steel helmets were worn and ammunition carried, but in the words of the regimental history: 'The miners in no way resented their presence and seemed glad to have them around.'[36] Amity, or worse still, fraternisation between soldiers and strikers was a matter for concern to the authorities and a matter of interest to Moscow too. In August 1921 a Scottish Communist, Tom Bell, reported to Lenin that in Buckhaven and Methil in Fife soldiers had been openly sympathetic to striking miners, and that in Fallin in Stirlingshire officers had even confiscated live ammunition from their men as a precautionary measure.[37]

In 1926 Scottish troops, often young recruits in training, were put on full alert in response to the General Strike.[38] No major show of strength by the army in Scotland was called for, however, as the civil authorities had been well prepared and had powers to enrol non- and anti-union labour to operate, or try to, some essential services. In the main, Scottish regimental journals thus had very little to say about strike duties. The Royal Scots noted the regrettable need that had arisen to call off the monthly summer garden party which its officers hosted in Edinburgh.[39]

In the meantime, members of the Territorial Army were urged to join a Civil Constabulary Reserve (CCR) force, although recruitment to it only got under way after the strike had started.⁴⁰ One Royal Scots Territorial battalion began to recruit for this force on 12 May and raised the target number of men in one hour and thirty-five minutes, with many having to be turned away. The strike was called off before they were needed, however, and the battalion's account of its role for the regimental journal noted that

> Our training was hardly interrupted by the industrial trouble. Many strange faces entered our [sergeants'] Mess when the CCR was embodied. These valiant guardians of the law made their presence felt by twice drinking us out of stock and that's where we really felt the strike.⁴¹

The General Strike was a bitter episode and memories of it were long. The overbearing behaviour and violence that was remembered and resented, especially in the coalfields, was, however, that of the police rather than the army. What might have been asked of the latter had the stoppage lasted nine weeks, instead of nine days, is of course another matter. The strike was called in support of a living wage for miners, just that. Writing of it later, A. J. P. Taylor said of those who answered the TUC's call, 'These were the very men who had rallied to the defence of Belgium in 1914. The voluntary recruitment of the First World War and the strike of 1926 were acts of spontaneous generosity, without parallel in any country.'⁴² A coalfield lock-out dragged on for many months after the strike with worsening hardship and hunger for mining communities. Yet not much of this impinged upon Scottish regimental histories. They were mainly compiled by officers with little empathy for the cause of labour, even when the miners' struggle was taking place just a short distance from their depots and messes.

A much bigger test for the army than strikes on Clydeside and elsewhere was provided by events in Ireland, a country of which Scottish regiments had long memories. Some of them during the Curragh crisis of 1914 were thought by their officers to have loyalties that would make it hard for them to take part in any action to impose home rule on protestant Ulster. 'The whole of the Sergeants and Lance Sergeants, with the exception of three, are heart and soul with Ulster', a Royal Scots major wrote at the time to Andrew Bonar Law, the Conservative leader. 'I feel equally certain,' he continued, 'that the same feeling pervades the other ranks from Corporals to Privates.'⁴³ Some Scottish regiments did indeed develop quite stong Protestant traditions though this could never define their actual recruitment policy.⁴⁴

The Curragh crisis passed and the reaction within the army of

Figure 20.3 A King's Own Scottish Borderer closes the gates of the Royal Barracks in Dublin after the Bachelor's Walk shootings, 1914.

those who supported Loyal Ulster was in fact out of proportion to any real military plans drawn up by the Asquith government to enforce home rule, as events were to show. Four months later, however, soldiers of the 2nd King's Own Scottish Borderers (KOSB) opened lethal fire on an angry Dublin crowd taunting and stoning them on a quay by the Liffey known as Bachelor's Walk. During Sunday 26 July, a day of high excitement after the Irish volunteers had illegally brought a shipment of German weapons ashore at Howth harbour, a KOSB detachment that had been on duty at Clontarf was ordered back to Dublin and during their three-mile march they were harassed by triumphant nationalist crowds. A young Sean O'Casey was there and wrote later of the visible fear of some of the youngest KOSB privates who would soon be facing much greater ordeals.[45] Two men and a woman were killed by the volley they fired on Bachelor's Walk. Another victim died later and thirty-seven people were injured.

During an inquest, which ruled that the use of live rounds had not been justified, the entire 2nd battalion was confined to barracks in Dublin until its orders to mobilise for war came on 4 August.[46] The incident was not forgotten, however. In 1971 the KOSB found themselves on crowd-control duty in the New Lodge area of Belfast where republican wall graffiti greeted them as the 'King's Own Scottish Murderers'. The regiment, in republican eyes, lived up to its reputation by shooting dead Danny O'Hagan, the first petrol bomber to be killed by the army in the Troubles.

Other Scottish regiments felt the burden of the past weighing on them, like the Highland Light Infantry as they began operations in 1920 against the Irish Republican Army (IRA) in County Clare. Their predecessors had been there too, the former 74th Regiment of Foot before it was renamed. 'They recollected,' the modern HLI's historian noted, 'that the 74th were on constant active duty in County Clare in 1831 and that it did not appear to have changed very much in the interval.'[47]

As Ireland's post-war Troubles worsened, Scottish regiments were deployed there in 1920 and 1921, along with many others. Their role was the standard one of aiding the civil power against the IRA, but the August 1920 Restoration of Order in Ireland Act, while it enlarged the army's powers of search and arrest, fell well short of imposing martial law. Even when that was ultimately applied to eight of Ireland's most insurgent counties, police primacy was still stressed. 'The Irish job', in Lloyd George's view, 'was a policeman's job, supported by the military and not vice versa. So long as it becomes a military job only, it will fail.'[48]

This view, in London's eyes, justified reinforcing the Royal Irish Constabulary with ex-soldiers in police units like the Black and Tans and the much larger Auxiliary Division, which comprised mainly ex-officers. These two irregular formations have often been conflated in accounts of the Troubles, and Scots certainly served in them.[49] They vied with each other in their brutality and the discredit they brought on the crown forces came to convince some senior officers that the army should take over policing functions in their entirety.[50]

Lloyd George's government flinched from this, though it increased Britain's military presence. Army units were seldom guilty of the excesses of the Black and Tans and Auxiliaries but, even so, in Scotland John MacLean campaigned for the withdrawal of Scottish regiments from Ireland. 'My desire,' he told a Motherwell audience in 1921, 'is to prevent Scotsmen being used to smash our sister race, the Celts of Ireland.'[51] In fact only three Scottish regiments were used in Ireland but MacLean had hopes that they might follow the example of the Connaught Rangers, who had mutinied in India that same year.[52] This was never likely to happen and the Highland Light Infantry's historian describes its rank and file as 'more than willing to oblige anyone wishing to die for Old Ireland'.[53]

The 2nd battalion of the Queen's Own Cameron Highlanders did a tour of duty in the south-west of Ireland in 1920 and the published record of its service offers no hint of any rebel sympathies, or resulting disciplinary problems, in a unit with a large element of post-war recruits. On the contrary, the fatal casualties they suffered in IRA attacks and ambushes stiffened their resolve:

> These and other dastardly outrages naturally caused great resentment amongst the troops, and it was only the fine sense of discipline of the Cameron Highlanders and other regiments which protected these despicable ruffians from retaliation and reprisals.[54]

Raids on houses and arms searches were described as 'a duty which was not made more pleasant by the extremely dirty conditions under which the Irish live'.[55]

One Scottish soldier who served with the Argylls in Ireland at this time was John Cormack. He may already have been prejudiced against the Irish, but he later wrote of what he claimed was the treachery of the population, and of the collusion of priests with the IRA, as well as of their sexual degeneracy.[56] He remained proud of his army service and later became the leader of the militantly anti-Catholic Protestant Action movement in Edinburgh.

British troops, Scots among them, continued to garrison Northern Ireland after partition in 1920. They were called onto Belfast's streets during the communal violence of 1935 and their bases came under intermittent attack before and during the border campaign which the IRA launched in December 1956. Scottish regiments were not among those deployed in Londonderry and Belfast in August 1969 but they were on active duty the following year as the situation worsened and the army took over policing pending the reorganisation of the Royal Ulster Constabulary (RUC). This, along with the creation of the Ulster Defence Regiment (UDR) to replace the police reserve force, embodied the wishes back in 1920 of some British officers who had pressed for overall army control of security in Ireland.[57]

The Sinn Féin president, Gerry Adams, has claimed in his memoirs that Scottish troops, 'amongst whom support for Orange bigotry was strong',[58] contributed directly to rising antagonism to the army in nationalist areas. Scottish regiments were certainly on the streets as the violent spring and summer of 1970 got under way and the Royal Scots and the Black Watch were involved in the Lower Falls cordon and curfew operation in Belfast in early July. Accusations of sectarian abuse and violence were predictably made against them, though one former Royal Scots officer has made the point that at that time 40 per cent of the battalion were Catholics.[59]

Figure 20.4 The King's Own Scottish Borderers man a barrier at Unity Flats, Belfast, 1970.

The Ministry of Defence, in its report to mark the conclusion of operations in Northern Ireland, concluded that this Lower Falls operation was a limited tactical success but that 'it handed a significant information operations opportunity to the IRA, and this was exploited to the full'.[60] Another Royal Scots officer wrote in sombre terms of what had happened:

> We left a city with a deep wound of hatred and suspicion which has been there for many centuries, but it was thought it had at least closed, if not healed. Now again it is wide open and will take many years to close and heal again. For a soldier it was an experience of great sadness which none of us will ever forget.[61]

Allegations against Scottish regiments continued to be orchestrated throughout the Troubles by the republican movement's propaganda machine, but there need be little doubt that they often resorted to tough and brutal measures against the population in nationalist areas. On 10 December 1973 the Queen's Own Highlanders had eighteen-year-old Private James Hesketh shot dead by the IRA in the Lower Falls. He was a Catholic from Clydebank who had been in the city for just one week. 'Paddy bashing took off for the next few days,' a former sergeant recalled:

> Our patrols would lie in wait at night outside the church youth clubs and discos for when the boys came out and they got the shite beaten out of them. You can get a fair head butt in with your helmet on and its visor down.[62]

In what was sometimes called a 'corporals' war' because of their key role in four-man infantry patrols or 'bricks', non-commissioned officers could act to stop abuse of the nationalist population. One former sergeant in the Argylls has spoken of this in his unit:

> As a battalion with heavy recruitment from the Glasgow area we were at times half and half Catholic and Protestant. Some boys were all the way Orange in sympathy and on house searches they'd mouth off about Fenian bastards. I'm a Catholic so I wouldn't take it, even when I was a private. I once hit a corporal over it, I chinned him on the spot and I talked myself out of a charge over it. There was no officer there but for most of them that stuff was way outside their own experience.[63]

The same former sergeant recalled the hold his upbringing had on him and the dilemmas it created:

> All my pals early on were for the Provos. I was home on leave in 1982 and some of them wanted me to go with them to a memorial event in honour of Bobby Sands. I didn't of course. I'd changed, they hadn't. Still, it began to worry me on later tours that here were people like me who were protecting the IRA, safe houses, observation, all that, helping them to kill us. The question in the back of my mind began to be, why am I here? My answer had to be, it's my job, I'm a soldier.[64]

'We were heavy-handed in 1971 and 1972,' a former KOSB sergeant admitted:

> We often went in too hard, but then we were taking casualties, boys were being killed. Ten years later I remember thinking that six-year-olds who had seen us dragging their brothers past a door we'd just kicked in were probably in the IRA themselves.[65]

Scots, of course, served in other units like the Royal Marines and the Parachute regiment and absorbed much of their ethos. One former Royal Marine commando did a tour of duty in West Belfast in 1981, the year of the republican H-Block hunger strikes:

Beating people up for the hell of it was a nightly occurrence. At the time I've got to say that I wasn't too unhappy about it. The fact that people were starving themselves to death in prison for a cause just didn't bother me. The trouble was that nothing in our training taught us to think of it as a political or moral problem.[66]

No Scottish regiment was involved in any operation that had as big a political fall-out as that of 'Bloody Sunday' in Londonderry on 30 January 1972, though Scots were part of the Parachute regiment's 1st battalion support company whose arrest operation on the day of a civil rights march went disastrously wrong. However, two sergeants of the Argylls were the first soldiers to be convicted of murder in the Troubles. In January 1981 a Belfast court gave them life sentences for murders committed more than eight years previously. A lance-corporal was found guilty of the lesser charge of manslaughter and a captain was given a one-year suspended sentence for concealing information about a crime. The case was a gruesome one, involving the frenzied and repeated use of a knife at a lonely farm near Newtonbutler in County Tyrone to kill a farmer and a simple-minded labourer, neither with any known IRA connections. Eight Argylls had already been killed in the area and this was advanced as a mitigating factor in an acrimonious correspondence about the case in one of Scotland's national newspapers.[67]

Scottish regiments took their fair share of deaths and serious injuries as the IRA stepped up its war of indiscriminate terror, and they also took their share of cleaning up after no-warning bomb attacks. Every unit and every soldier was exposed to regular provocation and abuse in nationalist areas, often from crowds gathered to give cover to IRA snipers. There could be similar provocation in Loyalist areas too, more often than many republican versions of the Troubles allow for. 'They could, when their blood was up, be even more antagonistic than nationalist people,' recalled the former KOSB sergeant. 'I suppose they thought of us as their army and that we shouldn't be used against them.'[68]

This was certainly the case during the vicious Loyalist blockade in 2001 to prevent Catholic girl pupils entering Holy Cross Primary School just inside the Protestant enclave of Ardoyne in North Belfast. The author of this chapter witnessed some of the Holy Cross blockade and heard from young Scots Guardsmen how shocked they were by what they had seen. They, as well as the Argylls,[69] risked their lives on a daily basis, sometimes under blast bomb attack, to keep the school open and get the children safely into it. There was never any

Figure 20.5 Soldiers of the 1st battalion, the Argyll and Sutherland Highlanders, man a barricade of Saxon armoured vehicles at the bottom of the Ardoyne Road during the sectarian stand-off at Holy Cross Primary School, Belfast, 2001.

acknowledgement of this from Sinn Féin spokesmen like Gerry Kelly, who was often on the scene to talk to the world's media.

By 1977 police primacy in security had been restored to Northern Ireland and the troops' role, as it had been initially in 1969, was to provide back-up and support for a retrained and much enlarged RUC, as well as to the UDR, though the latter's locally recruited units operated as an integral part of the army. Some Scots were seconded to it, sometimes for extended tours of duty. Others were recruited to special undercover units which drew much of their rationale from Brigadier (as he then was) Frank Kitson's 1970 book on counterinsurgency operations.[70] In this he had made the case for the army to win the intelligence war against terrorist organisations by infiltrating them and running agents within their structures.

This soon came to mean in practice running informers and agents within Loyalist paramilitary organisations like the Ulster Defence Association (UDA). One Scottish officer, Lieutenant-Colonel Gordon Kerr of the Gordon Highlanders, played a leading role in the work of the army's Force Research Unit (FRU). One of its key agents was Brian Nelson, who had served for a time in the Black Watch and later became the UDA's chief intelligence officer, feeding it information on targets for assassination within the nationalist community. Many of the victims were innocent of IRA involvement and Nelson's arrest in 1990 by the RUC was an acute embarrassment to the army, though it also posed questions as to whether police and army intelligence work was as highly integrated as republicans claimed.

Kerr's testimony at Nelson's trial in 1990, claiming that the defendant's regular briefing of the FRU about UDA operational plans had saved Catholic lives, certainly secured the latter a relatively lenient sentence. As a serving officer, Kerr's identity was concealed at the time but ten years later a Scottish newspaper named him as 'The Scot Behind Ulster's Dirty War'[71] and disputed his court version of his work with the FRU between 1987 and 1991. Claims about the level of army and police collusion with Loyalists have become a growth industry within the literature of the Troubles. They tend to rest on the assumption that Loyalists were incapable of operating on their own account against the IRA and the community that sustained it. Indeed if the levels of collusion claimed had been true, it is hard to see how the IRA could have survived at all.

The IRA did, of course, survive, despite itself being infiltrated to its highest levels by British intelligence. Yet by the year of its ceasefire, 1994, it was losing its war. Outside border areas its success rate against the security forces had become minimal and the Derry brigade had killed no soldiers since 1990. Even so, there were Scots who served in the worst of the Troubles who were prepared to accord some grudging respect to the IRA and its volunteers. One of them was a very senior KOSB officer, who agreed to talk about the IRA's military quality well ahead of the ceasefire. He drew something of a distinction between its rural and urban units, having himself served in border areas: 'I can actually identify with them as a soldier because, within the limits of their training, they operate with military skill. They know the ground and they use good fieldcraft.'[72] He spoke of Francis Hughes from Bellaghy in South Derry, who died on hunger strike in 1981, describing him as

> a real soldier and a skilled guerrilla. There's no question about that, he was capable of living rough for days and weeks at a time. He was a hard bastard of course and many of his victims were Protestant farmers or farm workers around his home in Bellaghy or across the Tyrone border, off-duty UDR men or RUC reservists there for the taking.[73]

A former sergeant in the Argylls agreed with him:

> We had to respect them, not for their cause, but what they were capable of. A lot of them were good and they got better but we had the training to win the shooting war. I think we did that quite early on but they could adapt, mortars, rocket-propelled grenades, all that came our way and of course car bombs. They never gave up on them. Omagh in August 1998 proved that. The ones who set it off had all learned the business with the Provos.[74]

Margaret Thatcher, when prime minister, was reluctant to use the word 'war' to describe the army's role in Northern Ireland, for fear it might ascribe some sort of legitimacy to the IRA. To this day, the republican movement demands that Britain should accept the word.[75] Some Scots who served in the Troubles still avoid the term because, they argue, conventional military outcomes remained outwith the army's reach. 'Did we win?', one former Royal Marines officer asked himself:

> I don't think it was ever about destroying the IRA or the other paramilitaries. We held the ring until constitutional politics could take over. We reduced violence to an acceptable level. Yes, I'll risk using that phrase. My view was that we were there to uphold the law. If we didn't we would have ended up no better than the IRA. Would we ever have followed the road the French took in Algeria? No, never.[76]

All armies who serve democracies are liable to be called upon to give aid to the civil power and Scots have played their part in doing this. They would still have to in any army formed in the future by a sovereign Scottish state. Over the course of the century covered here in outline Scottish soldiers on both sides of the Irish Sea were deployed in situations that could have severely tested their loyalties, and sometimes did, but a breaking point never came, not even during the army's longest commitment in Northern Ireland. Yet for many present and former Scottish soldiers of all ranks who served there, sometimes when very young, memories remain vivid and can be disturbing. Perhaps the final words here should be given to one of them:

> When I've had a few drinks, it all starts crawling back into my brain and I think, God Almighty, was that what really happened? Did I actually do things like that? Was there a different way without hurting people too much? It's too late for me to do anything about it now that I'm out of the army but at least I took no lives. That would have troubled me for a very long time. I might have killed in self-defence but never just for the hell of it. Conscience would have held me back before I pulled the trigger on someone put on this earth for a reason.[77]

Notes

My special thanks are due to Stuart Allan and his colleagues in the library of the National War Museum of Scotland at Edinburgh castle, and to the staff of the National Library of Scotland; in the preparation of this chapter their help has been indispensable. I am also deeply indebted to former members of Scottish regiments, and other units, who were willing to talk to me about their service in Northern Ireland, and to the regimental associations of the Royal Scots, the King's Own Scottish Borderers, the Argyll and Sutherland Highlanders and the Royal Highland Fusiliers for permission to use material from their journals.

1. A. Somerville, *The Autobiography of a Working Man* (London: Charles Gilpin, 1848), p. 277.
2. Ibid. p. 290.
3. Ibid. p. 248.
4. J. O. Baylen and N. J. Gossman (eds), *Biographical Dictionary of Modern British Radicals, vol. 2, 1830–1870* (Brighton: Harvester Press, 1984), pp. 470–4.
5. A. Babington, *Military Intervention in Britain: From the Gordon Riots to the Gibraltar Incident* (London: Routledge, 1990), pp. 5–6; K. Logue, *Popular Disturbances in Scotland 1780–1815* (Edinburgh: John Donald, 1979), passim.
6. W. Kenefick and A. McIvor, *Roots of Red Clydeside 1910–1914?* (Edinburgh: John Donald, 1996), pp. 1–18.
7. R. Page Arnot, *The Scottish Miners* (London: George Allen and Unwin, 1953), pp. 128–9.
8. J. Connell, *Wavell: Scholar and Soldier* (London: Collins, 1964), p. 85.
9. V. G. Kiernan, 'Conscription and society in Europe before the war of 1914', in M. R. D. Foot (ed.), *Historical Essays in Honour and Memory of J. R. Western 1928–1971* (London: Paul Elek, 1973), p. 141.
10. R. D. Challener, *The French Theory of the Nation in Arms 1866–1939* (New York: Columbia University Press, 1955), p. 39.
11. E. Weber, *Peasants into Frenchmen: The Modernisation of Rural France 1870–1914* (London: Chatto and Windus, 1979), pp. 292–303.
12. K. Demeter, *The German Officer Corps in Society and State 1650–1945* (London: Weidenfeld and Nicolson, 1962), pp. 339–40.
13. Challener, *The French Theory*, pp. 71–4.
14. T. Royle, *The Kitchener Enigma* (London: Michael Joseph, 1985), pp. 262–3.
15. A. G. Gardiner, *Pillars of Society* (London and Toronto: J. M. Dent & Sons, 1913), p. 333.
16. J. Alexander, *McCrae's Battalion: The Story of the 16th Royal Scots* (Edinburgh: Mainstream Publishing, 2003), p. 51.

17. I. S. Wood, *John Wheatley* (Manchester: Manchester University Press, 1990), p. 50.
18. H. McShane and J. Smith, *Harry McShane: No Mean Fighter* (London: Pluto Press, 1978), p. 67.
19. Ibid. p. 69.
20. G. Urquhart, 'Confrontation and withdrawal: Loos, readership and the "First Hundred Thousand"', in C. M. M. Macdonald and E. W. McFarland (eds), *Scotland and the Great War* (East Linton: Tuckwell Press, 1999), pp. 125–44.
21. I. Hay, *The First Hundred Thousand: Being the Unofficial Chronicle of a Unit of 'K(1)'* (Edinburgh: William Blackwood, 1915), pp. 19–20.
22. Ibid. p. 326.
23. Ibid. p. 310.
24. J. Buchan, *Mr Standfast* (Edinburgh: Thomas Nelson & Sons, 1919), pp. 99–102.
25. I. Hay, *Carrying On: After the First Hundred Thousand* (Edinburgh: William Blackwood, 1917), pp. 311–12.
26. C. Harvie, *No Gods and Precious Few Heroes: Scotland Since 1914* (London: Edward Arnold, 1981), p. 22.
27. W. Gallacher, *Revolt on the Clyde* (London: Lawrence and Wishart, 1936), pp. 233–4.
28. McShane and Smith, *Harry McShane*, p. 107.
29. Ibid. p. 108.
30. I. McLean, *The Legend of Red Clydeside* (Edinburgh: John Donald, 1983), p. 125.
31. McShane and Smith, *Harry McShane*, p. 109.
32. C. Townshend, *Britain's Civil Wars: Counterinsurgency in the Twentieth Century* (London: Faber and Faber, 1986), pp. 44–5.
33. Page Arnot, *The Scottish Miners*, p. 158.
34. 'The railway strike', *Argyll and Sutherland Highlanders Journal*, vol. 1, March 1921, p. 39.
35. Ibid. p. 39.
36. L. B. Oatts, *Proud Heritage: The Story of the Highland Light Infantry, Volume 4, The Regular and Service Battalions HLI and the HLI of Canada* (Glasgow and London: House of Grant, 1963), p. 31.
37. T. Bell, *Pioneering Days* (London: Lawrence and Wishart, 1941), p. 223. See also W. Kenefick, *Red Scotland: The Rise and Fall of the Radical Left c. 1872–1932* (Edinburgh: Edinburgh University Press, 2007), p. 165.
38. I. McDougall, 'Some aspects of the General Strike in Scotland', in I. McDougall (ed.), *Essays in Scottish Labour History: A Tribute to W. H. Marwick* (Edinburgh: John Donald, 1978), pp. 186–7.

39. 'Depot notes: General', *The Thistle: The Quarterly Journal of the Royal Scots (The Royal Regiment)*, vol. 2, no. 1 (July 1926), p. 16.
40. M. Stewart, *The General Strike* (London: Penguin, 1978), p. 256.
41. 'Sergeants' mess', *The Thistle*, vol. 2, no. 1 (July 1926), p. 19.
42. A. J. P. Taylor, *English History 1914–1945* (Oxford: Oxford University Press, 1965), p. 244.
43. I. F. W. Beckett, *The Army and the Curragh Incident* (London: Bodley Head, 1981), pp. 124–5.
44. I. S. Wood, 'Protestantism and Scottish military tradition', in G. Walker and T. Gallagher (eds), *Sermons and Battle Hymns: Protestant Popular Culture in Modern Scotland* (Edinburgh: Edinburgh University Press, 1990), pp. 112–36.
45. S. O'Casey, *Drums Under the Windows* (London: Macmillan, 1945), pp. 309–11.
46. R. Woollcombe, *All the Blue Bonnets: The History of the King's Own Scottish Borderers* (London: Arms and Armour Press, 1980), pp. 99–100.
47. Oatts, *Proud Heritage*, p. 24.
48. T. Jones, *Whitehall Diary*, 3 vols (Oxford: Oxford University Press, 1971), vol. 3, p. 73.
49. W. J. Lowe, 'Who were the Black and Tans?', *History Ireland*, vol. 12, no. 3 (Autumn 2004), pp. 47–51.
50. F. P. Crozier, *Impressions and Recollections* (London: T. Warner Laurie, 1930), pp. 254–5 and *Ireland For Ever* (Bath: Cedric Chivers, 1932), pp. 181–4.
51. N. Milton, *John MacLean* (London: Pluto Press, 1973), p. 240. See also G. Foster, 'Scotsmen, stand by Ireland: John MacLean and the Irish Revolution', *History Ireland*, vol. 16, no. 1 (January/February 2008), pp. 32–7.
52. S. Pollock, *Mutiny for the Cause* (London: Leo Cooper, 1969), passim.
53. Oatts, *Proud Heritage*, p. 32.
54. *Historical Records of the Queen's Own Cameron Highlanders*, 7 vols (Edinburgh: William Blackwood, 1909–1975), vol. 4, p. 416.
55. Ibid. p. 416.
56. T. Gallagher, *Edinburgh Divided: John Cormack and No Popery in the 1930s* (Edinburgh: Polygon, 1987), pp. 20–1.
57. C. Townshend, *Political Violence in Ireland: Government and Resistance Since 1848* (Oxford: Oxford University Press, 1983), p. 388.
58. G. Adams, *Before the Dawn: An Autobiography* (London: Heinemann, 1996), pp. 136–7.
59. Former lieutenant, Royal Scots, interview with author, 20 June 1989.
60. Ministry of Defence, *Operation Banner: An Analysis of Military Operations in Northern Ireland* (London: Ministry of Defence, 2006), para 217.

61. 'Emergency tour in Belfast', *The Thistle: The Journal of the Royal Scots (The Royal Regiment)*, vol. 14, no. 1 (1970), p. 22.
62. Former sergeant, Queen's Own Highlanders, interview with author, 13 August 1989.
63. Former sergeant, Argyll and Sutherland Highlanders, interview with author, 8 September 2007.
64. Ibid.
65. Former sergeant, King's Own Scottish Borderers, interview with author, 4 July 2007.
66. Former Royal Marine of 45 Commando, interview with author, 26 June 1986.
67. *The Scotsman*, 16 January 1981, p. 13; ibid. 20 January 1981, p. 10; ibid. 23 January 1981, p. 10.
68. Former sergeant, King's Own Scottish Borderers, interview with author, 4 July 2007.
69. *Thin Red Line: Regimental Magazine of the Argyll & Sutherland Highlanders (Princess Louise's)*, vol. 60, no. 1 (Spring 2002), pp. 34–6.
70. F. Kitson, *Low Intensity Operations: Subversion, Insurgency, Peace-Keeping* (London: Faber and Faber, 1971), passim.
71. *Sunday Herald*, 19 November 2000, pp. 1, 4. See also I. S. Wood, *Crimes of Loyalty: A History of the UDA* (Edinburgh University Press, 2006), pp. 160–1.
72. Senior officer, King's Own Scottish Borderers, interview with author, 16 May 1989.
73. Ibid.
74. Former sergeant, Argyll and Sutherland Highlanders, interview with author, 8 September 2007.
75. *An Phoblacht/Sinn Féin Weekly*, 10 January 2008, p. 5.
76. Former senior officer, 45 Royal Marine Commando, interview with author, 19 July 2007.
77. Former private, Royal Scots, interview with author, 18 February 1991. The story of Scottish soldiers in Northern Ireland has been discussed at chapter length by the author. See I. S. Wood, 'Thin red line? Scottish soldiers in the Troubles in Scotland and Ulster', in I. S. Wood (ed.), *Scotland and Ulster* (Edinburgh: Mercat Press, 1994), pp 150–71.

21
The Second World War

JEREMY A. CRANG

At noon on Monday, 16 October 1939 twelve German Junkers Ju-88 bombers took off from the island of Sylt and flew in loose formation over the North Sea to attack the Scottish naval base at Rosyth. The Spitfires of 603 (City of Edinburgh) squadron and 602 (City of Glasgow) squadron were ordered to intercept them. In combat over the Firth of Forth, Flight Lieutenant Patrick Gifford of 603 destroyed one enemy bomber and Flight Lieutenant George Pinkerton and Flying Officer Archie McKellar of 602 shared in the destruction of another. Although there was some rivalry as to which pilot had achieved the initial 'kill' – former Edinburgh University law student and Castle Douglas solicitor 'Patsy' Gifford was given official credit by the RAF authorities – these Scottish auxiliary squadrons accounted for the first German aircraft to be shot down over mainland Britain during the war. It marked an early victory in a long and bitter conflict in which Scotland was once again to play a significant role in the British military war effort.[1]

War production and supply

Scotland made a notable contribution to war production. Not only did heavy industry provide coal, iron, steel and ships for the war effort – with over a quarter of Britain's wartime shipbuilding taking place on the River Clyde – but also a host of factories manufactured arms and equipment for the forces. The Singer sewing machine factory at Clydebank, for example, produced 15,000 tank tracks, 60,000 rifle components, 250,000 sten guns, 1.25 million bayonets and 125 million bullets during the war. The Rolls-Royce plant at Hillington turned out 50,000 Merlin engines. The Barr & Stroud works at Anniesland supplied 27,000 field range finders. The Ferranti premises at Crewe

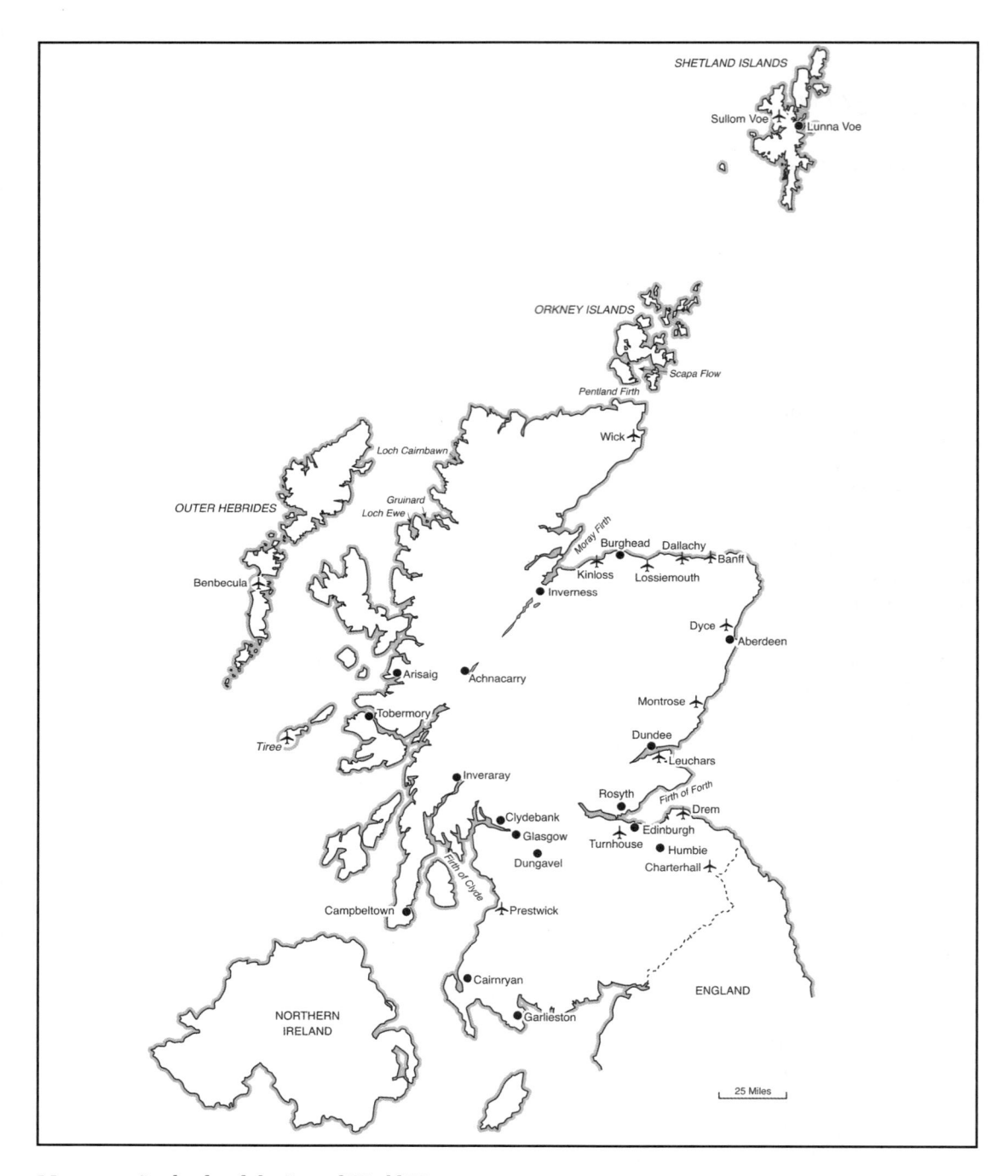

Map 21.1 Scotland and the Second World War.

Figure 21.1 The Singer sewing machine factory, Clydebank, in the 1930s.

Toll in Edinburgh furnished 10,000 gyro gun sights.[2] By 1942, 460,000 Scots, which was about a third of the workforce north of the border, were employed in the munitions industries.[3]

Among the most celebrated Scottish wartime military engineering projects were the Mulberry harbours: the artificial anchorages towed across the channel to aid the D-Day landings in 1944. The trials of several prototypes took place at Garlieston and eighteen of the twenty-three pierheads were built in Scotland under the supervision of Alexander Findlay & Co., a firm of bridge builders based in Motherwell. Of these eighteen structures, each comprising over 1,000 tons of welded steel, thirteen were assembled at Leith and four at Cairnryan.[4]

The country also became a vital supply hub. German control of the European coastline from the Baltic to the Bay of Biscay, and the heavy bombing of ports in England, heightened the strategic importance of the Clyde in maintaining Britain's Atlantic lifeline.[5] Fifty-two million tons of supplies and 2.4 million military personnel were landed along the river during the war.[6] The west coast of Scotland was a key air bridge too. Prestwick airfield served as the main UK terminal for aircraft flown across the Atlantic from factories in North America. Some 37,000 such aircraft had been delivered through this gateway by the end of the conflict.[7]

Home defence

Scotland played its part in home defence. After the fall of France and the Low Countries in 1940 the main invasion threat was to the south of England, but the German occupation of Denmark and Norway raised the possibility of a landing north of the border.[8] In order to counter this, records indicate that 113 Scottish beaches were protected by anti-invasion defences and, inland, 33 linear defence systems and 108 nodal defence points were established. The defence scheme for Edinburgh incorporated outer perimeter defences (the black line), main defences (the blue line) and inner defences (the red line). Each line was organised in depth and comprised a series of defended posts and localities.[9]

At the height of the invasion threat in 1940, approximately 181,000 British troops were located in Scottish Command. Of these, 33,000 were based in the Edinburgh area; 32,000 in the Glasgow area; 48,000 in the south Highland area; 36,000 in the north Highland area; 19,000 in Orkney and Shetland; and 13,000 in various 'non-regimental' stations.[10] Alongside the army, 169,000 members of the Home Guard stood ready to assist in the event of a landing. These included 28,000 in the Edinburgh area; 79,000 in the Glasgow area; 33,000 in the south Highland area; 27,000 in the north Highland area; and 2,000 in Orkney and Shetland.[11] In the Highlands many of these 'Dad's Army' volunteers were crofters, stalkers and ghillies who knew every inch of the ground. It was said that they could detect the presence of unseen German paratroopers by the movement of deer or grouse, and were able to communicate with one another by playing a code on the bagpipes, the sound of which travelled ten miles down the glen if the wind was in the right direction.[12]

During 1941 the prospect of invasion receded but vigilance had to be maintained. One German who did arrive in Scotland uninvited during this period was none other than the Deputy Führer, Rudolf Hess. On 10 May he set off from Augsburg in a long-range Messerschmitt Bf 110 on a secret freelance peace mission to Dungavel House in Lanarkshire, the residence of the duke of Hamilton. With the attack on the Soviet Union imminent, it seems that he hoped to enlist the help of the duke in negotiating an end to British hostilities with Germany in order to avoid a two-front war. Hess failed to land at Dungavel and was forced to bail out near Eaglesham in Renfrewshire, where he was swiftly apprehended by a local ploughman and escorted to Maryhill barracks in Glasgow. The British government then maintained official silence over this mysterious affair as part of a disinformation campaign to unnerve the Germans and create anxiety in the Soviet Union about German intentions.[13]

Training ground

The relative remoteness of Scotland from the preying eyes of the Germans, and the rugged and sparsely populated nature of much of the Highlands, made it a valuable training ground, especially for irregular units. The country north-west of the Great Glen was designated a protected area, which prohibited unauthorised access, and it was in this isolated location that in 1940 the Special Operations Executive (SOE) set up a network of training schools around Arisaig House to instruct its agents in the techniques of sabotage.[14] The commandos were also active in the region. In 1942 they established a basic training depot at Achnacarry House – the seat of Cameron of Lochiel, one of Prince Charles's leading supporters during the 1745 rebellion – where recruits were subjected to the notorious 'Tarzan course', 'toggle bridge' and 'death slide'. When a fire broke out at Achnacarry in 1943 as a result of a faulty boiler, the Cameron family wryly commented that it was the second time the British army had set light to their home, the previous occasion being in 1746. The following day the local postmistress refused to sell stamps to the English commandos because of their supposed repetition of this wicked act.[15]

Meanwhile, more conventional forces trained in Scotland in preparation for offensive operations overseas. The 51st (Highland) Division, for example, was put through its paces in Morayshire, Banffshire and Aberdeenshire before being sent to the Middle East in 1942.[16] It was replaced in the area by the 52nd (Lowland) Division, which carried out mountain warfare training in the Cairngorms – in anticipation of a possible strike on Norway – before being ordered to north-west Europe in 1944.[17] The British 3rd Division prepared for its D-Day assault on Sword beach north of the border. After amphibious instruction at the combined operations training centre at Inveraray, it moved to the Moray Firth where it conducted 'wetshod' invasion exercises during the winter of 1943–4. The Morayshire coast substituted for Normandy and the division splashed ashore at Burghead: the understudy for Ouistreham.[18] Overall, the number of British troops quartered in Scottish Command rose to a peak of 251,000 in 1942, fell back to 156,000 in 1943, increased again to 173,000 in 1944 and then declined to 82,000 by the end of the war in Europe.[19]

Various foreign contingents were also accommodated in Scotland

Figure 21.2 Commandos training at Achnacarry, 1943.

after the Germans overran their homelands. The largest group was the Poles. They arrived in 1940 and were soon deployed in Fife, Perthshire and Angus. In 1941 the 1st Independent Polish Parachute Brigade was formed and the following year the 1st Polish Armoured Division. Scottish symbols such as thistles and lions rampant were incorporated into Polish badges and some units even organised pipe bands. By 1943, 23,000 Polish troops were located in Scottish Command. After the war many decided to make the country their home.[20]

Naval operations

Scotland was an important centre of Royal Navy operations. Scapa Flow served as the main wartime base for the British home fleet. Although the warships were forced temporarily to abandon this anchorage in the early months of the war after a German U-boat crept undetected into the Flow on the night of 13–14 October 1939 and sank HMS *Royal Oak* with the loss of over 800 lives, its strategic position on the Pentland Firth, and the fact that it was considered less vulnerable to German bombing and mining, gave it the edge over Rosyth. On the west coast there were additional naval facilities on the Clyde, and at Loch Ewe, as well as a host of naval training establishments such as the Asdic school at Campbeltown and the convoy escort school at Tobermory. By 1942 there were twenty-nine naval bases of one type or another in Scotland, which represented over a quarter of all the Royal Navy bases around the world.[21]

The fleet patrolled off the north coast of Scotland in the hope of intercepting German surface raiders breaking out from the North Sea into the Atlantic to attack the convoys on which Britain depended. In May 1941 the pride of the German navy, the *Bismarck*, left her Norwegian fjord on such a mission. HMS *Hood* and HMS *Prince of Wales* were despatched from Scapa Flow to intercept her and they engaged the powerful German battleship in the Denmark Strait. The *Hood* was sunk and the *Prince of Wales* hit and forced to break off the attack but the *Bismarck*'s fuel tanks were damaged in the confrontation. This forced her to abort the mission and head for the French Atlantic coast to undertake repairs. Three days later she was sunk by the Royal Navy 600 miles west of Brest.[22]

Escort duty was a further task for naval forces in Scotland. Clyde warships met inward bound Atlantic convoys and accompanied those that were outward bound for the first stage of their voyage. For example, 2.1 million servicemen departed for overseas in troopships sailing from the Clyde.[23] Meanwhile, Loch Ewe became the chief UK assembly point for the Arctic convoys and Scottish-based naval escorts battled their way to northern Russia with the merchantmen. In April 1942 HMS *Edinburgh* – the fifth Royal Navy warship since the Act of Union in 1707 to bear the name of Scotland's capital – departed from Scapa Flow to escort convoy PQ14 on the perilous 2,000-mile passage to Murmansk. On her return journey with QP11 she was crippled by U-boat torpedoes and went down in the Barents Sea. In the ship's bomb room were ammunition boxes containing five tons of gold bullion: a down payment from the Soviet Union for its war supplies. In 1981 Stalin's gold, estimated to be worth £45 million, was recovered from the wreck and the treasure divided up between the salvage company and the British and Soviet governments.[24]

Naval strikes on German navy assets in Norway were also launched from Scotland. On 11–12 September 1943 a force of midget submarines, or X-craft, left Loch Cairnbawn to attack the *Tirpitz* – the sister ship of the *Bismarck* – which was anchored at Kåfjord. After being towed across the North Sea for eight days by conventional submarines, the X-craft were released by their 'parent' vessels when in range of the target. X-6 and X-7 managed to penetrate the fjord and lay explosive charges under the *Tirpitz*. These seriously damaged the ship's main turbines and put her out of action for several months. For his gallantry during this daring attack, the commander of X-6, Lieutenant Donald Cameron from Carluke, was awarded the Victoria Cross (VC).[25]

Air operations

There was a good deal of RAF activity in Scotland. Air operations were conducted from various air bases around the country. These included Prestwick, Tiree, Benbecula, Sullom Voe, Wick, Lossiemouth, Dallachy, Banff, Dyce, Montrose, Leuchars, Turnhouse and Drem. There were also a number of operational training units, such as 19 OTU at Kinloss and 54 OTU at Charterhall – the latter earning the sombre nickname of 'Slaughterhall' because of the number of fatal accidents among the trainees there. By 1945 there were ninety-five military airfields north of the border.[26]

Scotland's fighter squadrons saw a fair amount of action during the early months of the war as they defended the country against air attack. Apart from their exploits on 16 October 1939, 602 and 603 squadrons, based at Drem and Turnhouse respectively, shot down the first German aircraft to crash on mainland Britain (as opposed to landing in the sea). This was a Heinkel He-111 which fell to earth near Humbie on 28 October. Thereafter they were involved in a series of engagements with enemy intruders over the east coast. Such was the ferocity of the air defences around the Firth of Forth that the German pilots were said to have christened it 'suicide alley'.[27]

During the Battle of Britain 602 and 603 squadrons were ordered to airfields in the south of England to help meet the German onslaught and both scored highly. Indeed, it has been calculated that 603, under the command of Squadron Leader George Denholm from Bo'ness, was the top scoring squadron in the battle.[28] Although by the summer of 1940 it no longer consisted exclusively of Scots, 'Uncle George', as he was affectionately known, would serve his pilots Drambuie, rather than port, after dinner to remind them of 603's Scottish identity.[29] Scots were also prominent among the aircrew of other fighter squadrons that took part in this epic encounter. Archie McKellar, who had transferred from 602 to 615 (County of Warwick) squadron, became one of the top aces of the battle. The Paisley-born

Figure 21.3 The Heinkel He-111 shot down near Humbie, East Lothian, on 28 October 1939.

Hurricane pilot destroyed seventeen German aircraft – including five in a single day – before being killed in November 1940 whilst trying to make a forced landing at Adisham in Kent.[30] Another Scottish ace, Pilot Officer Wallace Cunningham from Govan, flew Spitfires with 19 squadron during the battle. Later in the war, whilst a POW in Stalag Luft III, he spent many hours jumping over a vaulting horse in order to assist in the renowned 'wooden horse' escape.[31]

Although Scotland avoided the worst of the Blitz, the west of the country did experience large-scale air raids. During the clear moonlit nights of 13–14 and 14–15 March 1941, German bombers mounted devastating attacks on Glasgow and Clydeside. On the first night, 236 raiders dropped 272 tons of high explosive bombs and 1,650 incendiary canisters; on the second, 203 aircraft returned to deliver 231 tons of bombs and 782 incendiaries. Over 1,200 people were killed in these raids. In Clydebank, which was badly mauled by the bombing, two-thirds of the town's 12,000 houses were destroyed or seriously damaged and 25,000 inhabitants left homeless. It is thought that 528 'Bankies' perished in the maelstrom.[32]

As the war went on German raids on Scotland became more sporadic and the focus of activity switched to the Coastal Command squadrons stationed north of the border. They flew sorties against German merchant ships and their escorts in Norwegian waters. In 1944 a strike wing was established at Banff to carry out such missions. The members of this wing included 333 (Norwegian) squadron. Its Mosquito pilots became an invaluable pathfinder force in the search for targets along their homeland's indented coastline.[33] German U-boats out in the Atlantic were hunted down too. On 17 July 1944 Flying Officer John Cruickshank, an Aberdonian Catalina pilot with Coastal Command's 210 squadron, took off from Sullom Voe on an anti-submarine patrol. Six hundred miles north of Shetland a U-boat was spotted on the surface. Despite being seriously wounded by anti-aircraft fire from the submarine, Cruickshank pressed home his attack with depth charges and sank the vessel. He then helped his surviving crew bring the damaged Catalina safely back to base after slipping in and out of consciousness during the five-hour return flight. When the medical team examined him he had seventy-two wounds on his body and required an urgent blood transfusion in order to survive. A few weeks later King George VI presented Cruickshank with the VC at Holyrood Palace.[34]

Bomber Command squadrons also utilised Scotland as a forward operating base for attacks on Norway. On 12 November 1944 a force of Lancasters from 9 and 617 (Dambuster) squadrons left Lossiemouth for Tromsø. Their objective was the *Tirpitz*. Over the anchorage the ship's fighter protection was mysteriously absent and the attacking aircraft were able to straddle her with 12,000-lb 'Tallboy' bombs. Two of these bombs penetrated the armoured deck and – this time – she capsized and sank. Among the Lancaster pilots who took part in the raid was Flying Officer Donald Macintosh of 9 squadron. In March 1941 he had been a young police telephonist in Clydebank during the Blitz.[35]

Clandestine operations

Scotland played a prominent part in the 'cloak and dagger' war. Commando raids were mounted from Scapa Flow against German installations in Norway. In December 1941 a force drawn from Nos 2 and 3 Commando was despatched to Vågsøy with the aim of destroying fish oil factories (the glycerine from which was used in munitions production) and eliminating the enemy garrison. Major John Churchill of 3 Commando was second-in-command of the raiding party. Although he hailed from an old Oxfordshire family, 'Mad Jack', as he was nicknamed by his men, had a passion for the Scottish way in warfare. Like a latter-day Rob Roy, he played the 'March of the Cameron Men' on his bagpipes as the landing craft approached the beach and led his commandos ashore armed with a claymore.[36]

Secret agents were infiltrated into Norway via Scotland. In July 1941 a fleet of Norwegian fishing boats was assembled at Lunna Voe on Shetland to ferry SOE and Secret Intelligence Service (SIS) operatives across the North Sea. The 'Shetland bus', as the flotilla became known, was crewed by Norwegian civilian volunteers who used their local knowledge to steal into the fjords in order to land and, when necessary, retrieve agents. Personnel from the two covert organisations even shared the same 'bus'. In February 1942 the *Arthur* sailed to Trøndelag with one SIS man, Bjørn Rørholt, and two SOE men, Arthur Pevik and Odd Sørli, on board.[37]

Scotland became a major element in the deception campaign for the D-Day landings. 'Operation Fortitude' was the codename given to the plan to deceive the Germans into deploying their forces where they would cause the least interference with the invasion of Normandy. 'Fortitude South' was the English dimension of this subterfuge and was intended to persuade the enemy that the main allied invasion would take place in the Pas de Calais. 'Fortitude North' was the Scottish arm of the enterprise. Its purpose was to create the impression of a concomitant invasion of Norway. This was to involve imaginary landings at Narvik, in order to open up road and rail communications with Sweden, and at Stavanger with the aim of advancing to Oslo in a series of coordinated land and amphibious operations. When southern Norway was secured an assault would be launched on Denmark. As part of this illusion, a mythical British 4th Army was established in Scotland under the commander-in-chief of Scottish Command Lieutenant-General Sir Andrew Thorne – with a headquarters at 15 Douglas Crescent in Edinburgh – and fake radio messages were transmitted to its imaginary formations. 'Real' divisions – including the 52nd (Lowland) Division, which, as we have seen, had been mountain trained for a potential attack on Norway – were merged into this fictitious army's order of battle and false information fed to the Germans by double agents such as 'Garbo' (Juan Pujol Garcia) and 'Brutus' (Roman Garby-Czerniawski). Ships were concentrated in the Firth of Forth, dummy aircraft were scattered around east coast airfields and one unit of the RAF regiment at Macmerry was actually issued with snowshoes.[38]

Highly classified military research was conducted in Scotland. In 1942 the government requisitioned Gruinard island off Ross-shire in order to carry out trials of biological weapons. Scientists attached to the Chemical Defence Experimental Station at Porton Down tested prototypes of anthrax bombs on sheep transported to the island. Unexplained anthrax deaths among livestock on the mainland, however, created disquiet among the locals. In order to dampen this down, the authorities invented the cover story that these were due to infected carcasses being thrown overboard by a Greek ship en route to a convoy assembly point. The contaminated island remained a prohibited area for many years after the war and was not declared 'safe' until 1988.[39]

The Scottish divisions

Military conscription was applied across Britain from the outbreak of hostilities and three-quarters of those who entered the wartime army were called up for service, the remaining quarter being volunteers.[40] By the end of 1944 2.8 million soldiers were serving in the British army of whom 263,000 were born in Scotland. This Scottish contingent included 20,000 officers, and 243,000 other ranks, and represented approximately 10 per cent of the total strength of the army (English-born soldiers made up 83 per cent, Welsh-born 4 per cent, Northern Irish-born 1 per cent, Eire-born 1 per cent, with the remaining 1 per cent born elsewhere).[41]

On the basis of a sample of 3,700 Scots who were medically examined in 1941 to assess their fitness for military service, it was found that the mean height of potential Scottish recruits was 66.82 inches and the mean weight 138.2 lbs. The equivalent figures for a sample of Englishmen were 67.14 inches and 135.9 lbs, and for Welshmen 66.55 inches and 133.7 lbs. This suggested to anatomists that the national stereotypes of the time – 'the short Welshman, the burly Scot, and the tall Southerner' – had some basis in fact.[42]

The largely conscript nature of the army, the introduction of intelligence and aptitude testing to assist in the allocation of recruits to the most appropriate arms and the need to cross-post soldiers in order to make up strengths, undermined the links between the Scottish regiments and their traditional recruiting areas.[43] Nevertheless, Scottish units served in all the major theatres. In the war against Japan, the 2nd Royal Scots, for example, fought at Hong Kong (1941), the 2nd Argyll and Sutherland Highlanders in Malaya (1941–2), the 1st Cameronians in the retreat from Burma (1942), the 1st Royal Scots in the Arakan (1943), the 1st Cameron Highlanders at Kohima (1944), and the 2nd King's Own Scottish Borderers (KOSB) in the advance on Rangoon (1945).[44] The 2nd Argyll's performance in the Malayan campaign was especially noteworthy. Led by Lieutenant-Colonel Ian Stewart, the thirteenth laird of Achnacone whose ancestors had fought for Prince Charles in the 'Forty-Five, it mounted a skilful rearguard action on the jungle peninsula before being eventually forced to surrender at Singapore. Nearly 200 Argylls were to die in captivity.[45] It was, however, the exploits of the Scottish divisions in the war against Germany that best caught the imagination of the Scottish public.

The 51st (Highland) Infantry Division became the most celebrated of these divisions. A pre-war Territorial formation commanded by Major-General Victor Fortune of the Black Watch, it was sent to France early in 1940 as part of the British Expeditionary Force (BEF).[46] Before embarking, its battalions were ordered to hand in their kilts. The War Office had decided that this customary Highland attire was unsuitable for modern warfare and decreed that battledress was to be worn.[47] This created consternation in Highland circles. A statement from the Glasgow Highland Societies declared that

> The ordinary Englishman cannot understand the sentimentalism and clannishness of the Scot, and is apt to sneer at it. But it is that sentimental love of the tartan and clannish spirit which have largely made the Highland regiments the dour fighters they are, and for which they are renowned.[48]

A delegation from the Highland societies travelled to Westminster to lobby the authorities, but with little effect.[49] Prior to being despatched overseas with the division, the 5th Gordon Highlanders burnt a kilt on their parade ground as a mark of protest against this assault on the highlanders' traditional dress.[50]

When the Germans launched their offensive in May 1940 the 51st was undertaking a tour of duty with the French army in the Saar sector of the Maginot line. The enemy breakthrough further north cut the division off from the main body of the BEF and instead of falling back on Dunkirk to be evacuated with the other British formations it was ordered to withdraw with its French allies to a line south of the River Somme. Here it fought a series of actions near Abbeville during 4–8 June under the French IX Corps. With the Germans now threatening to outflank the division, and its prospects of avoiding encirclement hindered by the procrastination of the French high command, it converged on St Valéry-en-Caux in the hope of rescue by the Royal Navy. A perimeter was set up around the town and the remnants of the Highland battalions, together with French units, sought to hold off the enemy. An armada was despatched to bring the

51st home but, by the time it was in position to lift the troops, thick fog prevented the ships from closing on the shore and the Germans had occupied the cliffs around the harbour, which made embarkation impossible. On 12 June the local French commander ordered his men to lay down their arms and Fortune was forced to follow suit. Major-General Erwin Rommel of the 7th Panzer Division took the surrender.[51] For many highlanders the British government's decision to shackle the 51st to the French during the campaign in the vain hope of keeping them in the war denied it the opportunity to escape across the Channel. 'It has always been abundantly clear to me,' opined the duke of Argyll (who, as Captain Ian Campbell of the Argylls, had been one of Fortune's staff officers), 'that no Division has ever been more uselessly sacrificed.'[52]

Over 10,000 soldiers from the 51st were taken prisoner at St Valéry and marched into captivity.[53] In the POW camps the internees sought to maintain their national customs. At Stalag 383, Highland gatherings were held, a Gaelic society was established and 'Scotland' versus 'England' football matches were vigorously contested.[54] A plucky few, however, managed to escape the clutches of the Germans and make their way back to Britain.[55] Among those who helped to repatriate fugitive highlanders was the Islay-born minister of the Scots Kirk in Paris: the Reverend Donald Caskie. He had fled south as the enemy approached the capital and had taken over the British and American Seamen's Mission in Vichy-controlled Marseilles. Caskie's Mission became a clearing house for servicemen on the run from occupied France, and he arranged for them to be smuggled to the UK through Spain and Gibraltar. In 1943 this 'Tartan Pimpernel' was incarcerated in the notorious Fresnes prison near Paris, sentenced to death by a Gestapo court and only saved from execution by the intervention of a kindly German pastor.[56]

The loss of the 51st was something of a national tragedy for Scotland and in the Highlands there was hardly a family that was unaffected by its demise. But such was the proud history of the division that it was decided to resurrect it. In the summer of 1940 the 9th (Highland) Infantry Division, which had been formed shortly before the war as a duplicate of its illustrious counterpart, was re-designated as the 'new' 51st and for the next eighteen months it trained in the north-east of Scotland.[57] From June 1941 it was commanded by Major-General Douglas Wimberley of the Camerons. 'Tartan Tam', as he was known to the 'Jocks', was a passionate highlander who was determined to foster a strong sense of Scottish national identity across the division. Kilts were to be worn whenever possible, pipe bands were to be turned out at the first opportunity and junior officers were to be taught Highland dancing at their divisional battle school. Wimberley also did his best to preserve the ethnic recruitment profile of the 51st. He was insistent that Scots – preferably highlanders but when necessary lowlanders – should be drafted to the division to bring it up to strength and was indefatigable in poaching his compatriots from other formations for this purpose.[58] When the 1st/7th Middlesex was assigned to the 51st as a machine gun battalion the regimental historian recorded the unit's frosty reception:

> The posting of a 'Sassenach' battalion to the Highland Division was certainly not greeted with a *feu de joie*, or with any other signs of delight, by the Scotsmen, but it was not very long before the Cockney soldiers made themselves appreciated.[59]

In the summer of 1942 the 51st was despatched to North Africa. Here it was to lock horns again with Rommel who by this time was the celebrated commander of the Panzerarmee Afrika. The 'Desert Fox' had been the target of an audacious assassination attempt by No. 11 Commando a few months earlier. This unit, which styled itself No. 11 (Scottish) Commando and wore a 'tam-o'-shanter' with a black hackle, had mounted a raid on his supposed rear headquarters at Beda Littoria in Libya only to discover that its intelligence was out of date.[60] Now Rommel and his panzers were deep inside Egypt, just 150 miles from Cairo, and the 51st arrived to reinforce Lieutenant-General Bernard Law Montgomery's Eighth Army defending the Nile Delta. The division quickly sought to acclimatise itself to desert conditions, learn the battlefield skills required in the theatre and become acquainted with the Commonwealth formations alongside which it would fight.[61] When Wimberley discovered that the commanders of these forces tended to consult their respective governments over 'difficult questions', he joked that if he was ordered to do something he did not agree with he would 'complain to the Secretary of State for Scotland'.[62]

On the night of 23–4 October 1942 the Eighth Army launched its long-awaited offensive at El Alamein and the 51st was in the vanguard of the assault. The division, at least 80 per cent of whose infantry battalions were said to be composed of Scots, codenamed its objectives after Scottish towns and cities connected to the attacking regiments – 'Inverness', 'Nairn', 'Aberdeen', 'Ballater', 'Dundee', 'Arbroath', 'Perth', 'Stirling', 'Forfar' – and Wimberley's order of the day to his Jocks was 'Scotland forever, and second to none!' The troops advanced towards

Figure 21.4 Douglas Wimberley in the North African desert, 1942.

the enemy lines with their bayonets glinting in the moonlight, white crosses of St Andrew attached to their back packs as an aid to identification and accompanied by the skirl of the pipes, the 5th Camerons moving forward to the strains of 'The Inverness Gathering', the 7th Argylls to 'Monymusk' and the 5th Black Watch to 'Highland Laddie'. The division took all of its objectives but suffered heavy casualties in the process.[63] Among them, Piper Duncan McIntyre of the 5th Black Watch was killed whilst playing his comrades into action at 'Montrose'. They found him with his beloved pipes still under his arm and his fingers 'rigid on the chanter'.[64]

The stirring deeds of the 51st during the Eighth Army's victory at El Alamein earned it widespread praise. Messages of congratulation flooded into divisional HQ from, among others, the town council of Inverness, the lord provost of Edinburgh and the Clyde shipyard workers, and its exploits were lauded in the newspapers and on radio. Such was the adulation that letters appeared in the Welsh press complaining about 'Scotsmania' at the BBC.[65] Meanwhile the division

Figure 21.5 The 'Highway Decorators', Sfax, Tunisia, 1943.

reorganised after the battle and replenished its depleted ranks. One new subaltern, Second Lieutenant Neil McCallum, found that the old clan system continued to operate in some parts of the desert. He and other replacement officers arrived at the encampment of the 2nd Seaforth Highlanders only to be turned away by the commanding officer because they had been commissioned into Lowland regiments. 'We had discovered in a twentieth-century Armageddon,' observed McCallum, 'a Highland Lieutenant-Colonel, desperate for reinforcements to replace his killed and wounded officers, who would not allow Lowland Scots to fight beside him. And the half-colonel spoke with the accents of Mayfair.'[66]

After El Alamein the 51st took part in the Eighth Army's pursuit of Rommel's forces back into Libya. In January 1943 the division – by this time nicknamed the 'Highway Decorators' because of its fondness for daubing the formation sign 'HD' on buildings along the line of its

Figure 21.6 Pipers of the 51st Highland Division parade in Tripoli, 1943.

advance – arrived in Tripoli. There it participated in a rousing victory parade for Churchill. All available kilts were on show for the occasion and immaculately turned out contingents from the Highland regiments marched through the Piazza Italia as the massed pipes and drums of the division struck up such tunes as 'The Campbells are Coming', 'The Cock of the North' and 'Pibroch O'Dhomnuill Dubh' (Black Donald's Pibroch).[67] For Wimberley, who by his own admission looked upon the 51st as an old Highland chief looked upon his clan, this event was one of the proudest moments of his life: 'my heart was very full, and there were tears in my eyes . . . as for Winston, the tears were running down his cheeks'.[68] McCallum, who along with his fellow waifish officers had been taken in by the 5th/7th Gordons, was told that he was to be excluded from the parade because orders had been given at a high level that only bona fide highlanders were to march past the prime minister: 'We complied with the instructions with relief, thankful for the unpredictable foibles of military vanity.'[69]

In the spring of 1943 the 51st pushed on into Tunisia.[70] On 6 April the 7th Argylls, under the command of Lieutenant-Colonel Lorne Campbell of Airds, were ordered to break through a minefield and capture an anti-tank ditch at Wadi Akarit. In spite of intense machine gun fire, they secured their objective and took 600 prisoners. They then held the ditch as the enemy launched determined counter attacks. With utter disregard for his own safety, Campbell moved around the battlefield rallying his men at points of greatest pressure. When one of the companies was compelled to fall back he went forward alone into a hail of enemy fire and personally reorganised its position. As reinforcements arrived to consolidate the gains, he was seen standing out in the open, continuing to direct operations under heavy fire, despite being painfully wounded in the neck by a mortar bomb. Campbell, who had already been awarded a Distinguished Service Order (DSO) and bar, won the VC for his heroism that day. 'This officer's gallantry and magnificent leadership,' recorded the medal citation, '. . . can seldom have been surpassed in the long history of the Highland Brigade.'[71]

The Axis armies in North Africa surrendered in May 1943 and the 51st was assigned a lead role in the subsequent invasion of Sicily. Wimberley scoured base camps and convalescent depots for Scots in order to bring his division up to strength and on 10 July it landed near Portopalo. The troops then advanced inland and fought a series of battles at Francofonte, Vizzini, Gerbini and Sferro during the thirty-nine-day campaign.[72] Up in the Sferro hills it was said that the officers of the 5th Camerons rallied their men with clan war cries before leading them in a bayonet charge against German positions.[73] In his account of these events in Sicily Major Hugh Pond indicates that the distinctive Scottish ethos of the 51st had by now earned it something of a maverick reputation within the Eighth Army:

> The Highland Division, from its tall gangling Commander 'Lang Tam' Wimberley, down to the humblest Jock private, was very much a law unto itself. One often had a feeling that they were fighting a Holy Crusade and at the end of the war they would return to Scotland, take Edinburgh by storm, put a Scottish king on the throne and form an independent country![74]

Indeed, the exploits of the division served as an inspiration to those of a nationalist persuasion. In the view of Captain Hamish Henderson, who was one of Wimberley's intelligence officers in Sicily

> it became a kind of symbol of Scotland. All the repressed nationhood of this luckless land broke out in spots at the mere mention of it. Here, at any

rate, was something distinctively Scottish, asserting its identity in the field with a bit of panache.[75]

Following the enemy withdrawal across the straits of Messina to mainland Italy, the 51st was ordered back to Britain. To mark its departure Henderson, who became the divisional bard, composed a ballad entitled 'The Highland Division's Farewell to Sicily':

> Then fareweel ye banks o' Sicily,
> Fare ye weel, ye valley an' shaw.
> There's nae Jock will mourn the kyles o' ye.
> Puir bluidy swaddies are weary.

This became a firm favourite among veterans and entered the canon of Scottish folk music.[76] As the formation prepared to leave the island, it was a testament to Wimberley's influence that after a year of fighting overseas 81 per cent of the officers and 72 per cent of the other ranks in its Highland regiments were still Scots.[77]

Back in North Africa some eighty soldiers of the 51st (along with others of the 50th (Northumbrian) Division) were tried for mutiny in October 1943. Their offence was to refuse to join the British 46th Division fighting with the Fifth Army at Salerno. These men had been plucked from a transit camp in Tripoli, where many had been sent after recovering from wounds or sickness, and shipped to Italy without informing them of their destination. They had fully expected to rejoin their division and were horrified to find themselves assigned to another formation at the beachhead. At the court martial in Algeria the defence team argued that the members of the 51st had been repeatedly told by their senior officers that they should not allow themselves to be drafted away from the division and compared its *esprit de corps* to a religion:[78]

> To these men . . . [contended one of the defending officers] General Wimberley is their military god and the sign 'HD' is the altar at which they worship. So much so, that to ask a soldier of the Highland Division to fight with another division is, in my mind, akin to asking a Hindu to worship Mohammed. Such a thing is unthinkable.[79]

The oratory fell on deaf ears. The mutineers were sentenced to lengthy periods of penal servitude, but these were later suspended on condition that they agreed to serve with units of the Eighth Army in Italy. Ironically, Wimberley did not hear about this episode for some time. At the end of the Sicilian campaign he had been appointed Commandant of the Staff College at Camberley. Although he was no longer in a position directly to influence events, the plight of his former Jocks weighed heavily on his conscience and he did what he could behind the scenes to mitigate their position. One Highland officer wrote to him that the affair was more than just a blunder on the part of the military authorities: 'a crime was committed in North Africa'.[80]

From late 1943 until the spring of 1944 the 51st was based in the south of England preparing for the forthcoming invasion of Normandy. A lowlander, Major-General Charles Bullen-Smith of the KOSB, had been summoned from the 15th (Scottish) Division to replace Wimberley and the troops participated in an intensive training programme. This included a street fighting exercise at Limehouse in the East End of London.[81] The division also took in reinforcements. Captain Alistair Borthwick of the 5th Seaforth Highlanders recalled how his unit calmly integrated these newcomers into its ranks and educated them in its peculiar language and customs: 'Our losses had been grievous and the soft vowels of the North were salted with many alien twangs; but we were, strangely enough, still very much a Highland battalion.'[82] On 5 June 1944 the leading elements of the formation set sail from the Thames Estuary for the invasion beaches.[83]

The 51st did not land with the first waves of assault troops on D-Day – the commandos of Brigadier the Lord Lovat's 1st Special Service Brigade were, however, accompanied into action on Sword beach that morning by Piper Bill Millin playing 'Highland Laddie' and 'The Road to the Isles' – but came ashore in stages between 6 and 13 June.[84] Thereafter it was in combat for six weeks against Rommel's forces among the woods and hedgerows around Caen.[85] During this period the performance of the division became a cause for concern and, after its 153 Brigade was unable to press home an attack on Colombelles on 11 July, Montgomery sent an exasperated cable to the Chief of the Imperial General Staff, Field Marshal Sir Alan Brooke, in which he reported that '51st Division is at present not – NOT – battleworthy'.[86] Bullen-Smith was subsequently relieved of his command.[87]

J. B. Salmond's 'authorised' history of the 51st described it as having 'met failure' in Normandy.[88] Bullen-Smith disputed this judgement. Although he admitted that the division had experienced problems adapting to the terrain in Normandy, and that he had not directed his subordinate officers as well as he might, he staunchly defended its record:

We were not set to fight an Alamein battle. Our job, firstly, was to plug holes, and then be offensive all with the object of holding and drawing enemy forces, particularly armoured forces, against us. In this, I contend the Division did not fail and I think it is unjust on the troops to record that finding. Our role was not spectacular but it was important . . . I took & am always willing to take *all* the blame. It hurts me to think that others should have to suffer.[89]

One of Wimberley's former brigadiers, Major-General Thomas Rennie of the Black Watch, took over from Bullen-Smith and the 51st was brought out of the line to regroup and receive new drafts. These included a party from the Duke of Wellington's Regiment, which was allotted to the 5th/7th Gordons, and another from the Oxfordshire and Buckinghamshire Light Infantry, which was sent to the 1st Black Watch. In August the division took part in the breakout from Normandy and seemed to recover its form. During its advance to Lisieux it fought continuously for seventeen days with every battalion participating in at least four main actions.[90]

The 51st – appropriately enough – liberated St Valéry in early September. As the leading infantrymen entered the town the pipers of the 5th Camerons struck up 'Blue Bonnets over the Border'.[91] It was then employed in the investment of Le Havre and Dunkirk before moving into Holland in October to man part of the corridor between Eindhoven and Nijmegan. Here it was involved in the clearance of the south and west banks of the River Maas as part of 'Operation Colin' and 'Operation Ascot'.[92] Among its visitors after these operations was the Moderator of the General Assembly of the Church of Scotland who conducted a service for the troops.[93] The division was rushed to Belgium in December to assist the Americans in containing the German offensive in the Ardennes. It subsequently returned to Holland and during 'Operation Veritable' in February fought through the southern end of the Reichswald forest and took part in the capture of Goch: a fortified German border town that was a key bastion in the Siegfried line.[94] Private Stan Whitehouse of the 1st Black Watch recalled that as his platoon made its way up to the frontline in the Reichswald some Gordon Highlanders were neatly stacking the dead head to toe: "'That's how I like to see the Jerries – piled high," said Beachy [Private Les Beach] to the Gordons, who were standing about, looking sullen. "Trouble is," said one of them, "they're our lads."'[95]

Following these battles the 51st enjoyed a brief period of recuperation away from the combat zone – the concert party of the 1st

Gordons, it might be noted, was by now named the 'London, Midland and Scottish' in recognition of the non-Scottish replacements in the battalion – before acting as one of the assault divisions during the Rhine crossing in late March.[96] On the night of 'Operation Plunder', 'Scotland the Brave' sounded out from the pipes of the 5th Black Watch amid the din of the preliminary bombardment as the troops prepared to board their Buffalo amphibious vehicles to traverse the 450 yards of river.[97] The division successfully landed on the far bank and established a bridgehead around Rees. Rennie was, however, killed by a mortar bomb whilst visiting his units during this period. The formation then advanced across the north German plain towards Bremen, dealing with pockets of enemy resistance as it went. When the war in Europe came to an end in May it was closing on Bremerhaven.[98]

Later that month soldiers from the 5th Black Watch were manning a bridge checkpoint at Bremervörde when a man sporting an eye patch and dressed in the uniform of a sergeant in the *Geheime Feldpolizei* caught their attention among the flood of refugees. They detained this suspicious individual, who was travelling under the name of Heinrich Hitzinger, and the field security police took him away for questioning. In custody the prisoner declared himself to be Heinrich Himmler, the notorious Reichsführer-SS. Shortly thereafter he went to meet his maker after biting on a capsule of cyanide concealed in his mouth.[99]

Ten years after the surrender of the original 51st at St Valéry a monument was erected near the French town to commemorate over 3,000 members of the division who had fallen during the war. Constructed from Aberdeen granite, it was sited on the east cliff above the harbour.[100] At the unveiling ceremony, Wimberley paid tribute to 'the brave men who fought and died for Britain and her Commonwealth, and for our own dear land of Scotland'.[101] It is, however, an indication of how diluted the ethnicity of the formation's infantry battalions had become by the end of the conflict that in June 1945, 484 of the 891 soldiers serving with the 5th Camerons – the one battalion of Wimberley's old regiment attached to the 51st – were English.[102]

The 52nd (Lowland) Infantry Division also fought in Europe. Another pre-war Territorial formation, it was sent to France via Cherbourg in early June 1940 as part of a 'second' BEF to stiffen the resolve of the French. After clashing with German forces south of the River Seine near Évreux, the division was forced to withdraw back to the coast and, with France on the point of collapse, was successfully evacuated through its port of entry.[103] Thereafter it was based in the UK for over four years, for a good deal of its time exercising in the mountains of north-east Scotland, before being ordered into Holland in the autumn of 1944.[104]

In late October and early November the 52nd played a prominent role in the assault on South Beveland and Walcheren in the Scheldt Estuary – the irony of a mountain-trained division being sent into battle below sea level was not lost on its personnel.[105] It then manned part of the line along the lower reaches of the Maas before being despatched to the Dutch-German border near Geilenkirchen towards the end of the year. Here it held back a number of enemy thrusts and participated in the clearance of the west bank of the River Roer under 'Operation Blackcock'.[106] In January nineteen-year-old Fusilier Dennis Donnini of the 4th/5th Royal Scots Fusiliers won a posthumous VC for his heroism at the hamlet of Stein during this operation. A Geordie-Italian from Easington in County Durham, he had been in the army for just six months and is reputed to be the youngest British soldier to win the VC during the war.[107]

The 52nd subsequently moved up to the Reichswald and during 'Veritable' passed through the 51st around Goch and helped to secure the west bank of the Rhine near Alpen.[108] It crossed the river as a follow-up formation to the 15th (Scottish) Division and pushed on towards Bremen where it assisted in the capture of the city during the closing days of the war.[109] In a final twist of fate, among the last acts of the Scottish mountain troops, who it turned out never fought at more than 300 feet above sea level, was to seize German submarines trapped in the muddy waters of the Weser estuary.[110] By this stage, though, there were many non-Scots among the Jocks. As the divisional historian admitted, 'It would be the merest sentimentality to gloss over the fact that, towards the end of the war, any Scottish unit might contain an actual majority of Englishmen in the ranks.'[111]

The 15th (Scottish) Infantry Division featured in Europe too. This formation came into being just before the outbreak of war as a duplicate of the 52nd. It spent most of the conflict in Britain, including a lengthy spell training in the north-east of England, before being despatched to Normandy shortly after D-Day. In late June the division spearheaded an attack west of Caen during 'Operation Epsom' and created a narrow wedge in the German line that extended across the River Odon. The ground taken became known as the 'Scottish corridor'.[112] It was subsequently involved in the breakout from the bridgehead and the pursuit of retreating enemy forces across northern France and into the Low Countries.[113]

Towards the end of September the 15th – a division, it should be remarked, that permitted all its troops, not just those in its Scottish

Figure 21.7 Led by their piper, men of the 7th battalion, the Seaforth Highlanders, 15th (Scottish) Division, advance during Operation Epsom, Normandy, 1944.

infantry battalions, to wear the 'tam-o'-shanter' – arrived in the Nijmegan corridor.[114] Here it participated in the capture of Tilburg under 'Operation Pheasant'. Its main opposition in this town came from the Dutch SS.[115] Thereafter it helped to secure the west bank of the River Maas near Blerick. During 'Veritable' it attacked north of the Reichswald and took Cleve before wheeling south to assist the 51st in the clearance of Goch.[116] Following these actions it was given a well-earned rest back at Tilburg where a Red Lion Club – named after the division's lion rampant emblem – was established as a social centre for the troops.[117]

The 15th, along with the 51st, was chosen to lead the British assault across the Rhine.[118] The fact that these two Scottish divisions formed the vanguard for 'Plunder' did not go unrecognised by the military chroniclers. 'Surely throughout her long martial history,' recorded one of the brigade historians, 'Scotland has never seen a day like this.'[119] The formation landed near Bislich, seven miles upstream from the 51st, and fought through to the River Elbe. When the war concluded it was in the vicinity of Hamburg.[120] A few weeks later the division was sent to man the area adjacent to the Soviet zone of occupation and contacts were established with the Red Army. Whisky and vodka were exchanged and a football match arranged – a team from the 8th Royal Scots convincingly defeating its Russian opponents – before the iron curtain descended.[121]

Scotland thus made an important contribution to the British military war effort. The sacrifices of its soldiers, sailors and airmen are testament to that. During the conflict it is estimated that some 34,000 Scottish-born service personnel died with the British armed forces. Of these, approximately 6,000 were serving with Royal Navy, 8,000 with the RAF and 20,000 with the army. In total, they represented about 11 per cent of the UK military war dead.[122] The Scots also managed, chiefly through their regiments and divisions, to retain a distinctive national identity within the armed services. Hamish Henderson described the 51st, for example, as the 'Scottish national army' and contended that through its efforts to defeat Nazism 'the men of our Highland Div. are doing more to solve Scotland's problems (social-economic-political) than Douglas [Young, chairman of the SNP, who had refused to be conscripted into an army of the British government] languishing in clink'.[123] Beyond their indigenous units and formations, combatants from north of the border were able to draw on the pugnacious reputation of their race. As George MacDonald Fraser recalled of his service in Burma with the Border Regiment

> Nothing put more heart into me, young and unsure as I was – most of all, fearful of being seen to be fearful – than the fact that, being a Scot, it was half expected of me that I would be a wild man, a head case. This age-old belief among the English, that their northern neighbours are desperate fellows, hangs on, and whether it's true or not it's one hell of an encouragement when you're nineteen and wondering how you'll be when the whistle blows and you take a deep breath and push your safety catch forward.[124]

The wartime exploits of the Scots could in turn inspire later generations of British servicemen. In November 1941 an attack by the 2nd Black Watch on an enemy strongpoint near Tobruk codenamed 'Tiger' stalled under heavy German fire. According to one of the battalion's officers:

> our Adjutant [Captain Mungo Stirling of Glorat], who had been wounded, crawled to where we were lying and got to his feet. 'Isn't this the Black

Watch?' he cried. 'Then-charge!' He waved us on with his stick and was instantly killed. We rose and took 'Tiger' with the bayonet.[125]

Forty years later, this Highland officer's actions influenced those of a young Welsh Royal Marines officer during the Falklands war. In June 1982 Lieutenant Clive Dytor of Z company 45 Commando was taking part in the assault on Two Sisters when the advance faltered. Pinned down by the Argentine defenders, he recalled reading about the deeds of the Black Watch adjutant in John Ellis's book *The Sharp End*. Galvanised by his example, he rallied his troops with shouts of 'Zulu!' and led them forward in what has been termed 'Dytor's charge'. The objective was taken and Dytor was awarded the Military Cross.[126]

Notes

1. H. Buckton, *Birth of the Few: 16 October 1939 – RAF Spitfires Win Their First Battle with the Luftwaffe* (Shrewsbury: Airlife, 1998), passim; D. Ross with B. Blanche and W. Simpson, *'The Greatest Squadron of Them All': The Definitive History of 603 (City of Edinburgh) Squadron RAuxAF*, vol. 1, *Formation to the end of 1940* (London: Grub Street, 2003), pp. 29–30, 55–92; H. MacLean, *Fighters in Defence: Memories of the Glasgow Squadron* (Glasgow: Squadron Prints, 1999), p. 76; B. Simpson, *Spitfires Over Scotland: 'First Blood to the Auxiliaries': The Life of Squadron Leader Patrick Gifford DFC* (Wigtown: G. C. Books, 2010), pp. 1–110. Gifford would drive between Kirkcudbrightshire and RAF Turnhouse in his Frazer-Nash sports car which he claimed could do 'ninety in third'. This became an unofficial squadron warcry. It might be recorded that on 26 September 1939 a Blackburn Skua of 803 squadron, operating from the aircraft carrier HMS *Ark Royal*, shot down a Dornier flying boat approximately 250 miles north west of Heligoland. On 8 October a Lockheed Hudson of 224 squadron, operating from RAF Leuchars, was said to have destroyed another Dornier flying boat some twenty miles off the coast of Aberdeen. See L. Taylor, *Luftwaffe Over Scotland: A History of German Air Attacks on Scotland 1939–1945* (Dunbeath: Whittles Publishing, 2010), pp. 4–6; T. Royle, *A Time of Tyrants: Scotland and the Second World War* (Edinburgh: Birlinn, 2011), pp. 34-6, 340-1.
2. T. M. Devine, *The Scottish Nation 1700–2000* (London: Allen Lane, 1999), pp. 547–8; Royle, *A Time of Tyrants*, pp. 188–97; 'Output of Scots shipyards', *The Scotsman*, 26 December 1945, p. 2; 'West Scotland war work', *The Scotsman*, 12 May 1945, p. 6; T. Steel, *Scotland's Story* (London: HarperCollins, 1994), pp. 360, 363; M. Moss and

I. Russell, *Range and Vision: The First Hundred Years of Barr & Stroud* (Edinburgh: Mainstream Publishing, 1998), p. 138; GEC Marconi Avionics, *Ferranti: 50 Years in Scotland* (Edinburgh: GEC Marconi Avionics, 1993), p. 5; J. F. Wilson, *Ferranti: A History: Building a Family Business 1882–1975* (Lancaster: Carnegie Publishing, 2001), p. 281.

3. The National Archives, Kew [hereafter TNA], BT 64/3343, Scottish council on industry, minutes of a meeting of the executive committee, 17 May 1943; TNA, BT 170/155, ministry of production, regional board for Scotland, report for September 1945.

4. G. Hartcup, *Code Name Mulberry: The Planning, Building and Operation of the Normandy Harbours* (Barnsley: Pen and Sword, 2006), pp. 29–30, 77, 83–4; Alexander Findlay & Co., *Mulberry Pier Heads: How they were Built by Findlay's of Motherwell* (Motherwell: Alexander Findlay & Co. Ltd, 1948). The eighteenth pierhead was the prototype built on the Clyde.

5. B. D. Osborne and R. Armstrong, *The Clyde at War* (Edinburgh: Birlinn, 2001), pp. 31–2; S. Allan and A. Carswell, *The Thin Red Line: War, Empire and Visions of Scotland* (Edinburgh: National Museums of Scotland, 2004), p. 74.

6. J. Shields, *Clyde Built: A History of Shipbuilding on the River Clyde* (Glasgow: William Maclennan, 1947), p. 157; Steel, *Scotland's Story*, p. 361; J. D. Drummond, *A River Runs to War* (London: W. H. Allen, 1960), p. 130.

7. D. Paton, 'Scotland in the air war 1939 to 1945', *History Scotland*, vol. 6, no. 4 (2006), pp. 51–2.

8. TNA, WO 277/37, 'Defence plans for the United Kingdom 1939–45', by Captain G. C. Wynne, 1948, p. 41; G. N. Thompson, 'Scotland's military role in the Second World War: A view from the Scottish Office' (unpublished MSc dissertation, University of Edinburgh, 2001), p. 13.

9. N. Redfern, 'Anti-invasion defence of Scotland, Wales and Northern Ireland, 1939–45: Insights and issues', *Defence Lines*, issue 12 (1999), article available through the website of the Council for British Archaeology, Defence of Britain project, www.britarch.ac.uk/projects/dob/dl12b.html, accessed on 7 November 2010. For a detailed study of one Scottish 'stop line', see G. J. Barclay, 'The Scottish Command Line: The archaeology and history of a 1940 anti-tank "stop line"', *Tayside and Fife Archaeological Journal*, vol. 17 (2011), pp. 114–56. It should be noted that there were significant differences between Scottish defence lines in that the Command Line covering the Clyde–Forth isthmus was a large barrier with many anti-tank ditches, road blocks and pill boxes, whilst other minor lines incorporated no artificial constructions.

Another aspect of home defence, which no doubt had an impact on local people, was the immobilisation of open spaces within a five-mile radius of an airfield or a listed port. This involved the strewing of vehicles or agricultural equipment across open ground and the digging of a checkerboard pattern of trenches or the erection of a pattern of wooden posts. I am grateful to Dr Gordon Barclay for this information. Further details can be obtained in his forthcoming book: *If Hitler Comes: Preparing for Invasion: Scotland 1940* (Birlinn).

10. TNA, WO 73/146, general return of the strength of the British army on 30 September 1940. It might be pointed out that these Scottish figures include approximately 80,000 infantry and 43,000 gunners, but also soldiers from the 'non-teeth' arms, such as the Auxiliary Military Pioneer Corps (11,000), the Royal Army Medical Corps (6,000) and the Royal Army Pay Corps (1,500).
11. TNA, WO 365/130, Home Guard, weekly return for week ending Thursday 12 September 1940, Director-General of Welfare and Territorial army, 14 September 1940. Also see B. D. Osborne, *The People's Army: The Home Guard in Scotland 1940-1944* (Edinburgh: Birlinn, 2009).
12. 'Defence of Scotland's open spaces', *The Times*, 12 August 1941, p. 5.
13. B. Collier, *The Defence of the United Kingdom* (London: HMSO, 1957), pp. 295, 432; D. Lindsay, *Forgotten General: A Life of Andrew Thorne* (Salisbury: Michael Russell, 1987), p. 150; J. Douglas-Hamilton, *The Truth about Rudolf Hess* (Edinburgh: Mainstream Publishing, 1993), pp. 135–81; D. Stafford (ed.), *Flight from Reality: Rudolf Hess and his Mission to Scotland 1941* (London: Pimlico, 2002), passim; Royle, *A Time of Tyrants*, pp. 204-6. It should be noted that the duke of Hamilton was a pre-war acquaintance of one of Hess's advisors, Albrecht Haushofer. The duke had never met Hess and knew nothing about his peace mission to Scotland.
14. S. Allan, *Commando Country* (Edinburgh: National Museums of Scotland, 2007), pp. 35, 166–220. SOE agents deemed unsuitable for operations, but whose knowledge of the covert organisation made it too risky to release them back into civilian society during the war, were required to 'live in retirement' at Inverlair Lodge near Spean Bridge. This was said to have inspired the 1960s cult television series *The Prisoner*. See S. Twigge, E. Hampshire and G. Macklin, *British Intelligence: Secrets, Spies and Sources* (London: The National Archives, 2008), p. 209 and C. J. Murphy, *Security and Special Operations: SOE and MI5 during the Second World War* (Basingstoke: Palgrave, 2006), p. 25.
15. Allan, *Commando Country*, pp. 17, 19, 111, 121–34; D. Gilchrist, *Castle*

Commando (Fort William: West Highland Museum Publishing, 2005), passim; TNA, DEFE 2/1134, 'The training of commandos in Scotland during the late war', by Major Chant, 17 October 1945.

16. J. B. Salmond, *The History of the 51st Highland Division 1939-1945* (Edinburgh: William Blackwood, 1953), pp. 19-25; P. Delaforce, *Monty's Highlanders: 51st Highland Division in the Second World War* (Barnsley: Pen and Sword, 2007), pp. 21-8.

17. G. Blake, *Mountain and Flood: The History of the 52nd (Lowland) Division 1939-1946* (Glasgow: Jackson, Son and Company, 1950), pp. 40-66; Allan and Carswell, *The Thin Red Line*, p. 77.

18. N. Scarfe, *Assault Division: A History of the 3rd Division from the Invasion of Normandy to the Surrender of Germany* (London: Collins, 1947), pp. 36-54; B. Bartlam and I. Keiller, *World War II in Moray* (Kinloss: Librario Publishing, 2003), pp. 32-8.

19. TNA, WO 73/154, general return of the strength of the British army on 30 September 1942; TNA, WO 305/1837, Scottish Command historical record book, 'Regular army in Scotland: strength of British army personnel', undated.

20. Allan and Carswell, *The Thin Red Line*, pp. 77-9; A. Carswell, *For Your Freedom and Ours: Poland, Scotland and the Second World War* (Edinburgh: National Museums of Scotland, 1993), pp. 5-9, 12; ibid. '"Bonnie fechters": The Polish army and the defence of Scotland, 1940-1942', in T. M. Devine and D. Hesse (eds), *Scotland and Poland: Historical Encounters, 1500-2010* (Edinburgh: John Donald, 2011), passim; Royle, *A Time of Tyrants*, pp. 225-38, 312; TNA, WO 73/157, general return of the strength of the British army on 30 June 1943.

21. S. W. Roskill, *The War at Sea 1939-1945*, 3 vols (London: HMSO, 1954), vol. 1, *The Defensive*, pp. 76-7; J. P. Levy, *The Royal Navy's Home Fleet in World War II* (Basingstoke: Palgrave Macmillan, 2003), pp. 40-1; B. Lavery, *Shield of Empire: The Royal Navy and Scotland* (Edinburgh: Birlinn, 2007), pp. 302-3, 355-86; J. Miller, *Scapa* (Edinburgh: Birlinn, 2000), pp. 80-95.

22. Levy, *The Royal Navy's Home Fleet*, pp. 82-107, 153; Roskill, *The War at Sea*, vol. 1, pp. 389-417; R. Jackson, *The Bismarck* (Staplehurst: Spellmount, 2002), p. 83.

23. Lavery, *Shield of Empire*, pp. 329-32, 342-5; Shields, *Clyde Built*, p. 157; Steel, *Scotland's Story*, p. 361; 'The Clyde in war-time', *The Scotsman*, 17 February 1945, p. 4.

24. Levy, *The Royal Navy's Home Fleet*, pp. 108-33, 160; Lavery, *Shield of Empire*, pp. 341-2; Miller, *Scapa*, pp. 149-50; F. Pearce, *Last Call for HMS Edinburgh: A Story of the Russian Convoys* (London: Collins,

1982), passim; B. Penrose, *Stalin's Gold: The Story of HMS Edinburgh and its Treasure* (Boston: Little, Brown & Co., 1982), passim.
25. S. W. Roskill, *The War at Sea 1939-1945*, vol. 3, *The Offensive*, part 1, *1 July 1943-31 May 1944* (London: HMSO, 1960), pp. 64-9; T. Gallagher, *Against All Odds: Midget Submarines Against the Tirpitz* (London: Macdonald, 1971), passim; Lavery, *Shield of Empire*, pp. 317-18; Royle, *A Time of Tyrants*, pp. 253-5; G. Ross, *Scotland's Forgotten Valour* (Skye: Maclean Press, 1995), pp. 71-2; M. Arthur, *Symbol of Courage: A History of the Victoria Cross* (London: Sidgwick and Jackson, 2004), pp. 455-6. The commander of X-7, Lieutenant Basil Place, was also awarded the VC. Both X-craft commanders were captured by the Germans.
26. Collier, *The Defence of the United Kingdom*, appendix xx, p. 474; Paton, 'Scotland in the air war', pp. 44-50; D. Lake, *Tartan Air Force: Scotland and a Century of Military Aviation 1907-2007* (Edinburgh: Birlinn, 2007), p. 187. Richard Hillary, the author of *The Last Enemy*, was killed at Charterhall in 1943. It should be recorded that there were Fleet Air Arm bases at such locations as Donibristle and Machrihanish.
27. Paton, 'Scotland in the air war', pp. 44-6; D. McRoberts, *Lions Rampant: The Story of 602 Spitfire Squadron* (London: William Kimber, 1985), pp. 52-75; D. Rowland, *Spitfires over Sussex: The Exploits of 602 Squadron* (Peacehaven: Finsbury Publishing, 2000), pp. 8-9; MacLean, *Fighters in Defence*, pp. 60-91; Ross et al., *'The Greatest Squadron'*, vol. 1, pp. 93-135. It should be noted that on 17 October 1939 a heavy anti-aircraft battery in the Orkney Islands shot down a Junkers Ju-88 bomber which crashed on Hoy. See Taylor, *Luftwaffe Over Scotland*, p. 11.
28. Ross et al., *'The Greatest Squadron'*, vol. 1, p. 292; J. Alcorn, 'Battle of Britain: Top guns', *Aeroplane*, souvenir issue, no. 1 (July 2000), pp. 24-9; Royle, *A Time of Tyrants*, pp. 89-90.
29. P. Addison and J. A. Crang, 'A battle of many nations', in P. Addison and J. A. Crang (eds), *The Burning Blue: A New History of the Battle of Britain* (London: Pimlico, 2000), pp. 247-8; D. Ross with B. Blanche and W. Simpson, *'The Greatest Squadron of Them All': The Definitive History of 603 (City of Edinburgh) Squadron RAuxAF*, vol. 2, *1941 to Date* (London: Grub Street, 2003), p. 9. A replica of the Spitfire that Denholm flew during the Battle of Britain ('Blue Peter' XT-D L1067) now guards the entrance to Edinburgh airport.
30. K. G. Wynn, *Men of the Battle of Britain: A Biographical Directory of 'The Few'* (Selsdon: CCB Associates, 1999), p. 329; C. Shores and C. Williams, *Aces High: A Tribute to the Most Notable Fighter Pilots of the British and Commonwealth Forces in WWII* (London: Grub Street, 1994), p. 436.
31. W. Cunningham, 'Memories of a British veteran', in Addison and Crang

(eds), *The Burning Blue*, pp. 129–37; Wynn, *Men of the Battle of Britain*, p. 116; Shores and Williams, *Aces High*, p. 202; D. Rowland, *Survivors: True Stories of Airmen Who Crashed – and Lived to Tell the Tale* (Peacehaven: Finsbury Publishing, 2004), pp. 88–96; private information.

32. Devine, *The Scottish Nation*, p. 545; I. M. M. MacPhail, *The Clydebank Blitz* (West Dunbartonshire Libraries and Museums, 1974), passim; J. MacLeod, *River of Fire: The Clydebank Blitz* (Edinburgh: Birlinn, 2010), passim; J. Hood, 'The Clydebank blitz', in J. Hood (ed.), *The History of Clydebank* (Carnforth: Parthenon Publishing, 1988), pp. 129–34; Collier, *The Defence of the United Kingdom*, appendix xxx, p. 504; Lake, *Tartan Air Force*, pp. 124–6; Taylor, *Luftwaffe Over Scotland*, pp. 61–73.

33. Paton, 'Scotland and the air war', pp. 46–9; Lake, *Tartan Air Force*, pp. 182–4; A. D. Bird, *A Separate Little War: The Banff Coastal Command Strike Wing Versus the Kriegsmarine and Luftwaffe September 1944 to May 1945* (London: Grub Street, 2003), passim; TNA, AIR 41/74, 'The RAF in the Maritime War', vol. 5, 'The Atlantic and Home Waters: The Victorious Phase June 1944–May 1945', Air Ministry, undated, p. 117.

34. Paton, 'Scotland in the air war', p. 47; Lake, *Tartan Air Force*, pp. 179–81; Ross, *Scotland's Forgotten Valour*, pp. 72–3; Arthur, *Symbol of Courage*, p. 496.

35. L. Peillard, *Sink the Tirpitz!* (London: Jonathan Cape, 1968; London: Granta, 1975), pp. 294–326; J. Sweetman, *Tirpitz: Hunting the Beast* (Stroud: Sutton, 2000), pp. 182–253; D. Macintosh, *Bomber Pilot* (London: Browsebooks, 2006), pp. 1–14, 135–85.

36. Allan, *Commando Country*, pp. 107–8, 112–13; J. H. Devins, *The Vaagso Raid* (Toronto: Bantam Books, 1983), passim; T. Moreman, *British Commandos 1940–46* (Oxford: Osprey, 2006), pp. 59–66; Allan and Carswell, *The Thin Red Line*, p. 132; D. Van Der Vat, 'Into battle with a bow and arrow: Obituary: Jack Churchill', *Guardian*, 29 March 1996, Features, p. 17; H. McCorry, *The Thistle at War* (Edinburgh: National Museums of Scotland, 1997), pp. 16–17; Royal Highland Fusiliers Museum, Glasgow, R. King-Clark, *Jack Churchill: 'Unlimited Boldness'* (Knutsford: Fleur-de-Lys Publishing, 1997), pp. 1–5.

37. Allan, *Commando Country*, pp. 204–6; J. Miller, *The North Atlantic Front: Orkney, Shetland, Faroe and Iceland at War* (Edinburgh: Birlinn, 2003), pp. 90–5, 150–2; I. Herrington, 'The SIS and SOE in Norway 1940–1945: Conflict or cooperation?', *War in History*, vol. 9, no. 1 (2002), pp. 93–4; D. Howarth, *The Shetland Bus* (London: Thomas Nelson, 1951), passim. The 'Shetland bus' base was later transferred to Scalloway.

38. TNA, WO 199/1378, 'Plan "Fortitude": Scottish Command instructions', 1944. I am grateful to Dr David Stafford for bringing this document to my attention; R. Hesketh, *Fortitude: The D-Day Deception Campaign* (London: St Ermin's Press, 1999), passim; M. Howard, *Strategic Deception in the Second World War* (London: Pimlico, 1992), pp. 103–32; D. Stafford, 'Scotland's secret war', *The Scotsman*, 14 February 2005, pp. 26–7; Lindsay, *Forgotten General*, pp. 166–9; Royle, *A Time of Tyrants*, pp. 184-7; The Scots at War Trust, available at www.scotsatwar.org.uk/AZ/dday.htm, accessed on 19 November 2008, and East Lothian at War, available at www.eastlothianatwar.co.uk/opfn.html, accessed on 19 November 2008. Some formations in Northern Ireland were also included in the 4th Army's order of battle.
39. 'Gruinard Island: The historical background 1942–1972', by G. B. Carter, Chemical Defence Establishment, Porton Down, 1981. I am indebted to Dr Stafford for providing me with a copy of this document; D. Powell, 'The mystery of Death Island', *Today: The New John Bull*, 19 May 1962, pp. 6–7; G. B. Carter, *Porton Down: 75 Years of Chemical and Biological Research* (London: HMSO, 1992), pp. 52–3, 80–2; R. Harris and J. Paxman, *A Higher Form of Killing: A Secret History of Chemical and Biological Warfare* (London: Arrow, 2002), pp. 68–74; E. A. Willis, 'Landscape with dead sheep: What they did to Gruinard Island', *Medicine, Conflict and Survival*, vol. 18, no. 2 (2002), pp. 199–210; ibid. 'Contamination and compensation: Gruinard as a "menace to the mainland"', *Medicine, Conflict and Survival*, vol. 20, no. 4 (2004), pp. 334–43.
40. J. A. Crang, *The British Army and the People's War 1939–1945* (Manchester: Manchester University Press, 2000), pp. 2, 144. It should be recorded that the Military Training Act of May 1939 required men of twenty years of age to undertake six months' training in the armed forces. This was superseded by the National Service (Armed Forces Act) of September 1939 which imposed a liability for military service on all males between eighteen and forty-one for the duration of the emergency. This Act did not apply to Northern Ireland.
41. TNA, WO 73/163, general return of the strength of the British army on 31 December 1944.
42. E. M. B. Clements and K. G. Pickett, 'Stature of Scotsmen aged 18 to 40 years in 1941', *British Journal of Social Medicine* [hereafter *BJSM*], vol. 6 (1952), pp. 245–52; ibid. 'Body-weight of men related to stature, age, and social status: Weight of Scotsmen measured in 1941', *BJSM*, vol. 8 (1954), pp. 99–107; ibid. 'Chest girth of men related to stature, age, body-weight, and social status: Chest girth of Scotsmen measured in 1941', *BJSM*, vol. 8 (1954), pp. 108–16; ibid. 'Stature and weight of men

from England and Wales in 1941', *BJSM*, vol. 11 (1957), pp. 51–60. I am grateful to Dr Paul Addison for bringing these articles to my attention.

43. D. French, *Military Identities: The Regimental System, the British Army and the British People c. 1870-2000* (Oxford: Oxford University Press, 2005), pp. 278–82; Crang, *The British Army*, p. 17; J. Moffatt and A. Holmes McCormick, *Moon Over Malaya: A Tale of Argylls and Marines* (Stroud: Tempus, 2002), pp. 37-8.

44. S. Wood, *The Scottish Soldier* (Manchester: Archive Publications, 1987), pp. 127-8; A. Leask, *Sword of Honour: Jocks at War* (Barnsley: Pen and Sword, 2006), pp. 166-8; P. Grant, *A Highlander Goes to War: A Memoir 1939-46* (Edinburgh: Pentland Press, 1995), pp. 69-95; T. Royle, *The Royal Scots: A Concise History* (Edinburgh: Mainstream Publishing, 2006), pp. 177-93; T. Royle, *Queen's Own Highlanders: A Concise History* (Edinburgh: Mainstream Publishing, 2007), pp. 178-82; T. Royle, *The King's Own Scottish Borderers: A Concise History* (Edinburgh: Mainstream Publishing, 2008), pp. 184-95; T. Royle, *The Cameronians: A Concise History* (Edinburgh: Mainstream Publishing, 2009), pp. 155-9; Royle, *A Time of Tyrants*, pp. 78-88, 164-6, 300-3.

45. C. Smith, *Singapore Burning: Heroism and Surrender in World War Two* (London: Penguin, 2006), pp. 30, 272-83; I. M. Stewart, *History of the Argyll & Sutherland Highlanders 2nd Battalion (The Thin Red Line): Malayan Campaign 1941-42* (London: Thomas Nelson & Sons, 1947), passim; Moffatt and McCormick, *Moon Over Malaya*, passim; A. Rose, *Who Dies Fighting* (London: the Right Book Club, 1945), passim. The experience of Scottish POWs in the Far East can be explored through such sources as E. Lomax, *The Railway Man* (London: Jonathan Cape, 1995), T. McGowran, *Beyond the Bamboo Screen: Scottish Prisoners of War Under the Japanese* (Dunfermline: Cualann Press, 1999) and A. Urquhart, *The Forgotten Highlander: My Incredible Story of Survival during the War in the Far East* (London: Little, Brown, 2010).

46. Salmond, *The History of the 51st*, p. 4; R. Doherty, *None Bolder: The History of the 51st Highland Division in the Second World War* (Stroud: Spellmount, 2006), pp. 8-10.

47. S. David, *Churchill's Sacrifice of the Highland Division: France 1940* (London: Brassey's, 2004), p. 10.

48. 'Abolition of the kilt: Glasgow Highland Societies' protest against War Office decision', *The Scotsman*, 15 December 1939, p. 7.

49. 'Kilt controversy: Protagonists interview Scottish members', *The Scotsman*, 16 February 1940, p. 9; 'The army kilt', *The Scotsman*, 8 March 1940, p. 6. I am indebted to Dr Addison for alerting me to these articles.

50. David, *Churchill's Sacrifice*, pp. 10-11. I am grateful to Jesper Ericsson of the Gordon Highlanders' museum for further details of the kilt burning.
51. E. Linklater, *The Highland Division* (London: HMSO, 1942), passim; L. F. Ellis, *The War in France and Flanders 1939-1940* (London: HMSO, 1953), pp. 20, 249-52, 257, 262-93; Salmond, *The History of the 51st*, pp. 5-18; David, *Churchill's Sacrifice*, passim; B. Innes (ed.), *St Valery: The Impossible Odds* (Edinburgh: Birlinn, 2004), pp. 1-39.
52. Quoted in E. Reoch, *The St Valery Story* (Inverness: Highland Printers, 1965), p. 22; David, *Churchill's Sacrifice*, p. 241; Royle, *A Time of Tyrants*, p. 75. See also S. Longdon, *Dunkirk: The Men They Left Behind* (London: Constable, 2008), p. 154; D. Young, *Scottish Voices from the Second World War* (Stroud: Tempus, 2006), pp. 21, 24.
53. David, *Churchill's Sacrifice*, p. 242.
54. Salmond, *History of the 51st*, p. 18; M. N. McKibbin, *Barbed Wire: Memories of Stalag 383* (London: Staples Press, 1947), pp. 78, 88; The Wartime Memories Project, Stalag 383 POW Camp, available at www.wartimememories.co.uk/pow/stalag383.html, accessed on 28 December 2008, and Australian War Memorial, available at http://cas.awm.gov.au/photograph/P03537.002, accessed on 28 December 2008; Allan and Carswell, *The Thin Red Line*, p. 130.
55. David, *Churchill's Sacrifice*, pp. 242-7.
56. D. Caskie, *The Tartan Pimpernel* (London: Oldbourne Press, 1957; Edinburgh: Birlinn, 1999), passim; 'Memorial to the 51st Highland Division: Unveiling ceremony on St Valery cliff-top', *The Scotsman*, 12 June 1950, p. 7; Innes, *St Valery*, pp. 85-139.
57. Linklater, *The Highland Division*, pp. 7-10; Allan, *Commando Country*, p. 72; Doherty, *None Bolder*, pp. 7, 55; Wood, *The Scottish Soldier*, p. 120. In his history of the Second World War, Churchill marked the loss of the 51st Highland Division, and its rebirth through the redesignation of the 9th (Highland) Division, by quoting a verse of Charles Murray's First World War poem 'A Sough o' War':

Half-mast the castle banner droops,
    The Laird's lament was played yestreen,
An' mony a widowed cottar wife
    Is greetin' at her shank aleen.
In Freedom's cause, for ane that fa's,
    We'll gleen the glens an' send them three
To clip the reivin' eagle's claws,
    An' drook his feathers i' the sea.
For gallant loons, in brochs an' toons,
    Are leavin' shop an' yard an' mill,

A' keen to show baith friend an' foe,
  Auld Scotland counts for something still.

See W. S. Churchill, *The Second World War*, 6 vols (London: Cassell, 1949; London: Penguin, 2005), vol. 2, *Their Finest Hour*, p. 135. My thanks to Dr Addison for drawing this to my attention.

58. National Library of Scotland, Edinburgh [hereafter NLS], Acc 6119, 'Scottish soldier: An autobiography', by Douglas Wimberley, 4 vols (1974), vol. 2, 'World War II', pp. 21–7; C. F. French, 'The fashioning of *esprit de corps* in the 51st Highland Division from St Valery to El Alamein', *Journal of the Society for Army Historical Research*, vol. 77, no. 312 (1999), pp. 275–92; Salmond, *History of the 51st*, pp. 20–5; Doherty, *None Bolder*, pp. 56–9; Delaforce, *Monty's Highlanders*, pp. 22–7.

59. Lieutenant-Commander P. K. Kemp, *The Middlesex Regiment (Duke of Cambridge's Own) 1919–1952* (Aldershot: Gale and Polden, 1956), pp. 128–9.

60. E. Keyes, *Geoffrey Keyes VC, MC, Croix de Guerre, Royal Scots Greys, Lieut.-Colonel 11th Scottish Commando* (London: WDL Books, 1957), pp. 219–302; M. Asher, *Get Rommel: The Secret Mission to Kill Hitler's Greatest General* (London: Cassell, 2004), passim; Allan, *Commando Country*, pp. 96–7. The raid took place on the night of 17–18 November 1941. The leader of the raiding party, Aberdour-born Lieutenant-Colonel Geoffrey Keyes (son of Admiral Sir Roger Keyes), was awarded a posthumous VC for his part in the operation.

61. Salmond, *History of the 51st*, pp. 25–32; Doherty, *None Bolder*, pp. 60–7. This integration into a multinational force was not always an edifying spectacle. On one occasion, Wimberley spotted a black South African sporting a Balmoral bonnet and personally removed it from the bemused man's head. 'No doubt he really meant no harm,' recalled Wimberley, 'but our morale was pretty high, and I was having no black Africans in a Highland Regiment, or wearing the uniform of a Highland Regiment.' See NLS, Acc 6119, 'Scottish soldier', vol. 2, p. 35. For his part, Montgomery did not always display a sure touch with his Scottish troops. It is said that when he visited the 7th Black Watch in the desert, and was told that the battalion hailed from Fife, he asked, to the amazement of the officers lined up to meet him, 'Where's Fife?' and admitted that 'You see, I have never been to Scotland'. See Delaforce, *Monty's Highlanders*, p. 33.

62. R. Ryder, *Oliver Leese* (London: Hamish Hamilton, 1987), p. 102; Delaforce, *Monty's Highlanders*, p. 39.

63. NLS, Acc 6119, 'Scottish soldier', vol. 2, pp. 25, 38–9; Salmond, *History*

of the 51st, pp. 32–52; Doherty, *None Bolder*, pp. 68–91; Delaforce, *Monty's Highlanders*, pp. 38–59; C. P. S. Denholm-Young, *Men of Alamein* (Stevenage: Spa Books in association with Tom Donovan Publishing, 1987), pp. 9, 36.

64. J. McGregor, *The Spirit of Angus: The War History of the County's Battalion of the Black Watch* (Chichester: Phillimore, 1988), p. 39. McIntyre was recommended for a posthumous VC but this was unsuccessful.

65. NLS, Acc 6119, 'Scottish soldier', vol. 2, pp. 51, 63; '51st Division in battle: Story of Scots' courage', *The Scotsman*, 18 November 1942, p. 4; A Military Correspondent, 'With the 51st at Alamein: Deeds of heroism and endurance which broke the Afrika Korps', *The Scotsman*, 26 December 1942, p. 4; An Australian Correspondent, 'Barrage like an earthquake', *The Times*, 26 October 1942, p. 4; 'Pipes of war', *The Times*, 27 October 1942, p. 5; S. O. Rose, *Which People's War? National Identity and Citizenship in Britain 1939–1945* (Oxford: Oxford University Press, 2003), p. 230.

66. N. McCallum, *Journey with a Pistol: A Diary of War* (London: Victor Gollancz, 1959), pp. 48–9; Delaforce, *Monty's Highlanders*, p. 59.

67. Salmond, *History of the 51st*, pp. 53–74; Doherty, *None Bolder*, pp. 93–102; Delaforce, *Monty's Highlanders*, pp. 59–77; NLS, Acc 6119, 'Scottish soldier', vol. 2, pp. 85–7.

68. NLS, Acc 6119, 'Scottish soldier', vol. 2, pp. 86, 202.

69. McCallum, *Journey with a Pistol*, p. 80; Delaforce, *Monty's Highlanders*, p. 59.

70. Salmond, *History of the 51st*, pp. 75–98; Doherty, *None Bolder*, pp. 102–16; Delaforce, *Monty's Highlanders*, pp. 78–98.

71. NLS, Acc 6119, 'Scottish soldier', vol. 2, pp. 114–15; I. C. Cameron, *History of the Argyll & Sutherland Highlanders 7th Battalion: from El Alamein to Germany* (London: Thomas Nelson, 1947), pp. 89–96. In civilian life Campbell was a wine merchant. It was said that he had 'the finest palate for wine in Britain'. See P. Warner, 'Campbell, Lorne Maclaine, of Airds (1902–1991)', *Oxford Dictionary of National Biography*, Oxford University Press, 2004. Available at www.oxforddnb.com/view/article/49552, accessed on 12 August 2011. A less heroic personal account of the Wadi Akarit battle appears in V. Scannell, *Argument of Kings* (London: Futura, 1987).

72. Salmond, *History of the 51st*, pp. 100–29; Doherty, *None Bolder*, pp. 116–38; Delaforce, *Monty's Highlanders*, pp. 98–115; NLS, Acc 6119, 'Scottish soldier', vol. 2, p. 120.

73. H. Pond, *Sicily* (London: William Kimber, 1962), p. 165.

74. Ibid. p. 152.

75. H. Henderson, 'Scotland's Alamein', *Voice of Scotland*, vol. 3, no. 4 (1947), p. 3.
76. H. Henderson, '"Puir bluidy swaddies are weary": Sicily, 1943', in P. Addison and A. Calder (eds), *Time to Kill: The Soldier's Experience of War in the West 1939-1945* (London: Pimlico, 1997), pp. 324-6; T. Neat, *Hamish Henderson: A Biography*, 2 vols (Edinburgh: Polygon, 2007), vol. 1, *The Making of a Poet (1919-1953)*, pp. 97-122; A. Calder, 'Obituary: Hamish Henderson', *Independent*, 12 March 2002, p. 6.
77. Salmond, *History of the 51st*, p. 133.
78. S. David, *Mutiny at Salerno: An Injustice Exposed* (London: Brassey's, 1995), passim.
79. Ibid. p. 148.
80. Ibid. passim; NLS, Acc 6119, 'Scottish soldier', vol. 2, pp. 209-10.
81. Salmond, *History of the 51st*, pp. 129, 135-7; Doherty, *None Bolder*, pp. 139, 145-9; Delaforce, *Monty's Highlanders*, pp. 115, 121-5.
82. A. Borthwick, *Battalion: A British Infantry Unit's Actions from El Alamein to the Elbe 1942-1945* (London: Bâton Wicks, 2001), p. 130.
83. Salmond, *History of the 51st*, pp. 138-9.
84. Ibid. pp. 139-41; B. Millin, *Invasion* (Lewes: the Book Guild, 1991), pp. 69-71.
85. Salmond, *History of the 51st*, pp. 141-9; Doherty, *None Bolder*, pp. 152-64; Delaforce, *Monty's Highlanders*, pp. 125-41.
86. N. Hamilton, *Monty: Master of the Battlefield 1942-1944* (Sevenoaks: Coronet, 1985), pp. 701-2; M. Hastings, *Overlord: D-Day and the Battle for Normandy* (London: Papermac, 1993), p. 173; C. D'Este, *Decision in Normandy* (London: Robson Books, 2000), pp. 271-8; Delaforce, *Monty's Highlanders*, pp. 141-5; T. Copp, 'The 21st Army Group in Normandy: Towards a new balance sheet', in J. Buckley (ed.), *The Normandy Campaign 1944: Sixty Years On* (London: Routledge, 2006), p. 17; Royle, *A Time of Tyrants*, pp. 280-2.
87. Delaforce, *Monty's Highlanders*, p. 145.
88. Salmond, *History of the 51st*, p. 149; NLS, Acc 6119, 'Scottish soldier', vol. 3, 'A new profession' (1970), pp. 108-9.
89. NLS, Acc 7380/78, letter from Charles [Bullen-Smith] to Douglas Wimberley, 14 April 1952; also see Copp, 'The 21st Army Group in Normandy', pp. 16-17.
90. Salmond, *History of the 51st*, pp. 150-71; Doherty, *None Bolder*, pp. 167-79; Delaforce, *Monty's Highlanders*, pp. 145-59.
91. Salmond, *History of the 51st*, pp. 172-3.
92. Ibid. pp. 175-204; Doherty, *None Bolder*, pp. 186-210; Delaforce, *Monty's Highlanders*, pp. 165-94.

93. W. Miles, *The Life of a Regiment*, vol. 5, *The Gordon Highlanders 1919-1945* (London: Frederick Warne, 1981), p. 319.
94. P. Stolte, *The 51st Highland Division in the Ardennes, December 1944–January 1945* (Arnhem: privately published, 1999), passim; Salmond, *History of the 51st*, pp. 205-28; Doherty, *None Bolder*, pp. 210-35; Delaforce, *Monty's Highlanders*, pp. 194-217; M. Lindsay, *So Few Got Through* (London: Arrow, 1968), pp. 167-207; R. Grant, *The 51st Highland Division at War* (London: Ian Allan, 1977), pp. 119-25.
95. S. Whitehouse and G. B. Bennett, *Fear is the Foe: A Footslogger from Normandy to the Rhine* (London: Robert Hale, 1995), p. 151.
96. Salmond, *History of the 51st*, pp. 230-1; Doherty, *None Bolder*, pp. 235-7; Delaforce, *Monty's Highlanders*, pp. 203, 217-19.
97. McGregor, *The Spirit of Angus*, pp. 179-80.
98. Salmond, *History of the 51st*, pp. 232-60; Doherty, *None Bolder*, pp. 237-59; Delaforce, *Monty's Highlanders*, pp. 220-34.
99. J. Hunt, 'The day we captured Himmler', *Sunday Mail*, 3 April 2005, p. 46; T. Renouf, *Black Watch: Liberating Europe and Catching Himmler – My Extraordinary WW2 with the Highland Division* (London: Little, Brown, 2011), pp. 289-94; R. Manvell and H. Fraenkel, *Heinrich Himmler* (London: Heinemann, 1965), pp. 244-5; P. Padfield, *Himmler: Reichsführer-SS* (New York: Henry Holt, 1990), pp. 608-9; Doherty, *None Bolder*, pp. 265-6. Apparently, it was Himmler's two impressively built male escorts who stood out from the crowd and first aroused suspicions.
100. 'Memorial to the 51st Highland Division: Unveiling ceremony on St Valery cliff-top', *The Scotsman*, 12 June 1950, p. 7; NLS, Acc 6119, 'Scottish soldier', vol. 3, pp. 144-5; Salmond, *History of the 51st*, pp. 269-72; Delaforce, *Monty's Highlanders*, p. 237.
101. Salmond, *History of the 51st*, p. 270.
102. NLS, Acc 8681/103, letter from Major-General Sir James Drew to Major-General J. F. Hare, 19 June 1945.
103. Blake, *Mountain and Flood*, pp. 1-35.
104. Ibid. pp. 36-82. It should be noted that, for a short period in 1944, the 52nd also trained as an 'air-portable' formation. Advance elements of the division fought briefly in the Nijmegan corridor before the main body arrived on the continent.
105. Ibid. pp. 82-115; P. White, *With the Jocks* (Stroud: Sutton, 2002), p. 8.
106. Blake, *Mountain and Flood*, pp. 116-45.
107. Ibid. pp. 131-3; J. C. Kemp, *The History of the Royal Scots Fusiliers 1919-1959* (Glasgow: Robert Maclehose, 1963), pp. 291-3; *The Register of the Victoria Cross* (Cheltenham: This England Books, 1988), p. 91;

British army website, www.army.mod.uk/infantry/regiments/4598.aspx, accessed on 6 April 2009.
108. Blake, *Mountain and Flood*, pp. 146–58; Salmond, *History of the 51st*, pp. 226–7.
109. Blake, *Mountain and Flood*, pp. 159–206.
110. Ibid. pp. 2, 205.
111. Ibid. p. 18.
112. H. G. Martin, *The History of the Fifteenth Scottish Division 1939–1945* (Edinburgh: William Blackwood, 1948), pp. 1–57; J. Keegan, *Six Armies in Normandy: From D-Day to the Liberation of Paris* (London: Penguin, 1983), pp. 143–81; M. Chappell, *Scottish Divisions in the World Wars* (Oxford: Osprey, 1994), pp. 54–5; P. Delaforce, *Monty's Northern Legions: 50th Northumbrian and 15th Scottish Divisions at War 1939–1945* (Stroud: Sutton, 2004), pp. 109–23; Royle, *A Time of Tyrants*, pp. 283–4.
113. Martin, *The History of the Fifteenth*, pp. 80–148; Delaforce, *Monty's Northern Legions*, pp. 130–47.
114. Martin, *The History of the Fifteenth*, pp. 15, 149–70; Chappell, *Scottish Divisions*, p. 55; D. Flower, *History of the Argyll & Sutherland Highlanders 5th Battalion 91st Anti-tank Regiment* (London: Thomas Nelson, 1950), p. 49; NLS, Acc 7380/54, letter from Major-General G. H. A. MacMillan to Major-General D. Wimberley, 14 October 1943. The division's dispute with the military authorities over the issue of non-Scottish units wearing the tam-o'-shanter became known as the 'battle of the bonnet'.
115. Martin, *The History of the Fifteenth*, pp. 171–84; Delaforce, *Monty's Northern Legions*, pp. 160–2.
116. Martin, *The History of the Fifteenth*, pp. 185–270; Delaforce, *Monty's Northern Legions*, pp. 163–85.
117. Martin, *The History of the Fifteenth*, pp. 271–3.
118. Ibid. pp. 274–5. The 1st Commando Brigade also assaulted that night.
119. Quoted in ibid. p. 282.
120. Ibid. pp. 282–336; Blake, *Mountain and Flood*, p. 162; Delaforce, *Monty's Northern Legions*, pp. 186–213.
121. Martin, *The History of the Fifteenth*, pp. 340–1.
122. These figures are estimates calculated from the following sources: data provided by the Scottish National War Memorial; *Army Roll of Honour – World War II: Soldiers Died in the Second World War*; TNA WO 305/1837, 'Personnel of Scottish domicile/birth and/or serving in Scottish regiments: officers and men who fell in the two world wars', undated [but 1953]; *Strength and Casualties of the Armed Forces and Auxiliary Services of the United Kingdom 1939 to 1945*, Cmd.

6832, June 1946, pp. 6–8. The total 'Scottish' war dead number nearly 58,000. This figure includes such categories as Scots killed whilst serving in the merchant navy, civilians killed in Scotland as a result of enemy action and non-Scots killed whilst serving in Scottish regiments. I am indebted to Lt.-Col. Ian Shepherd and the trustees of the Scottish National War Memorial for allowing me access to the data from the SNWM, and to Janie Corley for assisting me in my calculations. For a discussion of the IQ of the Scottish war dead, see J. Corley, J. A. Crang and I. J. Deary, 'Childhood IQ and in-service mortality in Scottish army personnel during World War II', *Intelligence*, vol. 37, issue 3 (2009), pp. 238–42.

123. Quoted in Neat, *Hamish Henderson*, pp. 59–60, 111; R. J. Finlay, *Independent and Free: Scottish Politics and the Origins of the Scottish National party 1918–1945* (Edinburgh: John Donald, 1994), pp. 224–8, 231–2, 235; D. Young, 'The anti-conscription position', *Scots Independent*, February 1941, p. 6; ibid. 'Towards a Scottish war effort', *Scots Independent*, July 1942, p. 7. After the war, Douglas Wimberley became principal of University College, Dundee, and he appointed Douglas Young to a lectureship in Latin at the institution. Not only did Wimberley regard him as the best scholar for the post, but he also admired his moral courage in being prepared to go to prison for his political beliefs. See T. Harrison Place, 'Wimberley, Douglas Neil (1896–1983)', *Oxford Dictionary of National Biography*, Oxford University Press, 2004. Available at www.oxforddnb.com/view/article/63740, accessed on 12 August 2011.

124. G. MacDonald Fraser, *Quartered Safe Out Here: A Recollection of the War in Burma* (London: HarperCollins, 1995), p. 35.

125. Quoted in J. F. MacDonald, *The War History of Southern Rhodesia*, 2 vols (Salisbury: Government of Rhodesia, 1947), vol. 1, p. 283; J. A. I. Agar-Hamilton and L. C. F. Turner, *The Sidi Rezeg Battles 1941* (Cape Town: Oxford University Press, 1957), pp. 193–4, 501; B. Fergusson, *The Black Watch and the King's Enemies* (London: Collins, 1950), pp. 59, 109–10. I am grateful to Thomas Smyth of the Black Watch museum for his assistance in tracing the adjutant's identity. Stirling in fact died of his wounds in Cairo a few weeks later.

126. M. Middlebrook, *The Falklands War* (London: Penguin, 2001), pp. 339–42; J. Ellis, *The Sharp End: The Fighting Man in World War II* (Newton Abbot: David and Charles, 1980; London: Pimlico, 1990), p. 225.

22

The Cold War and Beyond

NIALL BARR

John Connell, in his magisterial biography of Field Marshal Sir Archibald Wavell, wrote that Wavell's campaigns in the desert during the early, desperate years of World War II

> belong to an epoch of military techniques as remote as Wellington's. There seems only the most tenuous, temporal connection between the world of the Matilda tank and the Stuka and that of the Polaris submarine and the concept of overkill.[1]

Connell published Wavell's biography in 1964, twenty-three years after the brief but impressive triumph of 'Operation Compass' known at the time as 'Wavell's offensive'. This was during the height of the Cold War, when the confrontation between the United States and the Soviet Union still seemed likely to bring an end to the world through nuclear war. It is a fortunate irony that this chapter, which seeks to explore the impact and influence of the Cold War upon Scotland, is written some twenty years after the fall of the Berlin Wall in an era where the logic and assumptions of concepts such as nuclear counterforce strategies and mutually assured destruction seem more remote and improbable than those of Wavell's campaigns.

Yet the Cold War had a very real impact upon the people and landscape of Scotland as military installations and weaponry were deployed to counter the Soviet threat. Scotland's defence and security were intimately bound up within the government, military and security structures of the United Kingdom, which often gave Scotland little if any choice about the military developments which impacted directly upon it. At the same time, Britain's impoverished and weakened state after the exertions of the Second World War led to a decline in world power status, and Scotland, like the rest of the country, had to adjust to these two aspects of global politics: the Cold War and Britain's dependency upon the United States.

This chapter traces aspects of the Cold War confrontation with respect to Scotland, while recognising that its defence was contained within the broader context of the defence of the United Kingdom, of western Europe and of the NATO alliance as a whole. The Cold War was, of course, the war that never happened, but Scottish soldiers, sailors and airmen were still involved in the many proxy wars of the Cold War era as well as the numerous wars that flared up as part of Britain's retreat from empire. In many of these conflicts there was as much continuity with Britain's imperial past and experience of the two world wars as there was change. Also examined are the humorously named, but deadly serious, 'Cod Wars' fought between Britain and Iceland over fishing rights in the North Atlantic.

The full impact and implications of the deteriorating relations between the United States and the Soviet Union really only emerged after the Soviets imposed a complete blockade of the road and rail routes into West Berlin on 24 June 1948. This marked the real start of the confrontation between East and West that came to be known as the Cold War. The hastily organised airlift, which eventually lasted for over a year, preserved the Western position in Berlin. During the crisis, George Marshall, the US secretary of state, asked Ernest Bevin, the British foreign secretary, to give permission for two US B-29 bomber groups to deploy to British airbases. The cabinet in London gave immediate approval with few questions asked.

It was widely, although erroneously, believed that the B-29s were armed with atomic bombs at this time. But the rushed deployment during the Berlin crisis meant that there was never any clear diplomatic agreement over the status of these bomber groups, which meant that the British government had no control over their use.[2] By the summer of 1950 these bombers *were* armed with nuclear weapons and the decision to so arm the planes had been made by the United States Air Force without reference to the British. This meant that 'Britain became a United States strategic nuclear base not as a consequence of British or United States political policy but simply as a result of a change in the USAF's operational capability.'[3] The country had indeed become an advanced air base or aircraft carrier for the United States. In February 1951 Churchill warned the House of Commons that 'We must not forget that by creating the atomic bases in East Anglia we have made ourselves the target and perhaps the bull's eye of a Soviet attack.'[4] Yet, strangely, there was little public debate or outcry at the time about Britain's direct involvement in the stand-off between the superpowers.

Scotland became directly involved in the nuclear issue after Prime Minister Harold Macmillan and President Dwight Eisenhower had a series of meetings in 1960 concerning nuclear strategy. In common with all post-war British prime ministers, Macmillan considered it a 'matter of national pride and prestige' that the country should maintain an independent nuclear deterrent.[5] Britain had first tested a fission bomb in October 1952 and a thermonuclear device in May 1957.[6] Its independent nuclear deterrent was based on the V-Bomber Force, which became operational in 1956.[7] The cancellation of 'Blue Streak', the British ballistic missile, in February 1960, however, left the government without a credible successor to this bomber force.[8] Macmillan believed it imperative to find a new way forward for the country's independent nuclear deterrent and met with Eisenhower at Camp David in 1960 to thrash out a new deal. Eventually, the president agreed to provide the British with the proposed 'Skybolt' air-delivered nuclear missile. Its introduction would help to extend the life of the V-Bomber Force and bridge the embarrassing gap left by the cancellation of 'Blue Streak'. This American generosity, however, had a quid pro quo. In return, Macmillan agreed to the establishment of a base for the new US Polaris ballistic missile submarines in Holy Loch on the Firth of Clyde.[9]

It did not take long for a reaction against these decisions to develop in Scotland. When parliament was informed of the proposed US base at Holy Loch (but not the fact that the deal was essentially 'Skybolt for Holy Loch') in November 1960, thirty Labour MPs, the majority of them Scottish, including Emmanuel Shinwell, a former minister of defence, and Emrys Hughes, MP for South Ayrshire, tabled a motion opposing the new base. Their motion argued that there were 'grave dangers that might arise' from the base over which the government 'could have no adequate control'.[10] The motion raised legitimate concerns but the deal went ahead. In fact, these were the same concerns that could well have been raised about the deployment of the B-29 bombers to East Anglia in 1948.

Although Scotland cannot claim to have begun the protest movement that became the Campaign for Nuclear Disarmament (CND), the Scottish arm of the movement certainly developed its own character during the 1960s. The inspiration behind CND came from the churches, scientists and intellectuals; it began as a middle-class movement but quickly drew support from a much wider base of public opinion concerned about the nuclear threat.

CND derived its first wave of support from fears about the environmental impact of atmospheric nuclear testing and the British testing and development of the hydrogen bomb.[11] The organisation was officially launched on 17 February 1958, with meetings held at the Central Hall Westminster and four overflow halls.[12] Its purpose was to 'persuade the British people that Britain must renounce unconditionally the use or production of nuclear weapons and refuse to allow their use by others in its defence'.[13] Working within existing sympathetic groups to forward its aims, most notably the Church of Scotland, trade unions and the Labour party, the majority of CND supporters preferred peaceful demonstration to influence public opinion, while a minority favoured the use of 'sit-ins' and non-violent civil disobedience to highlight the cause.[14] CND's most famous early action was the march to the Atomic Weapons Establishment at Aldermaston on Easter Sunday in 1958. The Scottish movement, however, developed its own distinctive protest against nuclear weapons and, in particular, against the American Polaris submarine force based at Holy Loch. Ironically enough, the submarines carrying Polaris ballistic missiles were seen as an ideal platform for nuclear weapons by naval planners and nuclear strategists since, once at sea, they were virtually undetectable and practically invulnerable to counter attack. It was believed that they would most likely draw fire away from the UK, as the boats would be cruising the North Atlantic when operational.[15] Nonetheless, these submarines, and their Scottish bases, became far more symbolic and emotive issues than the V-Bomber Force.

While CND had found only a lukewarm response to its appeals for protests in East Anglia and the Midlands where the V-Bombers were based, and found it difficult to 'translate sympathy into action' amongst local trade union groups,[16] the response in Scotland was very different. With the 'militant left-wing traditions and national consciousness of Clydeside', the Direct Action Committee Against Nuclear War (DAC), which had a younger membership and a more militant approach than the mainstream CND, was able to put civil disobedience into practice as one element of local protest against the bases.[17] When the USS *Proteus*, the Polaris depot ship, sailed down the Clyde and into Holy Loch on 18 February 1961, DAC mounted a canoe-borne protest on its arrival. On the same day, a 'Committee of 100' organised a 4,000-strong 'sit-down' outside the Ministry of Defence in London.[18] The presence of these huge submarines, with their enormously powerful missiles, turned 'what had been a terrifying abstraction' for many of the CND campaigners into something

Figure 22.1 Demonstration against Polaris in Paisley, 1961.

that was 'now only too real, visible, menacing. We had a particular target which was of immediate and direct relevance.'[19] The active and vocal Scottish Communist party was also a major participant in protests against these submarines, as it viewed the United States and Britain as the originators of the Cold War threat.[20] While its politics may have been misguided, the Scottish Communist Peace Movement was able to produce some memorable protest songs, the most famous of which was 'Ding Dong Dollar', with the chorus of 'Oh, ye cannae spend a dollar when ye're deid.'[21]

CND attracted considerable support from within the Labour party, and the high point of its activism came in 1960 when the Labour party conference passed a motion demanding that Britain should unilaterally begin nuclear disarmament. Almost immediately, the party leadership distanced itself from the CND position and was able to have the resolution overturned the following year. Nonetheless, the momentum of CND protests continued in 1961. Scottish CND organised a march of 1,000 protesters from Dunoon to Holy Loch on 4 March, with supporting demonstrations on 14 and 20 May which involved nearly 2,000 people.[22] These disturbances reached a climax when simultaneous sit-downs were organised for Battle of Britain

Sunday in September 1961, which resulted in 1,314 protesters being arrested in Trafalgar Square and 351 at Holy Loch.[23]

While CND and associated peace activists saw the American Polaris base as a symbol of everything they stood against, the people of Dunoon had to learn to live with the presence of the US Navy's 14th Submarine Squadron and its 1,800 US Navy personnel and 2,000 dependants.[24] This presence could sharply divide local opinion. The base commanders were keen to place a human face upon the American nuclear deterrent by throwing Christmas parties for local children and supporting charity events, but peace campaigners also pointed out that '[t]he large number of bored single sailors in an alien country has raised crime levels, particularly rape, vehicle offences, drink and drugs . . . Fights on shore are a regular occurrence.'[25] The US military presence certainly could cause tension in the local community but, in common with most military bases, could bring benefits as well.[26]

Meanwhile, Macmillan had managed to convince President John F. Kennedy, during intense negotiations between 19 and 21 December 1962 at Nassau, that the British should be allowed to abandon the now doomed 'Skybolt' and purchase Polaris missiles from the US instead. Although the submarines and warheads would be built in the United Kingdom, critics of the deal questioned just how 'independent' Britain's nuclear deterrent would be.[27] Nonetheless, it would appear that the British government secured a bargain through the Nassau Agreement and it has been argued that 'Polaris was undoubtedly the most successful British weapon procurement project of the whole post-war period'.[28]

The resolution of the Cuban Missile Crisis in 1962, and the Partial Test Ban Treaty in 1963, which brought the testing of nuclear bombs in the atmosphere to an end, seemed to settle at least some of the major issues that had given rise to CND. When Harold Wilson's Labour government took the decision to continue the British nuclear deterrent, and deploy Britain's own Polaris armed nuclear submarines, CND appeared to melt 'away as a major political force'. The issue of the Vietnam War came to dominate the agendas of peace movements and protest groups, and the general public were found to be 'learning to live with the bomb'.[29] Yet although the CND campaign in Scotland stalled, the nuclear issue remained of distinct concern to some groups north of the border.

The first British Polaris boat, HMS *Resolution*, went on operational patrol in June 1968 and a year later the Polaris force, operating out of Faslane on Gare Loch, officially became Britain's independent nuclear deterrent.[30] Combined with the Glen Douglas nuclear storage facility, the two Polaris bases became major parts of the Cold War infrastructure in Scotland. With British and American Polaris submarines based within thirty miles of Glasgow there was 'a constant reminder of the nuclear threat'.[31] It might even be said that Scottish CND kept the movement alive with its yearly demonstrations on Clydeside from 1973 onwards. These demonstrations, however, had little wider impact upon the general public or the government, which remained firm in its determination to keep Britain's nuclear deterrent.

The Cold War itself seemed to thaw during the 1970s in the era of détente between the superpowers. But in the meantime Britain found itself involved in one of the strangest disputes in its diplomatic history. From the late 1950s there was a series of quarrels between the United Kingdom and Iceland that led to the firing of live ammunition, if only as warning shots, in what became known as the 'Cod Wars'. This conflict over territorial waters was 'fought' in the cold waters of the North Atlantic between Icelandic coastguard vessels and British trawlers supported by Royal Navy vessels. It was also linked, however tangentially, to the Cold War as the Icelanders used the strategic importance of the Keflavik airbase to exert pressure on the United States over the issue.

The first Law of the Sea Conference, held in Geneva in February 1958, proposed a six-mile limit to territorial waters. This conference, however, broke up without any general agreement on limits for fishery. In this atmosphere, Iceland unilaterally declared a twelve-mile limit that would preclude British trawlers from fishing in the fertile Icelandic waters. After fruitless negotiations, the British government decided that the trawler fleet must be protected by the Royal Navy while fishing in the disputed zones off the Icelandic coast. This led to the first Cod War, lasting from September 1958 to March 1961 and which saw eighty-four attempts by Icelandic coastguard vessels to arrest British trawlers and the successful protection of these boats by naval warships. Although the 1960 Law of the Sea Conference failed to resolve the dispute, both governments agreed in March 1961 to recognise the Icelandic twelve-mile fishing zone, along with British 'historic fishing' rights in the outer six miles of the zone for a period of three years.

This agreement was followed by ten years of relative quiet but the dispute was revived when a left-wing coalition government took power in Iceland in July 1971, aiming to cancel the 1961 agreement and extend Iceland's territorial waters to fifty miles. Again, negotiations collapsed and, in September 1971, the Icelandic government declared the fifty-mile limit. The Royal Navy protection of British trawlers thus resumed until both parties reached an interim agreement in November 1973. The Icelandic government, however, continued to press its advantage, announcing in July 1975 an extension of its territorial waters to 200 miles. In November of that year British trawlermen again demanded Royal Navy protection and the confrontation continued. During this period there were numerous incidents of warp cuttings, as well as fifty-six collisions, which resulted in serious damage to Royal Navy frigates, before the British government accepted defeat. The Icelandic arguments clearly influenced the international agreements, made during 1976 and 1977, to enshrine a twelve-mile limit on its territorial waters and to extend an economic exclusion zone to 200 miles.

From 1977 onwards the British distant water trawler fleet was rapidly paid off. While most of the fishing boats involved came from such English ports as Hull, Grimsby and Fleetwood, the Scottish inshore trawler fleet was badly affected. British agreements with the European Economic Community (EEC), in combination with the aftermath of the Icelandic disputes, meant that many traditional fishing grounds were now off limits to Scottish fishermen at the very same time that Scottish waters were open to fishermen from all EEC countries.[32] The Cod Wars were thus a series of conflicts that the United Kingdom, and Scotland, lost and, in some respects at least, they marked an end to the form of gunboat diplomacy that the Royal Navy had practised for over two centuries.

By the late 1970s James Callaghan's Labour government found itself on the horns of a dilemma over the issue of a replacement system for Polaris. Although the Labour party's declared policy was not to replace it, a secret committee composed of Callaghan, Denis Healey, the chancellor, David Owen, the foreign secretary, and Fred Mulley, the secretary of state for defence, decided to acquire a successor system if it could be afforded. Callaghan and President Carter discussed options at the Guadeloupe summit in January 1979, but it was Margaret Thatcher's new Conservative administration that took the final decision, in July 1980, to order the American Trident C-4 SLBM, an agreement that was altered in the following year to include the upgraded D-5 missile.[33]

The Trident programme continued throughout the Thatcher years and seemed an integral part of the 'second' Cold War. After a period of détente in the 1970s, relations between the United States and the Soviet Union deteriorated markedly, with the deployment of Soviet SS-20 missiles in 1978 and the Soviet invasion of

Afghanistan in 1979. Ronald Reagan's presidency was marked by an intensification of the arms race, such as the controversial American deployment of cruise missiles to Britain and Europe in 1982. This precipitated the Greenham Common peace camp in March 1982 after a series of demonstrations and sit-ins.[34] This was emulated in Scotland with a peace camp at Faslane which kept up a series of vigils and demonstrations against the British nuclear deterrent. During the 1980s Scottish CND worked with a number of groups, including Trident Ploughshares and the Scottish Campaign against Trident (SCAT), to build up opposition to the Trident submarines and their missiles.[35]

Although the deployment of American and British nuclear submarines to the Clyde was the most visible and controversial manifestation of the Cold War, this was certainly not the only impact of that conflict upon Scotland. From the late 1940s, existing bases and installations were joined by new ones which a decade later had made Scotland into a major bastion of NATO's 'Northern Flank'. Much of Scotland's military role concerned radar early warning, air defence, electronic listening posts and air and maritime patrolling of the Greenland–Iceland–UK 'gap' through which Soviet submarines could surge in the event of war. However, almost the entire range of military activity was to be found in Scotland, from army barracks and firing ranges to the nuclear research facilities at Dounreay in Caithness. Some bases were kept on twenty-four-hour alert, such as RAF Leuchars where pilots were always ready to 'scramble' their fighters to intercept the long-range Soviet bombers that played a game of 'cat and mouse' over the North Sea throughout the Cold War.

The impact of these installations can be illustrated by looking at the furthest flung military base in Scotland. The island of Unst, the most northerly of the Shetland islands, was first identified as an important site for radar in 1940. After its construction, RAF Saxa Vord, named after the highest peak on the island, became an important part of the 'Chain Home' radar system which provided radar early warning for the British Isles. With the run down of these radar stations in the latter part of the war, the base was closed in 1945.[36] In the aftermath of the Korean War, however, the air defences of the UK were revealed as inadequate to counter what became seen as a serious threat from Soviet long-range naval aviation.[37] An intensive period of scientific research and military planning resulted in a new integrated system of radar coverage for the United Kingdom, known as the ROTOR programme. A new radar station was thus constructed at Saxa Vord and became operational in 1956. Linked with new stations at Buchan and

Anstruther, RAF Saxa Vord once again became an integral part of the air defence of the United Kingdom. It was of particular importance as it provided radar coverage across a great span of the North Atlantic and provided a radar picture all the way from the Faroes to Norway. The station was progressively updated during the Cold War but, quite apart from its vital military function, its development also revealed the often ambiguous relationship between the military build-up of the Cold War and the Scottish people. On the one hand, there were few people who actually welcomed the cost and development of these military installations but, at the same time, local communities across Scotland, particularly in remote areas, became dependent upon the military for their livelihoods. RAF Saxa Vord became central to the local economy and provided the majority of jobs and income on the island. The RAF brought electricity to the islanders and provided them with their only doctor, dentist, fire brigade and cinema.[38] The military thus played an often overlooked role in not only sustaining but also changing communities across Scotland.

All of the defence and security assumptions which had held good for over forty years, however, became obsolete virtually overnight in 1989. The fall of the Berlin Wall in December of that year marked the unexpected beginning of the end of the Cold War. The rapid removal of the Soviet military threat led to an equally rapid drawdown of Western military forces in what became known as the 'peace dividend'. Bases across Scotland were closed or mothballed as the reason for their existence had disappeared. This posed severe challenges for communities that had become dependent upon military spending. When the US Navy pulled out of Holy Loch in 1992, it marked the end of a thirty-year relationship between the US Navy and Dunoon and the closure of that chapter resulted in real economic hardship in an area that had come to rely on US Navy dollars.[39] RAF Saxa Vord remained in operation for some considerable time but the final closure of the base in April 2006 was a serious blow to the island of Unst and its economy. The old RAF installations are now being reused in an innovative tourism venture,[40] but the steady income that the military had provided for over fifty years is no longer present. It is perhaps not too much to say that Scotland is still adjusting, in economic and social terms, to the end of the Cold War.

By the time that the first British Trident boat became operational on the Clyde in December 1994, the world had changed considerably. Britain still had its independent nuclear deterrent but there seemed to be no enemy which it was necessary to deter with such overwhelming nuclear devastation. Trident boats were now armed with thirty-six warheads which was half their maximum capacity.[41] Campaigners at the Faslane peace camp, and beyond, continued to use a wide variety of tactics to make their point. These included water-borne protests; attempts to stop road convoys carrying nuclear warheads; chaining themselves to railings; and illegal trespass.[42] Perhaps the most notorious incident took place in June 1999 when three activists gained access to a Ministry of Defence floating laboratory and destroyed property worth £80,000. When their case was brought to trial at Greenock Sheriff Court, their defence, which eventually led to their acquittal, was that Trident was illegal and that they had an obligation under international law to attempt to stop its use.[43] Despite this victory in the courts, neither Scottish CND nor any of the Scottish peace groups have been able to alter government policy on this sensitive issue. Nonetheless, research has shown that '[p]ublic attitudes on nuclear weapons are fluid, ambivalent and contradictory'.[44] This is just as true in Scotland as in the rest of the United Kingdom.

Nuclear devastation might have remained a threat rather than a reality, but throughout the period of the Cold War, and beyond, Scottish soldiers, sailors and airmen served in Britain's conventional armed forces just as they had in previous generations. Conscription remained in force after the Second World War, only to be superseded by National Service, which lasted until 1960. A generation of young post-war Scots thus gained experience of the armed forces whether they liked it or not. With the demise of National Service in 1960, the armed forces returned to a more traditional volunteer footing. Throughout the period of the Cold War, British forces remained in Germany, first as an army of occupation and, from 1949, as part of the British Army of the Rhine (BAOR). Thousands of Scottish soldiers and airmen served in the BAOR and garrison duty in Germany became a way of life as it had been for their predecessors in India in previous decades.

When the 2nd Black Watch marched through Karachi, now the capital of a newly independent Pakistan, on 26 February 1948, before embarking on one of the last British troopships to leave the subcontinent, it marked a very significant end of an era.[45] India had been the linchpin of the British empire, and 'second home' to the British army, and its loss divested the rest of Britain's possessions of much of their significance and value. It took a further twenty years before Britain had, sometimes reluctantly, withdrawn from all its major colonies and dependencies, in what became an inexorable process. However, as Correlli Barnett has pointed out, since the British government 'clung on successively to these pointless military bases' which were 'unwelcome to the local peoples', it often meant that the British army 'had to endure the consequences' in the form of nationalist movements that utilised guerrilla war and terrorism to persuade the British to leave.[46]

It is impossible to encapsulate neatly the experience of Scots who served in the armed forces all over the world during this period. It is perhaps sufficient to consider a small sample of that service in order to illustrate the changing and conflicting demands that were placed upon troops in these varied conflicts. The writer of a short regimental history of the Gordon Highlanders summed up the role of the British soldier since the end of the Second World War as 'not unlike that of a highly efficient repertory actor, prepared for tragedy or epic, farce or black comedy'.[47] He noted that the Gordons' experience up to 1968 included

> Three years of appalling conditions and perseverance in Malaya; over two years facing the sniper's bullet and the hatred of ordinary women and children in Cyprus; service in Germany, Kenya and other parts of the explosive south-east quarter of Africa; nine months spent patrolling the jungles of North Borneo and waiting for Indonesian infiltrators; these have left their scars and their casualties, often fatal.[48]

It was perhaps not surprising, given that Scottish soldiers had often been in the forefront of the imperial expansion, that many Scottish regiments were involved in the numerous conflicts throughout the world during the retreat from empire, as well as the 'proxy wars' of the superpowers.

The first 'shooting war' Britain became involved in as a result of the Cold War was the Korean War of 1950–3. The North Korean invasion of the South took the United States and its allies by surprise. The very fact that it was General Douglas MacArthur of Pacific war fame, commander of the American troops, who reversed the North's invasion with amphibious landings at Inchon, indicates the United States' military predominance in the theatre. Nevertheless, Britain managed to organise a Commonwealth division which took part in the intense fighting following the Chinese intervention in support of North Korea. In the resulting stalemate between the United Nations forces and the Chinese, the war resolved into bitter fighting for hill lines as the Chinese attempted to win minor objectives as bargaining counters for the ongoing armistice negotiations. It was during this period of static warfare that the 1st Black Watch found itself involved in a tough fight for an area of low hills known

Figure 22.2 Soldiers of the 1st battalion, the Black Watch, after the battle of the Hook, Korea, 1952.

as the 'Hook' in November 1952. The battalion took over responsibility for the area on 4 November and found itself repeatedly shelled and mortared for the following two weeks. On 18 November, in scenes reminiscent of the First World War, 4,000 Chinese shells pounded the Black Watch in a preliminary bombardment before numerous assaults were made on its positions.[49] The battalion suffered 107 casualties in one of the most intense engagements since the Second World War.[50]

While the fighting during the Korean War resembled that of the world wars, most of the conflicts that Scottish soldiers experienced after 1945 were less bloody but equally challenging battles against terrorists and guerrillas as Britain retreated from empire. Many Scottish regiments saw service during the long years of patrolling against the 'Communist Terrorists' in the Malayan Emergency of 1948 to 1960. The Scottish regiments that took part in this conflict fought in the era of National Service and, before the major defence cuts of the 1960s, included the Scots Guards, the Royal Scots Fusiliers, the King's Own Scottish Borderers, the Cameronians, the Seaforth Highlanders and the Queen's Own Cameron Highlanders.

Scottish troops also took part in the softly prosecuted, but deadly serious, undeclared war known as the 'Indonesian Confrontation'. The roots of this conflict lay in the aspirations of the Indonesian president, Dr Sukarno, who believed that the three British dependencies of Sarawak, Sabah and the Sultanate of Brunei on the northern coast of Borneo should be absorbed into his new pro-Communist Indonesia. Sukarno sponsored revolts which first broke out in Brunei on 8 December 1962, and subsequently Sarawak, both of which met with a rapid response from the British army, acting in the manner that had characterised its actions in many previous 'policing' actions throughout the empire. Although these internal risings were put down, the Indonesians then began to mount cross-border incursions to put pressure upon the three dependencies. These attacks intensified in 1963 when the newly independent Sarawak and Sabah decided to join the Federation of Malaysia rather than Indonesia. In 1964 the Indonesians launched raids on Singapore and the Malay peninsula, as well as mounting a full-scale invasion of Sarawak and Sabah through the inhospitable and remote jungles of central Borneo. It was during this dangerous situation that the 1st Gordon Highlanders were sent to Borneo where the soldiers had to live and work in the extreme conditions of the jungle. It was reported that '[a]ccommodation was dank and rotten, hygiene was hit-and-miss; in one location the only source of drinking water was the sky, and the other duplication a stream below the camp'.[51] While other British troops sent to the area, including the Brigade of Gurkhas, fought numerous skirmishes with the Indonesians, the Gordons only saw the enemy twice during a hard year of patrolling: their constant struggle was against the conditions they encountered in the jungle. Nonetheless, they had played their part in a campaign that eventually dissuaded the Indonesians from continuing their incursions into Borneo. This low-key campaign has been called 'one of the most efficient uses of military force'.[52]

Among the most controversial actions by a Scottish battalion in the post-war period was the retaking of Crater in Aden by the 1st Argyll and Sutherland Highlanders in July 1967. Aden had become the headquarters of Britain's Middle East Command and, even after fighting an intense war in the Radfan in 1964–5 against Yemeni opposition, the British intention had been to hold on to the base for future decades. However, opposition to British rule grew into armed resistance and terrorism in Aden and, in 1966, the British government announced its intention to leave the colony by 1968. With this apparent abdication of responsibility, the two rival factions of the National Liberation Front and the Front for the Liberation of South Yemen began to conduct a virtual civil war to decide who would take power once the British had left.

The deteriorating situation became even worse when, on 20 June 1967, the Aden armed police and the Aden Federal National Guard, both of which had been heavily infiltrated by the rival liberation groups, mutinied against British control and killed a number of soldiers from the Argylls and the Northumberland Fusiliers. This led to a humiliating British withdrawal from Crater, the old town of Aden, and a further deterioration in the security situation. Many Arabs in Aden and across the Middle East saw the occupation of Crater as revenge for the devastating Arab defeat by Israel in the Six Day War, which had taken place just two weeks before.[53]

In a well-planned operation on the evening of 3 July, codenamed 'Operation Stirling Castle', Lieutenant-Colonel Colin Mitchell led his Argylls back into Crater. In an echo of previous colonial campaigns, the skirl of the regimental pipes was to be heard as two companies reoccupied the town against limited opposition.[54] Mitchell's intent was to dominate and pacify Crater through the application of what he called 'Argyll Law'. There were, however, suspicions that the troops used excessive force in their attempt to keep order, and Mitchell was eventually reined in by the commander-in-chief, Admiral Le Fanu.[55] Nevertheless, he made full use of the British media in Aden to get his side of the story across and became something of a hero in the British press, being christened 'Mad Mitch', much to the embarrassment of the British government. Controversy aside, the Argylls did maintain order in Crater until, on the night of 25–6 November, they were finally withdrawn and then evacuated with the rest of the British force. Although their actions gave a shred of comfort to the British public, the conflict in Aden and the eventual British evacuation represented the 'most ignominious retreat' since the withdrawal from Palestine in 1947.[56]

Within months of their return from Aden, the future of the Argylls was threatened as Britain's conventional military forces were progressively reduced and regiments faced disbandment or amalgamation as a result of the decline in the country's global position. A vociferous public campaign to 'Save the Argylls' from disbandment was fought with parliamentary support organised by George Younger MP. The battalion was indeed broken up but was reformed in 1972 when more

Figure 22.3 Lieutenant-Colonel Colin 'Mad Mitch' Mitchell of the Argyll and Sutherland Highlanders at the wheel, Aden, 1967.

infantry was required for the growing number of patrols in Northern Ireland.[57] Other regiments accepted amalgamation quietly and with a certain degree of resignation. The Seaforth Highlanders, for example, had a distinguished history dating back to the raising of the regiment in 1778 but were selected for amalgamation in 1961.[58] They amalgamated with the Queen's Own Cameron Highlanders to become the 1st Battalion Queen's Own Highlanders (Seaforth and Camerons) with relatively little protest as the traditions of both regiments could be continued within the new organisation.[59]

One regiment, however, stands out as it elected to disband rather than see its traditions diluted through amalgamation. The Cameronians (Scottish Rifles) had first been raised in 1689 from the covenanters of the south-west of Scotland (who had only recently been engaged in a guerrilla war against the soldiers and dragoons of King James II) to fight for William of Orange against Bonnie Dundee.[60] It had, like many Scottish regiments, been involved in numerous campaigns after the Second World War. It had seen active service in Malaya, done garrison duty with the BAOR and taken part in the short Oman campaign in 1957–8. As a full-strength battalion it

Figure 22.4 Disbandment service of the 1st battalion, the Cameronians (Scottish Rifles), Douglas, Lanarkshire, 1968.

had undertaken a difficult but successful tour in Aden during 1966–7. There was thus considerable surprise when it was announced that the Lowland Brigade would be reduced by one battalion and that the council of colonels did not recommend amalgamation.[61] The Cameronians felt that their roots in the covenanting tradition were so distinctive that disbandment was preferable. It was decided to 'play things in typical Covenanter style, and fall back on dourness and silence rather than any attempts at generating widespread publicity'.[62] As a result, the regiment was disbanded where it had first been raised, at Douglas in Lanarkshire on 14 May 1968. With the last armed conventicle of the Cameronians, a distinctive strand of Scottish military tradition had ended.[63]

The Royal Scots Greys represented a further strand of that tradition. This regiment, which had first been raised in 1678 to deal with the covenanters in an echo of the deep religious and political divisions of the late seventeenth century, remained the only cavalry regiment recruited in Scotland, and the sole cavalry regiment in the British army that had never been amalgamated. After service in Libya and Egypt during the 1950s, it manned the Royal Armoured Corps Recruit Training Regiment at Catterick before returning to front-line duties preparing for the expected armoured clash between East and West on the plains of northern and central Germany. In 1961 it became the first regiment in the army to revert once more to an all-regular establishment. Just seven years short of its three hundredth anniversary, however, it was amalgamated with the 3rd Carabiniers (which itself was the result of an amalgamation of the 3rd and 6th Dragoon Guards in 1922) into the Royal Scots Dragoon Guards.[64] It has to be said, however, that it lost none of its Scottish character in the process, maintaining its recruiting base in Scotland as well as its regimental headquarters in Edinburgh castle.[65] Equipped with Challenger tanks, it then put its training, originally designed for the Central Front, into practice in the Kuwaiti desert during the First Gulf War of 1990–1.

While many of the campaigns conducted by the British army during the Cold War were low-key, 'low intensity' counter-insurgency campaigns that often did not register much public interest, the Falklands War of 1982 seems to stand out, alongside the First Gulf War, as an example of a rapid but intense operation that generated great popular support. When Argentine special forces landed near Port Stanley on East Falkland on 2 April 1982, they took the British government by surprise. The Argentine Junta, led by General Galtieri, aimed to settle a 150-year-old colonial dispute with Britain over the sovereignty of the Falkland Islands by seizing them. It hoped to divert growing protest and dissension within Argentina and calculated that the United Kingdom no longer possessed the military force or political will to recover the islands. Unlike many of the conflicts of the Cold War, the dispute seemed to represent a clear challenge to Britain's prestige and was answered with the formation and despatch of a Royal Navy task force to the South Atlantic.

It was in this context that the 2nd Scots Guards experienced one of the sharpest transitions from peace to war of any Scottish regiment during the twentieth century. In the spring of 1982 the battalion was conducting public duties in London when it was hurriedly selected to become part of the 5th Infantry Brigade, designated to support 3rd Commando Brigade in any possible ground campaign in the Falklands. The battalion was rapidly removed from public duties to enable it to undertake a hurried active service training programme in the Brecon Beacons of Wales. This was followed by a long shipborne journey to the South Atlantic, and by 2 June the battalion had reached San Carlos Water in the Falkland Islands. This was a demonstration of the global reach and mobility that the British army had taken for granted during the days of empire but which had become an increasingly rare occurrence in the 1970s and 1980s. The battalion was then transported by HMS *Intrepid* to Bluff Cove so that it

Figure 22.5 Celebrating the news of the Argentine surrender: Scots Guards on Mount Tumbledown, Falkland Islands, 14 June 1982.

could take part in the British drive upon Port Stanley, the capital of the Falklands.⁶⁶

Although their sister battalion, the Welsh Guards, had suffered grievous casualties when attacked while still onboard the logistic landing ships *Sir Galahad* and *Sir Tristram* at Bluff Cove on 8 June, the Scots Guards were ready to take a full part in the final battle for Port Stanley. On the night of 13 June, the battalion assaulted the Argentine positions on Mount Tumbledown. The left flank of the Scots Guards fought a tough seven-hour battle against determined and well-dug-in enemy marines. The leading elements, under their company commander Major John Kiszely, used grenades and bayonets to subdue the defence and reach the summit. The subsequent exploitation by the right flank of the battalion took the last key Argentine positions and the soldiers were able to look down and see the lights of Stanley in the distance. The attack was considered 'an epic battle when, against all the odds, a well prepared enemy, sited on dominating and often insurmountable crags, was overwhelmed

Figure 22.6 The colours of the 1st battalion, the Black Watch, being paraded during the Hong Kong handover ceremony, 1997.

by men determined to win.'⁶⁷ The attack on Tumbledown proved to be the last major action of the war and, on the morning of 14 June 1982, General Menéndez surrendered the Argentine garrison on the Falklands. The Scots Guards spent a further seven weeks on the islands before returning home to 'the greatest welcome any battalion of the Regiment has received for many a long year'.⁶⁸ By September, the battalion was back in London and preparing to resume its interrupted public duties. This remains a classic example of the unexpected demands that can suddenly be placed upon units of the British armed forces at any time. It also represented, in retrospect, a throwback to Britain's colonial wars of the past.

Despite the key role that the Royal Navy played in the recovery of the Falkland Islands, the change in Britain's post-war global position, as well as her relative economic decline, had serious consequences for Scottish naval shipbuilding. A shipyard on the Clyde had first built a warship for the Royal Navy in 1794, and shipbuilding for the navy had flourished there during the nineteenth and early twentieth centuries. By the time that HMS *Vanguard*, the last British battleship to be built, left the Clyde in 1946 that relationship was, however, in doubt.⁶⁹ The size of the Royal Navy was reduced, particularly in the wake of Denis Healey's 1966 Defence Review, which abandoned the defence role east of Suez, and the Nott Review of 1981, which focused Britain's armed forces almost solely on their NATO responsibilities within Europe. The 'peace dividend' at the end of Cold War saw further deep cuts. All this meant that there were far fewer orders for ships and the naval shipbuilding industry on the Clyde went into seemingly terminal decline. Warships are still being built there, most notably the Type 45 Daring Class,[70] but the numbers of vessels produced, and therefore the number of workers involved, are now a tiny fraction of what they once were. The decline of naval shipbuilding on the Clyde was just one aspect, although a significant one, of Scotland's painful adjustment to a post-industrial economy.

It fell to the Black Watch, as the oldest Highland regiment, to mark the end of another historic era. In 1997 the 1st battalion spent five months in Hong Kong before taking part in the ceremonies to mark the transfer of power from Britain to the People's Republic of China. When, on 30 June, Corporal James Macaulay lowered the Union flag to mark the termination of British rule in the colony it seemed to represent more than just the handing over of Hong Kong: it symbolised the end of an imperial age. The long association between Scotland's soldiers and the maintenance of Britain's empire had come to an end.[71]

By the turn of the millennium, many political theorists and thinkers were speculating on the role and utility of military force in the modern world. During the 1990s the main value of western armed forces had appeared to be in peacekeeping missions, policing and moderating the effects of civil wars and ethnic violence in failed states. Few people could have predicted the kind of strategic shock that occurred on 11 September 2001 with the terrorist attacks on the Twin Towers in New York and the Pentagon in Washington DC. These attacks, and the United States' response in the form of the 'war on terror', opened a new chapter in international relations. Britain, and Scotland, found itself committed as an ally of the United States to war in Iraq in 2003 in what was the most controversial and divisive conflict for Britain since the Suez crisis of 1956. In a strange, and possibly uncomfortable repetition of the past, the Black Watch, amongst other Scottish regiments, was involved in the 2003 invasion of Iraq; indeed, it led the advance into the southern Iraqi city of Basra. In October 2004 the regiment grabbed further headlines when it was moved into the American sector of Iraq to relieve US troops preparing for the assault on Fallujah. This deployment to Camp Dogwood proved especially emotive since plans were being mooted back in Britain to merge all of the remaining Scottish regiments into one

'Royal Regiment of Scotland' and thus subsume much of Scotland military identity into one organisation.[72] These emotions, and the experience of the Black Watch soldiers during the deployment, have been captured in Gregory Burke's acclaimed play *Black Watch*, which was first staged in 2006 at the National Theatre of Scotland. This play is only the latest cultural artefact to be inspired by the interrelationship between Scotland and its military forces.

In the new realities of the twenty-first century, the Cold War, and the superpower rivalry that underpinned it, seem part of a long-forgotten era. The fear of imminent nuclear war has been replaced by the anxiety of a far greater terrorist threat than that posed by the IRA for over thirty years. But whilst there is no longer an immediate external military threat to the UK, Scotland's young men and women in the British armed forces are still serving overseas as they have done for centuries. They will continue to add to the annals of Scottish military history.

Notes

1. J. Connell, *Wavell: Soldier and Scholar, to June 1941* (London: Collins, 1964), p. 15.
2. D. Dimbleby and D. Reynolds, *An Ocean Apart: The Relationship between Britain and America in the Twentieth Century* (London: Guild Publishing, 1988), pp. 177–8.
3. R. H. Paterson, *Britain's Strategic Nuclear Deterrent: From Before the V-Bomber to Beyond Trident* (London: Frank Cass, 1997), p. 8.
4. Quoted in C. Driver, *The Disarmers: A Study in Protest* (London: Hodder and Stoughton, 1964), p. 21.
5. A. J. R. Groom, *British Thinking About Nuclear Weapons* (London: Frances Pinter, 1974), p. 39.
6. Paterson, *Britain's Strategic Nuclear Deterrent*, pp. 10–11.
7. Ibid. p.11.
8. E. Grove, *Vanguard to Trident: British Naval Policy since World War II* (London: US Naval Institute Press, 1987), pp. 235–6.
9. Ibid. p. 237.
10. *The Times*, 3 November 1960, p. 12.
11. P. Byrd, 'The development of the peace movement in Britain', in W. Kaltefleiter and R. L. Pfaltzgraff (eds), *The Peace Movements in Europe and the United States* (London: Croom Helm, 1985), p. 64.
12. J. Minnion and P. Bolsover, *The CND Story: The First 25 Years of CND in the Words of the People Involved* (London: Allison and Busby, 1983), p. 9.

13. CND Resolution 1958 quoted in R. Taylor and C. Pritchard, *The Protest Makers: The British Nuclear Disarmament Movement of 1958–1965 Twenty Years On* (Oxford: Pergamon, 1980), p. 7.
14. Ibid. p. 7
15. Grove, *Vanguard to Trident*, p. 202.
16. Minnion and Bolsover, *CND*, p. 52.
17. Ibid. p. 52
18. Ibid. p. 21.
19. Ibid. p. 54.
20. W. Thompson, 'Scottish Communists in the Cold War', in B. P. Jamison (eds), *Scotland and the Cold War* (Dunfermline: Cualann Press, 2003), pp. 39–69.
21. For the full song, see B. P. Jamison, 'Will they blow us a' tae hell? Strategies and obstacles for the disarmament movement in Scotland', in Jamison, *Scotland and the Cold War*, p. 143; Minnion and Bolsover, *CND*, p. 54.
22. Ibid. p. 115.
23. Ibid. p. 22.
24. M. Spaven, *Fortress Scotland: A Guide to the Military Presence* (London: Pluto Press in association with Scottish CND, 1983), pp. 135–6.
25. Ibid. pp. 136–7.
26. See A. Messersmith, *The American Years: Dunoon and the US Navy* (Glendaruel: Argyll Publishing, 2003), pp. 43–50.
27. Ibid. p. 239.
28. Ibid. p. 243.
29. Minnion and Bolsover, *CND*, p. 52.
30. Grove, *Vanguard to Trident*, p. 242.
31. Minnion and Bolsover, *CND*, p. 32.
32. See A. Gilchrist, *Cod Wars and How to Lose Them* (Edinburgh: Q Press, 1978); H. Jonsson, *Friends in Conflict: The Anglo-Icelandic Cod Wars and the Law of the Sea* (London: C. Hurst & Co., 1982); Naval Staff History, *The Cod War: Naval Operations off Iceland in Support of the British Fishing Industry (1958–76)* (London: HMSO, 1990).
33. Grove, *Vanguard to Trident*, p. 349; Paterson, *Britain's Strategic Nuclear Deterrent*, p. 122.
34. Byrd, 'The development of the peace movement in Britain', p. 72.
35. Jamison, 'Will they blow us a' tae hell?', p. 118.
36. J. Gough, *Watching the Skies: A History of Ground Radar for the Air Defence of the United Kingdom by the Royal Air Force from 1946 to 1975* (London: HMSO, 1975), pp. 22–3; RAF Saxa Ford, site records, available at www.subbrit.org.uk/rsg/sites/s/saxa_vord/index.html, accessed on 24 July 2008.

37. Gough, *Watching the Skies*, p. 100.
38. *The Times*, 29 January 1973, p. 15.
39. See Messersmith, *The American Years*, pp. 108–12.
40. Saxa Vord resort, available at www.saxavord.com, accessed on 30 August 2011.
41. Paterson, *Britain's Strategic Nuclear Deterrent*, p. 123.
42. Jamison, 'Will they blow us a' tae hell?', pp. 126–7.
43. A. Zelter, *Trident on Trial: The Case for People's Disarmament* (Edinburgh: Luath Press, 2001), p. 69.
44. H. Berrington, 'British public opinion and nuclear weapons', in C. Marsh and C. Fraser (eds), *Public Opinion and Nuclear Weapons* (Basingstoke: Macmillan, 1989), p. 34.
45. E. Linklater and A. Linklater, *The Black Watch: The History of the Royal Highland Regiment* (London: Barrie and Jenkins, 1977), p. 208.
46. C. Barnett, *Britain and Her Army 1509–1970: A Military, Political and Social Survey* (London: Allen Lane, 1970), p. 481.
47. C. Sinclair-Stevenson, *The Gordon Highlanders* (London: Hamish Hamilton, 1968), p. 127.
48. Ibid. p. 128.
49. Linklater and Linklater, *Black Watch*, pp. 210–12.
50. The battalion suffered sixteen killed, seventy-six wounded and fifteen missing. A. Farrar-Hockley, *The British Part in the Korean War, Volume II: An Honourable Discharge* (London: HMSO, 1995), pp. 368–73; T. Royle, *The Black Watch: A Concise History* (Edinburgh: Mainstream Publishing, 2006), pp. 202–3.
51. C. Sinclair-Stevenson, *The Life of a Regiment: The History of the Gordon Highlanders, Volume VI, From 1945 to 1970* (London: Leo Cooper, 1974), p. 131.
52. Ibid. p. 138.
53. J. Walker, *Aden Insurgency: The Savage War in South Arabia 1962–1967* (Staplehurst: Spellmount, 2005), p. 264.
54. Ibid. p. 266.
55. Ibid. pp. 269–70.
56. T. R. Mockaitis, *British Counterinsurgency in the Post-Imperial Era* (Manchester: Manchester University Press, 1995), p. 66.
57. P. Mileham, *Fighting Highlanders! The History of the Argyll and Sutherland Highlanders* (London: Arms and Armour Press, 1993), pp. 167–9.
58. J. Sym, *Seaforth Highlanders* (Aldershot: Gale and Polden, 1962), pp. 1–2.
59. Ibid. p. 319.
60. See S. H. F. Johnston, *The History of the Cameronians (Scottish Rifles) 26th and 90th*, 2 vols (Aldershot: Gale and Polden, 1957), vol. 1.

61. J. Baynes, *The History of the Cameronians (Scottish Rifles)*, 7 vols (London: Cassell, 1971), vol. 4, p. 211.
62. Ibid. p. 212.
63. A conventicle was an open-air Presybyterian service with sentries posted to watch for government dragoons. This tradition was maintained throughout the Cameronians' existence. See Baynes, *Cameronians*, vol. 4, pp. 220–8.
64. M. Blacklock, *The Royal Scots Greys* (London: Leo Cooper, 1971), pp. 105–10.
65. P. Mileham, *The Scottish Regiments, 1633–1996* (Staplehurst: Spellmount, 1996), p. 40.
66. M. Naylor, *Among Friends: The Scots Guards 1956–1993* (London: Leo Cooper, 1995), pp. 132–9.
67. Ibid. p. 151.
68. Ibid. p. 155.
69. F. M. Walker, *Song of the Clyde: A History of Clyde Shipbuilding* (Cambridge: Patrick Stephens, 1984), p. 131.
70. Ibid. p. 7.
71. Royle, *Black Watch*, p. 211.
72. Ibid. pp. 214–16.

Part IV
The Cultural and Physical Dimensions

23
Scottish Military Dress

ALLAN CARSWELL

In March 2006, after months of debate, and in the teeth of fierce opposition, the six existing Scottish line infantry regiments were amalgamated to form a new Royal Regiment of Scotland. Although part of a wider army reorganisation designed to deal with very real problems affecting recruitment and operational effectiveness, the move was fiercely controversial in Scotland. For many Scots, who saw the Scottish soldier as an icon of their country's identity, the elimination of so many venerated regimental identities was an act of almost unimaginable vandalism. The army's plans had provoked public outcry and generated a political furore both at Westminster and at Holyrood, as well as a storm of protest in the Scottish media. Yet the Scottish regiments' recent difficulty in attracting sufficient recruits, although much disputed in terms of root causes, was a hard fact to counter. It was also not a new situation, and had given rise to a complaint that had dogged Scottish regiments for a very long time – that Scotland's actual contribution to the British army was exaggerated and that this fact was hidden behind a smokescreen of regimental tradition and sentiment. With the army heavily deployed in Iraq and Afghanistan and under strain, the New Labour government (which saw itself as the radical scourge of extravagant and outmoded custom) was not inclined to hold off on what it regarded as an essential reform. After some eleventh-hour tinkering with the titles of the new battalions, strengthening the emphasis on the old names, some of the less trenchant criticism was diffused and a sense of resignation crept in. Amidst much reassuring talk of the so-called 'Golden Thread' – the manner by which it was hoped the traditions of the former regiments would be perpetuated – the amalgamation went ahead. A page in Scotland's military history had most definitely been turned.

Symbols

Much of the outcry in 2005–6 had, of course, been heard before as the prelude to the amalgamation (or disbandment) of Scottish regiments, a process ongoing since the 1950s.[1] One issue, perhaps more than any other, that had exercised those responsible for carrying through these earlier mergers was the matter of the uniform of the new regiments. Great efforts had been made to retain as many elements of the dress of the old units as was possible – one regiment's tartan for kilts, the other's for trews; Gordon Highlanders' sporrans with Queen's Own Highlanders' Glengarries – so a little bit of everything had to be kept, not only to retain something of the varied character of the old regiments, but also to maintain the full panoply of the Scottish military image. In 2004–5, when plans were being made for the new Scottish 'super regiment', a slightly different view was taken, the 'Golden Thread' notwithstanding. Partly because the task of trying to represent key features of all six regiments in a single set of uniforms would have been near impossible (and prohibitively expensive), a more pragmatic approach emerged. With the exception of the individual battalion pipes and drums, which were to retain the 'full dress' uniforms of the old regiments, a single badge and tartan were to be adopted throughout the new regiment.

Significantly, this approach may also have been influenced by a recent trend in the army for wearing 'combat' clothing on almost all occasions. This preference for the internationally ubiquitous camouflage uniform can be seen as part of a shift in mood, a consequence of the frenetic pace of the army's post-Cold War operational history. Whether or not this change reflects an accurate recollection of the recent past, there is now a sense that this is a busy working army, not a static peacetime one; part of the modern world rather than something fixated with its past.[2] Although the kilt had not been worn on active service for nearly seventy years, it and other elements of Scottish military dress had still been in regular use by the post-Second World War army. Nowadays, by contrast, regimental (and national) distinctions have been largely reduced to the details of headwear, and the traditional finery of the Scottish military image is relegated to increasingly rare ceremonial occasions and occasional 'public duties'. This is not to say that the wearing of full dress is unpopular – most young 'Jocks' relish the opportunity (at least once in their career) to impress the tourists while on guard duty at Edinburgh castle. The deliberate choice, however, of 'desert' camouflage uniforms for recent public homecoming parades by Scottish battalions returning from either Iraq or Afghanistan does perhaps reveal how far the self-image of the Scottish soldier has shifted away from the tartan-clad symbol of the tourist postcard towards the frontline figure of the mass-media news report.[3]

Nevertheless, the new Royal Regiment had somehow to express its Scottish identity and the selection of a uniform tartan was an early consideration, even if its use was largely reduced to a 2½-inch-square badge backing. The choice, at least, was straightforward. Often known outside the army by the name of the regiment who first wore it – the Black Watch – the design had formed the basis for nearly all other regimental tartans developed since the mid-eighteenth century.[4] The fact that it was to be worn as a kilt on formal and ceremonial occasions by the new regiment, and thus based on the dress of a 'Highland' regiment, rather than as trews (still to be used, but in less formal orders of dress) as worn by the older 'Lowland' regiments, could have been more contentious had not the wider cultural status of Highland dress been so unassailable. It was decided, however, that the new regiment should have a completely new badge.[5]

In British military uniform, the regimental badge is a comparatively recent innovation. In earlier times, regiments were distinguished by other means – facing colours, design of button loop 'lace', heraldic emblems on regimental colours and grenadiers' caps, and even individual tartans for Highland regiments. It was only with the development of purpose-designed undress uniforms in the mid-nineteenth century, which in turn developed into field service clothing, that the need for regimental badges really arose. The small discreet symbol to be worn in a cap or bonnet as part of an otherwise relatively plain and functional universal uniform, soon, however, developed a life of its own, becoming a kind of prototype for the corporate logo of the modern world. Whether as part of a uniform, on a letterhead or signboard, or even carved into the hillside of some far-off imperial landscape, the regimental badge became the prime symbol of unit identity and cohesion. The choice of badge for the new Royal Regiment of Scotland was therefore of crucial importance, as the new symbol of Scotland's military tradition and as a 'brand' that would resonate with the people of contemporary Scotland, especially those soon to be serving as part of the new regiment. It was also going to be the principal piece of kit worn on a daily basis that would proclaim the identity of the new regiment to the world. The final design – a large lion rampant on a saltire (reminiscent of the formation sign of the old administrative Scottish Division), with the addition of a Scottish Crown and the motto of the Order of the Thistle,

Figure 23.1 Cap badge of the Royal Regiment of Scotland.

was an attempt to combine a mix of recognised national symbols in a way that suggests both military strength and Scottish identity. The decision to incorporate a representation of the Scottish crown, rather than the more conventional 'English' St Edward's Crown, as used by the rest of the armed forces (and by Scottish regiments prior to 2006), is revealing, reflecting as it does the resurgence of national confidence claimed to be prevalent in Scotland. Whilst all the elements of the new badge had been used before by Scottish regiments of the British army (the Scottish crown only very seldom), the intention to create a single national military symbol was almost unprecedented. In a world awash with visual imagery, it was vital that the public profile of the new regiment be prominent, especially as the need to attract more recruits was both an underlying issue behind its creation and one of its primary objectives. Unable to rely on the appeal of traditional images of the Scottish soldier, and now lacking the pulling power of the old regimental identities, the army in Scotland was investing much in this new symbol. Interestingly, the regimental badge the new device most resembles is that of the London Scottish, a part-time unit of the Territorial Army (TA) originally raised in 1859 from expatriate Scots living in London. This TA regiment and its handsome badge can be seen as an expression of a self-conscious and striving national identity, finding an outlet in a military form amidst a large and increasingly diverse and cosmopolitan mass. It would be stretching things to draw too direct a comparison between the two regiments, but perhaps parallels exist.

It was to be expected that when the new Royal Regiment came into existence in March 2006, the new badge would figure large. It certainly did but perhaps in rather unexpected ways. While full details of the dress of the new regiment were yet to be published, a section of 'Regimental Directive No. 1', marked 'Corporate Image', laid out, in a thoroughly modern way, how the new badge was to be used on signage, stationery and websites.[6] There was even a section on PowerPoint presentations. A full set of dress regulations have since appeared, specifying orders of dress appropriate for all occasions, from everyday wear to full ceremonial. While in no way an after thought, the sense remains, however, that the majority of these traditional style uniforms will seldom be worn and that their specification was a less pressing issue than the 'corporate image' of the new regiment. The fact that the uniforms (intended to be 'simple, stylish and quintessentially Scottish') have a slight look of having come straight from central casting does not help, conveying as they do an idealised image of how a Scottish soldier should look, while scrupulously avoiding too close a resemblance to what has gone before.

There is perhaps some irony in this – that the creators of one of the most widely recognised and influential military identities ever devised, the Scottish regiments, should have had to go to such trouble to manufacture a recognisable 'brand', and that it should have been reduced, in effect, to something as small as a bonnet badge (with a tartan backing). Those responsible for the creation of the Royal Regiment of Scotland had, of course, a difficult and unenviable task, pressured as they were by the demands of social change, politics (both civil and military), fashion, national feeling and military effectiveness (not least the need to attract more recruits). Yet the factors they had to contend with were not new. Indeed, they were the very ones that had been shaping Scotland's military identity all along.

Highlanders

The hallmarks of this historic identity in terms of dress – the tartans, kilts, trews, sporrans, broadswords, dirks and all the quaintly named items of headgear (feathered bonnets, Glengarries, tam-o'-shanters, Balmorals and Kilmarnocks) – each have their own particular origins and histories. Yet they all have at least two things in common. One is that none of them existed in its current form when Scottish soldiers first started wearing recognisable uniforms around 350 years ago.[7] The other is that they have all been adopted, outside their military use, either collectively or individually, as national symbols of Scotland: the external markers that have proclaimed Scotland's distinctiveness from the rest of the United Kingdom and the world.

It is no coincidence that these symbols trace their origins back to a time when a large part of Scotland, namely the Highlands, was seen as being dramatically different from the rest of Britain. This sense of difference, underpinned by geography, culture, language, history and dress, showed itself most threateningly in the region's capacity for insurrection and military activity. For the emerging British state, just as it had for the government of pre-union Scotland, the Highlands were seen as a problem that required particular solutions. By the early eighteenth century it was thought that the most pragmatic and economic way of dealing militarily with this Highland threat was for the area to police itself, using government money to pay highlanders to serve as officers and soldiers in 'independent companies' – an idea first used by the British crown in 1667. In this way well-affected highlanders – those whose support of the British government and the Protestant succession was well established – would profit through both income and patronage, thereby increasing their loyalty to the British state. In turn, the state would be spared the difficulty of sending its own conventional military forces to intervene in a difficult and alien environment. It was also recognised as a way in which the military potential of the Highlands could begin to be harnessed and thereby neutralised, while simultaneously forging a positive link between the fortunes of many Highland leaders, British military service and perceptions of the distinct nature of the region. It was therefore in the interests of these leaders to maintain the impression that only a Highland solution was workable for a Highland problem.[8] In consequence, a distinct British Highland military identity was born. When, in 1739, Britain needed to expand its army for war with Spain, six of these independent companies (originally sanctioned in 1725) were brought together to form the first Highland regiment in the British army. Four years later it departed for Flanders. The dress of the new regiment was central to this new Highland military identity and the perpetuation of the sense of 'difference' which created it. It was, however, a Highland identity at this stage, not a national one.

Scottish regiments had been a significant presence in the British army since its creation in the late seventeenth century. In 1739, however, their national origin was expressed largely in ways other than their dress. Excepting the use of obvious Scottish royal emblems – the insignia of the Order of the Thistle probably being the most common – these regiments were largely indistinguishable from the rest of the army, following the conventions of dress of their respective branches: guards, dragoons and line infantry. As for those earlier Scottish regiments that had existed before the creation of a British army, or that had continued to serve outside its control (for example, those on the strength of the Scottish parliamentary establishment until 1707), if their dress was distinguishable at all, it was marked by a preference for plain grey coats and blue woollen bonnets. Although there is strong pictorial evidence that certain features later associated with specifically Highland units, such as pipers, were used by all these Scottish regiments, and most would have accepted Highland recruits, there was no suggestion of a national military dress.[9] The fact that most of these regiments owed their origins to Scotland's civil strife of the seventeenth century, and by 1739 relied on British gold to pay their wages, inhibited any high-profile displays of Scottish national character.

At this early stage in its development, Highland military uniform (for that is what it had effectively become) was simply an adaptation of the traditional male costume worn throughout the Highlands, the main element of which was the *breacan an fheilidh*, or full belted plaid – a long length of tartan woollen cloth of double width, wrapped around the body and held in place by a waist belt.[10] The portion below the waist formed a kind of loosely pleated skirt, while the upper part could be wrapped around the body or looped up onto the shoulder depending on need. It was generally worn along with a long shirt and short jacket, cloth 'hose' to cover the lower leg and a flat bonnet. Altogether, this 'Highland dress' was seen as a practical, manly costume for a society which esteemed a vigorous life of hunting, warfare and physical resilience. The quality of the individual costume, whether through the brilliance of colour and complexity in the tartan, the style and decoration of the jacket or the opulence of the weapons carried, displayed the status of the wearer. Overall, however, regardless of class, the distinctive dress of the highlander was a source of enormous cultural pride and was frequently singled out for comment in the panegyric poetry of the Gaelic language.[11] By adopting the plaid (made from tartan of the standardised government sett probably already in use by the independent companies), accompanied by a short military jacket and waistcoat of scarlet cloth, and a flat blue bonnet, these first Highland soldiers of the British army were embodying a well-established part of the Highland military tradition.

The power of this tradition was demonstrated all too clearly a few

Figure 23.2 A private of the 43rd Highland Regiment (the Black Watch), 1742.

years later in 1745 when the Jacobite army of Prince Charles Edward Stuart came close to upending the Hanoverian British state. Although not exclusively Highland in its make-up, the army was dominated by the clan regiments. To instil a sense of cohesion, tartan and Highland dress were overtly encouraged throughout the army, as universal symbols of both Scottish identity and the Jacobite cause. The defeat of the 1745 rising led to an urgent reappraisal by a chastened British state of the Highland military threat. New legislation was enacted to disarm the Highlands (an old idea) and purge the region's culture of those aspects deemed to be vital to its military tradition. It was no accident that tartan and Highland dress should be part of this proscription or that the penalties for its breach (imprisonment and up to seven years' transportation) should have been so severe. In the years immediately after 1746, when the risk of further Jacobite insurrection was still thought to be high and there were enough British troops in the Highlands to enforce it, the Disarming Act of 1746 had real effect. Yet there was one important exception to the act – soldiers serving in Highland regiments of the British army. It was an exception set to grow.

Between the outbreak of the Seven Years War in 1756 and the end of the Napoleonic Wars in 1815, over fifty Highland regiments were raised for the British army. At a time when the distinctive culture of the Highlands was being undermined by legal, economic and social change, these Highland regiments provided both a refuge and an outlet for one of its most prominent manifestations – the warrior, and a precious sense of continuity for key elements of his dress and ethos. The formidable reputation attained by these regiments through their success on the battlefield projected this distinctive Highland image onto a much wider stage. For example, scrutiny of the colossal new 'history' paintings of the period commemorating the key battles in the wars against France, by artists such as Benjamin West and John Singleton Copley, reveals the frequent presence of a Highland soldier. In works such as *The Death of General Wolfe* (West 1770), *The Death of Major Peirson* (Copley 1784) and *The Siege and Relief of Gibraltar* (Copley 1791), the inclusion of a Highland soldier seems almost *de rigueur* in the military glorification of an ascendant British empire. Although his distinctive dress would have appealed to any artist, the frequent representation of a Highland soldier usually followed historic fact. Yet, as a distinctive figure, the Highland soldier was becoming understood as a form of visual shorthand for Scotland's commitment to the achievement of a British empire, even if this recognition distorted notions of a wider Scottish identity and inhibited understanding of other surviving facets of Highland culture. By the end of the eighteenth century, when the tide of the Jacobite threat had receded and intellectual interest in the Highlands and their culture was growing, the Highland regiments and their dress had become the most tangible and widely understood manifestation of the region's identity. As such, they became an easy point of reference for those keen to revive Highland dress, such as the Highland Society of London which drew its membership from the old Highland elite now following their fortunes in the British capital, and for whom the Highland regiments were a valued source of family income and prestige. The elaborate costumes seen in countless portraits of Highland gentlemen of the late eighteenth and early nineteenth centuries therefore owe almost as much to the military uniform of the period as they do to the authentic dress of the Highlands. Royal interest was also a highly significant influence. As early as 1789, only seven years after the repeal of the Disarming Act, the Prince of Wales attended a fashionable London ball in 'full Highland dress' – in effect a version of the uniform of a Highland regimental officer. Two of his brothers, including the duke of Kent, father to the future Queen Victoria, also had themselves fitted out in similar costumes, all under the guidance of Colonel John Small, a former officer of a Highland regiment.[12]

Meanwhile the development of Highland military uniform had acquired a momentum of its own, partly under the influence of utility and partly through a process of military formalisation. The full belted plaid was increasingly reserved for 'full dress' occasions, being considered too bulky and inconvenient for everyday use. Instead, the lower portion was split away and worn as a separate garment – the kilt, or *feileadh beag*. Arguments have raged over the origins of this item of dress, but most sources accept that the earliest reference to kilts dates to around 1730 when they were adopted by workers at a Highland ironworks. It seems fitting that the need for a simpler and more practical version of the picturesque full plaid among modern industrial process workers should have foreshadowed a similar requirement by the regimented Highland soldiers of the British army.[13] The kilt therefore became the standard dress of the Highland regiments even though the full plaid continued to be issued until around 1814. After that date a curious contrivance known as a 'fly plaid' crept into use. By attaching a triangular piece of tartan to a waist belt, and fastening it to the shoulder, the visual effect of the old full plaid could be simulated for special occasions. Individual regiments had also begun to adopt their own particular designs of tartan. Nearly all were simple variations on the government sett, achieved by adding one or more coloured over stripes. A few, however, were quite different, for example that adopted by the 79th Highlanders in 1793 and named 'Cameron of Erracht'. Furthermore, the Highland soldier's bonnet had begun to undergo a transformation, growing in stature alongside his reputation. From being a flat, knitted wool bonnet decorated with a silk cockade and perhaps a couple of feathers, it had became a stiffened round cap adorned with a profusion of ostrich feathers so tall as to require a wire structure to support them. The highlander's traditional weapons – basket-hilted sword, all-metal pistol and dirk – were now carried mainly by officers and usually reserved for 'dress' occasions. All were becoming more heavily ornamented, eventually reaching a point of near parody. The trials of active service and foreign climates, often far away from sources of regular resupply, had also forced Highland regiments to occasionally adapt their distinctive dress, for instance into tartan trews, or abandon it altogether in favour of plain breeches or trousers.

Whilst in the early days of the Highland regiments the opportunity to wear the traditional dress of their forefathers was seen as an incentive to potential recruits, the fast diminishing numbers of men available in the region forced the army to cast its net ever wider. By 1809, in the midst of the Napoleonic Wars, the fact had to be faced that there were now more Highland regiments in existence than there were Highland recruits to man them. The effects of land clearance, previous recruitment and emigration had taken their toll. In order to open up units to recruits from elsewhere (principally, it was hoped, from regiments of the English militia, for whom the dress of a Highland regiment was a serious disincentive to enlistment), the War Office instructed five regiments to give up their Highland dress.[14] There was also a growing (and occasionally much-frowned upon) habit among Highland officers to wear breeches rather than the kilt; a preference illustrative, in part, of the increasing 'Anglicisation' of the Highland gentry and of a contemporary view that associated the kilt with the dress of the Highland poor.[15]

A national dress

Yet just as the Highland regiments seemed to have passed their peak as a source of ready manpower, the transformation of the highlander's image into a national icon really began. Attempts after the union of 1707 to repackage Scotland as 'North Britain', encouraged by Scots keen to distance themselves from the country's turbulent recent past, had, unsurprisingly, failed to inspire. Something bold was required to project a sense of Scotland's recovering confidence in its own distinctiveness while simultaneously expressing the potency of the nation's contribution to the idea of Great Britain, demonstrated most recently by the nation's disproportionate military effort in the wars against Napoleon.[16] The Highland soldier fitted the bill perfectly, yet his appeal was even wider. By the early nineteenth century, Scotland was in the midst of a period of massive social and economic upheaval. To those nervous of the consequences of this process, the idealised image of the highlander represented a beacon of traditional values such as loyalty, steadfastness and individuality, all wrapped up in the recollection of a regimented and hierarchical society. More explicitly, for those in political power – the Tories of Pitt and Dundas – the Highland soldier appeared as an ideal model for a new Scottish identity, one inexorably linked to large-scale participation in war, empire and military service.[17] Encouraged by the Romantic novelist (and staunch Tory) Sir Walter Scott, a movement developed that popularised the wearing of tartan (especially the spurious new 'clan' setts) and Highland dress, both as an expression of this nostalgic view of the Highlands, and as an assertion of the new sense of national identity.

Figure 23.3 An officer of the 79th (Cameron) Highlanders, by William Spooner, c. 1833–6.

This movement reached its climax in the celebrated visit of King George IV to Edinburgh in 1822. Stage-managed by Scott and his friend General David Stewart of Garth (a former Highland officer and author of the first published history of the Highland regiments), the visit set the seal of both royal and popular approval on the new vision of Scotland. The debt it owed to the Highland soldier was obvious.

The enthusiasm for all things Highland naturally further enhanced the popularity of the surviving kilted regiments, issues of recruitment notwithstanding. It also pushed them up the ladder of social exclusivity when it came to the purchase of officers' commissions. In line with this fashionable status, the dress of Highland officers became ever more elaborate and expensive. In 1835 it cost a new officer of the 42nd Highlanders £136 17s 6d to kit himself out – equivalent to about £11,500 today.[18] This figure did not include the cost of his kilt and plaid, to be bought privately from the regimental quartermaster who would have carried out a complex and lucrative business with the main supplier of regimental tartan, the firm of Wilson of Bannockburn.[19] Although the cost to a junior officer joining a cavalry or a guards regiment would have been even higher, the expense of

Highland dress was a considerable outlay when a subaltern's annual salary was only £96. It was not only officers who were affected by such extravagance; the dress of other ranks in Highland regiments had become so elaborate that the overall cost was five guineas per man compared to just three for the rest of the line infantry. Until 1844 much of this expense was passed on to the soldier through the extra cost of his 'necessaries' – those items of clothing and equipment that had to be paid for by the soldier himself. For example, in 1830 the feathered bonnets of the men of the 93rd Highlanders were supplied by the colonel, but the feathers and the cost of mounting them had to be borne by the men as a 'necessary'.[20] It was finally recognised that this additional expense was a serious disincentive to potential recruits so an extra pound was added to the enlistment bounty for Highland regiments and an annual payment of eight shillings and sixpence was made to each man to help him buy and maintain his 'highland kit'.[21] While such solutions helped shift the expense away from the soldier, they simply transferred it to the tax payer. It is a mark of the prestige now enjoyed by the Highland regiments that the War Office should have been persuaded to bear this extra cost. Undoubtedly, growing royal enthusiasm, in the form of Queen Victoria's infatuation with the romantic vision of the Highlands, was a factor in overcoming any official reluctance. Royal approval would also play a part in the War Office's agreement, between 1823 and 1864, to reinstate Highland dress to three of the six regiments who had lost it in 1809. Although they had to wear tartan trews rather than the kilt, the 72nd, 74th and 91st Regiments adopted most of the other elements of Highland regimental dress, including newly designed regimental tartans. It should be stressed, however, that recruiting in the Highlands had not recovered since 1809; what had changed was that the nationalist aura surrounding the Highland regiments was now so intense that few questioned where the regiments actually found their recruits, whether it was in Lowland Scotland or even Ireland or England.

Questions were, nevertheless, being asked in the corridors of the War Office, where the supply of suitable manpower for the army was a constant theme as the nineteenth century wore on. Despite the attempt to repackage Scotland as a nation of tartan-clad imperial soldiers, the national contribution to the army was steadily falling – from 13 per cent in 1830 to 8 per cent by 1870.[22] Yet the number of regiments stayed the same. An undercurrent of resentment was also growing among other parts of the army at what was seen as the disproportionate popular attention paid to Highland exploits in battle, particularly in the Crimea and the Indian Mutiny. When these issues became clouded by royal favour and Scottish national feeling, trouble loomed. It came to a head around 1881 and it was the dress of the Highland regiments that provided the spark.

In 1881, in order to improve the supply of troops for overseas service and cut spending, the newly elected Liberal government decided to reform the army by pairing together around three-quarters of the line infantry regiments to form new large two battalion regiments. Prior to 1881, there were eighteen nominally Scottish regiments, of which five were kilted. Of the eighteen, the oldest three would be unaffected by the mergers. The remaining fifteen single-battalion regiments would be reduced to at least seven, making ten new large Scottish infantry regiments in total. In theory, the number of kilted regiments should also have been halved; it was not. Regimental intransigence (particularly from the 79th Queen's Own Cameron Highlanders) over the adoption of someone else's tartan, vehemently backed up by Queen Victoria's belief in the sanctity of 'clan' tartans, upset the plans. A suggestion to introduce a single universal tartan was met with utter scorn, and the proposed design mockingly referred to as the 'McChilders' in honour of the Liberal Secretary for War, Hugh C. E. Childers.[23] In the face of such strong royal opposition, the government had to give in. Instead of merging any of the kilted regiments with each other, four of the five were joined to non-kilted units whose previous identities were then largely subsumed. The remaining regiment, the 79th Highlanders (under extra royal protection through its particular association with the queen) was allowed to remain untouched. The number of kilted Highland regiments therefore remained unchanged, but the total of kilted battalions had jumped from five to nine. In October 1897 one of these battalions, the 1st Gordon Highlanders, achieved extraordinary fame when it stormed the Heights of Dargai on the north-west frontier of India. To the sound of the pipes, the kilted Gordons assaulted a formidable enemy position up a precipitous 200-metre mountain ridge.[24] Just a few years earlier this same battalion (the former 75th Regiment) had no Highland connection and only the very loosest affiliation to Scotland. Yet in the eyes of the public their action at Dargai seemed to epitomise the Highland fighting spirit.[25] The transformative power of the Highland image (coupled with an influx of recruits from the northeast of Scotland) was remarkable both for the rapid instillation of a powerful *esprit de corps* and in generating euphoric popular interest.

The influence of the Highland image did not end there. As part of the same reforms all the Scottish regiments were now to adopt tartan, pipers (if they did not already have them) and other distinctive items

Figure 23.4 Pipes and drums of the 2nd battalion, the King's Own Scottish Borderers, Dublin, 1914.

of 'Scottish' dress, regardless of their history or recruiting districts. Although the government sett was initially issued to these 'Lowland' regiments to be worn as trews (except for the newly authorised pipers who were to be kilted), it was not long before they each adopted their own 'regimental' tartans. Similarly, in 1903 new 'Scottish' bonnets, named 'Kilmarnocks', were designed and issued to the Royal Scots and the King's Own Scottish Borderers. Even if there were still distinctions after 1881 between 'Highland' and 'Lowland' regiments, the imposition of a national military dress finally made the Highland image synonymous with the Scottish soldier.

The Highland appeal was not just restricted to Scotland. Numerous part-time volunteer units which had sprung up amongst Scottish emigrant communities throughout the empire all chose to assert their origins by adopting the national military dress in one form or another. Elite regiments of the Indian army, such as the Gurkhas, whose British officers recognised in their men some affinity with the

Figure 23.5 Pipers of the 12th Indian Pioneers pose with their instructor, Pipe Major Duff of the 2nd battalion, the Royal Scots, c. 1904.

origins and culture of the Scottish highlander, also adopted pipers and kitted them out in tartan accordingly – a tradition that continues to this day. By the outbreak of the First World War, the Scottish military identity was embedded as perhaps the pre-eminent military expression of the British empire.

The wars of the twentieth century challenged this distinct identity, certainly as far as dress was concerned. The advent of camouflage and field service uniforms blunted the sartorial splendour of the Scottish regiments, hiding their tartans under drab kilt aprons and replacing feathered bonnets and Glengarries with steel helmets and khaki tam-o'-shanter bonnets. Still, the distinctive dress of the Highland regiments prompted some unknown German to dub them the 'Ladies from Hell' during the First World War – a nickname taken up with equal relish by the regiments and the copywriters of British propaganda. By the outbreak of the Second World War, the kilt was deemed unsuitable for modern warfare – it lacked obvious protection from chemical attack – and was withdrawn from field service use. Yet the traditional image still had enormous potency, both as a source of morale and as an enduring symbol of British arms. When the 51st Highland Division was re-formed after most of the original formation was forced to surrender at St Valéry in June 1940, the divisional commander Major-General Douglas Wimberley was adamant that the traditional dress of the Highland soldier should not be completely discarded. He believed strongly that it still had a role to play in inculcating a national military ethos into a conscript force drawn from all over Scotland and beyond. Whenever they were available, kilts were worn for special parades and guard duties, and the massed pipes and drums of the Division dominated the set-piece victory parades across North Africa, shown in newsreel footage across the world.[26] The Scottish military tradition had therefore continued to live up to the expectations of its early promoters by providing a national and cultural focus for a form of mass military service which might otherwise have been far more difficult to impose and manage. During times when Britain's very survival was in doubt, it simultaneously evoked and rekindled a unique sense of pride, resilience and fighting spirit.

As Britain began its long retreat from empire, so too did the Scottish military tradition. Disbandments and amalgamations removed famous regimental names even if public appeals saved a few. Yet these protests also polarised the argument. News pictures from 1967 of soldiers of the Argyll and Sutherland Highlanders, a regiment then under threat of amalgamation, proudly wearing their distinctive Glengarry bonnets as they reasserted control over the violent streets of Aden seemed to some a reaffirmation of both Britain's status and Scotland's military strength in the face of government weakness and indifference. Others saw it as outdated imperial bravado. Meanwhile a contemporary taste for revision in history was laying into the accepted symbols of Scottish identity, tapping into an older seam of post-Ossianic scepticism, and pointing out the fraudulence of cherished traditions such as clan tartans. In a similar vein, the old saw of the Scottish regiments being made up of Irishmen and Englishmen was again repeated. Such comments were, of course, intended as criticism, and were based on a stark truth – peacetime recruitment in Scotland had indeed often fallen short of the demands created by the number of Scottish regiments. However, a point the critics usually overlooked was that the ethos and reputation of these particular regiments, both individually and collectively, was so powerful that national origins were often immaterial in making a soldier a Gordon Highlander or a Royal Scot, just as being born a highlander had ceased to be a factor back in the nineteenth century. Vital to this ethos was the dress of the Scottish soldier. The simple act of wearing such a distinctive uniform (especially the kilt) generated such strong recognition that the soldier instantly saw himself as part of a unique and outstanding military tradition.[27]

Yet in the modern army opportunities for Scottish soldiers to appear in their traditional dress are increasingly rare. It remains to be seen what effect the tradition of Scottish military dress might still have in a world where utility, mass communication and global fashion have made even national armies largely indistinguishable in their dress. However, to those responsible for shaping Britain's army, attachment to such traditions has often appeared anachronistic and sentimental, perhaps because in the past so much that is unquantifiable has been claimed in their name. In February 1881, during the height of the controversy over the future of the Highland regiments, Childers, the secretary for war, vented his frustration with those resistant to his reforms. With heavy sarcasm, he wrote to a colleague:

> the tartan question is one of the gravest character, far more important . . . than the maintenance of the Union with Ireland. All the thoughts of the War Office are concentrated on it, and patterns of tartans past, present and future, fill our rooms. We are neglecting the Transvaal and the Ashanti for the sake of well weighing the merits of a few more threads of red, green or white.[28]

Childers's scathing words resurfaced in November 2004 when they were quoted in what, charitably, might have been intended as a bit of humour by the secretary of state for defence, Geoff Hoon, during a debate in the House of Commons on the proposed creation of the Royal Regiment of Scotland. Predictably, such levity was met with outrage from the opposite camp, campaigning against the merger of the Scottish regiments. They accused Hoon at best of insensitivity, at worst of deliberately belittling a proud tradition by portraying arguments in its defence as nothing more than squabbles over something as seemingly trivial as tartan. This might have been an understandable view to take in 1881, when the roots of Scotland's military tradition had yet to grip the popular imagination in a way that they did after two world wars, but by 2004 the Scottish regiments and their symbols mattered much more, to many more people. The two sides were therefore driven even further apart, reflecting in the process the timeless argument about what dominates the effective conduct of armies – the mercurial qualities of morale and personal response, or the measurable systems of matériel and control. Once again, it would seem, attitudes to Scotland's military dress continue to define different understandings of the nation's military tradition and perceptions of its future value.

Notes

1. H. Strachan, *The Politics of the British Army* (Oxford: Oxford University Press, 1997), pp. 195–233.
2. Sheer practicality has also been a factor in this shift. The current camouflage uniform is comfortable to wear and easy to maintain and therefore popular with soldiers.
3. Around 2006–7, a shortage of the new regimental 'dress' uniform may also have been a contributing factor in the use of 'combat' clothing for such formal parades, although the practice now seems well established.
4. The actual pattern of tartan selected is officially referred to as the 'No. 1A Government sett' and is a variant of the No. 1 sett, the tartan actually worn by the Black Watch before 2006, the difference being that the former has a slightly larger check. No. 1A was previously worn by the Argyll and Sutherland Highlanders.
5. In common with the rest of the modern army, the new regiment also wears a 'tactical recognition flash' (TRF) on the upper right sleeve of their combat clothing. This is an embroidered cloth patch bearing a version of the regimental badge. The individual battalions of the new regiment are also distinguished by coloured hackles worn in their Balmoral or tam-o'-shanter bonnets.
6. 'Regimental Directive No. 1', dated 31 January 2006, previously downloadable from the website of the Royal Regiment of Scotland: www.army.mod.uk/infantry/regiments/SCOTS.aspx.
7. The one possible exception is the broad blue woollen bonnet worn by Scottish soldiers since at least the early seventeenth century. It is most closely represented in modern dress by the Balmoral bonnet.
8. A. Mackillop, *'More Fruitful than the Soil': Army, Empire and the Scottish Highlands* (East Linton: Tuckwell Press, 2000), pp. 20–9.
9. Some of these regiments occasionally had 'Highland' companies temporarily attached to them while serving in Scotland prior to 1739. Like the independent companies, with which they may have been synonymous, it is probable that they wore a semi-uniform version Highland dress and not a recognisable regimental uniform. See C. C. P. Lawson, *A History of the Uniforms of the British Army*, 5 vols (London: Kaye and Ward, 1940–67), vol. 1, pp. 66–7.
10. An early military plaid required twelve yards of cloth, cut in two and stitched together to form a plaid six yards long.

11. H. Cheape, *Tartan: The Highland Habit*, third edition (Edinburgh: National Museums of Scotland, 2006), pp. 25–6.
12. A. V. B. Norman, 'George IV and Highland dress', *Review of Scottish Culture*, vol. 10 (1996–7), pp. 5–15. As colonel of the 1st Royal Scots between 1801 and 1820, the duke of Kent persistently tried without success to get official authority for the regiment to adopt tartan as part of their uniform; see J. T. Dunbar, *The Costume of Scotland* (London: Batsford, 1981), pp. 185–6.
13. J. T. Dunbar, *History of Highland Dress*, second edition (London: Batsford, 1979), pp. 12–14.
14. The original order actually lists six regiments – the 72nd, 73rd, 74th, 75th, 91st and 94th, but the last was not a Highland unit and it is unclear whether it in fact ever wore Highland dress, although some sources state that it was authorised to do so in 1807. See D. M. Henderson, *Highland Soldier 1820–1920* (Edinburgh: John Donald, 1989), p. 13, n. 34.
15. Henderson, *Highland Soldier*, pp. 121–2.
16. Scots had made up 17 per cent of the British army based on 10 per cent of the population; see J. E. Cookson, *The British Armed Nation 1793–1815* (Oxford: Oxford University Press, 1997), pp. 126–7.
17. J. E. Cookson, 'The Napoleonic Wars, military Scotland and Tory Highlandism in the early nineteenth century', *Scottish Historical Review*, vol. 78 (1999), pp. 60–75.
18. Henderson, *Highland Soldier*, pp. 143–5.
19. N. J. Mills and A. L. Carswell, 'Wilson of Bannockburn and the clothing of the Highland regiments', *Journal of the Society for Army Historical Research*, vol. 76 (1998), pp. 177–93.
20. Brigadier General A. E. J. Cavendish, *The 93rd Sutherland Highlanders 1799–1827* (Frome: privately published, 1928), pp. 354–5.
21. H. Strachan, *Wellington's Legacy: The Reform of the British Army 1830–54* (Manchester: Manchester University Press, 1984), p. 51; S. H. Myerly, *British Military Spectacle: From the Napoleonic Wars through the Crimea* (Cambridge, MA: Harvard University Press, 1996) p. 91 and n. 33; Clothing Account of Pte John Crichton, 93rd Highlanders, M.1961.156.2, National War Museum, Edinburgh castle.
22. H. Strachan, 'Scotland's military identity', *Scottish Historical Review*, vol. 85 (2006), p. 325.
23. In 1907 a design of dark green tartan with a red overstripe named 'Childers' was adopted for the pipers of the 1st Gurkha Rifles. This may have been the experimental design (the much ridiculed 'McChilders') prepared around 1880 for possible adoption as a new universal tartan for wear by all Scottish regiments. It is still worn by the regiment, part of the Indian Army since 1948.

24. E. M. Spiers, *The Scottish Soldier and Empire 1854–1912* (Edinburgh: Edinburgh University Press, 2006), pp. 120–8.
25. Although the 75th had been styled the Stirlingshire Regiment since 1862, in 1881 it had little real connection with Scotland, even though it was originally one of the Highland regiments that had lost their special status in 1809.
26. C. F. French, 'The fashioning of *esprit de corps* in the 51st Highland Division from St Valéry to El Alamein', *Journal of the Society for Army Historical Research*, vol. 77 (1999), pp. 275–92.
27. H. Streets, 'Identity in the Highland regiments: Soldier, region, nation', in S. Murdoch and A. Mackillop (eds), *Fighting for Identity: Scottish Military Experience c. 1550–1900* (Leiden: Brill, 2002), p. 230.
28. Strachan, *The Politics of the British Army*, p. 205.

24
Scottish Military Music

GARY J. WEST

The role of Scottish military music is a long and complex one, with some aspects of it being well documented, others remaining frustratingly vague. In his marvellously insightful volume, *Music of the Scottish Regiments*, David Murray attempts to provide a narrative that weaves together the story. As he asserts:

> The origins of military music derive from the demands of war itself. From the earliest times until the invention of the radio as a means of communication, it had three principal functions: to pass orders and give signals in battle; to regulate the military day in camp and garrison; and 'to excite cheerfulness and alacrity in the soldier'.[1]

Nowadays, the list can be expanded, for such music has played a prominent part in the army's success in transmitting its traditions and ethos to a much wider audience. Commercial recordings and tattoos have placed Scottish military music at the heart of a form of cultural iconography that reaches far beyond the troops themselves into a public consciousness that is truly international in scope. This chapter will address these issues, while recognising that Murray's three functions do indeed lie at the heart of the story of military music in Scotland.

Horn and drum

Amongst the earliest instruments that can be identified as having a specifically military purpose within Scotland are horns. Natural specimens from bulls and other animals were certainly pressed into action, but crafted forms were also constructed: a fragment of a side-blown bronze horn, dated to around the eighth century BC, and

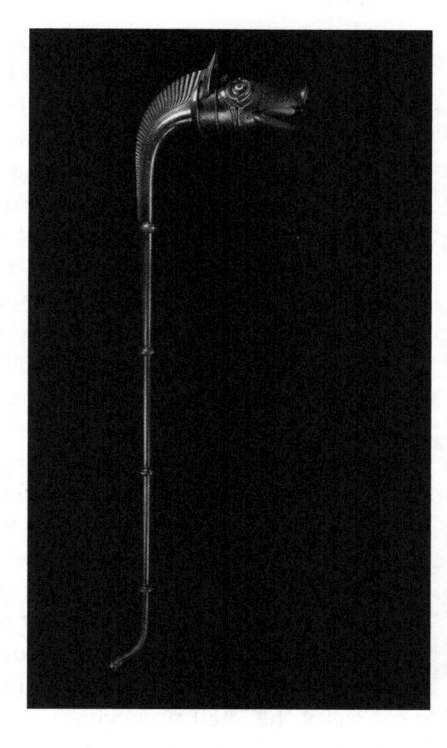

Figure 24.1
Reconstruction of a carnyx based on the head of the original instrument discovered at Deskford, Banffshire.

found in the south-west of Scotland, points to a shared tradition with Ireland, although a specifically martial function cannot be proven.[2] Within a wider European context, however, a much larger form of bronze horn – the carnyx – was clearly used for military purposes and a particularly fine example of the head of one such instrument was unearthed in Deskford in Banffshire in the early nineteenth century. Pictorial evidence from Roman coins and the magnificent first-century BC Gundestrup bowl in Denmark shows that these were very long-necked instruments which were sounded over the heads of the soldiers in front of the players. A recent reconstruction in Scotland suggests the carnyx was an instrument of immense power, producing a sound of prodigious volume and clearly ideally suited for communication in battle.[3]

While the Deskford carnyx has been dated to the period of Roman occupation, a thousand years later some form of horn was still being used to incite Scottish troops to battle. It was not the bagpipe that inspired the armies of Wallace and Bruce during the Wars of Independence – that icon of Scottishness had almost certainly yet to make its first appearance north of the Tweed – but rather the rousing tones of the horn. Later in the fourteenth century, the chronicler Froissart witnessed the scene at the battle of Otterburn in 1388:

> Lightly it is the usage of Scots, that when they be thus assembled together in arms, the footmen beareth about their necks horns in manner like hunters, some great, some small, and of all sorts, so that when they blow all at once, they make such a noise, that it may be heard nigh four miles off: thus they do to abash their enemies and to rejoice themselves. When the bishop of Durham with his banner and ten thousand men with him were approached within a league, then the Scots blew their horns in such wise, that it seemed that all the devils in hell had been among them, so that such as heard them and knew not of their usage were sore abashed.[4]

Effective as the horns may have been as an incitement to friend and as a warning to foe, as warfare increased in tactical complexity so too did the need for more subtle and precise modes of communication. Commanders required a reliable method of issuing instructions to their troops in the noise and confusion of battle, and by the early modern period the instrument that was considered to be best placed to achieve this was the drum. Portable and durable, it required minimum maintenance and could produce the necessary volume. In most cases the shell was cylindrical and constructed of wood, with heads of stretched animal skin, and beaten with heavy wooden sticks. From early in the eighteenth century, the addition of 'snares' became common: these were gut cords, reminiscent of a poacher's snare, strung against the bottom head, which raised the pitch of the drum and produced a more strident tone that cut through the noise of battle more effectively.[5] Compared to modern snare drums with very thin and highly tensioned heads that produce a sharp, almost gunfire-like 'crack' and are very responsive, allowing highly intricate beatings to be played, their pre-twentieth-century forebears could only support a simple style of rudiment. And yet, over time, the particular patterns and combinations of beatings that evolved were sophisticated enough to serve their key communication role effectively. Styles appear to have evolved along national lines and could even be 'decoded' by the enemy. Indeed, it became part of a drummer's job to learn the principal drum signals of the opposition and to keep his superiors informed of their intentions.[6] As the battle of Culloden moved towards its bloody conclusion on Drumossie Moor in 1746, one of the Jacobite commanders, Brigadier Walter Stapleton, ordered his drummers to beat the 'Chamade', a request for a 'time out' to discuss terms of surrender.[7] All those within earshot, on both sides, would have known what this meant, although for Stapleton himself the request was to little avail for he later died of his wounds.

It was important for successful communication that the drummer could be seen by his officers as well as heard, and so until the mid-nineteenth century his uniform was often distinct from that of his comrades in that the main colours of the tunic and facings were reversed. His special responsibilities were also recognised with a higher rate of pay.[8] In some Scottish regiments these special responsibilities included the unpleasant task of carrying out corporal punishment sentences on comrades. In March 1867 Private I. Mackay of the 42nd Highlanders (the Black Watch), having been found guilty at a court martial of 'disgraceful Conduct of a cruel and Felonious Nature', was imprisoned with hard labour for one year after he was stripped, tied up and placed in a square formed by his fellow soldiers standing two deep. Two drummers were then ordered to give him twenty-five lashes each.[9] A less violent, but still highly symbolic, ritual involved drummers 'drumming out' disgraced soldiers who were discharged from a regiment.

As late as the twentieth century, drummers continued to play a key role in battle, with several coming to prominence in the First World War. Drummer Walter Ritchie of the 2nd battalion, the Seaforth Highlanders, for example, was awarded the Victoria Cross during the battle of the Somme in July 1916. His citation clearly shows the musician's dual role of incitement and instruction when he 'stood on the parapet of the enemy trench and, under heavy machine gun fire and bomb attacks, repeatedly sounded the "Charge", thereby rallying many men of various units who, having lost their leaders, were wavering and beginning to retire.'[10]

The drums' central communicative role in war and peace led to their being elevated to icons of regimental identity and captured enemy drums became prized trophies. Regimental museums across Scotland proudly display such artefacts from a wide variety of campaigns: a caption reading 'Egyptian drum captured at Tel-el-Kebir, 13th September, 1882' accompanies one on show at the Highlanders Museum at Fort George. A good example of the importance placed on captured drums, or indeed the fear of their capture, relates to an incident that took place at St Valéry-en-Caux in June 1940. Once it became clear that the 51st Highland Division would be cut off there with no chance to escape, Captain Derek Lang, adjutant of the 4th Cameron Highlanders, ordered their drums to be hidden to avoid their capture. Mindful of the propaganda the Germans had made from the capture of the drums of the 2nd Gordon Highlanders at

Ostend in 1918,[11] Pipe Major Donald MacDonald thus sank them in a farm pond. The drums were not even their own regimental emblazoned set – these had been left in Britain to avoid this very scenario, and a plain brass ordinance-issue set had been taken in their place. That mattered little, however: the message was clearly that while there was no chance of escape for the highlanders themselves, the shame of having their drums taken too was to be avoided at all costs.[12]

Fife and bugle

Accompanying the drum, at varying points in history, have been two relatively simple instruments that have served to complement its percussive communications and also extend the aesthetic range through the introduction of melody. 'Tunes' were able to supplement the signals of the drummers, bringing added clarity to instructions in battle and added voice to drill and entertainment in camp. Common amongst Swiss and German mercenaries from the fifteenth century, the fife was soon adopted throughout much of northern Europe. By the late seventeenth century it had tended to be replaced in Britain by the hautbois (precursor to the oboe), only to make a comeback following the Jacobite defeat in the 1740s.[13] Because of its relatively low volume (though piercing tone), the fife was used primarily in garrison or field as the means of regulating the divisions and routines of the day. 'The Scotch Duty' was the standard fife and drum tunes and beatings arrangements used by Scottish regiments for this purpose and was said to date to the sixteenth century.[14]

The historical reliance on horns had returned to the Scottish military by the nineteenth century in the form of the bugle. Indeed, the semantic connection to horns is clear: the name derives from the Latin *buculus*, meaning a young bull. The development of the bugle went hand in hand with that of its close sister, the trumpet, and unlike those random cacophonies that had invoked 'all the devils in hell' at Otterburn four centuries earlier, the newly adopted brass instrument brought both volume and melody to the ranks.[15] Although limited to a range of five notes, an impressively large corpus of basic bugle tunes or 'calls' was developed, some of them probably the result of cross-fertilisation with American traditions during the War of Independence. These calls were first collected, arranged and published in 1799 by James Hyde, a 'Trumpet Major' with a London-based Volunteer unit, and they reveal a remarkably well-developed set of musical instructions relating to marching, drill, cavalry manoeuvres and the regulation of daily routines.[16] The instrument was widely adopted by regiments on both sides of the border,[17] and, by the early nineteenth century, bugle calls were often detailed in the standing orders of Scottish regiments. In 1819, for example, 'Rouse' was sounded by bugle in the 79th (Cameron) Highlanders.[18]

The bagpipe

Drums, fifes and bugles were not, of course, unique to Scotland, but if there is one feature of military music that sets the nation apart it is the bagpipe. As one of the 'icons' of Scottishness, this instrument has been as maligned as it has been celebrated. Yet despite the fact that it has been labelled the 'national' instrument since the early nineteenth century,[19] our understanding of its origins, arrival, adoption and development has been limited. There was little detailed scholarly study of the bagpipe and its music within Scotland until the last few decades of the twentieth century, the result being that the vacuum of understanding tended to be filled with myth, hyperbole, half-truth and, at times, outright nonsense. Claims that the bagpipe was first 'invented' in Scotland, or that it was introduced by the Romans, that it was the military instrument of choice for Bruce's army at Bannockburn and even that it was banned under the terms of the Act of Proscription following Culloden are all without foundation. So what *is* the story of the bagpipe in general and of its military use in particular?

The bagpipe has been known in many parts of Europe for at least a millennium, with a general spread through the continent appearing to coincide with the minstrel and troubadour culture that developed during the increasing urbanisation and trade of the twelfth and thirteenth centuries. First-millennium evidence tends to be restricted to pictorial representations of the non-bagged, mouth-blown form of pipe. These might be single, double or even triple pipes, all inserted into the mouth simultaneously and quite possibly played with a circular breathing technique that survives down to the present in the remarkable Sardinian *launeddas* tradition. In Scotland representations of triple pipes can be seen in Pictish carvings at Lethendy in Perthshire and Ardchattan in Argyll. We have to wait until the late fourteenth century for the first pictorial evidence of pipes with bags attached within Scotland although, like elsewhere in Europe, the depictions suggest that this was not an instrument befitting human endeavour: carvings in Melrose abbey and Roslin chapel show a piping pig and angel respectively. As Hugh Cheape has pointed out, these two contrasting images, one heavenly, the other a symbol of gluttony and sin, neatly capture the polar attitudes toward the bagpipe that have remained in currency.[20]

The paucity of early evidence suggests, therefore, that the bagpipe came comparatively late to Scotland, and only from the sixteenth century can we begin to see a pattern of diffusion and adoption of the instrument that points to it becoming firmly embedded within the sociocultural scene, and also the first hints of the military association that was eventually to help elevate it to a national icon. These military connections appear first in the context of the Highland clans, but only in the sense that a martial function was one element of a much wider cultural framework. When the bagpipe began to appear in Highland society, most likely in the early sixteenth century, it was as a newcomer to an already rich artistic scene played out within the homes of the clan chiefs whose patronage already supported the *bard*, *filidh* and *clarsair* (or harper).

That it quickly became established as an instrument fit for war was due in part to the timing of its arrival, for the abolition of the Lordship of the Isles in 1493 had opened up a political vacuum that many interests were trying to fill, resulting in an extended period of turbulent Highland history known as *Linn na Creach* or the 'Age of Forays'. The resulting inter-clan warfare introduced a demand for music that could incite men to battle, instruct and control them during it and afterwards celebrate their victory or mourn their loss. The great pipe, or *piob mhór*, with its loud and shrill tones, was perfect for the task and so began to replace the *clarsach*, which had emerged as the principal instrument of the Highland court in more peaceful times. The constant monotone of the bagpipe drone was the key to producing variety in 'mood', for the melody notes of the chanter could be arranged to either harmonise or clash against it, allowing the composer to evoke vibrant celebration or mournful lament equally well within the limited nine-note compass of the instrument. And evoke they did, producing a genre of music unique to Gaeldom which is still widely studied and performed.[21] *Ceòl mór* (great music), often now referred to in English as pibroch,[22] is, at least in part, martial music, with sub-genres such as 'gatherings', 'marches', 'salutes' and 'laments' often having military connotations.[23]

One of the earliest references to the use of bagpipes as an instrument of war appears in relation to the battle of Pinkie in 1547, when a French officer noted that 'the wild Scots encouraged themselves to arms by the sound of their bagpipes'.[24] These may have been men under the command of the earl of Argyll, although we cannot be sure exactly how many pipers there were, what form of bagpipe they were playing or indeed where they came from. What we can safely conclude, however, is that the practice was noteworthy enough to be highlighted by that witness and that the bagpipe was performing the same kind of role as ascribed by Froissart to that of the horns a century and a half earlier.

One of the most pervading myths is that the bagpipe was proscribed following the defeat of the Jacobites at Culloden. In fact, the instrument was not mentioned at all in the Disarming Act of 1746, nor in either of its amendments in 1747 or 1748.[25] John Gibson, who is so keen to prove the point that he reproduces the text of the main act in its entirety within his hugely detailed *Traditional Gaelic Bagpiping*, traces the development of the myth, which appears to date from the early nineteenth century and has been subsequently fuelled by generations of historians.[26] That the bagpipe was widely used by the Jacobite army is not in doubt,[27] nor that the spirit of the act discouraged any cultural practices with strong Highland associations, but an outright ban never took place. This is not a pedantic point for, as Gibson and others argue, the commonly held notion that piping disappeared in the mid-1700s only to be rescued by a combination of the Highland Society of London's piping competitions and the British army later in the century is a misrepresentation of Highland cultural history.[28]

That said, the integration of the bagpipe into the Scottish regiments of the British army undoubtedly moved both into a new phase of development. And while it is unclear exactly when this began to occur, one piece of visual evidence certainly indicates that a Lowland regiment, the 25th (later the King's Own Scottish Borderers), had adopted it by 1769, while the 1st battalion of the Royal Scots was said to have been authorised to keep a piper on its strength throughout the eighteenth century: a unique privilege accorded to no other Scottish regiment, either Highland or Lowland.[29] For most regiments, the appointment of pipers was a luxury that had to be privately financed and supported by the officers, and most did, recruiting at least one piper per company as well as a 'pipe major' with the rank of sergeant. The standard of player required was high – status was everything – and sometimes it was difficult to recruit such a piper. One regimental officer complained in 1778 that a possible candidate, 'John MacComie in Brakrie', 'might do for a recruiting party' but was certainly not of the standard required to be taken on full time.[30] Nevertheless, once a suitable piper was identified, he was an invaluable addition to any regiment and could be found leading the troops into battle. In a letter to his father describing the battle of Arroyo Molinos in March 1811

Figure 24.2 Piper George Findlater of the 1st battalion, the Gordon Highlanders, winning the Victoria Cross at Dargai, 1897. Painted by Vereker Monteith Hamilton, 1898.

during the Peninsular War, Lieutenant-Colonel John Cameron of the 92nd (Gordon) Highlanders mentioned that the first the French commander knew of their approach was the sound of their piper playing 'Hey Johnnie Cope are ye Waken Yet?'[31]

During the nineteenth century individual pipers began to establish themselves as great heroes for their feats of bravery while playing in the heat of combat. One of the first was Piper Kenneth Mackay of the Cameron Highlanders, who famously played the pibroch *Cogadh no Sidh* ('War or Peace') outside his regiment's defensive 'square' at the battle of Waterloo in June 1815. While Mackay's bravery was canonised in print and folklore alike, his exploits were to be overshadowed later in the century by those of George Findlater, a piper in the 1st Gordon Highlanders. Findlater took part in the assault upon the Dargai Heights on the north-west frontier of India in October 1897 and, whilst leading the charge with four other pipers, was wounded in both feet (and the chanter hit too). While one foot only took a glancing blow, the other injury was more serious and he was unable to advance any further. Yet propped up against a rock, and under enemy fire, he continued to play from a sitting position as the Gordons succeeded in storming the hill. His valour during the attack earned him the Victoria Cross and he was later able to capitalise on his fame by becoming a touring performer on the music hall stages of Britain.[32]

Most accounts of bravery in action suggest that pipers were playing alone, or occasionally in small groups, and there are few indications that pipers and drummers played together until the former received official recognition in 1854. Early that year, with war with Russia looking increasingly likely, the Horse Guards authorised a recruiting campaign that included (in the small print) an allowance for each Highland regiment to recruit a pipe major and five pipers.[33] With increasing numbers and central support, the way was now clear for the pipers to take on more official duties, play together in concert and work alongside the regiment's drummers. Only in the mid-nineteenth century, then, did the iconic sight and sound of the pipe band, now so closely associated with the military music of Scotland, begin to emerge.

The military band

Whilst eighteenth-century officers were dipping into their own pockets to support a piper, the tastes of the times demanded a greater variety of musical entertainment and they looked to the professional musician community to augment their needs in this respect. Again at their own expense, the 'band of musick' came into existence, consisting mainly of wood and brass wind instruments. At first these military bands were an unofficial part of the regiment, often contracted for a month at a time, and mainly provided music for indoor entertainment. From 1803, however, ten soldiers from each battalion were permitted by the military authorities to be employed as musicians and bands began to be used regularly on parade squares and on active service (when their members tended to act as stretcher bearers). Finding adequate numbers of skilled players who were willing to sign up remained problematic, however, and competent bandmasters were also in short supply. Many regiments were forced to look to Germany to recruit, including the 72nd and 79th Highlanders.[34]

During the first half of the nineteenth century the British army believed that it was falling behind its main European counterparts in terms of the quality of its bands, with both French and Prussian musicians leading the way. Something had to be done and so the Military Music Class was founded in 1857 at Kneller Hall in Twickenham, renamed the Royal Military School of Music on the occasion of Queen

Victoria's golden jubilee in 1887.[35] A generation later, pipers were provided with a similar high level of tuition with the founding of the Army School of Piping in 1910 at Cameron barracks in Inverness. The school subsequently moved to Edinburgh castle, where Pipe Major Willie Ross of the Scots Guards served as its head for many years, greatly influencing virtually all of the most celebrated players of the first half of the twentieth century.[36]

Repertoire

With so many different forms of instrument being adopted by the military in Scotland, it is difficult to generalise about the nature of the repertoire that emerged. Nonetheless, the issue of function remained central and the music that was composed, adapted and played on any of these instruments developed accordingly. 'Tradition' featured heavily too, as subsequent generations built upon the established practices of their forebears while adding their own preferences and innovations, reacting to new contexts as they met them.

This is reflected in the provision of music for marching. While the march may now be considered the very essence of military music it was actually a relative latecomer to the repertoire, for it was not until the late eighteenth and early nineteenth centuries, once roads were of sufficient standard to allow it, that marching in step became the norm.[37] 'Ordinary time' emerged as the slowest-paced standard at seventy-two paces to the minute – in replication of the average heart rate – and this evolved into the 'slow march'. The 'quick step', by contrast, was a more sprightly 108 paces per minute, and 'the quickest step' was set at 120, later to become the standard pace within the British army. Writing in 1784, the musician and collector of Gaelic music Patrick MacDonald clearly welcomed the faster pace that had recently been introduced:

> One of the greatest improvements in the military art that has been made in modern times, is the introduction of quick-step marches, by which the soldiers are made to advance not only quicker, but with more regularity and greater cheerfulness, than they would be made to do by any other contrivance.[38]

Whether provided by fife, drum, bagpipe or military band, the music clearly had to be conducive to being played at these tempos (although they did tend to vary between regiments). And so emerged the tradition of the regimental march, rousing and recognisable melodies that became key symbols of corporate identity for the troops, some tunes being adopted by several regiments, while others were 'owned' by one. The bagpipe quick march 'Highland Laddie', for example, was played by the Royal Scots Dragoon Guards, Scots Guards, Royal Highland Fusiliers, Black Watch and Argyll and Sutherland Highlanders. The Royal Scots, meanwhile, marched past to 'Dumbarton's Drums', the King's Own Scottish Borderers to 'All the Blue Bonnets over the Border' and the Gordon Highlanders to the 'Cock of the North'.[39]

Repertoires of 'duty tunes' for the regulation of daily routines developed along similar lines, with several transcending regimental boundaries. Reveille (the wake up call) was almost universally sounded with 'Johnny Cope' – although the Gordon Highlanders used 'Greenwoodside' – while meal times were variously marked with 'Bundle and Go', 'Brose and Butter' and 'Jenny's Bawbee'. The beating of the retreat, which signalled the end of the official day, brought rather more regimental variety. The Black Watch played 'Green Hills of Tyrol', the Royal Highland Fusiliers 'Banks of Allan Water' and the Royal Scots 'Heroes of Kohima'.[40] Many of these military tunes are nowadays in the repertoire of military and civilian pipers around the world.

The pipes in twentieth-century warfare

A month after the armistice in 1918, Sir Douglas Haig paid tribute to the role played by the pipers of the British army over the previous four years:

> The Pipers of Scotland may well be proud of the part they have played in this war. In the heat of battle, by the lonely grave, and during the long hours of waiting, they have called to us to show ourselves worthy of the land to which we belong. Many have fallen in the fight for liberty, but their memories remain.[41]

Many indeed had fallen. The First World War claimed the lives of over 500 pipers, with around 600 wounded, leaving the art form struggling to revive in the following years. Yet as Bruce Seton and John Grant carefully documented at the time, music had proved itself a crucial weapon in the thoroughly 'modern' warfare on the Western Front. The conflict had not begun that way, with few pipers being called upon to play during the winter of 1914–15, a severe shortage of manpower resulting in their being employed in the ranks instead. But from the spring of 1915 through to the end of the war, they played their comrades into action.

Figure 24.3 'The Piper of Loos': Pipe Major Daniel Laidlaw VC, 1934.

At the battle of Loos in September 1915 – the Scottish battle – the pipers followed in the footsteps of their nineteenth-century forebears and again earned themselves a reputation for reckless courage. Piper David Simpson of the 2nd Black Watch, Piper Charles Cameron of the 11th Argyll and Sutherland Highlanders and Piper Daniel Laidlaw of the 7th King's Own Scottish Borderers displayed such valour during the fighting that they were all later accorded the heroic sobriquet of 'the Piper of Loos'.[42] The best known of them, Piper Laidlaw, was awarded the Victoria Cross 'for most conspicuous bravery' in the fighting near hill 70. The *London Gazette* citation summarised his actions thus:

> During the worst of the bombardment, when the attack was about to commence, Piper Laidlaw, seeing that his company was somewhat shaken from the effects of gas, with absolute coolness and disregard of danger, mounted the parapet, marched up and down and played his company out of the trench [to the tune of the regimental march 'Blue Bonnets over the Border']. The effect of his splendid example was immediate, and the company dashed out to the assault. Piper Laidlaw continued playing his pipes till he was wounded.[43]

Figure 24.4 Commandos of the 1st Special Service Brigade landing at Sword Beach on D-Day. Brigadier the Lord Lovat can be seen striding through the water to the right of the column of men. Piper Bill Millin is the figure nearest the camera on the right.

By the time of the Second World War pipers were not supposed to play in action; however, they played the 51st Highland Division into battle at El Alamein in October 1942 – the pipes being given a prominent role in the Academy award-winning documentary film *Desert Victory* (1943) – and, famously, Lord Lovat of the 1st Special Service Brigade asked his piper, Bill Millin, to play the commandos ashore as they landed at Sword Beach on D-Day. As Millin later recalled

> I was so relieved of getting off that boat after all night being violently sick. I struck up the Pipes and paddled through the surf playing 'Hieland Laddie', and Lord Lovat turned round and looked at me and [gestured approvingly]. When I finished, Lovat asked for another tune. Well, when I looked round – the noise and people lying about shouting and the smoke, the crump of mortars, I said to myself 'Well, you must be joking surely.' He said 'What was that?' and he said 'Would you mind giving us a tune?' 'Well, what tune would you like, Sir?' 'How about The Road to the Isles?' 'Now, would

you want me to walk up and down, Sir?' 'Yes. That would be nice. Yes, walk up and down.'[44]

Millin continued to play whilst he and Lovat's commandos advanced inland to Pegasus bridge. Surprised not to have been shot by the enemy, he was later told by captured Germans that they had refrained from firing at him as 'they thought he had gone off his head'.[45]

Throughout the Cold War deployments and colonial conflicts of the post-war years pipers accompanied the Scottish regiments. In Aden in 1967 Lieutenant-Colonel Colin 'Mad Mitch' Mitchell of the 1st Argyll and Sutherland Highlanders ordered Pipe Major Kenneth Robson to strike up the regimental charge, 'Monymusk', as the troops reoccupied Crater. 'It is the most thrilling sound in the world to go into action with the pipes playing,' Mitchell recalled. 'It stirs the blood and reminds one of the heritage of Scotland and the Regiment. Best of all it frightens the enemy to death.'[46] During the more recent wars in Iraq and Afghanistan, musicians have continued to perform in a variety of ways. Major Bruce Hitchings, a former pipe major with the Queen's Own Highlanders, observed that 'The bagpipes are there – they're there as part of the war, there as part of the funerals, the remembrance, there as part of the ceremonial side of it. The bagpipe hasn't lost its position in warfare.'[47] On rare occasions, this still includes playing while in contact with the enemy, as was the case in Afghanistan when Corporal Ryan Pagnacco of the Royal Highland Fusiliers of Canada took up his instrument as 'nearby tanks fired at the enemy . . . and despite a lack of protective gear, started playing, even taking shouted requests for tunes from his comrades'.[48] In the same theatre of operations, Piper Phil Stevenson of Cumnock led the final patrol of a Scots Guards company back to base and remarked that 'it was a great honour for me to pipe home the company after the long and sometimes gruelling time we have spent in the deserts of Helmand province'.[49]

Much of the pipe music on contemporary operations, however, forms part of acts of commemoration and it is a sad truth that musicians are in regular demand for this purpose. The 'ramp ceremonies', whereby the coffins of fallen soldiers are taken to or from aircraft, are frequently carried out to the accompaniment of a bagpipe lament. Yet when the occasion calls for an upbeat celebration or a vibrant display of national identity, the instrument can still play its part. During the First Gulf War in 1991, Hitchings recalled that

> Actually in the fighting, when we went across the breach and we were advancing for about two or three days there was hardly any bagpipes

played, but as soon as we got into Kuwait city and the ceasefire was declared we actually played the pipes on top of the vehicles into the town . . . of course these days everyone's in combats and you all look the same, but once you get a piper playing people are going to know you're a Scottish regiment – it gives you that identification, it makes the guys proud.[50]

Taking the music to the public

Public entertainment is nowadays a common feature of military music, but this is by no means a new addition to the musicians' role. The regimental bands (the former 'band of musick') celebrated their increased numbers, repertoire and standards of musicianship in the early nineteenth century by putting on public recitals. These were common events in the open spaces of Edinburgh during the 1830s and 1840s, and in the same era the band of the Black Watch could regularly be heard in concert at the city's Assembly Rooms.[51]

In more recent times, however, it is the tattoo that has served a key role in taking military music to the public and has done so with considerable commercial success. The word 'tattoo' derives from the Dutch for 'last orders' (*doe den tap toe*, or 'put the tap to') and was adapted by the British army as the final duty call of the day, sounded to warn tavern owners to turn off their taps and send the troops back to their barracks. By the second half of the eighteenth century, the term appears to have taken on an extra meaning as an evening of musical entertainment, and two centuries later it was that concept that was translated into the public setting of the Edinburgh castle esplanade with the establishment, in 1950, of the Edinburgh Military Tattoo.[52] Although it grew to incorporate representations and performances of many aspects of military life, music has remained the central building block of the event. Witnessed live each year by well over 200,000 spectators, it is also watched on television by an estimated 100 million viewers worldwide.[53] As such, it has been hugely influential in constructing a particular representation of Scotland and Scottishness based firmly on the nation's military heritage and tradition.

Military music has also conquered the hit parade. The pipes and drums of the Royal Scots Dragoon Guards, in particular, have earned themselves a reputation as chart-toppers. Their version of 'Amazing Grace' went to number one in the popular music charts of the UK, Ireland, Australia, Canada and South Africa in 1972, while more recently their album, *Journey*, part of their *Spirit of the Glen* CD series, topped the UK classical album chart and won the Classical Brit award in 2009. The fact that part of the CD was recorded in extraordinary heat while on active service in Basra makes this success story all the more remarkable.

It can be seen, then, that music has played a prominent role in Scottish military history and the Scottish regiments have, in turn, brought considerable influence to bear on the wider musical landscape of the nation. In this brief overview it has only been possible to provide glimpses of this mutual relationship and hint at the complexities involved. Music instructs, inspires, celebrates and mourns, links past, present and future generations, and fosters emotions of identity and belonging. From the earliest localised soundings of bull horns to the global recognition of the massed pipes and drums, the military musical journey has been long and fruitful. It is a journey that looks set to continue for some time to come.

Notes

1. D. Murray, *Music of the Scottish Regiments: Cogadh no Sith (War or Peace)* (Edinburgh: Mercat Press, 1994), p. 1.
2. J. Purser, *Scotland's Music: A History of the Traditional and Classical Music of Scotland from Early Times to the Present Day* (Edinburgh: Mainstream Publishing, 1992), pp. 26–7.
3. The reconstruction was carried out in the early 1990s by a team comprising John Purser (musicologist), Fraser Hunter (archaeologist) and John Creed (craftsman) and was played by musician John Kenny. See www.carnyxscotland.co.uk, accessed on 6 September 2011.
4. J. Froissart, *The Chronicles of Froissart*, trans. John Bourchier, Lord Berners (1994). Available at www.fordham.edu/halsall/basis/froissart-full.html, accessed on 6 September 2011.
5. Murray, *Music of the Scottish Regiments*, p. 3.
6. Ibid. pp. 6–7. See also H. Barty-King, *The Drum: A Royal Tournament Tribute to the Military Drum* (London: The Royal Tournament, 1988).
7. Murray, *Music of the Scottish Regiments*, p. 7.
8. A. Fairrie, *Queen's Own Highlanders: Seaforths and Camerons* (Golspie: Queen's Own Highlanders Amalgamation Trust, 1998), p. 268.
9. Black Watch Regimental Museum Archive, Perth, 3591 (2), diary of Private A. W. McIntosh, 42nd, p. 149, and quoted in D. Henderson, *Highland Soldier: A Social Study of the Highland Regiments, 1820–1920* (Edinburgh: John Donald, 1989), p. 244.
10. *London Gazette*, 9 September 1916.
11. The drums were left by the Gordons in the care of the Belgian police at Ostend in 1914, but were subsequently captured by a German marine

battalion in 1918 and put on display in Berlin. I am grateful to Jesper Ericsson at the Gordon Highlanders Museum for this information.
12. The Highlanders Museum, Fort George, Inverness, display case caption 205-3-H.
13. Murray, *Music of the Scottish Regiments*, pp. 8–9. Army oral tradition suggests that the fife was reintroduced by a contingent of Hessians who joined the government forces as part of Cumberland's suppression of the Highlands.
14. Fairrie, *Queen's Own Highlanders*, p. 268.
15. For an in-depth discussion of the bugle's evolution, see A. Baines, *Brass Instruments: Their History and Development* (London: Faber and Faber, 1980). The best account of their military function from a Scottish perspective is once again provided by Murray, *Music of the Scottish Regiments*.
16. J. Hyde, *A New and Compleat Preceptor for the Trumpet and Bugle Horn* (London: Button and Whitakers, 1799).
17. Murray's analysis of the 1966 HMSO publication *Trumpet and Bugle Sounds for the Army* concludes that around a dozen calls still being used in modern times can be traced directly back to Hyde's *Preceptor* (Murray, *Music of the Scottish Regiments*, p. 155).
18. Henderson, *Highland Soldier*, p. 245.
19. The first such claim in print appears to have come from a Skyeman, Donald MacDonald, in 1819, in the preface to his *A Collection of the Ancient Martial Music of Caledonia Called Piobaireachd* (East Ardsley: E. P. Publishing Ltd, 1974). For a detailed discussion of the concept of the bagpipe as a national instrument, see H. Cheape, *Bagpipes: A National Collection of a National Instrument* (Edinburgh: National Museums of Scotland, 2008).
20. Cheape, *Bagpipes*, p. 30.
21. The word 'Gaeldom' is chosen carefully here, as some scholars (notably Cheape, *Bagpipes*, pp. 42–6) point towards the possibility that Scotland may not have had exclusive ownership of the *ceòl mór* tradition and that Irish input may have been stronger than has hitherto been recognised (or admitted!). This remains a contentious point.
22. The English form, pibroch, is derived from the Gaelic *piobaireachd*, which simply means 'piping', although both forms in modern usage tend to refer to *ceòl mór*. For a clear and accessible overview of this form of music, see R. Cannon, *The Highland Bagpipe and its Music* (Edinburgh: John Donald, 2002), and for detailed essays on specific aspects of piping development see J. Dickson (ed.), *The Highland Bagpipe: Music, History, Tradition* (Farnham: Ashgate, 2009).
23. The functions of these categories were not exclusively military, in that the concept of patronage to the chief was also paramount. Salutes and

laments, for example, would be offered by a piper to his chief and senior members of the clan irrespective of circumstance. Also, the term 'march' does not denote a regular paced movement in the modern sense.

24. J. Bain (ed.), *L'Histoire de la Guerre d'Écosse Pendant les Campagnes 1548–1549 par Jean de Beaugue* (Edinburgh: Maitland Club, 1830).
25. United Kingdom, *Statutes*, 19 Geo. 2, 1746; 20 Geo. 2, 1747; and 21 Geo. 2, 1748.
26. J. Gibson, *Traditional Gaelic Bagpiping, 1745–1945* (Montreal and Edinburgh: McGill-Queen's University Press and NMS Publishing, 1998), pp. 25–35. The texts of the acts appear in the appendices, pp. 258–72.
27. References to the use of bagpipes by the Jacobites in the 1745–6 campaign in particular are plentiful, but perhaps one succinct contemporary comment can illustrate the point. A note in the papers of the earl of Seafield from 17 September 1745 asserts that 'Edinburgh now full of highlanders and bagpipes instead of dragoons and drums'. See National Records of Scotland, Edinburgh [hereafter NRS], GD 248/168/7.
28. The other key text that argues against the standard interpretation is W. Donaldson, *The Highland Pipe and Scottish Society, 1750–1950: Transmission, Change and the Concept of Tradition* (East Linton: Tuckwell Press, 2000).
29. Murray, *Music of the Scottish Regiments*, p. 50. The pictorial evidence relating to the 25th is a painting commissioned by its commanding officer while stationed in Minorca showing a piper in full 'Highland' uniform standing alongside a fife player.
30. NRS, GD 44/43/203, letter from John Gordon, Laggan, to James Ross, 5 May 1778.
31. NRS, GD 1/737/122-123, letter from Lt.-Col. John Cameron, 2–5 Nov. 1811. Cameron was killed at Quatre Bras in 1815.
32. E. Spiers, 'Findlater, George Frederick (1872–1942)', *Oxford Dictionary of National Biography*, Oxford University Press, Oct 2008. Available at www.oxforddnb.com/view/article/96873, accessed on 6 September 2011.
33. Fairrie, *Queen's Own Highlanders*, p. 269; Murray, *Music of the Scottish Regiments*, p. 121.
34. Fairrie, *Queen's Own Highlanders*, p. 274.
35. See www.army.mod.uk/music/music.aspx, accessed on 15 August 2011.
36. Many of Ross's students went on to teach subsequent generations of top players, both military and civilian alike, and so the institution played a crucial role in the improvement of playing standards in recent times. The school (now the Army School of Bagpipe Music and Highland

Drumming) is currently based at Inchdrewer House at Redford barracks in Edinburgh.

37. D. Murray, 'Macadam's roads and the history of the march', *Piping Times*, vol. 52, no. 5 (2000), pp. 19–23.
38. P. MacDonald, *A Collection of Highland Vocal Airs* (Edinburgh: Muir Wood, 1784), p. 10.
39. Murray, *Music of the Scottish Regiments*, pp. 196–7. The slow march past air, *The Garb of Old Gaul*, which was associated initially with the Black Watch but was later played by other Scottish regiments, was composed by John Reid (1722–1807). He served as an officer in the Black Watch and was subsequently to reach the rank of general. It was his generous legacy to the University of Edinburgh that led to the setting up of the school of music and concert hall that bear his name.
40. Ibid. pp. 230–1.
41. Dated 6 December 1918 and reproduced in the foreword to B. Seton and J. Grant, *Pipes of War* (Glasgow: Maclehose, Jackson & Co., 1920).
42. Seton and Grant, *Pipes of War*, pp. 22–3.
43. *London Gazette*, 18 November 1915. For a succinct account of Laidlaw's life, see E. Spiers, 'Laidlaw, Daniel Logan (1875–1950)', *Oxford Dictionary of National Biography*, Oxford University Press, Oct 2008. Available at www.oxforddnb.com/view/article/89863, accessed on 6 September 2011. Interestingly, Laidlaw and Findlater marched together at the Cenotaph in 1932.
44. Quoted in www.pegasusarchive.org/normandy/bill_millin.htm, accessed on 27 June 2011.
45. 'Piper Bill Millin', obituary, *Daily Telegraph*, 19 August 2010.
46. Quoted in 'Lt.-Col. C. C. "Mad Mitch" Mitchell, obituary', *Daily Telegraph*, 24 July 1996.
47. Major B. Hitchings, recorded interview with author, August 2009.
48. Major R. Gunther, 'Pipers bring dignity and solemnity to ceremonies for fallen soldiers', *Piping Times*, vol. 62, no. 6 (2010), p. 13. Pagnacco was later wounded in action in a friendly-fire incident and his pipes were lost, but the Kilmarnock-based manufacturer, McCallum Bagpipes, presented him with a replacement set free of charge. Military piping on service in Afghanistan is by no means restricted to Scottish regiments. There is no clearer indication of how widely the instrument has been adopted internationally than the fact that pipers from Canada, Nepal, the USA, Australia, France and Germany have all played in the Afghan war zone.
49. Major R. Gunther, 'The British armed forces and their pipers cover old ground', *Piping Times*, vol. 62, no. 7 (2010), p. 41.

50. Recorded interview with Major Bruce Hitchings, August 2009.
51. Henderson, *Highland Soldier*, p. 241.
52. A smaller event, entitled 'Something About a Soldier', had been held at the Ross Bandstand in Princes Street Gardens the previous year.
53. See www.edintattoo.co.uk, accessed on 8 November 2010. See also R. Martine, *Edinburgh Military Tattoo* (London: Robert Hale, 2001). The event is now named the Royal Edinburgh Military Tattoo.

25
The Scottish Soldier in Literature

ROBERT P. IRVINE

The image of the heroic Scottish soldier, kilt and sporran displaying his nationality beneath a tunic of red or khaki, is an icon of Scottishness familiar from paintings, photographs, cartoons and films throughout the nineteenth and twentieth centuries. Many songs, too, have been written to celebrate this figure, but an equivalent in the literary writing of the same period is rare. What we find there instead is a range of types, all of them placed on the borderline between military life and some version of civilian society: the discharged soldier, mutilated, impoverished and disregarded by the country for which he fought; the highlander, committed to a native martial 'tradition' abroad even as his traditional way of life is being destroyed at home; and the career officer, for whom the army has become a substitute family, and thus a stage on which various private anxieties must be played out. These three types might be seen as characteristic of the eighteenth-, nineteenth- and twentieth-century texts respectively, and I will discuss them in this order. This chapter is not, however, a historical survey, and these modes of representing the Scottish soldier are not limited to the periods mentioned. For example, all of them crop up in Gregory Burke's play *Black Watch*, extracts from which will introduce each of the discussions in this chapter. First performed in the 2006 Edinburgh Festival simultaneously with, and within earshot of, the Edinburgh Military Tattoo, *Black Watch* is in part an anti-Tattoo, critiquing the traditional image of the Scottish soldier reproduced by its theatrical rival on the castle esplanade. It does this by telling the story of the famous regiment from the point of view of the soldiers who served in Iraq in 2004, while at the same time engaging in its own kinds of spectacle and nostalgia. But this is not a uniquely twenty-first century project: the heroic type of paintings and songs has always

Figure 25.1 A scene from the National Theatre of Scotland's *Black Watch* by Gregory Burke.

co-existed with its anti-type in fiction and poetry, and this is my subject in this chapter.

None of the texts I examine here was written before the second half of the eighteenth century. Clearly, this is not for a want of fighting men in the writing of earlier periods. John Barbour's verse biography of Scotland's hero-king, *The Bruce* (c. 1375), for example, is populated with little else. But they are not 'soldiers' in a way that makes sense in the context of this chapter. They are either noblemen whose identity as warriors is part of their identity as political rulers, or they are what Barbour calls 'the small folk', whose role is to run away whenever they are not given sufficiently heroic leadership by the nobles. The first Scot in literature who is a soldier in the modern, professional sense is probably Captain Jamy in *Henry V* (1599). But he is not in Shakespeare's play to represent a particular link between Scottishness and soldiering; rather, he is there, alongside the Welsh soldier and the Irish soldier, to indulge a Tudor fantasy of pan-Britannic hegemony. As far as Scottish literature is concerned, soldiering as a vocation is a modern phenomenon and, consequently, its representation necessarily evokes Scotland's place in a modern, commercial and imperial polity, the Great Britain dreamt of in *Henry V*.

Britons

> *Cammy*: See, I think people's minds are usually made up about you if you were in the army.
> *Beat.*
> They are though ay?
> *Beat.*
> They poor fucking boys. They cannae day anything else. They cannay get a job. They get exploited by the army.
> *Beat.*
> Well I want you to fucking know. I wanted to be in the army. I could have done other stuff. I'm not a fucking knuckle-dragger.[1]

Thus ex-Private Campbell, in civilian clothes, introduces *Black Watch* by evoking one version of the Scottish soldier: that of a victim of the army, of the British state and of modern economic and social systems generally. This figure is already there in Robert Burns's *Love and Liberty* (1785), with 'auld, red rags' remaining from his uniform, but lacking an arm and a leg, drinking and singing his sorrows away in the company of a whore, a pickpocket, a tinker, a fiddler and a poet. This veteran tells us that he has fought in some of the battles that established and maintained Britain's global dominance in the mid-eighteenth century: Wolfe's victory at the Heights of Abraham in 1759; in the storming of El Morro in Cuba in 1762; and in the Siege of Gibraltar under Eliott in 1779–83.

> And now tho' I must beg, with a wooden arm and leg,
>   And many a tatter'd rag hanging over my bum,
> I'm as happy with my wallet, my bottle and my Callet,
>   As when I us'd in scarlet to follow a drum.[2]

The soldier here is ready to return to duty at a moment's notice (if the army will have him back) in the service of Great Britain but, for just now, he inhabits the alternative nation of the eighteenth-century underclass. Burns's cantata ends with the chorus

> A fig for those by LAW protected,
>   LIBERTY's a glorious feast!

> COURTS for Cowards were erected,
> CHURCHES built to please the Priest.[3]

For the British propertied classes of this period, 'liberty' consisted in legal protection for property against the crown and a reformed established Church. This is the liberty that the soldier has spent his life defending from absolutist Catholic France and Spain. But since military service has left him with no property and little faith, the 'liberty' he enjoys on his return consists in his alienation from the norms of the modern commercial Britain for which he fought. The soldier thus performs a special function among Burns's cast of lowlifes: his fate suggests that their amorality is what makes them not different from but representative of a wider society capable of such ingratitude to those who have sacrificed so much in its defence.

We find a more complex version of the discharged Scottish soldier in another Rabelaisian text from this period, Tobias Smollett's epistolary novel *The Expedition of Humphry Clinker* (1771). In the eyes of Matthew Bramble and his family party on their tour of Britain, Lieutenant Obadiah Lismahago, with his tarnished scarlet coat and scalped cranium, at first appears merely grotesque: 'A tall, meagre figure, answering, with his horse, the description of Don Quixote mounted on Rozinante.'[4] But their laughter turns to pity when they hear his story: 'in the course of two sanguinary wars, he had been wounded, maimed, mutilated, taken, and enslaved, without ever having attained a higher rank than that of lieutenant'.[5] Lismahago is quite reconciled to his fate, but Bramble considers this an outrageous injustice and evidence of the corruption of modern Britain generally. Indeed, Lismahago plays an important role in the novel's representation of British society. As at once a Scot and a hero of Britain's wars with France, he stands in contrast to those in metropolitan England who Bramble discovers hiring French servants, imitating French fashions and even welcoming known French spies into their soirées. In a novel written, as Horace Walpole suggested, 'to vindicate the Scots' in the aftermath of Bute's ministry, Lismahago represents the possibility that a Scot might be a more patriotic Briton than an Englishman.

At the same time, he invites Bramble to reassess the imperial project within which the two nations had been united. In Bath and in London, Bramble recognised only the corrupting effects of imperial conquest, understood, in civic humanist terms, as the introduction of 'luxury' among the plebeians:

clerks and factors from the East Indies, loaded with the spoil of plundered provinces; planters, negro-drivers, and hucksters, from our American plantations, enriched they know not how; agents, commissaries, and contractors, who have fattened, in two successive wars, on the blood of the nation;[6]

and so on. Lismahago, like the veteran of *Love and Liberty*, conjures up a different version of empire as the defining horizon of modern Britain: not a source of corrupting wealth, but an arena for military heroism; an opportunity for self-sacrifice, rather than self-gratification. Lismahago also undercuts Bramble's fears about 'luxury', even though he shares them,[7] when he proposes, as many eighteenth-century philosophers had proposed, native Americans as living examples of republican political virtue, claiming that

> neither the simplicity of their manners, not the commerce of their country, would admit of those articles of luxury which are deemed magnificence in Europe; and that they were too virtuous and sensible to encourage the introduction of any fashion which might help to render them corrupt and effeminate.[8]

Lismahago says this, having already described the protracted and excruciating torture and mutilation to which these 'virtuous and sensible' people subjected him, by way of sport. Indeed, having survived this torture and been accepted into the tribe, Lismahago is the novel's reassurance that the imperial and commercial basis of modern Britain need not render it 'corrupt and effeminate' if only it can learn some lessons in self-command from an old Scottish soldier, and other beggarly-looking veterans.

Thus the figure of the Scottish soldier as a type first becomes visible in literary writing not as the embodiment of a tradition, but as the opposite: as an outcast, the battered product of modernity, but one whose marginal position allows him a critical perspective on the society to which he has returned. Something like this figure is revived in the last section of Lewis Grassic Gibbon's novel *Sunset Song* (1932), which chronicles the devastation (human, economic and ecological) wreaked on a Kincardineshire crofting community by the First World War. Its men join the local regiment (a fictional 'Northern Highlanders' standing in for the Gordons) either from a sense of outrage at German atrocities (Chae Strachan) or as a result of peer pressure (Ewan Tavendale) or of the more tangible economic pressures incurred by a stand against the war (Rob Duncan). None expresses any identification with a local or national tradition of military service. Chae, indeed, the only enthusiastic volunteer, is his community's spokesman for modernity, for scientific progress and socialism. On the eve of the battle of the Somme, home on leave, Chae clings to the prospect of a utopian outcome to this historical cataclysm:

> he still believed the War would bring a good thing to the world, it would end the armies and fighting forever, the day of socialism at last would dawn, the common folk had seen what their guns could do and right soon they'd use them when once they came back.[9]

In the segment that includes this declaration, the novel uses Chae, the returned soldier, as our point of view on Kinraddie, registering its transformation in his absence. In Smollett and Burns, the Scottish soldier returns to a country apparently unaffected by war (except in the profits it generates for a few) and thus indifferent to his suffering. In *Sunset Song*, the returned soldier, in the figure of Chae, is the one who has remained essentially the same, true to his original political principles; it is the country for which he is fighting that has changed in the meantime.

In the absence of a recognisable 'military tradition' which could rationalise the deaths of Chae, Ewan and Rob, *Sunset Song* offers a longer historical perspective. Chae's last visit to his homeland ends with a tipsy moonlit encounter on a moor with a man 'in strange gear, hardly clad at all, and something had flashed on his head, like a helmet maybe', tending to a basketwork chariot. A second look and he has vanished; Chae recognises him as 'a Calgacus' man from the Graupius battle when they fought the Romans up from the south'.[10] When a monument is erected to Kinraddie's dead, it takes the form of an inscription on an ancient standing stone, an inscription that repeats the form of the seventeenth-century memorial to the covenanters that Chris found in Dunnottar castle years before. *Sunset Song* thus represents Kinraddie as a palimpsest of thousands of years of war and suffering, into which the dead soldiers have now in turn been inscribed. But it does so without asserting any continuity between fighting in a Scottish regiment of the British army, Presbyterian resistance to Stuart absolutism and Pictish resistance to Rome. The ghostly warrior Chae thinks he sees does not welcome him into a brotherhood of fighting men whose shared experience of war transcends the historical gulf between them. Instead, each is a reiteration, in vastly different historical epochs, of the violence done to ordinary people by systems of state power. If the equation with the covenanters turns Rob, Chae and Ewan into martyrs, then they are martyred by forces that are millennia old. It will be left to the next generation, followed in the next two novels of Gibbon's trilogy, to decide what cause, if any, they were martyred for. The meaning of their deaths is not determined by the past, in the shape of 'tradition'; it will be determined by the future, in the prospect of revolution.

Celts

> *Cammy*: [. . .] So, aye, like I say, formed in 1739. By George the Second. And you can see why they wanted us on the firm ay. We're useful cunts tay hay on board. We're warriors. We're Celts.
> *Beat.*
> The thing about the Celts, apart fay being an oral culture and disappearing fay history, is that they looked upon warfare as sport. It was their fun. It was what they did to relax.
> *Beat.*
> Tay us, this . . . this is fucking relaxation.[11]

It was Walter Scott's generation of writers, the generation that watched Scottish regiments taking a prominent role in the war against Napoleon, that first tried to make sense of a link between the Highland clans and the Highland regiments of the modern British army. This is the project of Scott's 1827 story, 'The Highland Widow', from the collection *Chronicles of the Canongate*. Its hero, Hamish Bean MacTavish, is the son of an Argyll cateran, finally killed by government troops in the aftermath of Culloden, when Hamish is still an infant. His mother Elspat dreams of Hamish taking up his father's outlaw career; Hamish, recognising that times have changed, enlists in a Highland regiment instead. But the night before he is due to leave for his barracks in Dumbarton, Elspat puts a sleeping potion in his drink, he overstays his leave and shoots the sergeant sent to fetch him. He is captured, taken to Dumbarton and shot by firing squad. The narrator explains the background to this story in the context of the recruitment of Highland troops for the Seven Years War. For all their experience in arms, Highland men understood military service as an undertaking from which they could withdraw at any time, to return home with their booty from a victory or to recover from a defeat. Thus, 'the new-levied Highland recruits could scarce be made to comprehend the nature of a military engagement, which compelled a man to serve in the army longer than he pleased'.[12]

'The Highland Widow', however, finds a way of reconciling modern soldiering and Highland tradition by shifting responsibility for the tragedy from this historical contradiction to the old woman, Elspat MacTavish. Hamish's father makes two posthumous appearances in the story: once in his widow's imagination, to prevent her from urging Hamish to take up his father's career of banditry[13] and once as a ghost to his son, warning him off his final visit to Elspeth's bothy and pointing out instead the road to the south, to his regiment. The reader is thus reassured that in joining the British army, Hamish is not betraying the spirit of his father, even if he is abandoning his way of life. He is able to assert an abstract connection between father and son:

> Mother [...] you have taken my life; to that you have a right, for you gave it. But touch not my honour! – it came to me from a brave strain of ancestors, and should be sullied neither by man's deed nor woman's speech.[14]

Hamish understands his patrilineal inheritance not as a set of concrete social commitments (to his mother, to his clan) but as this usefully ideal quantity, 'honour', useful precisely because it can be withdrawn from a local account and invested instead in his regiment. 'The Highland Widow' thus promises that the manifest discontinuity between one social system and another can be reinvented as a continuity, via the abstraction of 'honour'. By Scott's own time, this imaginary resolution of a real social contradiction was long enough established that it could go by another name: 'tradition'. The idea that there was something vestigially 'celtic' in the Highland regiments was a long-lived one, as we can see from Cammy's comments at the start of this section.

Yet it is striking that when highlanders themselves write about war, the connection between the contemporary Highland soldier and the clan warrior is very rarely made. Donald Meek's recent anthology of nineteenth-century Gaelic verse includes a range of pieces celebrating Highland troops at Alexandria and Waterloo, and in the Crimea, but nowhere are ancient victories invoked as contexts for present glories. The note of protest at the poverty and depopulation of the homeland is never far away, however, so that Alexander MacDonald, in 'Cogadh a' Chrimea' ('The Crimean War') can turn from the glory of Sir Colin Campbell and his men at Alma to lines such as these:

Nach cluinn sibh, uaislean na Gàidhealtachd?	Will you not hear, you Highland aristocrats?
Nach èisd sibh an dàn seo le mùirn?	Will you not listen gladly to this song?
[...]	[...]
Nach builich sibh cuid de ur treud	Will you not assign part of your flock
A chumail nan laoch ann am freumh?	to keeping the heroes secure in their roots?
'S na fanadh an reothadh bhon cnàmhan,	If only frost would avoid their bones,
Gu bràth chan fhannaicheadh eud.	their zeal would never grow weak.[15]

It is this connection of the heroism of the Scottish soldier with wider social and political contexts that is the mark of the most distinguished war poetry Scotland has produced, that of the North African campaign in the Second World War. In Hamish Henderson's *Elegies for the Dead in Cyrenaica* (1948) we find the most unambiguous celebration of the traditions of the Highland regiments in his description of the 51st Highland Division advancing under the artillery barrage at El Alamein:

Is this all they will hear, this raucous apocalypse?
[...]
No! For I can hear it! Or is it? ... tell
me that I can hear it! Now – listen!
Yes, hill and shieling
sea-loch and island, hear it, the yell
of your war-pipes, scaling sound's mountains
guns thunder drowning in their soaring swell![16]

Yet this section of Henderson's poem ('Opening of an Offensive') is labelled 'Interlude', and its tone is very different from the ten elegies that surround it. In 'The Jocks', in the violence of this moment, it is possible to revel in the thought 'that many / German Fascists will not be going home/ [...] that many / will die, doomed in their false dream'[17] by the ferocity of the Highland infantry. Elsewhere, from the perspective of victory, the emphasis is on the equivalence of the British dead with the 'others', their German and Italian comrades in 'the proletariat / of levelling death' ('Third Elegy')[18]; and on the obligation their deaths place upon the survivors to build an equivalent solidarity among the living. As in *Sunset Song*, the soldiers' deaths will only make sense in the context of a wider future transformation of a whole society.

Figure 25.2 Hamish Henderson (on the left), who served as an intelligence officer with the 51st Highland Division in Sicily in 1943, interrogates a captured German paratroop commander, Captain Albrecht Guenther.

For George Campbell Hay, too, the war only makes sense as a radicalising experience. The Highland, and more broadly Scottish, tradition of military service abroad has amounted to a betrayal of the motherland in his wartime poem 'Ar Blàr Catha' ('Our Field of Battle'):

Rangan MhicAoidh is feachd Ghustàvais,	The ranks of Mackay, the campaigning of Gustavus the army of France, the guard of Louis,
arm na Frainge, geàrd nan Liuthais,	
a liuthad ceum sgìth is leòn is àrach,	so many weary steps and wounds and stricken fields,
's gun leas ar màthar an aon bhuille.	and no benefit to our mother in a single blow.
An e gun d'rinn sinn a dearmad,	Was it that we neglected her,
's gun d'fhàs i searbh is bochd is cruaidh dhuinn?	And that she grew bitter and poor and hard towards us?[19]

Like Henderson's *Elegies*, this poem ends with a call for a new type of social and political struggle at home in place of the military one abroad: 'is i Alba ar blàr Catha'; 'Scotland is our field of battle'. This discomfort with the Highland tradition of heroic soldiering, the sense that it is a distraction in the modern age, is there too in Sorley Maclean, as he looks at a dead English soldier in 'Curaidhean' ('Heroes'):

Chan fhaca mi Lannes aig Ratasbon	I did not see Lannes at Ratasbon
no MacGill-Fhinnein aig Allt Eire	nor MacLennan at Auldearn
no Gill-Iosa aig Cuil-Lodair,	nor Gillies MacBain at Culloden
ach chunnaic mi Sasannach 'san Eiphit	but I saw an Englishman in Egypt.
Fear beag truagh le gruaidhean pluiceach	A poor little chap with chubby cheeks
Is glùinean a' bleith a chéile,	and knees grinding each other,
aodann guireanach gun tlachd ann–	pimply unattractive face–
còmhdach an spioraid bu tréine.	garment of the bravest spirit.[20]

Contrast this to the ending of his 'Dol an Iar' ('Going Westwards'), where the speaker turns to his ancestors to give himself courage in the coming battle:

Agus biodh na bha mar bha e,	And be what was as it was,
tha mi de dh'fhir mhór' á Bhràighe,	I am of the big men of Braes,
de Choinn Mhic Ghille Chaluim threubhaich,	of the heroic Raasay MacLeods,
de Mhathanaich Loch Aills nan geurlann,	of the sharp-sword Mathesons of Lochalsh;
agus fir m' ainme–có bu tréine	and the men of my name–who were braver
nuair dh'fhadadh uabhar an léirchreach?	when their ruinous pride was kindled?[21]

This is something other than a falling-back on the legends of clan leaders such as Ruairidh MacLennan's heroic last stand against Montrose at Auldearn, or Gillies MacBain's against Cumberland's army at Culloden, evoked in 'Curaidhean', to explain the present moment. Courage here comes from the thought of more local, recent family connections. In particular, 'the big men of Braes' alludes to those who fought the police in 'the battle of the Braes' in April 1882, a turning point in opposition to landlordism in the *Gàidhealtachd* (the Gaelic-speaking Highlands and Islands). This is a different Highland tradition, one of resistance and social reform, in line with the hopes for post-war revolution raised by Henderson and Hay. Yet this tradition too is questioned in the poem's closing question: even in this context, courage depends on a pride that is ultimately 'ruinous'.

Fathers and sons

> *Cammy*: [. . .] you ken, I thought I kent why I was here. I really couldnay ever have seen myself behind the deli counter in Tesco or anything like that. I always wanted tay be a soldier. And this is way all due respect, sir . . .
> Beat.
> What the fuck are you doing here?
> *Officer*: What am I doing here?
> *Cammy*: Yes, sir.
> *Officer*: Well, I'm . . . I'm . . . what's the word . . .
> Pause.
> Cursed.[22]

In the twentieth century the Scottish military tradition began to be represented as a burdensome inheritance, as a 'curse', for an officer class in which military service was the expected career choice for the sons of soldier fathers. Cammy's officer in *Black Watch* explains:

> You see . . . my father, he was in Korea. Nineteen years old, Second Lieutenant. Got wounded. And promoted. And his father, he was at Loos. And his father, well he was more of a gambler than anything else, but you get my drift [. . .] Some of us . . . It's in the blood.'[23]

The two novels I discuss in this final section both imagine the career army officer in crisis and both were, coincidentally, published in the year of another sort of crisis, the Suez debacle of 1956.

Tony Chisholm, the hero of Eric Linklater's *The Dark of Summer*, wins a Military Cross on the retreat to Dunkirk, fights with the Highland Division from El Alamein to Tunisia, loses an arm in Korea and by the end of the novel is on the staff of NATO, planning for nuclear war. But this exemplary career, and indeed the clipped Buchanesque prose in which it is recounted, is rather at odds with the anxieties and disillusion that characterise Tony's inner life. This is shaped, we are told within the first few pages of the novel, by his sense of being unable to live up to the example of his father, a Great War VC:

> [W]hat I found particularly depressing was my mother's repeated assertion that the very best, the cream and the pride, of a generation had been lost. She herself, it appeared, had known a vast number of young men distinguished by the brilliance of their intellect, their personal courage, or their beauty – and all, all had gone. 'All but your father,' she would say, 'and he, thank God, remains to let you see the sort of men whom our politicians threw away!'[24]

The British army is the place where Tony's sense of belatedness is most cruelly amplified. Shortly after hearing that his younger brother was shot for cowardice while serving with the British Expeditionary Force in 1940, Tony finds himself sharing an overnight train compartment with a group of staff officers. He is immediately identified as his father's son by an army colonel: 'We don't breed 'em like that nowadays, more's the pity [. . .] I'm very glad to meet a son of his. I hope you'll be a credit to him.'[25] Tony spends the long journey to Scotland brooding on these men and his brother's death:

> It was their sort – the buffalo sort, the senior officers, the lions of the forest – who had turned on Peter and killed him; and I, in the confinement of their cage, felt rising in me a wave of panic, a momentarily insane desire to escape.[26]

He has to scramble over the dozing soldiers blocking the corridor to be sick in the toilet.

Tony eventually comes to terms with his destiny through his involvement in a wartime intelligence operation in the Northern Isles and the Faeroes, which occupies the first two-thirds of the novel. Here he encounters two men who, in effect, split the role of father figure between them. The first is Captain Silver, RN, who commands the converted trawler that takes Tony north from Scapa Flow. Silver is a man of Tony's own age, yet when he takes command of their expedition:

> I did not resent his assumption of authority. I welcomed and was glad of it. I have always wanted a leader – a man to say 'Do this' or an idea to compel my action with the authority of tradition – and when Silver took command

he did it with such an easy competence that almost immediately I fell into the position where I was told to go.[27]

Oddly enough, Silver owes some of his authority over Tony to his taste in literature. The books in his cabin are exclusively by women authors, and modern ones at that (Woolf, Colette, Rosamond Lehmann, Elizabeth Bowen). Silver explains his sexualised interest in them: 'All those books [. . .] contain a woman who is undressing herself. Oh yes, they do! Some of them only unwrap their sensibility and their intelligence, but even they give you the feeling that there's a bed behind the door.'[28] Silver is unaware, at this point, that Tony's mother is herself a novelist, two of whose books Tony has spotted in his collection. Because the novel has already shifted responsibility for Tony's feelings of inadequacy from his father to his mother, Silver's confident masculine appropriation of her kind promises Tony that, by subordinating himself to him, he can be liberated from the emasculating women in his life. When Tony falls asleep in the cabin, he dreams of a discussion with Silver about his wife's adultery. '"She looks at you like a spaniel," I said to him in my dreams, and in my dream he answered, "Beat her."'[29]

On the same trip, Tony and Silver 'kill' the 'bad' patriarch, in the figure of Shetland landowner Mungo Wishart. Wishart is a Yeats-quoting Nordic nationalist whom they suspect of being in contact with Quisling's puppet government in Norway. In person he is another version of the generals whom Tony still hates at this point: a red-faced late Victorian, '[s]omething like a picture of a hero of the Indian Mutiny',[30] and yet another for whom Tony is defined as a 'soldier, and the son of a soldier'.[31] The younger men, after confronting him with their suspicions, decide he is a harmless old buffer after all. But as soon as they set sail for Scapa, Mungo kills himself with a capsule of German cyanide. He leaves a son and daughter behind him, and Tony's feeling of guilt drives him to court his own death with the infantry in North Africa. He survives, and in effect takes Mungo Wishart's place with his children. First he acts as an alternative father figure for the son, Olaf, whom he finds serving with the Ulster Rifles in Korea, out of a desire to expiate his father's betrayal of Britain. Tony is with Olaf as he bleeds to death on the back of a Centurion tank in the retreat after the battle of the Imjin River, and his last words are 'Do you think – this – will make up – for him?'[32] Olaf has been destroyed by the burden of being his father's son, the curse that Tony has managed to evade. Then Tony finally escapes his own parents by marrying Mungo's daughter, Gudrun, and becoming a different sort of soldier, in the technocratic embrace of NATO High Command.

In *The Dark of Summer*, an army career is the stage on which the hero acts out a Freudian drama through which the son is enabled to take the father's place and is reconciled to the military hierarchy in the process. The other novel from 1956 enacts a similar drama, but one with a tragic ending, because the places of father and son are taken by men of the same wartime generation. In James Kennaway's *Tunes of Glory*, Lieutenant-Colonel Jock Sinclair is a war hero who has fought his way up from the ranks after starting in his regiment as a boy piper rescued from the Glasgow slums and Barlinnie. When the novel begins, he has been acting colonel of his battalion for four and a half years. He is its father figure, the object of equal measures of fear and love. After one drunken dinner in the mess, he dismisses his fellow officers with the words 'Get away with you, you bairns and cheeldron';[33] subalterns and peers alike are 'my babies!'[34] Under Jock, the battalion's tradition of piping is cultivated with precision, its traditions of dancing and drinking with more vigour than decorum.

His nemesis is Colonel Basil Barrow, an Oxford graduate, formerly of MI5 and Sandhurst, who has spent most of the war as a prisoner of the Japanese. He is sent to take Jock's place as permanent colonel, which Jock, of course, deeply resents. But what makes the clash between them so poignant is that, despite their differences, both men have the same deep stake in the battalion. Barrow had served in it before the war, and the prospect of return had been a consolation during his time as a POW: 'I said I'd get back to the Battalion: back to Scotland. I loved it here, you know, as a subaltern.'[35] He has swung this posting to give himself a new sense of home, not only after a divorce from his wife, but also (it is implied) after the dislocating trauma of Changi. In Jock, he faces at once the embodiment of the tradition and glory that he adores in the battalion (he is writing a history of it, in which Jock plays a central part) and an immovable obstruction to his own integration into it. So when Jock strikes an NCO whom he finds in a pub with his daughter, Barrow is torn by the necessity of proceeding to a court martial which would end Jock's career. Although they are the same age, Jock is to Barrow a father figure, just as he is to the rest of the battalion's officers, but he is a father figure whom he must, one way or another, displace if he is to come into his own:

> He seemed incapable of speaking the truth to Jock. He was almost like a son with a father too fierce: in order not to offend he told a half-truth,

Figure 25.3 Alec Guinness in the role of Jock Sinclair in the film version of *Tunes of Glory*, 1960.

until the time came when he found it more natural to lie. It was perfectly obvious to him why he did this. Everything about Jock frightened him.[36]

In the end, both men are destroyed: Barrow shoots himself and Jock, stricken with remorse, has a nervous breakdown, which ends the novel.

Unlike *The Dark of Summer*, *Tunes of Glory* suggests that there are particular national factors contributing to this crisis, both British and Scottish. British, because the class difference between the two men is always in the background, although this seems to be more of an issue for the NCOs (the Tory regimental sergeant major for whom Jock is simply not a 'gentleman', the 'Whig' pipe major who defends him) than for the officers themselves. Scottish, because the trappings of regimental tradition – the piping, the dancing, the uniforms – make the world within the barrack walls culturally absorbing, to the exclusion of other perspectives and commitments available in a wider society. What Kennaway's novel has in common with Linklater's is a sense of military tradition, as figured in the inimitable father-officer, as a burden that has the potential to crush whoever inherits it.

It is striking that, of all the texts discussed in this chapter, those that refer explicitly to a Scottish military tradition are twentieth- or twenty-first-century texts, which evoke that tradition as much to mourn its passing as to celebrate its survival. For Hamish Henderson, the skirl of the pipes as the 51st advances at El Alamein is a thrilling incitement to righteous violence but is hushed into silence by the dominant idea of the poem, the solidarity of German, Italian and empire dead in its prefiguring of a post-war new order of international socialism. In Kennaway's Campbell barracks, the same sound first resonates in the mess as a drug, working, like the whisky, to drown thought and feeling and produce a shallow, drunken solidarity of the living. Later in the same scene, pipe music figures as a genuine tradition, cultivated with care and passed from generation to generation, but that tradition is of pibroch, of lament, and the man to whom Jock Sinclair passes it is Corporal Fraser, the man he will later punch for dating his daughter.

Black Watch is an interesting text in this regard, because it offers two explanations for the ending of the tradition it describes. One is geopolitical, the nature of the campaign the regiment was fighting in Iraq. Cammy explains, in a scene named 'The Future': 'I enjoyed the war fighting, sir, I really did. [. . .] But this isnay the job, is it, sir? / [. . .] Sitting about daying camp security. Getting mortared all the time. Getting fucking ambushed.'[37] And his officer agrees: 'It takes three hundred years to build an army that's admired and respected around the world. But it only takes three years pissing about in the desert in the biggest western foreign policy disaster ever to fuck it up completely.'[38] There is a problem with this analysis. Iraq was not the first time the Black Watch found itself being mortared and ambushed by forces that melted into a hostile civilian population. Presumably Cammy is too young to have served in Northern Ireland, but that does not explain its absence from the regiment's battle honours that he recites in the middle of the play.[39] And if the regiment survived that deployment, the note of elegy, bagpipes and all, on which the play ends may seem premature.

But *Black Watch* offers another version of what exactly has been 'knackered'[40] in the recent history of the regiment. By telling the story mostly from the perspective of, and in the language of, its ordinary soldiers, Burke emphasises the extent to which the regiment is, as he says in the 'Author's Note' to the published play, 'a working class institution. As much a part of the social history of Scotland as mining, shipbuilding or fishing.'[41] The implication is that recruitment, at least in the twentieth century, depended upon the existence of an institutionalised working class, men who could carry the experience of shared danger from mine and shipyard and trawler into the army with them. Rather than being a last redoubt of such solidarity in a society where the alternative type of work is, as Cammy says, 'the deli counter in Tesco', the Scottish military tradition, Burke suggests, depended upon a certain sort of civilian society that has largely vanished. Like all the texts discussed here, *Black Watch* assumes that the meaning of soldiering can only be understood in its relation to wider social and political contexts. In that respect, Burke's play joins a tradition of literary representations of the Scottish soldier almost as long as the traditions of the regiments themselves.

Notes

1. G. Burke, *The National Theatre of Scotland's Black Watch* (London: Faber and Faber, 2007), pp. 3–4.
2. R. Burns, *Poems and Songs*, ed. J. Kinsley (London: Oxford University Press, 1969), p. 159.
3. Ibid. p. 169.
4. T. Smollett, *The Expedition of Humphry Clinker* (Oxford: Oxford University Press, 1984), p. 188.
5. Ibid. p. 189.
6. Ibid. p. 36.
7. Ibid. p. 204.
8. Ibid. pp. 194–5.
9. L. Grassic Gibbon, *A Scots Quair: Sunset Song, Cloud Howe, Grey Granite* (Harmondsworth: Penguin, 1986), p. 158.
10. Ibid. p. 158.
11. Burke, *Black Watch*, p. 31.
12. C. Lamont (ed.), *Chronicles of the Canongate by Walter Scott* (Edinburgh: Edinburgh University Press, 2000), pp. 98–9.
13. Ibid. p. 79.
14. Ibid. p. 106.
15. D. Meek (ed.), *Caran an t-Saoghail/The Wiles of the World: An Anthology of 19th Century Scottish Gaelic Verse* (Edinburgh: Birlinn, 2003), pp. 308–9.
16. H. Henderson, *Elegies for the Dead in Cyrenaica* (Edinburgh: Polygon, 2008), p. 32.
17. Ibid. p. 33.
18. Ibid. p. 25.
19. M. Byrne (ed.), *Collected Poems and Songs of George Campbell Hay*

(Deòrsa Mac Iain Dheòrsa) (Edinburgh: Edinburgh University Press, 2003), p. 199.
20. S. Maclean (Somhairle MacGill-Eain), *O Choille gu Bearradh/From Wood to Ridge: Dain Chruinnichte/Collected Poems* (Manchester: Carcanet; Edinburgh: Birlinn, 1999), pp. 208–9.
21. Ibid. pp. 205–6.
22. Burke, *Black Watch*, p. 70.
23. Ibid. p. 70.
24. E. Linklater, *The Dark of Summer* (London: Jonathan Cape, 1956), pp. 12–13.
25. Ibid. pp. 39–40.
26. Ibid. p. 44.
27. Ibid. p. 107.
28. Ibid. p. 62.
29. Ibid. p. 67.
30. Ibid. p. 110.
31. Ibid. p. 156.
32. Ibid. p. 253.
33. J. Kennaway, *Tunes of Glory* (Edinburgh: Canongate, 1988), p. 18.
34. Ibid. p. 106.
35. Ibid. p. 119.
36. Ibid. p. 105.
37. Burke, *Black Watch*, p. 70.
38. Ibid. p. 71.
39. Ibid. pp. 31–3.
40. Ibid. p. 71.
41. Ibid. p. viii.

26
The Scottish Soldier in Art

Peter Harrington

Visualise the archetypical Scottish soldier: fearless, loyal and courageous, a hunk of Highland masculinity, resplendent in his regimental kilt, bearing down upon an enemy in some distant corner of the empire, the glint of sun reflecting off his razor-sharp bayonet, shoulder to shoulder with the piper advancing through a storm of shot and shell, seemingly oblivious of the danger. Cliché or not, this 'ladies from hell' paradigm would have been familiar to many generations of Victorians schooled in Marryat, Henty, the poetry of Kipling and Newbolt, and the *Boy's Own Magazine*, and this powerful image still conjures up such perceived characteristics of Celtic soldiery even today. Truth be told, soldiers from northern Britain were prized for their tenacious courage and determination under fire, and it was the artist who helped to popularise their deeds through contemporary visual media. Even in death, the sight of a highlander moved observers: 'There is something in the sight of dead Highland soldiers which is peculiarly pathetic. The picturesque garb discloses the stalwart limbs, helpless in death, which are covered in the case of less picturesquely dressed infantry soldiers.'[1]

British artists were generally ambivalent towards martial themes, unlike their continental counterparts, especially the French. Although the numerous military campaigns from Waterloo onwards provided subjects rich in narrative and ideally suited for pictorial treatment, prior to 1815 the art establishment had not always embraced such visual military rhetoric. Nonetheless, there is a rich canon of artwork across the centuries and a gleaning of it reveals soldiers of Gaeldom in a range of ensembles.[2] To achieve an understanding of this requires a thematic approach in which ideas of rehabilitation, nationalism, costume and empire will be explored.

Early antecedents

A carving of vanquished warriors on a Roman legionary distance slab from the Antonine Wall may provide the first pictorial evidence of soldiers from Caledonia.[3] Pictish symbol stones from the seventh to the ninth centuries also occasionally portray armed men, the finest example being the Class II stone from Aberlemno, Angus, representing mounted and dismounted soldiers in battle.[4] This tradition of stone carving continued into the Anglo-Norman period and many tombstones bear detailed high-relief effigies of warriors in mail, bascinet helmets and the full panoply of medieval arms and armour. Such sculpted stones were still contemporaneous with the wars of Scottish independence, but no carvings of the battles have survived and the earliest known depiction of Bannockburn is a manuscript drawing in Walter Bower's *Scotichronicon* of the 1440s.[5] We then have to look to the sixteenth century, and such battles as Pinkie Cleugh in 1547, for further artistic confirmation of Scots in combat. In the case of Pinkie the clash of arms is represented diagrammatically and from an aerial perspective.[6]

A more realistic period to commence our survey might be the mid-seventeenth century with its burgeoning appetite for formal portraiture. The prominent Scottish artist George Jamesone, for example, took the likenesses of the covenanter generals, Alexander Leslie and David Leslie, as well as the renegade covenanter commander, the earl of Montrose. In these works, we glimpse the faces of martial Scots, but they are unremarkable for any semblance of the modern notion of 'Scottishness'. The tradition of formal military portraiture was continued in Scotland in the eighteenth century by Allan Ramsay, and into the early nineteenth century by Henry Raeburn. In such pictures what identifies Lowland soldiers as Scottish is invariably only their name, as in Ramsay's *Lieutenant John Abercrombie of the 1st Foot or the Royal Regiment* (1754), while military highlanders are more recognisable by their kilts and accoutrements, as in Raeburn's *Colonel Alastair Ranaldson Macdonell of Glengarry* (1812). It is the distinctive clothing that separates Highland soldiers pictorially from their southern counterparts and by the mid-eighteenth century a clearly representational Highland martial figure had emerged, portrayed as the 'enemy' in English prints of the Jacobite campaign and in the iconic representations of the 'Forty-Five rebellion by the Swiss artist David Morier, whose patron was the duke of Cumberland.[7]

The Jacobite army had given the government forces a good run for their money in 1745–6 and while the highlanders were punished, and the wearing of the tartan by civilians prohibited under the Disarming Act of 1746, there may still have been an underlying respect for the tenacity of the Scots. Indeed, in a piece traditionally attributed to Morier, entitled *An Incident in the Rebellion of 1745* (c. 1745–50), the artist represents the vigour and courage of the enemy facing the bayonets of the government troops. Clansmen were said to have been brought from Southwark gaol to pose for him. The same painter captured, perhaps for the first time, a formal image of a Highland soldier in a series of works depicting British infantry in 1751. In this case, it was a member of the 42nd Regiment.[8] Almost contemporary are a series of engravings, published around 1743, of four named Scottish soldiers who were involved in a mutiny of the same regiment, three of whom were shot for desertion in the Tower of London on 18 July 1743, while the fourth was transported to the American colonies.

As to how the Scots viewed themselves pictorially at this time, beyond some portraits of their military leaders, such as Lord George Murray, the only surviving evidence is a series of sixty contemporary ink sketches known as the 'Penicuik Drawings'.[9] These small, amateurish caricatures capture the immediacy of the 'Forty-Five, especially in their representation of Highland 'types' and their distinctive accoutrements, broadswords and targes. Loyalist volunteers from Edinburgh and government troops complete the series. Continental artists also portrayed Highland soldiers, including the German craftsman Martin Engelbrecht, who created a series of engravings in Augsburg around the mid-1700s entitled *Théâtre de la Malice Étrangère*. These included various Jacobites, along with Scots serving in the government forces.

The Highland 'presence' in grand history painting

By the late eighteenth century, history painting had taken a respectable place at the forefront of art in Britain. In particular, the London-domiciled American triumvirate of Benjamin West, John Singleton Copley and John Trumbull spearheaded the movement towards the creation of grand history pieces, often with military themes. Spurred on by their success, others began to emulate them, the result being a series of significant war scenes painted between 1770 and 1815. George Carter, Philippe Jacques de Loutherbourg, Thomas Stothard and Robert Ker Porter were just a few of the artists who produced large battle canvases.[10]

Close examination of these paintings reveals an interesting, if unique, phenomenon: a Highland 'presence', often denoted by a single figure, usually a high-ranking officer, attired in Highland dress. This can be traced back to West's ground-breaking composition of 1770 portraying General Wolfe's demise at Quebec in September 1759. In this case, a kilt blowing in the breeze betrays the presence of a lone Highland officer on the far left of the immortal 'thirteen'. The key accompanying the subsequent engraving identifies the soldier as 'Fraser' – Simon Fraser – who died at Saratoga and was himself the subject of a death tableau.[11] Other artists saw the compositional merits of West's piece and in Copley's *Death of Major Peirson* (1784), depicting the battle for Jersey, a tartan-clad figure is situated as a casualty on the ground, his Highland bonnet having rolled off into the right foreground while his broadsword lies across his left wrist. In Trumbull's case, the engraving of *The Sortie Made by the Garrison of Gibraltar* (1789) includes two Highland officers, Captain Alexander MacKenzie of the 73rd in pride of place next to General George Augustus Eliot, and Lieutenant-Colonel Hamilton Maxwell of the same regiment, although in two of the earlier oil versions Maxwell is

Figure 26.1 *The Death of General Wolfe* by Benjamin West, 1770.

absent. The same soldier, MacKenzie, appears on the extreme right of Carter's *The Siege of Gibraltar* (1784), while in Copley's better-known, but clearly derivative, scene seven years later a lone Highland officer, the Honourable Lieutenant-Colonel Lindsay of the 73rd, appears on the right margin of the main group. Subsequently, we see single kilted figures in scenes of the battle of Alexandria in 1801, especially surrounding the mortally wounded Scottish general, Sir Ralph Abercromby, in his final moments.

This deliberate inclusion of a single highlander, often on the margins, is more than mere coincidence and may be interpreted in several ways. There is the obvious picturesque element of Highland dress when an artist has attempted to include a range of costumes for artistic effect, contrast, tonality of colour or even movement. For West, the addition of a single Gael might have been part of an embodiment of the artist's rhetoric of the British empire. Perhaps, however, there is something more implicit at play. Is this a subtle, even reluctant, acknowledgement of the martial contribution of Scots couched in politically correct terms? The *Death of Major Peirson* might provide a clue. In April 1781, less than three months after Peirson's death at St Helier on Jersey, an aquatint print was published in London by Colley and Hedges depicting the 78th Highlanders advancing across the town square as the French retreated. Although Copley's painting included a distant view of highlanders firing from the heights of Fort Regent upon the French in the town, it featured only one Scottish soldier as a casualty, preferring instead to emphasise the contribution of the English troops. It has been suggested that the artist might have been influenced here by the mutual antipathy and suspicion at this time between the English and the Scots.[12] Aware that the market for the subsequent print would be primarily south of the border, Copley might not have wanted to offend English sensibilities, especially through the brush of an American artist. In similar terms, Sulzberger suggests that 'the token role played by both Highland officers in the siege of Gibraltar paintings suggests an artificiality to the "British" identity, in which an English identity still dominated'.[13] That being said, the representation of Scots in such works of art reflected the growing numbers of them serving in the British army and their 'presence' in the Seven Years War and the American War of Independence.

Waterloo

Wellington's victory in June 1815 can be seen as one of those defining moments in the history of Scottish soldiery. In many ways, it positioned them front and centre in the imagination of the public and transformed attitudes towards these soldiers.[14] The events of the battle, in which the Scots Greys famously charged at the French lines and Sergeant Charles Ewart captured the eagle standard of the enemy's 45th Regiment, certainly stirred the imagination of some artists. Richard Ansdell's *The Fight for the Standard* (1848) consolidated Ewart's heroic reputation, while later in the century Lady Elizabeth Butler portrayed the charge in *Scotland for Ever!* (1881) and Stanley Berkeley depicted the kilted Gordon Highlanders holding on to the stirrups of the Greys as they rode towards the French – an event almost certainly mythical – in *Gordons and Greys to the Front: Incident at Waterloo* (1898). Indeed, the kilt, once banned, had now been transformed into a metaphor for military strength, gallantry and loyalty, although disgruntled French print makers such as Genty poked fun at the dress in numerous satirical prints depicting Highland troops in Paris during the occupation of 1815.

Yet, while Scottish soldiers were feted and their deeds celebrated in song and on the stage, this did not necessarily translate into art in the years immediately following the events at Waterloo. Just as the earlier paintings had made veiled references to Scottish arms, so the Highland 'presence' featured in contemporary images of the battle. John Atkinson's *Battle of Waterloo* (1819) contained only a vignette of Scots fighting French cavalry on the right, while William Heath's portrayals incorporated similar representations. David Wilkie's immortal painting of Chelsea Pensioners reading the Waterloo despatch, commissioned by Wellington, included just a token Scottish veteran. Even in images of the battle painted in the succeeding forty years, the Scottish contribution was invariably given scant attention. Abraham Cooper, for example, included a vignette in his Royal Academy piece, entitled *Wellington at Waterloo* (1838), showing simply an unarmed Highland soldier assisting a wounded comrade. This theme of the highlander in a non-combative pose was taken further in several Waterloo pictures in which the Scots are portrayed as 'victims', especially in Joseph Turner's *The Field of Waterloo* (1818) and John Heaviside Clark's print of the evening of the battle (1817). The Irish artist Daniel Maclise chose Waterloo for his submission to the new Houses of Parliament fine arts competition in 1847 and his winning cartoon representing Wellington and Blücher meeting after the battle literally teemed with humanity. But in the spirit of the previous half-century, the Highland 'presence' for him devolved upon two figures in the right foreground assisting with the wounded and a dead piper on the left. For many artists,

Figure 26.2 *Wellington at Waterloo* by Abraham Cooper, 1838. Detail from left-hand side of the picture.

highlanders merely contributed some attractive contrast to the overall composition.

Art and national identity

Several native painters emerged from the burgeoning school of Scottish art in the first half of the nineteenth century to create impressionistic images of Celts in war as a defining statement in the re-emergence of national identity. In any consideration of the origins of this phenomenon, Sir Walter Scott is paramount. His writings sowed the seeds for the first flowering of a modern sense of Scottishness. One of Scott's friends, and a leading exponent of the school of Scottish history painting, was Sir William Allan. Born in 1782, he experienced the Napoleonic Wars, travelling extensively in Russia and Turkey during the first decade of the 1800s, and witnessed the Russian army on its way to Austerlitz. Returning to Scotland in 1814, he developed a close friendship with Scott that would serve him well throughout the rest of his career until his death in 1850. Although Allan chose to exhibit at both the Royal Academy in London and the Royal Scottish

Academy in Edinburgh, where he later became president, his pictures began to reflect an increasing interest in his homeland's history, especially during the last decade of his life. Several of these were scenes from Scottish wars, beginning with his portrayal of Robert the Bruce, *Heroism and Humanity* (1840). The battles of Prestonpans and Bannockburn also feature prominently in his *oeuvre*, as does Waterloo. The latter subject occupied the artist on several occasions. Yet it is interesting to note that for one so enamoured of the Scottish spirit and zeal his vast canvas depicting Wellington towards the close of the battle, painted in 1847, also for the Houses of Parliament competition, failed to single out the Scottish contribution beyond some distant soldiers wearing bonnets and trews. Perhaps the artist had been reluctant to illuminate the merits of Scottish martial prowess in his Westminster submission so as not to offend English sensitivities.

The half-century following Waterloo saw other Scottish artists portraying scenes from their country's military history, including Allan's younger contemporary, Sir George Harvey, who was especially attracted to the contribution of the seventeenth-century covenanters. He produced one significant picture pertinent to the present discussion, entitled *Drumclog* (1836), representing the battle between Claverhouse's troops and the covenanters in June 1679. Other relevant artists include Thomas Duncan, who painted *Prince Charles Edward and his Army Entering Edinburgh after the Battle of Prestonpans* (1840), and John Adam Houston, who produced *The Highlands in 1746* (1849). Ronald Robert McIan depicted *The Battle of Culloden* (1853), *Jacobite Hiding-place at Keppoch Brae, Lochaber* (1854) and numerous other military-themed scenes. The former epic is emblematic of Scottish pride in the face of English domination, with a lone highlander, Gillies MacBean, taking on several government soldiers. A century after the failed rebellion, the reviewer in the *Illustrated London News* hinted at a lingering contempt when commenting that 'the fire of the Royal troops [is] thinning the ranks of the rebel force in front of them'.[15]

The call of the plaid

By the mid-nineteenth century, the idea of Scottishness had been transformed. Scott, however, has been accused of distorting reality and institutionalising perceptions of the highlander, particularly in terms of costume and his 'plaided panorama' that first saw the light of day during the visit of George IV to Edinburgh in 1822.[16] This 'deception' was furthered by Queen Victoria's embrace of Scotland

and her eventual purchase of Balmoral castle in 1852. The 'Balmoral effect' cannot be overestimated in any analysis of the fascination of non-Scots for Scottish culture in the mid-1800s. Highland dress was now in vogue and artists from south of the border began 'discovering' the country, proclaiming its uniqueness in romantic words and pictures. James Logan's large, two-volume publication, entitled *The Clans of the Scottish Highlands* and published in London by Arthur Ackermann between 1845 and 1847, contained numerous full-page colour lithographs, after designs by McIan, depicting Highland warriors from various clans, some in combat.

The decade of the 1850s was a watershed in the visual emergence of the iconic Scottish soldier. Three Highland regiments participated in manoeuvres held at Chobham in 1853 and these units attracted considerable interest in southern England. A Hampshire-based artist, David Cunliffe, sketched members of the 93rd (Sutherland) Highlanders in a sword dance, yet the finished painting placed the dancers before a stark Highland landscape rather than the Surrey heathland.[17] Meanwhile, the 79th was the subject of four large canvases by McIan, mainly painted while the regiment was stationed at Edinburgh castle between February 1852 and March 1853.[18] These had been commissioned by Lieutenant-Colonel the Honourable Lauderdale Maule to celebrate the end of his ten-year colonelcy in December 1852; he was to die of cholera at Varna in August 1854. In order to include the portraits of thirty-nine members of the Camerons, McIan drew on a series of sixteen photographs, some of which were taken by David Octavius Hill, one of the pioneers of photography in Scotland. When the regiment moved to Portsmouth in the spring of 1853, the artist headed south for a month in order to complete his pictures.

The image of Highland military costume also became commonplace during this period through the mechanism of lithography. Rudolph Ackermann, the leading publisher of large colour plates representing British regiments and battles, published *Ackermann's Costumes of the British Army* between 1840 and 1854. This included several prints of Highland regiments after paintings by Henry Martens, who had also visited Chobham and sketched the 42nd and 93rd Highlanders for a series devoted to regiments on manoeuvres.

It was, however, the events in the Crimea that brought the exploits of the Highland regiments to a wider audience through the illustrated press and popular prints. Scottish troops were well represented in the battles and related genre scenes. Their departure for the war brought out the crowds who cheered them on the way to the docks, as

Figure 26.3 *The Departure of the Highland Brigade*, 1855, after Thomas Duncan.

portrayed in *The Departure of the Highland Brigade*. This was a coloured lithograph published in June 1855 showing a Highland soldier embracing his weeping wife and baby, her hand holding another infant while a third tugs at her dress as she watches the regiment march towards the harbour. The source of the print was actually a painting by Thomas Duncan and John Houston, dating from around 1840, entitled *Departing for Waterloo*, the only change being the background, which in the earlier piece had the highlanders marching through a city. Portrayals from the battlefront included John Millais's *News from Home* (1857), in which a soldier of the 42nd, resplendent in a clean uniform, pauses from the action to read a letter from home, while two of his comrades appear behind, one seated smoking a pipe, the other peering over the breastwork. The freshness of the highlander's clothing prompted John Ruskin to enquire sardonically whether the artist considered this to be a 'generally bright aspect of a Highlander on campaign? Or whether he imagines that Highlanders at the Crimea have dress portmanteaus as well as knapsacks and always put on new uniforms to read letters from home.'[19] In addition, Roger Fenton included photographs of several Scottish units among his numerous plates taken in the Crimea in 1855, some of which were published in a large portfolio, entitled *Incidents of Camp Life*.

The empire calls, 1857–1902

Scots were at the forefront of many battles of empire over the next four decades. These came to assume a prominent role in popular imagination, albeit sometimes embellished and exaggerated. Building on the Crimean exploits of the 42nd at the Alma and the 93rd at Balaclava, the gallantry of such regiments as the 78th at Lucknow, the Black Watch at Tel-el-Kebir and the Gordon Highlanders at Dargai further enhanced the martial reputation of the imperial Scottish soldiers, and their image was widely circulated through the visual media of the day.

The Highland 'presence' was nevertheless still evident in paintings of the sepoy revolt in India in 1857. Unlike in the Crimea, there were no large pitched battles so artists tended to focus upon the atrocities committed against British civilians. This presented challenges to those wishing to portray the horrors of the campaign to the Victorian public. Joseph Noel Paton was obliged to alter his moving *In Memoriam* (1858) by replacing enraged sepoys about to harm British women and children with two highlanders coming to their rescue. In Frederick Goodall's painting of the same year, *Jessie's Dream: The Campbells Are Coming, Lucknow, September 1857*, the highlanders are not seen but their imminent arrival to relieve the garrison is implied in the title and by the central female figure, Jessie, who apparently hears the approaching bagpipes. A year later, *The Relief of Lucknow*, by Thomas Jones Barker, included a lone dead or wounded highlander on the right of the picture. Alongside these, Henry O'Neil's fine pair of genre scenes, *Eastward Ho! August 1857*, and the following year *Home Again*, captured soldiers departing for India and their subsequent return. The latter included several members of a Scottish regiment wearing bonnets descending the gangplank of a ship and embracing their loved ones.

In the later Victorian period, however, the Scots increasingly began to take centre stage in the action. Scottish regiments played a leading role in the campaigns in Afghanistan and Egypt, in 1879 and 1882 respectively, and several paintings captured them in the heat of battle. The most celebrated is perhaps *The Storming of Tel-el-Kebir* (1883) by the French military artist Alphonse Marie de Neuville.[20] But other eminent works featured Scottish soldiery in combat, such as Richard Caton Woodville's *Kandahar: the 92nd Highlanders and 2nd Gurkhas Storming Gaudi Mullah Sahibdad* (1881). In such pictures, the Scots, once a conquered nation subjugated to the English, were themselves now seen to be conquering others at the behest of their former masters.[21] Other painters covered these campaigns more indirectly. Edinburgh artist Robert Gemmell Hutchison chose the recreational room of his home city's castle for the setting of *Under Orders* (1882). This is a narrative scene of soldiers of the Black Watch, the day prior to their departure for Egypt, talking with friends and loved ones.

Several other Scottish artists prominently featured their countryman in arms during this period, among them Robert Gibb, Allan Stewart, William Skeoch Cumming and William Lockhart Bogle. Gibb, in particular, built his reputation on four retrospective portrayals of the Highland Brigade in the Crimean War. In *Comrades* (1878), *The Thin Red Line* (1881), *Letters from Home* (1885) and *Alma: Advance of the 42nd Highlanders* (1888), we glimpse the face of Celts

Figure 26.4 *Kandahar: The 92nd Highlanders and 2nd Gurkhas Storming Gaudi Mullah Sahibdad* by Richard Caton Woodville, 1881.

at war through the eyes of one of their own. As a member of the Royal Scottish Academy, and with a growing reputation in the Edinburgh art world, Gibb had a clear Scottish agenda which would also be seen in his later works such as *Dargai* (1909) and *Backs to the Wall 1918* (1929).

For their part, the illustrated papers and magazines served up a steady dose of imperial imagery to feed the appetite of the reading public, and Scottish troops were frequently highlighted. A case in point is a scene from the second Afghan War as depicted in the pages of the *Illustrated London News* showing a piper and two men of the 72nd Highlanders (Duke of Albany's Own) performing a Tullochgorum reel before the camp bonfire at Kohat. In a rather condescending manner, the paper included the following note in the caption:

> [This] must delight the heart of every Scotchman. That 'smart, clean, and well behaved' Highland regiment a few days later had the opportunity at the Peiwar of showing its prowess by the smartest bit of fighting yet seen in this Afghan War.[22]

Away from the theatre of operations, artists continued to be attracted to the theme of Scottish troops leaving for, and returning from, war. In Frank Holl's *Ordered to the Front* (1880), Highland soldiers, accompanied by their wives and children, are assembled on the stark stone pavement of a railway platform. The expressions on the faces of the women and children speak of their anxiety as their men depart on another colonial enterprise, many of them never to return. In a smaller wash version of the same scene, a poster on the wall reads: 'Daily Telegraph. The Afghan War. Rumoured Submission . . . The Amir'. Holl painted a companion scene, *Home Again* (1881), showing kilted troops marching away from a harbour led by drummer boys. One stalwart soldier strides onward with his lady on his arm, while his comrade to his right is less fortunate as he leans on a crutch. Behind them, another soldier has taken off his feather bonnet and is parading it atop his rifle.[23]

There are few significant representations of Lowland regiments during this period, and the Scots Guards are pictorially indistinguishable to the untrained eye from other Guards regiments, but the latter came in for some artistic treatment, especially with regard to their action at the Alma in the Crimea. These included Lady Butler's *The Colours: Advance of the Scots Guards at the Alma River* (1899) and Louis William Desanges's *Captain Robert James Lindsay, Scots*

Fusilier Guards, winning the VC at the Alma, 20 September 1854 (1863). A corporal of the regiment returning from the war was the subject of Joseph Noel Paton's canvas *Home: the Return from the Crimea* (1859).

Scottish troops were not always victorious and their nobility in defeat was also portrayed through art. In Woodville's evocative *All That Was Left of Them: the Black Watch after the Battle of Magersfontein 1899*, the kilted survivors of the battle – an action in which the nerve of the Highland Brigade is alleged to have broken in the face of the Boers – are defiantly formed up in line as the dead and wounded are collected around them. The sergeant on the end of the line stands proudly at attention, his bayoneted rifle rigid at his side, as though manning a sentry box at the gates of Edinburgh castle.

Figure 26.5 Richard Caton Woodville's *All That Was Left of Them: the Black Watch after the Battle of Magersfontein 1899.*

Modern representations

In the twentieth century, the photograph and the moving image would largely replace representational art and, beyond the occasional anachronism, such as the 'stirrup charge' of the Scots Greys at St

Quentin, painted by both Woodville and Stewart, the war artists of the Great War were armed with a different agenda: one that emphasised total war's destructive hand over heroism or glory. Indeed, while the kilted soldier still held an attraction for some, as seen for example in Christopher Clark's *The Piper of Loos Playing the KOSB to the Attack* (1915),[24] Richard Jack's *Return to the Front: Victoria Railway Station* (1916) and William Orpen's *A Highlander Passing a Grave* (1917), Scottishness seemed less relevant.[25]

During the Second World War a good deal of Scotland's national identity was invested in the 51st Highland Division, and Dundee-born Ian Eadie became, in effect, the official divisional artist. A serving officer with the formation from 1943, he produced a number of wartime works detailing scenes from its campaigns. He was also commissioned to paint a retrospective study of Major-General Douglas Wimberley briefing his division's officers for the attack at El Alamein: *The 51st Highland Division Plans El Alamein* (1949). In order to compose the picture, Eadie had to obtain likenesses of all the twenty-one officers present at the briefing from tiny photographs.[26]

Scottish troops continued to feature in representations of post-1945 conflicts. Linda Kitson, a war artist during the Falklands War, depicted the 2nd battalion, the Scots Guards, resting in sheep sheds at Fitzroy.[27] David Rowlands was invited by the army to observe Operation Desert Storm and his portrayal of the Warrior vehicles of the 1st battalion, the Royal Scots, racing across the Iraqi desert was subsequently displayed in its warrant officers' and sergeants' mess.[28] Meanwhile, Peter Archer has produced notable historical studies of Scottish regiments. These include a painting of the 1st Argyll's re-entry into Crater in Aden with Lieutenant-Colonel Colin 'Mad Mitch' Mitchell directing operations and Pipe Major Robson playing the regimental march.

To summarise, in pictorial terms Scottish soldiers moved from being portrayed as the enemy to incorporation on the margins of grand history paintings produced in England in the late eighteenth century, a tacit acknowledgement of their contribution to British martial achievements. They then emerged from the fields of Waterloo with a new-found respect, yet they were still marginalised or represented as victims in contemporary representations. The portrayal of Scottish military heroes, such as the likes of Sergeant Ewart, provided visual confirmation of Scottish military prowess, but it was in the paintings from the late Victorian period that the full recognition of the soldiers of Gaeldom was truly embraced.

Notes

1. J. Luther Vaughan, *My Service in the Indian Army – and After* (London: Constable, 1904), p. 239.
2. The subject of Scottish soldiers in art has been considered in previous studies. See E. M. Spiers, *The Scottish Soldier and Empire, 1854–1902* (Edinburgh: Edinburgh University Press, 2006); P. Harrington, *British Artists and War: The Face of Battle in Paintings and Prints* (London: Greenhill, 1993); and J. Kestner, 'The colonized in the colonies: Representation of Celts in Victorian battle painting', in S. West (ed.), *The Victorians and Race* (Aldershot: Scolar Press, 1996), pp. 112–27.
3. I. Ferris, 'Suffering in silence: The political aesthetics of pain in Antonine art', in T. Pollard and I. Banks (eds), *Past Tense: Studies in the Archaeology of Conflict* (Leiden: Brill, 2006), pp. 66–92, and plate 1.
4. E. Mackie, *Scotland: An Archaeological Guide* (London: Faber and Faber, 1975), p. 33.
5. In Corpus Christi College, Cambridge, CCC, MS 171, f. 265. See M. Brown, *Bannockburn: The Scottish War and the British Isles, 1307–1323* (Edinburgh: Edinburgh University Press, 2008).
6. In the Bodleian Library, Oxford, is a series of contemporary drawings in pen and ink by John Ramsay depicting the battle of Pinkie. See Harrington, *British Artists*, pp. 12–13.
7. P. Harrington, 'Images of Culloden', *Journal of the Society for Army Historical Research* [hereafter *JSAHR*], vol. 63, no. 256 (1985), pp. 208–19; A. Sulzberger, 'Bringing Scotland into the fold: The highland military figure and the evolution of British imperial identity' (unpublished MA dissertation, Courtauld Institute of Art, 2008), pp. 3–7. A German print dating from the early seventeenth century depicts highlanders in the service of Gustavus Adolphus of Sweden, wearing the Scots bonnet, and two figures in the belted plaid. See British Library, 1750.b.29.
8. A. E. Haswell Miller and N. P. Dawnay, *Military Drawings and Paintings in the Royal Collection* (London: Phaidon, 1996), vol. 1, plate 70.
9. I. G. Brown, 'The 'Forty-Five in caricature: The Penicuik Drawings in their context', in I. G. Brown and H. Cheape (eds), *Witness to Rebellion: John Maclean's Journal of the 'Forty-Five and the Penicuik Drawings* (East Linton: Tuckwell Press in association with the National Library of Scotland, 1996), pp. 41–80.
10. See illustrations in Harrington, *British Artists*, chs 2 and 3.
11. As Kestner suggests, 'the kilt provided opportunities for colour tonalities and also for motion in paintings which might otherwise appear static in the manner of *tableaux vivants*'. See Kestner, 'The colonized', p. 113.

Fraser's death was painted by Samuel Woodford in 1800 (National Archives of Canada). See Harrington, *British Artists*, p. 40.

12. R. H. Saunders, 'Genius and glory: John Singleton Copley's *The Death of Major Peirson*', *American Art Journal*, vol. 22, no. 3 (1990), p. 31. Yet by the end of the eighteenth century many of the chiefs and clan gentry had been assimilated into the ranks of British aristocracy. See R. Clyde, *From Rebel to Hero: The Image of the Highlander, 1745-1830* (East Linton: Tuckwell Press, 1995), p. 160, and Sulzberger, 'Bringing Scotland', ch. 3. In all fairness to Copley, he did produce a fine portrait of a Highland officer, Hugh Montgomerie, twelfth earl of Eglinton, in 1780.
13. Sulzberger, 'Bringing Scotland', p. 35.
14. Clyde, *From Rebel*, p. 176; D. M. Henderson, *Highland Soldier: A Social Study of the Highland Regiments, 1820-1920* (Edinburgh: John Donald, 1989), p. 8.
15. *Illustrated London News*, 26 March 1853, p. 237 and engraving.
16. Clyde, *From Rebel*, p. 186.
17. T. H. McGuffie, '"The Sword Dance", the 93rd (Sutherland) Highlanders in 1853, as Portrayed by D. Cunliffe', *JSAHR*, vol. 42 (1965), pp. 167-8. Cunliffe painted other scenes of Highland regiments. See, for example, H. P. E. Pereira, 'Colonel Eyre Crabbe of the 74th, with Some Observations on D. Cunliffe as a Military Painter', *JSAHR*, vol. 33 (1955), pp. 143-6, and D. Henderson, 'A Group of the 79th Highlanders: A Cunliffe Rediscovered', *JSAHR*, vol. 60 (1982), pp. 191-5.
18. B. Morse, *A Women of Passion, a Man of Passion: The Pioneering McIans* (Lewes: the Book Guild, 2001), pp. 241-3 and plates 9-11. The four paintings (each measuring 72 x 48 inches), two of which formerly hung in the Queen's Own Highlanders' Regimental Museum at Fort George, Inverness-shire, and the other two in the mess of the Highlanders in Germany, are entitled *Group (Portraits) beside Mills Mount Battery, Edinburgh Castle*; *Guard of Honour of the 79th Cameron Highlanders at Holyrood*; *The 79th preparing for a Move, Foog's Gate, Edinburgh Castle*; and *Heavy Marching Order Group (portraits) on the Esplanade of Edinburgh Castle*.
19. J. Ruskin, *Notes on Some of the Principal Paintings Exhibited in the Rooms of the Royal Academy: 1857* (London: Smith, Elder & Co., 1857), p. 10; see Harrington, *British Artists*, illustration, p. 153.
20. Several French military artists included Scottish soldiers in their paintings, possibly alluding to the 'auld alliance'. De Neuville's friend Édouard Detaille visited Britain on several occasions and portrayed highlanders on manoeuvres at Aldershot in 1879 and the Scots Guards marching through Hyde Park in the following year. In 1875 Felix Philippoteaux exhibited his celebrated canvas of the French cuirassiers attacking

Highland troops at Waterloo. Another contemporary, Georges Scott, included members of the Highland Brigade in the background of his painting which portrayed the surrender of Cronje at Paardeberg.

21. Kestner, 'The colonized', p. 115; J. Kestner, *Masculinities in Victorian Painting* (Aldershot: Scolar Press, 1995), p. 207.
22. *Illustrated London News*, 18 January 1879, p. 54, illustration p. 56, after a sketch by Lieutenant Neville Chamberlain. The same paper included a subsequent note about the wearing of the kilt and trews in the scene. See *Illustrated London News*, 8 February 1879, p. 122.
23. *Ordered to the Front* (Walsall Art Gallery); *Home Again!* (National Gallery of Victoria, Australia); *Summoned to the Front* (wash drawing, Art Gallery of New South Wales, Australia). The latter was reproduced in *The Graphic*, 11 January 1879, pp. 32–3. Holl had also used the theme of Highland soldiers in his painting entitled *A Deserter* (1874), depicting a sergeant and a corporal of a Highland regiment about to apprehend a deserter in front of his wife and daughter outside their cottage. See Kestner, *Masculinities*, p. 215, and plates 5–17.
24. C. Clark, 'The piper of Loos playing the KOSB to the attack', *The Sphere*, 11 December 1915, p. 275.
25. Other artists portrayed the Scottish soldier during the Great War. While Lady Butler composed *The Black Watch at Aubers Ridge, May 1915* and *A 'VC' of the Seaforths* (1916), many of the other depictions were genre scenes, such as Fred Roe's *The Foster Parent* (1915), *Before the Dawn* (1916) and *The Fortune of War* (1916). For a wider discussion of First World War art, see J. Winter, 'Painting armageddon', in H. Cecil and P. H. Liddle (eds), *Facing Armageddon: The First World War Experienced* (London: Leo Cooper, 1996).
26. Information from Stuart Allan, Senior Curator, National War Museum, Edinburgh. Further details of Eadie's war art can be found in J. Y. K. Kerr, *Ian Eadie of Dundee 1913–1973* (London: J. Y. K. Kerr, 2000).
27. *The Falklands War: A Visual Diary by Linda Kitson, the Official War Artist* (London: Michael Beazley, in association with the Imperial War Museum, 1982), illustration p. 83.
28. Information on Rowlands' work is based on a letter from the artist to the author, 12 December 1991. See also the artist's website at www.davidrowlands.co.uk, accessed on 30 August 2011.

27
Castles and Fortifications in Scotland

Chris Tabraham

Castles are widely perceived as places of military strength. The very word conjures up in the mind a high-walled, multi-towered stronghold rising up behind a water-filled moat, its drawbridge raised and its battlements bustling with heavily armed defenders doing their utmost to repel the enemy ranged before them, equally massed and armed, and operating giant siege machines capable of hurling huge stones at the formidable walls. Whilst there is no doubt that most medieval castles, in Scotland as elsewhere, were built with defence firmly in mind, it must be questioned just how paramount such a consideration was in the minds of those building them. Take mighty Tantallon castle, rising from a cliff edge overlooking the Firth of Forth, in East Lothian: built around 1350 by the newly ennobled first earl of Douglas, it had to wait 150 years before withstanding its first siege, by James IV in 1491.[1]

Castles were first and foremost seats of lordship, the residences either of the monarchy or those lords holding their land of the crown in return for providing military service. These castles, whether royal or noble, were intended to accommodate a variety of functions, including primarily that of lordly residence, but also as guesthouse and place of hospitality, as estate office and as law court and prison. But in that feudal age, when the sword was generally mightier than the pen, such activities could not be expected to be carried out adequately without a secure shield.[2]

Formidable stone walls appear to have been built with more than defence in mind, however. Castles not only provided security, for both people and their possessions; they were visible statements of lordship, helping to reinforce the power and pomp of the lord within, in much the same way as the great cathedrals served to reinforce the overarching majesty of God. In addition to seeing those high castle walls as providing a defensive shield, we should also see them as screening prying eyes from the world of privilege lived behind them, again in much the same way as rood screens in churches prevented the laity in the nave from seeing the priests performing their wondrous rituals in the chancel beyond. Moreover, while a castle wall head arrayed with crenellations and turrets may give the appearance of being there solely for defence, it also made the 'outsider' look up, and not just physically, but also emotionally, to the mighty lord who had put them there – hence the expression 'looking up to one's superiors'.

Castles as fortifications

Castles started appearing in what is now Scotland in the early twelfth century. Militarily, each was designed to withstand the conventional armament and tactics of its day. Until the advent of gunpowdered artillery in the fifteenth century, the contemporary armament used in attacking a castle comprised longbows and crossbows, and assorted machines for lobbing large stones, firing large metal projectiles and battering down doors. Other tactics likely to be employed offensively against castles included the use of fire and sapping (undermining walls). The most common tactic, however, was that of investment, of laying siege to a castle to prevent its resupply, thereby slowly but steadily starving its garrison into surrender.[3]

The first castles appear by and large to have been built of earthwork and timber, with height providing the principal tactical advantage.[4] The popular image of these early castles is that of the motte-and-bailey design, comprising two raised platforms – the motte, normally the higher of the two, housing the lord's residence, and the lower bailey containing the ancillary, or service, accommodation – encircled by broad, deep ditches. Among the best preserved is Duffus, near Elgin (Morayshire), built around 1150 by Freskin, a Fleming who founded the powerful Moray (Murray) dynasty. The towering height of Freskin's motte would have provided sufficient defence against the projectiles of the day, assisted by the usual array of drawbridges, gates and timber palisades pierced by arrowslits.

There are around 300 mottes in Scotland.[5] Their distribution, however, suggests that they were by no means the norm. Although examples are known in east central Scotland, most are clustered in areas that in the twelfth and early thirteenth centuries were on the periphery of the realm, in regions such as Galloway and Moray which were militarily more unstable. The role of the motte-and-bailey castle in Scotland can thus be over-emphasised. Freskin himself, prior to becoming lord of Duffus, was peaceably serving his sovereign, David I, as lord of Strathbrock, in West Lothian, and there is no evidence that he needed such a formidable motte castle there.[6]

What is certain, though, is that Freskin and his peers would have required some form of suitably impressive residence from which to lord it over their people. So what were the choices? Some lords continued to occupy strongholds that had served their predecessors for centuries. The royal castles at Edinburgh (formerly Din Eidyn), and Dumbarton (Dun Breatann), were built on well-nigh impregnable rock outcrops that had respectively served the kings of Gododdin and Clyde Rock well in the aftermath of the Roman withdrawal, whilst archaeological excavations at Dundonald (Ayrshire) have shown that the Stewarts' castle there was the last in a long line of fortified residences reaching back far into prehistory.[7] Islands, whether natural or man-made crannogs, also served as lordly seats. It is perfectly possible that, before the de Vauxs built their impressive castle at Dirleton (East Lothian) in the mid-1200s, they were happily ensconced at Castle Tarbet, on the nearby Forth island of Fidra. Moreover, one need only visit Loch Finlaggan, Islay (Argyllshire), and gaze at its two small, unfortified islands, Eilean Mór and Eilean na Comhairle, that together formed the original residence of the chiefs of Clan Donald, the mighty Lords of the Isles, to dispel the notion that crannogs were only for those well down the 'pecking order'. Those lords in the heart of the realm building from new seem to have been content with less substantial residences of earthwork and timber – what archaeologists term ringworks and moated sites – than those of the motte-and-bailey form. Crookston (Renfrewshire), built by Sir Robert Croc, a vassal of the Stewarts, is a good example of the former, and Muirhouselaw (Roxburghshire), built by one of the de Normanvilles, of the latter. Both relied for defensive capability (not forgetting military show, of course) not on raised platforms but on more modest encircling earthworks (banks, ditches and water-filled moats) and timber palisades.

An obsession with motte-and-bailey castles has perhaps overshadowed the part played by masonry in castle construction in the twelfth century. Although stone was certainly not in short supply anywhere in Scotland, or the skills to hew it and use it, as the great churches from Jedburgh to Kirkwall majestically demonstrate, it seems not to have been a preferred material of choice for castles, and the number of twelfth-century masonry castles can be counted on the fingers of one hand. St Margaret's Chapel in Edinburgh castle, built around 1130 by David I, today reads as a free-standing building but may plausibly have formed part of a larger tower-keep similar to that at Bamburgh castle (Northumberland).⁸ Scotland's oldest datable stone castle is Cubbie Roo's castle (Orkney), constructed around 1150 by Kolbein Hrúga, when the Northern Isles were under Norwegian suzerainty. And masonry was found when excavating the motte built by Ralph Ruffus at Barton Hill (Perthshire), where it formed part of the enclosure wall.⁹

Yet there were likely to have been other examples. In addition to his putative tower-keep at Edinburgh, David I may well have built the imposing tower-keep at Carlisle castle (Cumberland), where he died in 1153. There may also be further keeps like Cubbie Roo, such as Old Wick (Caithness), and that embedded within Dunrobin (Sutherland), though in the absence of datable features and without archaeological excavation we cannot be certain. And almost lost amid the beguiling ruins at Aberdour castle (Fife) is another tower-keep that must surely date from the twelfth century, judging by the pilaster buttresses clasping two of the corners and the narrow round-headed slit windows. It was probably built by the same Lord de Mortimer who, around 1140, built the fine Romanesque parish church of St Fillan's close by.¹⁰

The use of stone in castle building certainly became far more widespread from the thirteenth century onwards. This was the age of the great curtain-walled castles, beginning, it seems, with Castle Sween (Argyll), built around 1200 by Suibhne (Sven) 'the Red', and ending with the earl of Douglas's Tantallon around 1350, and during which some of Scotland's mightiest castles were built. Why stone should suddenly come into its own at this time is not clear. The motive could have been military, for there is evidence that stone-throwing machines were becoming larger and more powerful, and siege-craft more cunning, thus calling into question the defensive capability of castles built chiefly of timber. But the change may equally have been motivated by show. As Geoffrey Stell has pointed out, building in stone and lime represented a huge financial undertaking, not lightly embarked upon nor speedily carried through.¹¹ The lord would have needed secure physical and legal tenure of his land, and settled political conditions also, if his investment was to pay off.¹² Because stone endures, it is possible to chart the development of defensive provision more precisely. The first curtain-walled castles consisted of a single thick, high wall enclosing a substantial area of ground, variously rectangular, as at Kinclaven (Perthshire), polygonal, as at Kildrummy (Aberdeenshire), and circular – uniquely – at Rothesay (Bute). They all had two entrances – the front entrance reserved for the lord and his peers, and a postern, or back gate, for use by servants, workmen and others. Openings through the curtain wall were few, restricted to narrow vertical slits that doubled up as air vents and arrowslits. Defence was largely carried out from the wall head, probably from behind a crenellated parapet that enabled archers to reload in comparative safety. Such parapets have rarely survived, but that at Rothesay has, immured in a later heightening. Rothesay also retains evidence for its timber hoarding, or temporary fighting gallery that oversailed the wall, thus allowing the defenders to deter sappers from undermining it.

During the course of the thirteenth and early fourteenth centuries, significant improvements were made to these rudimentary defensive arrangements. In the first generation of curtain-walled castles, entrances were relatively simple affairs, relying for defence on thick, wooden doors reinforced by sliding draw-bars, with or without a portcullis behind. The wall top directly overhead probably also had a projecting *bretasche*, or covered gallery, to help defenders 'cover' the entrance and deter battering rams. Over time, these entrances became considerably stronger, and of course far more impressive as 'front doors'. Portcullises came as 'standard', the entrance fronts were fitted with drawbridges, and their rears with long, stone-vaulted transes, or passages, furnished with a series of double-leaf folding doors and flanked by chambers serving either as guard rooms or porter's lodges.

Arguably the most significant development was the addition of circular towers boldly projecting outwards from the curtain wall. Where projecting towers existed in the earliest curtain-walled castles, as at Kinclaven, they were little more than shallow rectangles that served simply as latrines towers. Dirleton seems to have been the first to break the mould, if it was built, as seems likely, around 1240. Large circular towers were built at four of the five corners of its curtain wall, to house residential and service accommodation chiefly, but also to help improve defensive cover for the adjacent lengths of wall. Lord de Vaux's motive in adopting this design is unclear, but it must be doubted if a military objective was the chief reason. Dirleton could not have been more peacefully located, at the heart of the realm and in an area without a whiff of trouble in over a century. In the absence of evidence to the contrary, we must thus assume that de Vaux was attempting to keep up with the latest architectural fashion. He was well placed to do so. As steward to Marie de Coucy, Alexander II's French queen, he would have frequently accompanied her back to Coucy, near Amiens, where he would have seen one of the first of these new multi-towered castles, built in the 1220s by the queen's father, Enguerrand, lord of Coucy.[13]

Where de Vaux led, others followed. Those building castles anew incorporated such towers into the design as a matter of course, among

Figure 27.1 Dirleton castle, East Lothian, showing the great tower built by John de Vaux c. 1240. The castle, badly damaged in the Wars of Independence, was rebuilt in the late fourteenth century by the Haliburton family.

them Herbert Maxwell at his new castle at Caerlaverock, built in the 1270s, and Walter of Moray, a descendant of Freskin of Duffus, at Bothwell, probably begun in the 1270s but never completed. Both lords grasped the opportunity to incorporate a twin-towered gatehouse in the design, thereby significantly strengthening the castle's 'weak spot' – its entrance – as well as greatly enhancing the look of the place. Where lords already had an existing plain curtain-walled castle, they simply grafted towers on. This is no more evident than at Dunstaffnage castle (Argyll), which Ewen MacDougall had inherited from his father, Duncan, in the 1240s and to which he subsequently added three towers.[14] Rothesay's four towers were also added in the later thirteenth century.

A less conspicuous development, but one that must surely have been prompted by military considerations, was the improved provision of arrowslits. During the later thirteenth century, these evolved from simple slits into ones with 'fishtailed' bottoms (and occasionally tops), presumably to give the archer stationed behind an improved arc of fire and line of sight. An added refinement was the provision of horizontal slits midway up the arrowslit, to allow a better field of vision.[15] At Skipness castle (Argyll), in a major remodelling probably ordered by Walter Stewart, earl of Menteith, towards the close of the century, there is an impressive row of four crosslet-arrowslits along the west curtain wall, each with a wide rear-arch to allow two archers to operate together. Identical arrowslits have recently been discovered at two other Stewart castles – Brodick (Arran) and Doune (Stirlingshire).[16]

If Scotland's great thirteenth-century castles had been built for defensive purposes, then the outbreak of the Wars of Independence with England in 1296 was the time for them to prove themselves. They were found sadly wanting. The garrisons in the chief royal castles surrendered their charges with barely a fight. Edinburgh alone held out for three days and three nights. The great baronial castles fared little better. Dirleton initially resisted Bishop Bek's investment of 1298, but was taken as soon as better artillery arrived. Even mighty Bothwell was unable to withstand siege, no matter which side was holding it. In 1298–9 the beleaguered English garrison contrived to hold out for fourteen months before surrendering, whilst two years later the Scots garrison caved in after less than a month. That the English held out for so long is probably due to the fact that the Scots at that date lacked heavy siege artillery, unlike the English who had a formidable arsenal of machines, bearing such nicknames as 'War Wolf' and 'Parson', and a lofty siege tower known as 'Le Berefry'. Several stages high, this had a drawbridge at the top that could be dropped onto castle battlements, and was used successfully at Bothwell in 1301.

That most of Scotland's castles were found militarily wanting when put to the test suggests that defence against a fully pressed siege was not the primary concern of their builders. First and foremost, castles were seats of lordship requiring a measure of protection for the lord's family, household and retinue against a variety of threats – thieves, neighbours with whom they were at blood-feud, civil disorder and so forth. The aim of defence was to make life as difficult as possible for attackers for as long as possible. But no castle was impregnable.

One of the many consequences of the Wars of Independence was that scarcely any of Scotland's castles survived unscathed. Much of what we see today at Bothwell and Dirleton, for example, dates from the later fourteenth and early fifteenth centuries as the Douglases and the Haliburtons began to rebuild their newly acquired residences. The dendro-chronological dates for the drawbridge timbers found in the water-filled moat at Caerlaverock in 1962 mirror the fortunes of Scotland's great curtain-walled castles before, during and after the Wars. The original bridge was built in the 1270s, as Herbert Maxwell set about creating his impressive new residence. The bridge was patched up in the 1330s, when Eustace Maxwell repaired the castle and placed it at the disposal of 'King' Edward Balliol, but then was completely replaced in the 1370s as another Herbert Maxwell set about rebuilding the family's battered residence.[17]

After the Wars of Independence, castle building in Scotland took a different direction. Only the first earl of Douglas, it seems, chose to imitate the curtain-walled castles of Alexander III's 'golden age' when he built mighty Tantallon, probably to help celebrate his becoming an earl in 1358. With its formidable curtain, imposing centrally placed gatehouse and monumentally high flanking towers – the Douglas Tower housing the earl's private apartment had seven storeys – Tantallon was a Bothwell or a Kildrummy adapted to a promontory site, nothing more and nothing less.

But whilst Douglas at Tantallon was looking back nostalgically to the past, his peers were showing a preference for a new style of lordly residence – one where the chief focus was no longer on a great curtain wall studded with towers, but on one or more rectangular towers linked by a more modestly sized perimeter wall. The 'downsizing' may be attributable to the sheer ineffectiveness of the curtain wall as a defensive shield, so graphically demonstrated during the recent wars with England. An enclosing wall of middling strength would serve to deter all but a 'siege royal' as well as costing considerably less. By 1400 such 'tower-house castles' were being built as standard by the senior nobility. Even David II was persuaded to do so as he set about rebuilding Edinburgh castle following his return from captivity in England in 1357; although the Constable's Tower containing the front entrance and most of the perimeter wall has long gone, the stump of David's Tower, housing the royal apartment, still lurks deep within the later Half-Moon Battery. One of the finest examples to survive intact is Doune castle (Stirlingshire), largely rebuilt by Robert Stewart, duke of Albany, during his time as regent in the early 1400s. By 1450, tower-house castles were being built by lords the length and breadth of the realm.

Defensive elements were chiefly 'upgrades' of traditional features. Bishop Trail of St Andrews, for example, in rebuilding his episcopal castle around 1390, incorporated a new style of drawbridge into his gatehouse tower, one that was raised by two 'gaffs', or timber beams; whether it was any more effective defensively than the traditional drawbridge is debatable, but there is no doubting its power to impress.

Figure 27.2 Doune castle, Stirlingshire, substantially rebuilt between c. 1380 and 1420 by Robert Stewart, duke of Albany, younger brother of King Robert III.

After all, if it was good enough for the great castle builder Charles V of France, at the Bastille, Vincennes and elsewhere, then it was good enough for Scotland's leading cleric. James I was similarly impressed and incorporated one into his new palace at Linlithgow in the 1420s. Other defensive features, however, reflect the 'downsizing', most obviously the yett, a cross-barred wrought-iron gate, that replaced the larger, more bulky portcullis. Around fifty remain *in situ*, including a fine two-leaved example at Balvenie castle (Banffshire).

Perhaps the most noticeable changes to a castle's defences were those affecting its wall head. Up until this point, wall heads had been relatively simple affairs – plain parapets, or ones notched with alternating crenelles and merlons, carried up flush with the outside wall face. Fighting platforms oversailing the walls, where they existed, were temporary timber structures. Only over an entrance were they more permanent box-machicolations (small galleries projecting from the wall face with openings in their floors for firing down on the

Figure 27.3 Balvaird castle, Perthshire, a sophisticated tower house built c. 1500 by Sir Andrew Murray, of the Murrays of Tullibardine.

enemy), as atop Bothwell's great keep. Indeed, it was probably at Bothwell that wall heads began to acquire more permanent, and more comprehensive, machicolations, for Archibald, fourth earl of Douglas and first duke of Touraine (1400–24), crowned his new castle buildings with elaborate arcuated openings; they survive most spectacularly over the so-called 'Douglas Tower'. Earl Archibald doubtless saw them whilst fighting the English in France, for by then such machicolations were becoming highly fashionable on the continent (for example, at the castle of Pierrefonds, built by the duke of Orléans around 1400). The fashion caught on, and by the end of the fifteenth century it was seemingly *de rigueur* for every Scottish castle to have chequered tiers of corbels crowning the wall head, often sweeping around the corners as turrets or 'rounds', as, for example, around the wall head of Balvaird castle (Perthshire), built around 1500 by Sir Andrew Murray and Margaret Barclay, his wife.[18]

Such wall-head defences were not only highly visible on the castles, they were also prominent in 'licences to crenellate' granted by the crown. In the earliest surviving licence (1424), James I granted to James of Dundas permission 'to build, construct, fortify and erect on high the tower or fortalice of Dundas [West Lothian] in the manner of a castle with crenelles ('le kyrneles') and other manifestations'.[19] James II's 1449 licence to Herbert Maxwell of Mearns (Renfrewshire) granted him the right to erect on the top of his tower 'all warlike apparatus necessary for its defence',[20] and the triple row of projecting corbels, evenly spaced to allow the defenders to fire down through the gaps, proves that he did just that. What is not made clear in this latter licence, however, is whether defence by, and against, gunpowdered artillery was covered by the phrase 'all warlike apparatus'. If it was not, it should have been, for by 1449 the newfangled gun was beginning to make its presence felt.

Castles and artillery fortifications

Gunpowdered artillery appeared in western Europe in the early fourteenth century, and primitive 'crakes of war' may have been deployed by Edward III during the later Wars of Independence. In 1384 'an instrument called a gun' was purchased for Edinburgh castle, together with sulphur and saltpetre for making the gunpowder.[21] By then an 'arms race' was developing across Europe in which the Scottish monarchy played its part. James I is reported to have used 'fine large guns, cannon and mortars' at his siege of English-held Roxburgh castle in 1436. By the time of his son James II's death in 1460, also whilst laying siege to Roxburgh and tragically killed by one of his own guns which exploded, the crown had acquired an impressive siege train. This included the famous 'bombard' Mons Meg, gifted in 1457 by Duke Philip of Burgundy and still proudly on display in Edinburgh castle. By the end of the fifteenth century it was clear that the new weapon was here to stay. Owners of castles in future had no option but to take them into account.[22]

The continuing conflict between Scotland and England provided a theatre of war for those experimenting with the new technology. However, huge bombards such as Mons Meg (which weighed some six tons) soon proved inordinately cumbersome, both to haul around the country as well as to fire, with the result that by 1500 they had largely become redundant as siege guns; James IV took Mons Meg to the siege of Norham in 1497 but left her behind in 1513 as he set out on his ill-fated campaign that ended in disaster at Flodden. But there was another theatre of war within Scotland that provided an opportunity for military engineers to experiment with artillery fortification – the 'showdown' between James II and his over-mighty earls, the Black Douglases.

Between 1452 and 1455 King James carried out a Blitzkrieg-style offensive against the Douglases' numerous castles, in which we know bombards were deployed. The defences of some of those castles had been newly strengthened. Abercorn castle (West Lothian) was reportedly the most strongly fortified of all, requiring the king to 'remanit at the sege and gart strek mony of the towris doun with the gret gun, the quhilk a Francheman schot right wele'.[23] Unfortunately, nothing remains above ground of Abercorn. Another Douglas castle which James accused the Douglases of fortifying and arming does, however, survive. Around the base of the great tower house built c. 1370 on Threave Island by Archibald 'the Grim', third earl of Douglas, is the equally formidable artillery fortification built by William, the eighth earl, by 1450. James failed to take Threave by force, despite a three-month siege and the deployment of his 'great bombard'. The presence of that new artillery fortification, described in 1458 as *domus artilerie* ('artillery house'), doubtless contributed to Douglas's successful defence.[24]

Threave's artillery house mixed tradition with innovation – twenty narrow vertical slits in the two main walls for archers and eighteen gunholes (commonly known as 'murtherholes') in the three circular towers, shaped either like 'dumbbells' or 'inverted keyholes'. The three large crenelles at the top of each tower may also have served as gun emplacements, as was the case at the Cow Tower, Norwich, dated to 1398–9.[25] Threave's gunholes may have taken 'serpentines', breech-loading guns of forged iron, with an 80mm bore, mounted on wooden stocks.[26] This artillery house was innovative in one further respect – in most earlier castles defensive features, such as towers or gate-houses, also served a residential or domestic function, but Threave's outer defence was intended for use solely as an artillery fortification.

Nevertheless, despite its advanced concept of defence, Threave's artillery house was not immediately imitated. Indeed, it appears that no other free-standing artillery fortification was built until early the next century, probably because fifteenth-century guns were neither very accurate nor had a good range. The design of Threave's gunholes, however, caught on: as the fifteenth century drew to a close, other lords were inserting them into their castle walls, and James IV himself incorporated them into his foreworks at Stirling and Dunbar.[27]

King James's death at Flodden in 1513 brought the threat of English invasion closer to Scotland, and it was in preparing for that conflict that the kingdom acquired another purpose-built artillery fortification – the Dunbar castle blockhouse. Its inspirer was the next in line to the throne, John Stewart, duke of Albany, who arrived from France in 1515 to govern the country. He made Dunbar his chief base

– Berwick castle having by then been irrevocably lost to the English – and to ensure his greater safety he built there 'ane great staine house . . . callit the uttward blokehouse and garnist it witht artailzie pulder and bullatis'; it may have been ready for action by 1517.[28] The 'outer blockhouse' was built on an island-like promontory separate from, and flanking, James IV's rebuilt castle. The guns probably comprised serpentines firing through the seven ground-floor gunholes and heavier cannon emplaced at parapet level. Dunbar's horizontal, round-ended gunholes, of a type imported from France, soon became the standard adopted throughout the country, ousting Threave's 'dumbbells' and 'inverted keyholes'. So popular were the new wide-mouthed gunholes that Gilbert Balfour installed more than seventy at his Orkney lair, Noltland castle, in the 1560s.

By the time Albany finally returned to France in 1523, there was no doubting the fact that guns had achieved supremacy over more traditional weapons. Purpose-built artillery fortifications were no longer a luxury but a necessity. Within a generation of the construction of Dunbar's blockhouse, gun towers had been grafted onto existing castles (at St Andrews by Archbishop James Beaton), and added to them as free-standing structures (at Tantallon, by the sixth earl of Angus). Blockhouses were also built to help defend harbours (at Aberdeen, c. 1530) and towns (at Peebles, c. 1570). Such was the rapid pace of technological change, however, that it was not long before these too were becoming redundant.

The problem was that stonework, no matter how thick, was becoming increasingly vulnerable to the far higher velocity and largely horizontal trajectory of gunpowdered artillery. In response, military engineers, most of them Italians, had returned to earthwork as the main defensive ingredient, for it 'absorbed artillery fire like a sponge absorbing water'.[29] The upshot was the 'bastion' system of defence, where stone-faced earthen angled bastions interplayed with the lengths of rampart to provide complete flanking cover. Also known as *trace italienne*, the bastion system became the dominant factor in military engineering until the late nineteenth century.[30]

Scotland got its first angled bastion in 1547, during the so-called 'Wars of the Rough Wooing'. Built at Eyemouth (Berwickshire) by the English in late 1547, it was only the second to appear in the British Isles.[31] Sir Richard Lee's design for Eyemouth centred on a single bastion midway along a 15-metre-thick earthen rampart cutting off the promontory.[32] Lee then went on to design Berwick-upon-Tweed's formidable walled defences. Not to be outdone, the Scots built their own versions – or rather Italian engineers did with the king of France's money. Sadly, nothing now remains above ground of Pietro Strozzi's bastioned fortification at Leith, or of Migiliorino Ubaldini's 'forte of the castle hill', built to protect Edinburgh castle, both quickly thrown up in 1548,[33] though precious remains of the latter were recently uncovered during excavations on the castle esplanade.[34]

The supremacy of gunpowdered artillery and the appearance of bastioned fortifications effectively signalled the end of the private castle's role in military defence. Henceforth, defensive provision would be afforded by state fortresses incorporating some form of bastion defence. They included those developed around the cores of the principal royal castles at Edinburgh, Dumbarton, Stirling and Inverness, and those built during the various military crises of the mid-1600s, such as the redoubt on Duns Law (Berwickshire) and the redan (an arrow-shaped outwork) at Tantallon, built during the Bishops' Wars of 1639–40; the citadels at Ayr, Inverlochy and elsewhere, built by Cromwell in the 1650s; and Fort Charlotte (Shetland), built against a Dutch threat in the 1660s.[35] During the Jacobite troubles of the eighteenth century, the Hanoverian government built forts and barracks across the Highlands, from Inversnaid (Stirlingshire) to Bernera (Inverness-shire); they included Fort William and Fort Augustus (Inverness-shire), and culminated in mighty Fort George at Ardersier (Inverness-shire), one of the outstanding artillery fortifications of Europe.[36] The last fortifications built in Scotland incorporating Italianate models were three forts on Inchkeith, in the Firth of Forth, built in 1879–81 against a combined Franco-Russian threat, and subsequently upgraded.[37]

Castles in the modern era

What of castles during this period of increasingly purpose-built artillery defences? The last fortress-residence built from new in Scotland can be held to be Craignethan castle (Lanarkshire), constructed by Sir James Hamilton of Finnart in the 1530s. The illegitimate son of the earl of Arran, he had served in Albany's entourage and subsequently played a pivotal role in creating some of Scotland's earliest artillery fortifications. They included the major reinforcement of Blackness castle (Falkirk) in the 1530s.[38] At the same time, Finnart was building his own private castle in the Upper Clyde valley.[39] An articulate fusion of military and domestic architecture, it included a caponier, a covered gun gallery invented by yet another Italian around 1500. Only two caponiers appear to have been built in the British Isles in the sixteenth century, both by Finnart; the other is at Blackness.

Figure 27.4 Craignethan castle, Lanarkshire, built in the 1530s by Sir James Hamilton of Finnart. The main entrance of the tower house, seen here facing to the right, was originally protected by a massive wall, five metres thick, which may have mounted artillery.

The age of the Scottish castle can truly be said to have ended with Craignethan. Castles were the product of a feudal society. So long as they remained centres from which land and people were ruled, they remained essential military targets. But as the governance of the nation changed over the centuries, so fortified lordly residences became anachronisms. Henceforth, there would be only noble residences, with just the minimum defensive provision necessary to deter thieves and those coming lightly armed and with hostile intent. William Forbes, laird of Corse (Aberdeenshire), summed the situation up when, in 1581, he allegedly vowed to 'build me such a house as thieves will need to knock at ere they enter'.[40] So those iron yetts remained behind the front door, iron bars and cage-grilles were fitted to windows and small pistol holes replaced the old 'murtherholes'; these were the Jacobean equivalents of today's door chains, window

Figure 27.5 Tolquhon castle, Aberdeenshire. The elaborate gatehouse, with its proud display of heraldry, formed part of the rebuilding of the castle in 1586 by Sir William Forbes, seventh laird of Tolquhon.

locks and security lights. Charles McKean has suggested that we might be better calling these later castles 'châteaux', thus removing the misleading military connotation.[41]

But old habits die hard. Scottish lairds had fallen in love with all that 'warlike apparatus' referred to in the licences to crenellate. The age when faithful retainers manned the battlements and poured boiling oil onto the heads of the besiegers may have passed, but crenellations and other castle trappings were still seen as icons of lordship. When William Kerr was contemplating rebuilding his noble seat at Ancrum (Roxburghshire) in 1632, his father, Sir Robert, pleaded with him: 'do not take away the battlement . . . for that is the grace of the house, and makes it look lyk a castle'.[42] So they hung onto their crenellated battlements, even if these were now only used to admire the view.

The gatehouse at Tolquhon castle (Aberdeenshire), built by Sir William Forbes, the seventh laird, in 1586, wonderfully exemplifies this 'martial imagery'. It was the frontispiece of his brand-new residence. The arched doorway, flanking drum towers with their heavily grilled windows and fanciful gunholes combine to present an impression of defensibility. Yet this is illusory. Everything about that gatehouse facade proclaims a feudal display of pride rather than any stern military intention. All was designed to impress, not deter, the visitor. Any lingering doubt that it was not all for show is dispelled by the four fine bronze cannon Willie Forbes purchased in 1588 to go with his new gatehouse – their muzzles were too big to poke through the gunholes!

During the seventeenth century the process of change and decay accelerated as once-mighty castles were abandoned in favour of grand stately homes, and lofty tower houses gave way to more modest lairds' houses. Most lords would have relished the prospect of residing in brighter, more salubrious surroundings. Some, though, chose to stay put and upgrade rather than relocate, and the nineteenth-century architectural confections at Dunrobin (Sutherland) and Dunvegan (Skye), to name just two, have ancient walls entombed within them. Others had no choice but to remain. Throughout the Highlands the continuing unrest in the seventeenth and eighteenth centuries resulted in many castles seeing military action and serving as garrison strongholds. The Campbells built what are probably the two oldest surviving barracks on the British mainland, at their castles at Kilchurn and Mingary (Argyllshire) in the early 1690s, and Blair (Perthshire) has the distinction of being the last castle in Britain to undergo siege, by Lord George Murray's Jacobites in March 1746.[43] Only after the battle of Culloden (16 April 1746) were the majority of medieval Highland fastnesses finally abandoned to their fate.

As national government became stronger so the notion of a permanent standing army took root. Hitherto the national army, the host, had been raised only when the need arose and disbanded thereafter. That situation changed during Charles II's reign when Scotland acquired its first embryonic army establishment. Gone was the age of the private retainer fighting in the defence of the lord and his castle; the time of the professional soldier, housed in garrisons built at the nation's expense, had come. Edinburgh and Stirling castles became little more than military barracks. Even today, a century after the War Office handed over Edinburgh castle to the Office of Works, to be maintained thereafter as an 'ancient monument', the fortress still retains a significant army presence, and both Edinburgh and Stirling castles house the museums of the regiments whose depots they were – the Royal Scots and the Argyll and Sutherland Highlanders respectively.

This continuing attachment to the nation's royal strongholds was mirrored in the private sector. No sooner had castles begun to fall into ruin than they came to be seen as compelling features in the landscape.

Owners set about repairing their 'dungeons and embattled towers mantled with ivy' as romantic ruins; among the first was Hugh Hume-Campbell, third earl of Marchmont, at Hume castle (Berwickshire) some time before 1789. These eye-catching curiosities were now viewed as the stuff of legend and myth, inspired in no small measure by the writings of Sir Walter Scott. Scott wrote of his own ancestral seat, Smailholm tower (Roxburghshire), in the following terms:

> And still I thought that shatter'd tower-house
> The mightiest work of human power;
> And marvell'd as the aged hind
> With some strange tale bewitch'd my mind,
> Of forayers, who, with headlong force,
> Down from that strength had spurr'd their horse,
> Their southern rapine to renew,
> Far in the distant Cheviot blue,
> And, home returning, fill'd the hall
> With revel, wassel-rout, and brawl . . .
> Methought grim features, seam'd with scars,
> Glared through the window's rusty bars,
> And ever, by the winter hearth,
> Old tales I heard of woe and mirth,
> Of lovers' slights, of ladies' charms,
> Of witches' spells, of warriors' arms.[44]

So smitten were Scots by their medieval castles that they not only repaired them but also restored some back to use. Scotland's most photographed castle, Eilean Donan (Inverness-shire), is largely a recreation of the early twentieth century by a descendant of the castle's hereditary keepers. Scots even evolved an architectural style, Scots Baronial, whose debt to the tower houses built in Jacobean times is self-evident. The love affair continues to this day.

Notes

1. Standard textbooks examining Scottish castles include: S. H. Cruden, *The Scottish Castle* (Edinburgh: Nelson, 1960); J. G. Dunbar, *The Historic Architecture of Scotland* (London: Batsford, 1966); R. Fawcett, *The Architectural History of Scotland 1371–1560* (Edinburgh: Edinburgh University Press, 1994); D. MacGibbon and T. Ross, *The Castellated and Domestic Architecture of Scotland*, 5 vols (Edinburgh: D. Douglas, 1887–92); C. McKean, *The Scottish Chateau* (Stroud: Sutton, 2001); W. M.

Mackenzie, *The Medieval Castle in Scotland* (London: Methuen, 1927); C. Tabraham, *Scotland's Castles* (London: B. T. Batsford for Historic Scotland, 1997); J. Zeune, *The Last Scottish Castles* (Buch am Erlbach: Leidorf, 1992). In addition, the numerous *Inventories* published by the Royal Commission on the Ancient and Historical Monuments of Scotland give detailed descriptions and critical analyses of many castles and fortifications.

2. There were exceptions. Blackness castle, west of Edinburgh, seems to have been used almost from its outset in the 1440s as a garrison stronghold and state prison. There were also exceptional circumstances, such as in 1481, when James III directed that those 'castelles neire the Bordoures and on the Sea coaste . . . that is in maist danger, and sik uther castelles and strengthes, that may be keiped and defended fra our enemies of England' should be put into a state of readiness and be strengthened 'with victualles, men and artailzerie'. Quoted in G. Stell, 'Late medieval defences in Scotland', in D. H. Caldwell (ed.), *Scottish Weapons and Fortifications, 1100-1800* (Edinburgh: John Donald, 1981), p. 29.

3. H. W. Koch, *Medieval Warfare* (London: Bison Books, 1978), pp. 45–55, 77–85.

4. R. Higham and P. Barker, *Timber Castles* (London: Batsford, 1992).

5. G. Simpson and A. Webster, 'Charter evidence and the distribution of mottes in Scotland', *Château Gaillard*, vol. 5 (1970), pp. 175–92.

6. Not all the 300 or more mottes in Scotland were built in the first phase of castle building in the twelfth and early thirteenth centuries, as the excavations of a motte near Roberton (Lanarkshire) have demonstrated. See G. Haggarty and C. Tabraham, 'Excavation of a motte near Roberton, Clydesdale, 1979', *Transactions of the Dumfriesshire and Galloway Natural History and Antiquarian Society*, vol. 57 (1982), pp. 51–64. What was thought to have been the motte castle built by Robert the Fleming about 1160 could not possibly have been built any earlier than 1300, in which case it was probably hastily erected as a place of safety for the then landowner caught up in the civil war between the Balliols and the Bruces.

7. G. Ewart and D. Pringle, 'Dundonald castle excavations, 1986–93', *Scottish Archaeological Journal*, vol. 26, parts 1 and 2 (2004), pp. 21–48.

8. E. Fernie, 'Early church architecture in Scotland', *Proceedings of the Society of Antiquaries of Scotland*, vol. 116 (1986), pp. 400–3.

9. M. Stewart and C. Tabraham, 'Excavations at Barton Hill, Kinnaird, Perthshire', *Scottish Archaeological Forum*, vol. 6 (1974), pp. 58–65; Higham and Barker, *Timber Castles*, pp. 315–18.

10. J. Gifford, *The Buildings of Scotland: Fife* (London: Penguin, 1988), pp. 59–62.
11. Stell, 'Late medieval defences in Scotland', p. 25.
12. The move to stone castles in the thirteenth century was by no means universal, and timber continued to play a major part in the construction of lordly residences. In 1325 Robert I built a manor house at Cardross, near the royal castle of Dumbarton, where he lived until his death three years later. The records tell of painted plaster walls, glazed windows and thatched roofs – hardly the picture of a strong defence. His adversary, Edward I of England, renowned for his great stone castles of north Wales, was also content to build his numerous 'peels', or garrison strongholds, in southern Scotland – at Linlithgow (West Lothian), Lochmaben (Dumfriesshire) and elsewhere – mostly out of timber. See C. Tabraham, 'Scottorum Malleus: Edward I and Scotland', in D. H. Williams and J. R. Kenyon (eds), *The Impact of the Edwardian Castles in Wales* (Oxford and Oakville, CT: Oxbow Books, 2010), pp. 183–92.
13. MacGibbon and Ross, *The Castellated and Domestic Architecture of Scotland*, vol. 1, pp. 37–9.
14. J. Lewis, 'Dunstaffnage Castle, Argyll and Bute: Excavations in the North Tower and East Range, 1987–94', *Proceedings of the Society of Antiquaries of Scotland*, vol. 126 (1996), pp. 559–603.
15. As experiments at White castle (Monmouthshire), have demonstrated: P. N. Jones and D. Renn, 'The military effectiveness of arrow loops: Some experiments at White Castle', *Château Gaillard*, vols 9–10 (1982), pp. 447–56.
16. T. Addyman and R. Oram, *Doune Castle, Doune, Stirlingshire: An Assessment of the Evidence for Pre-existing Structures* (unpublished report for Historic Scotland, March 2010, by Addyman Archaeology).
17. I. MacIvor and D. Gallagher, 'Excavations at Caerlaverock Castle, Dumfriesshire, 1955–66', *Archaeological Journal*, vol. 156 (1999), pp. 112–245.
18. J. Gifford, *The Buildings of Scotland: Perth and Kinross* (New Haven, CT and London: Yale University Press, 2007), pp. 186–9.
19. J. M. Thomson et al. (eds), *Registrum Magni Sigilli Regum Scotorum*, 10 vols (Edinburgh: HM General Register House, 1883), vol. 2, no. 1.
20. W. Fraser, *Memoirs of the Maxwells of Pollock*, 2 vols (Edinburgh: n.p., 1863), vol. 1, pp. 167–8, n. 39.
21. Quoted in D. H. Caldwell, 'Royal patronage of arms and armour making', in Caldwell (ed.), *Scottish Weapons and Fortifications*, p. 89, n. 9.
22. A. Saunders, *Fortress Britain: Artillery Fortification in the British Isles and Ireland* (Liphook: Beaufort, 1989), pp. 15–33.

23. Stell, 'Late medieval defences in Scotland', p. 40.
24. C. J. Tabraham and G. L. Good, 'The artillery fortification at Threave Castle, Galloway', in Caldwell (ed.), *Scottish Weapons and Fortifications*, pp. 55–72.
25. Saunders, *Fortress Britain*, pp. 20–1.
26. I. MacIvor, 'Artillery and major places of strength in the Lothians and the East Border, 1513–1542', in Caldwell (ed.), *Scottish Weapons and Fortifications*, p. 97, fig. 43.
27. Ibid. p. 100. I have intentionally not mentioned the inner quadrangular curtain wall, with its four gunholed corner towers, at Craigmillar castle (Edinburgh). Although it has in the past been cited as the earliest dated artillery work in Scotland, built in 1427, this seems to have been a misreading of the armorial panel over the front entrance. See Stell, 'Late medieval defences in Scotland', pp. 45–6. Without that date, the wall, with its wall-head machicolations, could date from any time that century. An added complication is that the gunholes might not be integral features; certainly quite a number appear to be formed out of original arrowslits.
28. MacIvor, 'Artillery and major places of strength', pp. 104–19.
29. I. V. Hogg, *Fortress: A History of Military Defence* (London: MacDonald, 1975), p. 41.
30. Saunders, *Fortress Britain*, pp. 53–69.
31. Ibid. p. 55.
32. M. Merriman, *The Rough Wooings: Mary Queen of Scots, 1542–1551* (East Linton: Tuckwell Press, 2000), pp. 257–8.
33. Ibid. pp. 321–30.
34. G. Ewart, D. Gallagher et al., *Fortress of the Kingdom: Archaeology and Research at Edinburgh Castle* (Edinburgh: Historic Scotland, 2014), pp. 99–109.
35. Saunders, *Fortress Britain*, pp. 103–5, 128–9.
36. C. Tabraham and D. Grove, *Fortress Scotland and the Jacobites* (London: B. T. Batsford for Historic Scotland, 1995).
37. A. D. Saunders, 'The defences of the Firth of Forth', in D. J. Breeze (ed.), *Studies in Scottish Antiquity presented to Stewart Cruden* (Edinburgh: John Donald, 1984), pp. 472–3.
38. MacIvor, 'Artillery and major places of strength', pp. 128–32.
39. I. MacIvor, 'Craignethan Castle: An experiment in artillery fortification', in M. R. Apted, R. Gilyard-Beer and A. D. Saunders (eds), *Ancient Monuments and their Interpretation: Essays Presented to A. J. Taylor* (London: Phillimore, 1977), pp. 239–61; C. McKean, 'Craignethan: The Castle of the Bastard of Arran', *Proceedings of the Society of Antiquaries of Scotland*, vol. 125 (1995), pp. 1,069–90.
40. Quoted in Cruden, *The Scottish Castle*, p. 224.

41. McKean, *The Scottish Chateau*, p. 3.
42. D. Laing (ed.), *1875 Correspondence of the Earls of Ancrum and Lothian* (Edinburgh: Bannatyne Club, 1875), p. 64.
43. J. Sadler, *Culloden: The Last Charge of the Highland Clans 1746* (Stroud: Tempus, 2006), pp. 182–4.
44. Walter Scott, *Marmion* (1808), introduction to Canto Third, *The Works of Sir Walter Scott* (Ware: Wordsworth Poetry Library, 1995), p. 70.

28

The Archaeology of Scottish Battlefields

TONY POLLARD

Traditionally, the study of Scotland's long and varied martial past has been the domain of the military historian, with books on wars and battles drawing together documentary accounts and secondary sources to paint a picture of these violent and fortunately distant times (the last battle on British soil being fought at Culloden in 1746). More recently, however, the archaeologist, who might at first appear more attuned to the landscape than the library, has begun to play an increasingly important role in advancing our understanding of this military heritage.

The first seeds of battlefield archaeology, and the wider school of conflict archaeology, were sown in the UK in the 1970s when Peter Newman systematically recorded finds of musket balls at Marston Moor.[1] It was in the USA, however, that the archaeological investigation of battlefields really flowered, with the survey of Custer's fight at Little Bighorn in the early 1980s setting the benchmark for much of the work to follow.[2] In Scotland the first real attempt to subject a battlefield to archaeological investigation was at Culloden in 2000, as part of the BBC television series *Two Men in a Trench*.[3] Since those early days a number of battlefields and sites of other forms of conflict, such as sieges, have been subject to investigation, and in early 2006 the Centre for Battlefield Archaeology was established at the University of Glasgow.

Archaeology, artefacts and battlefields

Archaeology is concerned with the physical traces of past human activity, some of which survive within the modern landscape either as upstanding or buried archaeological remains. Over the century and a half or so in which archaeology has been a serious pursuit, attention in Scotland has tended to focus on the ancient past, ranging from hunter-gatherers operating in the wake of the retreating glaciers around 10,000 years ago to the early Middle Ages and then to the later medieval period. An extensive portfolio of sites, including graves, ritual monuments, rubbish heaps and settlements, has provided evidence for human activity in the same location stretching over centuries and even millennia, with plentiful finds of artefacts such as stone tools and sherds of pottery.

Battles, on the other hand, usually take place within very short timeframes, some of them lasting less than an hour from first encounter to the flight of the enemy from the field. Such events may leave behind very little, if anything, by way of archaeological evidence, particularly when compared to other types of site. But it is not just the challenge of finding evidence related to battle that has until recently discouraged archaeologists.[4] Despite the fact that conflict and violence represent a constant expression of human social behaviour, and that many of the pioneers in archaeology came from military backgrounds, there was for a long time a tendency to regard the study of battle and conflict disdainfully as the amateurism of the 'armchair general', at best unfashionable and at worst an expression of politically suspect militarism. A notable exception has been the study of the armies and wars of classical Rome, and perhaps too the study of medieval fortification, though even here there has been a marked backlash against 'military fundamentalism' in favour of analysing castles as 'symbols of power' rather than buildings designed for conflict. In the UK, this situation has changed dramatically over the past decade, and now archaeologists, no matter what their period of interest, seem keen to embrace conflict and warfare. This has been due in part to the success of a small number of projects, including some of those discussed below, but also to the belated acceptance in Britain of historical archaeology – a subject again pioneered in the USA, which is concerned with activity taking place in the modern era – as a valid intellectual pursuit.

It is important to note that the nature of the archaeological remains left behind by historic battles differ markedly from those related to the more traditional components of the archaeological record. It is an unfortunate reality that people die in battles and so graves of some sort are usually a result, but the evidence for the action itself can be much more ephemeral in nature. The most common types of artefact associated with battle are metal objects: iron arrowheads, lead musket balls and bullets, pieces of armour, broken weaponry and items of apparel such as buckles and buttons. Only in very unusual circumstances will non-metallic elements, such as wood, fabric and leather, survive. Arrowheads and bullets may be left to lie where they landed, whilst buttons and buckles were often ripped away during hand-to-hand fighting and objects dropped as one army pursued another from the field. Obviously larger objects, such as swords, muskets and, in many cases, arrows, were scavenged from the battlefield after the fighting was over, but the smaller of these would invariably be left behind and over time become incorporated into the soil matrix, from where they could be recovered by archaeologists hundreds of years later.

These artefacts generally exist in what an archaeologist would call an 'unstratified context' within the topsoil, which if the land has been farmed will often equate to the plough soil. Archaeological features, such as pits, ditches, floor deposits and graves, are found securely stratified in the soil horizon below the topsoil and of course artefacts may exist within them, this time within a 'stratified context'. Battle artefacts in the topsoil may be found on the surface, if the ground has been recently ploughed, or at depths of anywhere between forty and fifty centimetres beneath it. Ploughing does move objects around but studies have shown that the movement tends to be vertical rather than lateral, especially with small objects, and this is obviously important if the spatial distribution is to be used to draw conclusions about the activities they represent.[5]

The archaeological investigation of battle sites would not be possible without the metal detector, a tool that has its origins in the mine detectors developed during the Second World War.[6] Metal detecting has been a popular pastime for some thirty years, yet while battlefields have long provided hobbyists with interesting pickings, amateur enthusiasts rarely record the location of these finds.[7] Without this information, battlefield artefacts become worthless as far as their ability to add to our understanding of an historical event is concerned. Artefacts, moreover, are often hoarded, discarded as nothing more than 'hedge fodder' or, as is increasingly the case, appear for sale on internet auction sites. More positively, battlefield archaeologists have much to thank some of these detectorists for, as those with a keen interest in the past are often more than happy to offer their experience and time as volunteers on archaeological projects.[8]

Unstructured metal detecting, which some would argue represents little more than the looting of our national heritage, is clearly not the only threat that our battlefields and related artefacts and archaeological features have to face. Over time urban development has seen the disappearance of numerous battlefields, with Largs (1263) and Falkirk (1298) being just two examples of battle sites completely lost beneath later settlements. The pressures of modern living, which require more and more houses, roads, power lines and industrial estates, mean that historic battlefields are under increasing pressure, and given that the majority have little or nothing in the way of upstanding remains to signpost their importance, it may appear difficult to argue for their preservation. The ability to walk across and study the terrain, which to some extent has retained its original form, is, however, a visceral experience that can make a vital contribution to understanding how and why a battle unfolded in the way it did. To appreciate this one only has to visit the site of the battle of Dunbar, fought in 1650, and see the constricted nature of the ground on which the Scots were positioned to understand how Cromwell's cavalry managed to roll them up from the right; or to Falkirk Moor and see the slopes that restrict the line of sight and the ravine that partially separated the two armies, to understand why the Jacobite forces failed to act coherently and why only the government regiments on the right stood firm during the battle of 1746.

Some sites, of course, have been deliberately preserved, one of the most notable being the battlefield at Culloden, largely thanks to its ownership by the National Trust for Scotland and the central role it is perceived to have had in Scottish history. The equally iconic site of Bannockburn has not fared so well, for it was fought on the very outskirts of the medieval town which over time has expanded outward. The issue of how best to preserve such sites, which only recently have come to be regarded as valid elements of cultural heritage, is a vexed one and will be returned to at the end of this chapter. Before proceeding further, however, it is important to provide a brief introduction to the practice of archaeology as far as it relates to battlefields.

Battlefield archaeology in practice

In terms of battlefield finds, context – that is the location within the landscape where an object was found and its relationship to other objects in time and space – is of primary importance. There are a variety of techniques available to the archaeologist to help record the location of artefacts deposited during a battle. Among the most accurate are the Total Station, a device that utilises a laser to measure angle and distance and logs the data in a computer, and the subcentimetre GPS (Global Positioning System), which uses the same satellite technology to be found in the navigation systems in cars. Cheaper GPS systems, in the form of the handheld devices used by hill walkers, can also be used, though they can be far less accurate than the more advanced systems, and depending on satellite coverage can produce readings that range from one metre to twenty metres away from the actual location. At the most basic level measuring tapes can be used to take offsets from field boundaries.

Ideally, metal detecting on battlefield sites should be carried out as part of a formal archaeological project. During such a survey detectorists work along transects or within grids, which ensures full coverage and gives as much of an idea of where objects are absent as where they are present. Each object is given a unique reference number that, along with the rest of the data, helps to build up the distribution pattern, which has the potential to tell us so much about how a battle was fought. Firing lines can be redrawn; the location of individual units, perhaps horse and foot, identified; the site of hand-to-hand fighting pinpointed; and routes of retreat retraced.

Vital as it is, metal detecting is not the only technique utilised in battlefield investigation. Topographic survey provides a detailed insight into the nature of the terrain across which the battle was fought and geophysical survey may help to locate buried archaeological features, such as graves or trenches, which can then be subject to the more traditional techniques of excavation. Then, when the fieldwork is over, laboratory analyses may have much more to tell us about the recovered artefacts. Increasingly, experimental replication is also playing a role. The firing of musket balls at various targets, for example, can give us a good deal of information about what archaeologically recovered examples have impacted. Even the very act of handling the weaponry of the time can provide an insight not available via the more traditional investigations of the historian; anyone who has fired a Brown Bess will tell you that there is barely any recoil, despite the impression given in some published histories.[9]

Culloden

It was to Culloden that archaeologists turned for the first experiment in battlefield archaeology in Scotland.[10] The battle, fought on 16 April 1746, saw the defeat of a Jacobite army under Charles Edward Stuart by a government army under the duke of Cumberland, and marked a bloody end to the last of the Jacobite risings. The site provided distinct attractions for archaeological research, at least while techniques were still very much in the developmental phase. The site of the battle was known, with a number of reasonably detailed maps drawn up in its immediate aftermath, while the graves of the Jacobites were marked and memorialised.[11] Moreover, since the mid-twentieth century parts of the battlefield have been in the ownership of the National Trust for Scotland, which built a visitor centre there in 1970. In the 1980s trees planted in the nineteenth century were removed so as to return the site to the more open landscape it had been in 1746. A road that passed through the clan cemetery was also re-aligned and one of the contemporary enclosures reconstructed. Rows of flags were erected to show the initial location of the two armies and signposts displayed to mark the position of individual regiments. All of this, along with a rich body of contemporary accounts – in the form of letters written by combatants, official reports and eyewitness testimonies collected after the battle – provided, in theory at least, a framework within which recovered artefacts could be understood. However, one of the important outcomes of the archaeological surveys, which have taken place on several occasions since 2000, is that many of our preconceptions have been challenged by the results of this work.

The accepted understanding of the battle has a red-coated government army, which was some 8,000 strong, facing down a Jacobite

Figure 28.1 Culloden battlefield, 2009. The Jacobite line is in the foreground and the government line in the distance, with the visitor centre to the right. The Jacobite memorial cairn is visible in the centre of the battlefield.

> THE BATTLE
> OF CULLODEN
> WAS FOUGHT ON THIS MOOR
> 16TH APRIL 1746.
>
> THE GRAVES OF THE
> GALLANT HIGHLANDERS
> WHO FOUGHT FOR
> SCOTLAND & PRINCE CHARLIE,
> ARE MARKED BY THE NAMES
> OF THEIR CLANS.

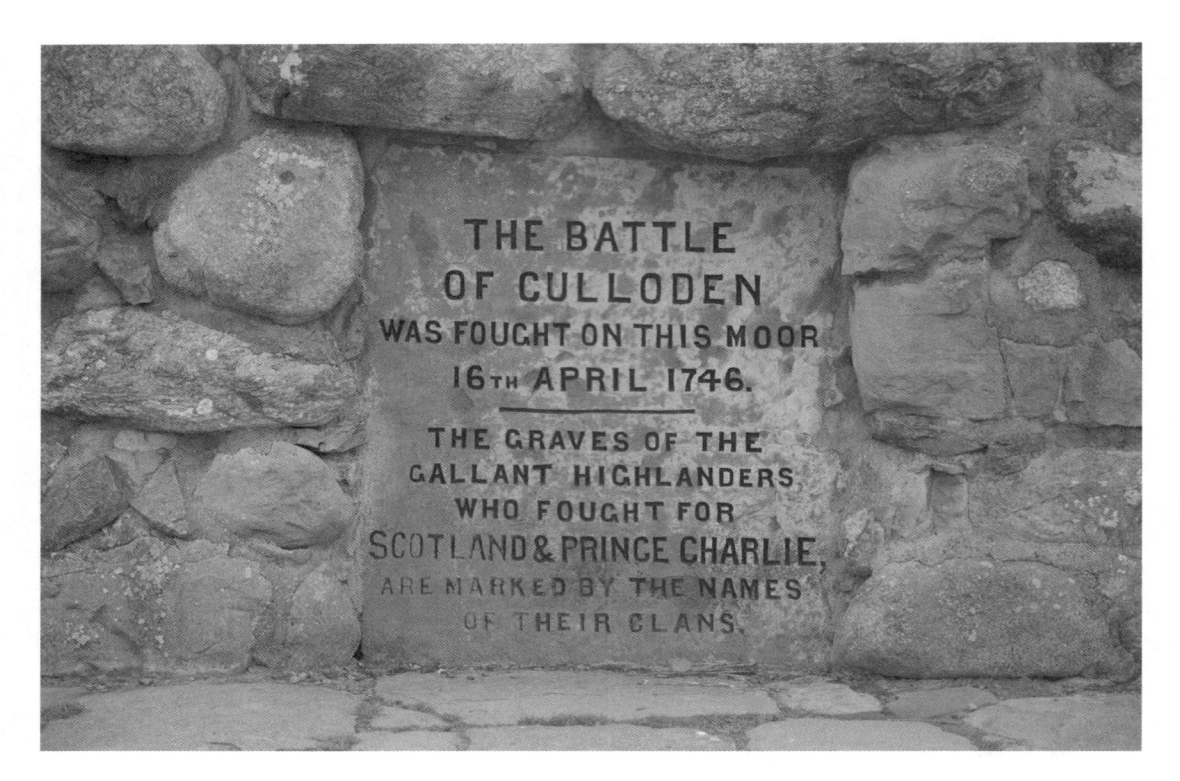

Figure 28.2 The Jacobite memorial cairn at Culloden battlefield.

army of approximately 5,500, first destroying their artillery with effective counter-battery fire and then using cannon shot and disciplined musketry to break the Jacobites as they charged with broadswords in hand. On the left of the government line the Jacobites came to hand-strokes but a newly introduced bayonet drill helped the redcoat ranks hold the charge.[12] Effective redeployment of troops in the reserve line, with Wolfe's regiment moving around the left flank to deliver devastating enfilade fire, sealed the government victory.

An alternative reading, and probably a more popular version (Culloden is perhaps the exception that proves the rule about history being written by the victor), tells the same story but from a different perspective. This is one of heroic sacrifice on the part of the Jacobites, who, despite the odds stacked against them, charged into a hail of lead and were only forced to leave the field after a fiercely fought hand-to-hand engagement on the government left. Their withdrawal was followed by a series of brutal reprisals, including the killing of the wounded. It is this bloody aftermath, as much as the battle itself, that has played a constant role in debates related to Scottish identity and the nation's perceived maltreatment by its English neighbour. It is also true to say that, despite attempts to correct the impression,[13] the 'Forty-Five is still popularly remembered as a straightforward struggle between Scotland and England, rather than as part of a pan-European war – the War of Austrian Succession – and, in part, as a Scottish civil war.

Although the Jacobite charge, and its rebuttal, are the most popular images of the battle and those that still fire the imagination of the visitor, there were other elements to the engagement, and historians have not overlooked these.[14] They include an important cavalry action to the rear of the Jacobite line, after government dragoons were given the freedom to pass through a stone enclosure thanks to breaches knocked in walls by the Campbell Highlanders in government service. The enclosure walls also provided cover for the Campbells when they fired on the Royal Écossais (Scots in French service) after they were brought forward to support the Jacobite charge.

Archaeology has not entirely rewritten or debunked these features of the battle, which have been continually rehearsed in the many books covering the subject. But what it has done is provide a much more nuanced, and perhaps objective, picture of the engagement and its choreography. An early and dramatic discovery was that the National Trust for Scotland's layout of the site – guidebooks, footpaths, line markers and interpretation panels – presented a battlefield that was markedly smaller than the reality. The cavalry action, for example, has never played much of a role in these interpretations, largely because the site of this action remains outside National Trust for Scotland ownership and therefore resides outside 'the battlefield'.

Furthermore, the position of the government left has been revised. Metal detector survey revealed a dense concentration of artefacts in the area known as the 'Field of the English'. These included musket balls, pistol balls, pieces of broken musket, buttons, buckles and other objects. Such a scatter of material is indicative of fierce hand-to-hand fighting: pistols were only fired at close range, muskets had been shattered by blows from edged weapons and buttons had been ripped from fabric in the struggle. There was little doubt that this material marked the position of the left wing of the government forces. It was here that Barrell's and Monro's regiments were posted and where they were hit by highlanders from the Jacobite right and centre, and where broadsword was pitched against bayonet. Yet this debris scatter stretched into the Field of the English for around eighty metres beyond (that is, to the south of) the position marked as the location of Barrell's regiment by an interpretation panel.

It was not just the position of the government left that the archaeology redefined. It has also forced us to reappraise the distance between the two armies. A distinct cluster of musket balls fired at close range (distinguishable by their high levels of deformation) was recovered from a location to the north of the Culwineach enclosure, against which the right flank of the Jacobite line was initially anchored. These were not far to the front of the Jacobite line, as delineated by marker flags. There seemed little doubt that these musket balls related to the exchange of fire between the Campbells, positioned behind the walls, and the Royal Écossais, who at the time were falling back after their move forward to support the failing charge. But this location seemed a little too close to the initial Jacobite line, with the fire-fight actually occurring some distance forward of this position – effectively in the no man's land between the Jacobite and government lines. Reference to the contemporary maps supported this observation: it was clear that the reconstructed Jacobite line was in the wrong location, and anything up to 100 metres too far to the east. This error appears to have originated from maps in histories published in the early 1960s when the locations (which fitted well with the Trust's limited land holdings) were first marked on the field by the National Trust for Scotland.[15]

Archaeology has also illustrated the influence of the terrain on the Jacobite charge. Topographic survey highlighted a spine of higher ground running across the moor, from roughly where the centre of the Jacobite line was located to the left of the government line. Until 1984 this ridge carried the road that ran through the clan cemetery. Back in 1746, however, it supported a track, which is marked on some of the contemporary maps. This feature undoubtedly had an impact on the nature of the Jacobite charge, with the right and centre veering to the right and engaging with the government left – a move that mirrored the alignment of the track and ridge. The track provided surer footing than the moor, and the spine of higher ground may have provided some cover from incoming fire as the Jacobites advanced. The Jacobite left, on the other hand, was faced with level, open ground which was also very wet. As a result, the left suffered very badly from government musketry and did not manage to close to hand-strokes. A traditional tale related to the battle is that the MacDonalds, located towards the left of the Jacobite ranks, did not press their charge with all due vigour as they were sulking about not being at the point of honour on the right.[16] A closer look at the terrain provides a far more logical explanation for Jacobite failure there.

Analysis of the artefacts has provided even more intimate battlefield insights. Broken pieces of Brown Bess furniture – the brass fittings – were recovered from the debris scatter on the govern-

Figure 28.3 Lead shot from Culloden battlefield: from left to right – grapeshot, 0.69 French musket ball (Jacobite), 0.75 Brown Bess musket ball (government), heavily impacted musket ball.

ment left. Several of these were back straps from the trigger guard. The largest piece bore a crescentic impact scar where it had been struck by the musket ball that had torn it from the weapon, perhaps injuring or killing the man holding it. If we assume that the Brown Bess was carried by a government soldier (though large numbers of these muskets were captured by the Jacobites after the battles at Prestonpans and Falkirk), then the musket ball that hit it was more than likely to have been Jacobite. This in itself forces us to reconsider some of our preconceptions about the battle, for traditional interpretations have the Jacobites armed with broadsword and targe and the government troops with Brown Bess and bayonet. What the archaeological work has brought to light is the strength of Jacobite firepower.

Indeed, the Jacobites had at their disposal several thousand French muskets imported by their continental allies.[17] These muskets had a calibre of 0.69 inches, which makes the musket balls slightly smaller than those fired by the Brown Bess (0.75 calibre), the standard weapon of the British army. This means that it is possible to distinguish between those fired by either side (although, as previously noted, the Jacobites also had access to the Brown Bess). Approximately half of the several hundred musket balls recovered were 0.69 calibre and therefore Jacobite.

Other conclusions may be drawn from the trigger guard strap, which must have been hit by a ball fired at close range. The highlander's normal practice was to fire a single shot while advancing and then to throw down the musket, draw the broadsword and close for combat.[18] Yet the Jacobite orders of the day at Culloden stated that 'no body to throw away their guns',[19] which was probably a reflection of Lord George Murray's desire to have the Jacobite army fight in the traditional European fashion, and the damaged strap seems to confirm this. Further evidence for this close-range use of muskets was the discovery of a socket from a bayonet recovered on the outer edge of the debris scatter on the government left. At Culloden the bayonet is usually associated with the government army. The recovered example, however, was French, of a type delivered in some quantities with the French muskets. The fact that the Jacobites were using their muskets at close quarters, and in some cases with bayonets fixed, does not negate the use of the broadsword, which is well documented. But it does provide for a more complex picture of events.

The archaeological investigations at Culloden have produced some striking results and have also contributed to the development of the tools and techniques most suited to this type of endeavour. The rich documentary evidence has helped us to make sense of the recovered data, but the archaeology has, in turn, helped to revise these accounts. In 2008 a new visitor centre was opened by the National Trust for Scotland at the battle site. Drawing on the new archaeological evidence, this incorporates a revised interpretation and layout of the battlefield. Culloden is one of the few battlefields in the world where full integrated archaeological data, rather than just written accounts, have been utilised to inform the visitor.

Other Jacobite battlefields

The experience gained at Culloden has since proven its worth at several other sites of Jacobite conflict, including the battlefields of Killiecrankie (1689) and Sheriffmuir (1715). At the former, a study of the terrain provided further explanation for why the Jacobite charge downhill was so successful – terraces kept them out of sight of the government musketeers for part of the time.[20] At the latter, archaeological survey and documentary research helped to pinpoint the actual location of the battle for the first time.[21]

The most recent site to be investigated is Prestonpans, where on 21 September 1745 the first battle of the 'Forty-Five saw a Jacobite army rout a government army under Major-General John Cope, both sides being around 2,500 strong.[22] After a lightning march through the Highlands the Jacobites had taken control of Edinburgh, leaving Cope and his redcoats in Inverness, and then Aberdeen, from where they were shipped to Dunbar. The Jacobites left the capital to confront them and on 20 September were positioned on the high ground at Tranent, with the government army on the coastal plain below, just to the east of the village of Preston (which is today part of

Prestonpans). A day of manoeuvre and counter-manoeuvre followed, with the Jacobites constantly probing for a suitable point of attack and the government army readjusting its position in response. The final effort came early in the morning of the 21st when the Jacobite army was guided through a marsh by a local man, a move that put them on the left flank of the government line.

In a very short time Cope managed to wheel his army round to face the Jacobites; both armies were now aligned north to south and the Jacobites positioned to the east. The Jacobites charged through the morning mist and almost immediately turned the government line, with cannon fire being ineffective and limited to one shot per gun as the gunners deserted their pieces. The dragoons were pushed back onto the infantry and the line broke from the right. The rout saw men trapped against the garden walls of Preston House where many were reported to have been killed. Cope, and what was left of his army, made it to Berwick, and the shockwaves quickly reached London. Six weeks later the Jacobites began their ill-fated march on London.

Today the town of Prestonpans and its environs are much changed since the time of the battle, with the settlement expanded to the east and west, the landscape intersected by roads and railways and a coal-fired power station located on the coast, just to the north of where the battle was fought. But these are simply modern manifestations of features already present in 1745; it was an industrialised landscape even then. One of the first railways in Britain, actually a horse-drawn tramway which carried coal from the pits at Tranent down to the port at Cockenzie, ran across the battlefield. Histories of the battle make much of the government army lined up either on the tramway or to the west of it, with the Jacobites charging across it from the east.[23] Today, a portion of the tramway is preserved as a footpath which runs between two fields close to the power station and its associated coal store. In 2009 this area was targeted by a metal detector survey as part of a Heritage Lottery funded community project that aimed to engage local people with their past. It was hoped that the survey would produce evidence for the battle. Only a small number of carbine balls (fired by the dragoons) were recovered, however.

This led to a reassessment of the contemporary maps, of which five at least are known to exist. Although detailed enough to show individual houses, only one of these maps showed the tramway; nor was it mentioned in any of the testimonies provided at the official inquiry into Cope's behaviour during the battle.[24] The exception is a sketch map drawn by Blakeney, the commander of the garrison at Stirling castle. This shows the government troops to the west of the tramway

Figure 28.4 Surveying Prestonpans battlefield.

and the Jacobites crossing it from the east. Blakeney, however, was not present at the battle but was told about it by a local man, Alexander Carlyle, the son of the minister at Prestonpans. We know from Carlyle's autobiography that he only witnessed the aftermath of the battle and not the initial encounter, which was watched from a distance by his father from his church tower.[25] Indeed, the 'fog of war' commonly associated with battle was also accentuated on this occasion by its meteorological equivalent as the Jacobites charged out of a morning mist. The reference to the tramway and the position of the troops in relation to it are therefore based on far from reliable sources.

Further metal detecting in the fields to the east of the tramway yielded no fewer than thirty musket balls, far more than during any other part of the survey. These included both 0.69 calibre Jacobite musket balls and 0.75 calibre government equivalents. The pattern suggested is very much in keeping with the battle taking place around 500 metres or more to the east of where it was presumed to have been fought. It is hoped that the fields in which the episode now seems to have taken place will be revisited and more evidence recovered. But even without another survey the recovered material strongly indicates that this is the correct battle site, an exciting conclusion as this part of the landscape is much better preserved than that further to the west. In truth, though, the battlefield has not been moved, merely extended. The government army was still pursued all the way back to Preston House and the Jacobites still charged over the tramway; now, however, we believe that it was while they were chasing the government troops, who had also run across it.

Siege sites

The bulk of this chapter has been concerned with the archaeological investigation of battlefields. It would, however, be remiss to overlook sieges, which, unlike battles, tended to be more static in nature and, importantly for the archaeologist, took place over a considerably longer timespan. Many of Scotland's numerous castles, forts, citadels and other defences have been the focus for attack and defence at some point in their history, and some of the most strategic sites suffered repeated siege. Stirling castle, for example, is known to have been invested at least sixteen times.

There have been attempts by archaeologists to investigate the remains of some of these actions.[26] Yet although protracted sieges should leave plenty of archaeological evidence, many siege fortifications have been encroached upon by the later development of the very towns or settlements they were constructed to besiege. For instance, any evidence for the late sixteenth-century siege works surrounding Edinburgh castle were long ago swallowed up by the expansion of the city around the castle.

Two notable examples of siege sites where urbanisation and its destructive tendencies have not put off the archaeologists are at Leith and Fort William. The citadel of Leith, held by a French garrison in the service of James V's widow, Mary of Guise, was besieged by the Protestant Lords of the Congregation and their English allies in 1560. A complex series of siege works, including trenches and earthwork fortifications, were constructed outside the impressive Italian-influenced defences and were the scene of some fierce fighting, in part because of the unwillingness of the French troops to shelter behind the walls and take what was thrown at them. Indeed, forays were made outside the citadel, resulting in a number of vicious engagements. The

Figure 28.5 The siege of Leith, 1560, from the contemporary Petworth map. Clearly depicted are the port's fortifications, built from 1548 by the Italian military engineer, Pietro Strozzi, employing the *trace italienne* system of defence with angled bastions for artillery.

siege ended only with the death of Mary and the signing of the Treaty of Edinburgh, a vital clause of which stipulated that all French troops were to depart Scottish shores within twenty days.

The town walls, slighted after the siege, have long since disappeared, and Leith itself has expanded to become effectively a continuation of Edinburgh. At first sight it would appear that there was very little chance of any physical evidence of the siege surviving. When a contemporary siege map was overlain with a modern street map, however, it was apparent that areas of battlefield archaeological interest coincided with modern open spaces, most notably Leith Links to the west of the old citadel and Pilrig Park to the south.[27] In 2006 a limited programme of excavation, directed by the present author, focused on anomalies resulting from geophysical survey. In both areas archaeological remains, consisting of banks and ditches related to the siege works, were uncovered, thus establishing that the archaeological investigation was viable in these areas.

In the Highlands, the town of Fort William is also much changed from the time it was besieged by the Jacobites in 1746. The fort there, first built by General Monck in 1654, was the most westerly of a chain of three government strongholds positioned along the Great

Glen. Fort George, at Inverness, and Fort Augustus, at the southern end of Loch Ness, had already fallen but Fort William proved to be a tougher nut to crack, not least because it was open to constant resupply from the sea and benefited from artillery support from Royal Navy ships.

Prior to investment, the garrison burned the settlement of Maryburgh (the civil settlement that had grown up beside the walls of the fort) in order to prevent the Jacobites from using the buildings as shelter from the elements and from the fort's guns. The siege lasted for no more than three weeks before the Jacobites withdrew, soon after to face their final showdown at Culloden. Since then, the fort has been largely destroyed, first by the railway and subsequently by a supermarket and car park. Excavation of what little remains of it, essentially elements of the walls and a demi-bastion in the north-west corner, revealed that the interior had been scoured clean of any relevant archaeology.[28] Fortunately, more information was forthcoming from part of Maryburgh which is now an open space near the centre of Fort William known as the Parade. This revealed a rich deposit of debris from the burning, including fragments of wine bottles, discoloured and twisted by high temperatures, and charred clay pipes.

Future challenges

The majority of sites discussed here relate to the Jacobite wars. Yet a survey carried out for Historic Scotland in advance of the preparation of an inventory of nationally significant battlefields has identified no fewer than 358 fields of conflict north of the border, which include battles, skirmishes and clan conflicts.[29] Clearly, many of these cannot claim great significance, but among those that may are sites of ancient conflicts such as the great battle fought between the Roman general Agricola and the Caledonii at Mons Graupius in AD 84, which is thought to be somewhere in Aberdeenshire. Then there are the battles between the Picts, the Scots and their southern neighbours, such as the victory of the Picts over the Anglian Northumbrians at Nechtanesmere (Dún Nechtain) in AD 685. Unfortunately, the precise location of these early sites remains unknown – in fact they represent something of a Holy Grail among battlefield archaeologists in Scotland. Nor is it just the ancient sites that have proved difficult to locate: to this day, not a single verified artefact has come from Bannockburn (1314), a battle that has been associated with no fewer than six possible locations around Stirling.[30]

As a result of the absence of contemporary maps of Bannockburn,[31] and all too vague chronicle accounts, the majority of which appeared decades after the battle, the exact location of this iconic encounter between Robert the Bruce's Scots and the English army of Edward II is today still open to debate. Of the half-dozen contenders, two sites are thought to be most likely: the first being the traditional location on the flatland of the Carse between the Pelstream and the Bannockburn; and the second being on the higher ground to the west, known as the Dryfield. But what little archaeological work there has been in the vicinity has yet to provide any firm evidence for either of them.

Battles that predate the widespread use of powder and shot provide special problems for the archaeologist. The fact that they took place so long ago does not assist artefact survival, as metals like iron are not likely to survive in most soils indefinitely. Even on the later sites, iron objects, unlike lead or copper alloy, can be highly degraded. The military technology deployed during earlier periods also has an influence on the nature of the archaeological signature left behind. As the sixteenth century progressed, so the bow and arrow was replaced by musket and shot. The musket ball is small, unlikely to be recovered once fired and made from lead, which generally survives well. Arrows, by contrast, were likely to be picked up after the battle to be used again. Only those arrowheads that entered bodies or were snapped have some sort of chance of being left behind to become part of the archaeological record. As an example we should perhaps look to Bosworth, where it has taken a team of archaeologists and metal detectorists five years to find any trace of the battle fought in 1485. When evidence did come to light it took the form of lead cannon shot fired by early artillery pieces. Although firearms would have been far outnumbered by bows, not a single arrowhead has been recovered.[32]

For a battlefield to attract the interest of the archaeologist it has to survive; yet many have not, or are currently under threat from development. Battlefields have not been regarded as heritage sites of national importance in the same way as prehistoric barrows, stone circles or castles. This situation, however, is changing and there are moves to produce an inventory of the most important sites, which will hopefully allow for conservation and management in a world where pressure on land for development can override all other considerations. But there is as yet no move to protect these sites by law or to put a stop to the activities of metal detectorists operating outwith the rigour of an archaeological project. Hopefully, these desirable outcomes will come to pass, though probably not before it is too late for some sites.

This chapter has given a brief indication of the contribution that battlefield archaeology can bring to the study of historic conflict in Scotland, and highlighted some of the important advances made over the past decade. The disciplines of battlefield and conflict archaeology, however, are still relatively young and, fortunately for the growing number of archaeologists interested in the subject, much work still remains to be done. It has not been argued here that archaeology has dramatically changed Scotland's military history – the Jacobites lost the battle of Culloden with or without an archaeological investigation. But what archaeology has done is to provide much needed additional information which in places has led us to question our preconceptions and the historical accounts. It has been said that archaeology is nothing more than the 'hand-maiden to history'.[33] The present author, however, who is not averse to a little crime fiction, believes its contribution makes it more akin to history's private detective.

Notes

1. G. Foard, 'The archaeology of attack: Battles and sieges of the English Civil War', in P. W. M. Freeman and T. Pollard (eds), *Fields of Conflict: Progress and Prospect in Battlefield Archaeology* (British Archaeological Reports, International Series, 958, 2001), pp. 87–104.
2. D. S. Scott, R. A. Fox, M. A. Connor and D. Harmon, *Archaeological Perspectives on the Battle of Little Bighorn* (Norman, OK: University of Oklahoma Press, 1989).
3. T. Pollard and N. Oliver, *Two Men in a Trench: Battlefield Archaeology, the Key to Unlocking the Past* (London: Penguin and Michael Joseph, 2002). This groundbreaking research was in part a legacy of an earlier landmark event in Scotland: the first international conference on battlefield archaeology, which was hosted by the University of Glasgow in 1999 (Freeman and Pollard, *Fields of Conflict*).
4. P. W. M. Freeman, 'Issues concerning the archaeology of battlefields', in Freeman and Pollard, *Fields of Conflict*, pp. 1–10.
5. C. Haselgrove, 'Inference from ploughsoil artefact samples', in C. Haselgrove, M. Millett and I. Smith (eds), *Archaeology from the Ploughsoil: Studies in the Collection and Interpretation of Field Survey Data* (Sheffield: Department of Archaeology and Prehistory, University of Sheffield, 1985), pp. 7–31.
6. It is interesting to note, however, that the first recorded use dates back to 1901 when Alexander Graham Bell tried to use an electronic coil to locate an assassin's bullet lodged in the fatally wounded body of the American president, William McKinley. It was not found, as the president was

lying on another new invention, a wire-sprung mattress, which masked the signal. See D. S. Scott, 'Shot and shell tell the tale: The rise of battlefield and conflict archaeology – a short retrospective' (unpublished paper presented at the Fourth Fields of Conflict Conference at the Royal Armouries Leeds, 29 September 2006).

7. T. Pollard, 'The rust of time: Metal detecting and battlefield archaeology', in S. Thomas and P. Stone (eds), *Metal Detecting and Archaeology* (Woodbridge: Boydell and Brewer, 2009), pp. 181–203.

8. A select number of hobby detectorists, under guidance from archaeologists, have made an important contribution, one being Jon Pettet who for years has been metal detecting the fields in which the battle of Sedgemoor took place in 1685, with each of his finds individually numbered and plotted on maps.

9. For instance, J. Sadler, *Culloden: The Last Charge of the Highland Clans* (Stroud: Tempus, 2006), p. 234: 'The report was loud, the recoil fierce'.

10. T. Pollard (ed.), *Culloden: The History and Archaeology of the Last Clan Battle* (Barnsley: Pen and Sword, 2009).

11. T. Pollard, 'Mapping mayhem: Scottish battle maps and their role in archaeological research', *The Scottish Geographical Journal*, vol. 125, no. 1 (2009), pp. 43–61; R. Woosnam-Savage, 'To gather the image whole: Some early maps and plans of the battle of Culloden', in Pollard, *Culloden*, pp. 163–87.

12. S. Reid, *Like Hungry Wolves, Culloden Moor 16 April 1746* (London: Windrow and Greene, 1994), p. 38.

13. For example, D. Szechi, 'The significance of Culloden', in Pollard, *Culloden*, pp. 218–39, and the displays in the new Culloden visitor centre.

14. For example, Reid, *Like Hungry Wolves*, and C. Duffy, *The '45: Bonnie Prince Charlie and the Untold Story of the Jacobite Rising* (London: Cassell, 2003).

15. Pollard, *Culloden*, p. 4.

16. The issue is discussed by Sadler, *Culloden*, p. 243.

17. Duffy, *The '45*, pp. 206–7.

18. Sadler, *Culloden*, p. 162.

19. Reid, *Like Hungry Wolves*, p. 58.

20. T. Pollard and N. Oliver, *Two Men In A Trench II: Uncovering the Secrets of British Battlefields* (London: Penguin and Michael Joseph, 2003), pp. 233–4.

21. T. Pollard, *Sheriffmuir Battlefield* (Glasgow University Archaeological Research Division Data Structure Report 2214, University of Glasgow, 2006).

22. T. Pollard and N. Ferguson, *Prestonpans Battlefield Project Report*

(Glasgow University Archaeological Research Division Data Structure Report 2815, University of Glasgow, 2010).
23. For example, F. Tomasson and F. Buist, *Battles of the '45* (London: Batsford, 1962), p. 69, and Duffy, *The '45*, p. 17.
24. Pollard and Ferguson, *Prestonpans Battlefield Project Report*.
25. A. Carlyle, *Autobiography of Dr Alexander Carlyle of Inveresk* (Edinburgh: Foulis, 1910), p. 116.
26. A good example is Leslie Alcock's excavation of Dunnottar castle, which included the investigation of a Cromwellian siege work on an opposing cliff top. L. Alcock and E. A. Alcock, 'Reconnaissance excavations on early historic fortifications and other royal sites in Scotland, 1974–84; 5', *Proceedings of the Society of Antiquaries of Scotland*, vol. 122 (1992), pp. 215–88.
27. T. Pollard, 'The archaeology of the siege of Leith, 1560', *Journal of Conflict Archaeology*, vol. 4 (2008), pp. 159–88.
28. T. Pollard, 'The archaeology of the siege of Fort William, 1746', *Journal of Conflict Archaeology*, vol. 4 (2008), pp. 189–229.
29. G. Foard and T. Perdita, 'Scotland's historic fields of conflict: An assessment for Historic Scotland by the Battlefields Trust' (unpublished, 2005).
30. F. Watson and M Anderson, 'The Battle of Bannockburn' (unpublished report for Stirling Council, 2001).
31. The earliest known maps or plans of a Scottish battle are those of Pinkie, fought in 1547, drawn up by Patten. See M. Merriman, *The Rough Wooing: Mary Queen of Scots, 1542–1551* (East Linton: Tuckwell Press, 2000), p. 9, which reproduces one of these woodcuts. These may be among the earliest maps of the British Isles.
32. G. Foard, 'Bosworth: Chasing the battlefield', *BBC History Magazine*, vol. 11, no. 3 (March 2010), pp. 28–30.
33. I. Noel Hume, 'Handmaiden to history', *North Carolina Historical Review*, vol. 41 (1964), pp. 215–25.

29
Scottish Military Monuments

ELAINE W. MCFARLAND

Monument raising is an ancient pastime. The escalating human cost of war is, however, a feature of modernity and it is hardly surprising, given the scale of its commemoration, that it is the Great War that has come to dominate both the popular consciousness and the work of professional historians.[1] Unfortunately, such attempts to evaluate the function of the twentieth-century war memorial have often taken place in isolation from the broader monumental tradition that shaped and sustained it.

The decision to make 'Scottish military monuments' rather than 'Scottish war memorials' the focus of this chapter is, therefore, quite deliberate. In this instance, a 'military monument' is defined in its most inclusive sense as

> any object, structure or scheme of endowment which has been created, installed or adapted to celebrate military victories and exploits in war and conflict, or to commemorate those who served or died as a result of disease or enemy action in time of war and conflict.[2]

These seemingly immutable physical and cultural markers, in fact, constitute a highly mobile and textured field of study. Their value to the historian lies in two long-term transitions, which in turn reflect broader developments in the culture of death and mourning.[3] The first is a democratising process that has rescued rank-and-file causalities from the anonymous collectivity of the mass grave. The act of 'naming' the dead, which began in the mid-nineteenth century, has allowed the common soldier to emerge as 'hero' in the dramatic narrative of war, formerly the preserve of monarchs and military leaders.[4] Paralleling this has been the replacement of celebration by commemoration as the dominant motive for memorialisation in the modern age, with the stereotype of hero ultimately giving way to 'victim' in the iconography of remembrance. Against this background, much of the historical debate has focused on the existential purpose of military monuments, either as sites for rituals of personal mourning or as conduits of political ideas, although recent interventions have attempted to bridge the dichotomy between the psychology of grief and the politics of mourning by mapping the shifting subjective layers of the commemorative experience.[5]

While often displaying similarities across cultures in their portrayal of the 'ideal warrior' and the transcendence of death, military monuments are also compelling as collective symbols of national and communal identities. In Scotland, this type of self-representation is particularly powerful given the historic association of Scottishness with a carefully nurtured martial tradition. Indeed, it is through this medium that the Scottish military identity has firmly imprinted itself upon the physical landscape, leaving a legacy of thousands of monuments in various shapes, sizes and locations. Ranging from the plaintive to the bizarre, these reveal not only changing images of the Scottish solider in popular culture, but also evolving attitudes towards military service, citizenship and war itself.

In order to capture this sense of change through time, the chapter adopts a broad chronological focus. It is inevitable that its approach is selective rather than comprehensive. For the sake of clarity, the analysis is organised sequentially in terms of the conflicts that the monuments commemorate. Here it soon becomes apparent that the lapse of time between fighting and memorialising can be highly variable, suggesting some of the challenges involved in shaping public memory on behalf of a 'stateless nation'.

'A monumental frame of mind'

Probably the earliest extant military monuments in Scotland are the symbol stones of the Picts. The battle stone at Aberlemno, carved in the decades around AD 700, possibly depicts the nearby battle of Nechtanesmere in AD 685, while the Sueno Stone at Forres, created in the tenth century, portrays another battle, perhaps that of Kinloss in AD 966.[6] Despite prominent elements of Christian symbolism, both can be firmly located in the ancient tradition of battle exploit memorials, offering a graphic narrative of triumph over the enemy. Through their brutal representation of fighting, decapitation and dead warriors, they proclaim an uncompromising message of power and military supremacy.

Unique to Scotland, these Pictish monoliths mark a high point of early historic European sculpture and in their own right form a vital part of the historical record.[7] Nevertheless, this indigenous tradition of memorialising seems to have subsided during the Middle Ages. Indeed, local monuments to mass death in battle were uncommon in medieval and early modern Europe generally, as battlefields themselves often remained contested political sites.[8] In the Scottish case, the continuance of a distinctive monumental tradition was further constrained by the relative poverty of the realm and the consequent lack of wealthy patronage. The individual funerary memorials of the military elite do, however, represent an important surviving medium of commemoration. These chantry tombs, carefully positioned within the sacred space of the church, are richly evocative of a cult of personal memory which imposed obligations of prayer and benefaction on the living to advance the spiritual welfare of the dead.[9] Sadly, given their aim of securing remembrance in perpetuity, many monuments, like the fourteenth-century knight's effigy at St Mary's Rothesay, are now worn and anonymous.[10] Of the tombs that can be identified, like the fourteenth-century Douglas memorials at St Bride's Church in Douglas, South Lanarkshire, their range of architectural references often underline the high social status of their patrons, a further motivation for this memorial form.[11]

The Wars of Independence may have created their own monument in securing national sovereignty through military victory, but Scotland's subsequently poor record on the battlefield was hardly the stuff of commemoration. The defeat of Flodden and the demise of much of the Scottish aristocracy in 1513 did, however, leave a distinct architectural impression by boosting the tradition of collegiate churches, created for the benefit of the founder's soul or the prestige of their family.[12] Typical is Castle Semple Collegiate Church, Lochwinnoch, enlarged to house the highly ornate tomb of its founder, Lord Sempill, who fell at Flodden, or the extension of Seton Church, near Tranent.[13] Although the Reformation in Scotland sundered this close identification between the worlds of the living and the dead more completely than elsewhere in Europe, the associated hunger for intra-mural commemoration would prove to be an abiding element of Scottish monumental design.

Far from constraining future commemorative enterprises, the lack of authentic military monuments from the medieval and early modern periods, in fact, offered an uncluttered landscape for later generations of Scots, who sought to embody national sentiment in physical form. It was the late Victorians who would prove the most

Figure 29.1 The National Wallace Monument, Abbey Craig, Stirling. The memorial was designed by John Thomas Rochead and opened in 1869.

prolific monument builders. As the national trade press in the shape of the *Undertakers' Journal and Monumental Masons' Review* commented in 1886, 'Scotchmen . . . seem just now to be in rather a monumental frame of mind.'[14] However, their efforts in this respect reflected a much broader process of cultural renegotiation in Scottish literature and art, which dated from the late eighteenth century onwards, entailing the rediscovery and re-evaluation of Scotland's history. The patriotic self-image that resulted has been interpreted as a form of heightened national consciousness, asserting a distinctive partnership role within the union and the empire. Rooted in the rising confidence and prosperity of Scottish urban elites, and reflecting their 'all pervasive' level of voluntary activity, nineteenth-century monument raising also benefited from a well-established infrastructure for fundraising and project management.[15]

The sequence of public meeting, committee formation, published appeal and public subscription became increasingly familiar during the course of the century, although the period from inception to completion could be highly variable depending on public generosity and squabbles over competing designs. The range of subjects selected for commemoration was extensive, but the vision of Scotland's heroic military past remained a staple theme. A favourite subject was the Wars of Independence, presented as the military success that provided the eventual key to equality in the union settlement.[16] From 1820 onwards, Wallace statues and monuments were raised at Falkirk, Ayr and Barnweill, Ayrshire, culminating in the construction of the national monument at Stirling during the 1860s.[17] The tercentenary of Flodden and its aftermath also, however, produced two fine monuments in Selkirk and Hawick, whose depiction of unbowed 'callants' is testament to the resilient quality of Scottish martial aspirations.[18] Indeed, the romanticism of Victorian monument builders even allowed them to accommodate the military misadventures of Mary Queen of Scots' reign, with monuments at Carberry Hill and Langside, where an elaborate Corinthian pillar was constructed, modelled on ancient victory columns.[19]

The most substantial and numerous groups of monuments commemorating Scottish conflicts of the early modern period are the covenanting memorials. These can be classed as 'war memorials', though their subjects in fact tend to be remembered more for their 'witness' and 'martyrdom' rather than any martial prowess. They fall into three main types: battlefield or event memorials; funerary monuments to those who died under persecution; and individual grave markers, or 'martyr stones', which are the most numerous.[20] Most relate to the period 1660–8 and are concentrated in the south-west, where the radical covenanting tradition was strongest and government repression most marked.

The covenanters may now have slipped to the edge of public memory, but this was not always the case. It is likely that none of their monuments is contemporary. Some, like the original Martyrs' Memorial in Greyfriars Churchyard, Edinburgh, were raised in the early eighteenth century by the continuing covenanting societies and thus have a direct link with events, but most are further products of the Victorian period, when 'our covenanting forefathers' had become entrenched as a theme in Scottish Presbyterian identity. The process of monument building again drew on the prevailing climate of historicism, evident in Walter Scott's covenanting novel, *The Tale of Old Mortality* (1816). A popular oral tradition had also persisted in localities such as east Ayrshire, Lanarkshire, and Dumfries and Galloway, as suggested by the simple covenanting memorial raised by local parishioners at Newmilns (1829).[21] A further powerful dynamic encouraging the larger monuments later raised by public subscription, such as the impressive tower at Mull of Deerness, Orkney (1888), was the ongoing schismatic tendency of Scottish Presbyterianism itself, as factions jostled to identify themselves with 'the covenanted work of reformation'.[22] It is ironic that these most intransigent of men and women created such a highly malleable tradition. Often heavily weathered, the monuments and their lonely locations have exerted their own emotional pull. It was indeed these same 'martyr graves' that haunted the expatriate Robert Louis Stevenson when his thoughts turned to home:

> Grey recumbent tombs of the dead in desert places,
> Standing stones on the vacant wine-red moor . . .[23]

While more firmly enshrined in current national consciousness, the Jacobite rebellions by comparison proved rather less prolific in terms of physical memorials. Yet, like the 'Killing Times', later generations also used their example to draw messages for their own age, with the romantic sensibility of Jacobitism and its associations of picturesque Highland valour forming another important strand in the developing sense of 'Scottishness' during the nineteenth century. The common enabling factor in these later projects was precisely that the Highlands had been pacified and Jacobitism was no longer a political threat. One of the most famous memorials, the Glenfinnan Monument, completed in 1815 as a result of private patronage, was only made possible by Telford's construction of a new military road from Fort William three years earlier.[24] The selectivity inherent in this process of memorialisation was also indicated by the 1853 obelisk at Prestonpans dedicated to the Hanoverian officer Colonel Gardiner, its subject honoured less for his military exploits than because he featured as a character in Scott's *Waverley* (1814).[25]

The empire's defenders

It was not only battles in Scotland's receding past that demanded the attention of nineteenth-century monument builders. The Napoleonic Wars were significant in shaping not only Scottish martial identity but also the Scottish monumental tradition, initiating a powerful partnership between civilian Scotland and the Scottish regiments in the business of military commemoration. Here, the keynote was glorious victory rather than gallant defeat.

This was a different type of war in scale and duration, placing new demands on Scottish military manpower both for home defence and overseas campaigns. By 1813, Scots comprised 15.3 per cent of the army, while constituting only 10 per cent of the population, a fact recognised by political elites who placed an increasing value on Scottish military service.[26] The extent of mobilisation, including the involvement of home-based Volunteer corps, also created a large ex-service constituency which regarded military participation as a touchstone of Scotland's role in the British imperial project.[27] The final ingredient was the battlefield performance of the Highland regiments in India and Egypt, hastening their cultural transformation into repositories of 'national character'.

The impact of these developments was felt both on memorial forms and on the themes of commemoration. The early nineteenth century witnessed a powerful restatement of traditional hero portrayal and elite memorialisation, as well as a more gradual movement towards the commemoration of collective sacrifice. Besides celebrating individual military achievements, the monument builders were eager to glorify the British nation in arms, while also increasingly underlining Scotland's distinctive contribution to military success.

The immediate legacy of the Napoleonic Wars was a plethora of memorials to officers whose graves were overseas. These followed the tradition of earlier intra-mural tributes, but their frequent location in Scottish Episcopal chapels, rather than local parish churches, reflects the progressive Anglicisation of the officer class in the early nineteenth century. Erected privately by relatives, friends or comrades, they usually take the form of simple wall tablets where expressions of Christian consolation are entwined with appropriately martial imagery.[28] For senior commanders, too, glorious death was the quickest route to commemoration, although in this case memorials usually assumed a more public and monumental form. Sir Ralph Abercromby, the fallen hero of Alexandria, for example, had an Edinburgh New Town crescent named in his honour, while a statue of Sir John Moore of Corunna was unveiled in Glasgow's George Square in 1819.[29] Proclaimed as Scottish national heroes by these tributes, both were also recognised in a series of monuments across Britain.[30] Indeed, further illustrating the overlapping of Scottish and British identities in the early nineteenth century, the death of Admiral Lord

Nelson particularly captured the popular imagination in Scotland. A standing stone erected by the ironworkers of Taynuilt following the news of Trafalgar in 1805 was reputedly the first of many such memorials in Britain.[31] A series of rival Nelson projects followed. In 1806, a 'chaste' Nelson Obelisk was erected by public subscription at Glasgow Green, and work began on an octagonal Nelson Tower at Forres, funded by prominent citizens in the local Trafalgar Club.[32] A year later, Edinburgh replied by commissioning its own 'Nelson Tower' in the form of an upturned stone telescope on Calton Hill.[33]

The celebration of British victory over Napoleon implicit in these projects also inspired the originators of the 'National Monument', which, it was hoped, would share the Nelson Tower's hillside space in Edinburgh. Begun in 1816, this was originally intended to be a British national monument located in Scotland, matched by a similar development in Dublin.[34] The project, however, also assumed a more specific local focus as its initial Tory sponsors quickly grasped that in order to raise the necessary funds Scottish military achievements in securing victory must be fully recognised.[35] The proposed monument can be further interpreted as an early attempt to address the collective human cost of war, since the classical structure was intended to serve both as a memorial to the 'Caledonian warriors' who had lost their lives and as 'a temple of gratitude to God' for the nation's deliverance.[36] Always an elite project, the lack of funds required to bring it to completion would haunt generations of future monument builders. Yet this failure did not necessarily imply a wider rejection of its ideological assumptions, but instead reflected a competition for funds with privately commissioned projects and other local enterprises.[37]

The theme of Scottish soldiers as the bulwarks of empire would continue to inspire military monument builders in the later nineteenth century. This was strengthened by an enthusiastic emphasis on the martial prowess of the highlander. The personal, intra-mural commemoration of junior officers continued in ecclesiastical settings, as did the erection of public statuary dedicated to successful Scottish commanders, like the veteran Lord Clyde.[38] These, however, were joined by a new collective monumental form, the regimental memorial, the popularity of which grew in step with the cult surrounding the kilted battalions. This had two main variants. The first was the regimental memorial at its simplest, raised by serving officers and men to commemorate fallen comrades in specific campaigns. Following the tradition of laying up the regimental colours in sacred space, these initially took the familiar form of memorial tablets in churches. St Giles, as the High Kirk of Edinburgh, and Glasgow Cathedral were focal points for these spontaneous commemorative acts, each accumulating dozens of tablets following the Crimean War, the Indian Mutiny and subsequent colonial expeditions.[39] From the mid-century onwards, larger free-standing monuments of this basic regimental type, usually obelisks or simple crosses, also began to be constructed, often situated in public spaces in regimental recruiting areas, or in symbolic sites in the capital, such as Edinburgh castle esplanade.[40]

Monuments have, of course, specific cultural meanings for both participants and observers. Here they served a double purpose, cauterising the emotions of survivors, while proclaiming the continuing vitality of the regiment and the values it had fought to uphold.[41] Indeed, it was through this medium that the ordinary Scottish soldier first emerged as a recognisable casualty of war. Unlike the nation's ancient battles which also inspired nineteenth-century monument builders, colonial campaigns were won at an immediate price. One of the first memorials to include individual names of the regimental dead, for example, was the Celtic cross inaugurated at Edinburgh castle in 1862 in memory of the officers and men of the 78th Highlanders who fell in the Indian Mutiny.[42] This practice subsequently grew to become a widely accepted element of military commemoration, fuelled by the more positive image of the rank-and-file soldier that had emerged from the Crimean War. Besides a growing concern for his individual welfare, this conflict had also established the cultural motif of the lonely soldier's grave, encouraged by sentimental descriptions of military cemeteries, including the Highland Brigade's burial ground at Kamara.[43] Similar developments were evident in the United States and Europe in the period, but in the Scottish case it would appear that the expansion of the heroic narrative to embrace the private soldier was again expedited by the hold that the 'heroic Highland warrior' had already assumed in popular culture.[44]

Popular militarism was embodied in ever more sophisticated form in the second type of regimental memorial which developed from the 1870s onwards. These were monuments to the regiment itself, rather than to its casualties in any single campaign. Originally inspired from within the serving officer corps, these projects were also able to draw on wider networks of communal patronage among the gentry and middle classes, even mobilising the subscribing potential of the Scottish diaspora.[45] Their historicism places them firmly in the context of the wider monumental impulse in Victorian Scotland, as their central motif was the 'thread of valour' that linked current

Figure 29.2 The Black Watch Monument at Aberfeldy, Perthshire. The monument was sculpted by William Birnie Rhind and unveiled in 1887.

battle exploits to a heroic past. In fact, many Scottish regimental identities were more fragile and impermanent than these monuments suggested. Unsurprisingly, it was the 42nd Highlanders, the Black Watch, which possessed one of the most impressive records of continuous service, that became one of the medium's chief exponents.[46] In 1872 a mural monument, then the largest ever constructed in Scotland, was unveiled at Dunkeld cathedral, depicting the history of the regiment since its inception.[47] This was followed in 1887 by the inauguration of a cairn at Aberfeldy, topped by the anonymous figure of a highlander in original regimental uniform in the act of drawing a sword.[48] Given the traditional rivalries of the Scottish regiments, such self-publicising techniques proved infectious. The riposte of the Cameronians, for example, was to mark their own bicentenary in 1892 by raising a statue to their founder, the earl of Angus, at Douglas Muir.[49] While this was a monument as much to the tenacity of the Lowland regimental tradition as to a covenanting hero, both statues shared a similar impulse in representing the regiment in ideal form, a reality greater than the sum of the unnamed men who had served or died in its ranks.

Figure 29.3 The Cameronians' Regimental Memorial at Douglas, Lanarkshire. Sculpted by Sir Thomas Brock, the memorial was erected in 1892.

Citizen soldiers

The range and volume of military monuments further increased in the wake of the South African War.[50] The task of memorialisation had, however, become an increasingly challenging and complex one, as many of Scotland's most prestigious regiments struggled to subdue the enemy in a costly and frustrating campaign. The defeat of the Highland Brigade at Magersfontein in 1899, for example, was particularly disastrous, resulting in the loss of over 700 officers and men, including the Brigade's commander, Major-General Andrew Wauchope.[51] In these circumstances, the response of the monument builders was a defiant restatement of Scotland's military tradition through the use of familiar memorial motifs, allowing the continuity of form and design to proclaim the survival of the tradition itself. Prominent casualties, such as Wauchope and Lord Airlie, colonel of the 12th Lancers, were thus recast as archetypal heroes, fallen at the head of their men.[52]

The conflict also produced the usual host of smaller, personal memorials from survivors and 'friends of the regiment' to their dead comrades, buried overseas. Besides the usual battalion tablet, these included stained glass windows and simple free-standing monuments – a large number of them originating from volunteer units.[53] Meanwhile, larger-scale commemoration persisted with a new wave of regimental memorials, again frequently raised by public subscription. These were symbolically sited not only across Scotland, but also on the South African battlefields and war cemeteries, now typically cast as romantic sites 'on which with silent eyes, the Southern stars look down'.[54] The latest figurative interpretations of 'the spirit of the regiment' reflected both the impact of continental influences on British figurative sculpture and recent practical advances in stone-cutting technology.[55] Their ambition and sophistication were further encouraged by the growing professionalisation of art and design, many of these commissions finding their way to the Edinburgh studio of the sculptor W. Birnie Rhind.[56]

Significantly, the scale of Scottish casualties now prompted these larger memorials to fuse corporate heroism and individual remembrance, further democratising the practice of commemoration. Again, the regimental dead were fully listed, albeit in rank order, with some regiments, such as the Royal Scots Fusiliers and the King's Own Scottish Borderers, using the opportunity to extend the memorial record back to previous imperial campaigns.[57] As General Leach explained on unveiling the Argyll and Sutherland Highlanders' memorial at Stirling castle in 1907:

> it would form a link between the present and the past. In the young soldier it would awaken a feeling of pride in his new regiment. To the older soldier . . . the long list of names engraved on its sides would bring back to them vivid reminiscences of many a hard fought struggle and perhaps sad and tender memories of lost friends and comrades.[58]

Yet, despite the rhetoric of continuity from within the military establishment, the Boer War marked a new junction point in the relationship between the army and civil society. This meant that some scope also existed for experimentation with new memorial forms. Most importantly, thousands of Scots joined the imperial yeomanry corps and Volunteer service battalions as 'citizen soldiers' for temporary duty overseas, their motives ranging from empire loyalty to financial expediency.[59] At a time when Scottish recruitment to the regular army was in decline, citizen service reduced the 'otherness' of military service and intensified popular identification with the figure of the Scottish soldier. The impact of this reduction in distance between the home front and the fighting front can be traced in greater civilian involvement in the raising of military monuments, prefiguring Great War developments. This was evidenced not only in a broader subscription base for the major regimental memorials, but also in a new range of opportunities for collective commemoration which drew on the school, the workplace or the locality. Civic memorials were particularly prominent, with examples at Hawick (1903), Alloa (1904), Dumbarton (1904) and Falkirk (1906), which paid tribute to the dead of the town and district, regardless of military formation.[60] A further new commemorative medium was the functional memorial, often associated with educational settings, where remembrance of the war dead could be linked symbolically with the rising generation. Prominent examples were the new library at Trinity College Glenalmond, or the Conan Doyle Transvaal Scholarship scheme inaugurated at Edinburgh University.[61] Indeed, Scotland's official national war memorial was 'the Queen Victoria School for the Sons of Scottish Sailors and Soldiers', opened at Dunblane in 1908, with some regiments, such as the Queen's Own Cameron Highlanders, preferring to direct the bulk of their memorial fundraising to this project.[62] Even in more conventional monuments there were subtle shifts in iconography, suggesting a greater familiarity with the actual experience of war. Now, the typical Scottish soldier was portrayed in khaki and in active service poses – on scouting duty, defending a wounded comrade or bareheaded with rifle at the ready – as if in capturing the 'heroic' there could be no escape from the destructive gaze of modern warfare.

The Great War

Scottish efforts to commemorate the dead of the Great War were fuelled by a hunger for permanence. Half a million unmarked British graves were left in the old frontlines, many hardly recognisable as resting places in the conventional sense. The need to confront the annihilation of war with an affirming tribute was captured in the unpolished rhetoric of 'The War Memorial', published by *The Scotsman* in 1919:

> Lay its foundation deep
> Here, where the heroes sleep;
> To meet the sky –
> Their name must never die! [63]

Figure 29.4
Remembering the fallen: a service of commemoration at the Scottish National War Memorial, Edinburgh castle, 1958. The memorial was designed by Sir John Lorimer and opened in 1927.

Compared with newer combatant nations such as Australia or Canada, Scotland was at least able to draw upon familiar rituals of memorialisation to give meaning to individual and collective sacrifice.[64] To date, most scholarly attention in this context has focused on the Scottish National War Memorial at Edinburgh castle. Described as 'the most flamboyantly monumental of British memorials', its use of Christian imagery and historical symbols of Scottishness, including chapels dedicated to the Scottish regiments, has been interpreted as reaffirming a unique imperial destiny.[65] Like its ill-fated predecessor on Calton Hill, however, this stylised, elite attempt to orchestrate a national tribute had also to take account of commemoration at a local level. Here the dynamics of this were immediate and personal. Reversing declining recruiting patterns, the war had left communities across Scotland in mourning for a new tragic generation of 'citizen soldiers'. The result was, in Lord Rosebery's words, 'a hurricane season of memorials'.[66] Indeed, Great War memorials remain Scotland's most widespread public monument, with a total of 1,545 currently listed in the *UK National War Memorials Inventory*.[67]

The novel scale of the war encouraged immediate memorialisation, with calls for 'rolls of service' to be established within a fortnight of its outbreak.[68] By early 1916, it was already clear that the focus of remembrance would be on those who had fallen in the 'Great European War', rather than mere participants. Tensions surrounding the appropriate level of commemoration had become evident even before the inception of the Edinburgh castle scheme, as rival 'Scottish' and 'National' schemes to honour the latest tragic hero, Lord Kitchener, placed demands on the subscribing public.[69] Even more controversial was the choice of appropriate memorial forms, as proponents debated the respective merits of the 'functional' and the 'artistic'. Although a scheme for the housing of widows and orphans had been one of the earliest proposed 'war memorials', this utilitarian approach was fiercely resisted by Scotland's arts establishment, who formed an Advisory Committee on War Memorials under the auspices of the Royal Scottish Academy in 1919.[70] 'The artistic monument, devoted to the sole purpose of doing honour to the dead', they claimed, embodied the feelings of the bereaved 'in a more direct and impressive manner' than in any utilitarian scheme that might masquerade under the title of 'war memorial'.[71] Equally to be feared was the absence of a cultured direction in the production and placing of such 'monumental' memorials, particularly given the poor quality of some of Scotland's recent specimens.[72] Clearly, professional vested interests were at stake, particularly voiced in the plea that construction should be 'entrusted to native artists and executed in Scotland'. But such sentiments also mirrored wider concerns amongst European combatant nations that the 'sacred' nature of remembrance should not become corrupted by the concrete needs of the living and the 'profanity' of modern technology.[73]

Although the incursion of mass production methods would prove impossible to resist, it was the artistic vision that triumphed. Remembrance did find practical expression through the endowment of church buildings and furnishings, with the gift of communion tables and vessels proving an ideal Presbyterian compromise with pre-Reformation tradition. Full-scale functional memorials of a secular type were less common, with notable exceptions making a vital link between commemoration and healing, such as the Arran War Memorial Hospital and the housing developments for disabled ex-servicemen at Callander and Longniddry, sponsored by the Scottish Veterans' Garden City Association.[74] In contrast, smaller functional schemes often elected to include a recreational dimension, in the form of village halls, parks and bowling clubs, while a few localities selected memorials with a more passive use, including fountains, clock towers, seats and sundials.[75]

The vast majority of memorials, however, followed the commemorative styles that had become firmly established in Scotland over the previous century. The simple plaque or tablet remained the most ubiquitous form, still found frequently in churches but also in village halls, post offices, railway stations and even a lifeboat station.[76] Despite their simple, standardised design, they capture the breadth of Scotland's Great War experience. In some cases the focus is collective, remembering workmates and fellow parishioners who enlisted together in doomed battalions, but an even greater number are dedicated to individuals. While officers still predominate, now other ranks could also claim their sacred space. The inscription commemorating Sergeant Robert Johnstone in Kingsbarns Parish Church is typically terse but full of meaning: 'An only child who died of wounds received in action in France on the 15th April 1917, aged 20'.

In contrast to these self-effacing tributes, it is the highly visible town and village memorials that have attracted the most critical attention. With the Scottish National War Memorial serving as the major focus for regimental commemoration, civic Scotland took over the business of raising military monuments. The mechanics of local procurement relied on the same machinery used in nineteenth-century public subscription projects. War memorial committees, however, while still limited in social profile, tended to be more broadly constituted than their elite predecessors, attracting municipal leaders, businessmen and other local interest groups. Designs were usually chosen by open or invited competition, or commissioned from pattern books and supplied direct from the Aberdeen granite yards, with lettering and erection completed locally. The total cost of Scotland's memorials has been estimated at £652,000 – equivalent to an expenditure of £6 per head of the fallen.[77]

Despite operating within the traditional idiom, their diversity is striking as many committees attempted to give Scotland's wartime contribution a distinctive physical expression. Crosses predominated, including many engraved Celtic types, but the popular abstract forms of obelisks, pillars and cairns also persisted, with architectural forms such as gates, walls and cenotaphs also well represented. In figurative terms, statues of servicemen outnumbered the allegorical sculptures. As in the Boer War, the ordinary Scottish soldier is shown in modern service dress, sometimes in action or on guard, but more often at rest or mourning his comrades.[78] These portrayals, accompanied frequently by the naming of the dead in alphabetical order, mark a further landmark in extending the scope of heroic commemoration. Nor were these tributes intended to stand alone. Rolls of Honour, lovingly and painstakingly compiled by local volunteer committees, were intended to make the memorials 'live' and assist in their interpretation. These often had a strong democratic ethos too, including not only women's wartime service but also the contribution of whole civilian communities.[79]

Criticisms of the 'visual bankruptcy' and 'mundanity' of Scotland's Great War monuments, and condemnation of their failure to engage with emerging experimental art forms, neglect their shared sense of purpose.[80] It was traditional art that alone appeared capable of providing an enduring statement of the magnitude of sacrifice. The need to emphasise continuity in terms of the values for which the war had been fought was equally vital for the monument builders. Anything less would devalue the memory of the dead and increase the pain of bereavement. Indeed, rather than a single finite act, the construction of a war memorial was intended to mark the beginning of the process of commemoration. As the marchioness of Ailsa commented at the unveiling of the Saltcoats War Memorial in 1922:

> This is a foundation stone on which to build the structure of a better, a cleaner, a wholesomer life for everyone . . . We have simply got to give the best we have in the memory of these men. It is the only memorial worth anything.[81]

Such ambitions would soon wither in the harsh conditions of postwar Scotland, but the memorials themselves remained a silent, insistent presence, inserting remembrance into the texture of everyday life. This perhaps was their success, rather than any pretension to artistic distinction.

'More than cold stone'

During the interwar decades Scottish regiments returned to the business of home defence and imperial soldiering. In the words of one recruitment call for the Royal Scots Fusiliers, 'there could be no finer memorial to the many men who have fallen than a living battalion'.[82] The Second World War, however, would test the resilience of the Scottish military identity as the specialisation and complexity of modern warfare expanded the possibilities of service beyond the traditional battalions. Coupled with a more visible UK national state, and a growing sense of 'Britishness' that developed out of common wartime experiences, the result was a new cultural climate for memorialisation.

By the end of the war civil servants noted that Scottish public opinion was still far from 'crystallised' on what form any specific national commemoration would take.[83] Nevertheless, a powerful consensus had developed that there should be a radical departure from Great War exemplars, since, as one correspondent to *The Scotsman* commented, 'the general revulsion against destruction and degradation of war has produced distaste for memorials of the older convention'.[84] For some, like the earl of Crawford, this distaste was based on the 'lack of dignity' displayed in these monuments, but a more general and heartfelt sentiment was expressed by one ex-serviceman, who commented that 'it is more than cold stone that is wanted'.[85] The fate of the Scottish War Memorials Advisory Committee was eloquent on the new spirit of the age. It was established in 1945 in order to mobilise the Scottish arts community in anticipation of 'a spate of ill considered war memorials', but was wound up four years later without any such flood materialising. Defiantly preaching 'the enriching power of beauty that is useless', its own scheme for the reconstruction of Stirling castle as a 'national shrine' singularly failed to rally popular enthusiasm.[86]

Instead, an alternative search had already begun for memorials that would be 'of a forward looking character more closely relevant to the needs of modern Scotland'.[87] As in the rest of the UK, two main methods of commemoration emerged. While neither was innovative in itself, their cumulative effect was to signal a major departure from older symbolic forms.[88] The first response was to make additions to existing memorials, followed by a simple ceremony of re-dedication. Here the naming of the dead was stripped down to its essentials. The majority of civic and regimental commemoration followed this practice, and while the Scottish National War Memorial remained unaltered as 'an integral work of art', a further 50,000 names were added to its Roll of Honour.[89] A small number of new visual memorials were also built, but like the Commando sculpture at Spean Bridge, or the Free French monument at Greenock, these tended to reflect Scotland's new strategic role as a remote training ground or a holding area for allied forces, rather than any distinctive Scottish military experience.

In the second mode of commemoration the balance between practicality and abstract remembrance shifted further as a new wave of functional memorials emerged, designed to 'look after the living'.[90] These included a range of small-scale, but imaginative, schemes, including the provision of a mountaineers' hut at Glen Brittle on the Isle of Skye.[91] In Ardrossan, the 'Welcome Home and Commemoration Fund' simply gave each returning serviceman or

Figure 29.5 The Commando Memorial, Spean Bridge, Inverness-shire. Sculpted by Scott Sutherland, the memorial was unveiled in 1952.

their relatives a gift of £6 – a perfect counterpoint to the previous generation's outlay on monumental tributes.[92] Meanwhile, a number of larger social welfare projects jostled to claim the status of 'national memorial' in the vacuum left by the lack of any conventional architectural scheme. Of these, the most interesting is perhaps the Thistle Foundation, established in 1944 by Sir Francis and Lady Tudsbery.[93] While the Second World War often appears as a caesura in military commemoration, this apparently utilitarian project is a reminder of the difficulty in breaking entirely with the traditional repertoire of memorial forms. The Foundation's self-contained housing complex at Craigmillar was designed as 'an entirely novel and unique provision for Scotland's most gravely disabled ex-servicemen'.[94] Yet at its heart was the Robin Chapel, built in memory of the Tudsberys' son, who had been killed during the last days of the war. Fusing practical public benefaction and Christian intercession, this was a Scottish 'chantry' for the twentieth century.

Figure 29.6 The Thistle Foundation's Robin Chapel, Edinburgh, built in memory of Lieutenant Robin Tudsbery. The chapel was designed by John F. Matthew and dedicated in 1953.

From heroes to victims

The changing post-war world did not favour the Scottish military establishment as its historic regiments faced both a withdrawal from empire and a dwindling local recruiting base. While retaining a grasp on public consciousness, not least through the process of regimental amalgamation and disbandment, the Scottish military tradition increasingly began to function as a convenient historical artefact in 'branding' Scotland, rather than as a living contribution to national identity. Yet, despite this background, Scotland's military monuments confounded gloomy prognoses of neglect and obsolescence.[95] Like the rest of the UK, new or revived modes of observance actually developed during the course of the later twentieth century – paradoxically as the numbers of actual veterans from the world wars became fewer. This development seems linked to the general growth of more expressive forms of mourning, itself reflecting the gradual erosion of the religious protocols of behaviour, which had traditionally prescribed 'appropriate' bereavement rituals.[96] Like roadside shrines and mass floral tributes, it would seem that modern war memorials have become part of a new stylised cult of 'community remembrance'.[97]

The second half of the century also witnessed a renewed burst of monumental construction. This featured some striking returns to nineteenth-century precedents in terms of type and form. For example, the Royal Scots Fusiliers' monument at Ayr (1951), with its anonymous figure in modern battledress, by the veteran sculptor Pilkington Jackson, is firmly located in the regimental memorial tradition, albeit representing a unit that had already been amalgamated to form a new Lowland infantry regiment.[98] Historic conflicts have similarly continued to fascinate civilian enthusiasts from a range of political and religious backgrounds. The most prolific in terms of new monuments have been the Wars of the Covenants and the Jacobite Rebellions, but the service of the International Brigade in the Spanish Civil War was also recognised by a burst of commemorative activity from the 1970s onwards, resulting in plaques and stones of remembrance.[99] Yet beneath this apparent continuity, there have been subtle, but fundamental, shifts in the nature of commemoration which have gathered ground in the early twenty-first century. A number of diffuse cultural processes have been at work here, evident across the UK and western Europe. Reflecting changing attitudes to class, gender and empire, as well as an awareness of the brutalising effects of modern warfare, the first can be interpreted as the continued extension of the scope of military commemoration to include not only service personnel but also marginalised social groups.[100] Typical is the 'Memorial to Women of World War Two', unveiled at Whitehall in 2005, featuring sculptures of women engaged in war work.[101] Frequently, this process has been reinforced by the portrayal of the subjects of commemoration as victims of war rather than active, heroic participants. Indeed, the drive towards 'inclusivity' found a particularly eloquent expression in another of London's new wave of war memorials. Dedicated to 'the millions of conscripted animals' who served in twentieth-century conflicts, it depicts two bronze mules with the legend 'They Had no Choice.'[102]

The temptation to replicate the latest types of collective or composite monument has so far been resisted in Scotland. Instead, local communities have preferred to join the quest to rescue the memory of 'forgotten VCs' or 'forgotten tragedies of war'.[103] Typical of this impulse is the 2007 memorial at Aberfoyle which honours the Women's Land Army Timber Corps as 'the forgotten corps of World War Two'.[104] It is, however, in the latest 'Scottish National War Memorial' that the current themes in military commemoration have found their greatest resonance. Unveiled in August 2007, on the site of the battle of Passchendaele, this is a granite Celtic cross dedicated to all the Scottish soldiers who died in the First World War. There is little attempt here to describe their exploits in battle, or to justify the cause they fought for. Nor are they depicted as products of a heroic military past. Instead, the memorial is simply inscribed 'Scotland'.[105] It is as if Scotland were mourning itself. The collective symbolism would be familiar to earlier generations of monument builders; the identification of nationhood with victimhood would not.

Notes

I am very happy to acknowledge the support of the Carnegie Trust for the Universities of Scotland in undertaking research for this chapter.

1. C. Moriarty, 'The material culture of Great War remembrance', *Journal of Contemporary History*, vol. 34, no. 4 (1999), pp. 653–62; J. Winter, 'The generation of memory: Reflections on the "memory boom" in contemporary historical studies', *Bulletin of the German Historical Institute, Washington*, vol. 27 (2000), pp. 69–92.
2. This definition is developed from M. Quinlan's more restrictive formula, *British War Memorials* (Hereford: Authors OnLine, 2005), p. xvi.
3. These include, for example, an increased role for memory in the grieving process, P. Jalland, *Death in the Victorian Family* (Oxford: Oxford University Press, 1996), p. 288.
4. A. Borg, *War Memorials from Antiquity to the Present* (London: Leo Cooper, 1991), pp. 104–7; T. W. Laqueur, 'Memory and naming in the Great War', in J. R. Gillis (ed.), *Commemorations: The Politics of National Identity* (Princeton, NJ: Princeton University Press, 1994), pp. 150–67.
5. Two classic, contrasting approaches are J. Winter, *Sites of Memory, Sites of Mourning: The Great War in European Cultural History* (Cambridge: Cambridge University Press, 1995) and G. L. Mosse, *Fallen Soldiers: Reshaping the Memory of the World Wars* (Oxford: Oxford University Press, 1990). For a new integrative treatment, see S. Goebel, 'Re-membered and re-mobilised: The "sleeping dead" in interwar Germany and Britain', *Journal of Contemporary History*, vol. 139, no. 4 (2004), pp. 487–501.
6. National Monuments Register of Scotland [hereafter NMRS], NO55NW 8.03; NMRS, NJ05NW 1.
7. See Royal Commission on the Ancient and Historical Monuments of Scotland [hereafter RCAHMS], *Pictish Symbol Stones: An Illustrated Gazetteer* (Edinburgh: RCAHMS, 1999); W. A. Cummins, *The Age of the Picts* (Stroud: Sutton, 1998); E. Sutherland, *A Guide to the Pictish Stones* (Edinburgh: Birlinn, 1997).
8. P. Morgan, 'Of worms and war', in P. Jupp and C. Gittings (eds),

Death in England: An Illustrated History (Manchester: Manchester University Press, 1999), p. 123.
9. P. Binski, *Medieval Death: Ritual and Representation* (London: British Museum Press, 1996), p. 9.
10. NMRS, NS06SE1. Note also the armed warriors' grave slabs at Knap Chapel, Kilmory, NMRS, NR77NW3.
11. NMRS, NS75NW6.00.
12. M. Glenndinning and A. Mackechnie, *Scottish Architecture* (London: Thames and Hudson, 2004), pp. 48–53.
13. NRMS, NS36SE 10; NRMS, NT47NW 4.00. In England the battle prompted a number of thanksgiving chantries and inspired one of its earliest war memorials – the stained glass window depicting English bowmen at Middleton, Lancashire.
14. *Undertakers' Journal and Monumental Masons' Review*, 22 September 1886, p. 185.
15. G. Morton, *Unionist Nationalism* (East Linton: Tuckwell Press, 1999), p. 95.
16. Ibid. p. 182.
17. Ibid. pp. 177, 181–4.
18. C. A. Strang, *An Illustrated Architectural Guide to the Scottish Borders and Tweed Valley* (Edinburgh: Royal Incorporation of Architects in Scotland, 1994), pp. 91, 142, 207. The battle site itself was marked by a more sober cross in 1910, dedicated to the dead of both sides.
19. 'Memorial monuments etc', *Undertakers' Journal and Monumental Masons' Review*, 23 May 1887, p. 56.
20. For a useful gazetteer, see T. Campbell, *Standing Witnesses: An Illustrated Guide to the Scottish Covenanters* (Edinburgh: Saltire Society, 1996).
21. J. H. Thomson, *The Martyr Graves of Scotland: Being the Travels of a Minster in his Own Country* (Edinburgh: Oliphant, Anderson and Ferrier, 1904), p. 131.
22. *The Orcadian*, 25 August 1888, p. 4.
23. R. L. Stevenson, 'To S. R. Crockett (On Receiving a Dedication)', in *Poems of Today: An Anthology* (London: Sidgwick and Jackson, 1918), p. 36.
24. See S. Smiles, *The Life of Thomas Telford, Civil Engineer. With an Introductory History of Roads and Travelling in Great Britain* (London: John Murray, 1867), p. 201.
25. For one of the few contemporary memorials of the period to another Hanoverian soldier, see A. Reid, 'The churchyards of Prestonpans', *Proceedings of the Society of Antiquaries of Scotland*, vol. 42 (1907), p. 27.

26. J. E. Cookson, *The British Armed Nation, 1793–1815* (Oxford: Clarendon Press, 1997), pp. 126–7; and by the same author, 'The Napoleonic Wars, military Scotland and Tory Highlandism in the early nineteenth century', *Scottish Historical Review*, vol. 78 (1999), pp. 60–1.
27. S. Allan and A. Carswell, *The Thin Red Line: War Empire and Visions of Scotland* (Edinburgh: National Museums of Scotland, 2004), p. 23.
28. The marble memorial in Wellpark Mid-Kirk, Greenock, dedicated to Captain George Stewart of the Black Watch, who fell at Bayonne in 1813, is typical with its carved trophy of arms, cannonballs and draped flag.
29. J. Cleland, *The Annals of Glasgow: Comprising an Account of the Public Buildings, Charities and the Rise and Progress of the City* (Glasgow: J. Smith, 1829), p. 40.
30. Abercromby is also commemorated in Westminster Abbey and in Liverpool. Moore has memorials in St Paul's Cathedral and an equestrian statue at Shorncliffe, Kent.
31. W. Thomson, 'Some antiquities in Benderloch and Lorn', *Proceedings of the Society of Antiquaries of Scotland*, 14 March 1927, pp. 130–1.
32. Cleland, *The Annals*, p. 45; W. Daniell, *A Voyage Round Great Britain*, 8 vols (London: Longman & Co and W. Daniell, 1821), vol. 5.
33. C. McKean, *Edinburgh: An Illustrated Architectural Guide* (Edinburgh: Royal Incorporation of Architects in Scotland, 1992), p. 103.
34. Edinburgh City Archives [hereafter ECA], National Monument of Scotland, Minute Book, 1816–47 (SL 103 1/1), 9 January 1816.
35. See *Edinburgh Evening Courant*, 23 April 1818, p. 3; 4 March 1819, p. 4; 8 March 1819, p. 4; 22 January 1820, p. 1.
36. ECA, National Monument of Scotland, Minute Book, 24 February 1819.
37. Defaulting subscribers proved a chronic problem for the organisers: ECA, National Monument of Scotland, Share Transfer Records (SL103/6/5). One of the alternative monuments was the Waterloo Tower at Peniel Heugh built by the marquis of Lothian between 1817 and 1824. Another memorial that offers an interesting counterpoint to the main currents of Napoleonic commemoration was erected at Penicuik in 1830, dedicated to French prisoners-of-war who had died locally in captivity: I. Macdougall, *The Prisoners at Penicuik: French and Other Prisoners of War 1803–1814* (Dalkeith: Midlothian District Libraries, 1989).
38. The High Church, Beith, Ayrshire, holds a particularly fine example of the smaller type of memorial, with a tablet depicting the death in battle of Captain Alexander Wilson at the Khyber Pass in 1842: *An Illustrated Guide to Beith High Church* (Beith: n.p., 1983). For the raising of Lord Clyde's statue in his Glasgow birthplace, see *The Scotsman*, 22 October 1863, p. 3.

39. Attempts at relocation in the former case caused fury in the Scottish military establishment, *The Scotsman*, 19 February 1887, p. 12.
40. An early example is the 79th Highlanders' Crimean monument in Dean Cemetery, Edinburgh, *The Scotsman*, 4 July 1857, p. 3.
41. Note, for example, the speech of Colonel Mathias on the unveiling of the monument to the Gordon Highlanders who fell in India, *The Scotsman*, 3 December 1900, p. 9.
42. *The Scotsman*, 9 July 1861, p. 2; 16 April 1862, p. 3. See, for example, *The Scotsman*, 8 July 1882, p. 6, for the memorial obelisk to the 72nd Highlanders in the Afghan Wars.
43. J. Colborne and F. Brine, *Memorials of the Brave or Resting Places of our Fallen Heroes in the Crimea and at Scutari* (London: n.p., 1857), pp. 42, 72, 79, 93.
44. E. M. Spiers, *The Scottish Soldier and Empire, 1854–1902* (Edinburgh: Edinburgh University Press, 2006), pp. 4–12. For an international perspective, see Mosse, *Fallen Soldiers*, pp. 45–6.
45. 'Memorial Monuments etc', *Undertakers' Journal and Monumental Masons' Review*, 22 January 1887, p. 8.
46. H. Strachan, 'Scotland's military identity', *Scottish Historical Review*, vol. 85 (2006), pp. 315–32.
47. *The Scotsman*, 3 April 1872, p. 8.
48. Ibid. 14 November 1887, p. 8. For selection of the design, see 'Memorial monuments etc', *Undertakers' Journal and Monumental Masons' Review*, 22 June 1887, p. 77.
49. *The Scotsman*, 9 September 1892, p. 4.
50. See Colonel Sir J. Gildea, *For Remembrance: South Africa 1899–1902* (London: Eyre and Spottiswoode, 1911). He lists fifty-two Scottish memorials, but this understates the true number, particularly of smaller and individual monuments, which is probably in the range of eighty to a hundred. Note also Spiers, *Scottish Soldier*, pp. 204–6.
51. *The Scotsman*, 14 December 1899, p. 5.
52. Airlie was commemorated by a massive Scottish baronial tower on his estate at Cortachy. Wauchope's memorials were less assuming, if more numerous, including a window dedicated to his memory in St Giles, Edinburgh, as well as monuments at Niddrie, Yetholm and York, and in South Africa, *The Scotsman*, 27 November 1900, p. 5; 21 May 1901, p. 8.
53. One of the first was the Celtic cross erected to the fallen of F Company of the 2nd Volunteer Battalion at Girvan Cemetery: Ayrshire Archives, Ayr, CO3/39/31, Minutes of the Girvan Cemetery Committee, 8 September 1904.
54. *The Muster Roll of Angus 1899–1901* (Arbroath: Brodie and Salmond, 1902). For examples of these memorials, see *Highland Light Infantry*

Chronicle, October 1906, p. 129, for the unveiling of the Highland Light Infantry memorial in Kelvingrove Park, Glasgow; *The Scotsman*, 7 July 1905, p. 5, for the Gordons' memorial at Edinburgh castle and 17 November, p. 11, for the Scots Greys' memorial at Princes Street, Edinburgh. South African examples include memorials to the Gordons at Bloemfontein and Doornkop, and to the Black Watch and the Highland Brigade at Magersfontein, the latter subscribed by readers of the *Glasgow Weekly Herald*, Gildea, *For Remembrance*, pp. 264–94.

55. Quinlan, *British War Memorials*, p. xx.
56. He had also designed the 1887 Black Watch statue, *Glasgow Herald*, 11 July 1933, p. 11.
57. *The Scotsman*, 3 November 1902, p. 11; 5 October 1906, p. 9. See also Spiers, *Scottish Soldier*, p. 206.
58. 'The Argyll and Sutherland war memorial', *The Thin Red Line*, February 1907, pp. 150–3.
59. E. W. McFarland, '"Empire enlarging genius": Scottish Imperial Yeomanry volunteers in the Boer War', *War in History*, vol. 13, no. 3 (2006), pp. 281–310.
60. See, for example, *The Scotsman*, 24 August 1904, p. 6, for the Hawick unveiling by Lord Roberts.
61. Gildea, *For Remembrance*, pp. 264–94. This bursary was funded by £1,000 in proceeds from Conan Doyle's history of the war, *The Scotsman*, 29 November 1902, p. 9.
62. Also a memorial to the late sovereign, over £50,000 was raised by public subscription, *The Scotsman*, 29 September 1908, p. 5. For the Camerons, see *The Scotsman*, 4 October 1904, p. 9. A further functional regimental tribute was the Gordon Highlanders' Memorial Institute in Aberdeen, *The Scotsman*, 25 August 1902, p. 6.
63. Ibid. 8 March 1919, p. 6.
64. P. Hoffenberg, 'Landscape, memory and the Australian war experience, 1915–18', *Journal of Contemporary History*, vol. 36, no. 1 (2002), pp. 111–31.
65. See A. Calder, 'Meditation on memorials', in A. Calder (ed.), *Disasters and Heroes: On War, Memory and Representation* (Cardiff: University of Wales Press, 2004) pp. 3–27, and A. Calder, 'The Scottish National War Memorial', in W. Kidd and B. Murdoch (eds), *Memory and Memorials: The Commemorative Century* (Aldershot: Ashgate, 2004), pp. 61–75. Note also I. Hay, *Their Name Liveth: The Book of the Scottish National War Memorial* (East Kilbride: Edinburgh Trustees of the Scottish National War Memorial, 1985).
66. *The Scotsman*, 20 February 1919, p. 6.
67. See www.ukniwm.org.uk, accessed on 8 September, 2011. One of

the best treatments of British memorials is offered by Alex King in *Memorials of the Great War in Britain: The Symbolism and Politics of Remembrance* (Oxford: Berg, 1998).
68. *The Scotsman*, 18 August 1914, p. 3; 14 September 1914, p. 4; 17 September 1914, p. 8; Winter, *Sites of Memory*, pp. 80–1.
69. *The Scotsman*, 7 August 1916, p. 8.
70. Ibid. 31 August 1914, p. 7.
71. Ibid. 27 March 1919, p. 4.
72. Ibid. 23 April 1919, p. 5.
73. Mosse, *Cult of the Fallen Soldier*, pp. 90–1.
74. *Ardrossan and Saltcoats Herald*, 26 August 1921, p. 3; 14 July 1922, p. 2; *The Scotsman*, 21 April 1919, p. 3. For a discussion of this link, see S. Goebel, 'Beyond discourse? Bodies and memory of two World Wars', *Journal of Contemporary History*, vol. 142, no. 2 (2007), pp. 377–85.
75. A prominent example of the latter type is the Heart of Midlothian War Memorial, Haymarket, Edinburgh (1921–2).
76. There are 497 of these listed for Scotland in the *UK National War Memorials Inventory*.
77. G. Bell, 'Monuments to the Fallen: Scottish war memorials of the Great War' (unpublished PhD thesis, University of Strathclyde, 1993), p. 463.
78. For Scotland, the *UK National War Memorials Inventory* contains 283 crosses, 108 obelisks, 99 columns and 18 cairns.
79. For examples of this much under-used source, see J. Minto Robertson (ed.), *The War Book of Turriff and Twelve Miles Around* (Banff and Turriff: n.p., 1926); S. Lindsay (ed.), *Coatbridge and the Great War* (Glasgow: Hay Nisbet, 1919).
80. See Bell, 'Monuments', pp. 235–8.
81. *Ardrossan and Saltcoats Herald*, 2 June 1922, p. 2.
82. Ibid. 16 April 1920, p. 1; 4 March 1921, p. 3.
83. National Records of Scotland [hereafter NRS], Edinburgh, Scottish War Memorials Advisory Council 1945–9 (SWMAC), HH1/668, note by Scottish Home and Health Department, 20 November 1945.
84. *The Scotsman*, 18 June 1949, p. 6.
85. NRS, SWMAC, HH1/668/50, Report of Meeting, 23 January 1945; *The Scotsman*, 3 November 1944, p. 4.
86. See NRS, SWMAC, *How Shall We Honour Them?* (Edinburgh: n.p., [1945]), pp. 5–8; SWMAC, First Annual Report, 1946.
87. This was the personal view of Joseph Westwood, Scottish Secretary of State: NRS, SWMAC, HH1/668, 27600/59.
88. For the wider context, see Winter, *Sites of Memory*, pp. 9–10; Berg, *War Memorials*, pp. 141–2.
89. *The Scotsman*, 16 June 1949, p. 5.

90. For the UK background, see *Parliamentary Debates (Hansard), House of Lords*, 14 February 1945, cols 1,016–54.
91. National Library of Scotland, Edinburgh, GB.1322 (9), Leaflet, *Glen Brittle Memorial Hut Appeal* (Stockport: British Mountaineering Council, 1959).
92. *Ardrossan and Saltcoats Herald*, 6 June 1947, p. 4. The small balance was handed over to the Council to create a garden of remembrance.
93. NRS, Thistle Foundation, HH1/671; *The Scotsman*, 6 September 1950, p. 7.
94. NRS, Thistle Foundation, HH1/671; *The Scotsman*, 22 August 1945, p. 1.
95. Bell, 'Scottish war memorials', p. 619.
96. E. W. McFarland, 'Working with death: An oral history of funeral directing in late twentieth-century Scotland', *Oral History*, vol. 36, no. 1 (2008), pp. 69–80.
97. D. L. Steinberg and A. Kear (eds), *Mourning Diana: Nation, Culture and the Performance of Grief* (London: Taylor and Francis, 1999), pp. 3–4.
98. R. Close, *Ayrshire and Arran: An Illustrated Architectural Guide* (Edinburgh: Royal Incorporation of Architects in Scotland, 1992), p. 23.
99. Note, for example, the work of the Covenanter Memorials Association, formed in 1966 (available at www.covenanter.org.uk, accessed on 8 September 2011); and the 1745 Association, formed in 1946 (available at www.1745association.org.uk, accessed on 8 September 2011). See also C. Williams, W. Alexander and J. Gorman, *Memorials of the Spanish Civil War* (Stroud: Alan Sutton Publishing Ltd, 1996); the UKNWMI lists thirteen of these in locations such as Aberdeen, Prestonpans and Kirkcaldy.
100. Mosse, *Cult of the Fallen Soldier*, pp. 219–21.
101. *Daily Telegraph*, 9 July 2005, p. 12.
102. *The Times*, 26 November 2004, p. 23.
103. See *The Scotsman*, 12 April 2007, p. 24, for the dedication of a new monument to Sergeant James McKechnie VC, a Crimean War hero, buried in a pauper's grave in Glasgow. An example of the latter type is the 1993 memorial unveiled at Ardrossan to mark the fiftieth anniversary of the sinking of HMS *Dasher* off Arran.
104. *Glasgow Herald*, 15 September 2007, p. 8.
105. *Sunday Herald*, 26 August 2007, p. 26.

30
Scottish Military Collections

STUART ALLAN

More than most walks of life, the profession of arms proliferates historic collections and museums to house them. It is in the nature of the military experience, and of the culture that surrounds this aspect of human behaviour, that individuals, families and institutions place value upon, and seek to preserve, objects associated with the practice of warfare. The connection between military prowess, status and prestige is an ancient, and perhaps a fundamental, one in most cultures. Among the powerful, one means by which such association is carried down the generations is through the inheritance of prized heirlooms. More democratically, military service for those of any rank in life connects individuals, living or remembered, directly with the fate of their own societies, with affairs of state and, intermittently, with the great events of world history. For those who experience war as an interlude in lives otherwise following more peaceful paths, material mementoes of what can be a profound personal experience take on a quality of preciousness which will see them survive while the other detritus of a life lived are worn out or disposed of. Add to this the antiquarian impulse to appreciate and collect military artefacts for their own sake, and the museum curator's task to inform and illustrate a society's understanding of its past, then the haul of treasure, one way or another, becomes considerable.

Worldwide, material culture looms large in the functioning of the military occupation. Its importance in practical terms, the equipment required to do the job, is all but matched by the relationship between objects and ideas about tradition, reputation and honour – the badge worn, the sword carried, the trophy won. Scotland is no different in this regard. Indeed, more than many places Scotland has been susceptible to the association between military service and a sense of self-worth, between war and reputation. Accordingly, the Scottish military tradition is represented today in terms of material culture in a wealth of public and private collections. These collections are not merely illustrative of the narrative of Scottish military service; they are of its essence. In no small measure it is in the iconography, in design and distinctions of dress and insignia, in relics, souvenirs and commemorative works of art that a military manifestation of Scottish identity has grown, been recognised and endured. Inevitably, the peculiarities of Scotland's history have influenced how and why such collections have formed. Their evolution and presentation says something in turn about how this cultural inheritance has been regarded, not only by the practitioners, but also across Scottish society and in the wider world.

One palpable influence in the practice of collecting Scottish history has been the desire to record and preserve that deemed to be distinctively Scottish. While a concern with distinctiveness of one kind or another would be a quality shared by many collections of historical artefacts, Scotland's constitutional context conditioned a preoccupation amongst collectors with defining and celebrating Scottish nationhood, ancient and cultural, over and above regional or local identities. This interest impacted in different ways on collecting activity in relation to Scottish artefacts dating from before the Unions of Crown and Parliament, and on collecting and representing the Scottish–British military identity that developed in the centuries thereafter.

Although antiquarian studies emerged in Scotland, as elsewhere, in the work of individual private scholars, military men among them, the beginnings of a broadly systematic approach to collecting may be found in the inception, in Edinburgh in 1780, of the Society of Antiquaries of Scotland and the founding of the Society's Museum of Antiquities the following year. While it clearly followed the lead of the Society of Antiquaries of London formed in 1707, of which body several of the leading lights of the Scottish society were also fellows, the Scottish society's approach was to be much influenced by the progress of antiquarian studies in the Nordic countries, and it set about creating, through its growing collections, a framework for a distinctively Scottish prehistory in a northern European context. However, from the first, medieval and 'modern' material was also collected.[1]

Within this collection, examples of military artefacts were secured, classified and displayed in different contexts. Prehistoric material included arrowheads, spearheads, axeheads and knife blades whose implicit function related not only to warfare but to hunting and other domestic activity and ritual. Such items were among some of the

Society's very first acquisitions: a hoard of bronze artefacts recovered from Duddingston Loch outside Edinburgh that included fragments of spearheads, swords and dagger blades.[2] In the museum displays and catalogues assembled by the Society such material would come to be categorised by typology, material and period, alongside other types of archaeological find. Among other outstanding Society accessions from the 1780s was a Roman era monumental stone commemorating a native soldier of the Brigantes, and a two-handed Scottish sword of the sixteenth century.[3] The original collection also extended its reach forward to touch on the military mobilisations of the modern era. A curio of Scottish service with the armies of foreign powers during the seventeenth century was acquired in the form of a pair of spurs said to have been removed from the corpse of King Gustavus Adolphus of Sweden by his Scottish aide-de-camp, Colonel Hugh Somerville, after his death at Lützen in 1632.[4] In 1781 the Society's founder, the eleventh earl of Buchan, presented to its new museum the painted guidon of a troop of dragoons raised in 1689 in the interest of William of Orange by Buchan's ancestor Lord Cardross.[5]

If in the ensuing years the Antiquaries were occasionally a little wary of rousing Scottish patriotic sentiment there was less circumspection when, during the 1820s, the Society's attention briefly turned towards a piece of historic heavy artillery.[6] National honour was invoked when prominent Fellows took up an informal initiative on the part of Sir Walter Scott and pressed for the return to Edinburgh castle of the fifteenth-century bombard known as Mons Meg, the great gun that had been removed to the Tower of London in 1754 along with other redundant ordnance in line with the demilitarising measures of the 1746 Disarming Act. The Antiquaries were careful to couch their formal request to the Master General of the Ordnance in terms that could not offend the king, to whose pleasure the matter of 'this curious relic of our antient [sic] fortifications in Edinburgh' was to be referred, but when royal assent was duly forthcoming, and in 1828 the gun shipped to Leith, its subsequent passage to Edinburgh castle was attended by crowds of spectators, the ringing of church bells and a procession that included pipers, members of Sir Walter Scott's Celtic Society and others bedecked in tartan, as well as a military escort.[7] The popular interest in this most formidable weapon of a fifteenth-century king of Scots was something of itself more potent than any strictly antiquarian enthusiasm.

One popular subject of collecting during the first decades of the nineteenth century was the Jacobite rising of 1745–6, an interest that sat within the wholesale rehabilitation of the martial traditions of

Highland culture following the post-Culloden period of persecution and stigma. The Antiquaries had entered their first Jacobite relic into the collection as early as 1783 and such material was becoming openly prized, the stuff of many Scottish private collections. By the 1820s any lingering political sensitivities around this subject were extinguished, not least by virtue of royal patronage for the growing nostalgic and antiquarian interest in the Stuarts and their Highland armies. In 1820 the Prince Regent made a personal presentation to clan chief Ranald MacDonald of Clanranald who, much to the future king's approval, was in the habit of attending at court in Highland dress. The gift Clanranald received was an elaborate silver basket-hilted back-sword, previously the property of Charles Edward Stuart and captured with the Pretender's baggage after Culloden.[8] An artefact of this quality and provenance was at the prestigious end of the recognition, acquisition and even manufacture of Jacobite relics. Broadswords, targes, powder flasks and pistols would number strongly among objects prized for their associations with the 'Forty-Five and earlier risings.

The assimilation of the Scottish Highlands into the British mainstream, and the new-found respectability and desirability of a Highland heritage, was the context for display, and indeed of collecting, in some of the great private houses of the realm. In Scotland, as elsewhere, it had become fashionable for aristocratic seats to be decorated with the arms, armour and portraiture that signified an ancestry of military service to the crown. For those who could again boast of chiefly origins, an array of Highland weaponry became an essential element of the domestic interior, as indeed of personal display on the right occasion. Always free from the taint of Jacobitism, and therefore ahead of the game in this respect, were the dukes of Argyll, chiefs of Clan Campbell. In 1745-6, while the family's Argyllshire Militia was in the field on crown service against the Jacobites, work had begun on building the third duke's elegant aristocratic residence at Inveraray. In the 1770s his descendant, Field Marshal John, the fifth duke, completed the castle interior and created in the great hall a display of ornamental weaponry. A contemporary visitor praised the impressive visual impact of the hall 'most nobly hung with armour in stars and every other species of pile'.[9] The array of wall-mounted weapons included pole-arms and broadswords of earlier centuries, but the displays relied for their geometric effect on quantities of British-issue Land Pattern muskets originally obtained to arm the Argyllshire Militia in 1745. To these were added in 1784 the arms of the Western Fencible Regiment, disbanded the previous year.[10]

Figure 30.1
The Armoury Hall at Inveraray castle.

The dual identity of hereditary clan chief and British army officer brought about similar accumulations in the ensuing years. The last decade of the eighteenth century and the first of the nineteenth were times of heavy military recruitment from Highland estates, and the formation of fencible, militia, yeomanry and Volunteer units across the country. Scotland was awash with weapons during the long wars against Revolutionary and Napoleonic France. As the seat of the lairds of Grant, Castle Grant in Strathspey had long had in its 'gun cage' examples of Highland guns and other weapons of the family and its retainers dating from before 1720, the remnant of those shared out to the clan for traditional 'wapinshawings'.[11] The Castle Grant armoury was, however, greatly filled out by the mass quantities of arms and accoutrements procured by Sir James Grant of Grant for issue to regiments he raised for the British army during the 1790s.

Decorative arrays of the weapons adorned the hall at Castle Grant in the years after the regiments were disbanded. This significant collection of eighteenth-century and earlier weaponry and military equipment was later acquired for the nation.[12]

For others, the trend for display of military antiquities was a little more challenging. The surviving evidence of a warlike past did not always live up to the ideal, and the wish to demonstrate martial ancestry and status could entail work and expense to acquire the necessary impedimenta. In 1812, the twelfth earl of Cassillis created at Culzean castle in Ayrshire a display that was by his own estimation the 'most Elegant Armoury belonging to any individual in the Kingdom'. It was constructed not from a family martial inheritance, but rather from some 500 pistols, 450 swords, 150 sword blades and 100 carbine bayonets that were redundant army stock purchased for the purpose from the Board of Ordnance.[13] Amidst the pageantry mounted in Edinburgh in 1822 for the visit of George IV, an event with a distinctly Highland flavour, one episode played out behind the scenes was the sudden demand for weapons and accoutrements. The domestic armouries of certain clan chiefs were not sufficiently stocked, where they existed at all, to supply even the small 'clan retinues' of tenants whom they were encouraged to parade before the king. The clansmen of Breadalbane, Sutherland and Drummond carried swords supplied by the Board of Ordnance from stores in Edinburgh castle, or made to order for the royal visit.[14]

The Highlands were not the sole source for historic romanticism in nineteenth-century Scotland. The current of medievalism brought along such extravaganzas as the 1839 Eglinton Tournament, an aristocratic experiment in public jousting where the 'knights' equipped themselves with replica weapons and armour purchased in London.[15] A more refined medievalist interest lay behind the collecting activity of Sir Joseph Noel Paton, a leading Scottish painter, illustrator and antiquarian. Paton's patriotic preoccupation with Scottish medieval history was reflected in much of his artistic output and in ambitious designs, never realised, for immense monuments to the Wars of Independence to be raised in Edinburgh and Stirling. Paton's collecting interests were not at all limited to Scotland, and the hoard of arms and armour that he assembled in his Edinburgh home reflected his regard for the wider European culture of chivalry, boasting such important pieces as the fifteenth-century Battle Abbey sword.[16] After his death, Paton's collection was acquired by the Royal Scottish Museum and has stood since as a core element of the national arms and armour collection.

Thanks to the endeavours of private collectors, arms and armour is a field in which Scotland is strong. The material preserved in Edinburgh is rivalled by the riches of Glasgow Museums, which can claim to have one of the foremost such collections in the United Kingdom. It has a wide range by place and period, allowing interpretive coverage of the subject in its European context from ancient to modern times. Its quality owes much to a core of private bequests received in the mid-twentieth century from the shipbuilder, big game hunter and collector Robert Lyons Scott, and from Charles Whitelaw, a Glasgow lawyer.[17] Whitelaw's interest was in traditional Scottish weapons, a subject on which he was an authority. His bequests to Glasgow and the national collection in Edinburgh include important pieces such as a Scottish longsword of the early fifteenth century, and the work of eighteenth-century gunsmiths making Scottish pistols in such centres of manufacture as Doune in Perthshire.

Whitelaw was not a man for Scottish military history; his principal interests lay in the workmanship and practices of Scottish arms makers, very much in the context of the broader crafts and manufactures of the burghs. The development of distinctly Scottish styles in weaponry has of itself been an important element shaping the private and public collecting of Scottish military artefacts. Broadswords, targes, axes, dirks and daggers, highland pistols and long guns and their various appurtenances have been, and are, prized for their intrinsic qualities. More than a few carry tantalising associations with noted historical figures, some of which may even be true, but all are redolent of a traditional Scottish past. Thus they were categorised and viewed with approval by the early Antiquaries, and later, in high Victorian enthusiasm, defined by such reverential works as *Ancient Scottish Weapons*, a handsome volume of James Drummond's illustrations published in 1881. An introduction was supplied by Joseph Anderson, Custodier of the National Museum of Antiquities, the public body that had taken over the Society of Antiquaries' collection in 1851. Anderson set out the stall with an endorsement born of his conviction that the function of his own and other museums was to define and preserve a national cultural inheritance:

> The distinctive character of the dress, the military equipments and the personal ornaments of the Highlanders of Scotland, has given a peculiar aspect to the most picturesque phases of our national history . . . They are almost the last surviving remnants of the old nationality of Celtic Scotland; and as they are distinguished from all other objects of the same kind by certain peculiarities of form and ornament, they form a group of relics which is especially national and wholly unique.[18]

Others, meantime, were instilling their own thoughts about the essence of national character into a different kind of military material. In 1883 a service of dedication was held at the High Kirk of St Giles in Edinburgh. This marked the hanging in the great church of a collection of colours that had been borne in past campaigns by Scottish regiments of the British army. Presented by the sovereign, and consecrated, these objects were instilled with the honour of the regiments that had carried them. By tradition, when new colours were presented to regiments, the old ones were retired and quietly laid up in churches or kept privately by colonels of regiments. By the 1880s the reputation of the Scottish regiments was, in the eyes of many, entwined with the good name of Scotland itself. Established in popular consciousness by the distinctive and fashionable appearance of the Highland regiments especially, and engrained by Scottish successes on the battlefields of empire, the regiments were a talisman for an idea of Scotland. They could be styled, and styled themselves, as the modern-day representatives of the ancient Scottish nation, one that could be held still to exist as a partner and a power in union and empire. The Old Colours Committee, formed by a small group of influential figures and chaired by the general officer commanding the army in Scotland, set about gathering together and securing the old colours in 'some suitable national edifice' in no doubt that they were about the business of the Scottish nation. Their accumulation in St Giles' 'in the presence of a great and representative assembly' was, by their own estimation, 'a great national event'.[19]

As with the old colours, so in time would such weighty significance be applied to other relics and trophies of Scottish endeavour in the armed forces of the crown, be it in the Lowland or Highland regiments, in the services of the East India Company or in the successes of Scottish senior officers in naval or army commands. Precedents for collections of this kind existed in London. At Greenwich the former Royal Hospital for Seamen had exhibited its gallery of naval painting to the public and, in 1873, opened an adjacent Naval Museum wherein relics of ships and great commanders celebrated the power and lore of the senior service. Trophies of the battlefield had long been placed in the Royal Hospital, Chelsea, and under the auspices of the Royal United Service Institution, there emerged a military museum of a similar celebratory feel in Whitehall, supporting the Institution's purpose in promoting the study of naval and military science.[20] Such metropolitan institutions enjoyed royal patronage and the support of the hierarchy of the armed services from which they grew. The situation of Scotland in all this was not, from the perspective of the highly centralised instruments of British hierarchy and administration, a matter of obvious concern.

The first stirrings of some equivalent in Scotland came as a private initiative and emerged from the national and international exhibition movement that burst intermittently into life in certain British cities in the wake of London's Great Exhibition of 1851. Edinburgh and Glasgow were two that vied with one another in staging these prestige-enhancing events that promoted industry, manufactures and art. Glasgow achieved the schemes of greatest grandeur, transforming Kelvingrove Park with fantastic temporary structures in 1888, 1901 and 1911 to accommodate hundreds of thousands of visitors.[21] One innovation of the Glasgow International Exhibition of 1888 was a historical and archaeological collection brought together inside a reproduction of the fifteenth-century Bishop's castle that had once stood near Glasgow Cathedral. Amongst what was billed as a 'national contribution to the History of Antiquities and a vivid picture of Scottish life' was a Military Section of loan exhibits drawn from private collections and great houses. This was largely concerned with the same overtly Scottish characteristics in arms and armour that formed, and would form, the basis of the Scottish public collections, but relics of more recent history also featured. These included a pair of pistols ascribed to the former possession of 'the American Privateer' John Paul Jones, the Scots-born founder of the US Navy, the colours of the Strathspey Fencibles from the Castle Grant collection and a drum of the Renfrewshire Militia.[22]

Meanwhile in Edinburgh a small but significant scheme was well under way. In the spring of 1888 a Military Exhibition opened in the Freemasons' Hall, organised by a Miss Emma Millar in association with the United Service Horticultural and Work Society. It shared with other collections a concern with the heroic figures and weaponry of pre-union Scotland but the content was more heavily concentrated in the British forces of the eighteenth and nineteenth centuries. In the relatively modest haul of exhibits may be seen the prototype for the classes of material that would in time come to make up the essential content of public military history collections: relics and trophies of the battlefield and of celebrated commanders, weapons, uniform and equipment, medals, paintings and prints. Contributors included private collectors, the representatives of the great landed families and, notably, the Scottish regiments themselves. The rationale for the exhibition was described in one approving press article:

> Scotland, in proportion to its size and population, has probably sent out a larger number of soldiers to fight her own and other people's battles than

Figure 30.2 A gallery in the Naval and Military Exhibition, Royal Scottish Academy, 1889.

any other country in the world . . . and it follows that few countries are richer in military memorials and remembrances than our own. It is curious that it should not long ago have occurred to some one that it might be worth while to give the public an opportunity of becoming acquainted with the nature and value of these memorials. The opportunity has come at length.[23]

Ambitious as it was, the exhibition was scheduled to run over only three days. The power of the sentiment behind it, and its apparent success with the public, quickly gave rise to a project for a bigger and better version the following year. The Naval and Military Exhibition, held in the galleries of the Royal Scottish Academy in Edinburgh through the latter six months of 1889, was supported by a list of subscribers comprising retired and service officers, aristocrats and military antiquarians, and steered by an executive committee including Andrew Ross, one of the Queen's Heralds, who had earlier been a key figure in the Old Colours Committee. The queen lent exhibits from the royal collection, and the official patronage of the commander-in-chief signified the approval of her army. The official opening, held on the anniversary of Waterloo, was attended by naval detachments from HMS *Devastation*, then at Leith, the Queen's Own Cameron Highlanders and the 15th Hussars, then in barracks at Edinburgh, and crowds of spectators turned out to see the military and civil dignitaries.[24]

With 5,062 exhibits crammed into the galleries, the scope was international, and included an American Section with exhibits lent by the US Military Service Institution and a private collection of North American Indian artefacts. The core was, however, Scottish, broken down into sections of fine art, arms and armour, colours, uniforms and accoutrements, medals, orders and decorations, autograph documents and 'naval and military relics'.[25] The exhibition was a roll call of the names whose naval and military services had reflected credit on Scotland in the pursuit and defence of the British empire. Tellingly, material reflecting such endeavour in the most recent centuries was for the first time placed in the same context as earlier artefacts, either in ready association or in straightforward chronological progression. Historical paintings and portraits competed for wall space with ornamental displays of weaponry in the traditional style. In one room devoted to colours, the Douglas Banner, said to have been carried at the battle of Otterburn in 1388, was displayed alongside stands of Napoleonic-era colours of Scottish militia regiments.[26] No great distinction was made in representing and celebrating Scotland's military experience and repute, ancient or modern.

The 1889 exhibition in Edinburgh might claim a notable reversal in the normal order of affairs either side of the Anglo-Scottish border, since the following summer saw a Royal Military Exhibition staged in the grounds of the Royal Hospital, Chelsea, a mighty demonstration of the heritage and current capabilities of the British army at the height of its power.[27] The Royal Navy got in on the act with its own 'expo' in the same location the very next year, an even greater enterprise that combined a celebration of British naval history with what might today be described as a defence industry trade fair.[28] Closer to home, the success of the Edinburgh exhibition prompted predictable suggestions that something of a permanent nature should be its legacy. One proposal was for a 'National Armoury for Scotland' to be created in some suitable accommodation in Edinburgh castle.[29] Something of the sort was eventually to be realised, but it would take a further forty years, and the impact of a major European war, to bring it into being.

It was in 1917 that an influential committee headed by the eighth duke of Atholl began meeting to develop proposals for a Scottish national war memorial which would incorporate a museum of the current war. The move was prompted by similar activity in London which was in time to produce the National (later Imperial) War Museum. The impetus in the Scottish scheme quickly moved into the creation of a monumental memorial in Edinburgh castle, and it

Figure 30.3 John Buchan MP, Lord High Commissioner to the General Assembly of the Church of Scotland, addresses veterans of the Guard of Honour at the opening of the Scottish National Naval and Military Museum, Edinburgh castle, 1933.

was not until 1930, after the opening of the Scottish National War Memorial, that collecting began for the museum that would complement and complete it. The interests of the prime movers in the scheme shaped a rather different museum from the one that was to develop in London. Not a museum of the Great War, the Scottish National Naval and Military Museum was conceived along similar lines to the idea of the Royal United Service Institution, a place to record systematically Scotland's military history, with especial reference to the Scottish regiments.[30] The task was to accumulate the kind of material presented in the Edinburgh and Glasgow exhibitions of previous decades, but to build comprehensive collections, and to subject them to the kind of serious scrutiny and considered presentation that might be associated with museums in more established disciplines.

The memorial and celebratory functions were not eschewed entirely, nor could they be. The record and sacrifice of Scottish people in the recent conflict had entrenched the position of the military profession as an embodiment of national feeling. More than ever, it came naturally to many to make the almost casual connection between Scotland's military reputation and something approaching the national soul. The museum's location within Edinburgh castle, and its proximity to the colossal memorial, was further suggestive of its nature as a place of pilgrimage. When the museum opened to the public in 1933, it was with a representative Guard of Honour formed

Figure 30.4 Regimental displays in the Scottish United Services Museum.

by Scottish veterans. One commentator was moved to describe the new museum as 'the altar of Scotland's heroism' and 'a monument to the courage of our race'.[31]

After the Second World War, the museum reopened as the Scottish United Services Museum, a title that recognised the development of the Royal Air Force as the third of the armed services. The museum continues to collect and interpret, now as the National War Museum, still occupying premises inside Edinburgh castle. As part of National Museums Scotland, the collections are today held in common with those developed by the kindred national museums in Edinburgh, uniting 'modern' military material with the Scottish historical and archaeological collections begun by the Antiquaries, and the arms and armour collected by the former Royal Scottish Museum. The scope of collecting has broadened with a view to representing dispassionately the place of war and military service in Scottish history and society, and in conceptions and perceptions of Scottish cultural identity. But the museum carries forward an inescapable relationship with its setting, and with it the powerful impulse for commemoration and tribute; many gifts to the collection are heavy with the donors' wish to see private treasures secured in such a hallowed place as Edinburgh castle.

The National War Museum, distinct as a civilian institution, is far from alone. In prominent locations across the country are the museums of the Scottish regiments, dedicated to preserving and representing the history and traditions of the parent regiments and their forebears. The origins of these museums lie in the day-to-day life of the regiments themselves, since they grew out of the silver, pictures, trophies and mementoes accumulated to furnish and endow the mess rooms used by officers for the communal living that was the norm of peripatetic imperial military service. These were always showpiece settings, ministering to prestige, pride and *esprit de corps* as well as to comfort in home and foreign stations. Their evolution into more public display spaces began with the army reforms of the 1870s and 1880s that sought to ground the infantry regiments in distinct home localities as centres of recruitment and support. This entailed the creation of regimental depots in each defined territorial area, permanent administrative bases that supported the serving regiments as they continued on their worldwide peregrinations.

The depots naturally took on the character of each regiment's 'home' and adopted the traditional mess style of furnishing and display, holding historical and decorative material over and above that which was required by the battalion messes. Over decades the depot displays developed into private museums attracting ever more material in donations from individuals who had served in the regiment, or from their families, seeking a place where their medals and other mementoes of service could be preserved and accrued to the honour of the regiment. The property of home service and temporary war service battalions was added to the haul. As a means of preserving tradition, and as a public face for each regiment in its territorial area, these museums were gradually recognised to be of some utility to the army in its relationship with civil society, and from the late 1950s a measure of support from the Ministry of Defence allowed them to extend their function to regular public opening.[32] By dint of the location of the depots or regimental headquarters, some enjoyed high visibility within significant historic monuments such as Fort George and the castles of Edinburgh and Stirling.

As much as anywhere in the United Kingdom, Scotland's regimental museums have sought to nurture and reflect local identification with a regiment and its traditions but, this being Scotland, they have

Figure 30.5 Regimental silver at the museum of the Argyll and Sutherland Highlanders, Stirling castle. This silver centrepiece was purchased by officers of the 1st battalion to commemorate the battalion's service in the South African War (1899–1902).

also had their place in relation to national feeling. The regiments they represent have carried forward strong popular support among elements of Scottish society that identify with military reputations, traditions and values in patriotic terms. In the post-imperial era the museums have helped to maintain such sentiments. Even as regimental amalgamations have impacted upon them, their essence of continuity and permanence has kept them as focal points for those who cherish each, and all, of the regiments. This has been one factor reinforcing the dominant position of the Scottish infantry regiments

Figure 30.6 Pipe banner in the Cameronians' regimental collection, Low Parks Museum, Hamilton.

in the popular appreciation of Scottish military history, a monolith that tended to overshadow historical experience in other arms of the services and attention to wider strategic, political and societal developments.

Like most military museums, the regimental museums have sought to broaden their appeal and meet interest among a wider public in family history, local history and twentieth-century conflict, the latter especially for study in schools. They have had to address more questioning attitudes towards war and military service than the respectful endorsement that might once have been taken for granted, and the material residue of mass volunteering, conscription and reserve service in the twentieth century have filled out their collections with a more egalitarian feel, conducive to this trend. But fundamentally their collections are what they are, and the museums are and must be about the regiment as something precious, as much a family inheritance as the arms, trophies and portraits on the walls of country houses.

Thanks to the regiments, Scotland is not short of military museums. The existence of discrete, specialist-interest public collections has arguably had a knock-on effect in reducing the visibility of military history in other history museums, compounding a hint of discomfort with the subject among some museum practitioners. With the notable exceptions of the Cameronians' regimental collection in the care of South Lanarkshire Council, and the Earl Haig collection in the Museum of Edinburgh, the subject has in the past not often been prominent, nor has it always been well integrated with other kinds of material in museum interpretation of historical trends and developments.[33] This is in the nature of how the various collections have come into being, but it need not necessarily be so. In recent years intellectual barriers around the interpretation of military history artefacts have looked less imposing. Politics, industry and commerce, migration, literature and art, religion, medicine, popular culture and national identity are among the subjects with which military artefacts can readily connect. Military history in itself is as popular as ever, and by means of cross-fertilisation of ideas, and of artefacts, military collections can progress further towards enhancing our understanding of how Scotland has come to be what it is.

Interpretation is one thing; there remains the other factor. The artefact associated with war still carries that powerful added charge of honour. The hard-earned campaign medal, the letter home from the front, the trophy wrested from the enemy, the wallet pierced by a fatal bullet, they are redolent not just with historical experience but with family honour: the honour of the individual's family, of the regimental family and of the family of the nation. In the period in which public museums have emerged the place of military affairs in Scottish society has waxed and waned. It continues to change, and is by no means over. Meantime, thanks to the mass conflicts of the twentieth century, the sheer quantity of collectable material still in private hands is immense, its long-term fate awaiting resolution at some point in the future. Such things as these cannot easily be thrown away.

Notes

1. H. Cheape, '"Contrived and anomalous conversations": The Society of Antiquaries and their museum', *Review of Scottish Culture*, vol. 21 (2009), pp. 3–14. The present author's use of the term 'prehistory' is anachronistic in this context, but the Society's intention was the same.
2. National Museums Scotland [hereafter NMS], accession number X.DQ 1-44.
3. NMS, X.FV 27, H.LA 6.
4. NMS, H.MM 3.
5. NMS, H.LF 1.

6. Cheape, '"Contrived and anomalous conversations"', quotes evidence of sensitivity on this point in the politically delicate years immediately following the French Revolution.
7. R. B. K. Stevenson, 'The return of Mons Meg from London, 1828–1829', in D. H. Caldwell (ed.), *Scottish Weapons and Fortifications, 1100–1800* (Edinburgh: John Donald, 1981), pp. 419–36. The Celtic Society was founded in 1820 to promote the wearing of Highland dress and preserve other Highland traditions.
8. NMS, H.MCR 2.
9. I. G. Lindsay and M. Cosh, *Inveraray and the Dukes of Argyll* (Edinburgh: Edinburgh University Press, 1973), p. 213. A proportion of the muskets was damaged in the fire of 1877, but others remain as part of the existing display in the Armoury Hall supplemented by Lochaber axes procured for the visit of Queen Victoria to Inveraray in 1844.
10. J. Cornforth and G. Hughes-Hartman, *Inveraray Castle* (Derby: Pilgrim, 1986) p. 9.
11. W. Fraser, *The Chiefs of Grant*, 3 vols (Granton: privately published, 1883), vol. 1, p. xli.
12. This, the Seafield collection, was acquired by National Museums Scotland in 1977. The military pattern weapons are displayed in the Grand Magazine at Fort George.
13. M. S. Moss, *The 'Magnificent Castle' of Culzean and the Kennedy Family* (Edinburgh, Edinburgh University Press, 2002), p. 115.
14. D. H. Caldwell, 'The re-arming of the clans, 1822', *Review of Scottish Culture*, vol. 22 (2009), pp. 67–84.
15. I. Anstruther, *The Knight and the Umbrella: An Account of the Eglinton Tournament 1839* (London: Geoffrey Bles, 1963).
16. A. V. B. Norman, *Arms and Armour in the Royal Scottish Museum* (Edinburgh: HMSO, 1972). The sword is NMS, A.1905.633.
17. T. Capwell, *The Real Fighting Stuff: Arms and Armour at Glasgow Museums* (Glasgow: Glasgow City Council Museums, 2007), pp. 5–7.
18. J. Drummond and J. Anderson, *Ancient Scottish Weapons* (Edinburgh: George Waterson, 1881), p. 1.
19. A. Ross, *Old Scottish Regimental Colours* (Edinburgh: William Blackwood, 1885), p. vii. The colours assembled in 1882–3 no longer hang in St Giles'.
20. E. Fraser, *Greenwich Royal Hospital and the Royal United Service Museum* (London: Wells, Gardner, Darton & Co., [1910]).
21. P. Kinchin and J. Kinchin, *Glasgow's Great Exhibitions, 1888, 1902, 1911, 1938, 1988* (Bicester: White Cockade Publishing, 1988).
22. J. Paton (ed.) *Scottish National Memorials* (Glasgow: James Maclehose, 1890), pp. 268–9.

23. *The Scotsman*, 17 March 1888, p. 9.
24. *The Scotsman*, 19 June 1889, p. 6.
25. *Catalogue of the Naval & Military Exhibition, historic, technical and artistic, held in the Royal Scottish Academy Galleries, Edinburgh, opened on Waterloo Day, June 18 1889* (Edinburgh: Frank Murray, 1889).
26. Lot 2619a lent by Captain Palmer Douglas of Cavers, now NMS H.LF 11. It is now thought to be of sixteenth- or seventeenth-century origin.
27. *Royal Military Exhibition 1890. Official report of the honorary director presented to the central committee of the War Office* (London: William Clowes, 1891).
28. J. Grego, *Royal Naval Exhibition. Illustrated Souvenir* (London: Sampson, Low, Marston, 1891).
29. *The Scotsman*, 16 November 1889, p. 12.
30. National Library of Scotland, Edinburgh, 'Notes on the Scottish Naval and Military Museum', Atholl Papers, Acc.4714.
31. L. Spence, 'The Scottish Naval and Military Museum, Edinburgh Castle', *SMT Magazine*, vol. xi, no. 2 (August 1933), pp. 46–51.
32. P. Thwaites, *Presenting Arms: Museum Representation of British Military History, 1660–1900* (Leicester: Leicester University Press, 1996), pp. 46–7.
33. The Scottish National Portrait Gallery is an exception that proves the rule.

Epilogue: Reflections on the Scottish Military Experience

Alistair Irwin

The preceding chapters have examined the history of the Scot at war. In these concluding pages we reflect on the nature of the Scottish military experience, with particular reference to the modern period. In doing so it might be supposed that this experience is in some way unique, different in character or intensity from the experience of other soldiers, whether British or foreign. At one level this is an ill-founded presumption; whether in barracks or on the field of battle the Scottish soldier's life has been very similar to that of any other. In barracks *la vie militaire* is characterised by predictable routine and by occasional forays to training grounds to hone the tactical skills on which, together with adequate numbers, sound leadership, high morale, logistics and quality of weapons and equipment, success in battle depends. In the face of the enemy the experiences so well described in such books as John Keegan's *Face of Battle* and Richard Holmes's *Firing Line* are experiences common to all, explaining in part why after the battle there is often so much comradeship between friend and foe.[1] At another level too, remarkable as it is, the fighting reputation of the Scots is not unique. Asked to name a short list of warrior nations it is likely that commentators would include Spartans, Mongols, Pathans, Gurkhas, Cossacks, Prussians and other more or less obvious candidates. Scots would take their place confidently in that list, for it is undeniable that the standing of the Scot as a fighting man is exceptionally high. But if we accept, as suggested above, that so much of his experience is not so noticeably different from that of others, why does the fighting Scot seem to capture the imagination of the onlooker in an unusually sharply defined way?

If only to counter accusations of bias this question might be better answered by someone other than a former Scottish soldier reared in the Scottish military tradition, for whom it is impossible to shake off the feelings of intense personal pride in the triumphs of Scottish regiments and the heroic deeds of individual soldiers. It is easy to empathise with Lord Rosebery, who wrote of the Scottish regiments in 1915 that 'United as clans, proudly conscious of the battles on their colours, holding their traditional reputation as a sacred trust, they are a brotherhood of honour on which the country confidently relies in peace and war.'[2] These are the sort of sentiments that help to create the *esprit de corps* that encourages the soldier to stride tall and confidently into battle. It may not be good or balanced history for this or that regiment to record its own battle honours while ignoring, or sometimes even diminishing, the glories of its rivals, but it is an essential element in the business of creating and maintaining the fighting spirit of several hundred men brought together to serve under the one banner. So perhaps a little bias can be both excused and justified.

Although this volume very properly recounts battles fought with the greatest skill, providing us with remarkable examples of personal and collective gallantry and fortitude in adversity, it would nevertheless be an unpersuasive argument to claim that others do not have a similar record. In fact to deny this is to rob the Scottish military record of some of its own lustre for it is always better to be compared favourably with excellence than with mediocrity. It is partly for this reason that descriptions of battles so often refer to the gallantry with which the enemy fought; the better the enemy the better the victory.[3] Equally, when things have not gone so well, it is important to attribute the cause of failure elsewhere; this is a particularly noticeable feature of regimental accounts of the battles on the Western Front during the First World War where failure to hold ground taken at great cost is frequently blamed on the failure of flanking units to achieve their own objectives. Such devices help to create and maintain pride in the past and confidence in the future. They are commonly used in all military cultures.

We shall return to the experiences and achievements of the Scottish soldier but first we need to establish what exactly a Scottish soldier is. He is, obviously, a lowlander or a highlander; but men from the rest of the United Kingdom have also served in Scottish regiments. Indeed for much of the history of the modern army the Scottish regiments, especially the Highland ones, placed noticeable reliance on recruits from outside their regimental areas, and from outside Scotland, to fill their establishments. Are they to be classified as 'Jocks'? From time to time, and particularly in the 1990s and early years of the twenty-first century, significant numbers of men from the Commonwealth

Figure E.1 A soldier of the 1st battalion, the Black Watch, shares a joke with children in Al-Zubayr, Iraq, 2003.

countries have added welcome numbers and character to the regiments; are they too to be classified as Jocks? The answer is of course an unqualified yes. As John Baynes and John Laffin have pointed out, the trustees of the Scottish National War Memorial in Edinburgh castle have ruled that a soldier's name may be recorded in the roll of honour there if he

> was either a Scotsman (i.e. had a Scottish father or mother) or served in a Scottish Regiment and was killed or died . . . as a result of a wound, injury or disease sustained (a) in a theatre of operations for which a medal has been awarded; or (b) whilst on duty in aid of the Civil Power.[4]

By extension, anyone who serves in a Scottish regiment immediately becomes 'one of us' wherever it is that he is from. With the words 'Ahve been a Jock longer than tha', one Lancashire soldier establishes his superiority over another,[5] and today men from Fiji proudly wear their bonnets and hackles, happy and proud also to be Jocks.

So for all Scottish soldiers, whether native born or Jocks by association, why is it, to repeat the earlier question, that they and their regiments are singled out as something special? The answer provides a useful boost to the strength and performance of the Scottish regiments and it lies in a mixture of well-conceived myth and the viscerally anxious preconceptions of outsiders. We might start on this idea by quoting Dr Johnson: 'The noblest prospect which a Scotchman ever sees, is the high road that leads him to England!' This points us straightaway to an attitude that persists to this day, that in some way Scotland and its inhabitants are beyond the pale. Enter any Ministry of Defence office, or any military headquarters in England, and it is more than likely that the obligatory map of the United Kingdom on the wall will come to an abrupt and unnaturally horizontal end somewhere just north of a line between Edinburgh and Glasgow. Although this decapitation is caused by nothing more sinister than the height of the surface to which the map has to be fixed, it is nevertheless a symbol of a mindset that emerges in different forms all too frequently.

At a trivial level it can be mildly amusing that staff officers planning a general's tour of troops in Scotland are surprised to discover that without a helicopter it is impossible to visit Fort George in the morning and Redford barracks in Edinburgh in the afternoon. Equally trivial is the tendency for some English soldiers to attempt to introduce some form of twisted Scots accent into their conversation when referring to matters north of the border. A particularly tiresome example was the officer who used habitually to refer to 'Glasgae' in a sentence otherwise entirely pronounced in Oxford English. Meanwhile, visitors to Scottish regiments are often confounded in their attempts to engage the troops in conversation by an inability to understand what is being said to them. The classic example of this is claimed as their own by all Scottish regiments, falsely so by all but one: 'You comfy here?' asks the brigadier visiting a base in Northern Ireland. 'No sir,' replies the dismayed soldier, 'come fae Dundee.' Light-hearted perhaps, but this sort of exchange is symptomatic of the nervousness with which the outsider approaches a platoon or battalion of Scots, for somehow he has been conditioned to think of them as a touch *autre monde*, to be feared almost as much as admired. Even in contemporary times an officer announcing that he serves in a Scottish regiment will often attract a response of profound respect, even envy, but respect and envy strongly flavoured with a misdirected mixture of pity and awe: awe that anyone could possibly control these wild men from a distant world; pity that anyone should even have to try.

This curious attitude was founded on a perception commonly held throughout the army that the Jocks were splendid in battle but a menace anywhere else; they could be relied upon, it was said, to have a record of ill-discipline that could not be matched by others. In fact the military crime statistics and indeed the testimony of onlookers rarely if ever supported this perception but over the years it proved very difficult to counter. The notion that the Jock was different was too firmly embedded in the public and military psyche. Because the well-established Lowland regiments had been such an integral part of the post-Restoration standing army, and because in uniformed appearance they were largely indistinguishable from the English regiments, it is probable that this perception of difference did not properly emerge until the appearance of the Highland regiments from 1739 onwards. Suddenly into the order of battle marched men dressed in uniforms and carrying weapons that were so distinct from everyone else's that they instantly stood out from the mass.[6] In the early days large numbers spoke Gaelic and no English. The 1715 uprising had given those so disposed plenty of evidence of latent danger about which to be anxious. Add Bannockburn, William Wallace and Black Douglas, and the preconceptions were already well established. Angus Konstam makes the point that 'For centuries the Lowlanders had portrayed them [the Highlanders] as rapacious thieves, lacking dignity, honour and a decent pair of breeches', but that 'it was recognised that with the right training and leadership, the ferocity and determination of these clansmen might well be a force for good'.[7]

This is a partial explanation for the authorities' reaction to the first of the six mutinies that occurred in Highland regiments in the eighteenth century, all of them caused by official insensitivity to a misunderstood culture. In 1743 the Highland Regiment had marched to London to be reviewed by the king, arousing extraordinary curiosity on their way. As one commentator outrageously put it:

> Their march through the English counties supplied a feast of wonderment to the eyes of all who looked at them. A highlander in full garb was a strange object to an Englishman. A gentlemanly, tastefully-dressed, and gracefully-mannered gorilla would not be more vacantly stared at in the crush of a crammed drawing-room.[8]

This is not the place to retell the circumstances of the mutiny and the subsequent court martial but the execution of three ringleaders and the deportation of others suggests that the authorities, led by the king himself, took a harsh line precisely because of their acute anxiety about what these men from the north, tough, strange and as yet of unproven loyalty, might do if not kept fiercely to heel.

Later, as Highland regiment after Highland regiment proved its loyalty and fighting prowess, the overt anxieties faded but however much they were relegated to the subconscious the unease was still there. In 1756, in response to General James Wolfe's request for more troops for North America, William Pitt advocated the despatch of highlanders to the war with the words 'they would do well in North America, and it would be a drain and not many would return'.[9] This more than hinted that highlanders, dead or alive, were better overseas than at home. In a similar vein the history of U Company of the Aberdeen University Officers' Training Corps records how, on mobilisation in 1914, the company was ordered from Aberdeen to Bedford:

> Sergeant Runcie, who came from Banff, recalled that Bedford people were a bit alarmed when they heard that a kilted army was to be quartered on them. They had visions of all kinds of savages armed with claymores descending on them. One girl asked him if he did not feel the cold at night sleeping out in the Scottish hills with only a plaid to cover him.[10]

Despite this scarcely believable ignorance, from the earliest days the surface anxieties and misconceptions were gradually replaced by admiration, high expectations and neverending curiosity as onlookers tried to fathom the mysteries of the great Highland bagpipe, Highland honours, men dancing reels with each other and, in the case of Highland regiments, what was worn under the kilt. These attitudes were not confined to the British. French cartoons dating from the allied occupation of Paris after Napoleon had been exiled in St Helena show buxom Parisian ladies swooning as Highland soldiers pass by showing far too much leg and, one assumes, other things besides.[11] The era of George IV and Sir Walter Scott, greatly boosted by Queen Victoria's abundant enthusiasm for all things Highland, added a thick layer of romance which, together with the appearance in the mid-nineteenth century of the first photographs of great bearded Highland soldiers in their feather bonnets, finally put the seal on the reputation of the fighting Scot as something special, something beyond the ordinary.

The aura thus acquired was an immeasurably important ingredient in the process that turned young Scots from field and street into integral members of proud and effective regiments. It always helps to cope with danger and adversity if the officers and men believe that they are comrades together in a regiment or division that is one step ahead of all the others. It does not matter if the aura is in part rose-tinted, for the creation of regimental pride is not an exercise in aca-

Figure E.2 The lure of the kilt: satirical engraving of Highland soldiers in Paris, 1815.

demic precision. The fact is that in all good corps a highly tuned sense of self-belief is a prerequisite to success in battle and any relevant evidence to sustain it, whether real or imaginary, is eagerly and quite properly brought into play. Almost as important is what the enemy thinks. In North America, Scottish regiments had proved themselves more than equal to the ugly demands of guerrilla warfare in the forests of the Pontiac.[12] As Stewart of Garth recorded, their French enemies referred to the Scots as *sauvages d'Écosse*: 'They believed that they would neither take nor give quarter . . . and that with a ferocity natural to savages they made no prisoners . . . they were always in the front of every action in which they were engaged.'[13] At the battle of Quatre Bras a Highland soldier noted 'how their strange bonnets and kilts suddenly rising out of the tall rye seemed to paralyse the French'.[14] Other Frenchmen at Waterloo recoiled in similar dismay as the distinctively mounted Royal Scots Greys charged through the ranks of the kilted Gordon Highlanders into the French line. And the high drama of Waterloo provides an example of another advantage of wearing a distinctive uniform. In the words of Elizabeth Longford, as the battle reached its climax:

> The highlanders above La Haye Sainte rushed down upon the farm and gravel-pit, 'like a legion of demons', driving the French before them and mingling with the first Prussian soldiers on the Brussels road . . .

Fortunately for the highlanders their bonnets and kilts distinguished them from the French. Other units in both Wellington's and Blücher's armies were cut up in error by their own allies.[15]

The Russians at Balaclava learned all about 'the thin red line' of Sutherland Highlanders and it was the Germans in the First World War who christened their Scottish opponents 'the ladies from hell'. The views of friends can be equally telling. According to Australian John Laffin:

> The Scots are different from other people – not in any peculiar way, but distinctively different. They have an innate pride of race, and, militarily, an intense pride of regiment. Not that this is peculiar in the British Army, but somehow the Scots have always been more fiercely aggressive in their traditions.[16]

This is an important thought. It would be difficult to find any British soldier who was not proud of his own regiment or who would not be prepared to roll up his sleeves to defend its reputation. There is, however, a sense that we Scots would roll up our sleeves that bit quicker and higher in defence of a reputation about which we mind that bit more.[17]

So year by year, campaign by campaign, Scotland's fighting units built up a reputation for excellence, based chiefly on what they did on the field of battle but greatly enhanced by the admiring attitudes that others had of them. There is a downside to this, manifest in the evident *Schadenfreude* of outside commentators when they have an opportunity to criticise. The recording of the alleged temporary failure of the battle-weary 51st Highland Division in France in 1944[18] is matched at a much lower level by the testimony of a platoon commander in the Somerset Light Infantry who reports an incident in April 1945:

> There was no hand-over because, before we arrived, the Scottish company had departed. Dug in, with their front facing a large wood, the siting of their positions was absurd. An attacker would have had total cover right up to their forward section posts. The tactical siting of their slit trenches was not the only factor that decreed a change of position. No latrines had been dug and their wretched soldiers had fouled many of their own trenches.[19]

There is an edge to these words that suggests an excess of zeal in cutting the Scot down to size (or is this just the surfacing of the Scot's sensitivity to censure?).

Nevertheless, the usually high regard that others had for the fighting Scot enhanced the intense sense of pride that Scots themselves had in belonging to their own particular regiments. The clearest evidence for this emerges every time that changes are made to the army's order of battle. In the period between 1660 and the Napoleonic Wars, regiments came and went with remarkable frequency but the great continental war and the expansion of empire that followed it resulted in a more stabilised force which permitted regimental loyalties to harden and mature. So the Cardwell-Childers reforms of the late nineteenth century led to changes that proved unpopular and controversial. The reforms converted the then 109 well-established single battalion infantry regiments in the British army into larger units of, typically, two regular battalions, a militia battalion (later expanded to two or more Territorial Army battalions) and a regimental depot.[20] Needless to say these changes were greatly resisted and criticised. When it was decreed that regiments were to be known by their names, rather than by their old numbers, there was much unhappiness; unhappiness that persisted for decades.[21] In Scotland the effect of these changes, deeply unpopular at the time, was to create a family of four Lowland regiments and no fewer than six Highland regiments.[22] Each of these regiments was allocated a regimental recruiting area within Scotland; other Scottish regiments, such as the Scots Guards and Royal Scots Greys, had recruiting rights throughout Scotland. In theory the men recruited into these regiments all came from well-defined geographical regions; in practice it was rarely possible to man all the battalions without bringing in men from other parts of Britain, but this did not stop the emergence of the conviction, only partly borne out by the evidence, that the men in each regiment were all of a homogenous type, that they had all grown up together and that they would therefore soldier even better together.

During the two world wars the vast expansion of the army, the introduction of conscription, the huge casualty rates and the need to cross-post soldiers between units in order to keep up strengths undermined the phenomenon of localised recruiting as men from all over the United Kingdom were drafted into Scottish regiments. As the Adjutant-General during the First World War, Sir Nevil Macready, recognised

> In a war in which the whole nation is engaged *esprit de corps* must be for the Army as a whole and for the nation, rather than for the smaller units whose names live in the history of the wars in the past.[23]

In the post-1945 national service era, however, the army was able to re-inject more localisation into its recruitment practices. A glance at any of the Scottish battalions in, say, 1958 would have shown that to all practical purposes all the men, but not all the officers, came from the relevant regimental recruiting areas. This gave a powerful lift to the perception of local regiments recruited locally and by implication being all the better for it.[24]

By the late 1950s the focus on Britain's nuclear deterrent, and the prospect of a return to an all-professional volunteer army, led to a planned reduction to sixty infantry battalions. The deputy chief of the Imperial General Staff at the time, Sir Richard Hull, and his predecessor, Sir Dudley Ward, used the reductions as an opportunity to advocate the forming of large regiments of between three and five battalions. The chief, Sir Gerald Templer, took a different line and preferred to leave the decision as to how to find the required cuts to the regiments themselves; this amounted to an abrogation of duty, for he should have issued orders one way or the other. The large regiment cause was nevertheless to find support among some of the army's best professional soldiers, including the commanding officer of the famous and distinguished Durham Light Infantry (itself to disappear as a result of the reductions and amalgamations), who pointed out that the 1881 Childers system might not be best suited to mid-twentieth-century needs.[25] As Hew Strachan has remarked, 'the single-battalion regiment was ill-adapted to this sort of [contemporary] warfare. The regimental system lacked the flexibility for the functions for which the army had now to prepare itself.'[26] Many English line regiments took the opportunity provided by Templer to create new larger entities, such as the Royal Anglian Regiment (1964) and the Queen's Regiment (1966).

This view did not, however, prevail in Scotland, where in 1959 the Highland Light Infantry (a Highland Brigade regiment) and the Royal Scots Fusiliers (of the Lowland Brigade) amalgamated to form the Royal Highland Fusiliers, and in 1961 the Seaforth and Cameron Highlanders came together to form the Queen's Own Highlanders. Later still in 1968, with a new planned target of fifty battalions, the Cameronians marched with great covenanting emotion into history, and the Argyll and Sutherland Highlanders, fresh from their highly publicised and popularly applauded actions in Aden, mounted their famous campaign to prevent the same thing happening to them. In the event they were saved not by the lobbying, or their widely supported petition, though these must undoubtedly have helped, but by the activities of the IRA which demanded the deployment to Northern Ireland of as many troops as could be found. None of these reductions was in any way popular either among the serving or veteran populations. Those regiments that escaped the axe told themselves they had done so because they were better, more senior or better recruited, and they put aside any grim thoughts that their day might also come.

Further cuts followed in the wake of the Conservative government's 1990 *Options for Change* defence review following the ending of the Cold War and, later, the 1994 *Front Line First – Defence Costs Study* initiated by the then secretary of state for defence Malcolm Rifkind. In the army at large, these reductions and reallocation of manpower led to a gradual imbalance of force, with too much in the firing line and too little at the rear to sustain it. In the short term they led in Scotland to the amalgamation in 1994 of the Queen's Own Highlanders and the Gordon Highlanders; the politically inconvenient amalgamation of the Royal Scots and the Kings Own Scottish Borderers was reversed in the light of the expanding operations in the Balkans. There were also yet more changes to the structure of the Territorial Army in Scotland, changes which had every appearance in retrospect of incoherence and muddle founded on nothing more substantial than a shortage of funds to sustain it. By the turn of the century it was obvious to those with their eyes open that the process of reduction was not yet finished.

In 2001 the then Colonel Commandant of the Scottish Division, by now consisting of no more than six regular and two Territorial infantry battalions, circulated amongst the Council of Scottish Colonels a paper entitled 'Thinking the Unthinkable'.[27] This paper was seen by fewer than a dozen people, despite one copy being inadvertently left on a commercial aircraft arriving in Belfast from which it was retrieved by an alert member of the military movements' staff. The paper asked what should happen in the event of further reductions in the numbers of battalions being ordered. No decisions were made but the paper achieved its purpose of provoking some preliminary thought on what would inevitably be a highly emotionally charged situation should further cuts occur. In the event the axe was sharpened much sooner than the paper feared. Despite the continuing operations in Iraq, and the plans to engage more fully in Afghanistan, the government of the day under prime minister Tony Blair, bankrolled by chancellor Gordon Brown, persistently declined to fund the armed forces to the extent needed to sustain them in the longer term. As a consequence of this political decision the army board was faced with a combination of two problems: the imbalances referred to above were by now urgently in need of repair but the budget was too small to contemplate remedying this by increasing the size of the army. This led to the painful but inevitable decision to cut four infantry battalions and reallocate the manpower to other parts of the army that were under even more strain.

One of the four battalion losses was to come from Scotland. The regimental colonels of the six regiments were set the task of achieving this within the context of two complementary factors. The first was an unwelcome but pragmatic view that it was no longer possible to go on weeding regiment after regiment out of the order of battle. In living memory the Scottish infantry regiments had declined from twelve to six. For how much longer would it be possible to disband or amalgamate and still persuade men to join the regiments that survived? How could men be persuaded to join when their local regiment no longer existed? The second factor was the army board's decision, in the spirit of Macready and Hull before it, that the circumstances had reached a point where the advantages of single-battalion regiments were outweighed by the advantages of larger regiments.[28] This time the decision was not left to the individual regiments; how the required cuts would have been achieved if it had been is impossible to know but at least this time people had their orders and, however unwelcome their orders may be, good soldiers know how to carry them out.

The announcement in 2004 that there was to be a new Scottish regiment of seven battalions, two of which were to be Territorial Army units, was welcomed by some, accepted gracefully as inevitable by others but characterised chiefly by a predictable outcry of protest, muted for obvious reasons within the serving community and deafening from elsewhere. There were also protests south of the border where other famous regiments such as the Royal Green Jackets (itself already a large regiment formed in the Templer era) and the Devons and Dorsets underwent similar changes. The outcry in Scotland was inevitably louder and more vociferous and there are still many who are unreconciled to what happened. To them it may be quietly observed that the regiments of which the protestors were rightly so proud were to a great extent themselves products of previous reorganisations, carried through, as we have observed above, to the sound of much protest at the time. From those reorganisations emerged regiments that served the nation brilliantly and we may be confident that the same will be said of the Royal Regiment of Scotland. Indeed, even in the first years of its life the men of the new regiment have excelled themselves in Iraq and Afghanistan in a way that should have drawn the unqualified admiration and respect of all, and especially of that generation of veterans whose operational experience had no more than a fraction of the danger or intensity being handled with such aplomb by the young men who followed them into the service. Today's young Scottish soldier is doing all this, furthermore, in the spirit and traditions of the old regiments, keeping the golden thread between past and present in appropriately good repair, not least in perpetuating the old names in the new titles.[29] In a letter to officers of the 3rd Battalion, Royal Regiment of Scotland, about to deploy to Afghanistan in 2009, the representative colonel included these words:

> Many of you will have started your careers in The Black Watch; some of you will have started in the sister Scottish regiments, each one of them with its own fine lineage and history; others still will have started your careers as officers in the Royal Regiment of Scotland. The same can be said of those under your command. All of you, however, will deploy to Afghanistan [as] part of the same team wearing the badge of the Royal Regiment of Scotland and the Red Hackle of the Black Watch Battalion. Both symbols are very important. The badge will remind you that the story of your tour will become one of the earliest chapters in the history of the new Regiment. The Red Hackle will remind you of one of the famous and distinguished antecedent regiments whose ideals, heritage and reputation you are carrying forward into a new era, and from whose example of courage, loyalty and *esprit de corps* you can take inspiration and pride.[30]

They did so with conspicuous success.

At the beginning of this chapter we asserted that the Scottish soldier's experience both in barracks and in action was not markedly different from any other soldier's experience.[31] Recollections of life on and off duty may be reported in different dialects and accents but they are all essentially the same mixture of numbing hours of boredom and predictable routine combined with high-energy activity, whether in battle, on the training ground or in the bar. It might have been possible at one time to claim that the Scot, especially if raised in the physically demanding mountains and glens, or in the mines and shipyards, was temperamentally and constitutionally more able to manage the pressures of combat than others. But it is now rather less likely that this is a characteristic that sets him apart from anyone else, and the extreme physical discomforts of cold, wet and shortage of sleep, overlaid by fear and an aching for home, are experiences shared with equal fortitude by all frontline soldiers. Of course in some superficial respects there were aspects of service life made unique to the Scot by the wearing of the kilt. The sun burning the skin off the backs of knees

Figure E.3 Recruiting poster for the Scottish regiments by Christopher Clark, 1919.

as men of the Highland Brigade lay face down all day under withering Boer fire at Magersfontein; or the intolerable chafing of the thighs under sodden, heavy kilts on the march up to the trenches in Flanders. Yet these were hardships that others were happy to do without and for all soldiers, whether kilted or trousered, the aching feet, the crack of the high-velocity bullet and the fizz of shrapnel were exactly the same.

Whilst their experiences might not be unique, Scottish soldiers have nevertheless earned their own special place in British military history on the back of a distinctive identity that has been prominently displayed on battlefields across the globe. A glance through a record of the battle honours of the British army confirms the popular perception that from 1660 to the present day Scottish regiments have been present at almost all the engagements that have punctuated modern British history.[32] Famous victories such as Waterloo and El Alamein keep company with lesser-known triumphs such as Dargai and Istabulat. The long, and largely unspectacular, counter-insurgency campaigns in Asia, the Middle East and Northern Ireland did not attract battle honours but were just as important an influence on the Scots' fighting reputation and their place in the evolution of Britain

Figure E.4 Soldiers from the Black Watch, 3rd battalion, Royal Regiment of Scotland (3 SCOTS), receive their gallantry awards for service in Afghanistan, July 2010.

and its empire. Not every attack has succeeded, not every defence has stood firm, but the failures merely underline the scale of professional and human achievement in the far larger record of success.

And the story of the fighting Scots continues in Afghanistan in the early twenty-first century. The Taleban, the heat, the intensity of combat, the relentless exposure to danger are common to all military personnel who serve there. But the regular battalions of the Royal Regiment of Scotland, reinforced superbly by volunteers from the two Territorial Army battalions of the regiment, have made their mark in their own particular and distinctive way. They have given every Scot cause to be immensely proud, for the new generation of Scottish soldier has proved himself to be at least the equal of his distinguished predecessors in the white heat of battle. In his fine memoir, *With the Jocks*, Peter White writes of his life as a platoon commander with the 4th King's Own Scottish Borderers in north-west Europe in 1944–5:

> If no words can convey the 'action', it would be an even harder task to express my appreciation, admiration and high regard for the wonderful

qualities of humour, compassion and 'guts' displayed by those with whom I had the privilege to serve.[33]

These words would be as appropriate now as they were then.

Given the subject of this book, and given that fierce pride in regiment may have prompted comparisons between the coverage given to one regiment or another, or indeed between the coverage given to the highlanders as compared to their lowland comrades, it might be appropriate to end with three balancing thoughts. First, as Tom Devine rightly reminds us, the Scottish contribution to British arms was by no means confined to the Highland regiments: the whole of Scotland, collectively and individually, has been prominent in the annals of British military history.[34] Yet the Highland contribution has been most noticeable because of the publicity it has attracted. The highlanders' identity, exemplified most obviously by the kilt, proved an infallible attraction to the outside observer, a fact recognised with deliberate intent by the decision to adopt the kilt for all seven battalions of the new Royal Regiment of Scotland. Second, the operational performance of all the Scottish regiments has been in the first class with little if anything to choose between them (except of course each man's own which is certain to be in first place). The third and concluding thought can be left to the Iron Duke. Pressed to attribute victory at Waterloo to one or other particular regiment, Wellington is reported to have replied: 'Oh I know nothing of the services of particular regiments, there was glory enough for all.'[35] After the Scots had claimed the lion's share of it, we might proudly suggest.

Notes

1. J. Keegan, *Face of Battle* (London: Jonathan Cape, 1976); R. Holmes, *Firing Line* (London: Jonathan Cape, 1985).
2. Quoted in the preface to *Scotland for Ever: a Gift-book of the Scottish Regiments* (London: Hodder and Stoughton, 1915), p. iii.
3. See, for example, P. Hart, *1918: A Very British Victory* (London: Weidenfeld and Nicolson, 2008), p. 362, but also more generally in the descriptions of the British victories from August 1918 onwards.
4. Quoted in J. Baynes with J. Laffin, *Soldiers of Scotland* (London: Brassey's, 1988), p. xv.
5. Quoted in Field Marshal Wavell's Introduction to B. Fergusson, *The Black Watch and the King's Enemies* (London: Collins, 1950), p. 13.
6. Broadswords, dirk, highland pattern pistols from Doune in Perthshire and, even as late as 1748, targes. See, for example, Peter Simpson,

The Independent Highland Companies 1603–1760 (Edinburgh: John Donald, 1996), pp. 26–7.
7. A. Konstam, *There Was a Soldier* (London: Hachette, 2009), p. 11.
8. Quoted in D. Herbert, *Great Historical Mutinies* (Edinburgh: W. P. Nimmo, Hay and Mitchell, 1876), p. 332.
9. Quoted in J. Corbett, *The Seven Years War* (London: the Folio Society, 2001), p. 112.
10. Quoted in J. McConachie, *The Student Soldiers* (Elgin: Moravian Press, 1995), p. 27.
11. For example, two unattributed prints on display in the Black Watch Museum bearing the inscription *Regiments Écossais, Armée des Souverains Alliés année 1815 No 6*.
12. T. M. Devine, *Scotland's Empire* (London: Allen Lane, 2003), p. 314.
13. D. Stewart of Garth, *Sketches of the Character, Manners and Present State of the Highlands of Scotland with Details of the Military Service of the Highland Regiments*, third edition, 2 vols (Edinburgh: Constable, 1825), vol. 1, p. 330.
14. Quoted in E. Longford, *Wellington: The Years of the Sword* (London: Panther Books, 1971), p. 518.
15. Quoted in ibid. p. 579. This is what would now be called a 'blue on blue' incident.
16. J. Laffin, *Scotland the Brave: The Story of the Scottish Soldier* (London: Cassell, 1963), p. 3.
17. Interestingly, this was an argument raised in 2004 when decisions had to be made about how further reductions in the number of infantry battalions would be achieved. Statistics and cold logic pointed to the loss of two of the six remaining Scottish battalions, but in the event only one was lost because the army board was persuaded that their passion for their distinctive status as 'Jocks' would prevent men for whom there was no longer room in the surviving Scottish battalions from remustering into regiments south of the border.
18. See, for example, A. Beevor, *D-Day* (London: Viking, 2009), p. 187.
19. S. Jary, *18 Platoon* (Carsholton Beeches: Sydney Jary Limited, 1987), p. 119.
20. By comparison, in 1815 there were 104 infantry regiments of which 17 were Scottish in name and origin. Helpful comparative lists of the order of battle can be found in P. Young and J. P. Lawford (eds), *History of the British Army* (London: Arthur Barker Ltd, 1970).
21. See, for example, E. C. Talbot-Booth, *The British Army* (London: Sampson Lowe, Marston & Co., 1922), p. 8, and E.W. Sheppard, *A Short History of the British Army to 1914* (London: Constable and Company Ltd, 1934), p. 218.

22. The Lowland regiments were: the Royal Scots, King's Own Scottish Borderers, Royal Scots Fusiliers and Cameronians. The Highland regiments were: the Black Watch, Highland Light Infantry, Gordon Highlanders, Seaforth Highlanders, Queen's Own Cameron Highlanders and Argyll and Sutherland Highlanders.
23. Quoted in H. Strachan, *The Politics of the British Army* (Oxford: Oxford University Press, 2001), p. 207.
24. It should be emphasised that these remarks refer to the regular army. The Territorial Army units were of necessity always recruited very locally.
25. Strachan, *The Politics of the British Army*, p. 219. The 1881 reforms are generally attributed to Cardwell alone but it was in fact Childers, the secretary of state for war, who introduced the finishing touches to a scheme of linked regiments originally devised by Cardwell a decade earlier.
26. Ibid. p. 223.
27. In the possession of the author.
28. A. Irwin, 'What is best in the regimental system?', *RUSI Journal*, vol. 149, no. 5 (October 2004), pp. 32–6.
29. For example, the Royal Highland Fusiliers, 2nd Battalion, the Royal Regiment of Scotland.
30. Letter from Lieutenant-General Sir Alistair Irwin to officers of the Black Watch, 3rd Battalion, the Royal Regiment of Scotland, 1 March 2009.
31. Stuart Allan and Allan Carswell argue, for example, that in Northern Ireland there 'seems to be little evidence that Scottish soldiers were regarded or treated on either side – loyalist or republican – in any distinct way from the British military presence as a whole, either of amity or animosity'. See S. Allan and A. Carswell, *The Thin Red Line: War, Empire and Visions of Scotland* (Edinburgh: National Museums of Scotland, 2004), p. 143.
32. See, for example, A. Rodger, *Battle Honours of the British Empire and Commonwealth Land Forces* (Trowbridge: Crowood Press, 2003).
33. P. White, *With the Jocks* (Stroud: Sutton, 2001), p. xx.
34. T. M. Devine, *Scotland's Empire*, p. 294.
35. Quoted in Longford, *Wellington: The Years of the Sword*, p. 586.

Select Bibliography

Abels, R. P., *Lordship and Military Obligation in Anglo-Saxon England* (London: British Museum, 1988)

Abler, T. S., *Hinterland Warriors and Military Dress: European Empires and Exotic Uniforms* (Oxford: Berg, 1999)

Aitchison, N., *The Picts and the Scots at War* (Stroud: Sutton, 2003)

Alcock, L., *Kings and Warriors, Craftsmen and Priests in Northern Britain AD 550–850* (Edinburgh: Society of Antiquaries of Scotland, 2003)

Alexander, J., *McCrae's Battalion: The Story of the 16th Royal Scots* (Edinburgh: Mainstream Publishing, 2003)

Allan, S., *Commando Country* (Edinburgh: National Museums of Scotland, 2007)

Allan, S. and A. Carswell, *The Thin Red Line: War, Empire and Visions of Scotland* (Edinburgh: National Museums of Scotland, 2004)

Anderson, A. O., *Early Sources of Scottish History, AD 500 to 1286*, 2 vols (Stamford: Paul Watkins, 1990)

Barbour, J., *The Bruce*, ed. and trans. A. A. M. Duncan (Edinburgh: Canongate, 1997)

Barrington, M., *Grahame of Claverhouse, Viscount Dundee* (London: Martin Secker, 1911)

Barrow, G. W. S., *The Anglo-Norman Era in Scottish History* (Oxford: Clarendon Press, 1980)

Barrow, G. W. S., 'The army of Alexander III's Scotland', in N. H. Reid (ed.), *Scotland in the Reign of Alexander III 1249-1286* (Edinburgh: John Donald, 1990), pp. 132–47

Barrow, G. W. S., *Robert Bruce and the Community of the Realm of Scotland* (Edinburgh: Edinburgh University Press, 2005)

Baynes, J., *Morale: A Study of Men and Courage: The Second Scottish*

Rifles at the Battle of Neuve Chapelle 1915 (London: Leo Cooper, 1967)

Baynes, J., *The Jacobite Rising of 1715* (London: Cassell, 1970)

Baynes, J. with J. Laffin, *Soldiers of Scotland* (London: Brassey's, 1988)

Bell, A. S., *The Scottish Antiquarian Tradition* (Edinburgh: John Donald, 1981)

Benitz, M., *Six Months Without Sundays: The Scots Guards in Afghanistan* (Edinburgh: Birlinn, 2011)

Bennett, H., *Fighting the Mau Mau: The British Army and Counter-Insurgency in the Kenya Emergency* (Cambridge: Cambridge University Press, 2013)

Bennett, M., *The Civil Wars in Britain and Ireland* (Oxford: Blackwell, 1997)

Bewsher, F. W., *The History of the 51st (Highland) Division 1914–1918* (Edinburgh and London: William Blackwood, 1921)

Black, J., *Culloden and the '45* (London: Grange, 1997)

Blake, G., *Mountain and Flood: The History of the 52nd (Lowland) Division 1939–1946* (Glasgow: Jackson, Son & Co., 1950)

Borg, A., *War Memorials from Antiquity to the Present* (London: Leo Cooper, 1991)

Breeze, D., *Roman Scotland: Frontier Country* (London: Batsford for Historic Scotland, 2006)

Brockington, W. S. (ed.), *Monro, His Expedition with the Worthy Scots Regiment called Mac-Keyes Regiment* (Westport, CT: Praeger, 1999)

Brown, I. G. and H. Cheape (eds), *Witness to Rebellion: John Maclean's Journal of the 'Forty-Five and the Penicuik Drawings* (East Linton: Tuckwell Press in association with the National Library of Scotland, 1996)

Brown, K. M., *Bloodfeud in Scotland 1573–1625: Violence, Justice and Politics in Early Modern Scotland* (Edinburgh: John Donald, 1986)

Brown, M., *The Black Douglases: War and Lordship in Late Medieval Scotland, 1300–1455* (East Linton: Tuckwell Press, 1998)

Brown, M., *Bannockburn: The Scottish War and the British Isles, 1307–1323* (Edinburgh: Edinburgh University Press, 2008)

Brumwell, S., *Redcoats: The British Soldier and War in the Americas, 1755–1763* (New York: Cambridge University Press, 2002)

Brumwell, S., *Paths of Glory: The Life and Death of General James Wolfe* (London: Hambledon Continuum, 2006)

Bryant, G. J., 'Scots in India in the eighteenth century', *Scottish Historical Review*, vol. 64 (1985), pp. 22–41

Buchan, J., *The History of The Royal Scots Fusiliers (1678-1918)* (London: Thomas Nelson & Sons, 1925)

Buckley, M. J., *Scarlet and Tartan: The Story of the Regiments and Regimental Bands of the NSW Scottish Rifles (Volunteers)* (Sydney: The Red Hackle Association, 1986)

Burke, G., *The National Theatre of Scotland's Black Watch* (London: Faber and Faber, 2007)

Calder, A., 'Scottish poets in the desert', *Southfields*, vol. 6 (1999), pp. 64–82

Caldwell, D. H., 'Scottish spearmen, 1298–1314: the answer to cavalry', *War in History*, vol. 19, no. 3 (2012), pp. 267–89

Caldwell, D. H. (ed.), *Scottish Weapons and Fortifications, 1100–1800* (Edinburgh: John Donald, 1981)

Cameron, E. A., '"They will listen to no remonstrance": Land raids and land raiders in the Scottish Highlands, 1886 to 1914', *Scottish Economic and Social History*, vol. 17 (1997), pp. 43–64

Cameron, J., *James V: The Personal Rule* (East Linton: Tuckwell Press, 1998)

Campbell, J., 'England, Scotland and the Hundred Years War in the fourteenth century', in J. R. Hale, J. R. L. Highfield and B. Smalley (eds), *Europe in the Later Middle Ages* (London: Faber and Faber, 1965), pp. 184–216

Cannon, R., *The Highland Bagpipe and its Music* (Edinburgh: John Donald, 2002)

Capwell, T., *The Real Fighting Stuff: Arms and Armour at Glasgow Museums* (Glasgow: Glasgow City Council Museums, 2007)

Carmen, J. and A. Harding (eds), *Ancient Warfare: Archaeological Perspectives* (Stroud: Sutton, 1999)

Cavendish, A. E. J., *An Reismeid Chataich: The 93rd Highlanders now 2nd Bn. the Argyll and Sutherland Highlanders (Princess Louise's), 1799-1927* (Frome: privately published, 1928)

Chalmers, M. and W. Walker, *Uncharted Waters: The UK, Nuclear Weapons and the Scottish Question* (East Linton: Tuckwell Press, 2001)

Cheape, H., *Tartan: The Highland Habit* (Edinburgh: National Museums of Scotland, 2006)

Cheape, H., *Bagpipes: A National Collection of a National Instrument* (Edinburgh: National Museums of Scotland, 2008)

Childs, J., *The Army of Charles II* (London: Routledge and Kegan Paul, 1976)

Childs, J., *The Army, James II and the Glorious Revolution* (Manchester: Manchester University Press, 1980)

Childs, J., *The British Army of William III, 1689-1702* (Manchester: Manchester University Press, 1987)

Conway, S., *The British Isles and the War of American Independence* (Oxford: Oxford University Press, 2000)

Conway, S., 'Scots, Britons and Europeans: Scottish military service, c. 1739-1783', *Historical Research*, vol. 82 (2009), pp. 114-30

Conway, S., 'The Scots Brigade in the eighteenth century', *Northern Scotland*, vol. 1 (2010), pp. 30-41

Cookson, J. E., *The British Armed Nation, 1793-1815* (Oxford: Clarendon Press, 1997)

Cookson, J. E., 'The Napoleonic Wars, military Scotland and Tory Highlandism in the early nineteenth century', *Scottish Historical Review*, vol. 78 (1999), pp. 60-75

Cookson, J. E., 'The Edinburgh and Glasgow duke of Wellington statues: Early nineteenth-century Unionist Nationalism as a Tory project', *Scottish Historical Review*, vol. 83 (2004), pp. 23-40

Cornell, D., 'A kingdom cleared of castles: The role of the castle in the campaigns of Robert Bruce', *Scottish Historical Review*, vol. 87 (2008), pp. 233-57

Cornell, D., *Bannockburn: The Triumph of Robert the Bruce* (New Haven, CT and London: Yale University Press, 2009)

Coss, E. J., *All For The King's Shilling: The British Soldier under Wellington, 1808-1814* (Norman, OK: University of Oklahoma Press, 2010)

Cowan, E. J. (ed.), *The Wallace Book* (Edinburgh: John Donald, 2007)

Cowan, E. J. and R. A. McDonald (eds), *Alba: Celtic Scotland in the Medieval Era* (East Linton: Tuckwell Press, 2000)

Craig, C., *Out of History: Narrative Paradigms in Scottish and British Culture* (Edinburgh: Polygon, 1996)

Croft, W. D., *Three Years with the 9th (Scottish) Division* (London: John Murray, 1919)

Cruden, S. H., *The Scottish Castle* (Edinburgh: Nelson, 1960)

Dalton, C., *The Scots Army 1661-1688* (London: Eyre and Spottiswoode, 1909)

David, S., *Churchill's Sacrifice of the Highland Division: France 1940* (London: Brassey's, 2004)

Davies, S., *Welsh Military Institutions, 633-1283* (Cardiff: University of Wales Press, 2004)

Devine, T. M., *The Scottish Nation 1700-2000* (London: Allen Lane, 1999)

Devine, T. M., *Scotland's Empire 1600-1815* (London: Allen Lane, 2003)

Devine, T. M., 'Soldiers of Empire, 1750–1914', in J. M. MacKenzie and T. M. Devine (eds), *Scotland and the British Empire* (Oxford: Oxford University Press, 2011), pp. 176–95

Devine, T. M., *To the Ends of the Earth: Scotland's Global Diaspora, 1750-2010* (London: Allen Lane, 2011)

Dove, H. M., 'The role of the police and other law enforcement agencies in their application of the law relating to popular disturbances in central Scotland, 1850–1914' (unpublished MPhil thesis, the Open University, 1994)

Duffy, C., *The '45: Bonnie Prince Charlie and the Untold Story of the Jacobite Rising* (London: Phoenix, 1997)

Duffy, S. (ed.), *The World of the Galloglass: Kings, Warlords and Warriors in Ireland and Scotland, 1200-1500* (Dublin: Four Courts Press, 2007)

Dunbar, J. T., *History of Highland Dress* (London: Batsford, 1979)

Duncan, A. A. M., 'The War of the Scots, 1306–23', *Transactions of the Royal Historical Society*, sixth series, vol. 2 (1992), pp. 125–51

Dunn-Pattison, R. P., *The History of the 91st Argyllshire Highlanders* (Edinburgh: Blackwood, 1910)

Dziennik, M. P., 'Imperial Conflict and the Contractual Basis of Military Society in the Highland Regiments', in C. Kennedy and M. M. Cormack (eds), *Men at Arms* (Basingstoke: Palgrave Macmillan, 2002), pp. 17–36.

Edwards, A., *Mad Mitch's Tribal Law: Aden and the End of Empire* (Edinburgh: Mainstream Publishing, 2014).

Erskine, D., *The Scots Guards, 1919-1955* (London: William Clowes, 1956)

Ewart G., D. Gallagher et al., *Fortress of the Kingdom: Archaeology and Research at Edinburgh Castle* (Edinburgh: Historic Scotland, 2014)

Ewing, J., *History of the 9th (Scottish) Division 1914-1919* (London: John Murray, 1921)

Fairrie, A., *'Cuidich 'N Righ': A History of the Queen's Own Highlanders (Seaforth and Camerons)* (Inverness: Regimental HQ, Queen's Own Highlanders, 1983)

Fissel, M. C., *The Bishops' Wars: Charles I's Campaigns against Scotland, 1638-1640* (Cambridge: Cambridge University Press, 1994)

Foran, S., 'A great romance: Chivalry and war in Barbour's Bruce', in C. Given-Wilson (ed.), *Fourteenth Century England*, vol. VI (Woodbridge: Boydell and Brewer, 2010), pp. 1–26.

Fraser, G. MacDonald, *The Steel Bonnets: The Story of the Anglo-*

Scottish Border Reivers (London: Barrie and Jenkins, 1971; HarperCollins, 1995)

Furgol, E., *A Regimental History of the Covenanting Armies* (Edinburgh: John Donald, 1990)

Gardyne, C. Greenhill, Gardyne, A. D. Greenhill, Falls, C., Miles, W., Sinclair-Stevenson, C. and Napier, D. M., *The Life of a Regiment: The History of the Gordon Highlanders*, 7 vols (London: The Medici Society, and other subsequent publishers, 1901–74)

Gentles, I., *The New Model Army in England, Ireland and Scotland, 1645–1653* (Oxford: Blackwell, 1992)

Gibson, J. S., *Playing the Scottish Card: The Franco-Jacobite Invasion of 1708* (Edinburgh: Edinburgh University Press, 1998)

Gildea, J., *For Remembrance: South Africa 1899–1902* (London: Eyre and Spottiswoode, 1911)

Glozier, M., *Scottish Soldiers in France in the Reign of the Sun King: Nursery for Men of Honour* (Leiden: Brill, 2004)

Goodare, J., *State and Society in Early Modern Scotland* (Oxford: Oxford University Press, 1999)

Goodwin, G., *Fatal Rivalry: Henry VIII, James IV and the Battle for Renaissance Britain: Flodden 1513* (London: Weidenfeld and Nicolson, 2013)

Grainger, J., *Cromwell Against the Scots* (East Linton: Tuckwell Press, 1997)

Grant, J., *The Scottish Soldier of Fortune* (London: George Routledge, 1889)

Gregory, D., *The History of the Western Highlands and Isles of Scotland, from A.D. 1493 to A.D. 1625* (Edinburgh: John Donald, 2008)

Grierson, J. M., *Records of the Scottish Volunteer Force 1859–1908* (Edinburgh: Blackwood, 1909)

Grosjean, A., *An Unofficial Alliance: Scotland and Sweden 1569–1654* (Leiden: Brill, 2003)

Gruber, I. D. (ed.), *John Peebles' American War: The Diary of a Scottish Grenadier, 1776–82* (Stroud: Sutton Publishing, for the Army Records Society, 1997)

Halsall, G., *Warfare and Society in the Barbarian West, 450–900* (London and New York: Routledge, 2003)

Hanham, H. J., 'Religion and nationality in the mid-Victorian army', in M. R. D. Foot (ed.), *War and Society: Historical Essays in Honour and Memory of J. R. Western 1928–1971* (London: Paul Elek, 1973), pp. 159–81, 318–20

Harrington, P., 'Images of Culloden', *Journal of the Society for Army Historical Research*, vol. 63 (1985), pp. 208–19

Harrington, P., *British Artists and War: The Face of Battle in Paintings and Prints* (London: Greenhill, 1993)

Harris, J. P., *Douglas Haig and the First World War* (Cambridge: Cambridge University Press, 2008)

Harris, T., *Restoration: Charles II and his Kingdoms* (London: Penguin, 2006)

Harris, T., *Revolution: The Great Crisis of the British Monarchy, 1685–1720* (London: Allen Lane, 2006)

Hay, I., *Their Name Liveth: The Book of the Scottish National War Memorial* (East Kilbride: Edinburgh Trustees of the Scottish National War Memorial, 1985)

Hayes-McCoy, G. A., *Scots Mercenary Forces in Ireland (1565–1603)* (Dublin: Burns, Oates and Washbourne, 1937)

Haythornthwaite, P., *The Armies of Wellington* (London: Arms and Armour Press, 1994)

Henderson, D. M., *Highland Soldier: A Social Study of the Highland Regiments, 1820–1920* (Edinburgh: John Donald, 1989)

Henderson, D. M., *The Scottish Regiments* (Glasgow: HarperCollins, 1996)

Henderson, H., *Elegies for the Dead in Cyrenaica* (London: John Lehmann, 1948; Edinburgh: Polygon, 2008)

Henshaw, V., 'A reassessment of the British army in Scotland, from the union to the '45', *Northern Scotland*, vol. 2 (2011), pp. 1–21.

Hichberger, J. W. M., *Images of the Army: The Military in British Art, 1815–1914* (Manchester: Manchester University Press, 1988)

Hill, J. M., *Celtic Warfare 1595–1763* (Edinburgh: John Donald, 1986)

Hill, J. M., 'The distinctiveness of Gaelic warfare, 1400–1750', *European History Quarterly*, vol. 22 (1992), pp. 323–45

Hill, J. M., 'Killiecrankie and the evolution of Highland warfare', *War in History*, vol. 1 (1994), pp. 125–39

Historical Records of the Queen's Own Cameron Highlanders, 6 vols (Edinburgh: Blackwood, 1909–32)

Hutchison, P. P., *Canada's Black Watch: The First Hundred Years 1862–1962* (Montreal: The Black Watch of Canada, 1962)

Hyslop, J., 'Cape Town Highlanders, Transvaal Scottish: Military "Scottishness" and social power in nineteenth and twentieth century South Africa', *South African Historical Journal*, vol. 47 (2002), pp. 96–114

Jackson, C., *Restoration Scotland, 1660–1690* (Woodbridge: Boydell and Brewer, 2003)

Jamison, B. P., *Scotland and the Cold War* (Dunfermline: Cualann Press, 2003)

Johnston, S. H. F., 'The Scots army in the reign of Anne', *Transactions of the Royal Historical Society*, fifth series, vol. 3 (1953), pp. 1–21

Johnston, S. H. F., Story, H. H., Barclay, C. N., Baynes, J., *The History of the Cameronians (Scottish Rifles)*, 4 vols (Aldershot: Gale and Polden, and other subsequent publishers, 1957–71)

Jones, M. K., 'The battle of Verneuil (17 August 1424): Towards a history of courage', *War in History*, vol. 9 (2002), pp. 375–411

Keeley, L. H., *War before Civilization* (New York and Oxford: Oxford University Press, 1996)

Kelly, F., *A Guide to Early Irish Law* (Dublin: Dublin Institute for Advanced Studies, 1988)

Kennaway, J., *Tunes of Glory* (London: Putnam & Co., 1956; Edinburgh: Canongate, 1988)

Kestner, J., *Masculinities in Victorian Painting* (Aldershot: Scolar Press, 1995)

King, A., *Memorials of the Great War in Britain: The Symbolism and Politics of Remembrance* (Oxford: Berg, 1998)

King, A. and D. Simpkin (eds), *England and Scotland at War, 1296–c. 1513* (Leiden: Brill, 2012)

Laffin, J., *Scotland the Brave: The Story of the Scottish Soldier* (London: Cassell, 1963)

Laidlaw, J. (ed), *The Auld Alliance: France and Scotland over 700 years* (Edinburgh: Edinburgh University Press, 1999)

Lake, D., *Tartan Air Force: Scotland and a Century of Military Aviation 1907-2007* (Edinburgh: Birlinn, 2007)

Lavery, B., *Shield of Empire: The Royal Navy and Scotland* (Edinburgh: Birlinn, 2007)

Lawrence, J. and R. Lawrence, *When the Fighting is Over: Tumbledown, a Personal Story* (London: Bloomsbury, 1988)

Leask, A., *Sword of Scotland: Jocks at War* (Barnsley: Pen and Sword, 2006)

Lenman, B., *The Jacobite Clans of the Great Glen, 1650-1784* (London: Methuen, 1984)

Lenman, B., *The Jacobite Risings in Britain 1689–1746* (Dalkeith: Scottish Cultural Press, 1995)

Linklater, E. and A. Linklater, *The Black Watch: The History of the Royal Highland Regiment* (London: Barrie and Jenkins, 1977)

Linklater, M. and C. Hesketh, *Bonnie Dundee: John Graham of Claverhouse* (Edinburgh: Canongate, 1992)

Logue, K. J., 'The Tranent Militia riot of 1797', *Transactions of the*

East Lothian Antiquarian and Field Naturalists' Society, vol. 14 (1974), pp. 37–61

Logue, K. J., *Popular Disturbances in Scotland, 1780–1815* (Edinburgh: John Donald, 1979)

McCorry, H. (ed.), *The Thistle at War: An Anthology of the Scottish Experience of War, in the Services and at Home* (Edinburgh: National Museums of Scotland, 1997)

Macdonald, A. J., *Border Bloodshed: Scotland and England at War, 1369–1403* (East Linton: Tuckwell Press, 2000)

Macdonald, C. M. M. and E. W. McFarland (eds), *Scotland and the Great War* (East Linton: Tuckwell Press, 1999)

McDonald, R. A., *The Kingdom of the Isles: Scotland's Western Seaboard, c. 1100– c. 1336* (East Linton: Tuckwell Press, 1997)

MacDougall, N., *James IV* (Edinburgh: John Donald, 1989)

MacDougall, N. (ed.), *Scotland and War, AD 79–1918* (Edinburgh: John Donald, 1991)

MacDougall, N., *An Antidote to the English: The Auld Alliance 1295–1560* (East Linton: Tuckwell Press, 2001)

McFarland, E. W., '"Empire-enlarging genius": Scottish Imperial Yeomanry volunteers in the Boer War', *War in History*, vol. 13 (2006), pp. 299–328

McFarland, E. W., 'Commemoration of the South African War in Scotland, 1900–10', *Scottish Historical Review*, vol. 89 (2010), pp. 194–223

McFarland, E. W., 'The Great War', in T. M. Devine and J. Wormald (eds), *The Oxford Handbook of Modern Scottish History* (Oxford: Oxford University Press, 2012), pp. 553–68

MacGibbon, D. and T. Ross, *The Castellated and Domestic Architecture of Scotland*, 5 vols (Edinburgh: D. Douglas, 1887–92)

Macinnes, A. I., *Clanship, Commerce and the House of Stuart, 1603–1788* (East Linton: Tuckwell Press, 1996)

McKean, C., *The Scottish Chateau* (Stroud: Sutton, 2001)

Mackesy, P., *British Victory in Egypt 1801: The End of Napoleon's Conquest* (London: Routledge, 1995)

Mackillop, A., *'More Fruitful than the Soil': Army, Empire and the Scottish Highlands 1715–1815* (East Linton: Tuckwell Press, 2000)

MacLeod, J., *River of Fire: The Clydebank Blitz* (Edinburgh: Birlinn, 2010)

McLeod, W. and M. Bateman (eds), *Duanaire na Sracaire: Song-Book of the Pillagers: Anthology of Scotland's Gaelic Verse to 1600* (Edinburgh: Birlinn, 2007)

McLynn, F., *Charles Edward Stuart: A Tragedy in Many Acts* (London and New York: Routledge, 1988)

McNamee, C. J., 'William Wallace's invasion of northern England in 1297', *Northern History*, vol. 26 (1990), pp. 40–58

McNamee, C., *The Wars of the Bruces* (East Linton: Tuckwell Press, 1997)

McNamee, C., *Robert Bruce: Our Most Valiant Prince, King and Lord* (Edinburgh: Birlinn, 2006)

MacPhail, I. M. M., *The Crofters' War* (Stornoway: Acair Press, 1989)

Manning, R. B., *Apprenticeship in Arms: The Origins of the British Army 1585–1702* (Oxford: Oxford University Press, 2006)

Martin, H. G., *The History of the Fifteenth Scottish Division 1939–1945* (Edinburgh: William Blackwood, 1948)

Martine, R., *Edinburgh Military Tattoo* (London: Robert Hale, 2001)

Maurice, F., *The History of the Scots Guards from the Creation of the Regiment to the Eve of the Great War*, 2 vols (London: Chatto and Windus, 1934)

Melville, M. L., *The Story of the Lovat Scouts 1900–1980* (Kinloss: Librario Publishing, 2004)

Merriman, M., *The Rough Wooings: Mary Queen of Scots 1542–1551* (East Linton: Tuckwell Press, 2000)

Mileham, P., *Fighting Highlanders! The History of the Argyll and Sutherland Highlanders* (London: Arms and Armour Press, 1993)

Mileham, P., *The Scottish Regiments 1633–1996* (Staplehurst: Spellmount, 1996)

Miller, J., *Swords for Hire: The Scottish Mercenary* (Edinburgh: Birlinn, 2007)

Mitchell, S., *Scattered Under the Rising Sun: the Gordon Highlanders in the Far East 1941–1945* (Barnsley: Pen and Sword, 2012)

Mosse, G. L., *Fallen Soldiers: Reshaping the Memory of the World Wars* (Oxford: Oxford University Press, 1990)

Murdoch, S. (ed.) *Scotland and the Thirty Years War 1618–1648* (Leiden: Brill, 2001)

Murdoch, S. and A. Mackillop (eds), *Fighting for Identity: Scottish Military Experience c. 1550–1900* (Leiden: Brill, 2002)

Murray, D., *Music of the Scottish Regiments: Cogadh no Sith (War or Peace)* (Edinburgh: Mercat Press, 1994)

Naylor, M., *Among Friends: The Scots Guards 1956–1993* (London: Leo Cooper, 1995)

Nicholson, R., *Edward III and the Scots: The Formative Years of a Military Career, 1327–1335* (London: Oxford University Press, 1965)

Norman, A. V. B., *Arms and Armour in the Royal Scottish Museum* (Edinburgh: HMSO, 1972)

Oatts, L. B., *Proud Heritage: The Story of the Highland Light Infantry*, 4 vols (London: Thomas Nelson, 1952–63)

Oram, R., *David I: The King who Made Scotland* (Stroud: Tempus, 2004)

Oram, R., *Alexander II: King of Scots, 1214–1249* (Edinburgh: Birlinn, 2013)

Osborne, B. D., *The People's Army: The Home Guard in Scotland 1940–1944* (Edinburgh: Birlinn, 2009)

Parker, J., *Black Watch: The Inside Story of the Oldest Highland Regiment in the British Army* (London: Headline, 2005)

Paterson, R. H., *Pontius Pilate's Bodyguard: A History of The First or The Royal Regiment of Foot, The Royal Scots (The Royal Regiment)*, 3 vols (Edinburgh: RHQ Royal Scots, 2000–7)

Paton, D., 'Scotland in the air war 1939 to 1945', *History Scotland*, vol. 6 (2006), pp. 51–2

Penman, M., *David II, 1329–71* (East Linton: Tuckwell Press, 2004)

Penman, M. A., 'Faith in War: the Religious Experience of Scottish Soldiery, c. 1100–1500', *Journal of Medieval History*, vol. 37 (2011), pp. 295–303

Pentland, G., *The Spirit of the Union: Popular Politics in Scotland, 1815–1820* (London: Pickering and Chatto, 2011)

Phillips, G., *The Anglo-Scots Wars 1513–1550* (Woodbridge: Boydell and Brewer, 1999)

Phillips, G., 'Strategy and its limitations: the Anglo-Scottish wars, 1480–1550', *War in History*, vol. 6 (1999), pp. 396–416

Pollard, T., 'Mapping mayhem: Scottish battle maps and their role in archaeological research', *The Scottish Geographical Journal*, vol. 125 (2009), pp. 25–43

Pollard, T. (ed.), *Culloden: The History and Archaeology of the Last Clan Battle* (Barnsley: Pen and Sword, 2009)

Pollard, T. and N. Oliver, *Two Men in a Trench: Battlefield Archaeology: The Key to Unlocking the Past* (London: Penguin and Michael Joseph, 2002)

Pollard, T. and N. Oliver, *Two Men In A Trench II: Uncovering the Secrets of British Battlefields* (London: Penguin and Michael Joseph, 2003)

Potter, H., *Edinburgh under Siege, 1571–1573* (Stroud: Tempus, 2003)

Prebble, J., *Mutiny: Highland Regiments in Revolt, 1743–1804* (London: Secker and Warburg, 1975)

Prebble, J., *Culloden* (London: Penguin, 1996)
Ralston, I., *Celtic Fortifications* (Stroud: Tempus, 2006)
Reid, S., *The Campaigns of Montrose* (Edinburgh: Mercat Press, 1990)
Reid, S., *1745: A Military History* (Staplehurst: Spellmount, 1996)
Reid, S., *Wellington's Highland Warriors: From the Black Watch Mutiny to the Battle of Waterloo, 1743-1815* (Barnsley: Frontline Books, 2010)
Reid, S., *Crown, Covenant and Cromwell: The Civil Wars in Scotland 1639-1651* (Barnsley: Pen and Sword, 2012)
Ritchie, R. L. G., *The Normans in Scotland* (Edinburgh: Edinburgh University Press, 1954)
Robbins, J., *The Jacobite Wars: Scotland and the Military Campaigns of 1715 and 1745* (Edinburgh: Edinburgh University Press, 2002)
Robertson, J., *The Scottish Enlightenment and the Militia Issue* (Edinburgh: John Donald, 1985)
Robinson, M., *The Battle of Quatre Bras 1815* (Stroud: Spellmount, 2010)
Rogers, C. J., 'The Scottish Invasion of 1346', *Northern History*, vol. 34 (1998), pp. 51-69, and the accompanying appendix: Rogers, C. J. and M. C. Buck, 'Three new accounts of the Neville's Cross campaign', pp. 70-82
Royle, T., *The Flowers of the Forest: Scotland and the First World War* (Edinburgh: Birlinn, 2006)
Royle, T., *A Time of Tyrants: Scotland and the Second World War* (Edinburgh: Birlinn, 2011)
Sadler, J., *Border Fury: England and Scotland at War, 1296-1568* (London: Longman, 2005)
Salmond, J. B., *The History of the 51st Highland Division 1939-1945* (Edinburgh: William Blackwood, 1953)
Schofield, V., *Highland Furies: The Black Watch 1739-1899* (London: Quercus, 2012), vol. 1 of new official history
Scouller, R. E., *The Armies of Queen Anne* (Oxford: Oxford University Press, 1966)
Seton, B. and J. Grant, *Pipes of War* (Glasgow: Maclehose, Jackson & Co., 1920)
Sheffield, G., *The Chief: Douglas Haig and the British Army* (London: Aurum Press, 2011)
Simms, K., 'Warfare in the medieval Gaelic lordships', *The Irish Sword*, vol. 12 (1975), pp. 98-108
Simms, K., 'Gaelic warfare in the Middle Ages', in T. Bartlett and

K. Jeffery (eds), *A Military History of Ireland* (Cambridge: Cambridge University Press, 1996), pp. 99–115

Simpson, G. (ed.), *Scotland and Scandinavia, 800-1800* (Edinburgh: John Donald, 1990)

Simpson, G. (ed.), *The Scottish Soldier Abroad 1247-1967* (Edinburgh: John Donald, 1992)

Snape, M., *God and the British Soldier: Religion and the British Army in the First and Second World Wars* (London and New York: Routledge, 2005)

Spaven, M., *Fortress Scotland: A Guide to the Military Presence* (London: Pluto Press in association with Scottish CND, 1983)

Speck, W., *The Butcher: The Duke of Cumberland and the Suppression of the '45* (Oxford: Basil Blackwell, 1981)

Spiers, E. M., *The Late Victorian Army 1868-1902* (Manchester: Manchester University Press, 1992)

Spiers, E. M., 'The Scottish soldier at war', in H. Cecil and P. Liddle (eds), *Facing Armageddon: The First World War Experienced* (London: Leo Cooper, 1996), pp. 314–35

Spiers, E. M., 'The Scottish soldier in the Boer War', in J. Gooch (ed.), *The Boer War: Direction, Experience and Image* (London: Frank Cass, 2000), pp. 152–65, 273–7

Spiers, E. M., *The Scottish Soldier and Empire, 1854-1902* (Edinburgh: Edinburgh University Press, 2006)

Spring, M. H., *With Zeal and Bayonets Only* (Norman, OK: University of Oklahoma Press, 2008)

Spurlock, R. Scott, *Cromwell and Scotland: Conquest and Religion, 1650-1660* (Edinburgh: John Donald, 2007)

Stanley, G. F. G., 'The Scottish military tradition', in W. S. Reid (ed.), *The Scottish Tradition in Canada* (Toronto: McClelland and Stewart, 1976), pp. 137–60

Steer, K. A. and J. W. M. Bannerman, *Late Medieval Monumental Sculpture in the West Highlands* (Edinburgh: The Royal Commission on the Ancient and Historical Monuments of Scotland, 1977)

Stell, G., 'The Scottish medieval castle: Form, function and "evolution"', in K. J. Stringer (ed.), *Essays on the Nobility of Medieval Scotland* (Edinburgh: John Donald, 1985), pp. 195–209

Sterling, A., *The Highland Brigade in the Crimea* (Minneapolis, MN: Absinthe Press, 1995)

Stevenson, D., *The Covenanters* (Edinburgh: Saltire Society, 1988)

Stevenson, D., *Highland Warrior: Alasdair MacColla and the Civil Wars* (Edinburgh: Saltire Society, 1994)

Stevenson, K., *Chivalry and Knighthood in Scotland, 1424–1513* (Woodbridge: Boydell and Brewer, 2006)

Stewart, J. L. M., *The Story of the Atholl Highlanders* (Blair Castle: The Atholl Highlanders, 2000)

Stewart, J. and J. Buchan, *The 15th (Scottish) Division 1914–1919* (Edinburgh and London: William Blackwood, 1926)

Strachan, H., *The Politics of the British Army* (Oxford: Oxford University Press, 1997)

Strachan, H., 'Scotland's military identity', *Scottish Historical Review*, vol. 85 (2006), pp. 315–32

Streets, H., *Martial Races: The Military, Race and Masculinity in British Imperial Culture, 1857–1914* (Manchester: Manchester University Press, 2004)

Strickland, M. J., 'Securing the north: Invasion and the strategy of defence in twelfth-century Anglo-Scottish warfare', in M. J. Strickland (ed.), *Anglo-Norman Warfare: Studies in Late Anglo-Saxon and Anglo-Norman Military Organization and Warfare* (Woodbridge: Boydell and Brewer, 1992), pp. 208–29

Stringer, K., 'Kingship, conflict and state making in the reign of Alexander II: The war of 1215–1217 and its context', in R. D. Oram (ed.), *The Reign of Alexander II, 1214–1249* (Leiden: Brill 2005), pp. 99–156

Sulzberger, A., 'Bringing Scotland into the fold: The Highland military figure and the evolution of British imperial identity' (unpublished MA dissertation, Courtauld Institute of Art, 2008)

Sym, J. (ed.), *Seaforth Highlanders* (Aldershot: Gale and Polden, 1962)

Szechi, D., *1715: The Great Jacobite Rebellion* (New Haven, CT and London: Yale University Press, 2006)

Tabraham, C., *Scotland's Castles* (London: Batsford, 1997)

Tabraham, C., 'Scottorum Malleus: Edward I and Scotland', in D. H. Williams and J. R. Kenyon (eds), *The Impact of the Edwardian Castles in Wales* (Oxford and Oakville, CT: Oxbow Books, 2010), pp. 183–92

Tabraham, C. J. and D. Grove, *Fortress Scotland and the Jacobites* (London: B. T. Batsford for Historic Scotland, 1995)

Terry, R., *Women in Khaki: The Story of the British Women Soldier* (London: Columbus Books, 1998)

Townshend, C., 'Martial law: Legal and administrative problems of civil emergency in Britain and the empire, 1800–1940', *Historical Journal*, vol. 25 (1982), pp. 167–95

Townshend, C., *Britain's Civil Wars: Counterinsurgency in the Twentieth Century* (London: Faber and Faber, 1986)

Usherwood, P. and J. Spencer-Smith, *Lady Butler: Battle Artists 1846–1933* (London: National Army Museum, 1987)
Van Emden, R., *Last Man Standing* (Barnsley: Pen and Sword, 2012)
Watson, F. J., *Under The Hammer: Edward 1 and Scotland 1286–1307* (East Linton: Tuckwell Press, 1998)
Watson, W. J. (ed.), *Scottish Verse from the Book of the Dean of Lismore* (Edinburgh: Scottish Gaelic Texts Society, 1937)
Watt, P., *Steel and Tartan: The 4th Cameron Highlanders in the Great War* (Stroud: The History Press, 2013)
Wedgwood, C. V., *Montrose* (Stroud: Alan Sutton, 1995)
West, S. (ed.), *The Victorians and Race* (Aldershot: Scolar Press, 1996)
Whitelaw, C. E., *Scottish Arms Makers* (London: Arms and Armour Press, 1977)
Wilkinson-Latham, R., *Scottish Military Uniforms* (Newton Abbot: David and Charles, 1975)
Wills, R., *The Jacobites and Russia, 1715–1750* (East Linton: Tuckwell Press, 2002)
Winter, J., *Sites of Memory, Sites of Mourning: The Great War in European Cultural History* (Cambridge: Cambridge University Press, 1995)
Womack, P., *Improvement and Romance: Constructing the Myth of the Scottish Highlands* (London: Macmillan, 1989)
Wood, I. S., 'Thin red line? Scottish soldiers in the Troubles in Scotland and Ulster', in I. S. Wood (ed.), *Scotland and Ulster* (Edinburgh: Mercat Press, 1994), pp. 150–71
Wood, S., *The Scottish Soldier* (Manchester: Archive Publications, 1987)
Wood, S., *In the Finest Tradition: The Royal Scots Dragoon Guards (Carabiniers & Greys): Its History and Treasures* (Edinburgh: Mainstream Publishing, 1988)
Wood, S., *The Auld Alliance: Scotland and France: The Military Connection* (Edinburgh: Mainstream Publishing, 1989)
Woollcombe, R., *All The Blue Bonnets: The History of the King's Own Scottish Borderers* (London: Arms and Armour Press, 1980)
Woosnam-Savage, R. C. (ed.), *1745: Charles Edward Stuart and the Jacobites* (Edinburgh: HMSO, 1995)
Young, D., *Forgotten Scottish Voices From the Great War* (Stroud: Tempus, 2005)
Young, J. R. (ed.), *Celtic Dimensions of the British Civil Wars* (Edinburgh: John Donald, 1997)
Zeune, J., *The Last Scottish Castles* (Buch am Erlbach: Leidorf, 1992)

Notes on the Contributors

Stuart Allan is Senior Curator of Military History at National Museums Scotland. He is the author of *Commando Country* (2007) and co-author (with Allan Carswell) of *The Thin Red Line: War, Empire and Visions of Scotland* (2004).

Niall Barr, a graduate of the University of St Andrews, is Reader in Military History, Defence Studies Department, King's College London, based at the Joint Services Command and Staff College. He has published extensively on British military history, including *Pendulum of War: The Three Battles of El Alamein* (2004) and *The Lion and the Poppy: Veterans, Politics and Society 1921–1939* (2005). His latest work, *Yanks and Limeys: Alliance Warfare in the Second World War*, will be published in 2012.

Martyn Bennett is Professor of Early Modern History, and Head of the Graduate School, Nottingham Trent University. He has published widely on the English civil wars and on the impact of war and revolutions on seventeenth-century Britain and Ireland. His books include *The Civil Wars in Britain and Ireland, 1638–1651* (1996), *The Civil War Experienced: Britain and Ireland, 1638–1661* (2000) and *Oliver Cromwell* (2006).

Stephen Brumwell is a freelance writer and historian. He is the author of *Redcoats: The British Soldier and War in the Americas, 1755–1763* (2002) and *White Devil: A True Story of War, Savagery and Vengeance in Colonial America* (2004). His most recent book, *Paths of Glory: The Life and Death of General James Wolfe* (2006), won the Distinguished Book Award of the Society of Colonial Wars, New York, and the C. P. Stacey Prize for Canadian Military History.

Ewen A. Cameron holds the Sir William Fraser Chair of Scottish History and Palaeography at the University of Edinburgh. He has published extensively on the history of the Scottish Highlands and on the political history of modern Scotland. His books include *Land for the People? The British Government and the Scottish Highlands, c. 1880–1925* (1996) and *Impaled on a Thistle: Scotland since 1880* (2010).

Allan Carswell is a freelance curator and museum consultant. He was formerly the Curator of the National War Museum of Scotland at Edinburgh castle. He is the author of *For Your Freedom and Ours: Poland, Scotland and the Second World War* (1993) and co-author (with Stuart Allan) of *The Thin Red Line: War, Empire and Visions of Scotland* (2004).

John C. R. Childs is Emeritus Professor of Military History at the University of Leeds. The author of several books on seventeenth- and eighteenth-century British and European military history, in particular a trilogy on the social and political history of the British army from 1660 to 1702, he is currently preparing biographies of Lieutenant-General Percy Kirke and the first duke of Marlborough. For ten years he was chairman of the English Heritage Battlefields Advisory Panel and is now chairman of the Royal Armouries Development Trust.

Jeremy A. Crang is Senior Lecturer in History at the University of Edinburgh. He is the author of *The British Army and the People's War, 1939–1945* (2000) and co-editor (with Paul Addison) of *The Burning Blue: A New History of the Battle of Britain* (2000), *Firestorm: The Bombing of Dresden, 1945* (2006) and *Listening to Britain: Home Intelligence Reports on Britain's 'Finest Hour', May–September 1940* (2010).

Christopher Duffy is a military historian and former lecturer at the Royal Military Academy, Sandhurst, and the Army Staff College. Between 1996 and 2001 he was Research Professor in the History of War at De Montfort University. He has published widely on aspects of military history, including *The '45: Bonnie Prince Charlie and the Untold Story of the Jacobite Rising* (2003).

Charles J. Esdaile holds a personal chair in History at the University of Liverpool. He has written extensively on the Napoleonic period and is the author of *The Wars of Napoleon* (1995), *Spain in the Liberal Age: From Constitution to Civil War, 1808–1939* (2000), *The Peninsular War: A New History* (2002), *Fighting Napoleon:*

Guerrillas, Bandits and Adventurers in Spain, 1808–1814 (2004), *Napoleon's Wars: An International History* (2007) and *Peninsular Eyewitnesses: The Human Experience of War in Spain and Portugal, 1808–1814* (2008).

James E. Fraser is Senior Lecturer in Early Scottish History at the University of Edinburgh. He is the author of *The Battle of Dunnichen 685* (2002), *From Caledonia to Pictland: Scotland to 795* (2009) and numerous articles on politics and identity in pre-Viking Scotland.

Matthew Glozier teaches in the Department of History, Sydney Grammar School, Australia, and is an Honorary Associate of the Medieval and Early Modern Centre at the University of Sydney. His research interests cover international soldiering in early modern Europe, the formation of state armies and the Scottish and Huguenot diaspora. His publications include *Scottish Soldiers in France in the Reign of the Sun King: Nursery for Men of Honour* (2004), *Marshal Schomberg (1615–1690): International Soldiering and the Formation of State Armies in Seventeenth-Century Europe* (2005) and, as co-editor, *War, Religion and Service: Huguenot Soldiering, 1685–1713* (2007).

Peter Harrington is Curator of the Anne S. K. Brown Military Collection at Brown University Library in Providence, Rhode Island, USA. His research focuses on artists and images of war and he has taught and published extensively on the subject, including *British Artists and War: The Face of Battle in Paintings and Prints* (1993). He is currently researching British war art, 1914–1918, and writing a book about the Scottish 'special' artist William Simpson in the Second Afghan War.

Fraser Hunter is the Principal Curator of Iron Age and Roman Archaeology at National Museums Scotland. He has published widely on aspects of Iron Age Scotland and on the impact of Rome, including *Beyond the Edge of the Empire: Caledonians, Picts and Romans* (2007). His current research includes a long-running project on the Iron Age carnyx, or war-trumpet, found at Deskford (Banffshire) and its European context.

Robert P. Irvine is Senior Lecturer in English Literature at the University of Edinburgh, specialising in Scottish literature of the eighteenth and nineteenth centuries. He has published on Smollett, Scott, Stevenson and Austen. He is currently editing *Prince Otto* for the Edinburgh Edition of the Works of Robert Louis Stevenson, and a new selection of the poems and songs of Robert Burns for Oxford World's Classics.

Lieutenant-General Sir Alistair Irwin was commissioned into the Black Watch in 1970 after graduating from the University of St Andrews. He commanded the 1st Battalion, the Black Watch, in Northern Ireland, Edinburgh and West Berlin, was General Officer Commanding Northern Ireland, and Adjutant-General on the Army Board. He retired from the army in 2005. He is President of the Royal British Legion Scotland, Veterans Scotland and the Officers' Association Scotland, and is Vice Chairman of the Commonwealth War Graves Commission.

Alastair J. Macdonald is Mackie Lecturer in History at the University of Aberdeen. His research focuses on later medieval Scotland, its place in European diplomacy and on Anglo-Scottish relations, as well as the study of European frontier societies. He has published a number of articles on Anglo-Scottish warfare in the later Middle Ages and is the author of *Border Bloodshed: Scotland and England at War, 1369–1403* (2000). His current research project examines the nature and impact of war on state and society in fourteenth- and fifteenth-century Scotland.

Martin MacGregor is Lecturer in Scottish History at the University of Glasgow. His principal area of research is the history of Gaelic Scotland in the later medieval and early modern eras, including the nature of clan- and kin-based society. His publications include, as co-editor, *Mìorun mòr nan Gall, 'The Great Ill-Will of the Lowlander'? Lowland Perceptions of the Highlands, Medieval and Modern* (2009). With Thomas Clancy, he is the editor of Edinburgh University Press's multi-volume *History of Gaelic Scotland*, to which he will contribute a volume on the later Middle Ages.

Elaine W. McFarland is Professor of History at Glasgow Caledonian University. Her publications include *Protestants First: Orangeism in Nineteenth Century Scotland* (1990), *Ireland and Scotland in the Age of Revolution* (1994), (co-editor) *Scotland and the Great War* (1999) and *John Ferguson 1836–1906: Irish Issues in Scottish Politics* (2004). She is currently working on a biography of Lieutenant-General Sir Aylmer Hunter-Weston.

K. A. J. McLay, a graduate of the University of Glasgow, is Head of the Department of History and Archaeology at the University of Chester. He has published articles on early modern military history in *Historical Research, Journal of Imperial and Commonwealth History, Journal of Mediterranean Studies* and *War in History*, and is completing a book on the British 'way in warfare' during the late seventeenth and early eighteenth centuries.

Gervase Phillips is Principal Lecturer in History at Manchester Metropolitan University. His research interests include Tudor armies and Anglo-Scottish warfare in the later fifteenth and sixteenth centuries. He is the author of *The Anglo-Scots Wars 1513–1550* (1999), as well as numerous articles on the development and transfer of weapons technology, and the role of the cavalry arm from the early modern period to the twentieth century.

Tony Pollard is Senior Lecturer in History and Director of the Centre for Battlefield Archaeology at the University of Glasgow. He has undertaken battlefield- and conflict-related archaeological projects in the UK, mainland Europe, Africa and South America, and has written widely on the subject. His publications include (with Neil Oliver) *Two Men in a Trench: Battlefield Archaeology, the Key to Unlocking the Past* (2002), (with Neil Oliver) *Two Men in a Trench II: Uncovering the Secrets of British Battlefields* (2003) and, as editor, *Culloden: The History and Archaeology of the Last Clan Battle* (2009). He is co-editor (with Iain Banks) of the *Journal of Conflict Archaeology*.

Michael Prestwich is Professor Emeritus in the Department of History at the University of Durham and a former Pro-Vice-Chancellor. He has published extensively on the political, constitutional and military history of thirteenth- and fourteenth-century England. His books include *War, Politics and Finance under Edward I* (1972), *The Three Edwards: War and State in England 1272–1377* (1980), *Edward I* (1988), *Armies and Warfare in the Middle Ages: The English Experience* (1996) and *Plantagenet England 1225–1360* (2005).

Trevor Royle is an Honorary fellow in the School of History, Classics and Archaeology at the University of Edinburgh. He has published widely on British military history. His recent books include *The Flowers of the Forest: Scotland and the First World War* (2006), *The Wars of the Roses: England's First Civil War* (2009), *Montgomery: Lessons in Leadership from the Soldier's General* (2010) and *A Time of Tyrants: Scotland and the Second World War* (2011).

Edward M. Spiers, a graduate of the University of Edinburgh, is Professor of Strategic Studies at the University of Leeds. His main works on military history include *Haldane: An Army Reformer* (1980), *The Army and Society, 1815–1914* (1980), *Radical General: Sir George de Lacy Evans, 1787–1870* (1983), *The Late Victorian Army, 1868–1902* (1992), *The Victorian Soldier in Africa* (2004), *The Scottish Soldier and Empire, 1854–1902* (2006) and *Letters from*

Ladysmith: Eyewitness Accounts from the South African War (2010). He also edited *Sudan: The Reconquest Reappraised* (1998).

Matthew J. Strickland is Professor of Medieval History at the University of Glasgow. His principal area of research is chivalric culture and conduct in medieval warfare, as well as the military and political history of the Anglo-Norman and Angevin periods. His books include *War and Chivalry: The Conduct and Perception of War in England and Normandy, 1066-1217* (1996) and (with Robert Hardy) *The Great War Bow: From Hastings to the Mary Rose* (2005). He is also the editor of *Anglo-Norman Warfare* (1992) and *Armies, Chivalry and Warfare in Medieval Britain and France* (1998).

Chris Tabraham was formerly Historic Scotland's Principal Historian and a Principal Inspector of Ancient Monuments. A specialist on the castles and fortifications of Scotland, his many publications include *Scottish Castles and Fortifications* (2000), *Castles of Scotland: A Voyage Through the Centuries* (2005), *Scotland's Castles* (2005), *The Illustrated History of Scotland* (2010) and (with Doreen Grove) *Fortress Scotland and the Jacobites* (1995). He has directed many archaeological excavations and is currently researching Scotland's Norman castles.

Wendy Ugolini is Lecturer in British History at the University of Edinburgh. She specialises in the field of war, memory and identities and is the author of *Experiencing War as the 'Enemy Other': Italian Scottish Experience in World War II* (2011).

Gary J. West is Senior Lecturer in Celtic and Scottish Studies, and Director of the European Ethnological Research Centre, at the University of Edinburgh. He has written and broadcast widely on Scottish cultural history, with particular emphasis on oral history, traditional music and revivalism. An active musician himself, he has recorded and performed in many parts of the world and since 2003 has presented the specialist piping programme, *Pipeline*, on BBC Radio Scotland.

Ian S. Wood taught history for many years at the Open University in Scotland and at Napier University in Edinburgh. His recent books include *Crimes of Loyalty: A History of the UDA* (2006) and *Britain, Ireland and the Second World War* (2010). He has been a regular contributor to *The Scotsman* and other newspapers on events in Northern Ireland, and, with Andrew Sanders, has co-authored *Times of Troubles: Britain's War in Northern Ireland* (2012).

Illustration Credits

Figures

I.1 © National Trust for Scotland/licensor www.scran.ac.uk
I.2 Courtesy of the Council of the National Army Museum, London
I.3 Courtesy of the Black Watch Museum Trust
I.4 Courtesy of the Regimental Museum of the Royal Highland Fusiliers
I.5 © National Museums Scotland
1.1 © National Museums Scotland
1.2 Courtesy of the Royal Commission on the Ancient and Historical Monuments of Scotland
1.3 © Historic Scotland/licensor www.scran.ac.uk
1.4 © National Museums Scotland
2.1 © Kilmartin House Trust/licensor www.scran.ac.uk
2.2 © Historic Scotland/licensor www.scran.ac.uk
2.3 © Royal Commission on the Ancient and Historical Monuments of Scotland/licensor www.scran.ac.uk
2.4 © Crown copyright reproduced courtesy of Historic Scotland. www.historicscotlandimages.gov.uk
3.1 © Royal Commission on the Ancient and Historical Monuments of Scotland/licensor www.scran.ac.uk
3.2 Courtesy of the Royal Commission on the Ancient and Historical Monuments of Scotland
3.3 © National Museums Scotland
3.4 © National Museums Scotland/licensor www.scran.ac.uk
4.1 © Estate of John Duncan. All rights reserved, DACS 2011
4.2 © Stirling District Tourism Ltd/licensor www.scran.ac.uk
4.3 © Crown copyright reproduced courtesy of Historic Scotland. www.historicscotlandimages.gov.uk

Illustration Credits

4.4 © Cumbria Archive Services/licensor www.scran.ac.uk
5.1 © Crown copyright reproduced courtesy of Historic Scotland. www.historicscotlandimages.gov.uk
5.2 © Culture and Sport Glasgow (Museums)
5.3 © Culture and Sport Glasgow (Museums)
5.4 © Royal Commission on the Ancient and Historical Monuments of Scotland/licensor www.scran.ac.uk
6.1 © Board of Trustees of the Armouries
6.2 © Crown copyright reproduced courtesy of Historic Scotland. www.historicscotlandimages.gov.uk
6.3 Courtesy of Getty Images
6.4 Courtesy of the Council of the National Army Museum, London
7.1 © Crown copyright reproduced courtesy of Historic Scotland. www.historicscotlandimages.gov.uk
7.2 © Crown copyright reproduced courtesy of Historic Scotland. www.historicscotlandimages.gov.uk
7.3 © Crown copyright reproduced courtesy of Historic Scotland. www.historicscotlandimages.gov.uk
7.4 © Culture and Sport Glasgow (Museums)
8.1 Courtesy of the National Archives, Kew
8.2 © Historic Scotland/licensor www.scran.ac.uk
8.3 Courtesy of Getty Images
8.4 © Crown copyright reproduced courtesy of Historic Scotland. www.historicscotlandimages.gov.uk
9.1 Courtesy of the British Library
9.2 Courtesy of the Trustees of the National Library of Scotland
9.3 © National Museums Scotland
9.4 © National Museums Scotland
10.1 © National Museums Scotland
10.2 Courtesy of Ken Welsh/Bridgeman Art Library
10.3 Courtesy of the Imperial Defence College, Camberley/Bridgeman Art Library
10.4 © Crown copyright reserved Historic Scotland/licensor www.scran.ac.uk
11.1 © Scottish National Portrait Gallery/licensor www.scran.ac.uk
11.2 © Scottish National Portrait Gallery/licensor www.scran.ac.uk
11.3 © Lennoxlove House Ltd/licensor www.scran.ac.uk
11.4 © National Museums Scotland
12.1 © Lennoxlove House Ltd/licensor www.scran.ac.uk
12.2 Reproduced from H. C. Wylly, *A Short History of the Cameronians (Scottish Rifles)* (Aldershot, 1924), opp. p. 6. Courtesy of the Trustees of the National Library of Scotland

12.3 Courtesy of the Royal Scots Dragoon Guards Museum
12.4 Courtesy of the Scottish National Portrait Gallery
13.1 © University of Glasgow/John S. Keltie (ed.), *History of the Scottish Highlands* (Edinburgh and London, 1875), vol. 1, p. 498/licensor www.scran.ac.uk
13.2 © National Museums Scotland
13.3 Courtesy of the Royal Collection and Her Majesty, Queen Elizabeth II/Bridgeman Art Library
13.4 © Scottish National Portrait Gallery/licensor www.scran.ac.uk
13.5 © National Museums Scotland
13.6 © National Museums Scotland
14.1 © National Museums Scotland
14.2 © National Museums Scotland
14.3 Courtesy of the Bute Collection at Mount Stuart. On loan to National Museums Scotland
14.4 © National Museums Scotland
15.1 Courtesy of the Gordon Highlanders Museum
15.2 © National Museums Scotland
15.3 Courtesy of the Royal Scots Dragoon Guards Museum
15.4 Courtesy of the Trustees of the Highlanders Museum
16.1 © Douglas Skelton/licensor www.scran.ac.uk
16.2 © National Museums Scotland
16.3 © University of Strathclyde/licensor www.scran.ac.uk
16.4 Courtesy of Getty Images
17.1 Courtesy of the Argory, County Armagh/Bridgeman Art Library
17.2 Courtesy of Getty Images
17.3 © National Museums Scotland
17.4 © National Museums Scotland
17.5 © National Museums Scotland
17.6 © National Museums Scotland
18.1 Reproduced from T. F. Wade-Ferrell, *In All Things Faithful: A History and Album of the 30th Battalion and New South Wales Scottish Regiment 1895–1985* (Sydney, 1985), p. 6
18.2 Courtesy of the Imperial War Museum, CO176
18.3 Courtesy of the Imperial War Museum, Q10675
18.4 Courtesy of the Imperial War Museum, E2987
19.1 © National Archives of Scotland/licensor www.scran.ac.uk
19.2 Courtesy of the Imperial War Museum, Q48957
19.3 Courtesy of the Imperial War Museum, Q4012
19.4 Courtesy of Fiona C. Douglas
19.5 © National Library of Scotland/licensor www.scran.ac.uk
19.6 © The Scotsman Publications Ltd/licensor www.scran.ac.uk

Illustration Credits

20.1 Courtesy of the Gordon Highlanders Museum
20.2 © Newsquest (Herald & Times)/licensor www.scran.ac.uk
20.3 Courtesy of Getty Images
20.4 © National Museums Scotland
20.5 Courtesy of the Argyll and Sutherland Highlanders Museum
21.1 Courtesy of the Royal Commission on the Ancient and Historical Monuments of Scotland
21.2 Courtesy of the Imperial War Museum, HO 26632
21.3 © The Scotsman Publications Ltd/licensor www.scran.ac.uk
21.4 Courtesy of the Imperial War Museum, EO 19364
21.5 Courtesy of the Imperial War Museum, NA 1918
21.6 Courtesy of the Imperial War Museum, E21974
21.7 Courtesy of the Imperial War Museum, B6000
22.1 © National Museums Scotland
22.2 Courtesy of the Imperial War Museum, BF 10875
22.3 Courtesy of Calvert/AP/Press Association Images
22.4 Courtesy of The Herald and Evening Times Picture Archive
22.5 Courtesy of the Imperial War Museum, FKD 314
22.6 Courtesy of the Black Watch Museum Trust
23.1 Courtesy of Allan Carswell
23.2 © National Museums Scotland
23.3 © National Museums Scotland
23.4 © National Museums Scotland
23.5 © National Museums Scotland
24.1 © National Museums Scotland
24.2 Courtesy of the Gordon Highlanders Museum
24.3 Courtesy of Getty Images
24.4 Courtesy of the Imperial War Museum, B 5103
25.1 Courtesy of the National Theatre of Scotland/Manuel Harlan
25.2 Courtesy of the Imperial War Museum, NA004759
25.3 Courtesy of Canongate/Kobal Collection
26.1 Courtesy of National Gallery of Canada, Ottawa
26.2 Courtesy of the Anne S. K. Brown Military Collection, Brown University Library
26.3 Courtesy of the Anne S. K. Brown Military Collection, Brown University Library
26.4 Courtesy of Christie's images/Bridgeman Art Library
26.5 © National Museums Scotland
27.1 © Crown copyright reproduced courtesy of Historic Scotland. www.historicscotlandimages.gov.uk
27.2 © Crown copyright reproduced courtesy of Historic Scotland. www.historicscotlandimages.gov.uk

27.3 © Crown copyright reproduced courtesy of Historic Scotland. www.historicscotlandimages.gov.uk
27.4 © Crown copyright reproduced courtesy of Historic Scotland. www.historicscotlandimages.gov.uk
27.5 Courtesy of the Royal Commission on the Ancient and Historical Monuments of Scotland
28.1 Courtesy of Scotavia Images.
28.2 © Crown copyright reproduced courtesy of Historic Scotland. www.historicscotlandimages.gov.uk
28.3 Courtesy of Tony Pollard
28.4 Courtesy of Natasha Ferguson
28.5 Courtesy of Lord Egremont and the Petworth House Archives
29.1 Courtesy of the Royal Commission on the Ancient and Historical Monuments of Scotland
29.2 © Colin J. M. Martin/licensor www.scran.ac.uk
29.3 © The National Trust for Scotland/licensor www.scran.ac.uk
29.4 © The Scotsman Publications Ltd/licensor www.scran.ac.uk
29.5 Courtesy of the Royal Commission on the Ancient and Historical Monuments of Scotland
29.6 © The Scotsman Publications Ltd/licensor www.scran.ac.uk
30.1 Courtesy of Heritage House Group Ltd
30.2 © National Museums Scotland
30.3 © National Museums Scotland
30.4 © National Museums Scotland
30.5 Courtesy of the Argyll and Sutherland Highlanders Museum
30.6 Courtesy of South Lanarkshire Council
E.1 © UK MOD Crown copyright 2011
E.2 Courtesy of the Anne S. K. Brown Military Collection, Brown University Library
E.3 © National Museums Scotland
E.4 Courtesy of Mark Owens/Army HQ2Div

Colour plates

1 © National Museums Scotland
2 Courtesy of Musée Condé, Chantilly/Bridgeman Art Library
3 Courtesy of the Bodleian Library, Oxford (MS. Bodl. 264, fol. 51v)
4 © National Museums Scotland
5 © National Trust for Scotland/licensor www.scran.ac.uk
6 Courtesy of the Royal Collection and Her Majesty, Queen Elizabeth II/Bridgeman Art Library

Illustration Credits

7 Crown copyright reproduced courtesy of Historic Scotland www.historicscotlandimages.gov.uk
8 Courtesy of Leeds Museums and Galleries (City Art Gallery)/Bridgeman Art Library
9 © National Museums Scotland
10 Courtesy of Mr Hew Blair-Imrie. On loan to National Museums Scotland
11 © National Museums Scotland
12 © By kind permission of Diageo. On loan to National Museums Scotland
13 Courtesy of Getty Images
14 Courtesy of the Argyll and Sutherland Highlanders Museum
15 © National Museums Scotland
16 Courtesy of Dundee Art Galleries and Museums (Dundee City Council)
17 Courtesy of York Museums Trust (York Art Gallery)/Bridgeman Art Library
18 Courtesy of the Imperial War Museum, ART 2995
19 Courtesy of Dundee Art Galleries and Museums (Dundee City Council)
20 © National Museums Scotland
21 Courtesy of the 51st (Highland) Division and Ross Bequest Trust. On loan to National Museums Scotland
22 Courtesy of the Argyll and Sutherland Highlanders Museum
23 © UK MOD Crown copyright 2011
24 © Marius Alexander/licensor www.scran.ac.uk
25 © The Scotsman Publications Ltd/licensor www.scran.ac.uk
26 © UK MOD Crown copyright 2011

Index

Abels, Richard, 77, 79
Abercrombie, Maj. James, 387, 393
Abercromby, Brig.-Gen. James, 393
Abercromby, Lt.-Gen. Sir Ralph,
    17–18, 692, 754
Aberdeen, 27, 172, 279, 369–70, 372,
    573, 585n1, 718, 738
  in the 'Forty-Five, 364, 369, 372,
    375, 738
  sacked (1336), 168
  seized (1644), 288
  University of, 354, 800
  Volunteers, 470
Aberdeenshire, 164, 172–3, 385, 563,
    709, 720–1, 743
  axehead find in Lumphanan, 112
  riots in, 437
Aberdour, Alan de Mortimer, lord of,
    709
Aberfeldy, Black Watch monument
    at, 757
Aberfoyle, war memorial at, 768
Aberlemno, 75–6, 81, 114, 689, 749
Aboyne, James Gordon, 2nd Viscount,
    279
Achnacarry, 516, 564
  House, 563
Achnacone, Lt.-Col. Ian MacAlister
    Stewart, 13th laird of, 571
Ackermann, Rudolph, 696
  *Ackermann's Costumes of the British
    Army* (1840–54), 696
Act of Settlement (1701), 339, 350
Act of Supremacy (1669), 306
Adam, John, 436, 438
Adams, Gerry, 548

Aden, 'Argyll Law' in, 614
  Crater reoccupied (1967), 614, 643,
    662, 702, 804
Admiralty, 449–52
Adomnán, 68–70, 72–3, 75, 83
  Life of Columba, 68, 71–2, 74, 77, 82
Æthelstan, king of Wessex, 80
Afghanistan, 500
  Second Afghan War (1878–80), 472,
    698, 700
  War in Afghanistan (2001–), 608,
    627, 629, 662, 805–7, 809
'Age of Forays', 654
Agricola, Gnaeus Julius, roman
    general and governor of
    Britannia, 55, 743
aid to the civil power, 2, 342, 465, 537,
    554
  in England and Wales, 19, 440,
    442
  in the Highlands, 327, 339, 359,
    415, 446–52
  Ireland, 19, 440–2, 546–8
  Northern Ireland, 548–55
  Scotland, 327, 339, 342–3, 409, 417,
    437–41, 444–5, 453, 542–4
Ailsa, Gertrude Millicent Cooper,
    marchioness of, 764
Airds, Lt.-Col. Lorne MacLaine
    Campbell of, 577, 595n71
Airlie, David Ogilvy, 11th earl of, 758
Airlie, James Ogilvy, 2nd earl of, 307
Aitkin, John, 327
Alba, 80, 82, 114
Albany, John Stewart, 2nd duke of,
    187, 193, 718–19

Albany, Robert Stewart, 1st duke of, 713–14
Albermarle, William Anne Keppel, 2nd earl of, 16
Aldermaston, Atomic Weapons Establishment, 603
Alexander I, king of Scots (r. 1107–24), 96, 111
Alexander II, king of Scots (r. 1214–49), 104, 107, 115
  defends Lothian (1216), 103
  forces of, 106, 109–10, 115
  invades England, 101–2,
  married to Marie de Courcy, 710
  meets Prince Louis of France at Dover (1216), 111
  seal of, 118–19
Alexander III, king of Scots (r. 1249–86), 106–7, 109, 114, 120, 138, 713
Alexander I, tsar of Russia, 304
Alexander, Capt. James, 466
Alexander Findlay & Co., 561
Alison, Gen. Sir Archibald, 2nd Baronet, 462, 477
Alison, Sir Archibald, 442–4, 446, 462
Allan, Stuart, 458
Allan, Sir William
  Heroism and Humanity (1840), 695
Allenby, FM Edmund Henry Hyman, 1st Viscount, 521–2
Alloa, 510
  find in, 53
  Boer War memorial, 760
Alnwick, 342
Amalgamated Society of Engineers, 542, 544
Ambeyla, expedition (1863), 471
American Revolutionary War *see* War of American Independence
Amherst, Maj.-Gen. (later FM) Jeffery, 1st Baron, 393–4, 397
Amiens, 526, 710
Ancrum, Sir Robert Kerr, 1st earl of, 721
Ancrum, William Kerr, 2nd earl of, 721
Ancrum Moor, battle of (1545), 10, 196–7
Anderson, Joseph, 782
Anderson, Cpl. Robert, 398
Anglo-Abyssinian War (1867–8), 472

Anglo-Burmese Wars, first (1824–6), 464
  second (1885–9), 472
Anglo-Dutch Brigade, 312–13, 317
  see also Anglo-Scottish Brigade, Scots Brigade
Anglo-Normans, 5, 96–7, 106, 108, 112, 115, 116, 689
  forces, 100, 103, 106, 110
  kings, 99, 111
  knights, 96, 101, 108
Anglo-Persian War (1856–7), 469
Anglo-Saxons, 65, 77, 79, 94, 110
Anglo-Scottish Brigade, 253, 266
  see also Anglo-Dutch Brigade, Scots Brigade
Anglo-Scottish wars (1093–1286 and 1357–1560), artillery, 161–2, 187–93, 198, 200–2, 716
  battle avoidance, 103, 120, 165, 189–90, 196–7
  cavalry, 185–6, 191, 194, 197–200
  cross-border raids, 101, 103, 105–6, 160, 163, 165, 168, 187, 189–94, 196–201
  diplomacy, 190, 193, 195, 197, 202–3
  engagements, 10–11, 164–5 184, 187, 190–4, 196–200
  English distractions, 99, 101, 103, 161, 165, 190
  savagery of, 5, 105–6, 115–18
  Scots invade England, 5, 94, 100–2, 104, 109–11, 120
  Scottish military leadership, 164–5, 169, 196–202
  Scottish resilience, 160, 176, 184, 192–3, 203
  siege warfare, 101–3, 110, 118, 161, 189–91, 193, 197–8, 202
  socio-economic effects of, 167–8, 201
  see also Wars of Independence
Anglo-Spanish War (1585–1604), 239
Anglo-Transvaal War (1880–1), 472, 644
Angus, Archibald Douglas, 6th earl of, 193–4, 197, 199–200, 202, 718
Angus, James Douglas, 3rd earl of, 317–18
  regiment of, 310, 317–18
Angus, Gillebridge, 2nd earl of, 109

Angus, William Douglas, 10th earl of, 12
Annandale, Robert de Brus, lord of, 97
  knightly quotas of, 137
Anne, Queen (r. 1702–14), 336, 339, 341, 350, 356
Ansdell, Richard, *The Fight for the Standard* (1848), 420, 693
'anti-Tattoo' critique, 26, 669
Anton, Quartermaster James, 19
Antonine Wall, 56–8
  carvings on, 689
Antrim, Randal (Ronald) MacDonnell, 2nd earl and 1st marquess of, 283, 287
Arbroath abbey, 114
archaeology, 41, 43–6, 48, 53, 59, 81, 728–9
  artefact analysis, 729–30, 735–7, 739
  battlefield, 2, 27, 428, 728–30, 743–5
  castle, 708–9, 729
  site investigations, 741–3
  surveys, 731–3, 735–6
Archer, Peter, 702
archers, 48, 75–6, 97, 100, 112, 137, 712, 717
  crossbow, 94, 186, 707
  English, 6, 137, 170, 186, 196, 770n13
  Highland, 200, 223–6
  longbow, 97, 158, 707
  Scottish, 5–6, 138–40, 169–70, 186, 198, 243
Arctic convoys, 565
Ardennes Offensive (1944–5), 580
Ardrossan, Welcome Home and Commemoration Fund of, 765–6
Argyll, 67, 71, 77, 81–2, 107, 196, 214
  Archatton carvings, 653
  earldom of, 219, 222
  hoards found in, 49
  king of, 78, 107
  military service in, 222
  Militia, 374–5, 735–6, 779
  raids in, 73, 196
Argyll, Archibald Campbell, 2nd earl of, 117
Argyll, Archibald Campbell, 4th earl of, at Pinkie, 198–9, 654
Argyll, Archibald Campbell, 5th earl of, 236
Argyll, Archibald, 7th earl of, 211
  at Glenlivet, 223, 226
Argyll, Archibald Campbell, 8th earl and 1st marquess of, 278, 280, 282, 285, 288, 291–3
  executed (1661), 311
Argyll, Archibald Campbell, 9th earl of, 311
  executed (1685), 312
  rebellion of (1685), 312–14, 317–18
Argyll, Archibald Campbell, 10th earl and 1st duke of, regiment of, 318
Argyll, Archibald Campbell, 3rd duke of, 386, 393
Argyll, Capt. Ian Campbell, 11th duke of, 572
Argyll, John of, 152
Argyll, Col. (later Lt.-Gen.) John Campbell, 2nd duke of, 326–7, 330, 337, 341
  as commander-in-chief, Scotland, 351–3, 355, 357
Argyll, Maj.-Gen. John Campbell of Mamore, 4th duke of, 16
Argyll, FM John Campbell, 5th duke of, 374, 416
Arisaig, 22
  House, 563
  landing (1745), 363
Arkinholm, battle of (1455), 11, 173
HMS *Ark Royal*, 585n1
armies, covenanters', 3, 12–13, 212, 262–4, 274n39, 280–1
  aristocratic officers of, 278–80, 286
  artillery of, 280–1, 283
  cavalry of, 276, 278, 280, 284–6
  conscripted, 263, 273
  engage Scottish royalists, 288–9
  funding of, 279–82, 284, 290
  invade north of England, 280–1, 284–7, 289–91
  invade Ulster, 282, 289
Armistice Day, 531
armour, 53, 114, 136, 146, 174, 186, 224, 286, 689, 729, 779–81, 784, 786, 788
  bronze, 48
  coat of mail, 185, 224
  leather, 44, 112
  light, 137, 170, 184, 224

Roman, 55
Scottish aristocratic, 170, 184–5
Scottish lack of, 103, 112, 137–8, 147
see also knights
Armstrongs, 242
Army School of Piping, 658
Armyre, Sir William, 285
arquebusiers, 185–7, 200–1
Arran, James Hamilton, 1st earl of (and duke of Châtelherault), 195–200, 202
Arras, 520, 526; *see also* battles, Arras
Asante War (1873–4), 472
Asquith, Herbert Henry, 1st earl of Oxford and, 509
government of, 546
HMS *Assistance*, 449
'assured Scots', 196, 198, 201
Ath, siege of (1697), 336
Atholl, David of Strathbogie, earl of, 166
Atholl, earldom of, 222
Atholl, John Murray, 2nd earl and 1st marquess of, 306, 312
Perthshire regiment of, 310
Atholl, John Murray, 1st duke of, 330, 343, 357
Atholl, John Stewart-Murray, 7th duke of, 19
Atholl, John Stewart-Murray, 8th duke of, 786
Atholl, Thomas of Galloway, earl of, 107
Atholl Highlanders, 19
Atholl raid (1746), 374
Atkinson, John Augustus, *Battle of Waterloo the 18th June 1815* (1819), 693
Atlantic convoys, 565
atomic bombs *see* nuclear weapons
Attwood, Thomas, Political Union of, 536
Auchintoul, Maj.-Gen. Alexander Gordon of, 352, 354
Auchleuchries, Gen. Patrick Gordon of, 268
Auld Alliance, 9–11, 133, 194, 202, 235
fraught relations in, 9, 165, 169, 193
French diplomatic support, 160, 203
French financial aid, 160, 166, 266–7, 718

French military/naval support, 169, 171, 187–8, 201–3, 235, 654, 741
French weapons/armour, 170, 188, 737
ordinances of war, 163
Scotland supports France militarily, 9–10, 169–70, 266
Scotland invades England, 10, 163, 165, 169, 190, 194, 202
Auldearn, battle of (1645), 288, 679
Australia, 20, 485, 487–92, 495, 499, 663, 761
Australian Imperial Force, 492–3, 499, 527
8th Australian Infantry Brigade, 500
in the South African War, 20, 491
Scots migrants in, 485–6, 488–9, 493, 497
see also New South Wales Scottish Rifles
Austria, 349, 356
Auxiliary Division, 547
Auxiliary Territorial Service, 23
axes, 108, 138, 170, 224, 239, 777, 782
Danish, 185
Irish, 112
Lochaber, 793n9
stone, 45–6
Ayr, 282, 304
fencibles, 305
monuments in, 752, 768
Ayrshire, 307, 383, 397, 508, 602, 753, 771, 781
finds in, 49, 708
monuments, 752, 771n38
Yeomanry, 470
Ayton, sacked (1497), 190

bagpipes, 478, 499, 666n27, 683, 685, 800
and Highland culture, 654–5
and recruiting, 485, 657
communications role of, 497–8, 562
icons of Scottish identity, 24, 500, 635–4, 663, 684
in daily military routines, 24, 659
inspirational role of, 19, 469, 569, 574, 581, 654, 659–63, 685, 698
marches, 659
mythology of, 649, 653, 655
origins of, 653–4
parades, 576, 643, 659

bagpipes (*cont.*)
   'ramp ceremonies', 662
   see also tattoo
Baillie, Lt.-Gen. William, 286, 288
Baines, Thomas, 465
Baird, John, 438
Baker, Rear Admiral John, 338
Balaclava, 468
Balcarres, Col. Alexander Lindsay, 1st earl of, 286
Balfour, Arthur James, 440, 449–50
Balfour, Gilbert, 718
Balfour, John, 448–9
Balfour-Melville, Evan W. M., 9
Balgonie, Lt.-Col. Alexander, Lord, 286
Ballach, Dòmhnall, 218
Ballimore, Capt. Colin Campbell of, 374–5
Ballindalloch, Maj. James Grant, laird of, 393–4
Balliol, Edward, 158, 166, 713
Balliol, John, king of Scots (r. 1292–6), 133
Balliol dynasty, 2, 158, 172
ballistic missiles
   'Blue Streak', 602
   Polaris, 600, 603
   'Skybolt', 602, 605
   SS-20, 608
   Trident, 607–10
Bambatha, rebellion of (1906), 492
Bamburgh, 71
   siege of (AD 704), 69–70, 74
bands, 21, 564, 572–3
   pipe, 21, 511, 564, 572–3
   entertainment role of, 657, 663
   massed pipes and drums, 576, 628, 641, 643, 657, 663–4
Banff, 133, 800
   RAF, 566, 568
banners, 75, 110, 114–15, 164; *see also Breccbennach*
Bannockburn, battle of (1314), 2, 7–9, 141, 143, 147, 152, 263, 517, 653, 799
   aftermath of, 7, 9, 150
   and siege of Stirling castle, 144
   armies at, 136–41
   battlefield disputes, 731, 743–4
   Bruce's tactics at, 7, 145
   celebrated, 1, 108, 135
   depictions of, 689, 695
   Gaels engaged at, 209
   infantry triumph over cavalry, 135, 145
   Scottish archers at, 139–40
Bannockburn, Wilson of, 638
Barbados, 463
Barbour, John, *The Bruce* (c. 1375), 136–41, 143, 145–7, 150, 670
Barbreck, Col. John Campbell of, 391
Barker, Thomas Jones, 698
   The Relief of Lucknow (1859), 698
Barnett, Corelli, 610
Barnweill, Ayrshire, Wallace statue at, 752
Barr, Niall, 190
Barr & Stroud works, 559
Barrington, William Wildman, Lord, 386
Barrymore, James Barry, 4th earl of, 342
Basra, 620, 664
Bass Rock, Jacobite surrender (1694), 348
battlefields, Scottish, 743
'battle of the Braes' (1882), 448, 680
battles (outside Scotland; all those fought in Scotland are listed separately under their place names)
   Abbeville (1940), 571
   Agincourt (1415), 9
   Alexandria (1801), 18, 419, 676, 692, 754
   Alma (1854), 1, 466–8, 676, 698, 700
   Almanza (1707), 337
   Amiens (1918), 527
   Ancre (1916), 495
   Ardscull (1316), 144–5
   Arras (1917), 509, 517, 520–3
   Arroyo Molinos (1811), 655–6
   Assaye (1803), 18
   Atbara (1898), 473
   Austerlitz (1805), 694
   Balaclava (1854), 4, 25, 466, 698, 802
   Bareilly (1858), 469
   Baugé (1421), 10, 169
   Benburb (1646), 289
   Blenheim (1704), 15, 328, 333–4
   Bosworth (1485), 744
   Brandywine Creek (1777), 396
   Breitenfeld (1631), 260–1

Brier Creek (1779), 396
Brihuega (1710), 337
Britain (1940), 566, 604
Brooklyn Heights or Long Island
    (1776), 394, 396
Brunanburh (AD 937), 80
Bunker's Hill (1775), 391
Bushy Run (1763), 394, 397, 401
Caen (1944), 579
Camden (1780), 396
Cawnpore (1857), 469
Charasiab (1879), 472
Chemin des Dames (1917), 520
Clithero (1138), 110
Colenso (1899), 475
Connor (1315), 144
Cravant (1423), 10, 169
Dardanelles (1915), 523-4
Delville Wood (1916), 495
El Alamein (1942), 1, 498, 573-5,
    580, 661, 677, 680, 685, 808
Elandslaagte (1899), 24, 474
El Teb (1884), 473
Faughart (1318), 9, 135, 143-4, 146
Flodden Field (1513), 10, 117, 182,
    184-6, 190-2, 198, 209, 716-17,
    750, 752
Fontenoy (1745), 17, 360, 374, 394
Fort Duquesne (1758), 385, 387,
    393-4
Fort Niagara (1759), 389, 400
Fort Washington (1776), 483
Francofonte (1943), 577
Geilenkirchen (1944), 582
Gerbini (1943), 577
Gingindlovu (1879), 472
Ginnis (1885), 473
Guilford Courthouse (1781), 392,
    396
Herrings (1429), 10
Hook (1952), 612
Humbleton or Homildon Hill
    (1402), 165
Imjin River (1951), 682
Inkerman (1854), 467
Istabulat (1917), 808
Jamestown (1781), 396
Jersey (1781), 691
Kabul (1879), 472
Kandahar (1880), 24, 472, 699
Khambula (1879), 472
Kirbekan (1885), 473
Kohima (1944), 570

Landen (1693), 15
Little Big Horn (1876), 728
Loos (1915), 1, 509, 513-17, 660,
    680, 702
Lützen (1632), 259
Lys (1918), 525
Magersfontein (1899), 19, 25, 474,
    477, 701, 758, 808
Majuba Hill (1881), 472
Malplaquet (1709), 15, 329-31,
    336-7
Marne, second (1918), 527
Marston Moor (1644), 286-9, 728
Minden (1759), 17
Modder River (1899), 474
Mome Gorge (1906), 492
Mons (1914), 20
Monte Cassino (1944), 499
Monte Sole (1945), 499
Mount Tumbledown (1982), 618-19
Myton (1319), 139, 143, 149
Nagpur (1817), 464
Naseby (1645), 288
Neuve Chapelle (1915), 21
Neville's Cross (1346), 163-5, 175
Newburn (1640), 280-1
Nieuwpoort (1600), 233
Nördlingen (1634), 261
Old Byland (1322), 9, 135, 139, 143,
    151
Omdurman (1898), 462, 473-4
Otterburn (1388), 163, 165, 175,
    650, 786
Oudenarde (1708), 15, 329, 331, 336
Paardeberg (1900), 475, 491
Pavia (1525), 189
Plains of Abraham or Quebec
    (1759), 16, 385, 387-9, 400, 671,
    691
Poltava (1709), 329
Port Stanley (1982), 618
Preston (1648), 291
Preston (1715), 352
Princeton (1777), 385, 394
Puerto de Maya (1813), 423
Quatre Bras (1815), 18, 434 n50,
    666n31, 801
Ramillies (1706), 15, 330, 332,
    334-6
Ravenna (1512), 189
Reichswald (1945), 497
Rorke's Drift (1879), 458
Saratoga (1777), 391, 395, 691

battles (outside Scotland; all those fought in Scotland are listed separately under their place names) (*cont.*)
  Schellenberg (1704), 333
  Sedgemoor (1685), 313
  Sferro Hills (1943), 1, 577
  Shrewsbury (1403), 165
  Sidi Rezegh (1941), 498
  Sollum (1941), 498
  Solway Moss (1542), 10, 182, 194–5
  Somme (1916), 26, 495, 509, 517–19, 523, 526, 651
  Standard (1138), 5, 100–1, 103, 108–10, 112, 114, 116
  Steenkirke (1692), 14–15
  Stormberg (1899), 474–5
  Taku Forts (1860), 471
  Tamai (1884), 473
  Tardenois (1918), 527
  Tel-el-Kebir (1882), 24, 472–3, 651, 698
  Ticonderoga (1758), 16, 387, 389, 396
  Trafalgar (1805), 413, 755
  Trenton (1776), 394
  Two Rivers (c. AD 671), 79
  Tyne (AD 918), 80
  Ulundi (1879), 472
  Verneuil (1424), 10, 169
  Vimeiro (1808), 421, 434n54
  Vimy Ridge (1917), 520–1
  Vizzini (1943), 577
  Wadi Akarit (1943), 577, 595n71
  Waterloo (1815), 1, 17–18, 25, 396, 418, 421–5, 427, 458, 656, 676, 688, 692–5, 702, 705n20, 785, 801, 808, 810
  Winwick (1648), 291
  Worcester (1651), 13, 294
  Wynendael (1708), 336
  Ypres, first (1914), 20
  Ypres, second (1915), 493
  Ypres, third or Passchendaele (1917), 523, 768
Batys, 242
Baynes, Lt.-Col. John, 22, 797
Beach, Pte. Les, 580
Beardmore, William, 508
Beaton, Cardinal David, 194–7
Beaton, Archbishop James, 718
Beatty, Vice-Admiral David, 1st Earl, 506
Beaumont Hamel, 518
Bechuanaland, expedition (1884), 471
  rebellion of (1897), 492
Bede, the Venerable, 68–70, 72, 74, 80, 82–4
Bedford, 800
Bel, Jean le, 136–7, 148, 163
Belfast, 548, 551, 805
  Holy Cross blockade (2001), 551–2
  Lower Falls (1970), 548–9
  New Lodge (1971), 546–7
  riot (1908), 440
  Unity Flats (1970), 549
  West (1981), 550–1
Bell, Gen. Sir George, 462
Bell, Thomas, 'Tom', 544
Bellaghy, 553
Bernera barracks, 719
Benbecula, RAF, 566
Bengal army, 18
Bergen-op-Zoom, siege of (1622), 253
  stormed (1747), 389
Berkeley, Stanley, 693
Berlin, blockade (1948–9), 601
  fall of the Wall (1989), 600, 609
Bernicia, 65, 67–8, 71, 74
  King Oswald of, 74
Berwick-upon-Tweed, 152, 163, 172, 191, 198, 201, 342, 365, 367, 739
  fortifications of, 162
  Pacification of (1639), 279
  sacked (1216), 103
  sieges of (1318), 151 and (1333), 168
Berwick-upon-Tweed, James Fitz-James, 1st duke of, 354, 387
Bevin, Ernest, 601
Birkenhead, 463–4
birlinn, 107, 152, 212–13, 223
  and naval Warfare, 214–15, 224, 226
Birmingham, 413, 537
  barracks, 536
  Scottish recruiting in, 24, 413
Biron, Jacques de la Carbonières de la, 'Chapelle de', 202
Bishops' Wars (1639–40), 14, 263–4, 279, 280–1, 288, 719
Bismarck, 565
Bismarck, Prince Otto von, 539
Blackader, Maj. John, 336
Black and Tans, 547
Black Rood of St Margaret, 164

'Black Week' (1899), 435
Blair, Adam, 436, 438
Blair, Tony, 805
Blair Atholl, 317
Blakeney, Maj.-Gen. William, 1st Baron, 739–40
Bland, Maj.-Gen. Humphrey, 375
Blàr Chàirinis, battle of (1601), 224
Blàr Chuilthionn, battle of (1601), 218, 223
Blitz (1940–1), 567–8
blockhouses, 718
Bloody Bay, battle of (c. early 1480s), 213–14, 222
Blücher, FM Gebhard Leberecht von, 419, 693
   army of 801–2
Bluff Cove, landing at (1982), 617–18
Boece, Hector, 211
Boer War, *see* South African War
Bogle, William Lockhart, 699
Bohemia, Elizabeth Stuart, 'Winter Queen' of, 255–7, 260
Bois de la Maison, 521
Bomber Command, 568
Bonar Law, Andrew, 545
bonnets, 430n12, 633, 636, 691, 695, 698, 797, 801–2
   Balmoral, 594n61, 631
   feathered, 460, 631, 636, 639, 642, 700, 800
   Glengarries, 511, 628, 631, 636, 642–3
   Kilmarnocks, 631, 641
   'tam-o'-shanter', 583, 631, 642
Bonnymuir, riot of (1820), 438
Bonnyrig, 544
Borders, 185–6, 201, 240, 339
   Border guard, 244
   Border Horse, 185
   feuds and reiving, 240–3, 256
   see also 'Jeddart Justice'
Borlum, William Mackintosh, laird of, 352, 355
Borneo, operations in (1964), 613
Borthwick, Capt. Alistair, 579
Borthwick, Robert, 188, 190–1
Borthwick, Col. William, 330
Botha, Gen. Louis, 493
Bothwell, Francis Stewart, 5th earl of, 12
Bothwell, James Hepburn, 4th earl of, 236

Bothwell Bridge, battle of (1679), 310–11, 323n70
Bouchain, siege of (1711), 337
Boudicca, 47
Boulogne, occupied (1544–50), 187, 202
   Treaty of (1550), 202
Bouquet, Col. Henri, 394
Bower, Walter, 171, 175
Bowes, Sir George, 197
Bowes, Robert, 194
Boys' Brigade, 470
   battalion, 511–12, 518–19
Boy's Own Magazine, 688
Breadalbanes, 781
Breccbennach [*Brecbennoch*], 114–15, 164
Bremen, 581
   capture of (1945), 582
Bridge of Alford, battle of (1645), 288
Bridge of Dee (Brig o' Dee), battle of (1639), 279
brigades *see* Anglo-Scots Brigade, Highland Brigades, Scots Brigade
British army, 2–4, 15, 22, 268, 326, 328, 339, 344, 356, 359, 391, 563, 613, 616–17, 619, 644, 655, 658
   former Jacobites join, 386–9
   purchase system of, 332, 461, 638
   reforms of, 23–4, 28, 459, 476, 537, 616, 640–1, 644, 789, 803–4
   Scottish contributions to, 267–9, 372–6, 458–9, 475, 478, 639;
   see also First World War, French Revolutionary Wars, Marlborough, Napoleonic Wars, North American Wars and Second World War
British Army of the Rhine (BAOR), 28, 610, 615
British Auxiliary Legion, 270–1, 460
British Broadcasting Corporation (BBC), alleged pro-Scottish bias of, 574
   television series, *Two Men in a Trench*, 728
British Expeditionary Force (BEF)
   in 1914, 20, 478, 510
   in 1939–40, 571, 581, 681
British Legion (1860), 271
British Socialist Party, 540
Bronze Age, 41, 44–6, 48, 50

Brooke, FM Sir Alan, 579
Broughty Craig, 201
Brown, Gordon, 805
Brown, Capt. James, 331
Brown, John, 508
Brown, Keith, 12, 243, 245, 302
Bruce, Edward, 141, 148
    and siege of Stirling castle, 141, 144, 146, 151–2
    in Galloway, 137, 141
    Irish campaign of (1315–18), 9, 117, 135, 137, 143–4, 149, 151–2
Bruce, Robert *see* Robert 1
Bruce dynasty, 158, 160, 166, 172
Bruce, Commissary-General of the Musters Thomas, 327
Brunei, 613
Brussels, 336, 419, 801
Buccleuch, Col. Francis Scott, 2nd earl of, 286
Buchan, Alexander Stewart, 1st earl of, 'Wolf of Badenoch', 219
Buchan, Colbán, earl of, 109
Buchan, David Erskine, 11th earl of, 778
Buchan, John (later 1st Baron Tweedsmuir), 22, 495, 517, 541
    Mr Standfast, 541
    war poetry of, xxi
Buchan, John Stewart, 2nd earl of, 10, 169
Buchan, Maj.-Gen. Thomas, 317
Buchan, RAF, 609
Buchanan, Duncan, 333
Buchanan, George, 215
Buckingham, George Villiers, 1st duke of
    expedition to La Rochelle (1627), 245, 264
bugle, calls, 652–3
Bullen-Smith, Maj.-Gen. Charles David, 579–80
Bunnock, William, 147
Burghead, 563
Burgos, siege of (1812), 428
Burgoyne, Gen. John, 385
Burgundy, John the Fearless, duke of, 225
Burgundy, Philip the Good, duke of, 162, 716
burial sites, 44–6, 52–4
Burke, Gregory, *Black Watch* (2006), 621, 669–71, 675, 680, 685

Burleigh, Sir Michael Balfour, later 1st Lord Balfour of, 239–40
Burleigh, Robert Balfour, 2nd Lord Balfour of, 286
Burma, 584
    retreat from (1942), 570
Burnet, Bishop Gilbert, 301, 303, 312
Burns, Robert, *Love and Liberty* (1785), 671–4
'Burnt Candlemas' (1356), 168
Bute, 104, 196
    Militia, 418
Bute, John Stuart, 3rd earl of, 400
    ministry of, 672
Butler, Lady Elizabeth, 24, 693
    Scotland For Ever! (1881), 693
    The Colours: Advance of the Scots Guards at the Alma River (1899), 700
Byng, Admiral Sir George, 338
Byron, John, 1st Baron, regiment of horse, 286

Cadiz, 356, expedition to (1706), 337
Cadogan, Maj.-Gen. William, 1st earl of, 338, 343, 352–3, 355
Caenn Tràigh Ghruineart, battle of (1598), 220–3
Cairnryan, Mulberry harbours assembled in, 561
Cairo, 573
Caledonian societies, 485, 487, 491, 493, 501
Callaghan, James, 607
Cambrai, 526
Cameron, Dr. Archibald, 34n51
Cameron, Piper Charles, 660
Cameron, Lt. Donald, 566
Cameron, Rev. Duncan, 511
Cameron, Lt.-Col. John, 423, 656, 666n31
Cameron, Richard, 'The Lion of the Covenant', 317
Cameron barracks *see* Inverness
Camerons, 215, 357, 363
    see also Lochiel
Campaign for Nuclear Disarmament (CND), 602–3
    Scottish, 606, 608, 610
Campbell, Capt. Alexander, 326
Campbell, Maj. Alexander, 401
Campbell, Lt.-Col. Archibald, 395

Campbell, FM Sir Colin (later 1st
    Baron Clyde), 29, 461-2, 465-6,
    468-9, 676
  statues of, 755
Campbell, Sir Colin, sheriff of Argyll,
    318
Campbell, Duncan, 151
Campbell, Lt.-Col. James, 336
Campbell, Col. John, 330
Campbell, Capt. Robert, 318
Campbells, 209, 219-20, 278, 288,
    312, 354, 374, 722
  lordships of, 214-15, 779
  at Culloden, 374-5, 735-6
  see also Argyll, earls and dukes of,
    and Argyll Militia
Campbeltown, Asdic school at, 565
Canada, 385, 389, 454, 478, 486, 761
  and the First World War, 492-6
  and the Second World War, 497-8
  and the South African War, 20,
    490-1
  and UN missions, 500
  Cameron Highlanders of Canada,
    497
  Canadian Expeditionary Force,
    492-5, 517, 520-1, 527
  Essex Scottish, 497
  expedition to (1709), 326
  Fenian raids in (1866), 472
  Glengarry Highlanders, 465
  48th Highlanders of Canada, 492
  91st Highlanders (later Argyll
    and Sutherland Highlanders of
    Canada), 488
  Militia Acts (1855 and 1859), 487-8
  pipers of, 495, 662-3, 667n48
  Royal Canadian Regiment, 490
  Royal Highlanders of Canada, 488,
    492-4, 497, 500
  Royal Highland Fusiliers of Canada,
    662
  Royal Scots of Canada, 490-1
  Scottish migrants in, 465, 478, 486,
    490, 495
  see also battle of Vimy Ridge,
    Cape Breton Highlanders, Nova
    Scotia, and regiments of the
    Commonwealth
Canmore dynasty, 2, 104; see also
    Malcolm III
Cannon, Col. Alexander, 317
Cantlie, Lt.-Col. S. S. T., 497

Cape Breton Highlanders, 485, 490
Cape Colony, 465
Cape Helles, landings/offensives
    (1915), 524
Cape Town Highlanders, 489-93, 498,
    500
Carberry Hill, battle of (1567), 236
  monument, 752
Carham, battle of (1018), 104
Carlingford, plundered and sacked by
    Scots (1388), 171
Carlisle, 99, 365, 464
  altar record in, 57
Cardross, Henry Erskine, 3rd Lord,
    778
Cardwell, Edward, 1st Viscount, 803,
    812n25
Carlyle, Alexander, 740
Carney, Capt. Charles, 315
Carnyx, 53, 649
Carpenter, Col. George, dragoons of,
    342
Carswell, Allan, 458
Carter, George, 690
  The Siege of Gibraltar (1784), 692
Carter, President Jimmy, 607
Caskie, Rev. Donald, 572
Cassillis, Archibald Kennedy, 12th earl
    of, 781
Cassillis, Col. John Kennedy, 6th earl
    of, 286
castle
  Abercorn, 11, 717
  Aberdour (Fife), 709
  Alnwick, 101, 109, 118
  Appleby, 102
  Ayr, 140, 148, 301, 719
  Balmoral, 19, 486, 696
  Balvaird, 715
  Balvenie, 714
  Bamburgh, 74, 149, 708-9
  Barnard, 111
  Barton Hill (Perthshire), 709
  Bastille, 714
  Berwick, 9-10, 31n22, 144, 146-7,
    161-2, 165-6, 280, 717-18
  Blackness, 235, 326, 719, 724n2
  Blair, 27, 722
  Bothwell, 118, 711-13, 715
  Brodick (Arran), 712
  Brough, 102
  Broughty, 201-2
  Caerlaverock, 146, 197, 711, 713

castle (*cont.*)
  Carisbrooke, 290
  Carlisle, 99–102, 111–12, 115, 118, 146, 149, 161, 365, 367, 709
  Carrickfergus, 146, 188, 342
  Cessford, 193
  Chillingham, 191
  Craigmillar, 726n27
  Craignethan, 719–20
  Crookston (Renfrewshire), 188, 708
  Cubbie Roo's (Orkney), 709
  Culzean, 781
  Dingwall, 213
  Dirleton, 118, 708, 710–12
  Douglas, 147
  Doune (Stirlingshire), 712–14
  Duchal, 188
  Duffus, 98–9, 707
  Dumbarton, 70, 162, 188, 214, 235–6, 301, 326, 338, 340, 361, 708, 719, 725n12
  Dunbar, 160, 193, 201, 717–18
  Dundas (West Lothian), 716
  Dundonald, 708
  Dunivaig, 214
  Dunnottar, 119, 674, 747n26
  Dunrobin, 709, 722
  Duns Law, 719
  Dunskeath (Ross-shire), 105
  Dunstaffnage, 107, 711
  Dunstanburgh, 149
  Dunvegan, 722
  Edinburgh, 7, 10, 27, 103, 143, 146, 148, 162, 187, 203, 223, 235, 237, 280, 300–1, 312, 315, 326, 338, 341, 350, 355, 361, 421, 438, 617, 628, 658, 663, 696, 701, 708–9, 712–13, 716, 719, 722, 756, 778, 781, 786–9, 797
  Eilean Donan (Inverness-shire), 357, 723
  Etal, 191–2
  Fast, 201
  Ferniehurst, 201
  Ford, 191, 202
  Forfar, 147
  Fort George (Ardersier), 16, 27, 361, 371, 438, 446, 651, 719, 789, 798
  Fort George (Inverness), 361, 370, 719, 743
  Grant (Strathspey), 780–1, 784
  Hailes, 201
  Home, 201
  Hume (Berwickshire), 723
  Inveraray, 779–80
  Inverlochy, 13, 147, 213, 719
  Inverness, 13, 147, 190, 213, 317, 719
  Jedburgh, 146, 162
  Kilchurn (Argyllshire), 722
  Kildrummy, 118, 709, 713
  Kinclaven, 709–10
  Langholm, 197–8
  Liddell, 118
  Linlithgow, 147–8
  Loch Leven, 236
  Lochmaben, 146, 161–2, 197
  Menzies, 417
  Mingary, 107, 722
  Mitford, 102
  Mote of Urr, 97–8
  Muirhouselaw (Roxburghshire), 708
  Nairn, 147
  Newark, 289–90
  Noltland, 718
  Norham, 102, 110, 146, 189–91, 716
  Norwich, 717
  Old Wick, 709
  Pembroke, 290
  Perth, 161
  Pierrefonds, 715
  Prudhoe, 102
  Redcastle, 105
  Rothesay, 104, 107, 709–11
  Roxburgh, 7, 31n22, 143, 146, 148, 161–2, 165, 201, 212, 716
  St Andrews, 198, 718
  Saltoun, 201
  Skipness, 712
  Slains, 350
  Smailholm Tower, 242, 723
  Stirling, 7, 103, 133, 141, 144, 146, 161–2, 235, 253, 288, 301, 307–8, 326, 338, 344, 350, 352, 363, 367–8, 371, 388, 717, 719, 722, 739, 741, 759, 765, 789
  Sween, 107, 214, 709
  Tantallon, 188, 193–4, 706, 709, 713, 718–19
  Tarbet, 107, 708
  Threave, 172, 174, 197, 717
  Tioram, 107
  Tolquhon, 721–2
  Tynemouth, 338
  Urquhart, 147, 213

Wark, 102, 110, 118
Warkworth, 149
castles, 69, 73, 94, 96–8, 103, 107, 120
   and artillery, 161–2, 187–91, 193, 237, 707, 709, 712, 716–19
   and galleys, 212–14
   as assertions of political/economic control, 97, 146, 161, 163, 196, 214
   as barracks, 27, 350, 722
   as icons of lordship, 214, 720–1, 729
   as lordly residences, 27, 706–8, 712, 720–2
   defensive improvements in, 102, 193, 237–8, 361, 709–18
   keeps/towers, 112, 118, 201, 237, 710–11, 713, 717–18, 721–3, 726n27
   motte and bailey, 97, 707–8, 724n6
   'Scots Baronial', 723
casualties, Scots military, 18, 20, 24, 261, 339, 549, 551, 612
   from disease, 459, 463
   in the Crimean War, 463, 468, 696
   in the First World War, 495, 509, 511, 517–19, 521–4, 526–7, 529–30, 659, 681, 760, 763, 768, 803
   in the French Revolutionary and Napoleonic Wars, 410, 424–6, 428
   in the Second World War, 584, 803
   in the South African War, 474, 477, 759–60
   in the War of the Spanish Succession, 329, 332–4, 336
Cawnpore massacre (1857), 469
Cecil, Sir Robert (later 1st earl of Salisbury), 239
Celtic charge *see* Highland charge
Cessford and Caverton, Sir Robert Ker, Lord Ker of, 240
Chalfont, Alun Gwynne Jones, Baron, 419
chaplains, 21–1, 36n78, 616
Charles I, king of England and Scotland (r. 1625–49), 13, 257, 298
   and Book of Common Prayer, 12–13, 261, 276
   employs mercenaries, 261–4
   executed, 291
   forces of, 279–80, 283, 285, 288
   strategy of, 279–83, 289–90
   'the incident', 278
Charles II, king of England and Scotland (r. 1660–85), 13, 294
   and Scotland, 292–3, 295, 301, 307, 310–11, 318
   armed forces of, 3, 300–1, 304, 307, 722
   uses military in Scotland, 301, 303, 305–7, 310–11, 318
Charles V, king of France, 714
Charles VII, king of France, 169
Charles XII, king of Sweden, 319
Charles Edward Stuart, 'Young Pretender' or 'Bonnie Prince Charlie', 218, 348, 362–70, 384, 386–8, 563, 571, 634
   at Culloden, 370, 375–6, 732
   at Derby, 366
   at Glenfinnan, 363
   ill health of, 368
   demoralised, 371
   escapes, 15–16
   sword of, 779
Charterhall, 54 operational training unit, 566
Chartism, 19, 438, 443
Cheape, Hugh, 653
Chelsea Pensioners, 446
Chemical Defence Experimental Station (Porton Down), 570
Cherokee Indians, two expeditions against (1760–1), 394
Cheyne, John, 450
Childers, Hugh Culling Eardley, army reforms of (1881), 23–4, 28, 459, 476, 640–1, 644, 789, 803–4
China, and Korean War, 611–12
   see also Second Opium War
Chitral relief expedition (1895), 473
chivalry, 7–9, 96, 101, 116–19, 136–7, 141, 167, 173–4, 189–90, 781
   and treatment of prisoners, 117–18, 150–1
   Anglo-French culture of, 118–19, 781
   see also James IV, Robert I and tournaments
chlorine gas, 513–14
Chobham manoeuvres (1853), 696
Christian IV, king of Denmark-Norway, 12, 245, 257

chronicles, 5, 140, 163, 174, 650, 655
  English, 100, 109, 112–13, 116, 136, 145, 148, 167–8, 182
  Irish, 69, 71, 82
  Scottish, lack of, 100, 136, 171
Churchill, Maj. John, 568–9
Churchill, Sir John *see* Marlborough
Churchill, Sir Winston Spencer, 20–1, 576, 593n57, 601
Church of Scotland, 3, 12, 21–2, 235, 243, 257, 263, 290, 292, 302, 349, 511, 572, 580, 603
citizen soldiers, Scottish, 19–20, 25, 758–9, 761
City of Paris, 463
Ciudad Rodrigo, retreat to (1812), 424–6
Civil Constabulary Reserve (CCR), force, 544–5
clan, 414
  as a military unit, 219–22, 239, 251, 263, 349, 368, 410, 426
Clan Cameron, 317
Clan Chattan, 193
Clan Donald, 708
Clan Donald South, 211, 214, 216, 218, 222
Clan MacDonald, 318
Clanranald, 215, 221
Clanranald, Ranald MacDonald of, 779
Clan Uisdein, 221
Clark, Christopher, *The Piper of Loos Playing the KOSB to the Attack* (1915), 702
Clark, Pte. George, 419
Clark, John Heaviside, 693
Claverhouse, John Graham *see* Dundee, 1st Viscount
Cleland, Lt.-Col. William, 309, 317
Clephane, Maj. James, 387
Clephane, Lt.-Col. William, 354
Cleve, capture of (1945), 583
Clifford, Sir Robert de, 1st Baron de, 145
Clinton, Admiral Edward, 9th Baron (later 1st earl of Lincoln), 199–200
  naval forces of, 200–1
Clyde, Robert, 416–17
Clydebank, 510
  bombed, 567–8

Clyde Rock, kingdom of, 67, 70–1, 708
Clydeside, 606, 619–20, 685–6
  shipyards, 506–8, 545, 559, 574
Cnoc Coirpri, battle of (AD 736), 81
coal-miners, army recruits from, 460, 507, 685–6
  strikes, 443–5, 537, 544–5
Cockburn, James, 327
'Cod Wars' (1958–61, 1972–3 and 1975–6), 601, 606–7
Colchester, siege of (1648), 290
Coldingham priory, 139, 193
Coldstream, 298
Cold War, 20, 22, 28, 600–1, 606, 610, 617, 621, 662
  defences in Scotland, 600–1
  ending of (1989), 609, 620, 805
  'peace dividend', 620
  protests, 603–4
  public support for, 601–2, 606
  'second Cold War', 607
Colquhouns, at Glen Fruin, 224, 226, 242
Coluim, Máel *see* Malcolm III
Colyear, Maj.-Gen. Walter, regiment of, 330–1
commandos, 563–4
  at D-Day landing, 661–2
  No. 2 Commando, 568
  No. 3 Commando, 568
  No. 11 (Scottish) Commando, 573
  raids of, 568–9, 573
  training of, 563–4
Committee of 100, civil disobedience of, 603
common armies, of Dál Riata, 81
  Picts, 81
  Scotland, 5, 80, 98, 108, 110, 238–9
  service, 79, 109, 111, 120, 182, 212, 235, 238
  soldiers, 138–9, 175–6, 220
  weapons of, 112–14, 138–9, 170, 184–5
Comyn, John, murdered, 7
  family of, 6
Connell, John, 600
conscription, 263, 278, 512–13, 538, 610, 791, 804
  Military Service Act (1916), 513, 803
  Second World War, 570, 584, 591n40, 643, 803
Conservatives, 23, 451–2, 805

Constantinople, 523
Constantius Chlorus, emperor of Rome, 59
Continental army, 385, 393
conventicles, 303, 307–8, 616
Cookson, John, 413, 415
Cooper, Abraham, *Wellington at Waterloo* (1838), 693–4
Cope, Lt.-Gen. Sir John, 364–6, 372–4, 738–9
Copley, John Singleton, 690
  The Death of Major Peirson (1784), 691–2
Corbett, A. F., 24
Corbridge, sacked (1312), 149
Corenewall [Cornwrall], Capt. Henry, 310
Cormack, John, 548
  and Protestant Action, 548
Cornell, David, 9
Cornwallis, Lt.-Gen. Charles, 1st Marquess, 396
Corse, William Forbes, laird of, 720–1
Corunna, 356–7
  retreat to (1808–9), 424–5, 754
Coss, Edward J., 412–13, 415, 418
Coucy, Marie de, 710
Council of Scottish Colonels, 805
counter-espionage, 541
counter-terrorism, 552
County Clare, operations in, 547
Couper, Col. James Elphinstone, 1st Lord, 286
Couper Angus, attacked (1186), 105
Covenant, National (1638), 13, 261, 263, 276, 278, 280, 290, 292, 295, 302–3, 317, 768
  Solemn League and (1643), 13, 227, 284, 289, 302–3
covenanters, 14, 209, 276, 290, 292, 309–10, 317, 327, 336, 343, 615–16, 674–5, 695, 804
  rebellion of *see* Presbyterian rebellion
  see also armies, covenanters' and conventicles
Cowdenbeath, 544
Cranston, Col. James, 336
Cranston, Sir Robert, 512
Crawford, David Lindsay, 1st earl of, 171
Crawford, John Lindsay, 4th earl of Lindsay and 20th earl of, 360
Crawford, Robert Lindsay, 29th earl of, 7
Crawford-Lindsay, Col. John, 10th Lord, 1st earl of Lindsay and 17th earl of Crawford, 286
Crieff, 368–9, 472
Crimean War (1854–6), 459, 463, 466–8, 639, 676, 696, 698, 700–1
  memorials, 756
Croc, Sir Robert, 708
crofters, protests of (1880s), 438–9, 442, 447–52
  Crofter Holdings (Scotland) Act (1886), 448, 450
  'Crofter MPs', 448
Cromartie, George Mackenzie, 3rd earl of, 370
Cromdale, battle of The Haughs of (1690), 317, 348
Cromwell, Oliver, Lord Protector (r. 1653–8), 12–13, 31n17, 33n41, 290, 293, 300, 311, 359–60
  cavalry of, 13, 286–7, 291, 293, 731
  conquers Scotland, 12, 292, 298, 719
  navy of, 14, 33n41
Cromwell, Richard, 298
Crovan, Godred, 107
Cruickshank, Flying Officer John, 568
cruise missile, 608
crusades, 112, 167, 175
Cuban Missile Crisis (1962), 605
Cuckoo, 447
Culblean, battle of (1335), 166
Culcairn, Capt. George Munro of, 16
Culloden, battle of (1746), 1, 17, 212, 366, 368, 385–6, 388–9, 400, 515, 679, 728, 738, 743, 745
  aftermath of, 15–16, 34n49–50, 348, 358, 375, 386, 653, 655, 689–90, 722, 734, 779
  artillery at, 372, 375, 734
  battlefield (Drumossie Moor), 27, 370, 731–8
  cavalry at, 375, 735
  drums at, 650
  government forces, 373–5, 733, 735
  Jacobite charge, 375, 384, 734–6
  Jacobite firepower, 737
  Jacobite graves, 732
  Jacobite infantry, 371–2, 374
  memorial cairn, 734
  mythology of, 734–6

Culloden, battle of (1746) (*cont.*)
    new visitor centre, 27, 733, 738
    site investigations, 735–6
Culloden, Duncan Forbes of, 359, 373, 374
Cumberland, 240
Cumberland, George Clifford, 3rd earl of, 241
Cumberland, Prince William Augustus, duke of, 'Butcher', 16, 355–6, 367–8, 372, 386, 689
    army of, 348, 369, 373, 679
    at Aberdeen, 369, 375
    martial qualities of, 373, 375
    tactics at Culloden, 375
Cumbria, 99, 100, 104, 109–10
Cumming, William Skeoch, 699
Cunningham, Brevet Maj. James, 343
Cunningham, Pilot Officer Wallace, 567
Curragh 'mutiny' (1914), 537–8, 545
Cutts, Maj.-Gen. John, 1st Baron, 330, 333
Cyprus, 500, 611

Dacre, Thomas, Lord, 191–2
    forces of, 192–3
Dalhousie, William Ramsay, 1st Lord and 2nd earl of, 286
Dalkeith, Sir James Douglas of, 173
Dallachy, RAF, 566
Dalriada, kingdom of, 67, 82
Dál Riata, 81
Dalrymple, Lt.-Col. John *see* Stair
Dalyell, Capt. James, 393
Dalyell, Gen. Thomas, 'Bluidy Tam', 267, 275n52, 304
    cavalry of, 304–6, 311
Dalzell, Sir William de, 175
Danish army, Scots serve in, 257, 259, 264
Dargai, storming of (1897), 24, 473, 640, 656–7, 698, 808
Darnley, Henry Stewart, Lord, assassination of (1567), 236
Darnley, Sir John Stewart of, 10
David I, king of Scots (r. 1124–1153), 96–8, 104–5, 108–10, 112, 115–18, 708–9
    and Normans, 97, 100, 108, 115–16
    invades England, 100–4, 110, 117
    land grants of, 5, 96, 98, 121n12
    military capacity of, 101, 108

David II, king of Scots (r. 1329–71), 160, 164–7, 171, 174
    bravery of, 175
    rebuilds Edinburgh castle, 713
    suppresses rebellion (1363), 172
D-Day landings (1944), 563, 579, 582, 661
    and Mulberry harbours, 561
    'Fortitude North', 569
    Pegasus bridge, 662
    Sword beach, 563, 579
Defence of the Realm Act (1914), 516
Defoe, Daniel, 329, 337, 342
Delhi, siege of (1857), 469
Dendermonde, siege of (1706), 336
Denholm, Squadron Leader George, 566
Denmark, 562, 569
    Gundestrup bowl, 649
Denmark-Norway, 254–5, 257, 263
Derby, Jacobite marches to and from (1745), 116, 365–7, 370
Derwenter, James Radcliffe, 3rd earl of, 354–5
Desanges, Louis William, *Captain Robert James Lindsay, Scots Fusilier Guards, winning the VC at the Alma, 20 September 1854* (1863), 701
desertion, 34n49, 81, 115–16, 202, 397, 413, 540
    among mercenaries, 267, 332
    Jacobite, 365, 368
    pre-Flodden, 190
Desert Victory (1943), 661
Deskford, Banffshire, carnyx found in, 649
d'Essé, André de Montalembert, Seigneur, 201–2
Detroit, siege of (1763), 393
HMS *Devastation*, 785
Devine, Tom, 1, 486, 810
Dieppe raid (1942), 497
Direct Action Committee Against Nuclear War (DAC), civil disobedience of, 603
Disarming Act (1716), 358
Disarming Acts (1746 and 1747), 16, 386, 634, 690, 778
    amendments (1747 and 1748), 655
    no proscription of bagpipes in, 653, 655
    repealed (1782), 635

Diss, Ralph of, 113
Dobbins, Lt.-Col. William, 342
Dog, Jamie, 201
Donaldson, Gordon, 202
Donaldson, Pte. Joseph, 426
Donnini, Pte. Dennis, 582
Douai, siege of (1710), 336
Douglas, Lanarkshire
  Cameronian's Regimental
    Memorial, 757–8
  disbandment of the Cameronians
    (1968), 616
  St Bride's Church, 750
Douglas, Archibald Douglas, 'the
  Grim', 3rd earl of *see* Galloway
Douglas, Archibald Douglas, 4th earl
  of (and duke of Touraine), 10,
  165, 169, 715
  bravery of, 175
Douglas, Archibald Douglas, 5th earl
  of (and count of Longueville), 10,
  169
Douglas, Archibald, Regent of
  Scotland, 143
Douglas, Reverend Dr. Fiona, 26
Douglas, Brig.-Gen. James, 330
Douglas, Lt.-Gen. James, 316
Douglas, James Douglas, 2nd earl of,
  164–5
Douglas, James Douglas, 9th earl of, 11
Douglas, Sir James, the 'Black
  Douglas', 136, 146–8, 150, 153, 799
  army of, 149–50
  captured Roxburgh castle, 143, 148
  'Douglas Larder', 143
  knighted on eve of Bannockburn,
    143
Douglas, Company Sergt.-Maj. John,
  26, 525
Douglas, Col. Sir Robert, 14
Douglas, William Douglas, 1st earl of,
  194, 706, 709, 713
Douglas, William Douglas, 8th earl
  of, 717
  knighted by French king, 174
Douglas Banner, 786
Douglas family, 160, 712
  estates ravaged (1455), 11, 172, 212,
    716
Doune (Perthshire), 782, 810n6
Dounreay, nuclear research facilities
  at, 608
Doutelle, 363

Drem, RAF, 566
dress, battle, 571, 628, 642
  and reforms of 1881, 640
  Highland, 24, 185, 398–400, 628,
    632–5, 637–9, 643, 779, 782
  medieval, 81
  Royal Regiment of Scotland, 628–31
  Scottish military, 640–4
  see also kilts
Drumclog, battle of (1679), 308–9, 695
Drumlanrig, ambush at (1548), 202
Drummond, James, *Ancient Scottish
  Weapons* (1881), 782
Drummond, Lord John, 367, 371
Drummond, Lt.-Gen. William (later
  Lord Drummond of Crombix and
  1st Viscount Strathallan), 267,
  275n52, 304, 315
Drummonds, 781
drums, 342, 641, 653, 658, 644
  communications role of, 650–1
  'drumming up' recruits, 391, 655
  entertainment role of, 663
  icons of regimental identity, 651–2
  in daily routines, 652
  The Drum (1938), 25
drummers, inspirational role of, 651
  drummer-boy images, 700
  heroism of, 657
Dryfe Sands, battle of (1593), 241
Dubh, Dòmhnall, 215, 222, 226
Dubh, Eoin, 218
Dublin, Bachelor's Walk shootings
  (1914), 546
  Royal Barracks, 107
Duddingston Loch, hoard found in,
  49, 778
Duguid, Pte. William, 460
Dumbarton, 67, 171, 416, 477, 510,
  675, 760
Dumbarton, Maj.-Gen. George
  Douglas, 1st earl of, 14, 266, 313,
  315
  horse and dragoons of, 312
  regiment of, 267, 304
Dumfries, 50, 56, 241
  and covenanters, 304, 308, 327,
    336, 343
Dun, John Erskine of, 186
Dun, Thomas, 152
Dunadd, 76
Dunbar, 67, 71, 203, 292, 364, 738
  sacked (1216), 103

Dunbar, battles of (1296), 133, 136, 143 and of (1650), 13, 292–4
Dunbar, Gospatric II, earl of, 109
Dunblane, Queen Victoria School for the Sons of Scottish Sailors and Soldiers, 760
Duncan II, king of Scots (r. 1094), 96, 105, 116
  seal of, 94
Duncan, Thomas, 695
  Departing for Waterloo (c. 1840), 697
Duncan, William fitz, 105, 110
Dundas, Henry, (later 1st Viscount Melville), 409–11, 637
Dundas, Robert, 438
Dundee, 201, 573, 798
  captured (1645), 288
  Great War casualties of, 530
  remembrance of Loos, 517
  sacked (1651), 13
  University College of, 23, 599n123
Dundee, John Graham, 7th laird of Claverhouse and 1st Viscount ('Bluidy Clavers' and 'Bonnie Dundee'), 15, 307–9
  raises Jacobite rebellion (1689), 316–17, 615
Dundrennan abbey, 119
Dunfermline, Col. Charles Seton, 2nd earl of, 286
Dunglass fort, 201
Dunkeld, 362
  battle of (1689), 317
  Cathedral, 757
Dunkeld, William Sinclair, bishop of, 137
Dunkirk, evacuation of (1940), 571
  siege of (1944–5), 580
Dún Leithfinn, 71
Dunoon, 604–5
  and Holy Loch base, 605
  economic costs of US base closure, 609
Dupplin Moor, battle of (1332), 158
Durham, 115, 281
  Bek, Antony, bishop of, 712
  sacked (1312), 149
  siege of (1006), 70, 80
  Simeon of, 94
Dury, Capt. Theodore, 350
Dutch army, 253, 255, 265, 269, 331–2, 348
  Scots serve in, 329–30, 391

Dutch Republic *see* United Provinces
Dutch Revolt (1568-1648), 12, 251–3
  Scots serve in, 12, 244–5, 249, 252–4, 256
Dwr, Owain Glyn, 171
Dyce, RAF, 566
Dytor, Lt. Clive, 585

Eadie, Ian, *The 51st Highland Division Plans El Alamein* (1949), 702
Eaglesham, 562
East India Company, 18, 270, 468–9
Eccles, Berwickshire, anti-militia riot in (1797), 417
Edgar, king of Scots (r. 1097–1107), 96
Edinburgh, 67, 103, 186, 189, 200–1, 252, 257, 265, 278–9, 281, 292, 295, 300, 304–5, 310, 342, 384, 392, 417, 440, 446, 530, 540, 548, 569, 577, 699, 759, 781, 798
  and the 'Forty-Five, 364, 367–8, 374
  bombed (1916), 508–9
  Chartism, 443
  Darnley assassinated in (1567), 236
  defences of, 562
  Festival, 669
  Flodden Wall, 193, 196, 364, 742
  French soldiers unpopular in, 202, 742
  George IV visits (1822), 4, 638, 695, 781
  Great War casualties of, 524, 529
  hoards, 49, 778
  Loyalist volunteers, 374, 690
  memorials in, 25, 477, 752, 754–6, 767, 782
  Military Exhibition of (1888), 784, 787
  military receptions in, 18, 421–4
  Militia, 343, 418
  museums, 27, 788, 792
  National Portrait Gallery, 108
  Naval and Military Exhibition (1889), 785–6
  police force of, 445
  recruiting in, 20, 270, 510–12
  Redford barracks, 798
  regiments of, 280, 288, 391, 512, 524
  riot control in, 343
  Royal Air Force units in, 559
  sacked (1544), 10, 196

St Giles, High Kirk of, 477, 756, 783
strikes, 544
Tattoo, 663
Treaty (ratified in Northampton, 1328), 135
Treaty (1560), 203, 235, 742
University of, 22, 559, 760
Volunteers, 470
war production in 561
see also parliament, Scottish
HMS *Edinburgh* (sunk, 1942), 565
Edward I, 'Hammer of the Scots', king of England (r. 1272-1307), 6-7, 99, 120, 146, 150, 152
army of, 6, 31n17, 133, 140
cavalry of, 114, 153
invades Scotland, 5-7, 31nn.17 and 18, 99-100, 114, 120, 133
occupies Scotland, 146, 148-9, 164
savagery of, 150
seaborne support for, 31n18, 152
Edward II, king of England (r. 1307-27), 7, 9, 143, 146, 149, 152
army of, 140, 143, 744
invades Scotland, 9, 135, 144
overthrown, 9
poor leadership of, 9, 135, 144
Edward III, king of England (r. 1327-77), 9, 135
defeats Scots in battle, 158, 168
harries raiding Scots, 149
preoccupied with French wars, 160-1
supports dynastic claims of Balliol, 158, 166
Edward IV, king of England (r. 1461-83), 11, 163, 166
Edward VI, king of England (r. 1547-53), 195, 198-9
Eglinton, Alexander Montgomery, 6th earl of, 286
Eglinton Tournament (1839), 781
Egypt, 616, 699
Arabi Pasha's revolt in, 473
expedition to (1801), 17, 754
in Great War, 509
in Second World War, 573
intervention in (1882), 472, 698
Eichorn, Gen. Hermann von, 539
Eighth Army, 573-4, 578
Eisenhower, President Dwight D., 602
Elgin, 133, 707

Eliott, Gen. George Augustus, 1st Baron Heathfield, 671
Elisabeth, 362-3
Elizabeth I, queen of England (r. 1558-1603), 235-7, 239
Elliots, 242
Ellis, John, *The Sharp End*, 585
El Morro, storming of (1762), 671
Emergency Powers Act (1920), 544
empire, British, 28, 270, 272, 489, 610, 617, 637, 673, 688, 692, 768, 803, 809
mission, 478, 486, 761
retreat from, 2, 601, 610-14, 620, 643
Scottish military identified with, 642, 698-701, 755, 759, 761, 783
see also imperial wars
'Engagement', 290-1
Engelbrecht, Martin, *Théâtre de la Malice Étrangère*, 690
Engels, Friedrich, 539
English army, 135-7, 140, 144, 148, 153, 160, 165, 189-90, 192, 198
Episcopalians, 302, 307
and Jacobitism, 348-9, 368
Erle, Lt.-Gen. Thomas, battalions of, 342
Erracht, Col. Alan Cameron of, 410
Erroll, Charles, 13th earl of, 350
Erskine, Col. Arthur, 286
Espec, Walter, 112
Essex, Lt.-Gen. Algernon Capell, 2nd earl of, dragoons of, 342
Essex, Walter Devereux, 1st earl of, 244
Ettrick forest campaign (1455), 212
Eure, Sir Ralph, 197
European Economic Community, 607
Evelyn, John, 300
Ewart, Sergt. Charles, 420-1, 702
Ewart, Gen. John Alexander, 461
Ewart, Lt.-Gen. Sir John Spencer, 22, 462, 477-8
Ewing, Sir Alfred, 22
Eyemouth, fort, 201-2, 718

Fairfax, Ferdinando Fairfax, 2nd Lord, 285
Fairfax, Gen. Thomas Fairfax, 3rd Lord, 290, 292
Falaise, Treaty of (1174), 101, 103
Falkenhausen, Gen. Ludwig von, 522

Falkirk, 438, 752, 760
Falkirk, battle of (1298), 114, 133, 139, 148
  battlefield built over, 730
  English army at, 140
  Scottish cavalry flee the battle, 136
  Wallace's tactics at, 6, 31n18, 143, 145
Falkirk, battle of (1746), 16, 368, 373–5, 389, 400
  Falkirk Moor, battlefield of, 731
Falklands War (1982), 585, 617–18
  5th Infantry Brigade in, 617
  surrender of Argentines, 619
Fallin, 544
Fallujah, assault on (2004), 4, 620
Fantosme, Jordan, 102, 118
Farnese, Elisabeth, queen of Spain, 356
Faslane, base, 605
  peace camp, 610
fencibles, 288, 304–5, 414–17, 436, 537, 779–80, 785
Fenians, 441, 472
Fenton, Roger, 697–8
Ferguson, Maj.-Gen. James, 328–9, 333
  battalion of, 339
Fergusson, Brig.-Gen. Sir Bernard, 29, 498
Ferranti, 559
Feversham, Louis de Duras, 2nd earl of, 316
Fife, 96, 136, 293, 302, 307, 350, 416, 468, 516, 544, 564, 594n61, 709
  burial sites in, 53, 55
  fencibles, 305
  Militia, 310, 316
  soldiers, 544
Fife, Duncan MacDuff, 2nd earl of, 97
fifes, 652–3, 658
Fifth Army, 578
Fiji, soldiers from, 797
films, imperial, 25, 669, 701
Findlater, Piper George, 473, 656–7, 667n43
Finglask, John Ogilvy of, 190
Finnart, James Hamilton of, 719–20
First Aid Nursing Yeomanry (FANY), 23
First Carlist War (1833–40), 270, 460

First Gulf War (1990–1), 617, 662, 702
First World War, 'Great War' (1914–18), 2, 20, 22–4, 28, 217, 452, 485, 492–6, 612, 642, 651, 659, 760, 796, 802–3
  and Scotland, 506–9, 529–31, 673–4, 681
  artillery in, 514, 518, 520, 522–4
  French allies in, 514, 519–20, 522, 526–7
  gas, 513–14, 518, 520, 532n16 and n19
  machine guns in, 514, 519, 522, 524
  memorials, 25–6, 748, 760–5, 768
  recruitment, 20, 506, 510–13, 545
  Scots on the Western Front, 21–2, 513–23, 526–7
  Scots serve in Gallipoli, 523–6
  Scottish military contribution to, 512–13, 529–30
  war artists of, 25, 702
First World War, battalions
  Argyll and Sutherland Highlanders, 514–15, 521, 526–7, 540, 660
  Black Watch, 513, 515, 517, 527, 530
  Border Regiment, 518
  Cameron Highlanders, 513, 515–16, 527
  Cameronians (Scottish Rifles), 515, 524, 527
  Gordon Highlanders, 513, 515, 521, 527, 530
  Highland Light Infantry (HLI), 511–13, 515, 518–19
  King's Own Scottish Borderers, 513, 521, 660, 702
  Lancashire Fusiliers, 519
  Royal Scots, 25–6, 512, 515, 517, 521–5, 529, 540
  Seaforth Highlanders, 513, 520
  see also New Army
First World War, divisions, 28, 514
  1st, 515
  2nd, 513, 515
  3rd, 521
  7th, 515
  9th (Scottish), 28, 495, 509–10, 513–14, 520–2, 527
  15th (Scottish), 28, 509–10, 513–15, 517, 523, 527
  32nd, 518

34th, 517, 523
47th, 515
51st (Highland), 20, 22, 28–9, 497, 509, 523, 527
52nd (Lowland), 28, 509, 524
fishing industry, decline of, 606–7, 685–6; *see also* 'Cod Wars'
Fitzroy, East Falkland, 702
Flanders, 20, 170, 181, 244, 249, 267, 333, 336–7, 339–40, 342, 360, 366, 371, 373, 410, 509, 513, 525, 632, 808
Flanders, Philip 1, count of, 101–2
Fletcher, Ian, 419
flogging, 463, 536, 651
Fontainebleau, Treaty of (1745), 365
Forbes, Brig.-Gen. John, 387, 393–4
Forbes, Lt.-Col. William, 13th Lord, 326
Forbin-Gardane, Claude, comte de, 338, 349–50
Force Research Unit (FRU), 552–3
Foreign Enlistment Act (1819), 270
Forfar, 106, 432n30, 573
Forglen, 114, 164
Forres, 749
  Nelson Tower at, 755
Forster, Thomas, 352–3
Fort Augustus, 361–2, 370, 710
Fort Charlotte (Shetland), 719
Fort Louis, Guadeloupe, capture of (1759), 387
Fort Peddie, defence of (1846), 465
Fort Regent, St Helier, 692
Fortune, Maj.-Gen. Victor M., 571
Fort William, 318, 338, 344, 350, 361–3, 364, 372, 719, 753
  Jacobite siege of (1746), 370, 743
  site investigation, 743
Foulkes, Maj.-Gen. Charles H., 22
'Foul Raid', 161
Foy, Gen. Maximilien, 407
Foyer, Sergt. James, 428
France, 10, 23, 94, 118, 151, 226, 264, 270, 318–19, 327, 411, 672, 717, 802
  and Jacobites, 266–7, 269, 338, 348–50, 352, 362–3, 365, 368, 370, 376, 388, 737–8
  and the Great War, 20, 509–10, 512, 523
  artists of, 688, 693, 698, 704–5n20

  at war with England, 10, 160–1, 165, 169, 187, 190, 194
  conscription, 538–9
  fall of (1940), 562, 581
  in the Second World War, 571–2, 582
  peace treaties, 197, 202
  refuge for Scots, 160, 172, 174, 193, 235, 316, 349
  see also Auld Alliance, French army and invasion scares
Francis I, king of France, 189
Francis II, king of France, married to Mary Queen of Scots, 235
Francis, William, 148
Franco-Irish Brigade, 267
Franco-Scottish alliance *see* Auld Alliance
Frankfurt Trench, 518
Fraser, George MacDonald, 584
Fraser, Capt. (later Brig.-Gen.) Simon, 395, 691
Fraser, Lt.-Col. Hon. William, 527
Frasers, 215, 221, 226, 354, 358; *see also* Lovat
Frederick V, Elector Palatine and (briefly) king of Bohemia, 244
Frederick the Great, king in Prussia, 354
French and Indian War (1754–63), 385; *see also* Seven Years War
French army, 17, 137, 161, 186, 419, 554, 571, 656
  Scots serve in, 10, 167, 169, 184–5, 250, 261, 263–7, 269, 329, 735
  see also La Garde Écossaise and Le Régiment Royal Écossais
French Revolution, 411, 417, 443
French Revolutionary War (1793–7), 3, 17, 407–9, 414, 416, 436, 438, 780
  Scottish military contribution in, 409, 412–13, 415
Freskin the Fleming, 98–9, 707–8, 711
Freuchie, John Grant of, 239
Froissart, Jean, 174, 650, 655
Frontier Wars, Sixth (1834–6), 465–6
  Seventh (1846–7), 465
  Eighth (1850–3), 465
  Ninth (1877–8), 472
Front Line First – Defence Costs Study (1994), 805

Gacé, Charles August Goyon de Motignon, comte de, 349
Gaelic warfare, 209, 211–12, 215–18, 220, 223–5, 227–8
  ambushes, 221
  and Stewart kings, 11, 172, 189, 197, 212, 217, 222, 226, 242, 258
  castle and galley, 107, 151–2, 196, 212–14, 224, 226
  confederal conflict, 222
  duels, 221
  dynastic disputes, 216, 221–2
  land disputes, 216–17, 220
  weaponry of, 185, 223–7
Gage, Gen, Thomas, 487
Gallacher, Willie, 542–3
galleys *see* birlinn
Gallipoli campaign (1915–16), 492, 495, 509, 523–6
  evacuation from, 525–6
  veterans of, 530
galloglass warriors, 113, 172, 218, 224, 227, 258
Galloway, 50, 96–8, 104–5, 110, 112, 115, 127, 137, 152, 303, 707
  and covenanters, 327, 336, 343
  destructive campaigns in, 104–5, 110, 115, 141
  lords of, 104, 107, 164
  rebellion of (1235), 104–5
Galloway, Alan, lord of, 104, 107, 111, 125n43, 128n95
Galloway, Archibald 'the Grim' Douglas, earl of Wigtown, 3rd earl of Douglas and lord of, 164
  builds Threave castle, 174, 717
Galloway, Fergus lord of, 118
Galloway, men of, 104, 106, 110, 113–14
  at battle of the Standard, 100–1, 114, 116
  at Clithero, 110
  in English army in Wales, 111
  savagery of, 115–17
Galloway, Roland, lord of, 105, 118–19
Galtieri, Gen. Leopoldo, 617
Garby-Czerniawski, Roman, 569
Garcia, Juan Pujol, 569
Gardiner, Alfred George, 539
Garibaldi, Giuseppe, 271
Garlieston, 561
Garth, Maj.-Gen. David Stewart of, 3–4, 396–8, 401, 421–2, 638, 801

Garth, Niall Stewart of, 222
Gawilghur, stormed (1803), 18
Geddes, Brig.-Gen. Sir Auckland, 1st Baron, 23
General Strike (1926), 544–5
George I, King (r. 1714–27), 344, 351, 356, 359
George II, King (r. 1727–60), 360, 372, 386–7, 400, 675, 799
George III, King (r. 1760–1820), 386, 400, 407
George IV, King (r. 1820–30), 800
  as Prince Regent, 779
  visits Edinburgh (1822), 4, 638, 695, 781
  wears Highland dress, 635
George VI, king (r. 1938–52), 568
George Watson's College, 509, 524
Georgia, expedition to (1778–9), 395
Germany, 94, 257, 259, 261, 265, 500, 507, 610–11, 616
  and First World War, 506, 509–10, 513–14, 518–23, 526–7, 673, 642, 802
  and Second World War, 559, 562, 566–8, 571–2, 580–2, 584, 662, 685
  band masters of, 657
  conscription, 539
  U-boats of, 509, 564–5, 568
Gesta Annalia, 116
Ghent, 331, 336, 342
Ghilleasbuig, Alasdair, 218
Ghilleasbuig, Colla mac, 218
Gibb, Robert, 24–5, 699–700
  Alma: Advance the 42nd Highlanders (1888), 699
  Backs to the Wall, 1918 (1929), 700
  Comrades (1878), 699
  Dargai (1909), 700
  Letters from Home (1885), 699
  The Thin Red Line (1885), 25, 699
Gibbon, Lewis Grassic (James Leslie Mitchell), *Sunset Song* (1932), 673–4, 677
  trilogy of, 675
Gibraltar, 327, 337, 473, 572
  great siege of (1779–83), 671, 691–2
Gibson, John, 655
Gifford, Flight Lt. Patrick, 'Patsy', 559, 585n1

Gladstone, William Ewart, 462
  government of, 448
Glanville, Ranulf de, 109
Glasgow, 237, 288–9, 302, 304, 307, 312, 342, 416, 450, 470, 476, 478, 507–8, 562, 606, 683, 798
  and covenanters, 308–10
  and the 'Forty-Five, 364, 367, 374
  bombed, 567
  casualties of, 518, 530
  Cathedral, 756, 784
  Corporation, 519
  George Square rally (1919), 542–3
  Highland Societies of, 571
  International Exhibition (1888), 784, 787
  Labour politics, 540
  Maryhill barracks, 445, 542–3, 562
  memorials, 25, 477, 754–6
  Militia, 315, 343
  museums, 27, 782
  police, 448, 542, 544
  recruiting in, 20, 270–1, 510–12, 518, 540, 550
  'Red Clydeside', 453, 537
  riots in, 343, 443
  Robert Wishart, bishop of, 150
  strikes, 442–3, 537, 542
  trade unions, 343, 540
  University of, 728
  Volunteers, 470
Glasgow Herald, 468, 510, 518
Glasgow Post, 512
Glenalmond, Trinity College, library of, 760
Glenbucket, John Gordon, laird of, 363
Glencairn, William Cunningham, 8th earl of, 294
Glencairn, Lt.-Col. William Cunningham, 12th earl of, 340
Glencoe, massacre of (1692), 318
Glendaruel, Colin Campbell of, 357
Glen Douglas, nuclear storage facility, 606
Glenfinnan, rallying point of Jacobite clans (1745), 363
  monument (1815), 753
Glen Fruin, battle of (1603), 218, 221, 226, 242
  10-mile rout, 223–4
Glengarry, 417, 421,
  see also bonnet

Glenlivet, battle of (1594), 209, 215, 223, 226
Glenluce abbey, 115
Glenshiel, battle of (1719), 358
Glorat, Capt. Mungo Stirling of, 584–5
Glorious, 'Bloodless', Revolution (1688), 316–18, 329, 348, 351
Goch, capture of (1945), 580, 582–3
Gododdin, kingdom of, 708
Godolphin, Sidney Godolphin, 1st earl of, 340–2, 344
Goodall, Frederick, 19
  Jessie's Dream: The Campbells Are Coming, Lucknow, September 1857 (1858), 698
Goodare, Julian, 239
Gordon, Gen. Lord Adam, 437
Gordon, Alexander Gordon, 4th duke of, 412
Gordon, Lt.-Col. Sir Charles, 462
Gordon, Maj.-Gen. Charles, 'Chinese', 470, 474, 488
  relief expedition (1884–5), 473
Gordon, George Gordon, 1st duke of, *see* Huntly
Gordon, 2nd Lt. Henry, 15
Gordon, Jane, 'Jean', Gordon, duchess of, 411–12
Gordon, Col. John, 264
Gordon, Lord Lewis, 371
Gordon, Mirabelle de, 367
Gordon, Capt. Patrick, 328
Gordons, 215, 288
  see also Huntly, earls of
Goring, George, Lord, 287
Gowrie, 96
Graham, Capt. David, 331
Graham, Sir Thomas (later 1st Baron Lynedoch), 411
Grahams, 256
Grand Alliance, 318–19
  Second, 327
Grange, Sir William Kirkcaldy of, 237
Grant, Alexander, 7
Grant, Col. Alexander Grant of, 327, 340
  battalion of, 336
Grant, James, 26
Grant, Col. James, 372
Grant, Maj. James, 393–4, 402n9
Grant, Sir James Grant of, 8th Baronet, 780
Grant, Gen, Sir James Hope, 471

Grant, John, 659
Grant, Lt. (later Maj.) John, 387, 401
Grant, Capt. William, 326
Grants, 340, 354
Gray, Sir Andrew, 256–7
Gray, Sir Thomas, 136
Great Glen, 105, 285, 370
  forts, 742–3
  restricted area, 506, 563
  strategic primacy of, 213, 215, 361–2
Great Michael, 188
Great Northern War (1700–21), 329
Greenham Common, peace camp, 608
Greening, Sergt. Will, 476
Greenock, Free French Movement in, 765
'Grey Dragoons' *see* regiments, British army, Royal Scots Greys
Gruinard Island, biological weapon tests on, 569–70
Guardians of Scotland, 6, 138
Guisborough, Walter of, 136, 145
Gurkhas, 473, 613, 795
  adopt Highland dress, 641–2, 646n23
  adopt pipes, 613
Gustav II Adolf, king of Sweden, 12, 255, 259–61, 678
  spurs of, 778

Habsburg, dynasty of, 256, 263
  Scots serve in armies of, 264
hackles, 797, 807
Haddington, 187
  fort, 201–2
  sacked (1216), 103
Haddon Rig, battle of (1542), 10, 184, 187
  English base at, 194
Hadrian's Wall, 56
Haig, FM Sir Douglas (later 1st Earl), 21, 462, 477–8, 514, 522, 528–9, 531, 791
  Earl Haig Collection, 792
Hakon IV, king of Norway, 107
Haldane, Richard Burdon (later 1st Viscount), 22, 477–8
Haliburtons, 712
Halidon Hill, battle of (1333), 158, 163, 166
Halkett, Maj. Edward, 330
Hall, Edward, 182, 184

Hamilton, Col. (General of Artillery) Sir Alexander, 286
Hamilton, Maj. Andrew, 333
Hamilton, Douglas Douglas-Hamilton, 8th duke of, and 82nd Foot, 391
Hamilton, Douglas Douglas-Hamilton, 14th duke of, 562
Hamilton, Brig.-Gen. George, 331
  regiment of, 329–30, 333
Hamilton, Lt.-Gen. Hugo, 329
Hamilton, Gen. Sir Ian Standish Monteith, 461, 477, 525
Hamilton, James, 3rd marquess and 1st duke of, 12, 276, 279, 290–1
Hamilton, Maj.-Gen. Malcolm, 329
Hamilton, Robert, 310
Hamilton, Sergt. William, 476
Hamilton, William Douglas, 3rd duke of, 307
Hamilton barracks, 444–5
Hamilton, battle of (1650), 293
Hardie, Andrew, 438
Hardie, Keir, 537, 539
Harlaw, battle of (1411), 172–3, 214, 217
Harry, Blind, 7
  The Wallace (c. 1477), 175
Harvey, Sir George, 695
  The Battle of Drumclog (1836), 695
Havelock, Maj.-Gen. Sir Henry, 18–19, 469
Hawick, Flodden monument in, 752
  Boer War memorial in, 760
Hawley, Lt.-Gen. Henry, 367, 373
  army of, 367–8, 372–3
Hay, George Campbell, 678, 680
  'Ar Blàr Catha' ('Our Field of Battle'), 678–9
Hay, Sir Gilbert, 173
Hay, Ian [John Hay Beith], 515, 540–1
  The First Hundred Thousand (1915), 540–1
Hay, Sir John, 488
Hay, Brig.-Gen. Lord John, 328, 333–4
Healey, Denis, 607
  defence review of (1966), 619
Heart of Midlothian Football Club, 22, 25, 512
Heath, William, 693

Hebrides *see* Western Isles
helmets, 112–13, 184
  bascinet, 138
  bronze, 48
  Roman, 55
  steel, 544, 642
Hemy, Thomas, 463–4
Henderson, Diana, 461
Henderson, Capt. Hamish, 577–8, 584, 678, 685
  Elegies for the Dead in Cyrenaica (1948), 677, 679
Henrisoun, James, 201
Henry I, king of England (r. 1110–35), 96, 100, 111
Henry II, king of England (r. 1154–89), 101–3, 111
  raids Scotland, 103
  receives Scottish military support, 111, 118
Henry II, king of France, 235
Henry III, king of England (r. 1216–72), 100, 109, 114
  receives Scottish military support, 120
Henry IV, king of England (r. 1399–1413), 160–1, 165
Henry V, king of England (r. 1413–22), 169
  victor at Agincourt, 9
Henry VII, king of England (r. 1485–1509), 10, 190
Henry VIII, king of England (r. 1509–47), 185, 195, 198, 238
  expeditionary forces in France, 187, 190, 194, 215
  forays in Scotland, 192–4, 196–7, 215
  see also 'Rough Wooing'
Henry, earl of Northumberland and son of David I, king of Scots, 100–1, 108–9
Henty, George Alfred, 688
Hepburn, Col. John, 256, 261, 266
Hepburn, Col. John, 330
  battalion of, 331
Hereford, Humphrey de Bohun, 4th earl of, 9, 150
Heritage Lottery Fund, 27, 739
Hertford, Edward Seymour, 1st earl of (and later 1st duke of Somerset), 196, 198–201
  armies of, 196–8
  fall from power, 202

Hesketh, Pte. James, 549
Hess, Rudolf, 562–3
Hexham, 110
  priory, 115, 149, 151
Hexham, Richard of, 110
Highland Brigades, 28–9, 462, 577
  in Crimean War, 465–6, 699, 756
  Egypt, 472
  Indian Mutiny, 469
  Napoleonic Wars, 28
  South African War, 19, 462, 474–5, 701, 705n20, 758, 773n54, 808
  The Departure of the Highland Brigade, 1855, 697
Highland charge, 3, 223, 278, 375–6, 400
  at Culloden, 384, 734–5
  Killiecrankie, 15, 317, 738
  preceding volley, 223–4, 400
  Prestonpans, 739–40
  terrain crucial, 223, 365, 736, 738
Highland Clearances, 217, 416, 427, 637
Highland Host, 307–8
Highland Independent Companies, 269, 326, 338–9, 344, 359–60, 372, 632–3
Highland Land Law Reform Association, 447
Highland regiments, 17, 19, 383–4, 386, 388–91, 396–8, 400, 408–9, 451, 462, 487, 571, 576, 579, 629, 696, 700, 783, 799–800
  amalgamations of, 803–6
  and reforms of 1881, 23–4, 28, 459, 476, 640, 644, 803
  distinctive imagery of, 633–7, 689–90, 696, 698, 810
  dubbed 'Ladies from Hell', 642, 688, 802
  fighting prowess of, 389, 394–7, 421–6, 466, 469, 472–3, 635, 639, 754, 800
  memorials, 755–6
  recruitment for, 359, 386–7, 389–91, 398, 407, 409–10, 412, 415–17, 426–7, 430n8, 431n26, 459–61, 573, 578, 637–40, 675, 780, 796
  resented by other regiments, 393, 422, 468, 639
  traditions of, 633, 677, 685, 778

Highland regiments (cont.)
  see also First World War and Second World War
Highland soldier, 227, 428, 500
  appearance of, 398–400, 427, 460, 633–4, 636, 643, 689, 697, 800–1, 810
  depictions of, 419, 423, 432, 635, 669, 673, 676, 679, 688–93, 696–701, 705n23
  images of, 3, 24–5, 396, 407, 412–19, 460, 478, 486, 496, 637, 640, 756
  'presence' in battle paintings, 690–3, 696, 698
  qualities of, 4, 15, 17, 19, 365, 389, 396–7, 408, 410, 422, 426–7, 649, 677, 698, 755
Highland Watch, 306, 398
Highlandism of Scottish military, 3–4, 476, 629, 640–1, 810
  and Scottish identity, 427, 486, 489
  mythology of, 3–4, 27, 211, 427, 486, 637–40, 639–4
Highlands, after Culloden, 16, 347, 375, 386, 486, 690, 753
  martial culture of, 3–4, 15, 17, 34n56, 215, 218–20, 226–7, 360, 386, 396–7, 633–5, 642, 756, 799
  public disorder in, 446–52, 679–80
Hill, David Octavius, 696
Hill, Maj.-Gen. John, 336
hill-forts, 4, 42, 46, 50–2, 56, 60, 69, 73, 75, 97
Himmler, Heinrich, Reichsführer-SS, capture of, 581
Hindenburg Line, 520
Historic Scotland, 743
Hitchings, Maj. Bruce, 662–3
hobelars, 139, 146
Hohenzollern Redoubt, 513
Hole, William, murals of, 108
Holl, Frank, *Ordered to the Front* (1880), 700
  Home Again (1881), 700
Holland, Col. A. E., 20
Holme Cultram abbey, plundered (1216), 115
Holmes, Richard, *Firing Line* (1985), 795
Holy Loch, US base at, 602–3, 605, 609
  protests at, 603–5

Holyrood Palace, 568
  sacked (1544), 196
Home, Alexander Home, 3rd Lord, 191–2
Home, Alexander Home, 6th Lord (later 1st earl of Home and Lord Dunglass), 241
Home, James Home, 3rd earl of, 281
home defence, 3, 17, 20, 338, 413–14, 427, 436, 478, 510, 562, 764
Hong Kong, 570
  ceremonial transfer of power (1997), 620
HMS *Hood*, 565
Hooke, Col. Nathaniel, 349
Hoon, Geoff, 644
Hope, Lt. James, 423
horns, 652, 664
  finds of, 648–9
  motivational effects of, 650, 655
Houston, John Adam, *The Highlands in 1746* (1849), 695
Howe, Gen. Sir William, 393
Hrúga, Kolbein, 709
Hughes, Emrys, 602
Hughes, Francis, 552
Hull, 342, 607
Hull, FM Sir Richard, 804, 806
Humbie, 566–7
Hundred Years War (1337–1453), 9–10, 161
hunting, 44–5, 48, 211, 226, 633, 650, 777
Huntly, Alexander Gordon, 3rd earl of, 191
Huntly, George Gordon, 4th earl of, 194, 197, 200, 221, 236
Huntly, George Gordon, 6th earl of (later 1st marquess of), 12
Huntly, George Gordon, 2nd marquess of, 279, 288
Huntly, George Gordon, 4th marquess of (later 1st duke of Gordon), 352
Huntly, George Gordon, 8th marquess of (later 5th duke of Gordon), 415
Huntly, earls of, 215
Hurry, Sir John, 288
Hutchison, Robert Gemmell, *Under Orders* (1882), 699
Hyde, James, 652
Hyndford, John Campbell, 1st earl of, 327
Hyslop, Jonathan, 492, 495, 500

Iceland, 601, 606–7
  Greenland–Iceland–UK 'gap', 608
  Keflavik air base of, 606
identity, 31n16
  British, 28, 476, 478, 632, 637, 684, 692, 754, 764
  Scottish, 1, 24, 28, 249–50, 260, 263, 272, 344, 427, 476, 478, 497, 500–1, 572, 577–8, 584, 627, 630, 632, 634, 637, 644, 653, 662–4, 669, 684, 734, 753, 767, 769, 776–7, 783
  'Scottishness', 25, 486–9, 498, 689, 694, 702, 749, 761
Illustrated London News, 695, 700
imperial wars, 344, 389, 401, 619
  adverse conditions in, 459, 463, 468–70
  diverse duties in, 464, 469, 471–6
  punitive actions in, 465, 469
  Scots earn renown in, 458, 466, 473, 476–7, 486, 637
Imperial Yeomanry, 20, 475, 759
Inchcolm abbey, 171
  fortifications of, 201
Inches, Robert Kirk, Lord Provost of Edinburgh, 512
Inchkeith, 202
  forts of, 719
Inchon, landings (1950), 611
India, 459, 461, 610, 698
  army of, 641–2
  mutinies in, 547
  north-west frontier of, 473, 477, 640, 656
  Scots serve in, 17–18, 25, 269, 458, 464, 469, 471, 473, 477, 487, 754
Indian Mutiny, 'sepoy revolt' (1857–9), 459, 462, 466, 468, 471, 698
  memorials, 756
  Scots in suppression of mutinous sepoys, 468–71, 639, 682
Indonesia, confrontation (1962–6), 611, 613
industry, 4, 85, 416
  decline of naval shipbuilding on the Clyde, 619–20
  disruption and strikes, 442–5, 537–8, 542–5
  wartime productivity of, 20, 506–8, 559, 561
Inglis, Capt. John, dragoons of, 308
Innes, Sheriff Cosmo, 446–7

intelligence services, 22, 569
  and war in Northern Ireland, 552–3
International Brigade, 768
HMS *Intrepid*, 617
invasion scares, 414, 470, 539
Inveraray, 312, 318, 338
  combined operations training centre at, 563
  see also castle, Inveraray
Invergordon, 506
Inverlochy, battles of (1431), 215, 218
  and of (1645), 215, 288
Inverness, 16, 105, 361–2, 391, 573
  and the 'Forty-Five, 364, 368–70, 372, 738
  Cameron barracks, 658
  sheriffs of, 190, 440
Inverness Courier, 516
Inversnaid barracks, 719
Iona, 68
  abbey, 224
  Statutes of (1609), 219
  Viking assault on (AD 806), 73
Iraq War (2003–11), 620, 627, 629, 662, 805–6
  soldiers' perspectives on, 669, 685
Ireland, 70, 75, 79, 107, 224–7, 263, 326, 351, 417, 441–2, 458, 461, 511, 545, 639, 649, 663
  agitation in, 448
  as a second front, 9, 11, 152, 171, 287
  atrocities in, 106, 117
  Catholic confederate forces of, 283, 287, 289
  chroniclers of, 69, 71, 82, 117
  Cromwell's impact in, 13, 292, 300, 359
  fleets of 104, 215, 223
  Gaels, 67, 209, 211–13, 215–20, 226–7
  home rule, 546
  invasion of Scotland, 279, 287–8
  Irish Brigade, 363, 388
  lordship in, 171, 216
  mercenaries from, 106, 139, 172, 185, 212, 216–18, 251, 254, 258, 264, 266–7, 270–1, 363, 367, 372, 388
  military tradition of, 2
  police primacy in, 547
  rebellions, 19, 282, 440
  recruitment in, 398, 408–9, 412, 413n19, 458–9, 639

Ireland (*cont.*)
  Scottish naval landings in, 171
  support for Jacobites, 267, 315, 362, 367–8, 372, 375
  Troubles, 547–8
  wars in, 72, 211, 220, 276, 281, 292, 316
  weapons, 46, 48, 112, 225
  'Wild Geese', 266
  see also Bruce, Edward, Irish Land League, Irish Republican Army, Northern Ireland and Ulster
Irish Land League, 439, 448
Irish Republican Army (IRA), 547–8
  Provisional IRA, 550, 553–4, 621, 804
Iron Age, 46–8, 50, 52, 54, 56, 67
Irwin, Capt. Alexander, 328
Islay, 77, 216, 223, 708
  naval battle off (1156), 213
  rising (1615), 211, 213–14, 218, 222, 245
Isles, Alasdair, 'Alexander of Islay', Lord of the, 218
Isles, Dòmhnall of Islay, Lord of the, 217
Isles, Eoin, 'John of Islay', Lord of the, 222
Isles, John MacDonald, earl of Ross and 4th Lord of the, 11, 189, 196
Isles, Lords of the, 11–12, 107, 152, 166, 172, 213–15, 708
  and English kings, 11, 196, 216
  lordship annexed by James IV, 217, 654
Israel, 614
Italy, 46, 94, 270–1, 498–9, 509, 526, 578, 685
  East African colonies, 498
  campaign (1943–5), 498–9, 578
Ivory, William, 440, 449–50

Jack, Gen. James, 527
Jack, Richard, *Return to the Front: Victoria Railway Station* (1916), 702
HMS *Jackal*, 450
Jackson, Charles d'Orville Pilkington, 768
Jackson, Pte. John, 515
Jacobite expedition (1708), 15, 338, 343, 350

Jacobite expedition (1719), 15, 356–8, 363
  government army, 358
  Jacobite army, 357
Jacobite rebellion (1689), 15, 316–17, 319, 348
Jacobite rebellion (1715), 15, 70, 268, 350–8, 363, 365, 799
  aftermath of, 355–6
  government army in, 354–5
  Jacobite army in, 352–4
Jacobite rebellion, 'the 'Forty-Five' (1745), 15, 116, 218, 350, 358, 360, 362, 384, 386–7, 392, 409, 563, 571, 652, 778
  divided Jacobite leadership, 365–6, 368, 371–2
  government forces, 363–70, 372–5, 689–90, 735
  Highland army, 225, 349, 363, 375–6, 385, 388, 634, 689, 722, 732–4, 736, 743, 745, 779
  naval role, 362–3, 370, 375
  romantic connotations of, 3, 216, 349, 353
Jacobites, 16, 27, 348–9, 355–6, 358, 384–5, 426, 655, 690
  and Tories, 351, 356
  conspiracies of, 34n51, 269, 355, 401
  English, 15, 349–50, 352, 355, 363, 366–6
  exiled, 267–8, 349, 353, 356, 387
Jacobitism, 436, 634
  memorials, 753, 768
  relics, 779
Jamaica, 463
James I, king of Scots (r. 1424–37), 161, 165–6, 170–2, 714–16
James II, king of Scots (r. 1437–60), 162, 164, 169, 173–4, 716
  accidental death, 716
  ravages Douglas lands, 11, 172, 212, 716–17
James III, king of Scots (r. 1460–88), 163, 172–3, 188, 724n2
James IV, king of Scots (r. 1488–1513), 706, 718
  annexes lordship of the Isles, 217
  artillery of, 188–91, 716
  bravery of, 182, 189
  chivalry of, 182, 189–90
  Gaelic soldiers of, 191, 212

killed at Flodden, 192, 717
navy of, 188
James V, king of Scots (r. 1513–42), 185, 193, 195, 225, 235, 240, 741
James VI, king of Scotland (r. 1567–1625) and I of England (r. 1603–25), 11–12, 211–12, 222, 236–8, 253–5, 257–8
   asserts internal authority, 239–43, 245
   foreign policy of, 239, 256
   limited naval and military assets of, 240, 243, 245
   see also Union of the Crowns
James VII, king of Scotland and II of England (r. 1685–8), 311, 349–50, 615
   as duke of York, 308
   crushes rebellions, 312–14
   defeated in Ireland and Scotland, 266
   flees for France, 266, 316, 348
   forces of, 266, 314–16
James Francis Edward Stuart, 'Old Pretender', 315, 339, 349–54, 356, 362, 371; *see also* Jacobite rebellion (1715) and Jacobite expedition (1719)
Jamesome, George, 689
Japan, 499
Jaurès, Jean, 539
Jedburgh, 146, 192, 708
   sacked (1523), 193
'Jeddart Justice', 242
Johannesburg, 477
John, king of England (r. 1199–1216), 100–1, 103, 105, 109, 111
Johnson, Dr Samuel, 798
Johnstone, James, 'Chevalier de Johnstone', 384–5
Johnstone, Sergt. Robert, 763
Johnstones, 240–1
Joiner, Clr.-Sergt. J., 467
Jones, John Paul, 784
Justice Mills, battle of (1644), 288

Kamara burial ground, 756
Karachi, 610
Keegan, Sir John, 28, 516
Keeley, Lawrence H., 43
Keith, George, 10th Earl Marischal of Scotland, 354, 356–7
Keith, FM James Edward, 268, 354

Keith, Sir Robert, Marischal of Scotland, 137
Kelhead, Col. Sir William Douglas of, 286
Kellie, Sir Thomas, 245
Kennaway, James, 683
   Tunes of Glory (1956), 683–5
Kenmure, Alexander Gordon, 5th Viscount, 317
Kenmure, William Gordon, 6th Viscount, 350, 355
Kennedy, President John Fitzgerald, 605
Kent and Strathearn, Prince Edward, duke of, 635
Kerch, expedition to (1855), 468
Kerr, Lt.-Col. Gordon, 552–3
Kerr, Lord Mark, regiment of, 327, 337
Kerrs, 240
Khartoum, siege of (1884–5), 473, 488
Killiecrankie, battle of (1689), 15, 317
   archaeological survey of, 738
Killigrew, Sir Henry, 244
Kilsyth, battle of (1645), 288
kilts, 407, 419, 427, 492, 515–16, 631, 641, 688, 800–2, 807
   and amalgamations, 628
   and recruiting, 24, 412, 431n19, 460, 491, 511, 636–8
   and reforms of 1881, 24, 640, 644
   and the Royal Regiment of Scotland, 24, 628–9, 810
   aprons, 24, 474, 496
   costs of, 490, 497, 638–9
   icon of Scottish identity, 24, 489–90, 500, 572, 643
   images involving, 419, 478, 486, 628, 689, 693, 700–2, 755, 801
   in parades, 576, 629–30, 643
   origins of, 636
   wartime practicality of, 24, 398–9, 434n54, 474, 571, 642
Kimberley, siege of (1899–1900), 491
King, Mary, 332–3
King, Capt. William Ross, 465–6
Kingsbarns Parish Church, 763
Kinlochlochy (Blàr nan Lèine), battle of (1544), 215, 221, 223
Kinloss, 19 operational training unit, 566
   battle of (AD 966), 85, 749
Kipling, Rudyard, 688

Kirkcudbright, Col. Thomas Maclennon, 2nd Lord, 286
Kirkwall, 708
Kirkwood, Robert, 397
Kiszely, Maj. (later Lt.-Gen. Sir) John, 618
Kitchener of Khartoum, FM Horatio Herbert, 1st Earl, 473, 509–10, 526, 539, 762
Kitson, Gen. Sir Frank Edward, 552
Kitson, Linda, 702
Kneller Hall, Royal Military School of Music at, 657
knights, 218
    armour of, 137, 170
    as elite forces, 100, 111–12, 116, 118, 136
    exchanged as prisoners, 150
    knighting ceremonies, 143, 173, 190
    knight service, 5, 79, 97, 108–9, 120, 137–8
    mounted role of, 96, 119–20, 136–7, 141, 145, 148
    see also chivalry
Knockando, Capt. Alexander Grant of, 16
Knox, John, 235
Konstam, Angus, 799
Korean War (1950–3), 500, 608, 611–12, 680, 682
Kuwait City, 663
Kynneries, Col. Hugh Fraser of, 286

Labour party, 540
    and Polaris, 602–4
Lachouque, Henry, *Waterloo* (1972), 419
Ladysmith, siege of (1899–1900), 19, 475–6
La Fère, 526
Laffin, John, 797, 802
La Garde Écossaise, 10, 169, 250
Laidlaw, Piper Daniel Logan, 660, 667n43
Laidlaw, Lt.-Col. David, 518
Lalaing, Jacques, 174
Lambert, Gen. John, 290
Lanarkshire, 508, 537, 562, 616, 719–20, 750, 753, 758, 792
    and covenanters, 304, 307
    excavations in, 724n6
    industrial protests in, 442–5
    Militia, 443
    sheriffs in, 6, 442–5, 462
    Volunteers, 470
    Yeomanry, 470
    see also Alison, Sir Archibald
Lancashire, 20, 290, 797
    and Jacobitism, 350, 366
    Scottish raids into, 110, 149
Lancaster, 342
Lancaster bombers, 568
Lang, Capt. (later Lt.-Gen. Sir) Derek Boileau, 651
Langdale, Marmaduke, 1st Baron, 290–1
Langside, battle of (1568), 237
    monument, 752
Largs, battle of (1263), 107–8, 112, 119–20, 730
Lauder, fort, 201
Lauder, Lt.-Gen. George, 330–1
    battalion of, 332
Lauder, Sir John, 315
Lauderdale, Col. Sir Maitland, Viscount, 2nd earl and 1st duke of, 286, 301, 303, 306–7
Law of the Sea Conferences (1958 and 1960), 606
Lawers, Sir James Campbell of, 306
Lawrence, Brig.-Gen. Charles, 397
Layton, Sir Brian, 197
Leach, Lt.-Gen. Edward Pemberton, 759
Leach, John, 422–3
Lee, Sergt.-Maj. George, 519
Lee, Sir Richard, 718
Leeds, 342
Le France, Admiral Michael, 614
Le Havre, 357; siege of (1944), 580
Leicester, Robert Dudley, 1st earl of, 236
Leipzig Salient, 518
Leith, 152, 171, 196, 280, 313, 315, 317, 327, 338–9, 561, 778, 785
    citadel of, 301, 741
    fortifications of, 202–3, 719
    siege of (1560), 203, 741–2
    site investigations of, 741–2
Lenin, Vladimir Ilyich, 544
Lenman, Bruce, 16, 301–2
Lennox, earldom of, 222
Lennox, Esmé Stewart, 1st duke of, 243
Lennox, Matthew Stewart, 4th earl of, 196, 198, 215

Le Régiment Royal Écossais, 267, 375, 388, 735
Leslie, Lt.-Col. Archibald Young, 459
Leslie, Lt.-Gen. David, 284–5, 293, 689
  at Dunbar, 292
  at Marston Moor, 286–7
  at Philiphaugh, 289
Leslie, John, 215, 220
Leslie, Maj. Walter, 264
Leuchars, RAF, 566, 585n1, 608
Leven, Alexander Leslie, 1st earl of, 12, 262, 268, 282, 289–90, 689
  armies of, 263, 278–81, 284–7, 289
  at Marston Moor, 286–7
Leven, Lt.-Gen. David Melville, 3rd earl of, 317–18, 326, 338, 341, 343
Lewis, 255, 357, 450
  burial sites, 46
  chessmen, 113
  protests in, 447, 450–2
Lewis, Torquil MacLeod of, 189
Libya, 616
Lille, siege of (1708), 336
Lindores, Patrick Leslie, 2nd Lord, 285
Lindsay, Lt.-Col. the Hon. John, 692
Lindsay, Lt.-Col. Martin, 497
Linklater, Eric, *The Dark of the Summer* (1956), 680–4
Linlithgow, George Livingston, 3rd earl of, 301, 308–10
  battalions of, 304, 306
Linlithgow palace, 714
Lintalee, battle of (1317), 139, 146, 150
HMS *Lion*, 362
Liverpool Scottish, 475
Livesay, Col. John, battalion of, 342
Livingstone [Livingston], Lord George (later 2nd earl of Linlithgow), 286, 316
Livingstone, Sir Thomas, 317
Lloyd George, David, 547
  cabinet of, 543, 547
Lochaber, 215, 217, 350, 360–1, 363, 695
Loch Cairnbawn, submarine base, 565
Loch Ewe, naval base, 565
Lochgarry, Donald MacDonell, 387
Lochgarry, Col. John MacDonell of, 387–8, 402n11

Lochiel, Donald Cameron of, 'Younger' or 'Gentle Lochiel', 116, 363, 379n19, 563
Lochiel, Donald Cameron, 24th chief of, 451
Lochiel, Lt.-Col. Donald Walter, 516
Lochiel, Sir Ewen Cameron of, 317
Lochiel, John Cameron of, 357
Lochwinnoch, Castle Semple Collegiate Church, 750
'Lockerbie licks', 241
Logan, James, 696
London, 29, 161, 170, 175, 192, 201, 256, 280, 304, 315–16, 340, 360, 421, 581, 603, 617, 619, 672, 690, 692, 696, 781
  and the Jacobites, 353, 355, 358, 366, 371, 739
  and the Restoration, 298, 300
  governments in, 3, 12, 269, 344, 410, 426, 542, 547, 601
  Great Exhibition (1851), 784
  Highland Societies of, 18, 635, 655
  military training in East End, 579
  museums, 783, 786–7
  radicals, 393
  Royal Academy, 693–4
  Royal Military Exhibition (1890), 786
  Society of Antiquaries, 777
  Tower of, 360–1, 690, 778
  war memorials in, 768
  see also London Scottish
Londonderry, 548, 551, 553
London Gazette, 304, 660
London Scottish, 475, 630–1
Longford, Elizabeth, 801
lordship, 78–84, 97, 138, 140, 211, 213, 216–17, 222, 239
Lords of the Congregation, 203, 212, 235, 741
Lorn, 71, 110, 221
Lossiemouth, RAF, 566, 568
Lothian, 33n41, 96, 104, 194, 196
  East, 50, 53, 236, 310, 436–7, 567, 706, 708, 711
  fencibles, 305
  fortresses, 103, 186
  men of, 101, 104, 110
  Militia, 310
  ravaged by war, 10, 101, 168, 196, 201
  Roman finds in, 56, 58
  West, 708, 716–17

Lothian, Schomberg Kerr, 9th marquess of, 452
Lothian, William Kerr, 1st earl of, 288
Lothian, William Kerr, 2nd marquess of, 327
   dragoons of, 336
Loudoun, Col. John Campbell, 2nd Lord and 1st earl of, 286
Loudoun, Maj.-Gen. John Campbell, 4th earl of, 369–70, 372–3, 393
   after Culloden, 16
   64th regiment of, 360, 372, 374–5
   North American command, 392–3
Loudoun Hill, battle of (1307), 133, 144–5
Louis VII, king of France, 9, 101
Louis XII, king of France, 190
Louis XIII, king of France, 264, 315, 678
Louis XIV, king of France, 315, 318–19, 349
Louis XV, king of France, 362, 365, 388
Louisbourg, siege of (1758), 384, 388–9, 396, 490
Loutherbourg, Philippe Jacques de, 690
Lovat, Simon Fraser, 11th Lord, 358–9
Lovat, Brig.-Gen. Simon Fraser, 14th Lord, 386, 391, 395
Lovat, Brig.-Gen. Simon Fraser, 15th Lord, 579, 661–2
Lovat, Gen. Simon Fraser, Master of, 395
Lovat Scouts, 20, 475
Lowland regiments, 459, 575, 629, 641, 783, 799, 810
   and bagpipes, 641, 655, 666n29
   and army reforms, 23–4, 476, 616, 641, 803, 805
   at Culloden, 34n55, 376
   images of, 3, 30n11, 632–3, 689, 700–2
   imperial service of, 463, 471–3
   in Napoleonic Wars, 18
   in Seven Years War, 17
   memorials, 757–9, 768
   origins of, 14, 304, 315, 317–18, 799
   serve under Marlborough, 328–9, 333–4, 336–7
Lucknow, siege of (1857–8), 18–19, 469, 698

Lucy, Richard de, 103
Ludendorff, Gen. Erich von, 526

Macartney, Gen. George, 327
   regiment of, 337
Macauley, Cpl. James, 620
McBane, Donald, 337–8
McBean, Pte. D., 468
MacBean [MacBain], Gillies, 679, 695
McCallum, 2nd Lt. Neil, 575–6
MacColla, Alasdair, 282, 287–8
McCrae, Lt.-Col. Sir George, 512, 540
   battalion of, 25, 512
MacDonald, Alexander, 676–7
MacDonald, Sir Alexander, 1st Baron, 391
MacDonald, Angus (Aonghas Òg), 152, 222, 225
MacDonald, Capt. Donald, 388, 393, 395
MacDonald, Pipe-Maj. Donald, 652
MacDonald, Donald Dubh, 189, 196–7
Macdonald, Maj.-Gen. Sir Hector, 462, 477
Macdonald, John, lord advocate, 452
MacDonald, James Ramsay, 539
MacDonald, Neil, 397
MacDonald, Patrick, 658
MacDonald, Sir Seumas, 211, 214, 218, 222, 225
MacDonalds, 209, 219, 222, 224, 226, 279, 288, 363
   at Culloden, 736
   lordship of, 214
MacDonalds of Glencoe, 318
MacDonalds of Glengarry, 224, 226
MacDonalds of Keppoch, 215
MacDonnell, Sorley Boy, 244
MacDonells of Keppoch, 363
MacDougall, Duncan, 711
MacDougall, Ewen, 711
MacDougalls, 222
MacGregor, Lt.-Col. Duncan, 462
MacGregors, 216, 218, 220
   at Glen Fruin, 224, 226, 242
McGuffie, T. H., 409
Macheth, Donald, 105
Macheths, family of, 105–6
MacIan, Ronald Robert, *Jacobite Hiding-place at Keppoch Brae, Lochaber* (1854), 695
   The Battle of Culloden (1853), 695
MacInnes, Alan, 15

Macintosh, Flying Officer Donald, 568
Macintoshes, 215
McIntyre, Piper Duncan, 574
Mackay, Maj.-Gen. Hugh, 312, 317
Mackay, Pte. I., 651
Mackay, Piper Kenneth, 424–5, 656
Mackays, 358, 370, 393, 678
McKean, Charles, 721
McKellar, Flying Officer Archie, 559, 566
Mackellar, Lt. Keith, 491
MacKenzie, Capt. Alexander, 691–2
Mackenzie, Compton, 22
Mackenzie, John, 491, 493
McKenzie, Malcolm, 395–6
MacKenzies, 220, 224, 353, 357
Mackillop, Andrew, 17
MacKinnons, 224
Maclain, Alastair, 317–18
Maclains, 216
MacLarens of Balquhidder, 222
MacLaurin, Col. Henry Normand, 492
MacLean, Brig.-Gen. Allan, 388–9, 401
MacLean, Lt.-Col. Allan, 437
MacLean, Sir Fitzroy, 23
MacLean, John, 540, 547
Maclean, Sorley, 679–80
MacLeans, 214–15, 219–20, 222, 226
MacLennan, Ruairidh, 679
MacLeod, Alasdair, 223
MacLeods, 372
MacLeods of Harris, 218, 234
MacLeods of Lewis, 216
MacLeods of Raasay, 679
Maclise, Daniel, 693
Macmillan, Harold, 602, 605
MacNaughtons, 225
MacPherson, Cpl. Malcolm, 360–1
MacPherson, Cpl. Samuel, 360
MacQuillans, 216
Macraes, 220
Macready, Gen. Sir Nevil, 803, 806
McShane, 540, 542, 544
MacWilliam, family of, 105–7
  rebellion of, 114
Madagascar, invasion of (1942), 501
Mafeking, siege of (1899–1900), 476
Maginot Line, 571
Mahratta (or Anglo-Maratha) Wars, Second (1803–5), 18
  Third (1817–18), 464
'Maid of Lilliard', 197

Maine, Maj. Edmund, 310
Mair, John, 209, 220
Maitland, Brig.-Gen. James, 326–7
  battalion of, 327, 338, 340, 344
Malakand Pass, storming of (1895), 473
Malaya, 570, 613
  emergency (1948–60), 611–12, 615
Malcolm II, king of Scots (r. 1005–34), 104
Malcolm III (Máel Coluim), Canmore or 'Big Head', king of Scots (r. 1057/8–93), 83, 94, 96, 100, 118
  invades England, 80, 94, 101
Malcolm IV, king of Scots (r. 1153–65), 96–7, 111, 118
  campaigns in Galloway, 104, 110
  yields Cumbria and Northumberland, 101
Malcolm, son of Alexander I, 108–9
'Mam Garvia', battle of (1187), 105–6
Man, Isle of, 104, 107, 152, 171, 213
Manchester, 20, 365, 413
Manchester, Edward Montagu, 2nd earl of, 285
Mann, Thomas, 537
Manton, Ralph, 146
Mar, Charles Erskine, 5th or 21st earl of, 308
  regiment of, 308, 311
Mar, Donald, earl of, 143, 150
Mar, John Erskine, 6th or 22nd earl of, 327, 340, 343, 351–3
  regiment of, 327, 333, 340
March, Agnes Randolph, 'Black Agnes', countess of, 160
March, George Dunbar, 10th earl of, 164–5
March, William Douglas, 2nd earl of, 341
Marchmont, Hugh Hume-Campbell, 3rd earl of, 723
Maria, Henrietta, queen of Charles I, 283
Marian civil war (1567–73), 11, 236–8, 252
Marlborough, Gen. John Churchill, 1st duke of, 15, 316, 319, 326–7, 330, 341–2, 355
  at Blenheim, 334
  at Oudenarde, 336
  at Ramillies, 336
  infantry of, 333
  Scots in his army, 327–9

Marryat, Capt. Frederick, 688
Marshall, George, 601
Martens, Henry, 696
martial culture, 754, 796
   51st Highland Division, 575, 577–8
   Scottish, 4, 27, 117–18, 171–5, 245, 251, 271–2, 318, 476, 490, 511, 643
   warrior ideal, 5, 47, 49, 52–3, 75, 104, 211, 778
Martinique, 410
   expedition to (1762), 387
Mary of Guise, 187, 194–6, 202–3, 235, 741–2
Mary Queen of Scots (r. 1542–67), 11, 195, 199, 202, 235, 243
   abdication of (1567), 236
   and religious disputes, 235–6
   executed (1587), 237
   flight to England (1568), 237
   monuments to, 752
Massie, Allan, 28
material culture, 226, 777–86, 792
Mathesons of Lochalsh, 679
Mauduit, Roger, 149
Maule, Lt.-Col. Hon. Lauderdale, 696
Maxwell, Eustace, 713
Maxwell, Lt.-Col. Hamilton, 691–2
Maxwell, Herbert, 711, 713, 716
Maxwell, John, 7th Lord, 241
Maxwell, Robert, 5th Lord, 194
Maxwell, Lt.-Col. William, 340
Maxwells, 240–1
Mearns, 96
Meek, Donald, 676
Meerut, sepoy revolt in (1857), 468
Melrose, abbey destroyed (1385), 168
   ambush at (1322), 146
   carvings in abbey, 653
Memorial to the Women of World War Two, 768
Menéndez, Gen. Luciano Benjamín, 619
Menin, 332
   siege of (1707), 330–1
Menteith, Sir John, 6
Menteith, Walter Stewart, earl of, 119, 140, 712
Menzies, Sergt. John, 460
Menzies, Maj.-Gen. Sir Stewart, 22
mercenaries, 105, 223, 248, 251, 257, 271
   Dutch, 352, 355, 358, 373

English, 253, 257
German, 251, 652
Hessian, 269, 373, 383
Highland, 258–9
Islemen, 106, 211, 216
Scots, 12, 111, 219–20, 222, 227, 263, 265, 276, 329–32, 341–2, 372, 384–5, 388, 391, 393, 395, 678
Swiss, 251, 352, 354, 394, 652
see also galloglass, Ireland and redshanks
mercenary service, 104, 250, 252–3, 255–6, 264–6, 269–72
   honoured abroad, 249, 254–5, 257, 265, 268, 271–2
   personal rewards, 167, 244, 248, 250–1, 253–4, 271
   political/religious motives for, 249, 251–7, 259–64, 270–2
   professional benefits of, 249, 251–4, 256–7, 263–5, 269–71
   recruitment, 211, 249, 251–4, 256–7, 263–5, 269–71
   veterans of, 184, 245, 262–3, 265, 276, 278, 280, 282, 284, 291, 301, 304, 354
Mercer, Capt. Cavalié, 421
Mercer, Hugh, 385
Mesopotamia, 509, 526
metal detecting, 730, 732, 735, 739–40, 744
Methven, Henry Stewart, 1st Lord, 187
Methven, battle of (1306), 133
Middleton, John, 1st earl of, 300–1, 303, 311
migration of Scots, 255, 270–1, 478, 485–6, 637
Miguelite War (1828–34), 270
military collections, 2, 776–7
   in Edinburgh museums, 781, 786–7
   in exhibitions, 784–6
   in Glasgow museums, 781–2
   in stately homes, 779–81
   of Jacobite relics, 779
   of regimental colours, 782–3
   see also regimental museums and Society of Antiquaries of Scotland
militia, 223, 250, 300, 387, 417–18, 436–7, 780

anti-militia riots, 417–18, 436–9, 446, 452, 803
   English, 313, 436, 637
   Scottish, 3, 301, 303, 305–7, 310, 312, 315–16, 318, 339, 354, 414, 416, 470
   Scottish Militia Acts (1663), 302 and (1797), 436
   see also Argyll, Bute, Edinburgh, Glasgow, Lanarkshire, Lothian, Perthshire and Renfrewshire
Millais, John Everett, *News from Home* (1857), 697
Millar, Miss Emma, 784
Millin, Piper Bill, 37n90, 579, 661–2
Ministry of Defence, 549, 603, 610, 789, 798
   defence reviews see *Front-Line First-Defence Costs Study* and *Options for Change*
Ministry of Munitions, 507–8
Minorca, expedition to (1708), 359
Mitchell, Lt.-Col. Colin, 'Mad Mitch', 614–15, 662, 702
Mohmand expedition (1908), 477
Monchy-le-Preux, 521–5
Monck, Gen. George (later 1st duke of Albemarle), 33n42, 293–4, 298, 742
   forces of, 300
Monmouth, James Scott, 1st duke of, 310–11
   rebellion of (1685), 312–14, 317
Monro, Gen. Sir Charles, 525
Monro, Col. Sir Robert, 258, 265, 265, 291
   forces of, 282, 287, 289–90
Monros, 358
Mons, siege of (1709), 336
Mons Graupius, battle of (AD 84), 55, 674, 743
Mons Meg, 162, 716, 778
Montcalm, Louis-Joseph, marquis de, 385
Montfort, Simon de, 120
Montgomery [Montgomerie], Lt.-Col. (later Gen.) Hon. Archibald (later 11th earl of Eglinton), 386, 391, 397
   and Montgomery's Highlanders, 386–7, 390, 393–4, 397, 400–1, 405n33

Montgomery, Lt.-Gen. (later FM) Bernard Law, 573, 579, 594n61
Montgomery, Capt. Thomas, 468
Montgomery, William, Horse Grenadier Guards of, 326
Monthermer, Ralph de, 151
Montreal, 465, 488
Montrose, amphibious assault on (1548), 186
   RAF, 566
Montrose, James Graham, 1st marquess of, 279, 282, 289, 292, 689
   renegade covenanter, 287–8
   victories of, 212, 218, 288, 679
Montrose, William Graham, 1st earl of, 191
monuments, 2, 5, 25, 41, 65, 75, 81, 175, 674, 748–54, 764, 767–8, 778
   as icons of national/communal identities, 749
   at St Valéry-en-Caux, 581
   failure of National Monument, 755
   see also Aberlemno, Sueno Stone
Monymusk reliquary, 115
Moodie, J. W., 460
Moore, Sir John, 424, 429n7, 754
Mòr, Alasdair, 218
morale, 21–2, 167, 518, 524, 643–4
   in medieval warfare, 114–15, 146, 148
Moray, 67, 85, 99, 105, 707
   Angus, mormaer of, 98, 105
   David I annexes, 99, 108
   firearms in, 239
   knightly quota of, 137
   warfare in, 105–6
Moray, Angus, of 98, 106, 108
Moray, James, earl of, 193
Moray, Lord James Stewart, 1st earl of (and Regent of Scotland), 11, 236–7, 239
Moray, Thomas Randolph, earl of, 143, 148, 153
   at Bannockburn, 143, 145
   forces of, 143, 149–50
Moray, Walter of, 711
Moray Firth, 16, 350, 371
   food riots (1847), 442, 446–7, 449, 451
   'wetshod' exercises, 563

Morier, David, 689–90
  An Incident in the Rebellion of 1745 (c. 1745–50), 690
Morrice, Roger, 309
Morrison, Sergt. W., 468
Morton, James Douglas, 4th earl of (and Regent of Scotland), 237–8
Mosquitos, 568
Motherwell, 547, 561
Mulley, Fred, 607
Munich Trench, 518
munitions industry, 507–8
Munro, Maj.-Gen. Sir George, 307–8, 315
Murmansk, 565
Murray, Andrew, 6, 133
Murray, Sir Andrew, 715
Murray, Charles, 493
Murray, David, 648
Murray, Lt.-Gen. George, 218, 357, 365–6, 368, 371, 384, 387, 690
  at Culloden, 737–8
  besieges Blair castle (1746), 722
Murray, Capt. (later Lt.-Gen.) James, 387–8
Murray, Gen. Lord John, 399
Murray, Lt.-Gen. Robert, 330–1, 341
Musselburgh, 198, 236, 315, 421, 476
mutinies, 398, 547, 799
  Black Watch, 17, 360, 690
  fencibles, 417
  First Mutiny Act (1689), 318
  First World War, 522
  Royal Scots, 15, 318
  Second World War, 578
  'white' (1859), 469

Nairn, 370, 573
Namur, siege of (1695), 15
Napoleon Bonaparte, emperor of the French, 18, 800
Napoleonic Wars (1799–1815), 3, 17, 28, 414, 416, 427, 458, 694, 753–5, 786, 803
  aftermath of, 270, 434n55, 438, 780
  highlanders in, 396, 407–8, 418–19, 421–8, 637, 675
  Scottish military contribution in, 412–13, 637, 646n16, 754
  see also battle of Waterloo
Narvik, 569

Nassau, Prince Maurice of, 251
  military reforms of, 251–4
National Museums Scotland, 788
National Service *see* conscription
National Service League, 478, 538–9
National Trust for Scotland, 731, 733, 735–6, 738
National Wallace Monument, 142, 751–2
National War Museum, 788–9
navies, English, 31n18, 103, 137, 152, 171–2, 198–9, 329
  and Lords of the Isles, 107, 172, 212–14
  Dutch, 329
  Norse, 106–8
  recruitment for, 3, 413
  Roman, 5
  Scottish, 107–8, 126n60, 151–2, 171–2, 188–9
  see also battle of Largs, *Great Michael*, Royal Navy
Nechtanesmere, battle of (AD 685), 76, 79, 114, 743, 749
Needham, Col. Francis, 397
Nelson, Brian, 552–3
Nelson, Vice-Admiral Horatio, 1st Viscount, Scottish memorials to, 754–5
Nemours, Gaston de Foix, duke of, 189
Neolithic period, 44–5, 60
Netherlands, 15, 240, 254, 263, 265, 269, 271, 278, 329–30, 332, 338, 582
  Dutch SS, 583
  see also United Provinces
Neuville, Alphonse Marie de, 698
  The Storming of Tel-el-Kebir (1883), 698
Neville, Ralph, 150
Neville, Robert, 146
New Army, 20–1, 28, 509–10, 513, 539–41
New Army battalions, 'pals', 511, 518
  'special service', 510, 512
Newbolt, Sir Henry John, 688
Newburgh, Sir James Livingston, 1st earl of, 301
Newburgh, William of, 106
Newcastle, 152, 202, 280, 285, 290, 444, 509
  and Jacobites, 350

captured (1644), 287
surrenders (1640), 281
Newcastle, William Cavendish, 1st earl, 1st marquess and 1st duke of, 285, 287
New Labour, government of, 627, 805
Newman, Peter, 286–7, 728
Newmilns, covenanting memorial at, 753
New Model Army, 12–14, 31n17, 33n41, 298, 300
Newry, stormed (1642), 282
New South Wales Scottish Rifles, 485, 488–92, 496, 499
newspapers, 396, 446, 466, 468, 536, 574, 614
  illustrated, 700
  North American, 396, 398
  Scottish, 1, 404n28, 468, 510, 516, 524, 544, 551, 553
  wartime censorship of, 516
Newtonbutler, 551
New York, 389
New Zealand, 485
  and South African War, 20
  Dunedin Highland Rifles, 488
  Highland rifle groups (of Wanganui, Wellington, Canterbury and Auckland), 488
  Militia Act (1858), 488
  Scottish migrants, 486
  Scottish Mounted Horse Rifles (Waipu), 488
  Wanganui Rifle Volunteers, 488
Nicoll, John, 300
Nijmegan corridor, 583, 597n104
Nine Years War (1688–97), 318–19, 329
Nithsdale, Robert Maxwell, 9th Lord Maxwell and 1st earl of, 258
Nithsdale, Sir William Douglas of, 175
Norfolk, Thomas Henry, 3rd duke of, 194
Norfolk, Pictish find in, 59
Norie, Orlando, 469
Normandy, 96, 100
  campaign (1944), 569, 579–80, 582–3
North American wars, 16–17, 355, 400–1, 800
  Highland battalions in, 383–4, 386–91, 393–8, 401–2n9

Scottish contribution to, 390–3, 403nn16 and 19, 412
North Atlantic Treaty Organization (NATO), 500, 601, 620, 680, 683
'Northern Flank' of, 608
Northern Ireland, army's role in, 548–50, 554, 615, 685, 805, 808
  allegations of sectarianism among Scots, 548, 550, 553
  intelligence war, 552–3
  'paddy bashing', 549–50
  police primacy, 552
  see also Ulster 'dirty war'
Northern Isles, 681, 709
  see also Orkney
Northumberland, 48, 170, 240
  barons of, 109
  Jacobites of, 352–3, 355
  Scots raid/invade, 94, 101, 110, 149, 165, 280–1
  Scottish claims on, 100–1, 104, 120
  veteran, 191
Northumbria, 65, 68, 72, 79, 94, 104
  and the Mercians, 71, 84
  forces of, 70, 73, 78–9, 82, 104
  kingdom of (AD 350–1100), 69, 78, 114
Norway, 106–7, 562–3, 568–9, 708
  forces at the battle of Largs, 107, 119–20
  King Magnus III of, 106
  Quisling's government of, 682
Nott, John, defence review of (1981), 620
Nottingham, Daniel Finch, 2nd earl of, 339
Nova Scotia, 389, 399, 465
nuclear weapons, 601–3, 610, 804
  submarine-launched, 603

O'Casey, Sean, 546
Ochiltree, Andrew Stewart, 3rd Lord, 225, 245
Officers' Training Corps, Aberdeen University, 800
Oglethorpe, Maj. Theophilus, 310
O'Hagan, Danny, 547
Oliphant, Capt. William, 315
Omagh, bombing (1998), 554
Oman, Sir Charles W. C., 426
Oman, campaign (1957–8), 615

O'Neil, Henry Nelson, *Eastward Ho! August 1857* (1858), 698
   Home Again (1859), 698
O'Neill, Owen Roe, 289
'Operation Ascot' (1944), 580
'Operation Blackcock' (1945), 582
'Operation Colin' (1944), 580
'Operation Compass' (1940–1), 600
Operation Desert Storm *see* First Gulf War
'Operation Epsom' (1944), 582–3
   'Scottish corridor' in, 582
'Operation Pheasant' (1944), 583
'Operation Plunder' (1945), 581, 583
'Operation Stirling Castle' (1967), 614
'Operation Veritable' (1945), 580, 582–3
Options for Change (1990), 805
Orange, John William Friss, prince of, 330–1
Order of the Thistle, 629, 632
Orkney, 107, 709, 718, 753
   rising in (1614), 245
Orkney, Lt.-Gen. George Hamilton, 1st earl of, 328, 331, 334, 340
   infantry of, 336
Orléans, siege of (1428–9), 10
Orléans, Louis, duke of, 715
Orléans, Philippe II, Regent of France and duke of, 352, 354
Ormonde, James Butler, 12th earl, 1st marquess and 1st duke of, 283
Ormonde, James Butler, 2nd duke of, 356–7
Orpen, William, *A Highlander Passing a Grave* (1917), 702
Orrery, Charles Boyle, 4th earl of, battalion of, 342
Oslo, 569
Ostend, capture of drums at (1918), 652, 664n11
Ostia, Alberic, cardinal bishop of, 117
O'Sullivan, John, 368
Otterburn, campaign (1388), 163, 165
Ottoman empire, 265, 269, 523
Ouistreham, 563
Owen, David, 607

Pagnacco, Cpl. Ryan, 662
Pakistan, 610
Palestine, 509, 614
panzers, 573
   Panzerarmee Afrika, 573
   7th Panzer Division, 572
Paris, 526, 572
   Commune (1871), 539
   surrender/occupation of (1815), 421, 693, 800–1
   Treaty of (1295), 9
Paris, Michael, 109
parliament, English, 264, 266, 280–1, 283–4, 289–91, 300–2, 313
   and the Ulster rebellion, 282
   'Committee of Both Kingdoms', 285
   Convention, 298
   Long, 298
   Rump, 298
parliament, Scottish (Estates), 235, 257, 279–80, 282, 284, 291, 300–3, 306, 316, 329, 339, 342–3
   and King Charles 1, 280–1
   committee of estates, 280, 289
   officers in, 340
Partial Test Ban Treaty (1963), 605
Pas de Calais, 569
Paton, Sir Joseph Noel, 698, 781
   Home: the Return from the Crimea (1859), 701
   In Memoriam (1858), 698
Patrick, Capt. J. R., 496
Patten, William, 184, 200
Patterson, Capt. John, 407–8
peacekeeping, 500, 620
Peck, Lt.-Col. Cyrus Wesley, 493
Peebles, 718
Peebles, Lt. John, 383–4, 394, 397–8, 401n1
Peking, sacking of the Summer Palace (1860), 471
Pembroke, Aymer de Valence, 2nd earl of, 144
'Penicuik Drawings', 690
Peniel Heugh, Waterloo Tower at, 771n37
Peninsular War (1808–14), 25, 407, 422, 424, 427, 431n21, 461, 656
Pentland Rising (1666), 304–6
Pepys, Samuel, 302, 304
Percy, Alande, 111
Percy, Sir Henry, 'Hotspur', 165

Percy, Lt-Gen Hugh, Earl, 393
Perth, 221, 288, 301, 305, 364, 391,
    402n9, 573
  evacuated (1716), 353
  Treaty of (1266), 108
Perth, James Drummond, 3rd duke
    of, 370
Perthshire, 411, 432n30, 564
  Barton Hill, 709
  Lethendy carvings, 653
  Militia, 427
  recruiting in, 427
Peterhead, landing at (1715), 352
Peterloo, 'massacre' (1819), 537
Peter the Great, tsar of Russia, 268
Pevik, Arthur, 569
Philip, Francis, Rhinegrave count of
    Salm, 201
Philiphaugh, battle of (1645), 289
Philippoteaux, Felix, 704n20
photography, 696–8, 701
Picts, 41, 59–60, 77–9, 81–2, 114, 674,
    743
  carvings of, 653, 689
  stones of, 25, 689, 749–50
Pienaar, Maj-Gen. Dan, 498
pikemen, 185, 197, 200
Pindar, Pte. John, 460
Pinkerton, Flight Lt. George, 559
Pinkie Cleugh, battle of (1547), 10–11,
    182, 184, 198–200
  bagpipes at, 654
  depiction of, 199, 689
  forces at, 186, 198
  Gaels at, 198, 200, 212, 223
  maps of, 747n31
pipers, 493, 683, 778
  bravery of, 24, 419, 421, 424–5, 473,
    495, 574, 656–7, 659–60
  costs of, 655, 657
  images of, 693, 700, 702
  'Piper of Loos', 660, 702
  prestige of, 24, 660
  wartime roles of, 497–8, 520, 574,
    576, 640, 661
Pitt, William, 'the Younger', 637
Pittenweem, landing at (1708), 350
Pocock, Col. John, 337
poetry, 75, 81, 215, 485, 493, 633
  Gaelic, 211, 218, 225–6
  imperialist, 473, 688
  radical, 679, 677–9, 685
  war, xxi, 485, 677, 760

Poland, 254–5, 265
  army of, 259, 329
  1st Independent Polish Parachute
    Brigade, 564
  1st Polish Armoured Division, 564
police forces, 537, 614
  in Ireland, 441, 537, 547
  in Northern Ireland, 548, 552–3
  in Scotland, 439–40, 443, 445,
    448–50, 452–3, 542–5, 568, 680
Pond, Maj. Hugh, 577
Pontiac's War (1763–4), 394, 801
Porter, Robert Ker, 690
Portmore, Gen. David Colyear, 1st earl
    of, 330, 337
  battalion of, 330
Port Stanley, 617–18
Portugal, 270, 337
  expedition to (1704), 337
Potchefstroom, siege of (1880–1), 472
Pratz del Rey, siege of (1711), 337
Prebble, John, 414
Premier, foundered (1843), 463
Presbyterians, 12–13, 261, 266, 291,
    302–3, 307–8, 311, 348, 436,
    752–3, 762
  'martyr graves', 752–3
  rebellion of (1679), 308–11, 674
  sufferings of, 303
  see also covenanters
Preston, Col. George, 336
Prestonpans, 198, 417, 739–40
Prestonpans, battle of (1745), 16, 365,
    375, 400, 737
  obelisk, 753
  print of, 695
  site investigation of, 738–41
Prestwick, RAF, 561, 566
Pretoria, siege of (1880–1), 472
  captured (1900), 476
  Highlanders, 501
Pride, Col. Thomas, 298
Le Prince Charles, 370
HMS *Prince of Wales*, 565
prisoners of war, 194, 311, 329, 337,
    419, 425, 527, 577, 592n45, 683,
    771n37, 801
  beheaded, 76, 84–5, 93n100, 106,
    150, 167
  enslaved, 5, 84, 117
  humiliated, 93n100, 150
  Jacobite, 34n49, 355
  killed, 5, 73, 84, 106, 117, 221

prisoners of war (cont.)
  mutilated, 76, 106, 150, 221
  POW camps, 567, 572
  ransomed, 84, 117–18, 150, 167
  released, 151
privy council, English, 309
privy council, Scottish, 12, 243–4,
  252–3, 256–7, 265, 304, 306,
  310–11, 339, 341
propaganda, 5, 12–13, 33n39, 149
  anti-war, 540
  British, 22, 642
  covenanter, 268
  German, 651
  IRA, 651
  Unionist, 441
USS *Proteus*, 603
Prussian army, 398, 413, 657, 795,
  801
  Scots serve in, 268–9, 354
public schools, 28

Quebec, 465
  campaign (1759), 385, 388–9, 395,
    487
  expedition to (1711), 336
Queensberry, James Douglas, 2nd
  duke of, 341–3

Radfan, operation (1964–5), 613
radicals, 270–1, 393, 438, 460
Rae, Col. James, 286
Raeburn, Henry, *Colonel Alastair
  Ranaldson Macdonell of
  Glengarry* (1812), 689
Raglan, FM FitzRoy James Henry
  Somerset, 1st Baron, 467–8
Ragnall, son of Somerled, 107, 119
raids, 3, 9, 43, 72, 74, 81, 102–3,
  106–7, 133, 135, 144, 165
  by Picts, 59, 73
  cattle, 89n42, 149, 216, 220
  English, 73, 103, 168, 191
  plunder, 7, 72–4, 78, 101, 149, 167
  savagery of, 5–6, 80, 105–6, 167
  small-scale, 56, 78, 165
  socio-economic impact of, 72, 105,
    150, 163, 158
Ramsay, Sir Alexander, 160
Ramsay, Allan, *Lieutenant John
  Abercrombie of the 1st Foot or the
  Royal Regiment* (1754), 689
Ramsay, Lt.-Gen. George, 326, 341

Rand, 491–2
Rangoon, advance on (1945), 570
Rannoch, 217
Rathlin Island, massacre (1575), 244
Rattray, Capt., 303
Reagan, President Ronald Wilson, 608
Reay, Sir Donald Mackay, later 1st
  Lord, 258
  regiment of, 259–60
Reay, George Mackay, 3rd Lord, 370
recruitment, 77, 84, 139
  process of, 408, 413–17, 426, 540,
    657, 789, 803–4
  of auxiliary forces, 3, 307, 339,
    374–5, 413–16, 478
  of non-Scots for Scottish units, 20,
    24, 28, 223, 337, 398, 408–9,
    412–13, 427, 459, 581–2, 639,
    643, 796–7
  of Scots, 3, 327, 409, 413, 415–16,
    418, 458–9, 461, 478–9, 510–11,
    545, 578, 627, 643
  of Scots for English/British units,
    18, 328, 391, 408, 458
Red Army, 584
'redshanks', 211, 227, 244, 258, 294
Reformation, 194, 211–12, 750
regimental museums, 651, 789–92
  Argyll and Sutherland Highlanders,
    722, 790
  Cameronians, 791–2
  Gordon Highlanders, 27
  Royal Scots, 722
regiments, British army (in order of
  precedence)
  Royal Horse Guards, 342, 344
  Royal Artillery, 408, 421
  Coldstream Guards, 298
  Grenadier Guards, 29
  Scots Guards, 24, 301, 303–4, 307,
    315, 326–7, 333, 337, 343, 408–9,
    418, 424, 458, 467–8, 551, 613,
    617–18, 659, 662, 700–2, 803
  Welsh Guards, 618
  Royal Scots Greys (formerly 'Grey
    Dragoons', Scots Dragoons or
    Royal North British Dragoons),
    15, 311, 333–6, 373, 409, 418,
    420–1, 433n43, 441, 458, 460,
    466–7, 536, 616–17, 693, 701–2,
    801, 803
  7th Royal Dragoon Guards, 491
  4th Queen's Own Hussars, 444

10th Royal Hussars, 438
15th The King's Hussars, 785
12th (Prince of Wales's) Royal Lancers, 758
1st (Royal Scots), 14–15, 18, 20, 274–5n49, 304, 314–15, 318, 333, 336, 343, 371, 373, 375, 391, 393–4, 408–9, 458–9, 462–4, 467–8, 471, 544–5, 548–9, 641–3, 655, 659, 689, 702, 805
2nd (Queen's), 330, 459
5th (Northumberland Fusiliers), 614
13th (Pulteney's, later Prince Albert's (Somerset Light Infantry), 373, 375, 802
21st (Mar's, later Royal North British Fusiliers and then Royal Scots Fusiliers), 15, 20–1, 24, 308, 333, 343, 374, 376, 391, 409, 458, 463, 466, 472, 613, 759, 764, 769, 804
22nd (Cheshire), 490
23rd (Royal Welch Fusiliers), 391–2
24th (Warwickshire), 458
25th (Leven's, later King's Own Scottish Borderers), 17, 318, 373, 375, 391, 458–9, 463, 472–3, 546, 549–51, 553, 579, 613, 641, 655, 659, 759, 805, 809
26th (Angus's, later 1st battalion, Cameronians [Scottish Rifles]), 15, 20–1, 317–18, 329–330, 333–4, 336, 344, 391–2, 398, 409, 413, 458, 472, 570, 613, 615–16, 757, 791, 804
27th (Inniskilling), 424
33rd (Duke of Wellington's), 443, 580
34th (Border), 518
35th (Royal Sussex), 461
42nd, originally 43rd (Royal Highland Regiment, 1st battalion, The Black Watch), 16–20, 29, 269, 359–60, 373–4, 383, 386–7, 390–1, 394, 396, 398–400, 407–9, 413, 415, 421, 424–5, 427–8, 434n50 and n54, 438, 458–62, 466, 468–9, 472–3, 478, 487, 490, 493, 496, 498, 538, 548, 552, 611–12, 620, 634, 638, 651, 659, 662, 669, 685, 690, 696–8, 757, 797, 799, 807

43rd (1st battalion, Oxfordshire and Buckinghamshire Light Infantry), 580
45th (Nottinghamshire), 460
47th (Loyal North Lancashire), 391
53rd (Shropshire Light Infantry), 438
55th (Perry's, later 2nd battalion, Border Regiment), 391
60th (Royal American, later King's Royal Rifle Corps), 385, 389, 392–4, 397, 473
68th (Durham Light Infantry), 408, 804
70th (Glasgow Lowland, later Surrey Regiment), 409
71st (Fraser's, later 1st battalion, Highland Light Infantry), 20, 390–1, 395, 398, 409, 413, 419, 425, 434n54, 441, 458–9, 464–5, 467–9, 471, 474, 476, 530, 543, 547, 804
72nd (Duke of Albany's Own, later 1st battalion, Seaforth Highlanders), 409, 412–13, 441, 458–9, 465, 468–9, 472–3, 477, 613, 615, 639, 657, 700, 804
73rd (MacLeod's Highlanders, later redesignated as 71st Regiment of Foot), 691–2
73rd (2nd battalion, The Black Watch), 35n60, 409, 412, 441, 458–9, 461, 463, 465, 469, 474–5, 477, 610, 660, 691–2, 701
74th (2nd battalion, Highland Light Infantry), 18, 20, 35n60, 391, 409, 412, 441, 463, 465, 469, 473, 547, 639
75th (Stirlingshire, later 1st battalion, Gordon Highlanders), 35n60, 409, 412, 458–9, 461, 465, 473–4, 497, 610, 613, 640, 656–7
76th (Harcourt's, re-raised as MacDonald's Highlanders, later 2nd battalion Duke of Wellington's Regiment), 391, 446
77th (1st Highland Regiment, Montgomery's Highlanders), 386–7, 390, 393–4, 397, 400–1, 405n33

regiments, British army (in order of precedence) (*cont.*)
78th (2nd Highland Regiment, Fraser's Highlanders), 386–90, 393, 395–7, 400
78th (Ross-shire Buffs, later 2nd battalion, Seaforth Highlanders), 'Saviours of India', 17–19, 24, 26, 391, 412, 413, 458–9, 469, 474, 477, 651, 692, 698, 756
79th (Queen's Own Cameron Highlanders), 19, 23, 408, 410, 412–13, 421, 424–5, 458–9, 463, 466, 469, 473, 477, 547–8, 613, 636, 638, 640, 651, 653, 656–7, 696, 760, 785, 804
80th (Gage's Light Infantry), 393
80th (second 80th Regiment, known as the Royal Edinburgh Volunteers), 391
82nd (Hamilton's), 391
88th (1st battalion, Connaught Rangers), 547
90th (Perthshire Volunteers, later 2nd battalion, Cameronians [Scottish Rifles]), 18, 411, 413, 458, 463, 468–9, 472, 476
91st (Argyllshire, later Princess Louise's Argyllshire Highlanders and 1st battalion, Argyll and Sutherland Highlanders), 20, 412–13, 425, 431n19, 458, 463, 465, 472, 474, 490, 544, 548, 550–4, 613–14, 639, 659, 662, 702, 759, 790, 804
92nd (Gordon Highlanders), 18–19, 24, 412–13, 415, 421, 423, 425, 433n43, 441, 458–9, 461, 468–9, 472, 474–5, 489, 510, 515, 538, 552, 613, 628, 643, 651–2, 656, 659, 673, 693, 698, 801, 805
93rd (Sutherland Highlanders, later 2nd battalion Argyll and Sutherland Highlanders), 20, 25, 412–13, 441, 458–62, 466–9, 471, 490, 514–15, 639, 696, 698, 802
94th (Scots Brigade), 18, 412–13
95th (Rifle Brigade), 422
99th (Lanarkshire, later Duke of Edinburgh's Lanarkshire and 2nd battalion, Wiltshire Regiment), 459, 469, 476
see also First World War, battalions and Second World War, battalions
regiments, British army amalgamated
Royal Scots Dragoon Guards, 617, 659, 663
Queen's Regiment, 804
Devonshire and Dorset, 806
Royal Anglian Regiment, 804
Royal Highland Fusiliers, 659, 804
Queen's Own Highlanders (Seaforth and Cameron), 549, 615, 628, 662, 804–5
Parachute Regiment, 550–1
Royal Green Jackets, 806
Royal Regiment of Scotland, 24, 621, 627–31, 644, 806–7, 809–10
regiments, covenanter
Balgonie's Lancers, 286
Clydesdale (Hamilton's) Foot, 286
Earl of Balcarres's Horse, 286
Earl of Dalhousie's Horse, 286
Earl of Eglinton's Horse, 286
Earl of Home's Foot, 281
Earl of Leven's Horse, 286
Edinburgh (Rae's) Foot, 286
Fife (Crawford-Lindsay's) Foot, 286
Fife (Dunfermline's) Foot, 286
Fraser's Dragoons, 286
Kyle and Carrick (Cassilis's) Foot, 286
Leslie's Horse, 286–7
Linlithgow and Tweeddale (Hay of Yester's) Foot, 286
Lord Couper's Dragoons, 286
Lord Kirkcudbright's Horse, 286
Loudoun-Glasgow (Loudoun's) Foot, 286
Midlothian (Lauderdale's) Foot, 286
Minister's (Erskine's) Foot, 286
Nithsdale and Annandale's (Douglas of Kelhead's) Foot, 286
Stirlingshire (Livingstone's) Foot, 286
Tweeddale (Buccleuch's) Foot, 286
regiments of the Commonwealth, affiliations, 485, 490, 498
aid civil power, 491–2, 500
in the two world wars, 492–500
see also Australia, Canada, New Zealand and South Africa
Reims, 522, 527

Reith, John Charles Walsham, 1st
    Baron, 478
reiving, Border, 12, 240–2
relics, 114–15, 164
religion, 21–2
    and mercenary service, 244,
        249–50, 252–7, 259, 261–4
    covenanting tradition, 615–16,
        752–3, 757
    in medieval wars, 114–15, 164
    rebellions in Scotland, 303–11
    see also Bishops' Wars, Thirty Years
        War
remonstrants, 293
Renfrew, 107
Renfrewshire, 107, 508, 562, 708, 716
    covenanters, 307
    fencibles, 305
    Militia, 784
Rennie, Maj.-Gen. Thomas, 580–1
Rescissory Act (1661), 302
HMS *Resolution*, 605
Restoration (1660), 14, 265, 300, 318,
        326, 339, 803, 808
    and Scotland, 3, 13, 295, 298, 301,
        311, 343
Restoration of Order in Ireland Act
    (1920), 547
Rhind, William Birnie, 757, 759
Rhine, Prince Rupert of the, 285–7
Richard II, king of England (r.
    1377–99), 160
Richardson, Piper James, 495
Rievaulx, Abbot Ailred of, 112, 114
Rifkind, Malcolm, 805
Riot Act (1714), 445, 481, 537, 542
riots, 343, 417–18, 436–9, 443–6, 452,
        465
    food, 442, 446
    Rebecca, 19
Ripon, Stephen of, 69
    Treaty of (1640), 280–1
Ritchie, Drummer Walter, 651
Rivers, Richard Savage, fourth Earl,
    337
Robert I, Robert Bruce, king of Scots
    (r. 1306–29), 2, 133, 138–9,
        141, 145, 150, 152, 217, 517, 695,
        725n12
    and slaying of Comyn, 7
    army of, 135, 140–1, 235, 649, 653,
        744
    at Bannockburn, 7–9, 145

battle avoidance, 7, 9, 144, 158, 160
capture/destruction of castles, 7. 9,
    147–8, 162
charters of, 137, 139
chivalrous, 7, 9, 150
family of, 6
invades England, 136
leadership of, 7, 153
limited naval assets, 151–2
raids of, 7, 9, 133, 135, 143–4,
    149–50
seizes throne, 7, 133, 150
Robert II, king of Scots (r. 1371–90),
    164, 172, 220
Robert III, king of Scots (r.
    1390–1406), 164, 173–4, 221, 714
Roberts, Paul, 286
Robertson, Capt. William, 510
Robertsons of Atholl, 220
Robin chapel, 766–7
Robson, Pipe Maj. Kenneth, 662, 702
Rœux, 522–3
Rogers, Robert, 393
Rolincourt, 521
Rolls-Royce plant, 559
Roman Catholics, 11–12, 253, 256,
    266, 282, 314–16, 348, 350, 360,
    363, 548
Rome, 41, 56, 58–60, 75, 271, 289,
    649, 708
    army of, 54–5, 57, 59–60, 674, 729
    Church of, 117, 271
    histories of, 47, 53, 59, 67
    invasions, 4–5, 41, 54–5, 649
Rommel, Maj.-Gen. (later FM) Erwin,
    572–3
    forces of, 579
Rørholt, Bjørn, 569
Rosebery, Archibald Primrose, 5th earl
    of, 761, 796
Roslin, ambush (1303), 146
Roslin chapel, 653
Ross, Andrew, 785
Ross, Maj.-Gen. Charles, 328
Ross, George, 11th Lord, 308–9
Ross, Isabella, 141
Ross, John Macdonald, earl of (and
    fourth Lord of the Isles), 11
Ross, Uilleam, 1st earl of, 107
Ross, Pipe-Maj. Willie, 658, 666n36
Ross, 105, 569
    Easter, 16, 438
    Wester, 447

Ross, earldom of, 11, 105, 217
Rosses, 493
Rosyth, naval base, 559, 565
Rothes, John Leslie, 7th earl (and 1st duke) of, 303–4, 306
Rothesay, David, duke of, 173
Rothesay, James, duke of, 188
Rothesay, St Mary's, 750
'Rough Wooing', 195–6, 199, 215, 718
Rowe, Brig.-Gen. Archibald, 328, 333–4, 339
Rowlands, David, 702
Roxburgh, 103, 124n37
 devastated by war, 168
 sacked (1216), 124n36
Roy, Pte. John W., 458
Roy, Rob, 569
Royal Academy, 693–4
Royal Air Force, 513
 bases, 566, 601, 608–9
 Regiment, 569
 Scottish casualties in Second World War, 584
 squadrons, 559, 566–8
Royal British Legion, 531
Royal Flying Corps, 509, 513
Royal Irish Constabulary, 547
Royal Marines, 449–50, 452, 550–1, 554, 585
 3rd Commando Brigade, 617
Royal Navy, 268, 356–7, 786
 and siege of Fort William (1746), 743
 and the Cod War, 606–7
 in Great War, 506, 509, 513
 in Second World War, 564–5, 571, 584
 task force in Falklands War, 617, 619
HMS *Royal Oak*, 565
Royal Scottish Academy, 694–5, 700, 785,
 Advisory Committee on War Memorials, 762
Royal Scottish Museum, 781, 788
royal standard, 164, 363
Royal Ulster Constabulary (RUC), 548, 582–3
Royal United Service Institution, 783, 787
Ruadh, Alasdair, 218
Ruffus, Ralph, 709

rule of the major-generals (1655–7), 300
Rullion Green, battle of (1666), 305–6
Runcie, Sgt., 800
Ruskin, John, 697
Russell, Pte. Jack, 515
Russell, William Howard, 467–8
Russia, 254, 265, 268, 488, 565, 657, 694, 719
Russian army, 25, 466, 488, 802
 Scots serve in, 267–8, 275n52, 329, 391
Russo-Japanese War (1904–5), 477
Rustenburg, siege of (1880–1), 472
Ruthven Raid (1582), 243
Rye House plot (1683), 311

Sabah, 613
Sabine, Brig.-Gen. Joseph, 338
St Andrews, 197–8, 201, 302, 306, 302, 713
 organisations, 487
 University of, 23
St Andrews, James, prior of, 201
St Andrew's Day celebrations, 383, 487, 491, 498, 713
St Clair, Maj.-Gen. Arthur, 385, 393
St Helier, Jersey, 691–2
St John's Newfoundland, expedition to (1762), 394
St Kilda, shelled (1918), 509
St Lucia, expedition to (1778), 394
St Quentin, 702
St Valéry-en-Caux, 651
 liberated (1944), 580
 monument near, 581
 surrender of 51st Division at, 571–2, 581, 643
St Wilfrid, 69, 82–3
Salerno, 578
Salonika, 509, 526
Saltcoats, War Memorial, 764
Saltoun, Andrew Fletcher of, 329
San Carlos Water, 617
Sandhurst, Royal Military College, 461
Sands, Bobby, 550
Sarawak, 613
Sauchieburn, battle of (1488), 172, 188
Savannah, siege of (1778), 395–6
'Save the Argylls', 614–15, 643, 804
Scandinavians, 67–8, 71–2, 80, 104, 106–8
Scapa Flow, 506, 564–5, 568, 681–2

INDEX 883

Scarborough, Scottish assault on (1378), 171
schiltroms, 3, 6–7, 139, 145, 153
Schomberg, Meinhardt Schomberg, 3rd duke of, 337
Scone, 28
Scot, John, 331
Scotland, anti-war tradition, 4, 539–41, 584, 603–4, 608, 610, 673
   military tradition, 2, 24, 176, 248–9, 344, 401, 458, 486, 500, 621, 627, 630, 632, 651, 749, 753, 757, 764
Scots Brigade, 15, 269, 300, 328–32, 341, 388–9, 393
   see also Anglo-Scottish Brigade, Anglo-Dutch Brigade
The Scotsman, 511–12, 760, 765
Scott, Robert Lyons, 782
Scott, Sir Walter, and visit of George IV to Edinburgh (1822), 3–4, 638, 800
   writings of, 240, 486, 637, 695, 723
      The Highland Widow (1827), 675–6
      The Tale of Old Mortality (1816), 753
      Waverley (1814), 3, 753
Scottish Campaign against Trident, 608
Scottish Command, 562–4, 569
Scottish Communist Party, 604
Scottish diaspora, 20, 485, 491, 496, 500, 756
   and Scottish regimental traditions, 486–90, 492–5, 497, 500
   units *see* Australia, Canada, New Zealand and South Africa
Scottish Division, 805
Scottish Horse, 19–20, 477
Scottish National Party, 584
Scottish National War Memorial, 27, 529, 761, 765, 786–7, 797
Scottish regiments, 674, 787, 796–8, 800, 802, 807–8
   amalgamations/disbandments of, 28, 470, 476, 612, 614–17, 627–8, 767–8, 790, 804–6
   'golden thread', 627–8, 800–1, 807
   memorials, 25–6, 759, 761, 768, 772–3n54
   museums, 27, 651, 722, 776, 789–91
   traditions, 2–4, 24, 26–9, 248–50, 254, 343–4, 458, 629, 643–5, 648, 686, 758, 776, 796
   see also 'Save the Argylls'
Scottish soldier, 'Jocks', and empire, 25, 630, 644, 692–701, 753–6, 758–9, 761
   and religion, 21–2
   as a victim, 671, 693, 749, 756, 768–9
   deaths of, 674, 677, 688, 748–9, 757–63, 765–6, 768, 795, 768
   fighting prowess of, 677, 755, 795, 800–1, 806, 808–9
   heroism, 669, 677, 679, 688, 749, 754, 756, 759–60, 762, 796
   sacrifice, 672–3, 764
   self-image, 629, 644, 751
Second World War (1939–45), 2, 20, 22–5, 28, 217, 497–500, 615, 642, 661, 730, 764–6, 788
   aerial operations from Scotland, 559, 566–8
   Atlantic lifeline, 561
   clandestine operations, 568–70
   D-Day landings, 561, 569, 579, 582, 661
   defence of Scotland, 559, 562–3, 586–7n9 and n10
   Scotland and naval operations, 564–6
   Scotland as a training ground, 563–4, 765
   Scottish military contribution in, 570, 584
   war production in Scotland, 559, 561
   see also Italy, Normandy and Sicily
Second World War, battalions
   Argyll and Sutherland Highlanders, 570–2, 574, 577
   Black Watch, 571, 574, 580–1, 584–5
   Cameron Highlanders, 570, 572, 574, 577, 580–1
   Gordon Highlanders, 571, 576, 580–1
   King's Own Scottish Borderers, 570, 809–10
   Middlesex, 573
   Royal Scots, 570, 584
   Royal Scots Fusiliers, 582
   Seaforth Highlanders, 575, 579, 583

Second World War, divisions
  3rd, 563
  15th (Scottish), 579, 582–4
  46th, 578
  50th, 578
  51st (Highland), 'Highway Decorators', 1, 563, 571–84, 643, 651, 677–8, 685, 702, 802
  52nd (Lowland), 563, 569, 581–2
Secret Intelligence Service, 22, 569
Segrave, Sir John de, 146, 150
Selkirk, Flodden monument at, 752
Sempill, John, 1st Lord, 750
Senior, Elinor, 465
Serbia, death rate in Great War, 529
serjeants, 5, 96–7, 108, 111
Seringapatam, stormed (1799), 18
Seton, Bruce, 659
settlement sites, 45, 49–50, 52
Sevastopol, siege of (1854–5), 467–8
Seven Years War (1756–63), 383, 389–90, 396–7, 400, 487, 692
Severus, Septimus, emperor, 56
Shah Najaf mosque, stormed (1857), 469
Sharp, James, Archbishop of St Andrews, 302, 308
Shaw, Private Farquharson, 360
Sheffield strike (1911), 538
Sheriffmuir, battle of (1715), 352, 357, 738
shields, 5, 43–4, 48–9, 75, 81, 112–14, 184–5, 225
  targe, 81, 112, 185, 225, 231n50, 372, 690, 737, 779, 782, 810n6
Shinwell, Emmanuel, 602
Sicily, 1, 94, 271, 577, 678
  Sicilian campaign (1943), 1, 577–9
siege warfare, 70–1, 102, 161, 201–2
  and artillery, 102, 161–2, 187–8, 190, 194, 237
  finances of, 7, 102
  Scots lack of siege engines, 5, 102, 146–7, 161, 712
  Scottish siege tactics, 70–1, 102, 146–8, 161
Siegfried line, 580
Sikandarbagh, stormed (1857), 469
Simms, Katharine, 211, 215, 218
Simpson, Piper David, 660
Sinclair, Archibald, 21
Sinclair, Oliver, 194
Sinclair, William, 137
Sinclairs, 288
Singapore, 613
  surrender of (1942), 571
Singer sewing machine factory, 559, 561
Sinn Féin, 548, 552
Sir Galahad, 618
Sir Tristram, 618
Six Day War (1967), 614
Skye, Isle of, 369, 447–8, 765
  expeditions to (1884–5 and 1886), 449–50
Sleat, Ronald Archibald Bosville, 6th baron of, 448
Small, Col. John, 636
Smith, William Alexander, 470
Smollett, Tobias George, *The Expedition of Humphry Clinker* (1771), 672–4
socialism, 445, 539, 674, 685
Society of Antiquaries of Scotland, 777–9, 782, 788
Somerled, king of the Hebrides, 107, 119
Somerset, duke of *see* Hertford
Somerville, Alexander, 460, 536–7
Somerville, Lt.-Col. George, 327
Somerville, Col. Hugh, 778
Sørli, Odd, 569
South Africa, 485, 488, 492, 501
  First City Regiment, 498–9
  Scottish immigrants, 486–7, 489, 491
  1st South African Infantry Brigade, 495, 498
  South African Scottish, 495
  see also Cape Town Highlanders and Transvaal Scottish
South African War (1899–1902), 22, 24–5, 462, 473–8, 490–1, 496–7, 509–10, 790
  Scottish citizen soldiers in, 19–20, 475, 758–60
  Scottish memorials, 477, 758–60, 763
South America, 270
Southey, Robert, 422
Soviet Union *see* Union of Soviet Socialist Republics
Spain, 239, 244, 249, 251, 256, 263, 270–1, 327, 337, 359, 428, 572, 672
  Civil War (1936–9), 270, 768

First Carlist War (1833–40), 270–1, 460
Spanish Armadas (1588, 1596 and 1597), 239
Spanish army, 252–3
  Scots serve in, 264, 268
Spean Bridge, Commando sculpture, 765–7
special constables, 443, 446
spears, 5, 47–50, 52–5, 71, 81, 136, 138, 170, 223, 230n49, 239, 777–8
  Gaelic use of, 224–5
  in hunting, 44–5
  Scottish long, 112, 114
  spearmen, 3, 75, 100, 114, 145–6, 153
  see also shiltroms
Special Operations Executive (SOE), 22, 563, 569
  training in Scotland, 587n14
Spens, Sir James, 254–5
Spitfires, 559, 567
Spynie, Alexander Lindsay, 2nd Lord, 258
Staff College, 462, 579
Stair, Sir John Dalrymple, Master, 2nd Viscount and 1st earl of, 318, 340, 343
Stair, Gen. John Dalrymple, 3rd Viscount and 2nd earl of, 336, 340
  regiment of, 15
Stalin, gold bullion of, 565
standing army, 265
  distrust of, 250, 300
  Scottish, 301, 303–4, 306–8, 312–15, 318–19, 326–7, 333–8, 343–4
Stanley, George, 494–5
Stanley, Henry Morton, 461
Stapleton, Brig.-Gen. Walter, 650–1
steel industry, 507
Stell, Geoffrey, 709
Stephen, king of England (r. 1135–54), 100–1, 103
Stevenson, Piper Phil, 662
Stevenson, Robert Louis, 753
Stewart, Allan, 699, 702
Stewart, Dubhghall, 221–2
Stewart, James, 143
Stewart, John *see* Buchan, second earl of
Stewart, Brig.-Gen. John, 337
Stewarts, lordship of, 214
Stirling, 352, 363, 368, 743, 781

Stirling Bridge, battle of (1297), 6, 108, 133, 136, 143
  English caught by surprise, 145
  post-battle atrocities, 150
Stirling, Col. (Archibald) David, 23
Stornoway, 451
  landing at (1719), 357
Stothard, Thomas, 690
Stracathro, battle of (1130), 108
Strachan, Hew, 3, 804
Strathallan, William Drummond, 4th Viscount, 367
Strathclyde, kingdom of, 104
Strathearn, Malise, earl of, 116
Strathnairn, Gen. (later FM) Sir Hugh Rose, later 1st Baron, 441, 469
Strathnaver, William Gordon, Lord (known as Master of), 327
  regiment of, 327, 329–30, 336
Strathnaver, battle of (1431), 220
Strathspey, anti-militia riots in, 417
  fencibles, 784
Strathspey, Sir James Grant of, 410
Stratton, Capt. Charles, 327
Strozzi, Leo, 198
Strozzi, Pietro, 201, 719, 742
Sudan, Mahdist revolt in, 473
  reconquest of (1898), 473–4, 509
Suez crisis (1956), 620, 680
suffragettes, 538
Suibhne (Sven), 'the Red', 709
Sukarno, 613
Sullom Voe, RAF, 566, 568
Sully, Henry de, 151
Surrey, John de Warenne, earl of, 6, 133, 136, 143
  army of, 145
Surrey, Thomas Howard, Lord Admiral, 1st earl of (later 2nd duke of Norfolk), 189, 193
  tactics at Flodden, 191
Sutherland, George Granville, William, 3rd duke of, 450
Sutherland, John, 419
Sutherland, John, 14th earl of, 245
Sutherland, John Gordon, 16th earl of, 327, 352
Sutherlands, 781
Suvla Bay, landing (1915), 525
Sweden, 252, 254, 259, 263, 329, 569
Swedish army, 259–61
  Scots serve in, 12, 252, 254–6, 259–65, 329, 391

Swinton, Lt.-Col. James, 331
Swinton, Sir John, 167
swords, 46, 48–9, 52–3, 81, 108, 119, 136, 138–9, 184, 200, 224–5, 239, 779
    Battle abbey, 781
    broadsword, 185, 369, 372, 386, 388, 399–400, 569, 690–1, 735, 738
    claymore, 474, 476, 509, 800
    double-hander, 185, 225–6
    longsword, 170, 782
    Roman, 55, 60
Sydney, 488
    Highland Society of, 488, 496–7
Szechi, Daniel, 353–4

Tacitus, 55
Taleban, 809
Tangier, defence of (1680–4), 14
tanks, 542–3
    Challenger, 617
    see also panzers
tartan, 398, 414, 486, 490–1, 495–6, 500, 628, 643–4, 690–1, 778
    Black Watch (government sett), 490, 496, 629, 641
    Cameron of Erracht, 636, 640
    'clan' setts, 637, 640
    objections to wearing, 646n12
    origins of, 633
    trews, 430n12, 461, 463, 476, 628–9, 631, 636, 639, 641, 695
Tascher, Capt. René de, 331
tattoo, 663
    anti, 26, 669
Taylor, A. J. P., 545
Taynuilt, Nelson stone at, 755
Templer, FM Sir Gerald, 804
Tennyson, Alfred, 1st Baron, 539
Territorial Army, 544, 630, 803, 805–6, 809
Territorial Force, 20–2, 28, 478, 509–11, 513, 539–40
Thatcher, Margaret Hilda, Baroness, 554, 607
Thermes, Paul de la Barthe, Maréchal de, 201
Thiers, Adolphe, 539
Thirty Years War (1618–48), 244, 248–9, 255, 265–6
Thistle Foundation, 766
Thomson, Neill, 395–6

Thorne, Lt.-Gen. Sir Andrew, 569
Thweng, Marmaduke, 150
Tilburg, capture of (1944), 583
The Times, 468
Tipperary, 441
Tippermuir, battle of (1644), 288
Tiree, RAF, 566
Tirpitz, 565, 568
Tito, Josip Broz, mission to, 23
Tobermory, convoy escort school at, 565
Tobruk, siege of (1941), 498, 584
Tolquhon, William Forbes, 7th laird of, 720–1
Tories, 311, 443
    promote Highlandism, 637
Toronto, 465, 488
Torphichen, James Sandilands, 7th Lord, 340
tournaments, 118, 174, 190, 781
trade unions, 443, 540, 603
Trail, Bishop Walter, later Archbishop of St Andrews, 713–14
Tranent, 738–9, 750
    anti-militia riots in (1707), 417, 436–9, 444–6, 452
HMS *Transit*, wrecked (1857), 463
Transvaal, 472
    Transvaal Scottish, 477, 485, 491–3, 498–500
trebuchet, 146
Trident Ploughshares, 608
Triple Alliance, 544
Tripoli, victory parade (1943), 576
Trumbull, John, 690
    The Sortie Made by the Garrison of Gibraltar (1789), 691
Tudsbery, Sir Francis and Lady Isabella, 766
Tudsbery, Lt. Robin, 767
Tullibardine, Col. John George Stewart-Murray, marquess of (later 8th duke of Atholl), 19, 491
Tullibardine, John Murray, marquess of, 330–1
    regiment of, 330–1
Tullibardine, William Murray, marquess of, 357
Tulloch of Assery B, 44
Tunisia, 576–7, 680
Turkey, 694
    and First World War, 523–5, 529
    soldiers of, 467–8

Turner, Lt.-Col. Sir James, 303–4, 308
Turner, Joseph Mallord William
   The Field of Waterloo (1818), 693
Turnhouse, RAF, 566, 585n1
Twin Towers, attack on (2001), 620

Ubaldini, Migiliorino, 719
Ulster, 107, 188, 290, 342, 538, 545
  'dirty war' in, 553
  expedition to (1642), 282–3, 287, 289
  loyalists in 538, 546
  plantation, 245, 255
  rebellion (1641), 282
  see also Northern Ireland, Ulster Defence Association, Ulster Defence Regiment
Ulster Defence Association (UDA), 552–3
Ulster Defence Regiment (UDR), 548, 552–3
Union of Soviet Socialist Republics, 565, 600, 607
  invades Afghanistan (1979), 607–8
  long-range-bombers of, 608
  submarines of, 608
  threat from, 600–1, 608–9
Union of the Crowns (1603), 12, 241, 243
Union of the Parliaments (1707), 329, 343, 351, 410, 413, 436, 565, 637
  Act of Union (1707), 3, 269, 328
  Jacobite opposition to, 349
  military support for, 15, 339–41, 343, 355
  popular opposition to, 342–3
United Irishmen, rebellion of (1798), 19
United Kingdom (UK), 600, 604, 606–8, 610, 613, 617, 796, 798, 803
  air defence of, 608–9
  independent nuclear deterrent of, 602, 605–6, 608–9, 804
  relationship with United States, 601–2, 605, 620
  V-Bomber force of, 602–3
United Nations, and Korean War, 611
  peacekeeping of, 500
United Provinces, 249, 256–7, 269, 298, 311–12, 318, 329–30
United Scotsmen, Society of, 417, 438
United States of America (USA), 600, 604, 606–7, 611
  Air Force, 601
  and archaeology, 728–9
  army, 526
  Polaris submarines of, 602, 605–6
  wages 'war on terror', 620
Unst, RAF Saxa Vord, 608–9
Urie, Sir Alexander Baird of, 510

Vågsøy, 568
Valence, Aymer de *see* Pembroke
Valois-Habsburg War (1557–9), 202
HMS *Vanguard*, 619
Vaux, John de, 708, 710
V-Bombers, 602–3
Venlo, siege of (1702), 330
Victoria, Queen (r. 1837–1901), 19, 635
  and 'Balmoral effect', 695–6
  golden jubilee of (1885), 657–8
  patronage of Highland regiments, 19, 486, 639–40, 800
  reviews the Scottish Volunteers, 470
Victoria Crosses, 469, 473, 494, 510, 566, 568, 577, 588, 594n60, 651, 657, 660, 681, 701
Vietnam War (1955–75), 605
Vikings, 73, 185; *see also* Scandinavians
Vitalis, Orderic, 109
Volunteers (part-time soldiers enrolled in British units), 20, 35n69, 413–16, 431n22, 436, 470, 478, 512, 539, 652, 754, 780
  and Highland dress, 24, 641
  and the South African War, 475–7, 759

Wade, Lt.-Gen. (later FM) George, 354–5, 359–62
  army of, 365, 367
  fortifications of, 361
  roads of, 363–4
Wales, 94, 99, 106, 111, 117, 152, 171, 280, 617
  conquest of, 133, 136
Wallace, 'Col.' James, 304–5
Wallace, William, 2, 133, 141, 799
  armies of, 649
  depicted as a 'war criminal', 150
  devastating raid of, 6, 149

Wallace, William (*cont.*)
  leadership, 6, 114, 141, 151, 153
  statues, 752
  see also battles of Falkirk and Stirling Bridge; National Wallace Monument
Wallace-Hadrill, John Michael, 78
Wallenstein, Count Albrecht von, 264
Walpole, Horace, 672
Walpole, Sir Robert, 359–60
Walsingham, Thomas, 168
Wanklyn, Malcolm, 286
wapinshawings (weapon showings), 170, 184, 238–9, 280, 780
war memorials, 25, 477, 674, 767
  and citizen soldiers, 758–60
  chantry tombs, 750
  'community remembrance', 767–9
  covenanting, 752
  First World War, 25–6, 748, 760–5, 768
  imperial, 753–9
  Second World War, 764–7
War of American Independence (1775–83), 269, 383, 390–1, 395, 397, 400, 410, 412, 487, 652, 692
War of the Austrian Succession (1740–8), 735
War of the Spanish Succession (1701–14), 15, 319, 326, 328, 332, 349
Ward, Gen. Sir Alfred Dudley, 804
Wardens of the Marches, 164, 192, 240
Warenne, John de *see* Surrey, earl of
warfare, ancient, 2, 4, 41, 43–6, 50, 52–4, 60
  chemical, 22, 493, 513–14, 520–1, 642, 660
  early medieval, 3, 5, 65, 72–85, 98, 104, 108–9, 115
  guerrilla, 5, 56, 146, 160, 289, 370, 417, 466, 475, 553, 611–12, 615, 801
War Office, 23, 445, 450–1, 462, 540, 571, 639, 644, 657, 722
Wars of Independence (1296–1328 and 1332–57), 1, 3, 6, 133, 152, 211, 649, 712–13, 750, 752, 781
  ambushes, 136, 146, 153
  battle avoidance, 9, 143–4, 153, 160, 165

castle destruction, 7, 9, 147–8
cavalry in, 3, 136–7, 145, 163
diplomacy, 135
English invasions/occupation, 6, 133, 135, 146, 148
French aid, 160, 166
Irish front, 135, 137, 141, 144–5, 149, 151–2
naval warfare, 151–2
savagery of, 149–51, 167
Scottish military leadership, 6, 136, 143, 145–6, 148–50, 153
Scottish raids, 6–7, 133, 134–5, 139, 143, 148–50, 153, 163, 165
sieges, 133, 143–4, 146–8, 152, 161–2
socio-economic impact of, 149–50, 167–8
see also Bannockburn, Falkirk, Stirling Bridge and Halidon Hill, Edward I, II and III, Robert I, David II and Wallace, William
Wars of the Roses (1455–85), 10
Wars of the Three Kingdoms (1639–51), 12, 226, 276
  artillery in, 280–1, 283
  cavalry in, 278, 280–1, 284–6, 288, 291
  conquest of Scotland, 12–13, 292–4, 298
  English civil wars, 283–9
  negotiations in, 278, 280, 284–5, 290–1
  rebellion in Ulster, 280, 283, 287–8
  see also Bishops' Wars, Charles I and Cromwell, Oliver
Warwick, John Dudley, 2nd earl of, 202
Watson, Fiona, 6
Watson, Dr Mary 'Mona' Chalmers, 23
Watson-Watt, Sir Robert, 23
Wauchope, Maj.-Gen. Andrew Gilbert, 29, 462, 474, 758
Wauchope, Col. John, 315
Wavell, FM Archibald, 1st Earl, 461, 538, 600
weapons, ancient, 4, 44–9, 52, 54–5, 60
  early medieval, 81
  Roman, 48, 54, 57
Weardale, campaign in (1327), 148
Webb, Maj.-Gen. Daniel, 393

Weekly Despatch, 536
Weir, Sir William Douglas, 1st Viscount, 508
Wellington, FM Sir Arthur Wellesley, 1st duke of, 18, 418–19, 431n21, 536, 692–3, 695, 810
　armies of, 427–8, 802
　Scottish statues of, 25
West, Benjamin, 690–1
　The Death of General Wolfe (1770), 691
West Indies, 360, 410, 463, 465
Western Fencible Regiment, 779
Western Front, 22, 493, 495, 509, 512, 517, 523, 525–7, 540–1, 659, 796
Western Isles, 104, 106–8, 120, 213, 226
　and Ireland, 215, 225–6, 258, 287
　'canon conquest' of, 189
　chieftains, 152
　disarming of, 225
　expedition, 225, 245
　men of, 11, 110, 113, 166, 185, 211–12, 220, 222, 226, 415
　naval warfare, 104, 107–8, 171–2
　potential second front, 11, 211
　Wimund, bishop of, 105–6
　see also Lord of the Isles
Westminster-Ardtornish, Treaty of (1462), 11
Wharton, Thomas, 1st Baron, 198, 202
Wheatley, John, 540
Whetham, Maj.-Gen. Thomas, 326
Whigs, 15–16, 311, 343, 374, 386, 443, 536
　in Glasgow, 364, 374
　in the Highlands, 341, 354–6, 358, 360, 364, 369–70, 372
White, Lt.-Col. John, 333
White, Peter, *With the Jocks* (2001), 809
Whitehouse, Pte. Stan, 580
Whitelaw, Charles, 782
Wick Harbour riot (1847), 446
Wick, RAF, 566
Wightman, Lt.-Gen. Joseph, 326, 355, 357, 363
Wigtown, earl of *see* Douglas, 5th earl
'Wild Geese', 266
Wilhelm II, Kaiser, 539
Wilkie, David, 693

William I, 'The Conqueror', king of England (r. 1066–87), 94
William II (known as William Rufus), king of England (r. 1087–1100), 96
William of Orange, later William III, king of England and William II, king of Scotland (r. 1689–1702), 15, 251, 315, 318–19, 339, 359, 615, 778
　conquers Ireland, 315
　forces of, 252, 266, 329
　invades England, 266, 316–17, 348
William the Lion, king of Scots (r. 1165–1214), 9, 96, 102, 105–6, 109, 114, 118
　captured, 100–1, 103–5
　invades England, 101, 104, 110, 116
Wilson, Harold, 605
Wilson, James, 438
Wilton, William Grey, 13th Baron, 198, 201
Wimberley, Maj.-Gen. Douglas, 'Tartan Tam', 1, 29, 578–80, 599n123
　fosters Scottish identity in 51st Division, 1, 572, 574, 576–8, 643
　plans El Alamein attack, 573–4
　seeks Highland recruits, 573
　unveils St Valéry monument, 581
Winchester, Roger de Quincy, 2nd earl of, 112
'Wolf of Badenoch' *see* Buchan, Alexander Stewart
Wolfe, Maj.-Gen. James, 388–9, 397, 400
　army of, 395
　at Culloden, 734
Wolseley, FM Sir Garnet Joseph, 1st Viscount, 472–3
women, in war, 23, 80, 160, 508, 764, 768
Women's Army Auxiliary Corps (WAAC), 23
Wood, Col. Sir James, 330
Wood, Thomas McKinnon, 543
Woodville, Richard Caton, 25, 474, 702
　Kandahar: the 92nd Highlanders and 2nd Gurkhas Storming Gandi Mullah Sahibdad (1881), 699

Woodville, Richard Caton (*cont.*)
  All That Was Left of Them: the Black Watch after the Battle of Magersfontein 1899 (1899), 25, 701
  At Last, the Bivouac at Omdurman (Gordon's Spirit at Rest) (1899), 474

Xhosa, 466

Yemen, 613–14
yeomanry, 414, 432n30, 478, 780
  Manchester and Salford, 537
  Pembrokeshire, 437
  Royal Cinque Ports Light Dragoons, 437
  Stirlingshire, 438
  see also Ayrshire, Imperial Yeomanry and Lanarkshire

Yester, Col. John Hay, Master of, 286
York, 56, 149, 283, 285–7, 316, 342
  Archbishop Thurstan of, 100
  Treaty of (1237), 100
York, Prince Frederick Augustus, the duke of, 410
Yorkshire, 20, 53, 59, 281, 285, 290, 342
  Scottish raids into, 100, 103, 110–11, 135, 149
Yorktown, surrender of (1781), 396
Young, Douglas, 584, 599n123
Young, Brig.-Gen. Peter, 286
Younger, George, 614
Yugoslavia, 23

Zakka Khel, expedition (1908), 477
Zululand, 471–2
  rebellion of (1906), 477